From a conference held under the auspices of
UCLA CENTER FOR MEDIEVAL AND RENAISSANCE STUDIES
HARVARD UNIVERSITY COMMITTEE ON MEDIEVAL STUDIES
26–29 November 1977 • Cambridge, Massachusetts

Commemorating the contribution by Charles Homer Haskins

A volume prepared for publication by the
UCLA CENTER FOR MEDIEVAL AND RENAISSANCE STUDIES

RENAISSANCE AND RENEWAL

IN

THE TWELFTH CENTURY

edited by

Robert L. Benson and Giles Constable

with Carol D. Lanham

HARVARD UNIVERSITY PRESS

Cambridge, Massachusetts

Library of Congress Cataloging in Publication Data
Main entry under title:

Renaissance and renewal in the twelfth century.

Papers presented at a conference marking the 50th
anniversary of the publication of Charles Homer Haskins'
Renaissance of the twelfth century and held in Cambridge,
Mass., Nov. 26–29, 1977.
Includes bibliographical references and index.
1. Twelfth century—Congresses.   2. Haskins, Charles
Homer, 1870–1937—Congresses.   I. Benson, Robert Louis,
1925–   II. Constable, Giles, 1929–
III. Lanham, Carol Dana.   IV. Haskins, Charles Homer.
1870–1937.
D201.8.R45   940.1'82   82-2999
ISBN 0–674–76085–9 (cloth)   AACR2
ISBN 0–674–76086–7 (paper)

Contents

Illustrations

Abbreviations

I. BOOKS, JOURNALS, SERIES

AASS	Acta Sanctorum
Abh	Abhandlungen (of the learned society indicated by the name of a city following, such as: Abh Göttingen = Abhandlungen der Gesellschaft der Wissenschaften in Göttingen, philologisch-historische Klasse)
AHDLMA	*Archives d'histoire doctrinale et littéraire du moyen âge*
AHR	*American Historical Review*
AKG	*Archiv für Kulturgeschichte*
Annales E.S.C.	*Annales: Economies, Sociétés, Civilisations*
Baldwin, *Masters*	John W. Baldwin, *Masters, Princes and Merchants: The Social Views of Peter the Chanter and His Circle* (2 vols. Princeton 1970)
BGPTMA	Beiträge zur Geschichte der Philosophie und Théologie des Mittelalters
BMCL	*Bulletin of Medieval Canon Law*
CCL	Corpus Christianorum: Series latina
cm	continuatio mediaevalis
CCM	*Cahiers de civilisation médiévale*
Chenu, *Théologie*	Marie-Dominique Chenu, *La théologie au douzième siècle*, EPM 45 (Paris 1957; 3rd ed. 1976)
Chenu, *Nature*	Idem, trans. Jerome Taylor and Lester K. Little, *Nature, Man, and Society in the Twelfth Century: Essays on New Theological Perspectives in the West* (Chicago and London 1968)
CIMAGL	*Cahiers de l'Institut du moyen âge grec et latin*
Coing, *Handbuch 1*	Helmut Coing, *Handbuch der Quellen und Literatur der neueren europäischen Privatrechtsgeschichte* (Munich 1973–) volume 1
CTSEEH	Collection de textes pour servir à l'étude et à l'enseignement de l'histoire
Curtius	Ernst Robert Curtius, *European Literature and the Latin Middle Ages*, trans. Willard R. Trask, Bollingen Series 36 (New York 1953)
DA	*Deutsches Archiv für Erforschung des Mittelalters*
DSB	*Dictionary of Scientific Biography*, ed. Charles C. Gillespie (15 vols. New York 1970–78)
Du Cange	Du Cange et al., *Glossarium mediae et infimae latinitatis*
EETS	Early English Text Society

EHR	*English Historical Review*
Entretiens	*Entretiens sur la Renaissance du 12e siècle*, ed. Maurice P. de Gandillac and Edouard Jeauneau (Paris 1968)
EPM	Etudes de philosophie médiévale
Faral, *Les arts poétiques*	Edmond Faral, ed., *Les arts poétiques du XIIe et du XIIIe siècle: Recherches et documents sur la technique littéraire du moyen âge*, Bibliothèque de l'Ecole des hautes études, Sciences historiques et philologiques 238 (Paris 1924)
GF	Otto of Freising (books 1–2) and Rahewin (books 3–4), *Gesta Friderici I imperatoris*, 3rd ed. Georg Waitz and Bernhard von Simson, MGH SS rer Germ (Hanover and Leipzig 1912)
Haskins, *Culture*	Charles Homer Haskins, *Studies in Mediaeval Culture* (Oxford 1929; repr. New York 1965)
Haskins, *Ren*	Charles Homer Haskins, *The Renaissance of the Twelfth Century* (Cambridge Mass. 1927)
Haskins, *Science*	Charles Homer Haskins, *Studies in the History of Mediaeval Science*, Harvard Historical Studies 27 (Cambridge Mass. 1924; 2nd ed. 1927)
IRMAE	Ius romanum medii aevi
Jaffé, *Bibl*	Philipp Jaffé, *Bibliotheca rerum Germanicarum* (6 vols. Berlin 1864–73; repr. Aalen 1964)
Jeauneau, *Lectio*	Edouard Jeauneau, "*Lectio philosophorum*": *Recherches sur l'Ecole de Chartres* (Amsterdam 1973)
JK, JE, JL	Philipp Jaffé, *Regesta pontificum Romanorum ab condita ecclesia ad annum post Christum natum MCXCVIII*, 2nd ed. rev. K. Kaltenbrunner (to 590), P. Ewald (590–882), and S. Loewenfeld (882–1198) (2 vols. Leipzig 1885–88; repr. Graz 1956)
JWI (JWCI)	*Journal of the Warburg* (*and Courtauld*) *Institute*(*s*)
Kuttner, *Repertorium*	Stephan Kuttner, *Repertorium der Kanonistik* (*1140–1234*): *Prodromus Corporis glossarum*, Studi e testi 71 (Vatican City 1937; repr. 1973)
LCL	Loeb Classical Library
Leclercq, *Love of Learning*	Jean Leclercq, *The Love of Learning and the Desire for God: A Study of Monastic Culture*, trans. Catharine Misrahi (New York 1961; 2nd ed. 1974)
ed. Leclercq	*Sancti Bernardi Opera*, ed. Jean Leclercq, C. H. Talbot, and Henri Rochais (8 vols. in 9 Rome 1957–77)
Manitius	Max Manitius, *Geschichte der lateinischen Literatur des Mittelalters* (3 vols. Munich 1911–31)
MGH	Monumenta Germaniae historica
AA	Auctores antiquissimi
Const	Constitutiones et acta publica imperatorum et regum
DD	Diplomata regum et imperatorum Germaniae
Epist sel	Epistolae selectae
Poetae	Poetae latini aevi Carolini

SS	Scriptores (folio)
SS rer Germ	Scriptores rerum Germanicarum in usum scholarum
M&RS	*Mediaeval and Renaissance Studies*
MIÖG	*Mitteilungen des Instituts für österreichische Geschichts-forschung*
Panofsky, *Ren & Ren*	Erwin Panofsky, *Renaissance and Renascences in Western Art* (Stockholm 1960; 2nd ed. 1965)
Pierre–Pierre	*Pierre Abélard, Pierre le Vénérable: Les courants philoso-phiques, littéraires et artistiques en Occident au milieu du XIIe siècle*, Colloques internationaux du Centre na-tional de la recherche scientifique 546 (Paris 1975)
PL	J. P. Migne, Patrologia . . . latina
RS	Rerum Britannicarum medii aevi scriptores: Rolls Series
RTAM	*Recherches de théologie ancienne et médiévale*
SB	Sitzungsberichte (of the learned society indicated by the name of a city following, such as: SB Vienna = Sitz-ungsberichte der kaiserlichen Akademie der Wissen-schaften zu Wien, philosophisch-historische Klasse)
Schramm, *KKP*	Percy Ernst Schramm, *Kaiser, Könige und Päpste* (4 vols. in 5 Stuttgart 1968–71)
Schramm, *KRR*	Percy Ernst Schramm, *Kaiser, Rom und Renovatio: Stu-dien und Texte zur Geschichte des römischen Erneuer-ungsgedankens vom Ende des karolingischen Reiches bis zum Investiturstreit*, Studien der Bibliothek War-burg 17 (2 vols. Leipzig 1929; vol. 1, 2nd ed. Darm-stadt 1957)
Settimane	Settimane di studio del Centro italiano di studi sull'alto medioevo
Smalley, *Study*	Beryl Smalley, *The Study of the Bible in the Middle Ages* (2nd ed. Oxford and New York 1952)
Southern, *Humanism*	Richard W. Southern, *Medieval Humanism and Other Studies* (Oxford and New York 1970)
Stock, *Myth and Science*	Brian C. Stock, *Myth and Science in the Twelfth Century: A Study of Bernard Silvester* (Princeton 1972)
TRHS	*Transactions of the Royal Historical Society*
Twelfth-Century Europe	*Twelfth-Century Europe and the Foundations of Modern Society*, ed. Marshall Clagett, Gaines Post, and Robert Reynolds (Madison Wisc. 1961)
ZRG	Zeitschrift der Savigny-Stiftung für Rechtsgeschichte
germ Abt	germanistische Abteilung
kan Abt	kanonistische Abteilung
rom Abt	romanistische Abteilung

II. MANUSCRIPTS

BL	London, British Library (formerly: British Museum)
BN lat	Paris, Bibliothèque nationale, Manuscrits latins

BN n.a.	Paris, Bibliothèque nationale, Nouvelles acquisitions latines
Clm	Munich, Bayerische Staatsbibliothek, Codex latinus monacensis
Vat lat	Vatican City, Biblioteca Apostolica Vaticana, Codices latini
Vat Pal	Vatican City, Biblioteca Apostolica Vaticana, Codices Palatini latini
Vat Reg	Vatican City, Biblioteca Apostolica Vaticana, Codices Reginenses

Introduction

By echoing the title of Charles Homer Haskins's best-known work, the title of this volume makes certain claims and, for anyone who has read his *Renaissance of the Twelfth Century*, arouses certain expectations. Haskins cast in enduring shape the problem of interpreting twelfth-century culture, which must still be approached through the portal of his book. Though more than fifty years have passed since it appeared, its audience and influence have scarcely diminished. The reader therefore deserves a brief explanation of why the editors chose a title which encourages comparison with a classic work familiar to a wide public as well as to every medievalist. By stressing equally ''renaissance'' and ''renewal'' in the twelfth century, however, the title of this volume also differs from Haskins's. The editors thereby implicitly promise not only a fresh survey of the terrain which Haskins charted, but also an inquiry which goes beyond the limits he set for himself. In diverse areas of cultural, religious, or social life, the twelfth century sometimes called for—and, just as often, thought that it had achieved—a renewal, revival, or reform. When twelfth-century thinkers sought a term for such sweeping change, or when they considered one of the great and distinctive achievements of their own age, they commonly identified it as a *renovatio*. Taken together, the terms ''renaissance'' and ''renewal'' reflect the intent of this volume.

The book's own history further illuminates its intent. It originated in an unusual collaboration between two universities, whose representatives agreed to celebrate together the semicentennial of Haskins's study. Various scholars from Europe and North America were invited to prepare papers on the twelfth-century renaissance, with each scholar treating a particular aspect. As a first step toward this volume, the organizers asked that the papers be presented for discussion at a conference in November 1977. Those who accepted the invitation received ''Guidelines for Authors,'' which stated the purpose of the conference and anticipated the structure of the volume. With a few minor omissions (principally of passages concerning the practical arrangements for the conference), these ''Guidelines'' may properly serve as the first part of this Introduction.

In 1927, Charles Homer Haskins published his *Renaissance of the Twelfth Century*. A conference marking this anniversary will be held in Cambridge, Massachusetts, on 26–29 November 1977 under the joint auspices of the University of California (Los Angeles) and Harvard University, in cooperation with the Mediaeval Academy of America.

Both as teacher and as scholar, Haskins was the most important American medieval historian of his time, and a leading figure in the foundation of the Mediaeval Academy. In a study of *The Renaissance in Historical Thought* (1948), Wallace K. Ferguson commented on Haskins's influence, then stated:

> His *Renaissance of the Twelfth Century*, limited though it was to Latin literature and learning, was the nearest approach to a general intellectual history of the High Middle Ages written during this age of monographic study. It was one of the most widely read works in the field—at least every scholar had read the title—and its impact upon historical thought was proportionately great. The idea of a medieval Renaissance, or of several such, was by no means new. Most often, however, the phenomenon had been treated as something exceptional, as one or more isolated rays of light in the medieval gloom, foreshadowing the true Renaissance. Or it had been studied in only one limited aspect. It was significant that Haskins treated his subject as a broad cultural movement; that he related it to contemporary economic and political developments, as well as to those in the allied fields of vernacular literature and art; and, above all, that he regarded the Renaissance of the Twelfth Century as something characteristically medieval.

With this work, in short, Haskins posed an important question in its classic form, and Ferguson has rightly assigned to the book the status of an historical classic.

The central purpose of the conference is to examine closely those aspects of the twelfth century which can be considered parts of a renaissance. Though we shall take as a point of departure and reference the contribution made by Haskins in his *Renaissance of the Twelfth Century* (1927) as well as his *Studies in the History of Mediaeval Science* (1924) and *Studies in Mediaeval Culture* (1929), the conference will not aim simply to honor Haskins, to supplement and correct his work, or to bring it up to date; rather, it will seek to assay the continuing vitality and importance of Haskins's historical vision. Our task is to assimilate the substantial advances of medieval research in the last fifty years, to deal with topics (such as painting, sculpture, architecture, and vernacular literature) which Haskins had to exclude from his account, and to emphasize certain elements (such as the role of religion in the process of cultural change) to which Haskins devoted little attention. One may hope that the conference will reflect new perspectives gained from deep shifts in thought and sensibility during the past half-century. Indeed, it might be said that the conference is designed to discover how a scholar of Haskins's insight and learning would present the phenomenon of a twelfth-century renaissance today. It is a measure of his success in opening up a major historical issue that it now takes a conference of scholars to do what a single scholar did fifty years ago.

The conference will produce a volume of scholarly studies, and the conference itself has been planned primarily as an indispensable step in the preparation of this book. We expect that the papers will be revised and coordinated in the light of the discussion so as to fit together into a scholarly collection which finds its legitimate place alongside Haskins's work, and which constitutes in its own right a basic contribution to this important topic.

In defining its task, the conference will draw as much on the last fifty years of scholarly inquiry as on Haskins's achievement. For there have been many important attempts, since 1927, to analyze and interpret twelfth-century culture afresh. Some of these are collaborative enterprises. In numerous articles as well as books, individual scholars have also ventured general essays on the culture of the twelfth century. In different ways and differing degrees, all of them—collaborative and individual efforts alike—have made worthwhile contributions to the study of this problem. Yet, as one can sometimes see from their titles or subtitles, none of them approached the problem with the intention of producing the particular kind of comprehensive synthesis at which we aim. For example, one of the collaborative volumes concentrates on twelfth-century education, whereas one of the pertinent books by an eminent scholar views twelfth-century intellectual history primarily under the rubric of theology.

Moreover, the time is ripe for a conference on this theme. That is, on most of the particular topics as well as on the larger subject, scholarly research has reached a point which renders a new large-scale synthesis possible. It is our hope that the volume produced by the conference will stimulate inquiry and redefine the problem as rewardingly for the next fifty years as Haskins's *Renaissance* has done for the past.

The most crucial aspect of the conference will be its collaborative character. Obviously, in gauging the probable results of a "working" colloquium of this kind, the planners looked first at the intellectual and scholarly quality of the prospective authors and other participants. Apart from this, however, there are two principal prerequisites to the success of this collaborative enterprise. First, though there must be enough participants to assure a certain diversity of specialization and expertise, the conference group must remain small enough to permit easy discussion. The planning committee has invited about fifty participants, twenty-five of whom will present papers; and there will be perhaps twenty auditors. Second, the papers must be distributed in advance in order to allow the participants to devote their time to discussion.

One of the main concerns of the organizers of the conference has been to give it a coherent structure. The papers should therefore deal with distinct but interrelated aspects of a single large subject, much like the chapters of Haskins's book, though not necessarily covering the same topics or approaching them in the same way. In particular, Haskins approached the subject largely through an examination of certain genres. Our conference will treat the twelfth-century renaissance less through genres than through themes and issues which appear in various kinds of literary and artistic production and which draw on a variety of cultural and social sources. Each paper is thus intended to be a fresh interpretative essay, studying its topic in the light of recent research, and not simply a survey of scholarly work done over the past fifty years.

Each working session of the conference will begin with a brief oral comment on the papers to be dealt with in that session. Among other possible and useful approaches, the comment may treat the congruences and tensions between the papers, and may also indicate any pertinent problems or topics with which the papers have not dealt sufficiently. But principally the comment should provide an informal agenda for the general discussion which follows it. There will be an opportunity for authors to reply at the end of each session. The final revision of each paper for publication will, one may hope, reflect in fruitful ways the discussions throughout the conference.

The striking qualities of Haskins's *Renaissance* include not only its durability (which one expects, after all, of a classic work) but also the remarkable range of audience which it can reach. Bright undergraduates find it exciting and fully intelligible, while seasoned scholars reread it with pleasure and profit. In short, the best of Haskins's chapters were superb *essais de synthèse*, incorporating the most recent scholarship, carefully selected texts and concrete information, and the most imaginative interpretative possibilities. These aspects of Haskins's achievement indicate an ideal at which we hope the authors will aim.

The most appropriate relation between Haskins's *Renaissance* and the individual papers may create problems for certain authors as well as for the planners of the conference. Should one, for example, treat topics which Haskins himself dealt with at length in the *Renaissance*? For some authors this question will be irrelevant, since Haskins did not touch upon all of the topics which will be examined in the conference. For other authors, however, the decision will be less easy. Two suggestions may help. First, every author should presuppose that the readers may have widely differing levels of knowledge about the twelfth century but are familiar with Haskins's *Renaissance*. Hence it will rarely be necessary to mention Haskins explicitly in the text of any paper. And second, though authors cannot and should not avoid the topics, persons, and texts treated in detail by Haskins, they should deal with these only when a substantially new interpretation is possible or when the familiar point is indispensable to the coherence and intelligibility of the account.

Much can be done to foster the overall coherence of the conference as well as the liveliness of its discussions, and to make the end-product more than a collection of disparate papers—that is, more than merely the sum of its parts. Among the general interpretative questions that can be asked of the entire subject, there are some that authors may wish to consider in relation to their particular topics. These questions are intended to stimulate rather than to limit thought and naturally should not be treated as all-inclusive or as in any way mandatory to answer. They are of differing degrees of importance and overlap at various points that are central to the main concerns of the conference. Taken together, these questions constitute a conceptual framework for advance reflection on the twelfth-century renaissance:

(1) *The defining characteristics of the renaissance*. What is meant by the term renaissance? Can it be said to have had a beginning or an end? In what areas of learning and knowledge was its impact primarily felt? Can it be understood exclusively in terms of a revival of classicism? Did it involve broad changes in point of view, such as attitudes toward God, the world, and the self? Was it associated with a new view of history? a new sense of change and progress? a willingness to accept innovation? Did these in turn contribute to the emergence of new secular values?

(2) *The problem of classicism*. What was meant by Antiquity and "the classics" in the twelfth century? Were there differing types and modes of revived classicism, such as the distinction between form and content? Was there an interaction of classical and nonclassical elements? Can developments that did not clearly involve classicism legitimately be seen as part of the renaissance?

(3) *The sources of the renaissance*. Did it draw on nonclassical as well as classical sources of inspiration? What was the contribution of non-Latin cultural traditions (Arabic, Celtic, Germanic, Greek, Jewish)? Did these influences, if any, come from inside or outside the Latin Christian tradition?

(4) *Religious elements in the renaissance*. What significance did the tradition of religious reform have for the renaissance? Did the feeling of revival in the twelfth century derive from religious rather than, or as well as, classical sources? Was the contemporary movement of religious renewal part of, parallel to, or in opposition to the renaissance?

(5) *Social, economic, and institutional setting*. What was the significance for the renaissance of such contemporary developments as the growth of population, the revival of towns, the emergence of the national monarchies, and the development of new social classes? To what extent was the renaissance linked to new sources of patronage, new kinds of audience, and new types of intellectual centers in twelfth-century society?

(6) *The chronological and regional framework*. Accepting the phenomenon of a renaissance, to what extent did it, or its component elements, fall chronologically into the twelfth century and cover all of Latin Europe? Did some features emerge before others? And were they more fully developed in some parts of Europe than in others? How can this chronological and regional diversity, if it existed, be explained? Did some features of the renaissance disappear and others persist? What was their relation, if any, to scholasticism and other aspects of later medieval learning and culture?

Although the conference took place largely as planned in these "Guidelines," things did not proceed smoothly in all regards. Two of the prospective contributors withdrew before the conference, and it proved impossible, because of the date, to replace one of them.[1] Two of the prepared comments, on the other hand, supplemented the distributed papers so valuably that their authors were asked to enlarge them for inclusion in the volume.[2]

The general questions posed in the "Guidelines" inevitably reflected our earlier views of the twelfth century's claim to be considered a renaissance. Many of the same questions could be applied, with minor changes, to other cultural movements in European history. Given the scope and stubbornness of these questions, we did not expect answers to all of them, or definitive answers to any. In retrospect, several of the questions seem less—or more—relevant than we had previously thought, and a few still seemed important but failed to find any answers in the conference. No doubt we would have framed some of the questions differently after the conference, and altered the list in other regards. Moreover, several papers raised significant questions which had not occurred to us before the conference, or which our list did not pose clearly. To what extent should one speak of survivals rather than revivals of Antiquity? Further, to what extent should either of these, in the sense of a simple persistence or borrowing from the past, be distinguished from a creative reuse, marked by an awareness of the difference between the present and the past? How, too, in contemporary as well as later terminology, were revival and renewal distinguished from rebellion and revolt? Some of the answers, finally, diverged markedly from our expectations. For, as we had hoped from so ambitious an enterprise, the papers not only reached many conclusions which most specialists would have anticipated, but also contained some startling surprises. The conference thus changed our thinking in important respects.

It would be impossible to summarize here the interpretations found in the twenty-six studies which this volume comprises, and even if we could do it, a reader facing a book of eight hundred pages might well be grateful for our restraint.[3] But a more modest goal may be both possible and appropriate in this Introduction. A reexamination of the general questions posed above may prove useful in two distinct ways. First, they constitute a set of criteria by which to judge this volume's success and limitations, thus also furnishing agenda for future research. Second, the questions help to indicate the principal respects in which the conference altered our picture of the twelfth century, and consequently to measure, or at least roughly estimate, the distance

[1] It was hoped that this contribution would discuss such themes in twelfth-century Latin literature as friendship and old age—both of which were popular literary topics in Antiquity— and would treat the rhetorical traditions and *dictamen*. This essay would thus have constituted a counterpart, dealing with the content of Latin literature, to Janet Martin's analysis of Latin style. It would have corresponded broadly to chapter 5 of Haskins's *Renaissance* ("The Latin Language"). Since significant scholarly progress has been made in these areas during the half century since Haskins wrote, this missing contribution marks a major lacuna in the volume.

[2] The papers by John W. Baldwin and Walter Horn originated as prepared comments.

[3] Nor shall we attempt to survey here the voluminous scholarly literature on the twelfth-century renaissance, of which an account up to the mid-1940s can be found in Wallace K. Ferguson, *The Renaissance in Historical Thought: Five Centuries of Interpretation* (Boston 1948) esp. ch. 10. See also the Bibliographical Note in Gerhart B. Ladner's contribution to this volume. The continuing attraction of the subject is shown by the recent appearance of a collection of essays edited by Peter Weimar, *Die Renaissance der Wissenschaften im 12. Jahrhundert* (Zurich 1981).

traversed by fifty years of scholarship. By pointing out the agreements and differences with Haskins, and by distinguishing surprises from expected conclusions, we may serve the reader's interest in the relations between the individual
papers, and thereby in the large configurations of the twelfth-century
renaissance.

Bearing the stamp of a single style, intelligence, and imagination,
Haskins's *Renaissance* constitutes a synthesis. Individually, most essays in this
volume offer syntheses on their particular topics, but it is not immediately
clear in what senses, if any, they collectively constitute a coherent and integrated unity. The statement in the "Guidelines," which aimed at a kind of
"comprehensive synthesis," was too sanguine in this respect. Though the
twenty-six studies overlap at some points, frequently supplement each other in
instructive ways, and are often mutually tangent, they also have quite different
approaches, present a number of divergent interpretations, and at a few points
disagree seriously. Such tensions are probably inescapable in a collaborative
volume of this sort. Yet it can still be called comprehensive in the sense that it
reflects the present state of historical thought and embraces the principal areas
of thought and action which might be considered to constitute a renaissance.
Moreover, since the individual studies—again, despite the tensions—agree and
interlock at many points, the volume has some of the features that one expects
of a synthesis. Still, if these studies can make any claim to offer a collective interpretation, the work of fusion and synthesis can take place only in the mind
of the reader.

Of the twelve chapters in *The Renaissance of the Twelfth Century*,
Haskins devoted the main parts of three—that is, almost a quarter of the
book—to the translations from Greek and Arabic and to their consequences for
the history of science and philosophy. Apart from his primary emphasis on the
classical tradition, he thereby assigned the largest role in the formation of the
renaissance to influences from outside Latin Christendom. Although no author
in this volume contests the important influence of non-Latin cultural traditions
on particular developments—of the Arabic translations, for example, or of the
Celtic background to French literature—equally no one maintains that the
confluence of Latin Christian civilization with other cultural traditions explains, in broad ways, the genesis and evolution of the twelfth-century
renaissance. Several authors, indeed, place their primary emphasis on the
creative reuse of artistic and intellectual elements lying dormant, as it were,
within Latin culture, such as Roman law and architecture. Others stress the
stimulating effect on culture of internal social and political developments, thus
tacitly playing down the importance of influences from outside. As perceived
here, therefore, the appropriations from other cultures furnished part of the
framework for the renaissance but were as much a result as an explanation of
its development. Differently stated, the renaissance made use of content
drawn from other cultures, but the central source of its energy lay within Latin
Christian culture. The key question for scholars, then, is not to show the existence of external elements but to explain the host culture's receptivity to them.

Rather than asking, as we did, whether the sources of the renaissance came from inside or outside the Latin Christian tradition, therefore, we might have asked a harder question: why was the twelfth century receptive to elements that had existed previously without, apparently, exercising much influence?

In 1927, Haskins presented a vision of a profoundly secular renaissance. It is difficult to say at this distance whether secularity reflected simply his style and interests or whether it seemed to him axiomatic as the recognition-mark of a renaissance. Both reasons may well apply. But the planners of the conference consciously departed from this approach and sought to integrate religious thought into the framework of the inquiry. Some of the studies in this volume, to be sure, examine the twelfth century's secularity and find elements of tension between classicism and traditional religion. At least one author stresses the progressive blurring between the secular and supernatural spheres and between this world and the next. Other authors, however, emphasize the vitality of religious life and ideals and note the ways in which the traditions of religious reform shaped and expressed ideas and ideals that indisputably belonged to the renaissance. Moreover, the twelfth century's sense of religious renewal—aspects of which can be traced back to the turn of the millennium—presupposed the consciousness of living in a new age, a *novus ordo saeculorum*. In this respect, religious thinkers echoed—or were the first to state—themes which one finds in literature, politics, and the arts, and which give new or heightened intelligibility to the twelfth-century renaissance. They contributed to the growing sense of individualism, or of individuation, both of people and of groups, which was founded on an examination of the inner life and an awareness of self; they contributed also to the emerging doctrine of the dignity of man, based far more on religious than on secular sources and attitudes. The concepts of experience, conscience, and virtue were the discoveries of the twelfth-century renaissance no less than of the later Italian Renaissance.

Several authors in this volume are inclined to stress rationalization more than secularization as a characteristic of the age. The distinction between theory and practice, the search for a rational order of society, and the emphasis on law rather than sacral authority as the basis of legitimate power were all aspects of this shift, as was the ever-growing effort to organize, clarify, and make accessible the heritage of both religious and secular thought.

Classicism inevitably plays a central role among the themes discussed in this volume. Architecture and the representational arts, various aspects of Latin writing, and the influence of ancient Rome on law and political thought come immediately to mind. In this respect, however, almost everyone at the conference expected a different interpretation of the twelfth century from that of Haskins, who in a revealing aside once referred to the twelfth-century cultural movement as "the Latin Renaissance."[4] This thematic limitation of his book was to a great extent self-imposed, accepted as a necessity rather than presented as implying a comprehensive account of twelfth-century culture,[5] since

[4]*Ren* 15.
[5]See the passage quoted below, at n. 18.

Haskins was fully aware that the renaissance encompassed much more than Latin culture and that its broad creative energy expressed itself through more than classicism. But he articulated a profound conviction, a controlling assumption, when he wrote: "From the fall of the Roman Empire down well into modern times the Latin classics furnished the best barometer of the culture of each period in Western Europe."[6] Behind this view lay a long tradition of historical thought, going back to the fifteenth century and culminating in Jacob Burckhardt's *Civilization of the Renaissance in Italy*, published in 1860, only a few years before Haskins was born. For Burckhardt, secularity and classicism were not only the twin *Leitmotiven* of the Italian Renaissance but also the liberating forces which made it possible. Without abandoning his view of twelfth-century culture as distinctively medieval, Haskins conceived his *Renaissance* at a time when one could not, in considering the idea of—and thereby the criteria for—a "renaissance," fully escape Burckhardt's overwhelming and ubiquitous influence.

Scholars in the 1930s and 1940s began to formulate more complex views of the place of Antiquity in medieval thought and feeling. Erwin Panofsky in particular challenged Haskins's interpretation of the twelfth-century renaissance by comparing the culture of the twelfth century with those of the earlier Carolingian and later Italian renaissances in terms of their attitudes toward Antiquity.[7] He argued three essential points. First, during the two earlier renaissances (or renascences, as he preferred to call them), works of art and literature tended to separate classical form and classical content.[8] Second, the medieval renaissances appropriated the bits and pieces—one might say *spolia*—of Antiquity but did not put them together. Third and perhaps most important, the principal distinction between the two medieval and the Italian renaissances lay in their differing sense of history: the fifteenth century, unlike the ninth and twelfth centuries, began to perceive the discontinuity of history, a cultural gap between Antiquity and the present. In the Middle Ages,

---

[6]*Ren* 93. One should note in this regard a tension implicit in Haskins's view. He states that twelfth-century culture, like the Italian Renaissance, "drew its life from two principal sources," one of them Latin, the other "an influx of new learning and literature from the East"; for the twelfth century, this Eastern infusion was Arabic as well as Greek (*Ren* 278). Similarly, the book falls naturally into two parts. Classicism constitutes an important strand in the first three chapters, which portray the historical background and setting of the movement, and is central to the next five chapters (chs. 4–8), which concern the main Latin literary genres in the twelfth century. The second part of the book, however, has little to do with classicism as he conceived it earlier, for the four final chapters, breaking sharply with the earlier themes, deal with the transmission of Greek and Arabic works (ch. 9), science (ch. 10), philosophy (ch. 11), and the nascent universities (ch.12). These topics constitute to some extent a catalogue of Haskins's research interests, which are naturally reflected in the overall structure of his book.

[7]He first presented his interpretation in an article, "Renaissance and Renascences," *The Kenyon Review* 6 (1944) 201–36, and reworked it on a much larger scale in *Renaissance and Renascences in Western Art* (Stockholm 1960) esp. chs. 1–2. Throughout these works he uses the term "renascences" for the two earlier cultural movements, thus emphasizing his sharp distinction between these and the Italian Renaissance.

[8]For example, a medieval sculptor might use a bust of Antoninus Pius as a model—but his statue represented St Peter, rather than an ancient Roman emperor (*Ren & Ren* 62–63).

Panofsky wrote, "The classical world was not approached historically but pragmatically, as something far off yet, in a sense, still alive and, therefore, at once potentially useful and potentially dangerous."[9] This statement, by suggesting the intricacy and ambivalence of the medieval attitude toward classical culture, as well as toward its uses, goes beyond Haskins and beyond the observation—significant as it is—that Antiquity was not only admired and imitated but also, for religious reasons, feared and condemned by some people in the twelfth century.

These points have been taken into consideration, at least implicitly, by many authors in the present volume. There is general agreement with Panofsky's first two points, though the imitation of classical style was in some areas, of both literature and art, so extensive that it became almost indistinguishable from content: some products of the twelfth century have been confused with those of Antiquity. On the question of the sense of cultural distance between Antiquity and the present, however, there is less agreement. A few authors have indeed noted the first appearance in the twelfth century precisely of the idea of historical discontinuity that Panofsky associated with the Italian Renaissance. Thinkers in the late eleventh and twelfth centuries began to perceive a break between Antiquity and "modernity" (or, as we would say, between ancient and medieval) and to feel a distance not only between themselves and Antiquity but also between the more recent past and the present.

In many of these essays, what marked the twelfth-century renaissance most distinctively was the consciousness of its position in history, its sense of time and of times, of change and innovation. As early as the turn of the millennium, religious reformers felt that a new day of quickened spirituality was dawning. This sense of a new age became widespread during the twelfth century, reflecting an awareness and acceptance of innovation in literature and the arts, in politics and society as well as in religion. It is emblematic of this new attitude that in the 1140s the commune of Rome officially inaugurated a new era and dated its documents by the years of this new age. In the eleventh and twelfth centuries the emerging idea of the crusade accompanied and occasioned a change in the status of the warrior from soldier to Christian knight to *chevalier*, and a heightened consciousness of such changes. *"In our time,"* wrote Guibert of Nogent, "God has instituted holy warfare so that the knightly order . . . should find a new way of deserving salvation." Bernard of Clairvaux in his treatise *In Praise of the New Army* rejoiced at the appearance of a new type of *milites Christi* in the form of the Knights Templar, and a generation later Chrétien de Troyes echoed these ideas in his statement that chivalry, after residing first in Greece and then in Rome, had finally settled in France.

Three further points concerning twelfth-century classicism emerge in this volume. First, since it was complex and diverse, it is only inadequately de-

[9]*Ren & Ren* 110–11. The same point was made, almost verbatim, in the earlier article (226).

scribed under such broad rubrics as admiration or rejection. Second, when it contemplated Antiquity, the twelfth century thought more commonly of Christian than of pagan Rome, and found its principal source and model in the civilization of the Christian Roman Empire from Constantine to Justinian. And third, the appropriation of Antiquity is only one among several central concerns in this volume. It is not accepted as "the best barometer" of culture in general or as the sole criterion for declaring the twelfth century a renaissance.

Reflecting this broadened sense of historical change, our volume includes a wider range of activities than are found in Haskins's *Renaissance*, and pays more attention to society and institutions and to the people by and for whom art and literature were created. Haskins was interested in schools, devoting a chapter of his book and also a smaller book to *The Rise of Universities*, but he paid relatively little attention to the society in which they developed or the social needs they served. Here, several authors examine the interaction between schools and society, which increasingly needed trained lawyers and rhetoricians and depended upon the skills acquired in the new universities. They study new types of patrons and consumers of culture as well as new and self-conscious kinds of producers, stressing the constant relation between what one author calls the material infrastructure of socioeconomic changes and the superstructure of cultural developments.

As the geographical locale of the renaissance, Haskins assigned the preponderant role to northern France, but recognized the considerable Italian contribution: "If Italy was the cradle of law and medicine, France was in this age superior in the liberal arts, and preeminent in philosophy, theology, and Latin poetry, not to mention the vernacular verse."[10] Today, however, the inclusion of topics omitted by Haskins—the arts, vernacular literature, political thought, and so forth—has enlarged as well as complicated the picture of the renaissance. Scholars would still maintain that the principal setting lay in the Francophone lands and in Italy—but they would quickly note that twelfth-century England's role almost equaled France's, and that in southern Italy, Sicily, and the Holy Land, as well as in England, the governing class spoke French.[11]

The authors in this work thus do not find the particular activities associated with the renaissance uniformly diffused throughout different parts of Europe. Classical models, for example, clearly influenced painting and sculpture south of the Alps more than north. In law and political thought as well as in some facets of the arts, furthermore, the *renovatio* of ancient Rome—whether or not it sprang from Rome itself—exerted a much greater

[10]*Ren* 24.

[11]On the crusades and the renaissance, Haskins claimed that "the two movements scarcely touch" (*Ren* 15). The Latin civilization of Outremer, however, though discussed by few authors in this volume, must be seen as a modification of the French culture that contributed so much to the renaissance. The historical writing, feudal law, and arts of Outremer in particular deserve further study.

appeal in Italy than elsewhere. The authors also disagree among themselves on the role of Rome in the twelfth-century renaissance. Some see it as a source of creative vitality in the thought and politics as well as in the art and architecture of the late eleventh and twelfth centuries. It can also be viewed, however, as a passive repository of an antique heritage from which artists, writers, and men of action coming from other parts of Europe, and inspired by contemporary concerns, drew in their own interests. The real contribution of Italy to the renaissance, however, like that of Sicily and further-flung parts of Latin Christendom, such as Spain and Hungary, remains something of an enigma.[12]

In historical thought, when one identifies a century with a movement, the boundaries of the century (like those of any historical period) must be seen as flexible and relative. The century becomes, as it were, a movable feast. In practice, this means that in reflecting on a discrete historical period, historians rarely treat the periodic century as identical with the chronological century. Viewed as a renaissance, the twelfth century confirms this familiar observation, and Haskins, with his usual acumen, fully grasped the problem:

By 1200 the mediaeval renaissance is well advanced, by 1250 its work is largely done. In a phrase like 'the renaissance of the twelfth century,' the word 'century' must be used very loosely so as to cover not only the twelfth century proper but the years which immediately precede and follow, yet with sufficient emphasis on the central period to indicate the outstanding characteristics of its civilization. For the movement as a whole we must really go back fifty years or more and forward almost as far.[13]

On several of these points, and especially the extension of the renaissance forward into the thirteenth century, the contributors to this volume disagree with Haskins—and their consensus is a source of surprise. The essays concentrate overwhelmingly on the period extending from the last third of the eleventh century through the second third of the twelfth.

By their self-imposed chronological limits, the authors imply that the renaissance was mainly bracketed in the century from the 1060s or 1070s to about the 1160s and that the *early* twelfth century was its center of gravity.[14] This in turn suggests two important propositions, both of which merit further study. First, although most of the authors could, by beginning their accounts in the eleventh century, simply be following Haskins's mandate to push the inquiry ''back into the eleventh century, that obscure period of origins which holds the secret of the new movement,''[15] deeper reasons may well underlie

[12]Since the humanism of the Italian Renaissance owed more to the rhetorical writing of the twelfth and thirteenth centuries than to the humanism of twelfth-century France, we shall grasp the relation between the twelfth- and fifteenth-century renaissances more fully only when the early Italian rhetorical tradition has been studied in sharper detail. This is another reason for regretting that there is no study of *dictamen* or of rhetoric in general in this volume (see n. 1 above).

[13]*Ren* 10.

[14]Among the notable exceptions to this generalization are the contributions of John Baldwin, who concentrates on the late twelfth and early thirteenth centuries, and of Richard and Mary Rouse, whose analysis points toward the thirteenth century rather than looks backward—like most of the essays—to the eleventh. The articles on law, while starting in the eleventh century, also tend to carry the story through the twelfth and into the thirteenth century.

[15]*Ren* 16.

their choice of chronological limits. The great ecclesiastical reform of the eleventh century—also, one suspects, the accompanying political struggles—played a larger role in the origins of our renaissance than we had anticipated, probably even larger than any of these essays has indicated. For surprisingly, the connections between the religious and ecclesiastical developments on the one hand, and on the other, the social and cultural developments, remain largely unexplored. Second, for reasons and in ways that are also not entirely clear, the phenomena which scholars identify collectively as the twelfth-century renaissance began to recede during the third quarter of the century, and their supersession appears to mark the beginning of a new period in cultural history—a period dominated by universities, high scholasticism, developed Gothic styles, and so forth. Some central aspects of this new period, most notably philosophy and science, had made their first great progress during the earlier twelfth century. Haskins remarked that

the force of the new humanism is largely spent before the twelfth century is over. The new science, on the other hand, . . . goes on into the thirteenth century in unbroken continuity. . . . The philosophical revival which starts in the twelfth century has its culmination in the thirteenth.[16]

Though concurring with much of what Haskins said here, one might question his assertion of an "unbroken continuity" in the history of philosophy and science. Beginning in the third quarter of the twelfth century, new directions were being charted there too.

It can be argued for the twelfth century, perhaps for other periods and even other civilizations, that a coherent account of any particular development, whether in the arts, literature, society, or other human activities, must take into consideration many other aspects, and that one cannot adequately describe any important expression of this culture without crossing disciplinary boundaries. To explain the genesis of early Gothic at St Denis, for example, one must deal with revivals in the theological tradition, with monasticism, popular piety, and royal politics, as well as with the survival and transformations of the late Roman basilica.[17] These propositions are corollaries of the more general assumption that a culture like that of the twelfth century is a seamless tunic, an indivisible unity. For this interlocking of the component parts, the static metaphor of a mosaic is inadequate: one will prefer the

---

[16]*Ren* 10.

[17]It is important to recall here that in the nineteenth century the idea of renaissance took a new shape in close connection with the study of the history of art, which oriented scholars to approach the problem primarily in terms of classicism and classical influence. The studies of the arts in this volume, like Panofsky's work, concentrate on the ways in which the twelfth century appropriated, or failed to appropriate, the legacy of Antiquity. Taken as a whole, however, St Denis—like much of twelfth-century architecture—owed little or nothing directly to Antiquity, and is therefore rarely mentioned in these pages. St Denis and early Gothic in general could find an accepted place in the renaissance only if nonclassical elements were successfully integrated into an interpretation of the twelfth-century arts. The point is also illustrated by the minor arts at St Denis, to which more attention might have been paid here. The reworking by abbot Suger's craftsmen of ancient works of art into distinctively medieval forms constitutes an interesting chapter in the use of Antiquity during the twelfth century.

dynamic analogy of a mobile, in which the movement of any part shifts all of the others.

These reflections point back toward the still intractable problem of defining *renaissance*, which no author in this volume attempts in relation to the full diversity of twelfth-century culture. Some writers see significant, though unspecified, links between the changes in artistic and literary production and those in other forms of activity, but these links remain principally within the framework of classicism. A few authors have, on the contrary, questioned the assumption of unity and interconnection and suggested that the development in their fields, though perhaps parallel with that in others, should be seen as distinct. Some of the changes in art and architecture, for example, may have resulted from purely technical problems unique to those genres and not from any broad spirit of revival or rebirth. It is therefore impossible to discern among these twenty-six papers a single conception of renaissance which might serve as a common denominator underlying the various approaches to the many topics treated. Only the most broadly framed statement can hope to suggest the unities underlying this diversity. We do not mean to imply by this that all new and important aspects of twelfth-century life properly belong to the renaissance. Throughout much of Europe, as every historian knows, the twelfth century witnessed monumental achievements in state-building, but this dramatic story pertains directly to the renaissance only insofar as princes fostered and exploited, limited and channeled the development of culture, or as culture constituted a mirror of politics.

What, then, was the twelfth-century renaissance? Quite simply, all that was new and vital in the culture of the age, and all that drew its inspiration, at least in part, from a desire to restore or return to a lost or buried past. We have signaled in this Introduction our conviction that classicism furnished many strands but not the entire fabric of the renaissance, which drew on a wide diversity of sources. In an important passage (not, to be sure, in full accord with his statements at other points), Haskins concurred. Since this volume commemorates his vision and imagination, we may conclude by invoking his name once again and by quoting this passage with enthusiastic agreement:

If we keep our eyes too close to the Latin and especially to the more classical types of Latin, we are in danger of viewing the age as one of a mere revival of learning and not a renaissance. . . . [But] it was also an age of new creation in literature and art beyond the mere imitation of ancient models. The . . . Latin phase of the movement . . . was only a part of something much larger. The analogy of the Italian Renaissance is again suggestive, a revival of ancient learning and also of ancient art, but still more an age of new life and new knowledge which carry us well beyond the ancients.[18]

Because so many elements of that culture interlock, we must regard the renaissance as the totality of that culture: its restless searching after ancient—and new—authorities, and its audacious criticism of authority; its tireless quest for new knowledge, and its insistence on restructuring knowledge new and old alike; its astonishing creativity in the arts and literature; its pro-

[18]*Ren* 190.

foundly innovative spirituality, balanced in part by its occasional secularity, sometimes earnest and sometimes laughing; its sense of renewal, reform, rebirth; its freshly positive assessment of nature, man, and the world; its heightened consciousness of the self and of society, of past and future; overall, its energy, and the general quickening of life.

It is no criticism of Haskins to say that his *Renaissance of the Twelfth Century* could not do full justice to the endless interest of this age. Even our volume, though more than twice the length of his, cannot treat all aspects of its culture. These observations simply recognize that readers and scholars in the future will correct and supplement what this volume has contributed, as the authors here have tried to supplement Haskins. For it is unlikely that the twelfth century—which in so many senses constitutes the beginning of the modern world—will cease to fascinate future students. Though we can guess at a few of the ways in which they will alter our portrait of the age, we should not try to anticipate here the agenda for a centennial conference on Haskins's *Renaissance*.

ROBERT L. BENSON   GILES CONSTABLE
Los Angeles   Washington, D.C.

October 1981

RENAISSANCE AND RENEWAL
IN
THE TWELFTH CENTURY

Terms and Ideas of Renewal

Gerhart B. Ladner

What place did the renaissance of the twelfth century occupy in the midst of almost continuous waves of renewal movements in the West? The principal forms of renewal, as I perceive them, are four: first, *restoration*—often in the sense of imperial renovation, for instance in Carolingian and Ottonian times; second, *reform*—as a continuation of spiritual regeneration by baptism, including both personal and ecclesiastical renewal, as in the Gregorian Church Reform; third, *rebellion*—a concept developed in imperial Rome to characterize the disturbers of the *pax Romana* and later transferred to revolutionary trends in the High and Late Middle Ages; and finally, *renascence*—rooted above all in the renewal of natural life, and related to cosmological reintegration.

Though it had been vaguely anticipated in 1840 by Ampère[1] and in 1873 by Walter Pater,[2] Haskins did coin the term "renaissance of the twelfth century." Yet he did not clearly distinguish "renaissance" from other terms and concepts of renewal. So, for instance, he says that the Carolingian renaissance "was a revival rather than a new birth"[3]—thus implicitly, and as we shall see with very good reason, attributing to the concept of "new birth" more importance in the twelfth century than in the ninth. But often he speaks of the twelfth-century renaissance simply as a revival, without trying to differentiate its newness from other forms and phases of renewal.[4]

Is there a way to transcend such indefiniteness? I believe there is: it is the relatively obvious, though likewise problematic, method of founding the study of renewal on contemporary formulations of renewal ideas rather than on our own. To use contemporary terms as guides to the history of ideas is not an infallible method; above all, it is not always sufficient. For not only words and ideas, but also nonverbalized, nonconceptualized actions, attitudes, and in-

---

[1]Jean-Jacques Ampère, *Histoire littéraire de la France avant le douzième siècle* (3 vols. Paris 1839–40) 3.457: "Le mouvement intellectuel qui se fait sentir en France vers la fin du XIe siècle offre tous les charactères d'une véritable renaissance. . . ."

[2]Walter Pater, *The Renaissance* (London 1925) 1–3.

[3]Haskins, *Ren* 17.

[4]This ambiguousness has been noted also by Norman Kretzmann in his essay in this volume.

fluences, which we can know only indirectly if at all, may have produced events which constitute a renewal. Lynn White's pithy statement, "world views are better judged by what people do than by what they say,"[5] certainly has truth in it. Nevertheless, to explore contemporary consciousness of renewal through its verbal and perhaps also its pictorial expressions, this I believe is a valid method which may be helpful for an *aggiornamento* of Haskins's epochal work. Of course, one must be careful not to cling too narrowly to individual terms: one should never see them in isolation but always in their context.

I have previously investigated the terminology and ideology of renascence encountered in the so-called Theodosian renaissance[6] and in the Italian Renaissance.[7] We find in both cases a prevalence of metaphors taken from the spontaneous processes of natural life such as birth and rebirth, growth and regrowth, flowering, spring, youth, warmth, light, indeed all of life itself. This is a quasi-"biological" or (to use a historically more appropriate Latinizing term) "vitalistic" imagery,[8] which may include cosmological elements.

To what extent does such a characterization of Renaissance ideology apply also to the renaissance of the twelfth century? To answer this question, it is necessary to compare—however briefly—the ideology of the twelfth-century renaissance with that of the so-called Carolingian and Ottonian renaissances on the one hand and on the other with that of the Gregorian Reform. Let us turn first to the latter, for taken in its wider sense it not only directly preceded, but also overlapped the beginnings of the twelfth-century renaissance.

Three significant texts concern a key figure of the Gregorian Reform, Lanfranc of Canterbury, and his role in the beginning cultural renewal of the age. One is found in the *Life* of Lanfranc by Milo Crispin of Bec; the biographer has personified *Latinitas* and has made her recognize this great man, Lanfranc, as her supreme master, who for her benefit had restored learning to its ancient state.[9] A second and earlier text is from Guitmund of Aversa's treatise on the eucharistic sacrament; the formulation is significantly different from the preceding text, for God is said to have made the liberal arts gain new warmth (*recalescere*) and excel in new life (*optime reviviscere*) through the most learned

⁵Lynn White, jr., "World View and Technology in the European Middle Ages," *World Views: Their Nature and Their Role in Culture*, Wenner-Gren Foundation for Anthropological Research, Symposium no. 41, Burg Wartenstein, August 2–August 11, 1968, 1.

⁶See my book *The Idea of Reform: Its Impact on Christian Thought and Action in the Age of the Fathers* (Cambridge Mass. 1959) 17–20.

⁷See my article "Vegetation Symbolism and the Concept of Renaissance," *De artibus opuscula XL: Essays in Honor of Erwin Panofsky*, ed. Millard Meiss (2 vols. New York 1961) 1.303–22.

⁸For such key concepts as *motus vitalis, vis*, and *virtus vitalis* in the fourth, ninth, and twelfth centuries, see below at n. 53.

⁹Milo Crispin of Bec, *Vita beati Lanfranci*, PL 150.29B: "Fuit quidam vir magnus, Italia ortus, quem Latinitas, in antiquum scientiae statum ab eo restituta tota, supremum debito cum amore et honore agnoscit magistrum, nomine Lanfrancus."

Lanfranc.[10] In the first case the context is that of reform to a supposedly better condition of the past; though the term *reformare* itself is not used, there is an implicit parallel between the restitution of the *status antiquus* of learning and the reform of the Church to its *forma primitiva*, an aspiration often expressed in writings of the Hildebrandine age.[11] In the second case, the process of renewal, though caused primarily by God, and secondarily by Lanfranc, is more spontaneous; it is not so much a reform as a rekindling, a revival of intellectual activity, something that comes closer to the concept of renascence.

This second text dates from the 1070s or 1080s, whereas the first belongs to the late 1130s. This means, not surprisingly, that reform ideology of the Gregorian type once formulated continued to be used, but it also means that renewal terms with renaissance overtones had been present in the Gregorian reform movement even in its early stages. This can likewise be seen from a third text concerning Lanfranc, in which Godfrey of Winchester writes of him at the end of the eleventh century, "Per te florentes artes valuere Latinae."[12] As a further example of a similar kind I mention the occurrence of the term *reflorere* in the language of St Peter Damiani.[13] Yet the reflourishing of which he speaks is always one of the Christian religion, and especially of the *disciplina* of the Church.[14] We shall soon see that the orientation of twelfth-century renaissance terminology and ideology continued in the line of Guitmund of Aversa rather than in that of Peter Damiani; even the language of religious renewal was to change to some extent.

A few remarks must suffice for the so-called Carolingian and Ottonian renaissances. In the Carolingian age renaissance ideology of a vitalistic and cosmological kind had formed enclaves, as it were, within a movement centered in the ideas of Christian personal reform and Roman imperial restoration. The most convincing example of a renaissance spirit is found in the verses of one of the younger poets at Charlemagne's court, Modoin (Muaduuinus), nicknamed Naso (Ovid), later bishop of Autun, in the oft-quoted line, "Golden Rome renewed is once more reborn to the world" (*Aurea Roma iterum renovata renascitur orbi*).[15]

---

[10]Guitmund of Aversa, *De corporis et sanguinis Christi veritate in eucharistia*, PL 149.1428B–C: ". . . cumque per ipsum D. Lanfrancum virum aeque doctissimum liberales artes Deus recalescere atque optime reviviscere fecisset."

[11]See, for instance, Giovanni Miccoli, *Chiesa gregoriana: Ricerche sulla riforma del secolo XI*, Storici antichi e moderni n.s. 17 (Florence 1966).

[12]Godfrey of Winchester, *Epigrammata historica*, ed. Thomas Wright, *The Anglo-Latin Satirical Poets and Epigrammatists of the Twelfth Century*, RS 59 (2 vols. London 1872) 2.150.

[13]See Hans Peter Laqua, "'Refloreat disciplina': Ein Erneuerungsmotiv bei Petrus Damiani," *San Pier Damiano: Nel centenario della morte (1072–1972)* (3 vols. Cesena 1972–73) 2.279–90; idem, *Traditionen und Leitbilder bei dem Ravennater Reformer Petrus Damiani, 1042–1052* (Munich 1976) 276.

[14]See Peter Damiani, *Epist.* 1.1, PL 144.205; *Disceptatio synodalis*, ed. L. von Heinemann, MGH LdL 1.94; *Epist.* 7.3, PL 144.441C. Professor Constable's essay in this volume gives many telling examples of religious vegetative symbolism of renewal, which point in the same direction.

[15]Nasonis (Muaduuini) *Ecloga* 1.27, ed. Ernst Duemmler, MGH Poetae 1.385.

In the Ottonian age, the Roman ideology of restorative renovation played, as is well known, a great role in the Empire and the Church,[16] with a strong admixture of ideas of reform—whereas I do not know of any explicit terms and concepts of rebirth. Nevertheless, the tenth and early eleventh centuries anticipated one of the most characteristic phenomena of the twelfth-century renaissance, its love poetry. One of the Cambridge Songs, the one beginning "A gentle west wind rises up," *Levis exsurgit zephirus*, is full of that vernal imagery which was later to serve as a favorite and characteristic expression of the consciousness of natural renewal.[17] Yet it is perhaps significant that the author of *Levis exsurgit zephirus* does not sing of the happiness and pleasure of love: the speaker, a woman,[18] contrasts her sad state of mind with the peaceful life of the animals in spring, with the joyful songs of the birds among the blossoming trees. She sees the beauty of spring with her eyes and hears it with her ears, but in the midst of it all she can only sigh, and she soon pales with sorrow; when she lifts up her head she no longer hears, no longer sees.[19]

The Cambridge Songs as a whole and, so far as I know, other contemporary poems contain little of the joyful tone achieved by so many twelfth-century songs of love and spring which have come down to us in the *Carmina Burana*[20] and in the corpus of troubadour poetry. The difference becomes clear if one compares the topos of seeing and hearing, as used in *Levis exsurgit*

---

[16]See the famous book by Percy Ernst Schramm, *Kaiser, Rom und Renovatio (KRR)*.

[17]*Die Cambridger Lieder*, ed. Karl Strecker, MGH (Berlin 1926) 95 no. 40 stanza 2, for instance:

> Ver purpuratum exiit,   ornatus suos induit,
> aspergit terram floribus,   ligna silvarum frondibus.

[18]I am very grateful to Professor Herbert Bloch for preventing me from overlooking that it is a woman who speaks. Whether she and the author are one is a separate problem.

[19]Strecker (n. 17 above) 95 no. 40 stanzas 3–5:

> Struunt lustra quadrupedes   et dulces nidos volucres,
> inter ligna florentia   sua decantant gaudia.

> Quod oculis dum video   et auribus dum audio,
> heu pro tantis gaudiis   tantis inflor suspiriis.

> Cum mihi sola sedeo   et hec revolvens palleo,
> si forte capud sublevo,   nec audio nec video.

[20]Most of the love songs in the *Carmina Burana* and in other collections of poems of the period are at the same time "vitalistic" celebrations of nature in spring. Among the many examples, I mention *Carmina Burana*, ed. Alfons Hilka, Otto Schumann, and Bernhard Bischoff (1 vol. in 3 pts. Heidelberg 1930–70) no. 74, "Letabundus rediit avium concentus" (1.2.46–47), no. 136, "Omnia sol temperat" (1.2.229), and no. 179, "Tempus est iocundum O virgines" (1.2.298–99); *Die Lieder Walters von Chatillon in der Handschrift 351 von St Omer*, ed. Karl Strecker (Berlin 1925) 33 no. 20, "Verna redit temperies," 41 no. 24, "Vetus error abiit, renovantur vetera," and 44 no. 26, "Anno revirente virentis est iuvente." A good nonpoetic example of the same feeling is the following text from Hugh of St Victor's *Didascalicon* 7.12, PL 176.821A–B: "Ecce tellus redimita floribus, quam iucundum spectaculum praebet, quomodo visum delectat, quomodo affectum provocat! Videmus rubentes rosas, candida lilia, purpureas violas. . . . Postremo super omne pulchrum viride, quomodo animos intuentium rapit, quando vere novo, nova quadam vita germina prodeunt . . . ad imaginem future resurrectionis."

zephirus, with its use in one of the oldest troubadour songs, William of Aquitaine's famous *Mout jauzenz me prenc en amar*, "Full of joy I begin to love."[21] There William calls his beloved the best any man could see or hear; no eyes could see, no mouth could speak of, a better one.[22] Probably both poets had in mind the image evoked by Matthew 13:13, "Seeing they see not and hearing they hear not," as well as Matthew 13:16, "But blessed are your eyes because they see and your ears because they hear." Yet in the case of the troubadour of around 1100, the negative aspect of the image has been completely absorbed by the positive, and his lines about seeing, hearing, and speaking almost directly precede three other lines which are, in their consciousness and assertion of vital renewal, among the earliest expressions of the spirit of the twelfth-century renaissance. William gives his reasons why he wants to keep his love for himself:

Per lo cor dedins refrescar	To refresh my heart in her
E per la carn renovellar	To renew my flesh in her
Que no puesca envellezir.	So that I shall never grow old.[23]

There is a deep and full tone of love—generally extramarital love—in many of the earlier troubadour songs, especially in the Albas or parting-at-dawn songs, with their refrains of painful separation.[24] One might think of it as love without benefit of clergy and religion, were it not that, for instance, an Arnaut Daniel says that he attends or offers a thousand masses for his success and happiness in this very kind of love,[25] and that a Giraut de Borneil prays to

---

[21]*Les Chansons de Guillaume IX, Duc d'Aquitaine (1071–1127)*, ed. Alfred Jeanroy (Paris 1913) 21–24 no. 9. Cf. Pierre Belperron, *La "joie d'amour": Contribution à l'étude des troubadours et de l'amour courtois* (Paris 1948) esp. 49–50; René Nelli, *L'érotique des troubadours* (Toulouse 1963) 85–87; Eugen Lerch, "Trobadorsprache und religiöse Sprache," *Cultura neolatina* 3 (1943) 214–30 at 216–19; Alexander J. Denomy, "*Jois* among the Early Troubadours: Its Meaning and Possible Source," *Mediaeval Studies* 13 (1951) 177–217; Raymond Gay-Crosier, *Religious Elements in the Secular Lyrics of the Troubadours* (Chapel Hill N.C. 1971) 51–53 § 3, "joy, joi < gaudium > "; Glynnis M. Cropp, *Le vocabulaire courtois des troubadours de l'époque classique* (Geneva 1975), and the review article by Jean-Charles Payen, CCM 21 (1978) 151–55 at 153. For the much debated question of the relationship between the content and form of the troubadour songs and Arabic poetry—as well as other sources of the troubadours—see the eminently reasonable remarks of Henri-Irénée Marrou, *Les troubadours* (2nd ed. Paris 1971) 114–71.

[22]Jeanroy (n. 21 above) ibid. lines 5–6, 31–32:

Quar mielhs onra·m, estiers cujar,
Qu'om puesca vezer ni auzir.
. . . .
Pus hom gensor no·n pot trobar
Ni huelhs vezer ni boca dir . . .

[23]Ibid. lines 34–36. Here, too, one can hear a biblical echo: Psalm 27:7 (Vulgate), "Et refloruit caro mea." Thus rightly Dimitri Scheludko, "Über die Theorien der Liebe bei den Trobadors," *Zeitschrift für romanische Philologie* 60 (1940) 191–234 at 197.

[24]See, for instance, Jonathan Saville, *The Medieval Erotic Alba* (New York and London 1972).

[25]See Arnaut's poem *En cest sonet coind'e leri*, beginning of stanza 3, ed. Joseph Anglade, *Anthologie des troubadours* (Paris 1927) 84: "Mil messas n'aug e'n proferi."

Christ for the same reasons.[26] This dialectic of human and divine love forms an important background of twelfth-century profane love poetry.[27]

With these texts, we have entered *in medias res*, into the renaissance of the twelfth century itself, and have encountered antinomies of life reflected in its ideology.

Few authors are as representative for the twelfth-century renaissance as Bernard Silvester, especially in his *De mundi universitate* or *Cosmographia*, the famous epic on the universe as macrocosm and man as microcosm. In our context, lines 35–36 of the first section of book 1 are particularly noteworthy: "Rursus et ecce cupit res antiquissima nasci / ortu Silva novo, circumscribique figuris," which may be translated, "and behold, matter, the oldest thing [in creation], wishes to be born again and in this new beginning to be encompassed in forms."[28] Here, then, we find expressed a wish for a new birth: *rursus nasci*, "renaissance." Yet this new birth is clearly part of the process of creation itself: chaotic unformed matter wishes to be born anew by receiving new forms. This whole conception is closely linked to the Platonic-Stoic-Hermetic, and to a lesser degree the Aristotelian-Arabic, strains in Bernard's world view.[29] This view envisages periodic renewals of the universe and of man: everything that exists in time was first born in eternity and will return to it, only to be born again: *ubi finiunt inde tempora renascuntur*, says Bernard.[30] The idea that such renewal consists of the bestowal of form on brute matter—in a sort of re-formation—is also of late ancient origin, both pagan and Christian.[31]

In Bernard Silvester's *Cosmographia* we find the term *reformare*, and even *reformare in melius*, several times; for instance, in the second section of book 1, the renewal of matter is explained as its reform and assimilation toward the eternal and divine ideas of created things.[32] In book 2, on man the

[26]Giraut de Borneil, *Aube*, stanzas 1 and 5, ibid. 81–82.

[27]See Peter Dronke, *Medieval Latin and the Rise of European Love-Lyric* (2nd ed. 2 vols. Oxford 1968) esp. 1.264–331.

[28]Instead of the old edition by Carl Sigmund Barach and Johann Wrobel (Innsbruck 1876; repr. Frankfurt 1964), see now Bernard Silvester, *Cosmographia*, Megacosmus 1.35–36, ed. Peter Dronke (Leiden 1978) 98; see also the translation by Winthrop Wetherbee, *The Cosmographia of Bernardus Silvestris*, Columbia University Records of Civilization 89 (New York 1973) 68.

[29]See the excellent and detailed analysis by Stock, *Myth and Science*, where earlier interpretations, especially those of Etienne Gilson, Ernst Robert Curtius, Theodore Silverstein, and Marie-Thérèse d'Alverny are also discussed. Cf. Gilson, "La cosmogonie de Bernardus Silvestris," AHDLMA 3 (1928) 5–24; Curtius 108–13; Silverstein, "The Fabulous Cosmogony of Bernardus Silvestris," *Modern Philology* 46 (1948) 92–116; d'Alverny, "Alain de Lille et la *Theologia*," *L'homme devant Dieu: Mélanges offerts au père Henri de Lubac*, Théologie 56–58 (3 vols. Paris 1964) 2.110–28 at 121 n. 39.

[30]*Cosmographia*, Megacosmus 4.11 (n. 28 above) 119.

[31]See Stock, *Myth and Science* 86 and passim; Ladner (n. 6 above) 167–73.

[32]*Cosmographia*, Megacosmus 2.8 (n. 28 above) 101: "Cumque quam fert Silva [= primitive matter] grossitiem elimatius expurgasset, [divine providence] ad eternas introspiciens nostiones [*sic*], germana et proximante similitudine rerum species reformavit." Cf. also the statement of *Noys* in Megacosmus 2.2 (99): "Usie [here another synonym for matter] pepigi, reformabitur in melius."

microcosm, Bernard again speaks of reform: just as the macrocosm, the microcosm must be re-formed from an inchoate state toward perfection, and such reformation can lead man, though mortal, to the realm of the divine.[33]

It is noteworthy that Bernard's renewal terminology in the *Cosmographia* leans at least as much toward *reformare* as toward *renasci*. This is due no doubt at least in part to the persistent strength and continued importance of the patristic and early medieval ideology of reform; but it must be emphasized that Bernard Silvester uses the term *reform*, too, in a cosmological and vitalistic context.

Alan of Lille, a generation or two later, was animated by an ethos of renewal directed toward reform of the world in his own times, but for the author of the *Cosmographia* reform, even the reform of man, occurs within the framework of the hexaemeral scheme of his epic of creation.[34] In fact, it is very remarkable that philosophers of nature and natural scientists of the twelfth century, such as Adelard of Bath and Herman of Carinthia—while they considered nature as an innovating force under God in generation and conservation[35]—do not seem to have designated their own time as an age of either rebirth or reform.

It is true that Adelard of Bath in his *Quaestiones naturales* energetically sets himself against those who do not trust their own reason but only the old authors.[36] This criticism implies at least a slight consciousness of newness of method.[37] Such consciousness may have been strong in St Anselm when he discovered his proof of the existence of God.[38] The writers in the arts of the

[33]Ibid. Microcosmus 12.55–58 (146):

> Humanumque genus, quamvis mortale trahatur
> Conditione sua,
> Tale reformandum, quod demigrare supernos
> Possit adusque deos.

Still in connection with cosmological renewal, Bernard calls Christ *reformantem secula nostra deum*, Megacosmus 3.246 (110).

[34]In this one respect, I cannot wholly share Stock's interpretation of the *Cosmographia*: see especially *Myth and Science* 236–37.

[35]See, for instance, Herman of Carinthia, *De essentiis*, ed. Manuel Alonso Alonso, Miscelánea Comillas 5 (Universidad Pontificia Comillas, Santander 1946) 63: "Est igitur . . . natura universe geniture proprietas sese propagandi et conservandi, quantum in ipsa est."

[36]In a passage edited and discussed by Haskins, *Science* 40 n. 99: "Quid enim aliud auctoritas est dicenda quam capistrum? . . . Non enim intelligunt ideo rationem singulis esse datam ut intra verum et falsum ea prima iudice discernant. . . . Amplius: ipsi qui auctores vocantur non aliunde primam fidem apud minores adepti sunt, nisi quia rationem secuti sunt quam quicunque nesciunt vel negligunt merito ceci habendi sunt."

[37]See also the prologue to the *Quaestiones naturales* in the more recent edition of Martin Müller, BGPTMA 31.2 (Münster 1934) 1, where Adelard complains: "Habet enim haec generatio ingenitum vitium, ut nihil, quod a modernis reperiatur, putet esse recipiendum. Unde fit, ut si quando inventum proprium publicare voluerim, personae id alienae imponens inquam: 'Quidam dixit non ego.'" Cf. furthermore the prologue, edited by Haskins, *Science* 191–93, to the Sicilian translation of Ptolemy's *Almagest*, which is attributed to Adelard by Franz Bliemetzrieder, *Adelhard von Bath* (Munich 1935) 154–262.

[38]*Proslogion*, prooemium, ed. F. S. Schmitt, *S. Anselmi Cantuariensis archiepiscopi opera omnia* (6 vols. Edinburgh 1946–61) 1.93: "in ipso cogitationum conflictu sic se obtulit quod

trivium, too, were aware of living in a new or modern phase of intellectual development,[39] although such terms as *logica nova* and *poetria nova* date from the thirteenth century.[40] For the twelfth century, the famous Chartrian topos of dwarfs who see farther because they stand on the shoulders of giants leads to a certain awareness of a modernity which is at the same time dependent on tradition.[41] Yet there were also ambivalent and unfavorable reactions—for example, John of Salisbury's bitter remarks in the *Metalogicon* about gratuitous fashionable innovations by ignorant and greedy young men, whom he called

---

desperaveram [i.e., of his simple proof of the existence of God], ut studiose cogitationem amplecterer . . .''; cf. also Eadmer, *Vita sancti Anselmi archiepiscopi Cantuariensis*, ed. and trans. Richard W. Southern (London 1962) 30: "Et ecce quadam nocte inter nocturnas vigilias Dei gratia illuxit in corde eius, et res patuit intellectui eius, immensoque gaudio et iubilatione replevit omnia intima eius.''

[39]See Marie-Dominique Chenu, "Notes de lexicographie philosophique médiévale: Antiqui, Moderni,'' *Revue des sciences philosophiques et théologiques* 17 (1928) 82–94; idem, *Nature* ch. 9, "Tradition and Progress'' (310–30); Walter Freund, *Modernus und andere Zeitbegriffe des Mittelalters* (Cologne 1957) 67–110; Wilfried Hartmann, " 'Modernus' und 'Antiquus': Zur Verbreitung und Bedeutung dieser Bezeichnungen in der wissenschaftlichen Literatur vom 9. bis zum 12. Jahrhundert,'' *Antiqui und Moderni: Traditionsbewusstsein und Fortschrittsbewusstsein im späten Mittelalter*, ed. Albert Zimmermann, Miscellanea mediaevalia 9 (Berlin and New York 1974) 21–39; Elisabeth Gössmann, *Antiqui und Moderni im Mittelalter: Eine geschichtliche Standortbestimmung*, Veröffentlichungen des Grabmann-Institutes zur Erforschung der mittelalterlichen Theologie und Philosophie n.s. 23 (Munich 1974) 63–101, and the important review of this book by Juliusz Domański in CCM 21 (1978) 174–83; Beryl Smalley, "Ecclesiastical Attitudes to Novelty c. 1100–c. 1250,'' *Church, Society, and Politics*, ed. Derek Baker, Studies in Church History 12 (Oxford 1975) 113–31.

[40]For *logica nova et vetus* see Carl von Prantl, *Geschichte der Logik im Abendlande* (4 vols. Leipzig 1855–70) 3.4 and 25–26; Martin Grabmann, *Die Geschichte der scholastischen Methode* (2 vols. Freiburg 1909–11; repr. Berlin 1956) 2.78 and 443; L. M. de Rijk, *Logica Modernorum: A Contribution to the History of Early Terminist Logic* (2 vols. in 3 Assen 1962–67) 1.14. The term *logica modernorum* does not seem to occur before the fourteenth century; see Neal Ward Gilbert, "Ockham, Wyclif, and the 'Via Moderna,' '' *Antiqui und Moderni* (n. 39 above) 111–15. For the *Poetria nova* of Geoffrey of Vinsauf (ca. 1208–13), see Faral, *Les arts poétiques* 27–33 and 194–262. See also Matthew of Vendôme, *Ars versificatoria* (ca. 1175) 4.5, ibid. 181: "Vetera enim cessavere novis supervenientibus.''

[41]See John of Salisbury, *Metalogicon* 3.4, ed. Clement C. J. Webb (Oxford 1929) 136: "Dicebat Bernardus Carnotensis nos esse quasi nanos gigantium humeris insidentes, ut possimus plura eis et remotiora videre, non utique proprii visus acumine aut eminentia corporis, sed quia in altum subvehimur et extollimur magnitudine gigantea.'' William of Conches was perhaps the first to make use of Bernard's simile of dwarfs and giants (which occurs also in several later authors of the twelfth century). He connected it with Priscian's saying about grammarians in the dedicatory letter of the *Institutiones grammaticae*, ed. M. Hertz in *Grammatici latini*, ed. Heinrich Keil (7 vols. Leipzig 1855–70) 2.1: *quanto sunt iuniores, tanto perspicaciores*; see Edouard Jeauneau, "Deux rédactions des gloses de Guillaume de Conches sur Priscien,'' *Lectio* 335–70 at 358 (= RTAM 27 [1960] 212–47 at 235): "Non dicit doctiores, sed perspicaciores. Non enim plura scimus quam antiqui, sed plura perspicimus. Habemus enim illorum scripta et, preter hoc, naturale ingenium quo aliquid novi perspicimus. Sumus enim nani super humeros gigantum, ex alterius qualitate multum, ex nostra parum perspicientes.'' (Jeauneau also prints another, longer version of the gloss.) Here too, then, ''modernity'' is indebted to ''antiquity'' and consists largely in its transmission to the contemporaries. However, there is at least one text of the period—drawn to my attention by Giles Constable—in which the topos of the *gigantes* and *nani* is combined with metaphors of the death and revival of learning; see Peter of Blois, *Epist.* 92, PL 207.290A–B: "Nos, quasi nani super gigantum humeros sumus, quorum beneficio longius, quam ipsi, speculamur, dum antiquorum tractatibus inhaerentes elegantiores eorum sententias, quas vetustas aboleverat, hominumve neglectus, quasi iam mortuas in quamdam novitatem essentiae

Cornificians.[42] A consciousness of newness is not necessarily the same as assertion of a renaissance.[43]

This, I think, is a point of great importance for understanding the relationship of the twelfth century to classical and Christian Antiquity. One need not waste many words to recall the greatly increased receptivity of the late eleventh and twelfth centuries toward the ancients in many diverse fields of human endeavor, from literature to law and from philosophy and science to art; I mention only the strongly classicizing poets of the turn of the century—Godfrey of Reims,[44] Marbod of Rennes,[45] Wido of Ivrea,[46] Baudri of Bourgueil,[47] Hildebert of Lavardin,[48] and Ralph Tortarius.[49] Yet how far was all this seen and felt as a *rebirth* of Antiquity? Certainly in the late eleventh and twelfth centuries the *antiqui*, whether long known or recently rediscovered, were often thought of as still alive rather than as reborn. Only in the fifteenth and sixteenth centuries was *antiquitas* consistently seen as reborn or regrown;[50] not before the seventeenth century, incidentally, was any serious attempt made to disparage or deny the ancients, as the moderns of the *Querelle des anciens et modernes* then tried to do.[51] In the twelfth century—though the

---

suscitamus." For these topoi of Priscian and Bernard of Chartres—*juniores/perspicaciores* and *nani/gigantes*—see also Edouard Jeauneau, "'*Nani gigantum humeris insidentes*': Essai d'interprétation de Bernard de Chartres," *Vivarium* 5 (1967) 79–99 and "Nains et géants," *Entretiens* 21–38, where the considerable literature on the subject is cited; Richard W. Hunt, "Studies on Priscian in the Eleventh and Twelfth Centuries," M&RS 1 (1943) 194–231 and 2 (1950) 1–56; and A. G. Molland, "Medieval Ideas of Scientific Progress," *Journal of the History of Ideas* 39 (1978) 561–77.

[42]*Metalogicon* 1.3 (n. 41 above) 11–12: "spretis his que a doctoribus suis audierant, cuderent et conderent novas sectas. . . . Ecce nova fiebant omnia: innovabatur gramatica, immutabatur dialectica, contemnebatur rethorica; et novas totius quadruvii vias, evacuatis priorum regulis, de ipsis philosophie aditis proferebant." For this much-discussed text see the excellent pages in Georg Misch, *Geschichte der Autobiographie* (4 vols. in 8 Frankfurt 1949–69) 3.2.2.1231–33, where a similar criticism by William of Conches is also discussed. For the Cornificians see also J. O. Ward, "The Date of the Commentary on Cicero's 'De inventione' by Thierry of Chartres (ca. 1095–1160?) and the Cornifician Attack on the Liberal Arts," *Viator* 3 (1972) 219–73.

[43]Many examples for the ambivalent estimation of newness and novelty are given by Chenu, *Nature* 310–30; they could be multiplied.

[44]John R. Williams, "Godfrey of Rheims, a Humanist of the Eleventh Century," *Speculum* 22 (1947) 29–45; F. J. E. Raby, *A History of Secular Latin Poetry in the Middle Ages* (2nd ed. 2 vols. Oxford 1957) 1.312–16.

[45]Manitius 3.719–30; Raby (n. 44 above) 1.329–37.

[46]Manitius 3.865–67; Raby (n. 44 above) 1.383–87.

[47]Baudri of Bourgueil, *Les oeuvres poétiques*, ed. Phyllis Abrahams (Paris 1926); cf. Manitius 3.883–98 and Raby (n. 44 above) 1.337–48.

[48]See Peter von Moos, *Hildebert von Lavardin 1056–1133* (Stuttgart 1965); Wolfram von den Steinen, "Humanismus um 1100," in his *Menschen im Mittelalter* (Bern 1967) 196–214; also Manitius 3.853–65 and Raby (n. 44 above) 1.317–29.

[49]Manitius 3.872–77; Raby (n. 44 above) 2.23–26.

[50]It was Erwin Panofsky who clearly demonstrated that the great Italian Renaissance was based on the realization of *distance* between the ancient past and the present: *Ren & Ren* 108–13; see also the earlier formulation in Erwin Panofsky and Fritz Saxl, "Classical Mythology in Mediaeval Art," *Metropolitan Museum Studies* 4 (1933) 228–80, esp. 274, on the "historical distance" separating the Greeks and Romans from the contemporary world.

[51]See, for instance, the introductions to Charles Perrault's *Parellèle des anciens et des modernes en ce qui regarde les arts et les sciences* (4 vols. Paris 1688–97) by Hans R. Jauss,

antiqui were open to attacks by the *moderni*—even John of Salisbury's anti-humanist Cornificians had probably not much more than a nuisance value.

In twelfth-century terminology and ideology the word *nasci*, with which *natura* is often closely linked, is more important than the term *renasci*, and the terminology of nature, birth, and growth represents one of the most characteristic aspects of the twelfth-century renaissance.[52]

It has often been suggested that not since late Antiquity had personified Nature been so strongly recognized as a vital world force[53] of almost supreme magnitude as it was in the twelfth century.[54] Nature was seen as the *mater generationis*, for instance by Bernard Silvester,[55] who adopted this concept for his own picture of the reform of still unformed material nature, whereby the ancient chaos became *suus ortus essentiis, sua nativitas elementis*.[56] Already at the turn of the century Hildebert of Lavardin had made *parens natura* state that a perfect man—who was none other than Hildebert's lamented though unorthodox master, Berengar of Tours—was being born to her: *nascitur iste mihi*, says Nature.[57] Later Herman of Carinthia connects *nascentes* with

---

"Ästhetische Normen und geschichtliche Reflexion in der 'Querelle des Anciens et des Modernes,'" and by Max Imdahl, 'Kunstgeschichtliche Exkurse," reprinted in the series Theorie und Geschichte der Literatur und der schönen Künste: Texte und Abhandlungen 2 (Munich 1964) 8–64 and 65–79. See also August Buck, *Die humanistische Tradition in der Romania* (Bad Homburg 1968) 75–91, "Aus der Vorgeschichte der 'Querelle des anciens et des modernes' in Mittelalter und Renaissance."

[52]This is my strong impression. In this instance, as in many similar ones, a computerized thesaurus of terms and concepts in medieval Latin literature would obviously be of great help. See my article "Gregory the Great and Gregory VII: A Comparison of Their Concepts of Renewal," with "A Note on the Computer Methods Used" by David W. Packard, *Viator* 4 (1973) 1–31, and Robert L. Benson, "A Proposed Thesaurus of Medieval Latin Writings," *Computers and Medieval Data Processing* 5 (1975) 10–14.

[53]The late ancient concepts of *motus vitalis* and *vis* or *virtus vitalis* (see my *Idea of Reform* [n. 6 above] 221 n. 28) reached the twelfth century through various channels—through John Eriugena, for instance, in the case of Honorius Augustodunensis's *Clavis physicae*, ed. Paolo Lucentini (Rome 1974) 216–17. For other related 12th-c. terms such as *motus* or *vis universalis* or *naturalis*, see Tullio Gregory, *Platonismo medievale* (n. 54 below).

[54] Chenu, *Nature*, esp. 18–24, "Dame Nature"; Tullio Gregory, *Anima mundi: La filosofia di Guglielmo di Conches e la Scuola di Chartres* (Florence 1955) ch. 4, "L'idea di natura" (175–246); also the same author's contributions to *La filosofia della natura nel Medioevo: Atti del terzo congresso internazionale di filosofia medioevale, Passo della Mendola . . . 1964* (Milan 1966), and esp. his *Platonismo medievale* (Rome 1958) 122–50, "Dall'*Anima Mundi* all'Idea di Natura." See also Curtius ch. 6, "The Goddess Natura" (106–27) and Gaines Post, *Studies in Medieval Legal Thought* (Princeton 1964) ch. 11, "The Naturalness of Society and the State" (494–561).

[55]*Cosmographia*, Microcosmus 9 (n. 28 above) 139. That Bernard's conception of nature as mother of generation was probably influenced by the Latin translation of Abū Maʿshar (*Introductorium in astronomiam* [Venice 1506] 1.2f.a.5) is suggested by Stock, *Myth and Science* 65 and 222; see also Richard J. Lemay, *Abū Maʿshar and Latin Aristotelianism in the Twelfth Century: The Recovery of Aristotle's Natural Philosophy through Arabic Astrology* (Beirut 1962) 258–84.

[56]*Cosmographia*, Megacosmus 2.8 (n. 28 above) 101.

[57]*Hildeberti Cenomannensis episcopi carmina minora*, ed. A. Brian Scott (Berlin 1969) 8 no. 18.35–36: "Quem Natura parens cum mundo contulit inquit / 'degenerant alii, nascitur iste mihi.'"

natura[58] and John of Salisbury speaks of created Nature as "the most kindly parent of all things," *clementissima parens omnium*,[59] as "a certain generative force implanted in all things," *vis quaedam genitiva rebus omnibus insita* (or *indita*).[60] Alan of Lille praises Nature as *Dei vicaria*[61] and *Dei proles*, God's regent or offspring, but also as the mother of things, *genetrix rerum*,[62] who summons *genius* to her side.[63] In Bernard Silvester's *Cosmographia* and in Alan's *De planctu naturae* these names and epithets belong together with the hymnic evocations of ever-young or reflourishing or reborn nature, which are related to the celebration of spring in goliardic and troubadour poetry.[64]

Alan's *Anticlaudianus* is of even greater interest.[65] Here Nature, desolate about the sad condition of man, which she feels is in part the fault of her own imperfection, decides to form a new man, who will be an example to future mankind and bring about a new golden age. She succeeds in her plan, for God agrees to grant a new soul to Nature's new handiwork, a soul shaped in accordance with a new idea of man in the divine mind. It has been a source of amazement to modern interpreters that in this entire poem, whose subject is the renewal of man, Alan did not find it necessary to harmonize the need which he perceives for renovation with the previous redemption of man by Christ.[66] Though a long passage in the *Anticlaudianus* extols Christ through Mary, it has little inner relation to the rest of the poem.[67]

It has been suggested that Alan's renewal of man takes place in a timeless cosmos.[68] It is true that he does not speak of that re-formation which for Bernard Silvester was a part of the six-day work of creation, but clearly the new man of whom Alan poetically dreams would be a creature of the here and now, of his own time.[69] In the two prologues, especially the one in verse, it is made

[58]Herman of Carinthia, *De essentiis* (n. 35 above) 63 (continuation of the text cited in n. 35 above): "Dico . . . habitudinem quandam omnium nascencium . . . naturam . . . a principali geniture motu. . . ."

[59]Cf. *Metalogicon* 1.1 (n. 41 above) 5.

[60]Ibid. 1.8 (23–24, and cf. 25).

[61]Alan of Lille, *De planctu naturae*, ed. Wright (n. 12 above) 2.450.5, 469.25, and 511.11.

[62]Ibid. 458.11.

[63]Ibid. 510–11.

[64]See Bernard Silvester, *Cosmographia*, Megacosmus 2.1 and 10, 3.285 (n. 28 above) 98–99, 101, 111; and Alan of Lille, *De planctu naturae*, ed. Wright (n. 12 above) 2.458–59; also *Anticlaudianus* 9.380–409 and 1.55–106 (about Nature's dwelling place), ed. Robert Bossuat (Paris 1955) 196–97 and 58–60 (also Wright 2.425 and 275–77).

[65]See the editions cited in the preceding note, and cf. Guy Raynaud de Lage, *Alain de Lille, poète du XIIe siècle*, Université de Montréal, Publications de l'Institut d'études médiévales 12 (Montreal and Paris 1951); Curtius 117–22; Wolfram von den Steinen, "Natur und Geist im zwölften Jahrhundert," *Die Welt als Geschichte* 14 (1954) 71–90; Marie-Thérèse d'Alverny, ed., *Alain de Lille: Textes inédits*, EPM 52 (Paris 1965).

[66]Cf. (n. 65 above) Raynaud de Lage 70, Curtius 121, and above all von den Steinen 88–90, whose interpretation is the most subtle and profound.

[67]*Anticlaudianus* 5.471–543, ed. Bossuat (n. 64 above) 137–39 (Wright [n. 12 above] 2.362–64).

[68]Raynaud de Lage (n. 65 above) 70 and 78.

[69]*Anticlaudianus* 1.216–17 and 236–39, ed. Bossuat (n. 64 above) 63–64 (Wright [n. 12 above] 2.280–81). Nature speaks:

quite evident that the poet is conscious of giving something new to his own time—even the old parchment, he says, rejoices in becoming young again through the newness of Alan's writing.[70]

In his earlier work, *De planctu naturae*, Alan ostensibly had wished to refute homosexuality; as a matter of fact, he wanted to condemn *all* deviation from that love which is natural and perfect in a Christian sense.[71] As far as sexual love was concerned, this meant love in marriage. It would seem, however, that homosexual and bisexual love were then somewhat more widespread than in the earlier Middle Ages, and that this almost by necessity led back to classical exemplars. A famous anonymous poetic dispute between Helen and Ganymede[72] about the primacy of heterosexual or homosexual love is set against an amazingly pagan mythological background.[73] Polyeroticism almost always goes with some avatar of polytheism, through a sort of euhemerism in reverse, a heroization and divinization of physical beauty and other human qualities.[74] In the twelfth century such attitudes began to be expressed more frequently, notwithstanding the normative and sacramental character of marriage and its model in the union of Christ and his Church, notwithstanding also the consummation of Christian sanctification and even deification in the ascetic-mystic spirituality of the monastic-religious life. There remains the question whether the twelfth century knew the erotic and sublimated motivation for the pursuit of the things of the spirit, which we know from the Platonic dialogues and—in a heterosexual form—from Dante.[75] If one thinks

---

> Sed nichil invenio quod in omni parte beate
> Vivat. . . . .
> Sed divinus homo nostro molimine terras
> Incolat et nostris donet solacia damnis,
> Insideat celis animo, sed corpore terris:
> In terris humanus erit, divinus in astris.

Linda E. Marshall, "The Identity of the 'New Man' in the *Anticlaudianus* of Alan of Lille," *Viator* 10 (1979) 77–94, attempts to identify the new *divinus homo* with the young king of France, Philip Augustus—an interesting, yet to me unconvincing hypothesis.

[70]*Anticlaudianus*, prologue 4–5, ed. Bossuat (n. 64 above) 57 (Wright [n. 12 above] 2.273: "Scribendi novitate vetus iuvenescere carta / gaudet. . . .''

[71]See Richard H. Green, "Alan of Lille's *De Planctu Naturae*," *Speculum* 31 (1956) 649–74.

[72]See the new edition by Rolf Lenzen, "'Altercatio Ganimedis et Helene': Kritische Edition mit Kommentar," *Mittellateinisches Jahrbuch* 7 (1972) 161–86; cf. Hans Walther, *Das Streitgedicht in der lateinischen Literatur des Mittelalters* (Munich 1920) 141–42, Manitius 3.947–48, Raby (n. 44 above) 2.289–90, Curtius 116–17 n. 26, and Dronke, in the introduction to his edition of Bernard Silvester's *Cosmographia* (n. 28 above) 11–12.

[73]Classical mythology in the Middle Ages is a vast and much explored subject. I refer only to Panofsky and Saxl (n. 50 above) and to Friedrich von Bezold, *Das Fortleben der antiken Götter im mittelalterlichen Humanismus* (Bonn 1922).

[74]See, for instance, "Altercatio Ganimedis et Helene" 4.3 (n. 72 above) 169, of Ganymede and Helen and implicitly of youthful beauty in general: "Tales deos fama est formas induisse."

[75]The problem and its age-old ethnosociological background has been thoroughly explored by Nelli (n. 21 above) 274–325. He distinguishes between blood-brotherhood of archaic origin and homosexuality, and between physical and spiritual friendship or love, be it homosexual or heterosexual.

of St Bernard of Clairvaux's spiritually seductive powers,[76] which brought
scores of his relatives and friends into his monasteries, and if one reads the
treatise of his disciple Aelred of Rievaulx, *De spiritali amicitia*, one can hardly
fail to answer the question in the affirmative.[77]

In spite of the very great importance which personified Nature, the imagery of natural birth, growth, flowering, and love in all its forms had assumed
in the thinking of the twelfth century, all this was still seen to be very much
under the sway of the triune God, who can of course reach far beyond Nature's
capacities in renewing man. Thus Alan in his *De planctu naturae* makes
Nature confess:

> Through my action man is born, through God's authority he is reborn. By me he is called
> from nonbeing into being; through (God) he is conducted to a better being. For
> through me man is propagated unto death, through Him he is re-created to life. But
> from the mystery of this second birth my ministry is kept away.[78]

It is in no way surprising that Alan contrasts with purely natural renewal the
mystery of the second birth, which in the Christian sense is first of all
sacramental regeneration by baptism, the starting point for further Christian
renewal. Rather, the surprising absence or at least transformation of the motif
of Christian regeneration in Bernard Silvester and in much of the new love
poetry amounts to a single-minded emphasis on natural life, which is not
found in the earlier Middle Ages and is characteristic of the twelfth-century
renaissance.[79] Nevertheless, a Christmas sermon of Guerric of Igny is very much
to the point here: *felicissime renasci* can still mean for men to be reborn as sons
of God.[80] If we look at life in the twelfth century as a whole, there can be no
doubt about its strong supernatural bent. One could refer here to the eschatological expectations, to crusaders' hopes, to the new religious orders (which,

[76]See William of St Thierry, *Sancti Bernardi Vita prima* 1.3.15, PL 185.1.235C–D:
"eo . . . praedicante, matres filios abscondebant, uxores detinebant maritos, amici amicos averte-
bant; quia voci eius Spiritus sanctus tantae dabat vocem virtutis, ut vix aliquis aliquem teneret
affectu."

[77]See Aelred of Rievaulx, *De spiritali amicitia*, esp. 3.1–2, ed. and trans. J. Dubois (Bruges
1948) 147–55. Cf. Adele M. Fiske, *Friends and Friendship in the Monastic Tradition* (Cuernavaca
Mexico 1970) ch. 18/1–49 (this chapter, "Aelred of Rievaulx," is reprinted from *Cîteaux* 13
[1962] 5–17, 97–132). See also the excellent pages in Colin M. Morris, *The Discovery of the Individual, 1050–1200* (London 1972) 96–107. This was written before the appearance of the book by
John Boswell, *Christianity, Social Tolerance and Homosexuality* (Chicago and London 1980),
which has some very good remarks on Aelred (221ff.), in spite of the unfortunate use of the term
and concept "gay" for him, which in my opinion here and elsewhere seriously distorts the picture.

[78]*De planctu naturae*, ed. Wright (n. 12 above) 2.455: "homo mea actione nascitur, Dei auctoritate renascitur. Per me a non esse vocatur ad esse; per ipsum, ab esse in melius esse perducitur.
Per me enim homo procreatur ad mortem, per ipsum recreatur ad vitam. Sed ab hoc secundae na-
tivitatis mysterio professionis meae ministerium [my emendation, which corresponds with the old
edition in PL 210.446A, of Wright's reading "mysterium"] ablegatur."

[79]In this respect see also the quite "naturalistic" allegory of nature in John of Hanville's *Architrenius*, ed. Wright (n. 12 above) 1.240–392, and its analysis by Winthrop Wetherbee,
Platonism and Poetry in the Twelfth Century (Princeton 1972) 242–55.

[80]Quoted by Chrysogonus Waddell in this volume.

incidentally, could regard their own origins and development as new spiritual growth and fruitbearing—so in the *Exordium magnum Cisterciense*[81] and in many other instances), and finally to the highest realms of theological and philosophical thought, where reform still meant renewal by the grace of God.

So, for instance, St Anselm of Canterbury, in the famous sentences closing the first chapter of his *Proslogion*, says that God created in him, Anselm, the image of God, so that Anselm could remember Him, think Him, and love Him. Yet the divine image is so darkened in man through vices and sins that he can no longer do what he was made to do, unless God renew and reform the image. Only then can man come to understand the God whom his heart believes in and loves. This is the old Pauline-Augustinian tradition of the reform of man to image-likeness with God, with its special Augustinian-Anselmian corollary, *credo ut intelligam*.[82]

Bernard of Clairvaux, in his *De gratia et libero arbitrio*, distinguishes sharply between the creational, natural-image relation of man to God and his likeness to God: the first consists in man's free will (that is to say, his freedom from necessity), the second is really man's progressive assimilation to Him through increasing freedom from sin and misery. This potential likeness to God, then, is no longer a creation through nature but a reformation through divine grace, to be consummated only in that freedom from misery that will be obtained in the glory of heaven.[83]

Bernard of Clairvaux and Anselm of Canterbury were clearly interested in reform as a renewal which belonged to the sphere of grace and which was quite distinct from the sphere of created nature, its formation and natural renewal, so long as that nature itself was conceived of in a relatively materialistic,

---

[81]Conrad of Eberbach, *Exordium magnum Cisterciense* 1.13, ed. Bruno Griesser, Series scriptorum S. Ordinis Cisterciensis 2 (Rome 1961) 65: "in diebus istis novissimis refrigescente iam caritate et abundante usquequaque iniquitate omnipotens et misericors Dominus . . . gratiae suae seminarium plantavit in heremo Cisterciensi, quod Spiritus sancti pluvia irrigatum, spiritalis pinguedinis largissimum sumpsit incrementum crescens et proficiens in arborem grandem, pulchram et fructiferam nimis. . . ." Other examples are cited by Giles Constable in his essay in this volume.

[82]*Proslogion* 1 (n. 38 above) 1.100: "Fateor, domine, et gratias ago, quia creasti in me hanc imaginem tuam, ut tui memor te cogitem, te amem. Sed sic est abolita attritione vitiorum, sic est offuscata fumo peccatorum, ut non possit facere ad quod facta est, nisi tu renoves et reformes eam. Non tento, domine, penetrare altitudinem tuam, quia nullatenus comparo illi intellectum meum; sed desidero aliquatenus intelligere veritatem tuam, quam credit et amat cor meum. Neque enim quaero intelligere ut credam, sed credo ut intelligam. Nam et hoc credo: quia 'nisi credidero, non intelligam.'"

[83]*De gratia et libero arbitrio* 3.7, PL 182.1005C: "Cum igitur . . . triplex sit nobis proposita libertas: a peccato, a miseria, a necessitate; hanc ultimo loco positam contulit nobis in conditione natura, in primam restauramur a gratia, media nobis reservatur in patria"; 9.28, 1016B: "Puto autem in his tribus libertatibus ipsam, ad quam conditi sumus, Conditoris imaginem atque similitudinem contineri: et imaginem quidem in libertate arbitrii, in reliquis autem duabus bipartitam quamdam consignari similitudinem"; 14.49, 1027D–28A: "Primo namque in Christo creati sumus in libertatem voluntatis; secundo reformamur per Christum in spiritum libertatis; cum Christo deinde consummandi in statum aeternitatis. . . ." The rest of this paragraph is also very important.

vitalistic sense. Precisely this sense appeared—as we have seen—in Bernard Silvester and in much of troubadour and goliardic poetry.

For William of St Thierry on the other hand (to whom Bernard of Clairvaux addressed his treatise on free will and grace), the natural life was that of the monks and hermits, for instance the Carthusians[84] or the Fathers of the Desert whose "conversation was in heaven."[85] In his explanation of Pseudo-Dionysius's *Celestial Hierarchy*, Hugh of St Victor likewise made it clear that created nature, though its beauty manifests its creator, receives its full illumination and illuminating power through Jesus, who by his teachings and his presence in the eucharistic sacrament enabled man to see the truth and to participate in it.[86]

On the opposite end of the scale from a Bernard Silvester we find that other great Anselm of the twelfth century, the bishop of Havelberg (died 1158 as archbishop of Ravenna): his conception of renovation is focused in the Church, which he saw as forever renewed by the Holy Spirit, like the eagle of Psalm 102.[87]

Should we then look at the ideology of the twelfth-century renaissance as the mere coexistence of naturalism with supranaturalism, or as an ambiguous attitude toward "this-worldly" and "other-worldly," an attitude which could be present in the same person, in a mode and mood of irony and relativization? Such an assumption would not be false.[88] And yet, even the "pagan" erotic naturalism of the twelfth century was influenced by Christian spirituality.[89] And the natural love of the moderns as well as of the ancients could apparently be valued—if only as a stepping-stone to a higher love—even by sincere Christians.

Abelard, in the midst of his personal tragedy, is here—as so often—a symbol of his time. The author of liturgical hymns,[90] he also wrote love

[84]William of St Thierry, *Epistola aurea* 4.2.151, addressed to the Carthusians of Mont-Dieu, ed. and trans. Jean-Marie Déchanet, *Lettre aux frères du Mont-Dieu (Lettre d'or)*, Sources chrétiennes 223 (Paris 1975) 262.6-7.

[85]Ibid. 4.3.158 (268); cf. Phil. 3:20. See also Déchanet, "Le 'Naturam sequi' chez Guillaume de Saint-Thierry," *Collectanea Ordinis Cisterciensium Reformatorum* 7 (1940) 141–48.

[86]Hugh of St Victor, *Commentariorum in Hierarchiam coelestem S. Dionysii Areopagitae* 2.1, PL 175.939A, 940B–C, 949–53.

[87]Anselm of Havelberg, *Dialogi* 1: *De unitate fidei et multiformitate vivendi*, PL 188.1149A: "sancta Ecclesia pertransiens per diversos status sibi invicem paulatim succedentes, usque in hodiernum diem, sicut iuventus aquilae renovatur [cf. Psalm 102:5] et semper renovabitur." For Anselm of Havelberg, Hugh of St Victor, and other representatives of 12th-c. consciousness of historical evolution, see Richard W. Southern, "Aspects of the European Tradition of Historical Writing: 2. Hugh of St Victor and the Idea of Historical Development," TRHS 5th ser. 21 (1971) 159–79.

[88]See Peter Dronke's study in this volume, and his remarks on Andreas Capellanus in *Medieval Latin* (n. 27 above) 1.83–85.

[89]Dronke (n. 27 above) 1.87–97 and passim; Robert Javelet, "L'amour spirituel face à l'amour courtois," *Entretiens* 309–36; Marrou (n. 21 above) 165–71.

[90]See Josef Szövérffy, *Die Annalen der lateinischen Hymnendichtung* (2 vols. Berlin 1965) 2.57–76.

poems.[91] His overall view of nature is very significant here. Not only did he identify reason with natural law,[92] but he also found the moral precepts of the Gospels to be nothing other than a reform of the natural law observed by the ancient philosophers.[93]

One might perhaps say that in developing the old teaching that nature is but the will of God,[94] the twelfth century enhanced the autonomy of both nature and man in relation to God.[95] The mentality of the twelfth century also included a new conception of friendship between God and man, in which the humanity of God was predominant, and this contributed to making the whole natural and supranatural universe appear more benign, more friendly to man.[96] We have seen in Alan of Lille's dream of a new man and a new world a profound if utopian concern for a renewal of man in which nature and God have an almost equal share.

A kindred, though significantly different, synthesis is contained in the work of Hildegard of Bingen, the mystic and prophetess whose vast exposure to natural science as well as to the twelfth-century myth of nature constitutes an unresolved enigma.[97] In the great work of her old age, the *Liber de operatione Dei*, Hildegard describes in the most detailed, elaborate, and ingenious way how the combined humors of the body and temperaments of the soul can lead man either to carnal enjoyment or to spiritual joy, and how giving in to the former leads to fatigue and subsequent dryness and coldness. She proceeds to explain how the soul—dissatisfied with the body's moral and physical weakness—can warm the blood, replenish the moisture of the marrow, and

[91]These may all be lost, but Dronke (n. 27 above) 1.313–18 has in my opinion strengthened the possibility that "Hebet sidus," one of the greatest poems in the *Carmina Burana* (n. 20 above, 1.2.285 no. 169) refers to Heloise and is by Abelard.

[92]See Tullio Gregory, "Considérations sur *ratio* et *natura* chez Abélard," *Pierre-Pierre* 569–84 at 574–81.

[93]*Theologia christiana* 2.44, ed. E. M. Buytaert, *Petri Abaelardi opera theologica* CCL cm 12.149: "Si enim diligenter moralia Evangelii praecepta consideremus, nihil ea aliud quam reformationem legis naturalis inveniemus, quam secutos esse philosophos constat." He thought especially of Plato, who he believed had a veiled knowledge of the Trinity: see Tullio Gregory, "Abélard et Platon," *Peter Abelard: Proceedings of the International Conference, Louvain, May 10–12, 1971*, ed. E. M. Buytaert, Mediaevalia Lovanensia ser. 1, Studia 2 (Louvain 1974) 38–64; Peter Dronke, *Fabula: Explorations into the Uses of Myth in Medieval Platonism* (Leiden 1974) 55–67; Jean Jolivet, "Abélard entre chien et loup," CCM 20 (1977) 307–22 at 319.

[94]See Augustine, *De civitate Dei* 21.8, CCL 48.771.33–34: "voluntas [Dei] . . . rei cuiusque natura"; Peter Damiani, *De divina omnipotentia* 13, ed. and trans. André Cantin, *Pierre Damien, Lettre sur la tout-puissance divine*, Sources chrétiennes 191 (Paris 1972) 450.46–48: "Ipsa quippe rerum natura habet naturam suam, Dei scilicet voluntatem." Abelard's language and conception are still very similar; cf. Gregory (n. 92 above) 574–80.

[95]Cf. above, p. 13, about Alan of Lille. John of Salisbury, though he still identifies the nature of things with God's will (and ascribes this doctrine to Plato), lays great stress also on nature's post-creational autonomous character as *vis genitiva*, which enables things to act and suffer: *Metalogicon* 1.8 (n. 41 above) 23–24; *Policraticus* 2.12, ed. Clement C. J. Webb (2 vols. Oxford 1909) 1.85.

[96]Richard W. Southern, "Medieval Humanism," *Humanism* 29–60, esp. 33–41.

[97]See the brief but excellent synthesis by Heinrich Schipperges, *Das Menschenbild Hildegards von Bingen* (Leipzig 1962), with bibliography.

thus reawaken and redirect the body toward the service of God.[98] In doing so, the soul impels the body to produce sighs and tears of regret and repentance and thus makes the body, whose virtues had dried up, reflourish by the moisture of divine grace.[99] Thus, she sees repentance and penitence as a process in which the physiological and spiritual causes and effects are inextricably mingled. No wonder then that Hildegard can designate virtuousness and penitence as a greening and regreening, as a *viriditas* and a *revirescere* of the life of man. Hildegard's work as a whole is an illuminating synthesis of the ideologies of renascence and reform.[100]

In order to evaluate the renewal terminology and ideology of the twelfth century more fully, it will be useful to return to Roman or Romanizing renovation-restoration on the one hand and to rebellion on the other.

Not long after 1066 the *Carmen de Hastingae proelio* calls William the Conqueror's victory a renovation of Caesar's conquest.[101] A little later, a Pisan poet speaks about his triumphant city in a similar manner,[102] and in a letter drafted for archbishop Theobald of Canterbury, John of Salisbury says that Henry II re-forms the golden age.[103] The communal rebellion and the restora-

---

[98]Hildegard of Bingen, *Liber de operatione Dei* (= *Liber divinorum operum simplicis hominis*) 1.4.19, PL 197.817D–18A: "Ipsa [i.e. *anima*] quoque multoties secundum gustum carnis tandiu operatur quousque sanguis per fatigationem in venis aliquantum exsiccetur, et sudor per medullam emittatur, et tunc per quietem se subtrahit, usque dum sanguinem carnis calefaciat et medullam repleat. Et sic corpus ad vigilandum excitat et ad laborem recreat, quia dum aliquando carnalibus concupiscentiis insistit, taedium illarum saepius incurrit, sed dum exinde vires suas reparaverit, ad servitium Dei se totam reflectit." For the role of the marrow (*medulla*), see also Hildegard, *Causae et curae*, ed. Paul Kaiser (Leipzig 1903) esp. 81–85; cf. Dronke (n. 27 above) 1.310.

[99]*Liber de operatione Dei* 1.4.57 (n. 98 above) PL 197.846B: "In hunc quoque modum cum anima corpus suum ab omni viriditate virtutum aridum senserit, in moerorem et luctum convertitur, et corpus suum per scientiam rationalitatis et per spiritum compunctionis ad suspiria et lacrymas impellit, quia opera eius prava esse cognoscit, et ita aridum corpus suum per humorem divinae gratiae revirescere facit." This text and the one quoted in the previous note were first drawn to my attention by a student of my colleague Professor Kees Bolle and of myself, Dr. Patricia A. North; see her unpublished Ph.D. thesis, "Mysticism and Prophetism in Hildegard of Bingen and in Rāmānuja: An Essay in History and Hermeneutics" (University of California, Los Angeles, 1977; cf. *Dissertation Abstracts International* 38.6 [1978] 6778A).

[100]The motifs of watering by tears and of the regreening of moral dryness occur many times in Hildegard's *Liber de operatione Dei* and are a part of her microcosmic-macrocosmic symbolism, which sees human dryness and human tears as analogues to dry earth and to the beneficial waters which make it green again; see 1.4.32 (PL 197.830A–31A) and 1.4.57 (846C–D). For the "physical" and "moral" theme of *viriditas* in Hildegard's works, see Adelgundis Führkötter in the introduction to her translation of Hildegard's letters, *Briefwechsel* (Salzburg 1965) 18–19, and Peter Dronke, *Poetic Individuality in the Middle Ages: New Departures in Poetry, 1000–1150* (Oxford 1970) 150–92.

[101]*The Carmen de Hastingae proelio of Guy, Bishop of Amiens*, ed. Catherine Morton and Hope Muntz (Oxford 1972) 4: "Iulius alter enim, cuius renovando triumphum / effrenem gentem cogis amare iugum." Its date and authorship are controversial; see now R. H. C. Davis, "The *Carmen de Hastingae Proelio*," EHR 93 (1978) 241–61.

[102]See p. 395 in this volume (Classen).

[103]Letter 101, ed. and trans. W. J. Millor, H. E. Butler, and C. N. L. Brooke, *The Letters of John of Salisbury* 1 (London 1955) 161.

tion of the Senate in mid-twelfth-century Rome used the language of renewal, and simultaneously the Staufer Empire strove for its own renewal and reform, particularly during the reign of Frederick Barbarossa.[104]

Frederick I was in contact with the greatest renovators of Roman law; he and those around him believed that he was to renew the prerogatives of the Empire, which, appropriating the vocabulary of the *Corpus iuris civilis*, he called a *sacrum imperium*, a *diva res publica*.[105] It is all the more interesting that his chancery seems to have preferred *reformare in pristinum* to other terms, when it wanted to express imperial as well as ecclesiastical restoration and renovation. Already in the notification which Frederick after his election sent to the pope, he proclaimed that through the steadiness of his zeal the Catholic Church should remain adorned (*decoretur*) with the privileges of its dignity, and the sublimity of the Roman Empire should with God's help be reformed to the original vigor (*in pristinum robur*) of its excellence.[106] This is reminiscent of the reform of the ecclesiastical *gloria pristini decoris* or *prisca libertas* or simply *pristinus status*, of which the papal chancery had spoken at least since Gregory VII.[107]

With regard to the terminology of rebellion, the term *revolution*—which is of astrological-astronomical origin—does not seem to have been used in a political sense until the fourteenth century.[108] But rebellion in the twelfth century ranged from feudal recalcitrance against rulers to the struggle of the new cities for independence, and from moral polemics and satirical invective against political or ecclesiastical institutions to heresy. The terms vary. In his autobiography Guibert of Nogent, for instance, speaks of the *coniuratio* (sworn conspiracy) and *seditio* of the commune of Laon[109] and of the *coniuratio* that led to founding the commune of Amiens; in this latter context he also uses the term *rebellis*.[110] The term *coniuratio* is found in many sources on

[104]See the essays by Robert L. Benson and Herbert Bloch in this volume.

[105]See MGH Const 1.224 no. 161, letter of Frederick I to Otto of Freising of 1157: "sacro imperio et divae rei publicae consulere debemus."

[106]MGH DD 10.11 no. 5: "quatinus per studii nostri instantiam catholica ecclesia suę dignitatis privilegiis decoretur et Romani imperii celsitudo in pristinum suę excellentię robur Deo adiuvante reformetur." See also Heinrich Appelt, "Die Kaiseridee Friedrich Barbarossas," SB Vienna 252.4 (1967) 1–32 at 9; Rainer Maria Herkenrath, *Regnum und Imperium: Das "Reich" in der frühstaufischen Kanzlei (1138–1155)*, SB Vienna 264.5 (1969) 1–62 at 26. Herkenrath refers to similar formulations of the same thought in diplomas of Conrad III after 1150; they were to continue through the reign of Frederick Barbarossa.

[107]See, for instance, *Gregorii VII Registrum* 4.5., ed. Erich Caspar, MGH Epist sel 2 (Berlin 1920; repr. 1955) 302, about the reform of a bishop's church (Dol in Brittany): "quatenus illa sedes . . . ad gloriam pristini decoris Deo opitulante vestris studiis reformetur." For influence of the papal on the imperial chancery in this period, see Karl Helleiner, "Der Einfluss der Pappsturkunde auf die Diplome der deutschen Könige im zwölften Jahrhundert," MIÖG 44 (1930) 21–56.

[108]See Matteo Villani, *Cronica* 4.89 and 9.34 (6 vols. in 3 Florence 1825–26) 2.285 and 4.209; see also Eugen Rosenstock-Huessy, *Out of Revolution: Autobiography of Western Man* (New York 1938) 500.

[109]Guibert de Nogent, *De vita sua* 3.7, 3.10, 3.13, ed. Georges Bourgin, *Guibert de Nogent, Histoire de sa vie (1053–1124)*, CTSEEH 40 (Paris 1907) 157, 174, 194.

[110]Ibid. 3.14 (198): "Videns itaque Ingelrannus urbis comes ex coniuratione burgensium comitatus sibi iura vetusta recidi, prout poterat, iam rebelles armis aggreditur." For Guibert's

urban revolutions of the period and also in the sources for the trial of Henry the Lion by Frederick Barbarossa,[111] where "contumacy" (*contumacia*) also appears, designating the duke's stubborn refusal to obey the summons to the imperial court or to recognize judgment.[112] Both *rebellis* and *contumax* are likewise frequently used by Frederick in his dealings with Milan and the Lombard League.[113] Otto of Freising used the ambivalent term *novitas* in connection with Arnold of Brescia's heretical or schismatic and generally rebellious activities.[114]

In an overall view of twelfth-century renewal, revolution and heresy would perhaps still have to be considered as fringe phenomena. The revolutionary ferment in Joachim of Fiore's new age of the Holy Spirit made itself felt strongly only in the thirteenth century.[115]

The closest link between the ideologies of renewal and rebellion in the twelfth century seems to exist in the area of moral indignation reflected in the large (and still not fully interpreted) body of moralizing and satirical literature.[116] Here we encounter cynicism as well as hope for reform in the face of real or apparent corruption and decline, which must have been felt as strongly by some as renewal was by others. This literature vigorously attacked the paradoxical materialism of some beneficiaries of the Gregorian Church Reform, and it also accused the intellectual and moral lightheartedness accompanying that vitalistic renewal which is perhaps the main justification for speaking of a renaissance of the twelfth century.

I cite two famous examples. First, a poem by Walter of Châtillon (or a pupil of his) against the abuses of the Roman Curia, which contains the oft-quoted punning verse *Roma mundi caput est, sed nil capit mundum* ("Rome is the head of the world [*mundus*], but it holds nothing that is pure [*mun-*

---

autobiography see also the annotated English translation and introduction by John F. Benton (including his emendations of the Latin text), *Self and Society in Medieval France: The Memoirs of Abbot Guibert of Nogent (1064?-c.1125)* (New York 1970).

[111]The *Annales Sancti Georgi in Nigra Silva*, for 1178, MGH SS 17.296; see Carl Erdmann, "Der Prozess Heinrichs des Löwen," in Theodor Mayer, Konrad Heilig, and Carl Erdmann, *Kaisertum und Herzogsgewalt im Zeitalter Friedrichs I*, MGH Schriften 9 (Leipzig 1944) 334, where other occurrences of *coniurare*—and of *conspirare*—are also mentioned.

[112]In the famous Gelnhausen charter, MGH Const 1.385 no. 279.23 and 28; cf. Erdmann, "Prozess" (n. 111 above) 358.

[113]See, for instance, MGH Const 1.312 no. 220, 325 no. 230, 346 no. 246, and 411 no. 293. See also the diploma of Frederick I for Pisa, of 1155, MGH DD 10.1.201 no. 119, where he praises the Pisans because they curb the *rebellandi audacia* of the peoples of Asia and Africa. See furthermore the Archpoet about Frederick I, *Die Gedichte des Archipoeta*, ed. Heinrich Watenphul and Heinrich Krefeld (Heidelberg 1958) 70 no. 9 stanza 16.3–4: "qui rebelles lancea fodiens ultrici/ representat Karolum dextera victrici."

[114]Otto, GF 2.30 (see list of abbreviations for this volume) 137.28. Similarly, Gerhoch of Reichersberg counted Arnold among the *novitates huius temporis* in a pejorative sense; see Peter Classen, *Gerhoch von Reichersberg* (Wiesbaden 1960) 175 and 177.

[115]The literature on Joachim and the Joachimites is enormous. Here it is sufficient to refer to the last part of Peter Classen's essay in this volume.

[116]Among the best recent discussions of this mentality are those found in Morris (n. 77 above) 122–33 and in the introduction to Ludwig Schmugge's edition of Ralph Niger, *De re militari et triplici via peregrinationis Ierosolimitane* (Berlin 1977).

dum]'').[117] The first two stanzas of this poem set the tone by speaking of rebellion in a twofold sense. Walter says that his song rebels against the prevailing corruption—*Utar contra vitia carmine rebelli*—but at the same time the poem fights against a different, though related, and likewise shameful kind of rebellious discrepancy, namely that between sweet faces and hearts full of gall: "Disputat cum animo facies rebellis / mel ab ore profluit, mens est plena fellis." All too often are faces and minds in rebellious discord, and Walter himself rebels against a world which is in rebellion against virtue.

The other example, even more famous, is the Archpoet's "Confession."[118] He begins in a sort of rebellion and bitterness against himself: "Estuans intrinsecus ira vehementi / in amaritudine loquor mee menti," and this tone persists, interlaced with two other equally important moods. One is the typically youthful and erotic naturalism of the twelfth-century renaissance:

> Hard beyond all hardness, this mastering of nature:
> Who shall say his heart is clean, near so fair a creature?
> Young are we, so hard a law, how should we obey it?
> And our bodies, they are young, shall they have no say in't?[119]

The second is a complement and palinode to the first:

> Now my old life I dislike and new manners please me;
> People see my outer face, in my heart God sees me.
> Virtue I now love, and vice I now hate and fear it,
> For I am renewed in mind and reborn in spirit.[120]

The Archpoet's Confession tells us that the spirit of vitalistic renewal through natural exuberance and the Christian belief in metanoia and spiritual regeneration were both alive and strong in the cultural phenomenon and the chronological era which Charles Homer Haskins called the twelfth-century renaissance.

Furthermore, it must never be forgotten that the twelfth century contained wide areas of renewal which do not clearly reveal either self-consciousness or

---

[117]This poem is contained in the *Carmina Burana* (n. 20 above) 1.1.76 no. 42.
[118]Likewise transmitted in the *Carmina Burana*, 1.3.6–8 no. 191.
[119]Ibid. 6 stanza 7.1–4:

> Res est arduissima   vincere naturam,
> in aspectu virginis   mentem esse puram;
> iuvenes non possumus   legem sequi duram
> leviumque corporum   non habere curam.

(The rather free English translation in the text is taken from Helen Waddell, *Mediaeval Latin Lyrics* [5th ed. London 1951] 175).
[120]Ibid. 8 stanzas 22.3–4, 23.1–2:

> vita vetus displicit,   mores placent novi;
> homo videt faciem   sed cor patet Iovi.
>
> Iam virtutes diligo,   vitiis irascor,
> renovatus animo   spiritu renascor.

an explicit ideology. This seems to hold true for certain aspects of social and economic life, including demographic change and its consequences, as well as technology and art. I can in this regard make only a few final suggestions.

In twelfth-century France, the aristocratic *iuvenes* constituted, in their origins, a merely societal group in the narrow sense of the term, without any articulate *prise de conscience* of its emotional and intellectual potentialities.[121] But after 1150 in southern France, though the practical purposes of maintaining and increasing the glory and wealth of noble lineage were never lost sight of,[122] the *iuvenes* embodied the exalted notion of *jovens* held by the troubadours.[123] Bertran de Born, in a poem about youth and old age, rejoices that the seigneurs who have become old must leave their estates to the young heirs, for the world is thus renewed even better than by the return of flowers and birds in spring.[124]

Georges Duby, in his contribution to this volume, makes further *rapprochements* between social and intellectual developments of the twelfth century. He has broached the fascinating possibility that the new conceptions of creation and nature, of birth and growth, of youth and love could have been influenced by such new facts as the more intensive exploitation and clearance of the land and a resulting awareness of the riches and the beneficial action of nature. It would be interesting also to examine more fully the related question whether there was an extension of the new ideas from the literate to the illiterate.[125]

We may also note the new esteem shown in the early twelfth century to the mechanical arts, including what we today call the fine arts,[126] for instance

---

[121]Georges Duby, "Les 'jeunes' dans la société aristocratique dans la France du Nord-Ouest au XIIe siècle," in his *Hommes et structures du Moyen Age* (Paris 1973) 213–25.

[122]Ibid. 222–23. See also Duby's *Medieval Marriage: Two Models from Twelfth-Century France*, trans. Elborg Forster (Baltimore and London 1978) 12–15, 105–10. I am very grateful to Professor Duby for allowing me to see the French manuscript of this book before publication, and to Professor John W. Baldwin and the Johns Hopkins University Press for making it available to me.

[123]Alexander J. Denomy, "*Jovens*: The Notion of Youth among the Troubadours, Its Meaning and Source," *Mediaeval Studies* 11 (1949) 1–22.

[124]*Anthologie des troubadours* (n. 25 above) 60:

> Bel m'es quan vei chamjar lo senhoratge
> E·lh velh laisson als joves los maisos
>
> . . . .
> Adoncs m'es vis que·l segles renovel
> Melhz que per flor ni per chantar d'ausel;
> E qui domna ni senhor pot chamjar,
> Velh per jove, be deu renovelar.

[125]See Duby, *Medieval Marriage* (n. 122 above) 85 and 106–09.

[126]See, for instance, Chenu, *Théologie* 45–49, and, among the more recent relevant studies by Lynn White, jr., "Theophilus Redivivus," *Technology and Culture* 5 (1964) 224–33 and "Medieval Engineering and the Sociology of Knowledge," *Pacific Historical Review* 44 (1975) 1–21, both reprinted in his *Medieval Religion and Technology* (Berkeley 1978).

by Hugh of St Victor in the *Didascalicon*[127] and by Theophilus, who in the prologue to the first book of his *De diversis artibus* actually says that he is offering new things to the reader's mind for his meditation.[128]

In architecture and the pictorial arts, the Gregorian Reform and its aftermath produced in Rome and South Italy a conscious reaching back to art forms of Christian and pagan Antiquity.[129] But this occurred in the context of ecclesiastical *reformatio* and Roman political *renovatio*—it had little to do with those aspects of the twelfth-century renaissance which were marked by a more comprehensive consciousness of spontaneous birth, growth, or even rebirth. One may indeed speak of the surface classicism of Italian art of the later eleventh and the twelfth centuries.[130] The even more important intrinsic renewal of architecture and art which went on at that time does not seem to have been aware of itself to the same degree;[131] nevertheless, there may have been some expressions of such awareness. There are texts in which the building of new churches or the renovation of old ones was perhaps more than usually praised—as already in the early eleventh century by Ralph Glaber[132] and then by Leo of Ostia,[133] Suger,[134] and Gervase,[135] in their famous descriptions of the new Monte Cassino, St Denis, and Canterbury, respectively.

More importantly, there are two illuminated manuscripts of the first half of the twelfth century whose half-naturalistic and half-symbolic approach to

---

[127]*Didascalicon*, ed. Charles H. Buttimer (Washington D.C. 1939); see also the English translation and introduction by Jerome Taylor, *The Didascalicon of Hugh of St. Victor: A Medieval Guide to the Arts*, Columbia University Records of Civilization 64 (New York 1961).

[128]Ed. and trans. C. R. Dodwell (London 1961) 1: "delectabili novitatum meditatione."

[129]The position of architecture and the pictorial arts within the self-consciousness of the twelfth century renaissance is a highly complex problem. See, for example, Ernst Kitzinger, "The Gregorian Reform and the Visual Arts: A Problem of Method,"TRHS 5th ser. 22 (1972) 87–102; idem, "The First Mosaic Decoration of Salerno Cathedral," *Jahrbuch der österreichischen Byzantinistik* 21 (1972) 149–62; also Hélène Toubert, "Le renouveau paléochrétien à Rome au début du XIIe siècle," *Cahiers archéologiques* 20 (1970) 99–154.

[130]See Ernst Kitzinger, in this volume, 669 and n. 96. For Panofsky's distinction between "surface" and "intrinsic" classicism, see *Ren & Ren* 62.

[131]In this sense—and only in this sense—Arthur Haseloff, "Begriff und Wesen der Renaissancekunst," *Mitteilungen des kunsthistorischen Institutes in Florenz* 3 (1931) 373–92 at 386, was right in criticizing Haskins's attempt at integrating Romanesque and early Gothic art with the twelfth-century renaissance.

[132]Ralph Glaber, *Historiarum sui temporis libri quinque* 3.4.13, ed. Victor Mortet, *Recueil de textes relatifs à l'histoire de l'architecture et à la condition des architectes en France au moyen âge*, vol. 1: *XIe–XIIe siècles*, CTSEEH 44 (Paris 1911) 4; but Ralph still belonged to an earlier, different age and ambience, the pre-Gregorian, Cluniac reform milieu.

[133]*Chronica monasterii Cassinensis* 3.10, ed. Otto Lehmann-Brockhaus, *Schriftquellen zur Kunstgeschichte des 11. und 12. Jahrhunderts für Deutschland, Lothringen und Italien* (2 vols. Berlin 1938) 1.475–76 no. 2274.

[134]*De rebus in administratione sua gestis* and *Libellus . . . de consecratione sancti Dionysii*, ed. and trans. Erwin Panofsky, *Abbot Suger on the Abbey Church of St.-Denis and Its Art Treasures*, 2nd ed. by Gerda Panofsky-Soergel (Princeton 1979).

[135]"Tractatus de combustione et reparatione Cantuariensis ecclesiae," *Chronica*, ed. William Stubbs, *The Historical Works of Gervase of Canterbury*, RS 73 (2 vols. 1879) 1.1–29; also Otto Lehmann-Brockhaus, *Lateinische Schriftquellen zur Kunst in England, Wales und Schottland vom Jahre 901 bis zum Jahre 1307* (5 vols. Munich 1955–60) 1.217–23 and 225–31.

Fig. 1. Gotha. Landesbibliothek, MS I.70 (early twelfth century). Thiofrid of Echternach, *Flores epitaphii sanctorum*, fol. 98: abbot Thiofrid. After Hanns Swarzenski, *Vorgotische Miniaturen: Die ersten Jahrhunderte deutscher Malerei* (2nd ed. Königstein im Taunus 1931) 27. Reproduced by permission of Karl Robert Langewiesche Nachfolger Hans Köster, Königstein im Taunus.

Fig. 2 (left). Ghent. Bibliothèque universitaire, MS 92 (ca. 1120). Lambert of St Omer, *Liber floridus*, fol. 140r: the Beatitudes. After *Liber floridus*, ed. Albert Derolez (Ghent 1968) 283. Reproduced by permission of E. Story–Scientia P.V.B.A., Ghent.

Fig. 3 (right). Ghent. Bibliothèque universitaire, MS 92 (ca. 1120). Lambert of St Omer, *Liber floridus*, fol. 230v: *lilium mysticum*. After *Liber floridus*, ed. Albert Derolez (Ghent 1968) 460. Reproduced by permission of E. Story–Scientia P.V.B.A., Ghent.

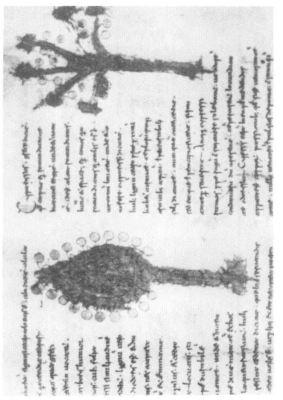

Fig. 4 (left). Ghent. Bibliothèque universitaire, MS 92 (ca. 1120). Lambert of St Omer, *Liber floridus*, fol. 76v: *palma virtutum*. After *Liber floridus*, ed. Albert Derolez (Ghent 1968) 156. Reproduced by permission of E. Story–Scientia P.V.B.A., Ghent.

Fig. 5. Monte Cassino. Biblioteca dell'Abbazia, MS 132 (early eleventh century). Rabanus Maurus, *De rerum naturis*, p. 461: cedar and cypress. After Fritz Saxl, *Lectures* (2 vols. London 1957) 2.167c.

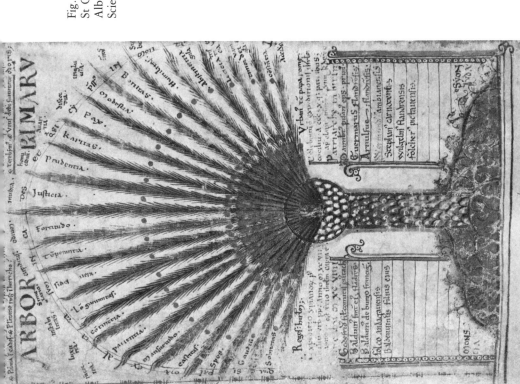

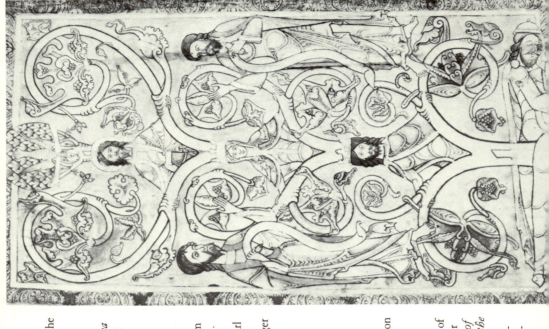

Fig. 6 (left). Munich. Bayerische Staatsbibliothek, MS Clm 4660 (thirteenth century). *Carmina Burana*, fol. 64v: landscape. After Albert Boeckler, *Deutsche Buchmalerei vorgotischer Zeit* (2nd ed. Königstein im Taunus 1959) 61. Reproduced by permission of Karl Robert Langewiesche Nachfolger Hans Köster, Königstein im Taunus.

Fig. 7 (right). London. British Library, MS Cotton Nero C.IV (ca. 1150). "Winchester Psalter," fol. 9r: the Tree of Jesse. After Roger Cook, *The Tree of Life: Symbol of the Centre* (London 1974) pl. 53. Reproduced by permission of the

the pictorial representation of vegetation[136] well suits their titles: the *Flores epitaphii sanctorum* by Thiofrid of Echternach[137] (fig. 1) and the *Liber floridus* by Lambert of St Omer.[138] Especially in the *Liber floridus* (ca. 1120) we find pictures of flowers and trees (figs. 2–4), which though still of symbolic intent[139] show the exuberant vitality characteristic of the twelfth-century renaissance. These miniatures—eclipsing by far the vegetation images in Rabanus Maurus's Encyclopaedia (fig. 5)[140]—foreshadowed a famous miniature in the thirteenth-century Munich codex of the *Carmina Burana* (fig. 6).[141] Both the *Liber floridus* and the *Carmina Burana* miniatures echo the spring and vegetation symbolism in the poetry of the age. Other twelfth-century examples of a new vogue of plant and especially tree symbolism are the flowering tree-cross of San Clemente in Rome[142] and the evolving iconography of the Tree of Jesse (fig. 7).[143]

Finally, there exist a few sculptures of the early and mid-twelfth-century Meuse School—above all the nude *baptizandi* on the font of Rainer of Huy, of ca. 1110 (see fig. 58)[144] and the head of pope Alexander I on Wibald of

---

[136]See Lynn White, jr., "Natural Science and Naturalistic Art in the Middle Ages," AHR 52 (1947) 421–35 at 426–27 (= *Medieval Religion and Technology* [n. 126 above] 23–41).

[137]For Thiofrid's work, see Manitius 3.95–96.

[138]Ed. by Albert Derolez (Ghent 1968) after the original, MS 92 of the University Library in Ghent.

[139]So, for instance, the trees on fols. 139v and 140r (Derolez 282–83) symbolize the eight beatitudes of Christ's Sermon on the Mount (fig. 2 shows the fifth through the eighth beatitudes, represented by an olive tree, a plane tree, a terebinth, and a vine); similarly the lily on fol. 230v, ibid. 460 (fig. 3), and the palm tree on fol. 76v, ibid. 156 (fig. 4), are explained by the inscriptions as *lilium mysticum* and *palma virtutum*. See also Fritz Saxl, "Illustrated Mediaeval Encyclopaedias 2: The Christian Transformation," in his *Lectures* (2 vols. London 1957) 1.242–54 at 244, 2 plates 167b and d, 166a.

[140]Rabanus Maurus, *De rerum naturis* (*De universo*). Fig. 5 reproduces the cedar and the cypress from p. 461 of Monte Cassino Cod. 132 (saec. XI in.); cf. Fritz Saxl, "Illustrated Mediaeval Encyclopaedias 1: The Classical Heritage," *Lectures* (n. 139 above) 1.228–41 at 234–41, 2 plate 167c.

[141]*Carmina Burana* (n. 20 above) 1.1 plate 3.

[142]See, in this volume, Kitzinger 642 and fig. 34, and Constable 39–40 at n. 13.

[143]Fig. 7 reproduces the Tree of Jesse in the so-called Winchester Psalter, BL MS Nero C.IV fol. 9r; cf. Francis Wormald, *The Winchester Psalter* (New York 1973) 9–10, fig. 12. The symbolism of the Tree of Jesse is probably a Western medieval invention and seems to date from the 11th c.; see Arthur Watson, *The Early Iconography of the Tree of Jesse* (Oxford 1934). Professor Kitzinger kindly drew my attention to the Tree of Jesse sketched on the verso of the last page of Cod. Vat gr 333, a richly illustrated 11th- or 12th-c. manuscript of the biblical Books of Kings. André Grabar, "Une pyxide en ivoire à Dumbarton Oaks," *Dumbarton Oaks Papers* 14 (1960) 123–46 at 132, is tempted, on the strength of Vat gr 333, to consider the possibility that the Tree of Jesse is of Byzantine origin, but I think Jean Lassus, *L'illustration byzantine du Livre des Rois: Vaticanus Graecus 333* (Paris 1973) 84 (to fig. 105) is much closer to the truth, when he recognizes here a Western and later hand. The Tree of Jesse among the frescoes in the Panagia Mavriotissa in Castoria seems early Palaeologan in style, not of the 11th c., as Stylianos M. Pelekanides, Καστορία 1 (Thessalonike 1953) plates 85–86, assumes. For tree symbolism, see also my article "Medieval and Modern Understanding of Symbolism: A Comparison," *Speculum* 54 (1979) 223–56.

[144]Now in St Barthélemy in Liège; see *Rhein und Maas: Kunst und Kultur 800–1400* (2 vols. Cologne 1972–73) 1.238–39, 2.237–50: Anton Legner, "Die Rinderherde des Reiner von Huy," esp.

Stavelot's reliquary of 1145–46 (see fig. 59)[145]—which are so deeply, classically human that they seem to have originated in a mentality similar to that of the great "naturalistic" thinkers and poets of the twelfth century and to be related to their new image of man. Perhaps, then, style as well as iconography may at times be equivalent to terminology and ideology in expressing newness.

Though language and ideology, even when contemporary, cannot encompass the entire life of an era, they can tell us something. In the case of Haskins's *Renaissance of the Twelfth Century*, this inquiry into terms and ideas has confirmed that Haskins, more clearly and comprehensively than anybody before him, had recognized what the twelfth century achieved and how it saw its own achievement. Since then many interpreters of the twelfth century have added to and modified Haskins's work.[146] What we have learned in the fifty years since Haskins conceived of a Renaissance of the Twelfth Century has on the whole confirmed that he had an authentic insight into the character of twelfth-century culture. Close to the core of the ideology of that age we find the great image of *Parens Natura* with its related terminology of *nasci* and *nativitas*, *generatio* and *genitura*, *genetrix* and *genius*.

At the end, one confronts again the much discussed and variously answered question: whether or not the term "renaissance" is appropriate for the twelfth century.[147] The answer must, it seems to me, be "yes and no." "Yes," if we think of that awareness of "newness," even of a metaphorical and secularized "new birth," which yet left a concomitant awareness of historical continuity untouched. "No," if we were obliged—as we actually are not—to understand by "renaissance" the same kind of "rebirth" which in the great Italian Renaissance linked the present to the past across a poignantly and nostalgically felt gap of *distance*—a concept of rebirth which created a new mode and mood in the awareness of renewal and finally shaped a new age of culture which is still called *"The* Renaissance."[148]

It is indispensable for historians to keep this distinction always in mind. If that is done, there seems to be no good reason to reject Haskins's title *The*

248–50; Peter Lasko, *Ars Sacra, 800–1200*, The Pelican History of Art (London 1972) 162–63, plate 169.

[145]Now in the Musées royaux d'art et d'histoire in Brussels; see *Rhein und Maas* (n. 144 above) 1.250; also Hanns Swarzenski, *Monuments of Romanesque Art* (Chicago 1954) 33 and 67, figs. 359–61. See, finally, the study by Willibald Sauerländer in this volume, at n. 43.

[146]My remarks obviously owe much, for instance, to Ernst Robert Curtius, to Père Chenu, to Erwin Panofsky, to Wolfram von den Steinen, and to Etienne Gilson.

[147]During the Conference it was raised most explicitly and clearly by Sir Richard Southern and by Morton Bloomfield.

[148]Panofsky, who first made the distinction here restated (see n. 50 above), has tried to conceptualize it in the title of his book *Renaissance and Renascences in Western Art*, where the medieval "renascences," of course, include Haskins's "renaissance of the twelfth century."

Renaissance of the Twelfth Century, which in any case seems now well protected by a tacit statute of limitations on changing widely accepted terms.

In sum, the term "renaissance of the twelfth century" reflects and expresses a new approach to life, the self-awareness of an epoch in which at least those who were literate possessed unprecedented consciousness of the natural processes of renewal, including among other things their own youth and the newness of the age. But let us also remember that the greatness of the twelfth century is perhaps most evident in the coexistence and partial fusion of the new ideas with the old but still evolving legacy of religious regeneration and reform and of political restoration and renovation.[149]

Bibliographical Note

The introductory character of this essay and its focus in terms and ideas entails noting here mainly works which explore and illustrate the phenomena of medieval renaissances, and especially of the twelfth-century renaissance, in their entirety, or which deal with the concepts of renaissance, humanism, and naturalism in general. Books and articles already cited in the footnotes will with a few exceptions not be mentioned here.

Among the "forerunners" of the renaissance of the twelfth century, the Theodosian renaissance—taken in its widest sense—is of particular importance in our context, because writers of the late fourth and early fifth centuries, such as Macrobius, Martianus Capella—see Claudio Leonardi, "I codici di Marziano Capella," *Aevum* 33 (1959) 443–89 at 470–78—and Claudianus, as well as certain works of the figurative arts of the period, exercised great influence in the twelfth century. A good survey of the cultural trends in the age of Theodosius the Great is found in *The Conflict between Paganism and Christianity in the Fourth Century*, ed. Arnaldo Momigliano (Oxford 1963), especially 193–218: Herbert Bloch, "The Pagan Revival in the West at the End of the Fourth Century"; cf. my *Idea of Reform: Its Impact on Christian Thought and Action in the Age of the Fathers* (Cambridge Mass. 1959) 17–21 (with further literature). For the art of the period see now Ernst Kitzinger, "A Marble Relief of the Theodosian Period," in his selected studies *The Art of Byzantium and the Medieval West*, ed. W. Eugene Kleinbauer (Bloomington and London 1976) 1–31.

Among the "established" medieval renascences, the Carolingian renaissance is the oldest; see Erna Patzelt, *Die karolingische Renaissance: Beiträge zur Geschichte der Kultur des frühen Mittelalters* (Vienna 1924; repr. Graz 1965) for the history of the term. More recently, Pierre Riché, *Education et culture dans l'Occident barbare, VI–VIII siècles* (Paris 1962) 410–72, has called certain anticipations of the Carolingian renewal of culture, which had occurred in the seventh and early eighth centuries among the Anglo-Saxons and in Italy, "renaissances." Even earlier, Pierre Courcelle, *Les lettres grecques en Occident, de Macrobe à Cassiodore* (2nd ed. Paris 1948) had spoken of ephemeral renascences of Hellenism in the West around 470 in Gaul (221–53) and during the Ostrogothic regime in Italy (257–400). Cf. also Eugenio Anagnine, *Il concetto di rinascita attraverso il Medio Evo (V–X sec.)* (Milan 1958).

---

[149] I know of few books in which the interaction between the old and the new in the twelfth century is described as well as in Dom Jean Leclercq's *Monks and Love in Twelfth-Century France* (Oxford 1979).

As far as the Carolingian renaissance is concerned, the older literature is now out-dated by *I problemi della civiltà carolingia*, Settimane 1 (Spoleto 1954), which contains two relevant articles: Paul Lehmann, "Das Problem der karolingischen Renaissance" (309–58), and Angelo Monteverdi, "Il problema del rinascimento carolino" (359–72); and by vols. 2 and 3 of *Karl der Grosse: Lebenswerk und Nachleben*, ed. Wolfgang Braunfels et al. (5 vols. Düsseldorf 1965–68), published on the occasion of the great ex-hibition on Charlemagne held in Aachen in 1965 under the auspices of the Council of Europe, which deal with literary and artistic culture in the Carolingian age. For the rela-tionship between personal and cultural renascence, political renovation, and religious regeneration and reform in the Carolingian era, see Friedrich Heer, "Die 'Renaissance'-Ideologie im frühen Mittelalter," MIÖG 57 (1949) 23–81; also Josef Fleckenstein, *Die Bildungsreform Karls des Grossen als Verwirklichung der Norma Rec-titudinis* (Bigge-Ruhr 1953); Percy Ernst Schramm, "Karl der Grosse: Denkart und Grundauffassungen—Die von ihm bewirkte 'Correctio' (nicht 'Renaissance')," in *KKP* 1.302–41 (first version published in *Historische Zeitschrift* 198 [1964] 306–45); Wolfram von den Steinen, "Der Neubeginn," in *Karl der Grosse: Lebenswerk und Nachleben* 2.9–27, and idem, "Karl und die Dichter," ibid. 63–94. For general orien-tation see also Jacques Boussard, *The Civilization of Charlemagne*, trans. Frances Partridge (New York 1968).

The term "Ottonian renaissance" is mainly used in art history, but it is frequently applied also to the whole culture of Germany and Italy in the period that reaches from Otto the Great (936–73) at least through the reigns of Otto III (d. 1002) and Henry II (d. 1024) or even through the reigns of the first two Salian emperors, to the death of Henry III in 1056. A renewal undoubtedly occurred in that age—see, for instance, Hans Naumann, *Karolingische und ottonische Renaissance* (Frankfurt 1927)—but there is little to be said for using the term "renaissance" for it: such usage is not supported by the sources, which generally persist in the terminology of *renovatio, reformatio*, and the like. See Schramm, *KRR*, and Heer, "'Renaissance'-Ideologie," cited above. Neverthe-less, Robert S. Lopez, "Still Another Renaissance?" AHR 57 (1951) 1–21, and *The Tenth Century: How Dark the Dark Ages?* (New York 1959), is right when he sees the tenth century as a turning point in medieval history. See also Henri Focillon, *L'an mil* (Paris 1952). However, this does not mean that that age defined itself as a "renaissance" or that we should see it so.

I refer only in passing to renaissances in Byzantine culture and art, which though hardly touched upon during the Conference are of great interest for purposes of com-parison with the West, all the more so because of recurrent waves of Byzantine influence on Western culture, and especially on Western art, during the Macedonian renaissance and its aftermath. Concerning Byzantine influence on Western culture in the twelfth century see, for instance, Chenu, *Théologie* 274–308. On Byzantine renaissances in art see Kurt Weitzmann, *Greek Mythology in Byzantine Art* (Princeton 1951) and *Geistige Grundlagen und Wesen der Makedonischen Renaissance*, Arbeitsgemeinschaft für For-schung des Landes Nordrhein-Westfalen, Geisteswissenschaften 107 (Cologne 1963), and, on their influence upon the West, Otto Demus, *The Mosaics of Norman Sicily* (London 1949) 423–25 and "Die Entstehung des Paläologenstils in der Malerei," *Berichte zum XI. Internationalen Byzantinisten-Kongress, München 1958* (2 vols. Munich 1958–60) I.IV.2.1–63; and Ernst Kitzinger, "The Byzantine Contribution to Western Art of the Twelfth and Thirteenth Centuries," *The Art of Byzantium and the Medieval West* (cited above) 357–88 (= *Dumbarton Oaks Papers* 20 [1966] 25–47).

Turning to the twelfth-century renaissance itself, and its relationship to the begin-nings of the great Italian Renaissance, I refer once and for all to four general studies: Johan Huizinga, "Das Problem der Renaissance," in his *Wege der Kulturgeschichte*

(Munich 1930) 89–139; Federico Chabod, "The Concept of the Renaissance," ch. 4 of *Machiavelli and the Renaissance*, trans. David Moore (London 1958) 149–247, including bibliography; Walter Paatz, "Renaissance oder Renovatio? Ein Problem der Begriffs-bildung in der Kunstgeschichte des Mittelalters," *Beiträge zur Kunst des Mittelalters: Vorträge der ersten deutschen Kunsthistorikertagung auf Schloss Brühl, 1948* (Berlin 1950) 16–27, with important bibliography; and Wallace K. Ferguson, *The Renaissance in Historical Thought: Five Centuries of Interpretation* (Boston 1948), especially ch. 11, likewise with ample bibliography. See also the recent presidential address of William J. Bouwsma, "The Renaissance and the Drama of Western History," AHR 84 (1979) 1–15.

I shall now list or very briefly characterize three kinds of studies: first, those which deal with the question of whether or not there really was a "renaissance" in the twelfth century; second, those which examine the role of humanism and of classical Antiquity in the twelfth century; and third, general works on the era, including also the acts of scholarly congresses and catalogues of important exhibitions.

A decisive new stimulus was given to the critical analysis of the concept of renaissance, and especially to the relationship between the great Italian Renaissance and medieval renascences, by Erwin Panofsky and Fritz Saxl in their paper "Classical Myth-ology in Mediaeval Art" (cited above, n. 50), a study which was later expanded by Panofsky in his well-known book *Renaissance and Renascences in Western Art* (see above, at n. 148). Panofsky and Saxl clearly perceived and explained the Italian Renaissance consciousness of historical *distance* between "moderns" and "ancients" as something distinct from the conception of continuity between them which had pre-vailed in the medieval renascences, including the renaissance of the twelfth century.

Fifteen years after Panofsky and Saxl's seminal study, William A. Nitze published a lively article focused on medieval literature, "The So-called Twelfth Century Renais-sance," *Speculum* 23 (1948) 464–71, in which he almost echoed the two Warburgian scholars (apparently without yet knowing their work) when he wrote, "The Middle Ages never knew that they were mediaeval. The men of the twelfth century had none of that awareness of a Cimmerian night from which . . . humanity had emerged" (466). A kindred view was taken by Eva M. Sanford, in her paper "The Twelfth Century—Renaissance or Proto-Renaissance?" *Speculum* 26 (1951) 635–42. Urban T. Holmes, Jr., in "The Idea of a Twelfth-Century Renaissance" in the same issue of *Speculum* (643–51) rightly speaks of the twelfth-century renaissance as "a vigorous awakening of cultural enthusiasm" (650) but "not necessarily the rebirth of anything" (643).

An approach similar to that of Holmes had been made already in 1931 by Karl Hampe, who (probably without knowing Haskins's book) gave a succinct and balanced account of the transformation of Western civilization in the twelfth century: "Der Kul-turwandel um die Mitte des zwölften Jahrhunderts," *Archiv für Kulturgeschichte* 21 (1931) 129–50, reedited in *Propyläen-Weltgeschichte*, ed. Walter Goetz (10 vols. Berlin 1929–33) 3.457–72. Somewhat along the same lines, Paul Lehmann wrote his essay "Die Vielgestalt des zwölften Jahrhunderts," *Historische Zeitschrift* 178 (1954) 225–50 (reprinted without notes in his *Erforschung des Mittelalters* [5 vols. Stuttgart 1959–62] 3.225–46). Bryce Lyon, too—not unlike the last-mentioned authors and Haskins himself—stressed the "wide-reaching movement" of the twelfth century in his article "Was There a Renaissance in the Twelfth Century?" *The Renaissance of the Twelfth Century*, Catalogue of an Exhibition, Museum of Art, Rhode Island School of Design (Providence 1969) 1–9 at 7 (see also Stephen K. Scher, "'The Renaissance of the Twelfth Century' Revisited," *Gesta* 9.2 [1970] 59–61); in searching for causes, Lyon follows Henri Pirenne, whose student he was, "in saying that without the western re-conquest of the Mediterranean, the renaissance of the twelfth century is inconceivable"

(9). Haskins himself, *Ren* vi, says that medieval renaissances were less wide-reaching than the Italian Renaissance, but only to point out in the next sentence how very wide the range of the twelfth-century renaissance actually was.

The historians so far mentioned stressed a certain discontinuity between the renaissance of the twelfth century and the great Italian Renaissance—except for Hampe and Lehmann, who did not discuss the problem, and also excepting Italo Siciliano, *Medio evo e rinascimento* (Milan 1936), who exaggerated the break between the Middle Ages and the Italian Renaissance as well as the contrast between northern Europe and Italy. Yet there were also historians who with good reason stressed (but sometimes over-stressed) the existence of strong humanistic and naturalistic trends in the twelfth century (see below), and others who were strongly aware of, or even exaggerated, the continuing vitality of medieval religious elements in the modern Renaissance. I mention in this con-nection Konrad Burdach, *Vom Mittelalter zur Reformation* (7 vols. Berlin 1912–35), which it is true deals chiefly with the thirteenth century and the late Middle Ages and considers the twelfth century only marginally. A serious shortcoming of this rich and stimulating work seems to me to lie in its lack of discrimination between early Christian ideas of rebirth and "naturalistic," "vitalistic" Renaissance ideology. Continuity be-tween the Middle Ages and the Renaissance was spun out into absurdity by some authors such as Johan Nordström, *Moyen Age et Renaissance*, trans. T. Hammar (Paris 1933), who tried to demonstrate that there was nothing worthwhile in the Italian Renaissance that had not been achieved previously, especially in the twelfth-century renaissance.

Compare to the contrary the exceedingly well-balanced statements by Paul Oskar Kristeller, "Humanism and Scholasticism in the Italian Renaissance," in his *Renaissance Thought: The Classic, Scholastic, and Humanistic Strains* (New York 1961) 92–119, and "The Medieval Antecedents of Renaissance Humanism," in his *Eight Philosophers of the Italian Renaissance* (Stanford 1964) 147–65.

Etienne Gilson, with the verve and esprit which were so characteristic of him, was one of the first to synthesize the more reasonable aspects of the view that the Middle Ages in some ways anticipated the Renaissance and that on the other hand the Renais-sance was in some respects a decline; see his essay "Humanisme médiéval et Renais-sance," first published in the *Revue trimestrielle canadienne* (March 1930) 1–17, and reprinted in *Les idées et les lettres* (2nd ed. Paris 1955) 171–96; cf. also his article "Le moyen âge et le naturalisme antique," AHDLMA 7 (1932) 5–37, and his later paper "Notes sur une frontière contestée," AHDLMA 25 (1958) 59–88, especially at 65–81, sect. 1, "In silvis et agris," and sect. 2, "Homo mediaevalis—Homo modernus."

This brings us to the role of naturalism and humanism and to the influence of classical Antiquity in the twelfth-century renaissance. I mention the following indepen-dent studies and parts of books to supplement those already quoted in the footnotes: Paul Renucci, *L'aventure de l'humanisme européen au moyen-âge, IVe–XIVe siècle* (Paris 1953) 54–133, well-balanced on the whole and useful as a survey of sources and literature; of greater weight is the volume *L'humanisme médiéval dans les littératures romanes du XIIe au XIVe siècle: Colloque organisé par le Centre de philologie et de littératures romanes de l'Université de Strasbourg . . . 1962, Actes,* ed. Anthime Four-rier (Paris 1964); the same holds true for the relevant chapter in Curtius ("Classicism," 247–72) and his remarks on the twelfth-century renaissance as a "youth movement" (ibid. 53 and 98); see furthermore Friedrich von Bezold's old but still helpful little book, *Das Fortleben der antiken Götter im mittelalterlichen Humanismus* (Bonn 1922), and the recent studies of Raymond J. Cormier on the "Romances of Antiquity" such as the *Roman d'Eneas,* especially his *One Heart, One Mind: The Rebirth of Virgil's Hero in Medieval French Romance* (University, Miss. 1973); Hans Liebeschütz, "Das zwölfte Jahrhundert und die Antike," *Archiv für Kulturgeschichte* 35 (1953) 247–71, and the same author's *Mediaeval Humanism in the Life and Writings of John of Salisbury,* which appeared under the auspices of the Warburg Institute of the University of London, Studies 17 (London 1950; repr. 1968), as did a very important work on the influence of ancient literature and art on French medieval art and culture by Jean Adhémar, *Influences antiques dans l'art du moyen âge français*, Studies of the Warburg Institute 7 (London 1939); Dom David Knowles, "The Humanism of the Twelfth Century," in his *The Historian and Character, and Other Essays* (Cambridge 1963) 16–30; August Buck, *Die humanistische Tradition in der Romania* (Bad Homburg 1968) ch. 3 of part 1, "Gab es einen mittelalterlichen Humanismus?"; Southern, *Humanism*, which besides the essay on "Medieval Humanism" contains several other studies dealing with the twelfth century, such as "Humanism and the School of Chartres" (61–85), which was much discussed during the Conference; Wolfram von den Steinen, whose illuminating essay "Natur und Geist im zwölften Jahrhundert" I have likewise cited above (n. 65), has a very good chapter entitled "Das neue Lied" (on Latin and vernacular poetry of the twelfth century) in his book *Der Kosmos des Mittelalters: Von Karl dem Grossen zu Bernhard von Clairvaux* (Bern 1959) 231–52; equally valuable is his study "Humanismus um 1100," in his *Menschen im Mittelalter* (Bern 1967) 196–214; see also his remarks on the role of art in the twelfth-century renaissance in his *Homo caelestis: Das Wort der Kunst im Mittelalter* (2 vols. Bern 1965) 1.64, 125–29. That the twelfth century, notwithstanding the intensity of its humanism and naturalism, was still religion-centered and law-directed, emerges nowhere more clearly than in two erudite and excellent books by Joseph de Ghellinck, *L'essor de la littérature latine au XIIe siècle* (Brussels 1946; 2nd ed. 1955) and *Le mouvement théologique du XIIe siècle* (2nd ed. Bruges 1948; repr. 1969). See also the brief, but truly synthetic book by Colin M. Morris, *The Discovery of the Individual, 1050–1200* (London 1972), and Amos Funkenstein, *Heilsplan und natürliche Entwicklung: Formen der Gegenwartsbestimmung im Geschichtsdenken des hohen Mittelalters* (Munich 1965).

To conclude, I list a few useful recent introductions or guides to twelfth-century history and culture, seen and described more often than not from the vantage point of Haskins's conception of a twelfth-century renaissance: Gérard M. Paré, A. Brunet, and P. Tremblay, *Le renaissance du XIIe siècle: Les écoles et l'enseignement*, Publications de l'Institute d'études médiévales d'Ottawa 3 (Paris and Ottawa 1933); Christopher Brooke, *The Twelfth-Century Renaissance* (New York 1970); C. Warren Hollister, *The Twelfth-Century Renaissance* (New York 1969), an instructive collection of readings taken from both primary and secondary sources; Sidney R. Packard, *12th Century Europe: An Interpretive Essay* (Amherst 1973), of which ch. 4, "The World of the Mind in Twelfth-Century Europe," opens with a section on "The Twelfth-Century Renaissance" (150–54); Bernard Levy and Sandro Sticca, eds., *The Twelfth Century*, The Center for Medieval and Early Renaissance Studies, State University of New York at Binghamton, Acta 2 (Binghamton 1975), especially "Sicily and Campania: The Twelfth-Century Renaissance," by Dorothy Glass (130–46).

Though I have already quoted them in the notes, I shall because of their importance draw attention once more to the publications of the acts of two French congresses on the renaissance of the twelfth century: *La filosofia della natura nel Medioevo* (see n. 54 above) and *Entretiens*; to these may be added *Twelfth-Century Europe*.

Finally, two great exhibitions of works of art and cultural monuments which chronologically straddled the twelfth and thirteenth centuries should be mentioned: "The Year 1200, The Metropolitan Museum of Art, New York, 1970," and "Die Zeit der Staufer, Stuttgart, 1977," at the Württembergisches Landesmuseum. Of both exhibitions multivolume scientific catalogues were published, richly illustrated and in both cases accompanied by scholarly essays; see *The Year 1200*, ed. Konrad Hoffmann and Florens Deuchler, Cloisters Studies in Medieval Art 1–2 (2 vols. New York 1970) and *The Year 1200: A Symposium* (New York 1975), and *Die Zeit der Staufer: Geschichte, Kunst, Kultur*, ed. Reiner Haussherr et al. (5 vols. Stuttgart 1977–79).

I

RELIGION

Renewal and Reform in Religious Life
Concepts and Realities

Giles Constable

The idea of renewal and reform was a major source of inspiration in both the personal and institutional forms of religious life throughout the Middle Ages, though it was expressed in different ways at different times.[1] In the New Testament it appears as an essentially personal ideal, especially in the writings of Paul, who exhorted men to let their minds be remade and their natures transformed and to be renewed inwardly every day.[2] In the early church, baptism and penance were seen as ceremonies of renewal and rebirth, and entry into monastic life as a means for men and women to recover their lost likeness to God.[3] The concept of renewal inspired not only the successive movements of

---

[1]See above all Konrad Burdach, *Reformation—Renaissance—Humanismus* (2nd ed. Berlin and Leipzig 1926; repr. Darmstadt 1963) 43, stressing the survival of what he called "the mystic image of rebirth and reformation" throughout the Middle Ages, and, more generally, 1–84, esp. 24–25, on the religious roots of the concepts of reform, renewal, rebirth, and regeneration; and Gerhart B. Ladner, *The Idea of Reform: Its Impact on Christian Thought and Action in the Age of the Fathers* (Cambridge Mass. 1959), which needs to be supplemented for the post-Patristic period by his articles cited below and in the Bibliographical Note. Various scholars have attempted, without success, to distinguish the contemporary meanings of the terms used to denote the concept of reform and renewal in the Middle Ages, and Charles Dereine, in *La vita comune del clero nei secoli XI e XII: Atti della [prima] settimana di studio, Mendola, settembre 1959*, Pubblicazioni dell'Università cattolica del Sacro Cuore 3rd ser.: Scienze storiche 2–3, = Miscellanea del Centro di studi medioevali 3 (2 vols. Milan 1962) 1.407 made the sensible suggestion (which has not been widely followed) to use the term "restoration" for all efforts to reestablish order in a traditional framework and "reform" for any real change of structure.

[2]Rom. 12:2 and 2 Cor. 4:16; see Burdach (n. 1 above) 30–31; Ladner (n. 1 above) 51–59, who wrote, "This [Pauline] reform leads to a complete renovation of the inner man which amounts to a new creation of man" (59), and his article "Erneuerung," *Reallexikon für Antike und Christentum* 6 (1966) 240–75 at 252–54.

[3]Philipp Oppenheim, "Mönchsweihe und Taufritus," *Miscellanea liturgica in honorem L. Cuniberti Mohlberg*, Bibliotheca "Ephemerides liturgicae" 22–23 (2 vols. Rome 1948–49) 1.259–82, esp. 263; Michael Marx, *Incessant Prayer in Ancient Monastic Literature* (Rome 1946) 93 and 99 (on the ascetic life as "return to paradise," "preservation of the primitive state of man before the fall," and "the restoration of the spiritual personality of Adam"); and Edward E. Malone, "Martyrdom and Monastic Profession as a Second Baptism," *Vom christlichen Mysterium: Gesammelte Arbeiten zum Gedächtnis von Odo Casel, O.S.B.*, ed. Anton Mayer, Johannes Quasten, and Burkhard Neunheuser (Düsseldorf 1951) 115–34.

messianism in the West[4] but also, in secular affairs, many of the most important developments in political thought and action.[5] Institutions as well as individuals began to be included within the concept of reform especially in the
post-Carolingian period. Whereas Gregory the Great used the term *reformare*
in his *Moralia* to refer to personal reform, it was applied by Gregory VII to the
reform of the Church as a whole.[6]

This emphasis on exterior or supra-individual renewal was a leading aspect
of reform ideology in the eleventh and twelfth centuries. Both religious and
secular texts of the period are filled with terms reflecting a sense of the renewal
of Christian society and institutions. Although many of these terms and images derived from traditional texts and rhetorical topoi going back to late Antiquity, their application reflected a new perception—that institutional change
was possible—which affected contemporary realities as well as attitudes.
Behind this imagery lay a belief in the decline and deformation of religious
and social institutions, a belief which fostered a sense of distance from the
past, and a confidence that the present state of affairs could be ameliorated.[7]
Not only churchmen and religious reformers but also laymen and heretics
sought to reshape contemporary society in accord with standards derived from
the past and, increasingly as time went on, projected into the future.[8] There
was a shift during the course of the twelfth century from what may be called a

[4]Paul Alphandéry, *Notes sur le messianisme médiéval latin (XIe–XIIe siècles).* . . , Ecole
pratique des hautes études: Section des sciences religieuses (Paris 1912) 8.

[5]See esp. Schramm, *KRR.*

[6]Gerhart B. Ladner, "Gregory the Great and Gregory VII: A Comparison of Their Concepts
of Renewal," *Viator* 4 (1973) 1–27. In the *Register* of Gregory the Great it referred to the restitution of rights and property. See also Ladner (n. 1 above) 423: "It was left to a later phase of
mediaeval history, to the age of Gregory VII, to formulate clearly and to initiate courageously a
reform of the *Ecclesia*, of the Church herself, as the mystical and hierarchical Body of Christ"; Jean
Leclercq, "The Bible and the Gregorian Reform," *Concilium: An International Review of
Theology* 7 (1966) 34–41 (= *Concilium: Theology in the Age of Renewal* 17 [1966] 63–77), commenting that "Gregory VII applied the Pauline vocabulary of personal reform to an institutional
reform" (38); Karl F. Morrison, *Tradition and Authority in the Western Church, 300–1140*
(Princeton 1969) 271–72, on Peter Damiani's sense of the renewal of the Church; and Glenn
Olsen, "The Idea of the *Ecclesia Primitiva* in the Writings of the Twelfth-Century Canonists,"
Traditio 25 (1969) 61–86, who stressed the importance during the Gregorian Reform of "the conscious wish to return to the antique, Biblical, patristic, and Roman models of the Christian life"
(61).

[7]This view differs from that of Panofsky in *Ren & Ren*, who distinguished the Renascence of
the eleventh and twelfth centuries from the Renaissance of the fourteenth to sixteenth centuries on
the basis of the existence of a conscious sense of distance and disjunction, saying (38): "The very
self-awareness of the Renaissance would have to be accepted as an objective and distinctive 'innovation' even if it could be shown to have been a kind of self-deception."

[8]The question of the extent to which (if at all) heresy itself should be considered an aspect
of the twelfth-century religious renewal cannot be fully considered here: see the remarks by Ladner
in his essay in this volume at n. 115. Many heretics used the ideology of renewal to criticize the
contemporary Church, but in a way that was parallel with rather than distinct from the use orthodox reformers made of similar concepts, such as the *ecclesia primitiva* and *vita apostolica*. Neither
Abelard nor Arnold of Brescia, for instance, advocated heterodox reforms in religious life and institutions: both got into trouble with the ecclesiastical authorities for entirely different reasons.

backward- to a forward-looking ideology of reform.[9] The ideals were often the same, but the reformers tended to look less to the past and more to the future for the models they sought to impose upon the present. The late Middle Ages in particular was marked by a ferment of prophetic speculation and apocalypticism that contributed to the emergence of a new concept of historical progress and acceptance of change and innovation.

In a celebrated passage describing the repair and rebuilding of churches all over Europe soon after the turn of the millenium, Ralph Glaber wrote, "It gave the world the appearance of having bestirred itself, of having cast off old age, and of having put on all over a white costume of churches."[10] The image of millenarian rebirth is here associated with that of baptismal renewal, represented by the white robe. In the first half of the eleventh century the Church took the lead in promoting the *reformatio pacis* by preaching, pilgrimage, and liturgical intervention and, more positively, through the Peace and Truce of God.[11] Later in the century the reformers concentrated their attention on the Church itself, which was turned by their efforts into new spiritual directions and institutional patterns. An extraordinary range of images indicating the process of renewal and reform was used at that time, including terms drawn from cosmology (*recreate*), religion (*convert*), instruction (*correct*), construction (*remake, restore, repair*), and travel (*return, revert*) as well as from the natural cycles of life (*regenerate, recover, recuperate, revive, resuscitate*), seasonal growth (*reflower, regrow, reflourish*), night and day, the weather, and fire (*rewarm, relight, rekindle*).[12] Visually, this concept was expressed in the early twelfth century by works like the Klosterneuburg candelabrum, of which the seven arms are shaped like branches sprouting leaves at every joint, and the San Clemente mosaic showing the Church as an

[9]See my article "Reformatio," *Ecumenical Dialogue at Harvard: The Roman Catholic–Protestant Colloquium*, ed. Samuel H. Miller and G. Ernest Wright (Cambridge Mass. 1964) 330–43.

[10]*Raoul Glaber, Les cinq livres de ses histoires (900–1044)* 3.4 (13), ed. Maurice Prou, CTSEEH 1 (Paris 1886) 62. See Amos Funkenstein, *Heilsplan und natürliche Entwicklung: Formen der Gegenwartsbestimmung im Geschichtsdenken des hohen Mittelalters* (Munich 1965) 77–84 on Glaber, whom he calls the first example of "einer reflektierenden Geschichtsschreibung, die sich um eine Gegenwartsbestimmung bemüht" (77).

[11]Georges Duby, "Les laïcs et la paix de Dieu," *I laici nella "Societas christiana" dei secoli XI e XII: Atti della terza settimana internazionale di studio, Mendola, 21–27 agosto 1965*, Pubblicazioni dell'Università cattolica del Sacro Cuore, Contributi 3rd ser.: Varia 5, = Miscellanea del Centro di studi medioevali 5 (Milan 1968) 448–61, esp. 448, 457, and 460.

[12]See especially the list of citations, referring mostly to regular and secular canons in the eleventh century, in Eusebius Amort, *Vetus disciplina canonicorum regularium et saecularium* (1 vol. in 2 Venice 1747; repr. Farnborough 1971) 1.67–74; Burdach (n. 1 above) 24, 30, and 196 n. 21, stressing the identity of many of these words in the terminology of the ancient mystics; Ladner (n. 1 above) 20, showing that *renasci* meant "to grow again" as well as "to be reborn," and his article on "Vegetation Symbolism and the Concept of Renaissance," *De artibus opuscula XL: Essays in Honor of Erwin Panofsky*, ed. Millard Meiss (2 vols. New York 1961) 1.303–22; and Robert Javelet, *Image et ressemblance au douzième siècle: De Saint Anselme à Alain de Lille* (2 vols. Strasbourg 1967) 2.239 n. 370 and 248 n. 445.

acanthus vine growing at the foot of a cross reaching from earth to heaven.[13] The idea of change for the better (*in melius*), which referred to the reform of the individual in the works of Tertullian and Augustine,[14] was applied to religious and secular institutions in the eleventh and twelfth centuries, and the prefix *re-* was increasingly accepted as meaning "new."[15] *Renovation, amelioration,* and *innovation* became almost interchangeable terms. St Norbert justified the introduction of regular canons into the church of Magdeburg in 1129, for instance, by his wish "to elevate it in religion, to complete [it] in immunity, and to reform what is incorrect" and by his effort "to reform it *in melius.*"[16]

The tendency to compare the present unfavorably with the past and to try to restore the good old days by abolishing subsequent deformities persisted throughout the eleventh and twelfth centuries and was only partially replaced by a more forward-looking and optimistic point of view.[17] The peace and prosperity of the tenth century (of all times!) were praised in a chronicle of the counts of Anjou written probably about the middle of the twelfth century, and the biographer of Robert of Knaresborough, who died in the early thirteenth

[13]Peter Bloch, "Der siebenarmige Leuchter in Klosterneuburg," *Jahrbuch des Stiftes Klosterneuburg* 11 [= n.s. 2] (1962) 163–73 attributed the nucleus of the candelabrum to the workshop of San Zeno ca. 1100 (see also his "Seven-Branched Candelabra in Christian Churches," *Journal of Jewish Art* 1 [1974] 44–49); *Mosaico di S. Clemente* (Rome 1975) 4; cf. Ladner, "Vegetation" (n. 12 above) 311. The image of the cross sprouting leaves from its base is frequent in Byzantine art: see Hans Belting, Cyril Mango, and Doula Mouriki, *The Mosaics and Frescoes of St. Mary Pammakaristos (Fethiye Camii) at Istanbul,* Dumbarton Oaks Studies 15 (Washington, D.C. 1978) pl. 3b. See also the illustrations from the *Liber floridus* of Lambert of St Omer (ca. 1120) in figs. 2–4 in this volume.

[14]Ladner, "Erneuerung" (n. 2 above) 259–60.

[15]Amort (n. 12 above) 70 and Gerhard Meissburger, *Grundlagen zum Verständnis der deutschen Mönchsdichtung im 11. und 12. Jahrhundert* (Munich 1970) 28–29 and n. 73. Some interesting examples of the use of reform terminology with reference to urban and social conditions are given by Gerhart B. Ladner, "Religious Renewal and Ethnic-Social Pressures as Forms of Life in Christian History," *Theology of Renewal,* ed. Laurence K. Shook (2 vols. Montreal 1968) 2.328–57 at 342–53.

[16] Charles-Louis Hugo, *Sacri et canonici ordinis Praemonstratensis annales* (1 vol. in 2 Nancy 1734–36) 1.2.cviii; cf. *Die Zwiefalter Chroniken Ortliebs und Bertholds,* ed. Luitpold Wallach, Erich König, and Karl Otto Müller, Schwäbische Chroniken der Stauferzeit 2 (Sigmaringen 1978) 166 (2.7: "in melius sunt reformata") and the late eleventh- or early twelfth-century account of the foundation of St Mary at York in William Dugdale, *Monasticon anglicanum,* ed. John Caley, Henry Ellis, and Bulkeley Bandinel (6 vols. in 8 London 1846) 3.545 ("ipsum locum in melius renovare").

[17]According to Harnack, "every really important reformation in the history of religion was primarily a critical reduction"; cited from *Das Wesen des Christentums* (Leipzig 1900) 160, in Wilhelm Pauck, *Harnack and Troeltsch: Two Historical Theologians* (New York 1968) 24. See also George Boas, *Essays on Primitivism and Related Ideas in the Middle Ages* (Baltimore 1948; repr. New York 1966) and Frances A. Yates, *Giordano Bruno and the Hermetic Tradition* (London, Chicago, and Toronto 1964) 1: "The great forward movements of the Renaissance all derive their vigour, their emotional impulse, from looking backwards. The cyclic view of time as a perpetual movement from pristine golden ages of purity and truth through successive brazen and iron ages still held sway and the search for truth was thus of necessity a search for the early, the ancient, the original gold from which the baser metals of the present and the immediate past were corrupt degenerations."

century, stressed that the examples of the saints were especially needed "in these final days" to arouse the frozen love and faith in the world.[18] Whether the deformation and decline were attributed to the evil propensities of mankind or to the cosmological aging of the world,[19] the state of affairs at present was worse than it had been in the past. For some, the work of reform would only put off the evil day by temporarily ameliorating present conditions, whereas for others it was seen as initiating a new age modeled on an earlier state of perfection.

Pessimists and optimists alike, however, agreed that reform was not only necessary but also to some extent possible. In the *Liber tramitis*, or *Consuetudines Farfenses*, dating from the second quarter of the eleventh century, Romuald was said to have "renewed the standard of ancient justice" and Hugh of Farfa to have "renewed the ancient ways of the holy fathers" in a society where clerical marriage and the heresy of simony were rampant.[20] William of Volpiano's renewal of the ancient abbey of St Evre at Toul was described in the *De instauratione coenobii S. Apri* by bishop Bruno of Toul, the future pope Leo IX, who was said in his own biography by Wibert to have stimulated a revival of the monastic religion "which had for a long time, alas, grown cold (*refriguerat*) throughout his own diocese."[21] The biographer of William of Hirsau, who died in 1091, likewise wrote that "By the effort of this holy man, the monastic religion, which among those who had assumed the religious habit had almost grown cold in the Teutonic regions, began to grow warm again (*recalescere*) and to recover (*recuperari*)."[22]

[18]*Chroniques des comtes d'Anjou et des seigneurs d'Amboise*, ed. Louis Halphen and René Poupardin, CTSEEH 48 (Paris 1913) 36; "Vitae S. Roberti Knaresburgensis," ed. Paul Grosjean, *Analecta Bollandiana* 57 (1939) 364–400 at 395.

[19]On the topos of the aging world, which went back to Antiquity, see Alphandéry (n. 4 above) 8, Chenu, *Théologie* 76–77, and Giovanni Miccoli, *Chiesa gregoriana: Ricerche sulla riforma del secolo XI*, Storici antichi e moderni n.s. 17 (Florence 1966) 301–03.

[20]*Consuetudines Farfenses*, ed. Bruno Albers, Consuetudines monasticae 1 (Stuttgart and Vienna 1900) 1: "Romualdus . . . normam priscae iustitiae . . . renovavit. . . . Hugo renovavit prisca sanctorum patrum" (= *Liber tramitis aevi Odilonis abbatis*, ed. Peter Dinter, Corpus consuetudinum monasticarum 10 [Siegburg 1980] 3–4). Maiolus of Cluny, who died in 994, was praised for "restaurationem . . . coenobiorum, pacem ecclesiis redditam, regum et principum concordiam," thus linking the restoration of monasticism with the return of peace, in his *Life* 2.10, PL 137.758B; and abbot Hugh was addressed as "totius religionis reformator" in the title to the *Ordo Cluniacensis* by Bernard of Cluny, ed. Marquard Herrgott, *Vetus disciplina monastica* (Paris 1726) 134. A monastery was given to Cluny in 1082 in the hope that "monasticus ordo reviviscat": *Recueil des chartes de l'abbaye de Cluny*, ed. Auguste J. Bernard and Alexandre Bruel, Collection de documents inédits sur l'histoire de France (6 vols. Paris 1876–1903) 4.756 no. 3598; cf. 5.69 no. 3724 (n. 39 below) and, for the ideal of personal reform, 5.255 no. 3905.

[21]Bruno of Toul, *De instauratione coenobii S. Apri*, PL 143.581C–582D; Wibert of Toul, *Vita Leonis IX* 1.11, in *Pontificum romanorum qui fuerunt inde ab exeunte saeculo IX usque ad finem saeculi XIII vitae*, ed. J. M. Watterich (2 vols. Leipzig 1862) 1.141; cf. Neithard Bulst, *Untersuchungen zu den Klosterreformen Wilhelms von Dijon (962–1031)*, Pariser historische Studien 11 (Bonn 1973) 90–100 and 108–14.

[22]William of Hirsau, *Vita* 21, MGH SS 12.218. Ebo, *Vita Ottonis episcopi Bambergensis* 1.19(20), ed. Jaffé, *Bibl.* 5.606–09 described the introduction of "the new order of the monks of Hirsau" into the abbey of St Michael at Bamberg. The spread of Cluniac monasticism in Germany

This dream of renewal after a period of decline came increasingly to seem a reality in the twelfth century. The lives of saints, chronicles, and charters contain countless references to the reform of religious houses by charismatic individuals and groups of monks.[23] The new orders of monks and canons used the imagery of renewal not only to legitimize their reforms but also, beginning in the 1130s, to celebrate the creation of new forms of religious life. Bernard of Clairvaux in the *De laude novae militiae* praised "the new type of army, unknown to the world" that had recently appeared in the East and which combined the vocation of a monk with that of a soldier in the service of God.[24] Cardinal Matthew of Albano combined the images of light and darkness, the seasons, and building, in his letter to the abbots assembled at Reims in 1131–32: they had been sent by God, he said, like "bright lights and shining stars" in order to banish the darkness obscuring the monastic order and had set up firm columns "in the ruined fabric of the monastic order in those frigid regions."[25] Matthew's friend Peter the Venerable rejoiced in a letter to the archbishop of Lyon that new religions had been founded and old ones renewed (*renovantur*) "throughout the entire region of the West and above all within this our Gaul." And to Matthew himself Peter exclaimed, "O how innumerable a crowd of monks has by divine grace multiplied above all in our days, has covered almost the entire countryside of Gaul, filled the towns, castles, and fortresses; however varied in clothing and in customs, the army of the Lord Saboath has sworn under one faith and love in the sacraments of the same monastic name."[26]

Philip of Harvengt used the cycle of life and death together with images of seasonal, vegetative, and igneous renewal in a notable passage in the *De*

---

by Morandus and his revival of the fervor of the monastic religion, "qui illo tempore pene refriguerat," are described in the *Vita Morandi*, in *Bibliotheca Cluniacensis*, ed. Martin Marrier and André Duchesne (Paris 1614) 503B–C and 506B.

[23]See the charter of bishop Alexander of Lincoln for Godstow in 1138, in Dugdale (n. 16 above) 4.362: "Benedictus Deus cuius nomen gloriosum in secula, qui sicut ecclesiam suam novo semper foetu multiplicat, ita eam nostris temporibus novo lumine sanctae religionis illustrat, dum fidelium devotione crescente, ad ipsius laudem novae fundantur ecclesiae"; Wibald of Corvey, *Epist.* 230–31, ed. Jaffé, *Bibl.* 1.348–51 (reform of Morbach in 1150); Goswin of Anchin, *Vita* 1.16, ed. Richard Gibbons (Douai 1620) 66 (reform of Anchin); Geoffrey of Vigeois, *Chronicon* 1.31 and 1.73, ed. Philippe Labbe, *Nova bibliotheca manuscriptorum librorum* (2 vols. Paris 1657) 2.296 and 328, on the decline of charity among monks and the "deformatio religionis" that preceded various reforms.

[24]Bernard of Clairvaux, *De laude novae militiae* 1.1 and 4.8, ed. Leclercq 3.214 and 221.

[25]Ursmer Berlière, *Documents inédits pour servir à l'histoire ecclésiastique de la Belgique* 1 (Maredsous 1894) 94–95.

[26]*The Letters of Peter the Venerable*, ed. Giles Constable, Harvard Historical Studies 78 (2 vols. Cambridge Mass 1967) 1.130 and 145 nos. 38 (1131/39) and 47 (1131/35). Peter referred to the new religious orders "per quos in Galliis, Germania, Anglia, Hispania, Italia, ac tota fere Europa, a multis annis arefacta religio refloruit, multorumque inveteratus tepor, divina praeeunte et comitante gratia recaluit," in his *Statutum* 22, ed. Giles Constable, *Consuetudines Benedictinae variae*, Corpus consuetudinum monasticarum 6 (Siegburg 1975) 60; see also *Statuta* 2 and 29, ibid. 43 and 65.

institutione clericorum, probably written in the 1140s. Thanks to the grace of God, he wrote, the monks of his own time

are seen to flower again (*reflorere*) and, after having been almost overwhelmed by the winter frost and desiccated by the constant northern winds, are restored (*revertuntur*) to their pristine state by the new sun and warmed by the favoring breezes. . . . When the new dew had fallen the claustral region flowered again (*reflorescit*). In the cloisters, as in trees, a rare fruit grew ripe. A workshop of total sanctity was set alight by the fire sent from above and fanned by violent winds.

Among the first of these workshops, according to Philip, was the abbey of Cîteaux, where "the monastic order, formerly dead, was revived (*suscitatur*); there the old ashes were poked; it was reformed by the grace of novelty, and by zeal it recovered (*revocatur*) its proper state . . . and the rule of Benedict recovered (*revocatur*) in our times the truth of the letter."[27]

This sense of satisfaction, almost self-congratulation, in the revival of monasticism is found in the works of many other writers in the twelfth and early thirteenth centuries.[28] Richard of St Victor compared the solitary places occupied by the thousands of monks, canons, and hermits to "the beautiful places of the wilderness" in Psalm 64.[29] Adam of Dryburgh referred to the many churches running forth like rivulets from the spring of Prémontré, which he called "a place of pleasure" not of the world but of God.[30] James of Vitry wrote, at the beginning of the chapter "On the Renovation of the Western Church" in his *Historia occidentalis*, "Every day the state of the western Church will be reformed for the better (*reformabitur in melius*)," and he went on to discuss the various groups of hermits and monks who, "placed like luminaries in the firmament of the western Church," illuminated the different parts of Europe. He described the Franciscans in particular as diligently striving "to reform in themselves the religion, poverty, and humility of the primitive church."[31] The decree of the Fourth Lateran Council requiring monks to establish chapters-general to treat "concerning the reformation of the order and regular observance" was likewise based on the assumption that

[27]Philip of Harvengt, *De institutione clericorum* 4 (*De continentia clericorum*) 125, PL 203.836A–37A; see also his *Epist.* 11 to Bernard of Clairvaux, ibid. 87D.

[28]See Gerhoch of Reichersberg, *Commentarium in Psalmos* 4, on Ps. 39:4, PL 193.1435D–36A: "Hinc post longam simoniae hiemem vernali suavitate spirante reflorescit vinea Dominica, constituuntur coenobia et xenodochia, et nova crebrescunt laudum cantica"; Wolfger of Prüfening, *Vita Theogeri abbatis S. Georgii et episcopi Mettensis* 1.11, MGH SS 12.452: "Tunc mirum in modum christiana religio, quae ab aliis conculcari iam coeperat, in aliis aucta refloruit"; and Robert of Torigny, *Tractatus de immutatione ordinis monachorum*, esp. c. 7 (*De reformatione quorumdam monasteriorum*), PL 202.1313B–C.

[29]Richard of St Victor, *Sermo* 72 *in anno novo*, PL 117.1127B (where it is attributed to Hugh of St Victor).

[30]Adam of Dryburgh, *De tripartito tabernaculo*, Proemia 6 and 10, PL 198.612D and 616A.

[31]James of Vitry, *Historia orientalis et occidentalis* 2.11–33, ed. Franciscus Moschus (Douai 1597) 294–357 (quotations on 294, 349, and 355).

the reform of religious life was possible—and must, indeed, be continuous.[32]

A Protestant historian writing in the seventeenth century likened the successive generations of monastic reformers in the Middle Ages to mercers who

when their old stuffs begin to tire in sale, refresh them with new names to make them more vendible; so when the Benedictines waxed stale in the world, the same order was set forth in a new edition, corrected and amended. . . . For commonly, once in a hundred years, starts up some pragmatical person in an Order, who out of novelty altars their old rules, . . . and out of his fancy adds some observances thereunto; to cry quits with whom, after the same distance of time, ariseth another, and under some new name reformeth his reformation, and then his late new (now old) Order is looked on as an almanac out of date, wanting the perfection of new and necessary alterations.[33]

There may be some truth in this view of natural cycles of monastic reform, but reformers in the twelfth century were less cynical and saw themselves not only as refurbishing old values but also as fostering genuinely new growth. In the foundation charter of the Cistercian abbey of Camp, issued in 1122, archbishop Frederick of Cologne expressed his desire "to insert spiritually into the garden of our church some branches of the new plantation of Cîteaux."[34] This horticultural image reflects the ideal of beauty and harmony that inspired many reformers. In 1160 archbishop Arnold of Metz issued a charter designed "to reform . . . the beauty" of the church of St Martin at Bingen.[35]

An important aspect of the reform movement was the rebuilding and repair of the ecclesiastical buildings that had been neglected or destroyed in the ninth and tenth centuries. Some of the reformers developed distinctive architectural and decorative styles designed to express both their break with the monastic traditions of the past and the beauty and simplicity of their religious ideals.[36] The new white costume of churches described by Ralph Glaber included repair as well as new construction, and many eleventh-century documents mention the restoration of churches.[37] The monks of St Jean d'Angély were given a church in about 1088 "on condition . . . that they rebuild and restore it to a better condition," and another one, about ten years later, that had been "burned by the fires of war and denuded of books and ornaments owing to the negligence of inexperienced priests," on condition that

[32]Concilium Lateranense IV, c. 12, ed. Giuseppe Alberigo et al., *Conciliorum oecumenicorum decreta* (3rd ed. Bologna 1973) 241; cf. cc. 7 and 14, ibid. 237 and 242.

[33]Thomas Fuller, *The Church History of Britain* 6.1.4.2 (3 vols. London 1837) 1.145–46. The first edition of this work appeared in 1655.

[34]Aubert Le Mire (Miraeus), *Opera diplomatica et historica*, 2nd ed. J. F. Foppens (4 vols. Louvain and Brussels 1723–48) 1.275–76.

[35]Heinrich Büttner, "Die Statuten des Binger St.-Martin-Stiftes von Jahre 1160," *Historisches Jahrbuch* 72 (1953) 169.

[36]The distinctive artistic style of the reformed orders is discussed elsewhere in this volume as an aspect of the renaissance in the arts, but the simple and uniform, though elegant, architecture of the Cistercians in particular also expressed their ideal of the renewal of religious life.

[37]See, among other secondary works, Emile Lesne, *Histoire de la propriété ecclésiastique en France*, Mémoires et travaux publiés par des professeurs des facultés catholiques de Lille 6, 19, 30, 34, 44, 46, 50, 53 (6 vols. in 8 Lille and Paris 1910–43) 3.95–96 and 6.36–37.

"what has been evilly destroyed should be built up into a good state, the ruins put together, the scattered property gathered."[38] Count William of Nevers rebuilt "from the foundation" the ruined monastery of St Stephen at Nevers.[39] To build or repair a church was a meritorious action,[40] and by occupying neglected churches many religious reformers and hermits achieved the double end of restoring to use previously consecrated buildings and of securing for themselves a church and habitation in a deserted place. Francis of Assisi rebuilt several churches with his own hands before devoting himself to the repair of the Church as a whole, and throughout his life he showed a concern for the proper upkeep of churches.[41]

Behind this need for material repair lay a deeper need for spiritual renewal, both of individuals and of institutions, and a growing confidence in the possibility of bridging the so-called "region of dissimilitude" between things as they had been created and as they had become and thus of recreating men and society into their original image and resemblance.[42] In the first chapter of the *Proslogion* Anselm thanked God for the creation within himself of the image of God but lamented, "It is so effaced by the rubbing of vices and so obscured by the smoke of sins that it cannot do that for which it was made unless You renew (*renoves*) and reform (*reformes*) it."[43] The terms *renovatio, reformatio, transformatio, reversio, recreatio,* and *reflectio* were applied by many writers in the twelfth century to the conversion or *transitus* of the soul from the state of dissimilarity into which it had fallen as a result of sin into the state of similarity or grace in which it had been created.[44] They also described the renewal of institutions, or re-forming in the literal sense of reshaping, back into their original forms. The personal and institutional uses of the concept were joined in a passage from the *Life* of William of St Thierry, who returned to his abbey after seeing a vision of the Virgin and taught the Christian life and monastic discipline there by both word and example. "By

---

[38]*Cartulaire de Saint-Jean d'Angély*, ed. Georges Musset, Archives historiques de la Saintonge et de l'Aunis 30, 33 (2 vols. Paris and Saintes 1901–04) 1.84 and 2.8–9 nos. 56 and 344; cf. the grant of a church to the abbey of St Alban by the archbishop of Mainz in 1090 "eo . . . pacto ut supradictus abbas destructa eius edificia per se repararet," *Mainzer Urkundenbuch* 1, ed. Manfred Stimming (Darmstadt 1932) 273 no. 374; and *La chronique de Saint-Hubert, dite Cantatorium* 79, ed. Karl Hanquet (Brussels 1906) 198.

[39]*Chartes de Cluny* (n. 20 above) 5.69 no. 3724.

[40]C. A. Garufi, "Il Tabulario di S. Maria di Valle Giosafat nel tempo Normanno-Svevo e la data delle sue falsificazioni," *Archivio storico per la Sicilia orientale* 5 (1908) 315–49 at 338 no. 1: "Scientes procul dubio quia quicumque construit domum ad laudem Dei in terris, preparat sibi sedem eternam in celis. . . ."

[41]*Scripta Leonis, Rufini et Angeli sociorum S. Francisci* 18, ed. and trans. Rosalind B. Brooke (Oxford 1970) 118.

[42]Javelet (n. 12 above) lists and discusses at length numerous secondary works on the doctrine of dissimilitude.

[43]Anselm of Canterbury, *Proslogion* 1, ed. F. S. Schmitt, *S. Anselmi Cantuariensis archiepiscopi opera omnia* (6 vols. Edinburgh 1946–61) 1.100.

[44]Javelet (n. 12 above) 2.239 n. 370 and 248 n. 445 cites several examples of writers using these terms.

the authority of his office he formed [this life and discipline] in beginners, strengthened [them] in the formed, reformed [them] in the deformed, and he enhanced his own reputation and improved his house."[45]

The process of deformation and reformation was often described by metaphors drawn from everyday life. Anselm pictured the soul as a rubbed medallion or smoky portrait. Hugh of St Victor, in describing the reformation into a new life by imitating good men, stressed that the softening action of humility was needed to make the individual responsive to the behavior of the example, which he compared to the projections and depressions of the matrix of a seal into which softened wax is pressed.[46] Peter of Celle also said that the image and similitude of God could be formed again in man, and his death assimilated to that of Christ, just as a seal is imprinted on wax that has been softened and yields to a seal.[47] Others used metaphors of clothing and instruction. Philip of Harvengt in *De dignitate clericorum* treated the clothes offered by a teacher to a pupil as the model shaping the behavior and character of the individual.[48] For Aelred of Rievaulx, the reading of Scripture, understanding of the sacraments, and daily practice of love were the means to repair the memory and "the perfect reformation of the image."[49]

This process was impossible without the aid of God and the exemplars sent by him, above all Christ himself, who in the eleventh and twelfth centuries was increasingly taken as a personal spiritual model whose least actions were to be imitated by the devout Christian. For Anselm it was the special role of Mary, "the mother of all that is recreated and of the restitution of all things," to remake everything that God had made.[50] This role was attributed

[45]A. Poncelet, "Vie ancienne de Guillaume de Saint-Thierry," *Mélanges Godefroid Kurth: Recueil de mémoires relatifs à l'histoire, à la philologie et à l'archéologie*, Bibliothèque de la faculté de philosophie et lettres de l'Université de Liège, Grand 8° 1–2 (2 vols. Liège and Paris 1908) 1.85–96 at 90. On the doctrine of teaching by word and example in the twelfth century, especially in relation to the spirituality of regular canons, see Caroline W. Bynum, *Docere verbo et exemplo: An Aspect of Twelfth-Century Spirituality*, Harvard Theological Studies 31 (Missoula Mont. 1979).

[46]Hugh of St Victor, *De institutione novitiorum* 7 (*De exemplis sanctorum imitandis*), PL 176.932D–33C. On the image of the seal in late ancient philosophy, see Stephen Gersh, *From Iamblichus to Eriugena: An Investigation of the Prehistory and Evolution of the Pseudo-Dionysian Tradition*, Studien zur Problemgeschichte der antiken und mittelalterlichen Philosophie 8 (Leiden 1978) 236 and, in the twelfth century, Javelet (n. 12 above) 1.83, 236, and 366–67.

[47]Peter of Celle, *Liber de panibus* 4, PL 202.949B–C (commenting on Genesis 1:26); see also his *Epist.* 1.43 (3.4), ibid. 463C–D–465, the passage by Thomas of Cîteaux quoted in n. 52 below, and Alan of Lille, *Elucidatio in Cantica canticorum* 8, PL 210.105A–06A at 105D (commenting on the *signaculum* in Cant. 8:6): "Signaculum dicitur cuius sigillum vel forma vel imago solet cerae imprimi ut cera recipiat formam sigilli. . . ."

[48]Philip of Harvengt, *De institutione clericorum* 1 (*De dignitate clericorum*) 16, PL 203.689–94.

[49]Aelred of Rievaulx, *Speculum caritatis* 1.5, ed. A. Hoste and C. H. Talbot, CCL cm 1 (1971) 18; cf. Herveus of Bourg-Dieu, *Commentaria in Epistolas Divi Pauli* 12, PL 181.765B (commenting on Rom. 12:2): "Reformatur autem sensus noster per exercitia sapientiae et emundationem verbi Dei, ac legis eius intelligentiam spiritualem."

[50]Anselm of Canterbury, *Oratio* 7, ed. Schmitt (n. 43 above) 3.22.

to the Holy Spirit by Rupert of Deutz, who said that "Although the Father, whose special task was to establish the nature of things, ceased, the Holy Spirit, whose special task was to improve nature, did not cease. Thus we properly distinguish God the Father and God the Holy Spirit in their tasks, since the Father founded, the Holy Spirit reformed the creation that He wished, and both Persons [act] through a third or middle Person, that is, the Son," whom Rupert described earlier in this passage as "this new man, this new creation."[51] Bernard of Clairvaux equated the stages of creation, reformation, and consummation with those in, through, and with Christ and those of liberty of will, the spirit of liberty, and the state of eternity. In his fourteenth and seventy-fourth sermons on the Song of Songs, Bernard described respectively the reformation of secular men "into the form of a new man" and the work of the Word within himself, waking, moving, softening, wounding, arousing, destroying, building, planting, irrigating, enlightening, warming, and affecting all his emotions and senses. "From the reformation and renovation of the spirit of my mind, that is, of my inner man," he concluded, "I have somehow received the semblance of His beauty."[52]

These and other contemporaries drew heavily on the Pauline image of the new man and on the doctrine of man's creation in the image of God. Hugh of St Victor in his sermon on the Circumcision stressed the need of monks to cut off their decadent ways, like a prepuce, and to renew themselves "in this world into a new man, by a new circumcision, in this new year" in order to deserve renewal in Christ in the next world.[53] Adam of Perseigne in his letter on novices stressed that through the action of the Holy Spirit, "the ways of life are recreated, the face of the earth is renewed" and the novices are made "participants in this marvelous novelty."[54] According to Adam of Dryburgh, a new canon must show by his way of life "the novelty of his sanctity" and his conversion "to a certain new rectitude."[55]

[51]Rupert of Deutz, *De sancta Trinitate et operibus suis* 34 (*De operibus Spiritus Sancti* 1), ed. Rhaban Haacke, CCL cm 24 (1972) 1824.

[52]Bernard of Clairvaux, *De gratia et libero arbitrio* 14, ed. Leclercq 3.201, and *Sermones super Cantica* 14.5 and 74.6 ibid. 1.79 and 2.243; cf. Isaac of Stella, *Sermones* 41, 51, and 54, PL 194.1828–29, 1865, and 1872–73 on the themes of renewal and revivification in and by Christ, and Thomas of Cîteaux, *In cantica canticorum* 8, PL 206.546C (commenting on Cant. 5:6, "Anima mea liquefacta est"): "Triplex est imago Christi: prima est carnis corruptibilis, secunda glorificatae humanitatis, tertia divinitatis. Primam debemus in corde sigillare, ut ei compatiamur; secundam, ut ad similitudinem eius suspiremus; tertiam ut eam in regno videamus." Alan of Lille, who became a Cistercian at the end of his life, was fascinated by the themes of rebirth, regeneration, and recreation: see his *Expositio prosae de angelis* in Marie-Thérèse d'Alverny, ed., *Alain de Lille: Textes inédits*, EPM 52 (Paris 1965) 200 and *De planctu naturae* 6 in Nikolaus M. Häring, "Alan of Lille, 'De planctu naturae,'" *Studi medievali* 3rd ser. 19 (1978) 797–879 at 829.

[53]Hugh of St Victor, *Sermo* 49, PL 177.1039B–C.

[54]Adam of Perseigne, *Lettres* vol. 1, ed. and trans. Jean Bouvet, Sources chrétiennes 66: Textes monastiques d'Occident 4 (Paris 1960) 122; see also his letter to abbot J. of La Couture, ed. Jean Bouvet, "Lettres d'Adam de Perseigne à ses correspondants du Maine (XIIe–XIIIe siècles)," *La Province du Maine* 2nd ser. 31 (1951) 155–77 at 170: "Revera Christi imitacio in conspicua vita pii pastoris, format et reformat Christum in subditis. . . ."

[55]Adam of Dryburgh, *Liber de ordine: Sermo* 6.2, PL 198.489D.

For institutions, too, the process of renewal required both divine inspiration and models to serve as exemplars for reform and to legitimize change and innovation. The reformers of the twelfth century found their models above all in the Bible and the early Church, and they looked back to the Garden of Eden, the primitive church in Jerusalem, and the beginnings of monasticism in Egypt and in Italy as the ideals by which to reshape the institutions of their own time. Each of these exemplars, like the metaphors of renewal, was to some extent a rhetorical topos and was probably not taken entirely seriously even by those who used it; but as models in a period of transition and experimentation they exercised a real influence on the forms of religious life in the central Middle Ages.

The idea of a return to the Garden of Eden was dear to the hearts of reformers at all times and crucial to the mystic experience of Christian "primitives."[56] Ecclesiastical writers had long applied paradisiacal imagery to the Church in general and to monasteries in particular and drawn on the topos of the *locus amoenus* that dictated the descriptions of natural beauty and paradise from Antiquity down to the sixteenth century.[57] In the eleventh and twelfth centuries there was a tendency to concentrate this imagery on the cloister rather than on the Church as a whole and to see the monastery as the *hortus conclusus* of Scripture.[58] Those who left the world at the urging of Odo of Anchin, later bishop of Cambrai, were said to have considered "their city . . . to be a prison, the monastery a paradise."[59] Alexander of Lewes, after becoming a Cluniac, was said to have regretted leaving "the house of the true paradise" at Witham.[60] For Peter of Blois the monastery, unlike the world and like paradise, was the home of virginity, "and by virginity the life and manners of the angels are reformed in man."[61] Hugh of Fouilloy specifically com-

---

[56]Mircea Eliade, *Images et symboles: Essais sur le symbolisme magico-religieux* (Paris 1952) 221.

[57]See Ernst Robert Curtius, "Rhetorische Naturschilderung im Mittelalter," *Romanische Forschungen* 56 (1942) 219–56 at 244–45; Stock, *Myth and Science* 133–37; Gregorio Penco, "Il senso della natura nell'agiografia monastica occidentale," *Studia monastica* 11 (1969) 327–34; Dagmar Thoss, *Studien zum locus amoenus im Mittelalter*, Wiener romanistische Arbeiten 10 (Vienna and Stuttgart 1972); Gabriella Lodolo, "Il tema simbolico del paradiso nella tradizione monastica dell'Occidente latino (secoli VI–XII): Lo spazio del simbolo," *Aevum* 51 (1977) 252–88.

[58]Henri de Lubac, *Exégèse médiévale: Les quatre sens de l'Ecriture*, Théologie 41, 42, 59 (2 vols. in 4 Paris 1959–64) 1.577; Jean Leclercq,"Le cloître est-il un paradis?"*Le message des moines à notre temps* (Paris 1958) 141–59; George H. Williams, *Wilderness and Paradise in Christian Thought* (New York 1962) esp. 38–48.

[59]Léopold Delisle, *Rouleaux des morts du IXe au XVe siècle*, Société de l'histoire de France 11 (Paris 1866) 175 no. 35.

[60]*The Life of St. Hugh of Lincoln*, ed. and trans. Decima L. Douie and Hugh Farmer (2 vols. Edinburgh 1961–62) 1.82.

[61]Peter of Blois, *Epist.* 239, ed. J. G. Giles, *Petri Blesensis bathoniensis archidiaconi opera omnia* (4 vols. Oxford 1846–47) 2.234. On the theme of the angelic life of monks, especially in the eastern monastic tradition, see Emmanuel von Severus, "'Bios angelikos': Zum Verständnis des Mönchslebens als 'Engelleben' in der christlichen Überlieferung," *Die Engel in der Welt und Heute: Gesammelte Aufsätze*, ed. Theodor Bogler, Liturgie und Mönchtum 21 (Maria Laach 1957) 56–70.

pared the monastery to paradise and monks to angels in his treatise *De claustro animae*: "The greenness of the lawn in the middle of the material cloister refreshes the eyes of the monks and makes them more eager to read," he said, pointing out that there was a similar green field with the tree of life in the middle of the heavenly monastery.[62]

Paradise and the cloister were often described in similar terms, as in the *Hexaemeron* of Arnold of Bonneval, who said that paradise

was called Eden, that is, pleasure, and a garden of delights because of the richness of the soil and the fruitful orchards. From the center there flowed a crystal spring, watering and moistening each plant at its roots, not overflowing too copiously, however, but by underground irrigation wetting the entire area of the garden. Spreading leaves in the tall trees shaded the grass beneath and both the moisture below and the equable atmosphere above nourished an everlasting greenness in the turf.[63]

Although this type of imagery was traditional and in certain respects commonplace, it took on a new meaning for the founders and reformers of religious houses in the eleventh and twelfth centuries. Peter Damiani called his hermitage "a paradise of pleasures" and compared it to a garden in which the colors and smells of each flower corresponded to a particular virtue.[64] William of Malmesbury described Thorney Abbey as "the image of paradise, which in its pleasantness already resembles heaven itself." Its beauty and fertility, he explained, were rivaled only by the virtues of its inhabitants.[65] William of St Denis, in a letter written in 1151/53, praised the beauty and fruitfulness of the hermitage at St Denis en Vaux in Aquitaine, where those who wished could be free for learning, "neither beaten by the tumult nor prevented by the crowd" and where no sound was heard "except that either made by the song of birds or roused by the breath of wind."[66] And the historian of Selby, writing in 1174 about the foundation of the abbey a century earlier, described its location as "a most pleasant place, both planted with many trees and surrounded by several abundant rivers, as if it were an earthly paradise."[67]

[62]Hugh of Fouilloy, *De claustro animae* 4.29–34, PL 176.1167B–72D (quotation on 1172D). On the symbolism of trees in the Middle Ages, see Gerhart B. Ladner, "Medieval and Modern Understanding of Symbolism: A Comparison," *Speculum* 54 (1979) 223–56, esp. 233–41.

[63]Arnold of Bonneval, *Hexaemeron*, PL 189.1535B–C; cf. Boas (n. 17 above) 72–75, who said that this passage "should be read in connection with the emphasis which the Franciscan school was to put upon natural beauty as evidence of God's goodness" (75 n. 38).

[64]Peter Damiani, *Liber qui appellatur Dominus Vobiscum* 19, PL 145.246D.

[65]William of Malmesbury, *De gestis pontificum Anglorum libri quinque* 4.186, ed. Nicholas E. S. A. Hamilton, RS 52 (London 1870) 326–27.

[66]William of St Denis, *Epist.*, PL 186.1472D–73A; cf. Hubert Glaser, "Wilhelm von Saint-Denis: Ein Humanist aus der Umgebung des Abtes Suger und die Krise seiner Abtei von 1151 bis 1153," *Historisches Jahrbuch* 85 (1965) 257–322 at 283–84.

[67]*Historia monasterii Selebiensis in Anglia* 11, ed. Joseph T. Fowler, *The Coucher Book of Selby*, Yorkshire Archaeological and Topographical Association: Record Series 10, 13 (2 vols. Durham 1891–93) 1.[12]. See also the descriptions of the locations of Rolduc in *Annales Rodenses*, MGH SS 16.700–01, and Marmoutiers in *Narratio de commendatione Turonicae provinciae*, ed. André Salmon, *Recueil de chroniques de Touraine* (Tours 1854) 294–95.

Some of the most sensitive descriptions of the natural beauty of monastic sites, and those most reminiscent of contemporary descriptions of paradise, were written by Cistercians. Their sense of the paradisiacal nature of their surroundings (in theory if not always in fact) was also shown by the names of their abbeys, which included the Court and Ladder of God and the Fountain of Salvation as well as innumerable shining, bright, beautiful, good, and golden valleys, springs, and meadows.[68] The sacred names of many Cistercian houses indicated to the historian Robert of Torigny "how great a blessedness is there."[69] For Walter Daniel, Rievaulx was "another paradise of wooded delight," surrounded by hills "clothed with a variety of trees" and by streams "softly sounding in a gentle murmur and joining their sweet notes in delightful songs."[70] Gilbert of Swineshead (Holland), addressing another Cistercian abbot, Roger of Byland, contrasted the location of his abbey with that of the ancient monks of Egypt:

A secret, cultivated, well-watered, and fertile place and a wooded valley resounds in springtime with the sweet song of birds, so that it can revive the dead spirit, remove the aversions of the dainty soul, soften the hardness of the undevout mind. These in brief either depict for you the signs of future happiness or show some remains of that first [happiness] which the integrity of the human condition received amid the pleasures of paradise.[71]

This passage is of special interest for two reasons. First, Gilbert looked for his model explicitly to the future as well as to the past and saw the paradisiacal features of the monastery both as a remnant of the happiness that once existed and as an anticipation of the happiness to come. Second, he defined three specific ways in which the paradisiacal site promoted the reform of the individual: by reviving the spirit, by overcoming aversions, and by softening resistance (again like the wax for a seal). The beauty of the site was not simply a by-product of the abbey's remote location or a rhetorical device to emphasize its resemblance to paradise but an essential factor in promoting its spiritual work of saving mankind.

William of St Denis, Walter Daniel, and Gilbert of Swineshead all drew attention to the sweet sounds of the birds and breezes, which contributed to the harmonious effect and roused the spirits of the listeners. Miro of Ripoll was

---

[68]Marie-Anselme Dimier, *Clarté paix et joie: Les beaux noms des monastères de Cîteaux en France*, La Clarté-Dieu 15 (Lyon 1944).

[69]Robert of Torigny, *Tractatus de immutatione ordinis monachorum* 1, PL 202.1311C.

[70]Walter Daniel, *The Life of Ailred of Rievaulx*, ed. and trans. F. M. Powicke (Edinburgh 1950) 12–13; Powicke compared this passage to Bernard's prefatory letter to the *Speculum caritatis* and to Bruno's account of his hermitage in Calabria but commented that "this lyrical rhapsody reveals a delight in natural beauty which is Walter's own" (13 n. 1). Cf. the description of the location of Meaux in *Chronica monasterii de Melsa*, ed. E. A. Bond, RS 43 (3 vols. London 1866–68) 1.76–77.

[71]Gilbert of Holland, *Tractatus VII ad Rogerum abbatem* 2.4, in Bernard of Clairvaux, *Opera omnia*, ed. Jean Mabillon (2 vols. in 6 Paris 1839) 2(5)376C; cf. Edmund Mikkers, "De vita et operibus Gilberti de Hoylandia," *Cîteaux* 14 (1963) 33–43 and 265–79 at 273.

said to have been inspired to leave the world by listening to the songs of birds at dawn. "Who except the Supreme Governor composed the melody of those birds?" he asked. "Who will give me the powers to concord in imitation of these animals? What an internal harmony is formed by the points of the virtues! Where, my beloved, do you desire me to make my nest in order to say farewell to the world?"[72] The same effect was produced for Walter Daniel by the sound of leaves: "And when the branches of lovely trees rustle and sing together and the leaves flutter gently to earth, the happy listener is filled increasingly with a glad jubilee of harmonious sound."[73] The sound as well as the sight of beauty touched the soul and roused it to seek God.

The peace and harmony of paradise also made it attractive to the reformers as a model for human society. For them the cloister was a microcosm of the cosmic harmony represented by the macrocosm of the universe.[74] William of Malmesbury stressed "the mutual endeavor of nature and cultivation" at Thorney, where man produced what nature forgot.[75] The idea of social harmony was praised in the biography of Gilbert of Sempringham, who brought together in his double monasteries men and women from varied walks of life. His houses were compared to the chariot of God and the chariots of Aminadab: "this miraculous unity both of persons and of churches, this unheard-of communion of all things which thus makes one thing all and all things one, in a diversity of so many hearts and of such great monasteries."[76]

The exemplar of social harmony as a spiritual ideal was found by many reformers in the description of the early church in Acts 4:32: "And the multitude of believers had but one heart and one soul. Neither did anyone say that aught of the things which he possessed was his own; but all things were common unto them." This text had been cited since the earliest days of Christianity as a spur to a common life not only of behavior and property but also of faith and prayer,[77] and for the reformers of the eleventh and twelfth centuries it embodied the concept of the primitive church as the golden age of the ideals of charity, poverty, and communality.[78] As time went on, the term *ecclesia*

[72]Miro of Ripoll, *Vita*, in *España sagrada* 28 (Madrid 1774) 305–12 at 306. On the importance of birds in twelfth-century paradisiacal imagery, see Charles Oulmont, *Les débats du clerc et du chevalier dans la littérature poétique du moyen-âge* (Paris 1911) 13–16.

[73]*Life of Ailred* (n. 70 above) 13.

[74]On the theological and philosophical theory of cosmological harmony in the twelfth century, see Tullio Gregory, *Anima mundi: La filosofia di Guglielmo di Conches e la Scuola di Chartres* (Florence 1955) and Stock, *Myth and Science*.

[75]*De gestis pontificum* 4.186 (n. 65 above) 326.

[76]Gilbert of Sempringham, *Vita*, ed. Dugdale (n. 16 above) 6(2)*x (after 945).

[77]Jonas of Orléans, *De institutione laicali* 1.20, PL 106.164A: "In primordio igitur sanctae Dei ecclesiae circa credentes ardor fidei ita vigebat, ut perseverarent in doctrina apostolorum, et communicatione fractionis panis, et orationibus, et haberent omnia communia; et sumerent cibum cum exsultatione, et simplicitate cordis, collaudantes Deum."

[78]See, among other works, the unpublished dissertation of Magnus Ditsche, "Die Ecclesia primitiva im Kirchenbild des hohen und späten Mittelalters" (Bonn 1958); Giovanni Miccoli,

primitiva was also applied to the church of Constantine, and even that of Gregory the Great, and increasingly it lost its ethical content and was used in a purely historical sense.[79] It was used as a political slogan by the Cathars, Waldensians, and other dissident religious groups who compared the contemporary church unfavorably with the church of the early Christians. By the late twelfth century, therefore, orthodox churchmen tended to treat the concept with a certain degree of caution, but among reformers and radicals it retained much of its power as a standard of reform.[80]

Among the most important references to the ideal of the primitive church in papal documents and conciliar decrees of the eleventh century was that of pope Urban II in his privilege of 1092 for the canons of Rottenbuch, who had "renewed (*renovatis*) the proven life of the holy fathers and revived (*suscitatis*) the institutions of the apostolic discipline which arose at the origins of the holy church but were almost obliterated as it grew." The pope went on to distinguish the monastic from the canonical way of life, which he equated with that of the early church, and concluded, "To revive (*suscitare*) this primitive life of the church . . . is therefore to be considered no less meritorious than to watch over the flourishing religion of monks."[81] This passage was used subsequently in a number of papal privileges and helped not only to fan the enthusiasm for reviving the life of the primitive church but also to establish that in principle the ways of life of monks and of canons were equal.[82] The example of the early church was cited as evidence of the superiority of canons over monks in a letter written by Lietbert of St Rufus, who argued, "This order of ours first flourished in Christ, in the apostles, in the primitive church, but subsequently, when love grew cold and persecution pressed, it withered away. Pope Urban the Martyr then began to revive it by his decrees; the blessed Augustine ordained it in his rules; St Jerome commended it in his letters."[83]

"'Ecclesiae primitivae forma,'" first published in *Studi medievali* 3rd ser. 1 (1960) 470–98 and republished in expanded form in his *Chiesa gregoriana* (n. 19 above) 225–99; and Olsen (n. 6 above). On the period down to the fifth century, see Pier Cesare Bori, *Chiesa primitiva: L'immagine della comunità delle origini—Atti 2.42–47; 4.32–37—nella storia della chiesa antica*, Testi e ricerche di scienze religiose 10 (Brescia 1974).

[79]Olsen (n. 6 above) 81–82.

[80]Ditsche (n. 78 above) 47–61 and, for the late Middle Ages, Gordon Leff, "The Apostolic Ideal in Later Medieval Ecclesiology," *Journal of Theological Studies* 2nd ser. 18 (1967) 58–82 and Scott H. Hendrix, "In Quest of the *Vera Ecclesia*: The Crises of Late Medieval Ecclesiology," *Viator* 7 (1976) 347–78. In the passage by James of Vitry cited in n. 31 above, however, the ideal of the primitive church was mentioned with reference to the Franciscans.

[81]PL 151.338C–D and, better, Jakob Mois, *Das Stift Rottenbuch in der Kirchenreform des 11. und 12. Jahrhunderts*, Beiträge zur altbayerischen Kirchengeschichte 3rd ser. 19 (Munich 1953) 76–77.

[82]PL 151.360B; cf. Wilhelm Levison, "Eine angebliche Urkunde Papst Gelasius' II. für die Regularkanoniker," ZRG kan Abt 8 (1918) 27–43; Peter Classen, "Gerhoch von Reichersberg und die Regularkanoniker in Bayern und Oesterreich, Beilage 3: Ein unbekanntes Mandat Papst Urbans II. fuer Rottenbuch," *Vita comune* (n. 1 above) 1.337–40; Dietrich Lohrmann, *Papsturkunden in Frankreich*, n.s. 7: *Nördliche Ile-de-France und Vermandois*, Abh Göttingen 3rd ser. 95 (Göttingen 1976) 248–50 no. 14.

[83]Lietbert of St Rufus, *Epist.* 1, PL 157.718D.

In 1124 the cardinals Pierleoni (the future antipope Anacletus II) and Gregory of St Angelo used almost the same words as Urban II in a document addressed to Norbert, thanking God that he had "renewed the proven life of the holy fathers and revived the institutions of the apostolic doctrine. . . . To revive this life of the primitive church. . . ," they continued, again almost repeating Urban, "is to be considered no less meritorious than to watch over the flourishing religion of monks."[84]

The example of the primitive church was cited as the basis for reform in many religious houses. The archbishop of Mainz in 1074 decreed that the canons of Ravengiersburg should live "in accordance with the example of those who in the primitive church . . . were said to have had nothing of their own but everything in common."[85] The founders of Chaumouzey, according to Seher, the first abbot, sought "to leave the broad path of their former way of life and as much as their strength allowed to renew (*renovare*) by penances the image of the Lord," which had been blotted out in the world. "There was among the brothers whom fear of hell and love of the eternal reward had gathered to live together," Seher continued, "one heart and one soul in God for restoring (*ad reparandum*) the condition of the primitive church."[86] The link between personal and institutional reform comes out clearly in this passage, which also underlines Seher's conviction that the renewal in individuals of the image of God was impossible in secular life and could be achieved only in an institution modeled on the early church. This ideal appealed to laymen as well as to monks and canons, and many reformers, both men and women, came from the ranks of the laity. According to Bernold of St Blaise (Constance), for example, the members of the lay religious groups in south Germany at the end of the eleventh century "appeared to live communally in the form of the primitive church."[87]

The *vita apostolica* offered an exemplary way of life corresponding to the institutional model proposed by the *ecclesia primitiva*, and in the early Middle Ages it was based on the same texts in the book of Acts.[88] According to Bede,

---

[84]Hugo, *Annales* (n. 16 above) 1.1.viii.

[85]Heinrich Beyer et al., *Urkundenbuch zur Geschichte der jetzt die preussischen Regierungsbezirke Coblenz und Trier bildenden mittelrheinischen Territorien* (3 vols. Coblenz 1860–74) 1.431 no. 374; cf. Johannes Wirges, *Die Anfänge der Augustiner-Chorherren und die Gründung des Augustiner-Chorherrenstiftes Ravengiersburg (Hunsrück) Diözese Trier* (Betzdorf 1928) 117 and Charles Dereine, "La réforme canoniale en Rhénanie (1075–1150)," *Mémorial d'un voyage d'études de la Société nationale des antiquaires de France en Rhénanie (juillet 1951)* (Paris 1953) 235–40 at 235.

[86]Seher of Chaumouzey, *Primordia Calmosiacensia* 1.1, *Documents rares ou inédits de l'histoire des Vosges*, vols. 1–2 ed. Léopold Duhamel (Paris 1868–69) 2.9.

[87]Bernold of St Blaise, *Chronicon* s.a. 1091, MGH SS 5.453.

[88]Among the many scholars who have studied the *vita apostolica* over the past thirty years, see especially Luchesius Spätling, *De apostolicis, pseudoapostolicis, apostolinis*, Pontificium Athenaeum Antonianum: Facultas theologica, Theses ad Lauream 35 (Munich 1947); Ernest W. McDonnell, "The *Vita apostolica*: Diversity or Dissent," *Church History* 24 (1955) 15–31; several articles in Chenu, *Théologie*; Marie-Humbert Vicaire, *L'imitation des apôtres: Moines, chanoines et mendiants, IVe–XIIIe siècles*, Tradition et spiritualité 2 (Paris 1963); Karl Suso Frank,

Augustine of Canterbury and his followers lived "the apostolic life of the primitive church," serving with prayers, vigils, and fasts, preaching the word of life, spurning worldly things, receiving support from those they instructed, living in accordance with their teaching, and willing to suffer for the truth.[89] Down to the eleventh century, the main feature of the *vita apostolica* was seen not as the pastoral activities but as the common life of the first apostles, and it was therefore generally equated with the life of monks.[90] The monastic ideal—a life of common customs, prayer, charity, and poverty, together with the manual labor and physical hardships resulting from poverty—inspired the reformers of the eleventh century, who sought to impose it on the entire Church. All clerics, according to the Roman council of 1059, "should live and sleep together, and hold in common what comes to them from churches . . . and should strive most greatly to achieve the apostolic, that is, the common life."[91]

For the better part of a century the apostolic life served as the ideal for communities of monks and canons. Countless charters, like that of archbishop Siegfried of Mainz cited above, required religious men and women to have nothing of their own and everything in common.[92] In a charter issued for Steinfeld in 1121, archbishop Frederick of Cologne said that he had "given heed to the rule of the canonical profession that was established by the apostles, was diligently observed by apostolic men, was then both made known in teaching and approved in use by the venerable father Augustine, [and] finally in modern times is spreading (*pullulantem*) far and wide through the church of Christ." The term *pullulantem* here suggests an image of growth and reproduction, and *modernis temporibus* shows an awareness of historical change and development. The ideal Frederick advocated was still the traditional one of withdrawal, however, and later in the charter he specifically excluded pastoral work from the community church and decreed that "the parochial care of which the disposition belongs to this monastery should be transferred to the chapel located in the atrium of the community."[93]

"Vita apostolica: Ansätze zur apostolischen Lebensform in der alten Kirche," *Zeitschrift für Kirchengeschichte* 82 (1971) 145–66; and Duane V. Lapsanski, *Perfectio evangelica: Eine begriffsgeschichtliche Untersuchung im frühfranziskanischen Schrifttum*, Veröffentlichungen des Grabmann-Institutes zur Erforschung der mittelalterlichen Theologie und Philosophie n.s. 22 (Munich 1974; English trans. St Bonaventure N.Y. 1977) esp. 1–43 on *vita apostolica* and *vita evangelica* in the pre-Franciscan movements.

[89]Bede, *Ecclesiastical History* (*Historia ecclesiastica gentis Anglorum*) 1.26, ed. Charles Plummer (2 vols. Oxford 1896; repr. 1959) 1.46–47, cf. 4.21[23] ibid. 1.254, where Bede said that in the primitive church no one was rich, no one was poor, and all things were common to all men.

[90]Chenu, *Théologie* 227–28, who stressed that the apostolic life at this time was a way of life rather than a function or *officium*.

[91]Mansi 19.898B, repeated almost verbatim by the Roman council of 1069, c. 4, ibid. 1025C. The authority of the primitive church was also cited in c. 1 of the council of Benevento in 1091, Mansi 20.738.

[92]See above at n. 85.

[93]Theodor J. Lacomblet, *Urkundenbuch für die Geschichte des Niederrheins oder des Erzstifts Cöln* (4 vols. Düsseldorf 1840–58; repr. Aalen 1960) 1.191 no. 292. Note the reference here to a

Already in the late eleventh century, however, there were signs of a shift away from this predominantly monastic conception of the *vita apostolica* and of a tendency to base it less on the ideal of communal perfection found in Acts 4:32 and more on the ideal of personal perfection found in Matthew 19:21.[94] In the *Epistola ad Fratres de Monte Dei*, William of St Thierry referred to "those saintly poor men in the primitive church" who gave up their property and were supported by alms given "to those preaching the Gospel . . . and living evangelically."[95] Especially in texts written by and for canons, there is an emphasis on preaching and teaching.[96] The ideal of the evangelical life, combining a stress on individual perfection with pastoral activity, thus increasingly overshadowed the older ideal of the apostolic life.[97] The precise nature and date of this shift is a subject of dispute among scholars, some of whom believe that it covered the entire twelfth century and others that it took place relatively quickly about the middle of the century.[98]

As the century progressed the concept of the apostolic life took on a more activist emphasis, and also heretical associations that tended to discredit it in the eyes of contemporaries. Guibert of Nogent, who died in 1124, spoke in his *Vita* of heretics who claimed to lead the apostolic life, and Peter the Venerable in the 1130s mentioned "false" monks who likewise claimed to live "the apostolic, that is, the common life."[99] Later in the century the monk Herbert warned against heretics "who say that they lead the apostolic life" and who won converts to their dualist beliefs. "No one is such a peasant," he wrote scornfully, "that within a week of joining them he is not so learned in letters that he can no longer be subdued by either words or examples."[100] Like the concept of the primitive church, therefore, the concept of the apostolic life was used to foment the growing discontent with the institutional structures of the

---

house of canons as *monasterium*. See also the bull of Innocent II for Berchtesgaden in 1138/43, PL 179.628D–29C, JL 8294.

[94]Miccoli (n. 19 above) 288–89.

[95]William of Thierry, *Un traité de la vie solitaire: Epistola ad Fratres de Monte Dei* 68, ed. Marie-Magdeleine Davy, EPM 29 (Paris 1940) 117.

[96]Charles Dereine, "La 'Vita apostolica' dans l'Ordre canonial du IXe au XIe siècles," *Revue Mabillon* 51 (1961) 47–53.

[97]Peter the Venerable, citing Isa. 52:7, substituted the term *aevangelizantis* for *adnuntiantis et praedicantis*, showing that the evangelical life had come to embrace missionary work and preaching: *Letters* (n. 26 above) 1.174 no. 54.

[98]For differing views on this question, see the works of Chenu and Vicaire cited in n. 88 above.

[99]Guibert of Nogent, *Vita* 3.17, ed. Georges Bourgin, *Guibert de Nogent: Histoire de sa vie (1053–1124)*, CTSEEH 40 (Paris 1907) 213; Peter the Venerable, *Letters* (n. 26 above) 1.129 no. 38.

[100]Herbert the Monk, *Epistola de haereticis Petragoricis*, PL 181.1722. For other examples of the use of the terms *vita apostolica* and *apostoli* for heretics in the twelfth century, see Herbert Grundmann, "Neue Beiträge zur Geschichte der religiösen Bewegungen im Mittelalter," AKG 37 (1955) 129–82 at 150–51, repr. in his *Ausgewählte Aufsätze*, vol. 1: *Religiöse Bewegungen*, MGH Schriften 25.1 (Stuttgart 1976) 38–92 at 60; Ernst Werner, *Pauperes Christi: Studien zu sozial-religiösen Bewegungen im Zeitalter des Reformpapsttums* (Leipzig 1956) 16 n. 41; Ladner (n. 1 above) 364 and 402 n. 64, who cites earlier examples.

medieval Church;[101] but in various circles, including the mendicant orders and pious lay groups, it continued to influence the revision of orthodox Christian values and ways of life.[102]

Both the monastic and the pastoral views of the *vita apostolica* appear in the works of Bernard of Clairvaux, who on this as on so many other issues stood at the crossroads of twelfth-century attitudes and institutions, pointing toward both the old and the new positions. In his sermons he more than once referred to the life of Cistercian monks as apostolic, and he wrote to king David of Scotland that the monks of Fountains had left St Mary's at York for "a deserted place" and had become poor religious men out of love for Christ, striving after "the apostolic life and true sanctity."[103] In his third sermon *De labore messis*, on the other hand, he equated evangelical perfection with the dominical injunction to leave all and follow Christ, which while compatible with traditional monastic views suggested a shift toward the new ideal, and in his *Life* of St Malachy, after emphasizing his itinerant preaching as well as his poverty, Bernard remarked that "This was the apostolic form. . . . He who does such things is indeed the true heir to the apostles."[104]

The third historical exemplar used as a model by reformers in the eleventh and twelfth centuries was the life of the desert fathers in Egypt and that of St Benedict's early followers. William of St Thierry in the *First Life* of St Bernard said that he followed in the steps of "the ancient Egyptian monks, our fathers" and dedicated "the first-fruits of his youth to resuscitating (*resuscitandum*) the fervor of the ancient religion in the monastic order, concentrating all his efforts on this by example and by word in the community of brothers within the enclosure of the monastery." William said that Bernard began to preach to the laity only when he was cut off by ill health from his community.[105] Geoffrey of Auxerre said that many others entered Cîteaux "in order to revive (*ad redivivam*) the profession of the observance of the rule of St Benedict."[106] When the Cistercian monk in the *Dialogus duorum mona- chorum* of Idung of Prüfening, written soon after 1154/55, asserted that the Cistercian *ordo* or *consuetudo* derived from the ancient monks, especially the Egyptian fathers and St Basil, the Cluniac retorted, "Since you Cistercians judaize, following the killing letter of the Rule, you therefore diligently ob-

---

[101]See especially Werner (n. 100 above) 198.

[102]Etienne Delaruelle, "La vie commune des clercs et la spiritualité populaire au XIe siècle," *Vita comune* (n. 1 above) 1.153, and Lapsanski (n. 88 above).

[103]Bernard of Clairvaux, *Sermones de diversis* 22.2 and 27.3, ed. Leclercq 6.1.171 and 200, and *Epist*. 519, ibid. 8.479.

[104]Bernard of Clairvaux, *Sermo de labore messis* 3.7, ed. Leclercq 5.226; *Vita sancti Malachiae* 19.43–44, ibid. 3.348–49.

[105]William of St Thierry, *Vita prima sancti Bernardi* 7.34 and 8.42, in Bernard of Clairvaux, *Opera omnia* (n. 71 above) 2(6)2118A and 2123B.

[106]Jean Leclercq, "Le témoignage de Geoffroy d'Auxerre sur la vie cistercienne," *Analecta monastica* 2, Studia Anselmiana 31 (Rome 1953) 174–201 at 193.

serve the authorities pertaining only to the letter, in order that through them you may defend your judaizing.''[107]

The charge of observing the letter rather than the spirit of the Rule was often brought against the Cistercians and other reformers who tried to impose on contemporary institutions a pattern of life found in earlier rules.[108] Literalism of this sort was not always criticized, as is shown by Philip of Harvengt's admiring reference, in the passage already cited, to the return in his time of the Rule of Benedict to the truth of the letter; but it has been interpreted as a criticism by modern scholars, who have pointed out that the phrase *ad litteram* is found in no official Cistercian text and that such terms as *arctius, perfectius, pure, simpliciter*, and *ex integro* indicate a concern for integrity and strictness rather than for the literal observance of the Rule.[109] The phrase *ad litteram* appears, however, in several nonlegislative texts of high authority and antiquity, including Bernard's *Apologia* and *De praecepto et dispensatione*, where he distinguished the Cistercians, who observed the Rule *pure ad litteram*, from less perfect monks whose customs had modified the Rule.[110] Orderic Vitalis likewise described the monks of Clairvaux under Bernard in 1130 as attempting to observe the Rule of Benedict *pure ad litteram*.[111]

For these writers literalism embodied the essence of their desire to reestablish a type of life that had existed in the past and had subsequently declined. They took as their models, after Christ himself, the prophets of the Old Testament, John the Baptist, and above all St Anthony and the desert fathers.[112] These ideals were combined with those of the apostolic life and the literal observance of the Rule of Benedict in a passage from the *Life* of Gerald of

[107]R. B. C. Huygens, "Le moine Idung et ses deux ouvrages: 'Argumentum super quatuor questionibus' et 'Dialogus duorum monachorum,'" *Studi medievali* 3rd ser. 13 (1972) 291–470 at 444.

[108]Gerd Zimmermann, *Ordensleben und Lebensstandard: Die Cura corporis in den Ordensvorschriften des abendländischen Hochmittelalters*, Beiträge zur Geschichte des alten Mönchtums und des Benediktinerordens 32 (Münster 1973) 204.

[109] Pierre Salmon, "L'ascèse monastique et les origines de Cîteaux," *Mélanges Saint Bernard: XXIVe Congrès de l'Association bourguignonne des sociétés savantes (8e centenaire de la mort de saint Bernard) Dijon 1953* (Dijon 1954) 268–83 at 278; Marie-Anselme Dimier, "Les concepts de moine et de la vie monastique chez les premiers Cisterciens," *Studia monastica* 1 (1959) 399–418 at 404.

[110]Bernard of Clairvaux, *De praecepto et dispensatione* 16.49, ed. Leclercq 3.286; see Dimier (n. 109 above) 411.

[111]*The Ecclesiastical History of Orderic Vitalis* 3.10, ed. and trans. Marjorie Chibnall (6 vols. Oxford 1969–81) 3.338. Philip of Harvengt, speaking of the Cistercians in the passage cited in n. 27 above, said: "Illius itaque Benedicti, sub qua degunt, regulae sic adhaerent, ut in omnibus, quae illa vel iubet ad litteram, vel admonet, perseverent: extimantes quod illam ad unguem aliter non tenerent, nisi tam parvis quam maioribus summam diligentiam adhiberent." Later in the twelfth century Robert of Torigny, *Tractatus de immutatione ordinis monachorum* 1, PL 202.1309B and 1310B, attributed the departure of Robert from Molesme to his study of the Rule of Benedict *ad litteram*.

[112] Jean Leclercq, "Saint Antoine dans la tradition monastique médiévale," *Antonius Magnus Eremita 356–1956: Studia ad antiquum monachismum spectantia*, ed. Basilius Steidle, Studia Anselmiana 38 (Rome 1956) 229–47, esp. 238.

Salles, who died in 1120 (though the *Life* was written considerably later) and was said to have founded nine houses in which he establish'ed

a way of life with regard to food and clothing scrupulously according to the Rule of St Benedict: nothing less, nothing more, nothing repeated, nothing omitted. . . . In all his deeds he was redolent of Hilarion, resembled Anthony; Christ really lived in him. He was totally on fire, and he set others on fire; he acted and spoke now [like] John in the desert, now [like] Paul in public; . . . he inflamed many, he summoned many into the desert, he built many places in which he ordained that the norm of St Benedict should be preserved down to the least iota. Why say more? He loved Christ, he preached Christ, he imitated Christ, he ascended to Christ.[113]

The first monks in the restored monastery of St Martin at Tournai were said to have modeled their lives on the *Institutes* and *Collations* of Cassian and on the *Lives of the Fathers*, and according to the *Life* of Bernard of Tiron "the vast solitudes" of northwestern France became "like another Egypt" owing to the number of hermits living there.[114]

Claims of this sort should not be taken literally. The desert ideal was part of a literary ideology or myth that was used, especially by the second generation of Cistercians, to support the claim of reformers to follow a type of monasticism that was stricter and purer than that of the old black Benedictines.[115] Even if such rhetoric did not describe reality, however, it reflects the desire to return to the authenticity of the sources—the movement of *resourcement*, as it is called in French. *Veritas* in the Middle Ages meant "authenticity" as well as "truth" and was the standard against which *consuetudo* was judged by reformers in the eleventh and twelfth centuries,[116] for whom the example of early monasticism was the basis for founding new religious houses and reforming old ones. The description of Carthusian monasticism in the *Life* of Hugh of Lincoln, written in the early thirteenth century, clearly depended upon that of the desert fathers, whose way of life, like that of the Carthusians (and by implication unlike that of some other monks) "encouraged solitude rather than singularity."[117] A late twelfth- or early thirteenth-century treatise on the eating of birds by monks referred to "the honest custom" of the ancient monks in Egypt and Palestine as a pure spring from which the monastic

---

[113]Gerald of Salles, *Vita* 2.12 and 18, AASS 23 Oct. 10.257C and 258D.

[114]Herman of Tournai, *Liber de restauratione monasterii sancti Martini Tornacensis* 39, MGH SS 14.291, cf. c. 68, ibid. 306, and Bernard of Tiron, *Vita* 3.19, PL 172.1380. See also Guy of Anderlac, *Vita* 1.3, AASS 12 Sept. 4.42A, who was inspired to the solitary life by the examples of Anthony and Arsenius and their followers; Theobald the Hermit, *Vita* 4, ed. Jean Mabillon, *Acta sanctorum Ordinis S. Benedicti* (9 vols. Paris 1668–1701) 6.2.160; Ulrich of Zell, *Vita* 3, AASS 10 July 3.160B, whose mortifications were compared to those of Anthony, Hilarion, and Jerome.

[115]Benedicta Ward, "The Desert Myth: Reflections on the Desert Ideal in Early Cistercian Monasticism," *One Yet Two: Monastic Tradition, East and West*, ed. M. Basil Pennington, Cistercian Studies Series 29 (Kalamazoo 1976) 183–99, esp. 188.

[116]Among the many works on this frequently cited theme, see Ladner (n. 1 above) 138, 139, 298, 410–11; and most recently, Jürgen Miethke, "Geschichtsprozess und Zeitgenössisches Bewusstsein: Die Theorie des monarchischen Papats im hohen und späteren Mittelalter," *Historische Zeitschrift* 226 (1978) 564–99 at 567–68.

[117]*Life of Hugh of Lincoln* (n. 60 above) 1.23.

discipline flowed.[118] The standard of life thus depended upon its closeness and similarity to its source.

The importance attached to *resourcement* by the Cistercians is shown not only by their concern for the purity and integrity of the Rule but also by their revision of the text of the Bible and their reform of the liturgy. This began in 1109, when Stephen Harding sent some monks to Metz in order to discover the authentic Gregorian tradition, and culminated in about 1175 with the compilation of the famous manuscript Dijon 114, designed to ensure liturgical uniformity throughout the Cistercian order. Within this period the basis of reform shifted significantly, from the authenticity of the manuscripts to the more radical authority of nature. The introduction to the reform of 1134 made several references to nature, and the reformers explicitly said that they were aiming at nature more than custom (*usus*). "Although emendations of this sort may appear contrary to custom," they wrote, "because, however, nature should prevail over custom, you should be less displeased by the change of custom than pleased by the integrity of nature that has been observed." The authors of the reformed Cistercian antiphonary of about 1147 also said in the preface that they had striven "more for nature than for custom."[119]

Such explicit appeals to nature as a justification for change raise important questions about the meaning of the term *natura* and its use by reformers in the twelfth century.[120] In some of the passages cited above, the concept of the beauty of nature, almost in the modern sense, was used to compare the reformed religious houses to paradise and was considered to play a role in preparing the soul for spiritual renewal. In a more positive sense it also referred to the divine plan as manifested in the visible world. The praise of natural beauty in the poems of Marbod of Rennes and in the letter of William of St Denis describing his hermitage—both of which have been seen as anticipations of later attitudes toward nature—reflect a view of nature as the image of divinity.[121] This attitude probably inspired Bernard's well-known statement in

---

[118]*Dialogus de esu volatilium*, ed. Bernhard Pez, *Thesaurus anecdotorum novissimus* (6 vols. Augsburg and Graz 1721–29) 2(2)564A.

[119]PL 182.1132A and 1152D–53A; cf. Solutor R. Marosszéki, *Les origines du chant cistercien: Recherches sur les réformes du plain-chant cistercien au XIIe siècle*, Analecta sacri ordinis Cisterciensis 8 (Rome 1952) 130 and the introduction by Chrysogonus Waddell to the translation of Bernard's "Prologue to the Cistercian Antiphonary" in *The Works of Bernard of Clairvaux: Treatises* 1, Cistercian Fathers Series 1 (Spencer Mass. 1970) 151–60. See also Waddell's essay in this volume.

[120]In addition to the works cited below, see Tullio Gregory, "L'idea di natura nella filosofia medievale prima dell'ingresso della filosofia di Aristotele: Il secolo XII," *La filosofia della natura nel Medioevo: Atti del terzo congresso internazionale di filosofia medioevale, Passo della Mendola . . . 1964* (Milan 1966) 27–65; F. J. E. Raby, "*Nuda natura* and Twelfth-Century Cosmology," *Speculum* 43 (1968) 72–77; Stock, *Myth and Science*; and, on the personification of nature, Ladner's essay in this volume at nn. 53–80. There is a learned and perceptive examination of the use of the term *nature* in C. S. Lewis, *Studies in Words* (2nd ed. Cambridge 1967) 24–74.

[121]Marbod of Rennes, *Carmina* 28, PL 171.1665D–66A and William of St Denis, *Epist.*, PL 186.1472D–73A (see n. 66 above); cf. on Marbod, Panofsky, *Ren & Ren* 82 and Boas (n. 17 above) 109 n. 60.

the introductory letter to Aelred's *Speculum caritatis* that monks might learn more in the woods and fields than from books and schools. What the monk, and presumably Bernard himself, learned there was the sweetness of contemplation and the spiritual sense of Scripture as revealed in nature.[122] William of St Thierry went a step further in his *First Life* of Bernard, of whom he said, "In him nature did not disagree with grace," and to whom he applied the text from Wisdom 8:19-20, "I was a witty (*ingeniosus*) child and had received a good soul. And whereas I was more good, I came to a body undefiled."[123] This implies a congruity between the individual and nature and a confidence in the natural powers and goodness of man that point toward a new and positive view of nature.

Nature was used as both a secular and a religious concept in the twelfth century. Philosophers and lawyers as well as theologians viewed it as a normative power. The law of nature was synonymous with divine law, under which man had lived in the Garden of Eden,[124] and it was equivalent to reason and the divine order of things.[125] It corresponded to the way things are and have to be, not always in a good sense. Abelard, for instance, cited the weakness of men in an aging world and the need to follow nature as reasons for relaxing the strictness of monastic regulations.[126] He cited Seneca's adage "Propositum nostrum est secundum naturam vivere," as did other contemporary writers, including William of St Thierry, who associated nature with the sobriety, discretion, and sufficiency found in the Garden of Eden.[127] Hildebert

[122]Bernard of Clairvaux, *Epist.* 523, ed. Leclercq 8.487; see Etienne Gilson, "Sur deux textes de Pétrarche," *Studi petrarcheschi* 7 (1961) 35-50 at 36-41, who studied the use of this text by Petrarch.

[123]William of St Thierry, *Vita prima sancti Bernardi* 4.21, in Bernard of Clairvaux, *Opera omnia* (n. 71 above) 2(6)2107A. John of Salisbury, in the *Metalogicon* 1.8, ed. Clement C. J. Webb (Oxford 1929) 26, suggested that nature is a quality that needs to be cultivated by study. Cf. Stock, *Myth and Science* 281-82 on Bernard Silvester's concept of the *homo naturalis*, whose "laws and institutions are the result of his own collective experience."

[124]See the opening words of the *Decretum* of Gratian, *Corpus iuris canonici*, ed. Emil A. Friedberg (2 vols. Leipzig 1879-81) 1.1, distinguishing the *ius naturale* from the customs or law of men, and the second prologue of the Two Anglo-Norman *Summae*, soon to be published by Brian Tierney and Robert L. Benson (to whom I am indebted for this reference), where the *lex naturalis* is distinguished from the *lex mosaica* and other laws following the first sin of man. Natural law is equated there with divine law and said to proceed from the uncorrupted nature of man before the sin of Adam.

[125]Cf. Alan of Lille, *De planctu naturae* 6 and 8, ed. Häring (n. 52 above) 826 ("Ego [Natura] illa sum, que ad exemplarem mundane machine similitudinem hominis exemplaui naturam, ut in ea uelut in speculo ipsius mundi scripta natura compareat.") and 840, where Nature is called the *pro-dea* and vice-regent of God. In the passage cited above at n. 51 Rupert of Deutz attributed the creation of nature to God the Father and its improvement to God the Holy Spirit.

[126]Zimmermann (n. 108 above) 226-28.

[127]Jean-Marie Déchanet, "Le 'Naturam sequi' chez Guillaume de Saint-Thierry," *Collectanea Ordinis Cisterciensium Reformatorum* 7 (1940) 141-48; Patrick Ryan, "The Influence of Seneca on William of St Thierry," *Cîteaux* 25 (1974) 24-32; and, more generally, Klaus-Dieter Nothdurft, *Studien zum Einfluss Senecas auf die Philosophie und Theologie des zwölften Jahrhunderts*, Studien und Texte zur Geistesgeschichte des Mittelalters 7 (Leiden and Cologne 1963) esp. 133-34 on Rupert of Deutz, 134-35 on Abelard, and 135-46 on William of St Thierry.

of Le Mans also urged men to follow nature, which he regarded as the order of creation willed by God.[128] "In nature no one [is] inferior, no one superior," according to a twelfth-century Cistercian text, "no one ahead, no one behind; no one noble, no one ignoble; but nature itself always creates us as equals."[129]

Nature and reason were linked in William of Malmesbury's account of the origins of the Cistercians, which is presented in the form of a speech by Stephen Harding, while he was still a monk at Molesme, questioning the monastic customs there:

By reason the Supreme Author of things has made all things; by reason he rules all things; by reason the fabric of the heaven is rotated; by reason even the stars that are called wandering [i.e. the planets] are turned; by reason the elements are moved; by reason and equilibrium our nature subsists. But since through neglect (*desidia*) it often falls away from reason, many laws have been proposed from time to time; most recently a rule came forth by divine inspiration through the blessed Benedict which was to bring back the vagaries (*fluxum*) of nature to reason; although it includes certain things of which I am unable to penetrate the reason, I consider it necessary to acquiesce to [its] authority. For reason and the authority of holy writers are one and the same thing, however much they may appear to differ; for since God created and recreated nothing without reason, how can it be that I should believe that the saintly fathers, that is the followers of God, declared anything against reason, as if we should put our trust in authority alone? Bring forth, therefore, either the reason or the authority for those things you are devising [i.e. the customs of Molesme], although not much credence should be given if some human reason is alleged that can be destroyed by arguments of equal force. Set examples, therefore, in conformity with the rule which is based on reason and authority, as it were dictated by the spirit of all just men. But if you cannot do this, you claim in vain the prerogative of him whose teaching you scorn to follow.

William went on to say that a number of the monks, including the abbot, were convinced by these arguments "that superfluous matters should be omitted and only the essence of the Rule should be observed" and that they should seek "the wish of the founder of the Rule." Others, however, "refused to accept the new things because they loved the old ones," and only eighteen, counting the abbot and Stephen Harding, decided "that they could not follow the purity of the Rule" at Molesme and therefore established a new monastery at Cîteaux.[130]

---

[128]Peter von Moos, *Hildebert von Lavardin, 1056–1133*, Pariser historische Studien 3 (Stuttgart 1965) 277–79 and Boas (n. 17 above) 80.

[129]H.-M. Rochais and R. M. Irène Binont, "La collection des textes divers du manuscrit Lincoln 201 et Saint Bernard," *Sacris erudiri* 15 (1964) 15–219 at 164 (Lc 58), cf. 199 (Lc 73): "Ergo omnes homines natura aequales genuit, sed variantur meritorum ordine."

[130]William of Malmesbury, *De gestis regum Anglorum libri quinque* 4.344–35, ed. William Stubbs, RS 90 (2 vols. London 1887–89) 2.381–82. It would require a full commentary on this remarkable passage to explain fully the role attributed to *ratio* (translated here as "reason"). The first sentence summarizes contemporary philosophical thought on the nature of the universe (the macrocosm) and on the position in it of man (the microcosm), whose nature is said to subsist in reason and equilibrium, a Ciceronian term used here probably as an equivalent for reason, meaning rational equilibrium or the equilibrium that comes from reason. Man reflects the reason of the universe and, like nature, subsists by the balance of the elements. This anthropocentrism provides

This account is for the most part fictional, but it shows how a perceptive and sympathetic contemporary saw the process of institutional reform, and it brings together several of the themes discussed in this paper. Stephen Harding emphasized in his speech above all the importance of reason and of the Rule, of which the purpose was to ensure that nature conformed to reason, as interpreted in the authoritative writings of the Fathers. William saw the Rule at the same time as part of history, the latest of several legal codes, and as above history, the embodiment of reason and authority and the basis for abolishing bad customs and for doing things a new way. It provided the means for man to recover his true nature and thus to bridge the region of dissimilitude between the condition in which he was created and that into which he had fallen as a result of sin.

For many contemporaries the new religious orders marked not only a recovery and renewal of a lost form of religious life but also, and increasingly as time went on, a new stage in God's plan for the reformation and recreation of men.[131] This progressive view of history was linked to the optimistic concept of nature found, for instance, in the works of Bernard Silvester, for whom nature was the heart of the constant process of creation and renewal both of the forms of religious life and of man the microcosm.[132] Already in the eleventh century Peter Damiani's use of the Augustinian idea that for God "there is no yesterday or tomorrow but an eternal today" implied an acceptance of the present and a forward- rather than backward-looking concept of reform,[133] and Bruno

---

the framework for William's view of the Rule of Benedict as designed to recreate the lost equilibrium in man by bringing back nature to reason, from which it had departed. The terms *revocare* and *recreare* suggest the later concept of the conserving or sustaining power of God, who maintains by recreation what he originally created. William's denial that reason and authority could ever differ shows a latent rationalism with which many contemporaries, including the early Cistercians, might have disagreed. William's refusal to believe that the Fathers declared anything "praeter rationem . . . quasi soli auctoritati fidem debeamus adhibere" suggests that he could conceive of no truth contrary to or beyond the bounds of reason, though there were doubtless truths that could not be proved by reason alone. In the phrase "ex regula quae ratione et auctoritate nixa utpote omnium iustorum spiritu dictata est" it is uncertain whether the *est* belongs with the *nixa* or the *dictata*. A somewhat different translation of this passage will be found at notes 58–59 in Fr Waddell's essay in this volume. The translation offered here, and this note, have been greatly improved by the assistance of Professor John Callahan of Georgetown University.

[131]See Richard W. Southern, "Aspects of the European Tradition of Historical Writing: 2. Hugh of St Victor and the Idea of Historical Development," TRHS 5th ser. 21 (1971) 159–79 on the idea of historical ages.

[132]According to Stock, *Myth and Science* 87, the allegory of Nature for Bernard Silvester was "the myth of how both the world and man emerged from the 'primal forest' into a new culture"; cf. 232–37, esp. 232: "For Bernard, the process of creation—which is for him the essence of the problem of creation—is continuous, having neither beginning nor end. From time to time the process submits to renewal, and at each stage, predictable from the stars, certain improvements are presumably made. Yet the creative changes proceed eternally; they consist of a displacement of God's creative energies down through the cosmic order." For a somewhat different view of Bernard Silvester's use of the concept of reform, see Ladner's essay in this volume at notes 28–34. See also Southern (n. 131 above) 172, stressing that Hugh of St Victor was "a prophet of a new age," who saw "upward movement in every department of life."

[133]Peter Damiani, *Lettre sur la toute-puissance divine*, ed. and trans. André Cantin, Sources chrétiennes 191 (Paris 1972) 428. In this work Damiani studied the question of how God can undo

of Segni's three ages of *umbra et figura, figura et veritas*, and *veritas* corresponded to those of the Synagogue, the Church, and the Celestial Kingdom.[134] A sense of *modernitas*—the present as a distinct historical period, not necessarily inferior to Antiquity—is found in the works of several eleventh-century papalist writers and became increasingly common in the twelfth century.[135] Archbishop Frederick of Cologne referred to modern times in the charter of 1121 cited above, and William of Malmesbury's use of *novissime* in reference to the Rule of Benedict implies both historical distance and progression. The ages of the prophets, apostles, and early monks, which were used as models of reform, came gradually to be seen as historical epochs, stages in the progressive and still unfolding history of the Church, rather than simply as exemplars of perfection to be refashioned in the present.[136]

Bernard of Clairvaux in his third sermon *De labore messis* saw the Cistercians as the third generation, in the words of the Psalmist, "of them that seek the face of the God of Jacob," following the generations of those who did not seek the Lord and those who were sought by Him.[137] Gilbert Foliot referred to Bernard himself as "the sun of his time," who surpassed the monks of Antiquity and whose name would live forever. "The church of Cîteaux," he wrote, "has flourished widely through the earth and, gathering from all sides the most gracious flowers of the world, it has taken them into itself and transformed (*transformavit*) them by some mutation into the flowers of celestial paradise."[138] Here, therefore, it is no longer a question of re-forming the Garden of Eden on earth but of transforming men into paradisiacal flowers. The past is projected into the future, and the Garden of Eden is seen as not only the beginning but also the end of creation.[139] Even more explicitly for Joachim of Fiore, who was himself a Cistercian before establishing his own reformed order, the Cistercians marked a new stage in the progression of

what has been done, but he looked forward as well as backward and pointed the way toward the optimistic view of the twelfth century in his combined emphasis on God's omnipotence (396: "Voluntas quippe Dei omnium rerum, siue uisibilium, siue inuisibilium, causa est ut existant.") and goodness (400: "Quod enim malum est, non potest facere Deus, quia nec potest etiam uelle. . . . Quod uero bonum est, et uelle potest et facere.") Cantin in his note and also in the introduction (170) compared this second phrase with Ockham's "eo ipso quod ipse uult bene et iuste factum est."

[134]Réginald Grégoire, *Bruno de Segni: Exégète médiéval et théologien monastique*, Centro italiano di studi sull'alto medioevo 3 (Spoleto 1965) 153.

[135]Walter Freund, *Modernus und andere Zeitbegriffe des Mittelalters*, Neue Münstersche Beiträge zur Geschichtsforschung 4 (Cologne and Graz 1957) 66–68 and Elisabeth Gössmann, *Antiqui und Moderni im Mittelalter: Eine geschichtliche Standortbestimmung*, Veröffentlichungen des Grabmann-Institutes zur Erforschung der mittelalterlichen Theologie und Philosophie n.s. 23 (Munich 1974). See also Stock, *Myth and Science* 228 and n. 81.

[136]Ditsche (n. 78 above) 62–75.

[137]Bernard of Clairvaux, *Sermo in labore messis* 3.2 and 9, ed. Leclercq 5.223 and 227.

[138]Adrian Morey and Christopher N. L. Brooke, *The Letters and Charters of Gilbert Foliot, Abbot of Gloucester (1139–48), Bishop of Hereford (1148–63) and London (1163–87)* (Cambridge 1967) 148–49 no. 108.

[139]On the association of the beginning and the end of time in patristic thought, see Ladner (n. 1 above) 68.

spiritual men which began with Benedict and will proceed to the stages of preaching and ultimately of contemplation. The rise of the Cistercian order was for him like the rise of Joseph in Egypt, and Bernard was like Moses, and in the Cistercians "Benedict lives and advances (*vivit et proficit*)."[140] Beyond them were to come other ages dominated by other types of spiritual men, according to Joachim, whose speculations on this point permanently influenced later views of history and religious development.[141]

This view of an historical progression in the forms of religious life is expressed most clearly in the first book of Anselm of Havelberg's *Dialogues*. He addressed himself directly to the question of the diversity of types of religious life and orders in the Church of his time, and justified them as part of God's unfolding plan for man.[142] Looking back over the history of monasticism, which was first renewed by Benedict, Anselm saw a progression of changes and innovations, which presented no fears for him either in the past or in the present. Camaldoli and Vallombrosa were novelties; the Cistercians were "another new congregation of monks, differing in order and habit from all who are called and are monks"; the military orders likewise were a "new institute of religion. . . . By a marvelous disposition of God," Anselm continued, using the celebrated image of rebirth in Psalm 102:5, "it happens that the youth of the Church is renewed (*renovatur*) like that of the eagle by a new religion [i.e. a new religious order] always arising from generation to generation."[143]

The process of change and innovation was less threatening for Anselm and those who saw things his way than it was for many contemporaries, including even otherwise innovative figures such as Abelard, who sharply attacked the novelties of the Cistercians. "Contrary to the entire custom of both clerics and monks . . . ," he wrote to Bernard, "you [who are] newly arisen and who greatly rejoice in your novelty have by some new decrees established otherwise among yourselves a divine office."[144] Innovation was even more abhorrent to those of a naturally conservative frame of mind, like the old

---

[140]Cipriano Baraut, "Un tratado inédito de Joaquín de Fiore: De vita sancti Benedicti et de Officio divino secundum eius doctrinam," *Analecta sacra Tarraconensia* 24 (1951) 33–122 at 43, 54–55, 60, 86, 117, cc. 1, 7, 11, 25, 45; cf. Herbert Grundmann, *Studien über Joachim von Floris*, Beiträge zur Kulturgeschichte des Mittelalters und der Renaissance 32 (Leipzig and Berlin 1927; repr. Darmstadt 1966) 68–69 and 114.

[141]Marjorie Reeves, "Joachimist Expectations in the Order of Augustinian Hermits," RTAM 25 (1958) 111–41 and "The Abbot Joachim and the Society of Jesus," M&RS 5 (1961) 163–81.

[142]Southern (n. 131 above) 174–76 and n. 28, where he said that Anselm adopted "the main lines of Hugh's view of religious development."

[143]Anselm of Havelberg, *Dialogi* 1.10, PL 188.1157A–B; cf. generally *Dialogues, Livre I: Renouveau dans l'Eglise*, ed. and trans. Gaston Salet, Sources chrétiennes 118 (Paris 1966) 96–106; cf. Wilhelm Berges, "Anselm von Havelberg in der Geistesgeschichte des 12. Jahrhunderts," *Jahrbuch für die Geschichte Mittel- und Ostdeutschlands* 5 (1956) 39–57, esp. 47–54, stressing Anselm's defense of novelty and progress against conservatives who esteemed "the old" for its own sake, and Funkenstein (n. 10 above) 60–67 on Anselm's view of historical diversity.

[144]Abelard, *Epist.* 10, to Bernard of Clairvaux, PL 178.339B. He went on to criticize what he called "haec vestra novitas aut singularitas."

abbot of St Mary's at York, who was shocked by "the novelty" of the Cistercian way of life.[145] Heretics were often accused of novelty,[146] and innovators were doubtless often suspected of heresy. It took a long time for novelty to be fully accepted and even admired, but the way was prepared by the religious reformers.[147] St Norbert was praised in his *Life* precisely for preaching "a new type of life on earth,"[148] and Marbod of Rennes said of Robert of La Chaise Dieu that "This new saint reversed for us the ancient order of sanctity."[149] In the thirteenth century the sense of novelty became in some reforming circles even stronger than the sense of reform. "The new commentators of the new religion and bearers of the new cross," according to the *Contra religionis simulatores*, must seek "the new Christ who promises us a new rest."[150]

This new attitude toward institutional development is in itself one of the most important changes of the twelfth century.[151] The concept of renewal and reform that started as an effort to recreate conditions that had existed in the distant—and often mythical—past came increasingly to be based on principles of nature and reason and to accept forms of religious life that had never existed

[145]*Narratio de fundatione Fontanis monasterii in comitatu Eboracensi*, ed. John Richard Walbran, *Memorials of the Abbey of St. Mary of Fountains*, Surtees Society 42, 67, 130 (3 vols. Durham 1863–1918) 1.8. For other examples of misoneism (an unreasoning fear and hatred of novelty) see Marie-Dominique Chenu, *L'éveil de la conscience dans la civilisation médiévale*, Conférence Albert-le-Grand 1968 (Montreal and Paris 1969) 14–15 and Beryl Smalley, "Ecclesiastical Attitudes to Novelty c. 1100–c. 1250," *Church, Society, and Politics*, ed. Derek Baker, Studies in Church History 12 (Oxford 1975) 113–31.

[146]See *Actus pontificum Cenomannis in urbe degentium*, ed. Gustave Busson and A. Ledru, Archives historiques du Maine 2 (Le Mans 1901) 409.

[147]Philip of Harvengt, in the passage cited at n. 27 above, praising the renewal of monastic life in his time, referred to *novo sole, vernalem novitatem, novo rore, nova disciplina, novitatis gratia*, and *nova incude*. See also the approving references to novelty in the passages by Bernard of Clairvaux (nn. 24 and 52), Peter the Venerable (n. 26), Gerhoch of Reichersberg (n. 28), Richard of St Victor (n. 29), Hugh of St Victor (nn. 46 and 53), Rupert of Deutz (n. 51), Adam of Perseigne (n. 54), and Adam of Dryburgh (n. 55).

[148]Norbert of Xanten, *Vita B* 5, PL 170.1276D.

[149]Marbod of Rennes, *Miracula b. Roberti ab. Casae-Dei*, in Labbe, *Nova bibliotheca* (n. 23 above) 2.652. Marbod also praised "the example of the new religion" in his letter to Robert of Arbrissel, PL 171.1481C and (with many differences) Johannes von Walter, *Die ersten Wanderprediger Frankreichs*, vol. 1: *Robert von Arbrissel*, Studien zur Geschichte der Theologie und der Kirche 9.3 (Leipzig 1903) 182.

[150]*Contra religionis simulatores* 65, ed. Marvin Colker, *Analecta Dublinensia: Three Medieval Latin Texts in the Library of Trinity College Dublin*, Mediaeval Academy of America Publications 82 (Cambridge Mass. 1975) 45. Colker suggests a date of the twelfth or thirteenth century for this text.

[151]Smalley (n. 145 above) suggested that "the pace of events" imposed this new attitude and that change became less threatening as men acquired more control over their environment. On the sense of change among writers of history in England after the Norman Conquest, see Richard W. Southern, "Aspects of the European Tradition of Historical Writing: 4. The Sense of the Past," TRHS 5th ser. 23 (1973) 243–63 at 246–48.

in the past and could be justified only as part of God's emerging plan for the present and the future. The confidence in the possibility of reforming religious institutions in this sense—that is, of reshaping and changing them in accordance with the requirements of successive historical ages—was a significant aspect of what has been called the optimistic outlook of the twelfth century.[152] People at that time were increasingly aware that, in spite of the evidence of corruption and decay in the world around them, both they and the institutions of their society could not only recover the image of perfection in which they had been created but could also be recreated into new forms adapted to the needs of mankind's progressive history.

Bibliographical Note

The basic works on the concept of renewal and reform in the Middle Ages are Konrad Burdach, *Reformation—Renaissance—Humanismus* (2nd ed. Berlin and Leipzig 1926; repr. Darmstadt 1963), especially Essay I, which was first published in 1910 and deals with the meaning and origins of the terms *renaissance* and *reformation*, and Gerhart B. Ladner, *The Idea of Reform: Its Impact on Christian Thought and Action in the Age of The Fathers* (Cambridge Mass. 1959), which should be supplemented, until the appearance of the next volume, by his articles on "Die mittelalterliche Reform-Idee und ihr Verhältnis zur Idee der Renaissance," MIÖG 60 (1952) 31–59; "Vegetation Symbolism and the Concept of Renaissance," *De artibus opuscula XL: Essays in Honor of Erwin Panofsky*, ed. Millard Meiss (2 vols. New York 1961) 1.303–22; "Reformatio," *Ecumenical Dialogue at Harvard: The Roman Catholic–Protestant Colloquium*, ed. Samuel H. Miller and G. Ernest Wright (Cambridge Mass. 1964) 172–90; "Erneuerung," *Reallexikon für Antike und Christentum* 6 (1966) 240–75; and "Religious Renewal and Ethnic-Social Pressures as Forms of Life in Christian History," *Theology of Renewal*, ed. Laurence K. Shook (2 vols. Montreal 1968) 2.328–57. A different but also interesting approach, stressing the backward-looking aspect of the medieval concept of reform, is found in George Boas, *Essays on Primitivism and Related Ideas in the Middle Ages* (Baltimore 1948; repr. New York 1966).

On the question of cosmological renewal in twelfth-century theological and philosophical thought, see Tullio Gregory, *Anima mundi: La filosofia di Guglielmo di Conches e la Scuola di Chartres* (Florence 1955) and Stock, *Myth and Science*.

The attitudes toward novelty and historical innovation have been studied in several essays by Richard Southern in *Humanism* and his four articles on "Aspects of the European Tradition of Historical Writing" published in TRHS 5th ser. 20–23 (1970–73). Southern emphasizes optimistic aspects of historical thought in the twelfth century. On the change from regarding new ideas as bad (misoneism) to regarding them as good, see Beryl Smalley, "Ecclesiastical Attitudes to Novelty c. 1100–c. 1250," *Church, Society, and Politics*, ed. Derek Baker, Studies in Church History 12 (Oxford 1975) 113–31. See also Amos Funkenstein, *Heilsplan und natürliche Entwicklung: Formen der Gegenwartsbestimmung im Geschichtsdenken des hohen Mittelalters* (Munich 1965).

The two most important works on the theme of personal reform in the image of God are Robert Javelet, *Image et ressemblance au douzième siècle: De Saint Anselme à*

---

[152]Southern (n. 131 above) 176–78.

Alain de Lille (2 vols. Strasbourg 1967) and Charles Trinkaus, *In Our Image and Likeness: Humanity and Divinity in Italian Humanist Thought* (2 vols. Chicago and London 1970), which although primarily concerned with the fourteenth and fifteenth centuries has some interesting sections on the Middle Ages.

The ideal of the *ecclesia primitiva* has been studied in particular by Giovanni Miccoli in an article on "'Ecclesiae primitivae forma'" that was first published in *Studi medievali* 3rd ser. 1 (1960) 470–98 and reprinted in a greatly expanded version in his *Chiesa gregoriana: Ricerche sulla riforma del secolo XI*, Storici antichi e moderni n.s. 17 (Florence 1966) 225–99, and by Glenn Olsen, "The Idea of the *Ecclesia Primitiva* in the Writings of the Twelfth-Century Canonists," *Traditio* 25 (1969) 61–86. See also, on the period down to the fifth century, Pier Cesare Bori, *Chiesa primitiva: L'immagine della comunità delle origini—Atti 2.42–47; 4.32–37—nella storia della chiesa antica*, Testi e ricerche di scienze religiose 10 (Brescia 1974). Among the many works on the *vita apostolica*, see in particular Luchesius Spätling, *De apostolicis, pseudoapostolicis, apostolinis*, Pontificium Athenaeum Antonianum: Facultas theologica, Theses ad Lauream 35 (Munich 1947); Ernest W. McDonnell, "The *Vita apostolica*: Diversity or Dissent," *Church History* 24 (1955) 15–31; Marie-Humbert Vicaire, *L'imitation des apôtres: Moines, chanoines et mendiants, IVe–XIIIe siècles*, Tradition et spiritualité 2 (Paris 1963), and several articles by Marie-Dominique Chenu reprinted in his *Théologie* and translated in *Nature*. On the ideal of wilderness and desert, see, in addition to the more general work of George H. Williams, *Wilderness and Paradise in Christian Thought* (New York 1962), the article by Benedicta Ward, "The Desert Myth: Reflections on the Desert Ideal in Early Cistercian Monasticism," originally given as a paper at the Orthodox-Cistercian Conference in Oxford in 1973 and printed in *One Yet Two: Monastic Tradition, East and West*, ed. M. Basil Pennington, Cistercian Studies 29 (Kalamazoo 1976) 183–99.

The Renewal of Theology

Jean Leclercq

Each term in this essay's title must be refined before we can portray its subject in detail. The very concept and even the term *theology* continue to hold surprises. In the last quarter of the twelfth century, the word *theologia* could still be used simply for the ''Word of God,'' transmitted by the Bible or the liturgy:[1] fifty years after Abelard, the meaning he gave the word had not taken over. Historians may legitimately apply it, however, to the reflections on the Revelation which have always been part of the Church's tradition.

Was there actually a *renewal* of theology in the twelfth century? It was certainly not a rebirth, as if theology had disappeared and died and had to appear anew. Since the era of patristic theology, the existence of which is undisputed, there had been no interruption. From late Antiquity through the Carolingian period of the ninth century there had been authentic theologians. If there was an eclipse, or at any rate a decline in this sphere, it came during the tenth century and the first half of the eleventh. But from the second half of the eleventh century, coincident with the Gregorian Reform, theological activity intensified. Two of its most important representatives—Bruno of Segni and Peter Damiani—have recently been the subjects of thorough studies.[2] John of Fécamp had written a ''Theological Confession'' expounding an authentic theology in the traditional sense of the word: reflection, more prayerful and contemplative than scientific, on Christian doctrine. Only half a century later, Abelard would give a new meaning to the word *theology*, by expressly associating it with intellectual research pursued according to a method calling more freely upon one of the liberal arts: dialectic. But this method had already been applied—without the new vocabulary—by St Anselm, at the end of the eleventh century and the beginning of the twelfth. Continuity, then, there was; renewal was not necessary.

---

[1] See the treatise on theoretical grammar, attributed to an English master named R. Blund, published by C. H. Kneepkens, ''The Relatio simplex in the Grammatical Tracts of the Late Twelfth and Early Thirteenth Century,'' *Vivarium* 15 (1977) 1–30 at 18, 22, 25.

[2] Réginald Grégoire, *Bruno de Ségni: Exégète médiéval et théologien monastique*, Centro italiano di studi sull'alto medioevo 3 (Spoleto 1965); André Cantin, *Les sciences séculières et la foi: Les deux voies de la science au jugement de S. Pierre Damien (1007–1072)*, Centro italiano di studi sull'alto medioevo 5 (Spoleto 1975).

There had been progress, however, in two respects. On the one hand, this preexisting, very much alive theology grew into a vaster and more coherent doctrinal whole, reaching a greater number of intellects and finding expression in more works than during the period immediately preceding. On the other hand—and this was its most striking characteristic—theology became diversified to the extent that the different spheres of Christian life acquired more distinct identities.

Within a given society, these spheres were located along a line between two extremes: at one end the hermits and recluses, of whatever persuasion, who separated themselves as much as possible from ordinary social life; at the other end the towns, in which schools, already in existence, experienced a new period of growth. The first pole, that of the hermits, can be symbolized by one of its representative institutions: Carthusian life. The Carthusians wrote relatively little; but Bernard of Clairvaux, William of St Thierry, Peter of Celle, and others wrote for them, bearing witness to a radical monasticism, for which the strictest monastic writings were composed—a kind of utopia achieved by few but influencing many. Between the two poles stood three kinds of intermediate spheres: first, that of traditional monasticism, represented by a Rupert of Deutz, a Peter the Venerable, a Peter of Celle, an Arnold of Bonneval; next, the new monasticism, best symbolized by the Cistercians; and last, the group of regular canons, itself diverse since it produced writers as varied as the authors of the Premonstratensian Order, those of St Victor of Paris over several generations, and a Gerhoch of Reichersberg.

A third preliminary question concerns chronology. First, does this period of progress in theology, through development and diversification, coincide with the "twelfth century"? Perhaps we should begin the periodization in the middle of the eleventh century?[3] This procedure has the advantage of including Bruno of Segni, Peter Damiani, and the theologians of the Gregorian Reform; and certainly the second half of the eleventh century was distinguished, in the realms of spirituality and psychology, by a growing appreciation of personal experience. Still, it is only with St Anselm that a new kind of theological thinking begins to appear. It is true that he died in 1109 and had produced most of his theological work before 1100. Anselm of Laon also taught before 1100. But these two truly mark the beginning of the growth of theology; even Lanfranc, master and predecessor of St Anselm, did not initiate it. Let us therefore place the beginning of this period during the last decades of the eleventh century—perhaps at 1076, the year of St Anselm's first great theological work, the *Monologion*.

Next, can one speak of the "twelfth century" as a *whole*? At least two periods are distinguishable, more or less coinciding with the two halves of the century. To the first period belong the greatest names: Anselm of Laon (d. 1117), Rupert of Deutz (d. 1129), Hugh of St Victor (d. 1141), Abelard (d.

[3]Colin M. Morris, *The Discovery of the Individual, 1050-1200* (London 1972).

1141), William of St Thierry (d. 1148), St Bernard (d. 1153), Gilbert of
Poitiers (d. 1154), Peter the Venerable (d. 1156), Peter Lombard (d. 1160). Its
high point was the twenty-five-year period from approximately 1125 to 1150,
when the crucial works appeared, the works of these masters, the initiators and
creators. The second half of the century belonged to their disciples, who
though less "great," endowed with less genius, carried on their work, and
sometimes went further than their predecessors.

To reflect even more precisely the complexity and fluidity of reality, it is
best to go by generations.[4] Thus, we have the generation of St Anselm; next,
that of St Bernard, William of St Thierry, Abelard, Hugh of St Victor, and
Gilbert of Poitiers; then the monasticism of Isaac of Stella, Guerric of Igny,
and Aelred of Rievaulx. Likewise, the schools of the early twelfth century must
be distinguished from those of the middle and the late twelfth century and of
the early thirteenth century. And just as we must distinguish different institutions and tendencies within monasticism, so, when dealing with urban schools,
we must remember that the towns did not develop in the same manner or at
the same pace in different countries, or even in the different regions of the
same country.

Finally, what chronological terminus should be assigned to the theological
renewal of the "twelfth century"? It includes Alan of Lille, who died after
1200,[5] while the *Porretani* and the disciples of Abelard continued to think and
write in the same vein as their masters; in monasticism, it was the era of
Thomas of Perseigne, called "of Cîteaux" (d. ca. 1190), Baldwin of Ford (d.
1191), Gunther of Pairis (d. ca. 1200), Geoffrey of Auxerre (d. after 1200),
Ogier of Locedio (d. 1214), Adam of Perseigne (d. 1221), John of Ford (d.
1224), and Hélinand of Froidmont (d. ca. 1235).[6] In this picture, the Lateran
Council of 1215 does not mark a significant date. In short, on the whole, if we
consider the death dates just cited as the extreme limit of the period, it extends
to include the first quarter of the thirteenth century. We can therefore claim
that the "theological renewal of the twelfth century" took place between approximately 1075 and 1224.

THEOLOGICAL DIVERSITY

Progress in theology came especially through diversification. How should we
formulate this diversity of theologies in the twelfth century? A convenient procedure, during the last thirty years, has been to distinguish between monastic

---

[4]A procedure followed in dealing with another era of 12th-c. literature, by Leslie T. Topsfield,
Troubadours and Love (Cambridge 1975).

[5]Robert Javelet, *Image et ressemblance au douzième siècle: De Saint Anselme à Alain de Lille*
(2 vols. Strasbourg 1967).

[6]Christopher J. Holdsworth, "John of Ford and English Cistercian Writing, 1167–1214,"
TRHS 5th ser. 11 (1961) 117–36.

theology and scholastic theology. Generally speaking, these two types of theology appeared linked to two types of milieux: the one was elaborated within and for the cloistered life in all its forms; the other was born and developed in the urban schools.

THEOLOGY IN THE CLOISTER

The term "monastic theology" has gained acceptance as more and more historians recognize its value.[7] It is interesting to note that whereas during Haskins's own time, most historians still combined all twelfth-century authors under the single heading "prescholasticism" (*Vorscholastik*) or "early scholasticism" (*Frühscholastik*), Haskins saw that a distinction within this group was needed, between "the theology of Anselm and Peter Lombard and the other early scholastics [and] the writings of St. Bernard and other monastic leaders."[8]

Today, however, we can better define the meaning of this distinction, and more clearly determine the relationships among the diverse "theologies" of the twelfth century. To recognize the existence of a theology different from that of the scholastics does not diminish the value of the latter; and to acknowledge the greatness and the predominant influence of St Bernard and the Cistercians does not imply a lesser esteem for the non-Cistercian monastic authors. Speaking of several theologies and comparing them does not imply opposing one to another; their enrichment was reciprocal. It must at least be understood that monasticism had its own theology. A formula such as "between a mystic like Bernard and a rationalist like Abaelard"[9] is obviously a simplification. It is equally revealing that the name of William of St Thierry never appears in Haskins's book, although he is today without a doubt after St Bernard the most written-about twelfth-century theologian.[10] This simply shows that in fifty years our knowledge of the twelfth century has progressed.[11] We have even begun to speak not only of monastic theology, but of a "plurality of monastic theologies,"[12] and the number of their representatives we are

---

[7]Evidence has been collected by Jean Leclercq, *Chances de la spiritualité occidentale* (Paris 1966) 184–224; idem, "A propos de 'la Renaissance du XIIe siècle': Nouveaux témoinages sur la 'théologie monastique,'" *Collectanea Cisterciensia* 40 (1978) 65–72; Réginald Grégoire, "Bulletin de théologie monastique," *Studia monastica* 10 (1968) 161–80, and 11 (1969) 149–68; idem, "Esiste una teologia monastica?" *Inter fratres* 27 (1977) 115–20.

[8]Haskins, *Ren* 7.

[9]Haskins, *Ren* 258.

[10]Jean Leclercq, "Etudes récentes sur Guillaume de Saint-Thierry," *Bulletin de la Société internationale pour l'histoire de la philosophie médiévale* 19 (1977) 49–55.

[11]The principal merit for having pointed out the theological interest of these 12th-c. monastic authors belongs to Etienne Gilson, particularly for his book *La théologie mystique de S. Bernard* (Paris 1934).

[12]Matthias Neuman, "Monastic Theology and the Dialogue with Cultural Humanism," *Monastic Studies* 12 (1976) 85–119 at 86.

interested in grows continually—St Hildegard has joined the once exclusively male company. The greatest figure, however, the one that dominates all the others, is that of a Cistercian: St Bernard.

WAS THERE A THEOLOGY OF THE SCHOOLS?

The last half-century has made it clearer that "scholastic" theology was linked to the development of urban schools.[13] Actually, the concept of "scholastic theology" should not be applied to the twelfth century: it is better perhaps to speak of a "theology of the schools," for it is not yet the classic scholasticism of the second third of the twelfth century on. In the case of Laon, for example, it would be better to describe the movement in thought, at the beginning of the twelfth century, as a "theology of *sententiae*,"[14] or as a nonscholastic theology in the schools. Its object was the practical problems raised by Christian life; it was "scholarly" without being "scholastic." It was expressed through *sententiae*, the maxims of Scripture and the Fathers, without recourse to searching theoretical reflection; it was not systematic. Such "schools without scholasticism" are attested in Poland, for example, throughout the twelfth century and even during the thirteenth.[15]

It is the meaning of "school" itself that is now in question.[16] Although the tendency used to be to identify each "school" with the academic milieu of a given town—Laons, Reims, Poitiers, Paris—it now appears more and more plain that we are dealing not with precise geographic centers but with personalities who could move from town to town; not so much with localized academic institutions as with "masters" influencing "circles" of disciples. Theology, therefore, was linked less to the name of a specific place, even if there was a school there, than to a person and his circle. Thus, we can speak of the teaching of Anselm of Canterbury, Bruno of Chartreux, Abelard, Hugh of St Victor, Gilbert of Poitiers, master Simon, Peter Lombard, Andrew of St Victor, William of Auxerre.[17] Similarly, we can distinguish between a "school *of* Laon" and a "school *at* Laon." There was indeed a school at Laon; however, it was not linked to the existence of this town and its cathedral, but to the fact that at a given moment two successive masters were there: Anselm, and then his brother Ralph (d. 1136). Again, there never was a "school of Bec," though there were, at Bec, some young monks and others who meditated on the faith with Lanfranc and Anselm of Aosta.[18]

[13]Gérard M. Paré, A. Brunet, and P. Tremblay, *La renaissance du XIIe siècle: Les écoles et l'enseignement*, Publications de l'Institut d'études médiévales d'Ottawa 3 (Paris and Ottawa 1933); Chenu, *Théologie*.

[14]Valerie I. J. Flint, "The 'School of Laon': A Reconsideration," RTAM 43 (1976) 89–110.

[15]Marian Rechowicz, "Origines et développement de la culture scolastique (jusqu'à la fin du XIVe siècle)," *Dzieje teologii katolickiej w Polsce*, ed. Marian Rechowicz (Lublin 1974) 89–91.

[16]Southern, *Humanism* 61–85, "Humanism and the School of Chartres."

[17]Artur M. Landgraf, *Einführung in die Geschichte der theologischen Literatur der Frühscholastik* (Regensburg 1948).

[18]Jean Leclercq, "Une doctrine de la vie monastique dans l'école du Bec," *Spicilegium Beccense* (Paris 1959) 477–88.

Thus, on the one hand, sometimes a school—that is, a group or circle of students—gathered around a master, and if he moved, as Abelard did, the circle moved with him. Of Abelard it could be said that during his lifetime there was a school *centered about* him; after his death, his dispersed disciples made up "the school of Peter Abelard."[19] On the other hand, there were towns which had a school but produced no theologian, because they lacked a master teacher. And if one can speak of a "school of St Victor," it is in the sense that there were several successive Victorines who influenced the groups of students they taught there; in this case, there was a certain local continuity. But this seems to have been an exception, arising from the fact that all the Victorines belonged to the same monastery. As for what some call "the Cistercian school"—which was actually a Claravallian school, and was neither in Clairvaux (as the Victorines were in Paris) nor gathered about St Bernard (as Abelard's disciples gathered about their master)—it was a part of the Cistercian Order, influenced by the person and works of St Bernard.

William of St Thierry offers yet another illustration. This Benedictine-turned-Cistercian wrote for the Carthusians, but these three orders had in common being *claustrales*, cloistered. A distinction must be made within his works.[20] Some treat dogmatic subjects and the nature of man; they are theoretical, written in technical language, and difficult to read. Consequently, their manuscript tradition was limited. But others, dealing with spiritual theology, brought the contents of those more difficult works within the grasp of a greater number of readers. Some works of this second group were soon attributed to St Bernard and widely diffused, especially perhaps in England, thanks to the influence there of Cistercian monasteries either founded by or linked to Clairvaux. One, which was both doctrinal and practical—the *Letter to the Brothers of Mont-Dieu*, called the *Epistola aurea*—became, so to speak, a "best-seller" of medieval literature, and remained so.[21] After William, the current of thought begun by him in his abbey was carried on there by Geoffrey of St Thierry.[22] Likewise, and almost certainly due to the stimulus he had given to the two successive communities in which he had lived, the libraries of St Thierry and Signy were enriched by works in patristics and general culture, as well as in monastic, pastoral, and speculative theology.[23]

All of this confirms two facts. First, different theologies developed: in the monasteries, according to the type of life that was led there; in the schools, out

[19]David E. Luscombe, *The School of Peter Abelard: The Influence of Abelard's Thought in the Early Scholastic Period* (Cambridge 1969).

[20]Jean Leclercq, "Pour un portrait spirituel de Guillaume de Saint-Thierry," *Saint-Thierry: Une abbaye du VIe au XXe siècle*, Actes du Colloque international d'histoire monastique, Reims–Saint-Thierry (1976), ed. Michel Bur (Saint-Thierry 1979) 413–28 at 419–20.

[21]Jean-Marie Déchanet, ed. and trans., *Guillaume de Saint-Thierry, Lettre aux Frères du Mont-Dieu (Lettre d'or)*, Sources chrétiennes 223 (Paris 1975) 50–121.

[22]Robert J. Sullivan, "The Sermons of Geoffrey of St. Thierry" (diss. Harvard University 1974).

[23]Leclercq, "Livres et lecteurs à Saint-Thierry au XIIe siècle," *Saint-Thierry* (n. 20 above) 101–11.

of the problems confronted there; and in certain intellectual circles. Second, there were fruitful exchanges among these three representative groups of religious thought, without any of them renouncing its own identity, message, or method: each master or writer remained deeply marked by the social milieu he belonged to and which he in turn influenced.

THE *RAISON D'ÊTRE* OF THE TWO THEOLOGIES

Why did two theologies exist side by side, each keeping its separate identity? Two explanations have been suggested. The first derives from sociopolitical considerations. According to this interpretation, the two theologies were those of town and countryside, and corresponded to two social and economic levels, indeed two "classes," of society: the theologians of the cloister and those of the schools belonged to groups that were all involved in the social evolution then taking place—those from the towns with groups which were fighting to gain their franchise and communal liberty, those of the monasteries with groups trying to maintain the feudal order.

But was it really so simple? First of all, what was "urban civilization" like in the twelfth century, and what relation could it have to a specific way of practicing theology? The urban population was a minority; even three hundred years later, in 1500, the great majority was classified as rural,[24] and the proportions must have been the same, or even less in the towns' favor, in the twelfth century. Here again, moreover, the evolutionary process was diversified; towns and rural areas, regions and countries, all followed different rhythms. The thirteenth-century   population   of   Troyes—important   because   of   its market—and its environs has been calculated at around 14,000 inhabitants; in 1172, in this same area, there were about 1,900 knights and lords, of various titles and degrees, living in twenty-six castellanies, several of which were centers of villages, sometimes important ones.[25] We speak of the "school of Troyes." But what did it produce? Peter Comestor was dean of the cathedral from 1147 to 1164, but it was at Paris, later on (between 1169 and 1173), that he composed his *Historia scholastica*, which was to become widely known. All the rest of the area's literary production came not from the town or the countryside, but, in the secular domain, from the court of Champagne and, in the theological domain, from the abbey of Clairvaux. Likewise, we refer to the "school of Reims," though the principal works came not from this town but from the abbey of St Thierry nearby. And when William of St Thierry reached Signy, in the Ardennes, theological ideas continued to flow from there.

In Paris, during the "twelfth" century (as defined earlier), there were many "circles" of students gathered around many masters, and in this sense

---

[24]Jean Delumeau, *Le christianisme va-t-il mourir?* (Paris 1977) 25.

[25]Theodore Evergates, *Feudal Society in the Bailliage of Troyes under the Counts of Champagne, 1152–1284* (Baltimore and London 1975) 53–61.

there were many schools, from that of the successive Victorines to those of Robert of Courson, Thomas of Chobham, and Geoffrey of Poitiers, at the beginning of the thirteenth century, not to mention those of Stephen Langton (most active around 1180) and Peter the Chanter, who died in 1197.[26] Certainly all, or nearly all (with certain nuances for the school of St Victor, especially in its early stages), had common preoccupations, in particular "practical morality";[27] their "academic life" did not pose the same economic problems, was not exposed to the same dangers and temptations, did not require the same rules and discipline as "monastic life" did. It did not produce the same kind of works, either. It is not apparent that *either* "monastic" or "academic" life was affected by the socioeconomic evolution then in progress.

That evolution, moreover, was a much more complex process than the sharply defined categories proposed by Marx and Engels would suggest and which some people naively project onto the twelfth century: it was not simply a case of oppressors (the nobles and feudal lords) and oppressed (the bourgeois of the towns)—a distinction which seems unaware of the existence, and importance, of the peasantry. For there were many types of settlement intermediate between the town and the peasant village, and great diversity in forms of serfdom and degrees of personal liberty. Faced with such facts, the historian who does not permit himself to be swayed by anachronistic a prioris rightly asks us to preserve our awareness of nuances.[28]

Judged according to Marxist history, the theology of the cloister and that of the schools would not be distinguished as contemplative and pastoral respectively. Monastic theology would be viewed as a "militant feudal theology," the "ideology of reaction"; as basically conservative, aiming to justify and to preserve for as long as possible the inherited feudal oppression. School theology would be seen as the theology of the bourgeois, in the medieval meaning of the word, expressing their need for "emancipation."[29]

Doubtless such categories can be applied to monastic economic policy; but such sociopolitical facts do not appear to have influenced either the monks' theology or that of the masters in the towns. William, while he was abbot of St Thierry, was actively involved in defending his monastery's lands against the claims of the Reims bourgeois, the peasants of St Thierry, and the nobles of the area. Peter the Venerable was obliged to take part in the same kind of conflict around Cluny. Neither man alluded to those disputes in his theological writings. The image of God in man, as William expounded it, knew no "class" distinctions; it was confirmed in all. Monastic theology would

---

[26]Baldwin, *Masters.*

[27]Baldwin, *Masters* 1.47.

[28]Lucien Musset, "Peuplement en bourgage et bourgs ruraux en Normandie du Xe au XIIIe siècle," CCM 9 (1966) 177–208.

[29]Ernst Werner, *Stadluft macht frei: Frühscholastik und bürgerliche Emanzipation in der ersten Hälfte des 12. Jahrhunderts,* SB Leipzig 118.5 (Berlin 1976) 39–41.

deserve to be called an "ideology of reaction" if it had sought to justify a sociopolitical situation, or opposed an emancipation movement. But this was not at all the case. Believing in the liberty of each individual makes it difficult to reduce everything to social pressures. The variety of talents and genius in so many thinkers is enough to account for the fact that each of them expressed himself according to the great passion which inspired his life, according to his vocation. The Christian historian of theology has the right to reckon with grace, which to him is a reality; to write history as if grace did not exist is to lack objectivity.

Furthermore, can we forget that monks such as Bernard of Clairvaux and Isaac of Stella devoted themselves to a radical criticism of the nobility and chivalry unequaled in the literature emanating from the town schools? Whereas Peter Comestor, dean of the cathedral of Troyes, gave the simplest of justifications for the violence of the crusaders and their successors in the Holy Land, St Bernard completely transformed the traditional motivations of the crusade. He went so far in condemning violence and oppression by the powerful that affinities, rather than opposition, have been seen between him and Marx.[30]

Another way to explain the existence of multiple theologies is to apply the concept of "a return to the sources," arguing that the school theologians went back to the Bible itself and to the works of the Fathers, while those of the cloister were content to use florilegia containing only extracts—not always well chosen. This may be true of the thirteenth century, but during the twelfth century, St Bernard, William of St Thierry, and many others certainly had a thorough knowledge of the Scriptures; their style shows that they had assimilated the sacred texts so well that they had no need for the concordances invented by the schools during the twelfth century.[31] For a single example, we may refer again to Troyes and its surroundings. What place, what school in this area possessed, in the first half of the twelfth century, a collection of St Augustine's works in eight folio volumes and a vast series of Origen's writings except the abbey of Clairvaux, where St Bernard had them copied?[32] At Cîteaux, the rabbis of the important Jewish community of Troyes had helped to establish a corrected text of the Bible;[33] the Cistercians' attitude toward exegesis, especially of the Song of Songs (so dear to monastic theologians), was close to the rabbinical tradition. And how many masters in town schools had an understanding of St Augustine equal to St Anselm's?[34]

[30]Karl Bertau, *Deutsche Literatur im europäischen Mittelalter* (2 vols. Munich 1972–73) 1.382.

[31]Richard H. Rouse, "Cistercian Aids to Study in the Thirteenth Century," *Studies in Medieval Cistercian History II*, ed. John R. Sommerfeldt, Cistercian Studies Series 24 (Kalamazoo 1976) 123–34 at 127 n. 10.

[32]Jean Leclercq, "Les manuscrits de l'abbaye de Liessies," *Scriptorium* 6 (1952) 51–62.

[33]Aryeh Grabois, "The *Hebraica veritas* and Jewish-Christian Intellectual Relations in the Twelfth Century," *Speculum* 50 (1975) 613–34.

[34]Gillian R. Evans, "St. Anselm's Images of Trinity," *Journal of Theological Studies* 2nd ser. 27 (1976) 46–57.

It was in the towns, more than in the cloisters, that the canonical collections—themselves in large part a kind of patristic anthology—were used.[35] And it was from the schools, not the cloisters, that the florilegium that became the Gloss emerged. Anthologies were compiled in the monasteries, of course, but of a different kind: those of John of Fécamp and others were drawn from the sources; those from the schools dispensed with referring to sources. In short, the difference between the theology of the schools and that of the monasteries is not explained any better by two different methods of using sources than by two types of sociopolitical conditioning. A valid explanation can only be reached by studying the particular orientation of each.

CHARACTERISTICS OF THE DIFFERENT THEOLOGIES

THE "CONTEMPLATIVE" MONASTIC THEOLOGY

One of the main characteristics of scholasticism was the search for systematization.[36] Certainly some monks had also sought to present the Christian mystery as a whole; Rupert of Deutz, for example, offered an interpretation of the entire history of salvation. St Bernard and, above all, William of St Thierry proposed comprehensive doctrines which are very "structured." Certain scholastics applied to theology the method of deducing a whole system from one principle, and some monks did the same: for William of St Thierry, the fact that man was the image of the Trinity explained everything. Nevertheless, in general, the scholastics' systematizations were more encyclopedic than the monks': they dealt with *all* the problems raised by Christian dogma and morality, faith and action. At first, such systems took the form of organized collections of sentences; these led, during the second half of the twelfth century, to the first *summae*. For the monks, it was rather a matter of synthesis, which always included a personal, subjective element that served as a point of departure for reflection.

This fundamental component was—to use a term St Bernard and the monks were fond of—experience.[37] This is already apparent in St Anselm, who initiated the entire renewal of monastic theology. The unity between his personal meditation on the Scriptures and his theological reflection on the Scriptures comes from the unity of his monastic life, and is reflected in the unity of

---

[35]Joseph de Ghellinck, *Le mouvement théologique du XIIe siècle* (2nd ed. Bruges 1948; repr. 1969) 131–249.

[36]Richard W. Hunt, "Manuscripts Containing the Indexing Symbols of Robert Grosseteste," *The Bodleian Library Record* 4 (1953) 241–55 at 249–50.

[37]Jean Leclercq, "St. Bernard and Christian Experience," *Worship* 41 (1967) 222–33; repr. in his *Aspects of Monasticism*, trans. Mary Dodd, Cistercian Studies Series 7 (Kalamazoo 1978) 251–65; idem, "Essais sur l'esthétique de S. Bernard," *Studi medievali* 3rd ser. 9 (1968) 688–728 at 695–705 ("De l'expérience à l'expression"); Brian C. Stock, "Experience, Praxis, Work, and Planning in Bernard of Clairvaux: Observations on the *Sermones in Cantica*," *The Cultural Context of Medieval Learning*, Proceedings of the First International Colloquium on Philosophy, Science, and Theology in the Middle Ages, ed. John E. Murdoch and Edith D. Sylla, Boston Studies in the Philosophy of Science 26 (Dordrecht and Boston 1975) 219–68 at 223–28.

his work. In his life as a monk, liturgy and devotion were primary. God, for him, was not a problem to be solved, but a reality to be loved and prayed to. His desire to know God better in order to be closer to him, and the cares of his position as abbot, were equally to Anselm opportunities to strive toward more light. His biographer, Eadmer, reports that one night, during the divine office, "the grace of God illuminated his heart"[38] and led him to understand what he then wrote about God in his *Proslogion*. This did not exempt him from an intellectual effort in which he made use of dialectical reasoning. But the writings which resulted from this illumination and this effort bear witness to the unity of his theoretical research and his spiritual experience.[39]

All this applies to monastic theology, and especially to that of the Cistercians, above all to their master and model, St Bernard. The analysis of life's experience required the use of reason; but, being less speculative and deductive than a systematization worked out by way of consequences derived from a principle, it was poetic rather than scientific in character, and it found expression through symbols and procedures dependent on esthetics. Even St Bernard's choice of vocabulary reveals the mode of thought. For him, images were more important than clear ideas. Studies by modern philosophers and linguists of how, through the use of symbols, the artist frees himself from conceptual rigidity are helping us to understand him.[40] Without giving up either the common meanings of words or the intelligibility which concepts make possible, St Bernard sought above all to translate an experience—to express, at least partially, a transcendence. He does not describe, he evokes. He does not prove that a beyond exists, he points it out and inspires a search for it. Such was the language God had chosen to convey his own revelation to the inspired scribes of the Old Testament, then to Jesus Christ, and later to the apostles and evangelists who spread his message in writing. This symbolism appeals to the imagination, at the junction between consciousness and body, and thereby draws the entire human being into sharing the experience from which proceeds the received and transmitted truth. No less than its intelligible content, its poetic content gives such reflection a dynamism which prepares the way for the religious experience, leads to and introduces it, and makes it available for sharing.[41]

Many monastic theologians could be adduced to illustrate these remarks. In brief, it can be said that their teaching is characterized by its origin, which

---

[38]*The Life of St. Anselm, Archbishop of Canterbury, by Eadmer*, ed. and trans. Richard W. Southern (London 1962) 30.

[39]James T. Gollnick, "The Monastic-Devotional Context of Anselm of Canterbury's Theology," *Monastic Studies* 12 (1976) 239–48 at 243–48.

[40]Charles A. Bernard, "La fonction symbolique en spiritualité," *Nouvelle revue théologique* 95 (1973) 1119–36.

[41]"Saint Bernard was a poet as well as a theologian and a politician," as Elizabeth T. Kennan rightly observed, "Rhetoric and Style in the *De consideratione*," *Studies* (n. 31 above) 40–48 at 40.

was experience, and by its expression, appealing largely to symbolism and the imagination.

THE PASTORAL THEOLOGY OF THE SCHOOLS

At the end of the eleventh century, in the aftermath of the Gregorian Reform, a new pastoral theology emerged. It was, however, the work neither of men of action nor of canonists, but of schoolmasters; and so it included both questions of Christian morality and the doctrine which underlay and justified it. Anselm and Ralph, the masters of Laon, as well as Manegold and others, have left glosses, commentaries, and *sententiae* in response to the moral concerns of everyday life: sin, the pursuit of happiness, God's presence in creation, God's will and man's free will, virtue and vice, scandals to avoid, love and sexuality, the sacraments—particularly baptism, marriage, and ordination of priests— clerical celibacy, relationships with the Jews, the final reward of human effort. These are the problems raised, not by the professionals of religious thought, but by the active, pastoral clergy and the faithful in their charge. As a theology oriented toward laymen, it relied mainly on the scriptural texts they were most familiar with, the texts which played the largest role in catechism and prayer: Genesis, the Gospel according to St Matthew, the Epistles of St Paul, the Psalms. When these *sententiae* were organized into collections, the order they followed was usually that of creation and salvation: the attributes of God, his works of creation, man's imperfection and its consequences, the remedies offered by the Ancient Law, redemption, the sacraments, moral life, the last things. The representatives of traditional monasticism who were most active in pastoral concerns and Church reform—as in southern Germany—obtained these maxims and used them: the separation between cloister and school was neither absolute nor uniform. Still, it can truly be said that "the world of the schools was the world of the reform."[42] What happened at Laon in the time of Anselm and Ralph was reflected in the teaching of most of the Paris masters throughout the twelfth century, and even later. It was indeed, for most of them, a question of "practical morality."[43]

SPECULATIVE THEOLOGY

Finally, masters who were powerful and original thinkers devoted themselves to theological activity of a different kind. Abelard was such a one; Thierry of Chartres and Gilbert of Poitiers were others. Their dominant characteristics were acuteness of judgment, a critical sense, the capacity for dialectic. They were neither contemplatives, like the monks, nor pastors, like the ordinary masters in the schools: they were intellectuals. A better understanding of the

[42]Flint (n. 14 above) 109.
[43]Baldwin, *Masters* 1.47.

sociology of religious knowledge today makes it possible for us to speak of a *third* theology. We may label it "speculative" or "theoretical," because logic and dialectic figured in it; it was organized in syntheses and *summae*, according to a systematic plan. It is the work of relatively few masters, but their efforts and writings served as a decisive guide for the growth of Christian thought which flowered in thirteenth-century scholasticism.

Another name can now be added to the list of known masters of this genre: William of Lucca, who taught at Bologna during the third quarter of the twelfth century. An important commentary of his on Pseudo-Dionysius has been found in Troyes, among the Clairvaux manuscripts—a new star in the twelfth-century sky, one that can be studied more closely when the work has been edited.[44] Meanwhile, it is interesting to note that the monks of St Bernard's abbey wished to own this text—another proof, if one were needed, that there were exchanges and influences, but not confusion, between the cloisters, the schools, and the intellectuals.

This speculative theology, though different from the pastoral theology of the schoolmasters, is nonetheless closer to it than to the theology of the cloister. Therefore, it will be justifiable here, for the sake of clarity, to set up our comparison with only two categories: on one hand, the theology of the canonical and monastic cloisters, and on the other, the theology of the masters—"masters" designating both the masters of the schools and the intellectuals, to be more precisely defined as necessary.

RELATIONSHIPS BETWEEN THE DIFFERENT THEOLOGIES

One can enumerate at least seven major differences which distinguish, without separating, the theological activity of the cloister from that of the schoolmasters.

The *audience*, even within the cloister, was diversified. Most of the new canonical and monastic orders that appeared toward the beginning of the century did not admit children offered by their parents; traditional monasticism, although it tended to reduce their numbers, continued to recruit such oblates. This difference in recruiting produced a profound difference in psychology. Adults who became monks, even if they were young adults, had a knowledge, and often an experience, of life's realities that was lacking in those who had been separated from their native environment since they were five to seven years old. Similarly, in the town schools, it was now not only children who learned the rudiments of faith and culture, but also, more and more, adult clerics—no longer "schoolboys" but "students."

The mental habits of each of these milieux are reflected in linguistic structures, the study of which belongs to psychology and stylistics; there is here a vast domain to be explored. Each experienced different problems and treated

---

[44]Ferruccio Gastaldelli, "La traduzione del De divinis nominibus dello Pseudo-Dionigi nel commento inedito di Guglielmo da Lucca († 1178)," *Salesianum* 39 (1977) 56–76, 221–54.

them differently: the problems raised by friendship, for example, as well as relationships between men and women, were different in each milieu; and it was the new orders that produced most of the works dealing with love of God and of man (and, in particular, the most commentaries on the Song of Songs), with numerous and extended comparisons borrowed from secular, chivalric life.[45] The monastic masters taught cloistered monks, concerned mostly with the problems of their own spiritual growth; the schoolmasters taught secular clerics and laymen who were expected to maintain or improve their faith and answer questions of daily morality in ordinary society.

Between each of these milieux, reciprocal influences were at work creating a true cross-fertilization. Henceforth we must study culture—including its theological expression—no longer in general, but in specific geographical and political areas: Norman England, the Rhineland, northern Italy, Languedoc, the region comprising the towns of Orléans, Poitiers, and Angers, and so forth. For Champagne, in particular, it is necessary to keep in mind the personal and cultural relationships that may have existed between the cathedral school of Troyes, the abbeys of Clairvaux and the Paraclete, the court of Marie de France, and the Yeshiva or rabbinical academy of Troyes.

The *subjects treated* were different, or approached from a different point of view. Monastic thought began with the experience of the self as a sinner, desiring God, striving to become one with him. Anthropological problems, problems of love, faith, the relationship of grace and free will, were its major concerns. The mysteries of the faith were considered, but mainly those associated with Christology and the Eucharist. Eschatology was dealt with, because the definitive and eternal possession of God was the ultimate goal for those who consecrated their lives to seeking God alone.

In the school, the subjective, personal aspect played a lesser role. All the mysteries of the faith, from the Creation to the last things —considered less in terms of an eschatological longing than of reward or punishment after this life—were subjects of meditation. For those masters who devoted themselves to speculation, the problems of the Trinity were of primary importance. As for secular morality, it too differed, of course, from what we might call "monastic morality,"[46] in that the problems raised were not the same in the cloister as in society.

Both milieux had a *pastoral tendency*. For abbots, "monastic pastoralism" (evoked, for example, by the very title of Aelred of Rievaulx's *Oratio pastoralis*)[47] consisted in caring for the spiritual development and training of their monks. In the schools, pastoralism taught how to practice Christian morality, in celibacy for the clerics, in marriage for the laity.

[45]Jean Leclercq, *Monks and Love in Twelfth-Century France* (Oxford 1979) 86–108.

[46]François Vandenbroucke, *La morale monastique du XIe au XVIe siècle*, Analecta mediaevalia Namurcensia 20 (Louvain 1966).

[47]Charles Dumont, ed., *Aelred de Rievaulx, La vie de recluse; La prière pastorale*, Sources chrétiennes 76 (Paris 1961) 184–203.

The permanent *reform of the Church* and the fight against heresies concerned all theologians. Although monks such as Peter the Venerable and St Bernard wrote against heretics, this polemical aspect was less important in the writings of the monks than in those of the secular masters; the same is true of the controversy with the Jews. In their reform writings, St Bernard and others attacked general abuses, with a certain universal goal: they sought reform of the Roman Curia, they denounced the pomp of prelates, the laxity of the old monastic orders, the violence and greed of the laity, the sinful behavior of clerics. The schoolmasters, on the other hand, grappled with concrete, specific problems that arose in the particular milieu in which they lived and taught.

The two theologies drew on different *sources*. While the masters depended mainly on texts with immediate applications to human action, the monks preferred more contemplative texts: in the Old Testament, the Song of Songs; in the New Testament, the Gospel according to St John rather than that of St Matthew. In the interpretation of Scripture, the Jewish tradition was made available to monks primarily through Origen, who owed a great deal to it,[48] and, in the town schools, sometimes also through contacts with contemporary rabbis.

Concerning knowledge of the Bible, a distinction must be made. How the Bible was used, referred to, reflected upon, differed according to whether it was meditated and prayed over in the *lectio divina* and sung daily in divine office, or whether answers to pastoral or speculative problems were sought in it. The type of memorization, and consequently the resultant literary use, was different in the two cases. In the cloister, a poetic type of spontaneous recollection was as important as exact quotation. In the schools, debate required one to reproduce exactly the *auctoritas* upon which the argument was based. These differences appear clearly in, on the one hand, monks like St Bernard and, on the other, masters like Peter Lombard and Gilbert of Poitiers. Can it be said that one group knew Scripture better than the other? It is a matter rather of a different way of assimilating it, and then of drawing upon it and referring to it. Nonetheless, it is a fact that the biblical psychology and the style of a Bernard of Clairvaux are more marked by the "biblical style," if not by scriptural doctrine itself, than is the case with the masters, pastoral or speculative.[49] Here again, it is not a case of preferring one group of authors over another, but of recognizing the special character of each.

The *intellectual methods* of monastic theology were based on the *lectio divina*, that is on reading accompanied by meditation and prayer; the methods

---

[48]Nicholas R. M. de Lange, *Origen and the Jews: Studies in Jewish-Christian Relations in Third-Century Palestine* (Cambridge 1976).

[49]Jean Leclercq, *Recueil d'études sur S. Bernard et ses écrits* (3 vols. Rome 1962–69) 3.213–66, "La Bible dans les homélies de S. Bernard sur 'Missus est,'" and "De quelques procédés du style biblique de S. Bernard."

of the schools were based on a *lectio* followed by a *disputatio*. In the cloister, there were "conversations," not debates.[50]

The monks—especially St Bernard, William of St Thierry, Isaac of Stella, and others—did not fail to make use of dialectic and reason. But the problems of speculative philosophy, as the special legacy of the Platonic tradition, were less important in the cloister than among the intellectuals. Likewise, whereas the monks' psychology started from the analysis of states of the soul and studied their growth, and was in that sense dynamic and "developmental," the psychology of the intellectuals strove rather to deduce logical consequences from principles related to the composition of the human being; it was more static and theoretical than dynamic and experiential.[51]

Canon law was not unknown to the monks,[52] but they referred to it less often than the schoolmasters. Sometimes they even claimed to distrust it. They were less concerned with the religious organization of society than with its spiritual reform; because of this preoccupation, a St Bernard was more demanding, more radical, but perhaps less realistic, than the masters who were accustomed to discussing actual cases.

The *modes of expression* might be either oral or written. The abbots spoke to the monks, of course, in order to teach them the daily observance; it is to these familiar conversations that we owe the words, the *dicta*, of St Bernard and St Anselm, comparable to the *apophthegmata*[53] of ancient monasticism. Their theological works, however, were written texts—that is to say, carefully composed and dictated. In the schools, the masters taught orally; they also had occasion to write, to compose works, but these works themselves sometimes betray the originally oral character of their teaching. This is why it is difficult to edit and identify the sentences of the masters of Laon and elsewhere, and to recognize all of Abelard's doctrine, through the successive drafts of his *Theologiae* and in the writings of his disciples on problems he himself had never written about.[54]

Perhaps it still bears repeating: this catalogue of differences records shades of difference, nuances rather than oppositions. Conflicts there were between the two groups, but we must take care not to exaggerate their importance—especially now that we understand better the points on which opinions

---

[50]Jean Leclercq, "La récréation et le colloque dans la tradition monastique," *Revue d'ascétique et de mystique* 43 (1967) 3–20.

[51]Jean Leclercq, "Modern Psychology and the Understanding of Medieval People," *Cistercian Studies* 11 (1976) 269–89 at 288–89.

[52]Bernard Jacqueline, *Episcopat et papauté chez Bernard de Clairvaux* (Sainte Marguerite d'Elle 1975).

[53]Benedicta Ward, "Apophthegmata Bernardi," *The Influence of Saint Bernard: Anglican Essays*, Fairacres Publications 60 (Oxford 1976) 135–43.

[54]Artur M. Landgraf, "Probleme um den Heiligen Bernhard von Clairvaux," *Cistercienser Chronik* 61 (1954) 1–16.

diverged, and that those differences sometimes existed more between individuals, their characters and their tendencies, than between doctrines.[55]

RENEWAL OF THEOLOGY AND "HUMANISM"

Was this renewal, then, a renaissance, in the sense in which before Haskins this
word was reserved for the Italian Renaissance in the West, and according to
which (even when Haskins applied it to the twelfth century) it meant above all
a rediscovery of Greco-Roman Antiquity and especially of classical writers?

This classical heritage was never lacking, and the greatest artisans of
Carolingian culture—Alcuin and others—had expressly wished to return to it.
What they knew of Antiquity had been passed on to the twelfth century,
which perhaps attached less importance to the classical heritage than had the
ninth century: literature and thought had become sufficiently autonomous
that they no longer needed to be propped up by so many quotations from ancient authors. Now, contributions from Antiquity were, in a sense,
filtered—which might be either an impoverishment or an enrichment. St Peter
Damiani is an example of an intermediary between the two periods. An Italian
who spent his formative years in a region of northern Italy where the ancient
Roman school traditions remained more vigorous than elsewhere, he reveals in
his vocabulary a surprising familiarity with classical Latin.[56] His thought was
vigorous enough, however, to separate from this matrix—of words,
mythological images, and ideas derived from the profane (and pagan)
world—an authentic Christian doctrine, original and coherent. This was the
direction in which more and more progress would be made in the course of the
twelfth century.

Monasticism, for example, used formulas borrowed from Ovid—but
transformed their meaning. Thus, the expression *amor socialis*, which Ovid
used to describe conjugal love, was interpreted as the charity practiced in conventual life. The idea that man was created with a face capable of looking at
the heavens was used to illustrate the theme of the image of God. From the
time, just before 1124,[57] when he read Cicero's *De amicitia*, St Bernard used it
freely in his treatise *On the Necessity of Loving God* and elsewhere; but
whereas Cicero said that friendship created equality in those between whom it
existed, Bernard went further: as a Christian, he spoke not only of equality,
but also of unity. In the same way, William of St Thierry adapted to his

---

[55]Thus, several recent works on Abelard have shown that on many issues he was in agreement
with the monastic tradition represented by St Bernard; see Jean Leclercq, "Notes Abélardiennes,"
Bulletin de la Société internationale pour l'histoire de la philosophie médiévale 8–9 (1966–67)
59–62, and 13 (1972) 68–71.

[56]Jean Leclercq, *Saint Pierre Damien, ermite et homme d'Eglise* (Rome 1960) 168–73; Cantin
(n. 2 above) 291–305.

[57]Remo Gelsomino, "S. Bernardo di Chiaravalle e il '*De amicitia*' di Cicerone," *Analecta
monastica* 5, Studia Anselmiana 43 (Rome 1958) 180–86.

teaching several concepts of Stoicism, acquired, it seems, from an assiduous study of Seneca.[58]

Other examples would show that in monasticism, the knowledge of classical Latin authors owed less to books than it had during the ninth century, and than it would in the sixteenth; it was more personal, better assimilated, influencing thought more than style—since style was in essence acquired from biblical, patristic, and liturgical sources. Even the debt owed to the Fathers, moreover, especially the Greek Fathers, by monastic theologians of the twelfth century seems today less significant than one thought thirty years ago.[59] In the domain of philosophical ideas, especially in anthropology, it is now accepted that the monks' theology owed less to Platonism, Neoplatonism, and Neostoicism than was even recently believed; such influences were probably greater in the theology of certain schoolmasters, especially, perhaps, at Chartres.

In short, the humanism of the monks consisted less in borrowing its means of expression from the writers of Antiquity than in preserving, developing, and analyzing Christian convictions about the dignity of man—a concept increasingly formulated during the Middle Ages in terms of "nobility."[60] To these basically optimistic intuitions writers gave expression suffused with beauty and poetry. This confidence in man, this refinement of sensibility, this quality of language: are these not so many tokens of a true humanism?

In any case, "the sources" do not explain, any better than socioeconomic and political conditions, the existence of such individualistic geniuses as St Bernard, William of St Thierry, Abelard, or Gilbert of Poitiers. The only important source they had in common was Holy Scripture. The monks drew their language mainly, but not exclusively, from this source; the others turned more to terms and concepts derived from other traditions. The most vigorous thinkers in the schools reflected on language; the most profound of the monks offered rather a theology of the imagination. Among the first, reasoning and dialectic dominated; among the second, intuition, born of experience and esthetics.

THE INFLUENCE OF THE THEOLOGICAL RENEWAL

At present one could offer no objective criterion for claiming that one of the two theologies is superior to the other. Each had its own grandeur, its own fruitfulness. One would like to be able to evaluate the influence each had, both on the milieu that produced it and on others. The theology of the schools

[58]Jean-Marie Déchanet, "Seneca noster: Des Lettres à Lucilius à la Lettre aux Frères du Mont-Dieu," *Mélanges Joseph de Ghellinck, S.J.* (2 vols. Gembloux 1951) 2.753–66.

[59]This is clear especially from the studies collected under the title *One Yet Two: Monastic Tradition, East and West*, ed. M. Basil Pennington, Cistercian Studies Series 29 (Kalamazoo 1976), and others I have surveyed in "Etudes" (n. 10 above).

[60]Jean Leclercq, "L'humanisme des moines du moyen âge," *Studi medievali* 3rd ser. 10 (1969) 69–113.

perhaps influenced the clergy, by whom it was elaborated, and the laity, whose problems it studied; to what degree laymen were aware of it remains to be determined. The theology of the cloister was aimed at a more limited audience, enclosed within the monasteries. It is however possible that, paradoxically, monastic theology was more accessible to nonspecialists, because its language was less technical. What seems certain is that the troubadours, trouvères, and other poets took more from St Bernard and the Cistercians than from the secular masters. Chrétien de Troyes did not attend the school in that town; but he could well have read St Bernard's sermons on the Song of Songs, whether in Latin—which he knew, since he translated some *Ovidiana*—or in one of the translations which circulated very soon after the death of the abbot of Clairvaux.[61] It is still uncertain whether the prose *Lancelot*, and, in the first half of the thirteenth century, the *Queste du Graal*, come from a Cistercian—or more precisely, Bernardian—milieu or were produced under its influence. Cistercian or not, direct or indirect, the influence of monastic thought on these works shaped them decisively. It was natural that monastic theology, because of the importance it gave to symbolism, and especially to the allegory of love, would find a greater echo among poets than the theories of the schoolmasters.

A more complete picture of the influences of the various theologies would include an account of the different kinds of social evolution undergone in the various parts of each European country. But, in a general way, two facts stand out.

First, the dialectical effort of the twelfth-century schoolmasters constituted a necessary step in the intellectual evolution of the medieval West. It set the stage for the "high scholasticism" (*Hochscholastik*) of the second half of the thirteenth century and the "late scholasticism" (*Spätscholastik*) of the fourteenth and fifteenth centuries. It was, however, of only temporary importance, and had to be supplanted. In fact, it scarcely held the interest of either the masters of that era or the humanists of the sixteenth and seventeenth centuries. It was not until between the twenties and fifties of our own century that doctrinal historians deciphered the *sententiae* and glosses in the manuscripts; and interest in this aspect of the twelfth century has already diminished greatly.

On the other hand, the theological literature of monasticism continues to be studied and reedited—for most of it had been published—translated, read, and (above all) meditated on and admired.[62] For many, both monks and others, it remains a source of inspiration. The literature of monastic theology

[61]Michel Zink, *La prédication en langue romane avant 1300*, Nouvelle bibliothèque du Moyen Age 4 (Paris 1976) 165–71, 478, and passim (see the Index, 562, s.v. *Bernard*).

[62]Its influence has been signaled by Giles Constable, "Twelfth-Century Spirituality and the Late Middle Ages," *Medieval and Renaissance Studies* 5, ed. O. B. Hardison, Jr. (Chapel Hill 1971) 27–60; idem, "The Popularity of Twelfth-Century Spiritual Writers in the Late Middle Ages," *Renaissance: Studies in Honor of Hans Baron*, ed. Anthony Molho and John A. Tedeschi (Florence 1970) 3–28.

owes its perpetual immediacy to its two characteristics: its appeal to human experience, which is the same in all ages, and its beauty, which endures. Its role can perhaps be compared to that of contemporary Christian existentialism, ''in the attempt to present Christ as the answer to the questions implied within existence. In earlier centuries a similar task was undertaken mainly by monastic theologians, who analyzed themselves and the members of their small communities so penetratingly that there are few present-day insights into the human predicament which they did not anticipate.''[63]

Bibliographical Note

Baldwin, *Masters*; Chenu, *Théologie*; Joseph de Ghellinck, *Le mouvement théologique du XIIe siècle* (2nd ed. Bruges 1948; repr. 1969); Robert Javelet, *Image et ressemblance au douzième siècle: De Saint Anselme à Alain de Lille* (2 vols. Strasbourg 1967); Artur M. Landgraf, *Einführung in die Geschichte der theologischen Literatur der Frühscholastik* (Regensburg 1948); Leclercq, *Love of Learning*; David E. Luscombe, *The School of Peter Abelard: The Influence of Abelard's Thought in the Early Scholastic Period* (Cambridge 1969); M. Basil Pennington, ed., *One Yet Two: Monastic Tradition, East and West*, Cistercian Studies Series 29 (Kalamazoo 1976); Colin M. Morris, *The Discovery of the Individual, 1050–1200* (London 1972); Gérard M. Paré, A. Brunet, and P. Tremblay, *La renaissance du XIIe siècle: Les écoles et l'enseignement*, Publications de l'Institut d'études médiévales d'Ottawa 3 (Paris and Ottawa 1933); Southern, *Humanism* 61–85, ''Humanism and the School of Chartres.''

[63]Paul Tillich, *Systematic Theology* (3 vols. Chicago 1951–63) 2.27.

The Reform of the Liturgy
from a Renaissance Perspective

Chrysogonus Waddell

The historian who addressed himself to the subject of twelfth-century liturgical reform in general would be either extremely naive or remarkably courageous, for the material at hand is simply vast. After all, liturgy in the twelfth century was still very much a meaningful part of the life of everyone from pope to peasant; and the creative ferment so evident in the schools, in the arts and crafts, in religious institutions, and in society at large was no less creatively at work in all that touched upon the worship of the Church.

The particular purpose of this volume fortunately restricts us to considering twelfth-century liturgical reform chiefly, indeed almost uniquely, from the perspective of renaissance ideology. "Renaissance" usually connotes at least two concomitant phenomena: first, a revival of interest in classical art and learning; and second, a deeper consciousness of man's dignity as man, together with a corresponding deeper appreciation of human genius. And so the question is: is it really possible to bring liturgical reform into common focus with a renaissance ideology such as this?

"Reform" and "renewal" admit of somewhat different acceptations from author to author. I shall use the term *reform* to cover almost every intentionally provoked or systematically implemented series of changes in liturgical books and rites. At Cluny, for instance, the liturgical changes introduced in the twelfth century were relatively minor; but they were the fruit of careful thinking and systematic choice. Here, however, "reform" is used in an admittedly elastic, weakened sense—especially if we consider the Cistercian program of liturgical reform, in which books and rites of an earlier period were totally reworked in the light of principles carefully formulated and mercilessly applied. And again, we are not interested in twelfth-century liturgical reform in general, but only in those aspects of it germane to renaissance ideology.

LITURGY AND CLASSICAL ANTIQUITY

No possible doubt that many of those most responsible for the shape of the liturgy in the twelfth century were as susceptible as any quattrocento *littérateur* to the silver magic of a Vergil or a Horace; no doubt, either, that more than one twelfth-century lover of classical learning felt something of an embarrassment that God should have chosen so uncouth a diction in which to reveal the mysteries of salvation—a particularly painful instance of God's foolishness being wiser than the wisdom of men.[1] But whatever the twelfth-century liturgist's nostalgia for classical Latin letters, his historical point of reference for liturgy went far deeper than the relatively superficial level of literary expression. As regards substance, the point of reference had to be the *in illo tempore* of biblical revelation, never the golden age of Greek and Roman Antiquity.[2]

Further, for the twelfth-century worshipper, the very concept of liturgy evoked a series of temporal and transtemporal relationships considerably more sophisticated than any renaissance return to the past. By means of the sacred texts and ritual actions, the past historic saving reality becomes somehow present and accessible in the here and now, and in such a way that something of the future eschatological fulfillment is anticipated and interiorized by the worshipper—provided, of course, that his spiritual and moral condition enables him to enter fully into the reality sacramentally present.

This is the real meaning of so many of the visions, dreams, and locutions sprinkled throughout the pages of twelfth-century hagiographical literature. When, for example, the illiterate Cistercian, Christian of Aumône, found himself transported into heaven, where he witnessed a liturgy choreographed by choirs of angels and centered on the cosmic Cross which was venerated with much the same rites practiced in the Palm Sunday liturgy,[3] Christian was simply experiencing (in a manner eminently suited to his own admittedly problematic psychology) the real content of the rather more prosaic liturgy being celebrated in a less spectacular manner by his brethren in their modest oratory.

For the medieval man, liturgy brought into sharp focus a symbolist version of his everyday reality: one can think of the perceptive twelfth-century man's world as bathed in a kind of diffused sacramentality, not unlike the world as experienced by individuals gifted with poetic intuition. For such people, the epiphenomenal world opened into a realm still more concrete and real. To illustrate the point by way of contrast, take sir Lancelot. Bogged down though he is in the quagmire of his adulterous passion for queen Guinevere, Lancelot becomes aware in his better moments of a mysterious Presence; still, his general condition remains characterized by a torpor in which the hero manqué lies "without speech or movement, as though in a trance." "Seek [the adventures of the Holy Grail] you may," the hermit priest tells him, "but find

---

[1]On the sacramental system as an exercise in humility, see the texts of the theologians of our period, analyzed by Innocenzo Colosio, "La prassi sacramentale come esercizio di umilità," *Rivista di Ascetica e Mistica* 9 (1964) 101–16.

[2]For a useful summary of the liturgical reality in terms of rite and symbol and human action, see Irenée H. Dalmais, *Introduction to the Liturgy*, trans. Roger Capel (Baltimore 1961) 1–26, esp. 8–12, "The Forest of Symbols."

[3]*Vita Christiani monachi* c. 15, "De signo Crucis in celo viso," ed. Jean Leclercq, "Le texte complet de la Vie de Christian de l'Aumône," *Analecta Bollandiana* 71 (1953) 21–52 at 34–35.

them you will not. For were the Holy Grail to appear before you, I do not think you would be able to see it.''[4] Whatever the content-reality we attach to the symbol of the *Sangreal*—grace, Eucharist, mystical experience, or what have you—the basic perspective remains the same: in the midst of our ordinary world there is present a reality of a higher order. One particularly efficacious way of entry into this reality is through the liturgy. What need, then, to hearken back to ancient Greece and Rome—pale adumbrators at best, and antagonists at worst, of the reality present and accessible in the here and now through the liturgy and the sacraments of faith?

THE EMERGING CONSCIOUSNESS OF MAN AS MAN

Mi pare rinascere, "I seem to be reborn"—words of the fifteenth-century Florentine architect, Antonio Averlino Filarete.[5] Could our twelfth-century man have said the same? Absolutely—and he did, almost *ad nauseam*. But though the formula was virtually the same, the meaning was different, utterly different.

It would be foolish indeed to suggest that, just because our quattrocento Florentine was convinced that classical Antiquity—eternally young because eternally human—was a source of richer life, he necessarily had to opt for pagan Antiquity as opposed to the dehumanizing supernaturalism of the ecclesiastical establishment. But in rejecting the equation "humanist, therefore godless," it would be equally foolish of us to overlook the fact that, since the twelfth century, the point of reference of much of Western civilization has changed; now less the cosmos and world history coming from God and leading back to him, it is rather man himself. Protagoras has come into his own: man has become at last the measure of all things—and with a vengeance!

The twelfth-century counterpart to *mi pare renascere* is actually its opposite number. "Ah, what bliss to be reborn," Guerric of Igny happily sighs—*felicissime renasci!* But the springtide rebirth which forms the theme of so much of Guerric's sermonizing is explicitly rooted in the unaging newness of the Ancient of Days, whose Son is born as man precisely to enable us to be reborn as sons of God. "How blissful, Child Jesus, how lovable your birth, that sets aright the birth of all mankind, and refashions our condition, . . . so that if anyone thinks it shameful to be born a reprobate, he can be reborn in total bliss.''[6] For Guerric and for the Christian twelfth century—and this

---

[4]*The Quest of the Holy Grail*, trans. Pauline M. Matarasso (London 1969) 140.

[5]From Filarete's *Trattato d'architettura* (between 1451 and 1464), as quoted by Vincent Cronin in the chapter "Florence of the Medici," *The Renaissance, Maker of Modern Man* (Washington D.C. 1970) 79.

[6]Guerric of Igny, *Sermo* 3.1: "Quam felix, quam amabilis nativitas tua, puer Iesu, quae nativitatem omnium emendat, conditionem reformat . . . ut si quem piget damnabiliter esse natum, possit felicissime renasci." PL 185.35B = ed. John Morson and Hilary Costello, Sources chrétiennes 166 (2 vols. Paris 1970–73) 1.186. For an extended analysis of the theme of rebirth in Guerric's Christmas sermons, see Thomas Merton, *The Christmas Sermons of Blessed Guerric of Igny* (Trappist Ky. 1959) 1–25.

means Abelard as well as Bernard, Peter Lombard as well as Matthew of Albano—man is more truly man the more divine he becomes. And in *this* context (there are, of course, other contexts), it is not to classical Greece and Rome that our *homo mediaevalis* is likely to look for regeneration.

Similarly, not even the acutest Renaissance perception of the dignity of man went beyond or even matched the twelfth-century perception of man's dignity. But here again, the point of reference tended to be different. What commanded the perspectives of our twelfth-century humanist was not only the fact that man had been created in the image and likeness of God, but that God himself had become man—no slight source of dignity for the thinking believer. Year after year, in the second nocturn reading of the Christmas Night Office, monks and clerics heard pope Leo the Great's *First Sermon for Christmas*, where the theologian of the Incarnation rings the changes on the theme, *Agnosce, o christiane, dignitatem tuam*—"O Christian, heed well your dignity."[7] Moreover, this was couched in a flawless Latinity so perfect that, despite occasional biblical citations and the specifically Christian vocabulary, the Latin stylist is left with little to learn from Cicero. But here the point is that, for Leo and his twelfth-century epigones, in any question of human dignity, "man" and "Christian" must be convertible terms. Can the same be said without serious qualification of even the more professedly Christian members of the later Florentine Platonic Academy? Once again, we would be falsifying perspectives were we to turn the members of the Academy into cryptopagans. They certainly kept high holiday with festive board on November 7, as the day made holy by the birth of Plato; but, rightly or wrongly, for them Plato was Moses talking Attic; and—worse still—*erôs* à la Plato was not all that different from New Testament *agapê*.

In brief, classical Antiquity had nothing to offer the twelfth century for the reform of liturgy as regards its *substance*—which is not to say that classical Antiquity had nothing to offer. Its contribution was, however, at the more superficial level. For rhetoric, for literary excellence, for beauty, for ideas, even for examples of moral excellence and virtue, one could and did look backward to classical Antiquity.

From our own vantage point in the twentieth century, we ourselves are much better placed to indulge our nostalgia for classical culture even in the area of liturgical research. Since the beginning of the present century (and even before), several generations of scholars have been victorious in their vindication of the principle that early Christianity (and therefore, by reason of its intrinsic continuity with the past, medieval Christianity) admits of no real or comprehensive understanding apart from a knowledge and appreciation of classical culture.[8] We are currently witnessing a no less fruitful compensatory

---

[7]Leo the Great, *Tractatus* 21.3, ed. Antoine Chavasse, CCL 138 (1973) 88.70–71.

[8]Among the leaders in this approach to the liturgy Odo Casel, Franz Dölger, Theodor Klauser, and Johannes Quasten are outstanding. Typical of the many scholarly fruits of this movement are the *Jahrbuch für Antike und Christentum* (Münster in Westfalen 1958–) and the still unfinished *Reallexikon für Antike und Christentum* (Stuttgart 1950–).

reaction, impelling scholars backward and beyond even Greco-Roman culture of the early Christian centuries into the Jewish and biblical roots of the Christian liturgy.[9] We shall probably have to wait several decades for a balanced synthesis of biblical, Jewish, Greek, and Roman contributions to the origins of Western liturgy and its early evolution. Our twelfth-century liturgist simply did not have available the tools of philology and archeology which the later Renaissance was to provide as a means for situating liturgical rites and formularies in their proper and original cultural milieu.

But though the Renaissance motifs of "back to classical Antiquity" and "man as man" admit of only uneasy application in the context of twelfth-century liturgical reform, they can nevertheless be said to have some sort of parallel in the period under investigation.

For "back to classical Antiquity," substitute "back to early Christian Rome," and for "man as man" read "local church as particular community." For there can be little doubt that the dynamism of liturgical reform was largely motivated by reference to (Christian) Antiquity, and by a reflective self-consciousness that enabled particular communities to become aware of themselves under the aspect of their unique identity—a self-awareness not without consequences for the liturgy. Besides these two renaissance-related tendencies there are still others which I shall touch upon briefly as germane to liturgical reform: a perception of the need for classification and systematization; an appreciation of *ratio* as arbiter of what is and is not tradition; and something of an urge toward subjective self-expression.

THE LITURGICAL SITUATION ON
THE EVE OF THE TWELFTH CENTURY

In matters touching on liturgy, Gregorian reform envisioned a general return to the earlier, more austere Roman liturgical practice as a means of attaining Gregory VII's ideal of a unified Western Christendom. But what did pope Gregory VII mean by "earlier Roman liturgy"? At the further distance of nine hundred years, we can see clearly (as Gregory could not) that the local Roman liturgy had never ceased to be in constant evolution; and as Peter Abelard pointed out in his Letter 10 to Bernard of Clairvaux, not only did Rome herself admit of a plurality of usages within the same capital of Christendom, but, of all the churches, only the Lateran basilica, "mother of all churches," remained true to the liturgy of the Rome of yore, *nulla filiarum suarum in hoc eam se-*

---

[9]See, for instance, as a rather typical example Louis Bouyer, *Eucharist: Theology and Spirituality of the Eucharistic Prayer*, trans. Charles Underhill Quinn (Notre Dame 1968), esp. the bibliography. Directly or indirectly, much of the current writing on the liturgy and its Jewish antecedents is based on the early and still valuable book by William O. E. Oesterley, *The Jewish Background of the Christian Liturgy* (Oxford 1925; repr. Gloucester Mass. 1965). Though interest centers on the Eucharist, the Office has also been a focus of attention; in this area, one of the most important contributions has been Clifford W. Dugmore, *The Influence of the Synagogue upon the Divine Office*, Alcuin Club Collections 45 (Oxford 1944; repr. Westminster 1964).

quente—"followed in this by not a single one of her daughter-churches."[10]
The preceding centuries had witnessed at Rome a liturgical evolution, brought
about by divers influences, that resulted in a pluralism of usage not only in
succeeding periods but in one and the same period and locale. Liturgists are
still attempting to sort out the bewilderingly complex history of what happened when Roman liturgical books and liturgical practices passed periodically
(perhaps uninterruptedly) from Rome, with its evolving, multiform liturgy,
into transalpine Europe, there to supplant, or modify, or fuse with liturgical
forms and formularies of other traditions. Ancient Roman brevity and
simplicity met with Gallo-Frankish depth of emotion, verbal prolixity, and
genius for a symbolism more extravagant and dramatic than what was familiar
and acceptable to the symbol-conscious but less demonstrative early Roman
community.[11] Charlemagne's earnest but unrealistic attempts in the direction
of a "pure" Roman liturgy for his realm did succeed in establishing the
"Gregorian" liturgy as normative in theory; but in point of fact, when the
dust finally settled, this liturgy really represented a fusion of Roman and
Frankish traditions—and a wonderful, mutually enriching fusion it was.[12]

Meanwhile in Rome herself, there was nothing if not confusion. From the
ninth century onward it was less a question of well-being than of mere survival
as *Sturm und Drang* closed in upon the See of Peter. It was now the turn of
Rome's daughters to come to the aid of the liturgically ailing mother; but the
result of the salutary assistance provided by Cluniac monks in the recently
founded or restored monasteries in and near Rome, and by the representatives
of the Ottonian emperors, was yet another amalgam of Roman, Frankish, and
Germanic elements—and (once again) a wonderful, deeply enriching fusion it
was.[13] Only in a few fiercely conservative Roman basilicas and churches did
elements of the older Roman tradition (or traditions) subsist in a more massive
way. But if we take, for instance, the twelfth- and thirteenth-century remains
of "Old Roman" chant and compare them to the chant popularly called
"Gregorian" or "standard"—the fruit of an eighth / ninth-century Carolingian reworking of the older Roman repertory[14]—we can only marvel at the

[10]PL 178.340BC.

[11]The most classic expression of the distinctive notes of Roman liturgy vis-à-vis its Gallo-
Frankish counterpart is the early (1899) essay by Edmund Bishop, "The Genius of the Roman
Rite," most accessible in his *Liturgica Historica: Papers on the Liturgy and Religious Life of the
Western Church* (Oxford 1918) 1–19.

[12]The fusion of Roman and Frankish traditions necessarily figures large in any general survey
of the extant liturgical sources for Western Europe. Particularly helpful for anyone wishing to study
the mutual exchange between Rome and countries to the north is Cyrille Vogel, *Introduction aux
sources de l'histoire du culte chrétien au moyen âge*, Biblioteca degli Studi medievali 1 (Spoleto
1966), esp. 43–203, "Epoque Romano-Francque et Romano-Germanique: De Grégoire I
(590–604) à Grégoire VII (1072–1085)."

[13]For the interaction between Cluny, Rome, and the Ottonian Empire, see the helpful article
by Cinzio Violante, "Il monachesimo cluniacense di fronte al mondo politico ed ecclesiastico
(secoli X e XI)," *Spiritualità cluniacense: 12–15 ottobre 1958*, Convegni del Centro di studi sulla
spiritualità medievale 2 (Todi 1960) 153–242.

[14]This is the working hypothesis adopted at present by the specialists in the field at the abbey
of Solesmes. For a recent summary of this position, see Eugène Cardine, "Vue d'ensemble sur le

cultural triumph scored by Frankish genius at work on Roman raw material of rather unpromising quality.[15]

Gregory VII was perspicacious enough to recognize and protest against what he considered the transmogrification of the ancient Roman liturgy through contamination from Germanic influences—a situation especially acute, he noted, "from the time that the government of our Church was given over to the Teutons";[16] but the "Roman" liturgy remained, for all that, essentially the "Romano-Franco-Germanic" liturgy.

Meanwhile, most of the particular regional liturgies in the more isolated areas of Western Europe were hastening toward extinction. Our contemporary climate of pluralism inclines us to view the extirpation of the ancient Hispanic liturgies (largely through the apostolate of Cluny in the Iberian peninsula), of the pre-Norman Conquest British usages, and of the Celtic rites as so many instances of Rome's ecclesiastical imperialism at work. But however fierce the pockets of resistance in some areas, Roman liturgical usage was not all that unwelcome in parts of Europe heretofore isolated but now interested in reaping the benefits of membership in the new spiritual and cultural commonwealth of nations. Further, conformity with Roman usage in no way meant absolute uniformity. The Roman *ordo missae* represented a flexible skeletal structure to be fleshed out at local and regional levels. As for the Office, there was a monastic *cursus*, with a characteristic distribution of psalms, as well as another *cursus* for canons and diocesan clergy; but whichever *cursus* was adopted, the content of the Office admitted of enormous diversity even within the same region.[17] Though the structure of the liturgical year was to be everywhere the same, and though there was general insistence on the same basic system of Mass readings, and on the same essential structure for baptism, confirmation, and the other sacraments, there was still room aplenty for distinctive regional and local particularities.

This, then, is how things stood on the eve of the twelfth century.

---

chant grégorien," *Etudes grégoriennes* 16 (1977) 173–92 at 173–74. For an older but still useful summary of other positions, see Stephen J. P. van Dijk, "Recent Developments in the Study of the Old-Roman Rite," *Studia Patristica* 8, = Texte und Untersuchungen zur Geschichte der altchristlichen Literatur 93 (Berlin 1966) 299–319, esp. 300–01.

[15]For an analysis and presentation of the Old-Roman melodies, accessible to the nonspecialist, see Robert J. Snow, "The Old-Roman Chant," in Willi Apel, *Gregorian Chant* (Bloomington Ind. 1958) 484–505.

[16]Gregory VII, *Regula canonica*, ed. Germain Morin, *Etudes, textes, découvertes*, Anecdota Maredsolana, 2e ser. 1 (Maredsous and Paris 1913) 459–60: "Romani autem diverso modo agere ceperunt, maxime a tempore quo teutonicis concessum est regimen nostrae aecclesiae. Nos autem et ordinem romanum et antiquum morem investigantes statuimus fieri nostrae ecclesiae sicut superius praenotavimus, antiquos imitantes patres."

[17]This principle of substantial similarity in the context of a certain pluralism is illustrated wonderfully well by René-Jean Hesbert's chart of manuscript relationships based on variants in the series of Advent Office responsories, in volume 5 of *Corpus Antiphonalium Officii*, Rerum Ecclesiasticarum Documenta, Series Maior: Fontes 7–11 (5 vols. Rome 1963–75). The variations on the same basic schema are virtually countless.

RENAISSANCE SELF-AWARENESS AND
TWELFTH-CENTURY LITURGICAL REFORM

The twelfth century is characterized by a tendency toward individuation of groups, with a concomitant sensitivity in those areas which render each group distinct. As *imperium* and *sacerdotium* each grew in self-awareness through opposition to each other, so did other units of society. The cleric was not to be confused with a layman; the canon regular was not a monk; and, clearly, the monk of Cluny lived in a world different from that of the monk of Cîteaux. Group individuation brought notable changes in the celebration of the liturgy.

TENSIONS BETWEEN CLERGY AND LAITY: CONSEQUENCES FOR THE LITURGY

The Gregorian reform of the clergy emphasized the distinction between cleric and layman, between their ways of life and the differing means of sanctification proper to each state. Humbert of Silva Candida (d. 1061) had expressed the principle nicely: "Just as within the walls of a basilica clerics have their own proper place and function, and laymen theirs, so also outside church ought they to be known and kept separate by their duties."[18] In the twelfth century, the architectural application of Humbert's formula led to the erection of higher and yet higher chancel partitions and rood screens, isolating the clergy in the sanctuary area but also cutting off the laymen from visual contact with the sanctuary and with the rites therein enacted[19] just as effectively as did the partitions in the rear of Cistercian and Carthusian oratories, behind which the lay brethren were present for the liturgy at the times appointed— albeit at a distance, and in a manner proper to their lay condition. "Light differs from darkness," wrote Honorius Augustodunensis (d. about 1156), "no less than the priestly order differs from the laity."[20] Honorius might have added that the priestly order was there precisely to bring light to the benighted lay folk. But here the point is that a distinction in order and function, intended of itself to make for the deeper unity of Church and society at large, actually resulted in a deepening cleavage between cleric and layman. What should have made for complementarity all too often made for mutual opposition.

---

[18]*Adversus simoniacos* 3.9, PL 143.1153C: "Sicut clerici a laicis etiam intra parietes basilicarum locis et officiis sic et extra separari et cognosci debent negotiis."

[19]This phenomenon has been studied by Jean Hubert, "La place faite aux laïcs dans les églises monastiques et dans les cathédrales aux XIe et XIIe siècles," *I laici nella "Societas christiana" dei secoli XI e XII: Atti della terza settimana internazionale di studio, Mendola, 21–27 agosto 1965,* Pubblicazioni dell'Università cattolica del Sacro Cuore, Contributi 3rd ser.: Varia 5, = Miscellanea del Centro di studi medioevali 5 (Milan 1968) 470–87.

[20]*De offendiculo* 38: "Quantum differt lux a tenebris, tantum differt ordo sacerdotum a laicis," MGH LdL 3.51, ed. I. Dieterich. Many similar texts are cited in the particularly useful contribution by Enrico Cattaneo, "La partecipazione dei laici alla liturgia," *I laici* (n. 19 above) 396–423.

The consequences for lay participation in the liturgy were, however, consistent with tendencies already centuries old. In the West, the transition from a Canon of the Mass proclaimed aloud to a "silent" Canon had occurred already in the course (probably) of the seventh century.[21] Though this transition had taken place at least in part as a spontaneous response to the sacred character of the mystery sacramentally reenacted in the Mass, the silent Canon tended to make the heart of the celebration the special preserve of the priest or bishop, and to reduce the liturgical role of the layman to that of attentive spectator. By the year 1000, the characteristic position of the priest at Mass was with his back to the faithful; and more and more, altars were shifted away from the worshipping assembly, toward the back wall of the sanctuary.[22] Forms of the offertory procession subsisted, but became increasingly occasional and vestigial.[23] Communion was infrequent—outside monasteries, a few times yearly at best.[24] Then, too, Latin was becoming less and less of a lingua franca for society at large, so that the language formed yet another obstacle to active participation in an exclusively Latin liturgy.

The devout but disadvantaged layman depended all the more on what John Beleth (d. 1182) called the "layman's book, consisting of two parts, painting and ornament."[25] Whereas the new breed of monk represented by the Carthusian or the Cistercian mistrusted emphasis on sensory perception in things liturgical—their own specialty being the "interiorized" liturgy—the ordinary layman depended precisely on what he could hear, feel, and smell. It was, then, part of the Church's pastoral practice that there be plenty to keep the layman's sense organs busy (thereby permitting some early twentieth-

[21]For a recent presentation of this much-studied phenomenon of a "silent Canon," see Josef Andreas Jungmann, "Heiliges Wort: Die rituelle Behandlung der Konsekrationsworte in den Liturgien," *Miscellanea liturgica in onore di sua Eminenza il Cardinale Giacomo Lercaro* (2 vols. Rome 1966) 1.307–19.

[22]See R. Kevin Seasoltz, *The House of God: Sacred Art and Church Architecture* (New York 1963), esp. the sections "Development of the Church Edifice: The Romanesque Period," 101–07, "The Gothic Period," 107–10, and the further notes on the altar scattered passim throughout the chapter "The Sanctuary—The Place for the Clergy," 146–200. This presentation is especially useful for the bibliographical references in the notes.

[23]The offertory rite calls for further study by liturgists; but consensus seems to be fairly general that, apart from rare exceptions, the processional offering of gifts had died out in most places by around 1200. For a useful summary (without references) see Theodor Klauser, *A Brief History of the Liturgy* (Collegeville Minn. 1953) 24–25; detailed survey in Josef Andreas Jungmann, *The Mass of the Roman Rite: Its Origins and Development*, trans. Francis A. Brunner (2 vols. New York 1951–55) 2.1–25.

[24]On the diminishing frequency of Communion of the faithful, see Jungmann (n. 23 above) 359–67.

[25]John Beleth, *Summa de ecclesiasticis officiis* c. 85e, ed. Herbert Douteil, CCL cm 41A (1976) 35–38: "nunc pauca dicenda sunt de laicorum scriptura. Scriptura autem laicorum in duobus consistit: In picturis et ornamentis. 'Nam,' ut ait Gregorius, 'quod est clerico littera, hoc est laico pictura.'" The quotation from Gregory's letter to Serenus, bishop of Marseille (*Registrum* 9.9), was well known, being incorporated into Gratian's *Decretum*, *De consecratione* D.3 c.27: "Nam quod legentibus scriptura, hoc idiotis prestat pictura cernentibus, quia in ipsa ignorantes uident quod sequi debeant, in ipsa legunt qui litteras nesciunt. Unde et precipue gentibus pro lectione picture est." *Corpus iuris canonici*, ed. Emil A. Friedberg (2 vols. Leipzig 1879–81) 1.1360.

century historians to discourse on the medieval liturgy almost wholly in terms of sensory perception).[26] Thus, Bernard of Clairvaux, taking amiss the liturgical humanism of Cluny (of which more later), castigates his Cluniac confrere for confusing a piety proper to the lay estate with a piety proper to monks: "[Bishops] . . . rouse devotion in carnal people by means of material ornamentation, for they cannot do it through things spiritual; but we [monks] have now gone forth from such a people."[27] As for the layman, he was caught between two conflicting tendencies: at the very time the rubrics, largely for his sake, were multiplying ritual gestures (bows, signs of the cross, osculations), and at the very time that liturgical appointments and decorations were more and more coming into their own (vestments, images, stained glass),[28] more and more of the liturgy was taking place behind the sanctuary partition.

Those scholars who see the proliferation of lay devotions and superstitions as a substitute for a more direct, active participation in the liturgy are surely correct.[29] But perhaps this theory of substitution is a bit simplistic, since popular devotions can also be interpreted in some instances as the *fruit* and further expression of an objective contact with the Mystery of Christ rendered present and accessible through the liturgical celebration. Once again, the twelfth-century distinction between cleric and layman was not meant (in theory) to deny the layman participation in the liturgy, but to ensure his participation in the manner best suited to his lay estate.[30] It would seem, too, that, in general, the layman had no serious complaints—though here the emphasis should be on *in general*. For in particular, the cleavage between layman and cleric, which crystallized so obviously in the celebration of the liturgy, surely contributed mightily to the rise of antiestablishment sects and movements such as those represented by the large variety of neo-Manichees—groups which tended to be not only antihierarchical and anticlerical, but antisacramentarian and antiliturgical as well.[31]

[26]Perhaps the best known representative of this approach is Johan Huizinga, in his popular *Waning of the Middle Ages*, trans. F. Hopman (London 1924).

[27]Bernard of Clairvaux, *Apologia ad Guillelmum abbatem* 12.28: "Scimus namque quod illi [episcopi] . . . carnalis populi devotionem, quia spiritualibus non possunt, corporalibus excitant ornamentis. Nos vero qui iam de populo exivimus. . . ." *Sancti Bernardi opera*, ed. Leclercq 3.104–05.

[28]Typical in this respect is the great rebuilder of the abbey church of St Denis, abbot Suger. His *Libellus . . . de consecratione ecclesiae Sancti Dionysii* can be said to sum up the liturgical esthetic of his century. For an edition of the Latin text with English translation and commentary, see Erwin Panofsky, *Abbot Suger on the Abbey Church of St.-Denis and Its Art Treasures*, 2nd ed. by Gerda Panofsky-Soergel (Princeton 1979) 82–121, 224–50.

[29]The multiplication of devotions as a substitute for liturgical devotion of a more traditional stamp is the theme of such classic studies as Edouard Dumoutet, *Le désir de voir l'Hostie et les origines de la dévotion au Saint-Sacrement* (Paris 1926); or the more comprehensive study by Peter Browe, *Die Verehrung der Eucharistie im Mittelalter* (Munich 1933; repr. Rome 1967).

[30]For a nuanced treatment of the interplay between private devotion, devotions, and the liturgy, see Jean Leclercq, "Dévotion privée, piété populaire et liturgie au moyen âge," *Etudes de Pastorale liturgique* (Vanves, 26–28 janvier 1944), Lex orandi 1 (Paris 1944) 149–83.

[31]The antiliturgical bias of some of these groups has perhaps been overstressed for lack of sufficient documentation about actual practice. A quite different picture is suggested, for instance, by

INDIVIDUALISM AND LITURGICAL BOOKS

The twelfth century witnessed codification projects on a massive scale. The same tendencies which resulted in the great theological summas and collections of canons were at work bringing forth monastic customaries and orderly, systematically revised liturgical codifications.[32] This was surely a function of that passion for order and systematization characteristic of the later Renaissance. But, with respect to the codification of liturgical books, more was at work than simply a spirit of good order.

Until the twelfth century, the normative form for the celebration of the Eucharist remained that of the assembled community: the celebrant with his ministers, the schola and clergy in stalls between altar and congregation, the assembly in the body of the church. Texts and music needed for the celebration were in separate books used by individuals whose separate ministries combined to create this complex communal act: sacramentary, epistolary, evangeliary, gradual, cantatorium. Progressively, however, the priest takes over the role of the other "actors" in the liturgical drama. The personal prebend with separate, noncommunal residence becomes widespread; the "private" Mass of earlier centuries becomes generalized; and the *missale plenum*, with all texts conveniently under one cover, now replaces the sacramentary as the characteristic book of the priest offering the Holy Sacrifice. Even in communal celebrations, the priest repeats in synchronous private recitation the Mass texts chanted by choir, schola, lectors, and deacons.[33]

A parallel trend obtains in the case of the Office books. The community celebration of the Hours called for psalter, Bible, collectarium, antiphonary, homiliary, legendarium, and hymnal. For individuals forced to pray the Office in a noncommunal context, the essential elements of the Office are excerpted and abbreviated so as to fit within one or two handy tomes. Melodies disappear, of course; and readings are represented only by a token *incipit*. But as time goes on, what was originally the exception—the individual recitation of the Office—becomes generalized. This tendency toward abbreviation and simplification now has a serious effect on the whole spirit of the celebration. So long as the elements constituting the Office were found in separate books, an "open-ended" approach to the celebration was possible: repertories of texts

---

the Cathar ritual recently edited and translated by Christine Thouzellier, *Rituel cathare*, Sources chrétiennes 236 (Paris 1977).

[32]These codifications often were connected with the rise of new Orders or reform groups (Carthusians, Premonstratensians, Cistercians, etc.); but quite independently of this, the twelfth century seems to have been when the liturgy found the characteristic shape it was to retain for centuries to come. It is instructive to read through the list of editions of monastic customaries catalogued in *Corpus consuetudinum monasticarum* 1, general editor Kassius Hallinger (Siegburg 1963) Introduction lix–lxxiv, and to note how many of these compilations either date from the twelfth century or else depend essentially on twelfth-century manuscripts.

[33]See François Vandenbroucke, "Aux origines du malaise liturgique," *Questions liturgiques et paroissiales* 40 (1959) 252–70.

and chants offered multiple choices of material, and it was always possible to add supplements of new texts and melodies. But the one-volume breviary means the reduction of the Office to its barest minimum, with the consequent elimination of variety and possibility of adaptation. Individualism here works to the disadvantage of creativity; and, once again, the individual cleric is farther and farther distanced from the worshipping assembly which should be his proper spiritual habitat.[34]

LITURGICAL REFORM IN RELIGIOUS GROUPS OLD AND NEW

The many new religious communities which arose in the period under study did so in a historical context that made them keenly aware of their own proper identity. A community which comes into existence in response to a new need, for example, or out of dissatisfaction with an established form of monastic or canonical life, perforce becomes aware of its own unique individuality. Reforming monks and canons generally have to be aware of their roots, and must be able to articulate and defend their particular form of life and their *raison d'être*. This in turn engenders among the older, more established communities a similar self-awareness—an awareness which can turn into defensiveness. Indeed, the twelfth century was a time of considerable defensiveness: reform monks and canons vis-à-vis nonreform monks and canons, canons vis-à-vis monks, Black Monks vis-à-vis White Monks. This heightened self-awareness often had important consequences for the liturgical life of the groups in question.

THE CANONS REGULAR

From a renaissance perspective, the liturgy of the canons regular offers only minor interest. Though it would be wrong to reduce to one type the great variety evident in twelfth-century forms of canonical life, it probably would not be far amiss to suggest that Norbert of Xanten (d. 1134) crystallized to a great extent the reforming spirit among the transalpine canons regular.[35] True, the Premonstratensian reform as a whole admits of a "renaissance interpretation" in the sense that it had a markedly historical point of reference in the past: a return to the classical sources of canonical life (chiefly the *Regula Augustini*) interpreted rather literally, and with the explicit intention of reviv-

---

[34]The connection between abbreviations of books and isolation of the cleric has been studied by Pierre Salmon most specifically in his two chapters, "L'office aux XIe et XIIe siècles" and "L'office à Rome aux XIe et XIIe siècles," in *L'Office divin au Moyen Age: Histoire de la formation du bréviaire du IXe au XVIe siècle,* Lex orandi 43 (Paris 1967) 86–123, 124–51.

[35]A useful study of the various forms of clerical life in common and the celebration of the liturgy has been made by Enrico Cattaneo, "La vita comune dei chierici e la liturgia," in *La vita comune del clero nei secoli XI e XII: Atti della [prima] settimana di studio, Mendola, settembre 1959,* Pubblicazioni dell'Università cattolica del Sacro Cuore 3rd ser.: Scienze storiche 2–3, = Miscellanea del Centro di studi medioevali 3 (2 vols. Milan 1962) 1.241–72.

ing the apostolic life of the Golden Age of the Church by means of a life in common, evangelical poverty, and manual labor as the sole means of subsistence. As for the liturgy, one cannot begin a reform from nothing; and it would seem that Norbert borrowed heavily from the canons regular of Springiersbach (ancient diocese of Trier). This primitive *ordo monasterii* soon gave way to the *usus receptus* more familiar to most communities of canons. Massive borrowings were made from the Cistercian usages and constitutional code. In spite of the early official codification of the Order's liturgical books and usages, however, the official ideal of liturgical uniformity admitted of no really systematic, Order-wide implementation. In general, the impression is that the liturgy of Prémontré, though of great interest to the historian of liturgy, was shaped by pragmatic and fortuitous considerations rather than a carefully thought out program of revision based on clearly articulated principles.[36]

THE CARTHUSIANS

The Carthusian experience was characterized by the utter consistency with which every aspect of the life—liturgy included—was transformed by the ideals of the community inaugurated by the former *scholasticus* of Reims, Bruno, in the mountainous desert of Chartreuse in 1084. *Quies*, silence, solitude. The prologue to the ancient Carthusian antiphonary gives off the characteristic resonance of their liturgy in its opening words: *Institutionis heremiticae GRAVITAS. . . .*[37] *Gravitas*, with all its implications of seriousness, austerity, simplicity, expresses both life style in general and liturgy in particular. Actually, the choice of raw material was eclectic in the extreme: usages inspired by Cluny, by Benedict of Aniane's *Codex regularum* and *Concordia regularum*, by an *ordinarium* of the canons of St Ruf (two of Bruno's companions had belonged to this congregation). The chant version seems to be that of the diocese, Grenoble and its environs.[38] Recent research suggests that the community followed the canons' *cursus* in its earliest years, only to adopt the monastic form of Office early in the new century.[39] The liturgical corpus

[36]A general spirit of eclecticism and a tendency to adapt to local practice seem to be characteristic of early Norbertine practice—which poses quite a problem for the liturgist intent upon discovering *the* normative Premonstratensian practice. Before a truly satisfactory synthesis of the White Canons' early liturgy can be made, it will be necessary to identify and date key documents as yet missing, and to study the sources drawn upon. In the meantime, it can be assumed that new acquisitions will not affect in a substantial way the main lines of the overview provided by Placide Lefèvre, *La Liturgie de Prémontré: Histoire, formulaire, chant et cérémonial*, Bibliotheca Analectorum Praemonstratensium 1 (Louvain 1957).

[37]Text cited *in extenso* in Charles Le Couteulx, *Annales Ordinis Cartusiensis, ab anno 1084 ad annum 1429* (8 vols. Montreuil 1887–91) 1.308.

[38]And not of Lyon, as has been the prevalent assumption until recent times. The question is touched upon, but without much detailed treatment, in the studies cited below in the Bibliographical Note, in the references to Carthusian practices.

[39]Hansjakob Becker, "War das Stundengebet der Kartäuser von Anfang an monastisch?" *Archiv für Liturgiewissenschaft* 13 (1971) 196–209.

which emerged bore the imprint of a draconian simplification both with respect to ceremonially inclined cenobites (simplified calendar, minimum of Mass and Office formularies, elimination of nonbiblical chants, purging of all "popular" elements—such as the use of three Passion deacons in Holy Week, the ringing of bells at the *Gloria in excelsis* in the Paschal Vigil, and so on—poverty of the extremest sort in liturgical appurtenances, rejection of musical instruments, no processions, well-nigh nothing by way of accretions to Mass and Office), and with respect to hermits of the Camaldolese type (no additional psalters over and above that of the Office, and no penitential exercises and votive prayers of the sort introduced at Camaldoli to compensate for the simplifications effected elsewhere in their life and liturgy).

Characteristic of the Carthusian liturgical reform is the same sort of biblicism characteristic of later Renaissance initiatives such as the immensely popular but short-lived Quiñonez Breviary (1535);[40] for only biblical texts were allowed to remain in the much-pruned traditional repertory of Mass and Office chants. There is nothing novel about such a biblicist approach; and, indeed, the antiphonary prologue, which formulates this stance, is simply rephrasing material borrowed from a characteristic figure of the earlier Carolingian renaissance, the deplorable Agobard of Lyon, whose *Liber de correctione Antiphonarii*, with all its antipoetic literalism, has to be read to be believed.[41] Another remarkable instance of the Carthusian return to sources is to be found in their unique patristic Night Office lectionary, compiled probably under prior Guigo (1109–36), and pieced together from carefully chosen texts excerpted from a mere handful of the most "authentic" Fathers—Ambrose, Augustine, Jerome, Leo, Chrysostom, with sixth-century Gregory the Great, coming as late as he does, introducing a note of modernity.[42] As regards monastic ritual, we find a similar sobriety: gestures, signs, and ritual actions are reduced to the minimum capable of fulfilling the function assigned them.

THE LITURGICAL HUMANISM OF CLUNY

Liturgical reform at Cluny consisted chiefly in keeping things essentially the same when poverty and simplicity *in re liturgica* were all the rage in the new monastic bodies proliferating right and left. It is true, of course, that a large number of the statutes framed by Peter the Venerable between 1122 and 1146/47 deal with liturgical particulars;[43] true, also, that many of these par-

---

[40]See Josef Andreas Jungmann, "Why Was the Reform Breviary of Cardinal Quiñonez a Failure?" *Pastoral Liturgy*, trans. Ronald Walls (London 1962) 200–14.

[41]PL 104.329–40, at 329–31.

[42]Robert Etaix, "L'homiliaire cartusien," *Sacris erudiri* 13 (1962) 67–112.

[43]Statutes 1–9, 31–32, 50–52, 54, 57–62, 65, 67–68, 71–76, A1, according to the numbers assigned in the edition by Giles Constable, "Statuta Petri Venerabilis abbatis cluniacensis IX (1146/7)," *Consuetudines benedictinae variae (saec. XI-saec. XIV)*, Corpus consuetudinum monasticarum 6 (Siegburg 1975) 37–106.

ticulars have their exact parallel in the Cistercian program of liturgical reform, and suggest something of the same mentality.[44] But if we situate these liturgical variations within the context of Cluny's liturgy as a whole, they do not loom large. Those statutes dealing with precise texts aim, in general, at eliminating apparent incongruities.[45] A dyed-in-the-wool Cistercian would have had no peace until the last textual incongruity had been eliminated or rendered inoffensive. As for Peter, he obviously prefers that there be no incongruities; but he also keeps his sense of proportion. Perhaps the statute most characteristic of his mentality in matters of liturgical reform is Statute 61, in which Peter arranges for Prime to be said in the chapel of the infirm at the proper time of day (the hymn for Prime begins, after all, "Now that the morning star has fully *risen*"). Splendid. But what about all the other dawn-allusions in those Lauds hymns sung, as often as not, long before dawn? "Well," says Peter, "I do indeed want everything of that sort to be corrected, both here at Cluny and elsewhere—if it can be done *peacefully.*"[46]

Meanwhile, Cluny enjoyed an extraordinary monastic culture.[47] The monastery was located at the theological point where earth opens directly onto heaven; and already the splendor, the *nitor*, of the heavenly Jerusalem was bathing Cluny in a spiritual luminosity translated even physically by the light-flooded spaciousness of the architecture.[48] It was a community of praise; and though the prolixity of their liturgy was notorious—even the brethren found it a *massa plumbea* at times—this prolixity was in imitation of the eternal uninterruptedness of the heavenly liturgy.[49]

[44]See R. Cortese Esposito, "Analogie e contrasti fra Cîteaux e Cluny," *Cîteaux* 19 (1968) 5–39.

[45]Typical are Statutes 5 (rank of Transfiguration raised in keeping with the intrinsic importance of the mystery); 9 (traditional gospel of Jesus' entry into Jerusalem replaced by another on the first Sunday of Advent, because of its "inappropriate" character); 58 (the Christmas *prosa* "Nostra tuba" is replaced by one better suited to Christmas); 59 (a new series of antiphons for Thursdays in Lent, in order to avoid the incongruity of reusing antiphons found elsewhere in the Office); 61 (Prime to be chanted at the corresponding time of day); 62 (wooden cross to be used in rites for the anointing of the sick, as more in keeping with those liturgical texts which speak not of a metal cross but of the *wood* of the cross); 68 (proper hymns for St Stephen, St John, the Holy Innocents, St Lawrence, and St Vincent, in keeping with the importance of their feasts, which heretofore had had hymns from the Common assigned them); 71 (emendation of several chant texts about the baptism of the Lord, to ensure their conformity with the biblical texts); and 74 (particularly solemn *Kyrie* chant for the five chief solemnities).

[46]"Quod si quis obiciat, cur non et in ceteris in quibus consimilis nota mendacii invenitur, istud correctum non est . . . respondeo, velle me quidem valde ut talia cuncta, si cum pace fieri posset, apud nostros et ubique corrigerentur." "Statuta" (n. 43 above) 93.

[47]The bibliography on Cluny and its culture is endless; but perhaps the best summary presentation is to be found in the relatively short article by Jean Leclercq, "Spiritualité et culture à Cluny," *Spiritualità cluniacense* (n. 13 above) 101–51.

[48]Ibid. 115.

[49]Philibert Schmitz, in his article "La liturgie de Cluny," in *Spiritualità cluniacense* (n. 13 above) 83–99, provides a useful description of the prolix liturgy at Cluny, but one which must be read with reservations. His point of reference is the liturgical season when the Office was at its most prolix; and he ignores the probability that not all the Offices over and above the canonical Office were obligatory for all the monks.

The feast most characteristic of Cluny was the recently introduced feast of the Transfiguration; its theme was not just the light of Divinity transfiguring the humanity of Christ, but the glory of the God-Man transfiguring in turn the created universe as well.[50] Nothing created, nothing human was foreign to this vision. Classical authors were not only well represented in the *armarium* of manuscripts, but were put to excellent use; and the many arts practiced at Cluny bear witness to influences received from Mediterranean regions and from the Christian East.[51] Specialists in the arts are impressed with the Cluniac craftsman's perfect assimilation of the most recent advances in anatomy and perspective, and with his mastery of the sciences ancillary to the arts.[52] Even the buildings that made up twelfth-century Cluny represented a symphony of number and proportion expressed in terms of space and mass; and anyone interested in the theme of mathematics as the basis of the arts would find at Cluny much to rejoice his heart.[53]

But if the more characteristic aspect of Cluny's culture is that of anticipated eschatology, it has also a strong historical point of reference, chiefly in a Romeward direction. It was a question not only of monastic exemption and direct dependence on the See of Peter, or of Cluny's important monasteries in and around Rome itself, but of a total vision embracing heaven and earth, with emphasis on the continuity between the Church in glory and the Church committed to the Apostle Peter.[54] Cluny's attachment to Peter's Rome was expressed even in the physical dimensions of Cluny III, which were those of the Roman basilica of St Peter.[55]

The holistic nature of Cluny's culture cannot be sufficiently stressed. If certain scholars have made capital of a few texts which portray Cluny as an enemy of studies,[56] it is due to their failure to realize that Cluny's bias was not against studies as such, but against a lopsided, exaggerated intellectualism irreconcilable with the more balanced catholic humanism implicit in Cluny's vision of a transfigured cosmos. Take away this vision, and the transparent luminosity of Cluny turns opaque, the institutional structure becomes an insupportable weight, and the marvelously choreographed liturgy degenerates into ritualism. The newer religious communities of the twelfth century, with

---

[50]The Transfiguration Office by Peter the Venerable has been edited, with helpful notes, by Jean Leclercq, *Pierre le Vénérable* (Paris 1946) 379–90.

[51]Leclercq, "Spiritualité" (n. 47 above) 111–12.

[52]Ibid. 112.

[53]Ibid. 112–15.

[54]On the exigency of beauty at Cluny, and the eschatological dimensions of Cluny's esthetic, see particularly Leclercq, "Spiritualité" (n. 47 above) 147–51.

[55]According to an observation by J. Hubert, quoted ibid. 114.

[56]Cluny's *Kulturfeindlichkeit* is a theme central to Kassius Hallinger's *Gorze-Kluny: Studien zu den monastischen Lebensformen und Gegensätzen im Hochmittelalter*, Studia Anselmiana 22–23 and 24–25 (2 vols. Rome 1950–51). It is a hypothesis which wins the votes of few historians. The article by Jean Leclercq, "Cluny fut-il ennemi de la culture?" *Revue Mabillon* 47 (1957) 172–82, touched on arguments developed more amply later on in the same author's "Spiritualité" (n. 47 above) in defense of Cluny as a center of spirituality and culture.

their mystique of poverty and simplicity, had difficulty understanding Cluny. They should not be blamed overmuch; for as the vision gradually waned at Cluny itself in the later Middle Ages, even Cluny no longer understood Cluny.

THE CISTERCIANS

For more than a decade the reform program inaugurated in 1098 at the New Monastery, some twenty kilometers south of Dijon, remained confined to a single monastery; but from 1113 onward, the new observance spread like wildfire. The Cistercian program seems to have had a special appeal in the university milieu, where significant numbers of students and teachers alike, disappointed in their experience of the twelfth-century intellectual breakthrough, turned disillusioned toward what we would nowadays speak of as "experience-oriented" monastic communities. The Cistercian reform program had a strong historical frame of reference, for it was based in large measure on a return to early sources: integral observance of the Rule of St Benedict, as well as on compliance with the decrees and canons concerning monastic life included in the compilations of Burchard of Worms and Ivo of Chartres.[57] But the text which best expresses the mentality characteristic of the fledgling Order is not by a Cistercian, but by a Black Monk admirer of the third abbot of Cîteaux, Stephen Harding. Writing shortly before 1124, William of Malmesbury slips into book four of his *De gestis regum anglorum* a finely drawn eyewitness account of early Cîteaux. In an obviously rhetorical literary fiction, William shows us Stephen, sometime before the founding of the New Monastery, already articulating at Molesme the rationale of the future observance. The two key words are *ratio* and *auctoritas*.

Reason it is, whereby the supreme Author of things has made all things; and reason it is, whereby he governs all things. By reason, too, the fabric of the pole revolves; and by reason are turned the stars that are said to wander; by reason the elements are moved. Through reason, too, and balanced ordering ought our own nature to subsist. But because nature, in its own slothfulness, often falls away from reason, in times past many laws were laid down; but in our own days there has come forth from God, through blessed Benedict, a RULE: a Rule to call wayward nature [*fluxum naturae*] back to reason.[58]

Is this really the twelfth century? Or is it the quattrocento? No reference to monastic life as the following of Christ; not a word about the monastery as

---

[57]Kolumban Spahr, in "Die Anfänge von Citeaux," *Bernhard von Clairvaux: Mönch und Mystiker*, Internationaler Bernhardkongress, Mainz 1953, ed. Joseph Lortz (Wiesbaden 1955) 215–24, esp. 221, is among the few historians who call attention to the importance of the collections of canons for the shaping of the Cistercian program of reform.

[58]*De gestis regum Anglorum libri quinque* 4.334, ed. William Stubbs, RS 90 (2 vols. London 1887–89) 2.381: "Ratione . . . supremus rerum Auctor omnia fecit, ratione omnia regit; ratione rotatur poli fabrica, ratione ipsa etiam quae dicuntur errantia torquentur sidera, ratione moventur elementa; ratione et aequilibritate debet nostra subsistere natura. Sed quia per desidiam saepe a ratione decidit, leges quondam multae latae; novissimi per beatum Benedictum regula divinitus processit quae fluxum naturae ad rationem revocaret."

the perpetuation of the first Christian community of believers in Jerusalem. Nor do Stephen's (or William's) further remarks about the relationship between faith and reason derogate at all the rights of reason:

In which [Rule], although there are things whose reason I cannot avail to penetrate, one should, I reckon, acquiesce in its authority. Because reason and the authority of the divine writings, though they may *seem* to be at odds, are one and the same: for since God neither created nor recreated anything except through reason, how could I ever be persuaded that the holy Fathers, docile followers of God that they were, would pass decrees wherein no part is had by reason, as though we ought to put our faith in authority alone?[59]

Who says "authority," says "authentic source." After Scripture, then, the Rule was the quasi-absolute point of reference. Since Benedict frequently refers to hymns by the technical term *ambrosiana*, this was taken to mean that only hymns composed by Ambrose himself should be admitted into the Cistercian hymn repertory. The traditional popular hymns were replaced by unfamiliar hymns taken from the Milanese tradition.[60] The sacramentary seems to have been based on the sacramentary of the papal chapel—a reasonably authoritative source, it was surely thought.[61] For Mass and Office chants, the White Monks went to Metz, long famous as the chief center for diffusing the authentic Roman chant in the days of Charles the Great. This so-called "authentic" Gregorian chant put the Cistercian's faith in authority to its cruelest test: for the ancient Metz tradition, by the time of the Cistercian reform, had long since degenerated into something of a Teutonic chant dialect, with the mischief compounded by the clumsiness of the scribes, who seem to have had difficulty in putting to proper use the newfangled method of notation on lines with a staff.[62] As for the Night Office readings, these too were brought into conformity with the prescriptions of the Rule: Scripture and commentaries by the well-known and orthodox Catholic Fathers.[63] Hagiographical readings were pruned away, and of the remaining readings, those by

[59]Ibid.: "In qua etsi habentur quaedam quorum rationem penetrare non sufficio, auctoritati tamen acquiescendum censeo. Ratio enim et auctoritas divinorum scriptorum quamvis dissonare videantur, unum idemque sunt: namque cum Deus nihil sine ratione creaverit, et recreaverit; qui fieri potest ut credam sanctos patres, sequaces scilicet Dei, quicquam praeter rationem edicere, quasi soli auctoritati fidem debeamus adhibere?" For a discussion of the entire passage, see note 130 of Giles Constable's essay in this volume.

[60]See Chrysogonus Waddell, "The Origin and Early Evolution of the Cistercian Antiphonary: Reflections on Two Cistercian Chant Reforms," *The Cistercian Spirit: A Symposium in Memory of Thomas Merton*, Cistercian Studies 3, ed. M. Basil Pennington (Spencer Mass. 1970), 204–06, where Benedict's references to hymns are tabulated and the encyclical letter affixed to the primitive Cistercian hymnary is transcribed. For a convenient inventory of the contents of the early hymnal, requiring only occasional corrections in the light of recent research, see M. Bernard Kaul, "Le psautier cistercien. Appendice: Tableau analytique de l'hymnaire cistercien," *Collectanea O.C.R. [Ordinis Cisterciensium Reformatorum]* 13 (1951) 257–72 at 264–66.

[61]An edition is currently in preparation, with detailed notes touching on the Cistercian text's points of contact with earlier forms of the "Gregorian" sacramentary.

[62]Waddell (n. 60 above) 190–223, esp. 209–18.

[63]Holy Rule 9.8: "Codices autem legantur in vigiliis tam veteris testamenti quam novi divinae auctoritatis; sed et expositiones earum, quae a nominatissimis doctoribus orthodoxis catholicis

less "authentic" ecclesiastical writers were abandoned.[64] This liturgical reform was characterized, however, not only by a passion for the authentic and by a return to sources, but also by a deeply experienced need for poverty and simplicity and functionality *in re liturgica*.

The truth of the matter is, nevertheless, that the average monk in the choirstall found this "authentic" liturgy well-nigh insupportable, chiefly because of the (for him) bizarre hymnal and Mass and Office chants. Tension was such that, sometime before 1147, Bernard of Clairvaux was designated by the abbots of the General Chapter to supervise a massive revision of the Order's liturgical books.[65] The normative authority of the Holy Rule evidently had to be respected; nor could there be any derogation of the principle of authenticity. But now *ratio* was to shape the Cistercian liturgy. Among those who had most suffered from the Order's official chant had been ecclesiastics well versed in the music theory taught as part of the quadrivium, and equally well versed in the writings of those theoreticians who had measured the Church's traditional music against the exigencies of their own inadequately formulated principles of musical composition, and had found the ancient repertory ripe for drastic rewriting.[66] This was perfectly in line with the Cistercian penchant for analyzing a thing in order to discover its real nature, and then setting about reshaping the existential phenomenon in the light of the essential definition—which was admirable, so long as the essential definition was reasonably accurate. In brief, Cistercian musicologists rewrote the entire repertory of Mass and Office chants in the light of their own rationally construed music theory. In the same operation, liturgical texts were revised with a view to removing apparent inconsistencies and even absurdities.[67]

The editors were unashamedly self-congratulatory about the finished product. The melodies were admittedly different from those of any other tradition; but what made the Cistercian version so different was precisely what was lacking to others: reason! *Nostrum ab aliis ratio fecit diversum.*[68] We are here

---

patribus factae sunt." Edition of Cistercian text by Eugene Manning, *Sancti Benedicti Regula Monasteriorum* (Westmalle 1962) 39.

[64]Detailed demonstration in Chrysogonus Waddell, "The Cistercian Night Office Lectionary in the Twelfth Century," to appear in the Cistercian Studies Series.

[65]Details in Bernard of Clairvaux, "Prologus in Antiphonarium," ed. Leclercq 3.515–16, with introductory notes 511–13. Translation and commentary by Chrysogonus Waddell, "Prologue to the Cistercian Antiphonary," *The Works of Bernard of Clairvaux: Treatises* 1, Cistercian Fathers Series 1 (Spencer Mass. 1970) 151–62.

[66]For the theoretical background of the Cistercian chant reform, the best survey remains that by Solutor Rodolphe Marosszéki, *Les origines du chant cistercien*, Analecta Sacri Ordinis Cisterciensis 8 (Rome 1952), esp. the principles of chant theory operative in the reform, discussed in detail in chapters 6–9 (49–79); and chapter 10 (81–90), on the sources of this chant theory in the writings of the theorists.

[67]Principles regarding the revision of the texts are formulated briefly (and incompletely) in the *justification* prefixed to the reformed antiphonary, and entitled, in the poor Mabillon edition, PL 182.1121C–32C, *Tractatus de Cantu seu Correctione Antiphonarii*. The paragraphs dealing more directly with the correction of the texts are in cols. 1122C–32B.

[68]PL 182.1132A.

face to face with a genuine Renaissance optic, and one automatically thinks ahead to the horrors of the Medicean edition of the Church's chant, when Renaissance musicians systematically revised the ancient melodies to make them conform to their own misconceptions about Latin prosody and the relationship between word and melody.[69]

These Cistercian reformers were explicit about their reasons for revising the earlier chant repertory, and they spelled out their main principles in detail in the preface affixed to the new antiphonary promulgated around 1147.[70] They were not at all explicit, however, about another major aspect of their reform which moved in a quite different direction. For in spite of the many changes made in the name of *ratio*, the vast majority of the revisions actually brought the peculiar Metz melodies (and often the texts, too) into closer conformity with the "standard" version current (with minor variants) throughout most of Western Europe.[71] What is more, a significant number of new texts and melodies were introduced; and these inevitably strike an attractive, rather popular note—the *Salve regina*, numerous Marian antiphons, a proper formulary for evangelists. The hymnal, too, was revised as to melody and was given a massive complement of Terce and Compline hymns (Benedict here does not use the term *ambrosianum*) drawn from the familiar, much-loved traditional repertoire. The White Monks could now sing *Vexilla regis, Conditor alme*, and *Ave maris stella*.[72] And if we look carefully, we can find that the revised hymnal contains a number of melodies apparently composed by the reformers themselves—wonderful melodies with a certain lyric exuberance, and yet well-proportioned and harmoniously structured, and with some of the qualities which characterize Bernard's splendid Latin style.[73]

In a word, the Cistercian liturgical reform, in its later stage, took into account not only *auctoritas* and *ratio*, but also the esthetic sensitivity of the twelfth-century monk—without, however, foreswearing the exigencies of monastic *gravitas*, simplicity, and evangelical poverty. This is, surely, humanism of a high order.

The twelfth-century liturgical scene is as complex as the century itself; and no one person or group of persons should be expected to mirror all the characteristic or significant features of the period.

[69]For the principles governing the "Medicean" revision of the Church's chant books, see the chapter "La 'révision' de l'Antiphonaire et du Graduel," in André Pons, *Droit ecclésiastique et Musique sacrée*, vol. 3: *Décadence et réforme du Chant liturgique* (St Maurice Switzerland 1960) 139–49.

[70]PL 182.1121–32. The treatise is sometimes referred to under its incipit, "Cantum quem Cisterciensis ordinis."

[71]See Waddell (n. 60 above) 218–22.

[72]See the entire list of hymns introduced under Bernard, and inventoried as "Hymni ex fundo Gallico additi" in Kaul (n. 60 above) 266–68.

[73]A list of the eight hymn-melodies of Cistercian composition is given in Waddell (n. 60 above) 220 n. 70.

Given the fact that the Christian liturgy is directly rooted in the Christian Mystery, and that the perspective is not "man as man," but "man as called to perfect communion with God," we should not expect to find much of a renaissance perspective informing the liturgy. Still, the Renaissance gazing backward to the Golden Age of Antiquity has a bit of a parallel in the tendency to look backward to the Fathers and to early Christian Rome as the norm for Christian worship. Also evident is an enormous concern for what is proper to a given segment of society or to a particular religious body, so that the course of liturgical reform is determined in part by a spirit of liberty and respect for human individuality—a stance not without ambiguity, since it can also help foster extremes of individualism and unrealistic subjectivism. Much of the later Renaissance passion for order and systematization can be found, too, in the twelfth century. And in at least some instances, as at Cîteaux, *ratio* was a determining factor in shaping a particular liturgical reform.

Bibliographical Note

No one seems to have studied the twelfth-century liturgical development explicitly from a Renaissance perspective, though Anton L. Mayer came close to doing so in his article, "Die Liturgie und der Geist der Gotik," in *Jahrbuch für Liturgiewissenschaft* 6 (1926) 68–97. For Mayer, however, "Renaissance" means chiefly a long list of -*isms* headed by "subjectivism," "individualism," "emotionalism." Moreover, his "Gothic" period is more the thirteenth than the twelfth century.

A survey of twelfth-century *liturgica* has to be situated with reference to the preceding centuries; and for the student less familiar with developments in the West, Theodor Klauser's minuscule *A Brief History of the Liturgy* (Collegeville Minn. 1953) is valuable as an outline around which to gather information drawn from lengthier surveys and more detailed studies. Similarly useful are the overviews in standard manuals such as *The Church at Prayer*, vol. 1: *Introduction to the Liturgy*, ed. Aimé-Georges Martimort, trans. Robert Fisher et al. (Shannon 1968) 32–41; or chapter 7, "Liturgy and History: The Development of Western Liturgy," in Irenée H. Dalmais, *Introduction to the Liturgy*, trans. Roger Capel (Baltimore 1961) 148–67.

For the Mass in the twelfth century, the chapter "The Gothic Period" in Josef Andreas Jungmann's classic, *The Mass of the Roman Rite: Its Origins and Development* (2 vols. New York 1951–55) 1.103–27, is invaluable not only by reason of the author's synthesis, but also for his many bibliographical references. (The translation, by Francis A. Brunner, is based on the corrected German edition [1949] of *Missarum Sollemnia: Eine genetische Erklärung der römischen Messe* [2 vols. Vienna 1948]; the fifth, and most recent, revised German edition dates from 1962.)

Though the twelfth century is treated only in passing, Pierre Salmon's *The Breviary through the Centuries*, trans. Sister David Mary (Collegeville Minn. 1962) provides useful background material; much more helpful is the same author's *L'Office divin au Moyen Age: Histoire de la formation du bréviaire du IXe au XVIe siècle*, Lex orandi 43 (Paris 1967), a systematic survey that includes two particularly useful chapters, "L'office aux XIe et XIIe siècles," 86–123, and "L'office à Rome aux XIe et XIIe siècles," 124–51.

Especially valuable, but to be recommended nonetheless only with serious reservations, are the several compilations by Archdale King: *Liturgies of the Religious Orders*

(Milwaukee 1955; London 1956) [Carthusians, Cistercians, Premonstratensians, Carmelites, Dominicans]; *Liturgies of the Primatial Sees* (Milwaukee and London 1957) [Lyon, Braga, Milan, Toledo]; *Liturgies of the Past* (Milwaukee and London 1959) [rites of Aquileia and Beneventum, Gallican rite, Celtic rite, medieval rites of England, and the Scandinavian rite of Nidaros]. All these volumes offer a wealth of citations and rich bibliographies. But the presentation is largely a collage of material translated or paraphrased by a scholar who was neither critical of his secondary sources nor discerning as a translator. Still, there is nothing comparable available in English; and the great advantage of these admittedly unscholarly compilations is that they bring together under one cover scattered material not easily obtainable in even the larger libraries.

With reference to the liturgy of the religious orders discussed briefly in the preceding pages, the best introduction to the Premonstratensian rite, though outdated in particular points, remains that of Placide Lefèvre, *La Liturgie de Prémontré: Histoire, formulaire, chant et cérémonial*, Bibliotheca Analectorum Praemonstratensium 1 (Louvain 1957). For the Carthusians, particularly helpful—at least in theory—is the anonymous [Maurice Laporte] *Aux sources de la vie cartusienne: Quatrième partie: Sources des "Consuetudines Cartusiae"* (In Domo Cartusiae 1965). I say "at least in theory" advisedly, since copies of this valuable work seem to be deposited only in charterhouses and a few other monastic libraries. For a concrete example of the Carthusian orientation in things liturgical, see Robert Etaix, "L'homiliaire cartusien," *Sacris erudiri* 13 (1962) 67–112. Hansjakob Becker argues in favor of a nonmonastic origin of the Carthusian breviary, in his study, "War das Stundengebet der Kartäuser von Anfang an monastisch?" *Archiv für Liturgiewissenschaft* 13 (1971) 196–209. For Cluny, Philibert Schmitz offers the standard itemization of the practices making up Cluny's sempiternal liturgy, in his "La liturgie de Cluny," *Spiritualità cluniacense: 12–15 ottobre 1958*, Convegni del Centro di studi sulla spiritualità medievale 2 (Todi 1960) 83–99; but to understand what the liturgy of Cluny really meant, one must read the next study in the same volume—Jean Leclercq's perceptive "Spiritualité et culture à Cluny," 101–51. For the Cistercians, Bede Lackner's "The Liturgy of Early Cîteaux," *Studies in Medieval Cistercian History*, Cistercian Studies 13 (Spencer Mass. 1971) 1–34 provides a useful overview marred chiefly by the author's uncritical dependence on secondary sources and by his unfamiliarity with recent literature dealing with his topic. For more recent advances in this field of studies, see Chrysogonus Waddell, "The Origin and Early Evolution of the Cistercian Antiphonary," *The Cistercian Spirit*, Cistercian Studies 3, ed. M. Basil Pennington (Spencer Mass. 1970) 190–223; and "The Early Cistercian Experience of Liturgy," *Rule and Life*, Cistercian Studies 12, ed. M. Basil Pennington (Spencer Mass. 1971) 77–116.

The best means of keeping abreast of new material concerning the liturgy of the twelfth century is the comprehensive "Literaturbericht" included in the annual publication *Archiv für Liturgiewissenschaft* (Regensburg 1950–   ).

Above all else, however, technical studies dealing with the specifics of the medieval liturgies should always be read against the proper cultural and spiritual background. Books such as Jean Leclercq's great classic, *Love of Learning*, and the same author's contribution, along with that of François Vandenbroucke, to *The Spirituality of the Middle Ages*, A History of Christian Spirituality 2, trans. Benedictines of Holmes Eden Abbey, Carlisle (London 1968) are enormously helpful in this respect, as is the collection of essays by Marie-Dominique Chenu, *Nature*.

II

EDUCATION

The Schools of Paris
and the School of Chartres

R. W. Southern

Some years ago I criticized the generally received view of the importance of the school of Chartres in the first half of the twelfth century.[1] If I return to the subject, my purpose is not to go over the old ground again, nor to spend much time answering objections—though this will sometimes be necessary—but to investigate some broader issues raised by a reinterpretation of the school of Chartres. I should begin by recalling the main points which I urged in 1970, and which, with modifications for which I have to thank my critics, I would still urge: first, that the importance of the school of Chartres has been very greatly exaggerated by scholars in the last hundred years; second, that after the death or retirement of the great master of the school, master Bernard, in or about 1124, there is no convincing evidence of a continuing intellectual tradition in the school of Chartres beyond what might be expected of any cathedral school; third, that the association of Chartres with a unique tradition of Platonism arose mainly from a mistaken identification of master Bernard of Chartres with Bernard Silvester, and that the whole theory of Chartrian Platonism requires radical revision; and fourth, that from the early years of the century Paris had far outstripped Chartres as a place of teaching and study, even in those areas of study which have been particularly associated with Chartres.

If the argument were only about geography it could be left to sleep in peace. But beneath the surface, there are two deeper and more important issues. The first concerns the circumstances in which scholastic thought developed, the environment which made it possible and profitable, and the

---

[1] "Humanism and the School of Chartres," Southern, *Humanism* 61–85. The main criticisms are: Nikolaus M. Häring, "Chartres and Paris Revisited," *Essays in Honour of Anton Charles Pegis*, ed. J. Reginald O'Donnell (Toronto 1974) 268–329, which is extremely valuable for its detailed information about masters of this period; and Peter Dronke, "New Approaches to the School of Chartres," *Anuario de estudios medievales* 6 (1971) 117–40. Roberto Giacone, "Masters, Books and Library at Chartres According to the Cartularies of Notre-Dame and Saint-Père," *Vivarium* 12 (1974) 30–51, has reviewed the problem and has made a number of new and interesting observations.

conditions of freedom and competition which led to the astonishing proliferation of new ideas and new methods of intellectual communication in the early twelfth century. The second question concerns the nature and extent of what is commonly called Chartrian Platonism.[2] It is with the first—the problem of circumstance, environment, and motivation—that I shall deal here.

I

The first step in studying these problems is to consider very broadly the respective roles of Paris and Chartres in the development of early twelfth-century scholastic thought, and the reason for the distinction between them. We may begin by noticing that the *place* of teaching had a very subordinate importance in the minds of contemporaries, compared with the *person* of the teacher. One sign of this is that students, who tell us with evident pride and particularity the names of the masters under whom they studied, very often fail to mention *where* they studied. We shall have later to consider three particularly striking examples of this habit. Second, we may notice that when contemporaries mention schools which are specially distinctive in their doctrines, they use group names such as *Albericani, Meludinenses, Montani, Porretani, Heliste, Parvipontani.*[3] None of these groups is called after a town or a well-established institutional school: they are called after masters or the neighborhoods in which these masters taught. Even the *Meludinenses* were not students in Melun but students in Paris of Robert of Melun, an Englishman who had once taught in Melun. The *Albericani* are named after master Alberic who taught on Mont Ste Geneviève in the 1130s and 40s, the *Meludinenses* after Robert of Melun who taught in the same area; the *Montani* are the pupils of one or other of the masters, or of a group of masters, on Mont Ste Geneviève; and the *Porretani, Heliste,* and *Parvipontani* are the pupils of Gilbert of Poitiers, Peter Helias, and Adam of the Petit Pont respectively.

In brief, it would seem that the most important, or at least the most distinctive, teaching of the period had become deinstitutionalized, detached from the corporate schools of the past and attached to a master who taught wherever he could find a place to teach. This state of private enterprise did not last long. New institutional ties and conventions were soon formed, which dominated the scholastic scene until the seventeenth century. After about 1170 the institutionalizing went ahead rapidly, and we begin to hear much about the *licentia docendi* and about scholastic jurisdiction, in phrases drawn

[2]For further discussion of this question, see Richard W. Southern, *Platonism, Scholastic Method and the School of Chartres,* Stenton Lecture 1979 (Reading University Press), where bibliographical references will be found.
[3]The names of these schools with the doctrines which they supported are collected and commented on by Richard W. Hunt, "Studies on Priscian in the Twelfth Century, Part II," M&RS 2 (1950) 1–56 at 50–51.

from the vocabulary of canon law as it took over the task of pressing unruly events into shape. But for a short time, broadly corresponding to the first half of the twelfth century, there was a wide opportunity for individual enterprise and for ruthless competition, which was never again so uncontrolled.

The reason for this relatively brief but profoundly important phase of scholastic development was simple: quite suddenly there were many individuals who wanted new skills and new knowledge, which few masters could supply and which traditional institutional schools were by their nature and functions not well adapted to provide. The traditional idea of a school had been an organized community providing instruction in its functions to beginners and practice and rehearsal for its more advanced members. The *schola* of a monastery or cathedral was originally the whole community at its work of worship in the choir. As the demands of the liturgy became increasingly exacting, the work of the master in his school grew in importance, but it was always dominated by the corporate needs of the community.[4] The large and rapidly increasing number of students in the early twelfth century did not fit into this pattern. They were not acting as members of a community: they were adventurers seeking rare and difficult knowledge which would lead to personal advancement or the perfecting of a personal gift. So too were the masters whom they sought. Of course such people had existed before the early twelfth century; the new feature was that they now existed in sufficient numbers to determine the shape of the organization and the procedures and subject matter of the teaching, in the schools which they helped to create. The students had committed a great deal of their available resources to their search for a master, and they wanted to be sure of success—as sure as the necessarily chancy nature of the business would allow. A kind of bush–telegraph rapidly developed to signal the masters who were worth finding and the places where they were to be found.

Curiously enough, one of the best pieces of evidence for this state of affairs is the collection of letters from the first quarter of the twelfth century which has been taken (wrongly as I think) to provide incontrovertible evidence for the importance of the school of Chartres.[5] Its real lesson is quite different: it provides evidence of the students' uncertainty about where to go for the teaching they wanted, and of the need to act quickly on up-to-date information if the master was to be caught before he was promoted to a higher dignity, or moved elsewhere, or died: "I give you this advice, that if you or any of your neighbors are thinking of coming here to profit from [the teaching of] master

[4]This is the meaning of *schola* for which numerous examples can be found from the time of Alcuin to Orderic Vitalis. I hope to return to the stages and significance of the shift of meaning which brought the independent master and his group of pupils into strong relief in the twelfth century, and prepared the way for the new institutional *scholae* of the later Middle Ages.

[5]Lucien Merlet, "Lettres d'Ives de Chartres et d'autres personnages de son temps, 1087–1130," *Bibliothèque de l'Ecole des Chartes* 4th ser. 1 (1855) 443–71.

Anselm you should come as quickly as you can, for it is doubtful if he will long have leisure to devote to clerks, and you may have come in vain if you delay.''[6] So, in one of these letters, wrote a student at Laon to his relatives at home, probably in about 1115. He was in the school of the most widely admired master of his day, the school of master Anselm, to whom students came from as far afield as Pisa and Milan, from Germany, and in unexpectedly large numbers from England. Master Anselm stayed long enough in one place for the school at Laon to become widely known throughout Europe, but there was always the risk that the light might go out at any moment. The master might move, be promoted, fall ill, or die; when this happened his school would fall to pieces, or survive only in the traditional form of a cathedral school without interest to an international body of students.

The great masters of this period were much sought after because the skills which they could impart were rare and difficult and (to put the matter at its lowest) commanded great rewards. Their skills commanded great rewards because they were needed for the highest places in the government and administration of the Church. These were not skills which were needed by local churches or liturgically oriented communities, except perhaps when they were involved in lawsuits. For the ordinary routine of life, even the greatest churches needed chiefly a high degree of proficiency in reading and writing Latin, in singing and in composing prose and verse. These skills could indeed be exquisitely developed and splendidly maintained, and they could become the expression of a high civilization; but it was not generally for these skills that students traveled to find famous masters. They traveled to hear of new techniques and new texts, and the manner of applying them to the study of law, medicine, the Bible, or the nature of the physical universe. They wanted to learn to argue and analyze, and to build up a stock of authoritative *sententiae* on the controversial questions of the day. None of these activities was a normal part of the functions of a local church. Consequently the cultivating of these skills fitted only awkwardly into the traditional pattern of a cathedral school.

When a cathedral school under a famous master expanded its activity beyond its local needs, an awkward situation arose, as we can see in Laon at the time when the letter I have just quoted was written. Laon was a small walled town of about twenty-five hectares with a population of perhaps 3,000, on a

---

[6]Ibid. 466: "De vobis vero vobis consulo quatinus, si vobis vel aliquibus vicinis vestris in proposito est adhuc magistro Anselmo frui, illum quam citius potueritis adeatis, ne tandem eum, quem dubium est diu vacare clericis, tarde aut frustra queratis." Note also from another letter, to a canon of Pisa, the following passage: "Unde rogo multumque vestram deprecor clementiam, ut de vestro adventu, et si apud nos Laudunum hiemare debetis, certis vestris notis per hunc mihi certificare curetis. Sum enim modo cum hospite meo non in propria domo; sed si certus fuero de vobis, proprium hospitium mihi et vobis locare curabo. Unde me firmum ad presens volo faciatis quia, multis clericis Laudunum adventantibus, vix inveniri valde cara poterunt. De apostolico, et aliis novis nostre patrie que scitis vel audistis, similiter mihi significate. Domnus Ildebrandus a Lauduno vos multum salutat; alii nostri socii adhuc sunt Parisius, quos de die in diem expecto."

constricted site which allowed no possibility of easy growth.[7] Master Anselm was the *magister scolae* of the cathedral, and later the chancellor, who (among his other duties) had the task of controlling the teaching in the cathedral and town. The core of the cathedral *schola* was the choir which needed instruction in the liturgical functions of the church. Then, perhaps distributed in different parts of the cathedral, there must have been classes of clergy being taught (in the words of Gregory VII's recent decree)[8] the *artes litterarum*, which were necessary for the well-being of the diocese as a whole. These were the permanent and inescapable functions of the cathedral. But in Laon there was also a cosmopolitan throng of students of all ages and levels of social and ecclesiastical consequence, who had been attracted to Laon by the reputation of master Anselm. Many had come with their own tutors, and these tutors were interested in making their mark in the scholastic world: it was probably they who chiefly benefited from Anselm's learning and from arguments with him and their fellow students.[9] How, or whether, they were organized we do not know, but at the height of Anselm's fame they must have numbered several hundreds, and their relations with both the town and the cathedral were uneasy.[10] Organically they had no connection with the permanent functions of the cathedral; they were a floating population held together only by the presence of master Anselm and by the advantages of being part of a large scholastic community.

A precisely similar situation existed in Reims a few years later, as we learn from the *Life* of Hugh, later abbot of Marchiennes. As a young man in about 1117–20, Hugh went with his tutor to the school of master Alberic at Reims.

[7]For the site of Laon, with plans and bibliography, see the magnificently produced work of Carlrichard Brühl, *Palatium und Civitas: Studien zur Profantopographie spätantiker Civitates vom 3. bis zum 13. Jahrhundert*, vol. 1: *Gallien* (Cologne 1975) 73–82. The walled area in the twelfth century contained (on my calculation) 25 hectares, which on the basis of 100 inhabitants per hectare would give a population of 2,500. To this some addition should be made for those living outside the walls, but there was little room for crowds of students.

[8]*Gregorii VII Registrum* 6.5b (Decree of 1078), ed. Erich Caspar, MGH Epist sel 2 (Berlin 1920; repr. 1955) 402 [XXXI]: ''Ut omnes episcopi artes litterarum suis ecclesiis doceri faciant et ornamenta ecclesie sine certa utilitate aut gravi necessitate nullo modo nulloque ingenio ecclesiis subtrahant ne periculum sacrilegii, quod absit, incurrant.'' The combination of care for the *artes litterarum* and the *ornamenta ecclesie* puts the duty of teaching in the correct liturgical context.

[9]Examples of tutors taking their young pupils to famous schools, as a step in their own studies, are Adelard of Bath (see *Quaestiones naturales*, ed. Martin Müller, BGPTMA 31.2 [Münster 1934] 4) and William of Corbeil (see Herman, *De miraculis S. Mariae Laudunensis* 2.6, PL 156.977), both at Laon; Walter of Mortagne, at Reims and Laon (see *Ex vita Hugonis abbatis Marchianensis*, in *Recueil des Historiens des Gaules et de la France* 14 (1806) 398–99; and the tutor who took his English pupil to study dialectic under ''magister T. universalis'' (master Thierry?) and became ferocious when his young pupil outshone him. (See the text of the letter describing his experiences in Marvin L. Colker, *Analecta Dublinensia* [Cambridge Mass. 1975] 132. This incident took place in about 1120; as a result of his ill-treatment the young pupil fell into despair and despondency, became a monk for sixteen or seventeen years, and died probably in 1139.)

[10]Signs of overcrowding are apparent in the letters quoted above, and a further example is given by K. M. Fredborg, ''The Commentaries on Cicero's *De inventione* and *Rhetorica ad Herennium* by William of Champeaux,'' CIMAGL 17 (1976) 1–39 at 13.

The town was crowded with students—so much so (his biographer tells us) that there were almost more clerks than citizens in the town, and peace could only be maintained by keeping them apart. The boy's tutor at once began to challenge the opinions of master Alberic and to collect pupils of his own.[11] Alberic reacted by forcing him to leave the town. He went first to the nearby precincts of St Remi, and then further afield to Laon, where there was by this time something of a gap left by the death of master Anselm. In these briefly recorded events we have as in a microcosm the situation of an overgrown cathedral school: the overcrowding, the tension between the single dominant master and potential rivals, the ambitious tutors with their pupils and their hopes of building up a following of their own, and the uneasy relations with the local people.

We may expect to find that the more successful a master became, the more he was irked by the restrictions of a local school. He looked for a place where his powers could be more freely exercised. Equally, as the number of students grew, the disadvantages of a small and constricted town became more irksome. These two pressures together led to a fairly rapid disengagement of "higher studies" from cathedrals, which existed primarily to provide education for a liturgical community or for the diocesan clergy. This process of disengagement has several contemporary parallels in other walks of life; for instance, it may be compared with the separation of the higher functions of government from the daily life of the English royal household in the early twelfth century, or the separation of governmental and liturgical functions in the papal Curia in the middle of the eleventh century and in episcopal households all over Europe a hundred years later. All are instances of the separation of general from local needs, and in all cases the general needs called for a high degree of scholastic training.

The most ambitious and able masters who could provide this training needed to be easily accessible to the pupils whom they wished to teach; they needed also to be free to teach only those pupils who had the capacity to understand and the resources to pay for what they heard, as well as the stamina to follow long and arduous courses of study. The ablest students needed the assurance that when they arrived at their destination they would find masters able and willing to teach them difficult subjects. Without this assurance they might better have stayed at home. The hazards of study far from home were great, and the basic requirements which needed to be met were, first, the assurance of finding masters; and second, the assurance of finding a plentiful supply of food and lodgings, and if possible friends from home. These were not easy requirements to meet.

---

[11]The tutor was Walter of Mortagne, who later became bishop of Laon. For him see Ludwig Ott, *Untersuchungen zur theologischen Briefliteratur der Frühscholastik*, BGPTMA 34 (Münster 1937) 126; Nikolaus M. Häring, "A Hitherto Unknown Commentary on Boethius' *de Hebdomadibus* Written by Clarenbaldus of Arras," *Mediaeval Studies* 15 (1953) 212–21 at 214.

II

How are Paris and Chartres to be compared as places where these requirements could be met?

In the middle of the eleventh century the advantages and limitations of the two towns were probably about equal. Both were small cathedral cities and centers of government in a fertile landscape. Paris, however, by about 1100 was beginning a period of very rapid growth. Recent studies have considerably increased our knowledge of the stages of this growth, and we begin to have a fairly substantial idea of the city's expansion southward across the Petit Pont into the area around the church of St Julien le Pauvre, the Clos Mauvoisin, and the vineyards which belonged to the Garland family; then out to the bourg St Germain on the west and St Victor on the east, and further south to St Hilaire du Mont and Mont Ste Geneviève. As a result of these extensions and a comparable extension on the north bank of the river, Paris grew in the course of the twelfth century from being a small town mainly confined to the Ile de Paris, to a city comparable in size and population to the largest urban centers in Europe: by 1215 it had a walled area of about 275 hectares and a population of at least 25,000–30,000.[12] No doubt much of the space within the walled area was unoccupied, but it was available for occupation, and this meant that there was plenty of room for schools and lodgings.

Everyone in the twelfth century who wrote about Paris—and a surprising number did—stretched his command of language to extol the advantages which Paris offered to masters and students alike. Not least among these advantages was the abundance of food and wine—amenities evidently felt to be so important that almost every prospectus for a new university in the Middle Ages inserted them among its chief claims.[13] Paris, everyone agreed, actually possessed them. Besides, it had another advantage: it was at the center of an area in which there were many schools. At least twenty-five well-known twelfth-century schools can be counted within a hundred miles of Paris. This was important, because students who looked for higher studies must always have had a good grounding in the skills which were cultivated in local grammar schools. Students would come from very far afield to find the best masters, but it must always have been an advantage to have a large supply of competent

---

[12]See once more the plans, discussion, and bibliography in Brühl (n. 7 above) 6–33. Calculations of the size of the walled area of Paris in 1210 differ, but a reasonable estimate (excluding uninhabited islets) is 252 hectares. On the basis of 100 inhabitants per hectare this would allow a population of 25,000, to which some addition (say 10% in 1210) should be made for those living outside the walls. This gives a total of 27,500. Most estimates are higher than this: Brühl, 19, gives 50,000–60,000.

[13]Frederick II's proclamation of 1224 establishing the university of Naples and promising prospective masters and students "locum . . . ubi rerum copia, ubi ample domus et spatiose satis, et ubi mores civium sunt benigni; ubi etiam necessaria vite hominum per terras et maritimas facile transvehuntur" set a pattern followed by most later foundation charters for universities. (See the text in J. L. A. Huillard-Bréholles, *Historia diplomatica Friderici secundi* [6 vols. in 11 Paris 1852–61; repr. Turin 1963] 2.450–53 at 451.)

students and ambitious masters near at hand who could easily be influenced by
the pull of the great city.

These were all considerable advantages, but more important than any
other was the wide freedom enjoyed by independent masters in Paris to set up
their own schools. The cathedral church of Paris, like other northern
cathedrals, enjoyed a monopoly of teaching in the city and perhaps also in the
diocese, and this monopoly was administered by the chancellor of the
cathedral. The exercise of any medieval monopoly was subject to many limitations, but in Paris the limitations are very conspicuous: there were ancient
churches in the suburbs (the abbey of Ste Geneviève in particular) exempt
from the chancellor's control; there were the canons of the chapter, who seem
from an early date to have had much freedom in letting their houses as schools
and lodgings for masters and students; and there must have been a real practical difficulty in supervising the large, sprawling developments of a growing
city. In practice, the chancellor's monopoly seems to have been exercised, if at
all, by charging a fee to masters who wished to set up a school of their own.[14]
To charge a fee to those whom it is impossible to restrain is one way of exercising a commercial monopoly, but it tended to reduce teaching to the level of
other commercial activities.[15] Alexander III forbade this commercial practice in
about 1170, but almost at once he had to withdraw his prohibition in the case
of the chancellor of Paris, who was perhaps the biggest offender of all in northern Europe.[16]

As for the chancellor's capacity to control his own colleagues, it seems that
the canons of Notre-Dame at the end of the eleventh century were already accustomed to letting their houses in the cathedral close and its neighborhood to
masters and their pupils for schools and lodgings, and by about 1120 this practice had become so great a nuisance that an agreement was made between the
bishop and the canons to limit their freedom in this respect.[17] This may have

[14]In 1170–72, Alexander III forbade the practice of taking a fee for allowing masters to teach,
and a commentator on this decree, Vincentius Hispanus, says that it was directed especially against
the chancellor of Paris, "qui a quolibet docente marcam unam exigebat." Heinrich Denifle and
Emile Chatelain, eds., *Chartularium universitatis Parisiensis* (4 vols. + supp. Paris 1889–97,
1937–64) 1.4–5.

[15]The too-often forgotten fact that schools were a commercial asset is emphasized in a number
of English twelfth-century charters in which the grant of a school is associated with the grant of a
market, e.g. Henry I's foundation charter for St Peter's Dunstaple (1131–33) giving the canons the
"manerium de Dunstaple . . . et mercatum eiusdem villae, et scolas eiusdem villae, cum omnibus
libertatibus et liberis consuetudinibus eidem villae pertinentibus" (William Dugdale, *Monasticon
Anglicanum*, rev. John Caley et al. [6 vols. in 8 London 1817–30] 6.240). In a practical context,
the association of markets and schools, however offensive it may be in ecclesiastical theory, was not
illogical: the right of setting up a stall or a schoolroom was a valuable commercial privilege for
which the monopolist could charge a fee.

[16]For Alexander III's letter of 29 October 1174 exempting Peter Manducator, chancellor of
Paris, from the rule which he had just laid down against taking a fee for the *licentia docendi*, so
long as his fee was moderate, see *Chart. univ. Paris.* (n. 14 above) 1.8–9.

[17]B. Guérard, ed., *Cartulaire de l'église Notre-Dame de Paris*, Collection de documents
inédits sur l'histoire de France (4 vols. Paris 1850) 1.338: the agreement limited the right of canons
to let their houses to scholars as schools or lodgings, and the bishop in return agreed to build a

had some effect in the immediate neighborhood of the cathedral, but by then it was too late to alter the general situation: the proliferation of schools and lodgings had spread too far into the suburbs on the left bank of the Seine to be halted.

If we compare the situation in Chartres with that in Paris, the great difference lay in the urban development of the two towns, and probably in the way in which the scholastic monopoly was operated. Chartres exhibits little significant growth in the twelfth century, and even in the sixteenth century it was still a small town almost totally enclosed within a walled area of about sixty hectares.[18] Politically the town sank in importance after 1125, when the county of Chartres was reintegrated into the commercially richer and more active county of Champagne, with its capital at Troyes.[19] We have no information about the way in which the monopoly of teaching was exercised by the cathedral of Chartres, but it is significant that the chancellor of Chartres was still enforcing his monopoly in the fourteenth century and still obtaining royal charters to support it as late as the sixteenth century.[20] We may conclude from this that whereas the teaching monopoly of the chancellor of Paris had broken down early in the twelfth century except as a source of fees, no similar breakdown took place in Chartres.

III

The practical effect of this breakdown of control in Paris can first be observed in Abelard's *Historia calamitatum*, a work which has been studied from almost every point of view, but not I think from this angle. It will be recalled that Abelard spent the years of his early adolescence going from school to school in the Loire valley within fairly easy reach of his home, probably like many other young men with a tutor as his companion. Then, as his abilities and ambitions unfolded, he made straight for Paris to study under William of Champeaux. He probably arrived in Paris about 1098 and he describes the next fifteen years

---

covered building for schools near the episcopal palace. It was probably in this building that Gilbert of Poitiers lectured "in the bishop's hall" in about 1140 (see n. 29 below), for it should be remembered that lectures, like lawsuits, seem often to have taken place in halls which could accommodate different classes in separate corners as need arose. A similar shortage of lodgings had brought about a similar letting of houses by the canons of Laon. See Fredborg (n. 10 above) 13 n. 36, quoting William of Champeaux: "Vere non est turpe Laudunensibus canonicis hospitia clericis locare, quia non est turpe clericis ea conducere."

[18]A plan of the town with its suburbs, made at the time of the siege of 1591 for lord Burghley by his emissary Edmund Yorke who was present at the siege, is reproduced in Eva M. Tenison, *Elizabethan England* (12 vols. in 13 Royal Leamington Spa 1933–60) 8.314: it shows little extensive building outside the walls.

[19]Ferdinand Lot and Robert Fawtier, *Histoire des institutions françaises au moyen âge* (3 vols. Paris 1957–62) 1.125–26.

[20]The chancellor's scholastic authority was defined in 1324 in a dispute with the master of the schools of St Jean en Vallée just outside the city walls, and was confirmed by royal charter in 1515. See E. de Lépinois and Lucien Merlet, eds., *Cartulaire de Notre-Dame de Chartres* (3 vols. Chartres 1862–65) 1.lxxxii.

of his career in terms of a military operation aimed at the academic capture of the stronghold of Paris. In Abelard's eyes, the stronghold was not held by the chancellor or by any other official person, but by a famous master, William of Champeaux, against whom he pitted himself in individual combat. In all his operations Abelard never mentions any overall authority. William, indeed, who was also archdeacon, could call on mysterious forces against the intruder, but these forces are always portrayed as working through personal influence.

Abelard's first aim was to appropriate William's fame, position, and pupils, but the ultimate prize was Paris. Abelard speaks of his career as a series of advances toward, and withdrawals from, this goal. He tells us how he first established himself in Melun, some fifty miles from Paris—just outside the bishopric of Paris and just beyond the long arm of the archdeacon, his enemy. At Melun he was in a royal town, where he had friends whom he could rely on to guard him against the enemy's attacks while he gathered strength for his first campaign. This is how he described his strategy:

> From this first trial of my schools [at Melun], my fame as a logician began to spread, so that the renown of my master—not to mention the reputation of my contemporaries—began to shrink and wither away. This led me to grow in confidence and to transfer my schools as soon as possible nearer Paris to Corbeil, from where I might launch more frequent and importunate dialectical assaults.[21]

At Corbeil Abelard was poised for a final assault when ill health suddenly forced him to call off his attack. This enforced withdrawal lasted a few years, probably from about 1105 to 1108. When Abelard returned, William of Champeaux had withdrawn from his school on the Ile de Paris and had installed another master in his place, while he himself continued to teach free of charge at St Victor on the south bank of the river. Here Abelard joined him once more, and very soon the battle was resumed. At first it seemed that Abelard was going to have an easy victory, since the master whom William of Champeaux had installed in his former premises on the Ile offered Abelard his school. Abelard says nothing about the details of the transaction, but he speaks of it as a deal freely entered into by the two parties, like transferring a lease.[22] But William objected to the transfer, and Abelard was obliged once more to return to his old retreat at Melun. Very soon, however, William also left Paris and Abelard at once came back, not to the city itself (where the school which he had taken over was still occupied by his rival) but to Mont Ste Geneviève. From this height Abelard began a regular siege of Paris: "I pitched my scholastic camp outside the city on Mont Ste Geneviève, to lay siege as it

[21]Peter Abelard, *Historia calamitatum*, ed. Jacques Monfrin (Paris 1959) 64–65: "Ab hoc autem scolarum nostrarum tirocinio ita in arte dialetica nomen meum dilatari cepit, ut non solum condiscipulorum meorum, verum etiam ipsius magistri fama contracta paulatim extingueretur. Hinc factum est ut de me amplius ipse presumens ad castrum Corbolii, quod Parisiace urbe vicinius est, quamtotius scolas nostras transferrem, ut inde videlicet crebriores disputationis assultus nostra daret importunitas."
[22]Ibid. 66.

were to the man who had seized my place.''[23] The threat brought William himself back once more to Paris, and the battle was resumed between the two principals supported by their rival troops. Abelard saw the ensuing conflict as a *conflictus disputationum* on a Homeric scale. He compared the battle to the fight between Ajax (Abelard) and Hector (William): "If you ask who won, I say with modest pride 'I was not defeated.'''[24]

With this quotation from Ovid, Abelard gave a final military stamp to his account of his long campaign for scholastic domination of Paris. He makes no secret of his motives: he was avid for fame, which could best be gained at the center of affairs, and for the wealth that could only come from having a large body of pupils. This was what the battle was about, and it was fought without any reference to an overriding authority exercised by the chancellor of the cathedral. William of Champeaux was indeed a power to be reckoned with, but even he could not prevent Abelard from occupying for a time his scholastic premises on the Ile de Paris itself or from continuing to plague him from the heights of Mont Ste Geneviève.

This picture of Abelard's experiences in Paris forms a strong contrast to his account of his attempt to pursue the same tactics at Laon against master Anselm that had succeeded at Paris against master William. At Laon when he attempted to lecture in opposition to master Anselm he was abruptly told to desist; and, with whatever indignation, he obeyed and left the city never to return.[25]

What we have been observing in the Paris of Abelard's struggle for fame is precisely that deinstitutionalizing of the *schola*, that separation of the schools from their corporate involvement and their attachment to an individual master, which I have already described as a symptom of the age. In this process of disengagement the place where teaching was done assumed a new kind of importance: it was no longer the importance of the institution that mattered, but the convenience of the place. The masters needed freedom to teach the subjects of their special interest, and a wide choice of pupils eager for the specialty they could offer; the students sought a place where they could find a choice of masters, the possibility of profiting from several masters, and plentiful supplies of lodgings and provisions. Paris offered these advantages more abundantly than any other town in northern Europe, and Abelard's plan of campaign is the earliest proof of its superiority. No doubt, when Abelard became famous, he could teach where he wished and draw pupils wherever he went; but when he was beginning he needed to be in Paris, and even when he was famous he returned to Paris because he needed to be sure of finding an eager audience already in existence.

[23]Ibid. 66–67: "extra civitatem in monte Sancte Genovefe scolarum nostrarum castra posui, quasi eum obsessurus qui locum occupaverat nostrum."

[24]Ibid. 67.

[25]Ibid. 70. Note the similarity between Abelard's experience at Laon and that of Walter of Mortagne at Reims, described above.

IV

Of the number of students in Paris when Abelard was conducting his great battle, we can make no estimate. That it was already large is suggested by a letter written probably in 1109. It comes from a German student writing to his patron back home:

I am now in Paris in the school of master William . . . who, though he was archdeacon and almost the chief adviser to the king, gave up all he possessed to retire last Easter to serve only God in a poor little church. There, like master Manegold of blessed memory, he offered his services to all comers free of charge, and he now directs a school of secular and sacred learning larger than any I have ever heard of or seen in my time anywhere in the world.[26]

The words are vaguer than we could wish. Nevertheless, they are early evidence of the large number of students in Paris who were prepared to take advantage of a free offer. We have to go on to about 1140 to get some more precise idea of the size of the local student body. The evidence comes from a writer, Everard of Ypres, whom I failed to notice in my earlier study.[27] What he tells us relates to the teaching career of Gilbert of Poitiers, who became chancellor of Chartres in 1126 and bishop of Poitiers in 1142, and it will make the context of the discussion clearer if I quote the passage in my earlier essay which needs revision. I wrote:

Gilbert became a canon of Chartres by 1124 and chancellor in 1126. He *may* have taught there, but there is a striking absence of pupils who can be shown to have studied under him during these years. His teaching career still needs to be elucidated, but for the moment the only certainty attaches to his teaching in Paris in 1141, and there is some evidence that his influence radiated from this centre.[28]

In writing these words I was certainly wrong on one point. Everard of Ypres heard Gilbert lecture not only in Paris, but also in Chartres. He adds that in Chartres he was one in a class of four, and in Paris in the bishop's hall he was one in an audience of nearly three hundred.[29]

---

[26]Jaffé, *Bibl* 5.285–87 at 286: "Parisius sum modo, in scolis magistri Gwillelmi. . . . Qui cum esset archidiaconus fereque apud regem primus, omnibus quae possidebat dimissis, in praeterito pascha ad quandam pauperrimam ecclesiolam, soli Deo serviturus, se contulit; ibique postea omnibus undique ad eum venientibus gratis et causa Dei solummodo, more magistri Manegaldi beatae memoriae, devotum ac benignum se praebuit. Iamque tantum studium regit tam in divinis quam in humanis scientiis, quantum nec vidi nec meo tempore usquam terrarum esse audivi."

[27]Nikolaus M. Häring, "A Latin Dialogue on the Doctrine of Gilbert of Poitiers," *Mediaeval Studies* 15 (1933) 243–89. For the bearing of this testimony on the school of Chartres, see Häring (n. 1 above) 302, 304–05, and Dronke (n. 1 above) 120–21.

[28]Southern, *Humanism* 71.

[29]Häring (n. 27 above) 252. The facts I have summarized are conveyed in a peculiar and ambiguous form, but my summary follows the general lines of Häring and Dronke. In addition to the articles already cited see Nikolaus M. Häring, "The Cistercian Everard of Ypres and His Appraisal of the Conflict between St. Bernard and Gilbert of Poitiers," *Mediaeval Studies* 17 (1955) 143–72, for Everard's career.

Everard's testimony gives an assurance that Gilbert taught in Chartres during the years from 1126 to 1142. It provides a similar assurance that he also lectured in Paris. How can this be explained? It has been suggested that he must have resigned his chancellorship at Chartres in order to teach in Paris, and that he was replaced as chancellor in 1137 by a certain Guido.[30] If he did this, his willingness to resign an assured position in Chartres to engage in free-lance teaching in Paris would be the strongest possible evidence for the superiority of Paris over Chartres as a teaching center. But the evidence does not support the suggestion and it seems very unlikely.[31] In the absence of any known successor, or any mention of a gap in his career between his being chancellor of Chartres and bishop of Poitiers, it is highly likely that he continued as chancellor until 1142, and that he taught in Paris as well as Chartres during this period.

Should this after all surprise us? Similar combinations have excited no surprise. We know that at this same time Robert Pullen was lecturing in Paris while holding the office of archdeacon of Rochester in England. His absence of several years from his official duties was indeed thought by his bishop to be a dereliction of duty and the bishop tried to force him to return, but Robert Pullen refused and was supported in his refusal by St Bernard.[32] The duties of an archdeacon were almost certainly more onerous and carried more pastoral responsibility than those of a chancellor, and Rochester was much more remote from Paris than Chartres, yet Robert Pullen successfully resisted the strongest pressure on him to return. A little later there is evidence that master Clarembald was writing and teaching in Laon for some considerable time in 1157–59

[30]Häring (n. 1 above) 274: "During the year 1137 Gilbert seems to have left Chartres, for charters dated 1137 and 1139 show that a certain Guido was given the office [of chancellor]"; and 302: "In 1137 Gilbert was still chancellor in Chartres. Before 1141 he must have left Chartres, for in 1141 John of Salisbury found him in Paris and studied logic and theology under him."

[31]His proposed successor Guido does indeed appear as *cancellarius* in witness lists of charters of the bishop and chapter of Chartres, but he appears with this title as early as 1136 and probably as early as 1135 (Charles Metais, ed., *Cartulaire de Notre-Dame de Josaphat* [2 vols. Chartres 1911–12] 1.116–17, 121–22), so he cannot have been the successor of Gilbert who witnessed as chancellor in 1137. Moreover, it seems likely that *Guido cancellarius* is the same witness who appears elsewhere as *Guido cancellarii* or *Guido nepos cancellarii*. Under one or another of these designations he is found in charters of Chartres from 1119 to 1139. The full list, so far as I have traced it, is as follows: *Guido cancellarii*, 1119–24 (René Merlet and A. Clerval, *Un manuscrit Chartrain du XIe siècle* [Chartres 1893] 196), 24 January 1139 (*Cart. N-D Chartres* [n. 20 above] 1.148; *Guido nepos cancellarii*, ca. 1137 (*Cart. Josaphat* 1.123–24); *Guido cancellarius*, ca. 1135 and 1136 (*Cart. Josaphat* 1.116–17, 121–22), 1137 (B. Guérard, ed., *Cartulaire de l'abbaye de Saint-Père de Chartres* [2 vols. Paris 1840] 2.384–85). All these forms are found only in transcripts of which the originals seem to be lost, except the document of 1139, with the form *Guido cancellarii*, of which the original exists. Unless we are dealing with two (or three) Guidos, a mistaken transcription of *cancellarius* for *cancellarii*, which would be easy, seems the only explanation. In any event, Guido cannot be Gilbert's successor as chancellor of Chartres.

[32]The documentary evidence for this curious and complicated incident is in Walther Holtzmann, *Papsturkunden in England*, Abh Göttingen n.s. 25 and 3rd ser. 14–15, 33 (3 vols. Berlin 1930–52) 2.177–79, 195–96; and see also 3.173; also St Bernard's letter no. 205 (PL 182.372).

while holding office as archdeacon of Arras;[33] and, later still, master Peter
Comestor seems to have lectured at and even become chancellor of Paris while
holding the office of dean of Troyes.[34] We find everywhere too many examples
of official duties being performed by deputy to be surprised at the absence of a
cathedral dignitary for several months of the year, and residence in the schools
was one of the commonest grounds of absence, sometimes for years on end.

We do not know the residence requirements of a chancellor of Chartres,
but it is very unlikely that they excluded the possibility of long periods of
absence. Even the chancellor of Paris, with all his real or nominal responsibility
for the schools, was not at this time bound by strict requirements of residence,
and it was not until 1207 that a new ordinance required him to reside in Paris
and to take an oath that he would do so.[35] Nor, for that matter, did a lecturer
at this time have any strict lecturing requirements which would have made it
impossible for him to interrupt his lectures when called upon to carry out his
official duties elsewhere. Indeed, there is some reason to think that this kind of
commuting between lecturing in one place and performing official duties at
another was not uncommon, for William of Tyre reports that students in Paris
in the 1140s had to plan their lectures with an eye to alternative courses when
their masters were called away by their other duties.[36] Altogether, therefore, it
appears quite unnecessary to suppose that Gilbert or his contemporaries would
have seen any objection to his dividing his time in a way which allowed him,
while chancellor of Chartres, to spend a large part of his year teaching in Paris.

How, in detail, Gilbert divided his time must remain unknown to us, but
Paris seems to have been the main center of his teaching and influence. We
have, first of all, Everard of Ypres's very marked contrast between the audience of four in Chartres and nearly three hundred in Paris; then John of
Salisbury's clear evidence that Gilbert was lecturing in Paris in 1141;[37] third,

[33]Nikolaus M. Häring, *Life and Works of Clarembald of Arras* (Toronto 1965) 9–20.

[34]Ignatius Brady, "Peter Manducator and the Oral Teachings of Peter Lombard," *Antonianum* 41 (1966) 454–90 at 483–90.

[35]*Chart. univ. Paris.* (n. 14 above) 1.65–66, "statuimus in capitulo Parisiensi ut quicumque
de cetero cancellarius Parisiensis fuerit, teneatur in persona propria bona fide Parisius residere, et
post institutionem suam teneatur iuramentum in capitulo exhibere, se facturum residentiam bona
fide in ecclesia Parisiensi, quamdiu cancellariam tenuerit, et quod per se vel per alium nullatenus
procurabit, quod relaxetur a iuramento predicto." The first chancellor to take this oath was Prepositinus (1206–10), who had taken it voluntarily at the bishop's request in 1206. It is clear from
this text that there had been a history of nonresidence before this date.

[36]For William of Tyre, see below at n. 53; in speaking of the three Parisian masters, Bernard
Brito, Peter Helias, and Ivo *genere et natione Carnotensis*, he says, "hos alternatim secundum
quod eorum negotia presentes eos nobis permittebant vel absentes annis audivimus circiter
decem."

[37]John of Salisbury, *Metalogicon* 2.10, ed. Clement C. J. Webb (Oxford 1929) 82: "Reuersus
itaque in fine triennii repperi magistrum Gilebertum, ipsumque audiui in logicis et diuinis; sed
nimis cito subtractus est." Everyone agrees that this refers to lectures given by Gilbert in Paris in
1141. Commenting on this passage, Dronke (n. 1 above, 123) lays great stress on the word *repperi*,
arguing that "*repperi* refers to a reunion, not to a first encounter," and that "*reversus* refers to a
return from some distance, not to a ten-minute walk." In his view, the sense of the passage is that
John found Gilbert, whom he had just left in Chartres, in Paris when he returned. It may,

the evidence of a writer who was well informed about Gilbert's career that he
was "first a master in Paris and then bishop of Poitiers";[38] and finally the fact
that there was a road on Mont Ste Geneviève known as the *rue des Porées* or
Poirées, probably because it was the place where the *Porretani*, the followers of
Gilbert, lived and were taught.[39] On the other hand, the evidence for
Gilbert's presence in Chartres during his chancellorship is extremely sparse.
During the years around 1126–27, when he first became chancellor, he witnessed three surviving charters; but during the next fifteen years, only two
more, in 1134 and 1137, although there were several occasions when the other
members of the chapter were present in some numbers.[40] Certainly it would be
unwise to attach too much weight to these facts, but they are consistent with
long periods of absence from Chartres.

If my general picture of the dissociation of teaching from the tenure of official positions during this period is acceptable, it will not be surprising to find
masters who have duties as canons and dignitaries in one church while lecturing elsewhere in the schools. On the other side of the coin, the loosening of
the corporate unity of the cathedral chapter can be seen in the declining
numbers of dignitaries who witness the charters of Chartres in the 1140s.[41]

One last point in the evidence of Everard of Ypres deserves a comment:
the very great difference between the number of students at Gilbert's lectures
in Chartres and in Paris. The small number in Chartres is perhaps not surprising, for Gilbert was a notoriously difficult lecturer;[42] but the very large
number in Paris is very surprising. Of course it is possible to give several dif-

---

however, be observed that, even if *repperi* refers to a reunion, it could equally well mean a reunion
with Gilbert, whom he had known earlier in Paris, after John's three-years' absence.

[38]The phrase occurs in a catalogue of twelfth-century scholars: "Gillebertus cognomento Por-
rata primum scholasticus Parisiensis post pictauensis episcopus." See Nikolaus M. Häring, "Two
Catalogues of Mediaeval Authors," *Franciscan Studies* 26 (1966) 195–211 at 210. The latest name
in the catalogue printed by Fr Häring is Peter Lombard, so it is unlikely that the list is much later
than 1160. The writer is well informed on Gilbert and his works.

[39]This road ran from the rue de la Sorbonne to the rue St Jacques. See H. Legrand, *Plans de
restitution: Paris en 1380* (Paris 1868) 48. Häring (n. 1 above) 303 n. 35 adds a reference to
Adolphe Berty and L.-M. Tisserand, *Topographie historique du vieux Paris*, Histoire générale de
Paris (6 vols. Paris 1866–97) 6.372–73, and comments that the name "probably denotes the street
where Gilbert was known to have resided or taught, at least temporarily."

[40]The charters witnessed by Gilbert as chancellor in his early years are *Cart. Josaphat* (n. 31
above) 1.29–30 (dated 1124–27), *Cart. S-P Chartres* (n. 31 above) 2.267 (27 November 1126), and
ibid. 2.307 (dated, surely wrongly, 1116–24, but certainly early). Thereafter we have only *Cart.
N-D Chartres* (n. 20 above) 1.142 (26 February 1134) and *Cart. Josaphat* 1.126–27 (1137).
Charters witnessed by a large body of canons without the chancellor Gilbert include *Cart. Josaphat*
1.114–15 (1 July 1134), 116–17 (ca. 1136), 121–22 (1136), 123–24 (ca. 1137); and *Cart. N-D
Chartres* 1.148 (24 January 1139).

[41]For the decline in the number of cathedral dignitaries witnessing the charters of the bishop
and canons of Chartres in the 1140s, and the increasing numbers of miscellaneous *magistri* and
household officers who act as witnesses, see the *Cart. Josaphat* (n. 31 above) 1.166–67, 170–74,
179, 188. On the significance and role of these masters, see Appendix 2 below.

[42]John of Salisbury, *Historia pontificalis*, ed. Reginald L. Poole (Oxford 1927) 28, summed up
this characteristic in a trenchant phrase: "Doctrina eius nouis obscurior sed prouectis compen-
diosior et solidior uidebatur."

ferent explanations of these figures, but since the authority for both numbers is the same and there was no obvious reason for distortion, they should, at least provisionally, be treated seriously.[43] It takes a very large student body to provide an audience of three hundred for a lecturer of well-attested obscurity. If this number is anywhere near the truth, the total number of students in Paris by about 1140 could scarcely have been less than two or three thousand, and various indications in the later years of the twelfth century support a figure of this order of magnitude.[44]

V

By 1140, then, Paris was in the full tide of its progress toward scholastic dominance over all other schools in northern Europe. This dominance rested on three sources of strength. First, it was based on the unique combination of practical advantages which had drawn masters to Paris in preference to all other places in northern Europe for the past forty years. Second, it was based on the presence of many independent masters, and not on the fame of a single school: we must not replace the "school of Chartres" with the "school of Paris," for that would miss the point that the strength of Paris lay in the free and confusing competition of many masters and not in the fame of a single school.[45] Third, the dominance of Paris rested on the simple fact that numbers alone could provide the interplay of specialized knowledge which was necessary for the general development of scholastic thought. John of Salisbury, who was a good judge in these matters, ascribed the strength of Gilbert of Poitiers to the number of disciplines which he could bring to bear on the discussion of any particular question: "He called all disciplines to his aid as the subject required, for he knew that all things are held together by the mutual support of all their individual parts."[46] Gilbert had acquired his widely ranging expertise

[43]Dronke (n. 1 above) 121, says with justice that the "relative audience sizes . . . may have something to do with the kind of *lectio* in question." This is true, but Everard gives us no clue on this point; he mentions only the bare contrast in numbers.

[44]Converging pieces of evidence suggest that there may have been 3,000 or 4,000 students in Paris by about 1200. Charles Samaran, "La vie estudiantine à Paris au moyen âge," *Aspects de l'Université de Paris*, ed. Louis Halphen et al. (Paris 1949) 103–32, has some wise words on the difficulties of making an estimate: as between the 1,000 to 1,300 of Charles Thurot and the 10,000 of Denifle (the latter for the fourteenth century) he gives a cautious assent to the latter. Two small pointers may be mentioned, which seem to me significant for the period around 1200. First, Innocent III in November 1207 evidently envisaged some difficulty in keeping the number of theological lecturers down to eight. This suggests a figure of at least 100 lecturers in Arts, and perhaps 20 in Law and Medicine (the comparable figures for 1349 were Theology 32, Canon Law 17, Medicine 46, Arts 514; or a ratio of 16:1 between Arts and Theology). Also, in 1213 a standing committee of Masters in Arts for the admission of new masters consisted of six Masters who were changed every six months. Since these were presumably senior Masters, it is hard to see how the system could have worked without a reservoir of about 100 Masters of Arts. See *Chart. univ. Paris.* (n. 14 above) 1.65, 76; 2.623–48.

[45]The judgment that "the school of Chartres was the most powerful force of the twelfth century" (Häring [n. 1 above] 329) would be equally misplaced if applied to the "school of Paris."

[46]John of Salisbury, *Hist. pontificalis* (n. 42 above) 28: "Utebatur, prout res exigebat, omnium adminiculo disciplinarum, in singulis quippe sciens auxiliis mutuis universa constare."

the hard way, by seeking masters in different subjects in several different places. But by 1140, it was possible to find nearly everything in Paris. True, it was necessary to go to Bologna for the higher flights of canon law, and to Montpellier for the latest and best in medicine; but for every branch of grammar, logic, philosophy, and theology, and even for a respectable level of law or medicine, Paris could provide everything that most ambitious students could desire. Nearly all the leading masters of this period were themselves men with several masters. A large number of these could be found without stirring from Paris. It was not just the convenience of proximity that Paris provided; it was also the possibility of an exchange of views between various disciplines. This last was the main cause of the intellectual as well as the numerical preeminence of the city.

The nature of this preeminence is well illustrated in three documents which give a vivid picture of Paris in the 1140s.

(1) The first document is John of Salisbury's well-known account of his ''nearly twelve years of varied study'' from the late summer of 1136 to the early spring of 1148.[47] The chronology and the location of the schools of the twelve masters under whom he studied during these years present problems of great, and in some cases insoluble, difficulty. He mentions the precise location of only three—Abelard, Alberic, and Robert of Melun, all on Mont Ste Geneviève. Of the remainder, he makes it clear that Gilbert of Poitiers, Robert Pullen, and Simon of Poissy also taught in Paris or on Mont Ste Geneviève. This leaves six masters unaccounted for, but we know from other sources that at least three of them (Adam of the Petit Point, Peter Helias, and Thierry) taught in Paris or its suburbs.[48] In total therefore at least nine out of John's twelve masters were teaching in or around Paris.

The main master whose position is in doubt is William of Conches, the *grammaticus de Conchis* as John calls him. The chief claimants for his school have been Chartres and Paris, but on present evidence neither can be strongly supported.[49] He may even have been at Conches in 1138; he certainly seems to

[47]*Metalogicon* 2.10 (n. 37 above) 77–83.

[48]For the evidence that Thierry was teaching in Paris in the 1130s and probably earlier, see Häring (n. 1 above) 272, 283, 287, quoting the *Vita Adalberti* in Jaffé, *Bibl* 3.589–90.

[49]I suggested in my earlier article that, when John of Salisbury says (*Metalogicon* 2.10 [n. 37 above] 80, and cf. 82) that he left the schools of Mont Ste Geneviève to study for three years under William of Conches, he may have meant no more than that he went down into the city of Paris itself. Dronke (n. 1 above) 122–23 points out that this is a strained interpretation of John of Salisbury's words and I do not press it. Nevertheless, as is often the case on matters of fact (cf. his treatment of the career of Vacarius in the *Policraticus*, and indeed the whole account of his student years), John of Salisbury's precise meaning is extraordinarily elusive, and there are contemporary precedents for speaking of Mont Ste Geneviève as distinct from Paris (e.g. Abelard, *Hist. calamitatum* [n. 21 above] 66: ''extra civitatem in monte Sancte Genovefe scolarum nostrarum castra posui''). The evidence for William of Conches's teaching at Chartres is at present no more than this: first, in his lectures on Priscian before 1125 he gives, as an example of simultaneity, the phrase ''me sedente hic, Secana currit Parisius,'' which implies that he was not in Paris but does not say where he is; second, he gives *Carnotum* as an example of a word signifying place; third, he mentions the choir of St Mary's, in a way which is consistent with his being in a church dedicated to St Mary (Edouard Jeauneau, ''Deux rédactions des gloses de Guillaume de Conches sur

have been in Normandy when he wrote the final version of his *Dragmaticon* at some time between 1144 and 1150. Like most great masters of the period, he was wholly individual in his range of learning and in the combination of subjects or texts on which he lectured. Paris was the place which gave such men the best opportunities for discussion with their equals and for finding and teaching the best pupils, but a master of William's eminence could draw pupils wherever he wished. Neither he nor John of Salisbury thought it important to mention the place where he taught. His own testimony is simply, ''I taught others for twenty years and more.''[50] That is all we know.

The other master on John of Salisbury's list who is of special interest to us is Thierry. On him I need do no more than repeat that the only place where we find him teaching before 1142 is Paris: he was certainly teaching there in the 1130s and probably a good deal earlier. It is possible that he was the Thierry who witnessed charters in the 1130s as archdeacon of Dreux in the diocese of Chartres.[51] If so, he is another example of a lecturer in Paris being at the same time an archdeacon in another diocese. In 1142 or shortly afterward he became chancellor of Chartres in succession to Gilbert of Poitiers, and held his office in conjunction with the archdeaconry of Chartres; but where or whether he taught after this date is unknown.[52]

(2) The second document is William of Tyre's account of his student years from 1145 to 1165.[53] William mentions sixteen masters under whom he studied over a period of nineteen years. Of these masters, he had ten in the liberal arts and theology, four in law, and two in classical literature and mathematics. The four lawyers, he tells us, taught in Bologna, and the two masters in classical literature and mathematics in a place or places not easy to deter-

---

Priscien,'' RTAM 27 [1960] 212–47 at 230–32). That William had a connection with Chartres as a student of Bernard is virtually certain: see *Metalogicon* 1.5 and 1.24 (16 and 57), where the fact is not directly stated (it is only stated that in his teaching of grammar he followed the same method as Bernard of Chartres, until its unpopularity caused him to give it up), but it seems to be implied. The only other point which should be mentioned here is that his teaching career probably started earlier than is generally accepted, probably at least by 1115. On this and other problems relating to William of Conches, see Southern (n. 2 above).

[50]''Per uiginti annos et eo amplius alios docui'' (William of Conches's preface to the second edition of his *Dragmaticon*, ed. André Wilmart, *Analecta Reginensia*, Studi e testi 5 (Vatican City 1933) 264.

[51]See Häring (n. 1 above) 272.

[52]I am glad to correct my earlier erroneous date of 1141 (Southern, *Humanism* 70) to 1142 or slightly later. Gilbert, whom he succeeded as chancellor, became bishop of Poitiers probably shortly after July 1142. At the same time, or shortly afterward, Thierry became archdeacon of Chartres, and held the two offices in plurality at least until 1149. Giacone (n. 1 above) 38–39 argues that Thierry's appearance, in some contemporary notes on the Council of Reims in 1148, in a group described as *magistri scolarum* proves that Thierry was teaching at Chartres at this time; but the classification of those present at the Council into archbishops, bishops, abbots, and *magistri scolarum* is intended to indicate the grounds on which those who are mentioned were qualified to take part in the dispute about the doctrines of Gilbert of Poitiers. It does not necessarily indicate the present employment of the *magistri*. Hence I retain my doubts about both the place and the fact of Thierry's continued teaching; and this doubt would extend also to some of the others in the list.

[53]R. B. C. Huygens, ''Guillaume de Tyr étudiant,'' *Latomus* 21 (1962) 811–29 at 822–24, where the chapter of William's *History* describing his student years was printed for the first time.

mine. But the remaining ten—all his masters in the liberal arts and theology—certainly taught in Paris. William of Tyre does not mention Paris, but the internal evidence suffices to identify it. The grounds for this assurance can be briefly stated. William divides his ten masters in the liberal arts and theology into three groups. The first group consists of three masters under whom he studied "alternately as their other duties made it possible for them to be present or absent." This certainly implies that they were all teaching in the same place; otherwise the students could not have switched from one to the other as the presence or absence of these masters required. Two of the three masters, Bernard Brito and Ivo of Chartres, are known to have taught in Paris.[54] We can therefore conclude with certainty that the third, Peter Helias, likewise taught there. The second group of masters consists of five to whom William went "only casually and mainly for practice in disputation." The way in which he speaks of his attendance at the lectures of these masters makes it clear that they were all in the same place.[55] Four of the five—Alberic de Monte, Robert of Melun, master Mainerus, and Adam of the Petit Pont—are known to have taught in Paris; so the fifth member of the group, Robert Amiclas, must have taught there also. The third group consists of two theologians, Peter Lombard and Maurice of Sully, who are well known to have been in Paris.[56] So here we have a list of ten masters in Paris between 1145 and 1165, of whom four are the same as the masters under whom John of Salisbury studied between 1136 and 1148.

(3) Finally, there is the *Metamorphosis Goliae*.[57] A penetrating study of this poem has recently dated it, rightly as I believe, between the late summer of 1142 and the early summer of 1143.[58] In this document fourteen modern masters are mentioned. What was it that qualified them for inclusion? I think this question can be answered in part at least by comparing its list of names

[54]See Häring (n. 1 above) 272. It may be worth noticing, as evidence of the vagaries of nomenclature at this time, that Ivo of Chartres was so called because he was a native of the county of Chartres (*genere et natione Carnotensis*), while Thierry who was a Breton does not appear as *Carnotensis* until he became chancellor in 1142.

[55]After speaking of Bernard Brito, Ivo of Chartres, and Peter Helias, whom he heard *alternatim*, William of Tyre goes on to say, "Audivimus et alios etsi non assidue, tamen sepius et maxime disputationis gratia," namely, Alberic de Monte, Robert of Melun, Mainerus, Robert Amiclas, and Adam of the Petit Pont. For these masters, see also Häring (n. 1 above) 324–28.

[56]For Peter Lombard's teaching career, see the *Prolegomena* to his *Sententiae*, ed. Ignatius Brady, Spicilegium Bonaventurianum 4 (Grottaferrata 1971) 21*–35*; for Maurice of Sully, see Victor Mortet, "Maurice de Sully, évêque de Paris (1160–1196): Etude sur l'administration épiscopale pendant la seconde moitié du XIIe siècle," *Mémoires de la Société de l'histoire de Paris* 16 (1889) 105–314. John of Cornwall's *Eulogium ad Alexandrum III papam* (PL 199.1041–86, esp. 1052–53) is especially valuable for his account of the relations between several of these masters in Paris in the 1150s: see Eleanor Rathbone, "John of Cornwall: A Brief Biography," RTAM 17 (1950) 46–60; Nikolaus M. Häring, "The Eulogium ad Alexandrum Papam tertium of John of Cornwall," *Mediaeval Studies* 13 (1951) 253–300 at 284, 286.

[57]For the text, see R. B. C. Huygens, "Mitteilungen aus Handschriften," *Studi medievali* 3rd ser. 3 (1962) 747–72 at 764–72 ("III. Die Metamorphose des Golias").

[58]John F. Benton, "Philology's Search for Abelard in the *Metamorphosis Goliae*," *Speculum* 50 (1975) 199–217. This is an indispensable commentary on the text, but less satisfactory on the principle of selection of the masters who are mentioned in it (see 210–11). Reginald L. Poole's

with those in the two documents just discussed. Twelve of the fourteen masters have already appeared as Parisian masters in the other two lists. The two who are unaccounted for, Reginaldus monachus and Bartholomew, have not been identified with any certainty, but it seems overwhelmingly likely that they, like the other twelve members of the group, taught in Paris.[59]

The main peculiarity of this list is that, at the time when the poem was written, three of the fourteen masters who are mentioned—the three most distinguished of them—had recently ceased, or at least interrupted, their teaching in Paris as a result of promotion or enforced exile. The two who had been promoted are identified by their new positions: Thierry, who had become chancellor of Chartres, is *doctor ille Carnotensis*;[60] Gilbert, who had become bishop of Poitiers, is *presul Pictavensis*. The third, the exile Abelard, is especially deplored.[61] The author had mixed feelings about those who remained: some were good, some bad; possibly none came up to the standard of the three who had gone. It may well have seemed that the glory had departed from the schools of Paris. The three great men had gone and their pupils were left to carry on as best they could: Mainerus, Robert of Melun, and Adam of the Petit Pont, the pupils or successors of Abelard; Peter Helias, Bernard Brito, and Ivo, the pupils of Thierry; Ivo the pupil also of Gilbert, and Peter Lombard the main continuer of the work of Gilbert and of Abelard.[62] There are a number of stubborn uncertainties about the author's attitude to the masters whom he mentions, but essentially he provides a group picture of the schools of Paris as they had recently been, and still were in 1142, with a hint of decline and of foreboding for the future: the three greatest had gone; their pupils and disciples were of varying quality; the enemies of promise were strong.

The result of combining these three lists is shown in Appendix 1. Certainly they do not give us a complete picture of the masters who were active in Paris in the 1140s, but they provide a reliable view of the range of talent available to students who had the ambition and resources to make use of the opportunities which Paris offered.

---

remarks in "The Masters of the Schools at Paris and Chartres in John of Salisbury's Time," EHR 35 (1920) 321–42, repr. in *Studies in Chronology and History*, ed. Austin L. Poole (Oxford 1934) 223–47 at 240–47 still retain their value.

[59]Master Bartholomew has often been identified with the canonist and bishop of Exeter: see Adrian Morey, *Bartholomew of Exeter, Bishop and Canonist* (Cambridge 1937) sec. 4.103, and Poole (n. 58 above) 244.

[60]This seems to be the earliest occasion on which Thierry is called *Carnotensis*, perhaps to emphasize his recent promotion and removal from Paris. Before this date, and generally also afterward, he was known simply as magister Terricus or Theodoricus, with the occasional addition of *Brito*, to denote his Breton origin.

[61]Professor Benton (n. 58 above) has shown conclusively that the *nupta* who sought Abelard in vain was not Heloise, but *Philologia* herself, and she sought him in vain because he had been driven away and silenced.

[62]At the time when the *Metamorphosis Goliae* was written, it is likely that Peter Lombard's only known work would have been his gloss on the Psalms (see *Prolegomena in Sent.* [n. 56 above] 31*), which was clearly in the tradition of Gilbert of Poitiers; and for his dependence on Abelard in the eyes of a contemporary, see John of Cornwall, *Eulogium* (n. 56 above) 1052–53.

Appendix 1

MASTERS IN PARISIAN SCHOOLS

Masters of John of Salisbury (1136–47)	Masters of William of Tyre (1145–ca. 1160)	Masters in the *Metamorphosis Goliae* (1142–43)
PROBABLY ELSEWHERE		
Peripateticus Palatinus	———	Abelard**
*Alberic	*Alberic de Monte	———
*Robert of Melun	*Robert of Melun	*Robertus theologus
Thierry	———	Doctor ille Carnotensis**
†Peter Helias	†Peter Helias	†Peter Helias
*Adam of the Petit Pont	*Adam of the Petit Pont	*Parvi Pontis incola
Gilbert	———	Presul Pictavensis**
Robert Pullen	———	———
Simon of Poissy	———	———
———	*Mainerus	*Manerius
———	Robertus Amiclas	Robertus Amiclas
———	†Bernardus Brito	†Bernardus
———	§†Ivo of Chartres	§†Ivo
———	§Peter Lombard	*§Lombardus
———	Maurice	———
PROBABLY IN PARIS		
———	———	Reginaldus monachus
———	———	Bartholomew
Hardewinus Teutonicus	———	———
CERTAINLY IN PARIS		
William of Conches	———	———
Richardus episcopus	———	———

† pupils of Thierry
§ pupils or followers of Gilbert of Poitiers
* pupils or followers of Abelard
** recently moved by force or promotion

Appendix 2

MASTERS IN GOVERNMENT

This paper has been concerned chiefly with the disengagement of masters and schools from their long-established association with the communities of cathedrals and collegiate churches; but it would be seriously incomplete without a brief note on contemporary developments within the cathedral communities. I shall deal only with one small part of this subject, that part which can be observed in the witness lists of charters of this period: an inconspicuous feature, but a keyhole through which a large landscape can be surveyed.

(1) If we look at witness lists of episcopal or cathedral charters of the early twelfth century, we shall, with very rare exceptions, see only one category of persons to whom the title *magister* is given. He is the official in charge of the school of a cathedral or other corporate church, and he is generally qualified very precisely as *magister scolae* or *scholasticus*. Thus we have *Bernardus scolae magister* (at Chartres), *Ansellus magister scolae* (at Laon), *Ibertus scholasticus* and *Robertus magister* successively (at Arras), *Guirinbaldus scholasticus* (at Cambrai), *Beclais magister scolarum* (at Tours), *Vasletus magister scolarum sancti Mauricii Andegavensis* (at Angers), *Baldwinus archdiaconus et magister scolarum principalis ecclesie Leodiensis* (at Liège).[63] In all these examples the man's function is added to his name and comes after his name. The last three examples also provide a clue to one part of the process whereby the plural form *scolarum* takes over from the singular *scola*, for these men were not only schoolmasters of a single community but also administrators of a scholastic monopoly in an area.

(2) This usage continued with few exceptions until about 1135. By then there are signs, few at first but growing more frequent as we approach the middle of the century, of a new system coming into existence. The following charters will give some examples of the new system. The first is a charter of William, bishop of Norwich, dated between 1146 and ca. 1150. Among the witnesses appear the following: *magister Stangrimus, magister Nicholaus, magister Godwinus, magister Walterus de Calna, magister Alanus capellanus*.[64] Or again, in a charter of Theobald, archbishop of Canterbury, to be dated between 1150 and 1153, the following appear among the witnesses: *magister Johannes Salesberiensis, magister Guido de Pressenni, magister de Tyleberia, magister Rogerus Species*.[65] Or again, among the witnesses of a charter of Geoffrey, bishop of Chartres, datable between 1133 and 1145, there is a group of men described as *clerici* of the bishop, and they include a *magister Guillermus Magdunensis* alongside *Guillermus medicus Aurelianensis*, and Ivo *legis doctus*.[66]

We are here in the presence of a new system of nomenclature. The *magistri* who witness these charters are not given this title in order to specify their function in the

---

[63]For Chartres, see Merlet and Clerval, *Un manuscrit Chartrain* (n. 31 above) 196; for Laon, *Cartulaire de Saint-Vincent de Laon*, ed. René Poupardin (Paris 1902; repr. from *Mémoires de la Société de l'histoire de Paris et de l'Ile-de-France* 29 [1902] 173–267) 204; for Arras and Cambrai, *Cartulaire de l'abbaye de Saint-Vaast d'Arras*, ed. E. Drival (Arras 1875) 64–67, 146–49, 175, 389–91; for Tours, *Cartulaire de l'abbaye de la Madeleine de Châteaudun*, ed. Lucien Merlet and L. Jarry (Châteaudun 1896) 12–14; for Angers, *Cartulaire de l'abbaye cardinale de la Trinité de Vendôme*, ed. Charles Metais (5 vols. Paris 1893–1904) 2.320–23, 344; for Liège, *Cartulaire de l'abbaye de Saint-Trond*, ed. Charles Piot (2 vols. Brussels 1870–74) 1.93–94.

[64]Barbara Dodwell, *The Charters of Norwich Cathedral Priory*, Pipe Roll Society n.s. 40 (London 1974) 70.

[65]Avrom Saltman, *Theobald, Archbishop of Canterbury* (London 1956) 482.

[66]*Cart. Châteaudun* (n. 63 above) 12–14.

community of the chapter, but to specify their status as professional men. To give a modern analogy, it is the difference between distinguishing a man's function by calling him a schoolmaster, and distinguishing his status by calling him M.A. or Dr. It is quite likely that none of the *magistri* in the second class was actually teaching when he witnessed a charter with the title *magister*: certainly the majority of those I have mentioned were not.

This change of usage has both a particular and a general application. The particular application relates to the school of Chartres; the general, to the position of masters in society. We will take them in order:

(1) From the time of Clerval to the present day, the number of masters alleged to have been teaching at the cathedral school of Chartres has been greatly swollen by counting among them all witnesses in the charters of the bishop and chapter of Chartres who have the title *magister*. In view of what has just been said it is clear that we must distinguish. Those who appear with the designation *magister scolae* after their names were either teaching or in charge of the cathedral or corporate school; those who appear with the simple designation *magister* before their names were not necessarily or even normally engaged in teaching, still less were they teaching in the cathedral school. The most important example in the first category is a document of 1119–24 which contains a very full list of the canons of Chartres, apparently in order of precedence, beginning with the dean and continuing through precentor, archdeacons, *praepositi*, chancellor, and so on to simple canons without designation. About halfway down the list there appears *Bernardus scolae magister*, and we can be sure that he was in charge of the cathedral school at that date. In the second category there are several charters, most of them after 1140 but a few earlier, in which masters appear with the designation *magister* before their names. In these cases the title denoted a status, not a function, and it cannot be assumed that any of them was teaching at the time when he was given this title. The great majority of those who have traditionally been given a place among the masters of the school of Chartres belong to this class.[67]

(2) The general application of this shift of meaning relates to the position of masters in society. The evolution of the word *magister* provides a parallel to the evolution of the word *schola*. Just as the word *schola* takes on new meanings which shift the emphasis from the corporate community to the individual master, so the word *magister* takes on a new meaning which shifts the emphasis from the office-holder in a community to the status-holder in an ill-defined social setting. This new emphasis reflects the growing importance and general usefulness of men with a scholastic training, and it is associated with the breakdown of the old solidarity of the corporate cathedral chapter, which is very evident if we compare the witness lists of Chartres charters of about 1150 with those of thirty years earlier. It is associated also with the transfer of the functions of government from the chapter to the households of the bishop and other officials. The most important men in the households of the great often had no formal office: they were advisers, advocates, writers of letters, and so on. Their claim to consideration rested on their expertise, their mastery, and the title *magister* became the sufficient indication of their authority. It was the sign that they had the weight of the schools behind them, and this was a distinction which they clung to, even when they had risen very high in the hierarchy of the Church.

[67]The twelve masters between 1133 and 1165 listed by Häring as evidence that ''the cathedral employed a number of teachers'' (n. 1 above, 274–78) are in this category. See also the remarks of Giacone (n. 1 above, 33–38) on the *magistri* in the cartularies of Chartres.

Bibliographical Note

This essay has its origin in a controversy for which the necessary bibliographical references will be found in the footnotes and need not be repeated here. The essential foundations were laid in works which are still important: Reginald L. Poole, *Illustrations of the History of Medieval Thought in the Departments of Theology and Ecclesiastical Politics* (London 1884) and "The Masters of the Schools at Paris and Chartres in John of Salisbury's Time," EHR 35 (1920) 321–42, repr. in *Studies in Chronology and History*, ed. Austin L. Poole (Oxford 1934) 223–47; and A. Clerval, *Les écoles de Chartres au moyen âge* (Paris 1895). More broadly, the work of Hastings Rashdall, *The Universities of Europe in the Middle Ages* (2 vols. in 3 Oxford 1895) still retains its value in the revised edition by Frederick M. Powicke and Alfred B. Emden (3 vols. Oxford 1936); and Gérard M. Paré, A. Brunet, and P. Tremblay, *La renaissance du XIIe siècle: Les écoles et l'enseignement*, Publications de l'Institut d'études médiévales d'Ottawa 3 (Paris and Ottawa 1933) is still the best account of schools and teaching of the period as a whole. Émile Lesne, *Histoire de la propriété ecclésiastique en France* (6 vols. in 8 Lille 1910–43) vol. 5, *Les écoles de la fin du VIIIe siècle à la fin du XIIe*, contains a mass of information about masters and schools, which needs to be supplemented by the information in Nikolaus M. Häring, "Chartres and Paris Revisited," *Essays in Honour of Anton Charles Pegis*, ed. J. Reginald O'Donnell (Toronto 1974) 268–329.

The greatest addition to our knowledge of the schools in the first half of the twelfth century has come from the large amount of material that has become available in the last thirty years, illustrating the teaching that went on within lecture rooms and the issues which divided leading masters and their pupils from rival groups. On the general outline of theological teaching in this period, Joseph de Ghellinck, *Le mouvement théologique du XIIe siècle* (2nd ed. Bruges 1948; repr. 1969) is full of important ideas, as also is the relevant part of Smalley, *Study*. For the main theologians, Artur M. Landgraf, *Einführung in die Geschichte der theologischen Literatur der Frühscholastik* (Regensburg 1948) is a valuable guide, especially in the French edition, *Introduction à l'histoire de la littérature théologique de la scolastique naissante*, rev. Albert M. Landry, trans. Louis B. Geiger, Université de Montréal, Publications de l'Institut d'études médiévales 22 (Montreal and Paris 1973). Odon Lottin, *Psychologie et morale aux XIIe et XIIIe siècles* (6 vols. Louvain 1942–60) vols. 1 (2nd ed. 1957) 12–50, 4.12–89, and 5.9–472, has much valuable information about the ramifications of the theological schools of this period. Bernhard Bischoff, "Aus der Schule Hugos von St. Viktor," *Mittelalterliche Studien* (2 vols. Stuttgart 1966–67) 2.182–87 has analyzed a document of the highest interest for the procedures of the school of Hugh of St Victor; and Heinrich Weisweiler, "Zur Einflussphäre der 'Vorlesungen' Hugos von St. Viktor," *Mélanges Joseph de Ghellinck, S.J.* (2 vols. Gembloux 1951) 2.527–81 has traced the influence of these lectures on various works of the period. Nikolaus M. Häring has produced important editions of the various forms of commentary on Boethius's *De Trinitate*: (1) by Thierry of Chartres and his followers, in *Commentaries on Boethius, by Thierry of Chartres and His School*, Pontifical Institute of Mediaeval Studies, Studies and Texts 20 (Toronto 1971); (2) by Clarembald of Arras, in *Life and Works of Clarembald of Arras* (Toronto 1965) 63–186; and (3) by Gilbert of Poitiers, in J. Reginald O'Donnell, ed., *Nine Medieval Thinkers: A Collection of Hitherto Unedited Texts* (Toronto 1955) 23–98. These have added greatly to our knowledge of the introduction of Boethius's Trinitarian speculations into the theological teaching of the schools. Fr Häring's "Bischoff Gilbert II. von Poitiers (1142–54) und seine Erzdiakone," DA 21 (1965) 150–72 also provides valuable information about the later career of Gilbert of Poitiers and about the schools of his diocese.

For the *artes*, the works of Richard W. Hunt are of primary importance; see especially "Studies on Priscian in the Eleventh and Twelfth Centuries," M&RS 1 (1941–43) 194–231; "Studies on Priscian in the Twelfth Century, Part II," M&RS 2 (1950) 1–56; "The Introductions to the 'Artes' in the Twelfth Century," *Studia mediaevalia in honorem . . . Raymundi Josephi Martin* (Bruges 1948) 85–112; and "Hugutio and Petrus Helias," M&RS 2 (1950) 174-78. Edouard Jeauneau's *Guillaume de Conches: Glosae super Platonem* (Paris 1965) is the most important publication of lectures on the Arts in the first half of the twelfth century outside logic, and his "Note sur l'Ecole de Chartres," *Studi medievali* 3rd ser. 5 (1964) 821–65 contains much of value on the masters commonly associated with this school. In logic, the editions of Peter Abelard by Bernhard Geyer, *Peter Abaelards philosophische Schriften, I. Die Logica 'ingredientibus,'* BGPTMA 21 (4 vols. Münster 1919–33); by L. M. de Rijk, *Dialectica* (Assen 1956; 2nd ed. 1970); and by Lorenzo Minio-Paluello, *Twelfth Century Logic: Texts and Studies* (2 vols. Rome 1956–68) vol. 2, *Abaelardiana inedita,* are of outstanding importance. To these must be added volume 1 of the last-named work, containing *The Ars disserendi of Adam of Petit Point*.

More recently, K. M. Fredborg has published several studies of lectures on the Arts in CIMAGL, notably "The Dependence of Petrus Helias' *Summa super Priscianum* on William of Conches' *Glose super Priscianum*," 11 (1973) 1–57; "Petrus Helias on Rhetoric," 13 (1974) 31–41; "The Commentaries on Cicero's *De inventione* and *Rhetorica ad Herennium* by William of Champeaux," 17 (1976) 1–39. In the same periodical, N. J. Green-Pedersen has studied "William of Champeaux on Boethius' *Topics* according to Orleans Bibl. Mun. 226," 13 (1974) 13–30. For the immediately preceding period there is a fund of valuable information on the study of the Arts in Margaret Gibson, *Lanfranc of Bec* (Oxford 1978).

Masters at Paris from 1179 to 1215

A Social Perspective

John W. Baldwin

The twelfth-century renaissance, it has long been agreed, was the product of an educational revolution. At the beginning of the century, numerous urban schools appeared in Western Europe to challenge the supremacy the monastic schools had enjoyed since the early Middle Ages. These new schools dominated the intellectual scene until the beginning of the next century, when those at Bologna and Paris were transmuted into universities. The first half of the twelfth century, therefore, was the pioneer age, epitomized by heroes such as Irnerius and Gratian at Bologna, Anselm at Laon, and Peter Abelard, Gilbert of Poitiers, Hugh of St Victor, and Peter Lombard, all at Paris, who by genius, inventiveness, and improvisation drew crowds of students to their classes. As is characteristic of innovative eras, their techniques were fluid, their writings sparse—and the resulting picture fragmentary.

This essay treats the twelfth-century schools by examining the case of Paris from 1179 to 1215. These admittedly arbitrary chronological limits span the period between the great Third and Fourth Lateran Councils when the papacy attempted to regulate the educational regime of Latin Christendom. The beginning date coincides with the opening of the reign of Philip Augustus, a pivotal epoch in the development of the French monarchy, and with the death of Peter Comestor (1178), the last of the heroic figures at Paris. The end is marked by Robert of Courson's statutes for studies at Paris (1215) and by the unmistakable appearance of the university of masters at Paris, now believed to have crystallized between 1208 and 1215.[1] Whatever the competition among the early schools of Laon, Reims, Chartres, and elsewhere, without doubt Paris had emerged supreme over all others north of the Alps by the end of the twelfth century. Although the Parisian masters were more numerous at this time, they did not enjoy the celebrity of an Abelard among the earlier heroes,

[1] *Chartularium universitatis Parisiensis*, ed. Heinrich Denifle and Emile Chatelain (4 vols. + supp. Paris 1889–97, 1937–64) 1.78–80. For the authoritative study on the emergence of the university see Gaines Post, "Parisian Masters as a Corporation, 1200–1246" *Speculum* 9 (1934) 421–45, repr. in his *Studies in Medieval Legal Thought: Public Law and the State, 1100–1322* (Princeton 1964) 27–60. Also, Pierre Michaud-Quantin, *Universitas: Expressions du mouvement communautaire dans le moyen-âge latin*, L'église et l'état au moyen âge 13 (Paris 1970) 54–57.

nor of a Thomas Aquinas among the later university professors.[2] Of lesser stature, they nonetheless perfected, regularized, and institutionalized the educational techniques of their predecessors. As a consequence, the later masters were more self-conscious and produced more writings—albeit never enough to satisfy modern historians. This self-awareness was conservative in character, looking back to the heritage of the twelfth century, rather than enunciating the innovations of its times. For these reasons Paris at the turn of the century represents a point of vantage for examining the twelfth-century schools.

Until recently, medieval historians have been largely concerned with the internal organization and institutions of schools and universities.[3] In the past decade or two, however, scholars, particularly those of the early modern and later periods, have become increasingly interested in the broader context in which schools and universities emerged and grew. Using matriculation registers and comparable sources susceptible to quantification, they have studied the recruitment of students and employment of graduates to measure the inter-action between politics, society, and the institutions of learning.[4] Making no effort to improve upon the well-established institutional history of the schools, this essay will explore three lines of inquiry to seek new perspectives on the Parisian schools at the turn of the twelfth century. First, it will probe the in-fluence of royal policy and action in creating a setting favorable to the advance-ment of learning. Second, it will attempt to delineate the interaction between schools and society in a double direction: by tracing the patterns of re-cruitment it will indicate social pressures on the schools, and by studying the employment of the graduates in Church and state it will measure the schools' impact on society. Finally, it will explicate some of the Parisian masters' theories advanced to legitimate their educational contributions to society and to give voice to their newly achieved sense of professional identity.[5] Unfor-tunately, the poverty of documentation, even at the turn of the century, will impede these three explorations from advancing as far as in the early modern period. The nature of the sources will reduce this essay, for the most part, to observations not about students but about masters—and chiefly theological masters at that.

[2] See the conclusion of David Knowles, *The Evolution of Medieval Thought* (London and New York 1962) 183–84, 223–24.

[3] Charles Homer Haskins was an early exponent of this approach in his *Ren* and *The Rise of the Universities* (New York 1923). The classic study remains Hastings Rashdall, *The Universities of Europe in the Middle Ages*, rev. ed. Frederick M. Powicke and Alfred B. Emden (3 vols. Oxford 1936).

[4] See the programmatic statement of John E. Talbott, "The History of Education," *Daedalus* 100 (1971) 133–50.

[5] See the perspective of Jacques Le Goff, "Quelle conscience l'université médiévale a-t-elle eu d'elle-même?" *Beiträge zum Berufsbewusstsein des mittelalterlichen Menschen*, ed. Paul Wilpert, Miscellanea mediaevalia 3 (Berlin 1964) 15–29, repr. in Le Goff's *Pour un autre moyen âge: Temps, travail et culture en Occident, 18 essais* (Paris 1977) 181–97.

THE CAPETIAN CONTRIBUTION

In those days [1210] the study of letters flourished at Paris. We read that there was never in Athens or Egypt or any other place in the world such a multitude of scholars as those who dwelt at Paris for the sake of learning. This came about not only because of the admirable pleasantness of the place and the superabundance of all goods, but also because of the freedom and special rights of defense with which king Philip and his father [Louis VII] before him endowed the scholars. And so, although in that noble city one found copious and excellent teaching about not only the trivium and quadrivium, but also about questions of canon and Roman law, and about how the body is healed and health preserved, nevertheless they were taught Scripture and theological questions with more ardent zeal.[6]

Thus did the royal chronicler, William the Breton, extol the schools of Paris in the opening pages of his continuation to the official biography of Philip Augustus. Of the three advantages enjoyed by scholars, one, the abundance of goods, was due to the natural fertility of the Seine basin; but the other two, the favorableness of the site and the rights of the scholars, could be credited to the king.

When Philip Augustus transformed Paris into the true capital of the kingdom at the turn of the twelfth century, the scholars benefited as well. After Philip acquired Artois, Vermandois, and Normandy, the royal domains were too extensive for the central court to encompass in periodic tourneys. Now the prévôts and baillis reported three times a year to the capital and the flow of government was reversed to pass from the provinces to Paris.[7] To embellish his new residence and make it more commodious for the expanded work of government, the king refurbished the royal city by paving the principal streets and squares, by erecting a new covered market place, and by encircling the right bank with enlarged walls, all of which favored the quarters inhabited by royal administrators and townsmen.[8] For the benefit of the scholars who increasingly overflowed the Ile de la Cité onto the left bank, he likewise enclosed that part with protective walls extending as far as the church of Ste Geneviève, which had sheltered schools since the early twelfth century. While the king had shared the expenses of the right bank walls with the townsmen, he bore the great cost (7,200 *livres Paris*) of the left alone.[9] Besides providing external

[6]"In diebus illis studium litterarum florebat Parisius, nec legimus tantam aliquando fuisse scholarium frequentiam Athenis vel Egypti, vel in qualibet parte mundi quanta locum predictum studendi gratia incolebat. Quod non solum fiebat propter loci illius admirabilem amenitatem, et bonorum omnium superabundantem affluentiam, sed etiam propter libertatem et specialem prerogativam defensionis quam Philippus rex, et pater eius ante ipsum, ipsis scholaribus impendebant. Cum itaque in eadem nobilissima civitate non modo de trivio et quadruvio, verum et de questionibus iuris canonici et civilis, et de ea facultate que de sanandis corporibus et sanitatibus conservandis scripta est, plena et perfecta inveniretur doctrina, ferventiori tamen desiderio sacram paginam et questiones theologicas docebantur." *Oeuvres de Rigord et de Guillaume le Breton, historiens de Philippe-Auguste,* ed. Henri François Delaborde (2 vols. Paris 1882–85) 1.230.

[7]On the significance of this shift see C. Warren Hollister and John W. Baldwin, "The Rise of Administrative Kingship: Henry I and Philip Augustus," AHR 83 (1978) 867–905 at 891–99.

[8]*Oeuvres* (n. 6 above) 1.54, 70, 105.

[9]Louis Halphen, *Paris sous les premiers Capétiens (987–1223): Etude de topographie historique* (Paris 1909) 28.

security, these encircling fortifications also stimulated a construction boom within. William the Breton noted that the walls encouraged landowners to build dwellings on their fields and vineyards for rental to new inhabitants until the "whole city was filled with houses up to the walls."[10] Although modern demographers have not yet been able to agree on the size of the Parisian population during this period (25,000 to 50,000),[11] the walls of Paris enclosed more than twice as much area as was found in any other French city containing important schools.[12] The royal city, therefore, offered an impressive amount of protected urban space to masters and students, who comprised perhaps as much as ten percent of the population.

In addition to providing a favorable site, Philip and Louis (according to the chronicler William) especially endorsed the clerical privileges of scholars.[13] Masters and students depended for their chief support on their status as members of the clergy. Not only did they occasionally enjoy ecclesiastical prebends,[14] but they could honorably seek alms from laymen. The two earliest charitable foundations for the benefit of poor students, the Collège des Dix-huit and the Collège du Louvre, originated under Capetian auspices. The former was endowed by Jocius of London, a rich English merchant, whom king Louis favored with unusual privileges and placed under the exclusive protection of the royal court; the latter was founded by Robert, count of Dreux, Louis's brother and Philip's uncle.[15] Thus the French kings took part in

---

[10]". . . ut tota civitas usque ad muros plena domibus videretur." *Oeuvres* (n. 6 above) 1.240–41.

[11]Josiah C. Russell, *Late Ancient and Medieval Population*, Transactions of the American Philosophical Society n.s. 48.3 (Philadelphia 1958), and Michel Robelin, "Cités ou citadelles? Les enceintes romaines du bas-empire d'après l'exemple de Paris," *Revue des études anciennes* 53 (1951) 301–11 at 302, 310. These two studies are based on the area enclosed by the walls. A similar disparity (60,000–210,000) has developed among demographers regarding the turn of the thir-teenth and fourteenth centuries, for which a hearth census exists. See Ferdinand Lot, "L'état de paroisses et des feux de 1328," *Bibliothèque de l'Ecole des Chartes* 90 (1929) 51–107 and 256–315; Philippe Dollinger, "Le chiffre de population de Paris au XIVe siècle: 210,000 ou 80,000 habitants?" *Revue historique* 216 (1956) 35–44; Roger Mols, *Introduction à la démographie his-torique des villes d'Europe du XIVe au XVIIIe siècle* (3 vols. Louvain 1954–56); Raymond Cazelles, "La population de Paris avant la Peste Noir," *Académie des inscriptions et belles-lettres, Comptes rendues* (Dec. 1966) 539–50; Jacques Heers, "Les limites des méthodes statistiques pour les recherches de démographie médiévale," *Annales de démographie historique* (1968) 43–72.

[12]The walls of Philip Augustus enclosed 250–272 square hectares, as compared with those of Orléans (142 hectares in 1450), Laon (68 hectares in 1411), and Tours (60 hectares in 1368). Carlrichard Brühl, *Palatium und Civitas: Studien zur Profantopographie spätantiker Civitates vom 3. bis zum 13. Jahrhundert*, vol. 1: *Gallien* (Cologne 1975) 17, 48, 79, 107. F. L. Ganshof, *Etude sur le développement des villes entre Loire et Rhin au moyen âge* (Paris 1943) 59. Ganshof notes that in Flanders and Brabant, where urbanism was more advanced, cities occupied larger spaces: 430 hectares at Bruges in 1572 and 644 hectares at Ghent in 1397.

[13]Louis VII's reputation for favoring the schools at Paris was recorded by Walter Map, *De nugis curialium*, ed. Montague Rhodes James, Anecdota Oxoniensia 14 (Oxford 1914) 226; English translation by Frederick Tupper and M. B. Ogle (London and New York 1924) 283.

[14]See below, pp. 158–59.

[15]*Chartularium* (n. 1 above) 1.49–50, 11, 15–16. See the discussion in Rashdall (n. 3 above) 1.501–03. For Louis VII's protection of Jocius see Charles V. Langlois, "Formulaires de lettres du XIIe, du XIIIe, et du XIVe siècle," *Notices et extraits des manuscrits de la Bibliothèque Nationale* 34.1 (1891) 1–32 at 13–14.

establishing the system of colleges that became an important means for supporting students in the subsequent universities.[16]

In the opinion of William the Breton, however, Philip Augustus's chief contribution to the scholars of Paris was his championing of their "freedom (*libertatem*) and special rights (*specialem prerogativam defensionis*)." Here the chronicler was alluding to the events of 1200 and the famous royal charter that resulted from them. In that year a typical tavern brawl provoked an overreaction by the police, who in quelling the disturbance killed several students. Fearing that masters and students might desert the city in protest, the king severely punished the responsible royal official, and also confirmed in a solemn royal charter to all Parisian scholars the protections afforded by their clerical status.[17] The first provision, designated the *privilegium canonis*, protected the clerics' bodies from physical harm. By declaring their persons sacrosanct, it made any assault or bodily injury upon a cleric a sacrilege, punishable by automatic excommunication. Philip ordered the police and townsmen henceforth to respect this protection for all scholars. The second provision of the royal charter, the *privilegium fori*, rendered all masters immune to the sanctions of secular courts, by placing them totally under ecclesiastical jurisdiction. Since the Church courts could not administer corporal punishment, but were limited to degradation (stripping of clerical status) as the ultimate penalty, clerics guilty of capital crimes thus escaped the death penalty. The king guaranteed this privilege to masters and students, although he later modified it to make it possible to deal with serious clerical criminals.[18] By recognizing and lending his enforcement to clerical privileges, Philip significantly contributed to the scholars' protection at Paris. Along with the city walls, this royal favor afforded the academic population a modicum of security in a chaotic world. While conflict and adversity were not entirely eliminated, the scholars of Paris enjoyed a degree of safety and stability which encouraged the progress of academic thought and institutions.[19]

SCHOOLS AND SOCIETY

If the Capetians provided the security conducive to nurturing learning at Paris, the masters themselves naturally engendered the schools. They, not the

[16]Rashdall (n. 3 above) 1.498.

[17]The incident is narrated by Roger of Hoveden, *Chronica*, ed. William Stubbs, RS 51 (4 vols. London 1868–71) 4.120–21. See also Rashdall (n. 3 above) 1.294–98. For the charter: *Chartularium* (n. 1 above) 1.59–61, and *Recueil des actes de Philippe Auguste*, ed. Henri-François Delaborde et al. (3 vols. Paris 1916–66) 2.200–03. The authoritative study on clerical privileges is Robert Génestal, *Le privilegium fori en France du Décret de Gratien à la fin du XIVe siècle*, Bibliothèque de l'Ecole des hautes études, Sciences religieuses 35, 39 (2 vols. Paris 1921–24). See also Baldwin, *Masters* 1.141–49.

[18]Baldwin, *Masters* 1.148–49; *Recueil . . . de Philippe Auguste* (n. 17 above) 2.488–89.

[19]Alan B. Cobban, "Medieval Student Power," *Past and Present* 53 (1971) 28–66 at 63 has pointed to the importance of relative security in the development of medieval universities.

students, were the dominant influence in education. Masters possessed full authority over their students, whose privileges were limited to the clerical status they shared with their teachers.[20] Technically speaking, in the twelfth century a master (*magister*) was one who had permission to teach (*licentia docendi*). In our period this license was conferred in Paris solely by the chancellor of Notre-Dame.[21] We have little notion of how the chancellor judged a prospective master's qualifications, but in the 1170s pope Alexander III confirmed his exclusive right to confer the license and requested him to grant it without charge to all qualified candidates. The pope's goals were scarcely followed. In 1174, as an exception, the celebrated chancellor Peter Comestor was allowed to accept fees for granting licenses, and in 1212 his successor was still enjoying the privilege.[22]

Those masters duly licensed by the chancellor taught all subjects by two general techniques: lecturing and disputing. By lecturing (*lectio*) they expounded the authoritative texts of their subjects; by disputing (*disputatio*) they argued the difficult questions. With the cooperation of designated students known as *reportatores*, they wrote down their expositions in the form of commentaries and glosses, and their debates in the form of *questiones*. If they were theologians, preaching was a third teaching technique. By these common pedagogical practices they devised what has been called the "scholastic" method simply because it was exercised in the schoolroom.[23]

In 1213, as the Parisian masters began to organize in opposition to the chancellor over issuing licenses, they divided themselves into four subjects: theology (*theologia*), canon and Roman law (*decreta et leges*), medicine (*phisica*), and arts (*artes*).[24] In the thirteenth century these four groups evolved into four faculties, but observers such as Guy of Bazoches and Alexander Neckam noted that the four were already flourishing at Paris by the end of the twelfth century.[25] Gerald of Wales, one of the very few autobiographers from the period, claimed that he had studied all these subjects except medicine during his two sojourns at Paris, around 1165 and from 1176 to 1179.[26]

[20]*Chartularium* (n. 1 above) 1.79.

[21]On the *licentia docendi* see Philippe Delhaye, "L'organisation scolaire au XIIe siècle," *Traditio* 5 (1947) 211–68 at 253–60, and Gaines Post, "Alexander III, the *Licentia docendi* and the Rise of the Universities," *Anniversary Essays in Mediaeval History by Students of Charles Homer Haskins* (Boston 1929) 255–77. The abbot of Ste Geneviève may have exercised this right early in the twelfth century and certainly did by the third decade of the thirteenth century, but little evidence of his jurisdiction has survived in the interval. Heinrich Denifle, *Die Entstehung der Universitäten des Mittelalters bis 1400* (Berlin 1885; repr. Graz 1956) 667–70.

[22]*Chartularium* (n. 1 above) 1.8, 73.

[23]Gérard M. Paré, A. Brunet, and P. Tremblay, *La renaissance du XIIe siècle: Les écoles et l'enseignement*, Publications de l'Institut d'études médiévales d'Ottawa 3 (Paris and Ottawa 1933) 109–36 ("Les méthodes d'enseignement"); and Baldwin, *Masters* 1.90–116.

[24]*Chartularium* (n. 1 above) 1.76.

[25]Ibid. 1.56. Alexander Neckam, *De naturis rerum . . .* and *De laudibus divinae sapientiae*, ed. Thomas Wright, RS 34 (London 1863) 413–14, 453.

[26]*Giraldi Cambrensis Opera*, ed. John S. Brewer, James F. Dimock, and George F. Warner, RS 21 (8 vols. London 1861–91) 1.54–58.

These contemporaries implied that masters abounded at Paris in unusual numbers. Our task will be to probe beneath the laudatory generalizations and to study the actual recruitment of masters by identifying specifically those who taught the four subjects at Paris between 1179 and 1215. Our search will be limited to those actively teaching (in medieval terminology, *regent masters*), as distinguished from those merely residing in the royal city for other reasons. Such a study is limited by the nature and availability of the sources. From the outset it is clear that we must abandon a search for precise numbers and be satisfied with general impressions. No local census of active masters has survived; nor is there any indication that the exercise was considered worth the effort. While John of Salisbury, William of Tyre, and the author of the *Metamorphosis Goliae* had reminisced about famous masters they had known in the early twelfth century, at the turn of the century no contemporary (with one enigmatic exception)[27] produced an extensive catalogue of celebrated scholars. To be sure, chroniclers from near or distant vantages named individual masters exemplary for their fame in the schools or their success afterwards. Notable bishops or abbots, for example, were remembered to have once taught at Paris. While all of this evidence should be collected assiduously, it naturally suffers from the bias of notoriety and neglects the ordinary cases. To this evidence of contemporary observers, however, we can add the hundreds of academic treatises produced in the classrooms that occasionally identify the responsible teacher. Though conditioned by the vagaries of survival, such documents nonetheless offer evidence that is more trustworthy about those active in the schools.

The available evidence varies significantly according to subject. Every indication from the end of our period confirms that masters who taught the liberal arts of grammar, logic, and rhetoric were the most numerous. When in 1213 the masters contested the chancellor over granting licenses, the chancellor negotiated directly with all the theologians, lawyers, and doctors, but the masters of arts were so many that they were obliged to choose a committee of six. Because they taught the elementary subjects, the statutes of 1215 fixed their minimum age lower (21) than for the other disciplines. By the 1220s their numbers had so increased that they divided themselves into groups called nations.[28] Early in the twelfth century, as well, the masters of arts were numerous

---

[27]For the early reminiscences see below at n. 102. The exception is the poet Giles of Paris, who on 3 September 1200 presented to Prince Louis, the heir to the French throne, a long Latin poem, entitled the *Karolinus* and devoted to the glories of Charlemagne and the French monarchy. Shortly thereafter Giles attached to this poem a sequel called the *Captatio benivolentiae* in which, to answer the calumny that Paris had produced no great scholars, he named fifteen figures who defended the contemporary reputation of the royal city. Unfortunately, because of the florid and obscure verse only six of these figures can be identified with any certainty: Giles of Corbeil, Anselm, bishop of Meaux, Peter of Poitiers, the chancellor Hilduin, Stephen, bishop of Noyon, and William the Breton. For the latest edition and commentary see M. L. Colker, ed., "The 'Karolinus' of Egidius Parisiensis," *Traditio* 29 (1973) 199–325 at 317–21.

[28]For the dispute of 1213 and the statutes of 1215 see *Chartularium* (n. 1 above) 1.76–78. For the nations see Pearl Kibre, *The Nations in the Mediaeval Universities*, Publications of the Mediaeval Academy 49 (Cambridge Mass. 1948; repr. 1965) 16–17.

enough to form schools around dominating personalities. The grammarians, for example, were associated with William of Conches, Peter Helias, and Ralph of Beauvais.[29] The logicians, who cannot always be distinguished from the grammarians, clustered either on the Petit Pont, where they followed Adam of the Petit Pont, or on Mont Ste Geneviève, where they heard Peter Abelard, Alberic, or Robert of Melun.[30] Attaching their names to their glosses and academic treatises, they also attracted the attention of contemporaries.

By the last quarter of the century, when these dominant figures had died, the picture had changed. Their successors did not elicit notice from contemporaries. While the statutes of 1215 show that the basic textbooks remained the same (Priscian for grammar, Aristotle, both *logica vetus et nova*, for logic),[31] the masters of arts ceased to identify themselves in their treatises. Of all the commentaries on Priscian, for example, only one author, the shadowy Petrus Hispanus, can be named.[32] It is true that two grammarians, Alexander of Villedieu and Everard of Béthune, whose treatises became authoritative in the later Middle Ages, flourished in this period, but their writings cannot be connected with Paris.[33] Among the logicians virtually no name surfaces at Paris between 1179 and 1215, since almost all treatises that can be dated from the period are anonymous.[34] Among those classified as rhetoricians only Matthew of Vendôme can be associated with Paris, in the decade ca. 1175–85; but his major work, the *Ars versificatoria*, was written at Orléans before he came to Paris.[35]

If at best only eleven masters of arts can be identified at Paris from 1179 to 1215 from contemporary observers and surviving writings, recent studies on medieval grammar and logic attest that work continued in these fields

---

[29]Richard W. Hunt, "Studies on Priscian in the Eleventh and Twelfth Centuries," M&RS 1 (1941–43) 194–231 and 2 (1950) 1–56.

[30]Lorenzo Minio-Paluello, "The 'Ars Disserendi' of Adam of Balsham 'Parvipontanus,'" M&RS 3 (1954) 116–69. L. M. de Rijk, "Some New Evidence on Twelfth Century Logic: Alberic and the School of Mont Ste Geneviève (Montani)," *Vivarium* 4 (1966) 1–57; idem, *Logica modernorum: A Contribution to the History of Early Terminist Logic* (2 vols. in 3 Assen 1962–67), esp. 2.1.281–91. See the observations of Geoffrey of St Victor ca. 1178: *Fons philosophiae*, ed. Pierre Michaud-Quantin, Analecta mediaevalia Namurcensia 8 (Namur 1956) 43–45.

[31]*Chartularium* (n. 1 above) 1.78.

[32]See Appendix for all regent masters who can be identified at Paris from 1179 to 1215. Hereafter those masters contained in the Appendix will not be cited in the footnotes unless additional information is furnished.

[33]Although Alexander studied at Paris, he taught in Brittany, where he wrote his famous *Doctrinale* around 1199. The career of Everard of Béthune, who wrote the *Graecismus* (before 1212), is too shadowy to be located anywhere. See Manitius 3.756–59, 747–51.

[34]The influential *Ars Meliduna* was most likely written before 1179. See de Rijk, *Logica modernorum* (n. 30 above) 2.1.279–90, and Richard W. Hunt, "*Absoluta:* The *Summa* of Petrus Hispanus on Priscianus Minor," *Historiographia linguistica* 2 (1975) 1–23 at 14, 18–19. The following anonymous treatises may only with difficulty be attributed to Paris between 1179 and 1215: *Fallacie Parvipontane*, in de Rijk, *Logica modernorum* 1.152; *Introductiones dialetice Parisienses*, ibid. 2.1.446–47; *Dialectica Monacensis*, ibid. 2.1.414; *Summe Metenses*, ibid. 2.1.451–52. The *Fallacie magistri Willelmi* might be attributed to William de Montibus. See ibid. 2.1.34–35.

[35]Faral, *Les arts poétiques* 2, 3, 14.

throughout the period.[36] Since modern scholarship on the medieval liberal arts is not so advanced as on other disciplines, it is possible that more grammatical and logical treatises will be uncovered; but it is not likely that new and important names will emerge. We know that the newly rediscovered works of Aristotle on physics and metaphysics became available at Paris precisely during this period. These writings may have distracted the masters of arts' attention from the more traditional texts and made the turn of the century a period of consolidation rather than innovation in grammar and logic.[37]

Surviving canonistic treatises attest to a flourishing group of canon lawyers at Paris from the middle of the twelfth century.[38] At the eve of our period (1176–79) the seldom reticent Gerald of Wales offered a grandiloquent account of his lectures on the *Decretum* in the school of Matthew of Angers before his teacher left to attend the Third Lateran Council and be elevated to the rank of cardinal.[39] At the same time Sicard of Cremona began his *Summa* to the *Decretum* at Paris, before he departed for Mainz to join other Parisian masters whom the archbishop of Mainz attracted with prebends. Undoubtedly interest in canon law at the royal capital was encouraged by the arrival in 1176 of Stephen of Tournai, newly elected abbot of Ste Geneviève.[40] Trained in the celebrated canon law school of Bologna, Stephen had already composed his influential *Summa decreti* before his appearance in Paris. It is possible that his duties as abbot prevented him from actively teaching in the schools, but his letters and sermons reveal lively interest in academic affairs before he left in 1191 to become bishop of Tournai. That canon law continued to thrive is indicated by four influential works on the *Decretum* datable to this period; like most of the writings of the Parisian canonists, however, they are anonymous.[41] The only names that emerge designate writers of minor treatises such as Everard of Ypres, Peter of Louveciennes, and Rodoicus and those mentioned

---

[36]Geoffrey L. Bursill-Hall, *Speculative Grammars of the Middle Ages: The Doctrine of Partes Orationis of the Modistae* (The Hague 1971) 29–30 and "Teaching Grammars of the Middle Ages: Notes on the Manuscript Tradition," *Historiographia linguistica* 4 (1977) 1–29 at 1–2. De Rijk, *Logica modernorum* (n. 30 above) 1.19 and 2.1.513. I should like to thank my colleague Nancy Struever for bibliographic help on the grammarians and logicians.

[37]The ecclesiastical opposition to the teaching of Aristotle's *Physics* and *Metaphysics* at the Council of Paris in 1210 and in the statutes of 1215 is well known. *Chartularium* (n. 1 above) 1.70, 78–79. See, for example, the discussions in Martin Grabmann, *I divieti ecclesiastici di Aristotele sotto Innocenzo III e Gregorio IX*, Miscellanea historiae pontificiae 5.7 (Rome 1941) 5–69 and Knowles (n. 2 above) 226–27.

[38]Stephan Kuttner, "Les débuts de l'école canoniste française," *Studia et documenta historiae et iuris* 4 (1938) 193–204 and *Repertorium* 168–207. Gabriel LeBras, Jacqueline Rambaud, and Charles Lefebvre, *L'âge classique, 1140–1378: Sources et théorie du droit*, Histoire du droit et des institutions de l'Eglise en Occident 7 (Paris 1965) 282–86.

[39]*Giraldi Cambrensis Opera* (n. 26 above) 1.45–48.

[40]Stephan Kuttner and Eleanor Rathbone, "Anglo-Norman Canonists of the Twelfth Century," *Traditio* 7 (1949–51) 279–358 at 293.

[41]For example: *Summa "Tractaturus magister"* (1175–91), *Summa "Omnis qui iuste iudicat,"* formerly called *Summa Lipsiensis* (ca. 1186), *Summa "Animal est substantia,"* formerly *Summa Bambergensis* (1206–10), *Apparatus "Ecce vicit leo"* (1202–10). Kuttner, *Repertorium* 184–87, 196–98, 206–07, 59–66.

in English sources such as Odo of Dover, Honorius of Richmond, Richard of Mores, and Simon of Southwell.[42] Because of their penchant for anonymity, therefore, the Parisian canonists left little trace of their identities. Our search has yielded only ten names.

Even less information survives about the Romanists and the physicians. The major canonistic treatises from the early thirteenth century show expertise in Roman law, but no name of a master teaching that subject has surfaced during our period. When pope Honorius III forbade the teaching of Roman law at the French capital in 1219, he did not suppress an active discipline.[43] Similarly, the instruction of medicine has left only faint traces at Paris. Guy of Bazoches omitted it from his description of the city at the beginning of the period, and the faculty never attained prominence in the thirteenth century.[44] One important master, however, was noticed by contemporary observers: Giles of Corbeil, whose teaching at Paris produced medical treatises and stimulated disciples to continue his work. Apart from Giles and one possible disciple other teachers of medicine have not yet come to light.[45]

In contrast to the masters of arts, law, and medicine, the theologians can be identified in significantly greater numbers. In his entry for the year 1194 the chronicler Otto of St Blaise remarked that Peter the Chanter, Alan of Lille, and Prepositinus were all active masters. These three represented the major doctrinal groups descended from the celebrated schools of St Victor, Gilbert of Poitiers, and Peter Lombard of the early twelfth century.[46] From available sources we can identify at least twenty-four regent masters of theology active in Paris from 1179 to 1215, nineteen of whom left academic writings. By comparison to their colleagues the theologians produced a veritable mountain of

---

[42]A *magister Albericus decretista* appears in a Paris charter of 1190. Dietrich Lohrmann, *Papsturkunden in Frankreich*, n.s. 7: *Nördliche Ile-de-France und Vermandois*, Abh Göttingen 3rd ser. 95 (Göttingen 1976) 617. He was probably the same as the *magister Albertus Lumbardus* who appears frequently between 1185 (Cartulary of St Germain l'Auxerrois, Paris, Archives Nationales LL 387, fol. 40v) and 1191 (*Cartulaire de l'église Notre-Dame de Paris*, ed. B. Guérard, Collection de documents inédits sur l'histoire de France [4 vols. Paris 1850] 1.45, 130). But we have no evidence that this master taught at Paris.

[43]*Chartularium* (n. 1 above) 1.90–93. See Baldwin, *Masters* 1.86–87.

[44]*Chartularium* (n. 1 above) 1.56; Rashdall (n. 3 above) 1.321–23, 435–37.

[45]Medical doctors are frequently found in the charters of Paris, but with no indication that they taught. For example: *magister Alexander medicus quondam canonicus Sancti Marcelli* (1195–1216) in the Cartulary of St Victor, Paris, Archives Nationales LL 145, fol. 29v. Karl Sudhoff, "Salerno, Montpellier und Paris um 1200," *Archiv für Geschichte der Medizin* 20 (1928) 51–62 at 60–61 has found some evidence for a school around Giles of Corbeil.

[46]Otto of St Blaise, *Chronicon*, ed. Roger Wilmans, MGH SS 20.326. The twelfth-century theologians have been classified largely in terms of doctrinal schools. See the fundamental study of Artur M. Landgraf, *Einführung in die Geschichte der theologischen Literatur der Frühscholastik, unter dem Gesichtspunkte der Schulenbildung* (Regensburg 1948), French ed. rev. Albert M. Landry, trans. Louis B. Geiger, *Introduction à l'histoire de la littérature théologique de la scolastique naissante*, Université de Montréal, Publications de l'Institut d'études médiévales 22 (Montreal and Paris 1973). Landgraf (159–67) classifies Peter the Chanter under the school of St Victor. Whether or not this is entirely accurate, the Chanter did represent a flourishing school to be distinguished from the descendants of Gilbert of Poitiers and Peter Lombard.

writings. The outstanding example was Stephen Langton, who wrote lectures on every book of the Bible, some in two to four versions, and innumerable theological questions, and preached hundreds of sermons during his Parisian career from the 1180s to 1206.[47] Nor was he an isolated case, because Peter the Chanter, Alan of Lille, Prepositinus, Peter of Poitiers, and Simon of Tournai have all bequeathed comparable quantities of academic works.[48] These two dozen identified masters, moreover, constitute a good statistical sampling of the total field of teaching theologians. In a letter of 1207 congratulating the bishop of Paris for the renown of theological studies in his city, pope Innocent III limited the number of regent theologians to eight, so that the quality of instruction would not be diluted.[49] Whether or not the restriction was respected, we can see that twenty-four is a representative number of a group that probably never exceeded twelve at one time over a period of thirty-five years.[50]

Indubitably less numerous than the masters of arts, but roughly on a par with the canonists, why were the theologians more visible? Not only were they noticed by chroniclers and other contemporary observers, but they were willing to be named in their works. Except for the greater prestige of theology over the arts, which were seen as mere handmaidens to the sacred science, and except for papal promotion of theology over law at Paris, the reasons escape us.[51] Nonetheless, as a group, the masters of theology offer the best insight into the social composition of the Parisian masters.

THE RECRUITMENT OF MASTERS

Despite the paucity of the evidence, the total of forty-seven names of regent masters at Paris from 1179 to 1215, if employed selectively and critically, illuminates two characteristics of the composition of this group: their geographic and social origins. Geographic origins are most readily discernible because medieval nomenclature nearly always discloses the place of origin. Table 1 summarizes the statistics on geographic origins derived from the Appendix to this study. In our group the origins of 89 percent (42/47) of the masters can be determined.[52] From those whose origins can be ascertained, our data yield two reasonably certain conclusions. The first is that between 24 and 28 percent of the regent masters originated from the French royal domain or lands near.[53] In the preindustrial era when mobility was difficult and most educa-

---

[47]See Baldwin, *Masters* 1.29–31 for a summary of research on Langton.

[48]Ibid. 1.12–16, 43–46.

[49]*Chartularium* (n. 1 above) 1.65.

[50]In 1218 pope Honorius III declared that Innocent's limitation was no longer observed: ibid. 1.85. See Rashdall (n. 3 above) 1.382.

[51]On the arts as handmaidens of theology see Baldwin, *Masters* 1.78–80. For the preeminence of theology at Paris, see ibid. 1.86–91.

[52]Stephen of Tournai is a rare case whose name (derived from his episcopal post) falsified his place of origin (Orléans).

[53]This proportion is derived from all of the samples: all masters whose origins can be determined: 10/42 = 24%; all masters whose origins can be determined and whose writings have sur-

Table 1

GEOGRAPHIC ORIGINS OF REGENT MASTERS AT PARIS, 1179-1215

	Arts	Law	Medicine	Theology	Total
Royal Domain	2	2 (2)	1 (1)	5 (4)	10 (7)
Normandy	1	-	-	-	1
Flanders	-	1 (1)	-	2 (2)	3 (3)
Poitou and Blois	2	-	-	3 (3)	5 (3)
England	5 (1)	5 (3)	1 (1)	5 (4)	16 (9)
Denmark	-	-	-	1	1
Provence	-	-	-	1	1
Spain	1 (1)	-	- ·	-	1 (1)
Italy	-	1 (1)	-	3 (3)	4 (4)
Undetermined	-	1 (1)	-	4 (3)	5 (4)
Total	11 (2)	10 (8)	2 (2)	24 (19)	47 (31)

( ) = masters who left writings

tional institutions drew preponderantly from their immediate hinterland, this is a significantly small proportion.[54] Three quarters of the Parisian masters, therefore, came from areas beyond the lands of which Paris was the natural center. The international character of the Parisian masters, of course, had been established since the first half of the twelfth century, when Peter Lombard arrived from Italy, Hugh of St Victor from Germany, and Robert of Melun and Adam of the Petit Pont from England. This trend continued through the turn of the century, when masters were drawn from the distant provinces of the French kingdom (Normandy, Flanders, Poitou) and from beyond the borders (Provence, Spain, Italy, England, and Denmark). The only surprising omission is the imperial lands of Germany—especially when a hostel of German students is well attested at Paris in 1200.[55]

Although the figures are too sparse to make meaningful comparisons among most foreign-born masters, our second conclusion reveals the preponderance of English masters. Thirty-eight percent (16/42) of the masters whose origins can be determined came from England. This figure is undoubt-

vived: 7/27 = 26%; all theologians whose origins can be determined: 5/18 = 28%; all theologians whose origins can be determined and whose writings have survived: 4/16 = 25%. Those lands counted are Louveciennes, St Denis, Corbeil, Bène, Vendôme, Orléans, Noyon, Beauvais, and Courlandon.

[54] Studies of early modern universities reveal that students were recruited largely from the vicinity. See Lawrence Stone, "The Size and Composition of the Oxford Student Body, 1580-1910," *The University in Society*, ed. idem (2 vols. Princeton 1974) 1.3-110 at 35-37, and Richard L. Kagan, *Students and Society in Early Modern Spain* (Baltimore 1974) 202-03 and "Law Students and Legal Careers in Eighteenth-Century France," *Past and Present* 68 (1975) 38-72 at 48-50. The geographical extent of recruitment of professors has not received the same attention.

[55] The hostel was involved in the riot of 1200. See p. 142 above.

edly exaggerated by the large number and accessibility of English sources.[56] If
we count, therefore, only those masters whose presence in Paris is attested by
academic writing, 33 percent (9/27) were English, and even if we limit our sample to the theologians the result remains high (25 percent: 4/16). A larger
proportion (25 to 38 percent) of the Parisian masters, therefore, came from
England than from the French royal domain and its environs. Some of this English preponderance can be explained by the conflicts between the English kings
and their churchmen that drove English clerics to the continent. During our
period, for example, the great interdict against king John (1208–13) emptied
England of its high prelacy, but the presence at Paris of only one of our regent
masters, Richard le Poer, can be accounted for in this way.[57] More than any
other group, therefore, English masters considered the schools of Paris to be
their own. When the masters of arts divided themselves into four nations in
the second decade of the thirteenth century, it is clear why the English
dominated and gave their name to that nation which drew from northern and
eastern Europe.[58]

Our sample yields less readily the social background of the regent masters.
To assess this influence we must know the individual biographies, which were
influenced by notoriety and later success. Here extremes such as high or low
birth were noteworthy. Only 16 (34 percent) indicate their social origins, and
no preponderant concentration emerges. Four were thought to be "lowly
born," either by self-confession or by contrast with subsequent success.[59]
Three were of illegitimate birth—meaning sons of priests—revealed when they
aspired to the prelacy and required a papal dispensation for defect of birth.[60]
Only one, an Italian, can be assigned to a town family.[61] Five came from
families of local knights and two from the ranks of local *domini*, possibly
castellans. One, the Dane Anders Sunesen, came from a family within the
highest ranks of aristocracy.[62] These figures are not large enough to make com-

---

[56]Not only were chronicles and other contemporary sources plentiful in England, but they
have also been well exploited by modern scholars for prosopographical purposes. See, for example,
Alfred B. Emden, *A Biographical Register of the University of Oxford to A.D. 1500* (3 vols. Oxford 1957–59).

[57]See C. R. Cheney, "King John and the Papal Interdict," *Bulletin of the John Rylands
Library* 31 (1948) 295–317 at 311.

[58]This conclusion, with examples mainly from the early twelfth century, is presented by Astrik
L. Gabriel in "English Masters and Students during the Twelfth Century," *Garlandia: Studies in
the History of the Mediaeval University* (Notre Dame Ind. 1969) 1–37.

[59]Giles of Corbeil asserted his lowly origins in his writings, and Alexander Neckam declared
that he was "milk brother" to king Richard, which makes his mother a wet-nurse. Local chroniclers characterized Peter of Corbeil as *de humili plebe* and John of Cella as *ex mediocri prosapia
oriundus*.

[60]The canonist Honorius and the theologians Richard le Poer and Thomas of Chobham.

[61]Sicard, from the family of Casellanus, Casalenus, or De Casalaschis of Cremona. Alan of
Lille and Simon of Tournai may have come from those towns since urbanism was more developed
in Flanders. It is less likely that William, Geoffrey, and Peter came from the town of Poitiers than
from the region of Poitou.

[62]Local knights' families: Hilduin, whose brother Simon of St Denis was canon of Notre-
Dame; Peter the Chanter from Hodenc-en-Bray in the Beauvaisis; Stephen Langton from Langton

parisons among the groups, but the major categories of society are here represented. At least half came from the landed "feudal" segment of society, but only one from baronial rank or above. The low percentage of masters drawn from the high aristocracy is fairly certain, because such status would most likely have been noticed.[63] Since a large proportion of the regent masters were successful in their careers and attained posts of prelacy in the Church, we are led to the conclusion that teaching at Paris was regarded as a vehicle of upward social mobility to improve one's standing in society.

THE EMPLOYMENT OF GRADUATES

In addition to reflecting recruitment, our sample of forty-seven regent masters at Paris sheds light on their employment. Since the subsequent careers of 83 percent (39/47) are known to us, the data are equally rich for this purpose. But here the biases of the sources are the most detrimental. Quite naturally, successful masters became better known than unsuccessful ones. This bias may be partially corrected by using the names of those who left writings from their teaching in Paris. (Sixty-seven percent [26/39] of those whose careers are known left academic treatises.) I shall use both figures, therefore, with the second as a modifier. It should also be remembered that careers both progressed and overlapped. Peter of Corbeil, for example, advanced successively as canon of Paris, archdeacon of York, bishop of Cambrai, and archbishop of Sens, and Stephen Langton was both archbishop of Canterbury and cardinal at the same time. For statistical purposes, therefore, I shall count only the last or most honorific post. Table 2 represents a résumé of the figures.

The weight of surviving evidence is clear: teaching at Paris often led to a high position in the Church. Forty-six (18/39) to 38 percent (10/26) of the regent masters became prelates (cardinals, archbishops, bishops, abbots, or priors); four of these became cardinals and twelve archbishops or bishops. A slightly smaller proportion (36 percent [14/39] to 35 percent [9/26]) were employed as dignitaries of collegiate chapters (dean, chanter, archdeacon, *officialis*, and chancellor). Among these positions those of *officialis* and archdeacon required the greatest legal expertise. That only four of our masters were at any time *officiales*, and four archdeacons, probably is due to the underrepresentation of the study of law. Eighteen (7/39) to 27 percent (7/26) ended their careers as monks or canons (holding only their prebends) without promotion to office. Everard of Ypres's and Alan of Lille's entry into the

---

by Wragby, Lincolnshire; William de Montibus, whose family from Wigford did not live in Lincoln, but outside. Local *domini*: Gerald of Wales, whose family were castellans at Manorbier, Pembrokeshire, Wales; and Michael of Corbeil/Courlandon, whose uncle was Adam from the family of Courlandon. Magnates: Anders Sunesen's father, Sune Ebbesen, was royal marshal and one of the wealthiest landholders in Denmark.

[63]In the seventeenth century, antiquarians and genealogists attempted to connect Michael and Peter of Corbeil with the family of the counts of Corbeil, but no medieval evidence has yet been found to support these claims. Baldwin, *Masters* 2.34–36.

Table 2

SUBSEQUENT CAREERS OF REGENT MASTERS AT PARIS, 1179–1215

	Arts	Law	Medicine	Theology	Total
Cardinal	-	-	-	4 (4)	4 (4)
Archbishop	-	-	-	4 (2)	4 (2)
Bishop	2	2 (2)	-	1	5 (2)
Abbot and Prior	2	1 (1)	-	2 (1)	5 (2)
Dean or Chanter	1	2 (2)	-	1 (1)	4 (3)
Archdeacon	-	1	-	-	1
Official	1	2 (1)	-	1 (1)	4 (2)
Chancellor	-	-	-	5 (4)	5 (4)
Prebendary	1 (1)	-	1 (1)	1 (1)	3 (3)
Monk	1 (1)	1 (1)	-	2 (2)	4 (4)
Undetermined	3	1 (1)	1 (1)	3 (3)	8 (5)
Total	11 (2)	10 (8)	2 (2)	24 (19)	47 (31)

( ) = masters who left writings

Cistercian order may well have been the result of genuine religious vocation,[64] but the three who ended as canon-prebendaries probably remained teachers for the rest of their lives. It was certainly true of master Simon of Tournai, who is a clear example of a career failure—a failure spectacular enough to attract widespread notice. Vain, belligerent, and outspoken, Simon was suspected of heretical opinions. When he ended his days felled by a stroke that deprived him of memory and speech, his fate was attributed to divine judgment.[65]

This sample indicates that the preferred way to remain a teacher was to become chancellor of the chapter. Of the six chancellors (five at Paris) only one advanced further into the prelacy. Teaching at Paris, therefore, was clearly (82 to 73 percent) rewarded by preferment in the Church. Again, because of scarce information for arts, medicine, and law, it is impossible to compare competition among the disciplines for posts outside the schools. The Parisian theologians, however, complained that their medical and legal colleagues were practicing the "lucrative sciences"—an epithet that became a current topos.[66] The allegations undoubtedly referred to the doctors' and lawyers' ability to charge high fees, but if we examine the theologians' own chances for promotion to high position, we can see that they had little reason for complaint. In our period 52 percent (11/21) to 43 percent (7/16) obtained prelacies and 33

---

[64]Peter the Chanter's becoming a Cistercian at the end of his life was a preparation for death. See Baldwin, *Masters* 1.11.

[65]*Les Disputationes de Simon de Tournai*, ed. Joseph Warichez, Spicilegium sacrum Lovaniense 12 (Louvain 1932) xviii–xxiii. Giles of Corbeil probably remained canon of Notre-Dame at Paris throughout his life.

[66]Baldwin, *Masters* 1.84–86.

percent (7/21) to 37 percent (6/16) became chapter dignitaries. Robert of Courson, a successful theologian himself, ruefully admitted that one could study theology not for God's sake but for advancement to the prelacy.[67]

The ultimate goal of the Parisian teachers was, of course, to train students who upon completion of their studies assumed the title of master whether they actually proceeded to teach or not. Once these graduates left the schools, however, we have no way of distinguishing where they studied nor in what subjects—unless, by chance, we know their biographical details. But these products of the schools can be readily identified within society because they almost invariably preceded their names with the title of *magister*, unless they also claimed a more honorific dignity such as bishop, abbot, dean, and so on.[68] In legal documents they rarely omitted the master's designation.[69] The prestige of the academic title at the eve of our period is well illustrated in a piece of humor composed by the English cleric Nigel Wireker about an ass, Daun Burnel, who spent ten years studying arts and theology at Paris before proceeding to law at Bologna. His goal was to be called *magister*:

> And so I'll have the title of "Master" placed
> Before Burnel, and I'll thus be called.
> If one should say Burnel, but perchance
> Leave "Master" off, he'll be my public foe.
> If thus my famous title goes before,
> I'll be a public speaker without peer.
> The Senate and people will rush forth,
> The rank and file will cry, "the master's here!"
> The bishops and monks will all agree
> To rule themselves by my advice and help.[70]

---

[67]"Eadem est obiectio de theologo, qui alia causa principali legit quam propter deum, qui, si intentionem ferat principaliter ad hoc quod promoveatur ad prelationem, mentalem committit simoniam." Robert of Courson, *Summa* VIII 9, BN lat 14524 fol. 37va.

[68]This includes all clerics who called themselves *magistri*, with the exception of heads of houses of knights Templars, of lepers, and of hospitals. Any layman using the title would generally be an artisan.

[69]For example, of the 26 occurrences of the name of master Roger the Norman known to me in the Norman sources only two omit the title of master. See John W. Baldwin, "A Debate at Paris over Thomas Becket between Master Roger and Master Peter the Chanter," *Studia Gratiana* 11 (1967) 119–32 at 124–25.

[70]Sicque meum nomen alio praeeunte Magister
Burnellus dicar nomine reque simul.
Si quis Burnellum non addens forte Magistrum
Dixerit, ille mihi publicus hostis erit.
Nominis ergo mei fama praeeunte celebri,
Subsequar orator publicus, absque pari.
Obvius adveniet populo comitante senatus;
Plebs ruet et dicet, "Ecce Magister adest!"
Praesulis et fratrum concors sententia, nostro
Se volet auxilio consilioque regi.

Nigel Wireker, *Speculum stultorum*, in *The Anglo-Latin Satirical Poets and Epigrammatists of the Twelfth Century*, ed. Thomas Wright, RS 59 (2 vols. London 1872) 1.3–145 at 53; *The Book of Daun Burnel the Ass*, trans. Graydon W. Regenos (Austin Tex. 1959) 73–74.

Because of the prominence of their titles, therefore, we can readily trace the penetration of masters into contemporary society.

The production of masters by the schools of Western Europe, including those of Paris, gained steadily throughout the twelfth century.[71] Masters were increasingly noticed by contemporary observers, and they began to appear in witness lists to charters and other legal documents—rarely in the early part of the century, in steadily growing numbers throughout the second half. By the end of the twelfth century, before the witness lists began to disappear in France, masters were frequently found in ecclesiastical charters.[72] As is confirmed by the subsequent employment of the regent professors at Paris, masters found service most readily in the Church. At the level of the episcopacy the number of masters who became bishops in France increased from three percent under king Louis VII (1137–79) to 13–16 percent under Philip Augustus (1179–1223), whose reign roughly corresponds to our period.[73] In the same period the English sees elected 29 percent of their bishops from the ranks of masters.[74] Since the bishop occupied the pinnacle of diocesan organization, his position may not be entirely representative. Yet masters penetrated steadily into the lower levels of episcopal entourages and chapters as well. At the turn of the century the witness lists on the charters of French bishops and chapters often included one or two masters in attendance; in English charters four to eight masters characteristically attested.[75] Studies of the composition of individual chapters also demonstrate the significant presence of masters. The chapter of Laon from 1179 to 1223, for example, contained 20 percent masters. Separate surveys of prebends taken in 1217 and

[71]In 1965–66 I attempted a quantitative study of the employment of learned personnel by the monarchy and Church of France at the turn of the twelfth and thirteenth centuries. The provisional results were published as "*Studium et regnum*: The Penetration of University Personnel into French and English Administration at the Turn of the Twelfth and Thirteenth Centuries," *L'enseignement en Islam et en Occident au moyen âge*, Colloques internationaux de La Napoule 1, ed. George Makdisi, Dominique Sourdel, and Janine Sourdel-Thomine (Paris 1977) 199–215 (= *Revue des études islamiques* 44 [1976] hors série 13). The chronological limits (1180–1223) of that study slightly exceed those of the present chapter.

[72]A list of approximate dates when the witness lists disappeared from French episcopal charters is offered in ibid. 212. They tended to disappear at later dates in England.

[73]For Louis VII: 8/300 = 3% of all the bishops of the kingdom. Data from Marcel Pacaut, *Louis VII et les élections épiscopales dans le royaume de France* (Paris 1957) 109. For Philip Augustus: 17/107 = 16% of the regalian bishops. Of these, 5/11 = 45% were from Normandy after the conquest of the duchy. It is apparent that the Norman bishoprics perpetuated the English pattern. If we reduce the regalian bishoprics by the Norman sees, the proportion becomes 12/96 = 13%. Data supplied from my forthcoming study of Philip Augustus. The increase of masters who became bishops continued into the reign of Louis IX: 37/90 = 41% of the regalian bishops. Data from Fernando A. Pico, "The Bishops of France in the Reign of Louis IX (1226–70)" (Ph.D. diss. Johns Hopkins University 1970) 245–323. Here I have counted only those found in the regalian sees included in the computations for Philip Augustus.

[74]10/35 = 29% of the bishops elected from 1180 to 1223. Data from John Le Neve, *Fasti Ecclesiae Anglicanae, 1066–1300*, ed. Diana Greenway (3rd ed. 3 vols. London 1968–77). Data are available only for the monastic cathedrals, plus London and Lincoln. When the other secular cathedrals are added, the proportion of masters may rise.

[75]See the tables in Baldwin, "*Studium*" (n. 71 above) 212–13.

1227 by the canons themselves produced 12 percent and 17 percent masters.[76] Although more difficult to ascertain, the number of masters in the chapter of Paris was roughly the same as at Laon.[77] In England, Hugh of Avallon, bishop of Lincoln (1186–1200), was especially eager to have his diocese served by well-trained men. He therefore searched the schools of England and other countries for masters on whom he conferred prebends. His policy undoubtedly contributed to staffing the chapter of Lincoln with 42 percent masters from 1180 to 1223, but it was not unusual among the English cathedrals. The chapters of London and York contained 47 percent and 46 percent masters during the same period. Two surveys of canons made at Salisbury in 1222 and 1225 yielded 27 percent and 31 percent masters. The entourage of the archbishop of Canterbury from 1193 to 1205 may have comprised as many as 63 percent masters.[78]

While these scattered examples from France and England demonstrate the significant presence of masters within the episcopal entourages and chapters, they do not shed light on their precise functions. One post created at the turn of the century appears to have been designed especially for men with academic training: that of the *officialis*, who served as the bishop's chief legal officer and attested with his seal legal documents of the diocese. Appearing first in 1180 at Beauvais and then throughout the French and English bishoprics, these positions were filled immediately or shortly thereafter by masters who styled themselves *magistri officiales*.[79] Not only did masters exercise legal functions at the diocesan level, but they also increasingly served the papacy in this capacity. As appeals to the papal Curia increased during the pontificate of Innocent III (1198–1216), more and more judges delegate were appointed to decide individual cases throughout Latin Christendom. These judges were appointed in panels of three: one member usually a prelate (bishop or abbot), the second a

---

[76]35/178 = 20% for the total chapter. Data from Fernando A. Pico, "The Cathedral Chapter of Laon, 1155–1318" (Unpublished mimeographed copy). The surveys of 1217 and 1227 are in the cartulary of the chapter of Laon, MS Arch. dép. Aisne G 180, fols. 201va and 206rb. See also Auguste Boxin, "Les prévôtés du chapitre de la cathédral de Laon au xIIIe siècle," *Bulletin de la Société académique de Laon* 30 (1899) 14–75.

[77]From an exhaustive search among the charters of the chapter of Paris from 1180 to 1223, I have been able to locate 35 masters, but I do not know the total size of the chapter during the period.

[78]On bishop Hugh's policy see *Life of St. Hugh of Lincoln*, ed. Decima L. Douie and Hugh Farmer (2 vols. Edinburgh 1961–62) 1.110. For Lincoln: 79/187 = 42%. For London: 63/133 = 47%. Data from Le Neve (n. 74 above) vols. 3 and 1. For York: 43/93 = 46%. Data from Charles T. Clay, *York Minster Fasti*, Yorkshire Archaeological Society Records Series 123, 124 (2 vols. Wakefield 1958–59). For the Salisbury surveys: 10/84 = 12% and 15/87 = 17%. Data from *Vetus Registrum Sarisberiense*, ed. William H. Rich-Jones, RS 78 (2 vols. London 1883–84). For Canterbury: 24/38 = 63%. Data from C. R. Cheney, *English Bishops' Chanceries 1100–1250* (Manchester 1950) 11.

[79]For the date of appearance of the *officialis* and the filling of the posts with masters in France see the table in Baldwin, "*Studium*" (n. 71 above) 212. On the *officialis* see Paul Fournier, *Les officialités au moyen âge* (Paris 1880). Unfortunately, there is no way of determining in what subject the *magistri officiales* were trained.

lesser dignitary (dean or archdeacon), and the third often a cleric designated only by his name and title of master.[80]

Kings also sought the services of masters. While our group of Parisian regent masters rarely participated in royal government, principally because of their preoccupation with theology,[81] other masters were drawn in growing numbers to the royal court. No master has been detected in French service before the reign of Louis VII. He may have had two or three in his employ, but Philip Augustus depended upon at least a dozen in our period.[82] These included master Bovo (or Boso), who specialized in administering churches that fell into royal custody.[83] Master Anselm, dean of St Martin of Tours, and master William of St Lazare were commissioned to negotiate with king Richard of England on different occasions.[84] In France the masters' most frequent function was to serve as envoys to the pope, as did master Fulk, dean of Orléans, and master William, treasurer of St Frambaud of Senlis, and master William the Breton, the royal chronicler.[85] *Magistri* were put to more widespread use, however, by the English kings. While no systematic study has been made of their employment, a rapid perusal of royal charters indicates their pervasive presence at the English court.[86] Kings Henry II, Richard, and John were rarely without the company of men like master Walter of Coutances, archdeacon of Oxford, master Roscelin, vice chancellor, and master Richard Marsh, archdeacon of Richmond, along with one or two other masters from the chancery.[87] Among the fifteen active itinerant justices of John, at least three were *magistri*.[88] This impression of large numbers of masters in English service is not

[80]For examples see Innocent III, *Regesta*, PL 214.962, 1098; 215.781, 1542; 216.267, 635, 717, 723. Jane E. Sayers, *Papal Judges Delegate in the Province of Canterbury, 1198–1254: A Study in Ecclesiastical Jurisdiction and Administration* (London 1971) 114–33 has noted the prevalence of masters among English judges delegate and especially the activities of the canonist Richard of Mores.

[81]Among the theologians only Anders Sunesen was chancellor (for the king of Denmark), before his election to the archbishopric of Lund. Nicholas of Farnham and possibly Giles of Corbeil were royal physicians.

[82]Eric Bournazel, *Le gouvernement capétien au XIIe siècle: 1108–1180, structures sociales et mutations institutionelles* (Paris 1975) 82, 171 has found one for Louis VII, to whom others undoubtedly will be added. I have found a little more than a dozen for Philip Augustus.

[83]Cartulary of Beaupré, BN lat 9973, fol. 93ra. Cartulary of St Remi of Reims, MS Arch. mun. H 1413, fol. 71v.

[84]Roger of Hoveden (n. 17 above) 3.254, 247, 260. Innocent III, *Regesta*, PL 214.197.

[85]Innocent III, PL 214.1014–15. On William the Breton's activities see *Oeuvres* (n. 6 above) 1.1xxix–1xxx and Colker (n. 27 above) 309, 320–321.

[86]The witness lists of the English royal charters fluctuated with the individuals who attended court, whereas those of the French were formalized to include only the five household officers.

[87]For a few examples among many, see *Recueil des actes de Henri II*, ed. Léopold Delisle and Elie Berger (3 vols. Paris 1916–27) 2.144, 147, 158, 192, 199, 232; Robert W. Eyton, *Court, Household, and Itinerary of King Henry II* (London 1878) 244–45; Lionel Landon, *The Itinerary of King Richard I*, Pipe Roll Society n.s. 51 no. 13 (London 1935) 124, 141, 143; J. Conway Davies and Lionel Landon, eds., *The Cartae Antiquae*, Pipe Roll Society n.s. 17, 33 (London 1939, 1957) 17.105, 112; 33.112, 113, 115. No masters have yet been discovered in the chancery of Philip Augustus.

[88]Ralph V. Turner, "The Judges of King John: Their Background and Training," *Speculum* 51 (1976) 447–61 at 454.

merely a product of more abundant governmental documentation. In 1202/ 03, the sole surviving French royal financial account yields the names of only two masters; the English roll for the same year contains twenty-two.[89] Between 1194 and 1214 the number of masters in the English pipe rolls never fell below fourteen, even during John's excommunication (1209–13), when the clergy were forbidden to associate with him. Despite the disparity in documentation, there is little doubt, therefore, that the English kings' use of masters far exceeded that of the French at the turn of the century.

These examples of masters employed by the Church and monarchies at the turn of the twelfth century are merely a few among thousands and cannot pretend to present the systematic investigation that the problem deserves. Moreover, they raise important questions that cannot be answered immediately. Not only are we ignorant of where masters studied and in what subjects they were trained, but we find it difficult to account for the evident contrast between France and England. Undoubtedly the French schools were producing more masters because of their greater number and celebrity, but English churchmen and kings were employing graduates at a strikingly higher rate. This phenomenon corresponds to the English preponderance among the regent masters of Paris previously noted. Perhaps the most ready explanation lies in the royal administrative precocity of England, almost a century in advance over France.[90] It can be argued that the more sophisticated English government required highly trained personnel earlier than the French, who did not catch up with their competitors until the mid-thirteenth century. But such reasoning is less cogent for the two churches, where the administrative contrast is less pronounced.

Despite these unanswered questions, one underlying impression will likely remain unchanged as further investigation proceeds. The schools of the twelfth and early thirteenth centuries trained graduates in greater numbers to provide services increasingly demanded by society, Church, and government. What services the four disciplines at Paris and elsewhere contributed beyond the teaching of their subjects, remains unclear. The teachers of medicine naturally promoted good health and the canon lawyers good administration for the Church. The Roman lawyers were of service in southern Europe where their law remained in force; in northern France and England—lands governed by customary law—the Romanist stimulated the analyzing, organizing, and formulating of the body of customary law.[91] But the expertise of the theologians and the numerous masters of arts bore no direct application to governing Church and kingdom. All who claimed to be masters of arts (including those

---

[89]*Le premier budget de la monarchie française: Le compte général de 1202–1203*, ed. Ferdinand Lot and Robert Fawtier, Bibliothèque de l'Ecole des hautes études, Sciences historiques et philologiques 259 (Paris 1932) cxlix (2) and clxix(2). *Pipe Roll 4 John (1202)*, ed. Doris M. Stenton, Pipe Roll Society n.s. 15 (London 1937) index s.v. *Magister*.

[90]See Hollister and Baldwin (n. 7 above) 867–905.

[91]On the use of Roman law in England see Eleanor Rathbone, "Roman Law in the Anglo-Norman Realm," *Studia Gratiana* 11 (1967) 253–71 at 262–64.

who advanced to other disciplines) could contribute to the furtherance of literacy. It is true that, since the early Middle Ages and in increasing numbers since the twelfth century, ordinary clerics and literate laymen had performed the basic services of reading and writing in French and English society.[92] But the master of arts, skilled in logic as well as in grammar and rhetoric, was trained to think rationally and systematically. He organized his material, discarded the irrelevant, and constructed an argument to suit whatever his purpose. By thinking better he also wrote better, and therefore contributed the higher quality of literacy demanded by an increasingly sophisticated society.

PROFESSIONAL IDENTITY

Ever proud of their *magister* title, the Parisian masters exhibited growing signs of maturity and self-awareness as a professional group. They sought to evaluate their proper functions, to distinguish their activities from those of other groups, and to legitimate their contributions to society. From the hundreds of teachers who flourished in Paris at the turn of the century insufficient writings survive from arts, law, and medicine to register these attitudes, but those of the theologians provide clear examples of professional consciousness. Peter the Chanter, Stephen Langton, and Robert of Courson did not hesitate to express themselves about their métier. Although their writings exhibited little concern with current innovations, such as the emergence of the university and the rediscovery of Aristotle's physical and metaphysical treatises,[93] they turned their attention to consolidating a position that had become well-established during the twelfth century. Let us examine three signs of their professionalization: the justification of their earnings, the awareness of their past, and the definition of their place in society.

By branding law and medicine as the "lucrative sciences," the theologians evoked the economic rivalry among the advanced disciplines taught at Paris. This competition led the theologians to probe into their own economic position as well as that of the masters of arts, whom they considered to be ancillary but necessary to their profession. Ideally, from Antiquity through the early Middle Ages, all learning was to be supported by ecclesiastical prebends. As clerics, both masters and students were eligible for regular incomes assigned to specific churches for their use. Thus the master was heir to the early medieval monk who taught his pupils in the security of his monastery and who, in turn, succeeded the free gentleman of classical Antiquity who had

[92]Most recently, on the advance of lay literacy in England, see Ralph V. Turner, "The *Miles Literatus* in Twelfth- and Thirteenth-Century England: How Rare a Phenomenon?" AHR 83 (1978) 928–45.

[93]Baldwin, *Masters* 1.75–76, 104–07. Both Peter of Corbeil and Robert of Courson, however, played a personal role in the ecclesiastical prohibitions against teaching the new Aristotelian writings at Paris in 1210 and 1215. *Chartularium* (n. 1 above) 1.70, 78, 79.

cultivated the liberal arts supported by his landed estates. The economic principle governing this teaching was derived ultimately from Socrates: "Knowledge is a gift from God and cannot be sold."[94] Teachers, therefore, should not accept fees. At the Lateran Council of 1179 pope Alexander III attempted to implement this principle of free education, first by prohibiting chancellors and *scholastici* from charging for licenses, and by commanding each cathedral chapter to provide a prebend for a master to instruct all poor students in the elementary liberal arts without cost. Admitting that the ordinance was poorly observed, pope Innocent III at the Lateran Council of 1215 extended the duty to all collegiate chapters as well, and required archepiscopal chapters to provide a master of theology.[95]

The papal program of free education hardly corresponded to the realities of Paris at the turn of the twelfth and thirteenth centuries. One master each from the chapters of Notre-Dame, Ste Geneviève, St Victor, and a few other collegiate churches was patently insufficient for the scores of masters of arts, and Notre-Dame was not required to provide a theologian, because it was not of metropolitan rank. Even the solution of assigning prebends to masters and students from distant churches was insufficient, and it raised the added problem of absenteeism.[96] In addition, the general rise of prices rendered the fixed incomes of the prebends inadequate and further encouraged pluralism (the holding of more than one prebend), in turn aggravating absenteeism. As Abelard had already discovered early in the twelfth century, masters were obliged to demand fees from their students.

Since the charging of fees violated ancient prescriptions, Peter the Chanter, Stephen Langton, and Robert of Courson agonized over a multitude of perplexing cases that arose in practice. In the end they arrived at a set of conclusions applicable to masters of arts and theology, the two prevailing disciplines at Paris. All were agreed that if a master, whether of arts or theology, held a prebend assigned for the sake of teaching, he could not, in principle, take money from his students, since he was already paid for his work. But if a master of arts enjoyed no prebend—the normal situation—he could contract with his pupils before his lessons to pay him fees for his teaching. A master of theology without prebend, however, could not engage his students by contract to pay fees, but he could accept gifts freely offered after his lessons. The normal situation envisaged for the theologian was to possess a prebend since he was performing a spiritual function for which church livings were appropriate.[97]

[94]Gaines Post, Kimon Giocarinis, and Richard Kay, "The Medieval Heritage of a Humanistic Ideal: 'Scientia donum dei est, unde vendi non potest,'" *Traditio* 11 (1955) 195–234.

[95]For the conciliar canons: *Chartularium* (n. 1 above) 1.10, 81–82. See the discussion by Post (n. 21 above) 255–77.

[96]For some examples see *Chartularium* (n. 1 above) 1.6–11, 14.

[97]For the many cases discussed by the theologians see Baldwin, *Masters* 1.124–27.

Of interest for the masters' self-image were the justifications devised for these practical solutions. The latest heir to the ancient ideal was the master of theology. Since theology was quintessentially the knowledge of God, to place it on sale was sinful. If, however, unfortunate circumstances impoverished the theologian, he could accept charitable gifts. The master of arts, on the other hand, was likened to a laborer, who, according to Scripture, "was worthy of his hire." Abelard confessed that "since I was 'not strong enough to dig and too proud to beg,'. . . I returned to the skill which I knew, and made use of my tongue instead of working with my hands."[98] Almost a century later, Robert of Courson equated the master who taught foreign languages or the liberal arts with the blacksmith and carpenter whose skills and labor should be remunerated at a contract price.[99] With justification of masters' fees came a change in professional image. No longer a classical gentleman nor a sacred monk, the Parisian master of arts became increasingly the urban artisan who fashioned intellectual wares in the atelier of his school and sold them for prices commensurate with his labor.[100]

Emerging as a new profession, the masters of the urban schools developed a sensitivity to their past that served to define their functions. The theologians not only identified and quoted the opinions of their predecessors, they also recognized their exemplary personalities. The earliest to be singled out were master Lanfranc of Bec (d. 1089) and master Anselm of Laon (d. 1117). The former's humility vanquished the heretical doctrines of the vainglorious Berengar of Tours. The latter's great learning won him respect and honor during the troubled times of his city. Abelard (d. 1142), Gilbert of Poitiers (d. 1154) and, most recently, Peter Comestor (d. 1178) were remembered as critics of monastic abuses.[101] These distinguished theological masters were divided into generations by Peter the Chanter: the "oldest" comprised Anselm of Laon and his brother Ralph; the "old" included Simon [of Poissy?], Alberic of

---

[98] ". . . cum 'fodere non valerem et mendicare erubescerem' [Luke 16:3]. Ad artem itaque quam noveram recurrens, pro labore manuum ad officium lingue compulsus sum." Peter Abelard, *Historia calamitatum*, ed. Jacques Monfrin (Paris 1959) 94; trans. Betty Radice, *The Letters of Abelard and Heloise* (New York 1974) 90.

[99] "Item queritur utrum licite possit locare operas suas magister artium sive magistri auctorum et facere collectas licite. . . . Videatur quod possint licite locare operas suas sicut rustici. Nam latina lingua idioma quoddam est. Ego possum inire tecum pactum ut doceas me linguam gallicanam vel teutonicam eadem ratione ut doceas me hanc linguam et ut elimes dentes meos et doceas me alphabetum aut in caldea aut in alia lingua. Nam possum locare operas si sum faber et per pactionem interpositam docere te artem fabrilem vel carpentariam. Quare ergo similiter artem geometricam vel arismeticam in quibus magnus labor est? Quare ergo in huiusmodi non possum laborem vendere sicut in aliis cum hec non sint spiritualia? . . . Solutio. Inter opera distinguendum est quedam enim sunt mecanica, et illa locare, vendi, et emi possunt. Alia sunt liberalium artium. Sed illorum quedam non sunt de moribus sed pocius quasi quedam idiomata in primis rudimentis que vendi possunt ut informatio alphabeti [et] eruditio lingue. In hiis enim magister potest locare operas suas tanquam in agro aret aut scriberet aut aliquid tale." Robert of Courson, *Summa* X 3, BN lat 14524, fol. 47ra.

[100] See Jacques Le Goff, *Les intellectuels au moyen âge* (Paris 1955) 66–68, 104–08.

[101] On these early masters see Baldwin, *Masters* 1.150–56.

Reims, Robert Pullen, and Gilbert [of Poitiers?], all of whom John of Salisbury observed at Paris in the 1130s and 1140s.[102]

Although the opinions of these masters deserved respect, they had to be distinguished from the fundamental sources that governed theological learning. For this reason the theologians of the late twelfth century created a dichotomy between *authentica* and *magistralia*. *Authentica* comprised Scripture and the writings of Church Fathers, whose authority (*auctoritas*) must be accepted, although they could be interpreted reverently. *Magistralia* included the works of the *magistri moderni*, whose opinions should be considered but could be accepted or rejected according to their merits.[103] By creating this separate category the theologians both defined and appreciated the tasks of their profession. Peter the Chanter, followed by others, expressed their function with a dental image. The apostles, who were with the Lord, were the front teeth of theology. The middle or canine teeth were the expositors of Scripture who barked against heretics. But most necessary were the back teeth or molars—the modern masters.[104] Their function fulfilled the last stage of preparing the food of sacred doctrine for the nourishment of the faithful.

To explain their origins and to legitimate their role in contemporary society, the Parisian theologians adopted a hallowed schema called the *translatio studii* that depicted the transmission of learning from the past.[105] The early bishops had devised the doctrine of apostolic succession by which divine authority was transmitted from Christ to the apostles and thence to all bishops. The papacy fashioned a parallel doctrine, the *translatio imperii*, to explain the transferral of imperial authority from the Roman emperors to Charlemagne and thence to the German kings.[106] In imitation of these venerable ideas, scholars in France created their own *translatio studii*. In the early twelfth cen-

[102]"Item in levitico (Lev. 26:10): Comedetis vetustissima veterum, id est, vetustissimorum modum legendi et morem intelligendi antiquorum doctorum, anselmi, scilicet, et fratris sui. Comeditis in usu, id est, imitabimi. Et vetera scilicet modum legendi veternorum [MS Ste G: modernorum], simonis, alberici remensis, roberti paulani [MS Ste G: pulani], gilleberti qui iam senuerunt, et ideo veteres novis, id est, vetustissimis veterum innovatis et item in usum supervenientibus proicietis." Peter the Chanter, *Verbum abbreviatum*, MS Vat Reg lat 106, fol. 2rb and MS Paris, Ste Geneviève 250, fol. 2va. For a short version see PL 205.27D and 373A. For the texts of John of Salisbury, see *Metalogicon* 1.5, ed. Clement C. J. Webb (Oxford 1929) 16–20 and *Historia pontificalis* (*Memoirs of the Papal Court*), ed. and trans. Marjorie Chibnall (London and New York 1956) 19. "Gilbert" may refer to either Gilbert of Poitiers or Gilbert "the Universal."

[103]Chenu, *Théologie* 324–29, 351–61; partial translation in *Nature* 272–79.

[104]Gloss (to Num. 3:18): "Sunt autem dentes anteriores apostoli, qui cum domino fuerint. Medii et cannii dentes sunt scripturarum expositores, qui latratum contra hereticos habuerunt. Posteriores dentes et magis necessarii, qui et molares sunt moderni doctores." Peter the Chanter, MS Oxford, Balliol Col. 23, fol. 10ra. The Chanter's text is followed closely in the distinction *De dentibus* of Peter of Poitiers, *Distinctiones super psalterium*, BN lat 425, fol. 68va.

[105]For the literature on this subject see Franz Josef Worstbrock, "Translatio artium: Über die Herkunft und Entwicklung einer Kulturhistorischen Theorie," AKG 47 (1965) 1–22 and David L. Gassman, *Translatio studii: A Study of Intellectual History in the Thirteenth Century* (Ph.D. diss. Cornell University 1973; repr. University Microfilms, Ann Arbor, Michigan).

[106]See Werner Goez, *Translatio imperii: Ein Beitrag zur Geschichte des Geschichtsdenkens und der politischen Theorien im Mittelalter und in der frühen Neuzeit* (Tübingen 1958).

tury the theory envisaged learning as originating in the East and passing by successive stages through Greece and Rome to the West where it finally reached Gaul. The poet Chrétien de Troyes in the 1170s fashioned a popular version in which learning was joined by chivalry in Greece and proceeded through Rome to France.[107]

Among the Parisian masters in the early thirteenth century this version was echoed by Gerald of Wales.[108] But Alexander Neckam was the first to focus specifically on Paris. In his account, the patriarch Abraham taught the quadrivium in Egypt, which Plato then transmitted to Greece where it was cultivated by Socrates, Aristotle, Zeno, and others. Later, Romans such as Cicero, Seneca, Lucan, and Vergil brought learning to Italy and joined it to their military prowess. In his own time Alexander celebrated Salerno and Montpellier for medicine, Italy for law, but gave highest honors to Paris for the study of Scripture and the liberal arts.[109] Peter the Chanter also alluded to the *translatio studii* in his biblical commentaries. Glossing Isaiah's lament over the succession of the Assyrian and Chaldean empires, he was reminded of how letters came from Athens to Rome and finally to Paris. For that reason, he explained, king Philip hesitated to evict the scholars from the royal city.[110] But it was the royal chronicler William the Breton who stressed the positive contributions of the French kings to fostering learning. For the year 1210, as we have seen, William celebrated the thriving studies in arts, law, medicine, and theology at Paris and exulted that nowhere at any time, not even in Athens or Egypt, had so many scholars gathered in one place for the sake of learning. This was the result not only of the favorableness of the place and the abundance of goods, but also of the special protection provided by king Philip and his father.[111] According to royal historiography, therefore, the Capetian kings joined the Parisian scholars to bring learning to France and to create one of the glories of the kingdom.

A little more than a half century later another royal chronicler, William of Nangis, integrated the tradition of *translatio studii* into royal symbolism. On the occasion of the great university dispersion in 1229–30, king Louis IX, like his grandfather Philip Augustus before him, feared that the great treasure of learning would depart from the kingdom. Both learning (*sapientia*) and

---

[107]*Les Romans de Chrétien de Troyes*, vol. 2: *Cligés*, ed. Alexandre Micha, Les classiques français du moyen âge 84 (Paris 1957) 2.28–37; trans. William W. Comfort, *Arthurian Romances* (London and New York 1914; repr. 1977) 91.

[108]*Giraldi Cambrensis Opera* (n. 26 above) 8.7–8, 259.

[109]Neckam (n. 25 above) 308–11, 414.

[110]Gloss to *talis populus non fuit* (Isa. 23:13): "*Usque ad mortem nobuchodonosor forciss[im]us homo. Unde non fuerunt assirii et caldei, post[ea] populus grecorum* quamdiu studium litterarum fuit athenis, post[ea] populus romanorum quamdiu studium rome [MS: reome] fuit, nunc francorum populus viget studium. Hic inquit exemplo motus est rex francorum philippus volens eicere scolares parisius.*" Peter the Chanter, MS Paris Mazarine 178, fol. 73va. The last sentence is somewhat ambiguous. It presumably refers to a student disturbance at Paris before the great riot of 1200, because the Chanter was dead by 1197.

[111]See above at n. 6.

chivalry (*militia*), the chronicler explained, came from Greece to Paris, where they were joined to a third element, faith (*fides*). So highly were these three virtues esteemed in France that the kings were accustomed to depict them on their arms and banners in the form of a fleur de lis. Faith stood as the central petal, supported on either side by learning and chivalry; but none could be removed without the destruction of the others.[112] As a royal symbol the fleur de lis dated from Carolingian times. Philip Augustus, however, placed it on the reverse of his seal and was probably the first king to carry it into battle on his banner, as he did at Bouvines in 1214.[113] Although the interpretation of the symbol as faith, learning, and chivalry did not appear in official historiography until later, the masters and students, who with the whole populace joyfully greeted the king on his triumphal entry into Paris after the great victory at Bouvines, may well have understood this significance. By bringing learning to the kingdom they shared in the triple glory of France, whose emblem was the fleur de lis emblazoned on the royal banner.

Bibliographical Note

Following the example of Haskins, subsequent scholarship on the schools and intellectual life of the twelfth century has largely concentrated attention on the first two-thirds of the century. This focus is well illustrated in the colloquium held in 1965 and published as *Entretiens*. Yet the educational regime of the early twelfth century remained in force through the turn of the century, and its corresponding scholarship applies to the later period as well. The twelfth century's educational institutions and techniques have been authoritatively established by the studies of Martin Grabmann, *Die Geschichte der scholastischen Methode* (2 vols. Freiburg 1909-11; repr. Berlin 1956); Gérard M. Paré, A. Brunet, and P. Tremblay, *La renaissance du XIIe siècle: Les écoles et l'enseignement*, Publications de l'Institut d'études médiévales d'Ottawa 3 (Paris and Ottawa 1933); and Philippe Delhaye, ''L'organisation scolaire au XIIe siècle,'' *Traditio* 5 (1947) 211-68. Hastings Rashdall, *The Universities of Europe in the Middle Ages*, ed. Frederick M. Powicke and Alfred B. Emden (3 vols. Oxford 1936), which remains the classic study on the universities of the thirteenth century, is also valuable for the preceding period. Emile Lesne, *Histoire de la propriété ecclésiastique en France* (6 vols. in 8 Lille 1910-43) vol. 5, *Les écoles de la fin du VIIIe siècle à la fin du XIIe*, Mémoires et travaux des Facultés Catholiques de Lille 50 (1940) contains a mine of information for the whole century, but must be used with care.

[112]William of Nangis, *Gesta sanctae memoriae Ludovici regis Franciae*, ed. M. Daunou, in *Recueil des historiens des Gaules et de la France* 20 (1840) 309-462 at 320 and *Chronique latine de Guillaume de Nangis de 1113 à 1300, avec les continuations de cette chronique de 1300 à 1368*, ed. Hercule Géraud, Société de l'histoire de France 33, 35 (2 vols. Paris 1843; repr. New York 1965) 2.181-82. On William of Nangis see Gabrielle M. Spiegel, *The Chronicle Tradition of Saint-Denis: A Survey*, Medieval Classics: Texts and Studies 10 (Brookline Mass. and Leiden 1978) 98-105.
[113]*Oeuvres* (n. 6 above) 1.281, 296-97 for the royal standard at Bouvines and the triumphal entry into Paris. For the fleur de lis see Percy Ernst Schramm, *Der König von Frankreich: Das Wesen der Monarchie vom 9. zum 16. Jahrhundert* (2nd ed. 2 vols. Weimar 1960) 1.214-15.

Twelfth-century theology has been studied in terms of doctrinal schools, an approach that was encouraged largely by Artur M. Landgraf. See his *Einführung in die Geschichte der theologischen Literatur der Frühscholastik, unter dem Gesichtspunkte der Schulenbildung* (Regensburg 1948), French ed. rev. Albert M. Landry, trans. Louis B. Geiger, *Introduction à l'histoire de la littérature théologique de la scolastique naissante*, Université de Montréal, Publications de l'Institut d'études médiévales 22 (Montreal and Paris 1973). David E. Luscombe, *The School of Peter Abelard: The Influence of Abelard's Thought in the Early Scholastic Period* (Cambridge 1969) is a recent application of this technique. Studies devoted to individual Parisian theologians at the turn of the century have been contributed by: Georges Lacombe, *La vie et les oeuvres de Prévostin*, Bibliothèque thomiste 11, sect. historique 10 (Le Saulchoir 1927); Frederick M. Powicke, *Stephen Langton* (Oxford 1928; repr. London 1965); Marcel and Christiane Dickson, "Le cardinal Robert de Courson, sa vie," AHDLMA 9 (1934) 53–142; Philip S. Moore, *The Works of Peter of Poitiers, Master in Theology and Chancellor of Paris (1193–1205)* (Washington D.C. 1936); Marie-Thérèse d'Alverny, *Alain de Lille: Textes inédits*, EPM 52 (Paris 1965); and Baldwin, *Masters*. Jean Longère, *Oeuvres oratoires de maîtres parisiens au XIIe siècle: Etude historique et doctrinale* (2 vols. Paris 1975) has explored sermons for their theological teaching.

Scholarship for the other disciplines at the turn of the century is less advanced. L. M. de Rijk, *Logica modernorum: A Contribution to the History of Early Terminist Logic* (2 vols. in 3 Assen 1962–67) has begun to assemble the logical treatises, which Jan Pinborg, *Logik und Semantik im Mittelalter: Ein Überblick* (Stuttgart 1972) has situated in the long-term developments. Kuttner's *Repertorium* remains still the only guide for the Parisian canonists of the period.

Two essays have been influential in relating theology and other currents of thought to the social context. They are Chenu's *Théologie*, partial translation in *Nature*, and Jacques Le Goff, *Les intellectuels au moyen âge* (Paris 1955). John W. Baldwin, *The Scholastic Culture of the Middle Ages, 1100–1300* (Lexington Mass. 1971) attempts to set scholastic institutions and thought within the urban context.

Palémon Glorieux has contributed repertories of masters of theology and of arts during the thirteenth century which are comprehensive in scope, but whose information for the earlier period must be checked for details: *Répertoire des maîtres en théologie de Paris au XIIIe siècle*, EPM 17–18 (2 vols. Paris 1933–34) and *La faculté des arts et ses maîtres au XIIIe siècle*, EPM 59 (Paris 1971).

The most recent and comprehensive study of twelfth-century Paris is Jacques Boussard, *Nouvelle histoire de Paris*, vol. 6: *De la fin du siège de 885–886 à la mort de Philippe Auguste* (Paris 1976). Anne Lombard-Jourdan, *Paris—Genèse de la 'Ville': La rive droite de la Seine des origines à 1223* (Paris 1976) treats the development of the right bank. The topography of the city is best seen in Adrien Friedmann, *Paris: Ses rues, ses paroisses du moyen age à la Revolution* (Paris 1959) and Carlrichard Brühl, *Palatium und Civitas: Studien zur Profantopographie spätantiker Civitates vom 3. bis zum 13. Jahrhundert*, vol. 1: *Gallien* (Cologne 1975).

Appendix

REGENT MASTERS AT PARIS, 1179–1215

Name	Academic Writings at Paris	Observed by	Geographic Origins	Social Status	Subsequent Career	References (follow table)
MASTERS OF ARTS						
Alan of Beccles		chronicle	Beccles, England		archdeacon of Sudbury, official of Norwich	A391, C1.145
Alexander Neckam (d. 1217)		self-testimony	St Albans, England	mother a wet-nurse	abbot of Cirencester (1213)	A81, D784
Amaury of Bène (d. 1206)		chronicle	Bène, near Chartres		condemned post-humously as heretic	A89, E98–105
John of Cella (d. 1214)		chronicle	Studham (Beds.), England	*ex mediocri prosapia oriundus*	abbot of St Albans (1195)	F28
Matthew of Vendôme		self-testimony	Vendôme			A256, G1–3, 14
Nicholas of Farnham (d. 1257)		chronicle	Farnham, England		royal physician, bishop of Durham (1241)	A391, C2.669
Petrus Hispanus	*Summa* on Priscian		Spain		monk of St Martial (1213)?	H1–23, I2.24. 25
Robert Blundus	*Summa* on Priscian	bishop's letter	England		canon of Lincoln	A324, C1.206. I2(1)256. 257
Roger the Norman (d. 1200)		chronicle, charters	Normandy		dean of Rouen (1199)	J124–26

Name	Academic Writings at Paris	Observed by	Geographic Origins	Social Status	Subsequent Career	References (follow table)
William of Blois (d. 1206)		letters, chronicles	Blois (Breton stock)	knights (small means)	abbot of Matina (Sicily), chanter (1197), bishop of Lincoln (1203)	A150, D1021–23, K339
William of Poitiers		Caesar of Heisterbach	Poitiers		subdeacon, condemned as heretic (1210)	A392, E101
MASTERS OF CANON LAW						
Everard of Ypres (d. 1191)	*Summula decretalium questionum*	self-testimony	Ypres		monk of Clairvaux (1185)	L187, M143–62
Gerald of Wales (d. 1223)		autobiography	Manorbier, Pembrokeshire, Wales	castellans	archdeacon of Brecon (St Davids)	A152, N379–90
Honorius (d. 1208/13)	*Summa decretalium questionum*		Kent, England	illegitimate birth	official of York (1195), contested archdeacon of Richmond	O304–16
Odo of Dover	*Summa*		Dover			L172, O293
Peter of Louveciennes (d. 1185)	prologue to *Decretum*, grammatical opinions		Louveciennes, near Paris		dean of St Germain l'Auxerrois (1175)	L183, P2.80, 81
Richard of Mores (d. 1242)	*Questiones decretales, Summa*	chronicle	Lincoln		prior of Dunstable (1202)	O335–39
Rodoicus Modicipassus (d. 1204/07)	*Questiones, Summa?*	Robert of Courson			chanter of Sens?	Q701, 702

Name	Writings	Sources	Origin	Family	Career	References
Sicard of Cremona (1215)	*Summa decreti*		Cremona	family: Casellanus	bishop of Cremona (1185)	L151, O314, R1008
Simon of Southwell		self-testimony	England		canon of Lincoln, official of Canterbury	O326, 327
Stephen of Tournai (d. 1203)	sermons, letters	charters, letters	Orléans		abbot of St Euvert (1167), Ste Geneviève (1176), bishop of Tournai (1191)	S2–40
MASTERS OF MEDICINE						
Giles of Corbeil (d. 1224)	didactic medical verse	Giles of Paris, chronicle	Corbeil	"lowly"	canon of Paris? royal physician?	P1.41
Richard the Englishman	commentaries to Giles of Corbeil		England			T61
MASTERS OF THEOLOGY						
Alan of Lille (d. 1203)	theological treatises, biblical commentaries, sermons	chronicle	Lille		monk at Cîteaux	A69, U11–29
Anders Sunesen (d. 1228)		chronicle, charters	Knardrup, Denmark	wealthiest aristocracy	royal chancellor (1195), archbishop of Lund (1201)	A91, V240–44
Bernard Chabert (d. 1235)		charters			chancellor of Paris (1206), bishop of Geneva (1206), archbishop of Embrun (1212)	B1.260, AA16
Geoffrey of Poitiers	*Questiones*	papal letters	Poitiers			B1.298, P1.31. 32

Name	Academic Writings at Paris	Observed by	Geographic Origins	Social Status	Subsequent Career	References (follow table)
Geoffrey of St Victor (d. 1194)	academic verse	charters			sacristan at St Victor (1194)	W2.33
Hilduin (d. 1193)	sermons	charters	near Paris	knights, family of St Denis	deacon, canon, chancellor of Paris (1180)	X1.21, 22
Humbert of Pirovano (d. 1211)	biblical treatise	chronicle	Pirovano, Italy		archbishop of Milan (1206), cardinal	Y878
John de la Chandleur		charters	Noyon?		canon of Noyen (1206), chancellor of Paris (1209)	B1.270
John of Matha (d. 1213)		chronicle	Provence		founder of Trinitarian Order	Z10, 11
Martin	Questiones					B1.269, P1.44
Michael of Corbeil / Courlandon (d. 1199)	Distinctiones	chronicle	Corbeil or Courlandon	*domini*; uncle: Adam of Courlandon	dean of Meaux (1166), Laon (1191), Paris (1192); archbishop of Sens (1194)	P1.45, 46
Peter the Chanter (d. 1197)	lectures, *questiones*, manuals	chronicle, charters	Hodenc-en-Bray, Beauvaisis	knights	chanter of Paris (1183), bishop elect of Tournai (1191), dean of Reims (1196)	P1.3–16

Name	Works	Documentation	Origin	Personal	Positions	References
Peter of Capua (d. 1242)	*Questiones*	papal letter	Capua, Italy		patriarch of Antioch (1218), cardinal (1218)	B1.265, P1.45
Peter of Corbeil (d. 1222)	scriptural commentaries, *questiones?*	chronicle, papal letters, charters	Corbeil	*de humili plebe*	canon of Paris, archdeacon of York (1198), bishop of Cambrai (1199), archbishop of Sens (1200)	P1.46
Peter of Poitiers (d. 1205)	theological sentences, *distinctiones*, sermons	chronicle, charters	Poitiers		deacon, chancellor of Paris (1193)	B1.229, AA1–24
Prepositinus (d. 1210)	*Questiones*, *distinctiones*, sermons	chronicle, charters	Cremona, Lombardy		chancellor of Paris (1206)	B1.266, Z4–46. P1.44, 45
Ralph Ardent	sermons, encyclopedia		Beaulieu, near Bressuire			B1.234, P1.39. 40
Richard le Poer (d. 1237)		papal letter	England	illegitimate birth	dean of Salisbury (1198), bishop of Chichester (1215), Salisbury (1217), Durham (1228)	C3.2189
Robert of Courson (d. 1219)	*Questiones*	papal letters, charters	England: Derbyshire?		canon of Noyon, Paris, cardinal (1213)	B1.235, P1.19–25
Simon of Tournai (d. 1201)	*Summa*, *disputationes*	chronicle, charters	Tournai		prebend from Tournai	B1.232, P1.44. BBx–xxiii
Stephen Langton (d. 1228)	lectures, *questiones*, sermons	papal letters, charters	Langton near Wragby, Lincolnshire, England	knights, father Henry de Langton	canon of Paris, York; cardinal (1206), archbishop of Canterbury (1207)	B1.238, C3.2187, P1.25–31
Thomas of Chobham (d. 1233/36)	*inceptio*, sermons	John of Garland?	Chobham, Surrey, England	illegitimate birth	subdean and official of Salisbury	B1.275, P1.34–36

Name	Academic Writings at Paris	Observed by	Geographic Origins	Social Status	Subsequent Career	References (follow table)
Walter of St Victor	theological polemic, sermons				prior of St Victor	CC187
William de Montibus (d. 1213)	logic? theological manuals, *distinctiones*	chronicle	Wigford near Lincoln, England	knights, de Montibus family near Lincoln	chancellor of Lincoln (1192)	A168, DD32–33

REFERENCES

(A)   Palémon Glorieux, *La faculté des arts et ses maîtres au XIIIe siècle*, EPM 59 (Paris 1971).

(B)   Palémon Glorieux, *Répertoire des maîtres en théologie de Paris au XIIIe siècle*, EPM 17–18 (2 vols. Paris 1933–34).

(C)   Alfred B. Emden, *A Biographical Register of the University of Oxford to A.D. 1500* (3 vols. Oxford 1957–59).

(D)   Manitius, vol. 3.

(E)   Germaine C. Capelle, *Autour du décret de 1210*, vol. 3: *Amaury de Bène: Etude sur son panthéisme formel*, Bibliothèque thomiste 16 (Paris 1932).

(F)   Richard W. Hunt, "English Learning in the Late Twelfth Century," TRHS 4th ser. 19 (1936) 19–42 at 19–35.

(G)   Faral, *Les arts poétiques*.

(H)   Richard W. Hunt, "*Absoluta*: The *Summa* of Petrus Hispanus on Priscianus Minor," *Historiographia linguistica* 2 (1975) 1–23.

(I)   L. M. de Rijk, *Logica modernorum: A Contribution to the History of Early Terminist Logic* (2 vols. in 3 Assen 1962–67).

(J)   John W. Baldwin, "A Debate at Paris over Thomas Becket between Master Roger and Master Peter the Chanter," *Studia Gratiana* 11 (1967) 119–32.

(K)   André Boutemy, "Thèses nouvelles et travaux en cours," *Revue du moyen âge latin* 1 (1945) 338–42 at 339.

(L)   Kuttner, *Repertorium*.

(M)   Nikolaus M. Häring, "The Cistercian Everard of Ypres and His Appraisal of the Conflict between St. Bernard and Gilbert of Poitiers," *Mediaeval Studies* 17 (1955) 143–62.

(N)   Michael Richter, "Gerald of Wales: A Reassessment on the 750th Anniversary of His Death," *Traditio* 29 (1973) 379–90.

(O)   Stephen Kuttner and Eleanor Rathbone, "Anglo-Norman Canonists of the Twelfth Century: An Introductory Study," *Traditio* 7 (1959–61) 279–358.

(P)   Baldwin, *Masters*.

(Q)   Stephan Kuttner, "Rodoicus ou Rotbertus Modicipassus (Parvipassus)," *Dictionnaire de droit canonique* 7 (1965) 701–02.

(R)   Charles Lefebvre, "Sicard de Crémone," *Dictionnaire de droit canonique* 7 (1965) 1008–11.

(S)   Joseph Warichez, *Etienne de Tournai et son temps (1128–1203)* (Paris 1937).

(T)   Karl Sudhoff, "Salerno, Montpellier und Paris um 1200," *Archiv für Geschichte der Medizin* 20 (1928) 51–62.

(U)   Marie-Thérèse d'Alverny, ed., *Alain de Lille: Textes inédits*, EPM 52 (Paris 1965).

(V)   Niels Skyum-Nielsen, *Kvinde og Slave* (Copenhagen 1971).

(W)   Geoffrey of St Victor, *Microcosmus*, ed. Philippe Delhaye, Mémoires et travaux des Facultés Catholiques de Lille 56–57 (2 vols. Lille 1951).

(X)   Jean Longère, *Oeuvres oratoires de maîtres parisiens au XIIe siècle: Etude historique et doctrinale* (2 vols. Paris 1975).

(Y)   Alberic of Trois-Fontaines, *Chronica*, ed. Paul Scheffer-Boichorst, MGH SS 13.631–950.

(Z)   Georges Lacombe, *La vie et les oeuvres de Prévostin*, Bibliothèque thomiste 11, sect. historique 10 (Le Saulchoir 1927).

(AA)   Philip S. Moore, *The Works of Peter of Poitiers, Master in Theology and Chancellor of Paris (1193–1205)* (Washington D.C. 1936).

(BB)   *Les Disputationes de Simon de Tournai*, ed. Joseph Warichez, Spicilegium sacrum Lovaniense 12 (Louvain 1932).

(CC)   Palémon Glorieux, "Le *Contra Quatuor Labyrinthos Franciae* de Gauthier de Saint-Victor," AHDLMA 19 (1952) 187–335.

(DD)   Hugh MacKinnon, "William de Montibus: A Medieval Teacher," *Essays in Medieval History presented to Bertie Wilkinson*, ed. T. A. Sandquist and M. R. Powicke (Toronto 1969) 32–45.

Commentary and Hermeneutics

Nikolaus M. Häring

Although the custom of writing commentaries is by no means an invention of the twelfth century, the remarkable urge of twelfth-century scholastics to compose commentaries produced a vast number and variety of such works. It is impossible here to present more than a general outline of the achievements in this branch of education.[1]

The writing of commentaries presupposes the recognition of an authoritative text, known as *littera*, which the commentator endeavors to elucidate without, if possible, altering the letter of the original. In the Christian era the Bible has been such a text—a collection of writings whose very wording came to be considered the work of divine inspiration. Classical authors continued to receive commentaries, of course. Thierry of Chartres has been identified as the author of commentaries on Cicero's *De inventione* and on the *Auctor ad Herennium*, both transmitted anonymously.[2] His contemporary, William of Conches, commented on Plato's *Timaeus*,[3] wrote *glose* and *glosule* on Boethius (*De consolatione*),[4] Juvenal,[5] Macrobius,[6] and Priscian.[7] Another contemporary, Peter Abelard, commented on Porphyry's *Isagoge*, Aristotle's *Categories* and *De interpretatione*, on *De divisionibus*, *De syllogismo*

---

[1]Not included in this study is the immense multitude of twelfth-century sermons, most of which can be classified as miniature commentaries on biblical themes. See Johannes Baptist Schneyer, *Repertorium der lateinischen Sermones des Mittelalters*, BGPTMA 43.1–8 (8 vols. to date Münster 1969–78).

[2]Karin M. Fredborg, "The Commentary of Thierry of Chartres on Cicero's *De inventione*," CIMAGL 7 (1972) 1–36.

[3]*Guillaume de Conches: Glosae super Platonem*, ed. Edouard Jeauneau, Textes philosophiques du moyen âge 13 (Paris 1965).

[4]Jeauneau, *Lectio* 127–92 at 135 ("L'usage de la notion d'*integumentum* à travers les gloses de Guillaume de Conches").

[5]Ibid. 148.

[6]Ibid. 267–308 at 267, 301 ("Le 'Commentaire' de Macrobe sur le 'Songe de Scipion'"). He refers to it as *commentarius* (271, 272).

[7]Ibid. 335–70 ("Deux redactions des gloses de Guillaume de Conches sur Priscien"). See Leclercq, *Love of Learning* 116–31; Walter Stack, "Mitteilungen zur mittelalterlichen Glossographie," *Liber Floridus: Mittellateinische Studien Paul Lehmann gewidmet*, ed. Bernhard Bischoff and Heinrich Suso Brechter (St Ottilien 1950) 11–18 at 12–16; Richard W. Hunt, "Studies on Priscian in the Eleventh and Twelfth Centuries," M&RS 1 (1943) 194–231 and 2 (1950) 1–56.

categorico, and the *Topica*.[8] And, from the middle of the twelfth century on, many commentaries on Gratian's *Decretum* and Peter Lombard's *Sentences* were produced;[9] these have been carefully catalogued by modern scholars.[10] Indeed, scholars of the twelfth century were so fond of adding their comments that they even enriched glosses with new glosses;[11] an example is the extensive commentary on Gilbert's explanation of the Pauline Letters preserved in the twelfth-century MS Boulogne-sur-mer 24, fols. 136v–210v.[12]

TITLES AND INSCRIPTIONS OF COMMENTARIES

Modern authors often employ the Greek term *exegesis* to describe the task of explaining scriptural texts. Medieval exegetes or librarians had a much larger choice of technical terms for this sort of literature. Some of the terms they adopted were hallowed by long tradition, while others can be classed as novelties. The variety and lack of uniformity can lead to confusion.

St Augustine's commentary on the Psalms was titled *Enarrationes in Psalmos*. Some historians consider Geoffrey Babion (fl. 1110) the author of a commentary entitled *Enarrationes in Matheum*, elsewhere referred to as *Glose super Matheum*.[13] Under the name of Anselm of Laon a student will find *Enarrationes in Cantica Canticorum* and *Enarrationes in Apocalipsin*.[14] But in MS BN lat 568 (fols. 1–64) he will be faced with the title *Glosule super Cantica Canticorum Salemonis secundum magistrum Anselmum*, and in two other manuscripts (Le Mans 218 and BN lat 712) with the title *Glose in Apocalipsi secundum lectionem magistri Anselmi Laudunensis*.[15] Which of these inscriptions is authentic?

---

[8]Bernhard Geyer, *Peter Abaelards philosophische Schriften*, BGPTMA 21 (4 vols. Münster 1919–33); Mario dal Pra, ed., *Pietro Abelardo: Scritti filosofici* (Rome 1954). See also Nikolaus M. Häring, "Abelard Yesterday and Today," *Pierre-Pierre* 395–402.

[9]Artur M. Landgraf, "The First Sentence Commentary of Early Scholasticism," *The New Scholasticism* 13 (1939) 101–33 at 127–31.

[10]Stephan Kuttner, *Repertorium*; Friedrich Stegmüller, *Repertorium commentariorum in Sententias Petri Lombardi* (2 vols. Würzburg 1947); idem, *Repertorium biblicum medii aevi* (11 vols. Madrid 1940–80).

[11]Smalley, *Study* 65: "So far as we know, the earliest example of a gloss on the *Gloss* is a series of lectures on the Gospels by Peter Comestor, given probably before he became Chancellor in 1168."

[12]See Nikolaus M. Häring, "Chartres and Paris Revisited," *Essays in Honour of Anton Charles Pegis*, ed. J. Reginald O'Donnell (Toronto 1974) 268–329 at 312. The strong urge to write commentaries is also apparent in the *Glosa in historiam ecclesiasticam* by Stephen Langton: see Artur M. Landgraf, *Der Sentenzenkommentar des Kardinals Stephan Langton*, BGPTMA 37 (Münster 1952) xv; George Lacombe, "Studies on the Commentaries of Cardinal Stephen Langton (Part 1)," AHDLMA 5 (1930) 5–151 at 18–57.

[13]See Léopold Delisle, *Le cabinet des manuscrits de la Bibliothèque impériale* (3 vols. Paris 1868–81) 2.491 no. 111: *Glose magistri Anselmi Laudunensis super Matheum*; Damien van den Eynde, "Autour des 'Enarrationes in Evangelium S. Matthaei' attribuées à Geoffroi Babion," RTAM 26 (1959) 50–84.

[14]PL 162.1187–1228 and 1499–1586; Jean Leclercq, "Le commentaire du Cantique des cantiques attribué à Anselme de Laon," RTAM 16 (1949) 29–39.

[15]Artur M. Landgraf, *Introduction à l'histoire de la littérature théologique de la scolastique naissante*, rev. Albert M. Landry, trans. Louis B. Geiger, Université de Montréal, Publications de

St Augustine's commentary on the Gospel of St John bears the title *Tractatus in Evangelium Iohannis*. Thierry of Chartres twice refers to his own commentary on Genesis as *tractatus*.[16] In the footsteps of his master, Clarembald of Arras wrote a similar work which he classified as *tractatulus* based on Thierry's *lectio*.[17] Clarembald himself calls his own commentary on Boethius *tractatus*[18] but the manuscript labels it an *expositio*.[19] Moreover, the title *Tractatus in Hexameron* heads the commentary on Genesis by Hugh of Amiens.[20] What was the reason for adopting the inscription *tractatus*?

In the list of works by Hugh of St Victor there is a *Commentum Hugonis super De consolatione*.[21] According to Clarembald, Boethius wrote a *Commentum* on Aristotle's *Categories*.[22] The same Clarembald designates Gilbert's commentary on the *opuscula sacra* of Boethius as *glose*[23] and, in keeping with the general custom, the text of Boethius as *littera*.[24]

How authentic are these titles? The answer is perhaps very simple: for authors of the twelfth century it is wise to assume that their commentaries were published anonymously and without what we might call an authentic title or inscription.

To substantiate this assumption let us turn to Peter Abelard's commentary on St Paul's Letter to the Romans, of which three manuscripts and as many different titles have survived. The oldest of them (MS Angers 68, saec. XII) has no proper inscription, though its colophon (fol. 26) describes it as *Abaelardi commentariorum liber*.[25] The second copy (Vat Reg lat 242), originally without an inscription, dates back to the twelfth or thirteenth century; a later librarian (thirteenth/fourteenth century) chose to characterize it as *exposicio*. In the last and latest manuscript (Oxford, Bodl. 296) the same work is designated as *glose*. The reader can hardly be accused of rash judgment if he concludes that none of these inscriptions is authentic.

---

l'Institut d'études médiévales 22 (Montreal and Paris 1973) 71; André Wilmart, "Un commentaire des Psaumes restitué à Anselme de Laon," *RTAM* 8 (1936) 325–44 at 326.

[16]*Tractatus de sex dierum operibus* 46–47, ed. Nikolaus M. Häring, *Commentaries on Boethius, by Thierry of Chartres and His School*, Pontifical Institute of Mediaeval Studies, Studies and Texts 20 (Toronto 1971) 574–75.

[17]Nikolaus M. Häring, *Life and Works of Clarembald of Arras*, Pontifical Institute of Mediaeval Studies, Studies and Texts 10 (Toronto 1965) 226: "Cui operi *Tractatulum* quendam supposui quem ab ipsius lectione ita collegi."

[18]Clarembald, *De Trinitate* 1.11 and 4.6, and *De hebdomadibus* 1.61, ed. Häring (n. 17 above) 90, 149, 191.

[19]Ibid. 64 n. 1.

[20]Francis Lecomte, ed., "Un commentaire scripturaire du XIIe siècle: Le *Tractatus in Hexameron* de Hughes d'Amiens (Archevêque de Rouen 1130–1164)," *AHDLMA* 25 (1958) 227–94; PL 192.1247–56.

[21]Manitius 3.117.

[22]Clarembald, *De Trinitate* 4.11.1, ed. Häring (n. 17 above) 147.

[23]Clarembald, *Epistola ad Odonem* 2, ibid. 63.

[24]Clarembald, *De Trinitate*, intro. 23 and prol. 3, ibid. 74, 76.

[25]*Petri Abaelardi opera theologica*, ed. E. M. Buytaert, CCL cm 11 (1969) 41. His commentary (PL 178.731–84) on the *Hexameron* is called *expositio*. The same term is used for his commentaries on the Lord's Prayer (PL 178.611–18), the Apostles' Creed (617–30), the Athanasian Creed (629–30), and St Paul's Letter to the Romans (783–874).

In a similar fashion, Gilbert, bishop of Poitiers (1142–54), must have published all his commentaries anonymously and without inscription. This assumption would account for the fact that most copies circulated without attribution to Gilbert and that the titles, if provided at all, are far from uniform. The most common inscription seems to be *glosa* (or *glose*) *super.* . . .[26] Other manuscripts introduce his expositions as *Epistole (Pauli) glosate*[27] or *Psalterium glosatum.*[28] Instead of *glose* we encounter the diminutive *glosule.*[29] Less frequent than one might expect is the use of *commentarius,*[30] *commentarium,*[31] and *commentum.*[32] In addition we meet *expositio,*[33] *explanatio,*[34] *lectura,*[35] and *postilla.*[36] Of special interest is the term *glosatura*[37] because of the distinction made between the *glosatura parva* or *antiqua* of the early period,[38] the *glosatura media* or *minor* by Gilbert of Poitiers, and the *glosatura magna* or *maior* of Peter Lombard.[39]

---

[26]MSS Brussels Bibl. Roy. 131, fol. 265; Cambrai 308, fol. 1; Leipzig 427, fol. 1 and 428, fol. 1; St. Florian, Stiftsb. VI.44, fol. 4; Zwettl, Stiftsb. 38, fol. 1v; Troyes 488, fol. 1: *Glosa et expositio super psalterium*; Valenciennes 42, fol. 1: *Glose super psalterium collecte de dictis sanctorum.*

[27]MS Cambridge, Pembroke 78, fol. 1 (saec XII).

[28]MS Lincoln, Cathedral Lib. 174, fol. 1v (saec. XII).

[29]MS Reims 149, fol. 4 (saec. XII). See also the *Glosule glosularum* attributed to Ralph of Laon, analyzed by Artur M. Landgraf, "Familienbildung bei Paulinenkommentaren des 12. Jahrhunderts," *Biblica* 13 (1932) 61–72, 169–93; and idem, trans. Paul G. Gleis, "Some Unknown Writings of the Early Scholastic Period," *New Scholasticism* 4 (1930) 1–22 at 10.

[30]MS Bourges 56, fol. 1 (saec. XII): *Commentarius in psalmos*; MS Oxford, Magd. Coll. 118, fol. 33 (saec. XII): *"Commentarius cum prologo.* . . . *Incipiunt glose.* . . ."

[31]MS Vat lat 89, fol. 1 (saec. XII–XIII): *Commentarium in psalterium.*

[32]MS Oxford, Univ. Coll. 62, fol. 65 (saec. XII): *Commentum super epistolas Pauli.* On the strength of manuscript evidence, the large commentary on St John (CCL cm 9.1–789: *Commentarius*) by Rupert of Deutz, written ca. 1115, is a *commentum*, not a *commentarius.*

[33]MS Monte Cassino 235, fol. 11 (saec. XII); MS Rome, Vallicelliana C. 36, fol. 54 (saec. XII): *Expositio psalmorum.*

[34]MS Troyes 764, fol. 1 (saec. XII): *Explanatio in psalmos.* The diminutive *explanatiuncula* is used by Andrew of St Victor: Smalley, *Study* 120. A commentator on Boethius (MS Munich Clm 14689) speaks of both *explanatiuncula* and *explicatiuncula*; Jeauneau: *Lectio* 312, 325.

[35]MS Prague, Univ. 524, fol. 1 (saec. XV).

[36]MS Cambridge, Univ. Lib. Kk.I.21, fol. 1 (saec XIII); MS Florence, Plut. VII dext. cod. 9, fol. 1: *Psalterium cum postilla continua.*

[37]MS Oxford, Ball. 36, fol. 1v (saec XII): *Glosatura Porretani super psalterium.* See also *Chronicon Turonense*, in *Recueil des historiens des Gaules et de la France* 12 (1781; rev. ed. 1877) 461–78 at 472B: "Compactam edidit glosaturam," and *Chronicon Nicolai Trivetti*, in Luc d'Achéry, ed., *Spicilegium*, 2nd ed. S. Baluze, E. Martène, and L. F. J. de la Barre (3 vols. Paris 1723; repr. Farnborough, Eng. 1967–68) 3.143–231 at 144.

[38]Landgraf (n. 15 above) 74; idem, "Untersuchungen zu den Eigenlehren Gilberts de la Porrée," *Zeitschrift für katholische Theologie* 54 (1930) 180–213 at 197; Smalley, *Study* 73.

[39]Landgraf (n. 15 above) 75n. Ignatius Brady, ed., *Magistri Petri Lombardi Parisiensis episcopi Sententiae in IV libris distinctae*, Spicilegium Bonaventurianum 4 (Grottaferrata 1971) *Prolegomena* 47*. Ermenegildo Bertola, "Il commentario paolino di P. Lombardo," *Pier Lombardo* 3 (Novaro 1959) 75–90. Artur M. Landgraf, "Zur Methode der biblischen Textkritik im 12. Jahrhundert," *Biblica* 10 (1929) 445–74 at 453 n. 3.

The question whether Peter Lombard himself adopted the expression *glosa*, now commonly used of his scriptural commentaries,[40] is still worth investigating. The chronicler Alberic of Trois-Fontaines mentions the Lombard's commentary on the Psalms as *opus super psalterium*.[41] An earlier reference classifies his commentaries as *libri*.[42] Gerhoch of Reichersberg denounces the Lombard and reminds pope Alexander III of errors he discovered in Peter's *glosis psalterii et in sententiis*.[43] An anonymous commentary on Peter's fourth book of *Sentences* is entitled *notule super quartum librum sententiarum*;[44] another exposition of the same book has survived as *Lectura super quartum sententiarum*.[45] The term *notule* occurs also in a gloss on a commentary attributed to Peter Comestor: *Notule quedam super psalterium glosatum*.[46]

Historians have noticed that in his commentary on Romans, Peter Abelard has inserted the occasional *questio*.[47] Its later expansion produced a new literary genre under the title *questiones*. About the middle of the century the English scholar Robert of Melun expounded the Pauline Letters in the form of *Questiones de epistolis Pauli*.[48] The work was preceded by Robert's *Questiones de divina pagina*.[49] The *Questiones* attributed to Hugh of St Victor[50] are now considered to belong to one of Robert's followers. As a rule, the *questio* begins with the formula *Queritur utrum*; the answer is often introduced as *solutio*.

Later the term *distinctiones* became more fashionable. In 1186, Garnier of Rochefort compiled his alphabetical *Distinctiones 'Angelus'*, published as the *Allegoriae* of Rabanus Maurus.[51] Peter of Poitiers (d. 1205) is the author of

---

[40]Brady, *Prolegomena* (n. 39 above) 46*–71*.

[41]Alberic of Trois-Fontaines, *Chronica*, ed. Paul Scheffer-Boichorst, MGH SS 23.843. The printed edition (PL 191) calls it *In totum psalterium commentarii*.

[42]Brady, *Prolegomena* (n. 39 above) 46*. The current title *Collectanea* is of much later date.

[43]Gerhoch of Reichersberg, *Epist.* 17, PL 193.565A. See Peter Classen, *Gerhoch von Reichersberg* (Wiesbaden 1960) 391.

[44]MS Vat Reg lat 411. Landgraf (n. 15 above) 137, 138.

[45]MS Vat lat 78, fols. 152–79v. Landgraf (n. 15 above) 175.

[46]MS Rouen 129. Landgraf (n. 15 above) 142. See also MS Vat Ottob lat 86, fols. 1–228v, containing glosses on Lombard's commentary on the Psalms collected from Gilbert's commentary.

[47]See Smalley, *Study* 66–74 and Landgraf (n. 15 above) 48–50.

[48]Raymond M. Martin, ed., *Oeuvres de Robert de Melun*, Spicilegium sacrum Lovaniense 13, 18, 21, 25 (4 vols. Louvain 1932–52) 2.1–318.

[49]Ibid. 1.3–62; Franz Bliemetzrieder, "Robert von Melun und die Schule Anselms von Laon," *Zeitschrift für Kirchengeschichte* 53 (1934) 117–70; Artur M. Landgraf, "Quelques collections de 'Quaestiones' de la seconde moitié du XIIe siècle," RTAM 7 (1935) 113–28 at 122–26.

[50]*Quaestiones et decisiones in epistolas d. Pauli*, PL 175.431–1088.

[51]*Allegoriae in universam sacram scripturam*, PL 112.849–1088; André Wilmart, "Les allégories sur L'Ecriture attribuées à Raban Maur," *Revue bénédictine* 32 (1920) 47–56; MSS Troyes 32, fols. 1–157, and 396, fols. 1–169, analyzed by Clemens Baeumker, ed., *Contra Amaurianos*, BGPTMA 24 (Münster 1926) xxxvi. Arnulf of Orléans is the author of *Allegoriae super Ovidii methamorphosin*; Jeauneau, *Lectio* 128–29.

Distinctiones super psalterium, and Peter the Chanter (d. 1197) the compiler of the *Distinctiones 'Abel'*.[52] William of Ramsey (fl. 1200) is known as the author of *Distinctiones super Cantica*.[53]

Several scriptural commentaries ascribed to Hugh of St Victor have been published as *Allegoriae* and *Adnotationes*.[54] The inscription *Summa super psalterium* heads a commentary by Prepositinus,[55] but perhaps it would be more accurate to call it *Distinctiones*.[56]

Finally, simple prepositions such as *de, in*, and *super* often denote a commentary. Thus, St Augustine wrote *De Genesi ad litteram*, and the title *Anselmus super psalterium* means a commentary on the Psalms by Anselm.[57]

It must be conceded that, for whatever reasons, expositors in the twelfth century were not overly concerned about the titles to be bestowed on their works. In the manuscripts, commentaries written by Andrew of St Victor are entitled *notule, compilationes*, and *exposicio historica*, while Andrew himself refers to them more modestly as *expositiuncula, explanatiuncula*, or *libri exposicionum*.[58]

This multiplicity of synonyms for what we would generally call "commentaries" was by no means restricted to biblical works. I have already noted that Gilbert of Poitiers cannot be the author of the numerous titles given to his scriptural commentaries. The same is true of Gilbert's exposition of the *opuscula sacra*. Most copies are anonymous. An early codex (MS Valenciennes 197) bears the title *Gilebertus super libros Boetii. Prologus cum commentario*.[59] According to its *explicit* the same commentary is a *tractatus*.[60] Other manuscripts call the work *commentum*.[61] A later inscription in a copy preserved at Bologna defines it as an *expositio*.[62] In MS BN lat 16341 the word *explanatio* is used.[63] The inscription *commentarius* occurs in MSS Bruges 133 and Paris BN lat 18093.[64] In MS Zwettl 314 the verb *glosauit* is employed.[65] The inscription *glosa* is found in MS Arras 967.[66]

[52]Landgraf (n. 15 above) 162, 180.

[53]Jean Leclercq, "Les *Distinctiones super Cantica* de Guillaume de Ramsey," *Sacris erudiri* 10 (1958) 329–52; see also Richard H. and Mary A. Rouse, "Biblical Distinctions in the Thirteenth Century," AHDLMA 41 (1974) 27–37.

[54]*Allegoriae*, PL 175.633–924; *Adnotationes*, ibid. 87–99.

[55]Landgraf (n. 15 above) 143, 155.

[56]See MS Munich Clm 4784: "Collecta ex distinctionibus Prepositini."

[57]Landgraf (n. 15 above) 72; MS Arras 626, fol. 2.

[58]Smalley, *Study* 120, 376.

[59]Nikolaus M. Häring, *The Commentaries on Boethius by Gilbert of Poitiers*, Pontifical Institute of Mediaeval Studies, Studies and Texts 13 (Toronto 1966) 53.

[60]Häring, *Commentaries/Gilbert* (n. 59 above) 364. See also MS Dublin, Trin. 303 (ibid.).

[61]Häring, *Commentaries/Gilbert* (n. 59 above) 364: MS Munich Clm 18478.

[62]MS Bologna, Univ. 1509, fol. 1.

[63]Häring, *Commentaries/Gilbert* (n. 59 above) 56.

[64]Ibid.

[65]Ibid. 364. Other equivalents used are *exponere, explicare, explanare*, and *glosulare* (see Tullio Gregory, "Note e testi per la storia del platonismo medievale," *Giornale critico della filosofia italiana* [1955] 346–84 at 348).

[66]Häring, *Commentaries/Gilbert* (n. 59 above) 186.

All commentaries composed by Thierry of Chartres are anonymous.[67] Originally they too circulated without an inscription.[68] In one case the heading *glosa* has been entered by a later hand;[69] in another instance the inscription *commentum*, by a later hand, is found.[70]

Which of these numerous titles enjoyed the greatest popularity? *Glosa* seems to have been the noun most commonly used to designate a commentary. William of Conches explains why *glosa* was preferred to *commentum*: "Nowadays," he declares, "we call *commentum* only an explanatory text. Hence it is different from the *glosa*, for a *commentum* deals only with the *sententia*. It says nothing about the *continuatio* or the *expositio* of the *littera*. But a *glosa* takes care of all these factors. That is why it is called *glosa*."[71] In other words, according to William of Conches, *commentum* is a sort of résumé (*in unum collectio*) describing the author's doctrine (*sententia*),[72] while the *glosa*[73] explains individual words and pays attention to the context (*continuatio*).[74] William's remark also aims at an entirely new genre called *sententie*.[75]

A later generation of commentators (Peter Comestor and Peter the Chanter) distinguished with care between *expositor* and *glosator* or *ordinator glose*. The *expositor* was the patristic and postpatristic authority quoted in the gloss.[76] The *glosator* or *ordinator glose*, on the other hand, was one of those masters who while putting together the gloss added his personal comment. In this sense Peter Comestor contrasts Rabanus Maurus, the *expositor*, with the

[67] An exception is Thierry's *Heptateuchon*, the prologue of which has been edited in Jeauneau, *Lectio* 90: "Incipit prologus Theodorici. . . ."

[68] Häring, *Commentaries/Thierry* (n. 16 above) 57.

[69] Ibid. 257.

[70] Ibid. 405. The motives for anonymity were not always unselfish. Honorius Augustodunensis, *Elucidarium* (PL 172.1110A, or ed. Martin Grabmann, *Miscellanea Giovanni Mercati*, Studi e testi 121–126 [6 vols. Vatican City 1946] 2.247), concealed his name to escape the adverse effects of jealousy: "Nomen autem meum silentio subtegi, ne invidia tabescens suis iuberet lectionibus utile opus contempnendo negligi." See also Paul Lehmann, "Mittelalterliche Büchertitel," *Erforschung des Mittelalters* (5 vols. Stuttgart 1959–62) 5.1–93.

[71] *Glosae super Platonem* (n. 3 above) 67: "Non hodie uocamus commentum nisi alterius libri expositorium. Quod differt a glosa. Commentum enim, solam sententiam exequens, de continuatione uel expositione littere nichil agit. Glosa uero omnia illa exequitur. Vnde dicitur glosa i.e. lingua." See also Häring, *Commentaries/Thierry* (n. 16 above) 57; Jeauneau, *Lectio* 111–12, 238.

[72] The exact meaning of *sententia* is difficult to determine. Leclercq, *Love of Learning* 171 writes: "In monastic tradition, however, the primitive meaning of *sententia* is also the text being commented."

[73] Conrad of Hirsau, *Dialogus super auctores*, ed. R. B. C. Huygens, Collection Latomus 17 (Brussels 1955) 19.232–34, declares that, "when we clarify the meaning of one word by another word, it is called glosa in Greek, lingua in Latin." See also Isidore of Seville, *Etymologiae* 1.30.1, ed. W. M. Lindsay (2 vols. Oxford 1911); Jean Leclercq, "Le 'De grammatica' de Hugues de Saint-Victor," AHDLMA 14 (1943–45) 263–322 at 299.

[74] Jeauneau, *Lectio* 341–42 concerning William of Conches; concerning Thierry's use of *continuatio* see Häring, *Commentaries/Thierry* (n. 16 above) 599. Smalley, *Study* 70, interprets it as "meaning 'the sequence of thought.'" Its use among the canonists is listed in Kuttner, *Repertorium* 521, s.v. *continuationes*. See also Marie-Dominique Chenu, "L'homme et la nature: Perspectives sur la Renaissance du XIIᵉ siècle," AHDLMA 19 (1952) 39–66 at 58 n. 1.

[75] Landgraf (n. 15 above) 68–70.

[76] Smalley, *Study* 225.

glosator.[77] Peter the Chanter warns his reader, "This gloss has been put in by the *ordinator*, not by Jerome."[78]

THE BIBLICAL *GLOSA ORDINARIA*

In the twelfth century, theologians begin quoting a *glosa* as doctrinal authority. As a rule, they mean the biblical *Glosa ordinaria*, which is a combination of interlinear and marginal elucidations of the text or *littera.*[79] Compared to commentaries of the Carolingian period, the *Glosa ordinaria* generally has shorter patristic extracts[80] and leaves more room for the glossator's personal views. The interlinear gloss clarifies the meaning of individual words. A well-known nonbiblical example of this kind is the Carolingian gloss on the *opuscula sacra* of Boethius edited as a work of John the Scot.[81]

The biblical *Glosa ordinaria* was long considered the work of Walafrid Strabo (d. 849), but recent research has established Anselm of Laon and his brother Ralph as its principal originators and promotors.[82] The first efforts were concentrated on the Psalms and the Pauline Letters.[83] Their work became known as the *glosatura parva* and was soon held to be too short to satisfy the students.

The chronicler Robert of Auxerre recorded the evolution which took place in the first half of the twelfth century. Peter Lombard, he related, "has given a clearer and more detailed exposition of the *glosatura* on the Psalms and the Pauline Letters which Anselm had divided into short interlinear and marginal glosses and which Gilbert then transformed into a coherent text."[84] (Perhaps, however, it would be more accurate to credit Abelard with this development.) To identify Gilbert's commentaries scholars began to cite it as *glosatura media.*[85]

---

[77]*Glosses on the Gospels*: MS Oxford, Bodl. Laud Misc. 291, fol. 6v.

[78]*Commentary on Isaiah*: MS Brussels, Bibl. Roy. 252, fol. 26v.

[79]Landgraf (n. 15 above) 72–76.

[80]Carolingian exegesis consisted largely of lengthy extracts collected from the writings of the (available) Church Fathers. By the twelfth century, Carolingian exegetes enjoyed an authority similar to that of the earlier writers.

[81]Glosses on Boethius's *opuscula sacra* in Edward K. Rand, ed., *Johannes Scottus*, Quellen und Untersuchungen zur lateinischen Philologie des Mittelalters 1.2 (Munich 1906).

[82]*Glossa ordinaria*, PL 113–114 (= Basel 1498 ed.). Smalley, *Study* 57, notes with resignation, "The myth of Walafrid Strabo's authorship dies hard." See Jean de Blic, "L'oeuvre exégétique de Walafrid Strabon et la *Glossa ordinaria*," RTAM 16 (1949) 5–28.

[83]Beryl Smalley, "Gilbertus Universalis, Bishop of London (1128–34), and the Problem of the 'Glossa Ordinaria,'" RTAM 7 (1935) 235–62 and 8 (1936) 24–60; Landgraf, "Familienbildung," (n. 29 above) 67. Some "forerunners" have been pointed out by Beryl Smalley, "La Glossa Ordinaria: Quelques prédécesseurs d'Anselme de Laon," RTAM 9 (1937) 364–400.

[84]Robert of Auxerre, *Chronicon*, ed. O. Holder-Egger, MGH SS 26.237 (ad. ann. 1153): "Hic etiam glosaturam super psalterium et epistolas Pauli ab Anselmo per glosulas interlineales marginalesque distinctam, post a Gisleberto continuative productam, latius apertiusque explicuit." See also Vincent of Beauvais, *Speculum historiale* 29.1, in *Bibliotheca mundi* (4 vols. Douai 1624) 4.1185; Alberic, *Chronica* (n. 41 above) 840, recommends Gilbert's "minorem glossaturam continuam in psalterium et epistolas Pauli."

[85]Landgraf (n. 15 above) 108.

The chronicler describes Gilbert's gloss as *continuative productam*; this means that he wove the words of his sources, his own views, and the words of Scripture into a single unit.[86] In most manuscripts the scriptural words are marked by underlining. The names of the patristic and postpatristic (Carolingian) authors from whose writings the glossator gathered his exegesis are often indicated in the margins. Gilbert adopted the same procedure in his commentary on the *opuscula sacra*, where the words of Boethius are treated with the same high regard for accuracy.[87]

The *explicit* in MS Oxford, Balliol Coll. 36 suggests that Gilbert composed his commentary on the Psalms before Anselm of Laon died.[88] Methodically it still follows the pattern popularized by the Carolingians. In his commentary on St Paul, written much later,[89] Gilbert interspersed brief discussions of theological problems, frequently introduced by such expressions as *Notandum* or *Attendendum*. But by this injection of personal, perhaps controversial, views a gloss ceased to be the neutral voice of tradition and became the source of hostility.

As early as 1141 Gerhoch of Reichersberg began to attack Anselm, Gilbert, and later Peter Lombard, all of whom he accused of inserting falsehoods into their glosses.[90] Commenting on Psalm 38, Gerhoch cites a lengthy passage from Gilbert's exposition of Eph. 4:10, "Hic dicendum quod inter personam et eius substantiam ratio dividit. . . ."[91] The point had been loudly debated at the consistory of Reims in 1148. Only at a later date did Gerhoch realize that the author of the passage was not Augustine but Gilbert.[92] Yet despite his fierce denunciation of the French expositors, Gerhoch often borrowed long paragraphs from Gilbert's commentary on the Psalms without acknowledgment, just as the Lombard had done in explaining the Letters of St Paul.[93]

---

[86]Such a gloss is also described as *glosa continua* or *perpetua*. See Alberic, *Chronica* (n. 41 above) 840, quoted in n. 84 above.

[87]Häring, *Commentaries/Gilbert* (n. 59 above). The extract-type of gloss made up almost exclusively of patristic quotations is represented in Nikolaus M. Häring, "The Tractatus de Trinitate of Adhemar of Saint-Ruf (Valence)," AHDLMA 31 (1964) 111–206.

[88]Manuscripts are listed by Stegmüller, *Repertorium biblicum* (n. 10 above) 2.345–46 no. 2511. See also Maria Fontana, "Il commento ai Salmi di Gilberto della Porrée," *Logos* [Rivista internazionale di filosofia] (Palermo 1930) 283–301.

[89]For manuscripts see Stegmüller, *Repertorium biblicum* (n. 10 above) 2.349–50 no. 2528. See also Vincenzo Miano, "Il commento alle lettere di S. Paolo di Gilberto Porretano," *Bibliotheca pontificii Athenaei Antoniani* 7 (Rome 1951) 171–90; Maurice Simon, "La glose de l'Epître aux Romains de Gilbert de la Porrée," *Revue d'histoire ecclésiastique* 52 (1957) 51–80.

[90]Damien van den Eynde, *Gerhohi praepositi Reichersbergi: Opera inedita* (2 vols. in 3 Rome 1955–56) 1.70–71.

[91]*Commentarium in Psalmos*, PL 193.1412B–D. See Classen (n. 43 above) 117, 436–38.

[92]*Commentarium* (n. 91 above) 1412D.

[93]Van den Eynde (n. 90 above) 2.674; Brady, *Prolegomena* (n. 39 above) 75*. For modern readers the evaluation accorded a medieval author by his contemporaries should help avoid a one-sided judgment. A twelfth-century cataloguer, for instance, preferred the Lombard to all other expositors: "magistris sui temporis et scripturarum expositoribus eo maxime preferendus iudicatur quod ingenio sagaci et usu assiduo tanta in exponendis Scripturis luce claruerit ut pene magisterio doctoris non egeat qui glosarum ipsius lectioni animum intendere uoluerit." Nikolaus M. Häring,

The expositor could also use his skill to display his knowledge of cosmology, a less controversial branch of medieval learning. Thierry of Chartres referred to his commentary on Genesis as a *tractatus*, and about the year 1142 his contemporary, Hugh of Amiens, published a similar work under the title *Tractatus in Hexameron*.[94] The choice of the word *tractatus* may not have been accidental, for the opening chapters of Genesis afforded a welcome opportunity to expound and enlarge on the principles and teaching of cosmology.[95]

Both Hugh of Amiens and Thierry begin with a full-fledged *accessus ad auctorem*. Hugh, a former Benedictine abbot, proceeds in a traditional manner, systematically presenting the scriptural *littera* in the form of *lemmata* and interpreting their meaning. Thierry's commentary, on the other hand, displays all the characteristics of the *glosa continua*; his use of nonbiblical authors such as Trismegistus, Plato, and Vergil is another distinctive novelty in biblical commentaries. Thierry interprets the text *secundum phisicam* and deliberately disregards the allegorical and moral meanings expounded, as he says, by earlier commentators.[96]

Doctrinally the two expositors differ considerably. Hugh prefers the traditional exegesis. Since Genesis attributes the creation of the world to God, Thierry chose the first verse to enlarge on the deity and the Trinity.[97] Here he calls on the quadrivium (arithmetic, music, geometry, and astronomy) rather than Scripture and the Fathers to assist him. His basic thesis is surprisingly simple: God created matter, i.e. the four elements (earth, water, air, light). Thereupon the evolution of the universe followed without further divine intervention in accordance with the physical laws of nature. Thus Thierry shows how plants and animals came into existence. But he is silent concerning the origin of human beings. This silence is understandable in view of the human soul, whose spiritual nature could hardly be explained by recourse to the four elements. (The same silence prevails in the *tractatulus* on Genesis written by Thierry's disciple, Clarembald of Arras.)[98] Opposition to the transformation of biblical books into treatises on cosmology is already registered by Arnold of Bonneval.[99]

CANONISTIC GLOSSING AND COMMENTARIES

In the field of canon law the need of, and call for, clarifications became equally pressing after the publication (about 1140) of Gratian's *Concordantia dis-*

"Two Catalogues of Mediaeval Authors," *Franciscan Studies* 26 (1966) 195–211 at 211 (*Catalogus scriptorum ecclesiasticorum* 13). The same author holds that Gilbert's gloss is "prolixior et euidentior" (210).

[94]Lecomte (n. 20 above). See also Arnold of Bonneval, *Tractatus de operibus sex dierum*, PL 189.1507–70.

[95]Ceslaus Spicq, *Esquisse d'une histoire de l'exégèse latine au moyen âge*, Bibliothèque thomiste 26 (Paris 1944) 29, 118, 125, 323.

[96]Häring, *Commentaries/Thierry* (n. 16 above) 555: *Tractatus* 1.

[97]Ibid. 568–75: *Tractatus* 30–47.

[98]Häring, *Life and Works* (n. 17 above) 225–49.

[99]Arnold of Bonneval, *Tractatus* (n. 94 above) 1507A–1516C.

cordantium canonum, better known as *Decretum Gratiani*. Before long, interlinear and marginal glosses began to surround the canons collected by the monk of Bologna,[100] and gradually led to what was (and is) known as the decretistic *Glosa ordinaria*.

The historical development shows certain features in common between the biblical *Glosa ordinaria* and the method of commenting on Roman law. Interlinear glosses on Roman law can be traced back to the end of the eleventh century; in the middle of the twelfth the system was extended to the canons of ecclesiastical law. In time, these two types of annotations developed into what historians of canon law designate as *apparatus*, written in the wide margins provided for this purpose on all sides of the text. The *apparatus* clarified individual words and included references to similar canons, *notabilia, contraria*, and sources. Its initially short elucidations grew into larger doctrinal summaries. Frequently sigla indicating the names of glossators were added.[101]

In order to classify the different forms of glosses that emanated from Bologna, modern canonists distinguish three successive types. The first is ascribed to Paucapalea and consists essentially of citations of parallel or contrary texts, occasionally accompanied by solutions. Glosses of the second type are more discursive in nature and of higher quality, with summaries and schematized distinctions. The third type, which begins in the sixties, shows an increasing amount of material and progressively more thorough treatments of the text.[102]

Toward the end of the century, canonists strove to collect and organize the steadily spreading and growing *apparatus glosarum*. The most popular collection of this kind became known as the decretistic *Glosa ordinaria*; it was edited shortly after 1215 by Johannes Teutonicus, and revised some thirty years later by Bartholomew of Brescia.[103]

While the interlinear and marginal method of commenting established the earlier types of *apparatus*, a more systematic elaboration soon resulted in the canonistic *summa*. The *Summa* of Paucapalea, a disciple of Gratian, was composed between 1140 and 1148.[104] Its *continuationes* introducing the *Causae* are the most extensive part of the work. Before 1148 Roland Bandinelli, later

---

[100]Kuttner, *Repertorium*; Hermann Kantorowicz, *Studies in the Glossators of the Roman Law* (Cambridge 1938; 2nd ed. rev. Peter Weimar [Aalen 1969]).

[101]An alphabetical list of sigla has been compiled by Kuttner, *Repertorium* 10–12. A similar recognition of modern authors is not found in the biblical *Glosa ordinaria*. The canonical meanings of *casus, notabilia, contraria, questio*, and other terms are explained in *Repertorium* 228–39 (*casus, notabilia*), 243–56 (*questio*). A lucid description of the canonical *glosa, summa, questio*, and *distinctio* is also given by Leonard E. Boyle, s.v. "Decretists," in *New Catholic Encyclopedia* 4 (1967) 711–13.

[102]Kuttner, *Repertorium* 3–8.

[103]Ibid. 93–115.

[104]Johann Friedrich von Schulte, ed., *Die Summa des Paucapalea über das Decretum Gratiani* (Giessen 1890); Kuttner, *Repertorium* 125–27, describes its contents as follows: "Sie enthält fast nur Auszüge aus den Dicta Gratiani, Paleae und Historiae, ist also (in der Terminologie der Theologen des 12. Jahrhunderts) eigentlich ein Sentenzenwerk" (126). Roland Bandinelli calls it *rationes*: Josef Juncker, "Summen und Glossen," ZRG kan Abt 14 (1924) 384–474 at 412.

pope Alexander III (1159–81), wrote his *Stroma ex decretorum corpore carptum*.[105] The sigla "R" and "r" in MS Vat lat 3529 are now considered to mean glosses derived from Roland Bandinelli.[106]

In its combination of a synthetic and an analytical approach to the *littera*, the *Summa* composed by master Rufinus between 1157 and 1159 represents the mixed type of *apparatus* which served as the model for many later glossators.[107] It was used by Stephen of Tournai, whose *Summa* dates to the sixties.[108] Although in the prologue to his *Summa*, completed after 1171, John of Faenza (Faventinus) openly admits that he borrowed from Rufinus and Stephen, he was perhaps the most popular commentator before Huguccio. Simon of Bisignano, one of Gratian's direct pupils, is believed to have composed his *Summa* between March 1177 and March 1179. The fact that the *Summa* written between 1179 and 1181 by Sicard of Cremona contains numerous *questiones, distinctiones, solutiones,* and arguments *pro* and *contra*, clearly indicates that devices practiced in philosophy and theology were being applied to canon law.[109] All these commentators were surpassed by master Huguccio, the future bishop of Ferrara (1190–1210), whose huge *Summa* was completed about 1189.[110]

To the decades just mentioned belong such anonymous commentaries as the *Summa "Animal est substantia"* (formerly called *Summa Bambergensis*),[111] *Summa Parisiensis*,[112] *Summa "Omnis qui iuste iudicat"* (formerly *Summa Lipsiensis*),[113] and others. More details are known about the compilers and glossators of the five *compilationes*, collections of decretals in

[105]Friedrich Thaner, ed., *Die Summa magistri Rolandi, nachmals Papstes Alexander III., nebst einem Anhange* (Innsbruck 1874); Kuttner, *Repertorium* 127–29.

[106]Kuttner, *Repertorium* 55–56; Juncker (n. 104 above) 428.

[107]Johann Friedrich von Schulte, ed., *Die Summa magistri Rufini zum Decretum Gratiani* (Giessen 1892); superseded by Heinrich Singer, ed., *Die Summa decretorum des magister Rufinus* (Paderborn 1902). Kuttner, *Repertorium* 59 and 123 distinguishes between "Glossen-Apparate" and the more systematic "Apparat-Summen." The former may be found with the *Decretum* (as marginal glosses) or independently.

[108]Johann Friedrich von Schulte, ed., *Die Summa des Stephanus Tornacensis über das Decretum Gratiani* (Giessen 1891), incomplete. Kuttner, *Repertorium* 133–35.

[109]Terence P. McLaughlin, "The Extravagantes in the Summa of Simon of Bisignano," *Mediaeval Studies* 20 (1958) 167–76; Kuttner, *Repertorium* 143–46 (Ioh. Faventinus), 148–49 (Simon), 150–53 (Sicard of Cremona). The literary genus of the canonistic *distinctiones* is described in *Repertorium* 208–27 and Boyle (n. 101 above). Juncker (n. 104 above) 413, quotes a definition, "Commentum est generalis expositio super textum," and points out that extensive theoretical explanations were called *documenta* by Rufinus, while *summa* was used for a compilation of (shortened) sources (Stephen of Tournai). A *glosa* meant a brief explanation.

[110]Kuttner, *Repertorium* 155–60.

[111]Ibid. 206; Landgraf, "Zur Methode" (n. 39 above) 450.

[112]Terence P. McLaughlin, ed., *The Summa Parisiensis on the Decretum Gratiani* (Toronto 1952); Kuttner, *Repertorium* 177–78. See also the *Summa "Elegantius in iure divino" seu Coloniensis*, now being edited by Gerard Fransen, with Stephan Kuttner, Monumenta iuris canonici, ser. A: Corpus glossatorum 1.1–2 (New York 1969–78); *Repertorium* 170–72.

[113]Johann Friedrich von Schulte, "Die Summa Decreti Lipsiensis des Cod. 986 der Leipziger Universitätsbibliothek," SB Vienna 68 (1871) 37–54; Kuttner, *Repertorium* 196–98.

use at Bologna. Between 1188 and June 1192 Bernard Balbi of Pavia put together and glossed his *Breviarium extravagantium*, which the school of Bologna honored as the *Compilatio prima*.[114] The authoritative *apparatus* of glosses (that is, the *glosa ordinaria*) to the first three *Compilationes* was published in 1210–15 by Tancred of Bologna. The compiler of the *Glosa ordinaria* on the *Decretum*, Johannes Teutonicus, collected the glosses on the fourth (1217) and (probably) James of Albenga those on the fifth *Compilatio*.[115]

Since large sections of Gratian's *Decretum* were made up of canons with considerable theological import, commentators could not cope with their subject without previous training in theology. It was natural that this training should influence their views. Being compelled to debate divergent theological opinions, Bologna and Paris did not always agree.[116] It was also to be expected that part of the canonistic terminology (*continuatio, distinctio, questio, summa*, etc.) should witness to the interaction between canon law and other academic disciplines.

THE *ACCESSUS AD AUCTORES*

The *accessus ad auctorem* found in many biblical commentaries of the twelfth century seems to have originated in Abelard's philosophical writings. The introduction to his *Editio super Porphyrium* begins, "Intentio Porphyrii est. . . ." Then he turns to *materia* and *finis*, the title and usefulness of Porphyry's treatise. In his commentary on Aristotle's *De interpretatione* he follows the same pattern: "Intentio Aristotilis . . . materia . . . finalis causa . . . titulus."[117] His commentary on the *De divisionibus* opens with the statement, "Intentio Boetii est. . . ." Then Abelard points out the book's *materia, finis*, and position in the order of sciences. The explanation of *Topics* is introduced in the same manner: "Topicorum intentio est . . . materia auctoris . . . tituli inscriptio . . . modus . . . utilitas. . . ," and it ends with the place of the tract in the discipline of logic.[118]

---

[114]The five *compilationes* are described by Kuttner, *Repertorium* 322–85.

[115]Alfonso M. Stickler, *Historia iuris canonici latini institutiones academicae* (Turin 1954) 233–36; Kuttner, *Repertorium* 327 (Tancred), 373 (Ioh. Teutonicus), 383 (James of Albenga).

[116]Nikolaus M. Häring, "The Interaction between Canon Law and Sacramental Theology in the Twelfth Century," *Proceedings of the Fourth International Congress of Medieval Canon Law, Toronto, 21–25 August 1972*, ed. Stephan Kuttner, Monumenta iuris canonici, ser. C: Subsidia 5 (Vatican City 1976) 483–93.

[117]Dal Pra (n. 8 above) 3–4 (Porphyry) and 69–73 (Aristotle). For standardized patterns see R. B. C. Huygens, ed., *Accessus ad auctores*, Collection Latomus 15 (Brussels 1954); Edwin A. Quain, "The Medieval accessus ad auctores," *Traditio* 3 (1945) 215–64; Richard W. Hunt, "The Introductions to the 'Artes' in the Twelfth Century," *Studia mediaevalia in honorem . . . Raymundi Josephi Martin* (Bruges 1948) 85–112. Some *accessus* to the *Timaeus* are analyzed by Gregory (n. 65 above).

[118]Dal Pra (n. 8 above) 155–57, 205–08.

Later Abelard transferred this schema to his biblical commentaries. In his *Hexameron* he explains *materia* and *intentio*.[119] In commenting on Romans he had already formulated the general rule that, in accordance with the laws of rhetoric, every book of Holy Scripture intends either to teach or to cause emotion.[120] Abelard was convinced that St Paul wrote according to the rules of rhetoric to make his readers attentive (*attentos*), docile (*dociles*), and well-disposed (*benivolos*).[121] Each Letter, we learn, has its own *intentio, materia*, and *modus tractandi*.[122] In the previous century, scholars like Othloh of St Emmeram (d. ca. 1070) had taken exception to this trend and politely begged to disagree with such claims made by the "dialecticians."[123]

We have already seen that Abelard's exposition is to be classified as *glosa perpetua* or *continua*, with the occasional insertion of a *questio*.[124] The inroads of the liberal arts upon theology are confirmed by the fact that among Abelard's *auctoritates* we encounter Plato, Cicero, Horace, Juvenal, Lucan, Ovid, Terence, Vergil, and Quintilian.[125]

The Abelardian approach was soon adopted by other commentators.[126] In his exposition of the Song of Songs, Honorius Augustodunensis states: "At the beginnings of books three things are investigated: author, subject matter, and intention"; then he discusses the title of the work.[127] Explaining the Psalms, he speaks of title, intention, matter, author, usefulness, and final cause.[128] In his *Hexameron* he discusses only intention and subject matter.[129]

By 1145 the device was a common practice, as we learn from Gerhoch of Reichersberg. To Gerhoch's mind it is worthwhile to examine four aspects: *materia, intentio, modus tractandi,* and *titulus libri*; he notes that the question whether the *modus tractandi* varies in different Psalms had been under discussion.[130]

Peter Lombard, who is thought to have composed his commentary on St Paul after the Council of Reims in 1148,[131] writes in his prologue, "Having

---

[119]*Expositio in Hexameron*, PL 178.732D.

[120]*Commentaria in epistolam Pauli ad Romanos*, PL 178.783B (CCL cm 11.41): "Omnis scriptura diuina more orationis rethorice aut docere intendit aut mouere."

[121]*Expositio in Romanos*, PL 178.787D (CCL cm 11.47); Cicero, *De inventione* 1.16.22.

[122]*Expositio in Romanos*, PL 178.785B (CCL cm 11.43).

[123]Othloh of St Emmeram, *Dialogus de tribus quaestionibus*, preface: PL 146.60B; Smalley, *Study* 46.

[124]E. M. Buytaert, ed., CCL cm 11.17–18; see above at notes 47 and 86.

[125]Ibid. 17.

[126]There is, for instance, no sign of an *accessus* in the commentary written by Rupert of Deutz (n. 32 above) 1.

[127]*Expositio in Cantica Canticorum*, PL 172.347D: "In principiis librorum tria requiruntur, scilicet, auctor, materia, intentio. Auctor, ut noueris nomen scriptoris utrum ethnicus, an fidelis, utrum Catholicus an haereticus fuerit. . . . Auctor libri huius est Spiritus sanctus." He intends to interpret the text *historice, allegorice, tropologice, anagogice* (349A), and he explains the *titulus* (350A).

[128]*Selectorum psalmorum expositio* PL 172.270C–71A.

[129]*Hexameron*, ibid. 253B, 254A.

[130]*Commentarium in psalmos*, PL 193.630C, 633A.

[131]Brady, *Prolegomena* (n. 39 above) 88*.

given the reason for this work, the number and order, the whys and wherefores of the Letters, it remains to delineate subject matter, intention, and *modus tractandi*," and he goes on to say, "Commendat enim personam suam et negotium et auctorem negotii in quibus congrue captat benevolentiam."[132] He copied this Ciceronian pattern from Gilbert's commentary on Romans.[133] In his introduction to the commentary on the Psalms the Lombard deals with *materia, intentio, modus tractandi,* and *ordo.*[134] In addition he explains title, subject matter, intention, and *modus tractandi* of each Psalm.

Hugh of Amiens advises his readers, "pensa auctorem operis, opus auctoris, modum operis, intentionem auctoris."[135] Later he mentions *materia, fructus,* and *utilitas.*[136] In his dedicatory letter to Arnulf, bishop of Lisieux, Hugh declares that he is interested in the *historia* of the text rather than in its allegorical or moral interpretation.[137] He notes that he discussed these aspects in the second book of his *Dialogues.*[138] This shift of emphasis is even more pronounced in Thierry's commentary on Genesis.

In the course of this development, commentators did not lose sight of those elements in scriptural exegesis which separated it from other disciplines. In his *De scripturis et scriptoribus sacris* Hugh of St Victor has a special chapter under the heading "Quod diuina Scriptura ab aliis distinguitur in materia et modo tractandi."[139] And the *accessus ad auctorem* carefully outlined by Herveus of Bourg-Dieu contains a classification according to which his "tractate" on St Paul belongs to ethics: "Et idcirco ad ethicam pertinet tractatus earumdem epistolarum."[140]

---

[132]*Collectanea in omnes D. Pauli Apostoli Epistolas,* PL 191.1302A.

[133]See Gilbert's *accessus* to the Letters of St Paul (MS Bruges 78, fol. 1): "More scribentium epistolas premittit salutationem in qua commendat personam suam et negotium suum et auctorem negotii." Simon (n. 89 above) 56. Cicero, *De inventione* 1.16, 23. Gilbert's *accessus* to the Psalms, ed. Fontana (n. 88 above) 284: "Christus integer, caput cum membris, est materia huius libri. . . . De hac autem materia agit et hoc modo agit hac intentione ut. . . . Titulus libri est: Incipit liber hymnorum. . . . Habent autem singuli psalmi singularem et materiam et modum et finem et titulum. . . . Nunc de genere prophetie dicendum uidetur"; 285: "Post materiam, modum, finem, titulum, et genus prophetie non est pretermittendum. . . ."

[134]*In totum psalterium commentarii,* PL 191.59C: "Materia itaque huius libri est totus Christus. . . . Intentio, homines, in Adam deformatos, Christo novo homini conformare. Modus tractandi . . . de ordine quoque psalmorum. . . . Praeter haec autem in singulis psalmis quaedam specialia consideranda sunt"; 60B (concerning the first Psalm): "Materia autem . . . Christus integer . . . similiter intentio. Modus autem tractandi. . . ."

[135]*Tractatus in Hexameron* 1.3, ed. Lecomte (n. 20 above) 237 (PL 192.1249C).

[136]Ibid. 1.4 and 8, ed. Lecomte 238 (PL 192.1250B–C).

[137]Ibid. 236 (PL 192.1248D): "Nunc autem in hoc opusculo nostro magis historiam exquirendo tractamus, quam sensus allegoricos seu morales attingamus."

[138]*Dialogorum seu quaestionum theologicarum libri septem* 2, PL 192.1153–66.

[139]PL 175.11A; see Nikolaus M. Häring, "The Lectures of Thierry of Chartres on Boethius' De Trinitate," AHDLMA 25 (1958) 113–226 at 119.

[140]Herveus of Bourg-Dieu, *Commentaria in Epistolas Divi Pauli,* PL 181.595A–98D at 595A. See G. Morin, "Un critique en liturgie au XIIe siècle: Le traité inédit d'Hervé de Bourgdieu *De correctione quarundam lectionum*," *Revue bénédictine* 24 (1907) 36–61. Honorius Augustodunensis begins his *Selectorum psalmorum expositio* by dividing philosophy into *physica, ethica,* and *logica* (PL 172.270B). Then he declares, "Ad physicam pertinet Genesis que de naturis lo-

Occasionally commentators felt called upon to rearrange the *littera* of Sacred Scripture. Herveus of Bourg-Dieu, for instance, corrects the word order in St Paul, saying "Ordo est, *An ignoratis. . . .*"[141] Abelard introduces such corrections of word order with the formula *Sic construe.*[142] But not only the *littera* was the object of such scrutiny. Robert of Melun remarks, with an unmistakable touch of sarcasm, "They dispute often very sharply whether the *glosa* is construed in proper order, correctly divided, rightly punctuated, fittingly placed."[143] He even warns against an exaggerated cult of the gloss to the detriment of the *littera.*[144]

What kind of *auctor* did commentators prefer? In the faculty of theology the works of St Augustine did not, for some unknown reason, attract commentators. Boethius was the undisputed favorite. The *opuscula sacra* were so short that the average student could afford his own copy and furnish it with information gathered in the classroom. The two treatises on the Trinity offered the commentator an opportunity to air his views on matter and form, on the ten categories, and many other preliminaries necessary to penetrate into the trinitarian mystery. The christological tract against Nestorius and Eutyches served to expound the concepts of nature, substance, person, and others. Commenting on the *De hebdomadibus*, the third *opusculum*, they enlarged upon the notion of transcendental goodness. The *De consolatione philosophiae*[145] invited commentators to digress on ethics, cosmology, predestination, time and eternity, the purpose of life, and other topics. By far the most popular commentary (still unpublished) on the *De consolatione* was the work of William of Conches.[146]

---

quitur; Epistolae Pauli ad ethicam pertinent, quae de moribus tractant; Psalterium ad logicam, quae et theorica dicitur, eo quod de ratione diuinae scientiae memorat."

[141]*Commentaria* (n. 140 above) PL 181.681A.

[142]*Commentaria* (n. 120 above) CCL cm 11.60, 143, 293.

[143]Smalley, *Study* 219; Robert of Melun, *Sententie*, preface, ed. Martin (n. 48 above) 3.11. See also Raymond M. Martin, "L'oeuvre théologique de Robert de Melun," *Revue d'histoire ecclésiastique* 15 (1914) 456–89 at 474–77.

[144]*Sententie*, preface, ed. Martin (n. 48 above) 3.12.

[145]Pierre P. Courcelle, *La consolation de philosophie dans la tradition littéraire: Antécédents et postérité de Boèce* (Paris 1967) 302–15; R. B. C. Huygens, "Mittelalterliche Kommentare zum O qui perpetua," *Sacris erudiri* 6 (1954) 373–427. A *Commentum Hugonis super De Consolatione* is listed in an ancient catalogue of the works of Hugh of St Victor: Manitius 3.117. William of Conches refers to his own commentary as *Glosule super Boecium:* Jeauneau, *Lectio* 148.

[146]Courcelle (n. 145 above) 408–10. An interesting *accessus* to the *Consolation of Philosophy* is found in MS Troyes 1381 (olim Clairvaux G.78; saec. XIII): "Materia Boetii est philosophica consolatio. Et hec dicitur demonstratio rationabilis rei temporalis de cuius presentia non est gaudendum nec de eius absentia dolendum. Ostendit quid sit summum bonum et ubi situm sit et bonos esse potentes et malos impotentes. Ad ultimum de prouidentia et libero arbitrio. Intentio huius (libri) est non debere desperari de amissione rerum temporalium nec de earundem adeptione gaudere. Utilitas est non extolli prosperitate nec frangi aduersitate. Iste Boecius in fide catholicus conflictum habens cum duobus hereticis, scilicet Nestorio et Euticen, utrumque confutauit. Nestorius Alexandrine urbis episcopus fuit. Euticen abbas in eadem ciuitate. Nestorius duas personas in Christo esse dixit." Then follows information on the life of Boethius: "Boetius iste nobilissimus ciuis Romanus fuit. . . . Deinde tempore Theodorici regis Gothorum rempublicam optinentis et omnes bonos sine alicuius contradictione crudeliter deprimentis, Boecius iste uirtute

Commentators also turned their attention to liturgical texts, and composed commentaries on the Creed attributed to St Athanasius,[147] on the Creed of the Mass and on the so-called Apostles' Creed,[148] on the Lord's Prayer[149] and liturgical texts of minor importance.[150] Alan of Lille was even able to spare the time for a poem on the Pseudo-Athanasian Creed.[151]

Even the field of medicine attracted commentators. The *Versus Egidii de pulsibus*, extant in a thirteenth-century manuscript, may serve as an example: the expositor first investigates the author's intention and his reason for writing the work, then its usefulness and position in the faculty of philosophy, its division and title; mindful of the precepts of rhetoric, he points out the *captatio benivolentie*, the means by which the reader's *attentio* and *docilitas* are won (fol. 28v).[152]

---

fidei armatus." Finally, the epitaph on the wife of Boethius is added: "Heu malus ille sapor. . . ." See Johann A. Fabricius, *Bibliotheca latina* (3 vols. Hamburg 1721–22) 3.203.

[147]Gilbert of Poitiers, *Expositio in symbolum Quicumque uult:* Nikolaus M. Häring, ed., "A Commentary on the Pseudo-Athanasian Creed by Gilbert of Poitiers," *Mediaeval Studies* 27 (1965) 23–53 at 30–53. Idem, "Simon of Tournai's Commentary on the So-Called Athanasian Creed," AHDLMA 43 (1976) 135–99. Gerhoch of Reichersberg, *Expositio in symbolum*, ed. Franz Scheibelberger, *Oesterreichische Vierteljahresschrift für katholische Theologie* 10 (1871) 565–68. See also Nikolaus M. Häring, "Commentaries on the Pseudo-Athanasian Creed," *Mediaeval Studies* 34 (1972) 208–54 at 239–40, concerning Alan of Lille.

[148]See the commentaries edited by Nikolaus M. Häring: "A Commentary on the Apostles' Creed by Alan of Lille (O. Cist.)" and "A Commentary on the Creed of the Mass by Alan of Lille (O. Cist.)," *Analecta Cisterciensia* 30 (1974) 7–45 and 281–303; "Two Redactions of a Commentary on a Gallican Creed by Simon of Tournai," AHDLMA 41 (1974) 39–112; "Zwei Kommentare von Huguccio, Bischof von Ferrara," *Studia Gratiana* 19 (1976) 355–416 at 365–98. Gerhoch wrote an *Expositio super Canonem*, ed. Damien van den Eynde (n. 90 above) 1.5–61. Cardinal Lotario, the future pope Innocent III (1198–1216), commented on the entire text of the Mass in his *De missarum mysteriis*, PL 217.763–916. At the beginning of the twelfth century Odo of Cambrai (d. 1113) wrote *Expositio in canonem Missae*, PL 160.1053–70.

[149]Nikolaus M. Häring, "A Commentary on the Our Father by Alan of Lille," *Analecta Cisterciensia* 31 (1975) 149–77; idem, "Huguccio" (n. 148 above) 399–416. See also Pseudo-Bernard, *Expositio in orationem dominicam*, PL 184.811–18; Stephen of Baugé, *Tractatus de sacramento altaris* 19: *Expositio orationis Dominicae*, PL 172.1303–07; and Honorius Augustodunensis, PL 172.819–23.

[150]Other commentaries by Alan have been edited by Marie-Thérèse d'Alverny, *Alain de Lille: Textes inédits*, EPM 52 (Paris 1965).

[151]Nikolaus M. Häring, "A Poem by Alan of Lille on the Pseudo-Athanasian Creed," *Revue d'histoire des textes* 4 (1974) 225–38.

[152]MS BN lat 6882A, fols. 27–34 at 28v: "Investiganda occurrunt que sit auctoris intentio, que causa, que utilitas, ad quam partem philosophie spectat, quid modus agendi, que libri diuisio, quis ordo tractandi et quis titulus." The following *accessus* is found in the margin of MS London, Lambeth Palace 67, fol. 1 (saec. XII) to the *Arithmetica Boetii*: "Materia huius libri est numerus tam per se acceptus quam per relationem. Intentio est tractare de ui et potentia numeri. Potentia quantum ad procreationem uel multiplicationem. Et secundum hoc intitulatur liber. Dicitur enim: Incipit arithmetica. Ares grece, uirtus latine. Rithmus numerus. Vtilitas est cognitio numeri que ualet ad omnes artes. Si quis enim sciret naturam numeri, omnes questiones per eum posset soluere. Hic Boetius facit prologum siue epistolam ad Simachum socerum suum siue ad alium, ubi captat eius beniuolentiam et promotionem sui operis. Solo enim iudicio eius poterat opus eius promoueri ad utrumque punctum. Officium est congruus actus uniuscuiusque persone secundum mores ciuitatis. Sed hic pro beniuolentia accipitur." Fol. 2 marg.: "Intentio huius prologi est conmendare arithmeticam. Et hoc fit duppliciter, scilicet communiter et simpliciter: communiter quando laudat quadruuium, simpliciter" (here the text breaks off). We are then told:

By the end of the twelfth century, the commentary had become an integral part of the educational system. In the liberal arts, texts prescribed in philosophy,[153] rhetoric,[154] and grammar,[155] in mathematics, music, and law, circulated with attached comments and glosses of varying length and quality. In theology, the biblical *glosa* was the indispensable manual for all aspirants to an ecclesiastical career, and the systematic *accessus* approach was adopted for a wide variety of commentaries on Scripture.

THE SINGULAR CONTRIBUTION
OF THE ABBEY OF ST VICTOR, PARIS

Did some centers of learning contribute more than others to promoting the commentary as a means of education? The steps taken by the scholastics of Laon would seem to rank high in the evolution of the biblical gloss:[156] the high reputation of this school challenged the audacity of Abelard[157] and inspired the industry of Gilbert, the future bishop of Poitiers,[158] and we can hardly overestimate the influence of these two masters on the doctrinal level of Scripture studies.

The flourishing cathedral school of Reims, directed by master Alberic (1118–36), was famous enough to attract Peter Lombard, but its masters were not outstanding as commentators.[159] Bologna was the seat of legal studies, while Salerno and Montpellier were growing centers of medical research. The role played by Chartres may be gauged by the achievements of such scholastics as Thierry, Gilbert, and William of Conches—although the question whether or to what extent their glory should be credited to Chartres or Paris is obscured by uncertainties regarding the time and schools at which they taught.

"Sapientia est integra conprehensio rerum que sunt. Sed res que sunt conprehenduntur quadruuio. Ergo sapientia conprehenditur quadruuio." Fol. 5: "Ostendit unitatem non esse numerum quia non est posita inter extimos numeros."

[153]Martin Grabmann, "Aristoteles im 12. Jahrhundert," *Mittelalterliches Geistesleben*, ed. Ludwig Ott (3 vols. Munich 1956) 3.64–127.

[154]Charles Thurot, *Notices et Extraits de divers manuscrits latins pour servir à l'histoire des doctrines grammaticales au moyen âge*, Notices et extraits des manuscrits de la Bibliothèque impériale 22.2 (Paris 1868). Thierry, as we have seen, commented on Cicero, *De inventione*, and the *Ad Herennium*.

[155]The commentary on Priscian by Peter Helias remained the leading manual for a long time. According to Grabmann (n. 153 above) 3.115, Peter was the originator of speculative grammar.

[156]Speaking of the school of Laon, Smalley, *Study* 74, remarks: "It seems, indeed, that glossing had become second nature to Anselm's pupils, and that they glossed whatever literature came within their reach."

[157]Peter Abelard, *Historia calamitatum*, ed. Jacques Monfrin (Paris 1959) 69.

[158]The explicit of MS Oxford, Balliol Coll. 36 speaks of the "glosatura magistri Gilberti Porretani super psalterium quam ipse recitauit coram suo magistro Anselmo. . . ."

[159]John R. Williams, "The Cathedral School of Reims in the Time of Master Alberic, 1118–1136," *Traditio* 20 (1964) 93–114.

When Peter Lombard decided to move from Reims to Paris,[160] the abbey of St Victor in Paris, which received him at the request of St Bernard, was beyond doubt a most promising scholastic center. In those years, individual masters attached to the cathedral of Notre Dame produced very creative works. The grammarian Peter Helias, for instance, raised Priscian commentary to higher levels, and the *Psalterium glosatum* of the future dean of Chartres, master Ivo, a disciple of master Gilbert, was already available at Durham's library under prior Laurence (1149–53).[161] But the multitude of classrooms scattered among the growing communities of the Latin Quarter still lacked the institutional structure and unity to merit the name "university."[162]

Quite understandably, therefore, the Lombard preferred attending the lectures offered by Hugh of St Victor, whose reputation for learning and orthodoxy was not confined to the monastery. A twelfth-century catalogue of ecclesiastical authors describes Hugh as a devout man and well versed in the liberal arts as well as in theology.[163] The list of his theological works includes many exegetical commentaries such as "little notes" (*Notule ad litteram*) on Old Testament books from Genesis to Judges (extant in two redactions);[164] nineteen homilies, preached to his confreres, on Ecclesiastes;[165] a threefold exposition of Lamentations;[166] commentaries on the Magnificat,[167] the Lord's Prayer,[168] the "Celestial Hierarchy" of Pseudo-Dionysius;[169] on Noah's Ark interpreted according to the moral and mystical meanings;[170] and others. In the opinion of a thirteenth-century reader, Hugh interpreted the "Hierarchy" *subtilissime.*[171]

[160]Brady, *Prolegomena* (n. 39 above) 13*–14*. St Bernard's letter of recommendation to abbot Gilduin is still extant: PL 182.618–19 (*Epist.* 410). The date 1139 is suggested by Elphège Vacandard, *La vie de Saint Bernard, abbé de Clairvaux* (2 vols. Paris 1895) 2.45 n. 4.

[161]Beryl Smalley, "Master Ivo of Chartres," EHR 50 (1935) 680–86; Stegmüller, *Repertorium biblicum* (n.10 above) 3.507–09 nos. 5337–40; Häring, "Chartres" (n. 12 above) 313–17.

[162]Information on Parisian schoolhouses about the middle of the century is assembled in Häring, "Chartres" (n. 12 above) 327–29.

[163]*Catalogus scriptorum ecclesiasticorum* 7, "Vir religiosus et in utraque litteratura adprime disertus," ed. Häring, "Two Catalogues" (n. 93 above) 209. Jean Châtillon, "Les écoles de Chartres et de Saint-Victor," *La scuola nell'Occidente latino dell'alto medioevo*, Settimane 19 (2 vols. Spoleto 1972) 2.795–839.

[164]Smalley, *Study* 80; Hugh of St Victor, *Notule ad litteram*, PL 175.29–44.

[165]*In Salomonis ecclesiasten, homiliae XIX*, PL 175.113–256. He calls his exposition a *lucubratiuncula* (115C).

[166]*In Threnos Ieremiae*, PL 175.255–322.

[167]*Explanatio in Canticum Beatae Mariae*, PL 175.413–32. He calls it *expositio* (414B) and *explanatio* (414C). The commentary begins: "Si circumstantiam rei gestae perpendere velimus. . . ."

[168]BN lat 15315A, fols. 79v–81 (saec. XIII): "Expositio dominice orationis. . . ."

[169]*Commentariorum in hierarchiam coelestem S. Dionysii Areopagitae*, PL 175.923–1154. See also the *Liber magistri Hugonis*, analyzed by Ludwig Ott, "Sententiae magistri Hugonis Parisiensis," RTAM 27 (1960) 29–41: Damien van den Eynde, "Le *Liber magistri Hugonis,*" *Franciscan Studies* 23 (1963) 268–99.

[170]Smalley, *Study* 95–96; Heinrich M. Köster, *Die Heilslehre des Hugo von Sankt-Viktor* (Emsdetten 1940) 2–7.

[171]*Catalogus virorum illustrium* 25, ed. Häring, "Two Catalogues" (n. 93 above) 201.

Some commentaries long ascribed to Hugh have been shown to be the work of others. The commentaries on Joel, Obadiah, and Nahum, and parts 1–4 of the *Allegories* are now considered to belong to Richard of St Victor.[172] The *Questiones super Epistolas Pauli* and parts 5–8 of the *Allegories* depend on Robert of Melun.[173] Nevertheless, Hugh's influence in grammar, exegesis, canon law, theology, and spirituality was so far-reaching[174] that St Bonaventure, not given to exaggerations, ventured the sweeping comparison: "Anselmus in ratiocinatione, Bernardus in praedicatione, Richardus in contemplatione—Hugo vero omnia haec."[175]

Richard of St Victor, who praises his teacher Hugh as "that foremost theologian of our day,"[176] continued the Victorine tradition in his explanations of certain passages of St Paul's Letters,[177] in the enormous *Liber exceptionum*,[178] and in his exegesis of *Misit Herodes rex manus* (previously ascribed to Fulbert of Chartres).[179] His prolific skill as commentator shines in his *Beniamin minor* and *maior*, which deal with the twelve Patriarchs; in his work on Emmanuel, critical of Andrew of St Victor; on the Mystical Dream, the Psalms, and the Apocalypse; on the *Visions of Ezekiel* and the Song of Songs; in his tracts on the Tabernacle and the Temple.[180] To these we may add his

[172]*Adnotatiunculae elucidatoriae in Ioelem Prophetam*, PL 175.321–72, and *Expositio moralis in Abdiam*, 371–406. André Wilmart, "Le commentaire sur le prophète Nahum," *Bulletin de littérature ecclésiastique* 23 (1922) 253–79. The Nahum commentary was formerly attributed to Julian of Toledo (PL 96.705–58). Damien van den Eynde, "Les commentaires sur Joel, Abdias, et Nahum, attribués à Hugues de Saint-Victor," *Franciscan Studies* 2nd ser. 17 (1957) 363–72. H. J. Pollitt, "The Authorship of the Commentaries on Joel and Obadiah Attributed to Hugh of St Victor," RTAM 32 (1965) 296–306.

[173]*Quaestiones et decisiones in epistolas d. Pauli*, PL 175.431–634, and *Allegoriae in Vetus Testamentum*, 681–734. Landgraf (n. 15 above) 92, 97.

[174]Roger Baron, "L'influence de Hugues de Saint-Victor," RTAM 22 (1955) 56–71.

[175]St Bonaventure, *Opusculum de reductione artium ad theologiam* 5, *Opera omnia*, Quaracchi ed. (11 vols. in 28, 1882–1902) 5.321.

[176]Richard of St Victor, *Beniamin maior* 1.4, PL 196.67D, and *Tractatus de spiritu blasphemiae*, 1189A–B.

[177]*Explicatio aliquorum passuum difficilium apostoli*, PL 196.665–84; Smalley, *Study* 106. Richard reveals his problems saying: "Videtur namque (Paulus) esse contrarius sibi ipsi, contrarius rationi, contrarius veritati, et quod his omnibus amplius est, sententiae ipsius Domini" (668A–B).

[178]*Liber exceptionum*, ed. Jean Châtillon, Textes philosophiques du moyen âge 5 (Paris 1958) 97–517. Idem, "Les écoles" (n. 163 above) 830.

[179]*Tractatus in illud Actorum 12.1: Misit Herodes rex manus*, PL 141.277–306; it is attributed to Richard of St Victor in *Catalogus virorum illustrium* 26, ed. Häring, "Two Catalogues" (n. 93 above) 201. See also Jean Châtillon, "*Misit Herodes Rex Manus*: Un opuscule de Richard de Saint-Victor égaré parmi les oeuvres de Fulbert de Chartres," *Revue du moyen âge latin* 6 (1950) 287–98.

[180]*Beniamin minor* and *Beniamin maior*: PL 196.1–64 and 63–202; *De Emmanuele*, 601–66; *De eruditione hominis interioris*, 1229–1366; *Mysticae adnotationes in psalmos*, 265–403; *In apocalypsim Ioannis*, 683–888; *In visionem Ezechielis*, 527–600 (with diagrams); *In Cantica Canticorum explicatio*, 405–528; *Expositio difficultatum suborientum in expositione Tabernaculi foederis*, 211–42.

treatises entitled *De contemplatione*,[181] *De exterminatione mali*,[182] *De statu interioris hominis*,[183] and *Super exiit edictum*,[184] all dominated by scriptural themes. Richard's general purpose is neatly summed up by a medieval author: "Omnia moraliter et subtilissime in contemplatiuam uitam dirigens semper intentionem disputationis sue."[185] The consensus of historians still agrees with this evaluation.

It may surprise the student to discover among Richard's writings a work entitled in the manuscript *Inuectio . . . contra Andream socium suum super illud Ecce uirgo concipiet. . . .*[186] The disagreement between Richard and master Andrew arose from conflicts between Christian and Jewish interpretations of certain biblical passages.[187] Andrew has been characterized as "an unusual person" who could have flourished only in the Victorine circle.[188] He studied under Hugh and taught in Paris before 1147. Later he was elected prior, then abbot, of Wigmore (Herefordshire) but returned to Paris to teach there until he was recalled (about 1161–63) to Wigmore, where he died in 1175.[189]

As a commentator Andrew chose to expound passages of special interest or difficulty, stressing the *sensus litteralis* rather than the spiritual and theological significance of the text under consideration. His training in the liberal arts reveals itself in quotations from Cicero, Lucan, Seneca, Sallust, and

---

[181]However, Roger Baron questions its authenticity: "Richard de Saint-Victor: A-t-il écrit le *De contemplatione et ejus speciebus?*" *Recherches de science religieuse* 50 (1962) 409–24.

[182]*De exterminatione mali et promotione boni*, PL 196.1073–1116; Jean Châtillon, "De Guillaume de Champeaux à Thomas Gallus," *Revue du moyen âge latin* 8 (1952) 139–62 and 247–72 at 259.

[183]PL 196.1115–60; or Jean Ribaillier, ed., "Richard de Saint-Victor: *De statu interioris hominis*," AHDLMA 34 (1967) 7–128.

[184]Richard of St Victor, *Sermons et opuscules spirituels inédits*, ed. Jean Châtillon and William J. Tulloch (Paris 1951): *Super exiit edictum*. Some 56 manuscripts are still extant. For smaller tractates on scriptural texts see Ribaillier (n. 183 above) 32 n. 14, 36 n. 42, 41 n. 76, 49 n. 125.

[185]*Catalogus virorum illustrium* 26, ed. Häring, "Two Catalogues" (n. 93 above) 201.

[186]MS BN lat 13432, fols. 65–83. Richard of St Victor, *De Emmanuele*, PL 196.601–04; Ribaillier (n. 183 above) 44 n. 94 (Isa. 7:14–16); Smalley, *Study* 110, 163.

[187]Richard's verdict (*De Emmanuele* prologus, PL 196.601) is quite severe: "In quemdam magistri Andreae tractatum, quem in Isaiae explanationem scripserat, simul et ediderat, incidi, in quo nonnulla minus caute posita, minus catholice disputata inveni. In multis namque scripturae illius locis ponitur Iudaeorum sententia quasi sit non tam Iudaeorum quam propria, et velut vera. Super illum autem locum: *Ecce Virgo . . .* Iudaeorum obiectiones et quaestiones ponit, nec solvit, et videtur velut eis palmam dedisse. . . . In eiusmodi itaque positionibus scandalizantur peritiores, infamantur imperitiores."

[188]Smalley, *Study* 112.

[189]Beryl Smalley, "Andrew of Saint-Victor, Abbot of Wigmore: A Twelfth-Century Hebraist," RTAM 10 (1938) 358–73; Raphael Loewe, "Herbert of Bosham's Commentary on Jerome's Hebrew Psalter," *Biblica* 34 (1953) 44–77, 159–92, 275–98; idem, "The Mediaeval Christian Hebraists of England: Herbert of Bosham and Earlier Scholars," *Transactions of the Jewish Historical Society of England* 17 (1951–52) 225–49.

Vegetius, from Vergil, Ovid, Horace, Juvenal, and others.[190] Remarkable is his use of Jewish sources and personal contacts with Jewish exegetes,[191] whose views he occasionally followed to such a degree that Richard openly accused him of judaizing.[192] But Andrew did not fail to impress the commentators of his time. References to his opinions, less critical than Richard's, are numerous in the works of Peter the Chanter and Stephen Langton.[193]

Andrew's expositions of Jonah and Ecclesiastes have been edited.[194] Extant in manuscripts only are his comments on the Pentateuch, Joshua, Judges, Samuel, Kings, Chronicles, Maccabees, the Prophets, and Proverbs.[195] His prologues introducing the Pentateuch, the Prophets, Isaiah, Daniel, and Ezekiel, his notes on Genesis 2:5-6, on Daniel 7:7-8 and 9:24-27, on Jeremiah 1:4-5, Ezekiel 1:1 and 9:2-11, and Isaiah 1:16-18, 9:2-11, 51:5, and 53:2-12 have been edited with translations.[196]

The biblical learning and advanced Hebrew scholarship shown by Herbert of Bosham, who is believed to have been a pupil of Peter Lombard and Andrew,[197] should be mentioned, although his large commentary on the Psalter apparently went unnoticed. But in Paris the Victorine tradition was carried on by three masters of great renown: Peter Comestor, the famous *magister historiarum*,[198] Peter the Chanter, the leading moralist and exegete of his time,[199] and master Stephen Langton, the future cardinal (1206-28). Of Stephen it was written, "Totam scripturam primus medullitus et moraliter cepit exponere."[200] The same historian was well aware that the method of commenting was undergoing a change: "Scripsit et in XII prophetas, ipsos moraliter et subtiliter secundum modum scolastice lectionis exponens."[201]

[190]Smalley, *Study* 125.

[191]Ibid. 145-56. The necessity of Hebrew studies is well illustrated in a commentator's remark, "Deus hebreum nomen est. Latine dicitur timor." Nikolaus M. Häring, "Four Commentaries on the *De Consolatione philosophiae* in MS Heiligenkreuz 130," *Mediaeval Studies* 31 (1969) 287-316 at 301.

[192]Richard of St Victor, *De Emmanuele*, PL 196.601-04.

[193]Martin Grabmann, *Die Geschichte der scholastischen Methode* (2 vols. Freiburg 1909-11; repr. Berlin 1956) 2.476-501.

[194]Angelo Penna, "Andrea di S. Vittore: Il suo commento a Giona," *Biblica* 36 (1955) 305-31; Gregorio Calandra, *De historica Andreae Victorini expositione in Ecclesiasten*, Pontificium Athenaeum Antonianum, Facultas theologica, Thesis ad lauream 56 [1940] (Palermo 1948).

[195]Stegmüller, *Repertorium biblicum* (n. 10 above) 2.100-06 nos. 1295-1329; Landgraf (n. 15 above) 159.

[196]Smalley, *Study* 375-94; MSS Cambridge, Pembroke Coll. 45; Oxford, Corpus Christi Coll. 30; BN lat 356 and 14432; Mazarine 175; and Vat lat 1053.

[197]Smalley, *Study* 186-95.

[198]Peter Comestor, *Historia scholastica*, PL 198.1049-1722. The chronicler Robert of Auxerre praises Comestor as "vir facundissimus et in scripturis diuinis excellenter instructus" (*Chronicon*, MGH SS 26.240 [n. 84 above]). See also Alberic, *Chronica* (n. 41 above) 874 (ad ann. 1197).

[199]Grabmann, *Geschichte* (n. 193 above) 2.476-501, speaks of "die von Petrus Cantor ausgehende biblisch-moralische Richtung der Theologie." Peter may well be classified as the Father of Casuistry.

[200]*Catalogus virorum illustrium* 27, ed. Häring, "Two Catalogues" (n. 93 above) 201.

[201]Ibid.

HERMENEUTICS

Hugh of Amiens, we may recall, restricted his efforts to elucidating the *historia* or literal meaning of the Hexameron.[202] At about the same time, Thierry of Chartres adopted a similar attitude and deliberately refrained from discussing the allegorical and moral meanings because, as he claimed, "the saints" had sufficiently elaborated them. Accordingly, he made up his mind to interpret Genesis *secundum phisicam et ad litteram*.[203]

Traditional exegesis of the Bible had detected at least three or four meanings or senses: literal, allegorical, tropological, anagogical.[204] Thus, the student was told that according to the literal sense the word "lion" means a beast but allegorically symbolizes Christ.[205] When the monks asked St Gregory (d. 604) for an interpretation of the Book of Job, he had conformed to their wishes and, reducing the literal exposition to a bare minimum, emphasized instead the mystical and moral message of the text.[206] And as to the liberal arts, he strongly opposed the application of grammatical rules to the word of revelation.[207]

By the twelfth century, times and tastes were definitely changing. Accentuating the literal sense gradually compelled exegetes to pay more attention to the laws of hermeneutics—the science of interpretation and explanation. The new emphasis on the historical and literal meaning of the *littera* coincided with the development of speculative grammar, which advocated strict rules governing philosophical and theological language.[208] These grammarians distinguished between concrete and abstract terms and defined their functions within the framework of a logically construed sentence. These rules were not confined to the linguistic analysis of scriptural texts but were applicable to any written document.

---

[202]*Tractatus*, ed. Lecomte (n. 20 above) 236: "magis historiam exquirendo tractamus, quam sensus allegoricos seu morales."

[203]*Tractatus de sex dierum operibus* 1, ed. Häring, *Commentaries/Thierry* (n. 16 above) 555.

[204]Smalley, *Study* 87–88. Honorius Augustodunensis, *De anime exsilio et patria* 12, PL 172. 1245C–D, ingeniously links the four senses to the liberal arts. The grammarian Arnulf of Orléans interpreted Ovid's *Metamorphoses* according to three senses, *allegorice, moraliter, historice*: Jeauneau, *Lectio* 128–29. See also Conrad of Hirsau, *Dialogus* (n. 73 above) 18–19.

[205]Hugh of St Victor, *De scripturis* 5, PL 175.13B. See Smalley, *Study* 93.

[206]See Smalley, *Study* 33; Gregory, *Homiliarum in Ezechielem prophetam* 2.10, PL 76.1072.

[207]Gregory, *Moralium libri* (*Expositio in librum B. Iob*) 5, PL 76.516B. See Peter Abelard, *Theologia 'Scolarium'* [*Introductio ad theologiam*] 2.10 and *Theologia christiana* 3 and 4, PL 178.1062C, 1255B, 1285B; Gratian, *Decretum*, (palea) D.38 c.13, *Corpus iuris canonici*, ed. Emil A. Friedberg (2 vols. Leipzig 1879–81) 1.143. See also Henri de Lubac, "Saint Grégoire et la grammaire," *Recherches de science religieuse* 48 (1960) 185–226 at 206.

[208]Nikolaus M. Häring, "Sprachlogische und philosophische Voraussetzungen zum Verständnis der Christologie Gilberts von Poitiers," *Scholastik* 32 (1957) 373–98; idem, "Petrus Lombardus und die Sprachlogik in der Trinitätslehre der Porretanerschule," *Miscellanea Lombardiana* (Novara 1957) 113–27; Lauge Nielsen, "On the Doctrine of Logic and Language of Gilbert Porreta and His Followers," CIMAGL 17 (1976) 40–69.

In addition, Gilbert, later bishop of Poitiers, introduced an important distinction between the grammatical meaning of a word and the writer's intention.[209] It was believed that Hilary of Poitiers (d. 367) had initiated the exegetical principle of examining the author's intention: he declared that heresy flows not from the words used but from the user's intention or interpretation of the words.[210] After quoting St Hilary's statement, the anonymous author of the *Liber de uera philosophia* concludes: "Therefore, words must be interpreted according to the intention of the writer, not according to their grammatical sense."[211]

Simon of Tournai also insists that words must be understood in harmony with the writer's intention.[212] For that reason he distinguishes a twofold meaning: the proper meaning of the word and the meaning intended by the author. Accordingly, he holds that words express a twofold truth. To illustrate this he notes that when we see the sentence "The meadow smiles," we know exactly what the writer wishes to express but, strictly speaking, the meadow cannot smile.[213] Adjusted to the often highly figurative and metaphorical language of the Sacred Scriptures, this sort of clarification contributed a great deal to a more competent exegesis of the Bible.

St Hilary had also pointed out that our understanding (*intelligentia*) of an object (*res*) is limited and that the word (*sermo*) is not an adequate expression of its *res*.[214] Implying this progressive diminution, he wrote: "naturae sermo succumbit, et rem ut est verba non explicant."[215] Hilary's hermeneutical principle was first adopted by Gilbert of Poitiers. In his commentary on Boethius he reminds his readers that in approaching an object (*res*), human understanding (*intellectus*) fails to grasp it in its entirety, and that, moreover, the linguistic expression lags behind both reality and our understanding.[216] The distinction between the grammatical meaning of a word and the author's intention[217] induced Gilbert to correct certain statements made by Boethius. He maintains, for instance, that Boethius occasionally uses *diuinitas* where he

---

[209]Of Hugh of St Victor, Smalley, *Study* 101 writes: "Living over a century before St. Thomas, Hugh seems to have grasped the Thomist principle that the clue to prophecy and metaphor is the writer's intention; the literal sense includes everything which the sacred writer meant to say."

[210]*De Trinitate* 2.3, PL 10.51B: "De intelligentia enim heresis, non de Scriptura est: et sensus, non sermo fit crimen."

[211]*Liber de uera philosophia* 4: MS Grenoble, Bibl. publ. 290 (1085), fol. 75v: "De intelligentia . . . crimen. Verba ergo interpretanda sunt ex sensu ex quo fiunt, non ex sensu quem faciunt."

[212]Joseph Warichez, ed., *Les Disputationes de Simon de Tournai*, Spicilegium sacrum Lovaniense 12 (Louvain 1932) 32 (6.3): "Ex sensu ex quo fiunt uerba ab auctore. . . ."

[213]Ibid. 167–68 (59.2).

[214]*De Trinitate* 4.14, PL 10.107C: "Intelligentia enim dictorum . . . sed rei est sermo subiectus." See Peter Lombard, *Sententiae* 1.5.1 (10) (n. 39 above) 84.

[215]*De Trinitate* 2.7, PL 10.56B. See Palémon Glorieux, "La somme *Quoniam homines* d'Alain de Lille," AHDLMA 20 (1954) 112–364 at 140; Häring, "Two Redactions" (n. 148 above) 55 and 93: *Expositio super Symbolum* 1.60 and 2.75.

[216]Häring, *Commentaries/Gilbert* (n. 59 above) 67: Gilbert, *De Trinitate* 1.3.21.

[217]Ibid. 54: 1.1.7.

intended to write *deus*, or employs the word *homo* where he meant *humanitas*.[218] Immaterial and harmless as such emendations may appear to the modern reader, they caused considerable misgivings among contemporary theologians.[219]

There is no need to prove that neither the Bible nor the writings of the Church Fathers fully conformed with these rules. Their terminology, therefore, required the clarification of the writer's intention whenever the grammatical term was thought to conflict with doctrinal considerations.

The heavier stress on the literal and historical sense of the *littera* also promoted linguistic studies. Herbert of Bosham, a pupil of Andrew of St Victor and Peter Lombard, claimed to be the first to expound Jerome's *Hebraica*, neglected for centuries.[220] Although he shows an unmistakable interest in Greek, he does not seem to have been proficient in it.[221]

Herbert's efforts to investigate and examine Hebrew sources stemmed from endeavors that dated back to the inspirational initiative of Hugh of St Victor. Andrew of St Victor remarked that his master "learnt the literal sense of the Pentateuch from the Jews."[222] There is ample evidence to show that Hugh mastered Hebrew well enough to discriminate between linguistic nuances.[223] Richard of St Victor also consulted Jewish scholars and compared their views with his own,[224] but—as we have noted—he rebuked Andrew for judaizing and accepting Jewish sources in an uncritical way.[225]

Gilbert of Poitiers and his students advocated a more intensive study of the theology of the Greek Church Fathers. Translations made by Cerbanus (in Hungary), Hugo of Pisa, his brother Leo, and Burgundio of Pisa were eagerly and gratefully received.[226] But despite the increasing respect for Greek learning the knowledge of Greek was not widespread among the Latins.[227] Paradoxically, it was perhaps because their knowledge of Greek was meager that scholastics took special delight in such titles as *Proslogion* (Anselm), *Didascalicon* (Hugh), *Metalogicon* (John of Salisbury), and *Dragmaticon*

---

[218]Ibid. 298: *Contra Eutychen* 4.53.

[219]Nikolaus M. Häring, "Die ersten Konflikte zwischen der Universität von Paris und der kirchlichen Lehrautorität," *Miscellanea mediaevalia* 10 (1976) 38–51.

[220]Beryl Smalley, "A Commentary on the *Hebraica* by Herbert of Bosham," RTAM 18 (1951) 29–65.

[221]Smalley, *Study* 187.

[222]Ibid. 102. Stephen Harding corrected the text of the Old Testament with the help of Jewish scholars. For the same purpose the Cistercian Nicholas Manjacoria (d. ca. 1145) wrote a *Libellus de corruptione et correptione psalmorum*. See André Wilmart, "Nicolas Manjacoria: Cistercien à Trois-Fontaines," *Revue bénédictine* 33 (1921) 136–43; Landgraf, "Zur Methode" (n. 39 above) 445–74.

[223]Hugh of St Victor, *Adnotationes elucidatoriae*, PL 175.29–114.

[224]Smalley, *Study* 110.

[225]Ibid. See above at note 192.

[226]Nikolaus M. Häring, "The Porretans and the Greek Fathers," *Mediaeval Studies* 24 (1962) 181–209; Haskins, *Ren* 294–96; Peter Classen, *Burgundio von Pisa: Richter, Gesandter, Übersetzer*, SB Heidelberg, Philos.-hist. Kl. 1974 no. 4.

[227]John of Salisbury (*Epist.* 194) asked John Sarrasin of Poitiers for an explanation of the word *usia* he had encountered in St Ambrose (*The Letters of John of Salisbury* 2, ed. and trans. W. J.

(William of Conches). Manuscripts are still-eloquent illustrations of the fact that scribes often labored hopelessly in their attempts to copy the unfamiliar Greek characters.[228]

Readers needed assistance to understand the relatively numerous Greek words, phrases, and sentences scattered through the *opuscula sacra* of Boethius. But Latin commentators faced with Greek terms were hard put to deal with and elucidate a language they did not understand. Thierry of Chartres, for example, took *prosopa* to be a feminine noun whose accusative forms he thought to be *prosopam* and *prosopas*. He must have been embarrassed when he wrote, "*Prosopa* i.e. ad faciem posita. Hoc sonat istud Grecum."[229] His poorly concealed uneasiness is equally obvious in the admission, "Hoc dixit et ponit Grecum."[230] Thierry was not prone to concede shortcomings.

Everard of Ypres, who became a Cistercian, boasts that he taught Gilbert Greek while he learned Latin from Gilbert.[231] However, the writings of neither Everard nor Gilbert will incline the student to hold that they were proficient in Greek. A brief illustration may suffice. The Greek phrase *para toy pros toys opas tithesthai* in Boethius appears in Gilbert's commentary in Latin characters as *paratoy prostoy sopaste ty testay*, with the following clarification: "*Para* namque sonat ab. *Pros* sonat in vel ante. *Sopas* sonat faciem, *Testay* ponendo. *Toy* vero et iterum *toy* et *ty* articuli sunt."[232] His desperate dilemma is not disguised by the translation provided by Boethius.

Millor, H. E. Butler, and C. N. L. Brooke [Oxford 1979] 272, = PL 199.162C–D no. 169). The ritual for the dedication of a church required the bishop to write the Hebrew, Greek, and Latin alphabets in the ashes spread on the ground for this purpose. However, reasons were found to reduce the three tongues to one (*pro modulo ecclesie*) for the bishop's spoken role: Honorius Augustodunensis, *Sacramentarium* 101, PL 172.803A–B.

[228]See Arthur Allgeier, "Exegetische Beiträge zur Geschichte des Griechischen vor dem Humanismus," *Biblica* 24 (1943) 261–88; Bernhard Bischoff, "Das griechische Element in der abendländischen Bildung des Mittelalters," in his *Mittelalterliche Studien* (2 vols. Stuttgart 1966–67) 2.246–75; Milton V. Anastos, "Some Aspects of Byzantine Influence on Latin Thought," *Twelfth-Century Europe* 131–87 at 141–54; Haskins, *Culture* 160–69 and *Science* 141–54.

[229]*Contra Eutychen* 3.2–7 (quotation at 3.7), ed. Häring, *Commentaries/Thierry* (n. 16 above) 236–37. Landgraf, "Zur Methode" (n. 39 above) 455 shows how in MS BN lat 4286, fols. 112 and 113, the scribe mixed Latin and Greek letters.

[230]*Contra Eutychen* 3.14 (238).

[231]Nikolaus M. Häring, "A Latin Dialogue on the Doctrine of Gilbert of Poitiers," *Mediaeval Studies* 15 (1953) 243–89 at 252; Johannes Gründel, *Die Lehre des Radulphus Ardens von den Verstandestugenden auf dem Hintergrund seiner Seelenlehre*, Veröffentlichungen des Grabmann-Institutes 27 (Munich 1976) 18 writes of the Porretan Ralph Ardens (d. ca. 1200): "Es ist anzunehmen, dass Radulfus Ardens auch der griechischen Sprache kundig war; denn die häufigen Worterklärungen und Ableitungen lateinischer Vokabeln aus dem Griechischen setzen . . . sehr wohl einige griechische Kenntnisse voraus." The same might well be said of his contemporary, the Porretan Alan of Lille. But a detailed examination is needed to show how genuine such "knowledge" was.

[232]Boethius, *Contra Eutychen* 3, *The Theological Tractates*, ed. and trans. Hugh F. Stewart and Edward K. Rand, LCL (1918) 86; Gilbert, *Contra Eutychen* 3.25, ed. Häring, *Commen-*

As a teaching method, the commentary ranged over the entire educational system of the twelfth century. One cannot help perceiving it as a reflection of the profound reverence and respect of the age for the giants from whose shoulders its scholars professed to pierce more deeply the distant horizons of learning.[233]

Bibliographical Note

A history of commentaries in the Middle Ages is still to be written, though partial studies of excellent quality have become available. Very little has been done, however, to examine the hermeneutical principles adopted or advocated by twelfth-century commentators. The following works merit being consulted:

Chenu, *Théologie*; Heinrich Denifle, *Die abendländischen Schriftausleger bis Luther über die Iustitia Dei* (Mainz 1905); Joseph de Ghellinck, *L'essor de la littérature latine au XIIe siècle* (2nd ed. Brussels 1955); idem, *Le mouvement théologique du XIIe siècle* (2nd ed. Bruges 1948; repr. 1969); Palémon Glorieux, *Répertoire des maîtres en théologie de Paris au XIIIe siècle*, EPM 17–18 (2 vols. Paris 1933–34); Martin Grabmann, *Die Geschichte der scholastischen Methode* (2 vols. Freiburg 1909–11); Nikolaus M. Häring, "Commentaries on the Pseudo-Athanasian Creed," *Mediaeval Studies* 34 (1972) 208–54; Ludwig Hödl, *Die Geschichte der scholastischen Literatur und der Theologie der Schlüsselgewalt*, BGPTMA, Texte und Untersuchungen 38/4 (Münster 1960); Richard W. Hunt, "Studies on Priscian in the Eleventh and Twelfth Centuries," M&RS 1 (1943) 194–231 and 2 (1950) 1–56; idem, "The Introductions to the 'Artes' in the Twelfth Century," *Studia mediaevalia in honorem . . . Raymundi Josephi Martin* (Bruges 1948) 85–112; R. B. C. Huygens, *Accessus ad auctores*, Collection Latomus 15 (Brussels 1954); idem, ed., *Conrad de Hirsau, Dialogus super auctores*, Collection Latomus 17 (Brussels 1955); Jeauneau, *Lectio*; Hermann Kantorowicz, *Studies in the Glossators of the Roman Law* (Cambridge 1938; 2nd ed. rev. Peter Weimar [Aalen 1969]); Kuttner, *Repertorium*; Artur M. Landgraf, "Familienbildung bei Paulinenkommentaren des 12. Jahrhunderts," *Biblica* 13 (1932) 61–72 and 169–93; Odon Lottin, *Psychologie et morale aux XIIe et XIIIe siècles* (6 vols. in 8 Louvain 1942–60); Artur M. Landgraf, *Dogmengeschichte der Frühscholastik* (4 vols. Regensburg 1952–56); idem, *Introduction à l'histoire de la littérature théologique de la scolastique naissante*, rev. Albert M. Landry, trans. Louis B. Geiger, Université de Montréal, Publications de l'Institut d'études médiévales 22 (Montreal and Paris 1973); idem, "Untersuchungen zu den Paulinenkommentaren des 12. Jahrhunderts," RTAM 8 (1936) 350–65; Manitius, volume 3; Gabriel Le Bras, Jacqueline Rambaud, and Charles Lefebvre, *L'âge classique, 1140–1378: Sources et théorie du droit*, Histoire du droit et des institutions de l'Eglise en Occident 7 (Paris 1965); Johannes Baptist Schneyer, *Repertorium der lateinischen Sermones des Mittelalters*, BGPTMA 43.1–8 (8 vols. to date Münster 1969–78); Johann Friedrich von Schulte, *Zur Geschichte der Literatur über das Dekret Gratians*, SB

---

taries/Gilbert (n. 59 above) 276–77. Landgraf, "Zur Methode" (n. 39 above) 474 states: "Im Pauluskommentar des Gilbert von Porrée ist zudem noch—ähnlich wie in demjenigen des Petrus Lombardus—nichts von einer Kenntnis der griechischen Sprache zu verspüren." Gilbert's references to the Greek text are secondhand, derived mainly from Jerome and Augustine. See the examples Landgraf gives on 458–67.

[233]Jeauneau, "*'Nani gigantum humeris insidentes': Essai d'interprétation de Bernard de Chartres*," *Lectio* 53–73.

Vienna 63 (1869) 299–352, 64 (1870) 93–142, esp. 93–114, "Die Summa Coloniensis des Cod. Bamberg. D.II.17," and 65 (1870) 21–76; Smalley, *Study*; idem, "La Glossa ordinaria: Quelques prédécesseurs d'Anselme de Laon," RTAM 9 (1937) 364–400; Ceslaus Spicq, *Esquisse d'une histoire de l'exégèse latine au moyen âge*, Bibliothèque thomiste 26 (Paris 1944); Friedrich Stegmüller, *Repertorium commentariorum in Sententias Petri Lombardi* (2 vols. Würzburg 1947); idem, *Repertorium biblicum medii aevi* (11 vols. Madrid 1940–80); Lynn Thorndike and Pearl Kibre, *A Catalogue of Incipits of Mediaeval Scientific Writings in Latin* (2nd ed. Cambridge Mass. and London 1963).

Statim invenire

Schools, Preachers, and New Attitudes to the Page

Richard H. Rouse and Mary A. Rouse

Twelfth-century scholarship is characterized by the effort to gather, organize, and harmonize the legacy of the Christian past as it pertained to juris-prudence, theological doctrine, and Scripture. The products of this effort, the *Decretum*, the *Sentences*, and the Ordinary Gloss to the Bible, were in existence by about 1150. In a certain sense the "twelfth century" can be said to close with the achievement of these goals and the emergence of a new mode of scholarship characterized by efforts to penetrate these great mosaics of the twelfth century, to gain access to the whole works of authority, and to ask fresh questions of them.[1] Major products of this second effort, the verbal concordance to the Scriptures and the theological summas, were in existence by about 1250.[2] While the *Glossa ordinaria* and the verbal concordance are the most important tools of biblical scholarship devised in the Middle Ages, these two works embody strikingly different approaches to written authority, each created in response to the needs of its own time.[3] The change in approach represented by the contrast between the Gloss and the concordance has hither-to been attributed to the coming of the mendicant orders, the institutionaliza-tion of the university, and the introduction of the new Aristotle. This explana-tion has never satisfactorily come to grips with the problem of the transition

[1] See Richard W. Hunt, "Manuscripts Containing the Indexing Symbols of Robert Grosseteste," *Bodleian Library Record* 4 (1953) 241–55 at 249–50.

[2] Thirteenth-century scholarly apparatus was the subject of the A. S. W. Rosenbach Lectures in Bibliography given by Richard H. Rouse at the University of Pennsylvania in 1975. See also Richard H. Rouse, "Cistercian Aids to Study in the Thirteenth Century," *Studies in Cistercian History II*, ed. John R. Sommerfeldt, Cistercian Studies Series 24 (Kalamazoo 1976) 123–34; idem, "La diffusion en Occident au XIIIe siècle des outils de travail facilitant l'accès aux textes autoritatifs," *L'enseignement en Islam et en Occident au moyen âge*, Colloques internationaux de La Napoule 1, ed. George Makdisi, Dominique Sourdel, and Janine Sourdel-Thomine (Paris 1977) 115–47 (= *Revue des études islamiques* 44 [1976] hors série 13); and, with Mary A. Rouse, *Preachers, Florilegia and Sermons: Studies on the Manipulus florum of Thomas of Ireland* (Toronto 1979) ch. 1, "Thirteenth-Century Sermon Aids."

[3] See Richard H. and Mary A. Rouse, "The Verbal Concordance to the Scriptures," *Archivum Fratrum Praedicatorum* 44 (1974) 5–30.

from one mode of thought to another, shaped by events taking place in the decades before Francis and Dominic. We should like to investigate the transitional period that lies between the completion of the Gloss and the making of the verbal concordance, using as evidence changes in the apparatus that scholars created to serve their needs.

This study will deal, then, with the evolution of scholarly apparatus in the second half of the twelfth century: the forms that such instruments took, and the causes of their creation. The explanation of both forms and causes has much to do, of course, with the twelfth-century growth of the schools and the needs of formalized instruction. It has probably more to do with the growing need—or, rather, a growing perception of the need—for a pastoral ministry of preaching, in the service of a new, rootless urban society and in the face of the most widespread and successful challenges to orthodoxy that the Church had faced in many centuries. The explanation also has to do with the emergence of a new form of sermon. Throughout, it was the needs of the intellectual community that determined the shape of their scholarly tools. By identifying these needs, we hope to illuminate as well the changes in society that gave rise to them.

We shall discuss the transition from memory to page layout, as a means of locating material in the codex; the impetus for this change came, at least initially, from the needs of the schoolroom. And we shall examine the background to the first works that are alphabetically organized for searchability, the "distinction" collections; the force that underlay their creation was a newly aggressive preaching ministry, which used that new device the *distinctio* to preach in a new way. Finally, we shall observe that the interrelationships between classroom and pulpit led to combining the best techniques of both, to produce a new generation of tools for a new generation of scholar-preachers.

FROM MEMORY TO ARTIFICIAL FINDING DEVICES

Before the idea of searchability came the idea of putting into order. Order is not a twelfth-century creation, but it certainly was reemphasized in the first half of that century. This includes not only such obvious examples as the Lombard's *Sentences* and Gratian's *Decretum*, but also such works as Peter Abelard's *Sic et non*, and the Gloss—the "ordering" of patristic exegesis according to the order of Scripture; the makers of the Gloss were referred to as *ordinatores glose*.[4] One of the most explicit advocates of order was Hugh of St Victor. The *Didascalicon* is much concerned not only with why and what and how one studies, but equally with the order of study. Of course, if one's study is logically ordered, one may use one's recall as a finding device, rather than "thumb the pages of books to hunt for rules and reasons" (*Didascalicon* 3.3). "We ought, therefore, in all that we learn, to gather brief and dependable

[4]See Smalley, *Study* 225.

abstracts to be stored in the little chest of memory" (*Didascalicon* 3.11). Hugh's *De tribus maximis circumstantiis gestorum*[5] discusses mnemonic devices, and includes historical tables to be memorized. Hugh of St Victor seems to be the last major figure to propose memory as the sole or principal means of retrieving information.[6]

Hugh stands in the tradition of memory training or "artificial memory" that reaches back to Antiquity.[7] Yet there were various sporadic attempts, throughout the era in which one literally searched one's memory, to provide artificial devices as a supplement, not so much to aid the memory as to perform tasks for which the memory was unsuited. Let us examine three such devices, beginning with the mid-eleventh century: those of Papias, Deusdedit, and Gilbert of Poitiers.

Papias's dictionary, the *Elementarium doctrinae erudimentum* (saec. XI med.), was a milestone in itself, as the first alphabetically arranged work of any magnitude.[8] Moreover, in order to help readers find their way through his complicated lexicon, Papias describes in the prologue a system of signposts that would appear in the manuscript. The breaks of the alphabet were to be marked by three sizes of letters: the first word beginning with a given letter was to be marked by a large A, B, C, etc. in the text; each successive change in second letter (words beginning Ab——, Ac——, etc.) was to be marked in the margin by a middle-sized B, C, etc., and each change in third letter (Aba——, Abb——, etc.) by a small marginal *a, b,* etc. Genders of nouns were to be designated (m., f., n.); and the names of authors cited were to be given in abbreviated form—he lists the abbreviations—in the proper place in the margin (Hisidorus, *hi*; Augustinus, *aug*; and so forth). Papias's apparatus, with its use of letter size and marginalia, was far ahead of its time; and contemporary copyists, to whom such features were unknown and, presumably, of no interest, disregarded the instructions of the prologue. Papias's instructions began to be honored in practice largely in copies of the dictionary made after the twelfth century (see, for example, Paris, BN lat 17162, saec. XIII[1]), when scribes were familiar with, and readers appreciated the value of, such signposts. Papias's major innovation, that of organizing a large work alphabetically, inspired no emulation among his contemporaries.

---

[5]Discussed by William M. Green, "Hugo of St. Victor, *De tribus maximis circumstantiis gestorum*," *Speculum* 18 (1943) 484–93. The *Didascalicon* is cited from Jerome Taylor, trans., *The Didascalicon of Hugh of St. Victor: A Medieval Guide to the Arts*, Columbia University Records of Civilization 64 (New York 1961).

[6]This is not to say that memory training as such ceased to be of interest; but from this time forward, memory was aided by artificial finding devices.

[7]Concerning artificial memory, see Frances A. Yates, *The Art of Memory* (Chicago and London 1966).

[8]Concerning this dictionary see Lloyd W. and Betty A. Daly, "Some Techniques in Mediaeval Latin Lexicography," *Speculum* 39 (1964) 229–39; and Lloyd W. Daly, *Contributions to a History of Alphabetization in Antiquity and the Middle Ages*, Collection Latomus 90 (Brussels 1967) 71–72.

The technique for searching devised by cardinal Deusdedit for his collection of canonical texts (1083–87)[9] points up a curious problem. Beginning with the Gregorian Reform, when the first great canon law compendia were assembled, the canon lawyers faced the same need to search through written authority that would confront the school of theology over a century later; why did not the former, as did the latter, produce elaborate reference tools? Perhaps the difference lies in the fact that canon law as a field of study evolved before, and outside of, the universities. For whatever reason, the canonists depended upon rational classification by subject, with little apparatus to aid in searching before the late thirteenth century. Deusdedit was an exception: he compiled a subject index, in rational rather than alphabetical order, as an aid to searching his collection of 1,173 canonical texts, divided into four books. Deusdedit explained his motives in a preface: he did not arrange the material itself according to subject, because this would have required him to violate the integrity of the documents, recording portions under one heading, other portions under other headings; therefore, to enable one to find information concerning a specific topic, he provided a list of subjects for each of the four books (a total of roughly 800), with reference by number to the appropriate chapters, or books and chapters. What looks, at first glance, like a chapter list at the head of each book is in fact a primitive subject index. In the early thirteenth century, similar subject indexes in rational order would appear at the schools, where they were part of the rapidly increasing and evolving body of searchable tools; cardinal Deusdedit's index, in contrast, occurred in isolation, and it was neither imitated nor improved upon by other canonists.[10]

The third example dates from the first half of the twelfth century. The manuscripts of Gilbert of Poitiers's Commentary on the Psalms contain marginal indexing symbols—twelve different ones, each occurring a varying number of times, and employed to group the psalms by theme. Gilbert's classification of the psalms is derived from Cassiodorus; and it is possible that he found there as well the notion of marginal symbols, although Cassiodorus uses quite different symbols, applied for different purposes.[11] Gilbert's symbols consist of Greek letters, conventional signs and the like—for example, **8**, ∿, Ψ, Φ, ζ. The symbol **8** refers to the two natures of Christ, ∿ to the Passion and Resurrection, Ψ identifies the penitential psalms, and so on. To take as an example an early dated manuscript of the Commentary, Oxford, Balliol College MS 36 (saec. XII; written before 1166, when it was given to Lincoln Cathedral

[9]Edited by Victor Wolf von Glanvell, *Die Kanonessammlung des Kardinals Deusdedit* (Paderborn 1905); see the discussion of Paul Fournier and Gabriel LeBras, *Histoire des collections canoniques en Occident* (2 vols. Paris 1931–32) 2.37–54. We are grateful to Robert Somerville, Columbia University, for drawing our attention to Deusdedit's index.

[10]Not until the time of Martinus Polonus (d. ca. 1279) do we have a subject index to the *Decretum*.

[11]See Cassiodorus, *Expositio psalmorum*, CCL 97 (Turnhout 1958) 3; Cassiodorus's notes or symbols are on this model: GEO (= hoc in geometrica), Ṁ (= hoc in musica), ⊕ (= hoc in astronomia), etc.

by Robert de Chesney):[12] on fol. 3, beside the beginning of Gilbert's gloss on Psalm 2, there is the marginal symbol 8. This tells one that Psalm 2 is the first psalm that treats *De duabus naturis in Christo*, and that the next psalm with the same theme is Psalm 8. On fol. 8v, beside the beginning of Psalm 8, is the symbol 8; and it goes on—at Psalm 20 we find 8; at Psalm 71, 8; and so on to the last, at Psalm 138, 8; which has no figure at the bottom, thus indicating that it is the last. Gilbert has devised a finding system in chain fashion—that is, one is referred not to all the psalms on a given theme, but merely to the next "link," which will direct one in turn to the next. The principal drawback is obvious: this is a one-way chain, that leads forward only. Therefore, if one were reading Psalm 138, for example, the symbol 8 tells one only that there are seven other psalms concerning the dual nature of Christ, without identifying any of them. These symbols were used in twelfth-century manuscripts of Gilbert's Commentary, but even by the end of that century new manuscripts ceased to include them, or included them only sporadically; copyists evidently found them of no use, and quite likely had forgotten their significance. We have seen the symbols (including the top and bottom numerals) in the margin of the psalms in one early thirteenth-century manuscript (Oriel College MS 77), and others may turn up. But Gilbert's indexing method was too eccentric for acceptance by any significant number of people; and at the time of its creation, there was insufficient interest for anyone to imitate and improve upon it. The use of marginal symbols for indexing was not tried again until the independent development of indexing symbols or "concordantial signs" by Grosseteste and his circle at Oxford, in the middle of the thirteenth century.[13]

LAYOUT AS A FINDING DEVICE OF THE SCHOOLS

The devices of Papias, Deusdedit, and Gilbert of Poitiers failed to inspire emulation principally because they were created at the wrong time and place, where need or demand for them was lacking. The insufficiency of memory as a finding device—and, hence, the need for artificial devices—became crucial only with the growth of the schools and, especially, with the emerging prominence of theology at Paris in the course of the twelfth century. The number of

---

[12]The volume was kindly brought to our attention by Malcolm Parkes. It is described by R. A. B. Mynors, *Catalogue of the Manuscripts of Balliol College Oxford* (Oxford 1963) 26. MS 36 can be identified with no. 60 in the twelfth-century catalogue of the cathedral; ed. Reginald M. Woolley, *Catalogue of the Manuscripts of Lincoln Cathedral Chapter Library* (London 1927) vii.

[13]S. Harrison Thomson, "Grosseteste's Topical Concordance of the Bible and the Fathers," *Speculum* 9 (1934) 139–44; idem, "Grosseteste's Concordantial Signs," *Medievalia et humanistica* 9 (1955) 39–53; Hunt (n. 1 above). We have identified two additional MSS containing versions of the Grossetestian symbols: San Marino, California, Huntington Library MS 26061, kindly shown us by Jean Preston in 1972; and BN n.a.1. 540, kindly brought to our attention by François Avril in 1977. The latter is a concordance to the Fathers and a key to the symbols different from that in Lyon MS 414.

students to be instructed was large, in comparison for example with the number at such cathedral schools as Laon. The time for instruction was limited, in comparison with the lifelong immersion in prayerful reading that distinguished monastic learning. And the very subject matter of theology was itself in the process of being defined and redefined, with the *Glossa ordinaria* and Peter Lombard's *Sentences* standing out as towering landmarks. In this context, the deficiency of memory as the principal means for finding was glaringly apparent: one cannot remember what one has not read, and one may well wish to find a part without reading the whole.

The major collections of the twelfth century—the Gloss, the *Decretum*, the *Sentences*—were in effect "finding devices" in themselves. For example, one did not need to search all the literature, both patristic and canonical, on a given question of law, because Gratian had already done the job. Peter Lombard is explicit on this point: he has compiled the *Sentences* "so that it will not be necessary for the seeker to turn through numerous books; for the brevity [of the *Sentences*] offers him, without effort, what he seeks" ("ut non sit necesse quaerenti librorum numerositatem evolvere, cui brevitas quod quaeritur offert sine labore").[14] These compilations were a new kind of literature in many ways, not the least of which is that they are designed, not for reflective reading, but for seeking out specific information.

This leaves, of course, the problem of how to locate a given sort of information within the compilations themselves. As we have implied above, the original impetus was the needs of the schools, where teaching took the form of commentary on a text, with the written page as its point of departure. The original response was well tailored to these needs: scholars of the mid- and late twelfth century employed the physical arrangement and appearance of the manuscript book and page as an aid to finding. Many of the devices used were not new; the change lay in their systematic and increasingly sophisticated application.

The simplest finding device was the list of chapter headings prefaced to a work. Tables of chapters can be found in earlier books. But with the mid-twelfth century such tables in new works become the norm, rather than the exception; and at this date we may safely assume that chapter lists are intended not only as an overview or summary of the contents but also as a device to facilitate searching. Peter Lombard, in the prologue to the *Sentences*, puts the implicit into words: "Ut autem quod quaeritur facilius occurrat, titulos quibus singulorum librorum capitula distinguuntur praemisimus."[15] Here the compiler himself makes provision for a finding device. It is instructive to contrast the Lombard's language with the words of another "prologue," the first of Bernard's *Sermones in Cantica canticorum*, only a few years earlier in time but

---

[14]*Magistri Petri Lombardi Parisiensis episcopi Sententiae in IV libris distinctae*, ed. Ignatius Brady, Spicilegium Bonaventurianum 4 (Grottaferrata 1971) 4 (= PL 192.522).
[15]Ibid.

far removed in spirit. Bernard hopes that his auditors or readers will delight in the hard work of difficult inquiry: "Ut quod in ea latet, delectet etiam cum labore investigare, nec fatiget inquirendi forte difficultas."[16] The Lombard's hopes are quite other: "Quod quaeritur offert sine labore . . . , ut quod quaeritur facilius occurrat." Peter Lombard's is the language of the new *instruments de travail*, reiterated in virtually every twelfth- to fourteenth-century aid to study that has a prologue—expressions like *sine labore, facilius occurrere, presto habere*, and *citius* or even *statim invenire*.

While a list of chapters could help one to single out the chapter that contained the information sought, the actual locating of information in the text was facilitated by the layout of the page.[17] Innovations in layout of the manuscript page are surely the most highly visible of all the twelfth-century aids to study—such techniques as running headlines, chapter titles in red, alternating red and blue initials and gradation in the size of initials, paragraph marks, cross-references, and citation of authors quoted. One cannot give a precise *terminus ante quem* for general acceptance of the individual elements, save to say that by about 1220 they were all standard; most can be seen on the pages of any late twelfth-century glossed Bible or manuscript of the *Sentences*. Twelfth-century manuscripts of the *Sentences*, for example, have the chapter titles in red, and a two-line majuscule begins the first word of each chapter. Subdivisions of the chapter's topic (*prima causa, secunda, tertia*) are entered as marginal rubrics. Authors quoted in the text have their names in red in the margin, tied neatly to the precise words of the text, beginning and end, by *puncti*—usually two dots (. .) above the words at the beginning, and two vertical dots (:) above the end. These functioned like quotation marks, accompanied by rudimentary footnotes.

In biblical study the great product of the twelfth-century schools was the development of the commentaries to be applied to the Scriptures, the *Glossa ordinaria*, and its corollary in the book—namely, the layout of the glossed page. If the Gloss became the main vehicle for the accumulation and transfer of thought, clearly the book would have to undergo a marked alteration in the process of being adapted, first to accommodate, and then to focus on, the commentary. The exegesis of earlier centuries had been continuous works, physically independent of the text of the Bible. Adaptation of exegesis to the biblical text was worked out probably in Paris in the course of the twelfth century, a change that is currently being reconstructed by Christopher de Hamel.[18] His researches have identified several successive steps in the develop-

---

[16]*Sancti Bernardi opera*, ed. Leclercq, 1.5.13–15 (= PL 183.787).

[17]See Malcolm B. Parkes, "The Influence of the Concepts of *Ordinatio* and *Compilatio* on the Development of the Book," *Medieval Learning and Literature: Essays presented to Richard William Hunt*, ed. J. J. G. Alexander and M. T. Gibson (Oxford 1976) 115–41.

[18]See his unpublished D.Phil. diss. (Oxford 1979) on the layout of the glossed Bible in the twelfth century. We are grateful to him for having shared with us his firsthand knowledge of these books.

ing layout of the Gloss. By mid-century or slightly after, it had reached the stage in which the text of the Scriptures shrank in width from the two columns of an unglossed Bible to a single column in the center of the page, written on widely separated lines in a bold or enlarged script. The glosses were entered on either side in separately ruled sections, written in smaller script with two lines of gloss for every line of text. The connection between gloss and text was made precise by the inclusion of lemmata (usually underlined in red) in the gloss; and tie marks either linked gloss to text or, more commonly, linked a gloss that was incomplete at the end of one column to its continuation (in the next column, or on the next page). This three-column format became standard by the middle of the century, with Gilbert of Poitiers's commentary on the Psalms and Peter Lombard's commentary on Psalms and the Pauline epistles. It is seen in hundreds of surviving glossed books of the Bible.[19]

At a later stage, Gilbert's and the Lombard's commentaries, initially written continuous in columns flanking a column of Scripture, were presented on the page as two columns of commentary interspersed with, and virtually engulfing, the text of the Scripture written in large letters. This stage, in existence by 1166, is marked by the appearance of several techniques important to locating material, in particular the marginal citation of authorities that were quoted. Herbert of Bosham produced an "edition" or restructuring of the layout of the Lombard's *Magna glosatura* about 1170–76, which is a splendid example of the techniques available by the last quarter of the century to assist the reader in finding his way about a glossed text.[20]

Let us take as an example Bosham's edition of the Lombard on Psalms. Each "quinquagena" or group of fifty psalms is preceded by a chapter list, that is, the number of each psalm followed by a four-to-six-line summary of its content. The work is written in two columns per page. In each column, in large script, is a passage from the Gallican Psalter; to its left, in half-size script, is the same passage from the Hebrew Psalter; and to its right and above and below, again at half size, is the Lombard's commentary. In the outside margins (that is, to the left of the left-hand, to the right of the right-hand column of glossed text) are three columns of marginal apparatus. In the first or inner column are cross-references within the book of Psalms, written in very small script, on this model: "S. i. super fructum suum," meaning "See above, Psalm 1, at the passage *fructum suum."* In the second column are the

[19]A good example is plate 43 in R. A. B. Mynors, *Durham Cathedral Manuscripts to the End of the Twelfth Century* (Oxford 1939), fol. 4v of MS A.III.4 (3rd quarter of the twelfth century) containing I–IV Kings. Cf. Smalley, *Study* pl. 1.

[20]See Ignatius Brady, "The Rubrics of Peter Lombard's Sentences," *Pier Lombardo* 6 (1962) 5–25. Our description of Bosham's edition is based on Oxford, Bodleian Library MS Auct. E infra 6 (S.C. 2051) and Cambridge, Trinity College MSS 150, 152–53, which were given by Bosham to Christ Church, Canterbury; see Montague Rhodes James, *The Ancient Libraries of Canterbury and Dover* (Cambridge 1903) 85 nos. 855–57, and Beryl Smalley, *The Becket Conflict and the Schools* (Oxford 1973) 81–83.

author citations in red, with both *puncti* (corresponding to identical *puncti* in the text) and, where necessary, an inclusive vertical line marking the beginning and end. This device is the Lombard's own, but it is Herbert who explains the necessity of these quotation marks: he wishes to distinguish clearly the words of the glossator (the Lombard) from those of the expositors (the patristic commentators) and to distinguish the latter one from another, "lest you be led to mistake Cassiodorus for Augustine or Jerome, or the glossator for an expositor, a matter in which we have seen, not just the unlettered, but very learned readers fall into error."[21] (Compilers must have given much thought to the matter of how and where to cite their sources; some seventy years later, Vincent of Beauvais stated that he had decided to cite his sources in the text, as Gratian had done, rather than in the margins in the style of the *Magna glosatura*, because marginalia tended to be lost in copying.)[22] The third or outside column contains cross-references to books of the Bible other than the Psalms. At the top of the page is a running headline, in alternating red and blue, giving the number of the psalm contained on that page; the running headline changes over the proper column, where the text of a new psalm begins. Herbert's manuscripts of the revised *Magna glosatura* are the earliest we know that employ cross-references and running headlines in a deliberate and consistent fashion. Bosham's layout, *mutatis mutandis*, is typical of that employed for glossed Scripture in the course of the 1170s and '80s.[23] De Hamel has recorded a great many examples of this format, demonstrating that it spread across Europe with great speed.

The utility of the devices of layout worked out in the twelfth century is evident: we still use virtually all of them today, save that we have moved the marginalia to the foot of the page.[24] And whenever one has occasion to turn directly from use of a well-laid-out twelfth- or thirteenth-century manuscript to look for something in the exceptional modern printed text that does *not* have, for example, running headlines or clear paragraph divisions, one has an annoying sense of lost ground. By the end of the twelfth century, then, we might assume that the needs for a "finding technique" for classroom use were being met by the development of the clearly displayed text, with its chapter lists, running headlines, and marginal apparatus. With the teaching of the *sacra pagina* wedded to the order of the text, why should artificial tools for retrievability be developed?

[21]"Verba expositorum inter se et etiam a verbis glosatoris distinxi, ne Cassiodorum pro Augustino sive Ieronimo, vel glosatorem inducas pro expositore, in quo interdum non simplices sed eruditiores etiam vidimus lectores erasse"; quoted by Brady (n. 20 above) 10–11.

[22]"Nequaquam in margine sicut sit in psalterio glossato et epistolis Pauli vel in sentenciis, sed inter lineas ipsas sicut in decretis ea inserui"; cited and discussed by Parkes (n. 17 above) 133.

[23]A number of fine examples appear among the books acquired in Paris, probably in the 1180s, and left to Durham cathedral by Robert of Adington; see Mynors (n. 19 above) 78–82 and pl. 48, showing fol. 4v of MS A.III.17 (glossed Isaiah).

[24]The word "footnote" seems to date only from the nineteenth century; the earliest citation for the word in the *Oxford English Dictionary* is "1841. Savage, *Dictionary of Printing* p. 88: *Bottom notes . . . are also termed Foot Notes.*"

ALPHABETIZATION AS A FINDING DEVICE FOR PREACHERS

And yet, the limitations of layout as a finding device are obvious: they are imposed by the physical limits of the page. This will be true of any work in any age; for the glossed Bible, the limits had been reached by the end of the twelfth century. Although we sometimes overlook the fact, the late twelfth-century masters who lectured on the Gloss were themselves aware of its insufficiencies and of the need to go beyond it.[25] It was therefore inevitable that alternative methods of retrieving information must eventually be devised, methods that would require different notions of order, as opposed to ordering information according to the text. Such a change was bound to be difficult, for it involved not merely creating a new ordering of ideas, but also consenting to break with an already established order. It is perhaps for this reason that canon law, with its early and carefully ordered body of topics, produced no artificial tools (until the late thirteenth century, when the notion was borrowed from others). For theologians, the order of topics was defined by the order of the Scriptures; as new information accumulated, the natural inclination was to force it into the mold of the Gloss, so that the Gloss, and glosses on the Gloss, swelled to unwieldy proportions. Despite the strains, it seemed impossible to conceive of any other method of making accessible to students the information necessary to the study of the sacred page.

Therefore the need, already apparent in the twelfth century, to create tools for teaching purposes was initially held back by the barrier of tradition. Instead, the first tools that successfully employed artificial order as a finding device, in contrast to reliance on layout, emerged in response to a different need, in a field unencumbered with established conventions. These were the late twelfth-century collections of biblical "distinctions," created in response to the need for sermon material. This innovation illustrates how need shapes response: for the very same masters who, in their teaching, were glossing the Gloss in traditional fashion—such men as Peter the Chanter, Peter of Poitiers, Prepositinus, Alan of Lille, Peter of Capua—felt free to create new structures when responding to the needs of preaching. Before we go on to discuss the what and the why of distinction collections, therefore, we must consider structure and arrangement.

One immediately striking aspect of these new tools, and surely the most influential in the long view, is the fact that certain of the late twelfth-century distinction collections, as well as all significant thirteenth-century ones, were arranged in alphabetical order to facilitate searching. They were the first tools so organized;[26] and they were, insofar as we have been able to determine, the

---

[25] See below at n. 62.

[26] Alphabetical order was of course used before the distinction collection; the main medieval example is the glossary, in particular Papias's dictionary. It belongs to a separate tradition, however, akin both to older glossarial works and to the later works of Huguccio, Alexander of Villedieu, the *Graecismus*, and Brito, the composition and use of which were narrowly confined to the *artes*. Alphabetical apparatus, at least for the faculty of theology, began with alphabetized distinction collections.

direct ancestor of all later alphabetical and searchable tools—beginning with the alphabetical verbal concordances to the Scriptures and the first alphabetical subject indexes before the middle of the thirteenth century, and continuing through the thirteenth and fourteenth centuries with alphabetical indexes to the Fathers and Aristotle, collections of *exempla* and *florilegia* alphabetized by topic, tenant and tax rolls alphabetized by name, and so on. The adoption of the alphabet to order ideas, by a handful of men in the late twelfth century, implies on their part a major change in attitude toward the written word. "The Middle Ages did not care much for alphabetical order," because they were committed instead to rational order.[27] The universe is a harmonious whole, whose parts are related to one another. It was the responsibility of the author or scholar to discern these rational relationships—of hierarchy, or of chronology, or of similarities and differences, and so forth—and to reflect them in his writing.[28]

Given this predisposition, therefore, the acceptance of alphabetical order was reluctant and proceeded at an uneven pace, even within the confines of a single literary form. Peter the Chanter (about 1190) and Alan of Lille (before 1195), for example, arranged their distinction collections alphabetically; but the contemporary collections of Peter of Poitiers (about 1190) and Prepositinus (1196–98) were arranged in the order of the Psalter, while others, such as Peter of Cornwall (about 1189–1200) and Peter of Capua (about 1220), combined alphabetical with rational order. Complete alphabetization (alphabetization throughout the word) never became *de rigueur* in distinction collections. Moreover, the adoption of alphabetical order in one set of circumstances obviously influenced but by no means ensured its acceptance in another where, from our viewpoint, it would seem to have been equally applicable. Thus, for example, while the Chanter alphabetized his distinctions, it would not have occurred to him to equip his *Verbum abbreviatum* with an index. In the thirteenth century the earliest subject indexes, and a good many later ones, were arranged in rational rather than alphabetical order. At a time (just after mid-century) when Robert Kilwardby was making alphabetical indexes to the works of the Fathers, Grosseteste's intellectual heirs were still compiling a concordance to the Fathers arranged in rational order. And shortly after the Dominicans under Hugh of St Cher had compiled a massive alphabetical con-

---

[27]Haskins, *Ren* 78: "The Middle Ages did not care much for alphabetical order, at least beyond the initial letter, and they would have faced a telephone directory with the consternation of an American office boy." Haskins made this statement merely as an aside, and it would be unjust to fault him for it; however, it typifies the assumptions of many historians, of his day and of our own. Moreover, one can still take only minor exception to the statement as it applies to the Middle Ages up to the second half of the twelfth century.

[28]Possibly the nicest example of the conflict between the two sorts of order, and of the scholastic's estimate of alphabetical order, comes from Albertus Magnus, who, in his commentary on the *De animalibus*, apologizes for using alphabetical order after having said "hunc modum non proprium philosophie esse"—but he uses it nonetheless, for the benefit of the unlearned reader; *Opera omnia*, ed. Auguste Borgnet (38 vols. in 90 Paris 1890–99) 12.433. We are grateful to Lynn White, jr., for this reference.

cordance of the words in the Bible, other Dominicans were compiling biblical subject indexes or "real" (as opposed to "verbal") concordances in rational order; in some of these—for example, the *Concordantiae morales bibliorum* mistakenly attributed to Anthony of Padua—the order is so well thought out, with rational subdivision of books into parts further subdivided into chapters, that they are not difficult to use as finding devices.[29]

The use of alphabetical order, then, was not inevitable; once introduced, its acceptance was neither immediate nor widespread; and it never, during the Middle Ages, succeeded in supplanting the use of rational order, even for those tasks for which alphabetical order would have been more efficient. Nevertheless, in the subsequent discussion we emphasize the alphabetical aspect, for two reasons. First is the obvious one, that the alphabetical principle eventually won out, as the device for making information retrievable. The second is that such tools document the emergence of a different attitude to written tradition. Prior to this time, alphabetization had been largely restricted to lists of things which had no known or discernible rational relationship: one alphabetized lapidaries, for instance, because no classification of stones existed. For the alphabetized distinction collections, such a rule did not hold: one was in no sense compelled to use alphabetical order, as witness those collections organized according to the order of the Scriptures or some other rational order. Rather, the use of alphabetical order was a tacit recognition of the fact that each user of a work will bring to it his own preconceived rational order, which may differ from those of other users and from that of the writer himself. Applied to distinction collections, this notion meant recognition that, while one might teach in the order of the text of the Bible, one did not preach thus. Applied, for example, to the Bible itself, this notion produced the verbal concordance. Alphabetization was not simply a handy new device; it was also the manifestation of a different way of thinking.

BIBLICAL DISTINCTION COLLECTIONS

It is ironic that, of all the useful alphabetical tools descendent from the burgeoning "need to find" of the twelfth-century schools, the collection of biblical distinctions has the role of progenitor. The distinction is an oddity, of quickly passing importance, one of those ideas whose time has come and, long

---

[29]Concerning the development of distinction collections see Richard H. and Mary A. Rouse, "Biblical Distinctions in the Thirteenth Century," AHDLMA 41 (1974) 27–37, and in the text below; concerning Kilwardby's indexes see D. A. Callus, "The 'Tabulae super Originalia Patrum' of Robert Kilwardby O.P.," in *Studia mediaevalia in honorem . . . Raymundi Josephi Martin* (Bruges 1948) 243–70; idem, "New Manuscripts of Kilwardby's 'Tabulae super originalia patrum,'" *Dominican Studies* 2 (1949) 38–45; idem, "The Contribution to the Study of the Fathers made by the Thirteenth-Century Oxford Schools," *Journal of Ecclesiastical History* 5 (1954) 139–48; concerning Grosseteste's concordance see n. 13 above; concerning the *Concordantiae morales bibliorum* see Arduinus Kleinhans, "De concordantiis Biblicis S. Antonio Patavino aliisque fratribus minoribus saec. XIII attributis," *Antonianum* 6 (1931) 273–326.

since, gone. In discussing layout we were content merely to say "the *Sentences*" or "the Gloss," confident that these names would be immediately recognized and understood. Here, we must consider what distinctions were, why and when collections of them were compiled, and what function the distinction performed that made it, however briefly, a matter of importance.[30]

A biblical *distinctio* distinguishes (hence the name) the various figurative meanings of a word in the Bible, supplying for each meaning a text of Scripture in which the word is used with that meaning. Let us take as an example a late twelfth-century *distinctio* on the word *nubes:*[31]

Tres sunt nubes: obscuritas in prophetis, profunditas in divinis consiliis, occulta et inaudita fecunditas virginitatis. De nube prophetarum scriptum est, "Tenebrosa aqua in nubibus aeris" [Ps. 17:12 = AV 18:11]; de nube consiliorum Dei legitur, "Rorate, celi, desuper, et nubes pluant justum" [Isa. 45:8]; de nube virginitatis et fecunditatis absconditae dicit propheta, "Super nubem levem et candidam ingredietur Dominus Aegyptum" [Isa. 19:1].

Clearly, the *distinctio* is stated in highly compressed language; for most of us, this "explanation" of the meaning of *nubes* is no explanation at all. One would need to know in advance, for example, the standard (or a standard) interpretation of "tenebrosa aqua in nubibus aeris" as a reference to prophetic ambiguity. As stated in a distinction collection, the language was likely to be more compressed still; in the early collections (some of the oldest manuscripts of the Chanter's, for example) distinctions were often displayed schematically, so that our distinction would have looked like this:

obscuritas in prophetis. Unde, Tenebrosa aqua in nubibus aeris.
nubes — profunditas in divinis consiliis. Unde, Rorate celi desuper et nubes pluant justum.
occulta et inaudita fecunditas virginitatis. Unde, Super nubem levem etc.

Within the compass of a decade, beginning around 1189 or 1190, the twelfth century produced at least five major collections of distinctions, containing up to 1,500 biblical terms and distinguishing as many as six or eight meanings for each: the *Pantheologus* of Peter Cornwall, Peter the Chanter's *Summa Abel*, the collection of Alan of Lille, and the distinctions on the Psalms of Peter of Poitiers and Prepositinus. Distinction collections continued to be produced, with undiminished enthusiasm, through most of the thirteenth century.

Such instant and continued popularity demonstrates that these collections met a need. It has sometimes been assumed that the source of this demand lay in the field of exegesis—that these were tools for teaching, or tools for com-

---

[30]The term *distinctio*, "distinction," has many other meanings in the language of the twelfth century (as in the twentieth). For example, *distinctiones* as employed in the organization of legal compendia have a quite separate history, which does not concern us here; and *distinctiones* meaning "chapter divisions" is mentioned below, following n. 66.

[31]From Peter of Blois, Sermon 2, PL 207.565. Other examples, and a discussion of the thirteenth-century evolution of the *distinctio*, are found in Rouse and Rouse, "Biblical Distinctions" (n. 29 above).

posing works of theology.[32] The collections of Peter of Poitiers and
Prepositinus, arranged in the order of the biblical text, could have served as
the basis for classroom lectures (though the *distinctiones* of Prepositinus may
have been delivered as a series of sermons).[33] Also, one certainly finds distinctions being used in commentaries of the late twelfth century: in the Chanter's
Verbum abbreviatum, for example, or in Gilbert Foliot's commentary on Can-
ticles, which opens with a detailed consideration of several interpretations of
the word *osculetur*.

The major demand for a ready supply of distinctions, however, arose from
the making of sermons. More specifically, one can say both that the demand
originated with preachers, and that the preponderant use of the distinction,
throughout its brief but busy life, was for the composition of sermons. We
have traced elsewhere how, subsequent to the appearance of the first distinction collections, the *distinctio* became a standard device used in sermons
throughout the thirteenth century and beyond. But actually, as we shall see,
the employment of distinctions in sermons precedes by perhaps twenty-five
years and more the compilation of the earliest collections—although the
distinctio could not be called a commonplace in sermons until the turn of the
century. Such a pattern of development is reflected in all the searchable tools
of the thirteenth century: the needs of users motivate the making of the tool
which, by virtue of its accessibility, increases the use. Others have said that *distinctiones* appeared in the generation following the death of the Lombard; and
the single case of Gilbert Foliot has been cited repeatedly.[34] A few specific examples will provide a clearer idea of who and when and, eventually, why.

There are rare *distinctiones* in the sermons of Peter Lombard himself (d.
1160), surely among the earliest uses of this device; see, for example, in an Advent sermon on the text "Aspiciebam ego in visione noctis . . ." (Dan.
7:13), the distinction of *visio*: "Est enim triplex visio, scilicet visio noctis, visio
diei, visio lucis . . . ," which goes on to expound each sort of vision, with a
biblical quotation supporting each one.[35] Peter Comestor (d. 1179) was an
early large-scale user of *distinctiones*, with much amplification of each mean-

[32]See, for example, Joseph de Ghellinck, *L'essor de la littérature latine au XIIe siècle* (2nd ed.
Brussels 1955) 81: "Instruments de travail, qui nous font entrer de plus près dans l'atelier de composition des oeuvres théologiques de cette fin du XIIe siècle: la *Summa quae dicitur Abel*. . ."; cf.
also 232–34.

[33]Georges Lacombe, *La vie et les oeuvres de Prévostin*, Bibliothèque thomiste 11, sect. historique 10 (Le Saulchoir 1927) 112–30. Concerning the collection of Peter of Poitiers and its use, see
Philip S. Moore, *The Works of Peter of Poitiers, Master in Theology and Chancellor of Paris
(1193–1205)* (Washington D.C. 1936) 79–81.

[34]Richard W. Hunt, "English Learning in the Late Twelfth Century," TRHS 4th ser. 19
(1936) 19–42 at 33–34, 40–41. Hunt's example of Peter of Cornwall's enthusiastic description of
Gilbert's use of distinctions is also cited by Smalley, *Study* 248; by Hugh MacKinnon, "William
de Montibus: A Medieval Teacher," *Essays in Medieval History presented to Bertie Wilkinson*, ed.
T. A. Sandquist and M. R. Powicke (Toronto 1969) 32–45 at 38 n. 16; and, obliquely, by ourselves
(n. 29 above) 30 n. 10.

[35]PL 171.373–74, under Hildebert's name.

ing; see, for example, in a sermon on the text "Convertit me ad viam portae sanctuarii exterioris. . ." (Ezek. 44:1), the detailed *distinctio* on the word *via*: "Quatuor enim sunt viae hominis: via infirmitatis, . . . via necessitatis, . . . via vanitatis, . . . via veritatis." He explains each *via*, supporting each with a biblical quotation (*via necessitatis* with a quotation from Horace!); and he tells whether it leads north, south, east, or west, and why.[36] The Comestor is the first preacher for whom one can say that the *distinctio* was a favorite rhetorical device.[37] Peter of Blois (ca. 1135 to after 1204) used *distinctiones* in preaching: the example "Tres sunt nubes" cited above is his. Marie-Thérèse d'Alverny has documented the use of *distinctiones* in the sermons of Alan of Lille (d. 1203).[38] And we know that Gilbert Foliot, bishop of London, was using *distinctiones* to great effect in his preaching by the 1170s, for Peter of Cornwall describes his "exhilaration" at hearing Gilbert preach according to this new form, when Peter was but a *novus canonicus* (he is thought to have joined the Austin Canons of Aldgate about 1170).[39] There is no need to give further names—not that the list would be endless, but that it would be imprecise; we lack both accurate dating and printed editions for so many twelfth-century sermons. The examples cited will suffice as evidence that twelfth-century preachers, from before 1160, had begun to employ *distinctiones* in their sermons.

This new fashion created a need for preachers to have available a body of distinctions from which to choose, a need that was met by the creation of the new tools. Circumstantial evidence clearly indicates as much; and, fortunately, Peter of Cornwall explicitly describes the progression, from the use of distinctions in preaching to the making of a distinction collection for further preaching. He states, on the one hand, that he was inspired to compile his *Pantheologus* by hearing Foliot's use of distinctions in a sermon; and, on the other, he explains that his collection was fashioned so that sermon-makers (*sermonem facientes*) need not so much make sermons, as to form sermons already made for them ("non tam sermonem facere quam iam factum formare").[40]

The *Pantheologus* illustrates, as well, the reluctant but steady shift from rational to alphabetical order, in response to the preachers' demand for quickly accessible sermon material. The distinctions in the *Pantheologus* were

---

[36]Sermon 2, PL 198.1725–28.

[37]On this point, see the blunt assessment of Jean Longère, *Oeuvres oratoires de maîtres parisiens au XIIe siècle: Etude historique et doctrinale* (2 vols. Paris 1975) 1.55: "Pierre Comestor est parmi ceux qui ont le plus usé et abusé des distinctions."

[38]Marie-Thérèse d'Alverny, ed., *Alain de Lille: Textes inédits*, EPM 52 (Paris 1965), esp. 242–45 and nn., 270 and nn., 276–77 and nn.

[39]For the details of Peter's career see Richard W. Hunt, "The Disputation of Peter of Cornwall Against Symon the Jew," *Studies in Medieval History presented to Frederick Maurice Powicke*, ed. Richard W. Hunt et al. (Oxford 1948) 143–56, esp. 143–45.

[40]From the prologue to part 4, as seen in Oxford, Lincoln College MS lat. 83 fol. 1r–v; we thank Richard Hunt for making available to us his transcript of this prologue. Virtually the same words occur in the prologue to part 1, edited by Hunt (n. 34 above) 38–42, esp. 40.72–76 ("sermones facientem").

divided into four parts, according to the text of the Bible: part one contained distinctions of words in the Psalms, and in other books "tam veteris quam novi testamenti"; part two, distinctions of words in the four sapiential books; part three, distinctions of words in the major and minor prophets; and part four, a catchall in rational order (beginning with *Deus*) "from all the books of both Old and New Testament," containing distinctions of words "which the other parts omitted." Peter of Cornwall completed the *Pantheologus* about 1189, relying on his *capitula* or lists of words being distinguished, at the head of each part, to make the work searchable ("Capitula . . . disposuimus ut . . . sine difficultatis mora que querit inveniat,"[41] language reminiscent of the Lombard's in similar circumstances). But not long after the work was completed, he realized that the *capitula* were not adequate, particularly for the collection in part four, to enable one to find immediately (*statim invenire*) what was wanted. Therefore, he made a second list, containing the same *capitula* rearranged in first-letter alphabetical order, with a brief prefatory paragraph explaining "how to find quite easily what is sought, according to a new method, alphabetical order."[42] The surviving copy of this alphabetical list is dated about 1200. Peter's list may be regarded as a proto-index. More important, it documents with clear and datable evidence one man's conscious shift, within some ten years' time, from rational to alphabetical order to make his work searchable for preachers.

We should like to be able to describe the procedures by which Peter of Cornwall and his fellows compiled their collections of distinctions—the sources of their interpretations, and the means by which they located multiple biblical usages for each of several hundred words. But the present state of research does not provide any certain indications, and the compilers themselves do not say. At any rate, the problem of how to find a variety of passages that use the same word was eventually solved, in the thirteenth century, by the alphabetical verbal concordance, and it seems likely that the continuing demand for distinctions was no small factor among the needs that produced the concordance: the flyleaf of the oldest datable copy of the concordance contains distinctions, employing the concordance reference system and written in the hand of the manuscript's original owner.[43]

THE THEMATIC SERMON

Whatever may have been the mechanics of compiling twelfth-century distinction collections, the cause was the use of distinctions in preaching. But why did

---

[41]Ibid. 42.131–34.

[42]Oxford, St. John's College MS 31 fol. 2: "Explanatio qualiter facillime inveniuntur que queruntur in quarta parte Pantheologi secundum novum modum scilicet per litteras alphabeti. Quia per capitula que primitus ante initium quarte partis Panteologi apposuimus non potest qui vis statim invenire que in libro illo invenire desiderat . . . ideo hic eadem capitula, sed non eodem ordine quo ibi, disposuimus. Hic enim eadem secundum ordinem alphabeti disposuimus. . . ."

[43]Rouse and Rouse (n. 3 above) 23.

distinctions begin to be used in sermons? Lacking a thorough survey of the evolution of sermon form during the twelfth and thirteenth centuries, we offer a tentative conclusion: the origin of the distinction seems to be closely linked with the emergence of the thematic sermon.

By the fourteenth century the form of the scholastic sermon, the so-called thematic sermon, had become pretty well standardized: theme, protheme, statement of divisions of the theme, confirmation of the divisions, amplification of the divisions.[44] In a group of Parisian sermons for the academic year 1230–31,[45] the majority already incorporate the principal elements of this structure; that is, most of them take a "theme"—meaning, not a topic, but a verse of Scripture—which is then divided, usually into three but also into two or four or more components, each of which divisions is then amplified to produce a three-part (or two- or four-part) sermon. Frequently, in these sermons of 1230–31, the divisions of the theme consisted of a *distinctio* on a key word in the biblical quotation, with each meaning, duly amplified, serving as one part of the sermon.

The use of *distinctiones* in earlier sermons, in the last half of the twelfth century and on into the early thirteenth, coincides with the origin of what would later become the thematic sermon. The form of the sermon was not yet systematized: one does not find in the twelfth century a division, stated or implicit, of the sermon into an imposed number of parts.[46] But one does begin to find sermons with a true "theme," that is, one selected scriptural passage, usually brief enough to be reiterated from time to time by the preacher and to be retained by his auditors. In the established sermon form—the form eventually displaced (at least among school-trained preachers) by the thematic sermon—there appear to have been two main methods of procedure: either (1) the preacher took a selected passage of Scripture, and used its subject matter as a springboard or topic for discourse; or (2) he took a lengthy passage, perhaps from the *lectio* for that Sunday or feastday, and commented upon its symbolic meaning, a word or phrase at a time.[47] In the newly emerging thematic sermons, the preacher stayed with his brief selected passage, giving, not one symbolic meaning, but rather an investigation of the layered wealth of meanings to be found there. The usefulness, the near inevitability, of the

---

[44]Concerning the elements of the full-blown thematic sermon, see Thomas-Marie Charland, *Artes praedicandi: Contributions à l'histoire de la rhétorique au moyen âge*, Publications de l'Institut d'études médiévales d'Ottawa 7 (Paris 1936) 107–226.

[45]Marie-Magdeleine Davy, ed., *Les sermons universitaires parisiens de 1230–1231*, EPM 15 (Paris 1931).

[46]However, see Longère (n. 37 above) 1.55, who assumes that Peter of Poitiers's fourfold explanation of his theme is meant as a statement of divisions—although, as Longère adds, Peter's sermon does not adhere to the stated plan.

[47]For purposes of comparison see J.-P. Bonnes, "Un des plus grands prédicateurs du XIIe siècle: Geoffroy du Loroux, dit Geoffroy Babion," *Revue bénédictine* 56 (1945–46) 174–215; he prints two sermons based on the same biblical text: the one, by Babion, is discursive in style; the other, by Peter the Chanter, is quasi-thematic and uses distinctions.

distinctio in such a procedure is obvious. Moreover, as the thematic sermon evolved, the *distinctio* served as a nascent structure. See, for example, the sermon of Innocent III on the same theme cited above for the Lombard, "Aspiciebam in visione noctis, et ecce cum nubibus celi quasi filius hominis veniebat" (Dan. 7:13); the entire sermon consists of a distinction on the word *nox* ("in scriptura divina septem modis intelligitur"), followed by a brief distinction of *nubes* (five meanings).[48] This is not yet a formal *divisio thematis*, but we can sense its presence just over the horizon.[49]

THE THIRTEENTH-CENTURY FUSION

The thematic sermon's need for material motivated the creation of the first tools in searchable order, rational and alphabetical. The needs of teaching from the page motivated the development of the techniques of layout. But the distinction between preaching and classroom, though indispensable to a theoretical discussion, is largely artificial. The masters who taught also preached, and made preaching tools; the students they taught were being prepared to spend much of their time in the pulpit.[50] Therefore it is not surprising to see that the makers of distinction collections utilized the techniques created in the development of the great glossed page.

The distinction collection of Peter of Capua[51] reveals, as clearly as any work could, the close interrelationship between classroom lectern and pulpit, between theology lecture and sermon, between university preparation and parish application—however one cares to put it; Peter calls them respectively the contemplative and the active life (a novel use of this terminology), and likens them to Rachel and Leah, two wives of one man. Peter of Capua himself embodies the interrelationship: he was a master of theology at Paris from at least 1202, and then went to Rome as cardinal-deacon of San Giorgio in 1219

---

[48]PL 217.323–28.

[49]See also Longère (n. 37 above) 1.57: "Les sens de l'Ecriture peuvent fournir le cadre autour duquel s'organise le déploiement d'un thème."

[50]Good descriptions of the relationship of preaching and teaching as seen by the Chanter and Stephen Langton are found in Baldwin, *Masters* 1.110–11, and Smalley, *Study* 207–09.

[51]The description of Peter of Capua's *Alphabetum* is based on an examination of fourteen manuscripts, all but one (Trier) written in the thirteenth century: Bruges, Bibl. mun. MS 253 (Ter Duinen, O.Cist.); Chalon-sur-Saône, Bibl. mun. MS 15 (La Ferté-sur-Grosne, O.Cist.); Charleville, Bibl. mun. MS 230 (Signy, O.Cist.); Douai, Bibl. mun. MS 433 (Marchiennes, O.S.B.); Hereford Cathedral MS P.VI.6; Paris, Bibl. Maz. MSS 1007 (Royaumont, O.Cist.) and 1008 (Paris Carmelites, 1550/1); Paris, BN MSS lat 16984 (St-Germain-des-Prés, O.S.B.) and lat 16986 (St-Jacques, O.P.); St-Omer, Bibl. mun. MS 217 (Clairmarais, O.Cist.); Toulouse, Bibl. mun. MS 211 (Toulouse, O.F.M.); Trier, Stadtbibl. MS 721 (saec. XIV–XV; Germany); Troyes, Bibl. mun. MS 114 (Clairvaux, O.Cist.); Vienna, Öst. Nat.-bibl. MS 1380. There are at least two other surviving MSS not seen by us: Monte Cassino MS 255 (O.S.B.) and Vatican, MS Vat lat 4304. Virtually all of these look to have been written in the first half of the century, many if not most of them in Italy. Of the eleven manuscripts whose medieval owners are known, six belonged to Cistercian houses—indicating, as we have noted in "Cistercian Aids" (n. 2 above), the importance of this order to developments in preaching in the late twelfth and early thirteenth centuries.

until his death in 1242.[52] He began his collection of distinctions at the instance of his students in Paris, and completed it in the south after he was named cardinal: "a magistro Petro in scholis inchoatum et post modum ab eodem sancte romane ecclesie cardinali licet indigno, correcto ipso principio, consumatum."[53] It is likely that he completed the work not long after he changed positions, roughly 1220–25; the wording of the prologue implies that he was nagged by the responsibility of this unfinished task, and pressed on to get it done.[54] He addressed the work jointly to the clergy of Rome and his students at Paris, and expressed the hope that it would be useful to both, the former in their preaching, the latter in their studies.[55]

It is evident, however, that the work was principally designed for the composition of sermons, a task already incumbent upon the *venerandus clerus romanus* and soon to be so for most of Peter's *viri scolastici*. Peter entitled the collection "Alphabetum in artem sermocinandi"; and his explanation of its use is headed, "Qualiter debet quis de hoc opere texere sermonem." From this explanation we can see that Peter had in mind some form of thematic sermon: "When one wishes to make a sermon, he should lay as his foundation some scriptural passage, since . . . one builds more suitably on a stable foundation. He should then consider carefully how many key words are contained in the passage," look them up in Peter's collection, and construct a sermon from them "according to his own discretion."[56]

To make his work searchable, Peter of Capua first of all combined two techniques used in earlier collections of distinctions, that is, alphabetical and rational order. His words are arranged alphabetically by first letter; but internally, among those beginning with a given letter, the words are arranged in a descending hierarchy, according as they deal with nine topics: God, angels,

[52]Regarding Peter's life see Baldwin, *Masters* 1.45, 2.34. He is to be distinguished from Peter of Capua, papal legate, card.-diac. S. Maria in via lata (1193), card.-pr. S. Marcello (1201), d. 1214; and he is not to be conflated with Pierre de Mora, card.-diac. S. Angelo (1205), d. 1213, as is done by Palémon Glorieux, *Répertoire des maîtres en théologie de Paris au XIIIe siècle*, EPM 17–18 (2 vols. Paris 1933–34) 1 no. 108.

[53]Another rubric speaks of his "responsio . . . facta scolaribus in ipsis scolis insistentibus pro presenti opere inchoando."

[54]"Curavimus tamen contra negotiorum importunitatem luctando . . . illud opus ipsum correcto primo principio prosequi, ne forte illud de nobis irrisorie diceretur quia hic homo cepit edificare et non potuit consumare."

[55]"Dilectis plurimum et diligendis semper in visceribus Ihesu Christi venerando clero romano, et viris scolasticis prophetarum filiis . . . ," the opening words of the prologue. And later, ". . . in quo et venerandus clerus exercitetur facilius ad loquendum, et sollicitudo scolastica presto et ad manum pleniorem habet copiam ad scrutandum."

[56]"Cum ergo placuerit alicui sermonem proponere, auctoritatem [*scil.* sancte scripture] aliquam iaciat in fundamento, ut basis sub columpna firma subsistat et super stabile fundamentum commodius valeat edificare. Consideret etiam diligenter quot dictiones in ipsa auctoritate ponuntur, et a quibus litteris ipse dictiones incipiunt, quibus etiam rebus conveniant proprie dictiones ipse; quo diligenter prenotato, secundum premissam duplicem ordinem de facili poterit in hoc opere de singulis dictionibus tractatus singulos invenire, quibus inventis, facile erit lectori ipsos coniungere et ex ipsis sermonem texere iuxta suam discretionem." We discuss this "duplex ordo" below.

the firmament, the air, man, beasts, the earth, the waters under the earth, and the abyss. To take an example of how this nonalphabetical hierarchy works: under the first letter *Altissimus* comes before *Aer, Avis* before *Adam*, and *Abissus* comes eighty-first and last of the words that begin with *A*.

Along with the techniques of searchable order derived from the tradition of preaching tools, Peter added the techniques of layout developed in the classroom for teaching from and commenting upon the written page. Peter calls each alphabetical section simply *littera*, and refers to the sections by number—*littera iii* (= C), *littera v* (= E), and so on. Running headlines across both pages of the opening read like this: left-hand page, "F L [ittera]," right-hand page, "VI." At the head of each *littera* is a numbered list of *capitula*, the words that are distinguished; the list for each successive *littera* recommences with the number *i*. The number of each chapter is written in the margin beside its beginning, in large Roman numerals with heavy red and blue paragraph marks. In the text at the head of each chapter is a tally of the distinctions, in red: *Altissimus vi modis in bono, uno in malo; Altitudo viii modis in bono, tribus in malo*; and so on. The initial of the opening word in chapter one of each *littera* is very large (sometimes the whole first word is in twelve-line capitals), with the initials of subsequent chapters two lines in height, alternating red and blue. Marginal rubrics, marked with smaller paragraph marks, indicate subtopics within a distinction; for example, in the chapter *Altitudo* are these marginal rubrics: "Qualis sit quelibet altitudo," "Unde sit altitudo," "Quid agitur per altitudinem." Finally, in the margin just below each chapter number is a list, in small and highly abbreviated script, of from two to ten cross-references to similar or contrasting chapters; Peter notes in his prologue that, when preaching on the word *rosa*, one might also want to use the material on *flos* or *lilium*; or when preaching on "fasting" (*ieiunium*), one might use the material against "gluttony" (*gula*). Not only the idea, but the physical appearance of these cross-reference notes is patterned on the notes in Bosham's edition of the *Magna glosatura*. Take for example the cross-references for the first chapter, *Alpha*:

I. lit. iii. C. lxx co[a]
I. lit. v. C. xxxviii
I. lit. vi. C. xxxiii 7 xxxviii co[a]
I. lit. xi. C. xii
I. lit. xv. C. xxxii

These are to be interpreted as follows: "Infra, littera iii (= C), capitulum lxx (= Cauda), contra," with the others referring respectively to *Elementa, Fimbrie, Festinatio* (*contra*), *Littera*, and *Primogenitus*. Later chapters will, of course, have cross-references that begin "S." (*supra*) as well.

Peter of Capua's *Alphabetum* was a response to the needs of those who composed thematic sermons. His biblical distinctions were arranged alphabetically and subdivided rationally, to make them easier to find. The searchability of his work was enhanced by his use of the devices of layout—numbered chapter lists, running headlines, marginal rubrics, color, graduated letter size, paragraph marks, and extensive cross-references. And all of this, both the intricate and sophisticated form of his response and the need itself, Peter inherited from the twelfth century.

We have, thus far, investigated the twelfth-century origins of the effort to make information accessible in the layout of the glossed Bible and in the alphabetical collections of biblical distinctions. Let us now look ahead, to examine how this effort would affect the Bible of the twelfth century and transform the very attitude to written texts that was prevalent then.

The Bible, which in the twelfth century had invariably been in multiple volumes (one each for the Pentateuch, Psalter, Gospels and Epistles, and so on), in the early thirteenth century was reduced to a single thick but portable volume, via compression of letter form and layout, and the preparation of thinner parchment.[57] It descended from the communal altar to become the private property of the priest, a personal possession of the friar; few priests of the twelfth century owned a whole Bible, we should think. The numerous and varying chapter structures found in the twelfth-century Bible gave way slowly to a single standard structure, when Stephen Langton's divisions (before 1203)[58] were adopted by and popularized through the verbal concordance and other Dominican tools in the 1230s. Eusebius's canon tables and the marginal concordances in the Gospels, common to Bibles from late Antiquity on, disappeared in the early thirteenth century when they were made redundant by the concordance. Conversely, Jerome's *Interpretations of Hebrew Names*, which had enjoyed only a limited circulation before 1200, was thoroughly revised around the turn of the century to become part of the biblical canon, appearing in virtually all Bibles thereafter.[59] Whereas Jerome's *Interpretations* go through the Bible book by book, the revised versions integrate the names into a single list alphabetized by the first two letters, to make them searchable; their purpose quite clearly was to serve preachers, with the interpretations being used in sermons very much as distinctions were. Early thirteenth-century Bibles not infrequently contain, as well, brief indexes, in rational or alphabetical order, of biblical "themes" for preachers—for example, the index of texts useful for preaching against the Manichees (that is, the Cathars) that is found in early Dominican pocket Bibles.[60]

---

[57]This subject has not to our knowledge been studied in print. The art-historical aspects of it are examined by Robert Branner, *Manuscript Painting in Paris during the Reign of St. Louis*, California Studies in the History of Art 18 (Berkeley 1977).

[58]Smalley, *Study* 222–24.

[59]For example, of some 91 whole Bibles of the thirteenth century described in the Bibliothèque Nationale's *Catalogue général des manuscrits latins* 1 (Paris 1939), 81 contain one or more versions of the revised *Interpretations*.

[60]For example, BN lat 174 (saec. XIII) fols. 181v–203, and University of California, Los Angeles, Research Library MS Δ 170/348 fols. 383v–385v, a French or English Dominican Bible of

By mid-century two concordances, one in alphabetical order, the other in rational order, existed in numerous copies to serve as an apparatus to the Scriptures.[61] Concording, relegated to the gloss in the twelfth century, now had a book of its own. At this juncture we have come to the type of book that can only be searched, for it cannot be read.

What transformation in attitude to written authority do these new Bibles and concordances reflect? Or to put it another way: What route has one traveled, starting with the snippets of Augustine contained in the twelfth-century Gloss, to reach the massive alphabetical indexes to Augustine's major works compiled by Robert Kilwardby in the middle of the thirteenth century?

One inescapable "product" of the Gloss, if we may call it that, was a keen awareness of its inadequacies. Masters "accepted [the Gloss] as a necessary evil";[62] basic instruction often requires a textbook. The glossed Bible was the major effort of the schools to order the legacy of the past, biblical and patristic, via juxtaposition; but it was insufficient, and the masters knew this. On the one hand, they decried the superfluity of glosses that tended to obscure, rather than to illuminate, the biblical text. On the other, they realized that the Gloss inadequately represented patristic thought. This latter concern was no mere matter of logistics, of squeezing more and longer extracts onto the page. Rather, it was a fundamental discontent with extracts as such.

One can see, before mid-century, an acknowledgment of the higher authority of the full text, as opposed to that of extracts taken out of context. Geoffrey of Auxerre describes how Gilbert of Poitiers, in his defense at the consistory of Reims in 1148, arrived armed with the *codices integri*, to the consternation of Bernard and his other accusers who had brought with them only a sheet of extracts as their documentation; and the accusers returned, the next day, equipped with their own whole texts.[63]

The emphasis on the authority of the whole work, and on the necessity of reading statements in context, grew during the second half of the century, to the point of generating a significant change in terminology. Geoffrey used the expected term, *integri*, to designate the full texts; the new term, or rather an old one put to new use, was *originalia*.[64] Previously, one had used phrases such

---

the second quarter of the thirteenth century. The index begins, "*I° quod pater et filius et spiritus sanctus una substantia et unus Deus*. Io. ca. i. In principio et vidimus gloriam eius; Io. ca. i. . . . ,'' and ends, "Explicit summa breviata contra Manicheos et Paterinos, et contra Passaginos et cirumcisos, et contra multos alios hereticos qui nituntur subvertere veritatem quorum dampnatio iam olim non cessat et eorum perditio non dormitat de qua dampnatione ille custodiat suos qui ad dexteram maiestatis residet in excelsis super novem ordines angelorum. Amen." It is followed in MS Δ 170/348 by a second subject index with additional scriptural citations, fols. 385v–386v.

[61] Concerning the great alphabetical verbal concordance see Rouse and Rouse (n. 3 above); regarding the real concordance see Kleinhans (n. 29 above), and Friedrich Stegmüller, *Repertorium biblicum medii aevi* 2 (Madrid 1950) 119–20 no. 1382.

[62] Smalley, *Study* 226.

[63] See Nikolaus M. Häring, "Notes on the Council and the Consistory of Rheims (1148)," *Mediaeval Studies* 28 (1966) 39–59, esp. 48–49.

[64] Joseph de Ghellinck, " 'Originale' et 'Originalia,' " *Archivum latinitatis medii aevi (Bulletin Du Cange)* 14 (1939) 95–105.

as *originalia rescripta, originalia documenta*, to refer to the original documents, that is, those with signature and seal, issued by an official. By 1191 Ralph Niger was using the phrase *originalia scripta* in a new sense, meaning the whole work of an author in contrast to extracts from the work. Niger says that, from the very brevity of the gloss, his students must understand the necessity of turning to the whole works, "intelligant ad originalia scripta fore recurrendum."[65] In the contemporary usage of Stephen Langton the word was a noun, *originale* or *originalia*—as when he contrasts *glosa Ieronimi* with *Ieronimus in originali*, or simply *in glosa* with *in originali*. Niger and Langton are the earliest that we have found to use *originale* in this sense; and in both instances, the word is used in a context indicating the insufficiency of the Gloss. In their choice of *originalia* rather than *integri*, moreover, there is a deliberate implication that the whole works possess the authority or authenticity of the originals, lacking in mere excerpts. The noun forms, *originale* and *originalia*, were universally accepted by the middle of the thirteenth century; and accepted along with them was the idea they represent, that the intent of a writer is best grasped through reading his words in context. This is not by any means to imply that one dispensed with the Gloss, but rather that one went beyond, to search out the *originalia*.

The emergence of a concept of whole work in contrast to extracts was accompanied by a parallel interest in the proper division of the whole work into its components—parts, books, chapters, *distinctiones, quaestiones*, and the like. Such divisions and subdivisions had to constitute coherent units, so that the process of division would aid the reader to understand the organization of the whole work and the intent of its author; and the units had to be small enough to serve for reference purposes. Not surprisingly, the Bible was the first text to receive such attentions; as we noted above, the standard capitulation of the Bible has been ascribed to Langton, on the basis of slender but suggestive evidence. And one sees elsewhere Langton's interest in the matter of chapter divisions, "which are very necessary for finding what you want and for remembering"; in an early Langton gloss on Jerome's prologue to the book of Joshua, he observes, "Here you have authority for chapter division."[66] In the early thirteenth century, the chapters of the Lombard's *Sentences* were further broken down by Alexander of Hales into subdivisions, called *distinctiones*, of more manageable length; and during the course of the thirteenth century other scholars provided chapter structures for *originalia* that lacked them, such as Gregory's *Moralia*.[67]

---

[65]Cited from Smalley, *Study* 226 and n. 4; regarding Niger see G. B. Flahiff, "Ralph Niger: An Introduction to His Life and Works," *Mediaeval Studies* 2 (1940) 104-26 and Ludwig Schmugge's introduction to his edition of *De re militari et triplici via peregrinationis Ierosolimitane* (Berlin 1977) esp. 3-14.

[66]". . . que valde necessaria sunt ad inveniendum quod volueris et ad tenendum memoriter. Hic habes auctoritatem distinguendi capitula"; cited from Smalley, *Study* 224 and n. 1.

[67]Concerning Hales see Brady ed. 1.1 (n. 14 above) 143*-44*; concerning Gregory see Neil R. Ker, "The English Manuscripts of the *Moralia* of Gregory the Great," *Kunsthistorische*

Fairly early on, just as with the shift from *libri integri* to *originalia*, a change in attitude is manifest in a change of terminology. By about 1220 one has explicit acknowledgment of the importance of division and subdivision of works: Jordanus of Saxony, in the introduction to his Priscian commentary, states (for the first time, in the tradition of *accessus* literature) that the form of a work includes both its *forma tractandi* (the way in which a book treats its subject matter) and the *forma tractatus*, "the separation into books and chapters, and their order."[68] At virtually the same date Peter of Capua, in the prologue to the *Alphabetum*, describes in the same sequence these two aspects of his own work, *De modo tractandi* and *De ordine tractatus*. Attention to a fixed, and meaningful, division of the whole into manageable units had rapidly become an accepted part of scholarship, in the *artes*, in biblical study, in patristics, in preaching tools.

The concept of whole work permitted, and the emphasis on use of the whole works required, the creation of tools with which to search the *originalia*. In the thirteenth century, indexes to the *originalia* were compiled, borrowing the devices of alphabetical or rational order created for the twelfth-century preaching tools and utilizing the divisions into chapters as their reference system. Even before the mid-thirteenth-century *tabulae originalium*, this fruitful conjunction of ideas—notion of the whole work, sensible division into chapters, alphabetical arrangement—produced the finest achievement of thirteenth-century toolmaking, the verbal concordance to the Bible.

Scholars in the early twelfth century did not need the devices used by thirteenth-century preachers to organize their materials. The learned community was small in numbers, and its methods of instruction not yet formalized; the legacy of Antiquity and of the monastic church sufficed: rote familiarity with a finite body of authority, arranged according to rational principles and retained by memory. Little more was needed, given the lack of institutionalized procedures of instruction for clergy or for lay Christians. It is the supplying of these procedures that accounts for the transformation in scholarship discussed here. The Church, faced with diversity (both heterodoxy and heresy), accepted the need actively to present and interpret a common faith to Western

---

Forschungen: Otto Pächt zu seinem 70. Geburtstag, ed. Artur Rosenauer and Gerold Weber (Salzburg 1972) 77–89. The famous manuscript of Lactantius, Bodleian Library MS Canon. pat. lat. 131, written in France probably in the third quarter of the twelfth century, has chapter divisions added by an early thirteenth-century writer. The text of Glanvill, written ca. 1187–89 in continuous sequence, undergoes several restructurings in the next generation to render it more usable; see George D. G. Hall, ed. and trans., *The Treatise on the Laws and Customs of the Realm of England commonly called Glanvill* (London 1965) xl–lvi.

[68] The passage is discussed by Martin Grabmann, *Mittelalterliches Geistesleben: Abhandlungen zur Geschichte der Scholastik und Mystik* (3 vols. Munich 1926–56) 3.234; and Jan Pinborg, *Die Entwicklung der Sprachtheorie im Mittelalter*, BGPTMA 42.2 (Münster 1967) 25–26.

Christendom; this resulted in the attention paid to the schools for the instruction of clergy, in an emphasis upon the instruction of the laity through preaching, and in the eventual nurturing of the Mendicant Orders. This is the context in which the emergence of an apparatus to scholarship is to be seen.

Chenu states, in an oft-quoted passage introducing the evangelical return to the Gospel, "What interests us more than the actual results of these ventures, however, is the spirit that animated the men who undertook them, their taste for quenching their thirst at original sources, and also their anxious faith-inspired search for appropriate tools."[69] Unquestionably, it was the thirteenth century, not the twelfth, that produced, developed, adapted, and continually improved the tools for mining the patristic and biblical heritage. But it owed no small debt, in spirit and in sheer technology, to the intellectual and scholarly ferment of the twelfth century.

[69]Marie-Dominique Chenu, *Toward Understanding Saint Thomas*, trans. A.-M. Landry and D. Hughes (Chicago 1964) 46.

III

SOCIETY AND THE INDIVIDUAL

Urban Society and Culture
Toulouse and Its Region

John Hine Mundy

Broadly defined, the history of the twelfth-century renaissance comprises both intellectual innovations in academic and literary subjects and changes in underlying social and institutional structures and attitudes. Twelfth-century Toulouse, for example, though it had as yet no university, saw the emergence of a secular, vernacular literature, and was notably inventive in the revival of scribal culture and secular law. At the same time, the evolution of secular paradigms was slowed, at Toulouse as elsewhere in Europe, by the pervasive dominance of religious over civil institutions. This essay examines the social structure of twelfth-century Toulouse and its environs in order to argue that popular forms of intellectualism in law, letters, and religion were consonant with, and suited to, this society's evolution during the rapid economic growth of the age.

SOCIETY

In the decades around 1100, and in regions where central states were weak, substantial towns of some antiquity began to undermine princely authority, reduce the service and taxes owed by their inhabitants, and obtain increasing autonomy. This movement was part of a general search for liberty that, animated by Gregorian churchmen seeking freedom from state churches and by a general revolt of the secular and ministerial service cadres, led to a partial dismantlement of states and monarchies in much of Western Europe. This change—to which, if to anything, the term ''revolution'' may be felicitously applied—had profound effects on the political and social structure of town and countryside.

In accord with this, the Gregorian age saw the start of a movement toward political liberty in Toulouse. After a troubled period of civil war and foreign intervention in the decades around 1100, Toulouse evolved in the manner of an Italian city, and began to usurp the prerogatives of its prince, the count of Toulouse. From the late 1170s, the count tried to restore his authority, but eventually, in 1189, was forced to capitulate. His ancient county and town council became the increasingly independent board of consuls, and for two decades Toulouse was a kind of Italian city republic. True to its model, the town was beginning to move toward popular government when, in 1202, new men pushed their way onto the board of consuls, then more or less dominated by a quasi-oligarchical group of families, themselves of rather recent origins. This radical change, soon mitigated by compromises, may well have been initiated by the count, whose populism was inspired by hostility to the independence of the town's ruling elite. If so, the prince was quickly disabused, because, from 1202 to 1205, the popular consulate launched wars against twenty-three towns and villages of the Toulousain, clearly designing to conquer a *contado*, the *patria Tolosana*.

Although well begun, Toulousan expansionism was stopped in 1209 with the start of the Albigensian crusade. This northern French invasion of the Midi combined with civil war, and lasted until the capitulation of the southern side at the Peace of Paris in 1229. Thereafter (to look ahead for a moment), the mixed constitution created by the shrinking authority of the count or prince and the growing power of the town's consuls was gradually overturned as the central monarchy grew stronger, and the town's incipient hegemony over its province was destroyed.[1]

This temporary—about half a century long—achievement of a real measure of political liberty or republicanism would have been impossible without a parallel social unification. Communities like Toulouse often united through oath associations rooted in the idea of the Peace of God. Such communes proposed that all inhabitants were to be judged by the same law, were equal before it, and had the same right to its protection. This change transformed society by weakening ancient distinctions based on function or service, in favor of an emphasis on common citizenship and law. Thus merchants and artisans became town citizens, and the distinction between *milites* and *pedites*, between mounted and foot militias, became less marked in community law. Furthermore, the income or means possessed by an individual or family and derived from the performance of service, either by or for others, necessarily diminished as people won personal freedom from such obligations. Ideally, this freedom included the establishment or confirmation of a hereditary right to properties, incomes, or goods previously held in return for service. Similarly, although to a lesser extent, a like uniformization of the inhabitants and generalization of hereditary rights took place in the villages of the countryside.[2]

---

[1]Throughout this essay, the political history largely derives from my *Liberty and Political Power in Toulouse, 1050–1230* (New York 1954), and the social history from my book on the social history of Toulouse now in preparation. Unless otherwise specified, archival references in this study are to documents in the departmental archives of the Haute-Garonne, cited by series, collection, *liasse*, document number and/or date. All dates are modernized.

[2]Familiar materials about the knights of Toulouse and the unification of the City and Bourg have been surveyed anew by Philippe Wolff, in "La noblesse Toulousaine: Essai sur son histoire

The economic regime under which Toulousans lived in the twelfth and early thirteenth centuries was therefore one of private property—family exploitation of land, other means of production, and other sources of income, including monopolies, tolls, and (typically medieval) seigneurial rights. Simultaneously, new methods of family identification were appearing, especially or initially among the leading families of town and countryside: surnames, particularly family names. Introduced around 1100 and gradually generalized, such family names never became universal during the Middle Ages. Certain categories—Jews, for example—never bore family names in Latin charters at Toulouse, and Christians of all social levels continued to appear in the documents identified only by a somewhat rare Christian name or by two given names. On the whole, however, surnames were becoming a normal means of identification, even for people of modest station.[3]

The commonest family names derived from localities, either those whence immigrants had come to town or, on a higher social level, those where families possessed substantial properties and rights. Such names were used with or without the particule *de*, which was itself rarely aristocratic in this period. But family names derived from almost anything, rare first names, for example, and especially trade and craft designations: when we see a Willelmus Faber *notarius* in 1230, we have spotted a scribe whose name was Wm Smith. At first on the upper social levels, family names gained a measure of stability, reflecting the strength of family self-awareness and identification. Naturally enough, the adoption and continued use of family names was especially a mark of the middle and upper classes of society and not of the lower. Still, around 1200, not a few simple craftsmen or tradesmen bore surnames and had identifiable family names.

To judge from the charters, families from the middle and lower ranges of the population were usually smaller, and certainly less durable, than those from the middle and upper ranges. Around 1200, the average Toulousan family household consisted of a man and wife, their children, and sometimes one or more siblings or older relatives, especially widows. The greater, richer, or older families, on the other hand, were often much larger and more cohesive than ordinary ones. Their homes were larger and could house additional relatives or clients, and it is easy to prove that such space rarely went

médiévale," *La noblesse au moyen âge: Essais à la mémoire de Robert Boutruche*, ed. Philippe Contamine (Paris 1976) 153–74, and "*Civitas et burgus*: L'exemple de Toulouse," *Die Stadt in der europäischen Geschichte: Festschrift Edith Ennen*, ed. Werner Besch et al. (Bonn 1972) 200–09. The Italian analogy may be seen in Gerhard Dilcher, *Die Entstehung der lombardischen Stadtkommune* (Aalen 1967).

[3]Important studies of French family names and surnames are Hildburg Weber, *Die Personennamen in Rodez (Aveyron) um die Mitte des 14. Jahrhunderts* (Jena and Leipzig 1934), and especially Karl Michaëlsson, *Etudes sur les noms de personne français d'après les rôles de taille parisiens* (Uppsala 1927). Very useful comparative materials are to be had in Augusto Gaudenzi, *Sulla storia del cognome a Bologna nel secolo XIII*, = *Bullettino dell'Istituto storico italiano* 19 (Rome 1898) and Hermann Reichert, *Die deutschen Familiennamen, nach Breslauer Quellen des 13. und 14. Jahrhunderts* (Breslau 1908).

unused. The documents often speak of such houses having stone halls, towers, even private chapels, as well as attached and rented-out stores or workshops. Just as flies cluster around the honey pot, the members of successful clans loved to rub shoulders with their collaterals, and viewed them with a benignity not divorced from the hope of gain.

All the same, there was nothing like a really communitarian or extended family at this time. Division of inheritance among heirs was not only common, but equally frequent among rich and poor. Even though real property, shares in the mills on the river, and seigneurial rights were often held in common, the members of great urban families preferred to divide their housing and live as separate units. Even the *fratrisca* (the joint administration of an inheritance) did not create enlarged families. Although it sometimes crossed generational lines, the typical twelfth-century *fratrisca* rarely lasted more than a decade and was usually imposed in order to educate or marry children left in minority by deceased parents. In fact, the common ownership of property by siblings and *parentes* was no more durable than the similarly shared ownership by business partners (*socii*).

Having thus "identified" their families, the leaders of Toulousan society found in their names a sufficient claim to worth and authority. Nothing shows this better and nothing is more consonant with the political unification of Toulouse in the twelfth century than the remarkable absence from the charters of honorific social identifications. Naturally, there are some: the count of Toulouse was always identified by his title, and so were occasional foreign notables; the various grades of the clergy were specified, as were those of the actual officers of the civil government, even short-term ones. But these are functional titles, of no more significance than the identification of a craftsman by the name of his craft.

Apart from these functional designations, the social vocabulary of Toulouse was almost wholly devoid of titles around 1200, and remained so for some time thereafter. Officially speaking, the word *burgensis*, for example, meant someone living in the Bourg, *civis* someone in the City. This usage persisted in public documents and was seen in private ones into the late 1200s. Again, in private documents drawn by public notaries, occupation or status titles, save those of the crafts, trades, and professions, were very rare indeed. The title of "knight" was not used in the charters before 1200 and rarely thereafter, becoming common only in the last third of the thirteenth century; that of "squire" (*domicellus*) waited even longer. This does not mean that knighthood was undesirable. We know of knights and scions of seigneurial families who were citizens, and of burghers who intended their sons to be knighted. Besides, vernacular literary sources—always more advanced than legal or Latin ones—use *cavaer* and *donzel* to describe both individuals and groups. It was nevertheless a telltale mark of a modestly republican and patrician society that private and public charters in both Latin and the vernacular did not describe individuals as knights—or, for that matter, as nobles—in this period: for the mixed burgher and knightly leaders of this community, it was enough to boast a good name. Other honors were not yet needed.

The families of Toulouse inhabited an expanding world of economic growth. Although the first statutes regulating an industry (cloth) are from 1227, the charters show the crafts growing apace in the later twelfth century. Toulousans frequented the fairs of the Champagne, and numerous instruments attest the spread of vineyards well before 1200, when the down-river wine trade to Bordeaux began. Ample evidence shows that urban entrepreneurs not only tried to exploit the small towns and villages around their city (even undertaking to conquer them in 1202–05), but also made fortunes by acquiring rural properties, including seigneuries. Others came from seigneuries to town to profit there. Both groups used similar methods. If most of those fingered as usurers in the attack on that "sin" in the early 1200s came from the middle and lower ranges of the population, members of the best families, and not merely male ones, had long lent money by the usurious *mutuum* and derived much revenue from the usurious *pignus* or mortgage. Around 1200, then, impeded by few institutional restraints—enjoying, for example, a near monopoly of government, limited by no craft or trade guilds, and suffering from no serious attack on usury—Toulouse's leading families were characterized by something like the ethos of the economic individual. Those Toulousan families about which we know a fair amount usually boasted individuals especially active in politics and business, and sometimes famous (or notorious) for economic aggression or compensatory charity. A world, in short, of *laissez faire*.

What seems strange about these lively businessmen and their families is that they also possessed what moderns might call a "feudal" ethos. Quite apart from the seigneuries and knighthood held by a few families, Toulouse itself was a visual representation of "feudal society." As Michelangelo later called San Gimignano, it was a "città turrita." Toulousans loved towers and substantial families wanted towered town houses and stone halls—patrician names such as de Turribus reflect their pride of possession—and a *nouveau riche* found his ascension incomplete until he acquired them. Because, however, the town enjoyed only a relatively brief period of republicanism during which family vanity was able to express itself freely, Toulouse never matched skyscraper cities like Siena or Bologna. The northern French who conquered or absorbed the Midi disliked the Italianate urban landscape where the towers of families equally at home in town and countryside dominated the *aspectus ville*. The Albigensian war resulted in a holocaust of such constructions, and the later Capetian monarchy was not hospitable to such manifestations of family self-assertion.

INTELLECTUALISM

The scientific and academic disciplines already flourishing elsewhere were but little represented in twelfth-century Toulouse. There was, however, a lively popular intellectual life. What was its relationship to the society just described? Paralleling the expansion around 1100 of family ownership of private property was the appearance of secular scribes, public officers who answered the need and desire of families to possess and amass documents concerning their property and to record the suddenly multiplying testaments, sales, loans, and other contracts characteristic of economic growth and individual ownership. The evolution of the public notariate, at first under the count and then under the consuls, is significant in two cultural areas. One is the spread of a vulgar Latin culture which, however haltingly, began to renew Latin studies and to expunge the vernacular from the charters. The other was the development of lay professionalism. Although ecclesiastics instrumented for private parties into the late 1100s, the secular character of the scribal profession was established early and had altogether triumphed by 1200. Nor was this a small constituency: over thirty public notaries are known to have been instrumenting in 1200.

A smaller but quite as significant a profession is that of the lawyers. Lawyers begin to appear at Toulouse in the last third of the twelfth century, a quarter to half a century behind those of Italy or Provence. Emerging from the old judicial and advocatorial offices of the county administration, these *causidici*—one of the early words used to describe them—were made into a bar by the multiplying litigation that, as the count's authority in civil and criminal matters weakened, came before the consuls or the courts delegated by them. The need for such specialists also reflected the increased participation by middling and lower elements of society in the community's economic and legal life around 1200, for which groups the old method of private arbitration—whereby substantial families had settled their civil disputes without recourse to any governmental forum at all—was peculiarly unsuitable. Now that cases between people of widely differing classes came before the consuls or their subordinate courts, the parties needed someone learned in the law to guide them and speak for them, a *racionator* as one lawyer was called in 1186. Suitably, all of this came to a head just after 1202 when popular elements found their first large-scale representation among the consuls. Consular regulation from 1208 instructs us that lawyers with *patrocinium* in their court existed in Toulouse, ruling that no one litigant could employ all or a majority of the five named *allegatores* of the town bar.

Legal professionalism advanced but slowly. Admitting lawyers, Toulouse's leading families still resisted the professionalization of the judges, either the consuls themselves sitting in judgment or those who sat on their delegated courts. Only in the latter half of the thirteenth century was the judicature largely professionalized, and then under auspices notably hostile to Toulousan self-government. Still, however much the relatively older and established families resisted professionalization, the economic growth of the town and the natural evolution of republican institutions around 1200 encouraged the development of professional legal services. Precisely from this time comes the first evidence of the study of Europe's *ius commune*, the Roman law of the medieval schools. Admittedly first in an ecclesiastical court, the civil law was alleged in a case as early as 1181 and, by around 1200, some lawyers began to parade the evidences of their schooling by bearing the titles of *magister* and *legista. Jurisperitus* and *legum professor* appear first in the mid-1200s.

The expansion of scribal and legal services helped to improve and spread the use of Latin in the town. Although the language of business and of testimony before the court of the consuls was the vernacular, charters and court decisions were in Latin. We may therefore presume that lay businessfolk could read a bit of Latin, and that notaries and lawyers wrote and probably spoke it passably. Moreover, notarial and advocatorial service spread from the town to the countryside in the decades around 1200 and, to a lesser extent, effected the same change there. Although things were to change radically a century later when the vernacular rose again, we witness everywhere around 1200 a vigorous growth of legal, if somewhat vulgar, Latin.

Simultaneously, the vernacular language was enjoying a golden age, one in which, although town gentle- and businessfolk were happy to have their documents in Latin, they also participated as both authors and audiences in the expansion of vernacular culture. The vehicles carrying the vernacular were of two kinds, literary and religious.

The literature was that of the troubadours, and the twelfth century was their great age.[4] Occitanian authors drew on much the same body of models that Atlantic and northern French artists did, and, in fact, translated into their tongue some of the more important pieces of these provenances. Poets of the Midi commented at length on political events and particularly on the Albigensian war and the consequent northern French conquest of the Midi. The *Chanson* of the Albigensian crusade, the livelier part of which, at least, was written by a Toulousan, is really a magnificent verse history or epic of that great combat.[5] After the defeat, some of these authors emigrated to Italy and elsewhere,

---

[4]The information given here derives chiefly from Reto R. Bezzola, *Les origines et la formation de la littérature courtoise en Occident (500–1200)* (3 vols. in 5 Paris 1944–63), Joseph Anglade, *Les troubadours de Toulouse* (Toulouse and Paris 1928), René Nelli, *L'érotique des troubadours* (Toulouse 1963), and especially Alfred Jeanroy, *La poésie lyrique des troubadours* (2 vols. Toulouse and Paris 1934).

[5]Eugène Martin-Chabot, ed., *La chanson de la croisade albigeoise*, Les classiques de l'histoire de France au moyen âge 13, 24, 25 (3 vols. Paris 1931–61) 1.vii–xi notes that William of Tudela, author of the first half, was a Navarrese canon who lived ten years in Montauban, and was not the author of the second and better half of the work. His and others' argument is based on the different versification and different ideology of the two parts of the epic, and seems convincing. It is to be noted, however, that the name de Tudela existed in Toulouse: H, Malte, Toulouse 1, 18 and 19, both dated November 1211, mention an Arnold William de Tudela and his brother John. In ibid. 1, 110, ii, February 1215, copied in 1225, we hear of Arnold William again, and of his sons Arnold Bernard and William de Tudela. That this family was domiciled in, and were citizens of, Toulouse is shown by E 501, i, March 1214: Arnold William served as a judge in a court deputized by the consuls. None of this necessarily conflicts with the information about the poet in Martin-Chabot's edition, except to show, perhaps, that the family was at Toulouse.

there aligning themselves to those hostile to the Capetians and to the Roman see and its allies, the mendicants.

Besides offering commentaries on the times, the main business of these singers and poets was to entertain, a function they sometimes performed with such brio as to stagger the morally stiff. But the capacity to shock was a necessary part of exploring what is still today the basic topic of popular song, the agony and delight of being in love. As in other romantic literature, the lover's condition monopolized the bulk of poetic attention, but social themes—"from love alone comes virtue," for example, and quite several others—were regularly present. Furthermore, because a lover's desires often conflict with the interests of family and affront his duties to prince or government, romantic literature is ideally suited to survey the frontiers between the individual, the family, and the social order generally, a matter of intense interest in an age when individuals and families had emerged to play independent and powerful roles in society.

Readers of these poets and their *vidas* may well argue that, if these entertainers had any social sense at all, it was a very "feudal" one. The *vidas*, for example, mention few *amice* except great ladies or princesses, and they stress the patronage of great notables, especially the counts of Toulouse and various kings. Furthermore, the artists themselves, as typified by the great Toulousan Peire Vidal, often dilated on their prowess in arms and achievement of knighthood. A careless reader of the *vidas* might think that the world of these writers was simply that of a "feudal culture."[6]

Up to a point, he is right. A peculiarity of this age in the Midi is that hereditary right, that is, private ownership, extended to seigneury and governmental rights. In the Toulousain, as town liberty grew, so did the enfranchisement of the local seigneuries and of the families dominating them. Also, despite dissimilarities and conflicts, there were profound similarities between townsfolk and countryfolk. Both in town and in the countryside, many leading families derived from a onetime service cadre devoted to martial and administrative services; in this age when such clans had become relatively free from their local prince, the capacity of each seigneurial or urban unit to defend itself exalted the martial ideal to an extraordinary degree. As a result, in town and even in the villages, those who were rising socially had their hearts set on sharing the style of life, and even the domestic architecture, of seigneurial and knightly families. It is therefore no wonder that the poets' ideal lover is a soldier and gentleman and not a public notary or businessman-usurer.

Besides, being professional entertainers as well as authors, the troubadours wanted butter on their bread. Both the old leading families of the town and the new rich and entrepreneurial groups regarded land as a prime object of investment; seigneurial and knightly families sat on that stable and

---

[6]The *vidas* are published by Jean Boutière and A.-H. Schutz, *Biographies des troubadours* (Paris 1964).

profitable commodity. At Toulouse around 1200, excepting a few very rich *ar-rivistes*, the most expensive marriage contracts are those among landed families, urban or rural in domicile. It is therefore not merely curious that nearby petty princes and seigneurs, those of Armagnac, l'Isle-Jourdain, Lanta, or Lautrec, engaged and even educated artists. Lower on the social scale, when a somewhat impoverished knight, Aimeric de Castelnau, at Issel in 1255 alienated property to an inhabitant of Mas-Saintes-Puelles by reason of poverty, he saw fit to include among his witnesses a *joculator* named Peire Gasc.[7]

Although, then, "feudal" or aristocratic patronage meant much to poetry and song, we may remind ourselves that what was done individually by notables like the above was also done collectively by the citizens of Toulouse. Many troubadours, including some of the most famous, were raised and trained there. Of the eight Toulousan poets listed in the biographies or *vidas* compiled in the thirteenth century, one was the son of a poor *cabalarius*, two were said to have been solid burghers, including the prolific Aimeric de Pegulhan, the son of a cloth merchant, and the unspecified social origins of two others, including [domi]Na Lombarda, may have been about the same. The remaining three were probably humbler. In spite of what his *vida* says about his origins, Guillem de Montanhagol was the brother-in-law of a modest burgher, and the remaining two were sons of craftsmen. One, the vehement and polemical Guillem Figuera, was the son of a tailor and a tailor himself, and the other, perhaps the most celebrated of all the Toulousan troubadours, was Peire Vidal, the son of a furrier.[8] Other literary sources record four more authors. One was among those whose origins cannot be discerned, two others were from about the level of a public notary, and the last was Pelardit, of whom more later.

The modest average social level of the artists mentioned in these literary sources fits the evidence found in the archives, evidence which, in turn, inspires a conviction that literacy in the vernacular was quite widespread at this time. *Joculatores* are usually seen in documents describing the property of middling and lower burghers, notaries, craftsmen, and the like. In an instrument dated 1192, Pelardit witnessed the sale of a house by Maria, widow of the cutler Raymond Faber deceased in 1189, and by Jordan *joculator*, her present husband, to a dairyman.[9] Wholly typical, the act is remarkable only for the presence of Pillusardid, to use its "Latin." And what is curious about this poet (none of whose verses are extant) is that, although omitted by the *vidas* and only once described by a later contemporary, Pelardit was singled out by his concitizens for the rare honor of having a street named after him, the "carraria

---

[7]Petrus Vasco, in the Latin charter in BN, Collection Doat, LXXXIV, 315v, November 1255.

[8]A brief appendix to this essay summarizes the information concerning Toulousan troubadours.

[9]H, Malte, Toulouse 3, 147, iv, July 1192, copied in 1225. Pilisarditus had a small property at Lardenne near St Cyprien: H, Daurade 149, May 1203.

Pilisarditis joculatoris'' in the City.[10] Was he, perhaps, the anonymous author of the liveliest part of the *Chanson* of the Albigensian war, that dealing with the rising of Toulouse against de Montfort and the successive and unsuccessful sieges of that city?

Quite apart from the passion evoked by works on topical events and their many songs suitable for both the courts and the streets, these entertainers appealed to the mass of the people partly because of their careers and lives. The mere existence, indeed, of the somewhat fictional and often exaggerated *vidas* is almost as significant as the testimony of these artists' ideas and work itself. By singing, loving, and fighting, he rose up from the furs in his father's shop to seize the crown of empire—along with the princess, of course. Peire Vidal's boastful and fictional career made his *vida* a positive caricature or paradigm of the hope and desire for social advancement characteristic of the inhabitants of his home town.

RELIGION

Catharism, the only sect really to flourish in Toulouse and its immediate region, was an expression of vernacular culture. Its members' habit of treating sacred matters in a language other than Latin was pointedly deplored by a legatine and Cistercian mission to Toulouse against them in 1178.[11] It is true, of course, that, not wishing to be *idiotae*, Cathar intellectuals were drawn toward Latin, wrote tracts in that language of learning, and would have written more had their cult survived; but the sacred text, ritual, and preaching of Catharism were in the vernacular.[12] What is worthy of mark here is a seeming contradiction about language on the part of the leading Toulousan families. On the one hand, they wanted their scribes and lawyers to expound their legal culture in Latin; on the other, they were sometimes proponents of, and often tolerant toward, a religion one of whose most express arguments was the need to teach and serve the cult in a language the people could understand. But this

[10]The passage about Pelardit by Uc de Lescura is in Alfred Pillet and Henry Carstens, *Bibliographie der Troubadours* (rev. ed. Halle 1933) 331, no. 368. An early reference to the street is in the national archives, J 327, 4, xiii, dated June 1274, and one also notes that this part of the present rue des Filatiers was often called Pelardit.

[11]See my "Une famille Cathare: Les Maurand," *Annales E.S.C.* 29 (1974) 1211–23 at 1212, the report of an outraged cardinal who may have had the curious idea that the Scriptures had been written in Latin.

[12]Carrying on the work of the Dominican Antoine Dondaine, who published the Italian Cathar *Liber de duobus principiis* (Rome 1939), Christine Thouzellier has issued another Latin text from Occitania in her *Un traité cathare inédit du début du XIIIe siècle d'après le "Liber contra Manicheos" de Durand de Huesca*, Bibliothèque de la Revue d'histoire ecclésiastique 37 (Louvain 1961), and her *Une somme anti-Cathare: Le "Liber contra Manicheos" de Durand de Huesca*, Spicilegium sacrum Lovaniense 32 (Louvain 1964). If many Cathar clergy lacked Latin, some, like Guilabert of Castres, bishop of Toulouse, had it. Nor is there any reason to doubt the information collected by the indefatigable Arno Borst, *Die Katharer*, MGH Schriften 12 (Stuttgart 1953) 107–08, including Matthew Paris's reference to Cathars seeking out the University of Paris.

contradiction is more apparent than real, because of a common denominator. Legal Latin was an expression of secular professionalism, whose proponents, having stolen both their language and their robes from the clergy, were implicitly in competition with the priesthood. The Cathar sect was overtly anticlerical. Laicism was the common denominator.

Anticlericalism aside, Catharism had its doctrines, its theology. The persistence and frequent revival of varieties of gnostic dualism in Antiquity, the Middle Ages, and today confirm the continuing appeal of such intellectualized or spiritualized religions. Furthermore, the Cathar's rigorous separation of things heavenly and things earthly preached a severely rigorist morality, propagating a thoroughly skeptical evaluation of human institutions that is not without charm. To cite an exaggerated example, the famous doctrine that carnal marriage is little more than legalized whoredom smacks of an appalling, if only sometime, truth. Still, this dour teaching put not a few potential adherents off, especially women, and it is doctrines like this that make the appeal of Catharism as against Waldensianism all the more puzzling.[13] The Waldensians and similar sects not only preached a similar or even stronger laicism by their doctrine of the priesthood of all true believers, but, far more consequential, rested a large part of their case on the hope of reliving the shared poverty and communism of the ideal found in the Acts of the Apostles. Their revolution was to take place in historical time, when what had once been perfectly realized only by a few could be, if not quite so perfectly, lived by the many. Here were teachings that naturally attracted members of the lower classes, encouraged guild corporatism, and even moved those of the wealthy whose social consciences or fears were stirred by their curious relationship to those they exploited. None of this, save for an attack on the purported luxury of the orthodox clergy and an undoubted aspiration to imitate the legendary simplicity of the apostles both in their liturgy and style of life, was available to Cathar missionaries.[14]

---

[13]Secondary literature usually accents the appeal of Catharism to women in spite of the facts that, although they were spiritually equal to men in that faith and could be *perfectae*, they were never in the hierarchy, the bishops and deacons, and were not active missionaries, at least, no more than some Catholic religious and Beguines. The antisocial quality of Cathar morality is also a commonplace, expressed by both Protestants and Catholics, by Henry C. Lea and Jean Guiraud, for example. A balanced view on the latter and related matters is to be found in Paul Alphandéry, *Les idées morales chez les hétérodoxes latins au début du XIIIe siècle* (Paris 1903). A successful attempt to show that women were not especially important in Catharism: Richard Abels and Ellen Harrison, "The Participation of Women in Languedocian Catharism," *Mediaeval Studies* 41 (1979) 215–51.

[14]On this question, see Christine Thouzellier's many works, notably her *Catharisme et Valdéisme en Languedoc* (Paris 1966) and the lively debates involving the historian of Waldensianism Kurt-Victor Selge in *Vaudois languedociens et Pauvres catholiques*, Cahiers de Fanjeaux 2 (Toulouse 1967). Almost all older historical work on Catharism was marked by a clear bias against this cult, even to denying it the status of a "religion." Nowadays things have changed, as we see in Jean Duvernoy, *Le Catharisme: La religion des Cathares* (Toulouse 1976), and not only because of the Neo-Cathar movement.

In spite of these apparent weaknesses, Cathar intellectualism and faith flourished in Toulouse and its region, and even largely excluded the Waldensians. One is therefore forced to the conclusion that its peculiar meld of anticlericalism and spiritualism gave it power. But why was its asocial spiritualism so appealing? Both older research and my own nearly completed study of the town of Toulouse show pretty clearly that Catharism was concentrated in the middle and upper ranges of the population, that is, from rural and urban knights through patrician commoner families to the solid middle ranges of the burghers.[15]

Attempts to go beyond these bare facts have led scholars to seek a direct economic motivation for the adoption of Catharism. It is commonly asserted that, owing to the subdivision of inheritances and the rise of urban wealth, landed families were being impoverished and were therefore markedly inclined to heresy.[16] In line with this argument, there is clear evidence from the town that some knightly and burgher clans were moved to attack usurers, that is, to attack new wealth and economic individualism. Furthermore, economic hardships may well have created a climate of discontent with the social institutions of the time, and especially with the Church, the greatest of all such institutions. A difficulty here is that such discontent evoked not only heresy but also orthodox extremism, promoting those, for example, who aided the ecclesiastical assault on both heresy and usury that began with the accession to the see of Toulouse of the onetime troubadour Fulk of Marseille in 1206. In addition, there is no real proof that landed families were being impoverished any more than were occasional urban ones, and, as we have seen, much to show that the landed interest was strong and flourishing around 1200. Although, then, there was undoubtedly some heartbreak and consequent discontent, the basic proposition of this economic argument seems unsound.

But perhaps the shoe fits the other foot. It has been asserted that usurers favored Catharism, a doctrine that (unlike those of the Waldensians and some orthodox groups) had no teaching favoring apostolic community or even poverty except as applied to the *perfecti*, the mixture of priest and monk that, under bishops and deacons, led the Cathar faith.[17] To oversimplify, the or-

---

[15]Concerning the town, I hope to prove this proposition in my forthcoming social history (n. 1 above). The idea that the landed aristocracy was most prone to heresy was long ago expressed in Célestin Douais, "Les hérétiques du comté de Toulouse," *Compte rendu du [second] Congrès scientifique international des Catholiques* (Paris 1891) 142–62, and in the works of Jean Guiraud, summed up anew in his *Histoire de l'Inquisition au moyen âge* (2 vols. Paris 1935–38).

[16]To cite references for this commonplace would be otiose, but see the works cited in n. 15 above. Not only are the Marxist sectarians inclined to see economic motivation everywhere, but also the polemists of orthodoxy—whatever it may be—are always willing to tar their enemies with being economically determined. Both are right, but they often clutch at straws.

[17]Mireille Castaing-Sicard, "Le prêt à intérêt à Toulouse aux XIIe et XIIIe siècles," *Bulletin philologique et historique* (Paris 1953–54) 273–78 at 278. I denied it in my *Toulouse* (n. 1 above) and a subsequent article, as did this excellent legal historian in her *Les contrats dans le très ancien droit Toulousain, Xe–XIIIe siècle* (Toulouse 1959), but now, on second thought, feel that the truth lies somewhere in between.

dinary *credens* could do as he wanted, and may have been drawn to a kind of antinomianism by the only too rigorous skepticism of his sect about the moral taboos of ordinary society. We certainly know that the orthodox clergy thought this the Achilles heel of the Cathars, and, as we see with bishop Fulk, they successfully joined the attack on heresy to that on usury, appealing both to some of the older rich and to the crafts and trades that were beginning to form associations to protect themselves from entrepreneurial exploitation just after 1200. On the other hand, usurers were often conscience-stricken or afraid of social censure, and therefore hyperorthodox. Although we know of some Cathar usurers, we know of more Catholic ones. A spectacularly successful usurer and *arriviste* businessman was Pons de Capitedenario, the original *patronus* of the Dominican order founded at Toulouse in the first decade of Fulk's episcopate. Still, there may be something to this argument. In history, some men have profited, and those often the most, from circumstances created by others who have had the courage to take the risk, to drain the contents of the cup. As it stands thus starkly, however, the argument "usury equals heresy" is too simplistic to stand alone, and has to be placed in the larger social context of the time to be meaningful.

There is also the matter of the ecclesiastical tithe. It has been said that the "recuperation" of tithes by the Church in the twelfth century offended landlords, both large and small.[18] Several Cathar families of the town are known to have had trouble with the Church over tithes. Here again, however, real history is more nuanced. The great period of the "return" of tithes—and of churches themselves, for that matter—lay in the last quarter of the eleventh century through the first two-thirds of the twelfth. What remained to be done thereafter was difficult, but essentially mopping up. Furthermore, although Catharism or its preliminary forms were already growing in that early period, it was probably profitable for landed families in Toulouse and its environs to "return" churches and tithes to the Church in exchange for ideological support and material capitalization. Materially, landed families in Toulouse, then capital-poor and land-rich, were aided by the ecumenical agencies of the "reformed" Church. Not to speak of the capitalization provided by the Cluniac Benedictines, Cîteaux, and Fontevrault around 1100 and thereafter, this alliance is strikingly exemplified by the joining of landed families with the Templars and Hospitalers to found *salvetats* or new communities and villages in both town and countryside during the first half of the twelfth century. Doubtless—indeed, certainly—this harmony was disintegrating in the later twelfth century as the land filled up and the Gregorian political alliance lost its reason for being, and some families were therefore much exercised by ecclesiastical pressure about tithes. It is nevertheless hard to see how this conflict

---

[18]This point has been made from the days of Bernard of Clairvaux's secretary Geoffrey of Auxerre through Elie Griffe, *Les débuts de l'aventure cathare en Languedoc 1140–1190* (Paris 1969) 172.

could affect more than a few, the scions of families that were not keeping up. Tithes were significant, then, but they do not seem decisive, especially in an economy that was generally expanding.

What seems more significant about Cathar spiritualism was its congruence with the general tenor of life. Although, like many religions, implicitly totalitarian or monopolist, Catharism spread in circumstances that deprived it of either ideological or practical police. Its demanding morality applied principally to the *perfecti*; the *credentes* were principally required only to convert on their deathbeds by the *consolamentum*, an act without confession. There was no confessional police, such as was coming to be the practice among Catholics. The lack of a firm social conscience such as that taught by the Waldensians also helped make Catharism suitable for a family-based society in which aggressive individuals gained new wealth or amplified family fortunes, often at the expense of their humble neighbors. Catharism's dour view of human institutions may even have appealed to the many Catholics who tolerated this divergent faith, surely a substantial part of the population. Cathar critical rigorism had the inadvertent function of weakening faith in dominant institutions, and men were thereby enabled to live according to the rather open *mores* of the time. Just as the political authority of the local prince had been limited by a measure of seigneurial independence and by the implicit republicanism of the town's leading families, so likewise was Catholicism weakened by the tolerance or acceptance of a faith that had the great advantage of desacralizing the established Church. Catharism, in fine, was another church—indeed, one of three competing churches, although the Waldensians were so weak in the Toulousain as to appear for a time to be allied to the Catholics.[19]

To examine the balance of the rival religions before 1200, one may turn to art. The rise of Catharism in the late twelfth century coincided with a marked *rallentando* of orthodox building. The Cluniac priories and parishes of the Daurade and St Pierre des Cuisines, the urban and rural foundations of the Templars and Hospitalers, the old great nave of the cathedral, and particularly the famous Romanesque basilica of St Sernin date from the late eleventh century through the first half of the twelfth. A renewed spurt of building was not

---

[19]For the weakness of the Waldensians in Toulouse and the Toulousain generally (save just outside the frontiers at Montauban, Lavaur, Castres, Carcassonne, etc.), see the article by Yves Dossat cited in my appendix, no. 7. As to the Lauragais, just southwest of Toulouse, see Municipal Library of Toulouse, MS 609, where, in the depositions taken by the inquisitors in 1245/46, several Waldensian missionaries are mentioned (fols. 234v and 249). Folio 198 refers to a debate at Lavaur that took place around 1208 between the celebrated Cathar Isarn of Castres and the famous Waldensian Bernard Prima. An aged witness from Avignonet said that about 20 or 30 years ago "Valdenses persequebantur dictos hereticos [Catharos], et multociens fecit [ipse testis] helemosinam dictis Valdensibus, quando querebant hostiatim amore Dei; et quia ecclesia sustinebat tunc dictos Valdenses, et erant cum clericis in ipsa ecclesia cantantes et legentes, credebat eos esse bonos homines" (fol. 136). But most of the later witnesses merely repeated what one at Villeneuve-la-Comptal said (fol. 183v): "De Valdensibus dixit se penitus nichil scire." None of this means, however, that the Catholics were really tolerant about Waldensians. When, according to Peter de Vaux-de-Cernay, *Historia Albigensis* 513 (ed. Pascal Guébin and Ernest Lyon

to occur until after about 1250, when the many mendicant churches and cloisters, the new colleges of the university, and the new and Gothic cathedral, were started.[20]

One cannot, however, speak of a collapse of religion during this hiatus. Not only were the Cathars there and increasing, but public charity developed significantly in the town around 1200, in this regard a time probably greater than that of the Gregorians which preceded it and nearly as ample as the later thirteenth century. It is also indicative of the social character of the age around 1200 that, unlike either the earlier or later periods of charitable foundation, several hospitals and leperhouses were founded by, and named after, private persons and families of the town.[21] Charity, one guesses, had the advantage not only of appearing to be religious, but also of being relatively unattached to any one form of religion. It was altogether fitting that this kind of endeavor should flourish at a time when two rival religions were fighting it out.

In spite of the lack of academic learning, the twelfth century was an exciting age at Toulouse in the history of language, literature, law, and religion, and the kind of intellectualism there implanted suited the social institutions of the town and its region. Temporary though it was, a kind of balance of contraries had engendered a tolerant kind of society. Two religions, Catharism against Catholicism; two political forms, urban republicanism and rural decentralization against princely power; and two moralities, Cathar and Catholic rigorism against *laissez faire* and indulgence of the individual—all balanced admirably for a moment to fit a little world where families and their individual members believed themselves capable of directing society for its betterment without the supervision or police of externally imposed institutions or authorities. This belief—and the freedom to protect it—was to fade during the thirteenth century.

[3 vols. Paris 1926–39] 2.208), the crusaders under no less a person than the legate Robert of Courson took Norlhon (Aveyron) in 1214, they burned seven Waldensians "cum ingenti gaudio." As we see in ibid. 28 (1.18–19), however, even Peter admitted about Waldensians that "mali erant, set comparatione aliorum hereticorum longe minus perversi: in multis enim nobiscum conveniebant, in aliquibus dissentiebant." Their crimes were that they wore sandals "more apostolorum," believed in apostolic poverty, took no oaths, altogether eschewed the sword, and espoused the priesthood of all true believers.

[20]A sketch of the history of Toulousan art and building, with bibliography, may be seen in the sections written by Marcel Durliat in Philippe Wolff et al., *Nouvelle Histoire de Toulouse* (Toulouse 1974) 80–94 and 136–56.

[21]See my "Charity and Social Work in Toulouse, 1100–1250," *Traditio* 22 (1966) 203–87.

Appendix

TROUBADOURS OF TOULOUSAN ORIGIN FOUND IN LITERARY SOURCES

The references below are to Jeanroy's book in n. 4 above, Anglade's in the same note, Pillet-Carstens in n. 10, the edition of the *vidas* in n. 6, and Camille Chabaneau's earlier edition of the *vidas* and his catalogue of the troubadours published in Claude Devic and J. Vaissete, *Histoire générale de Languedoc* (éd. Privat, 15 vols. Toulouse 1872–92) 10.Note 38. The authors are arranged in rough chronological order, and I omit all late thirteenth-century figures. I also omit Cadenet, called Baguas (masc. for *bagassa*, "whore") when in training in Lanta near Toulouse (*vidas* 500, no. 80), and who lived until 1239 (Jeanroy 1.128 and 355), but who was a Provençal and had most of his career there, and William of Tudela for reasons given in n. 5 above.

(1) "Guiraudos [Gerald] lo Ros si fo de Tollosa, fils d'un paubre cavalier" (*vidas* 345, no. 54). The authorities say he was associated with a prince of the Toulouse line who died ca. 1185, but he may have been earlier. A family living north of the Bourg at Castillon is variously named de Castilone, de Ros, or, collectively, the Rocenses, for which see Célestin Douais, *Cartulaire de Saint-Sernin de Toulouse (844–1200)* (Paris 1887), via the index, and H, Saint-Sernin 600 (Cresty: 10, 36, 8), iii, July 1200, recording the loss of tithings held forty years before by the Rocenses, and vii, January 1164, containing the testament of a Gerald de Castilone.

(2) "Peire Raimons [sometimes simply Raymond] de Tolosa lo Viellz si fo filz d'un borges" (*vidas* 347, no. 55), fl. ca. 1180–1225 (Jeanroy 1.409; for a question, see below), was associated with princes in Catalonia, Montpellier, and Toulouse, and married a woman in Pamiers. Although surely not of the main line of the knightly family of Toulouse called de Tolosa, he may have been of a perhaps related line seen in the charters. Two brothers, Raymond and Arnold, inherited from a Peter de Tolosa (mentioned in a destroyed act of 1174). Rendering his (much obliterated) testament in 1201, Raymond left his property in *fratrisca* with his brother Arnold to his children Peter Raymond and Arnalda. In 1215, Peter Raymond, obviously no longer a minor, ended the *fratrisca* with his uncle. We hear of Peter Raymond once again in 1218, and of Arnold's son Peter by his wife Bernarda from 1210 to 1221. What gives this linkage likelihood is that the families regularly chose the same Christian names, that the old Peter Raymond was also called simply Raymond in literary sources, and that he was there called *vetus* or *senior* as we see above or "lo pros," *probushomo*, all words usually used to describe a senior member of a family when a younger member carried the same surname and Christian name. The archival references are H, Grandselve 7, seven acts on the same membrane running from January 1174 to June 1218, copied in 1227; ibid. 4, January 1210; ibid. 5, August 1213; E 510, two acts dated respectively August 1205 and May 1214; and D, Saint-Bernard 138, 84–85v, January 1221.

(3) "Peire Vidals si fo de Tolosa. Fils fo d'un pelicer. E cantava meilz c'ome del mon. E fo dels plus fols omes que mais fossen. . . . E'l meiller cavaillier del mon crezia estre e'l plus amatz de donnas" (*vidas* 351–52, no. 77), fl. ca. 1180–1206 (Jeanroy 1.411). Active in Provence, Cyprus, and Spain, this was a wonderful character, but one with a very common name. He pretended that he had married a daughter of the emperor of Constantinople, and much else.

(4) Pelardit, for whom see above at note 9.

(5) "Aimerics de Peguillan si fo de Tolosa, fils d'un borges qu'era mercadiers, que tenia draps a vendre" (*vidas* 425–27, no. 68). He fell in love with a "borgesa, soa visina," tangled with her husband, and agreed to "issir de Tollosa e faidir." Fl. ca.

1195–1230 (Jeanroy 1.331–32). His prolific career, at home and in Catalonia and Castile, was marked by great hostility to the crusade and ended in exile in Lombardy: "e lai definet in eretgia segon com ditz," according to one version of the *vida*, which seems reasonable. Quite apart from charters concerning the de Pegulano at Toulouse, not a few members were consuls: a Pons in 1202–03, Arnold 1203–04, Raymond 1207–08, and William Aimeric in 1215–16, in office, in short, always when the popular party dominated.

(6) "Na Lonbarda si fo una dona de Tolosa, gentil e bella et avinens de la persona et insegnada. E sabia bien trobar e fazia bellas coblas et amorosas" (*vidas* 416, no. 60). The *vida* tells us that she had a relationship with a scion of the house of Armagnac who succeeded to that county in 1219, and mention of a Jordan in a verse has encouraged some to link her with a lord of l'Isle-Jourdain. This inspires in me the notion that Lombarda was either a lady or a hetaira. That she was called "dona" means nothing because all women, no matter how low their social state, are called *domina* or *na* in the Latin and vernacular charters of this period. Lombarda was also a frequent name at Toulouse, and it therefore seems that Chabaneau's pointing (Note 38 279b) to a Lombarda in the charter from the national archives, J 321, 51, dated June 1206, as being the same person, is a mere shot in the dark.

(7) "Guillems Figuera si fo de Tolosa, fils d'un sartor, et el fo sartres. E quant li Franses aguen Tolosa, si s'en venc en Lombardia. E saup ben trobar e cantar; e fez se joglars entre los ciutadis. Non fo hom que saubes caber entre'ls baros ni entre la bona gen; mas mout se fez grazir als arlotz et als putans et als hostes et als taverniers" (*vidas* 434–35, no. 65). In spite of these observations and one tale about him to the effect that, in a brawl, he nearly lost an eye, William (fl. ca. 1215–45; Jeanroy 1.140 and 378–79) wrote a most famous *sirventès* against Rome while still at Toulouse on the side of Raymond VII. That this circulated in Toulouse is shown in Yves Dossat, "Les Vaudois méridionaux d'après les documents de l'Inquisition," *Vaudois languedociens et Pauvres catholiques*, Cahiers de Fanjeaux 2 (Toulouse 1967) 207–26 at 221–22: a Waldensian Bernard Raymond Baranonus was questioned in 1274, and noted that he had long had copies of William's "D'un sirventes far," and translations of St Brandon's life, the *Bible* of Guiot of Provins, and much of the New Testament. In Italy, William supported—and occasionally castigated—Frederick II, especially congratulating him on crushing the Milanese. In short, here as elsewhere, and quite apart from their political bias, the *vidas* show themselves to be interested in nothing but romances and commentaries on *mores*. A family with William's surname was known at Toulouse. A Stephen Figera is mentioned in February 1163 and May 1164, and his heir was clearly an Arnold Figuera, first seen in July 1202 (E 501, acts ii, iv, and v on this membrane) and again as Figueria in E 504, April 1214. An interesting charter is D, Saint-Bernard 138, 74v–76, April 1214, where we learn that Arnold was either the brother or father of Willelma, the wife of Peter Vitalis *macellarius*, a butcher. Lastly, a Peregrin Figuerius is seen in E 501, ii, dated October 1231, copied in 1233.

(8) Raimon Escriva wrote a pro-southern work containing a dialogue—in the 1968 sense—between a cat and a trebuchet, the latter being the artillery that killed Simon de Montfort while he was defending the former siege instrument. Nothing can be done with a name like this except to record the familiar information in Jeanroy 1.420 and 2.258, to the effect that the famous Raymond Scriptor (Scriba, Escriba, etc.) was a canon of St Etienne and *officialis* who was assassinated along with the inquisitors at Avignonet in 1242 by some heretics and their fautors. Hardly a likely candidate for this poet, although men have been known to change their minds.

(9) "Peire Guillems si fo de Tolosa, cortes hom e ben avinenz d'estar entre las bonas genz. . . . e fez sirventes joglaresc[s] et de blasmar los baros. E rendet se a l'or-

dre de la Spaza'' (*vidas* 436–37, no. 66). Jeanroy 1.407 dates him in the first half of the thirteenth century, and that seems right because cursing the barons usually had to do with Raymond VII's failure to break free of the Capetians in 1242. The mention of the Spanish Order of the Sword (Santiago) makes it seem that Peter William was a gentleman, but not necessarily. The *vidas* seem to me to show that, as in twentieth-century New York, every southern four-flusher pretends to be plantation aristocracy.

(10) "Guillem de Montangnhagout si fo uns chavaliers de Proenza, e fon bon trobador e grant amador'' (*vidas* 518–19, no. 90). In spite of this, Jeanroy 1.380 seems right when he remarks that he was a Toulousan who fl. ca. 1233–58. The name Montanhagol is known at Toulouse, for which see D, Saint-Bernard 4, March 1261, copied in 1695 (!), where we see a Gerald de Montanhagollo. Besides, although he had a distinguished career in Catalonia and Castile, Montanhagol is known to have been the brother-in-law of our next troubadour.

(11) Pons or Peter Santolh, according to Anglade 147–49, has only one extant piece, a *planh* about the death of his brother-in-law Montanhagol. He is almost certainly a member of a family called Centullus in Latin, but whether he was from the Centulli of nearby Castelsarrasin or those of Toulouse is not known. The line at Toulouse had produced one consul who held office during the popular consulate of 1202–03, and, although other members were artisans, it boasted one active notary, Sancius Centullus, who instrumented from at least 1205 to 1235.

(12) Guiraut d'Espagne from Toulouse is described by Anglade 134, following Chabaneau, Note 38, 352b. Gerald, active between 1245 and 1265, was distinctly unusual among Toulousans because he supported Charles of Anjou. Chabaneau had the idea that a family de Hispania was frequently represented among the consuls, but there are no consuls de Hispania or Ispanolus in extant lists, at least not until after 1280. There was, however, a family of modest distinction that took its name from a miner named Ispaniolus who became vicar of Toulouse in the twelfth century, for whom see my *Toulouse* (n. 1 above) 53. Among a gaggle of children, the vicar had a son named Gerald, last seen in a charter in E 501, March 1199. It is possible that the family emancipated itself from the name of this fortune-maker, but, if so, it took time, one of his sons being called Ispanus Ispanolus until at least 1230. The old vicar's daughter was named Ispaniola.

(13) Atz de Mons was, according to Jeanroy 1.339, active in Aragon and Castile in the second half of the thirteenth century. As does Anglade 154, he argues that this is a Toulousan of the knightly line of the de Montibus. They are probably right. De Montibus filled the consular office at least ten times from 1180 to 1259, including two terms for an Ato de Montibus in 1198–99 and 1201–02, therefore before the inclusion of the popular party. This patrician family also used the given name Ato in conjunction with other Christian names such as Raymond.

This figure, who is not included in the social evaluation given in the article above, is indicative of the drift of troubadour poetry. Not only is his work didactic, but also, like the majority of the late thirteenth- and early fourteenth-century Toulousan versifiers, he was from a self-conscious and defensive upper class. It is therefore not surprising that, written at this period, the *vidas* do not quite do justice to fellows like Guillem Figuera. When we add to this the fact that many *vidas* were redrafted by Italians who were largely Guelph in sympathy, and therefore did not enjoy the natural antipapal bias of many Toulousan poets, we understand why they cleave to literary values and do not appreciate political *sirventès* or epics like the *Chanson*.

JOCULATORES OF TOULOUSE FOUND IN THE CHARTERS

This checklist of references found in charters already catalogued is obviously a skimming of what could be found in the documents. Slim though the sample is, it shows the modest level of the average *joculator* and, at the same time, the fact that he rented or owned property from time to time.

Arnold, a property holder next to a cutler, in H, Grandselve 1, September 1172, copied in 1190.

Pelardit, see above at note 9.

Jordan, ibid.

Galaubetus purchased a house from the wife of William John Auriollus *textor* in E 510, February 1201.

Tolosanus rented an apartment or house from the heirs of the minter Pons David in H, Malte, Toulouse 1, 21, June 1214.

Peter, deceased, had rented a small property sold to Pons de Capitedenario in D, Saint-Bernard 138, 181v, May 1218.

William held property next door to that of a broker in H, Grandselve i, November 1253.

The Culture of the Knightly Class
Audience and Patronage

Georges Duby

A major problem facing the social sciences today is the relationship between cultural phenomena and socioeconomic structures, or, to put it in different terms, the interaction between material infrastructures and the superstructures: in the present case, the production and reception of cultural entities which are considered—by contemporaries or by ourselves—the expression of a renaissance.

There are two main difficulties. There is no theoretical foundation on which to construct a formulation of the problem before proceeding to the inquiry. And the task is considerably complicated by the present compartmentalization of disciplines in universities and research institutes, by the boundaries which unfortunately keep economic and social historians separate from the historians of thought, literature, and art. Between these territories so jealously delimited and defended, communication is rare. In this respect, conditions have not appreciably altered since the time of Charles Homer Haskins. One significant and promising change, however, is our growing dissatisfaction, upon rereading *The Renaissance of the Twelfth Century*, at finding in this admirable book scarcely any reference to the considerable changes in social relationships within Latin Christendom during this period: we want to correlate those patterns of change with concurrent changes in mental attitudes and with the cultural forms which both express and govern these attitudes. I shall illustrate some of the possibilities from French history of the period, organizing my remarks around three sets of questions, which may be taken as research proposals.

I. GROWTH AND ITS EFFECTS

The process of cultural development which since Haskins has been called the renaissance of the twelfth century is inseparable from the long movement of material progress then taking place in Western Europe. This movement had neither beginning nor end, nor did the renaissance we speak of, no more so than the Renaissance of the quattrocento. The manifestations of cultural development are easier to place chronologically, thanks to the nature of the available sources, than those of material change. Since, however, they lack a series of quantifiable indicia, they do not permit close monitoring of the social and economic evolution. Of this, we perceive little more than tendencies.

The twelfth century seems indeed to have been, in France at least, the height of this advance. We can judge by three criteria:

(1) *The diffusion of the monetary medium:* The first signs of its diffusion appear around 1080 in documents from the countryside of the Mâcon region;[1] a hundred years later currency was everywhere, dominating everything, and nobody, from the greatest prince to the humblest peasant, could dispense with its daily use.

(2) *The extension of land under cultivation:* Statistical analyses for Picardy place the greatest increase between 1150 and 1170.

(3) *The increase in population:* In Picardy, population growth reached its greatest intensity in the last quarter of the twelfth century.[2]

This growth, primarily agricultural in nature, took place in what then constituted the basic framework for the profits of production—the rural seigneury. Originating in France about 1000, the institutions of the seigneurial fiscal system were perfected during the last two decades of the eleventh century; they functioned perfectly throughout the twelfth century. To meet the demands of their lords—masters of their bodies, of the land they cultivated, and of the power to control them—the peasant households continually had to increase their output. Their own standard of living, however, does not seem to have risen perceptibly before the 1180s: the system of rents and taxes transferred to the lords the bulk of the increased resources created by the expansion of agricultural land, by the raising of rents, and by the enlarged work force. The nobility was virtually the only class to profit from the enrichment of the countryside.

The lay aristocracy appears to have benefited more from the general progress than did the great ecclesiastical establishments. In fact, during the eleventh century the aristocracy had succeeded in effectively protecting the source of its revenues, the manors, from the disruptive tendencies which severely affected them until about 1050. This was achieved in two ways: by appreciably reducing the donations of lands and rights to the churches, and especially by limiting the birth rate, thus preventing the family stock from branching out and, in so doing, dividing the inheritances. The exclusion of married and dowered daughters from sharing in inheritances, and the practice

<hr>

[1]Georges Duby, *La société aux XIe et XIIe siècles dans la région mâconnaise* (Paris 1953) 275ff.

[2]Robert Fossier, *La terre et les hommes en Picardie jusqu'à la fin du XIIIe siècle* (2 vols. Paris 1968) 1.283, 305ff.

of keeping all but the eldest sons celibate, assured the numerical stability of noble lineages during this entire period, and hence the stability of their patrimony, the profits of which were constantly being increased by economic growth and the improvement of manorial fiscal policy. The princely houses, like the knightly families, lived for the most part in ease. They spent more and more, using money more often.

This increased consumption on the part of the aristocracy stimulated both the specialized handicrafts and commerce. It favored urban growth—quite vigorous in twelfth-century France—to the extent that by the last two decades of the century the centers of growth had moved to the cities. Henceforth, the town prevails over the countryside, dominates and exploits it. This change supported the rise of two social classes: the elite of the merchant bourgeoisie, and the servants of the great lords. They grew rich, and some of them became wealthier than many of the nobles. Their goal remained, however, to integrate themselves into the rural nobility, to be accepted into its circle, to share its way of life and its culture.

These major trends in socioeconomic evolution directly concern our subject, because they had repercussions on mental constructions. Two facts, determined by economic growth and the transformation of society, merit special attention.

First, there emerged an ideological system peculiar to the secular aristocracy, developed around the concept of chivalry. Throughout the twelfth century, the spectrum of values encompassed by this term was affirmed and enhanced through the entertainments, tournaments, and *joutes amoureuses* directed at that dynamic segment of the nobility which reinforced its matrimonial politics—the *iuvenes* or "bachelors," the unmarried knights. We see evidence of it, in northern France after 1160, in the elaboration of the ritual of dubbing and, more plainly, in the resurgence in secular literature of the old concept of a trifunctional society.[3] This concept was transformed and desanctified, however, and the "order" of knights was granted preeminence not only over that of the "serfs" but also over that of the clergy.

The cultural monopolies until then retained by the Church were now clearly challenged: the chivalric society too intended to participate in high culture. Its dream was to appropriate "clerisy"—meaning the knowledge of the schools. Thus the cultural distinction between the ecclesiastical sector and the lay aristocracy tended to blur, and interpenetration took place. It is precisely at this point that the phenomena of patronage and audience are found.

Second, the spectacle of a world transformed by man's efforts, and the constantly rising value attached to the natural environment, produced—and this is, in my opinion, an essential point—an awareness of progress. The intensified perception of progress is visible first among the intellectuals who were

---

[3]Georges Duby, *The Three Orders: Feudal Society Imagined*, trans. Arthur Goldhammer (Chicago 1980).

most closely allied with the secular aristocracy: the members of the cathedral chapters. Bernard Silvester is a typical example. These men of learning, men of written culture and reflection, undertook to celebrate nature, a rehabilitated nature. Ever more clearly, they portrayed man, his deep structure homologous to that of the created universe, as capable of acting upon this universe, as summoned by God to cooperate with all his powers in this work—henceforth conceived as continuing in time—of creation. Here, together with the improvement of technology, with the labor of settlers ceaselessly clearing new land, was born the idea that civilization grows like a plant, that each generation takes up the task from the hands of its predecessors and must carry it further toward its goal. This concept constitutes a complete reversal in the view of human history. It ceased to be regarded pessimistically, as a process of progressive corruption, and appeared rather as a conquest. Its meaning changed. Its progress, from now on parallel to the history of salvation, no longer seemed to lead implacably toward decay but to ascend—step by step, from era to era—toward greater perfection.

Of course, such an inversion of the value system operates imperceptibly. Let us consider, for example, the Cistercians. The gaze of the monks of Cîteaux remained fixed upon the past. Convinced that all things deteriorate with the passage of time, they saw themselves as reformers, but in a retrogressive or, more precisely, a reactionary sense. They determined to return to the original principles of Benedictine life. Faithful to the spirit of *contemptus mundi*, the greatest expression of an ideology framed in times of decline and stagnation, they chose to separate themselves from the flow of life, to flee to the desert.

For them, the manual labor to which their decision compelled them remained a negative value, an act of humiliation and penance. Yet these men assiduously put into practice the most modern technological innovations; they worked persistently to increase the productivity of the underdeveloped land where they had established themselves. Thus they took part—without actually being aware of it—in the most vigorous aspect of the general movement of progress, ultimately moving their agricultural holdings to the forefront of economic successes. Above all, in putting the mystery of the Incarnation at the center of their meditation, they affirmed ever more strongly that, in man, the spirit's struggles for perfection cannot be separated from those of the body, and so aligned themselves with the rehabilitation of the flesh as well.

A decisive turning point was therefore reached in the intellectuals' concept of the world and its history during the middle of the century, between the region around Chartres, the Ile de France, and Champagne. The meaning of the word *renovatio* was fundamentally modified. Each previous renaissance had set out to rescue from inevitable deterioration works that were admired as the heritage of an earlier and therefore better age, to renew them and to restore their original brilliance. Renewal was an exhumation. From now on, every renaissance would be regarded as a creative process. The legacy of the past was taken up, but with the purpose of exploitation, as settlers exploited virgin lands, in order to take more from them. As in all the noble families the heir in each generation felt himself chosen to make the ancestral patrimony bear fruit, and confident of being able to increase its yield, so the moderns judged themselves capable, not only of equaling the ancients, but of surpassing them.

II. PATRONAGE

The continuously growing surplus from manorial exploitation was, in part, used for culture; evidently the part so used was larger in the ecclesiastical seigneuries. Here, the Reform of the Church succeeded on two levels. On the one hand, it brought about the reorganization of ecclesiastical revenues. Plundering by the laity declined, as did the administrative negligence which caused a large part of the profits to be lost. One learned to keep accounts and to plan. The administrative arrangements made by abbot Suger of St Denis and by Peter the Venerable, abbot of Cluny, bear witness to that concerted effort which revitalized the Church domains. The gains resulting from reorganization largely offset the losses caused by the decline of alms in the form of lands donated by the lay aristocracy. Protected, better administered, ecclesiastical wealth produced more abundant resources. Churches established in urban areas became particularly prosperous. They shared in the profits from the lucrative taxes levied on the circulation and exchange of money in the growing towns. They collected the pious donations of the bourgeoisie, all the more generous because businessmen were uncertain of their salvation.[4] Through its offerings, the urban population soon became the principal benefactor.

Second, the Reform placed able prelates in decision-making positions. Having triumphed over the secular power, these prelates believed that the resources of their houses should be employed to promote learning, to support the activity of scriptorium and chantry, and to adorn the liturgy more sumptuously. As long as it was a question of enhancing the musical embellishments of the Office, enriching the bookshelves, maintaining the school, and sending emissaries in search of new knowledge, the cost remained light. It became very heavy when one decided to build. Nevertheless, most bishops, abbots, and priors did not hesitate. Rivalry spurred them to outdo each other. For a time, St Bernard resisted his companions, who urged him to rebuild the monastery of Clairvaux; finally he yielded, and authorized emptying the coffers to hire workmen.

Plans were often too extravagant, and to carry on with the enterprise exceeded the community's ordinary means; subsidies had to be found from outside. We know the difficulties with which Peter the Venerable struggled as,

---

[4]See Jacques Le Goff, "The Usurer and Purgatory," in *The Dawn of Modern Banking*, UCLA Center for Medieval and Renaissance Studies (New Haven 1979) 25–52.

besieged with debts, he was obliged to finish building the immense abbey of Cluny.[5] Usually, however, lay benefactors came to the rescue just in time. Generous subsidies by the count of Champagne, for example, allowed the Cistercians to renovate conventual buildings in that province. King Alfonso VI of León–Castile and Henry I of England, in turn, were regarded as the "true builders" of the "great church" of Cluny, before the prudent generosity of Henry of Blois, bishop of Winchester, temporarily rescued the community.

When chroniclers of the year 1000 described the rebuilding of churches, they often invoked miracles—the fortuitous discovery of hidden treasures. This was their way of accounting for the real circumstance which actually permitted such projects to be carried out: an end to hoarding brought back into circulation the reserves of precious metals accumulated in the sanctuaries. Twelfth-century sources, though—Arnold of Bonneval in his *Vita Bernardi*, for example —make it very clear that ecclesiastical building projects were financed in large part by lay patrons.[6] Their contribution was made possible chiefly by the economic growth and the mechanisms for collecting seigneurial dues. Money piled up in their hands. They felt obliged to consecrate their new wealth to this kind of enterprise above all.

In the early Middle Ages, kings were expected to participate in the embellishment of religious buildings. The Alfonso and Henry who aided Cluny were kings, as was Robert the Pious, who was especially praised by his biographer Helgaud and by Odorannus of Sens for having contributed generously to the adornment of many churches.[7] Such activities were part of the mission of royalty, and in earlier times the largest monetary revenues had in fact been in the hands of monarchs. The sovereign was obliged to participate in ecclesiastical culture, beginning with the ceremony of his consecration and coronation, which placed him among the *oratores*, among the celebrants of the liturgy. Kings collaborated directly in the flowering of that culture, by supporting in their *palatium* the main center of creativity, the chapel, and its associated ateliers of art, writing, and thought; by conferring benefactions on cathedrals and royal abbeys; and lastly by maintaining peace, which favors works of the mind.

In its origin, then, patronage was the specific function of the king, God's lieutenant on earth. But in the twelfth century, the entire aristocracy aspired to play this role. Three phenomena explain this diffusion of the functions of patronage.

First, the feudal system—that is, the appropriation by a growing number of princes of the prerogatives of sovereignty. These princes took on the powers

[5]Georges Duby, "Economie domaniale et économie monétaire: Le budget de l'abbaye de Cluny entre 1080 et 1155," *Annales E.S.C.* 7 (1952) 155–71.

[6]Arnold of Bonneval, *S. Bernardi vita prima* 2.5, PL 185.267–302 at 283–85.

[7]Helgaud of Fleury, *Epitoma vitae regis Rotberti pii* 15 and 22, ed. and trans. Robert-Henri Bautier and Gillette Labory (Paris 1965) 84–90, 106–14; Odorannus of Sens, *Opera omnia*, ed. and trans. Robert-Henri Bautier and Monique Gilles (Paris 1972) 100–06.

of the king; they also wanted to clothe themselves in his virtues. In particular, they wished to occupy the place at the heart of religious culture which the king had previously been the only layman to hold. This happened very rapidly. In the year 1000, the duke of Aquitaine wished it to be known that he too was educated, read books, and meditated on the mysteries of the Faith.[8] One hundred and fifty years later, this claim had gained considerable ground; an increasing number of princes wished not only to imitate the king in this sphere, but also to set him an example. An anecdote added about 1155 to the second version of the *History of the Counts of Anjou* attests to this wish naively but eloquently. Its subject is count Fulk the Good (who died about 960): the intimates of the king laughed when they saw the count singing the Office in the midst of the canons, but they could soon hear the answer he himself had written, that "an illiterate king is a crowned ass"; and the monarch himself had to admit that "*sapientia*, eloquence, and letters are as appropriate for counts as for kings."[9]

At the time of this interpolation, the king had lost his monopoly on participation in learned culture, and on the patronage implied by that participation. All the lords who were responsible for the physical safety of the people considered themselves also responsible for their general well-being. Their duty was therefore to combine, as formerly only kings had done, the learning of the schools and the practice of arms. Count Fulk was admired because, it was said, "although he was thoroughly and discerningly initiated in letters, in the rules of grammar, and in the arguments of Aristotle and Cicero, he nonetheless surpassed the strongest, best, and most valiant of the knights."[10] In the twelfth century everyone was convinced that the goods appropriated by the secular lords from the fruits of peasant toil should not be employed solely to conduct war for the defense of the realm. These fiscal levies seemed justified only if they were partly applied to the advancement of knowledge and the cultivation of religious art. The patronage of high culture became one of the missions of the nobility.

At the same time, a summons to austerity rendered more important that portion of baronial revenues consecrated to intellectual works. The preaching of penitence, an appeal to the spirit of poverty, to the renunciation of worldly riches, to banish the excesses of luxury from the courts, was gaining ground all through the twelfth century. Such preaching certainly encouraged works of charity and care for the destitute. But it eventually called into question the very form of patronage that sustained the great artistic enterprises. When Peter the Chanter denounced as robbery the taxes levied on the "poor" of Paris—which, thanks to the generosity of Louis VII, went to supporting the

---

[8]Ademar of Chabannes, *Chronique*, ed. Jules Chavanon, CTSEEH 20 (Paris 1897) 209.

[9]*Chronica de gestis consulum Andegavorum*, ed. Louis Halphen and René Poupardin, *Chroniques des comtes d'Anjou et des seigneurs d'Amboise*, CTSEEH 48 (Paris 1913) 25–171 at 140–41.

[10]Ibid.

chantries founded by Maurice of Sully—he condemned royal patronage. It is, however, certain that insofar as the exhortations to austerity were heeded, some at least of the money that the great had formerly spent on their own pleasure and on sumptuous living was channeled toward the religious establishments—that is, toward culture. These pleas thus contributed to furthering the "renaissance." An example: Arnold of Bonneval congratulated St Bernard on knowing how to convince the count of Champagne to part with the jewels in his treasure—he donated them to the Cistercians, who, finding liturgical display repugnant, sold them to Suger, who used them in goldsmiths" work, while the Cistercians used the money thus obtained for building.[11]

Lastly, an irresistible process of imitation, having first popularized the royal model of behavior, inspired a progressive mimicry, down to the lowest levels of aristocratic society, of the attitudes of the princes—which is to say, those of the kings. To the extent that chivalry became sanctified, acquired the allure of an "order," to which a "sacrament"—the dubbing or "accolade"—permitted entry, all the adults of the military caste felt themselves called upon henceforth not merely to prove their physical bravery, but to cultivate the virtue of *prudentia*—to conduct themselves not only with valor, *en preux*, but also as *prud'hommes*—and to participate in some way in high culture, as did the *proceres* and the kings, and to patronize it with their generosity. In this evolution, and of particular interest for analyzing the phenomena of patronage and audience, three principal traits are distinguishable.

(1) Like the count of Anjou in the legend, all the knights wished to be regarded as *litterati*. From the end of the eleventh century on, there is mounting evidence of young men who neither belonged to the ranking nobility nor were destined for the Church, and yet were taught at home by private tutors or duly sent off to schools—who, at any rate, learned to read and understand a little Latin. The custom of entrusting to clerics the education of boys continued to flourish, and at the end of the twelfth century it was beginning to spread beyond the chivalric society. It won over certain newly rich parvenus, such as Durand de Blanot, an obscure village provost and brother of a peasant freeholder, who around 1220 sent his son to Bologna to study law.[12]

(2) Such intellectual demands gave rise to investments. Money was spent to maintain clerics, who were expected to help with the instruction of family members as well as with the administration of the seigneury. Lords of moderate rank were not content, like the count of Champagne, with helping to finance Cistercian buildings, as had, for example, the lord of Simiane at Senanque and the lord of Baux at Silvacane in the second half of the century.

[11]Arnold of Bonneval, *S. Bernardi vita prima* 2.8.55, PL 185.301–02; Suger, *De rebus in administratione sua gestis* 32, ed. Albert Lecoy de La Marche, *Oeuvres complètes de Suger*, Société de l'histoire de France 139 (Paris 1867) 195.

[12]Duby (n. 1 above) 436.

They preferred instead to found colleges of canons, if they did not already exist, near their residences. In this way, centers of learning grew up everywhere. In Champagne, members and officials of the comital dynasty alone created more than 320 prebends for canons during the 1150s.[13]

(3) Most significant, the generosity of the lay aristocracy much increased the number of positions, assuring to men whom I shall categorize as "intellectuals" the means to work and to spread culture around themselves. It would be an instructive inquiry (and one less difficult to carry out than many others in this field) to examine the increasing numbers of canons, of the men who gradually acquired the title of "master," and of all those clerics who found temporary or permanent employment in noble households.[14] The importance of these men, who played a decisive role in the "renaissance," could better be measured if we could monitor more closely the rapid development—paralleling that of the "courtly" troops of *iuvenes*, the "young" unmarried knights—of these other, clerical *iuvenes*. This equally dynamic clerical class was itself almost entirely an outgrowth of the aristocracy, and for the same reasons. These clerks, berated by Stephen Langton because they made a career in the service of the secular powers rather than meditating on holy texts,[15] were the principal agents of this acculturation which, embracing the concept of chivalry, transmitted to the aristocratic ideology certain values and techniques of scholarly culture.

Particular attention should be directed toward the schools where these intellectuals were trained, and toward the movements which brought these educational institutions out of their torpor and caused them to multiply and consolidate, and, in some cases, to grow enormously large. The social and economic study of scholarly institutions during this period has scarcely been broached, and would not be impossible. It would permit closer observation of the material growth, the role of money—begged by scholars from their families and earned by the teachers, sometimes copiously (Abelard boasts of the rewards his knowledge brought him)[16]—and of the role of patronage, the subsidies granted by prelates and princes, whose conscientious largesse was deployed to this sector well before the first colleges for poor students were founded at the very end of the century. It could be demonstrated that the scholarly milieu, along with that of the *ministeriales* and wholesale trade, was the scene of the liveliest social mobility. Like the chivalric "youth," the "young men" of the intelligentsia engaged in competitions analogous to tournaments (again, Abelard is our source), where some won glory and the "prize" and all strove to wield better the formidable arms of reason. They

[13]Michel Bur, *La formation du comté de Champagne, v. 950–v. 1150*, Mémoires des Annales de l'Est 54 (Nancy 1977) 478.

[14]Examples of this approach are the essays by John W. Baldwin and Richard W. Southern in this volume.

[15]Duby (n. 3 above) 319.

[16]Abelard, *Historia calamitatum*, ed. Jacques Monfrin (Paris 1959) 70, 63–64.

rank among the adventurers of their era, more certain than many others of rising in the social hierarchy if they had even a little will and ambition.

If the number of students continued to increase during the twelfth century, it was because more and more careers were opening up for those who had finished their studies. The most accessible and most attractive careers were not ecclesiastical. Lay society clamored for the services of men who possessed such training, and it was ready to pay them handsomely. The money that the greater and lesser aristocracy paid to attract such large numbers of young men—men who could handle words and figures, could reason, and had a superficial knowledge of the quadrivium—entitles it to be regarded collectively as the true patron of the expansion and diffusion of knowledge. Demand was so pressing, and the response so enthusiastic, that during the last decades of the century the leaders of the Church began to reconsider the purpose of the cathedral schools and thought of taking measures to stem the flight of their graduates into more or less secular professions. Hired in ever growing numbers by the courts, where their function—increasingly judged essential—received ever greater rewards, these intellectuals were the artisans who brought the lay and learned cultures together, and the most effective propagators of a "renaissance" for which the school was the great studio.

III. AUDIENCE

In the twelfth century a new type of culture took shape, accessible to all members of the aristocracy, and also to the newly rich who sensed that adopting it would be the best way to obscure their origins and blend with the well-born. In *The Art of Loving "Honestly,"* by Andreas Capellanus, a *litteratus* at the court of Philip Augustus, the *plebeius* is sharply distinguished by his birth and the sources of his wealth from the *nobilis*, the *nobilior*, and that *nobilissimus* the clerk. But he prides himself on sharing their tastes, speaking their language, and scrupulously conforming to the rules of behavior they observed.[17] This culture was largely a reflection of the knowledge and forms of expression which were being "reborn" in the creative centers of the Church. To examine its formation and expansion poses the problem of audience, inseparable from that of patronage, since we are dealing with two complementary aspects of the same phenomenon, itself inseparable from economic and social evolution. I shall limit myself to a few remarks on the location and chronology of the reception of this culture.

The culture can certainly be characterized as courtly: the courts, both large and small, were the site of its enrichment and its diffusion. The court is the expanded form of the seigneurial household. It developed as the nobility's profits grew. Largesse, the principal virtue of the aristocracy's value system,

---

[17] *De amore libri tres* 2.6, ed. Emil Trojel (Copenhagen 1893; repr. Munich 1964); trans. Claude Buridant, *Traité de l'amour courtois* (Paris 1974).

created a lord's authority and prestige; it compelled him to attract as many table companions as he could support and to treat them well. Since it was essential to his prestige that his guests feel at ease in his household, he endeavored to entertain them—with intellectual as well as physical games. Thus the code of generosity made the court a center of cultural creativity. It was likewise a school, a permanent gathering in which good manners were learned. In the establishments of the most magnificent princes, this initiation was the most elaborate, fashioned the greatest *prud'hommes*. From the rivalry of the *iuvenes*, both knights and clerks, each burning to eclipse the others, to win for himself the favors of his patron by demonstrating his excellence in arms or in letters, came the animation of courtly life.

But it also came from women. Let us not forget them. All the evidence shows that their participation in the learned culture was more precocious, more extensive, than that of males in the secular aristocracy. Adjoining the noble residence was a cloister of nuns, in which the daughters of the lord were educated. They emerged doubtless less superficially *litteratae* than the knights, their brothers. They played a central role in the cultural competition whose theater was the court. This competition took place before them; the young men wished to shine in their eyes; it was their duty to bestow the "prize." Did they not constitute one of the essential links between the renaissance and secular high society?

In this society the encounter between knights and clergy took place. The *senior*—and the lady, his wife—were at the center of the court, each incarnating in complementary fashion the courtly virtues. Like the kings before them, they were also supposed to set an example for the people of their household, to appear as models of lay piety. They made room in their life for religious observances. Through them, close communication was established between their entourage and the monastery where their ancestors reposed, the convent of nuns to which the widows and unmarriageable daughters withdrew, the collegiate church to which the master went regularly "in clerical vestments" to perform the Office with his confreres the canons, reading from a book, ritually distributing alms, as did Fulk the Good of Anjou in the legend or count Charles the Good of Flanders in reality. In this manner, the court was linked to the chapel, and practices grew up in the courtly society of the time which fostered a closer connection between laymen and the Church's liturgy.

This osmosis between sacred and profane obviously facilitated the high society's acceptance of the forms whose flowering in the ecclesiastical world was a result of the "renaissance." The renewal of religious art and music, which adorned the liturgical celebrations attended by the knights, had repercussions on the embellishments of secular festivities, inspiring a renewal here also. Likewise, the *exempla* which illustrated sermons communicated to secular thinking something of the logical processes of scholarly thought, of its perceptions of nature, history, and the supernatural. Significant relationships can be discerned between the little left to us of literary production in the vernacular and what little we know of the preaching aimed at the people of the courts. An example is the earl of Chester's chaplain, described by Orderic Vitalis: in his sermons to the earl's household, the young knights and the not so young, he kept the attention of his audience by combining the word of God with stories of warrior-saints and the tale of William of Orange—stories which would captivate these military men.[18] A careful reading of the *Song of Roland* reveals that it could have been understood on several levels at court, and that it was composed for an audience at least part of which, though lay, remembered more fragments of Holy Scripture than one might think. Audience? Of the "renaissance of the twelfth century," what the lay aristocracy perceived came to it first through the sermon.

The renaissance came to it also in entertainments. The members of courtly society—exclusive and strictly protected against intrusions of *vilains*, the "serfs," scornfully looking down from their superior position, entrenched in their wealth and in the idleness it sanctioned—lived at first without obligations, for games and pleasure. Their principal entertainment was storytelling: the people of the court listened to works composed by clerks, but in a form accessible to them, in verse and the vernacular. The form we call the romance (*roman antique*) clearly represents the most striking expression of the effort then being made to adapt to the lay audience the *auctores* whom the school grammarians explicated, but no genre of chivalric literature was immune from the strong influence of the trivium. Nevertheless, during the twelfth century, the Latin literary production addressed to courtly circles was so abundant that we must examine the manner in which it reached its audience.

Among the lords and ladies to whom Hildebert of Lavardin and Baudri of Bourgueil dedicated their sophisticated poems, were there really so few who could enjoy these works without an interpreter? The canon who composed the history of the lords of Amboise about 1160,[19] specifically citing Boethius, Horace, Lucan, Sidonius Apollinaris, and Seneca, and who strove to make the affective bond forged by vassalage resemble Ciceronian *amicitia*—did he not expect that the grace and vigor of his Latin composition would be appreciated by persons other than his clerical colleagues? Must we not assume a significant enlargement of the lay audience, people sufficiently cultured to be able to communicate with and appreciate the language and knowledge of the schools without an intermediary? What could have been the practical function of a work such as the *Historia Gaufredi ducis*, in Latin? Was it read? Where, in what circumstances? How—in translation, with annotations? This work shows Geoffrey Plantagenet besieging the castle of Montreuil-Bellay: the "educated count" (*litteratus consul*) requested that a copy of Vegetius be brought from the abbey of Marmoutier. To be sure, it was not claimed that he read this book himself; he had it read to him by a monk. In Latin? Translating, commenting

[18]*The Ecclesiastical History of Orderic Vitalis* 6.2, ed. and trans. Marjorie Chibnall (6 vols. Oxford 1969–81) 3.216.
[19]*Gesta Ambaziensium dominorum*, ed. Halphen and Poupardin (n. 9 above) 74–132.

on the text? At any rate, the following day, the count put into practice what he had learned.[20] Whether this story is true, or—more probably—invented, it demonstrates what was expected of a lord of this rank during the 1180s in Touraine: like a man of the Church, he should consult the classical authors. This is a good example of a state of mind, of how one imagined the achievements of the "renaissance" made their way into the aristocrat's daily life.

It is clear that the social sphere capable of absorbing these gains was expanding throughout the entire twelfth century. Doubtless it is impossible to date precisely the stages of this progressive extension. But a chronological analysis—not yet attempted—would be a worthwhile endeavor. Using some scattered indications, I can offer some preliminary impressions of the development in France.

This movement appears already well advanced in the last decades of the eleventh century. Certainly the lesser nobility (the family of Guibert of Nogent, for example), as well as the great lords, still chose between two types of education for their sons, depending on whether they were destined for knighthood or ecclesiastical status. Younger sons were either placed in collegiate churches or entrusted to private tutors. First-born sons were expected only to become skilled at physical exercises and faithful to the warrior's code. Educating the mind through study carried the risk, or so it was thought, of spoiling the body. On the other hand, from what we know of Abelard's father or St Bernard's youth, it is plain that the barrier between these two types of upbringing was not impenetrable. The future knights profited from the lessons their brothers took, and some of them knew how to read and write. It sometimes happened, moreover, that the death of an older brother obliged a cleric to abandon his status and rule the seigneury—as happened to a canon who, about 1100, became head of his family and assumed the military command of the castle of Berzé in the Mâcon region.[21]

In the middle of the twelfth century, the connection between the secular and scholastic cultures seemed to be well established in certain privileged, influential places where the nobility of an entire region periodically assembled. These were the great courts, which set the tone, dictating the fashions and showing how well-born people should behave if they wished to be worthy of their rank. At first, these courts were the gatherings around the feudal princes, the Capetians' rivals: Henry Plantagenet, the count of Flanders, the count of Champagne. In disseminating the culture produced and codified around them, these men clearly perceived a sure means of raising their prestige relative to that of the king. Paris appeared to be in retreat. Actually, though the adaptation of the scholarly culture to the secular seems less advanced there, it is nonetheless true that the actions of the king of France—directly responsible for

[20]*Historia Gaufredi ducis Normannorum et comitis Andegavorum*, ibid. 172–231 at 218.

[21]*Recueil des chartes de l'abbaye de Cluny*, ed. Auguste Bernard and Alexandre Bruel, Collection de documents inédits sur l'histoire de France (6 vols. Paris 1876–1903) 4.184 and 417–18, nos. 2985 and 3324–25.

the scholarly concentration from which Paris profited—caused the diffusion, more vigorous here than anywhere else, of the forms of the renaissance directly associated with the spiritual realm. In the south, this leading role was filled by the cities—Avignon, Arles, Narbonne, Toulouse. But the expressions of the renaissance which spread out from these urban centers were much more lay, more secular in nature. Cultural structures peculiar to the southern provinces explain this trait: following the Gregorian Reform, the Church and the lay powers were more widely separated; concomitantly, ecclesiastics did not retain their monopoly on writing, and an important stratum of civic high society—the judges and notaries—had direct access to scholarly culture.[22]

The documents at our disposal permit a clearer understanding of the system of relationships between the creative centers of the intellectual renaissance and the places of its reception at the end of the century. Unusually precise information is furnished by *The History of the Counts of Guines*, written in a small principality—a satellite of the county of Flanders—at the very beginning of the thirteenth century.[23] Its author, Lambert of Ardres, is precisely one of those household clerics who were the most effective agents of acculturation. He boasted of being a *magister*, a school graduate, and he used the books kept in the collegiate church founded in 1069 near the residence of his lords. His work bears the most convincing witness to the cultural encounter: in Latin, it is nourished by a reading of the classics; it shows expertise in the most learned rhetoric; and it also echoes the most modern expressions of secular literature (showing, for example, the renown already enjoyed by Andreas Capellanus in this small provincial court).

But above all, the priest Lambert, composing a double panegyric to the glory of his two patrons—the lord of Ardres, master of the household he served, and the father of this lord, the count of Guines, to whom the work is dedicated—demonstrates the two levels of the structure in whose midst the mechanisms of cultural reception operated: the stratum of the *iuvenes*, to which the lord of Ardres still belonged—where the military values of chivalry prevailed and where culture remained purely oral, preserved in the memory of the *commilitones* of the young hero who recounted, for the company's amusement in the intervals between their war games, tales of the Holy Land, fables of the "matter of France" and the "matter of Brittany," and exploits of the family's ancestors—and the level of the *seniores*, whose preeminent representative is count Baldwin.

Proud of having been knighted by Thomas Becket, this petty *princeps* Baldwin, who fought to preserve the autonomy of his domain wedged in between more powerful principalities, remained *illiteratus*; he endeavored however to attain *sapientia*. He was quite aware of how the intellectual activity he inspired in his household could augment his prestige, and he spared no ex-

---

[22]See the study by John Mundy in this volume, at "Intellectualism."
[23]*Historia comitum Ghisnensium*, ed. Joh. Heller, MGH SS 24.550–642.

pense to stimulate that activity. He supported among the members of his household a team of masters; he debated with these *doctores artium*, they initiated him into theology, and he in exchange taught them what secular narratives he knew. He flattered himself with having penetrated, though a mere listener, to the "mystical virtue" of the holy texts, with being able to take a creditable part in the exercise of the *disputatio*, and because people wondered, hearing him discourse, how "he could know letters without ever having learned them." He also loved the fact that, thanks to the nuns of his proprietary convent, his chapel was graced with splendid music. He filled it with books, the writings of the Fathers and the fables of the poets. He paid translators generously, for he wanted to hear read, in the language he understood, not only the Song of Songs, St Augustine, and the *Life of St Anthony*, but also treatises summarizing what was then known about physics.

Eventually he commissioned the work which celebrates the brilliance and antiquity of his lineage. But he desired that this dynastic monument, from which his descendants would learn to encourage learning by following his own example, be written in Latin, in the most classical, the most "renascent" Latin. Where, among these nobles of modest grandeur whose castles dot the French landscape as the twelfth century draws to a close, can we more clearly perceive the links between the renaissance, its patronage, and its audience?

Bibliographical Note

Michel Bur, *La formation du comté de Champagne, v. 950–v. 1150*, Mémoires des Annales de l'Est 54 (Nancy 1977).

Georges Duby, "Economie domaniale et économie monétaire: Le budget de l'abbaye de Cluny entre 1080 et 1155," *Annales E.S.C.* 7 (1952) 155–71.

————, *La société aux XIe et XIIe siècles dans la région mâconnaise* (Paris 1953).

————, "La vulgarisation des modèles culturels dans la société féodale," *Niveaux de culture et groupes sociaux: Actes du colloque réuni du 7 au 9 mai 1966 à l'Ecole normale supérieure* (Paris 1967) 33–40.

————, *Guerriers et paysans, VII–XIIe siècle: Premier essor de l'économie européenne* (Paris 1973).

————, *Saint Bernard: L'art cistercien* (Paris 1976).

Jean Flori, "La notion de chevalerie dans les chansons de geste du XIIe siècle: Etude historique du vocabulaire," *Le moyen âge* 81 (1975) 211–44 and 407–45.

————, "Sémantique et société médiévale: Le verbe adouber et son évolution au XIIe siècle," *Annales E.S.C.* 31 (1976) 915–40.

Robert Fossier, *La terre et les hommes en Picardie jusqu'à la fin du XIIIe siècle* (2 vols. Paris 1968).

Urban T. Holmes, Jr., "The Arthurian Tradition in Lambert d'Ardres," *Speculum* 25 (1950) 100–03.

Brian C. Stock, *Myth and Science in the Twelfth Century: A Study of Bernard Silvester* (Princeton 1972).

Consciousness of Self
and Perceptions of Individuality

John F. Benton

"Consider how, when you recently blundered before the brethren by saying one antiphon for another, your mind sought how it might blame the fault on something else, either on the book itself or on some other thing. For your heart was unwilling to behold itself as it was." So Guigo, prior of the Grande Chartreuse, writing for his own benefit in the desolate and windswept mountains near Grenoble, noted early in the twelfth century.[1] The "you" is Guigo himself, trying to stand apart from his "heart" or "mind" and to be aware of inner drives of which he had not before been conscious. Even an apparently trivial slip in the choice of a liturgical formula was an occasion for self-examination. How far we are here from the barren internal world of the literary Roland and Oliver, who question each other, but who unselfconsciously follow their own imperatives, without reflecting on either the wisdom or the morality of their own acts.

Bernard of Clairvaux, preaching to his monks on the seven steps of confession, explained that the first was expressed in the celestial precept, "Know thyself."[2] The attempt to follow the Delphic command, "Know thyself," had a long and by no means linear evolution from the time of Socrates to the twelfth century.[3] Consciousness of self and of the inner life and motives of

For discussion and criticism which have greatly aided the revision of this essay, I am indebted to the members of the Conference on the Renaissance of the Twelfth Century (especially the editors of this volume) and of the Group for Psychology in the Humanities at the California Institute of Technology. Among other friends who have made major contributions to my thinking, I should name in particular Elizabeth Brown, Gerard Caspary, the late Max Delbrück, and S. D. Goitein.

[1]*Meditationes Guigonis prioris Cartusiae: Le recueil des pensées du B. Guigue* no. 282, ed. André Wilmart, EPM 22 (Paris 1936) 114–15; trans. John J. Jolin, *Meditations of Guigo, Prior of the Charterhouse* (Milwaukee 1951) 41 (slightly altered here).

[2]*De diversis*, sermo 40.3, ed. Leclercq 6.1.236.

[3]Pierre Courcelle, *Connais-toi toi-même: De Socrate à saint Bernard* (3 vols. Paris 1974–75). Courcelle states (1.231) that in the West consideration of the topic faltered during the seventh and eighth centuries, and that John the Scot, who translated large portions of Gregory of Nyssa, was the only ninth-century Occidental author to treat the precept at length.

others in the twelfth century differed from what we find in Antiquity, but it would be hard to say that any authors in the Middle Ages understood their subjective world better than Catullus or Augustine of Hippo. Evidence does exist, however, which suggests that the practice of self-examination was deeper and more widespread in twelfth-century Europe than at any time since the fifth century. The twelfth century was not a time of the "discovery of self" or "discovery of the individual."[4] The origin of consciousness as we know it in the human species, the beginning of introspection, of the reflective remembering of the self in relation to things past and imaginative projection into the future, surely occurred in the distant past.[5] In the century and a half which included the lives of Gregory VII and Francis of Assisi there did occur, however, a renewed commitment to the examination of the inner life and a development of modes of thought about the self and others which have profoundly affected our civilization. It was prompted by new values and new forms of material life, rather than being a revival of the self-examination of Antiquity, but in its own way it was a renaissance.

The central matter of this essay is not to demonstrate that a shift in attitudes toward the self and other individuals occurred in the period centering on the twelfth century, for that interpretation of the available evidence has been amply presented elsewhere.[6] Instead, my major concern will be to assess the nature and comparative level of self-awareness, concluding with some theories of why and how the psychology of the twelfth century differed so much from even so stable and wealthy an age as the Carolingian renaissance.

EXAMINING THE SELF

FORMS OF AUTOBIOGRAPHY

Throughout the earlier Middle Ages, clerics continued to read the *Confessions* of St Augustine, a work of such profound self-examination that a "history of

---

[4]I have treated the issue of "individualism" in "Individualism and Conformity in Medieval Western Europe," *Individualism and Conformity in Classical Islam*, ed. Amin Banani and Speros Vryonis, Jr. (Wiesbaden 1977) 145–58. The present essay is intended to complement that lecture, delivered at a conference where the theme and the effort at cross-cultural comparison were determined by an Orientalist, S. D. Goitein.

[5]In *The Origin of Consciousness in the Breakdown of the Bicameral Mind* (Boston 1976), Julian Jaynes argues that consciousness is not an inherent attribute of the human condition but has had specific, historical origins in what he calls the breakdown of the bicameral mind, occurring at different times in different cultures ("bicamerality" being a condition in which the right hemisphere of the brain dictates to an "unconscious" left hemisphere). While I have found Jaynes's book heuristically stimulating, his theories that "consciousness" in humans developed relatively recently on the evolutionary scale and is closely related to a highly developed, metaphorical language are not in accord with the findings of current split-brain research; cf. Roger W. Sperry, "Changing Concepts of Consciousness and Free Will," *Perspectives in Biology and Medicine* 20 (1976) 9–19 and "Forebrain Commissurotomy and Conscious Awareness," *Journal of Medicine and Philosophy* 2 (1977) 101–26.

[6]See in particular Colin M. Morris, *The Discovery of the Individual, 1050–1200* (London 1972).

human self-awareness'' in Antiquity which concludes with Augustine has been said to end "where it should begin."[7] Until the beginning of the twelfth century no reader of the *Confessions* dared or was moved to write a self-examination in the same mode.[8] About 1115, however, Guibert of Nogent, an ambitious author and abbot of an obscure Benedictine abbey near Laon, began to write in his *Monodiae* or memoirs, "I confess to Thy Majesty, O God, my endless wanderings from Thy paths." In that opening word *confiteor*, Guibert invited a comparison with Augustine, and he starts his work in the confessional mode.[9] But the correspondences between these two confessional autobiographies are verbal, formal, topical; the two books are in no way equivalent in the quality of self-examination. Augustine stripped back the flesh and bared his soul to his God. Though Guibert begins bravely, as the story of his life comes closer to the time of his writing, he hides himself from the monks he knows will be his readers in a mist of anecdotal history about external events. Where Guibert is most openly revealing, in what he writes of his mother, his long-dead father, his dreams and fantasies, he appears to be naive rather than self-aware. He is perhaps most revealing in what he hides, in what he fails or does not dare to tell us about himself.

While the confessional tradition which influenced Guibert had few followers, many medieval authors developed the classical epistolary genre and wrote of themselves and their reflections in letters. From Bernard of Clairvaux and Peter the Venerable to quite obscure correspondents, some of the most revealing authors of the twelfth century expressed themselves in letters.[10] Closely related genres were the *apologia*, like the defense against his detractors Guy of Bazoches dedicated to his mother, and the *otium*, of which a good example is the collection of meditations Hugh Farsit of Soissons sent to his sister.[11] The most famous autobiography since that of Augustine, Abelard's

---

[7]Arnaldo Momigliano, *The Development of Greek Biography* (Cambridge Mass. 1971) 18, referring to Georg Misch, *Geschichte der Autobiographie* (4 vols. in 8 Frankfurt 1949–69). The first volume of Misch has been translated as *A History of Autobiography in Antiquity* (2 vols. London 1950 and Cambridge Mass. 1951). Misch says (*History* 1.8, *Geschichte* 1.11), "In a certain sense the history of autobiography is a history of human self-awareness" (*menschlichen Selbstbewusstseins*).

[8]Pierre Courcelle, *Les confessions de saint Augustin dans la tradition littéraire* (Paris 1963) esp. 272–75.

[9]My own views on Guibert appear in the introduction to *Self and Society in Medieval France: The Memoirs of Abbot Guibert of Nogent (1064?–c. 1125)* (New York 1970); a slightly different version appears in "The Personality of Guibert of Nogent," *Psychoanalytic Review* 57 (1971) 563–86. See also Frederic Amory, "The Confessional Superstructure of Guibert of Nogent's *Vita*," *Classica et Mediaevalia* 25 (1964) 224–40. The most recent edition of the Latin text is *Guibert de Nogent, Histoire de sa vie (1053–1124)*, ed. Georges Bourgin, CTSEEH 40 (Paris 1907).

[10]For a general survey with bibliography see Giles Constable, *Letters and Letter-Collections*, Typologie des sources du moyen âge occidental 17 (Turnhout 1976). Excellent studies of the collected letters of two major authors are the introduction to *The Letters of Peter the Venerable*, ed. Giles Constable, Harvard Historical Studies 78 (2 vols. Cambridge Mass. 1967) and Jean Leclercq, "Lettres de S. Bernard: Histoire ou littérature?" *Studi medievali* 3rd ser. 12 (1971) 1–74.

[11]On Guy's *apologia*, of which only extracts have been edited, see Wilhelm Wattenbach, "Die Apologie des Guido von Bazoches," SB Berlin (1893) 395–420. Guy's letters have recently

history of his calamities, appears as a letter, overtly of consolation but more accurately of self-criticism and justification. Whether this "letter" was actually
sent to an anonymous friend or was composed as the introduction to a unified
literary composition, and whether any portion of the work was reworked by
another hand, are questions not yet resolved.[12] What is clear is that Abelard
did set down for posterity his own errors (or at least some of them), his shame
and his glory, as well as recounting the envy and hostility of his critics, the only
explanation for opposition he and many other medieval authors were willing
to admit. Part of Abelard's genius lies in his literary skill and ability to record
evocative detail, part in his awesome sense of the importance of his own feelings and position. But while Abelard's autobiography stands out as an unparalleled masterpiece, it is also important to remember that in their letters
many of his contemporaries matched or even exceeded his capacity for self-
examination.

History provided a medium for other autobiographical writers, such as
Gerald of Wales, who in his third-person account of his exploits revealed much
of his fiery and tempestuous personality.[13] Such distancing or reification of the
self, writing as if one were one's own biographer rather than autobiographer,
was not used to obtain greater objectivity of analysis, but rather made the
author appear as an actor in his own account. The *Commentaries* of Pius II are
no more personal than the *Commentaries* of Julius Caesar, and the histories of
Villehardouin and Joinville tell us little of the authors' subjective awareness of
their historical roles. Margery Kempe regularly referred to herself as "this
creature," and in all the torrent of words this fifteenth-century woman released upon her harassed secretaries, she never revealed even the nature of the
secret sin which she could not confess and which drove her out of her mind.[14]
Any reader who expects the frankness of a Rétif de la Bretonne from medieval
authors will be sorely disappointed, for a great leap in subjectivity separates
medieval Europe from the eighteenth century.[15]

been edited by Herbert Adolfsson, *Liber epistularum Guidonis de Basochis*, Studia latina Stockholmiensia 18 (Stockholm 1969). On the largely unpublished *Otium ad Helvidem* of Hugh Farsit
in MS Troyes, Bibl. mun. 433, fols. 49–106v, see André Vernet, "'Loisirs' d'un chanoine de
Soissons," *Bulletin de la Société nationale des Antiquaires de France* (année 1959) 108–11.

[12]Since publishing "Fraud, 'Fiction, and Borrowing in the Correspondence of Abelard and
Héloise" in *Pierre–Pierre* 469–511, I am much more willing to accept the view that the *Historia
calamitatum* and the other letters in the correspondence attributed to Abelard are indeed his own
compositions. My reasons for this change appear in "A Reconsideration of the Authenticity of the
Correspondence of Abelard and Heloise," *Petrus Abaelardus: Person, Werk und Wirkung*, ed.
Rudolf Thomas, Trierer Theologische Studien 38 (Trier 1980).

[13]Passages from a number of works in which Gerald wrote about himself, notably *De rebus a
se gestis*, have been edited and translated by Harold E. Butler, *The Autobiography of Giraldus
Cambrensis* (London 1937).

[14]*The Book of Margery Kempe* c.1, ed. Sanford Brown Meech, EETS 212 (London 1940);
modern version by William Butler-Bowdon (New York 1944); cf. Louise Collis, *Memoirs of a
Medieval Woman: The Life and Times of Margery of Kempe* (New York 1964).

[15]In *The Value of the Individual: Self and Circumstance in Autobiography* (Chicago and London 1978), Karl Joachim Weintraub states, correctly, I believe, "The full convergence of all the

Dreams are today such a powerful tool for analysis of the self that the modern reader might expect medieval dream reports to be closely tied to autobiography or self-examination. On the whole, they are nothing of the kind. Guibert reports frankly on a few of his dreams or visions, as did Gilbert of Sempringham and Rupert of Deutz. The eleventh-century monk Othloh of St Emmeram relates some in his *Book of Visions*, but in the *Book on the Temptations of a Certain Monk*, Othloh can never bring himself to record the specific content of the vivid, erotic dreams which tormented him from early childhood and made him wish an angel would pluck "from his viscera the fiery tumor" that was inciting his flesh.[16] Most dreams or visions were recorded by others, as Orderic Vitalis reported the vision of the priest Walchelin, who on the night of 1 January 1091 was terrified by a hellish troop of the dead, including women riding on saddles covered with red-hot nails as a punishment for their mortal "obscene delights and seductions" and his own brother with fiery spurs to which he had been condemned because of his eagerness to shed blood in battle.[17] Hundreds of reports of such experiences are extant, providing fascinating, if difficult, material for the psychohistorian. But though dreams may be used to examine the inner life of the dreamer, in the Middle Ages they were normally considered not psychologically creative but imposed experiences, originating from such causes as poor digestion, carnal prompting, irritating anxiety, or demonic or other external influences.[18]

Dreams or visions, sometimes troublesome or indeed terrifying, could also be accepted positively as divine inspirations, as they were for abbess Hildegard of Bingen. Hildegard was an effective administrator as well as an intelligent student of science, a talented poet, and a devout contemplative, though from childhood until her death at 82 she suffered from repeated and protracted illness which has been described as "a functional nervous disorder" or "hystero-

---

factors constituting this modern view of the self [i.e., the emergence of individuality as a self-conscious concern] occurred only at the end of the eighteenth century" (xv). The viewpoint of his survey of autobiographical literature from Augustine to Goethe differs significantly from mine, primarily because his major concern is individuality, not self-awareness. As he says on p. xiv, "St. Augustine produced in the *Confessions* an autobiographical form and a view of the self (though not of individuality) of extraordinary power for the subsequent story."

[16]Othloh, *Liber de tentatione cuiusdam monachi*, PL 146.47C, and *Liber visionum*, ibid. 343–88. The religious rather than the psychological aspects of his life are stressed by Helga Schauwecker, *Otloh von St. Emmeram*, Studien und Mitteilungen zur Geschichte des Benediktiner-Ordens und seiner Zweige 74 (Munich 1964).

[17]Orderic Vitalis, *Ecclesiastical History* 8.17, ed. and trans. Marjorie Chibnall (6 vols. Oxford 1969–81) 4.236–50; cf. xxxviii–xl.

[18]Paul Gerhard Schmidt provides a recent bibliography concerning medieval visions in his edition of the *Visio Thurkilli* (Leipzig 1978) xi–xiv; see also Carolly Erickson, *The Medieval Vision: Essays in History and Perception* (New York 1976). Ellen Karnofsky Petrie is now preparing a *catalogue raisonné* of dreams and visions from the period 1050–1150. In his classification of dreams, in the immensely influential *Commentarii in Somnium Scipionis* 1.3.1–8, ed. James A. Willis (2nd ed. Leipzig 1970) 8–10, Macrobius is interested only in oracles or visions, because they allow one to deal with or foresee future events; dreams which arise *ex habitu mentis* are of no concern because they have "no utility or significance."

epilepsy,'' or what today might be diagnosed as temporal lobe epilepsy.[19] Hildegard read widely in the best scientific works available—Hugh of St Victor, Bernard Silvester, the translations by Gerard of Cremona. She incorporated this knowledge and then perceived it in visions which seemed to her more "real" than her own thoughts: "From my infancy . . . I have always seen this light in my spirit and not with external eyes, nor with any thoughts of my heart nor with help from the senses.''[20] Hildegard, who combined with intelligence and a passion for learning a fascination with deterministic systems and a comparative lack of subjective consciousness, understood herself in terms of *in*spiration rather than personal *ex*pression, and is comparable to Joan of Arc, who believed her life was directed by voices today called "hallucinatory.''[21]

Terms like "hystero-epilepsy" or "hallucinatory" may shock when applied to functionally effective people like Hildegard and Joan. They remind the reader that in the application of psychology to history there is an ever-present danger of concentrating only on pathology or imposing modern Western values on another culture. If, as in the Middle Ages, a significant portion of a population sees visions or hears "voices" and is indeed honored for doing so, there is no historical, moral, or psychological value in labeling either the individuals or the society as "sick" or "pathological." Nevertheless, when medical or psychological diagnoses can explain a person's inability to carry out a desired act, or thoughts or behavior which otherwise seem strange, they can be a useful tool for the historian. If Guibert of Nogent's treatise on relics was shaped by an excessive fear of sexual mutilation, if Bernard of Clairvaux suffered from an acute gastritis which interfered with his duties as abbot and may have caused him such pain that when he rode a mule all day along Lake Geneva this unusually observant man did not notice the scenery (a limitation of sight which John Addington Symonds blamed on his monk's cowl, not his physical condition), or if Abelard, after calling for a confrontation at the

---

[19]The quoted diagnosis is that of Charles J. Singer, M.D., "The Visions of Hildegard of Bingen," *From Magic to Science: Essays on the Scientific Twilight* (New York and London 1928) 199–239. Much research on temporal lobe epilepsy, which produces visual hallucinations of structured images, has been done since the time of Singer's essay.

[20]PL 197.18B, quoted by Singer (n. 19 above) 233–34 in his section on "The Pathological Basis of the Visions."

[21]The highly structured, geometric forms revealed to Hildegard suggest the value of comparison with similar figures produced by visionary mystics like Joachim of Fiore (see Marjorie Reeves and Beatrice Hirsch-Reich, *The Figurae of Joachim of Fiore* [Oxford 1972]) and Ramón Lull (see Frances A. Yates, "The Art of Ramon Lull: An Approach to it through Lull's *Theory of the Elements*," JWCI 17 [1954] 115–73), or a "certified" hysterical neurotic like Opicinus de Canistris (see Richard Salomon, *Opicinus de Canistris*, Studies of the Warburg Institute 1A and 1B [1 vol. + atlas London 1936] and Ernst Kris, *Psychoanalytic Explorations in Art* [New York 1952] 118–27). Joan of Arc is mentioned here, not because her well-documented accounts of her voices are particularly unusual, but because she is the only medieval individual named by Jaynes (n. 5 above, 74, 79), who suggests an explanation for those voices as right-hemispheric messages perceived (or "heard") by the left side of the brain.

Council of Sens, failed to defend himself because of either acute depression or Hodgkin's disease, then the accurate diagnosis and understanding of either physiologic or psychogenic conditions can enrich history without turning it into a form of anachronistic autopsy.[22]

BIOGRAPHY

An egocentric logic suggests that greater awareness of the self precedes and permits greater awareness of the individuality, the special characteristics, and indeed the motives of others. Possibly, however, the process works in the opposite direction, or is more likely reciprocal, for greater understanding and more acute observation of others may permit by comparison deeper understanding of the subjective self. Despite the example of Augustine, clearer delineation of individuality appears in twelfth-century biography than autobiography. The limitations of biography in the Carolingian renaissance are demonstrated by the most notable attempt of that period, the *Life of Charlemagne*, in which Einhard follows Suetonius both in what he feels free to record and in his very choice of words.[23] Einhard's sparkling image of Charlemagne is like a mosaic created by rearrangement from tesserae taken from the work of another author, comparable to a *cento* on Christ restricted to phrases from Vergil. The saints' lives of the earlier period—formulaic, didactic, and inspirational—reveal even less of "personality." By contrast, in the renaissance of the twelfth century we see a multicolored flowering of biography. Eadmer's *Life of St Anselm*, "the first intimate portrait of a saint in our history," tells us much more of Anselm than Einhard ever conceived of writing about Charlemagne, and in the process tells us much of the author himself.[24]

One could continue for pages with the great biographies, some but not all of saints: the *Life of Aelred of Rievaulx* by Walter Daniel, the *Chronicle* of Jocelin of Brakelond, which records the life of his abbot Samson of Bury St Edmunds, the *Magna Vita* of St Hugh of Lincoln by Adam of Eynsham, to name

---

[22]On Guibert, see Benton, *Self and Society* (n. 9 above) introduction, esp. 29–30; a psychological problem which troubled Guibert consciously was his inability to speak out in the face of opposition (20). Elphège Vacandard, *Vie de Saint Bernard, abbé de Clairvaux* (4th ed. 2 vols. Paris 1910) 1.76–79 and 232–35 deals with Bernard's illness. The story of the ride along Lake Geneva is told by Alan of Auxerre in the *Vita secunda* c. 16 and is (mis)used by Symonds at the beginning of his *Renaissance in Italy* (3rd ed. 5 vols. in 7 London 1926–29). On Abelard at the Council of Sens see Jean Jeannin, M.D., "La dernière maladie d'Abélard: Une alliée imprévue de Saint Bernard," *Mélanges Saint Bernard*, XXIVe Congrès de l'Association bourguignonne des sociétés savantes (Dijon 1954) 109–14.

[23]Louis Halphen, *Etudes critiques sur l'histoire de Charlemagne* (Paris 1921) 91–95. In the twelfth century, William of Malmesbury avoided the annalistic style by following the structure of Suetonius, but he clearly felt much freer to digress than Einhard had; see Marie Schütt, "The Literary Form of William of Malmesbury's 'Gesta Regum,'" EHR 46 (1931) 255–60.

[24]*The Life of St. Anselm, Archbishop of Canterbury, by Eadmer*, ed. and trans. Richard W. Southern (London 1962) vii. Southern discusses "intimate biography," in contrast to other forms of biography, in *Saint Anselm and His Biographer: A Study of Monastic Life and Thought 1059–c. 1130* (Cambridge 1963) 320–36.

only a few.[25] These books are so untraditional, so personal, that we can even see the individual proclivities of their authors. Jocelin, for example, is humorous and enamored with words: he notes Samson's reputation as a "disputer," praises the abbot's eloquence in Latin, French, and the dialect of Norfolk, himself fakes a Scottish accent as a disguise in Italy, or repeats with bemusement a weak pun on the name of the Muses.[26] Adam, on the other hand, is both more pious and more visually oriented, achieving his best effects through images of actions, showing us Henry II at Woodstock angrily sewing a bandage on his finger in silence "instead of doing nothing" and then, pierced by a daring jest, lying on the ground dissolved in laughter; or an infant, entranced by bishop Hugh, chuckling with delight and stretching out his arms as if to fly. Adam also reveals his own attitude toward "personality" as he explains the baby's pleasure: "What could the infant have seen in the bishop which gave it so much delight, unless it were God in him?"[27]

Both abbot Samson and bishop Hugh were outstanding individuals, but perhaps the most interesting new departure in biography comes in the lives of rather ordinary men who happened to be saintly. Stephen, first abbot of Obazine in the region of Limoges, sprang from a family of modest means and had only a rudimentary education. The verbose author of his *Vita* meets the obligatory hagiographic requirements by telling us of his virtues and miracles, but the anecdotes he reports build up a realistic portrait of a man who laughed vindictively when fire broke out in a house of canons who had turned him away, wandered about the cloister picking up scattered vegetables, could terrify two playful bakers with a cough, punished breaches of discipline severely, was also quick to extend the consoling arm of charity, and criticized "indecent" spitting and showing one's teeth while laughing. Religious zeal and piety aside, Stephen must have been like a great many other rough, emotional, and authoritarian leaders of his day. His biographer showed the everyday side of a man he considered a saint.[28]

---

[25]As an indication of merit and for the convenience of readers of English I have limited these examples to volumes edited and translated in the Nelson-Oxford Medieval Texts, except for *The Life of Christina of Markyate, a Twelfth-Century Recluse*, ed. and trans. Charles H. Talbot (Oxford 1959).

[26]*The Chronicle of Jocelin of Brakelond, concerning the Acts of Samson, Abbot of the Monastery of St. Edmund*, ed. and trans. Harold E. Butler (London 1949) 34, 40, 48, 130; in the final example, to decline *musa, musae* was commonplace, for it was a paradigm in the *Ars minor* of Donatus.

[27]*The Life of St. Hugh of Lincoln* 3.10, 14, ed. and trans. Decima L. Douie and Hugh Farmer (2 vols. Edinburgh 1961–62) 1.117, 130. Discussing contrasts between guilt and shame, Herbert Morris, *On Guilt and Innocence: Essays in Legal Philosophy and Moral Psychology* (Berkeley 1976) 62 states that "shame connects with sight and guilt with hearing." Although this suggested contrast has a certain *a priori* plausibility, it is not supported by the two authors cited here, for the more visual Adam seems to be more concerned with guilt than the verbal Jocelin.

[28]*Vie de saint Étienne d'Obazine* 1.25, 2.11, 53–55, 59, ed. and trans. Michel Aubrun, Publications de l'Institut d'études du Massif Central 6 (Clermont-Ferrand 1970) 80, 110–12, 178–86. For comparable details, see "Le texte complet de la Vie de Chrétien de l'Aumône," ed. Jean Leclercq, *Analecta Bollandiana* 71 (1953) 21–52. For a discussion of "ordinary" characteristics in the

GUILT, SHAME, AND INTENTION

The profundity of spiritual meditations like those of Guigo or Bernard of Clairvaux, the confessional nature of the most revealing autobiography, and the religious function of so much biography lead us to examine with special attention the spiritual climate which nourished these works, particularly by a growing and institutionalized concern with confession and penance.[29] In the setting of examination of conscience, either by private meditation or with the aid of a confessor or spiritual director, we find our clearest evidence of the twelfth-century Church's contribution to the nurturing and propagation of introspection. The term "introspection" as used here does not mean exactly the same thing as "self-awareness," for a person may ruminate compulsively on a thought or fault without learning anything from the experience. For Freud and his followers, guilt is one of the greatest inhibitors of self-awareness, but in the march toward an increased understanding of the subjective self, guilt may be a necessary stage, either culturally or individually. A person who obeys the directions of authoritative internal voices may not feel guilt, nor does one whose actions are determined solely by the shame or honor bestowed by his peers. Examination of conscience and reflection on one's own faults, fostered by both the immediate family and the Church, must have helped to cause the apparent shift which changed medieval Europe from a "shame culture" to a "guilt culture," to use the terms once favored by anthropologists, or more precisely, from a shame-dominated culture to one in which guilt played a rapidly increasing role.[30]

The concepts of "shame" and "guilt" cultures conveniently and attractively summarize many of the differences observable between earlier and later medieval society, and yet there is a danger in their uncritical use, for human societies are not homogeneous and individuals are motivated by both shame and guilt. The aristocratic audience of the *Song of Roland* enjoyed that great

lives of twelfth-century saints, see Chrysogonus Waddell, "La simplicité de l'ordinaire: Note dominante de la première hagiographie cistercienne," *Collectanea Cisterciensia* 41 (1979) 3–28.

[29] On the larger subject, see Paul Anciaux, *La théologie du sacrement de pénitence au XIIe siècle* (Louvain 1949) and Jean-Charles Payen, *Le motif du repentir dans la littérature française médiévale (des origines à 1230)*, Publications romanes et françaises 98 (Geneva 1967). A short guide to the new confessional literature which became popular in the later twelfth century is Pierre Michaud-Quantin, *Sommes de casuistique et manuels de confession au moyen âge (XII–XVI siècles)*, Analecta mediaevalia Namurcensia 13 (Louvain 1962). John W. Baldwin shows how these ethical concepts were actually applied in his *Masters*.

[30] The concepts were popularized by Ruth F. Benedict, *The Chrysanthemum and the Sword* (Boston 1946) and have since been subjected to severe criticism, e.g. Gerhart Piers and Milton B. Singer, *Shame and Guilt: A Psychoanalytic and a Cultural Study* (Springfield Ill. 1953; repr. New York 1971). For a sensitive assessment of the strengths and weaknesses of Benedict's theories by a Japanese psychiatrist see Takeo Doi, *The Anatomy of Dependence*, trans. John Bester (Tokyo 1973, New York 1977) 48–57. For a recent application to medieval literature see Josef Szövérffy, "'Artuswelt' und 'Gralwelt': Shame Culture and Guilt Culture in 'Parzival,'" in his *Germanistische Abhandlungen: Mittelalter, Barock und Aufklärung*, Medieval Classics: Texts and Studies 8 (Brookline Mass. and Leiden 1977) 33–46 (= *Paradosis: Studies in Memory of Edwin A. Quain* [New York 1976] 85–96).

epic at the same time that Guigo wrote his meditations and Guibert confessed his sins to God.[31] How many medieval authors, including churchmen, ascribe their misfortunes, not to their own weaknesses, but to the envy of their rivals, to the jealousy of *losengiers*! Honor continues today to challenge moral virtue as a major determinant of human behavior.[32] Nevertheless, in the twelfth century, guilt and its expiation became increasingly dominant themes, and the values and judgments of European society were never again to be as simple as they had been in the shame-conditioned world of Gregory of Tours.

For us, the determination of guilt is closely tied to the concept of intention. Intention was a matter of legal and moral concern to jurists of the late Roman Empire and some Fathers of the Church, but when Germanic culture became dominant, the importance of intention was significantly reduced. In Anglo-Saxon law, a principle of simple behavior modification prevailed: "He who sins unknowingly shall pay for it knowingly."[33] The assessment of early medieval wergeld had been based on both the gravity of the offense and the rank of the injured party. A new attitude can be seen forming in the argument made about 1080 by master Pepo, the legendary founder of the school of law at Bologna, that the punishment for homicide should not be determined by the status of the victim, for what was at stake was the value of a human life. But Pepo, though critical of earlier Germanic practice and fascinated by what could be learned from Roman law, did not make an issue of intention, of a *mens rea*.[34] Throughout the early Middle Ages intention was the concern of authors of penitentials, not of law codes and commentaries, and even in the penitentials far more attention was concentrated on sinful actions than on thoughts. With the Gregorian Reform and the great expansion of penitential literature in the twelfth century, which brought an increased emphasis on penance to ever-widening circles of the laity, intention—the choices and

---

[31]On the "shame" cultural content of the *Song of Roland* see George F. Jones, *The Ethos of the Song of Roland* (Baltimore 1963). The conflict of differing values derived from both parents is discussed by Anne Parsons, "Is the Oedipus Complex Universal? The Jones–Malinowski Debate Revisited and a South Italian 'Nuclear Complex,'" *The Psychoanalytic Study of Society* 3 (1964) 278–328.

[32]See Jean G. Péristiany, ed., *Honour and Shame: The Values of Mediterranean Society* (Chicago 1966).

[33]On intention in ancient (particularly Hebrew and Greek) law see David Daube, *Roman Law: Linguistic, Social and Psychological Aspects* (Edinburgh and Chicago 1969) 163–75; on 173–74 Daube discusses a case of unintentional homicide in *Beowulf*. For the precept "qui inscienter peccat, scienter emendet," see *Leges Henrici primi*, ed. and trans. Leslie J. Downer (Oxford 1972) c. 88.6a (p. 270), c. 90.11a (282), and cf. c. 70.12b (222). King Alfred's well-known ordinance (Alf., c. 36) that a man who killed another while carrying his spear in a "safe" manner over his shoulder owed payment to the victim's family but could purge himself of *wite* owed to the king seems more to be an assessment of a degree of criminal negligence than a judgment of innocence by virtue of an absence of criminal intent. Moreover, Alfred's distinction is most significant because exceptional.

[34]Ludwig Schmugge, "'Codicis Iustiniani et Institutionum baiulus'—Eine neue Quelle zu Magister Pepo von Bologna," *Ius commune* 6 (1977) 1–9, esp. 6. Francis B. Sayre, "Mens Rea," *Harvard Law Review* 45 (1932) 974–1026 at 981 concludes that "up to the twelfth century the conception of *mens rea* in anything like its modern sense was nonexistent."

desires of the conscious self independent of specific actions—again became a central issue.[35]

The way in which one twelfth-century man weighed the ancient literature on intention is laid bare in the dialectical presentation of Gratian's *Concordance of Discordant Canons*, significantly, in the "Treatise on Penance" (= C.33 q. 3). Here the old, conflicting authorities are mustered and called forth, on the one hand "A vow is treated as a deed," on the other the *Digest*'s "No one shall suffer punishment for a thought." Midway through his discussion, Gratian states as a provisional conclusion, "It appears clearer than light that sins are remitted not by oral confession but by inner contrition." But such an emphasis on an inner state of mind, revealed only to the subjective self and the deity who knows "the hearts and reins of men," could also be opposed on both practical and theoretical grounds. In the end Gratian left the question of the necessity of oral confession to his readers' judgment, "for both sides are supported by wise and pious men." Within a few years Peter Lombard used many of the same authorities to reach the conclusion that confession to God alone is not sufficient if it is possible to make oral confession to a man, preferably a priest. By the early thirteenth century the role of the priest as confessor was settled and a new style of *Liber penitentialis*, such as that of Robert of Flamborough, specified how penance should be weighted according to the individual characteristics of the penitent.[36]

Gratian's initial emphasis on inner contrition and the primacy of intention accorded with a powerful current of thought in his age. For twelfth-

[35]Charles M. Radding, "Evolution of Medieval Mentalities: A Cognitive-Structural Approach," *American Historical Review* 83 (1978) 577–97 makes stimulating use of modern theories of the stages of moral development in children, as studied by Jean Piaget, Lawrence Kohlberg, Elliot Turiel, and others, but seems to me to underestimate the concern with intention exhibited in early medieval law. Impressed by the fact that penitentials commonly quoted or paraphrased earlier authorities, he also places less emphasis on the importance of penitential literature than I am inclined to do. In contrast, I believe that the availability of patristic and other "authorities" dealing with intention and examination of conscience meant that, unlike children, twelfth-century Europeans did not have to create a *new*, previously unexperienced moral stage, but instead renewed or increased a concern with interiority already known in late Antiquity. Thomas Pollock Oakley's still useful *English Penitential Discipline and Anglo-Saxon Law in their Joint Influence*, Columbia University Studies in History, Economics, and Public Law 107.2 (New York 1923) concludes (200) with an approving quotation from Henry Charles Lea, *A History of Auricular Confession and Indulgences in the Latin Church* (3 vols. Philadelphia 1896) 2.107: "It was no small matter that the uncultured barbarian should be taught that evil thoughts and desires were punishable as well as evil acts."

[36]The citations from Gratian are *De pen.* D.1 c.5 ("Augustine"); c.14 (= *Dig.* 48.19.18); dict. p. cc.30, 89 (Gratian); *Corpus iuris canonici*, ed. Emil A. Friedberg (2 vols. Leipzig 1879–81) 1.1159, 1161, 1165, 1189. Although Gratian wrongly attributes to Augustine "Votum enim pro opere reputatur," the statement is a fair summary of much patristic thought; it is a paraphrase of Cassiodorus, *Expositio psalmorum* 31.5, PL 70.220 or ed. M. Adriaen, CCL 97 (1958) 278. For Peter Lombard see *Sentences*, 4.17.1–4, PL 192.880–82 or ed. Ignatius Brady, Spicilegium Bonaventurianum 4 (2 vols. Grottaferrata 1971–81) 2.342–55. On Gratian, Lombard, and Robert of Flamborough see Anciaux (n. 29 above) 122–26, 196–208, 223–31. Robert of Flamborough's *Liber poenitentialis* has been edited by J.J. Francis Firth, Pontifical Institute of Mediaeval Studies, Studies and Texts 18 (Toronto 1971).

century scholars concerned with either classical or patristic authors, determining the intention of the writer became a powerful tool of literary analysis.[37] In the realm of moral philosophy, conscience and intention were topics of intense debate at Laon and Paris, and the subject found its most daring exposition in Abelard's *Ethics*, called in the manuscripts *Know Thyself*. Abelard went too far, as he often did, and carried an idea of Anselm of Bec beyond the pale in arguing that the crucifiers of Christ were innocent of unjust action (*culpa*), for they knew not what they did.[38] Were Abelard's extreme conclusions the product of his relentless logic alone? We may well ask, for an anonymous twelfth-century poem states that Heloise was innocent of crime, since she did not "consent."[39] We are reminded here of the growing canonistic agreement that consent rather than coitus makes a marriage.[40] Abelard never mentions Heloise in his *Ethics*, but we would see him at his most human if we could think that his doctrine of intention, which earned him an article of condemnation at the Council of Sens, was an extended defense of the innocence of his beloved wife before man and before God. Few Christians could excuse the killers of Christ, but the anonymous poet absolved Heloise on the basis of her intention rather than her actions.

MODES OF INDIVIDUALIZATION

PORTRAITURE

In the visual arts, a similar decline and then reemergence of interest in the individual are apparent, though on the whole artists lagged behind authors in the renewed concern with personal representation. Individualized portraiture had been widespread in Antiquity, in the busts of the Greek philosophers and rulers, the widely disseminated statues of the Roman imperial family, the haunting painted faces of quite common people found on the mummies of Fayum.[41] But as individualization receded from biography with the Germanic

[37]Bernard of Utrecht, writing at the end of the eleventh century, is the earliest author of an *accessus* known to have replaced the seven formal questions mandated by Priscian (*quis, quid, ubi*, etc.) with three new questions, of which one was the intention of the writer; see Conrad of Hirsau, *Dialogus super auctores*, ed. R. B. C. Huygens, Collection Latomus 17 (Brussels 1955) 11. On the treatment of *intentio* by such commentators as Abelard, Honorius Augustodunensis, Gerhoch of Reichersberg, and others, see the study in this volume by Nikolaus M. Häring, 185–87, 196–97.

[38]*Peter Abelard's Ethics*, ed. and trans. David E. Luscombe (Oxford 1971) 56–67 and notes; see also xxxv–xxxvi. On canonistic discussion of Abelard's problem see Stephan Kuttner, *Kanonistische Schuldlehre von Gratian bis auf die Dekretalen Gregors IX.*, Studi e testi 64 (Vatican City 1935) 137–40.

[39]MS Orléans, Bibl. mun. 284 (*olim* 238), p. 183: "Sola tamen Petri coniunx est criminis expers, / Consensus nullus quam facit esse ream." The poem is partially edited and translated with commentary by Peter Dronke, *Abelard and Heloise in Mediaeval Testimonies*, W. P. Ker Memorial Lecture 26 (Glasgow 1976) esp. 45–46.

[40]See Rudolf Weigand, *Die bedingte Eheschliessung im kanonischen Recht* (Munich 1963) 47–58; Piero Rasi, *Consensus facit nuptias* (Milan 1946); and Michael M. Sheehan, "Choice of Marriage Partner in the Middle Ages: Development and Mode of Application of a Theory of Marriage," *Studies in Medieval and Renaissance History* n.s. 1 (1978) 1–33.

[41]I am aware that many of the Egyptian mummy "portraits," particularly from the third century A.D. and beyond, are not actual portraits, but there are some which seem to have been

invasions, so it was also reduced to a modicum in art. Even the exquisite Carolingian statue of a mounted emperor now in the Louvre cannot be identified with certainty as Charlemagne, so unsure are we of the physical appearance of this preeminent man.[42] In the elongated Romanesque statues of the west façade of Chartres, one king of Israel looks like the next. How radical is the change in style in the differentiated faces of Reims, carved in the early thirteenth century! Here again is a "renaissance" phenomenon, for it is hard to treat as coincidental the resemblance of St Peter at Reims to the official imperial bust of Antoninus Pius.[43] In the visual arts this fascination with individualization becomes evident late in the twelfth century and rushes forward through the thirteenth century, through the awesomely mimetic statues of the long-dead male founders of the cathedral of Naumburg,[44] to the tomb statue of Rudolf of Habsburg at Speyer, carved during his lifetime, whose sculptor was said to have hastened to alter his work after he had noticed a new line in the king's face.[45] But such funerary effigies made from living subjects, which indicate a desire to remember the dead as they actually were, appear only at the end of the thirteenth century.[46]

Change toward individualization was not only slow in the twelfth century, as compared to the thirteenth, but it was also uneven in the work of an individual artist. Just as an early medieval artist could use a late antique style to represent angels and a "Byzantine" style for other figures,[47] so in the later twelfth century Herrad of Landsberg, abbess of Hohenbourg (or her illustrator), drew the faces of the damned at the Last Judgment with more differentiation than she gave to familiar people, herself included. In the "group

---

painted from life. See David L. Thompson, *The Artists of the Mummy Portraits* (Malibu Calif. 1976) 12. On antique portraiture in general see James D. Breckenridge, *Likeness: A Conceptual History of Ancient Portraiture* (Evanston Ill. 1968).

[42]Percy Ernst Schramm, "Karl der Grosse im Lichte seiner Siegel und Bullen sowie der Bild- und Wortzeugnisse über sein Aussehen," *Karl der Grosse*, ed. Wolfgang Braunfels et al. (5 vols. Düsseldorf 1965-68) 1.15-23, esp. 21; and *Charlemagne: Oeuvre, rayonnement et survivances*, ed. Wolfgang Braunfels (Aachen 1965) 39-40.

[43]On the movement toward naturalism and the classicizing tendencies of art toward the end of the period we are considering there is ample illustration in *The Year 1200*, ed. Konrad Hoffmann and Florens Deuchler, Cloisters Studies in Medieval Art 1-2 (2 vols. New York 1970). On St Peter at Reims see Panofsky, *Ren & Ren* 62-63.

[44]Willibald Sauerländer, "Die Naumburger Stifterfiguren: Rückblick und Fragen," *Die Zeit der Staufer: Geschichte, Kunst, Kultur*, ed. Reiner Haussherr et al., Württembergisches Landesmuseum, Katalog der Ausstellung (5 vols. Stuttgart 1977-79) 5.169-245, citing earlier literature. It is worth noting that the male faces in the choir at Naumburg show greater "individuality" than the three women.

[45]*Ottokars Österreichische Reimchronik*, lines 39,125-59, ed. Joseph Seemüller, MGH Deutsche Chroniken 5.1.508-09, cited with literature in Bruno Gebhardt, *Handbuch der deutschen Geschichte*, 9th ed. by Herbert Grundmann (4 vols. in 5 Stuttgart 1970-76) 1.490-91.

[46]It is curious that the tomb of Rudolf of Habsburg is, as far as I know, the earliest for which there is direct, independent evidence of funerary sculpture made from life, since death masks were made at the beginning of the period we are considering; for the death mask of Hildegard of Büren (d. 1094), now in the Musée de l'Oeuvre Notre-Dame at Strasbourg, see *Die Zeit der Staufer* (n. 44 above) 1.270 no. 385 and 3.344.

[47]For example, contrast the "classical" style of the attendant angels with the "Byzantine" style of the Virgin and Child at Santa Maria in Trastevere at Rome, illustrated in this volume, fig. 36.

portrait'' of her convent (fig. 8), Herrad represented herself at full length, but her face is similar to the faces of sixty equally similar nuns who stare away from her. Except for two nameless nuns who bracket the congregation like parentheses, each of these women has her name written above her head, her only identifying distinction. Herrad could address her flock as individuals, but she did not choose to portray them as such.[48] Nevertheless, the beginning of medieval "portraiture" appeared in a few isolated instances in the twelfth-century renaissance.

The most famous artistic representation of an individual made in the twelfth century is the gilded bronze head, probably created in the 1160s, which Frederick Barbarossa presented to his godfather, count Otto of Cappenberg. The artist made use of symbolic and unrealistic conventions, but his representation of the emperor accords with the cut of the hair described by Rahewin, and there is no reason to doubt that his contemporaries could recognize his work as a likeness of Frederick. The significance of the Cappenberg head is twofold, or indeed double-edged. It exists, and therefore shows that in the classicizing environment of Frederick's court the antique tradition of imperial portraiture could be revived, providing an example of true *renovatio*. On the other hand, the uniqueness of the head, and our consequent inability to compare it with other "portraits" of even such a prominent figure as Frederick I, emphasize the comparative rarity of naturalistic likeness in twelfth-century art.[49]

To attribute the scarcity of portraiture to the incompetence of artists would be improper, for eleventh- and twelfth-century artists knew perfectly well how to depict recognizable individuals. The proof of this statement is to be found in the representation of certain prominent saints. The convention that St Peter had a short, rounded, curly beard and the balding St Paul a

---

[48]Herrad of Landsberg, abbess of Hohenbourg, *Hortus deliciarum*, ed. Rosalie Green et al., Studies of the Warburg Institute 36 (2 vols. London and Leiden 1979) 2.505 (= fol. 323r of destroyed MS). This plate reproduces a hand-colored copy of Christian Moritz Engelhardt, *Herrad von Landsperg, Aebtissin zu Hohenburg, oder St. Odilien, im Elsasz, im zwölften Jahrhundert; und ihr Werk: Hortus deliciarum* (Stuttgart 1818) plate 12. This same plate was reproduced in the partial edition of the *Hortus* by Alexandre Straub and Gustave Keller (Strasbourg 1901) plate 80, and its English reproduction by Aristide D. Caratzas (New Rochelle N.Y. 1977), the source of the reproduction given here as fig. 8. The fidelity of the Engelhardt plate is attested by the tracing in Paris, BN, Cabinet des Estampes, Coll. Bastard, Ad 144a folio, fol. 323r p. 122 (kindly located for me by Prof. James Greenlee), reproduced by Green, 1 no. 334. For the damned at the Last Judgment see 2.434 (= fol. 253v). On fol. 38r–v the faces of Pharaoh and King David are practically identical. In his introduction Canon Keller remarks (p. vi) that "les physionomies en général se rassemblent et n'ont pas de caractère individuel." The colored reproduction reveals, nevertheless, that in the painted original the variety of colors somewhat mitigated the similarity of the drawing of the faces in the "group portrait."

[49]On this uncommon effigy see Herbert Grundmann, *Der Cappenberger Barbarossakopf und die Anfänge des Stiftes Cappenberg* (Cologne 1959) and Horst Appuhn, "Beobachtungen und Versuche zum Bildnis Kaiser Friedrichs I. Barbarossa in Cappenberg," *Aachener Kunstblätter* 44 (1973) 129–92 (with bibliography), and Willibald Sauerländer's essay in this volume, at n. 76; the head is reproduced as fig. 73. For Rahewin's description see n. 52 below.

longer, pointed beard, to pick the most common example, was established in early Christian art and never disappeared (fig. 9).[50] The two saints who crown Otto III in the early eleventh-century Bamberg Apocalypse (fig. 10) have precisely the same faces as the images of Peter and Paul which unchangingly represent the papacy on the bulls of Pascal II and all his medieval successors (fig. 11).[51] In short, artists *could* produce "portraits" as instantly recognizable as those of a modern cartoonist when they saw a reason to do so, and their preference for the conventional and symbolic representation of living individuals was a matter of choice. In the twelfth century, historians and other authors frequently described individuals in a detailed, personal, and naturalistic fashion, and though these verbal portraits were heavily influenced by literary sources and sometimes by flattery, they were probably reasonably accurate.[52] That artists of the same period so rarely showed the same concern with individualized depiction of their subjects is apparently due to differences between the traditions and functions of the two forms of expression.

NAMES

Interest in the presentation of character is an outstanding development in twelfth-century imaginative literature.[53] Even a name, a simple phonemic expression, can evoke an individual human being, a specific character. In

[50]The medallions illustrated in fig. 9 are from a late fifth-century mosaic in the archiepiscopal chapel at Ravenna, but a wealth of other early representations could have been used, such as the sixth-century Syrian silver vase found at Emesa (now in the Louvre) or the sixth-century ivory diptych from Constantinople (now in the Staatliches Museum in Berlin), both illustrated in *Age of Spirituality: Late Antique and Early Christian Art, Third to Seventh Century*, ed. Kurt Weitzmann (New York 1979) 528–30 no. 474 and 615–17 no. 552.

[51]On the Bamberg Apocalypse see Heinrich Wölfflin, *Die Bamberger Apokalypse: Eine Reichenauer Bilderhandschrift vom Jahre 1000* (Munich 1918). The bulls illustrated in fig. 11 are of popes Pascal II and Innocent III, but the choice is inconsequential, for the representations of Peter and Paul remained practically static from Pascal II (1099–1118) to Pius II (1458–64); see Camillo Serafini, *Le monete e le bolle plumbee pontificie del Medagliere vaticano* (4 vols. Milan 1910; repr. Bologna 1965) 1.25 and 125 and plates H and M.

[52]Most of Rahewin's "portrait" of Frederick I is drawn from the descriptions by Sidonius Apollinaris of Theodoric II, by Einhard of Charlemagne, and by Jordanes of Attila the Hun, with a few words of his own on Frederick's hair; see GF 4.86 (342–44). Far more realistic and concerned with character is Peter of Blois, writing of Henry II, see *Epist.* 66, PL 207.195–210 and the curious dramatic dialogue between the king and the abbot of Bonneval, ibid. 975–88. Erich Kleinschmidt has gathered material on the conventions of the *descriptio personarum* and its application to rulers in *Herrscherdarstellung: Zur Disposition mittelalterlichen Aussageverhaltens, untersucht an Texten über Rudolf I. von Habsburg*, Bibliotheca Germanica 17 (Bern 1974) 11–90. For the highly formalized conventions of personal descriptions in literature see Alice M. Colby, *The Portrait in Twelfth-Century French Literature: An Example of the Stylistic Originality of Chrétien de Troyes* (Geneva 1965).

[53]For a treatment which deals with "inner awareness" as well as individuality, see Robert W. Hanning, *The Individual in Twelfth-Century Romance* (New Haven and London 1977). The change from epic to romance, the growth of "poetic individuality," are subjects both too large and too familiar to be treated here. See, for example, the concluding section, "From Epic to Romance," in Richard W. Southern, *The Making of the Middle Ages* (London 1953) 219–57, and Peter Dronke, *Poetic Individuality in the Middle Ages: New Departures in Poetry, 1000–1150* (Oxford 1970).

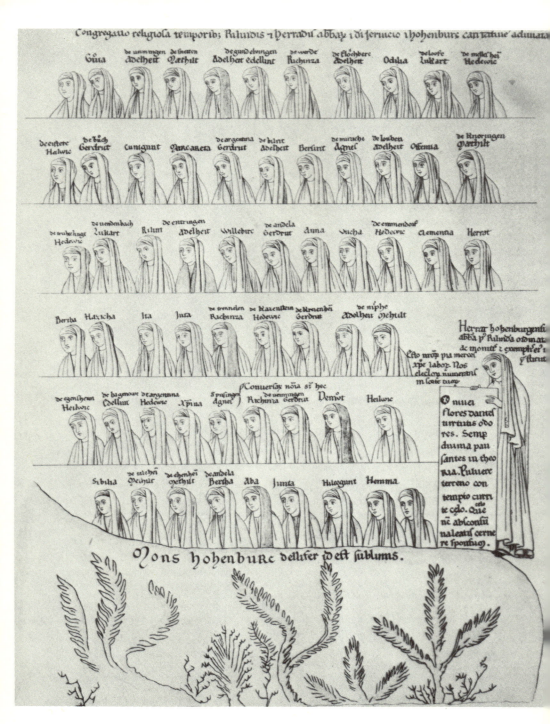

Fig. 8. Strasbourg. Bibliothèque publique. Herrad of Landsberg, *Hortus deliciarum* (late twelfth century), fol. 323r: "group portrait" of the Hohenbourg convent under abbess Herrad. The library and codex were destroyed in the 1870 fire; figure after *Herrad of Landsberg, Hortus deliciarum (Garden of Delights)*, ed. Aristide D. Caratzas (New Rochelle, N.Y. 1976) 323r (= *Hortus deliciarum*, ed. Alexandre Straub and Gustave Keller [Strasbourg 1901] pl. 80). Reproduced courtesy Caratzas Brothers, Publishers, New Rochelle.

Fig. 9. Ravenna. Cappella Arcivescovile. Mosaics (late fifth century): SS Peter and Paul.
Photos: Angelo Longo Editore, Ravenna.

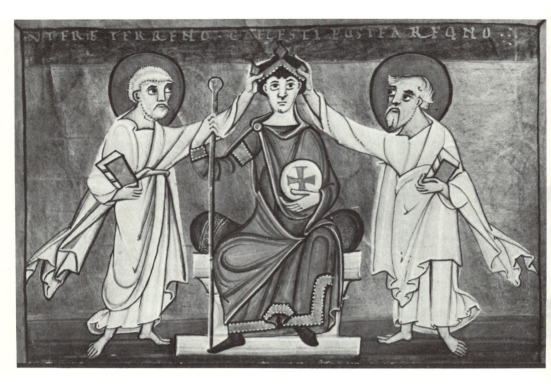

Fig. 10. Bamberg. Staatsbibliothek, MS 140 (early eleventh century). "Bamberg Apocalypse," fol. 59v: the coronation of Otto III. Photo: Staatsbibliothek Bamberg.

Fig. 11. Paris. Archives nationales. Papal bulls: left, Pascal II (1103); right, Innocent III (1200). Photo courtesy of Yves Metman, Archives nationales.

literature a prophetic "baptismal" name, a "Tristan," can easily encapsulate character, but real life is not so simple. At first it seems contradictory that as we move forward from the Dark Ages to the twelfth century, the variety of names given at birth decreases. So much diversity exists in the jumble of tongues we find in Gregory of Tours, the combination and recombination of meaningful syllables in Germanic "leading names," and so little in the baptismal names of the twelfth century, when a banquet in Normandy was limited to knights named Guillaume and 110 men of the same name jammed into the hall.[54] We may be reminded of a similar shift in another culture, when under the conformity-producing influence of Islam the onomastic richness of the early desert Arabs was reduced to the routine Muḥammads and ʿAlīs.[55]

In Western Europe the paradoxical shift proves more apparent than real, for the complex names of Germanic Europe were often created to indicate lineage rather than personal characteristics, as today breeders name horses and dogs. As conformity to a relatively restricted list of the names of saints and recognized heroes became more general, the need for accurate individualization produced added appellations, frequently indicating not family or locale (though these too were part of a "person") but recognizable characteristics. In the 1140s three canons of the cathedral of Troyes named Peter sat in the stalls together; their colleagues distinguished them as Peter the Squinter (*Strabo*), Peter the Drinker (*Bibitor* or *Potator*), and Peter the Eater (*Comestor* or *Manducator*).[56] Burghers and peasants too developed highly distinctive, personalized names through the use of *cognomina* or nicknames, often more personalized than those used by the aristocracy: Lipestan Bittecat, Robert Bontens, Herbert Gidi, Godewin Clawecuncte, and William Mordant, to pick a few of the more colorful from the Winton Domesday.[57] As family names for peasants

[54]For the Norman banquet see the *Chronicle of Robert of Torigni*, in *Chronicles of the Reigns of Stephen, Henry II, and Richard I*, ed. Richard Howlett, RS 82 (4 vols. London 1884–89) 4.253, and James W. Greenlee and John F. Benton, "Montaigne and the 110 Guillaumes: A Note on the Sources," *Romance Notes* 12 (1970) 177–79. On the earlier diversity of names in Gaul alone see Marie-Thérèse Morlet, *Les noms de personne sur le territoire de l'ancienne Gaule du VIe au XIIe siècle* (2 vols. Paris 1968–72). Karl Ferdinand Werner, "Liens de parenté et noms de personne," *Famille et parenté dans l'Occident médiéval*, ed. Georges Duby and Jacques Le Goff, Collection de l'Ecole française de Rome 30 (Rome 1977) 13–34 at 13–18 and 25–34 provides a succinct survey of current literature and research on given names in relation to lineage.

[55]S. D. Goitein, "Individualism and Conformity in Classical Islam," *Individualism and Conformity* (n. 4 above) 3–17 at 6 and 14.

[56]Jacques Laurent, *Cartulaires de l'abbaye de Molesme* (2 vols. in 4 Paris 1907–11) 2.379 no. 334, incorrectly dated 1125 instead of 1145. Unless we assume that Petrus Potator was known for imbibing knowledge, it is hard to believe that the more famous Petrus Comestor received his name because he devoured books.

[57]See Olof von Feilitzen, "The Personal Names and Bynames of the Winton Domesday," *Winchester in the Early Middle Ages: An Edition and Discussion of the Winton Domesday*, ed. Martin Biddle, Winchester Studies 1 (Oxford 1976) 143–229 at 207–17. Feminine bynames rarely appear here or in the Canterbury rentals published by William Urry, *Canterbury under the Angevin Kings,* University of London Historical Studies 19 (London 1967). For comparison I note, from a thirteenth-century French serf-list (BN lat 5993 A, opening 293–94), Odeline la mignote, Emeline la fadoule, Odeline called Queen (*dicta Regina*), and Isabelle la lardone.

became more routine, characterization in naming was reduced, but we should not forget that it grew in the twelfth century and flourished in the thirteenth.

"What's in a name?" is a question which lies at the heart of the debate over the meaning of universals. That question could rise, inflated with logic and learning, to explode catastrophically against the mystery of the Trinity, but in the schoolroom the most concrete topic for debate was the observable reality of personalized differences between individuals who still had *something* in common. How can the words *homo* or *albus* be predicated of Socrates or Plato? If we take "Socrates is white" to be the locating of the individual (*individuum*) Socrates among other individuals, such as Plato, that are white, the statement makes no sense, for if Socrates is altogether individable, there is nothing that is common to both Socrates and Plato and no ontological basis for locating the two white things in a single group. And if we take "Socrates is white" to be the locating of whiteness in Socrates, we have pulled a thread that leads to the unraveling of the individual to an aggregate of properties, for "he" will turn out to be only an inexplicable congeries of universals. The problem faced by Abelard and his fellows was that the first approach erodes the universal, the second the individual.[58] Though they phrased their arguments with ancient referents, early scholastic philosophers were as deeply concerned with the contemporary problem of understanding the relationship of the individual self to others as was the more mystical Bernard of Clairvaux, preaching to his monks to know themselves.

THE EMERGENT AWARENESS OF SELF

THE MONK IN HIS COMMUNITY

The monasteries fostered humility and obedience and based self-fulfillment on contemplation and community life; the schools of the secular clergy thrived on intellectual pride and questioning. The contrast should not be overstressed, however, for Abelard spent the last and highly productive third of his life as a monk, and the brilliant Benedictine theologian Rupert of Deutz daringly asserted his reliance on his personal talents (*proprium ingenium*).[59] Moreover, one may wonder if the questions of interiority so sharply debated in the twelfth-century schools by such masters as Gratian, Lombard, and Peter the Chanter could have been developed as they were if monastic culture had not prepared the way. The monasteries not only transmitted the learning and literature of Antiquity but had applied themselves to examining the inner life in their own special way. Such profound psychologists as John Cassian and

---

[58]Abelard's investigation of the problems of predication is discussed in detail in Norman Kretzmann's contribution to this volume. The preceding four sentences summarize a memorandum kindly prepared for me by Prof. Kretzmann.

[59]Rupert's introduction to his commentary on the Apocalypse, PL 169.827–28.

Evagrius Ponticus had directed early monastic contemplation to questions of will and the human passions, and the regular reading of these authors, coupled with the discipline of community life, must have had a continuing effect on those prepared to be receptive. In many ways the twelfth-century concern with the self and others can be seen as a spreading of monastic habits of thought to a larger world.[60]

"The first degree of humility is obedience without delay," St Benedict had written in his Rule, citing the Psalmist, "At the hearing of the ear he hath obeyed Me."[61] In a Benedictine community the commands of the abbot could be treated as the voice heard by the Psalmist, and the Rule prescribed instant, unreflective obedience as the first step toward a life of Christian charity. Benedict expected that his monks had renounced their own wills; the authoritative voice of the abbot should ring out louder than the murmuring of monks discussing their interpretations of a written Rule. The Rule of St Benedict is not simply an expression of a sixth-century mentality; it dominated the religious structure of monastic Europe till the twelfth and thirteenth centuries, when it was partially replaced by new forms of organization.

Why did thirteenth-century men and women flock to the new mendicant orders? One reason may be found in simple economic reality, for the religious expansion of the twelfth century had put heavy pressure on the resources of monasteries and collegiate churches, and it was much cheaper to establish a house for urban mendicants than to provide for monks, even hardworking Cistercians, or canons. But while financial considerations may have affected both benefactors and converts to the religious life, the new Rules reveal an altered ideal of the relationship of the individual to a religious community. A comparison of the Rule of St Benedict and the various redactions of the Rule of St Francis shows dramatically how much had changed in the twelfth century. Francis of Assisi stressed vocation rather than organization, and he reveled in an absence of hierarchy in his "order." "Through spiritual charity let them render services willingly and obey each other mutually," he wrote in his first brief precepts. In the more formalized Rule of 1221, when organizational requirements seemed to make "ministers" necessary, he limited their authority: "If any one of the ministers gives to his brothers an order contrary to our rule or to conscience, the brothers are not bound to obey him, for obedience cannot command sin." Francis was readier to accept authority than Peter Waldo, who eventually suffered excommunication for disobedience; he used commands as well as admonitions in his Rule, but he was reluctant to impose

---

[60]Owen Chadwick, *John Cassian* (2nd ed. Cambridge 1968) 82–109; Adalbert de Vogüé, "Les relations fraternelles et le souci de la subjectivité," *La communauté et l'abbé dans la Règle de saint Benoît* (Paris 1961) 438–503; and Leclercq, *Love of Learning*, trans. from *L'Amour des lettres et le désir de Dieu* (Paris 1957).

[61]*La règle de saint Benoît*, text ed. by Jean Neufville, introduction, trans. and notes by Adalbert de Vogüé, Sources chrétiennes 181–86 (6 vols. Paris 1971–72) 1.464 c. 5, citing Ps. 17:45; on obedience and hearing see 4.262–63 and cf. 6.1231.

authority on the consciences of others.[62] The Dominicans, adopting a modified form of the Augustinian Rule, found another, innovative way to limit the authority of superiors, introducing the election by majority vote of officers to serve for specific periods of time.[63]

TWELFTH-CENTURY CONCEPTIONS

The idea of order itself is a human construction—a metaphor—and therefore mutable. Language and metaphor both limit and stimulate the ways we think, even about ourselves. Though there is a perfectly good Latin word for "self," so that Fulbert of Chartres could write a poem *Ad se ipsum de se ipso*,[64] there is no medieval word which has anything like the meaning of "personality," and *persona* was still defined in the twelfth century primarily in its etymological sense as a mask held before an actor.[65] In this essay the word "personality" has always been enclosed in quotation marks as a reminder that a medieval person could never verbalize the idea of having a "personality." Nevertheless, one feature of the renaissance of the twelfth century is the growth of precision in language and definition and the propagation of metaphoric terms like "microcosm" and "macrocosm" which facilitated new conceptualizations, indeed, new forms of consciousness. The treatises *De anima* which were recovered or written in this period encouraged and permitted a collective language of awareness.[66]

Whatever the causes, European authors in the twelfth century had a clearer sense of their own inner life and their relations to others than their Carolingian predecessors. A heightened sense of history is a form of self-consciousness, and in both theology and in the study of *res gestae* the twelfth century was a great age of historical awareness.[67] Investigation of the concept of

---

[62]See the article by P. Cyprien, "Franciscaine (règle)," in *Dictionnaire de droit canonique* 5 (1953) 884–96, and Lothar Hardick, Josef Terschlüssen, and Kajetan Esser, *La règle des Frères Mineurs*, trans. Jean-Marie Genvo (Paris 1961).

[63]Georgina R. Galbraith, *The Constitution of the Dominican Order, 1216 to 1360* (Manchester 1925) 46–47, 103.

[64]*The Letters and Poems of Fulbert of Chartres*, ed. and trans. Frederick Behrends (Oxford 1976) 242–44.

[65]In his theological dictionary Alan of Lille followed Boethius in his definition of *persona*: "Etiam apud illos qui tractant comoedias vel tragoedias persona dicitur histrio, qui variis modis personando diversos status hominum repraesentat, et dicitur persona a personando" (PL 210.899A), cited by Hans Rheinfelder, *Das Wort "Persona,"* Beihefte zur Zeitschrift für romanische Philologie 77 (Halle 1928) 19.

[66]Harder to evaluate, because linguistic interaction had existed before, is the heightened consciousness of different "selves" which occurs when one speaks different languages, as well as the enrichment of vocabulary created by works like Burgundio of Pisa's translation of *De natura hominis* by Nemesius of Emesa, ed. Gérard Verbeke and J. R. Moncho (Leiden 1975).

[67]See the lucid chapter by Marie-Dominique Chenu, *Théologie* 62–89, "Conscience de l'histoire et théologie," trans. as "Theology and the New Awareness of History" in *Nature* 162–201.

"experience" also forces special consideration of the role of the self.[68] In scientific cosmology, Man self-consciously marked out his place in the universe. Perhaps increased political stability and material wealth encouraged an optimistic humanism, but the self-esteem, the positive view of the powers of human reason which we see in the best scientific and theological writing, may also have helped to create a collective consciousness of human dignity.[69]

These compressed pages have attempted to illustrate from a variety of fields a striking growth of self-awareness in the twelfth century, without suggesting that these people had a sense of subjectivity anywhere nearly as fully developed as our own. Two great limiting restraints in the mentality of the twelfth century are readily apparent.

In the first place, the conceptualization of the nature of self and of what we call "personality" differed from our own. To state the matter in a metaphor of direction, in the Middle Ages the journey inward was a journey toward self for the sake of God; today it is commonly for the sake of self alone.[70] In the modern secular world, when a person sets out to "find himself," his quest is usually conceived of as a stripping away of the layers of conformity and contrived artifice and the psychological defenses which encrust, hide, and even smother the "true self." It is as if each wondrously unique infant were wrapped by its social environment in thick swaddling clothes which must be broken or cut away in order for the individual "personality" to appear most fully. In medieval thought the *persona* was not inner but outer, and looking behind the individualized mask eventually brought one closer to the uniqueness, not of self, but of God. Modern readers more concerned with personality than the soul find Dante's *Inferno* far more interesting than his *Paradiso*, but Dante's own pilgrimage was away from both hell and personality.

A second restriction was the availability of very limited and mechanical theories of what creates individuation or "personality"—and it should be noted that what creates individuality, not conformity, was the major question examined. When Matthew of Vendôme wished to explain why one of his aca-

---

[68]See the works cited by Jean Leclercq in n. 37 of his essay in this volume.

[69]See Robert Javelet, *Image et ressemblance au douzième siècle: De saint Anselme à Alain de Lille* (2 vols. Strasbourg 1967) and Richard C. Dales, "A Medieval View of Human Dignity," *Journal of the History of Ideas* 38 (1977) 557–72, who cites the important articles of Robert Bultot. For the relationship of developments in medieval science to self-awareness see Lynn White, jr., "Science and the Sense of Self: The Medieval Background of a Modern Confrontation," *Daedalus* 107 (1978) 47–59. Our two essays were written without knowledge of the other's work, and our remarkable agreement therefore provides a form of independent and mutually gratifying confirmation.

[70]Hugh of St Victor, for example, equated "ascent to God" with "entry into oneself" in *De vanitate mundi*, PL 176.715B. On the soul as a mirror of God in patristic literature see Jean Daniélou, *Platonisme et théologie mystique: Doctrine spirituelle de saint Grégoire de Nysse*, Théologie 2 (2nd ed. Paris 1944) 210–22, and Régis Bernard, *L'image de Dieu d'après saint Athanase*, Théologie 25 (Paris 1952) 72–74. A variety of stimulating essays appears in *Images of Man in Ancient and Medieval Thought: Studia Gerardo Verbeke . . . dicata* (Louvain 1976).

demic rivals was a treacherous and scandalous scoundrel, the matter was simple: Arnulf of Orléans had red hair.[71] This conclusion had all the authority of proverbial wisdom, "Never trust a redhead" (*In rufa pelle nemo latitat sine felle*). Other differences were created by "national character." Early in the thirteenth century James of Vitry reported the mutual "national" insults exchanged in the schools of Paris: the English were said to be great drinkers and had tails; the French were proud, delicate, and womanizers; the Germans were mad and given to obscenity at social gatherings.[72]

Such simplistic views were too crude for the better scientific minds of people who observed differences among Germans, French, and English or even the redheaded. Physiological theories inherited from Antiquity, which find their modern counterpart in Sheldonian somatotyping, explained differences of character in terms of the balance of the four bodily fluids or cardinal humors, blood, phlegm, and black and yellow bile, which when dominant produced the sanguine, phlegmatic, melancholic, and choleric temperaments. Different balances, and the new combinations in children engendered by men and women of different humoral types, could create quite a sophisticated variety of physiologically determined character traits, as Hildegard of Bingen explained in one of her treatises.[73]

Alternatively, our fates could be found in the stars, as we are reminded by such terms for temperament as mercurial, martial, saturnine, or jovial. Since both humoral theory and astrology were developed in Antiquity and transmitted, often by means of translations, to the twelfth century, this revival of learning must also be considered a "renaissance" phenomenon.[74] Since it was obvious to any reasonably informed scholar that the celestial bodies had an effect on climatic conditions, agriculture, and the movement of the tides, it is not surprising that most people believed that they also influenced mutable human beings, and astrology was simply an attempt to set that belief on a sound theoretical foundation. Nevertheless, though physiological or astrological explanations of character differences satisfied a large percentage of the population, they posed both a social and a spiritual threat, one that was met by recourse either to free will or to the will of God. Hildegard placed her ultimate deterministic faith not in the power of the planets but in the permission and decree of God; and Abelard, more conscious of the element of human choice, criticized humoral prediction and noted that astrologers would foretell on the basis of the stars what others would do, but were unable to predict intention and feared to make such a forecast directly to the person in-

---

[71]See Berthe M. Marti, "Hugh Primas and Arnulf of Orléans," *Speculum* 30 (1955) 233–38.
[72]*The Historia Occidentalis of Jacques de Vitry* c. 7, ed. John Frederick Hinnebusch, Spicilegium Friburgense 17 (Fribourg 1972) 92.
[73]*Causae et curae*, ed. Paul Kaiser (Leipzig 1903) 70–76, 87–89.
[74]Haskins begins his chapter in *Science* on Hugh of Santalla, the translator of Albumasar and Messahala, with a reference to "the renaissance of the twelfth century" (67). He used the same term in the first version of that essay, "The Translations of Hugo Sanctelliensis," *Romanic Review* 2 (1911) 1–15 at 1.

volved because he might prove them wrong by deliberately following an alternative course.[75]

In determining the characteristics and destinies of humans, the concept of free will, which gives the greatest incentive for self-awareness and the choice of one's destiny, lies at one extreme.[76] Mechanistic explanation of individual differences occupies a middle ground, and in its medical form, with its possibility of altering the balance of the humors through diet or other means, it offers the hope of some conscious control of the differentiated self. We must not forget, however, that throughout the renaissance of the twelfth century a dark and ancient substratum persisted, the belief that Fate determines all and can be discovered by magical practices, that individual selves have no meaning in a world where neither choice nor chance exists.

The survival of an ancient, unselfconscious system of belief can be seen in the practice of fortune-telling or sortilege. It was, like witchcraft, condemned repeatedly by the Fathers of the Church, successive church councils, and the medieval canonists, and was eventually forced underground though never eliminated. Its open practice in the twelfth century is clearly revealed in an English scientific miscellany. After illustrating the ancient "sphere of Pythagoras" and other predictive devices, the manuscript continues in a bold hand with a mass for telling fortunes by lot, including an episcopal benediction. The supplicant then casts three dice which determine one of fifty-six "fortunes," the *sortes sanctorum*, apparently derived from texts of the Hellenistic East, including such vague wisdom as "The winds are cruel" or "You have honey and seek vinegar." What is striking is not the banality of the "fortunes," but that in the twelfth century such a denial of conscious decision-making could be considered to have episcopal sanction. That such practices eventually lost their official approval is shown by the same manuscript, since a late fourteenth-century hand has added a new litany and a set of rules for this form of sortilege, beginning with the instruction, "Whoever wishes to administer these fortunes should go into a secret room or a field, so that no one may disturb or come upon him. . . ."[77]

TWENTIETH-CENTURY PERSPECTIVES

The twelfth century was not so brilliantly self-conscious, or even interested in the search for self-awareness, as an isolated reading of Abelard's *Know Thyself*

[75]Hildegard, *Causae et curae* (n. 73 above) 19–20, and Abelard, *Expositio in Hexaemeron* (4th day), PL 178.754–55. A new edition of Abelard's commentary is being prepared by Mary Romig.

[76]A fine historical survey, amply supported by quotations from the sources, is given by Odon Lottin, "Libre arbitre et liberté depuis saint Anselm jusqu'à la fin du XIIIe siècle," *Psychologie et morale aux XIIe et XIIIe siècles* (6 vols. in 8 Louvain 1942–60) vol. 1 (2nd ed. 1957) 11–389; cf. vol. 3 (1st ed. 1949) 606–20.

[77]MS Köln, Schnütgen-Museum, Ludwig XIII 5, fols. 48–50; on the practice, see Pierre Courcelle, "Divinatio," in *Reallexikon für Antike und Christentum* 3 (1950) 1235–51 and Richard Ganszyniec, "Les sortes sanctorum," *Congrès d'histoire du christianisme* 3 (Jubilé Alfred Loisy), ed. Paul-Louis Couchoud (Paris 1928) 41–51.

would suggest, but it is unquestionable that changes, dramatic changes, did occur in spite of all the limiting factors. Qualitative judgments about a culture based on the examination of a few individuals are always tentative; if asked whether Augustine understood himself and his feelings better than Guibert of Nogent or Rousseau, we might well answer in the affirmative, but we would have to add that Augustine is a thoroughly unrepresentative figure of his own period, a mountain, as it were, surrounded only by hills. But if we look comparatively at the relative, quantitative indications of self-examination and concern with the inner life of oneself and of others, it is easy to see that there was significantly more of such interest in the twelfth century than in earlier medieval times. A quantitative graph, if one could be constructed accurately, would probably show a decline from the time of Augustine—roughly coincident with the Germanic invasions—only a slight increase in the Carolingian renaissance, a rise in the eleventh century which sharply increases in the twelfth, and then a continuing though perhaps irregular increase up to the present.

Comparison of this sort is relatively easy within one cultural tradition. Comparison between differing cultures is much more difficult, for it is by no means clear what weight and significance to attach to different indications of the awareness of self. We have seen, for example, that twelfth-century Europe produced practically no individualized portraiture and that most evidence of concern with individual differences appears in writing. We have some grounds for comparing the levels of awareness of self and the determinants of individual differences found in Carolingian and twelfth-century Europe, but how could we compare either culture with the Merovingians' contemporaries in Peru? There, Moche artists have left us stunningly differentiated sculptured pots, some of them apparently authentic portraits, but no written records at all.[78] This extreme case is cited only to illustrate the nature of the comparative problem. Even where extensive written records exist, the difficulty of comparing the level and nature of self-awareness of medieval Western Europe with the culture of Islam, Mediterranean Judaism, or even Christian Byzantium seems immense, though perhaps not insurmountable.[79]

Where comparison is difficult, explanation is too, and yet some attempt at explanation should be made. For such complex phenomena as those dis-

---

[78]Although Christopher B. Donnan, *Moche Art of Peru: Pre-Columbian Symbolic Communication* (rev. ed. Los Angeles 1978) is concerned with art as a means of symbolic communication and does not discuss individuation in his catalogue, some of the portrait-head bottles in figs. 1–9 illustrate my point.

[79]The possibilities as well as some of the difficulties of comparative treatment can be seen in the essays collected in *Individualism and Conformity in Classical Islam* (n. 4 above) and *East-West Studies on the Problem of the Self*, ed. Poolla T. Raju and Alburey Castell (The Hague 1968). Alexander Altmann has collected material on "The Delphic Maxim in Medieval Islam and Judaism" in *Biblical and Other Studies* (Cambridge Mass. 1963) 196–232, a study to be compared with that of Pierre Courcelle cited in n. 3 above. For recent literature on Islamic autobiography (and to some extent biography) see Rudolf Sellheim, "Gedanken zur Autobiographie im

cussed here we can scarcely expect a single explanation, for influences must surely have been reciprocal, but it should still be useful to consider explanations under separable headings. A change in psychology invites first a psychological explanation. If twelfth-century Europeans were more interested in themselves, more ready to take the risks of turning inward, then they probably had more self-esteem, or a different sense of self-worth, than their Merovingian and Carolingian predecessors. A sense of self-esteem, we know today, is most easily formed in childhood, and we attribute that process in large part to the role of parents or their surrogates. Was love or "marital affection" between spouses more likely to be found in twelfth-century families than in earlier centuries?[80] Did social restraints on infanticide leave surviving children with a greater sense of security?[81] Were parents or nurses, or at least some of them, more nurturing in the late eleventh and twelfth centuries than they had been in a previous age?[82]

Evidence of an increased concern with family life and the nurturance of children in the twelfth century can be found, though it is scanty and sometimes contradictory. In his discussion of the disadvantages of marriage in his autobiographical letter, Abelard assumed that a child would be a noisy bother precisely because the baby would be cared for by a nurse in his own home and not sent out to a wet-nurse, and in one of his hymns he pointed out that the infant Jesus was more favored than the sons of kings because he was suckled by his own mother.[83] Though the first biographer of Bernard of Clairvaux reported that the saint was nursed by his mother (for William of St Thierry was writing an idealized work of hagiography), he quickly added that Aleth did not pamper her children with delicate food but toughened them with a coarse

---

islamischen Mittelalter," *Zeitschrift der deutschen morgenländischen Gesellschaft* supp. 3.1 (1977) 607–12. The richest treatment of personal life in medieval Mediterranean Judaism is vol. 3 (1978) of S. D. Goitein's *A Mediterranean Society* (4 vols. projected, Berkeley 1967–   ), which deals with the family; vol. 4 will conclude with a section on "The Mediterranean Mind."

[80]In spite of all that has been written about "courtly love" and adultery, what seems to be most interesting about new developments in the twelfth century is the growing attention paid to love between married spouses; see John T. Noonan, Jr., "Marital Affection in the Canonists," *Collectanea Stephan Kuttner* 2, = *Studia Gratiana* 12 (1967) 479–509, and John F. Benton, "Clio and Venus: An Historical View of Medieval Love," *The Meaning of Courtly Love*, ed. Francis X. Newman (Albany 1968) 19–42. Literary specialists, who often seem to be surprised that adultery is a relatively minor theme in their sources, should now see William D. Paden, Jr., et al., "The Troubadour's Lady: Her Marital Status and Social Rank," *Studies in Philology* 72 (1975) 28–50.

[81]The idea has been developed by Lloyd deMause, ed., *The History of Childhood* (New York 1974) 1–73 at 25–32, "The Evolution of Childhood"; see also Barbara A. Kellum, "Infanticide in England in the Later Middle Ages," *History of Childhood Quarterly* 1 (1974) 367–88.

[82]On child-rearing practices in the twelfth century see Mary M. McLaughlin, "Survivors and Surrogates: Children and Parents from the Ninth to the Thirteenth Centuries," in deMause (n. 81 above) 101–81.

[83]*Historia calamitatum*, ed. Jacques Monfrin (Paris 1959) 76, and *Hymnarius Paraclitensis*, ed. Josef Szövérffy (2 vols. Albany N.Y. and Brookline Mass. 1975) 88 hymn 32; Abelard underlines the mercenary or even servile character of wet-nurses by the phrase "subacta nutricum ubera."

and common diet.[84] The mother of Guibert of Nogent indulged her son with fine clothes, but he called her "cruel and unnatural" because she abandoned him when he was about twelve. Both men probably absorbed a sense of guilt along with whatever self-esteem they derived from their mothers, and as has been suggested before, guilt rather than shame may be an important stage in the development of introspection. An evolutionary psychogenic theory of the development of personality fits much of the observed evidence and deserves serious attention.[85] Such a theory is hard to test by traditional historical methods, however, for the central issue here may not be "causation" but "function," the question of how cultures in the past "used" childhood "to synthesize their concepts and their ideals in a coherent design for living."[86]

A second theoretical approach is political, tied more, it should be said, to the development of individual liberties, the passage from subject to citizen, than to the growth of self-awareness, though the two phenomena may well have an intimate relationship. If civil society is to remain coherent, recognition of individual differences cannot easily be dissociated from a right for those differences to exist, or at least for individuals to have a certain equality before the law. In twelfth-century Europe a notable increase in codified or customary liberties occurred—the *libertas ecclesie*, the granting of town and communal charters, the rights of free men as they were set down in Magna Carta and other great charters. These political developments had traceable political antecedents in the practices of the Germanic right of resistance and in the contractual aspects of feudal relations, and in the view of at least one theorist they created the conditions for a greater sense of self-worth among certain groups of men.[87] But it does not seem likely that widespread and large-scale changes in attitudes toward the self were solely or even primarily produced by political changes. It is hard to believe that Guigo the Carthusian wrote his meditations because of changes in the political world from which he had fled, or that the sculptures of the façade of Reims differ from those at Chartres because of the communal liberties possessed by the burghers of Reims.

An economic theory for the growth of "individualism" has also been developed.[88] Since specialization of labor provides economic benefits, internal

---

[84]*Vita prima* 1.1, PL 185.277C; on the issue of this report's accuracy Jean Leclercq raises questions rather than answering them in *Nouveau visage de Bernard de Clairvaux: Approches psychohistoriques* (Paris 1976) 20–27.

[85]I am particularly impressed by the approach taken by Lloyd deMause in his introduction to *A History of Childhood* (n. 81 above).

[86]Erik H. Erikson, *Childhood and Society* (2nd ed. New York 1963) 185.

[87]Walter Ullmann, *The Individual and Society in the Middle Ages* (Baltimore 1966), in part developing ideas expressed by Sidney Painter, "Individualism in the Middle Ages," repr. in his *Feudalism and Liberty*, ed. Fred A. Cazel, Jr. (Baltimore 1961) 254–59.

[88]These ideas of the effect of increasing wealth and specialization of labor on "individuation" are presented in my own formulation. They require no special annotation, for they are commonplaces of late nineteenth-century economic and sociological theorists, such as Karl Marx in *Formen, die der kapitalistischen Produktion vorhergehen*, written in 1858, published in Berlin in 1952 and interpretatively translated by Eric J. Hobsbawm and Jack Cohen as *Pre-Capitalist Economic Formations* (London 1964, New York 1965); Emile Durkheim, *De la division du travail*

economic forces produce a growing social differentiation of labor. Not only do some fight, others pray, and others work, but among those who work a growingly differentiated economy supports the smiths, farmers, bakers, fletchers, tanners, weavers, carters, and others whose names, now capitalized, remind us that a specialized occupation is a form of identity. What effect the growing towns of the twelfth century had on the people who lived in them is indeed uncertain. Did they produce urban alienation or urban freedom and self-fulfillment? Probably both, depending on class and personal differences. It is obvious that wealth facilitated the expression of self-awareness in durable form. It is equally clear, however, that great wealth was not essential for psychological development. Iceland was one of the poorest and least urbanized countries of Greater Europe, but by the thirteenth century it was producing literature crammed with finely drawn, highly individualized portraits of great psychological profundity. The first settlers of Iceland knew who they were, as we can see from the *Book of Settlements* or Landnámabók; by the thirteenth century their best authors could perceive and express what manner of people they were in all their multifaceted diversity.

What was the influence of religion over such a luxuriantly diverse economic, political, and cultural area as that which stretched from Iceland to the Mediterranean? Although all the evidence discussed so far has been taken from the dominant Christian culture, in evaluating the role of religion we should avoid the unwarranted assumption that the Christian religion was uniquely capable of fostering the development of consciousness and increased psychological awareness. If by some chance the Jewish Khazars or the Moslem Moors instead of the Catholic Franks had created an empire in early medieval Europe, interest in the examination of the subjective self might have recovered at the same rate, or perhaps even faster. This conclusion is based on the existence of a form of "control group," the small Jewish communities which shared much of the same cultural, economic, and even political environment as their Christian neighbors, though they differed both through the effects of exile, hostility, and persecution and in a greater devotion to learning, which one of Abelard's students observed with envy.[89]

---

social (Paris 1893; 5th ed. 1926), trans. from both editions by George Simpson as *The Division of Labor in Society* (New York 1933; incomplete repr. 1964); and Georg Simmel, *Über sociale Differenzierung*, Staats- und socialwissenschaftliche Forschungen 10.1 (Leipzig 1890).

[89]Detailed, comparative study should be made of self-awareness in medieval Christian, Jewish, and Islamic cultures, with particular attention to points of intercommunication and influence. In a private communication, Professor S. D. Goitein has suggested to me that the Jewish pietists in Germany were influenced by their environment and that in the matter of self-awareness something new really did begin in Western Christendom in the twelfth century. If Jewish introspection and self-awareness was significantly more advanced in northern Europe than in the world revealed by the records of the Cairo Genizah (and in fact Maimonides seems to have had no time for introspection), then the northern European environment, including its particular forms of Christianity, played a determining role in the development of consciousness of self. For the remark of Abelard's student on Jewish learning, see *Commentarius Cantabrigiensis in Epistolas Pauli e Schola Petri Abaelardi*, ed. Artur M. Landgraf (4 vols. Notre Dame Ind. 1937–45) 2.434, cited by Smalley, *Study* 78.

Some four centuries before the time of Christ, the prophet Joel had recorded the Lord's command to "rend your hearts and not your garments." Judaism maintained and developed its own institutions for both inner contrition and public atonement, and twelfth-century Jews, like their Christian contemporaries, practiced examination of conscience and suffered from a sense of guilt. Following traditional liturgical forms, they questioned whether their own faults were the cause of their exile, and even internalized the epithets hurled at them by Christians, as can be seen in a liturgical poem composed by rabbi Eleazar ben Nathan of Mainz for the Sabbath between the New Year and the Day of Atonement:

> Let us return to our God in the sorrow of our exile,
> For Thou art righteous in all that befalls us.
> We have been sent away from Thy face for our sin of avarice.
> Cause us to return and we shall return.
> "Exiles the son of exiles," they call us with enmity,
> "Filthy lucre," they name us in condemnation. . . .[90]

Whatever effect another religion might have had if it had prevailed, in fact Christianity triumphed in medieval Europe, and we must therefore examine its influence on the majority of the population. A central problem, however, is that Christianity is and has been many things to many people. One can find in the Gospels a stress on intention ("who looks at a woman lustfully has already committed adultery with her in his heart"); a private and personal relationship to God ("and when you pray, you must not be like the hypocrites"); a rejection of form and ritual ("this people honors me with their lips, but their heart is far from me"—this last a quotation from Isaiah). And on the other hand, the same Gospels provide an ample and express textual basis for a concern with the power of baptism, salvation by faith, respect for the law, and external miracles.

Emphasis on ritual, sacraments, relics, collective worship, and community life is as much a part of the Christian religion as concern with interiority and individual self-examination.[91] When Gregory of Tours recounts how a priest drove away a demonic fly with a sign of the cross or that oil consecrated at the tomb of St Martin cured a rash of pimples, his *pura credulitas* may today seem rank superstition,[92] but by the standards of his own time he was nonetheless

[90]Text in Seligmann Baer, *Die Piutim für alle Sabbathe des Jahres* (Rödelheim 1854) 254–56, trans. rabbi Michael Signer of Hebrew Union College (Los Angeles), who informs me that Baer's German translation avoids much of the self-condemnatory nuance of the Hebrew. For a comprehensive study of Jewish thought see Haim Hillel Ben-Sasson, "The Uniqueness of the Jewish People in Twelfth-Century Thought" (in Hebrew) in *Perakim: Yearbook of the Schocken Institute for Jewish Research of the Jewish Theological Seminary of America* 2 (1969–74) 145–218, and the same author's medieval chapters (in English) in his *History of the Jewish People* (Cambridge Mass. 1976).

[91]On changing attitudes toward liturgy and communal worship see Louis Bouyer, *Liturgical Piety*, Notre Dame University Liturgical Studies 1 (Notre Dame Ind. 1954).

[92]*Liber miraculorum* c. 106, ed. Bruno Krusch, MGH SS rer Mer 1.2.561, and *Historia Francorum* 8.15, 2nd ed. Krusch and Wilhelm Levison, MGH SS rer Mer 1.1 (1951) 380–83. The quite

Christian and could devoutly worship a thaumaturgic Savior who had cured a speech impairment by spitting and touching the tongue of the afflicted man. Paul and even more Augustine stressed the interiority of their religion; many other Christians did not. Augustine readily acknowledged his own personal responsibility—"I, not fate, not fortune, not the devil"—and he put so much trust in informed Christian virtue that he could even advise, "Love, and do what you wish," a statement often quoted in the twelfth century.[93] If Christianity in the renaissance of the twelfth century once more served to foster self-awareness, it must have been because of changes in that religion itself.

We are therefore brought back to a problem of historical change. Why and how did Christianity develop a renewed concern with the interior life? The reasons behind the change require deep examination, but very likely they are associated with other cultural changes already discussed—political, economic, and probably particularly psychological. The means of propagating a change in religion are far clearer, for with the Gregorian Reform the Christian Church became better organized and effective in spreading and indeed enforcing whatever modes of religious thought were then dominant. The effect of that reform was felt most strongly by the clergy in the late eleventh and early twelfth century, and in the course of the twelfth and thirteenth centuries the Christian beliefs and practices of the time were institutionalized and came to have more and more effect on a receptive European populace.

Different readers will weigh these, and perhaps other, explanatory theories differently, and far more must be known about self-awareness and consciousness of others in both medieval European and other cultures before solid statements about the relative importance of various causative influences can be seriously proposed. At this point, however, I may state briefly my own tentative and personal conclusions. Germanic Europe's political tradition of "individualism" provided a fertile ground in which concern with the self and others could grow, though it is hard to see that early Germanic culture as a

---

common view that Gregory's *pura credulitas* (H.F. 1, pref.) should be considered a "system of superstition" is that of one of his translators, Ernest Brehaut, *History of the Franks, by Gregory, Bishop of Tours: Selections*, Columbia University Records of Civilization 2 (New York 1916) xxi. Gregory's story about the fly reported only a simple exorcism, but William of St Thierry records that St Bernard actually excommunicated some flies (*Vita prima* 1.11, PL 185.256B–C), and the debate over the excommunication of animals continued long into the modern period; see, for example, Jules Desnoyers, "Excommunication des insectes et d'autres animaux nuisibles à l'agriculture," *Bulletin du Comité historique des arts et monuments* 4 (1853) 36–54, and Ernest Gelée, "Quelques recherches sur l'excommunication des animaux," *Mémoires de la Société académique . . . de l'Aube* 29 (1865) 131–71.

[93]"Ego, non fatum, non fortuna, non diabolus," in *Enarrationes in psalmos* 31.16, PL 36.268. The Latin text in *Tractatus in Epistolam Iohannis ad Parthos* 7.8, PL 35.2033, is "Dilige, et quod vis fac." The quotation is cited in its original and correct form by Abelard in *Sic et non*, prologue, ed. Blanche B. Boyer and Richard McKeon (Chicago 1977) 98.221. The possible ambiguity of *dilige* was avoided in the version quoted (or created?) by Ivo of Chartres, prologue to *Decretum*, PL 161.48B: "Habe caritatem, et fac quidquid vis." This reworking was preferred by Abelard, Hugh of St Victor, and other twelfth-century authors; see *Sic et non*, prologue, 98.217–18 and notes, and Benton (n. 4 above) 150 n. 22.

whole provided an environment favorable to self-awareness. Changing attitudes were nurtured, and in some cases probably produced, by changing economic conditions, particularly specialization of labor, greater wealth, and the growth of towns. Intellectual support was provided by both a "classical renaissance" and "reformed" religion, and while intellectual arguments on the nature of the individual were more likely influenced by other changes in society than their fundamental cause, the development of a richer and more precise vocabulary for the discussion of the self surely had a cumulative effect on European consciousness. A shift from a culture in which shame and worth accorded by peers predominated to one in which a sense of both guilt and self-esteem became far more common profoundly affected the way in which individuals perceived themselves.

Here we should distinguish between childhood and adult influences. For children, changes in family structure, marital love, and maternal nurturance must be considered fundamental; for adults the most important influences encouraging self-awareness and examination were the institutions of the reformed Church. Childhood and adult influences surely were reciprocal, for the institutions of the Church affected family life and child care, and every adult who legislated and enforced changes, exhorted and gave moral instruction, or nurtured children more or less well had been a child subject to the shaping influence of family life. The two stages of life cannot be separated, and as we seek to know more about the growth of self-awareness in the renaissance of the twelfth century we should look most closely at the influence of Mother Church and biological mothers.

Bibliographical Note

For evidence of medieval self-awareness the best large-scale work, which goes beyond the apparent limits of its title, is Georg Misch, *Geschichte der Autobiographie* (4 vols. in 8 Frankfurt 1949–69). Briefer and more recent is Karl Joachim Weintraub, *The Value of the Individual: Self and Circumstance in Autobiography* (Chicago and London 1978), which for its medieval chapters is based on material already treated by Misch.

Pierre Courcelle covers an immense range of philosophical and theological literature in *Connais-toi toi-même: De Socrate à saint Bernard* (3 vols. Paris 1974–75), as does Robert Javelet, *Image et ressemblance au douzième siècle: De Saint Anselm à Alain de Lille* (2 vols. Strasbourg 1967). Particularly important for the theme of this essay are a small gem, Marie-Dominique Chenu, *L'éveil de la conscience dans la civilisation médiévale*, Conférence Albert-le-Grand 1968 (Montreal and Paris 1969) and Paul Anciaux, *La théologie du sacrement de pénitence au XIIe siècle* (Louvain 1949).

A recent cluster of books has treated the theme of the "individual" or "individualism," which should be carefully distinguished from the topic of this essay: Colin M. Morris, *The Discovery of the Individual, 1050–1200* (London 1972); Walter Ullmann, *The Individual and Society in the Middle Ages* (Baltimore 1966); *Individualism and Conformity in Classical Islam* (which also goes beyond its title for comparisons), ed.

Amin Banani and Speros Vryonis, Jr. (Wiesbaden 1977); Peter Dronke, *Poetic Individuality in the Middle Ages: New Departures in Poetry, 1000–1150* (Oxford 1970); Robert W. Hanning, *The Individual in Twelfth-Century Romance* (New Haven and London 1977); and Steven Lukes, *Individualism* (New York and Oxford 1973).

Among the many fine recent contributions to the study of twelfth-century thought two may be cited as stimulating introductions for readers of English: Southern's *Humanism* and Chenu's *Nature*. Two especially stimulating articles are Peter Brown, "Society and the Supernatural: A Medieval Change," *Daedalus* 104 (1975) 133–51 and Lynn White, jr., "Science and the Sense of Self: The Medieval Background of a Modern Confrontation," *Daedalus* 107.2 (1978) 47–59.

Good samples of anthropological papers of value for medievalists are collected by Douglas G. Haring, ed., *Personal Character and Cultural Milieu* (3rd ed. Syracuse N.Y. 1956) and Robert A. LeVine, ed., *Culture and Personality: Contemporary Readings* (Chicago 1974). Psychohistory itself is a new field for medievalists, and a pioneering study of great interest is *A History of Childhood*, ed. Lloyd deMause (New York 1974). Recent developments can be followed in the articles and reviews in *The Journal of Psychohistory* (formerly *The History of Childhood Quarterly*), *The Psychohistory Review*, and *Psychohistory: The Bulletin of the International Psychohistorical Association*.

An introduction to twelfth-century ideas of the self and of others can, however, probably best be gained from careful attention to biographical studies and the work of medieval authors and artists themselves, such as Guigo the Carthusian, Bernard of Clairvaux, Hildegard of Bingen, Guibert of Nogent, Hermannus Judaeus, Peter Abelard, Jocelin of Brakelond, Christina of Markyate, Gerhoch of Reichersberg, Rupert of Deutz, and many, many others. For the visual arts, two fine works by Erwin Panofsky have excellent plates which permit long-range comparisons: *Ren & Ren*, which is particularly recommended, and *Tomb Sculpture* (New York 1964).

IV

LAW, POLITICS, AND HISTORY

The Revival of Jurisprudence

Stephan Kuttner

In the cultural universe of the twelfth century the new jurisprudence is a major component of that intellectual achievement which allows us to give the century the name of a renaissance. Hardly any legal historian has been able to discuss our period without speaking of "rebirth and renewal." For it was indeed the period that rediscovered "law"—Roman law at first—as both an object and a result of scientific endeavor; and it happens rarely enough in history that we can connect such a rediscovery with a single fact or event in the stream of time. Medieval philosophy would have blossomed—though the flower might have looked different—even if Aristotle's Posterior Analytics had never been found. But it is unthinkable that a science of law could have taken shape in the medieval West without the rediscovery of Justinian's Digest, about 1070 A.D. The central monument of ancient Roman jurisprudence presented a model and a challenge to the medieval mind for which the eleventh-century reader was rather ill prepared. To be sure, relics of the imposing structure of the laws of Rome existed. Above all, there was the Visigothic *Breviarium* (*Lex Romana Visigothorum*, 506 A.D.), which combined a small selection of abridgments of some classical school texts and commonplace books with pre-Justinian imperial legislation taken from the Theodosian Code (438 A.D.): this and other "barbarian" adaptations had retained currency in the Frankish kingdom; elsewhere they had become amalgamated with national laws. Lombard Italy and the formerly Byzantine regions of the peninsula had preserved portions of Justinian's Code (*Codex Justinianus*), his elementary *Institutiones*, and an abridged Latin version of his Greek *Novellae* (the *Epitome Juliani*).

Much progress has been made over the eighty-odd years since the appearance of Max Conrat's classic *Geschichte der Quellen und Literatur des römischen Rechts im früheren Mittelalter* (1891). But when we browse through the pertinent chapters which today's experts have thus far contributed to the collective enterprise entitled *Ius Romanum Medii Aevi*, we find little reason to revise the judgment of Savigny (d. 1861), Conrat (d. 1911), or Hermann Kantorowicz (d. 1940): any "continuity" of Roman jurisprudence between the sixth and eleventh century in the West remains a dream, if by "jurisprudence" we understand an intellectually coherent discipline, a mastery of the sources which can give rational guidance to legal thinking—as distinct from professional routine.[1] It is not to belittle the notaries, *iudices, defensores, legisperiti*, and other worthies of eleventh-century Italy if we maintain that theirs was a prescholarly grasp of the everyday needs of legal business. "Tradition, not reflection, determined everything."[2] As for the literary efforts represented by such early medieval writings as the primitive summary of Justinian's Code known as *Summa Perusina*,[3] or the grammatical and etymological glosses of his Institutes and the shortened Codex in some early Italian manuscripts, there seems little point today in continuing a debate which in its heyday—between the late nineteenth century and the last decade before the Second World War—was more often than not influenced by national prejudices. All things considered, the literary relics from before the mid-eleventh century do not prove more about legal learning than does the study by schoolboys of Cicero's forensic speeches,[4] or the use of material from the Institutes in the curriculum of rhetoric.

I. THE REAPPEARANCE OF THE DIGEST

"Potentissima pars est unius cuiusque rei principium": thus Peter of Blois began the first chapter of his *Distinctiones* (ca. 1180), slightly paraphrasing one of the opening sentences of old Gaius for his commentary on the Twelve Tables as found in the title *De origine iuris* of the Digest.[5] This dictum on "the mightiest part" may fittingly be applied to the reappearance of the Digest itself, which marked indeed "the beginning of everything," a new epoch. In some respects this reappearance was unique. First, everything "hung by a slender thread,"[6] since only a single complete manuscript of the book had

---

[1] For a summary and exhaustive bibliography of the long-drawn discussion on the continuity of Roman jurisprudence—proclaimed mainly by Hermann Fitting in several impressive publications of the 1870s and 1880s—see Peter Weimar in Coing's *Handbuch* 1.132-36. The following titles in *Ius Romanum Medii Aevi* (= IRMAE, on which see the Bibliographical Note below) are pertinent: Pierre Riché, *Enseignement du Droit en Gaule du VIe au XIe siècle*, IRMAE 1.5.b *bb* (Milan 1965); Rafael Gibert, *Enseñanza del Derecho romano en Hispania durante los siglos VI a XI*, IRMAE 1.5.b *cc* (Milan 1967); Ugo Gualazzini, *Trivium e quadrivium*, IRMAE 1.5.a (Milan 1974). Collected essays by two scholars representing different schools of thought: Federico Patetta (d. 1945), *Studi sulle fonti giuridiche medievali* (Turin 1967); Carlo Guido Mor, *Scritti di storia giuridica altomedievale* (Pisa 1977). The former was one of the early critics of Fitting.

[2] Haskins, *Ren* 195.

[3] See Conrat, *Geschichte* (see Bibliographical Note below) 182-87.

[4] The remark is Hermann Kantorowicz's, "Über die Entstehung der Digestenvulgata," ZRG rom Abt 30 (1909) 196 n. 9 (= separate edition [Weimar 1910] 14 n. 9). Only the separate edition in book form will hereafter be cited (originally two installments in ZRG rom Abt 30.183-271 and 31 [1910] 14-88).

[5] *Opusculum de distinctionibus in canonum interpretatione adhibendis, sive, ut auctor voluit, Speculum iuris canonici* 1.1, ed. Theophilus Augustus Reimarus (Berlin 1837) 8. "The most powerful part of every thing is its beginning." In the classical text, *Dig.* 1.2.1, the word order differs, and the *codex Florentinus* (on which more presently) reads *potissima pars*, "The principal part" instead of *potentissima*, which is the common medieval reading.

[6] Haskins, *Ren* 198.

survived, and lay unused until the latter part of the eleventh century. Second, no other scholastic discipline could boast that its chief *auctoritas* existed, physically, in a book that was copied down at about the time the *auctoritas* itself was compiled, approved, and promulgated. For the complete text of Justinian's *Digesta seu Pandectae* is extant in the sixth-century book the Florentines carried off as war booty from Pisa in 1406 and which—whatever one may think of the doubtful story that the Pisan fleet had brought it home from a raid on Amalfi—is certainly attested at Pisa in the twelfth century. Third, each and every extant copy of the Digest (with the exception of one ninth-century fragment) is ultimately derived from the *codex Florentinus* (**F**).[7] This was first seen by that incomparable Spanish humanist and churchman, don Antonio Agustín (d. 1586); Cujas (d. 1590) thought otherwise. After more than three centuries of debate, Theodor Mommsen's studies, culminating in his *editio maior* of 1870, demonstrated that all the differences from **F** which are common to the so-called vulgate manuscripts or *littera Bononiensis* can be reduced to a single, lost archetype, the *codex secundus* (**S**), and that this itself was an emended copy of **F**, written in Beneventan script.[8] At times the "redactor" of **S** erred in his conjectures, but on the whole his emendations show a respectable standard of critical and philological insights, which would place the book's presumable origin at the threshold of the "new times": they bespeak an urge for learning and harmonization that would have been out of context before the last third of the eleventh century. The intellectual effort involved even made some modern historians think of Guarnerius/Irnerius himself as the person who revised the text of the Digest[9]—but this remains an unsupported conjecture.

Somewhere between the completion of codex **S** and the early years of the twelfth century we ought to place the beginnings of the Bolognese School, that is, of Irnerius's teaching.[10] That there was a Master Pepo before him is no longer doubtful, but apart from one early quotation and some literary notices almost a century later, we know very little about him.[11] It is, however, worth

---

[7]Full bibliography in Weimar, in Coing, *Handbuch* 1.158–60. See especially Juan Miquel, "Mechanische Fehler in der Überlieferung der Digesten," ZRG rom Abt 80 (1963) 233–86.

[8]See Theodor Mommsen's *praefatio* to his *Digesta Iustiniani Augusti* [editio maior] (Berlin 1870) lxiiii–lxxii; cf. Kantorowicz, *Digestenvulgata* (n. 4 above) 29–37; Miquel (n. 7 above) 273–77.

[9]Kantorowicz, *Digestenvulgata* (n. 4 above) 88–116; the hypothesis was generally not accepted.

[10]On Irnerius (Wernerius, Guarnerius) see especially Kantorowicz, *Studies in the Glossators* (Bibliographical Note, below) 33–65; Gero Dolezalek, "Irnerius," *Handwörterbuch zur deutschen Rechtsgeschichte* 2.10, ed. Adalbert Erler and Ekkehard Kaufmann (Berlin 1973) 439–42.

[11]On Pepo, see Hermann Kantorowicz and Beryl Smalley, "An English Theologian's View of Roman Law: Pepo, Irnerius, Ralph Niger," M&RS 1 (1943) 237–52; also in Kantorowicz, *Rechtshistorische Schriften*, ed. Helmut Coing and Gerhard Immel, Freiburger rechts- und staatswissenschaftliche Abhandlungen (Karlsruhe 1970) 231–44; André Gouron, "Die Entstehung der französischen Rechtsschule," ZRG rom Abt 93 (1976) 138–60 at 140.

noticing that Ralph Niger in the 1180s, in calling Pepo a *baiulus* of the Institutes and the Codex of Justinian, also states that Pepo was as yet not acquainted with the *Pandectae* ("utpote pandecte nullam habens noticiam").[12] We do not know the source of this information, but if he is correct it shows that the process of reading, absorbing, and assimilating this enormous bulk of highly sophisticated legal thought was rather slow in the period between about 1070 and 1100.

Other evidence of the slow pace at which the Digest was being absorbed wherever the book would be consulted in this period comes from two sides: writings of the pre-Bolognese school of Lombard law, and a series of excerpts, possibly of ecclesiastical origin, from Institutes and Digest which was utilized twice by canonists in the 1090s.

Let us first consider the school of Pavia, the only true precursor of Bologna, the only center at which serious scholarly reflection on legal texts can be found during the period in question.[13] A set of Lombard glosses on the Institutes (in a manuscript now at Cologne) and, even more important, many glosses as well as the running commentary, called *Expositio*, of the *Liber Papiensis* show a quite respectable use of the formal precepts of rhetoric and the dialectic process of *distinctio* in expounding the texts. The *Liber Papiensis*, as a compilation of royal ordinances and statutes, established law for the Lombard (Germanic) population, whereas under the early medieval principle of "personality" or *lex originis*, Roman law—such as there was of it—governed the legal status of the Italians in the kingdom. Now it is remarkable to what an extent the glosses and the author of the *Expositio* applied rules from the Roman sources to the Lombard statute, especially by introducing the doctrine that Roman law as the "lex omnium generalis" must supply the rule where Lombard law is silent.[14] In its own day, this fascinating statement was that of a voice crying in the wilderness; it was to have a great future in European legal history, down to the threshold of modern codification.

If we look, however, at the number of texts actually cited from the Digest by the Lombard writers, it is very small. Only exceptionally would they go beyond the first of the three parts into which the redactor of codex **S** had arbitrarily divided the fifty books of the Digest, that is, beyond the part which the

---

[12]Ludwig Schmugge, "'Codicis Iustiniani et Institutionum baiulus'—Eine neue Quelle zu Magister Pepo von Bologna," *Ius commune* 6 (1977) 1–9 at 3. The medieval usage of *baiulus* (class. "bearer") is ambivalent. Here a messenger, a tutor, a standard bearer could be meant.

[13]Summary and bibliography on the school of Pavia in Gerhard Dilcher, "Langobardisches Recht" section VI, *Handwörterbuch* (n. 10 above) 2.15 (1977) 1614–18. Also, Pietro Vaccari, *Diritto longobardo e letteratura longobardistica intorno al diritto romano*, IRMAE 1.4.b *ee* (Milan 1966).

[14]*Liber Papiensis* with glosses and *Expositio*, ed. Alfred Boretius, MGH Leges 4 (Hanover 1868, repr. 1965) 290–606. For qualities and tendencies of the *Expositio* see Conrat, *Geschichte* (Bibliographical Note, below) 404–12 (on "lex omnium generalis": 407 with n. 4), and see now the monograph by Giovanni Diurni, *L'Expositio ad Librum Papiensem e la scienza giuridica preirneriana*, Biblioteca della Rivista di storia del diritto italiano 23 (Rome 1976); also the observations on Pavia by Margaret Gibson, *Lanfranc of Bec* (Oxford 1978) 4–11.

twelfth-century schools, for reasons still insufficiently explained, called the *Digestum vetus* (books 1–24, title 2).[15] The same basic limitation to texts from the *vetus*—ninety out of ninety-three chapters—characterizes the series of excerpts, mentioned above, which became a source for certain canonical collections before the end of the eleventh century. Indeed, it was a very slow pace at which the overwhelming riches of the new and difficult sourcebook were explored. But this should not tempt us to give credence to certain medieval tales about a piecemeal reappearance of the three parts, whose sobriquets—*Digestum vetus, Infortiatum, Digestum novum*—had become a riddle to the glossators themselves a hundred years later.[16]

There remains one important but unsolved question concerning the rediscovery of the Digest: where was the *codex Florentinus* found, copied, and emended? In other words, where was the *codex secundus* written? Paul Fournier in 1917 advanced the hypothesis that all this was connected with the Gregorian Reform; more precisely, with the intense search for old texts of the sacred canons and *decreta sanctorum patrum* that was evidently conducted in the papal archives and elsewhere during the pontificate of Gregory VII (1073–85).[17] The search was aimed at recovering old materials for new canonical collections that would better reflect the spirit of the reformers: could not the finding of the Digest have been a byproduct of this movement? Fournier argued from the *Collectio Britannica* of papal letters (ca. 1090), which was indeed partly based on fresh investigations in the registers of the papal archives but includes also two sets of *Varia*, among them the series of ninety-three excerpts from the Digest mentioned above.[18] The collector of the *Britannica* (the misleading name is derived from the British Museum, in whose library it had been found) was certainly an Italian with access to the records kept in the *scrinium* of the Roman church.

The second canonist to make use of the excerpts from the Digest was Ivo of Chartres, who assembled much of the material for his *Liber decretorum* during his Roman visit of 1093–94. Moreover, as Max Conrat already suggested, a

[15]Conrat, *Geschichte* 72, 408. Bibliography on the tripartite division of the Digest in the schools and the unresolved controversy concerning its explanation: Weimar, in Coing, *Handbuch* 1.158–61. Kantorowicz, *Digestenvulgata* (n. 4 above) 116 called it one of the most infamous (*verrufensten*) problems in the history of legal sources. The parts are *Dig.* 1–24.2 (*Digestum vetus*), 24.3–38 (*Infortiatum*), and 39–50 (*Digestum novum*).

[16]Kantorowicz, *Digestenvulgata* (n. 4 above) 124–29. Differently Weimar in Coing, *Handbuch* 1.158.

[17]Paul Fournier, "Un tournant de l'histoire du droit, 1060–1140," *Nouvelle Revue historique de droit français et étranger* 41 (1917) 129–80 at 151–53; cf. Fournier and Le Bras, *Histoire* (see Bibliographical Note, below) 2.13–14. For Gregory VII and jurisprudence in general see now Horst Fuhrmann, "Das Reformpapsttum und die Rechtswissenschaft," *Investiturstreit und Reichsverfassung*, ed. Josef Fleckenstein, Vorträge und Forschungen 17 (Sigmaringen 1973) 175–203.

[18]Max Conrat (Cohn), *Der Pandekten- und Institutionenauszug der brittischen Dekretalensammlung, Quelle des Ivo* (Berlin 1887); also Conrat, *Geschichte* (Bibliographical Note, below) 351–54, 370–72. A revised survey of the excerpts in Mor, "Il Digesto nell'età preirneriana e la formazione della 'Vulgata,'" *Scritti* (n. 1 above) 83–234 (first publ. in *Per il XIV Centenario delle Pandette e del Codice di Giustiniano* [Pavia 1934] 559–697) at 163–81, with an edition, 215–34.

judgment given by pope Urban II in 1088, the first year of his pontificate, may contain an implied reference to this series of excerpts.[19] All these observations seem to support the assumption of a link between the *Pandektenauszug* and the circles of the Reform papacy. They have recently been taken up again by Juan Miquel, whose closely argued paper on errors in the transmission of the Digest persuasively pleads for the great library of Montecassino under abbot Desiderius as the place where the *codex Florentinus* may have been found and copied. The close connection of the Abbey with the Reform papacy is well-known; Desiderius himself was a Roman cardinal (1059–86) and pope for a few months as Victor III (d. 1087).[20]

Such conjectures linking Church reform and the beginnings of the new jurisprudence may of course never be proved by more substantial evidence. They are, on the other hand, not *a priori* improbable at a moment of history when a new intellectual curiosity, a passion for discovery and for a better-organized understanding appeared in every area of learning and thought.

II. THE TWELFTH CENTURY: THE INTELLECTUAL CLIMATE

We have dwelt at some length on these beginnings of the renewal of Roman jurisprudence in the eleventh century, since they are the foundation for the achievements of the twelfth—and this not only in the new discipline of exploring Justinian's law. Certain synchronisms are striking: in the same span of years, St Anselm wrote his *Monologion* (1076), the opening statement of a renewed theology. Only a few years later his namesake, bishop Anselm of Lucca, would compose his canonical collection, which expressed more perfectly and succinctly than any other the ecclesiology of the Gregorian Reform with its emphasis on a well-ordered, centralized system of papal governance.[21] In the same generation, Bernold of Constance, Alger of Liège, and Ivo of Chartres— all before the turn of the century—began a new and imaginative search for rational principles of hermeneutics; that is, for methods of interpreting difficulties and contradictions in the oddly stratified mixture of authoritative texts presented by the canonical books. Next to the exciting discovery of sources, it was the concern of these churchmen with principles of interpretation which would become a powerful element, a *potentissima pars*, in the beginnings of the new jurisprudence and a seminal force even beyond that field. To name

---

[19]Urban II's letter JL 5382 is preserved only in part in the *Britannica*, Ivo *Decr.* 8.23, and Gratian C.31 q.2 c.1. Conrat, *Geschichte* 353 n.5.

[20]Miquel (n. 7 above) 282–84. He goes too far, however, when he speaks of "the mention of the Digest" in a letter of Urban II; Conrat (as cited in n. 19 above) cautiously suggested no more than a possibility, and this merely with regard to the excerpts attested by the *Britannica*; see also his *Pandektenauszug* (n. 18 above) 18 n.6.

[21]Ronald Knox, "Finding the Law: Developments in Canon Law during the Gregorian Reform," *Studi Gregoriani* 9 (1972) 419–66; Horst Fuhrmann, *Einfluss und Verbreitung der pseudoisidorischen Fälschungen von ihrem Auftauchen bis in die neuere Zeit*, MGH Schriften 24 (3 vols. Stuttgart 1972–74) 2.509–22.

only a few of the categories of their thought: the discerning reader should place a canonical rule in its context; he should explore the differences between strict law and the law that may be relaxed by dispensation, between justice and mercy, precept and counsel, divine immutable and human changeable laws; he must distinguish an absolute rule from that which ought to be understood according to the circumstances of time, place, persons, motives, and the like. Such intellectual devices would make it possible for Gratian, two generations later, to create the *Concordia discordantium canonum*: harmony out of dissonance in the collected *auctoritates* of canon law.[22]

New texts of authority discovered, traditional texts reorganized, modes of interpretation more sharply defined: out of these premises came the developments and accomplishments of the new century in the *droit savant*, the new jurisprudence that took shape in the school of Bologna and rapidly spread to other centers in northern Italy, France, the Rhineland, and England. Not only were these developments rich in literary production, to an extent still largely unknown to the great legal historians of the nineteenth century. They are also more complex than the older historiographic tradition would have it which believed in such convenient classifications as: an age of mere academic exegetes of Roman law (the glossators), followed by an age of more philosophically oriented but also more practical-minded "post-glossators" (or commentators); or—in the field of canon law—an age of "decretists" after Gratian, overtaken by "decretalists" in the thirteenth century.

There are good reasons for not attempting to present a neat miniature painting of jurisprudence in the twelfth century. For one, it is obvious (and Haskins himself was the first to acknowledge it) that centuries are mere conveniences for the calendar:[23] our history of a "renaissance" of law not only begins before the year 1100 but also reaches beyond 1200 A.D. and clearly includes the first third of the next century. Second (and this point has been somewhat neglected in modern times), there are not only the "two laws," Roman and canon, that were professionally explored by the scholars of the twelfth century. There were the statutes and customs of feudal law, codified and acknowledged by the end of the twelfth century as a subject of legal study.[24] Some of the new learning found its way into the *Usatges* of Barcelona with their far-reaching influence in the western Mediterranean,[25] some found its way into the treatise on the laws and customs of England that goes under

[22]This paragraph is an attempt to sum up the insights formulated in the last chapter of Fournier and Le Bras, *Histoire* (see Bibliographical Note, below) 2.334–52. Some further remarks in Stephan Kuttner, *Harmony from Dissonance: An Interpretation of Medieval Canon Law*, Wimmer Lecture 10 (Latrobe Pa. 1960), esp. at 21–26; idem, "Urban II and the Doctrine of Interpretation: A Turning Point?" *Studia Gratiana* 15 (1972) 53–85.

[23]Haskins, *Ren* 8–9.

[24]Bibliography in Weimar, in Coing, *Handbuch* 1.166–67, 186–88.

[25]A full bibliography in Armin Wolf, "Die Gesetzgebung der entstehenden Territorialstaaten," in Coing, *Handbuch* 1.517–800 at 689–90.

the name of Glanvill.[26] There was above all Lombard law, now systematically reorganized from the *Liber Papiensis* as (*lex*) *Lombarda* in the age of the Glossators. "The early sets of glosses remain unexplored":[27] a sad comment on the fate of the only legal order from which the jurists could have formed a true "common" law, a viable fusion of Roman and Germanic elements, by consistently applying the doctrine of the *Expositio* on the *lex Romana* as common to all and therefore suppletory to their own statute. But a strange emotional aversion to the *Lombarda* must have existed among the Bolognese, who would even indulge in the gross pun of calling it the Lombard crap (*faex* for *lex*).[28] In all these areas of twelfth-century law that essentially were outside the Roman and canonistic jurisprudence, much remains to be explored about the way legal doctrines took shape and almost unwittingly absorbed—some more, some less—terms and methods of the new learning.

III. SCHOLARSHIP SINCE HASKINS: NEW DIRECTIONS

Rereading today the pages Haskins wrote on our topic, one is struck by the intuitive insights of a historian whose access to the source material was only indirect. At a time when little had been done even in the civil-law countries to study the work of the glossators in the light of general medieval history, he could write that this work "constitutes a large and highly important part of the mental activity of the twelfth century, and at the same time has its place in the general history of the European intellect"; or that the civilian glossators' "dialectical analysis [was] peculiarly suited to a logical age working on a rigidly limited body of material."[29] He also saw that the process of making canon law into a discipline on the same intellectual level began, in a way, from the opposite end: a book of authority had first to be created; and "unlike the Roman law, the canon law did not constitute a closed *corpus*, but continued to grow."[30] What I just called intuitive insight was of course determined by a close reading of some great standard manuals, from Savigny to Schulte to Rashdall, supplemented by some special studies among which it is interesting to note Singer's analytical monographs on two decretal collections in the Vienna Academy's *Sitzungsberichte* of 1914. He also knew of Paul Fournier's ongoing work toward a history of pre-Gratian collections of canon law, and of Père

---

[26]See the Introduction (and earlier bibliography there cited) of George D. G. Hall to his edition and translation of the *Tractatus de legibus et consuetudinibus Angliae qui Glanvilla vocatur* (London 1965).

[27]Weimar, in Coing, *Handbuch* 1.186: "Die älteren Glossenapparate sind unerforscht." For bibliography on the *Lombarda* see also ibid. 165–66.

[28]See for instance Huguccio, *Summa* C.32 q.4 c.15. The extent to which the *Lombarda* was studied by the Bolognese before 1200 is controversial. See references in Weimar, in Coing, *Handbuch* 1.165 n. 1, and the interesting material discussed and edited by Giuliana D'Amelio, "Notizie di letteratura longobardistica," *Studi economico-giuridici* 46 (1971) 89–116.

[29]Haskins, *Ren* 204, 205.

[30]Haskins, *Ren* 214–15.

de Ghellinck's pioneering studies on the connection between canon law and theology in early scholasticism, *Le mouvement théologique du XIIe siècle* (1914).[31] But Haskins seems not to have known Seckel's fundamental review article of 1900 on recent editions of some writings of medieval jurists nor his *Distinctiones Glossatorum* (admittedly no easy reading),[32] nor the much more esoteric yet very informative studies of Franz Gillmann and Josef Juncker on the glossators of the canon law that were available by 1927.[33]

But this is less important than the fact that on both the civil and the canon law schools of the twelfth century our knowledge has increased by leaps and bounds since Haskins wrote. This became apparent even before the Second World War. The great *Histoire des collections canoniques* by Fournier and Le Bras appeared in 1931–32;[34] Erich Genzmer's masterful paper on Justinian's codification and the glossators was presented in 1933 at the Congress of Bologna and Rome commemorating the Digest of Justinian:[35] it provided the first true survey after Savigny on the scholarship of the civilian glossators. An unexpected wealth of new material from a London manuscript prompted Hermann Kantorowicz, a refugee in England from Hitler's Germany, to publish in 1938, two years before his death, his *Studies in the Glossators of the Roman Law*, which has since become a classic.[36] Concerning the glossators of the canon law, the writer of this paper as a brash young man proposed to produce single-handedly a *corpus glossarum* which would include all the extant glosses on Gratian antedating the *Glossa ordinaria*, together with an edition of the latter. In 1937 he published a preliminary *Repertorium* of materials—glosses as well as other writings on Gratian's book and on early collections of decretals—recovered in the manuscript tradition preceding the official compilation of Gregory IX. This volume was the main fruit of his efforts before the war interrupted them.[37]

Since the war, studies in both laws have intensified wherever we turn. They have resulted in fresh discoveries and added much to the dossier of our knowledge, be it on legal science in general during the twelfth century, be it on individual glossators and their work in particular. The Institute of Medieval

---

[31]Haskins, *Ren* 223 (bibliographical note).

[32]Emil Seckel, "Über neuere Editionen juristischer Schriften aus dem Mittelalter," ZRG rom Abt 21 (1900) 212–338; "Distinctiones Glossatorum," *Festschrift der Berliner Juristischen Fakultät für Ferdinand von Martitz* (Berlin 1911) 277–436 (separate repr. Graz 1956).

[33]No adequate bibliography exists of the enormous literary output of Franz Gillmann (d. 1941), most of which appeared as articles or brief notes in the *Archiv für katholisches Kirchenrecht* between 1907 and 1941 (over 30 papers before 1927). Josef Juncker (d. 1938), "Die Collectio Berolinensis," ZRG kan Abt 13 (1924) 284–426; "Summen und Glossen," ibid. 14 (1925) 384–474; "Die Summa des Simon von Bisignano und seine Glossen," ibid. 15 (1926) 326–500.

[34]See Bibliographical Note, below.

[35]Erich Genzmer, "Die iustinianische Kodifikation und die Glossatoren," *Atti del Congresso internazionale di Diritto Romano, Bologna e Roma 1933* (4 vols. Pavia 1934–35) *Bologna* 1.345–430.

[36]See Bibliographical Note, below.

[37]*Repertorium der Kanonistik*: see Bibliographical Note, below.

Canon Law now at Berkeley endeavors to provide information in its annual Bulletins; for the glossators of the Roman law, Peter Weimar's comprehensive chapter in Coing's *Handbuch* brings us up to date as far as the published information is concerned.[38] In the program of the Max-Planck-Institut für europäische Rechtsgeschichte this survey is to be followed by a *Repertorium* based on the manuscript evidence collected over the years by a team in Frankfurt. In addition to Frankfurt and Berkeley, other centers have intensified their research in the history of medieval legal science—Siena, Louvain, Milan, Montpellier, Leiden, Salamanca, and Würzburg, to name only a few. The magnitude of work still to be done is fortunately recognized today in a spirit of international cooperation and an endeavor to coordinate these researches.

NEW TOOLS, NEW APPROACHES

The need for cooperation is undeniable. With all the progress made, one must remember that ours is a much younger field of investigation than theology, philosophy, liturgy, or letters in the twelfth century. In all of these, modern scholarship had a headstart over the history of legal science: it suffices to take a look at shelf after shelf of Migne's *Patrologia latina* where about 60 out of 220 volumes cover twelfth-century texts. This reflects the simple fact that for the areas just mentioned the abbé Migne could lay his hands on a large number of volumes produced by learned editors between the sixteenth century and the nineteenth; he would have had next to nothing available in print to reproduce the literary output of the glossators of both laws. Publications of texts and textual studies by the great legal scholars of the sixteenth and the seventeenth century—Agustín, the Pithou brothers, Cujas, Baluze, and others—had shown the deep concern of their age for reconstructing ancient and medieval legislative sources;[39] their interest in the glossators of the two laws was rather limited. As for the antiquarians, from Diplovatatius (d. 1541) to Sarti (d. 1766) they had been primarily interested in the prosopography of the glossators, not in exploring their writings.[40] As a result of all this (if one may sum up three important centuries in a few lines) these writings were as good as nonexistent for Migne, who could, and did, reproduce only certain canonical collections, down to and including Gratian, while collections of secular law by and large remained outside the scope of his enterprise.

So much for the historical gap between the exploration of jurisprudence and of other areas in twelfth-century culture. It had already been considerably

---

[38]See ibid.

[39]On these scholars the historiographical introduction of Friedrich Maassen to his *Geschichte der Quellen und der Literatur des canonischen Rechts im Abendlande* 1 [un.] (Graz 1870; repr. 1956) xvii–lxvi, is still worth reading.

[40]Thomas Diplovatatius, *Liber de claris iuris consultis*, Pars posterior, ed. †Fritz Schulz, †Hermann Kantorowicz, and Giuseppe Rabotti, = *Studia Gratiana* 10 (Bologna 1968); Maurus Sarti and Maurus Fattorini, *De claris Archigymnasii Bononiensis professoribus a saeculo XI usque ad saeculum XIV* (2 vols. Bologna 1769–72; 2nd ed. Bologna 1888–96).

reduced by the time Haskins wrote, and today there is much that points to an accelerated pace of "catching up" with the accomplishments in other fields. The steady progress of microphotography makes it possible to place before the student the entire surviving output of the glossators, and to have him compare and collate the manuscript tradition to an extent never realized before. In this he is moreover assisted by the technological progress of electronic data storage and retrieval which allows him to record frequencies of glosses and gloss combinations in any number of manuscripts, patterns of variant readings, patterns of vocabulary, and the like. Obviously the need for coordinating research among the various centers becomes more urgent because of these technological developments. Intercommunication of microfilm holdings, if only in order to avoid the deterioration of the world's manuscripts by repeated exposure to photography; mutual information and consultation on ongoing projects, rather than competitive duplicating of research—these are some of the steps which will lead to a rewarding use of the means and the techniques at our disposal.[41] In particular, we should not forget that new methodological problems have been created by our seeking the aid of computers in the critical study of texts, especially of such composite "living" texts as an apparatus of glosses, a *lectura*, or a series of variously reported *quaestiones*. Some admirable pioneering work in this area has been done at the Max-Planck-Institut in Frankfurt. Further experimentation, and scrutiny of the statistical results, may one day tell us to what extent critical problems in the *textes vivants* of the jurists are quantifiable. Here is a field in which coordination of efforts among the major centers is particularly desirable.[42]

IV. ASPECTS OF THE NEW JURISPRUDENCE

If new vistas are opened up by new technical aids to research, one should not forget that these devices must be applied to a given body of knowledge, to a body of source material that is on record somewhere. It would be a great challenge to take stock, even merely to put out a bibliography of all that has been done in the last fifty years to make that body grow. But it may be more helpful, in preference to such a survey, to take up a few selected points which I think are characteristic of new insights into the jurisprudence of the twelfth century.

---

[41] *Conservation et reproduction des manuscrits et imprimés anciens: Colloque international* organisé par la Bibliothèque Vaticane à l'occasion de son Ve centenaire 21–24 octobre 1975, Studi e testi 276 (Vatican City 1976).

[42] See Gero Dolezalek, "Computers and Medieval Manuscripts of Roman Law," BMCL n.s. 4 (1974) 79–85 and "Computer und Rechtsgeschichte: Einführung und Literaturüberblick," *Rechtsgeschichte und quantitative Geschichte: Arbeitsberichte*, ed. Filippo Ranieri, Ius commune Sonderheft 7 (Frankfurt 1977) 36–116.

THE METHODS OF THE NEW JURISPRUDENCE[43]

They grew out of the application to the higher disciplines of what people had learned in the trivium (grammar, rhetoric, dialectic). In this, nothing distinguishes the new scholarly (or scholastic) approach to law from what happened at the same time in theology: the old controversy on priority—were the lawyers or the theologians the first to apply these devices of logic and argumentation to their *auctoritates?*—has been quietly put to rest. It was a mistaken question, based on the search for "influences" where the reality was that of an intellectual climate which became apparent at the same time but in different ways north, west, and south, wherever the need for organizing knowledge in a comprehensive, rational manner was felt. We may call it a climate of desire for learning: it manifested itself in what was more than a search, rather an impassioned quest for understanding the universal order that must exist behind the accumulated, fragmentary, and often contradictory authorities of the past. The quest was not less intense where it concerned a body of *auctoritates* dealing with contingent realities rather than the eternal order of salvation; especially so if these were considered texts of authority because they rested, ultimately, on the authority of Rome: the imperial Rome of Justinian's *Corpus*, and the Apostles' Rome in the texts of canon law. While the great political confrontations, both in theory and in action, that were to grow out of the topos of the two Romes, are not our concern here, it is probably correct to say that the idea of Roman *auctoritas* was always in the back of the mind of those who first endeavored to transform the individual *auctoritates*, in both laws, into a coherent whole.

As for Irnerius and his school, Justinian's own assertion that no contradictions existed in his legislative work was enough incentive to use dialectic devices for harmonizing the texts. The apparently dull strings of references (*allegationes*) to parallel or adversative texts which make up a considerable part of the early glosses are actually an admirable record of the mastery of all parts of the *Corpus* achieved at an early time. They also gave occasional solutions for the conflicting references (*contraria*) and thus provided the first point of contact with the scholastic maxim, "diversa sunt, non adversa," which was to become one of the most powerful elements in the lawyer's mode of argumen-

[43]See in general Biagio Brugi, "Il metodo dei glossatori bolognesi," *Studi in onore di Salvatore Riccobono* (4 vols. Palermo 1936) 1.21–31; Albert Lang, "Rhetorische Einflüsse auf die Behandlung des Prozesses in der Kanonistik des 12. Jahrhunderts," *Festschrift Eduard Eichmann zum 70. Geburtstag*, ed. Martin Grabmann and Karl Hofmann (Paderborn 1940) 69–97; Kuttner, *Harmony from Dissonance* (n. 22 above); Georges Chevrier, "Sur l'art de l'argumentation chez quelques Romanistes médiévaux au XIIe et au XIIIe siècle," *Archives de philosophie du droit* 2nd ser. 11 (1966) 115–48; Bruno Paradisi, "Osservazioni sull'uso del metodo dialettico nei glossatori del sec. XII," *Atti del Convegno internazionale di studi Accursiani, Bologna 1963* (3 vols. Milan 1968) 2.619–36; Peter Weimar, "Die legistische Literatur und die Methode des Rechtsunterrichts der Glossatorenzeit," *Ius commune* 2 (1969) 43–83; Gerhard Otte, *Dialektik und Jurisprudenz*, Ius commune Sonderheft 1 (Frankfurt 1971); Harold J. Berman, "The Origins of Western Legal Science," *Harvard Law Review* 90 (1977) 894–943.

tation.[44] One could indeed reduce many of the literary forms employed by the glossators (of both laws) to *solutio contrariorum* as a common denominator.

Methodical assembling of references to parallel texts and *contraria* also characterizes the early glosses on Gratian's *Concordia*.[45] But this was more than a generation after Irnerius, in the 1140s: we are obviously faced with the transfer of a method from one discipline to another. From then on, the methods used in the schools of the civilian and the canonist glossators were to develop in very close relation to each other. But before recording these parallels, one should pause to remember what the lag of forty-odd years means: until Gratian, no comprehensive book of canons existed that had a standing of authority. Neither Burchard's collection from the beginning of the eleventh century, nor any of the collections from the circle of Gregory VII, nor the *Panormia* of Ivo of Chartres, from the century's last years, had ever become a focal point for organized teaching. And yet, in these last decades before 1100 the canonists had developed general doctrines of interpretation for which no parallels exist in that first generation then beginning to study Justinian's books at Bologna. Thus, when Gratian's *Concordia* was to become, forty years later, the "Digest" of a new school of canonists, the basic principles of hermeneutics were already there for them to use, as Gratian had used them in his connecting *dicta*. It cannot be far from the truth if we assume that the prologue of the *Panormia*—the most widely copied canonical collection before Gratian—was more instrumental than other treatises of the same period in disseminating these methods and principles.[46]

LITERARY FORMS[47]

Significance and development of the forms of writing used by the glossators of the two laws had only rarely been studied in any detail at the time Haskins wrote. Seckel's important monograph on *distinctiones* (1911) and the study on canonistic *summae* in relation to glosses by his pupil Juncker (1925) were the only major contributions since the times of Savigny and Schulte.[48] Likewise, on the relationship between the glossators' lectures and their writings not much

[44]Joseph de Ghellinck, *Le mouvement théologique du XIIe siècle* (2nd ed. Bruges 1948) 517–23; Henri de Lubac, "A propos de la formule: *diversi sed non adversi,*" *Recherches de science religieuse* 40 (1952) 27–40.

[45]For an early example see n. 52 below.

[46]References in n. 22 above. A tentative list of manuscripts for Ivo's *Panormia*, from printed library catalogues alone, was compiled by Peter Brommer, "Unbekannte Fragmente von Kanonessammlungen im Staatsarchiv Marburg," *Hessisches Jahrbuch für Landesgeschichte* 24 (1974) 228–33 at 232 n. 13 and could easily be enlarged.

[47]Besides writings cited below in the Bibliographical Note, see also Genzmer (n. 35 above); Alfons M. Stickler, "Sacerdotium et regnum nei decretisti e primi decretalisti: Considerazioni metodologiche di ricerca e testi," *Salesianum* 15 (1953) 575–612; Eduard M. Meijers, "Sommes, lectures et commentaires (1100 à 1250)," *Atti* (n. 35 above) *Bologna* 1.431–90, repr. in his *Etudes d'histoire du droit* (4 vols. Leiden 1956–73) 3.211–77; Weimar, "Die legistische Literatur" (n. 43 above). Genzmer's article remains unsurpassed as a general statement.

[48]See notes 32 and 33 above.

work had been done since Savigny's chapter on "Die Glossatoren als Schrift-steller." Comparative studies in the two branches of learned writing had hardly begun. On all these aspects scholarship has made considerable advances in the last fifty years. The late Erich Genzmer, in his paper for the Roman Congress of 1933, was the first to survey the work of the Roman law glossators by literary genres rather than by the personal dossiers of individual legists, and this ap-proach proved very fruitful for new research in the canonists as well.

It had long been known that all, or nearly all, these literary genres—*casus, summae, notabilia, brocardica, distinctiones*, and others—had their origin in different types of glosses. But modern technical facilities for ex-amining and recording all available manuscripts of the schools' "books of authority"—Justinian, Gratian, the Decretals—that contain twelfth-century glosses have made it possible in recent times to obtain better insights into the genesis of the early *apparatus* of glosses than could have been obtained by earlier scholars. These insights have also helped to establish much closer con-nections between the forms of lecturing and the types of glosses included in the *apparatus* of a professor. Both for the legists and the canonists it now ap-pears that we must abandon earlier conceptions which assumed a gradual de-velopment, from scattered single glosses by several authors down to the coherent *apparatus* of glosses published by an individual author as we know them for the end of the twelfth and the thirteenth century. This view had been largely determined by the difference of density (the early layers of glosses are more thinly spread), by the presence of *sigla* of different authors in the same layer, by the often fluctuating transmission of glosses in manuscripts whose layers of glosses on the whole seem to be related. These phenomena are un-deniable, but they only go to show that for the early generations of masters—and students—an *apparatus glossarum* did not yet mean what it meant at the time of Azo and Hugolinus or (among the canonists) an Alanus or Laurentius or Johannes Teutonicus. It could still have that looseness which comes from the connection with the lecture room, where the teacher will incor-porate quotations from others into his exegesis, will change a gloss in another year, dwell with preference on one text in the book and bypass another, and so on. In short, the early *apparatus* was a *texte vivant*.

These insights were developed in recent years by the Roman law scholars of the Max-Planck-Institut and by the parallel investigations of several canonists.[49] They are still far from solving all the complexities of the

---

[49]Gero Dolezalek, "Der Glossenapparat des Martinus Gosia zum Digestum Novum," ZRG rom Abt 84 (1967) 245–349; Weimar in Coing, *Handbuch* 1.168–71. For the canonists, see Jiří Kejř, "La genèse de l'apparat 'Ordinaturus' au Décret de Gratien," *Proceedings of the Second In-ternational Congress of Medieval Canon Law, Boston . . . 1963*, ed. Stephan Kuttner and J. Joseph Ryan, Monumenta iuris canonici, ser. C: Subsidia 1 (Vatican City 1965) 45–53, the first of a series of recent studies on "Ordinaturus"; see Alfons M. Stickler, "Zur Entstehungsgeschichte und Verbreitung des Dekretapparats 'Ordinaturus Magister Gratianus,'" *Studia Gratiana* 12 (1967) 111–41; idem, "La genesi degli apparati di glosse dei Decretisti presupposto fondamentale

manuscript tradition, but definitely bring us a step closer to the ideal goal of a *Corpus glossarum*. One must, however, not stop here. In both laws the literary production that detached itself from the *lectio* or *apparatus*, as well as the production that had its origin outside the *lectio*, has become much better known during the last fifty years, and our understanding has undoubtedly profited from the typological approach. New works and new manuscripts of known or imperfectly known works have been discovered at a rapid pace, and in most cases—more perhaps for the canonists than the legists—it has been possible to assign (at least provisionally) places or regions of origin and approximate times of origin. Only a few of such writings will be briefly mentioned here.

Summae have always attracted the modern student of medieval doctrines because they are more compact than the unwieldy *apparatus* or *lecturae*, and are not beset with the same problems of transmission: a single manuscript may suffice for study, and some of them at least exist in adequate editions. While the legists' *summae* presented the subject matter of a given *titulus* in a formally organized, comprehensive fashion, the canonists' *summae* in the twelfth century in most cases combined the general presentation of a section (*distinctio, quaestio*) of Gratian's work with an exegesis of individual *capitula*, attached, not differently from a gloss, to lemma after lemma within the text. They thus fulfilled the function of *summae* and *apparatus* in one—and often indeed only the prevailing form of manuscript tradition will allow us to decide whether a work was meant to be a *summa* or an *apparatus*.[50] On the other hand, *summae* which were meant as general treatises at times abandoned the legal order of the law book, reorganizing the subject matter in a "system" of their own. All works of this type thus far attested for the twelfth century seem to be connected with the French and Rhenish schools.[51]

Solutio contrariorum as a principle of harmonizing interpretations first made its modest appearance in the chains of *allegationes* characteristic already of the earliest marginal glosses. From the often terse explanation of the *contrarium* in those glosses,[52] the methodical application of the principle grew into a basic element of several literary types. Thus we have collections of

---

della critica del loro testo," *La critica del testo*, Atti del secondo Congresso Internazionale della Società Italiana di Storia del Diritto [1967] (2 vols. Florence 1971) 2.771–81; and four articles by Rudolf Weigand: "Der erste Glossenapparat zum Dekret: 'Ordinaturus magister,'" BMCL n.s. 1 (1971) 31–41; "Die Glossen des Cardinalis (Magister Hubald?) zum Dekret Gratians, besonders zu C.27 q.2," BMCL n.s. 3 (1973) 73–95; "Frühe Glossen zu D.12 cc. 1–6 des Dekrets Gratians," BMCL n.s. 5 (1975) 35–51; and "Welcher Glossenapparat zum Dekret ist der Erste?" *Archiv für katholisches Kirchenrecht* 139 (1970) 459–81.

[50]Kuttner, *Repertorium* 122–24, 161–63, etc.

[51]Stephan Kuttner and Eleanor Rathbone, "Anglo-Norman Canonists of the Twelfth Century: An Introductory Study," *Traditio* 7 (1949–51) 279–358 at 314.

[52]Thus a very early gloss on Gratian's opening statement, "Humanum genus duobus regitur, naturali uidelicet iure et moribus" (Mankind is governed by two things: natural law and moral conventions) notes a *contrarium*, Dist. 96 c. 10 *Duo*, i.e. the famous saying of Gelasius on royal power and pontifical authority; the solution couldn't be shorter, six words: "regitur ab illis set per hec": it [mankind] is governed by those [powers] but through these [rules] (BN lat 3888, fol. 10r).

distinctiones, especially among canonists, where a quoted text, followed by an adversative *auctoritas*, is the subject matter of the distinction. *Solutio contrariorum* was applied at an advanced stage to the collections of *brocardica* or *generalia*, on which much work has been done in recent years.[53] If an *argumentum generale* was a maxim of which the contrary also found support in the sources, a dialectic solution would have to be found—differently from the *regula iuris* which suffered only an *exceptio* but no *contrarium*. Thus at least the theory: actually, the boundary line between *regula* and *generale*, rule and commonplace, was not at all clear to every medieval writer—to say nothing of the often erratic qualification as "universal" of a maxim that was really only "general."[54] In any event, *solutio contrariorum* was the answer to the dilemma.

The literary category of *quaestiones legitimae—quaestiones decretales* to the canonists—was virtually unexplored when Haskins wrote. Writings in this class are, however, among the most accomplished, one may even say elegant, *solutiones contrariorum*. From simple antinomies in the sources to hypothetical cases, from real difficulties in interpreting a legal term to the didactic device of formulating statements as questions, the *quaestio decretalis* or *legitima* offered a broad area of dialectic *solutiones contrariorum*. They were sometimes clad in the Socratic dress of a dialogue, sometimes presented as a more elementary question-and-answer catechism, sometimes made into structural elements of a *summa*. The dialogues of Rogerius, the *Quaestiones de iuris subtilitatibus* (of still controversial authorship), the frequently copied *Summa decretalium quaestionum* by Honorius of Richmond present different aspects of this important species of writing.[55]

The boundary between this type of *quaestio*, ultimately based on a technique in lecturing, and the *quaestio disputata* is not always easy to draw, except that the latter, as far as we can determine, had its origin in the practical exercises of disputation in the classroom, which from the times of the second generation of Roman law glossators (Bulgarus) supplemented the *lectio* and took place under the master's direction. The *quaestiones* were collected mostly by student reporters (*quaestiones reportatae*), while collections arranged and edited by the professors themselves (*quaestiones redactae*) were the exception at the beginning. On the problems of transmission, formal structure (only rarely maintained in its entirety), and historical development, Kantorowicz's pioneering study of 1939 remains fundamental. Much supplementary informa-

---

[53]Kuttner, "Réflexions sur les brocards des glossateurs," *Mélanges Joseph de Ghellinck* (2 vols. Gembloux 1951) 2.767–92; Severino Caprioli, "Tre capitoli intorno alla nozione di 'regula iuris' nel pensiero dei glossatori," *Annali di storia del diritto* 5–6 (1961–62) 221–374; Peter Weimar, "Argumenta brocardica," *Studia Gratiana* 14 (1967) 89–123; D'Amelio (n. 28 above).

[54]Genzmer (n. 35 above) 424–25; Kuttner, "Réflexions" (n. 53 above) 788–92.

[55]Kantorowicz, *Studies* (see Bibliographical Note) 122–44 and 181; Kuttner, "Zur neuesten Glossatorenforschung," *Studia et documenta historiae et iuris* 6 (1940) 275–319 at 304–08; Kuttner and Rathbone (n. 51 above) 304–16; Weimar in Coing, *Handbuch* 1.222–26 (with full bibliography on the *Quaestiones de iuris subtilitatibus* at 225).

tion has since become available; a series of studies preliminary to a complete *repertorium* of the canonists' *quaestiones* has been published by Gérard Fransen in the course of the last two decades.[56]

One last observation with regard to the typology of the glossators' works: without doubt the writers consciously chose one or another form of writing for presenting their subject matter. The reasons for their choice we may not always be able to see, but it was certainly not playfulness if they sometimes went over the same ground in different forms.[57] On the other hand, there was nothing slavish in their observance of set forms. For instance, the lecture on a given *lex* or canon or decretal traditionally began with the *casus*, that is, a summary of the contents of that particular text, giving first an outline of the facts (if they are reported) underlying the decision or ruling, then the ruling itself. But when *casus* came to be detached from the glosses of a law book and to be published in sequence, so as to provide students and practitioners with a handy survey of the individual *leges* or *capitula*, elements of exegesis began to enter into what had first been a purely descriptive device. The *Casus Codicis* of Willielmus de Cabriano (only recently rediscovered in their entirety) or the *Casus Decretorum* of Benencasa of Arezzo illustrate this expansion into an interpretive approach. Thereby they border on a literary form the school called a *commentum*: an exploration of the contents and problems of a given text by all the familiar dialectic means, but attached to the individual *lex* or *capitulum* as a whole, not to individual lemmata as one would do in a gloss. This style of writing was to become dominant in all commentaries by the mid-fourteenth century; it has only recently been given some attention for the earlier period.[58] (We may note in passing that where the lawyers of the twelfth century define the contrast between *commentum* and *glossa*, they do it in the terms coined by William of Conches in his commentaries on the *Timaeus* and on Priscian: an illustration of the intellectual bond between the scholastic fields of learning.)[59]

---

[56]Hermann Kantorowicz, "The Quaestiones disputatae of the Glossators," *Tijdschrift voor Rechtsgeschiedenis* 16 (1939) 1–67, reprinted in *Rechtshistorische Schriften* (n. 11 above) 137–85; Kuttner, "Glossatorenforschung" (n. 55 above) 286–89; idem, "Bernardus Compostellanus antiquus," *Traditio* 1 (1943) 277–340 at 320–27; Gérard Fransen, "Les 'questiones' des canonistes" (I–IV), *Traditio* 12 (1956) 566–92; 13 (1957) 481–501; 19 (1963) 516–31; and 20 (1964) 495–502; and other papers on individual collections, ibid. 21 (1965) 492–510, 519–20; 23 (1967) 516–34; and BMCL n.s. 6 (1976) 29–46; Charles Lefebvre and Gérard Fransen, "Quaestiones," *Dictionnaire de droit canonique* 7 (1965) 407–18.

[57]Thus Ricardus Anglicus in his several writings on Gratian (*Summa brevis, Distinctiones,* etc.) and on the *Compilatio prima* (*Generalia, Casus, Apparatus*).

[58]Meijers, "Sommes" (n. 47 above) 464–65 (= *Etudes* 3.236–37); Kuttner, *Repertorium* 229–30, 397–99; and his introduction to Johannes Andreae, *In quinque Decretalium libros Novella commentaria* (5 vols. in 4, Turin 1963, repr. of Venice 1581 ed.) 1.v–xiv at xi; idem, "Johannes Andreae and his *Novella* on the Decretals of Gregory IX," *The Jurist* 24 (1964) 393–408 at 404 (J. A. on *commentum*); Weimar, in Coing, *Handbuch* 1.212–14; Gero Dolezalek, "Die Casus Codicis des Wilhelmus de Cabriano," *Studien zur europäischen Rechtsgeschichte*, ed. Walter Wilhelm (Frankfurt 1972) 25–52 (rediscovery of the work).

[59]Compare the definitions of Huguccio's *Derivationes* and the anonymous *De verbis quibusdam legalibus*, quoted by Weimar in Coing, *Handbuch* 1.214 n. 1, with *Guillaume de*

NEW LAW: THE DECRETALS

There existed, of course, one major difference between the two branches of the *droit savant* in the way of developing new insights and fresh interpretations. Civilian glossators dealt with a completed corpus of sources: since contemporary statutes and custom remained outside their academic concerns, theirs was a "closed revelation," ending with the *Authenticum*, the accepted Latin version of Justinian's *Novellae*. The Staufen emperors, Frederick Barbarossa and Frederick II, ordered the insertion into Justinian's Code of certain of their legislative enactments; but that was high politics rather than concern for the growth of the law. For the canonists, on the other hand, creation of new law in the Church was an ongoing process. Gratian's book was the capstone of the traditional "canons and decrees of the holy fathers," but his *Concordia* could by no means provide firm answers to all the problems of their interpretation, still less to the new problems that the canons did not cover at all. It is a matter of common knowledge that it was the greatly enhanced magisterial and judicial authority of the papal office in the twelfth century that provided such answers in an ever-growing number of *epistolae decretales*.[60] These letters might be answers to inquiries sent by bishops on difficult points of law (*consultatio*), or they might be decisions on cases that had been appealed or directly submitted to the apostolic see by aggrieved parties; and these decisions might be final sentences, simply to be carried out by the prelates abroad to whom they were addressed (*mandatum*), or they might state the terms of the sentence as contingent upon the facts to be ascertained by the judges whom the pope delegated, and instructed in the letter, to gather the evidence and terminate the case (*commissio*).

Over seven hundred decretal letters from the chancery of Alexander III (1159–81), a production rapidly outgrowing that of his predecessors, can still be traced today. More generalized, unsolicited papal rulings establishing new law (*decreta, constitutiones*), rarely issued in the twelfth century, were to become more frequent in the thirteenth. Important new general legislation, however, came from papal councils, above all Alexander III's Lateran council

---

Conches: Glosae super Platonem, ed. Edouard Jeauneau, Textes philosophiques du moyen âge 13 (Paris 1965) c.10 p. 67 with note *c*, and introduction p. 16 n. 2. The observation was first made by Raymond Klibansky, as quoted by Richard W. Hunt, "Hugutio and Petrus Helias," M&RS 2 (1950) 174–78 at 174 n. 2.

[60]For what follows, see now in general Charles Duggan, *Twelfth-Century Decretal Collections and Their Importance in English History* (London 1963); Jacoba J. H. M. Hanenburg, "Decretals and Decretal Collections in the Second Half of the Twelfth Century" (review article), *Tijdschrift voor Rechtsgeschiedenis* 34 (1966) 552–99; Charles Lefebvre, "Ius novum: Le droit pontifical," in *L'âge classique* (see Bibliographical Note, below) 133–48; Knut Wolfgang Nörr, "Päpstliche Dekretalen und römisch-kanonischer Zivilprozess," *Studien zur europäischen Rechtsgeschichte* (n. 58 above) 53–65; Gérard Fransen, *Les décrétales et les collections de décrétales*, Typologie des sources du moyen âge occidental 2 (Turnhout 1972); see also the remarks in Kuttner, *Harmony from Dissonance* (n. 22 above) 27–30.

of 1179 (commonly designated as Lateran III) and, early in the following century, the great council of Innocent III (Lateran IV).

Decretal letters, like the imperial rescripts of late Antiquity, were originally meant as responses to individual inquiries or rulings on individual issues. The initiative for transforming them into "precedents," that is into *auctoritates* that could be cited as belonging to the general body of canon law, came entirely from the schools. Reference to individual letters of Alexander III appeared in commentaries on Gratian by the late 1160s, and by the end of his pontificate, the collecting of decretals had progressed from small appendices, placed on the flyleaves of copies of Gratian's book, to separate collections, often circulated together with copies of the legislation enacted in the Third Lateran Council, and eventually to collections organized topically into systems of *tituli*.[61] With the adoption at Bologna of one of these, Bernard of Pavia's *Breviarium extravagantium*, as a text for lecturing on the new law side by side with Gratian's *Concordia*, a new stage in the teaching and writing of the canonists was reached.

This brings us to the end of the twelfth century. The next step would be that the popes themselves directed the choice, from the copious output of the chancery, of those decretals that were to serve as texts of authority "in judgments and the schools," and published them in official collections. The first of such formal law books was promulgated by Innocent III in 1209. We cannot follow here the further course of papal "codifications" throughout the thirteenth century; but their academic matrix remains apparent in that they all were officially addressed to the masters and students of the universities, not to the hierarchy of the Church.

Already the medieval canonists showed a certain interest in the history of the decretal law, and some of the collections between Gratian and Gregory IX were printed as early as the sixteenth century.[62] Considerable progress in decretal research had been made by the time Haskins wrote; but that was before the great leap forward which the lifelong work of the late Walther Holtzmann has made possible in our knowledge of twelfth-century decretals and their collections. The first of his many papers appeared in the same year as

---

[61]The starting point for modern research on the collections (some of it cited in the preceding note) is Walther Holtzmann, "Über eine Ausgabe der päpstlichen Dekretalen des 12. Jahrhunderts," *Nachr Göttingen 1945*, 15–36; cf. Kuttner, "Notes on a Projected Corpus of Twelfth-Century Decretal Letters" (review article) *Traditio* 6 (1948) 345–51. Holtzmann published his final list of collections in "Kanonistische Ergänzungen zur Italia Pontificia I," *Quellen und Forschungen aus italienischen Archiven und Bibliotheken* 37 (1957) 58–67 (= separate edition [of pts. 1 and 2] Tübingen 1959, 4–13). It is now superseded by the list in the posthumous *Studies* cited below, n. 64. For the systematic collections see *Index titulorum decretalium ex collectionibus tam privatis quam publicis conscriptus*, ed. Kuttner, IRMAE, Subsidia 2 (Milan 1977) vi–xiv and, most recently, Peter Landau, "Die Entstehung der systematischen Dekretalensammlungen und die europäische Kanonistik des 12. Jahrhunderts," ZRG kan Abt 66 (1979) 120–48.

[62]References in the *Index titulorum* (see preceding note) vi, x; also Kuttner, "Antonio Agustín's Edition of the Compilationes antiquae," BMCL n.s. 7 (1977) 1–14.

Haskins's book;[63] by the time of his death (1963) he had laid the groundwork for a *Corpus decretalium*, the completion of which remains a major task for the future. Meanwhile, much of the preparatory materials and drafts he left unfinished is now being revised and edited for publication.[64]

CENTERS AND MASTERS

This much on the making of new law in the Roman curia. Turning again to the history of the schools, one can observe that the proud tradition of Bologna as *mater legum* led already in the Middle Ages to a more than antiquarian interest in the succession of the masters (*doctores, magistri*) of her *studium* and the record of their writing. The history of the early civilians and canonists in Bologna may contain a certain number of legendary elements but provides us all the same with a great wealth of material that allows us to connect documented names with extant writings, signed glosses, and so on. Historians less than a hundred years ago were still not free from the spell of Bologna. From Johannes Andreae (d. 1349) down to Mauro Sarti's posthumous book on the professors of the *Archigymnasium Bononiense* (1769),[65] bibliographical information was so much richer than for any other center of legal studies that even the discovery of twelfth-century writings in the two laws which obviously originated elsewhere did not change the general image. For some writings, such as the set of epitomizing books around the *Petri Exceptiones legum Romanarum*, denial of their Provençal or rather Dauphinois origin continues even today (one had better not analyze the partly emotional reasons).[66] As regards canon law, the spell of Bologna still remained powerful after more than half a dozen writings on Gratian had been found and recorded that were demonstrably of French, Anglo-Norman, or Rhenish origin. In his *Geschichte der Quellen und Literatur*, J. F. von Schulte—who had discovered some of these works himself—made no attempt at grouping them together or asking the question whether there might have been schools of law in France.

[63]Walther Holtzmann, "Beiträge zu den Dekretalensammlungen des zwölften Jahrhunderts," ZRG kan Abt 16 (1927) 37–115; he published four decretals at the same time in "Papst Alexander III and Ungarn," *Ungarische Jahrbücher* 6 (1926) 397–426, reprinted in his *Beiträge zur Reichs- und Papstgeschichte des hohen Mittelalters*, Bonner historische Forschungen 8 (Bonn 1957) 139–67; a bibliography of his papers up to 1956, ibid. 235–38.

[64]See the notice by the present writer in "Annual Report" on the research materials Holtzmann left in his will to the Institute of Medieval Canon Law, *Traditio* 20 (1964) 491–95. Since the lines above were written, *Studies in the Collections of Twelfth-Century Decretals*, from the papers of the late Walther Holtzmann, edited, revised, and translated by C. R. Cheney and Mary G. Cheney, has appeared, Monumenta iuris canonici, ser. B: Corpus collectionum 3 (Vatican City 1979); a volume of *Decretales ineditae* and two volumes of *Regesta decretalium* are being readied for the printer by Stanley Chodorow and Charles Duggan.

[65]Johannes Andreae: references in the "Introduction" cited in n. 58 above; Sarti: n. 40 above.

[66]Bibliography in Weimar, in Coing, *Handbuch* 1.254; for the latest Italian claim, by Giovanni Santini, *Ricerche sulle "Exceptiones legum Romanarum"* (Milan 1969), see the reviews by Peter Weimar, ZRG rom Abt 88 (1971) 488–92 and André Gouron, *Tijdschrift voor Rechtsgeschiedenis* 40 (1972) 286–92; idem, *La science juridique française aux XIe et XIIe siècles: Diffusion du droit de Justinien et influences canoniques jusqu'à Gratien*, IRMAE 1.4.d–e (Milan 1978) 8–10, 42–78.

Additional discoveries and studies of the last fifty years have helped to change the simplified picture that gave Bologna to the lawyers and Paris to the artists and theologians. The history of universities is outside my assignment; the legal historian can only establish that a number of canonistic treatises of all sorts were written in the last third of the twelfth century in or around Paris, Cologne, Rouen, Mainz, Oxford, Northampton, and perhaps Troyes and Reims.[67] This goes to show that "centers" of teaching the sacred canons from Gratian's book were developing in many places in the West; but in the absence of records of organized *studia* for most of these places, or of any records of a college of *doctores* (or *magistri*) *decretorum* even for *studia* such as Paris, we should see those schools or centers as unstructured groups of students around individual masters. This might also explain the anonymity of most of the preserved *summae, apparatus,* and other writings from outside Bologna. Where names—and especially names traceable in other sources—are recorded in these writings, we are perhaps entitled to assume the existence of a school in the formal sense. This was probably true of Oxford for the teaching of canon law at the turn of the twelfth century; and it was probably true for the teaching of Roman law in Montpellier in the 1160s.[68] Civilian learning had been brought to the Dauphiné a generation earlier. The probable connection of the circle of the *Petri Exceptiones* with Valence has been strengthened by the recent discovery of a *Summa Institutionum* which proves that an active center existed at Die between 1120 and 1130.[69] The canons regular of St Ruf in Avignon seem to have had an important share in this first bloom of Roman law in which the influence of both the Bolognese glossator Martinus Gosia and the earlier school of Pavia can be discerned, as the latest investigations of André Gouron have shown.[70]

Much research remains to be done on all these centers and schools in southern and central France, Normandy, the Rhineland, and England. But if we turn once more to Bologna, as we should, we shall find that some of the most significant contributions of modern scholarship center around the beginnings of the canonistic jurisprudence, that is, around Gratian and the first generation of his school.[71] We find here in recent writing some of the fascina-

[67]See e.g. Kuttner, "Les débuts de l'école canoniste française," *Studia et documenta historiae et iuris* 4 (1938) 193–204; idem, "Réflexions" (n. 53 above) 783–88; Kuttner and Rathbone (n. 51 above) passim.

[68]The teaching of Placentinus in Montpellier and his death there (1192) are certain, but this may not have been a formal "school"; see André Gouron, *Les juristes de l'école de Montpellier*, IRMAE 4.3.a (Milan 1970) 3–4; for Placentinus's disciples see Gouron, *La science* (n. 66 above) 107–10. For Oxford see Kuttner and Rathbone (n. 51 above) 321–27.

[69]*La Summa Institutionum "Iustiniani est in hoc opere"* (*Manuscrit Pierpont Morgan 903*), ed. Pierre Legendre, Ius commune Sonderheft 2 (Frankfurt 1973). Legendre discovered the text in 1963.

[70]Gouron (n. 11 above).

[71]The renewed interest found expression in the 1948 issue of *Apollinaris* (vol. 21; contributions by Van Hove, Le Bras, Vetulani, Kuttner, Battelli, et al.) and in the series of *Studia Gratiana* launched by G. Forchielli in 1953.

tion the sixteenth-century humanists experienced when they first began to scrutinize Justinian's codification *more gallico* as a historical document, in contrast to its juristic construction, *more italico*, as part of the common law of their time. Or to put it differently, studies on Gratian are now going through the phase of *Interpolationenkritik* and *Textstufenkritik* that has characterized much of the Roman law scholars' work for nearly a hundred years.

The need for a more satisfactory critical edition than that produced by Friedberg of the *Concordia discordantium canonum* has been voiced before, during, and after the eighth-centenary celebrations of 1952 in Bologna and Rome. Work undertaken toward a classification of the hundreds of manuscripts in existence, especially the work of Jacqueline Rambaud and her collaborators in Paris, has brought out that the "internal" history of Gratian's text presents much more intricate problems than textual corruptions at the hands of its copyists. It has brought out, for instance, that occasional misgivings of earlier historians about the disproportionate *tractatus de penitentia* (which bursts the framework of the topic proposed in C.33 q.3) or about the *tractatus de consecratione* (where Gratian's dialectic method is abandoned) are justified by the somewhat erratic manuscript tradition of these sections, and that Gratian's book in the beginning may have included at those points only some parts of the vulgate text.[72]

Pride of place in the new movement of textual criticism belongs to the late Adam Vetulani of Cracow (d. 1976). In a brilliant paper, drafted under most difficult conditions during the war and published in France in 1947, he demonstrated, with little more at his disposal than a copy of Friedberg's text and apparatus, that most of the clusters of Roman law excerpts found in Gratian were not part of the Magister's original text. The evidence consists primarily of irregularities of transmission in the manuscripts, combined with signs of obviously deficient redaction in the vulgate text. Other instances of imperfect coordination and fitful reworking, indicating several stages of redaction, have been pointed out in the wake of Vetulani's pioneering studies also for areas of the *Concordia* outside the Roman law excerpts. Some of these inconsistencies had already been noticed by the early glossators of Gratian's book.[73]

---

[72]Jacqueline Rambaud-Buhot, "L'étude des manuscrits du Décret de Gratien conservés en France," *Studia Gratiana* 1 (1953) 119–45; "Plan et méthode de travail pour la rédaction d'un catalogue des manuscrits du Décret de Gratien," *Revue d'histoire ecclésiastique* 48 (1953) 211–23; "L'étude des manuscrits du Décret de Gratien," *Congrès de droit canonique médiéval, Louvain et Bruxelles, 22-26 Juillet 1958*, Bibliothèque de la Revue d'histoire ecclésiastique 33 (Louvain 1959) 25–42, with a discussion (42–48) and sample description (49–63); and her general statement in *L'âge classique* (see Bibliographical Note, below) 78–99. See also Louis Guizard, "Manuscrits du 'Decretum Gratiani' conservés à l'Université de Paris," *Studia Gratiana* 3 (1955) 17–50; Karol Wojtyła [pope John Paul II], "Le traité 'de penitentia' de Gratien dans l'abrégé de Gdańsk Mar. F. 275," *Studia Gratiana* 7 (1959) 355–90.

[73]Adam Vetulani, "Gratien et le droit romain," *Revue historique de droit français et étranger*, 4th ser. 24–25 (1945–47) 11–48, and "Encore un mot sur le droit romain dans le Décret

Wherever textual studies reach the point at which stages of reworking, accretion, or elimination can be convincingly demonstrated, the question of how to interpret such evidence will often remain controversial. We should not expect studies on Gratian today to differ in this respect from higher biblical criticism or the critical analysis of Justinian's Digest. The case for Gratian himself, or for Gratian together with a team of students, having revised the original draft of the *Concordia* more than once over the years and finally circulated it with all its imperfections, cannot be disproved as long as no manuscript evidence of an "Ur-Gratian" turns up. On the other hand, fascinating historical perspectives open up for those who accept "internal" evidence without transcriptional support. In his later years, and basing himself on his reading of the twelfth-century *Abbreviatio "Gratiani opus egregium"* in an Italian manuscript now at Gdansk, Vetulani arrived at postulating an original state of Gratian's work—without the Roman law texts, without the summaries (rubrics) of the individual chapters, without the Second Lateran Council of 1139, perhaps even without the First of 1123—written by Gratian in the first quarter of the century, with the purpose of strengthening papal against imperial jurisdiction, very much in the spirit of the Investiture Conflict before Worms. This hypothetical Master Gratian probably was no longer alive when his book was revised, enlarged, "romanized," and provided with rubrics about 1140 by the author of the Gdansk *abbreviatio*.[74]

Vetulani's theories have proved attractive for a younger generation today probing further into Gratian's background, his ecclesiology, the acceptance of his work, and its first expositors at Bologna.[75] We should keep an open mind

---

de Gratien," *Apollinaris* 21 (1948) 129–34. See further on Gratian and the Roman Law: Jacqueline Rambaud-Buhot, "Le 'Corpus juris civilis' dans le Décret de Gratien," *Bibliothèque de l'Ecole des Chartes* 111 (1953) 54–64, "Le Décret de Gratien et le Droit Romain: Influence d'Yves de Chartres," *Revue historique de droit français et étranger* 4th ser. 35 (1957) 290–300, and "Les textes de droit romain," *L'âge classique* (Bibliographical Note, below) 119–28; Kuttner, "New Studies on the Roman Law in Gratian's Decretum," *Seminar* 11 (1953) 12–50 and "Additional Notes on the Roman Law in Gratian," ibid. 12 (1954) 68–74; Giuseppe Rabotti, "Le interpolazioni dei testi romanistici nel 'Decretum Gratiani' secondo Diomede Brava," *Studia Gratiana* 8 (1962) 115–58; Jean Gaudemet, "Das römische Recht in Gratians Dekret," *Österreichisches Archiv für Kirchenrecht* 12 (1961) 177–91.

[74]Adam Vetulani, "Le Décret de Gratien et les premiers décrétistes à la lumière d'une source nouvelle," *Studia Gratiana* 7 (1959) 273–354 (trans. of *Dekret Gracjana i pierwsi dekretyści w świetle nowego źródła* [Warsaw 1955]); "Nouvelles vues sur le Décret de Gratien," *La Pologne au Xe Congrès international des sciences historiques à Rome* (Warsaw 1955) 83–105, and other papers; summing-up in "Autour du Décret de Gratien," *Apollinaris* 41 (1968) 43–58.

[75]Stanley Chodorow, *Christian Political Theory and Church Politics in the Mid-Twelfth Century: The Ecclesiology of Gratian's Decretum* (Berkeley 1972); John T. Noonan, Jr., "Was Gratian Approved at Ferentino?" BMCL n.s. 6 (1976) 15–27, "Who Was Rolandus?" *Law, Church, and Society: Essays in Honor of Stephan Kuttner*, ed. Kenneth Pennington and Robert Somerville (Philadelphia 1977) 21–48, "Gratian Slept Here: The Changing Identity of the Father of the Systematic Study of Canon Law," *Traditio* 35 (1979) 145–72, and "The True Paucapalea?" *Proceedings of the Fifth International Congress of Medieval Canon Law, Salamanca, 21–25 September 1976*, ed. Stephan Kuttner and Kenneth Pennington, Monumenta iuris canonici, ser. C: Subsidia 6 (Vatican City 1980) 157–86.

for such revisionist interpretations of history, even though we might find the evidence inconclusive.[76] The exasperating lack of verifiable information on the "father of the science of canon law" made him an object of legend before the end of the twelfth century. We ought not to be surprised if the elusive *magister* still invites speculation in the twentieth.

Bibliographical Note

To the student of twelfth-century civilian and canonistic jurisprudence, the classics of the nineteenth century, although overtaken in numerous details by modern research, remain indispensable. Friedrich Karl von Savigny's *Geschichte des römischen Rechts im Mittelalter* (2nd ed. 7 vols. Heidelberg 1834–51; repr. Bad Homburg 1961) has not been surpassed in its breadth of scope by any single later treatise. For the pre-Bolognese centuries of medieval Roman law, the work of Max Conrat (Cohn), especially his *Geschichte der Quellen und Literatur des römischen Rechts im früheren Mittelalter* (Leipzig 1891; repr. Aalen 1963), completed and confirmed Savigny's basic insights. In important modern treatises of a wider scope, such as Francesco Calasso, *Medio Evo del diritto*, vol. 1: *Le fonti* (Milan 1954), or Franz Wieacker, *Privatrechtsgeschichte der Neuzeit* (2nd ed. Göttingen 1967), substantial sections are given to the beginnings and first achievements of the renascence of Roman law. "Roman and Canon Law in the Middle Ages," by Harold D. Hazeltine, chapter 21 in the *Cambridge Medieval History*, vol. 5 (1929), still remains useful reading; chapters 2–6 of Walter Ullmann, *Law and Politics in the Middle Ages* (London and Ithaca N.Y. 1975, in the series The Sources of History, ed. Geoffrey R. Elton) provide a solid introduction to the *droit savant* as well as to non-Roman secular law. But to appreciate the great progress made after Savigny in the history of the Roman law glossators at Bologna and elsewhere, one must turn to the far-flung monographic and periodical literature. Some of the writings that mark major steps of this progress have been indicated in section III of this paper. Among these, the work of Hermann Kantorowicz, *Studies in the Glossators of the Roman Law*, with the collaboration of William W. Buckland (Cambridge 1938; repr. with Addenda et corrigenda by Peter Weimar, Aalen 1969) presents a happy combination of critical research and a preliminary synthesis. A full bibliography is now available in the chapter on "Die legistische Literatur der Glossatorenzeit" which Peter Weimar contributed to the *Handbuch der Quellen und Literatur der neueren europäischen Privatrechtsgeschichte*, ed. Helmut Coing, vol. 1: *Mittelalter (1100–1500)* (Munich 1973) 129–260. This comprehensive, critical, and carefully documented survey has become the indispensable guide to all we know at present of the methods and writings of the civilian glossators.

We should mention here the great collective enterprise of the *Ius Romanum Medii Aevi* (Milan 1961–   ), conceived as a "New Savigny" by its originator, the late Erich Genzmer (d. 1970), directed by an international committee, and organized as a systematically arranged series of contributions written by a large international group of scholars. Their individual studies on the topics assigned have appeared thus far as separate fascicles in the order of completion (not of their place in the systematic order); this makes it difficult to survey the present state of the whole project. Over thirty

---

[76]See Peter Classen, "Das Decretum Gratiani wurde nicht in Ferentino approbiert," BMCL n.s. 8 (1978) 38–40. The writer of these pages plans a critical study on revisionism in the history of canon law.

fascicles—some short essays, some of book length—have been published to date for the first and the fifth part of IRMAE, that is for the parts dealing with the pre-Bolognese history on the one hand, and the influence of Roman law and civilian learning from the thirteenth century on in individual countries, on the other. But as for the core of the projected work, on the universities (part 2) and the writings of the glossators (part 3) and the commentators after Accursius (part 4), completion of nearly all the major contributions remains a hope for the future.

For the history of the collections and writers of the canon law in the formative period, the nineteenth-century classic remains the first volume of Johann Friedrich von Schulte, *Die Geschichte der Quellen und Literatur des Canonischen Rechts von Gratian bis auf die Gegenwart* (3 vols. in 4 pts. Stuttgart 1875–80; repr. Graz 1956). No comparable major treatise on the developments of the last three hundred years before Gratian existed to replace the works of the eighteenth and the early nineteenth century, largely outdated by later research, until Paul Fournier and Gabriel Le Bras published the monumental *Histoire des collections canoniques en Occident depuis les Fausses Décrétales jusqu'au Décret de Gratien* (2 vols. Paris 1931–32). For the century after Gratian, which saw the most intense growth of canonistic learning and writing, the present writer's *Repertorium der Kanonistik (1140–1234): Prodromus Corporis glossarum*, vol. 1 [un.], Studi e testi 71 (Vatican City 1937; repr. 1973) has in most respects replaced Schulte's volume 1; it in turn needs revision in the light of more recent progress. The state of information available by the end of the Second War was reported in the tersely written and fully annotated book by Alphonse Van Hove, *Prolegomena*, Commentarium Lovaniense in Codicem iuris canonici 1.1 (2nd ed. Malines and Rome 1945). In the great series in progress, Histoire du droit et des institutions de l'Eglise en Occident (Paris 1955–   ), founded by the late Gabriel Le Bras (d. 1970), volume 7 is the fruit of collaboration by Le Bras, Jacqueline Rambaud, and Charles Lefebvre: *L'âge classique, 1140–1378: Sources et théorie du droit* (Paris 1965). Part 1, "Le legs de l'ancien droit: Gratien" (47–129), by Rambaud, and part 2, "Formation du droit classique" (131–345), by Lefebvre, present very substantial, original surveys of the sources and the writers for our period and beyond. An annual bibliography of publications in the field appeared from 1955 to 1970 in the Bulletin of the Institute of Medieval Canon Law as part of *Traditio*, vols. 11–26, thereafter in the *Bulletin of Medieval Canon Law*, new series 1–   (1971–   ).

Institutional Foundations of
the New Jurisprudence

Knut Wolfgang Nörr

This essay undertakes to describe the institutions connected with the rise of scientific jurisprudence and with its practical effectiveness in the twelfth century. Its subject, in other words, is the universities and, broadly speaking, the institutions of justice. The institutions established for legal praxis were commonly both a creation shaped in part by scientific jurisprudence and at the same time the vehicles of its further propagation. This does not mean that it will be possible to examine all the ways in which the new jurisprudence affected legal practice. Important as they are for the complete history of its effects, certain subjects must be omitted: the royal chanceries; the imperial chancery with its use of Roman legal terminology to present the Empire's public image;[1] legal writings which, like Glanvill's, show contact with scientific jurisprudence;[2] and notarial practice (to which, for this period alone, an entire lecture could be devoted). In this brief sketch I shall concentrate instead—since a focus is necessary—on the seat of ecclesiastical authority in Rome.

I. THE UNIVERSITIES

Among those universities which emerged slowly without any single moment of foundation (and one finds only this kind of university in the twelfth century), Bologna was preeminent in jurisprudence. At the beginning of the new discipline was the glossing of the Digest; that is, classical Roman law in the form given it by Justinian. The Bolognese renaissance of Roman law began at the end of the eleventh century. Its first important representative (with Pepo as a forerunner) was Irnerius, who attracted a circle of students about him, the most important of whom were the *quattuor doctores*; even before the middle of the century scholars were drawn from across the Alps and the British Isles.[3]

---

[1] See Robert L. Benson's study in this volume.
[2] See Stephan Kuttner's study in this volume.
[3] Eleanor Rathbone, ''Roman Law in the Anglo-Norman Realm,'' *Studia Gratiana* 11 (1967) 253–71 at 259ff.

Instruction was still free of civic, ecclesiastical, or secular control and had no fixed institutional form or organization. In this respect too the instruction of the Bolognese jurists resembled that of classical Roman law, which took the form of a private, loosely organized course of studies. Students in Bologna entered into agreements with specific teachers. Since these agreements led to a legal relation with the features of a corporation, they were no different from other pacts concluded for more than a single exchange of services and involving several persons or *socii*. Such agreements were typical of the Middle Ages, with its multiplicity of corporate ties. Whether these structures arose according to local Bolognese law need not be decided here; one must in any case be cautious in applying Roman or modern notions of contract, since these were only then in the process of developing—and at most, appeared simultaneously with the new forms themselves.

With the scholarly study of Gratian's *Decretum*, about the middle of the century, ecclesiastical law also became a subject of instruction in this new mode. The great powers of the time soon established contact with the Bolognese *studia*, not yet in the sense of systematically influencing them, but to some extent through recognizing them; emperor Frederick Barbarossa, for instance—above all through the Magna Carta of privileges, the *Authentica "Habita"* of 1158[4]—and in 1159 pope Alexander III, through the announcement of his election to the bishop, canons, *doctores*, and *magistri* of Bologna (intended perhaps in part as a countermove to the former).[5]

The actual establishment of the university and its legal organization began in the last decades of the twelfth century, at a time, that is, when modern Bolognese legal instruction as such had gained full acceptance. Windmills, after all, are built only where the wind blows. It follows that the way in which the teaching of law was now institutionalized and outside powers exerted their influence upon it was of secondary importance for the emergence of the new scientific jurisprudence: this topic belongs mainly to the history of the university.

The constitution of the *studium* resulted essentially from two initial developments. One was the joining together of students from a particular land to achieve solidarity in a foreign city far from home. Thus in 1174 the English "nation" erected an altar in San Salvatore in Bologna to honor Thomas Becket, and the Lombards appear as purchasers of a tract of land in 1191.[6] These compatriotic student associations also served for protection against the incipient monopolistic demands of the city of Bologna. The structuring of the

---

[4]On the date, see Winfried Stelzer, "Zum Scholarenprivileg Friedrich Barbarossas (Authentica 'Habita')," DA 34 (1978) 123–65.

[5]JL 10587. A decree of 1176–77 by a papal legate concerning the protection of student tenants also belongs in this context. See Peter Landau, "Papst Lucius III. und das Mietrecht in Bologna," *Proceedings of the Fourth International Congress of Medieval Canon Law, Toronto, 21–25 August 1972*, ed. Stephan Kuttner, Monumenta iuris canonici, ser. C: Subsidia 5 (Vatican City 1976) 511–22.

[6]See Coing, *Handbuch* 1.52.

university was completed in the thirteenth century. Each "nation" comprised a corporate body of students with an elected rector, and the nations combined into two *universitates* of *ultramontani* and *citramontani* with a common body of statutes and separate rectorates. The statutes, the earliest of which (1252) was recently discovered, specified among other things precisely which texts the lecturer had to cover in his principal lectures, and when (*forma per doctores in punctis servanda*).[7]

The other impetus to the development of the *studium*'s constitution lay in the formalization of examinations and of the conferment of the *licentia docendi*. In our period, this directly affected only those jurists who sought a career in academic teaching, though of course it also introduced a certain guarantee of the quality of juristic training. At this point we begin to find a connection between the teaching staff and the ecclesiastical authorities, a development which for the twelfth century is known primarily from France[8] and was thus not peculiar to the law school of Bologna. Examinations were the responsibility of the doctors, and in Bologna, as pope Honorius III decreed in 1219, the *licentia docendi* was conferred by the archdeacon (to whom the same pope later addressed his collection of decretals, the *Compilatio quinta*—a precedent that was not followed).

Paris, the other great center of studies in the twelfth century and the stronghold of the *artes liberales* and theology, played an uneven role in jurisprudence. Here Roman law served primarily as a discipline merely supplementary to canon law, so that Honorius III's constitution of 1219—forbidding clerics to teach or study Roman law in Paris—had a rather marginal effect and in its consequences did more harm to canon law.[9] The considerable cultivation of canon law in the twelfth century led to the emergence of an independent French school of decretists.[10] In Paris's development into a university, ecclesiastical institutions must be taken into account: the cathedral and collegiate schools as well as the traditional supervision by the *scholasticus* or chancellor. At the center of the university's structure stood not the organization of students, as in Bologna, but that of the *magistri*, the majority of whom were, to be sure, young masters in the faculty of arts. From the beginning of the thirteenth century, the corporation of *magistri* in Paris developed hand in hand with the pertinent rules of the new canon law.[11] Demarcation of author-

---

[7]From the statutes we learn that the *puncta* system itself was older. See the edition by Domenico Maffei, "Un trattato di Bonaccorso degli Elisei e i più antichi statuti dello Studio di Bologna nel manoscritto 22 della Robbins Collection," BMCL n.s. 5 (1975) 94 line 32.

[8]See Philippe Delhaye, "L'organisation scolaire au XIIe siècle," *Traditio* 5 (1947) 211–68.

[9]From the abundant literature on *Super speculam*, see Stephan Kuttner, "Papst Honorius III. und das Studium des Zivilrechts," *Festschrift für Martin Wolff: Beiträge zum Zivilrecht und internationalen Privatrecht*, ed. Ernst von Caemmerer et al. (Tübingen 1952) 79–101.

[10]Stephan Kuttner, "Les débuts de l'école canoniste française," *Studia et documenta historiae et iuris* 4 (1938) 193–204.

[11]Gaines Post has described this process in exemplary fashion: "Parisian Masters as a Corporation, 1200–1246," *Speculum* 9 (1934) 421–45 (= *Studies in Medieval Legal Thought: Public Law and the State, 1100–1322* [Princeton 1964] 27–60).

ity between examination by the *magistri* and the merely formal conferment of the *licentia docendi* by the chancellor followed in 1213. Two years later, the first reform regulations, recalling guild rules, were issued by the papal legate, Robert of Courson.[12] No further dates are needed; in sum, the universities of Paris and Bologna were constituted at about the same time: both received fixed form in approximately the first two decades of the thirteenth century.

In the twelfth century the new scientific law was already being fostered in many other places in Europe besides Bologna and Paris. Indeed, this local multiplicity, particularity, and variety mark the development of education in that century. New *studia* appeared both within and outside existing ecclesiastical schools, flourishing around either a single teacher or a group of teachers. To be sure, only a very few of these centers of learning succeeded in growing beyond a course of instruction in one or several subjects to become organized universities in the thirteenth century.[13] This holds true for juridical studies as well. A school of decretists, for example, flourished briefly in Cologne beginning about 1170. In other places law schools became established in the thirteenth century, but without any obvious continuity with the legal instruction of the twelfth; the best known of these is Montpellier, where Placentinus, one of the most famous glossators, taught in the last third of the twelfth century. The subject of Oxford as a center of legal training in the twelfth century has recently been taken up again, and doubt has been cast on the view that Vacarius read Roman law there even before the middle of the century; the continuity of academic instruction can be affirmed beyond question only from the last decade of the century.

II. SECULAR INSTITUTIONS OF JUSTICE

The study of the *Digest* was inspired largely by practical needs. We have only to mention Irnerius, whom the sources call *causidicus* and *iudex*. The laws taught in the schools were at once introduced into practice. The degree to which this occurred of course varied according to time and place; in general we can say that this usual sequence was considerably less marked in the ecclesiastical realm than in the secular. The process could be traced from different vantage points: from that of legal history, for instance, in the penetration of scientific jurisprudence into medieval law—that is, its reception; or sociohistorically, in the rise of a new professional class (which, as the example of England shows, does not necessarily presuppose Bolognese jurisprudence as its starting point). In the twelfth century, developments were still largely connected with single individuals, and the institutions with which they were

---

[12]Peter Classen, "Die ältesten Universitätsreformen und Universitätsgründungen des Mittelalters," *Heidelberger Jahrbücher* 12 (1968) 72–92 at 80.

[13]Discussed by Haskins, *Ren* 376–77, and Peter Classen, "Die hohen Schulen und die Gesellschaft im 12. Jahrhundert," AKG 48 (1966) 155–80 at 160–61 and 174–75, using Chartres as their example. See Richard W. Southern's study in this volume.

associated were not yet as a rule influenced or transformed by the new juridical thought and subject matter. Even at the end of the twelfth century much was just beginning which would develop fully only in the decades after 1200.

For the secular sphere, we must look chiefly at northern Italy. There we find the new jurist smoothly taking his place within the traditional institutions of justice at court and in the Church; participating in the commune in every capacity, as judge, *assessor*, advocate, or legal consultant; engaged in drafting statutes; or in political office as consul, as *podestà* or a member of his staff, as envoy, and so forth. For contemporaries, in contrast to us who look back, the emergence of a new title such as *legis doctor* or *causidicus* did not signify any change of direction. Recent scholarship has traced the practical activities of numerous trained jurists named in various sources; the appearance of the *quattuor doctores* at the Diet of Roncaglia remains a classic example. The new jurist appears as a counselor in the circle of the "literate" (*literati*) outside Italy as well. Still, even in Bologna one can scarcely speak of a new professional class of lawyers much before the turn of the century—one which could, for instance, hold its own alongside the nobility of the commune.[14] In many cities the guilds of doctors, judges, lawyers, and notaries served, within the guild system, as both professional and political organizations—another striking example of the corporative structuring of the medieval world. In Florence, the "guild of judges and notaries" (*arte dei giudici e notai*), which emerged about 1200 beside the older guild of merchants, attained the highest standing.

The guilds were among those institutions which scientific jurisprudence subsequently helped to shape. The judicial court of the *podestà*, although initially uninfluenced by scientific jurisprudence, constitutes another example: the new Roman law eventually shaped, in various ways, the conception of this court as objective and neutral; and in the *praeses provinciae* mentioned by the Roman law sources the legist recognized the *podestà* of his own time.[15] One example of an institution spreading hand in hand with Roman law takes us to southern France, where, about 1130, the Italian consular form of government—which in itself had developed uninfluenced by legal science—began to penetrate into the cities together with Roman law.

An important mediator between scientific jurisprudence and Italian legal practice was the *consilium sapientum* of the law court, though it only later developed into a well-defined legal institution, frequently in connection with the system of government by a *podestà*. That its antecedents are to be found in ancient Roman law is as unlikely as that it reflects the Frankish distinction between judge and "judgment-finder" (*rachinburgus*, "Urteiler"). What we see was more likely the result of an autochthonous development—especially in the civic and ecclesiastical domains—for which the trained jurists then found some

---

[14]See Johannes Fried, *Die Entstehung des Juristenstandes im 12. Jahrhundert: Zur sozialen Stellung und politischen Bedeutung gelehrter Juristen in Bologna und Modena* (Cologne 1974).
[15]Woldemar Engelmann, *Die Wiedergeburt der Rechtskultur in Italien durch die wissenschaftliche Lehre* (Leipzig 1938) 58.

indications in Justinian. The role of the judicial *consilium sapientum* varied not only regionally but also according to the matter at issue: it was different, for instance, in commercial cases, just as in general the influence of scientific law on commercial law was of a distinctive kind. Besides the *consilium sapientum*, it was especially the citation (*allegationes*) by advocates that introduced the substance of the new jurisprudence into the practice of the law courts.

III. THE CHURCH

THE ROMAN CURIA

Within the Church, Rome was likewise in early contact with scientific Roman law, if for no other reason than because in the *patrimonium Petri* judgments were passed in accordance with Roman law, and because in practice no precise distinction was made between the ecclesiastical and the secular-territorial jurisdictions of the pope. For a long time, however, this contact had no influence on the organization of the Roman Curia. It was only under Urban II and Paschal II that the Curia, by looking either to its own tradition or to various secular curias, found a structure suitable to the Reform papacy. The college of cardinals was formed, and a new group, the papal chaplains, made its appearance. The first administrative offices took form, even though personal factors still prevented a clear separation between the different branches. A chamberlain was appointed, probably with an eye on Cluny, to deal with financial matters; he held a position of special trust, and it soon became a rule for each new pope to appoint his own chamberlain. It is uncertain whether the chamberlain already had permanent assistants at this early date. In any case, his sphere of activity was loosely structured; if a comparison to the Anglo-Norman monarchy may be drawn, it was rather on a level with the informal *camera curie* than with the more institutionalized Exchequer.[16]

The chancellor is more important for our discussion. The title *cancellarius* already appears about the year 1000, but the foundation for the powerful office of the future was laid only by the Reform papacy. The debate over Kehr's "*scrinium* and *palatium*" need not be taken up here; what is certain is that from the time of John of Gaeta, who served as chancellor from 1088 until his election as pope Gelasius II in 1118, numerous decisive changes are observable in the script and form of documents, evidence that the chancery was being reshaped. Important signs are the gradual replacement of Roman scribes by non-Roman scribes, who were always available to the chancellor; the accompanying transition from the Roman Curial hand to the minuscule generally legible outside Rome; and the changes that took place in the *cursus*. The papal chancery became independent of the diplomatic (that is, documentary) procedures of the city of Rome, and to that extent gained autonomy; at the same

---

[16]See S. B. Chrimes, *An Introduction to the Administrative History of Mediaeval England* (3rd ed. Oxford and New York 1966) 27–32, with further references.

time it formed close ties with the new papal chaplains, as well as with the sub-deacons, a group subordinate to the cardinals. These changes are part of a more sweeping process: the orientation of the papacy toward the Church as a whole. Whether before Innocent III notaries and scribes were already differentiated within the chancery by their particular tasks is not clear from the sources. Also, the way in which a deputy was empowered when the chancellor's office was vacant shows that initially the chancery was a loosely structured institution.

Among the chancellors (who were always cardinals) in the first half of the century, Aimeric stands out: during his long term in office (1123–41) he was the dominant figure at the Curia and in Church politics. To him the chancery owes a number of programmatic *arengae*; and in the context of our discussion it is important to note that, so far as we know, he was the first to establish contact between the Roman see and Bolognese jurisprudence. At his request, Bulgarus, one of the *quattuor doctores*, composed and sent to him a concise survey of procedural law and some of the *regulae iuris* of the *Digest*. Presumably Aimeric had requested clarification of terminology pertaining to procedural rules and to the participants in lawsuits, addressing certain ambiguous terms and concepts customarily employed, for instance *arbiter* and *iudex* (Bulgarus begins his answer by distinguishing between these two) and *advocatus*. Still, it would be difficult to prove that this instruction about litigation procedures exercised an influence on the Curia.

In 1153 Roland Bandinelli became the first Bolognese canonist[17] to assume the office of chancellor; after becoming pope in 1159 he left the office unfilled until 1178, when he appointed Albert of Morra, also a canonist and the author of a *forma dictandi*,[18] who in turn became pope in 1187 and left the office vacant. It was presumably under him that a vice-chancellor was first appointed as permanent representative of the unfilled office of chancellor. With the accession of Honorius III to the papacy in 1216, the vice-chancellor presided alone over the chancery, chancellors with the rank of cardinal no longer being appointed. Two decretals from the time of pope Alexander III[19] contain the first use of the term *cancellaria* in the sense of a chancery where the papal "litterae fuerunt compositae" (not with the meaning of the *office* of the chancellor, as the word is used in the second half of the century in some European states[20] to express, possibly under canonistic influence, the abstraction of the office from the person).

Roland Bandinelli brought the papal chancery into close contact with Bolognese canon law when the new field was scarcely a dozen years old. Scien-

[17]Recently doubted by John T. Noonan, Jr., "Who Was Rolandus?" *Law, Church and Society: Essays in Honor of Stephan Kuttner*, ed. Kenneth Pennington and Robert Somerville (Philadelphia 1977) 21–48.

[18]But see Ann Dalzell, "The *Forma dictandi* attributed to Albert of Morra and Related Texts," *Mediaeval Studies* 39 (1977) 440–65.

[19]JL 14139 = 1. Comp. 2.15.3; JL 14142 = X 2.22.3 p.d.

[20]Hans-Walter Klewitz, "Cancellaria: Ein Beitrag zur Geschichte des geistlichen Hofdienstes," DA 1 (1937) 44–79 at 72–74.

tific jurisprudence first affected the style and language of pertinent papal documents in those places where the text delivers the papal decision; but elsewhere as well, presumably also in the *arengae*. Changes, however, in the structure of the chancery or in the conduct of its business, cannot yet be shown; even under Innocent III, as we shall see, they were still only indirect. The jurisdictional competence of the chancery was likewise unaffected; as before, it played no part in actual legal decisions. Since the end of the Reform papacy, as we know, legal disputes were brought to the pope in ever increasing numbers from all parts of the Church; though welcomed by the Roman see, the tendency was clearly disapproved of elsewhere, and even by many churchmen. In these cases the pope reached his decision after consulting with the cardinals, *de communi fratrum nostrorum consilio*, and calling on others who were learned in the law. The trial and the preparation of the decision were entrusted chiefly, although not exclusively, to one or several cardinals, later more often to subdeacons and chaplains. Thus anyone at the Curia, including of course the chancellor or a chancery notary, might still participate in the administration of justice; to regard the papal court of law as a firmly structured institution for dispensing justice we must look far into the thirteenth century, to the *audientia sacri palatii*, the *Rota romana* as it was later called.

But the pope could not only unburden himself of legal chores by assigning them to members of the Curia, he could also relieve the Curia by commissioning outside prelates, through delegation, to settle local quarrels in their own regions. Alexander III made liberal use of this possibility, employing for the purpose the rescript of delegation, which, like other mandates and similar documents, passed through the Roman chancery. Legal questions in the rescript were similarly decided by the pope after the traditional consultation, in accordance with the old and the new laws.

Different concepts of "correctness" may perhaps underlie this division of labor between legal decision-making on the one hand and the preparation of documents on the other. For the chancery clerk, a papal letter was correct if it was drafted according to the rules of the *ars dictaminis*, the *cursus*, and the rest; for the jurist, however, it was correct if its contents conformed to the rules of law. In a certain sense, the formal validity of a papal rescript depended upon adherence to stylistic rules, as today the validity of a law or judicial decision depends upon adherence to procedural norms. Whether the rescript was substantially correct or not worried the jurist, but did not concern the chancery clerk. This attitude can also be seen among the recipients. Alexander III, for example, had to answer a question from the bishop of Hereford concerning a rescript procured on the basis of inaccurate or omitted information: should the judge delegate proceed *secundum formam* regardless of the misstatements—that is, according to the given wording and instructions—or *secundum rigorem iustitie*?[21] For the *forma*, after all (and this was probably in part

---

[21]JL 13950 = 1. Comp. 1.21.11. Somewhat close to this is JL 13877 = X 1.29.13.

why the question was posed) is valid according to every chancery rule; the rescript does offer *this* guarantee of correctness. The pope, naturally, answered as a jurist would. The two lines of thought would eventually be reconciled in the jurist's favor, most clearly perhaps in the future *audientia litterarum contradictarum*.

IURISDICTIO DELEGATA

Papal delegation of judicial authority is among those institutions which, though they were known in the Church for ages, were given new impetus and developed under the influence of scientific jurisprudence. When a litigant appealed from the provinces, the pope delegated the case to one or more neighboring church dignitaries. From the time of Alexander III, such delegation became a factor of primary importance in ecclesiastical policy and Church law. Only then did the juridical instruments become available to give a thoroughgoing legal form to the delegation of judicial authority and to the rescript connected with it, from the fundamental principles down to the smallest details. The new jurists accomplished this by interpreting and developing the *leges* and *canones* in the schools and in practice, with the prominent collaboration of the popes themselves, insofar as they were trained in the new school. Standardization was attained largely by drawing upon Roman laws pertaining to the delegation of legal proceedings, whether the emperor delegated to a judge, or an "ordinary judge" delegated to the *iudices pedanei* of late Antiquity or to other officials. The *commissio*, by which the pope charged a delegated judge with a legal case, granted him narrower or broader jurisdiction according to circumstances; for this reason, too, it belongs to the same legal-historical type as, for example, the order given by the praetor to the judge to pass judgment (*iudicare iubere*) within the civil procedure of classical Roman law. The *commissio* could contain decisions on new legal questions raised by the case, and thereby contribute to the further development of canon law.

Together with the other kinds of papal mandates, and especially the pope's answers to *consultationes* from prelates, the mandates of delegation constitute that large body of legal sources, the papal rescripts. The subject of delegated jurisdiction thus touches on that of the papal decretals, and with it on one of the most exciting juristic phenomena of the twelfth-century renaissance—a subject, however, which cannot be pursued here. To the extent that the rescripts of delegation contributed directly to shaping the institution of delegated jurisdiction, they are to be found in the decretal collections of the schools and popes from the time of the *Compilatio prima* (about 1190), under the titles *de rescriptis, de officio et potestate iudicis delegati*, and *de appellationibus et recusationibus*.

The delegation rescripts, which dealt with legal questions and proceedings of every kind and thereby promoted the spread of Romano-canonical law, at the same time presupposed knowledge of the prevailing law on the part of their recipients, so that the particular issues in question either fitted into the existing body of law—which at this point means the new scientific law—or else grew directly out of it. When occasion demanded, the judge delegate availed himself of the advice of jurists, sometimes from his own *familia*. In this connection there exist decretals which expressly, and occasionally reprovingly, address themselves to the legal knowledge of delegated judges (and elsewhere, of advice-seeking bishops)[22] or mention consultation with *prudentes* by non-Italian addressees as well.[23] Some recipients, because of their expertise, were consulted particularly often: for example, bishop Bartholomew of Exeter[24] and bishop Roger of Worcester.[25] From the procedural point of view, the linking of delegated jurisdiction to regular diocesan jurisdiction served above all to ensure execution of the judgment passed by the judge delegate.

Delegation in turn affected the organization of the papal chancery, although this becomes fully evident only from the time of Innocent III. The compartmentalization of the Curia observable during his pontificate gave the chancery a more defined structure; required by the steadily increasing flow of legal cases to Rome, it was probably also intended to safeguard against the forgery of papal letters discovered in Rome during his reign and even under his predecessor. Some of the chancery notaries—the vice-chancellor, the *corrector*, and the *auditor litterarum contradictarum*—were entrusted with special tasks.

The last is of particular interest here. To relieve the pope, the chancery assumed the responsibility of drafting those letters which contained recurring and thus juridically clarified decisions; if the opposing party raised objections to the letters—the majority of them rescripts of delegation—the case was taken to the *audientia litterarum contradictarum* for a decision by the *auditor*. Judicial functions thus came to be exercised by a regular chancery official; in this way the chancery, to which the *auditor* remained attached, came for the first time to play an institutional role in the papal dispensation of justice on cases concerning the Church as a whole. In this context we can observe that the emerging formularies of the *audientia litterarum contradictarum* show only limited continuity with the older *ars dictandi*, and are in the main an outgrowth of the chancery's legal practice.[26] In the *audientia* we see clearly the institutionalization of the chancery: a permanent department was duly formed, having its own distinct and defined competency with respect to its parent organization, and with written rules to ensure uniformity of practice and to

---

[22]Examples are: Alexander III, JL 13984 = X 2.13.3 p.d.; Lucius III, JL 15189 = X 5.32.1 p.d.; JL 15208 = X 1.3.10 p.d.

[23]Examples are: Alexander III, JL 14009/14175 = X 1.29.14 p.d. and App. 46.4; Lucius III, Coll. Brug. 44.7.

[24]See JL 12180 = X 5.12.6 p.d.; JL 13899 = X 3.32.4.

[25]See Mary G. Cheney, "Pope Alexander III and Roger, Bishop of Worcester, 1164–1179: The Exchange of Ideas," *Proceedings* (n. 5 above) 207–27 at 226.

[26]Peter Herde, *Audientia litterarum contradictarum: Untersuchungen über die päpstlichen Justizbriefe und die päpstliche Delegationsgerichtsbarkeit vom 13. bis zum Beginn des 16. Jahrhunderts* (2 vols. Tübingen 1970) 1.18–19.

prevent legal uncertainty. Although the papal chancery in its developed form (including the *audientia*) took shape from within, it was nevertheless indirectly influenced by scientific jurisprudence, through the mechanisms of delegated jurisdiction and the rescript.

THE OFFICIALIS

On the diocesan level, the *officialis*, as one of the early professional judges, is linked especially closely with the development of scientific jurisprudence. How and when he replaced the earlier synods and cathedral chapters in the episcopal administration of justice varied considerably from region to region, as did his emergence in connection with judges delegated by the bishop. *Officiales* were initially assistants of the bishop, or of other prelates, to whom various business was assigned. In this sense, the title appeared in England, for example, about the middle of the twelfth century. One finds the new trained canonists among these *officiales* as well as within the bishop's *familia*. It is difficult to discover how the term came to be restricted to the office of the episcopal judge. *Officialis* in that sense possibly occurs first in Reims toward the end of the twelfth century (but the question with respect to France needs to be reexamined). In the course of the thirteenth century, this form of diocesan tribunal became common throughout large parts of the European Church as the institution exercising both contentious and voluntary jurisdiction; it thus became one of the most effective agents for disseminating the new scientific jurisprudence.

Bibliographical Note

No attempt has been made at completeness. The list is restricted to literature appearing since Haskins's book of 1927 and, moreover, consistently to the most recent titles. Its organization follows that of the essay.

THE UNIVERSITIES

Hastings Rashdall, *The Universities of Europe in the Middle Ages*, rev. ed. Frederick M. Powicke and Alfred B. Emden (3 vols. Oxford 1936).

Herbert Grundmann, *Vom Ursprung der Universität im Mittelalter*, SB Leipzig, Phil.-hist. Kl. 103.2 (Berlin 1957).

Sven Stelling-Michaud, "L'histoire des universités au moyen âge et à la renaissance au cours des vingt-cinq dernières années," *XIe Congrès international des sciences historiques, Stockholm 21–28 août 1960, Rapports* (6 vols. Stockholm 1960) 1.97–143 (with additional bibliography).

Jacques Le Goff, "Quelle conscience l'université médiévale a-t-elle eu d'elle-même?" *Beiträge zum Berufsbewusstsein des mittelalterlichen Menschen*, ed. Paul Wilpert, Miscellanea mediaevalia 3 (Berlin 1964) 15–29; repr. in Le Goff, *Pour un autre moyen âge: Temps, travail et culture en Occident, 18 essais* (Paris 1977) 181–97.

Laetitia Boehm, "*De negotio scholaris*: Zur Entstehung von Berufsbewusstsein und Rechtsstand des Universitätsgelehrten im Mittelalter," *Festiva Lanx: Studien zum mittelalterlichen Geistesleben* (Festschrift for Johannes Spörl), ed. Karl Schnith (Munich 1966) 29–52.

Pearl Kibre, *Scholarly Privileges in the Middle Ages* (Cambridge Mass. 1962).

Peter Classen, "Die hohen Schulen und die Gesellschaft im 12. Jahrhundert," AKG 48 (1966) 155–80.

Peter Classen, "Die ältesten Universitätsreformen und Universitätsgründungen des Mittelalters," *Heidelberger Jahrbücher* 12 (1968) 72–92.

Helmut Coing, "Die juristische Fakultät und ihr Lehrprogramm," in Coing, *Handbuch* 1.39–128 (with additional bibliography).

BOLOGNA

Studi e memorie per la storia dell'Università di Bologna n.s. 1 (1956) and 2 (1961), including Giovanni de Vergottini, "Lo Studio di Bologna, l'Impero, il Papato," 1 (1956) 19–95, and Guido Rossi, "'Universitas scholarium' e Comune (sec. XII–XIV)," ibid. 173–266.

Giorgio Cencetti, "Studium fuit Bononie: Note sulla storia dell'Università di Bologna nel primo mezzo secolo della sua esistenza," *Studi medievali* 3rd ser. 7 (1966) 781–833 (with additional bibliography).

Gina Fasoli, the section "Per la storia dell'Università di Bologna" in her *Scritti di storia medievale*, ed. F. Bocchi et al. (Bologna 1974) 567–642.

Domenico Maffei, "Un trattato di Bonaccorso degli Elisei e i più antichi statuti dello Studio di Bologna nel manoscritto 22 della Robbins Collection," BMCL n.s. 5 (1975) 73–101.

PARIS

Gaines Post, "Parisian Masters as a Corporation, 1200–1246," *Speculum* 9 (1934) 421–45, repr. in his *Studies in Medieval Legal Thought: Public Law and the State, 1100–1322* (Princeton 1964) 27–60.

Louis Halphen, "Les origines de l'Université de Paris," *A travers l'histoire du moyen âge* (Paris 1950) 286–98.

John W. Baldwin, *Masters, Princes and Merchants: The Social Views of Peter the Chanter and His Circle* (2 vols. Princeton 1970).

Astrik L. Gabriel, "Les origines de la Faculté de Décret de l'ancienne Université de Paris," *L'année canonique* 17 (1973) 507–31.

OXFORD

H. E. Salter, "The Medieval University of Oxford," *History* 14 (1929–30) 57–61.

H. G. Richardson, "The Oxford Law School under John," *Law Quarterly Review* 57 (1941) 319–38.

Stephan Kuttner and Eleanor Rathbone, "Anglo-Norman Canonists of the Twelfth Century: An Introductory Study," *Traditio* 7 (1949–51) 279–358.

M. B. Hackett, *The Original Statutes of Cambridge University: The Text and Its History* (Cambridge 1970) ch. 3, "The Origin of the Cambridge Statutes."

Ralph V. Turner, "Roman Law in England before the Time of Bracton," *Journal of British Studies* 15 (1975) 1–25.

Richard W. Southern, "Master Vacarius and the Beginning of an English Academic Tradition," *Medieval Learning and Literature: Essays Presented to Richard William Hunt*, ed. J. J. G. Alexander and M. T. Gibson (Oxford 1976) 257–86.

Peter Stein, "Vacarius and the Civil Law," *Church and Government in the Middle Ages: Essays Presented to C. R. Cheney on His 70th Birthday*, ed. C. N. L. Brooke et al. (Cambridge and New York 1976) 119–37.

MONTPELLIER AND SOUTHERN FRANCE

Actes des journées internationales tenues en commun par la Société d'histoire du droit et la Société d'histoire du droit et des institutions des anciens pays de droit écrit, Montpellier, 24–26 mai 1966, Recueil de mémoires et travaux publié par la Sociéte d'histoire du droit et des institutions des anciens pays de droit écrit 6 (Montpellier 1967).

André Gouron, *Les juristes de l'école de Montpellier*, IRMAE 4.3.a (Milan 1970).

André Gouron, "Die Entstehung der französischen Rechtsschule," ZRG rom Abt 93 (1976) 138–60.

SECULAR INSTITUTIONS OF JUSTICE

Ius Romanum Medii Aevi (1961 ff.).

Mario Sbriccoli, *L'interpretazione dello statuto: Contributo allo studio della funzione dei giuristi nell'età comunale* (Milan 1969) part 1, ch. 2, "L'impegno politico dei giuristi."

Johannes Fried, *Die Entstehung des Juristenstandes im 12. Jahrhundert: Zur sozialen Stellung und politischen Bedeutung gelehrter Juristen in Bologna und Modena* (Cologne 1974).

Antonio Padoa Schioppa, "Le rôle du droit savant dans quelques actes judiciaires italiens des XIe et XIIe siècles," *Confluence des droits savants et des pratiques juridiques*, Actes du Colloque de Montpellier, 1977 (Milan 1979) 341–71.

André Gouron, "Diffusion des consulats méridionaux et expansion du droit romain aux XIIe et XIIIe siècles," *Bibliothèque de l'Ecole des Chartes* 121 (1963) 26–76.

Jean-Pierre Poly, "Les légistes provençaux et la diffusion du droit romain dans le midi," *Mélanges Roger Aubenas*, Recueil de mémoires et travaux publié par la Société d'histoire du droit et des institutions des anciens pays de droit écrit 9 (Montpellier 1974) 613–35.

ARTI

Antonio Padoa Schioppa, "Giurisdizione e statuti delle arti nella dottrina del diritto comune," *Studia et documenta historiae et iuris* 30 (1964) 179–234.

Santi Calleri, *L'arte dei giudici e notai di Firenze nell'età comunale e nel suo statuto del 1344* (Milan 1966).

Lauro Martines, *Lawyers and Statecraft in Renaissance Florence* (Princeton 1968) ch. 2, "The Guild."

Gina Fasoli, "Giuristi, giudici e notai nell'ordinamento comunale e nella vita cittadina," *Atti del Convegno internazionale di studi Accursiani, Bologna 1963* (3 vols. Milan 1968) 1.25–39.

CONSILIUM SAPIENTIS

Aldo Checchini, "I consiliarii nella storia della procedura" (1909), in his *Scritti giuridici e storico-giuridici* (3 vols. Padua 1958) 2.3–65.

Woldemar Engelmann, *Die Wiedergeburt der Rechtskultur in Italien durch die wissenschaftliche Lehre* (Leipzig 1938).

Guido Rossi, *Consilium sapientis iudiciale: Studi e ricerche per la storia del processo romano-canonico, secoli XII–XIII* (Milan 1958).

Mario Ascheri, *Consilium e res iudicata* (lecture given in 1976; forthcoming).

THE ROMAN CURIA

Hans-Walter Klewitz, "Cancellaria: Ein Beitrag zur Geschichte des geistlichen Hofdienstes," DA 1 (1937) 44–79.

Rudolf von Heckel, "Studien über die Kanzleiordnung Innozenz' III.," *Historisches Jahrbuch* 57 (1937) 258–89.

Karl Jordan, "Die Entstehung der römischen Kurie: Ein Versuch," ZRG kan Abt 28 (1939) 97–152.

Reinhard Elze, "Die päpstliche Kapelle im 12. und 13. Jahrhundert," ZRG kan Abt 36 (1950) 145–204.

Jürgen Sydow, "Untersuchungen zur kurialen Verwaltungsgeschichte im Zeitalter des Reformpapsttums," DA 11 (1954–55) 18–73.

Walter Ullmann, *The Growth of Papal Government in the Middle Ages: A Study in the Ideological Relation of Clerical to Lay Power* (London 1955) ch. 10, "The Court of the Pope."

Franz-Josef Schmale, *Studien zum Schisma des Jahres 1130* (Cologne 1961).

C. R. Cheney, *The Study of the Medieval Papal Chancery* (Glasgow 1966).

Johannes Fried, "Die römische Kurie und die Anfänge der Prozessliteratur," ZRG kan Abt 59 (1973) 151–74.

Horst Fuhrmann, "Das Reformpapsttum und die Rechtswissenschaft," *Investiturstreit und Reichsverfassung*, ed. Josef Fleckenstein, Vorträge und Forschungen 17 (Sigmaringen 1973) 175–203.

Edith Pásztor, "La curia romana," *Le istituzioni ecclesiastiche della "Societas Christiana" dei secoli XI–XII: Papato, cardinalato ed episcopato*, Atti della quinta Settimana internazionale di studio, Mendola, 26–31 agosto 1971 (Milan 1974) 490–504.

Paul Rabikauskas, "Cancellaria Apostolica (In eius memoriam: saec. XI – die 31 martii 1973)," *Periodica de re morali, canonica, liturgica* 63 (1974) 243–73.

C. R. Cheney, *From Becket to Langton: English Church Government 1170–1213* (Manchester 1956) ch. 3, "England and Rome."

Peter Herde, *Beiträge zum päpstlichen Kanzlei- und Urkundenwesen im dreizehnten Jahrhundert* (2nd ed. Kallmünz Opf. 1967).

Peter Herde, *Audientia litterarum contradictarum: Untersuchungen über die päpstlichen Justizbriefe und die päpstliche Delegationsgerichtsbarkeit vom 13. bis zum Beginn des 16. Jahrhunderts* (2 vols. Tübingen 1970).

Othmar Hageneder, *Die geistliche Gerichtsbarkeit in Ober- und Niederösterreich: Von den Anfängen bis zum Beginn des 15. Jahrhunderts* (Graz, Vienna, Cologne 1967).

Jane E. Sayers, *Papal Judges Delegate in the Province of Canterbury, 1198–1254: A Study in Ecclesiastical Jurisdiction and Administration* (London 1971).

Knut Wolfgang Nörr, "Päpstliche Dekretalen und römisch-kanonischer Zivilprozess," *Studien zur europäischen Rechtsgeschichte*, ed. Walter Wilhelm (Frankfurt 1972) 53–65.

Mary G. Cheney, "Pope Alexander III and Roger, Bishop of Worcester, 1164–1179: The Exchange of Ideas," *Proceedings of the Fourth International Congress of Medieval Canon Law, Toronto, 21–25 August 1972*, ed. Stephan Kuttner, Monumenta iuris canonici, ser. C.: Subsidia 5 (Vatican City 1976) 207–27.

ON THEORY

Ennio Cortese, *La norma giuridica: Spunti teorici nel diritto comune classico* (2 vols. Milan 1962–64).

Pierre Legendre, *La pénétration du droit romain dans le droit canonique classique de Gratien à Innocent IV (1140–1254)* (Paris 1964) ch. 4, "L'application du mandat à la justice."

Charles Lefebvre, "Formation du droit classique," part 2 of Gabriel Le Bras et al., *L'âge classique, 1140–1378: Sources et théorie du droit*, Histoire du droit et des institutions de l'Eglise en Occident 7 (Paris 1965) 131–345.

Jacoba J. H. M. Hanenburg, "Decretals and Decretal Collections in the Second Half of the Twelfth Century," *Tijdschrift voor Rechtsgeschiedenis* 34 (1966) 552–99, sect. 1, "The Nature and Authority of the Decretal Letter."

THE OFFICIALIS

Edouard Fournier, *L'origine du vicaire général et des autres membres de la curie diocésaine* (Paris 1940) part 2, "Le fonctionnement des premières officialités."

C. R. Cheney, *English Bishops' Chanceries 1100–1250* (Manchester 1950).

Odile Grandmottet, "Les officialités de Reims aux XIIIe et XIVe siècles," *Bulletin d'information de l'Institut de Recherche et d'Histoire des Textes* 4 (1955) 77–106.

Winfried Trusen, "Die gelehrte Gerichtsbarkeit der Kirche," Coing, *Handbuch* 1.467–504 (with additional bibliography).

Political *Renovatio*:
Two Models from Roman Antiquity

Robert L. Benson

Twelfth-century political thought was preoccupied with the legitimacy of political institutions and of governing authority. Though the problem of legitimacy never strays far from the center of the political theorist's attention, the twelfth century felt this concern with a new intensity, rarely matched during the centuries intervening since the death of Augustine in 430. More: twelfth-century statesmen and thinkers responded to the problem with a new urgency, gave new shapes to the question and furnished fresh answers to it. Not surprisingly, the revival of concern with legitimacy reflects important new developments on the European political and intellectual scene between the mid-eleventh century and the mid-twelfth:

First, new political forms as well as new states and new dynasties had emerged. Of this, the two most dramatic examples were Norman: William I's conquest of England in 1066, and the culmination of Norman expansion in the south under Roger II (1101–54), who fused Sicily and southern Italy into a unified realm. During the second quarter of the twelfth century, the rulers of both Sicily and Portugal began to claim kingly status. In northern Italy, many towns had become wealthy, powerful, and virtually autonomous communes. The Latin Kingdom of Jerusalem and the other new crusading principalities held the eastern edge of the Mediterranean.

Older monarchies, moreover, sought new bases for their authority. In 1100, the Investiture Struggle was being fiercely fought. A quarter-century later, radical reformers within the Church had largely succeeded in stripping sacral elements from the anointed kings of Europe, and had even limited the traditional royal domination of the Church. As a consequence, in the second half of the twelfth century a new mode of kingship began to define its pre-

Both on large questions and on small points of detail, this study profited greatly from generous help by many colleagues and friends, at the Conference and subsequently. With warm thanks to all, I must single out three who especially helped to make this a better essay than it would otherwise have been: the late Peter Classen, Giles Constable, and Stephan Kuttner. In addition, several other friends and colleagues read an earlier draft, and discussed various problems with me: Gerard E. Caspary, Richard Krautheimer, Glenn W. Olsen, and Bernhard Schimmelpfennig. I am deeply grateful for their suggestions and criticisms.

rogatives in juristic terms: law-centered monarchy came to replace the sacral kingship of the early Middle Ages. And even during the later eleventh century, the papacy had developed into a monarchy and a *curia*, a royal and feudal court, with substantial claims to dominion over the secular world.

Between the mid-eleventh and the early twelfth century, as the papal Reform movement and the Investiture Struggle fractured the traditional foundations of medieval government, thinkers of all persuasions began to subject government itself to a new and intense scrutiny, to rational analysis and a thoroughgoing critique. For this purpose, formidable intellectual tools had become increasingly available: not only the methods of early scholasticism, but also the full corpus of Roman law (ca. 1080), and finally Gratian's *Decretum* (ca. 1140), which offered a definitive compilation of earlier canon law as well as techniques for reconciling the contradictions in the earlier tradition. At any time after the mid-twelfth century, in short, the new schools played a central role in the evolution of political thought.

But this study will not retell the familiar story of these developments, nor attempt a full account of twelfth-century political thought. The goal of this study is more modest: to assay the influence of certain texts and models from Antiquity on twelfth-century conceptions of legitimacy, and to examine some of the ways in which twelfth-century statesmen and thinkers perceived or reconstructed political ideas drawn from Antiquity.

I. RENOVATIO SACRI SENATVS

Rebelling against the bishop of Rome as lord of the City in 1143, the Roman Commune followed a pattern already familiar in the North Italian communes since the later eleventh century. By the mid-twelfth century, the Lombard and Tuscan cities had largely overthrown the temporal rule of their bishops and of feudal lords, and had been, for two generations or more, largely free of intervention by German monarchs, who were also the kings of Italy and usually Roman emperors as well. In Lombardy and Tuscany, a powerful bourgeoisie drew its wealth from commerce, requiring—and winning—substantial autonomy to pursue concrete and limited goals both economically and politically. Like the Lombard and Tuscan cities, Rome wanted to dominate its *contado*, to subject Latium as its own territory of surrounding towns and countryside. When the Romans revolted in 1143 and reconstituted the Senate, territorial politics furnished the impetus: after pope and Commune together had defeated Tivoli, the pope's lenient terms angered the Romans by frustrating their wish to crush the small neighboring city. Though short-lived, the revolt of 1143 was merely a prelude: in 1144 Rome rebelled again, and again reestablished the Senate.[1]

---

[1] Antonio Rota, "La costituzione originaria del Comune di Roma: L'epoca del Comune libero (luglio 1143–dicembre 1145)," *Bullettino dell'Istituto storico italiano per il medio evo* 64 (1953)

But several things distinguished Rome from the North Italian communes. First, the City's lord held a uniquely important position, since the bishop of Rome had opportunities and political resources which lesser bishops could not hope for. Elsewhere in Italy, the papacy often backed communes against their bishops, against feudal magnates, or against the emperor, but obviously could not support autonomy for Rome. Further, Rome differed in its social composition. The City lacked a commercial base and a large bourgeoisie. Following the second rebellion, the Commune took on a more democratic cast as it destroyed the power of the nobles, many of whom had close ties to the papacy and the Curia. Above all, Rome's history was unique. From 1144 to 1155, far from having concrete and limited goals, the Romans relied on Antiquity as a political model, and claimed to exercise in the present the undiminished prerogatives of the ancient Roman Senate and people. As a case-history, the Commune holds particular interest, for it furnishes the twelfth century's only example of political classicism at the very center of a historical movement.[2]

After October 1144, with powerful enemies—the pope, his ally the king of Sicily, and the Roman nobles—arrayed against the Commune, the revolutionaries urgently needed an ally, and they turned for support to the Staufer kings of Germany. Though representatives of the Commune must have elaborated their political ideology on many occasions, their communications to the German kings remain the principal surviving records. Between 1144 and 1149, the Senate sent a number of letters—now lost—to king Conrad III. Then in 1149 they sent three more letters to Conrad.[3] In 1152, Wezel, a supporter of Arnold of Brescia, wrote to Frederick Barbarossa, ostensibly to congratulate him on his accession.[4] Finally, in June 1155, as Barbarossa approached Rome

---

19–131 and esp. 41–63; other scholarly literature on the Commune can be found below (nn. 19–20, 25) and in the Bibliographical Note. Part I of this study will consider only a single episode of the Commune's history: the revolutionary development from 1144 to 1155, from the second and definitive reconstitution of the Senate to Frederick Barbarossa's coronation. For it was principally during this period that Antiquity served the Romans as a political model. Though the Senate continued to seek independence from popes and emperors long after 1155, Antiquity did not again play the central role in Roman ideology till Cola di Rienzo formulated his fantastic programs in the 1340s.

[2]For an eloquent epitaph on the Commune as well as on the medieval Empire, see Peter Classen, "*Causa imperii*: Probleme Roms in Spätantike und Mittelalter," *Das Hauptstadtproblem im Mittelalter: Festgabe zum 90. Geburtstag Friedrich Meineckes*, Jahrbuch für Geschichte des deutschen Ostens 1 (Tübingen 1952) 225–48 at 238–39, 244–45: "um Haupt der Welt zu sein, . . . versäumte Rom die Möglichkeit, Stadt zu werden. . . .Wie das Römisch-Deutsche Reich nicht zum Staat werden konnte, weil sein König zugleich universaler Kaiser war, so konnte Rom nicht zur selbständigen Stadt werden, weil sein Bischof zugleich universaler Papst war" (245).

[3]Franco Bartoloni, ed., *Codice diplomatico del Senato Romano dal MCXLIV al MCCCXLVII* 1, Fonti per la storia d'Italia 87 (Rome 1948) (hereafter: Bartoloni) 3–9 nos. 5–7 (= Jaffé, *Bibl* 1.332–36 nos. 214–16). One of these (Bartoloni no. 5; Jaffé no. 214) was also transmitted by Otto of Freising (and Rahewin), GF 1.29 pp. 45–47; in this letter, the Senate complained that Conrad had not replied to previous letters.

[4]Jaffé, *Bibl* 1.539–43 no. 404 (not in Bartoloni).

to receive his imperial coronation, envoys from the Commune delivered an address to the monarch.[5]

THE PROGRAM OF THE COMMUNE IN 1149

Using an ancient formula, the Senate defined the Commune as the *senatus populusque Romanus*, and they revived the ancient abbreviation S.P.Q.R.[6] Moreover, they anticipated the slightly later definition of the Empire as the *sacrum imperium* by referring to the "holy Senate" (*sacer senatus*).[7] But there is an apocalyptic note in their self-perception, for the "renewal" or "restoration of the holy Senate" in October 1144 inaugurated a new era, according to which the Senate dated its documents. Indeed, "renewal of the holy Senate" (*renovatio sacri senatus*) and "restoration of the Roman Empire" (*restauratio imperii Romani*) might well be regarded as the twin mottos of the Commune's new era.[8]

In 1149, the Romans announced to Conrad III their intention to restore the Empire to the golden age it had enjoyed under Constantine the Great and Justinian, "who, by the vigor of the Senate and the Roman people, held the entire world in their hands."[9] It is striking that the senators did not invoke the name of Augustus or of any other pagan emperor. Rather, they singled out Constantine's reign as a high-point in the Empire's history, perhaps also Constantine himself as the architect of the Empire's conversion to Christianity, and Justinian as the great legislator. In short, they looked to the Christian Roman Empire of the fourth, fifth, and sixth centuries as an ideal and model.

Within the Senate's thought in 1149, there was a marked tension between a visionary conception of the renewal of the ancient Roman Empire and more realistic concerns. On the one hand, the representatives of the Commune showed a lively interest in local Roman politics and in such concrete questions as the strategic value of the Castel Sant'Angelo,[10] as well as in the dangers arising from the accord between the papacy and Roger II of Sicily, which they

[5] Otto, GF 2.29 pp. 135–36.

[6] Much of the Senate's program is visible in the salutations of their letters: "Excellentissimo atque preclaro Urbis et orbis totius domino Conrado Dei gratia Romanorum regi semper augusto senatus populusque Romanus salutem et Romani imperii felicem et inclitam gubernationem" (Bartoloni 1.4 no. 5; Jaffé, *Bibl* 1.332 no. 214); "Excellentissimo et magnifico domino Urbis et orbis Conrado Dei gratia Romanorum regi semper augusto Sixtus, Nicolaus et Guido consiliatores curiae sacri senatus et communis salutis rei publicae procuratores, pro posse in omnibus fidelia servitia et Romani imperii restaurationem" (Bartoloni 1.7 no. 6; Jaffé 1.334–35 no. 215); "Illustrissimo atque magnifico terrarum orbis domino Conrado Dei gratia Romanorum regi semper triumphatori augusto. . ." (Bartoloni 1.8 no. 7; Jaffé 1.335 no. 216). Cf. also Otto, GF 2.29 p. 135.

[7] Bartoloni 1.7 no. 6; Jaffé, *Bibl* 1.335 no. 215; "sacer sanctae Urbis senatus" (Otto, GF 2.29 p. 136). The theme of the *sacrosancta Urbs* appeared also in Wezel's letter (Jaffé 1.539 no. 404). On the Staufer chancery's conception of the *sacrum imperium*, see n. 113 below.

[8] Bartoloni 1.13, 25, 27 nos. 11, 17, 18. In general: Pietro Fedele, "L'êra del senato," *Archivio della R. Società romana di storia patria* 35 (1912) 583–610; Rota (n. 1 above) 63–77.

[9] Bartoloni 1.4 no. 5; Jaffé, *Bibl* 1.332 no. 214.

[10] Bartoloni 1.4–5 no. 5; Jaffé, *Bibl* 1.333–34 no. 214.

rightly saw as a major threat not only to the Commune but also to the Staufer king's claim to rule in Italy.[11] Further, they accepted the notion that the German kingship carried with it the kingship of Italy and especially the expectation of receiving the imperial crown. The Romans regarded the German *regnum* and the *imperium Romanum* as linked, and both as having been conferred on Conrad by God[12]—two major concessions to the policies and ideology of the Staufer. Finally, the Senate saw "all Italy and the German kingdom" (*tota Italia ac regnum Teutonicum*) as the principal sphere of Conrad's governance.[13] On the other hand, claims to world dominion and the language of universal rule fill the Senate's communications to Conrad III and Frederick Barbarossa. In terms drawn from Antiquity, the representatives of the Senate addressed Conrad as *semper augustus*, as *triumphator*, and as "lord of the City and of the world" (*urbis et orbis dominus*).[14] Describing Rome as the *caput mundi*,[15] they urged Conrad to move the seat of government to the City, and to rule the world "as Justinian did."[16]

Seeking to explain the Roman revolution, Otto of Freising found the moving force in the figure who was and remains the best known of its leaders. According to Otto, Arnold of Brescia believed that

Neither clerics owning property nor bishops holding *regalia* nor monks having possessions can on any account be saved. All of these things belong to the prince and should from his beneficence be granted for the use of laymen alone.

Moreover, Otto considered Arnold responsible for the City's political classicism as well as for its antipapal rebellion:

He held out the example of the ancient Romans, who . . . had made the entire earth their own. Therefore he urged that the Capitoline be rebuilt, the senatorial dignity restored (*renovanda*), the equestrian order reformed (*reformandus*). Nothing in the administration of the City should pertain to the Roman pontiff.[17]

In this respect, Otto's testimony has deceived many historians.[18] In fact, the Roman revolution against papal rule had already begun in 1143 with the in-

---

[11]Bartoloni 1.4–7 nos. 5–6; Jaffé, *Bibl* 1.333–35 nos. 214–15.

[12]Bartoloni 1.4 no. 5; Jaffé, *Bibl* 1.332 no. 214: "regnum et imperium Romanum vestro a Deo regimini concessum exaltare atque amplificare cupientes. . . ."

[13]Bartoloni 1.5 no. 5; Jaffé, *Bibl* 1.333–34 no. 214. Though the precise meaning of the expression is not clear, in all likelihood the Senate directed the notion of *tota Italia* against the Normans in the South. A study of twelfth- and early thirteenth-century conceptions of *Italia* would be welcome.

[14]Above, n. 6. These formulae and titles will be discussed in Part II.

[15]Bartoloni 1.5 no. 5; Jaffé, *Bibl* 1.333 no. 214; in 1152, "domina mundi" (n. 41 below).

[16]Note especially the verses near the end of the Senate's letter (Bartoloni 1.6 no. 5; Jaffé, *Bibl* 1.334 no. 214): "Imperium teneat, Romae sedeat, regat orbem / Princeps terrarum, ceu fecit Iustinianus; / Cesaris accipiat Cesar, que sunt sua presul, / Ut Christus iussit, Petro solvente tributum."

[17]GF 2.28 pp. 133–34.

[18]For example: Robert Folz, *The Concept of Empire in Western Europe from the Fifth to the Fourteenth Century*, trans. Sheila A. Ogilvie (New York 1969) 95, suggests that Arnold's "main contribution" probably lay in giving "the Romans a political doctrine." Equally exaggerated is

stallation of the Senate on the Capitoline, then institutionalized itself in 1144 with the reconstitution of the Senate and the inauguration of the Senate's new era. Thereupon the Romans had proceeded to the election of a "patrician," who replaced the "prefect of the City" (*praefectus urbis*) in the government of Rome. This *patricius* should have all of the pope's revenues as well, except for tithes and the offerings of the faithful. The appeal of the title *patricius* is evident. Considering the "patriciate" an ancient Roman office, the Romans conceived the *patricius* as the emperor's vicar for the immediate governance of the City, and probably also assumed that his charge included the oversight of papal elections.[19] Thus the Commune's claim to autonomy, its political revival of Antiquity, and its antipapalism were firmly established by October 1144.

But Arnold arrived in Rome, at the earliest, only late in 1145 or in 1146.[20] Nor did he come, like Lenin at the Finland Station in 1917, to take command of a revolution which had begun without him. First and foremost a religious reformer, Arnold led a deeply ascetic and exemplary life, and had great gifts as a preacher. At Brescia, he may well have grown up in the tradition of the *Pataria*, for he advocated a Church not only stripped of its property, but also freed from the tasks of worldly government and committed to apostolic poverty: a Church without power, pomp, or high office. Like the Lombard cities, where the Patarine movement still flourished in the early twelfth century, Rome had a populace easily stirred to evangelical fervor. But in Rome, protest against the laxity of priesthood and hierarchy inevitably entailed antipapalism. In antipapal Rome, Arnold quickly found a receptive audience for his views: the college of cardinals is "a den of thieves," the pope is "a man of blood, . . . a tormentor of churches and oppressor of the innocent." Whatever political ideas he held before coming to the City, he apparently found the imitation of Antiquity a congenial alternative to the hierarchical Church, just as he supported imperial authority in place of papal theocracy.

---

the view that he played no political role whatsoever; cf. Raoul Manselli, "Grundzüge der religiösen Geschichte Italiens im 12. Jahrhundert," in *Beiträge zur Geschichte Italiens im 12. Jahrhundert*, Vorträge und Forschungen, Sonderband 9 (Sigmaringen 1971) 5–35 at 15–16, 31–32.

[19]Principal sources: Otto of Freising, *Chronica sive Historia de duabus civitatibus* 7.27, 31, 2nd ed. Adolf Hofmeister, MGH SS rer Germ (Hanover 1912) 352–53, 359; John of Salisbury, *Historia pontificalis* c. 27, ed. and trans. Marjorie Chibnall, *Memoirs of the Papal Court* (London and New York 1956) 59–60. *Auctarium Laudunense* anno 1145 (*recte*: 1144), MGH SS 6.447: "[patricius] rei publicae curam gerat et vices imperatoris eo absente suppleat." The *patricius* is mentioned in Roman law (*Cod.* 3.24.3 pr., 12.3.3, 5) and by Isidore of Seville, *Etymologiae* 9.3.25, ed. W. M. Lindsay (2 vols. Oxford 1911); also below, at n. 75.

On the Commune's constitution in 1144–45 and particularly on the *patricius*, whose office was suppressed in December 1145: Louis Halphen, *Etudes sur l'administration de Rome au moyen âge (751–1252)*, Bibliothèque de l'Ecole des hautes études, Sciences historiques et philologiques 166 (Paris 1907) esp. 53–76; Rota (n. 1 above) 77–93; Schramm, *KRR* 1.59–63, 229–38, 253.

[20]On the date: Arsenio Frugoni, "Sulla *Renovatio Senatus* del 1143 e l'*Ordo equestris*," *Bullettino dell'Istituto storico italiano per il medio evo* 62 (1950) 159–74 at 170; Helmut Gleber, *Papst Eugen III. (1145–1153) unter besonderer Berücksichtigung seiner politischen Tätigkeit*, Beiträge zur mittelalterlichen und neueren Geschichte 6 (Jena 1936) 27–31, argues for 1146.

Rome is, he asserted, "the seat of Empire, the fountain of liberty, the mistress of the world" (*sedes imperii, fons libertatis, mundi domina*).[21] Undoubtedly he played an important political role—"He was frequently heard on the Capitoline and in public gatherings"[22]—and his religious passion surely left an imprint on the communal movement, intensifying popular support for the revolution. One may argue that his political engagement grew, and that his leadership had become explicitly and primarily political by 1152. But beyond this, one can say little about his part in the twelfth-century Roman *renovatio*.

In the letters of 1149, the Commune's double program of a *renovatio sacri senatus* and a *restauratio imperii Romani* was linked to the Romans' antipapalism, while at the same time Arnold's views are visible in the Romans' vehement opposition to a secularized clergy engaging in litigation and warfare.[23] Conrad should recall—the Senate urged—how gravely the papacy had damaged his predecessors, "and now, together with the Sicilian [Roger II], they are trying to do worse things to you." For the Roman clergy has always been an "obstacle" to strong and effective government.[24] Moreover, the Senate suggested to Conrad that the clock could be turned back to the period before the papal Reform, and that an enlarged imperial prerogative could include the right to veto any papal election.[25] Three years later, in even more indignant tones, Wezel denounced the reigning pope and his predecessors as "blind heretics and apostate clerics and false monks," dismissing the Donation of Constantine as "that lie and heretical fable" which no longer deceives "even servants and simple women" in Rome.[26] A member of the Commune's radical wing, Wezel was undoubtedly expressing the religious preoccupations of Arnold's circle when he filled the larger part of his long letter with references to the Old Testament and with quotations from Pseudo-Isidore as well as from

[21]John of Salisbury, *Historia pontificalis* c. 31 (n. 19 above) 64–65. On Arnold, see the literature cited in the Bibliographical Note.

[22]John of Salisbury, *Historia pontificalis* c. 31 (n. 19 above) 64.

[23]Bartoloni 1.9 no. 7; Jaffé, *Bibl* 1.336 no. 216.

[24]Bartoloni 1.5 no. 5; Jaffé, *Bibl* 1.333–34 no. 214. The pope should be required to pay tribute to the emperor (n. 16 above).

[25]Above, n. 23. In this proposal, Gottfried Koch, *Auf dem Wege zum Sacrum imperium: Studien zur ideologischen Herrschaftsbegründung der deutschen Zentralgewalt im 11. und 12. Jahrhundert*, Forschungen zur mittelalterlichen Geschichte 20 (Vienna 1972) 202, sees a probable reference to Nicholas II's decree on papal elections (1059). Undoubtedly. But the senatorial spokesman has twisted the sense of the decree, which noted that Gregory I had actually administered the papal office while awaiting the emperor's permission to be consecrated; in 1149, however, the statement stressed that Gregory had recognized the lawfulness of the emperor's right to approve. See MGH Const 1.540 no. 382 §8 (= D.23 c.1 §6).

[26]Jaffé, *Bibl* 1.539, 542 no. 404. Otto III's well known charter of 1001 (MGH DD 2.2.820 no. 389; MGH Const. 1.56 no. 26) did not deny the Donation's authenticity, but simply asserted that the deacon "Johannes digitorum mutilus" had fabricated a copy of the Donation, making it appear to be the original charter issued by Constantine himself; Horst Fuhrmann, "Konstantinische Schenkung und abendländisches Kaisertum," DA 22 (1966) 63–178 at 128–42, and his *Einfluss und Verbreitung der pseudoisidorischen Fälschungen von ihrem Auftauchen bis in die neuere Zeit*, MGH Schriften 24 (3 vols. Stuttgart 1972–74) 2.389–91. Thus Wezel's statement remains the earliest recorded attack on the Donation's authenticity.

the New Testament.[27] And in 1155, the Commune restated its determination to shake off the "yoke of the clerics" (*clericorum iugum*).[28]

THE CLAIM TO CREATE AN EMPEROR

Throughout the three letters of 1149, however, the Senate's tone remained amicable and deeply respectful toward the Staufer king. Indeed, the Senate even promised Conrad its obedience.[29] Needing Conrad's support, the Senate asked him to hasten to Rome, assured him that he could have whatever he wanted in the City, and offered him the coronation—offered "to place," in their words, "the imperial crown on the royal head."[30] Yet the offer claimed little for the Senate, which had conceded that Conrad, in some sense, already held the *regnum et imperium Romanum* as divine gifts.[31] In 1149 the representatives of the Senate correctly addressed Conrad as "king of the Romans" (*rex Romanorum*),[32] a title which, in the Staufer view, indicated the German king's right to Italy and to the imperial office. In short, here the Commune accepted the Staufer conception of the title and office of the *rex Romanorum* as virtually indistinguishable from the imperial office. Hence there is no reason to assume that in 1149 the senatorial spokesmen considered the Roman coronation constitutive with respect to anything other than the imperial title: after the coronation, Conrad would be rightly entitled *imperator Romanorum*, and would govern as emperor what had already been rightly his as *rex Romanorum*.

Thus the Commune's letters of 1149 offered king Conrad an unorthodox alternative to the customary coronation and consecration of an emperor by the Roman pontiff. By envisioning the creation of an emperor as a secular act—that is, without an anointment and without the active collaboration of the papacy—the Romans perceived correctly, and attempted to revive, a central feature of constitutional procedure in late Antiquity.[33] Moreover (though the Romans could scarcely have known this), the notion of an essentially

---

[27]Wezel's heavy reliance on these authorities contrasts sharply with the more secular style in the letters of 1149.

[28]Otto, GF 2.29 p. 135.

[29]Bartoloni 1.5 no. 5; Jaffé, *Bibl* 1.334 no. 214; "sumus enim per omnia vestre voluntati semper obtemperare parati."

[30]Bartoloni 1.4 no. 5; Jaffé, *Bibl* 1.333 no. 214.

[31]Above, n. 12.

[32]The title *rex Romanorum* is discussed below, at nn. 176–80.

[33]In the making of an emperor during late Antiquity, the constitutive element was election, which in practice usually took the form of acclamation (see below, at nn. 52–53). The senior emperor might crown a new co-emperor (as still occurred in twelfth-century Byzantium); or, following the precedent set with emperor Leo I (457–74), the patriarch of Constantinople could crown the emperor, but coronation by the patriarch was never viewed as constitutive or indispensable. On all this, see A. H. M. Jones, *The Later Roman Empire 284–602: A Social, Economic, and Administrative Survey* (3 vols. Oxford 1964) 1.321–29; W. Ensslin, "The Government and Administration of the Byzantine Empire," *The Cambridge Medieval History* 4 (2nd ed. 2 vols. Cambridge 1966–67) 2.1–54 at 2–7.

secular monarchy was not entirely foreign to the history of the German kingship, for in 919 Henry the Fowler had chosen to be an "unanointed king."[34] Still, by the mid-twelfth century, long-standing custom and the powerful position of the Church within the German kingdom had rendered a truly secular accession inconceivable to the rulers of Germany.

Though the sixth-century chronicler Malalas reports that the Senate crowned the emperor Leo in 457, there is no trustworthy evidence for such a procedure in Antiquity.[35] But in making their offer to Conrad, the leaders of the Commune did not necessarily have to invent the idea of an imperial coronation by the Senate, since Peter the Deacon of Monte Cassino had already created a tradition of pseudohistorical precedents for this.[36] According to Peter's fiction, in late Antiquity rulers were elected in "new Rome,"then went to "golden Rome" for their imperial coronation by the Senate. In this fashion, the Senate had enthroned and crowned not only Justinian I as *monocrator* but also his successors Justin II, Maurice, and Heraclius. Peter clearly conceived the Senate's coronation as a central part of a constitutive ceremonial which conferred the "imperial prerogatives" (*imperialia iura*).[37] But Charlemagne's imperial coronation by pope Leo III altered a procedure which had become standard, "for till that time the emperor was crowned by the Roman Senate."[38] Within the history of the imperial constitution, thereby, Peter marked the coronation of 800 as the break between two periods, that is, as the end of Christian Roman Antiquity—including early Byzantium, for he noted that Maurice was "the first *monocrator* from the race of the Greeks."[39] Political ideas current at Monte Cassino may have influenced twelfth-century Rome. But even if one does not assume such influence, the twelfth-century Senate undoubtedly saw in its claim to crown the Roman emperor a *renovatio* of pre-Carolingian constitutional practice.[40]

[34]Carl Erdmann, "Der ungesalbte König," DA 2 (1938) 311–40 (repr. in his *Ottonische Studien,* ed. Helmut Beumann [Darmstadt 1968] 1–30).

[35]Milton V. Anastos, "*Vox populi voluntas Dei* and the Election of the Byzantine Emperor," *Christianity, Judaism, and Other Greco-Roman Cults: Studies for Morton Smith at Sixty,* ed. Jacob Neusner, Studies in Judaism in Late Antiquity 12 (4 vols. Leiden 1975) 2.181–207 at 192.

[36]On Peter in general, see Erich Caspar, *Petrus Diaconus und die Monte Cassineser Fälschungen* (Berlin 1909).

[37]*Epitome chronicorum Casinensium,* ed. L. A. Muratori, *Rerum italicarum scriptores* 2 (Milan 1723) 353: "Iustinianus ob coronationem suam a nova Roma ad auream Romam pervenit, et a senatu populoque Romano susceptus et in augustali solio collocatus, a senatu Romano coronatus, monocrator constituitur. Postquam autem imperialia iura suscepit, ad reparandum reipublicae statum animum intendit." On Justinian's successors: ibid. 2.354. See Peter Classen, "Die Komnenen und die Kaiserkrone des Westens," *Journal of Medieval History* 3 (1977) 207–24 at 210–12.

[38]*Epitome* (n. 37 above) 2.364: "Papa . . . [Carolum] coronavit in imperatorem Romanum. Nam usque ad tempora illa a senatu Romano imperator coronabatur." But even after 800, Peter assigned an important and apparently still constitutive role to the Senate. On Louis the Pious, he states: "Ludovicus . . . [veniens] ad auream Urbem a papa Valentino coronatur et a senatu populoque Romano monocrator constituitur" (2.365).

[39]*Epitome* (n. 37 above) 2.354.

[40]Above, n. 33.

After 1149, perhaps in part under the increasing influence of Arnold's radical religious ideas, the Commune grew politically more radical: there is a sharp break. The change in the political climate becomes evident in a letter of 1152, addressed by Wezel to Frederick Barbarossa following his accession to the German kingship. Nothing is known about Wezel, who is usually assumed to have been German, and who was manifestly a spokesman for the Arnoldists. From the text of his letter, however, it is not absolutely certain that Wezel wrote as an official representative of the Commune. He began his letter with a calculated affront: in the salutation he did not address Frederick with his royal title, but used only the title *clarissimus*.[41] Since *clarissimus* indicated senatorial rank in the constitutional language of late Antiquity, and since this was well known in the twelfth century,[42] Wezel was demoting Frederick to the level of a Roman senator. Then Wezel congratulated Barbarossa "that your people (*gens vestra*) has elected you as their king." In Wezel's view, thereby, Frederick's election as German king had only local significance. By avoiding the title *rex Romanorum*, Wezel denied any connection between Rome and the German kingship. Thus Frederick's election by the German princes conferred no claim on either the Italian kingship or the imperial office: it gave merely the kingship over an extra-Italian *gens*.

Correspondingly, Wezel implied that the papacy had never had the right to summon Frederick or his predecessors to Rome for the imperial coronation. The Senate had recently offered Conrad III an imperial coronation, and—since he had little else to offer—Wezel could scarcely have intended to offer Frederick less than that. Nor would anyone in the twelfth-century West have dispensed with coronation as an element in an emperor's accession. But Wezel insisted that as the City is "the creator and mother of all emperors" and since the emperor is the City's "son and minister," Frederick was obligated to con-

---

[41]Jaffé, *Bibl* 1.539 no. 404: "Clarissimo Dei gratia Friderico Wezel, ad summa animae et corporis leta undique proficere. Inmensa laeticia, quod gens vestra vos sibi in regem elegerit, moveor. Ceterum, quod . . . sacrosanctam Urbem, dominam mundi, creatricem et matrem omnium imperatorum, super hoc sicut deberetis non consuluistis, et eius confirmationem, per quam omnes et sine qua nulli umquam principum imperaverunt, non requisistis, nec ei sicut filius matri, si tamen filius et minister eius esse proposuistis, non scripsistis, vehementer doleo. . . . Vocatio vestrorum olim predecessorum et vestra adhuc a cecis, id est a Iulianistis, hereticis et apostatis clericis dico et falsis monachis . . . et, legibus tam humanis quam divinis reclamantibus, aecclesiam Dei et secularia disturbantibus, facta est. . . ."

[42]Though one might be tempted to regard "clarissimo" as a simple adjective in this salutation (like "preclaro" in the Senate's letter of 1149; n. 6 above), the full salutation—"Clarissimo Dei gratia Friderico," without the addition of "Romanorum regi" or even of "regi" alone—implies that Wezel was using *clarissimus* as a title. Cicero identified senators as "clarissimi," and *equites* as "splendidissimi" (RE Suppl. 6 [1935] 761). One finds *clarissimus* and *clarissimatus* in Roman law (*Cod.* 3.24, 5.33, 12.1.11, 12.19.5). But in late Antiquity, the senatorial rank of *clarissimus* had declined in status (Jones [n. 33 above] 2.528–31). Twelfth-century thinkers were familiar with the remark by Isidore of Seville, *Etymologiae* 9.4.12 (n. 19 above): "Primi ordines senatorum dicuntur inlustres, secundi spectabiles, tertii clarissimi." Further, a twelfth-century jurist ranked different kinds of *iudex*, with the *illustres* highest, followed by *spectabiles*, *clarissimi*, and *pedanei* (Hermann Fitting, ed., *Juristische Schriften des Mittelalters* [Halle 1876] 148).

sult Rome and to request its "confirmation." For without this *confirmatio*, "no prince (*princeps*) has ever ruled as emperor." The "confirmation" is thus the portal to the imperial office. Here, Wezel referred to an indispensable juridical act which would express, in some sense, the City's approval—undoubtedly, approval of Frederick's suitability as a candidate for the *imperium*. But through what kind of juridical act? Since Wezel believed that the royal election by the German princes had no constitutional significance for the Romans, this *confirmatio* cannot have meant a "confirmation" of Frederick's election in Germany.[43] In all likelihood, the *confirmatio* simply indicated the imperial coronation by the officials of Rome.[44] And in fact, a contemporary jurist described an imperial coronation by the pope as a *confirmatio*.[45] From this, one can briefly summarize Wezel's argument: Frederick should have requested the coronation by Senate and people, for only that can bestow Romanness and can transform the king of a mere *gens* by conferring on him dominion in Italy and imperial status.[46] As Wezel stated his general point in a rhetorical question: "What law, what reasoning prevents the Senate and the people from creating an emperor?"[47]

Wezel's letter to Frederick evidently reflects the direction of events in Rome during 1152, as one sees from a secret communication by pope Eugene III to the imperial adviser, Wibald of Corvey, on 20 September 1152.[48] Both Eugene and his friend Bernard of Clairvaux had tried unsuccessfully to persuade Conrad III to march against the Commune. But despite Eugene's understandable hostility toward the Roman revolutionaries, there is nothing improbable in his report: under Arnold's leadership, he wrote, a "rustic mob" of about 2,000 gathered and swore to "create" on 1 November 1152 a hundred senators (Eugene's pun refers to them contemptuously as *sectatores*),

[43]For a different view, cf. Koch (n. 25 above) 204. To be sure, the Commune would have found precedents for the "confirmation" of a German king's election: on 17 May 1152 Eugene III "approved" Frederick's royal election (MGH Const 1.194 no. 139), and there were earlier precedents. But within Wezel's letter, there is no mention, even implicitly, of an *imperial* election.

[44]Two arguments suggest this: (1) Wezel implicitly contrasted the City's *confirmatio* with the popes' unlawful summoning (*vocatio*) of German kings to Rome for the imperial coronation. (2) Since Wezel's letter does not explicitly mention an imperial *coronatio*, the *confirmatio* is best construed as a veiled reference to that.

[45]Rufinus, *Summa decretorum* ad D.22 c.1 v. *terr. s. et cel. imper. iura comm.*, ed. Heinrich Singer (Paderborn 1902) 47–48; written between 1157 and 1159. On this passage: Robert L. Benson, *The Bishop-Elect: A Study in Medieval Ecclesiastical Office* (Princeton 1968) 76–77.

[46]Consequently, one cannot assert—as Koch does (n. 25 above, 204)—that Wezel drew no sharp distinction "zwischen Königs- und Kaisererhebung." Cf. Eugenio Dupré Theseider, *L'idea imperiale di Roma nella tradizione del medioevo* (Milan 1942) 143, suggesting that here the Romans claimed the right to bestow the title *rex Romanorum*; there is no evidence to support this, nor is it probable that in 1152 the radical Romans would have appropriated the title *rex Romanorum*, which embodied a constitutional tradition whose implications they could not accept. But Dupré Theseider rightly sees in this *confirmatio* a claim to make "la designazione all'impero."

[47]Below, n. 81.

[48]Jaffé, *Bibl* 1.538–39 no. 403; note that in Wibald's collection, this letter immediately precedes Wezel's.

two consuls, one with authority inside the City and the other outside (reflecting the division of responsibility between the ancient *praetores urbanus* and *peregrinus*), and "one whom they want to call emperor." Eugene concluded ominously by urging that Wibald secretly inform Frederick, who should then do "what the situation requires." If this papal account is accurate, Arnold and a group of poorer and less eminent Romans had taken control of the communal movement in 1152. In all likelihood, they anticipated—correctly—that the new German king would refuse their crown and their offer of a Roman alliance; hence the decision to elect an emperor soon and, undoubtedly, to choose one of the Commune's leaders as emperor. By assuming that the German king had no inherent claim on the imperial office, Wezel expressed a central conviction of this new group: the Roman people is free to elect as emperor whomever it wishes. In any case, the episode was brief, cooler heads seem to have prevailed, and the election planned for 1 November 1152 evidently never took place.

In June 1155, envoys from "the Senate and the Roman people" met and addressed Barbarossa on the road from Sutri to Rome. In their address, the envoys pretended to speak with the voice of *Roma* herself, telling Barbarossa that he would soon be "prince, emperor, and lord" (*princeps, imperator et dominus*) of the City.[49] After calling for the return of "ancient times," when the City's power stretched to the ends of the earth and beyond, and for the return of the City's "ancient magnificence," *Roma* imagines that she has already granted the crown to Frederick: "You were a visitor, I made you a citizen. You were a stranger from across the Alps, I established you as *princeps*. I gave to you what was rightly mine." As in Wezel's letter, here the City's grant of the imperial office is presented as a constitutive act. Though *Roma*'s address contains flattering promises to Frederick in high-flown language, he would never have accepted the notion that he had been made "citizen" and *princeps* by free grant of the City.[50] Nor would he ever have agreed to the conditions which *Roma* imposed as the price of the imperial office. The address concludes in tones as imperious as those of Wezel's letter, for *Roma* demands the payment of 5,000 pounds, the confirmation of ancient rights, the assurance of protection, and guarantees by oath.[51]

---

[49]Otto, GF 2.29 pp. 135–36. Although Otto—who did not accompany Frederick on this expedition—has certainly not given verbatim the text of the envoys' address, his reconstruction presumably presents their position and their arguments with general accuracy. As Otto renders it, the content of the address is, after all, broadly congruent with Wezel's letter (Koch [n. 25 above] 205–06 n. 174). There are no grounds for radical skepticism; but cf. Ernst Schoenian, *Die Idee der Volkssouveränität im mittelalterlichen Rom*, Frankfurter historische Forschungen n.s. 2 (Leipzig 1919) 63 n. 2, and Edmund E. Stengel, *Abhandlungen und Untersuchungen zur Geschichte des Kaisergedankens im Mittelalter* (Cologne 1965) 93 n. 7.

[50]To be sure, in 1111 Henry V described himself as a Roman *civis* and the Romans as his *concives* (MGH Const 1.134 no. 82). In 1239, Frederick II similarly wrote "suis conromanis"; J.-L.-A. Huillard-Bréholles, ed., *Historia diplomatica Friderici secundi* (6 vols. in 11 Paris 1852–61) 5.1.307.

[51]GF 2.29 p. 136. Noting that "earlier emperors" had confirmed and sworn to observe the City's "bonae consuetudines legesque antiquae," *Roma* was essentially right: the contemporary

In the envoys' address, *Roma* remarks that the "officials" of the City will "acclaim" Barbarossa on the Capitoline.[52] An unbroken tradition of such "acclamations" or *laudes* went back to the first-century Empire: when the Senate and the army—or, more typically, the army alone—hailed the candidate with the title *augustus*, they represented the *populus*, and expressed the people's recognition of and consent to the new ruler. Moreover, these hails normally counted as the emperor's election. In their early development, such *laudes* may be summed up as a secular liturgy endowed with the highest constitutional significance. Nor did the particular mode of succession—inheritance, adoption, designation, or violence—affect the requirement: the acclamations remained indispensable as well as constitutive.[53] To mention only the example most familiar to historians, when the "entire Roman people" hailed Charlemagne as emperor in 800, their acclamations were constitutionally decisive.[54] Here, the point is that in the envoys' address, by calling for the restoration of the Senate and of the army (in the form of the City's "equestrian order"),[55] and by promising the acclamations to Barbarossa, *Roma* has invoked this ancient constitutional tradition. From the perspective of this tradition, the *laudes* on the Capitoline would have been Barbarossa's *imperial* election. From the Romans' perspective in 1155, the acclamations and coronation sufficed to create an emperor.[56]

GRAPHIA AVREAE VRBIS ROMAE

With their reference to acclamations on the Capitoline, the envoys were invoking at the same time the mystique of ancient Rome, a mystique which not only hallowed the Capitoline and many of the Roman buildings and monuments still surviving from Antiquity, but also underlay a programmatic myth about the universal authority of the City and of the imperial office in Antiquity. This

---

coronation *ordo* "Cencius II" prescribed that the emperor-elect take such an oath three times as he entered the City; Reinhard Elze, ed., *Ordines coronationis imperialis* 14.57–59, MGH Fontes iuris Germanici antiqui 9 (Hanover 1960) 47. In 1133, Lothar III swore to maintain the "Urbis honores" (Rahewin, GF 3.10 p. 177).

[52]GF 2.29 p. 136: ". . . officialibus meis, a quibus tibi in Capitolio adclamandum erit. . . ."

[53]In general, see n. 33 above, and Ernst H. Kantorowicz, *Laudes regiae: A Study in Liturgical Acclamations and Mediaeval Ruler Worship* (Berkeley 1946) 76–78. Of course, *laudes* were offered not only at the ruler's accession but on other ceremonial occasions as well.

[54]*Annales regni Francorum* anno 801 (*sic*), ed. Friedrich Kurze, MGH SS rer Germ (Hanover 1895) 112; Schramm, *KKP* 1.234–39. On the early medieval development generally: Karl Heldmann, *Das Kaisertum Karls des Grossen* (Weimar 1928) 258–89. The acclamations by the Romans in 800 and at subsequent occasions should not be confused with the *laudes* chanted by the clergy (Kantorowicz [n. 53 above] 84).

[55]GF 2.29 p. 136: ". . . ad sacrum sanctae Urbis senatum equestremque ordinem instaurandum, quatinus huius consiliis, illius armis Romano imperio tuaeque personae antiqua redeat magnificentia." Frugoni (n. 20 above) 172–74: the *ordo equester* was the Romans' "army."

[56]Cf. Helmold of Bosau's account of the Roman envoys' address to Frederick: "quem electio principum regni creavit regem, auctoritas senatus perficiat cesarem" (*Chronica Slavorum* 1.80, 3rd ed. Bernhard Schmeidler, MGH SS rer Germ [Hanover 1937] 152); this text nicely fits the Commune's position in 1149, but not that of 1155. Equally in 1149 or 1155, the Senate's program excluded a papal coronation.

enthusiasm for ancient Rome found its most remarkable twelfth-century expression in the "Description of the Golden City of Rome" (*Graphia aureae Urbis Romae*), a composite work which was probably put together in Rome during the first five months of 1155, just before—and, one may assume, in anticipation of—Barbarossa's arrival.[57] The *Graphia* consists of three distinct parts: (1) a brief and fantastic "history" of the region of Rome from Noah till the founding of the City by Romulus;[58] (2) a learned guidebook to the "Wonders of the City of Rome" (*Mirabilia urbis Rome*), that is, to the topography and monuments of Rome in Antiquity, composed by Benedict of St Peter's between 1140 and 1143, and lightly reworked for inclusion in the *Graphia;*[59] (3) a treatise on the imperial court (*Libellus de cerimoniis aule imperatoris*), which dealt with Roman offices and the insignia of the emperor as well as with ceremonials. The original version of the *Libellus* was composed by a layman of Rome, perhaps by a judge, before the mid-eleventh century.[60] Thus the twelfth-century Roman adherents of *renovatio* did not create the *Libellus*, but rather appealed to its "ancient" authority, just as others invoked the Donation of Constantine.

The character of the *Graphia* emerges from the juxtaposition of the three works, especially of Benedict's *Mirabilia* and the anonymous *Libellus*. The short history of the region reflects a general quickening of the contemporary Romans' interest in the City's glorious past, most notably in pre-Christian Rome as well as in the myth of Rome's Trojan origins.[61] Read together in the light of Rome's history, the *Mirabilia* and the *Libellus* chart a program for the City's *renovatio*. The *Mirabilia* rendered manifest the Romans' reverence for the visible past of the City. But this reverence went far beyond *campanilismo*, beyond any interest in or mere attachment to the ancient stones. Indeed, it could even verge on an eschatological vision, as one sees from a charter in which the Senate asserted that the column of Trajan "should remain undamaged and uncorrupted so long as the world lasts," for the column is a representation of the world, a *figura mundi*.[62] The *Mirabilia* provided not only

---

[57]There are two scholarly editions of the *Graphia*: Roberto Valentini and Giuseppe Zucchetti, eds., *Codice topografico della città di Roma* 3, Fonti per la storia d'Italia 90 (Rome 1946) 67–110, and Schramm, *KKP* 3.313–53 (on the dating: 3.355–56).

[58]It is not clear whether this history was composed specifically for the *Graphia*, or was an older work.

[59]See Herbert Bloch's valuable analysis in this volume (632). Schramm does not regard Benedict's authorship as proven beyond all possible doubt (*KKP* 3.354–55).

[60]In general: Schramm, *KRR* 1.193–217, who dates the *Libellus* around 1030; for a brief account, Folz (n. 18 above) esp. 67–69. Cf., however, Ernst Mayer's review of Schramm's first edition (ZRG germ Abt 50 [1930] 426–32), arguing for composition in the period 966–72, a dating which Schramm rejects but which Valentini and Zucchetti are inclined to prefer (n. 57 above, 71). Schramm formulated the title of the *Libellus*, which has no separate rubric in the only complete surviving manuscript of the *Graphia*.

[61]Paolo Brezzi, *Roma e l'impero medioevale (774–1252)*, Storia di Roma 10 (Bologna 1947) 510–11; Schramm, *KKP* 4.1.28–33.

[62]Bartoloni 1.27 no. 18 (27 March 1162): "ut est ad honorem . . . totius populi Romani, [columpna Traiana] integra et incorrupta permaneat dum mundus durat, sic eius stante figura." On this text: Classen (n. 2 above) 236–37.

a concrete enumeration of gates, arches, baths, palaces, theaters, temples, and so forth, but also illustrative legends about the various sites and ruins. Sometimes the little anecdote linked the monument to the Christian past ("the Appian gate, outside of which, as it is told, Jesus appeared to St Peter"),[63] but more frequently the story identified the monument or place in relation to Republican or imperial Antiquity (Marcus Agrippa built the Pantheon in fulfillment of a vow to the goddess Cybele, who spoke to him in a dream and who, together with Neptune, gave him victory in a battle).[64]

To these dimensions of the *Mirabilia*, the *Libellus* added an idealized—and, needless to say, largely imaginary—portrait of the ancient emperorship as well as of the Roman administration.[65] The author of the *Libellus* described in detail the many offices at the imperial court, the emperor's ten crowns and other insignia, and the various processions and ceremonials. One may say that with its emphasis on symbols, vestments, and ceremonies, the *Libellus* presents the imperial office and government in an essentially liturgical mode. The anonymous author confirms this impression by couching his entire account in the present tense, ignoring any differences or distance between "Antiquity" and the imagined present. Thus the tendency of the *Mirabilia* is archeological and historical, while the *Libellus*, by rendering Antiquity as though it were present, is timeless: its portrayal refers to *any* ancient emperor.

From a medieval perspective, the most striking difference between the two works would have been religious: Christianity has no overt existence within the *Libellus*, which represents the emperor as a devout pagan. On the other hand, in his *Mirabilia* Benedict notes a profusion of places sanctified "by the passions of the saints" and a fair number of churches. Though primarily concerned with the pre-Constantinian topography of the city, Benedict has unmistakably shown his reader a Christian Rome, a Rome in which time and Christianity have superimposed a layer of historical experience over the ruins of the pagan period. But Benedict gives scarcely a sign that Rome was also the City of the popes: he briefly mentions two popes, one of them—his contemporary, Innocent II—only to identify the emperor Hadrian's porphyry tomb and to note that Innocent had taken it for himself.[66]

The Middle Ages, we are often told,[67] were interested not in Republican Rome, but in the imperial City. Though incontestable at most times and

---

[63]*Mirabilia* c. 2, ed. Schramm, *KKP* 3.322.

[64]*Mirabilia* c. 18, ed. Schramm, *KKP* 3.330.

[65]It forms a conglomerate picture, drawn from ancient and contemporary Rome, also from Byzantine and Ottonian practice. The most important written sources for the *Libellus* were Isidore of Seville's *Etymologiae* and the *Constitutum Constantini.*

[66]*Mirabilia* cc. 14, 16, ed. Schramm, *KKP* 3.328–29. The compiler of the *Graphia* added a reference (c. 16) to the porphyry sepulcher of Anastasius IV, who died on 3 December 1154. Contemporaries were aware that porphyry had symbolic significance, and surely understood that by appropriating the porphyry sarcophagi of Hadrian and of St Helen, Innocent and Anastasius were exercising an imperial prerogative; Josef Deér, *The Dynastic Porphyry Tombs of the Norman Period in Sicily*, trans. G. A. Gillhoff, Dumbarton Oaks Studies 5 (Cambridge Mass. 1959) 146–54.

[67]For example, by Paul Koschaker, *Europa und das römische Recht* (Munich 1947) 39 n. 2.

places, the generalization does not hold true in twelfth-century Rome. Still, in asking whether Benedict and the anonymous author of the *Libellus* owed their first loyalty to the Republic or the Empire, one may be posing an unanswerable question. Certainly both had a particular reverence for the Capitoline, with its senatorial tradition. For Benedict, "The Capitoline was the chief place of the world, where the consuls and senators stayed to govern the world,"[68] and the *Libellus* refers to it as the *caput orbis*. The anonymous author stressed the Capitoline's sacred precincts, for even the emperor must put on special garments before entering the temple of Jupiter Capitoline.[69] But Benedict also says of the purely imperial Palatine that one finds there the "throne and chief place of the entire world."[70] Both the *Mirabilia* and the *Libellus* are populated with figures from Rome's Republican past as well as from the pagan Empire, but probably they most frequently mention Julius Caesar and Augustus—indeed, every emperor is the "imitator of Julius Caesar."[71] On the other hand, though eleventh- and twelfth-century people could distinguish between the various traditions—Republic and Empire,[72] Senate and emperor, pagan Rome and Christian Rome—easily enough when they wanted to, this did not always suit their purposes. One of Benedict's legends illustrates the point. The Senate wished to pay divine honors to Augustus, who refused them and consulted the Sibyl. While he was listening to her oracle, he had a vision of the Virgin and the Savior in heaven.[73] It is characteristic of Benedict's thought that all three—senators, Augustus, and Christ—could come together without tension in a brief anecdote.

Both Benedict and the anonymous author were preoccupied with Rome's historic achievement in conquering and governing the world. As described in the *Libellus*, the emperor is "the lord of all" (*omnium dominator*), his office has "universality," his power comes from God (not from the people!), and all must salute the emperor by prostrating themselves before him in the Byzantine fashion.[74] When the *Libellus* gave a formula in which the absolute monarch invests a *patricius* as his "deputy" (*adiutor*), the anonymous author drew on a tradition which the Commune also appropriated.[75] In a formula for the investiture of a judge, the emperor hands over Justinian's *Code* and says:

[68]*Mirabilia* c. 20, ed. Schramm, *KKP* 3.331.

[69]*Libellus* c. 19, ed. Schramm, *KKP* 3.351.

[70]*Mirabilia* c. 5, ed. Schramm, *KKP* 3.323.

[71]*Libellus* c. 19, ed. Schramm, *KKP* 3.351.

[72]*Mirabilia* c. 24, ed. Schramm, *KKP* 3.335: "Tempore, quo consules et senatores rempublicam aministrabant. . . ." Also, n. 68 above.

[73]*Mirabilia* c. 21, ed. Schramm, *KKP* 3.332.

[74]*Mirabilia* c. 20, and *Libellus* cc. 1, 4, 13, 19, ed. Schramm, *KKP* 3.331, 339, 341–42, 347–48, 351. Since the *Libellus* was a manual on liturgical kingship, one should not dismiss its emperor as merely "a brilliant ornament" or criticize the treatise's "lack of political substance" (cf. Folz [n. 18 above] 90, 68). Within the *Libellus*, after all, the emperor's power is summed up as virtually absolute (c. 19). And to cite an analogy: Constantine VII Porphyrogenitus's *Liber de caerimoniis* was also not intended to instruct its readers on "real" politics in Byzantium. Or, from a different perspective, this *was* real politics.

[75]*Libellus* c. 20, ed. Schramm, *KKP* 3.352; see also n.19 above.

"Judge Rome and the Leonine City and the entire world according to this book."[76] Here too, by stressing the validity of Roman law throughout the Empire, the *Libellus* anticipated the Commune's views.[77] Above all, with the assumption that the emperor resides in Rome and rules the Empire from there, the *Libellus*'s account matched the Commune's stated hopes.

In various ways, then, the two treatises glorified the physical City, the ancient Roman people, and the ancient emperors with their administrative hierarchy. One might say that from the Commune's perspective in 1155, the *Mirabilia* presented the historical background of the story and the stage-setting, while the *Libellus* furnished a cast of characters as well as a scenario for the Roman *renovatio*: the two treatises supplement and reinforce each other, they converge to become a program truly designed for the Romans. Of course, the *Graphia* could not have served as a detailed blueprint for the reconstruction of Rome's constitution, but it must have seemed an authoritative picture of Roman Antiquity—the *Libellus* would have been perceived as itself an ancient work. Thereby the *Graphia* defined an ideal which accurately reflected, in broad outlines and on some points of detail, the Commune's goals: it offered the Romans a heightened consciousness of their own past, an image of Rome without papal domination, and a Rome imagined in its greatness as an imperial capital.

LEX REGIA

But the *Graphia* could not provide the juridical foundation of the Commune's claims. Roman law was to furnish this: concluding his letter of 1152, Wezel stated that to define the relations between Frederick and the City, jurists trained in Roman law (*periti legum*) would be needed.[78]

A generation earlier, Roman aristocrats supporting the antipope Anacletus II had written to king Lothar III: "If you wish to be our *princeps* and that of the clergy, if you want to claim for yourself the insignia (*fasces*) and glory of the Roman Empire, you must conform to the Roman laws."[79] Near the close of his letter to Frederick, in a clever argument Wezel incorporated the much quoted first sentence from Justinian's *Institutes*—"The imperial majesty must be not only distinguished in arms but also armed with laws"—in order to

---

[76]*Libellus* c. 21, ed. Schramm, *KKP* 3.353: "imperator . . . det ei [iudici] in manum librum codicum et dicat: 'Secundum hunc librum iudica Romam et Leonianam orbemque uniuersum.'"

[77]A third formula prescribes the procedure for the creation of a Roman citizen—the revival of an ancient form, though obviously without its ancient content; *Libellus* c. 22, ed. Schramm, *KKP* 3.353 (also: Schramm, *KRR* 1.213).

[78]As soon as possible, Frederick should send certain envoys to Rome, "qui, assumptis peritis legum qui de iure imperii sciant, et audeant tractare" (Jaffé, *Bibl* 1.543 no. 404).

[79]Baronius (Cesare Baronio), *Annales ecclesiastici* (rev. ed. 37 vols. Paris 1864–83) 18.422: "necesse est Romanis te legibus coaptari"; Wilhelm Bernhardi, *Lothar von Supplinburg*, Jahrbücher der deutschen Geschichte (Leipzig 1879) 322. In this letter of 18 May 1130, the *Romanae urbis potentes* hint that they will play a certain role in Lothar's receiving the *imperii culmen*, but do not assert the right to confer or withhold the imperial coronation and office.

prove that as Roman emperor, Frederick should be *legum peritus*, fully familiar with Roman law.[80] Then Wezel asserted that emperors acquire the power "to rule and to establish laws" (*imperare et leges condere*) from Roman law itself, for as Roman law states, "What the prince has decided has the force of law, . . . since the people has conferred on him all of its *imperium* and power."[81] This is the famous *lex regia*, the doctrine of popular sovereignty embedded in Roman law. Though Wezel quoted the *lex regia*, with slight alterations, in the form offered by the *Institutes*, he could also have found it in the *Digest* and the Justinian *Code*.[82] Within the corpus of Roman law, the *lex regia* referred only to the emperor's legislative authority, and professional jurists usually confined their discussions of the *lex regia* to the issue of legislation, but—like Wezel—other twelfth-century thinkers readily interpreted the *lex regia* as a general statement on the emperor's entire prerogative. And

[80]Since Barbarossa undoubtedly had little conception of Roman law, here Wezel's hopes were too sanguine; but Wezel could not have known the thirteenth-century maxim *raro princeps iurista invenitur* (on which, see Ernst H. Kantorowicz, *The King's Two Bodies: A Study in Mediaeval Political Theology* [Princeton 1957] 153–54).

In this text (n. 81 below), Wezel seems to intimate a doctrine which became common in the following century: that the prince or pope has *iura omnia in scrinio pectoris sui* (deriving from *Cod.* 6.23.19.1). In other words, since the prince is presumed to know all pertinent laws, when he issues a law or charter, no one can take exception by asserting the law-giver's ignorance of certain earlier laws. On this formula, see Kantorowicz 28 n. 15, 153–54; Gaines Post, *Studies in Medieval Legal Thought* (Princeton 1964) 352–53, 470. But Wezel's principle that the ruler *should* know Roman law is distinguishable from the idea that the prince is *presumed* to know the relevant laws.

[81]Jaffé, *Bibl* 1.542 no. 404: "Imperatorem non silvestrem set legum peritum debere esse, testatur Iustinianus imperator . . . dicens: 'Imperatoriam maiestatem non solum armis decoratam set etiam legibus oportet esse armatam, ut utrumque tempus, et bellorum et pacis, recte possit gubernari' (*Inst.* pr.). Idem etiam, unde princeps Romanus imperare et leges condere habeat, paulo post ostendit: 'Set et quod principi placuit, legis habeat vigorem,' et quare, subinfert, 'cum populus ei et in eum omne suum imperium et potestatem concessit' (cf. *Inst.* 1.2.6). Set cum imperium et omnis rei publicae dignitas sit Romanorum, et dum imperator sit Romanorum, non Romani imperatoris, quod sequatur considerantibus [patet]. Quae lex, quae ratio senatum populumque prohibet, creare imperatorem?"

[82]The idea of popular sovereignty left traces in other texts as well; R. W. and A. J. Carlyle, *A History of Mediaeval Political Theory in the West* (6 vols. New York 1903–36) 1.63–70. But the *lex regia* appears explicitly in *Inst.* 1.2.6: "Sed et quod principi placuit, legis habet vigorem, cum lege regia, quae de imperio eius lata est, populus ei et in eum omne suum imperium et potestatem concessit"; in *Dig.* 1.4.1 (adapted from Ulpian): "Quod principi placuit, legis habet vigorem: utpote cum lege . . . (as in *Inst.* 1.2.6) . . . potestatem conferat"; and in *Cod.* 1.17.1.7: ". . . cum enim lege antiqua, quae regia nuncupabatur, omne ius omnisque potestas populi Romani in imperatoriam translata sunt potestatem. . . ." See the analysis by Fritz Schulz, "Bracton on Kingship," EHR 60 (1945) 136–76 at 153–56.

A well-known text embodying such a transfer of *imperium* to an ancient emperor has survived on a bronze tablet, which Cola di Rienzo discovered about 1346. For the inscription's original significance, see P. A. Brunt, "Lex de imperio Vespasiani," *Journal of Roman Studies* 67 (1977) 95–116. W. S. Heckscher, *Sixtus IIII aeneas statuas Romano populo restituendas censuit* (The Hague n.d.) 10–11, 36, has argued that master Gregorius, an English traveler in Rome (probably late twelfth century), had seen this *enea tabula* but could not decipher it: Magister Gregorius, *Narracio de mirabilibus urbis Rome* c. 33, ed. R. B. C. Huygens (Leiden 1970) 31. Though there are grounds for doubting that what Gregorius saw was the *Lex de imperio*, the question cannot be pursued here.

precisely the *lex regia* constituted the fundamental law justifying the Commune's aspirations.[83]

For Wezel, the meaning of the *lex regia* was clear: because "the *imperium* and every office in the State belongs to the Romans, . . . not to the Roman emperor," the Senate and people have the right to "create an emperor." There is no reason to believe that Wezel was a jurist,[84] but twelfth-century jurists commonly discussed the interpretation of the *lex regia*: had the Roman people made an irrevocable grant? Or could the people reclaim their legislative and governmental rights? As the immediate question which implied the *lex regia* and usually provoked the discussions of it, glossators asked whether popular usage can abrogate statutory law. That is, can the people's custom itself become law and thereby override an imperial statute?[85] Wezel and the Romans would have recognized their own position—that the people can take back their *imperium* and power—in the view attributed to the contemporary legist, master Bulgarus, and later in the century to Johannes Bassianus, both of whom argued that under certain conditions, custom abrogates statute. Not long after 1200, Azo maintained that the Roman people "had not utterly renounced" its authority, and making the same point a few years later, Hugolinus added that the people had appointed the emperor merely as their "deputy" for legislation (*procurator ad hoc*).[86] The argument could scarcely have been carried further. Probably a majority of twelfth-century glossators accepted the *lex regia* as an irrevocable grant by the people, an historical event whose consequences would remain final.[87] But the Commune's insistence on the Roman people's imprescriptible rights rested finally on contemporary jurisprudence as well as on the Roman law of late Antiquity.

In summing up, one can argue that the Roman revolutionaries were the victims of three illusions.

The first illusion concerned the Germans. The Romans were deferential toward the weak Conrad III, and arrogant toward the powerful Barbarossa. Misperceiving the German monarchy, they could not estimate how minute

---

[83]Though not explicitly mentioned or cited in the three letters of 1149, the *lex regia* must be inferred as the legal basis of the claims made there. But cf. Koch (n. 25 above) 201, who remains uncertain about this.

[84]Familiarity with *Inst.* pr. and 1.2.6 did not require a legal education: the passages were widely known (see n. 101 below). Again, cf. Koch (n. 25 above) 203–04 and n. 160, who exaggerates Wezel's knowledge of and reliance on Roman law.

[85]Carlyle (n. 82 above) 2.56–67.

[86]These legistic sources and others on the *lex regia* are conveniently assembled in: Carlyle (n. 82 above) 2.57–66; Dupré Theseider (n. 46 above) 255–69; Sergio Mochi Onory and Gianluigi Barni, ed., *La crisi del sacro romano impero* (Milan 1961). See Armin Wolf, in Coing, *Handbuch* 1.547–48. Though twelfth-century canonists also had interesting views on the *lex regia*, they cannot be discussed here.

[87]Below, at n. 119.

were the chances that a German king would accept a crown from the Senate and the Roman people. For the German monarchy had already committed itself to an ideology which derived the kingship and Empire from God and from the election of the German princes.[88] Indeed, it is unlikely that either Conrad III or Barbarossa ever seriously considered an alliance with the Romans.[89] Proud and conservative, Frederick refused "to buy the *imperium*" and "to swear oaths to a mob."[90] Though Frederick was equally unwilling to owe his imperial crown to the Roman pontiff, he could—and did—receive the crown from the pope's hands while rejecting the papacy's interpretation of that act.

The second illusion concerned power, and it was fatal. Without a commercial base, Rome depended for its income on the papacy, on the City's status as the ecclesiastical capital of Christendom, and therefore lacked the resources necessary to maintain its antipapal policy. The Commune could not long survive without the German alliance—a fact which the Romans clearly saw till 1149, but perhaps forgot thereafter. Yet since the Romans had nothing, apart from the imperial coronation, to offer Conrad or Frederick in return, the basis for an alliance did not exist. Further, no twelfth-century German king could have preserved his power if he had tried to govern the Empire from Rome: the foundations of power lay in Germany. Finally, because the Romans saw the City's glorious past as the warrant for their universal claims, they inevitably came into simultaneous conflict with the papacy and the German monarchy: both of them also claiming a universal role, both also bound to Rome. Since the Romans could not hold out against an alliance between Frederick and the papacy, the Treaty of Constance in 1153 meant the end of their hopes.

The third illusion concerned Antiquity. The Roman revolutionaries' program of *renovatio* clothed itself in Republican rhetoric, and they imagined that they were restoring the rights of "the Senate and the Roman people." But like the *Graphia*, which orbited principally around its memory of the Empire, the Romans gave no sign of having envisioned a restoration of the ancient

---

[88]Otto, *Chronica* 4 pr. (n. 19 above) 182: "Dum enim ab eis querimus, quo iure reges id habeant, respondere solent: ex ordinatione Dei et electione populi."

[89]Cf. Koch (n. 25 above) 203, arguing that Conrad took the proposals seriously; against this view: Dupré Theseider (n. 46 above) 39–40, and—with less certainty—Brezzi (n. 61 above) 336–37. Undoubtedly Conrad negotiated with the Senate; Friedrich Hausmann, *Reichskanzlei und Hofkapelle unter Heinrich V. und Konrad III.*, MGH Schriften 14 (Stuttgart 1956) 106–17, 208, 227–29. Exasperated by the alliance between Eugene and Roger II, Conrad apparently entertained the possibility of including the Commune—along with the Byzantine emperor—in a common front against the Norman king. Still, Conrad may simply have intended to put pressure on the pope. Nor do his negotiations with the Romans prove that Conrad was even briefly willing to accept the imperial crown from the Senate. It is significant that his only letter to the Romans was not addressed to the Senate (MGH DD 9.455 no. 262; after 17 September 1151). In any case, Otto—who was Conrad's half-brother—characterized the proposals as fairy tales (*neniae*) and rightly reports that Conrad rejected them (GF 1.29 p. 47).

[90]GF, Epistola Friderici p. 3.

Roman Republic, with all government carried on by the Senate and the elected magistrates. Their *renovatio* aimed to restore sovereignty to the Roman people, but aimed to do so in only one respect: only "the Senate and the Roman people" could grant the imperial crown, could confer legitimacy upon a Roman emperor. In short, although they surely expected that the Senate would rule the Roman *contado*, have an enlarged prerogative, and generally play a prominent role, they could not imagine Rome without an emperor. Here too, their program did not correspond to the realities of Antiquity. At least until 1149, the Commune regarded election by the German princes as the effective designation of the future Roman emperor, and was eager to confer the Roman crown on a German king. Between 1152 and 1155, though the Commune had grown more radical, it did not fully abandon—or, at most, only briefly gave up—the hope that a German king would willingly adopt their model of emperorship. Of course, by 1152 the revolutionaries had conceived at least the possibility of detaching the imperial crown from the German kingship. Still, throughout the Commune's short career, its program represented a fusion of ancient elements and present political realities. Differently stated, Antiquity furnished the form, the twelfth century provided the substance.

Of the three illusions, the third was decisive, for the Romans' intoxication with Antiquity encouraged them in the other two.

II. RENOVATIO IMPERII ROMANI

The idea had a long history before the twelfth century: on their imperial seals, both Charlemagne and Otto III had proclaimed the "Renewal of the Roman Empire."[91] No twelfth-century German king or emperor announced the *renovatio imperii* on his seals or coinage. Yet between the later eleventh and the mid-twelfth century, the idea of a *renovatio imperii Romani*—that is, the acceptance of Roman imperial Antiquity as a political and constitutional model—gained fresh momentum, acquired new meaning, and filled new needs. Though the Roman Commune included the "renewal" of the Roman Empire among its central goals, also in mid-twelfth-century Rome the concept of a *renovatio imperii* was far from new. And like the Roman Commune, the German monarchy took as the principal model for its *renovatio imperii* the period of late Antiquity and the Empire of the Christian emperors from Constantine to Justinian, but not the Empire of Augustus.

Still, in the late eleventh- and twelfth-century Empire—in Germany, Burgundy, and imperial Italy—the impulse toward a *renovatio imperii* did not come from the Commune's extravagant ideas.[92] Rather, after 1125 the Ger-

[91]From the ninth century till the early eleventh, not all rulers were equally eager to stress the Romanness of their regimes. One finds *Renovatio regni Francorum* on imperial bulls from Louis the Pious to Henry II; Schramm, *KKP* 2.51, 56, 294, 3.173, 178.

[92]Cf. Koch (n. 25 above) 195, 200–02 and elsewhere, who believes that the Senate substantially influenced German conceptions of the imperial office.

man monarchy was, in fact, seriously weakened, and its rulers had to reconstruct the theory of monarchy which justified their governance in Germany and Italy, since the papal Reform and the Investiture Struggle had successfully challenged the older ideological foundations of kingship and Empire. Overall, the twelfth-century German kings had to face a formidable constellation of potential threats to their power: the imperial princes in Germany, the communes of North Italy, the papacy with its diplomatic initiatives and theoretical claims, the Norman realm in the South, and the rival pretensions of the Byzantine emperors. In differing degrees and in different ways, the program of a *renovatio imperii Romani* constituted a response to each of these dangers.

What most sharply distinguished the *renovatio imperii* of the twelfth century from the earlier "renewals" was the role played by Roman law. To a remarkable extent, this twelfth-century *renovatio* was coterminous with the revival of Roman jurisprudence, which furnished much of its program and its style.[93]

ROMAN LAW AND THE EMPEROR'S PREROGATIVE

The origins of the twelfth-century *renovatio imperii* must be sought in the Investiture Struggle, for the juridically oriented idea of *renovatio* found its first advocates in Italy among the imperialist writers replying to papal claims.[94] In the early 1080s, juristic interests and a substantial familiarity with Roman law informed the publicistic writings of Peter Crassus and his Ravenna circle, who backed Henry IV against "the enemy of the laws," Gregory VII. Peter considered Henry the legitimate successor of the ancient emperors, and he used Roman private law to defend the heritability of Henry's realm. Drawing on Roman public law, moreover, a member of Peter's circle resurrected the *lex regia*: from the people's bestowal of power on the emperor, he inferred that the duly installed ruler cannot be deposed.[95] Undoubtedly because the Justi-

---

[93]From the 1080s through the reign of Barbarossa, one can usually distinguish between the *renovatio imperii* and the growing influence of Roman law on the theory and practice of rulership (Koch [n. 25 above] 230–31). But since the two developments were—especially from the late 1140s—increasingly interwoven, much of Part II will consider the *renovatio* in its relation to Roman law.

[94]In Germany, to be sure, Roman law's definition of justice (*Inst.* 1.1.1; *Dig.* 1.1.10) appeared in royal charters of the 1060s and 1070s, again under Lothar III, and was cited with greater accuracy under Conrad III; Heinrich Fichtenau, *Arenga: Spätantike und Mittelalter im Spiegel von Urkundenformeln*, MIÖG Ergänzungsband 18 (Graz 1957) 53–54, 119.

In eleventh-century Italy, some exponents of *renovatio*—bishop Benzo of Alba, for example, who compiled his treatise *Ad Heinricum IV.* around 1085—did not reflect the juristic tradition; on Benzo, see Schramm, *KRR* 1.258–74, and *KKP* 3.380–94; Koch (n. 25 above) esp. 42–43, 115–18. Benzo failed to influence contemporaries.

[95]Peter's *Defensio Heinrici IV. regis* can be found in MGH LdL 1.434–53. For the use of the *lex regia*, see MGH Const 1.667, 673 no. 449. In general: Karl Jordan, "Der Kaisergedanke in Ravenna zur Zeit Heinrichs IV.: Ein Beitrag zur Vorgeschichte der staufischen Reichsidee," DA 2 (1938) 85–128 and esp. 110–16; Robert Folz, *Le souvenir et la légende de Charlemagne dans l'Empire germanique médiéval* (Paris 1950) 126–31; Koch (n. 25 above) esp. 37–40, 105–06, 119–22.

nian corpus portrayed the imperial prerogative as virtually absolute, the twelfth-century Italian glossators tended to be—despite disagreements on many other questions—strong supporters of the emperor. Even before the Investiture Struggle had ended, one finds master Irnerius by Henry V's side, serving as imperial counselor, judge, and envoy. But the glossators' support could significantly affect political thought and action only under a monarch who regarded the *renovatio imperii* as a major goal of his policy.

Toward the end of Conrad III's reign, royal letters display a concern for the reform of the Empire.[96] Four days after Conrad's death on 15 February 1152, duke Frederick of Swabia held conversations with the bishops of Bamberg and Würzburg "on reforming and ordering the state of the realm" (*de reformando et componendo regni statu*).[97] On March 4th and 9th, the young duke was elected and crowned as Conrad's successor. Soon thereafter, in a letter informing Eugene III of his accession to the German kingship, Frederick stated what one may consider the central theme of his reign: "The majesty of the Roman Empire should be reformed, with God's help, to the former strength of its preeminence."[98]

As a formulation of Frederick's ideological commitments, the letter to Eugene must be judged a masterpiece. From its opening words, the program of a *renovatio imperii*—clearly inseparable from the *reformatio imperii*—is fully visible: "It is fitting for the father of the fatherland to maintain the venerable decrees of earlier kings and to adhere with persistent effort to their sacred laws, so that he may know how to provide the kingdom—which has been conferred on him by God—with laws and customs, as well as to defend it with arms and warfare."[99] As *pater patriae*, Frederick appropriated a title which can be traced back to pre-Christian Antiquity, but which the twelfth century could readily have found enshrined in Roman law.[100] By linking "laws and customs" with "arms and warfare" as the monarch's principal instruments, Frederick echoed the first sentence of the *Institutes*—a popular topos in the world of the Staufer.[101] His statement on "laws and customs" (*leges ac mores*) announced

---

[96]MGH DD 9.395, 407 nos. 222, 230; DD 9.455 no. 262, to the Romans, mentions their efforts toward the Empire's reform. Wibald composed these letters in 1150–51. The Senate also wanted a *restauratio imperii Romani* (n. 6 above).

[97]Henry Simonsfeld, *Jahrbücher des Deutschen Reiches unter Friedrich I.* 1, Jahrbücher der deutschen Geschichte (Leipzig 1908) 21.

[98]MGH DD 10.1.11 no. 5: "per studii nostri instantiam catholica ecclesia sue dignitatis privilegiis decoretur et Romani imperii celsitudo in pristinum sue excellentie robur deo adiuvante reformetur." On the letter: Heinrich Appelt, *Die Kaiseridee Friedrich Barbarossas*, SB Vienna 252.4 (1967) 7–11; Rainer Maria Herkenrath, *Regnum und Imperium: Das "Reich" in der frühstaufischen Kanzlei (1138–1155)*, SB Vienna 264.5 (1969) 24–30. The letter was composed by Wibald.

[99]MGH DD 10.1.10 no. 5: "Patrem patrie decet veneranda priscorum instituta regum vigilanter observare et sacris eorum disciplinis tenaci studio inherere, ut noverit regnum sibi a deo collatum legibus ac moribus non minus adornare quam armis et bello defensare."

[100]*Dig.* 48.22.19. Cicero, Caesar, and Augustus had borne the title *pater* (or *parens*) *patriae*. It was also applied to Henry I and Otto I (Schramm, *KRR* 1.80–81).

[101]The *Institutes'* first sentence (n. 81 above) was repeatedly cited in eleventh-century Italy (Anselm the Peripatetic, Peter Crassus and his circle); Schramm, *KRR* 1.282. In the twelfth cen-

that Roman and Germanic law would furnish the juridical foundations of his reign. Finally, Barbarossa quoted the famous dictum by pope Gelasius I: "There are two things by which this world is chiefly ruled, namely the sacred authority of the pontiffs and the royal power."[102] For his future relations with Church and papacy, he thereby pledged himself to dualism as a controlling principle.

Frederick continued to stress the two kinds of law as the twin supports of his government. Early in 1158, a manifesto defined a basic constitutional axiom: "There are two things by which our Empire must be ruled, the holy laws of the emperors and the good customs of our predecessors."[103] This did not, of course, imply that Frederick ever intended to impose the Justinian corpus as a binding legal system in Germany, or even in Italy. Rather, such statements recognized the high authority inherent in Roman law, and they belonged to the *Romanitas* of his office. Even more, they justified Barbarossa's occasional appeal to Roman law or invocation of Romanistic principles—especially in the governance of Italy.[104]

Since the Christian Roman Empire and Byzantium regarded as sacred everything which touched the emperor's person and office, it is not surprising that the Justinian corpus defined the imperial laws as *sacrae constitutiones* and *sanctae leges*.[105] "Sacred" was virtually a synonym for "imperial." Barbarossa borrowed this usage from the Justinian corpus: the "laws of the emperors" are "holy."[106] But as his reign began, Frederick had mentioned the "sacred laws" of earlier kings—that is, the *sacrae disciplinae* of his German (perhaps also Frankish) predecessors.[107] Frederick once summed up laws of Frankish and an-

---

tury, moreover, the church of Bamberg had two copies of the *Institutes* (Schramm, *KRR* 1.277–78; Appelt [n. 98 above] 20). Scholars have not noticed that Wibald was familiar with this topos as early as March 1151 (MGH DD 9.426 no. 244: "et in pace legibus honestant et in bello armis defensant"); Wezel's letter therefore did not constitute Wibald's source (cf. Koch [n. 25 above] 204, 238). For later echoes of this sentence: MGH DD 10.1.247 no. 147 (1156); Otto, *Chronica*, Epistola dedicatoria (n. 19 above) 1; Rahewin, GF 4.4 p. 236 (in Frederick's address at Roncaglia).

[102]Even apart from its accessibility in canonical collections, the Gelasian formula was widely diffused and certainly known at Bamberg (MGH DD 3.468 no. 366 [1017]; DD 8.13 no. 11 [1127]). But the dictum's appearance in Eugene III's letter of 27 January 1152 to the German bishops and nobles (Jaffé, *Bibl* 1.490–91 no. 362) probably inspired its use here (Herkenrath [n. 98 above] 26–27; cf. Appelt [n. 98 above] 10–11, Koch [n. 25 above] 161, and others, arguing for a source in Bamberg).

[103]Rahewin, GF 3.17 p. 188: "Duo sunt, quibus nostrum regi oportet imperium, leges sanctae imperatorum et usus bonus predecessorum . . . nostrorum." This manifesto followed the terrible clash between emperor and papal legates at Besançon in October 1157. With its unmistakable paraphrase of Gelasius's dictum, the statement suggested the exclusion of the papacy from any role sharing the Empire's governance.

[104]In 1162, the theme of *lex* and *consuetudo* reappeared in two charters: at Genoa, justice should be done "secundum leges nostras Romanas et bonas consuetudines" (MGH DD 10.2.222 no. 367), at Cremona "secundum leges et bonos mores" (DD 10.2.228 no. 369).

[105]*Heumanns Handlexikon zu den Quellen des römischen Rechts*, 9th ed. rev. E. Seckel (Jena 1907) 522, 525.

[106]Above, n. 103. Note also that in 1155, the law *Habita* (n. 114 below) designated Roman law as the *divinae atque sacrae leges*.

[107]Above, n. 99. Though *sacrae disciplinae* reflects Romanistic usage (Heumann-Seckel [n. 105 above] 151), a reference to *prisci reges* could not refer to the emperors of Antiquity; MGH DD 9.529 Heinrich (VI.) no. 9 (1149).

cient Roman emperors as *sacrae leges,*[108] and repeatedly applied epithets of sacredness to his own charters.[109] When he stated that to understand and observe the *sacrae leges* is preeminently a duty of the Roman *princeps*, he evidently referred to law in general.[110] For Barbarossa, in short, not only Roman law but *all* law had a numinous character.[111]

From Charlemagne to Conrad III, Western chanceries were generally reluctant to ascribe sacredness to the ruler or the realm. In 1157, Barbarossa broke with this tradition. Going beyond the sacredness of the laws, he asserted that his realm was a "sacred Empire."[112] Without ever becoming a fixed or official title for the German king's dominions, thereafter *sacrum imperium* was a standard term—and a major step toward the title "Holy Roman Empire of the German Nation," which appeared in the fifteenth century. Seen within the political context of 1157, however, the sacralization of the Empire is a barometer, for it indicates the approaching storms in Frederick's relations with popes Hadrian IV and Alexander III. Sacredness implied an office given by God: perhaps only the ruler of a *sacrum imperium* could effectively claim independence from the papacy and the *sancta ecclesia.*[113]

Near Bologna in May 1155, on the way to his imperial coronation in Rome, Frederick met the leading professors of Roman law—the "four doctors": Bulgarus, Hugo, Jacob, Martin. There, by forging close links to the chief representatives of the new jurisprudence, Frederick began to fulfill the promise made at his accession, to rule by Roman law as well as Germanic custom. When one of the professors complained that Bolognese students were oppressed by unjust debts, Frederick issued the law *Habita*, which extended imperial protection to professors of law and also, with certain immunities as well, to students of law.[114] Further, it placed each student under the jurisdiction either of the local bishop or (a simultaneously alluring and sobering prospect!) of his professor.

Because *Habita*'s wording displays an unmistakable juristic virtuosity, the professors themselves certainly composed it. In its formulation, they hand-

---

[108]MGH DD 10.2.416 no. 492 (1165); this privilege also cites as *sacratissimus* a law of Valentinian I.

[109]MGH DD 10.1.324 no. 193 (1157); DD 10.2.286, 289, 298 nos. 406, 408, 413 (all 1163). Cf. the *sacratissimae constitutiones* of Charlemagne, mentioned in the confirmation of a forged charter of Charles (DD 10.2.433 no. 502 [1166]).

[110]MGH DD 10.1.129 no. 77 (1154).

[111]The point is commonly overlooked by historians.

[112]MGH DD 10.1.280 no. 163 (March 1157): the full expression here is *sacrum imperium et diva res publica*. But the chancery never attached an epithet of sacredness to Frederick personally.

[113]On *sacrum imperium*: Appelt (n. 98 above) 11–17; Koch (n. 25 above) 259–79; Walther Kienast, *Deutschland und Frankreich in der Kaiserzeit (900–1270)*, Monographien zur Geschichte des Mittelalters 9 (2nd ed. 3 vols. Stuttgart 1974–75) 2.274–76, 3.675–82. Though there were medieval precedents for this usage (as there were for his notion of the "sacred laws"), Frederick's term created a new and durable tradition, and thus remains a significant innovation. Cf. Koch (204 n. 167), who maintains unconvincingly that the Senate, with its idea of the *sacer senatus*, influenced the imperial chancery in this respect.

[114]Till recently, most scholars have assumed that *Habita* was issued first in 1155 and—some assert, with an addition—again in 1158. But Winfried Stelzer, "Zum Scholarenprivileg Friedrich Barbarossas (Authentica 'Habita')," DA 34 (1978) 123–65, has argued persuasively that it was

somely repaid Frederick's support. The end of *Habita* orders that "this law be inserted among the imperial constitutions in the Justinian *Code*."[115] Considering the corpus of Roman law still open, still susceptible of additions, the jurists placed Barbarossa—and his enactment—in the tradition of Justinian and the earlier emperors. On this idea of continuity, more later. In the issuance of a "generally and eternally valid law," since Frederick as *rex Romanorum* possessed the legislative authority of a Roman emperor, his prerogative did not depend on the imperial coronation or the papacy: he was already the beneficiary of the *lex regia*. Above all, *Habita* states—in Frederick's voice—that knowledge of Roman law illuminates the world and shapes the life of subjects "to obey God and ourself, his minister."[116] With this hopeful claim, and with its assurance that Frederick holds his authority directly from God, *Habita* could scarcely have served him better.

RONCAGLIA 1158

These expressions of the *renovatio imperii* might be dismissed as essentially theoretical, remote from the realities of power. But in November 1158, when the imperial court met at Roncaglia on the Po River, the *renovatio imperii* merged with Barbarossa's most urgent political concerns, as he sought to reconstruct the royal prerogative within the *regnum Italicum*. Italy lay at the center of Frederick's policy. If he could control the rich cities of the Lombard plain, he could tranquilly accept his political limitations in Germany to the north, and need not fear the papacy or the Normans to the south. Correspondingly, apart from the army and entourage accompanying him, he summoned only Italians to this meeting of the court.

At Roncaglia, the assembly devoted a day to orations, the first by Frederick and the last by archbishop Hubert of Milan—both of them resonant with quotations and echoes from Roman law. Speaking for all, the archbishop said to Barbarossa, "Know that all of the people's authority to establish laws has been conferred on you," and before quoting the *lex regia* at length, he summed up its doctrine in a single sentence: "Your will is law" (*Tua voluntas ius est*).[117] Though Frederick himself apparently never mentioned the *lex*

---

promulgated in May 1155, and had no connection with the *Reichstag* of Roncaglia in November 1158. For the text, see MGH DD 10.2.39–40 no. 243, or Stelzer 165. Of the voluminous earlier literature on *Habita*, one can still profitably read H. Koeppler, "Frederick Barbarossa and the Schools of Bologna: Some Remarks on the 'Authentica Habita,'" EHR 54 (1939) 577–607.

[115]Stelzer (n. 114 above) 138–41; *Cod.* post 4.12.4 or post 4.13.5. The jurists also inserted into the *Codex* (post 2.27 [28].1) a law issued at Roncaglia in 1158, on the right of minors to bind themselves by sworn contract; see Peter Weimar, in Coing, *Handbuch* 1.161, and cf. Haskins, *Ren* 207.

[116]"Dignum . . . existavimus, ut . . . eos, quorum scientia illuminatur mundus ad obediendum deo et nobis, eius ministris, vita subiectorum informatur, . . . ab omni iniuria defendamus" (MGH DD 10.2.39 no. 243; see Stelzer [n. 114 above] 158). In a similar vein, Frederick said of an imperial abbey: "nulli . . . servicium debeat nisi deo viventi et post eum Romano imperatori" (DD 10.1.324 no. 193 [1157]; Koch [n. 25 above] 241–42).

[117]Rahewin, GF 4.5 p. 239; the *lex regia* was quoted from *Inst.* 1.2.6 (n. 82 above).

regia,[118] he surely understood Hubert's remark as implying that the people's grant of legislative authority was definitive and irrevocable. Since many jurists—from Peter Crassus's circle and master Irnerius to 1200 and beyond—accepted the doctrine of the grant's irrevocability, the *lex regia* could serve the Staufer conception of emperorship as well as it supported the Roman revolutionaries.[119] Other texts from Roman law also exalted Barbarossa's prerogative. Dedicating his *Chronicle* to Frederick in 1157, Otto of Freising asserted, "Since they are set above the laws, only kings . . . are not constrained by the laws of this world."[120] This view presupposed another statement from the Justinian corpus, equally famous: "The prince is not bound by the laws."[121] According to Godrey of Viterbo in the 1180s, at Roncaglia the four doctors told Frederick: "As the living law, you can give, abrogate, and establish laws. . . . As the animate law, you do whatever you want."[122] Though the idea of the emperor as a *lex viva* or *lex animata* originated in the Hellenistic world, the Bolognese professors would have taken it from Justinian's *Novels.*

In his address, Frederick promised "lawful rule" (*legitimum imperium*) which would "preserve to each his liberty and right."[123] This was no mere rhetorical flourish: few monarchs have shown such consistent concern for the legality of their acts as Barbarossa.[124] Then he came to the main purpose of the meeting at Roncaglia, as he summarized his new policy by closely paraphrasing a sentence from the *Institutes:* Italian law, "wherein that which previously prevailed was afterward obscured by neglect, must be clarified by an imperial remedy and by your wisdom."[125] There can be no doubt about the "imperial

---

[118]But his grandson, Frederick II, found important uses for the *lex regia* (E. H. Kantorowicz [n. 80 above] esp. 103–07).

[119]On the Ravenna circle, see n. 95 above. Master Irnerius opposed the doctrine that custom can abrogate statutory law (discussed above, at nn. 85–86), though he admitted that through custom, the people had once had the authority to make law. Then he explained: "Today"—and by *hodie* he meant the entire period since Justinian—"this power has been transferred to the emperor"; Hermann Kantorowicz, *Studies in the Glossators of the Roman Law,* 2nd ed. rev. Peter Weimar (Aalen 1969) 135. For Roger, Placentinus, and others, see H. Kantorowicz 279, and the works cited in n. 86 above.

[120]*Chronica,* Epistola (n. 19 above) 1.

[121]*Dig.* 1.3.31: "Princeps legibus solutus est." On the emperor as *legibus solutus* and *super leges* in first-century constitutional thought, see Brunt (n. 82 above) 107–09.

[122]*Gesta Friderici* vv. 386–90, MGH SS 22.316: "Omnis honor mundi te constituente tenetur; / . . . Tu lex viva potes dare, solvere, condere leges. / Stantque caduntque duces, regnant te iudice reges; / Rem quocumque velis lex animata geris." For the source: *Nov.* 105.2.4.

[123]Rahewin, GF 4.4 p. 236. Showing Sallust's influence, the style is clearly Rahewin's, but since he was present at Roncaglia, one must trust his rendering of the substance.

[124]Heinrich Appelt, "Friedrich Barbarossa und das römische Recht," *Römische historische Mitteilungen* 5 (1961–62) 18–34 at 34.

[125]GF 4.4 p. 237: "Nostis autem, quod iura civilia, . . . regnorum leges, in quibus quod ante obtinebat postea desuetudine inumbratum est, ab imperiali remedio vestraque prudentia necesse habent illuminari [*Inst.* pr. 5]. Sive ergo ius nostrum sive vestrum in scriptum redigatur, in eius constitutione considerandum est, ut sit honestum, iustum, possibile, necessarium, utile, loco temporique conveniens; ideoque tam nobis quam vobis, dum ius condimus, cautius previdendum est, quia, cum leges institutae fuerint, non erit liberum iudicari de eis, sed oportebit iudicare se-

remedy'' which Frederick had in mind. He promised here the recovery of the royal rights which the North Italian cities had seized for themselves during the preceding century, that is, the recuperation of those *regalia* "which, for a long time, had been lost to the empire either through the audacity of usurpers or through royal neglect.''[126] Though the *lex regia* would have authorized Frederick to legislate on the *regalia*, he preferred a typically Germanic procedure: to establish and restore the old law.[127] To determine the valid law and set it down in writing, the emperor appointed a commission of jurisprudents: the four doctors of Bologna, who asked that twenty-eight judges representing fourteen cities be added to their number. This sworn commission of thirty-two found for the emperor, agreeing that the cities must restore all regalian rights which could not be defended by royal or imperial charter.

In fulfilling their instructions, the commission prepared four decrees on the *regalia*.[128] Since the Roncaglian decrees presented declaratory judgments, findings of law, rather than legislative enactments by the emperor, the procedural form was traditional and appropriate.[129] Identified by their opening words, the four decrees were:

(1) *Regalia sunt* enumerates specific rights.[130] But the list was subsequently regarded neither as complete nor as fully and equally applicable to all cities: it was more a legal framework than a law generally valid throughout the kingdom of Italy.[131]

(2) *Omnis*: "All jurisdiction belongs to the emperor. All judges must receive [the right to exercise] their office (*administratio*) from the emperor, and all must take the oath [to the emperor] which is prescribed by law."[132] With the mention of "judges," one should recall that medieval people conceived governance itself primarily in terms of judicial authority.

---

cundum ipsas.'' Reliance on *Inst.* pr. 5 was no novelty (Koch [n. 25 above] 238): MGH DD 10.1.282 no. 165 (1157); GF, Epistola Friderici p. 1; GF 3.53 p. 228 (specifically on Roncaglia).

[126]GF 4.7 p. 240.

[127]But in Frederick's address (n.125 above), the Romanistic expression "ius condimus" implied that his *imperiale remedium* would be an act of legislation.

[128]The text of the first decree (*Regalia sunt*) has long been known, but the full texts of the other three have only recently been identified by Vittore Colorni, *Die drei verschollenen Gesetze des Reichstages bei Roncaglia, wieder aufgefunden in einer Pariser Handschrift (Bibl. Nat. Cod. Lat. 4677)*, trans. Gero Dolezalek, Untersuchungen zur deutschen Staats- und Rechtsgeschichte n.s. 12 (Aalen 1969) (hereafter: Colorni). Though studies published before 1967 (when Colorni's discovery appeared in Italian) must be consulted with caution, the article by Paul W. Finsterwalder, "Die Gesetze des Reichstags von Roncalia vom 11. November 1158," ZRG germ Abt 51 (1931) 1–69, remains fundamental, and is valuably supplemented by Appelt (n. 124 above).

[129]Certainly the first decree, presumably the second and third as well, simply aimed to summarize the existing law.

[130]Text of *Regalia sunt*: Colorni 3–4; MGH Const 1.244–45 no. 175.

[131]Finsterwalder (n. 128 above) 62–63: "ein Rahmengesetz." See also Alfred Haverkamp, *Herrschaftsformen der Frühstaufer in Reichsitalien*, Monographien zur Geschichte des Mittelalters 1 (2 vols. Stuttgart 1970–71) 1.93–94.

[132]"Omnis iurisdictio et omnis districtus apud principem est et omnes iudices a principe administrationem accipere debent et iusiurandum prestare quale a lege constitutum est" (Colorni 26). In the translation, *iurisdictio* and *districtus* have been summarily rendered together as "jurisdiction." On *Omnis*, see Finsterwalder (n. 128 above) 29–56; the prescribed *iusiurandum* appears in *Nov.* 8. In Roman law, the *iurisdictio* of all officials derived from the emperor (Finsterwalder

(3) *Palacia*: "The emperor must have palaces and fortresses in whatever places he chooses."[133]

(4) *Tributum* was, strictly speaking, not a law at all, since it contains no prescriptive statement. Rather, it surveys historically the ancient Roman system of taxation as mirrored in the Justinian corpus: "Taxes were paid per capita, and were paid on land. . . ."[134] Though *Tributum* could have had no effect without an enactive clause, it undoubtedly suggested that taxation belonged to Frederick's prerogative in Italy whenever he decided to exercise this right.

Among the political claims made at Roncaglia, the most important consisted of a broad principle: all jurisdiction derives from the emperor. According to *Regalia sunt*, Frederick had "the power to appoint magistrates for the furthering of justice."[135] Emphasizing the ruler's direct authority over urban officials, this provision reflected not only ancient Roman law but also contemporary Romanistic thought.[136] But in the twelfth century, terms like "judge" or "magistrate" often applied indiscriminately to all bearers of public authority. Thereby the great feudal magnates were not considered exempt from the decrees, for Barbarossa also claimed the free disposition of "dukeships, margraviates, and countships" as well as of urban "consulships."[137] Or as the four doctors reportedly said to Barbarossa: "With you as judge, dukes stand and fall."[138] As their net effect, such provisions aimed to transform both the urban magistrate, hitherto accountable only to his city, and the great feudal lord into imperial officials. Finally, the right to maintain palaces and fortresses anywhere was designed to guarantee political control: the emperor's deputies and soldiers would enforce the prerogative.

But in *Regalia sunt*, the emphasis is overwhelmingly fiscal. Though *Tributum* presents only in historical terms—hence only programmatically—the ruler's right to tax persons and real property, Rahewin saw both forms of taxa-

---

40–41). But *districtus* indicated a Germanic king's authority (*Königsbann*). In Roman law, *administratio* meant either a public office or a magistrate's exercise of one; in canon law around 1158, it was emerging as a synonym for jurisdiction (Benson [n. 45 above] 65–67, 71; Finsterwalder ignores the Romano-canonical uses of *administratio*). Apart from the word *districtus*, which had no significance in Roman public law (cf. Colorni 30 n. 95, arguing unconvincingly that at least the substance of *districtus* was ancient), one could have read *Omnis* from either a Romanistic or Germanic perspective: from both perspectives, it was self-evident that "all judges must receive their *administratio* from the emperor." And equally from both, a "judge" who was appointed by the emperor automatically had the *administratio* (in Germanic law: *Bannleihe*, the right to exercise the jurisdiction entrusted to him). But under Germanic law, a different situation pertained if the "judge" was elected by a commune, for then he had to get his *administratio* or *Bannleihe* as a separate grant from the emperor. No matter how one construed the law, it powerfully reinforced Frederick's prerogative.

[133]"Palacia et pretoria habere debet princeps in his locis in quibus ei placuerit" (Colorni 26).
[134]"Tributum dabatur pro capite, tributum dabatur pro agro. . . ." (Colorni 26).
[135]Colorni 4: "potestas constituendorum magistratuum ad iustitiam expediendam."
[136]*Summa Trecensis* 1.17.1, ed. Hermann Fitting, *Summa Codicis des Irnerius* (Berlin 1894) 21: "necesse ergo est ab eo exordium sumi qui caput est omnium magistratuum, immo omnium hominum, id est Romanus princeps." On this work: Weimar, in Coing, *Handbuch* 1.198–99. See also *Dig.* 48.14.1 pr.
[137]Rahewin, GF 4.7 p. 240.
[138]Above, n. 122.

tion as part of the prerogative which Frederick actually imposed at Roncaglia.[139] Listing such rights as "mints, tolls, fodder, imposts," and so forth, Rahewin estimated that North Italy subsequently brought overall as much as 30,000 pounds silver annually into Frederick's treasury.[140] Roncaglia made Barbarossa rich.

Many scholars, perhaps most, have concluded that at Roncaglia, Roman law furnished only an ornament, a veneer, a façade. "The leading lawyers of Bologna" were "appointed only to put imperial pretensions into legal shape."[141] True, the procedure at Roncaglia was medieval, Germanic rather than Roman: the appointment of a commission could simply represent the duty of any medieval monarch to take counsel while judging on matters of law. Even the term *regalia* went back only to the eleventh century.[142] And since the specific *regalia* claimed at Roncaglia can be traced back to the customary prerogative which earlier kings of the *regnum Italicum* had exercised,[143] the crucial precedents for these *regalia* evidently belonged to Lombard law, the prevalent legal tradition in North Italy, rather than to Roman law.[144]

On the role of Roman law at Roncaglia, the jury is still out—scholars are far from agreement. But one can argue a few large points: since the lapsed *regalia* could be lastingly recovered only by legal definition and action, it is misleading to assert that the Roncaglian decrees *merely* "put imperial pretensions into legal shape." Apart from arms, what other shape could imperial policy have taken? Given the need for legal definition, the consequent question—did the decrees derive principally from Roman or Lombard law?—is inappropriately formulated. Clearly they drew on both.

Addressing the Italians at Roncaglia, Frederick envisaged that when he decreed his "imperial remedy" for the problems "obscured by neglect," the written instrument might embody "either our law or yours." In the exclusively Italian context of this statement, *ius nostrum* must refer to Roman law, *vestrum* to Lombard law.[145] And when he initially commissioned only the four doctors to determine his regalian rights, Barbarossa must have expected them

---

[139]GF 4.7 p. 240; along with other narrative sources, he confirms the reality of these taxes *de terra* and *de capitibus*.

[140]GF 4.8 p. 240.

[141]Koeppler (n. 114 above) 587. For some equally skeptical statements, see Appelt (n. 124 above) esp. 33–34, and Haverkamp (n. 131 above) 1.90–93; other names could easily be added.

[142]Johannes Fried, "Der Regalienbegriff im 11. und 12. Jahrhundert," DA 29 (1973) 450–528 at 483–95, 500–14.

[143]Haverkamp (n. 131 above) 1.91–93.

[144]Here, the term "Lombard" designates the complex tradition of North Italian customary law which one finds in royal charters as well as in the *Lombarda* (compiled in the second half of the eleventh century). On this tradition: Weimar, in Coing, *Handbuch* 1.165–68, and Wolf, ibid. 1.566–68. See Appelt (n. 124 above) 25 n. 24, criticizing Finsterwalder's nonspecific term "germanisch" for this tradition (since there were other "Germanic" legal traditions) and preferring "langobardisch-italisch." One must also agree with Appelt's view that scholarly studies of the decrees have not taken sufficient account of canon law and Italian communal law.

[145]Above, n. 125. For his notion of "our" Roman law, see n. 104 above.

to cast their opinions entirely in terms of Roman law, as he would subsequently have expected the twenty-eight Lombard "judges" to apply Italian customary law.

In both their language and their substance, the decrees reveal Romanistic background. They apply the title *princeps* to the emperor, as Roman law commonly does.[146] Most of the specific regalian rights can be found in the Justinian corpus.[147] Verbatim appropriation from the *Code* requires no comment.[148] One sees Romanistic sources not only in such provisions as the emperor's claim to treasure trove or to "the property of those committing lèse majesté,"[149] but also in the sweeping constitutional principles stated by the laws *Omnis* and *Palacia*. With its claim to an imperial monopoly on jurisdictional authority—conceived partly in Romanistic terms, partly in terms of customary law—and with its purely Roman oath of office, *Omnis* presents a clever fusion of elements deriving from the two traditions.[150] Similarly, both Roman law and Italian custom justified the rights asserted by *Palacia*.[151]

Since reliance on Italian custom alone in the four decrees would need no explanation, the preferable formulation of the question must be: why did the decrees draw, in more or less equal measure, on Roman as well as Lombard law? Frederick repeatedly stated his intention of ruling by Roman and customary law. The most salient feature of the Roncaglian decrees lay precisely here, in the interlocking of two legal traditions and in their striking consensus, and nothing else in his reign reflects this intention so well. During the Middle Ages, programs of reform typically looked back to older models, aimed to restore a real or mythic ideal embodied in an earlier period. Though Frederick's program of reform at Roncaglia was no exception, this point is most visible and explicit in *Tributum*, where sixth-century Rome furnished the model for sovereign rights which would radically enlarge the resources of his government. But in seeking the recovery of the lost *regalia*, Barbarossa envisioned *two* earlier models: the imperial prerogative in ancient Roman law, and the royal prerogative in Italy before the Investiture Struggle. At the very least, the recourse to Roman law at Roncaglia constituted a crucial part of the larger attempt to dramatize, publicize, and heighten, in terms that carried authority for many Italians, the legitimacy of a monarchy imposing a tough and unpopular policy. The policy's eventual failure does not lessen the importance of the attempt.

[146]Above, nn. 132, 133. *Regalia sunt* refers to the emperor as "Cesar" (thus also *Tributum*) and as "regale numen" (n. 148 below).

[147]Finsterwalder (n. 128 above) 66–68. But the jurists did not aim to present the *regalia* systematically as Roman in origin: in *Regalia sunt*, the list begins with *arimannie*, which derives from early Lombard law and has no Roman equivalent.

[148]*Regalia sunt* (Colorni 4): "extraordinaria collatio ad felicissimam regalis numinis expeditionem" (cf. *Cod.* 1.2.11). On this phrase, see Appelt (n. 124 above) 25–26.

[149]*Regalia sunt* (Colorni 4); Finsterwalder (n. 128 above) 67.

[150]Above, n. 132.

[151]Colorni 33–35; Haverkamp (n. 131 above) 1.92.

THE CLAIM TO ROMANNESS

Within twelfth-century German and Italian imperial thought, an inescapable logic placed Roman law at the center of the *renovatio imperii Romani*. This logic started from the premise that the twelfth-century Empire, with a German king at its head, was indeed still truly Roman. The premise was relatively new. In the tenth century, though Otto II and especially Otto III identified themselves with the title *imperator Romanorum augustus*, the Ottonian emperors styled their realm simply the *imperium*. Only in 1034 did Conrad II begin to designate the Empire itself officially and regularly as the *imperium Romanum*.[152]

By 1100, many believed that there had been, despite periods of decline, continuity from the founding of the Empire to the present. At the end of the historical narrative in his *Chronicle*, Otto of Freising listed the "Roman pontiffs" and "emperors" in parallel columns from St Peter and Augustus to the mid-twelfth century, mentioning just above Charlemagne's name that "From this point the Empire has been transferred to the Franks," and tersely noting "Germans" just before Otto I's name begins a line of German rulers.[153] Here Otto was invoking the theory of a "transfer of the Empire" from the Greeks in Constantinople to the Franks in the West. For the notion of an unbroken historical continuity presupposed a fiction which rendered a Germanic ruler the legitimate successor of the Caesars, and the doctrine of a *translatio imperii*—when Charlemagne became emperor in 800—served this purpose. Some attributed the *translatio* to the pope's initiative in crowning Charles, others ascribed it purely to the valor of the Franks.[154]

But contemporaries also stated in other contexts—and sometimes specifically with regard to the emperor's legislative authority—the twin themes of historical continuity and the consequent Romanness of the German monarch's Empire. This tendency is already apparent in the *Libellus de cerimoniis*: in the formula for the investiture of a judge, the emperor warns him "not to subvert the law of Justinian, our most holy predecessor."[155] For Frederick, to insert his own laws into the Justinian *Code* clearly implied continuity and Romanness, and dovetailed nicely with his view that they were "our Roman laws."[156] Frederick accepted the same broad assumptions when he decreed that "what is prescribed in the laws of the Roman emperors" should regulate the succession to the property of those dying childless and intestate.[157]

---

[152]Carl Erdmann, "Das ottonische Reich als Imperium Romanum," DA 6 (1943) 412–41 at 413–14 (repr. [n. 34 above] 174–203 at 175–76).

[153]*Chronica* 7 post c. 35 (n. 19 above) 374–85.

[154]Werner Goez, *Translatio imperii: Ein Beitrag zur Geschichte des Geschichtsdenkens und der politischen Theorien im Mittelalter und in der frühen Neuzeit* (Tübingen 1958) esp. ch. 5–7.

[155]*Libellus* c. 21, ed. Schramm, KKP 3.353.

[156]Above, nn. 104, 115.

[157]MGH Const 1.378 no. 275 (1177).

In a privilege on the testamentary rights of clerics, however, Barbarossa stated the two themes explicitly when he cited the *divi imperatores* Constantine, Justinian, Valentinian, Charlemagne, and Louis the Pious. "Venerating their sacred laws as divine oracles," he quoted two of those laws at length.[158] But he drew no distinction between the Christian Roman and the Frankish emperors, considering both equally his "predecessors," not least in their legislative authority, and in Italy, he regarded not only Roman and Frankish emperors but also the Lombard kings as "predecessors."[159] Addressing the Synod of Pavia in 1160, Frederick claimed the right to summon a Church council, "for it is recorded that the emperors Constantine, Theodosius, Justinian, and in more recent times, Charlemagne and Otto also did this."[160] Also in this facet of Frederick's imperial prerogative, the conception of historical continuity is unmistakable.

To be sure, a German emperor could hardly claim Romanness if he left the City itself out of account. No emperor after Otto III contemplated making Rome the governmental center of the Empire, but at least in a symbolic sense, it had to be the capital of a truly Roman Empire. In 1033, a bull of emperor Conrad II proclaimed that "Rome the capital of the world holds dominion over the entire earth" (ROMA CAPVT MVNDI TENET ORBIS FRENA ROTVNDI),[161] and thereafter this leonine hexameter reappeared on the metal bulls of German monarchs through the twelfth century and beyond. Writing to the Romans in 1111, Henry V defined the City as "the capital and seat of our Empire."[162] And a half-century later, stressing his obligation to maintain order in "the City, which is the capital of our Empire," Barbarossa believed that—among other grounds—this duty justified his intervention in the papal schism.[163]

Such statements become fully intelligible only as answers to those who contested the German monarch's ties to Rome. For example, twelfth-century Byzantine emperors had not reconciled themselves to purely symbolic links to Italy and Old Rome. Though Alexius I Comnenus strove to make his influence felt in South Italy,[164] his son and grandson directed more ambitious policies toward the West. Around 1141, John II Comnenus proposed to Innocent II that the Greek and Latin churches be reunited, and that within a reunited Roman Empire, he and Innocent hold respectively the two swords of earthly and spiritual power. After briefly invading South Italy, Manuel I Comnenus used only diplomacy to pursue his Italian goals. Although Rahewin reports

[158]MGH DD 10.2.416 no. 492 (1165); the quoted laws were *Cod.* 1.2.1, 1.2.14.1.

[159]MGH DD 10.2.95 no. 284 (1159).

[160]Rahewin, GF 4.64, 74 pp. 309, 319.

[161]Schramm, *KRR* 1.203–04. A virtually identical verse ("regit" for "tenet") appeared on the imperial crown and mantle described in *Libellus* cc. 4, 5, ed. Schramm, *KKP* 3.343, 345.

[162]MGH Const 1.134 no. 82.

[163]Rahewin, GF 4.65 p. 310.

[164]In 1112; on this, see Classen (n. 37 above) 207–10.

that Frederick persuaded Manuel to "call himself emperor of New Rome, not of Rome,"[165] the story is scarcely plausible, for subsequently Manuel not only intensified his diplomatic initiatives in the West but retained the traditional Byzantine claim to a universal authority.[166] By 1166, he was negotiating with Alexander III over the union of the churches and seeking papal recognition as sole Roman emperor. But when Manuel insisted on ruling over the City, the negotiations collapsed, since Alexander "demanded that he himself rule as emperor in Rome."[167]

More dangerous, however, were the rivals close by. To the envoys of the Commune in 1155, Barbarossa replied that Rome is "also ours," just as he referred to the pope as the bishop "of our City of Rome."[168] The forged Donation of Constantine purported to grant the City—among other territories and rights—to Silvester I and his successors, promising that the papacy should have no lord over itself: "It is not just that an earthly emperor should have power there, where . . . the head of the Christian religion was established by the heavenly Emperor."[169] Fortified by the Donation, the twelfth-century Roman pontiffs offered the most consistent and serious challenge to the German monarchs' rights in the City. In 1159, after Frederick sent envoys to the Roman Commune, Hadrian IV protested that he must not do this without papal permission, "since every magistrate there is subject to St Peter."[170] To this, Frederick countered: "Since by divine decree I am called and am Roman emperor, I show only the appearance of ruling and bear an utterly empty title, without substance, if power over the City of Rome is torn from my grasp."[171] Though there is no reason to believe that Barbarossa doubted the authenticity of the Donation, obviously he denied its continuing validity. In diverse ways

---

[165]GF 4.86 p. 345. The story probably has a basis in the arrival of an embassy from Manuel to Frederick in 1157 (GF 3.6 pp. 170–71); apparently, at first the Greek envoys did not address Barbarossa respectfully—which undoubtedly means that initially they failed to greet him as a universal Roman emperor. Since the envoys assumed a more accommodating posture, they must have recognized the Romanness of Frederick's office, and the German court may have interpreted the incident along the lines of Rahewin's statement. Nettled by a similar incident more than 30 years later, Frederick recalled that Manuel—though they were enemies—had treated him with respect: "nec in aliquo dignitatibus nostrae maiestatis derogavit" (*Chronicon Magni presbiteri* anno 1189, MGH SS 17.510).

[166]Classen (n. 37 above) 214–20.

[167]John Cinnamus, *Epitome rerum gestarum* 6.4, ed. August Meineke, Corpus scriptorum historiae Byzantinae 15 (Bonn 1836) 262; Classen (n. 37 above) 212–14. Some scholars give a fantastic meaning to this passage: Manuel refused because Alexander "demanded that [Manuel] rule in Rome" (Charles M. Brand, trans., *Deeds of John and Manuel Comnenus*, Columbia University Records of Civilization 95 [New York 1976] 197); the same interpretation is accepted—though with reservations—by J. M. Hussey, "The Later Macedonians, the Comneni, and the Angeli, 1025–1204," *Cambridge Medieval History* 4 (n. 33 above) 1.193–249 at 231.

[168]Otto, GF 2.30 p. 137: "Roma tua, immo et nostra." MGH DD 10.1.266 no. 155 (1156–57): "pontifex alme nostre urbis Rome"; similar: DD 10.2.298 no. 413 (1163).

[169]Horst Fuhrmann, ed., *Constitutum Constantini* c. 18, MGH Fontes iuris Germanici antiqui 10 (Hanover 1968) 94–95.

[170]Hadrian's complaint is related in a letter from Eberhard II of Bamberg to Eberhard I of Salzburg (GF 4.34 p. 276): "cum omnis magistratus inibi beati Petri sit cum universis regalibus."

[171]Rahewin, GF 4.35 p. 278.

Constantine served the twelfth century as a model emperor, but his "Donation" found no place within the Staufer *renovatio imperii.*[172]

The twin themes—historical continuity, and the Romanness of the contemporary Empire—left an imprint on language, which furnishes a mirror of twelfth-century political consciousness and self-perception. In historical writing, the German princes might be called *optimates* or a *senatus* or "the foremost in Roman valor" (*Romanae virtutis proceres*). Similarly, German knights could be identified as the "Roman soldiers" or "army" (*milites Romani* or *exercitus Romanus*). A German castle might even be termed the *arx Capitolii.*[173] But as a mirror of politics, chancery usage is more instructive for it is official, and, though conservative, sensitive to new currents of thought. No imperial title expressed continuity better than *augustus* or *semper augustus*, which derived from Antiquity and was applied to medieval emperors beginning with Charlemagne. Another ancient title, *triumphator*, reappeared during the second half of the eleventh century, and survived into the twelfth. It can be found in charters and publicistic treatises, even in a work designed for teaching. Charters in which Henry IV or Henry V bore titles like *caesar* or *triumphator* were usually addressed to Italian recipients: ancient usage of this kind found greater resonance in Italy than in Germany.[174] When an Italian notary drafted for Lothar III a law forbidding the alienation of fiefs, Lothar's title read: "Romanorum imperator, pius, felix, inclitus, triumphator, semper augustus"—a remarkable set of echoes from Antiquity.[175]

In royal charters and other writings since the early eleventh century, the German king who had not been crowned in Rome was often simply entitled *rex*, occasionally *rex Romanorum*. Under Henry V before his imperial coronation, "king of the Romans" was becoming a standard title in the chancery and remained so thereafter. The title *rex Romanorum* not only implied the German king's claim to Italy and the imperial office, but also vividly manifested the increasing fusion of the *regnum* and the *imperium*, of the German kingship and of the emperorship.[176] Differently stated, the *rex Romanorum* was already, in some sense, the Roman emperor.[177] Correspondingly, since the tenth century, a German king might also be entitled *augustus*, and after March

[172]Herwig Wolfram, "Constantin als Vorbild für den Herrscher des hochmittelalterlichen Reiches," MIÖG 68 (1960) 226–43 at 234–35.

[173]Richard Schlierer, *Weltherrschaftsgedanke und altdeutsches Kaisertum* (Tübingen 1934) 19, 34.

[174]Schramm, *KRR* 1.283–84; Koch (n. 25 above) 115.

[175]MGH DD 8.170 no. 105 (1136). With similar effect, Otto of Freising added *victor inclitus triumphator* to the emperor's usual titles (*Chronica*, Epistola dedicatoria [n. 19 above] 1).

[176]Rudolf Buchner, "Der Titel *rex Romanorum* in deutschen Königsurkunden des 11. Jahrhunderts," DA 19 (1963) 327–38, with some corrections by Koch (n. 25 above) 111–13.

[177]First under Conrad III and then under Barbarossa, the chancery occasionally applied the title *imperator Romanorum* to the king before his imperial coronation. For both, this usage reflected the rivalry with Constantinople and asserted that the king was the equal of the *basileus*. For Barbarossa, this practice was also directed against the papacy's claim to an effective and discretionary role in the creation of an emperor. But since this usage was not appropriated from Antiquity, it need not be discussed here.

1147 the chancery frequently listed *augustus* among the epithets attached to the "king of the Romans."[178] One final example: When Conrad II's motto— *Roma caput mundi regit orbis frena rotundi*—was repeated on a golden bull from the beginning of Barbarossa's reign, its lofty claim did not depend on the German ruler's imperial coronation and imperial title. On the obverse, a bust of Frederick, with crown, orb, and scepter, rises out of the circular wall of the city; the inscription reads FREDERICVS DEI GRA(tia) ROMANOR(um) REX. Displaying the hexameter around the outside, the reverse of the bull represents the City with an image of the Colosseum girded by towers, and with the inscription AVREA ROMA on the foremost tower.[179] Within this iconographic program, even as German king—that is, as *rex Romanorum*—Frederick defined his office as Roman, and claimed dominion over the City.[180] In all this, one sees the progressive Romanization both of the Empire in its territorial sense— the three kingdoms taken together—and even, to some extent, of the German kingship, since the title "king of the Germans" scarcely existed in the eleventh- and twelfth-century German chancery.[181] For although *rex Romanorum* was not actually an ancient title, contemporaries can only have considered it an expression of continuity with ancient Rome.

But when an ancient title was revived, the *renovatio* could serve concrete political purposes. Since the reign of Hadrian, emperors had designated their successors by conferring on them the title *caesar*, and commonly made the Caesar a junior co-regent as well. In 1169, Barbarossa's four-year-old son Henry VI was elected and crowned as *rex Romanorum*. Hoping also to secure Henry's succession to the imperial dignity, Frederick asked Lucius III and later Urban III to crown the young king as *imperator Romanorum*.[182] But after the

---

[178]Herkenrath (n. 98 above) 8–11; Koch (n. 25 above) 215–17. In March 1147, composing an important letter from Conrad III to Eugene III, Wibald introduced the title *Romanorum rex et semper augustus* (MGH DD 9.332 no. 184). The letter announced (a) the election and imminent coronation of Conrad's son Henry as German king, and (b) Conrad's decision, in late December 1146, to take part in the Second Crusade. Herkenrath (10) assumes that Conrad's enhanced prestige as crusader explains the appearance of the classicizing epithet *semper augustus*. But one might suggest a more mundane explanation: since the election and royal coronation gave Conrad's son the same title which Conrad himself held, the addition of *semper augustus* or *augustus* to the title *rex Romanorum* clearly distinguished Conrad's superiority of rank. In fact, the charters of Conrad's son entitle him consistently *Romanorum rex* (once: *iunior Romanorum rex*) but never *augustus*; see DD 9.521–31 Heinrich (VI.) nos. 1–11.

[179]Rainer Kahsnitz, "Siegel und Goldbullen," *Die Zeit der Staufer: Geschichte, Kunst, Kultur*, ed. Rainer Haussherr et al., Württembergisches Landesmuseum, Katalog der Ausstellung (5 vols. Stuttgart 1977–79) 1.17–107 at 21–22 no. 29 (reproduced in vol. 3 Abb. 2).

[180]Josef Deér, *Byzanz und das abendländisches Herrschertum: Ausgewählte Aufsätze*, ed. Peter Classen, Vorträge und Forschungen 21 (Sigmaringen 1977) 225–28.

[181]Two exceptions: the title *rex Teutonicorum* can be found in a charter of Henry II and one of Henry V, as well as in a charter of Henry III which was almost certainly forged; Eckhard Müller-Mertens, *Regnum teutonicum: Aufkommen und Verbreitung der deutschen Reichs- und Königsauffassung im früheren Mittelalter*, Forschungen zur mittelalterlichen Geschichte 15 (Berlin [East] 1970) 64–69, 83–87, 359. In unofficial usage, historians and other contemporaries frequently referred to the *rex teutonicus (Teutonicorum)*, *rex Alamannie*, and so forth.

[182]In this, Frederick's efforts began as early as 1169; *The Letters of John of Salisbury*, ed. and trans. W. J. Millor, H. E. Butler, and C. N. L. Brooke (2 vols. London 1955, Oxford 1979) 2.656–58 no. 289.

papacy had consistently refused to crown Henry while Frederick still held the imperial office, ancient usage gave Barbarossa a momentary substitute for the unattainable coronation. At Milan in 1186, when the patriarch of Aquileia crowned Henry as king of Italy, Frederick designated his son to succeed him in the imperial office, for "from that day he was called Caesar."[183]

THE CLAIM TO UNIVERSALITY

"Hail, lord of the world!" So begins the panegyric which the Archpoet addressed to Barbarossa soon after the emperor's victory over Milan.[184] Court poets and jurists rarely speak the same language. But the Archpoet's phrase recurred later at Bologna, as generations of professors retold and embroidered an apocryphal story about Barbarossa. While riding with masters Bulgarus and Martin at Roncaglia in 1158, Frederick asked whether he was, by law, "the lord of the world." The two lawyers disagreed. Though Martin replied that the emperor was *dominus mundi* "with respect to property," Bulgarus displeased Frederick by denying this, for (as thirteenth-century jurists explained) Bulgarus believed that the emperor was "lord of the world" only "with respect to jurisdiction." Thereupon Frederick presented his own horse to Martin as a gift.[185]

---

[183]Ralph of Diceto, *Ymagines historiarum* anno 1186, *Opera historica*, ed. William Stubbs, RS 68 (2 vols. London 1876) 2.39: "Aquileiensis patriarcha coronavit Henricum regem Teutonicum, et ab ea die vocatus est Caesar"; Theodor Toeche, *Kaiser Heinrich VI.*, Jahrbücher der deutschen Geschichte (Leipzig 1867) 515–18, argues convincingly that in 1186, Henry was crowned as king of Italy, not as *rex Teutonicus*. See also *Annales romani*, in *Le Liber pontificalis*, ed. Louis Duchesne, 2nd ed. rev. Cyrille Vogel (3 vols. Paris 1955–57) 2.349: "Fredericus . . . fecit Heinricum filium suum Cesarem." Though charters often used the title *caesar* as a synonym for *imperator*, the chancery apparently never applied it to king Henry before his father's death (Kienast [n. 113 above] 2.277–78 n. 696). As a term for a junior co-regent, however, *caesar* may have had Carolingian precedents (Schramm, *KKP* 2.77–78, 90–91).

Cf. Toeche (518) and Kienast (2.277), who maintain that Henry VI first took the title *augustus* at this time; but Henry appears as *Romanorum rex augustus* in 1183 (MGH Const 1.411 no. 293: Peace of Constance). Here, the application of *augustus* to Barbarossa's son contrasts with the titulature of Conrad's son (n. 178 above).

[184]Heinrich Watenphul and Heinrich Krefeld, eds., *Die Gedichte des Archipoeta* (Heidelberg 1958) 68 no. 9: "Salve mundi domine, Cesar noster ave!" (commentary: 127–31). Milan fell on 1 March 1162.

[185]Otto Morena, *Historia Frederici I.*, ed. Ferdinand Güterbock, *Das Geschichtswerk des Otto Morena und seiner Fortsetzer über die Taten Friedrichs I. in der Lombardei*, MGH SS rer Germ n.s. 7 (Berlin 1930) 59; the relevant passage was added to a later version ca. 1221 (Einleitung xxviii). Accursius (*Gl. ord.* ad *Cod.* 7.37.3.1 v *omnia principis*) clearly assumed that the story was well known, as did Odofredus (*Lectura super Codice* ad 7.37.3 v. *cum omnia principis* [2 vols. Lyon 1552; repr. Bologna n.d.] 2.11va). See Friedrich Karl von Savigny, *Geschichte des römischen Rechts im Mittelalter* (2nd ed. 7 vols. Heidelberg 1834–51; repr. Bad Homburg 1961) 4.180–83; Kienast (n. 113 above) 2.297–98, 367–68, 3.682–83. The tale spread far beyond the lawyers' lecture halls.

But this extremely popular anecdote derived from a true—and juridically more technical—story told about Henry VI and the Bolognese masters Azo and Lothar. When Henry asked the two professors whether he alone had supreme jurisdiction (*merum imperium*), the two disagreed along the same lines, and with the same result, as in the apocryphal story (Odofredus, *Lectura super Digesto veteri* ad *Dig.* 2.1.3 [2 vols. Lyon 1550–52; repr. Bologna n.d.] 1.38rb–va; Myron P. Gilmore, *Argument from Roman Law in Political Thought 1200–1600*, Harvard Historical Monographs 15 [Cambridge Mass. 1941] 17–19; Kienast 2.284–85, 302–04). Azo himself confirms that his answer cost him a horse (*Summa Codicis* ad 3.13 no. 17 [Venice 1581] 179).

Yet despite the emperor's displeasure, even Bulgarus's answer expressed—and this is the interesting point here—a truly exalted conception of the Roman imperial dignity, for both answers presuppose a sovereign with universal jurisdiction based on a universal system of law. Considering the German rulers the successors of the ancient Roman emperors, most twelfth-century legists held comparable views of the contemporary imperial office.[186]

In his *Chronicle*, after asking "why the whole world was subjected to the *imperium* of a single City," Otto of Freising argued that "the Lord of the world wanted the entire world to be instructed by the laws of that one City."[187] Thus universal government is Providence's vehicle for the diffusion and preservation of a universal body of law. A similar concept could appear in a quite different setting. Probably composed at the Bavarian monastery of Tegernsee around 1160, *The Play of Antichrist* presents in its first half an elaborate political allegory of the Roman emperor's universal authority over the kings of Christendom. Three times the emperor's envoys approach a different king to demand service, each time with the same statement:

> We know that Your Majesty is aware
> That you should be subject to Roman *ius*.[188]

With the word *ius*, the poet capitalized on ambiguity, for *ius* meant equally "law" and "authority" or "jurisdiction." If one construes the verses as referring to both, the author was suggesting a twofold obligation, to receive Roman law and to serve the Roman emperor. But the poet's Christian mysticism set him apart from most other exponents of the *renovatio imperii*, for he was not primarily interested in the authority of ancient Rome *per se* or of ancient Roman law. Rather, his ideas drew on an apocalyptic tradition: the German monarch as Roman emperor has a providential mission to protect the Church and to stave off the coming of Antichrist.

Inevitably the theme of a twofold universality emerged also within canon law, the sister discipline of Roman law at Bologna. A single example will suffice. Around 1190, master Huguccio began a gloss on Gratian's *Decretum* by noting that "only Romans and those subject to the Roman Empire" seem bound by Roman law.

---

[186]In this, Placentinus and the author of the *Questiones de iuris subtilitatibus* (perhaps Placentinus himself; n. 205 below) were striking exceptions. On the views of the legists in general: Kienast (n. 113 above) 2.282–309.

[187]*Chronica* 3 pr. (n. 19 above) 133: "Hic . . . solvendum puto, quare unius urbis imperio totum orbem subici, unius urbis legibus totum orbem informari Dominus orbis voluerit." According to the *Libellus de cerimoniis*, Roman law's authority extended throughout the *orbis universus* (n. 76 above).

[188]*Ludus de Antichristo* vv. 63–64, post 110a, post 116, ed. Wilhelm Meyer, *Gesammelte Abhandlungen zur mittelateinischen Rythmik* (3 vols. Berlin 1905–36) 1.153–55: "Tuae discretioni notum scimus esse, / quod romano iuri tu debeas subesse" (also: ed. Karl Young, *The Drama of the Medieval Church* [2 vols. Oxford 1933] 2.373, 375). And see Antichrist's statement (vv. 185–86): ". . . regna subiugabo, / deponam vetera, nova iura dictabo" (Meyer 1.158; Young 2.378). In general: Haskins, *Ren* 175–77; Klaus Aichele, *Das Antichristdrama des Mittelalters, der Reformation und Gegenreformation* (The Hague 1974) esp. 15–20, 27–33.

But what about the French and the English and the others on the far side of the Alps? Are they bound to Roman laws and obligated to live by them? Answer: Yes, since they are or must be subject to the Roman Empire, for there is one emperor in the world, . . . but in various provinces there are various kings under him. . . . Moreover, all those who use the Latin language are called Roman, . . . and therefore all Latins are understood here [in the text which Huguccio was glossing] to be "Romans.". . . At least by reason of the [authority of the Roman] pontiff, they are subject to the Roman Empire, for all Christians are subject to the pope, and therefore they are obligated to live according to Roman laws, at least those which the Church approves.[189]

Clearly he recognized that in reality Roman law did not govern non-Italians. On the other hand, a layman's subjection to the Empire implied—so Huguccio believed—his acceptance of Roman law; and vice versa.

To defend the universality of the Empire and of its law, Huguccio presented three distinguishable arguments. First, implicitly contrasting *de facto* independence with *de iure* subjection, he maintained that kings should be subordinate to the emperor's uniquely preeminent office. They rule merely over "provinces" of the Empire. Second, he invoked the idea of Christendom, and identified all Latin Christians as "Romans," inferring from this the universal obligation of Latin Christians to obey Roman law. His final argument— "by reason of the pontiff"—rested on the fact that the Church had found it necessary, for purely juristic reasons, to accept Roman law in those areas which canon law did not adequately treat. Here, Huguccio probably had in mind the final version of Gratian's *Decretum*, which had incorporated many texts from Roman law.[190] But even apart from these *leges canonizatae*, and specifically for the clergy, Lucius III had officially prescribed that Roman law should be used subsidiarily in ecclesiastical proceedings.[191]

Huguccio's position—all are subject to Roman law and the Roman emperor—remained generally typical of later twelfth- and early thirteenth-century canonists from Italy or Germany, whose king was, after all, also the Roman emperor. But by the beginning of the thirteenth century, an increasing

---

[189]*Summa* ad D.1 c.12 v. *in eos solos:* ". . . Sed quid de Francis et Anglicis et aliis ultramontanis, numquid ligantur legibus romanis et tenentur vivere secundum eas? Resp.: Utique, quia subsunt vel subesse debent romano imperio, nam unus imperator in orbe, . . . sed in diversis provinciis diversi reges sub eo. . . . Praeterea quicumque utuntur lingua latina dicuntur romani, unde et lingua romana dicitur, . . .et ideo Romani hic intelliguntur omnes Latini, unde et hoc omnes Latini astringuntur. Item saltem ratione pontificis subsunt romano imperio, omnes enim Christiani subsunt apostolico et ideo omnes tenentur vivere secundum leges romanas, saltem quas approbat ecclesia. Item quid de clericis? numquid et ipsi ligantur legibus romanis? Sic, illis quae approbantur ab ecclesia et non obviant canonibus, sed non ideo quia sint promulgate ab imperatoribus, sed quia sunt confirmate a domino papa . . ." (Gaetano Catalano, *Impero, regni e sacerdozio nel pensiero di Uguccio da Pisa* [Milan 1959] 61–62).

[190]Jacqueline Rambaud, "Le legs de l'ancien droit: Gratien," part 1 of Gabriel Le Bras et al., *L'âge classique, 1140–1378: Sources et théorie du droit*, Histoire du droit et des institutions de l'Eglise en Occident 7 (Paris 1965) 47–129 at 119–28.

[191]JL 15189 (1181–85); 2 Comp. 3.26.3; X 5.32.1. On Roman law as *lex suppletoria* for clerics, see Stephan Kuttner, "Papst Honorius III. und das Studium des Zivilrechts," *Festschrift für Martin Wolff: Beiträge zum Zivilrecht und internationalen Privatrecht*, ed. Ernst von Caemmerer et al. (Tübingen 1952) 79–101 at 92–95.

number of Spanish and English canonists defended their kings' freedom from subjection to the emperor.

Even when one admitted the *de facto* independence of the various kings, one could still imagine that a twelfth-century German monarch would extend imperial authority once again over all the lands of the ancient Empire. Celebrating Barbarossa's Italian triumph, the Archpoet interpreted it in this vein: "The commonwealth is restored to its ancient state."[192] In an apocalyptic mode, *The Play of Antichrist* described a Roman emperor's reestablishment of his rule throughout the Mediterranean world.[193] Later in the century, the same idea reappeared in an invented letter from Barbarossa to Saladin. Since the fiction formed part of an English propaganda campaign for the Third Crusade, it depicted Frederick as the leader of a unified Christendom. In the letter, Frederick enumerates the African and Asian provinces of the ancient Empire—including Parthia, where "our *dictator* Crassus met a premature death" —and asks Saladin, "Do you pretend not to know" that these "and innumerable other lands are subject to our rule?"[194]

In reality, Frederick never envisioned either the reconquest of the provinces subject to the ancient Empire, or the exercise of lordship over the Western monarchies: France, England, and Spain. But he undoubtedly perceived the imperial dignity as, in some sense, preeminent among the kings of Europe. In a moment of anger, Barbarossa and his chancellor Rainald of Dassel called the rulers of England and France "the kings of provinces" (*provinciarum reges*).[195] Though the term was clearly disparaging, it surely did not imply, in Huguccio's sense, that *de iure* the two kings owed subjection to Frederick.[196] When Rainald ridiculed Louis VII of France as a "kinglet," *regulus* meant something like *rex provinciarum*, and though Louis was understandably indignant over Rainald's insult, he could not have construed either term as a direct claim to lordship.[197]

In only one setting did the "universality" of Frederick's *imperium* have concrete consequences: As Roman emperor, he claimed and exercised a special

[192]*Archipoeta* (n. 184 above) 71 no. 9 (stanza 30.1–2): "Iterum describitur orbis ab Augusto, / redditur res publica statui vetusto" (cf. Luc. 2:1). See also 69–70 no. 9 (stanzas 8.4, 17.3).

[193]*Ludus* (n. 188 above) vv. 53–54, 105–06, post 114d (Meyer 1.152, 154–55; Young 2.373, 375), mentioning the loss—and recovery—of the Empire's *potestas*. Also, v. 50: "totus mundus fuerat fiscus Romanorum" (cf. v. 102).

[194]The letter was widely diffused, in chronicles as well as in separate transmission. Most recent edition: Hans Eberhard Mayer, *Das Itinerarium peregrinorum: Eine zeitgenössische englische Chronik zum dritten Kreuzzug in ursprünglicher Gestalt*, MGH Schriften 18 (Stuttgart 1962) 281. The list of provinces (wrongly mentioning Ethiopia) is representative, rather than complete. Mayer, "Der Brief Kaiser Friedrichs I. an Saladin vom Jahre 1188," DA 14 (1958) 488–94, has authoritatively proven the letter's spuriousness, but cf. Kienast (n. 113 above) 2.365–66, considering its authenticity discussible.

[195]Saxo Grammaticus, *Gesta Danorum* 14.28, ed. J. Olrik and H. Raeder (2 vols. Copenhagen 1931–57) 1.443.

[196]But cf. Kienast (n. 113 above) 2.336–39, who is uncertain about the meaning of this expression.

[197]John of Salisbury, *Letters* (n. 182 above) 2.228 no. 186 (1166).

prerogative in matters concerning the Roman Church.[198] When the long papal schism began in 1159, he intervened, convoking the synod of Pavia. His letter of summons to the German prelates spoke of "one God, one pope, one emperor, . . . and one Church of God."[199] The implication of universality was unmistakable. Announcing the synod of Pavia to the English king, however, he tactfully omitted such offensive phrases.[200] Frederick may well have believed that as Rome formed part of his Empire, the Roman Church was the greatest of his imperial churches—but shrewdly he never explicitly claimed more than a special duty to defend and protect the Roman Church.

IMPERIVM TEVTONICORVM: THE NON-ROMAN EMPIRE

"Who appointed the Germans to be the judges of nations?"[201] Posing this rhetorical question in 1160, John of Salisbury summed up his deep hostility not only to Barbarossa and the "barbarism" of the Germans, but also to the claims of preeminence growing out of Frederick's *renovatio imperii.* Eight years earlier, when Eugene III received Frederick's letter announcing his accession and his intention to reform the Empire, John had been in the pope's entourage. In 1160, he attacked Frederick's *reformatio imperii* as a shameless scheme of world-domination.[202] When John denounced Frederick's program of 1152, the lucidity of hindsight undoubtedly sharpened his view, for he stood bitterly opposed to Frederick's intervention in the papal schism and his support of the antipope Victor IV. Far from being a Roman emperor and thereby the successor to the ancient imperial dignity, Barbarossa emerges in John's letters as—at best—the "German emperor," later as the "German tyrant" and "ex-emperor."[203]

John was not the first to regard a German emperor as a barbarian. Around 1090, bishop Bonizo of Sutri deplored the times in which he lived. "By the neglect of emperors and bishops," by the vices of rulers and subjects, "the Roman Empire has been in large part destroyed," leaving "only the Empire of New Rome at Constantinople" effectively resisting the barbarians. Since Bonizo—an unshakably loyal Gregorian—could not, in any case, have considered the excommunicate Henry IV a legitimate Roman emperor, his belief

---

[198]Above, at nn. 160, 163.

[199]MGH DD 10.2.95 no. 284 (October 1159).

[200]MGH Const 1.254–55 no. 183 (October 1159).

[201]John of Salisbury, *Letters* (n. 182 above) 1.206 no. 124 (1160): "Quis Teutonicos constituit iudices nationum?"

[202]*Letters* (n. 182 above) 1.207 no. 124: "Promittebat enim se totius orbis reformaturum imperium et urbi subiciendum orbem." Apart from Frederick's letter of 1152 (nn. 98–99 above), oral messages by his envoys may have contributed to John's reaction. See also Arnulf of Lisieux's summary of Frederick's intention "ut . . . pristinam reformet imperii maiestatem" (Frank Barlow, ed., *The Letters of Arnulf of Lisieux,* Camden Society 3rd ser. 61 [London 1939] 41 no. 28 [1160]); Arnulf had evidently seen the letter of 1152. In general: Kienast (n. 113 above) 2.363–64.

[203]*Letters* (n. 182 above) 1.205 no. 124 (*Teutonicus imperator*); 2.52 no. 152, 102 no. 168 (*Teutonicus tyrannus*); 2.458 no. 240 (*Christianorum hostis* and *ex-Augustus*); 2.216 no. 184 (*scismaticus et haereticus*).

that "the Roman Empire has perished . . . in the West" interlocked with his political convictions. "Old Rome," he lamented, "serves barbarians, and does not use its own laws."[204] With its admiration for the Christian Roman Empire and its resistance to German domination, the papal Reform movement entailed the idea of historical discontinuity and decline between late Antiquity and the present. In this respect, the Reform and the Investiture Struggle created a new historical consciousness. When he ascribed the decline of Rome and of Roman law to the conquest by Germanic barbarians, Bonizo strikingly reflected this new mode of thought.

Other routes could lead to the same view of history. In his *Questions on the Subtleties of the Law*, a Roman lawyer of the mid-twelfth century complained about the diversity of legal systems in Italy: "We have almost as many laws as households."[205] As remedy, the Italian jurist urged that Roman law should be imposed throughout the Empire.

Whoever bears the imperial title must sustain its authority. Those laws which have issued from the imperial authority should always be protected by it. One or the other of these points must be conceded: Either there must be one law, since there is one Empire. Or if there are many diverse laws, many kingdoms exist. . . . Our emperors . . . should strive to be the imitators of those whose successors they want to be considered.[206]

Italians had grounds not only for bitterness against the Germans, but also for grave doubts about the chances of successfully reforming the law in a world where the king of Italy and Roman emperor was, in fact, a semiliterate German king. As "new legislators," the author of the *Questions* remarked, "these transalpine kings can apparently, by their statutes, abrogate Roman laws, since they long ago began to rule in Rome."[207] But after considering this proposition, he concluded by dismissing the past and present *reges transalpini* with a contempt verging on pity:

The transalpine kings have taken power, but they could not have knowledge of law and of the laws, for in earlier times not only the schools but also the books of legal science had almost disappeared. I pass over in silence the fact that in their usual fashion they would have been unwilling to exert themselves for the laws, even if these were at hand. Therefore it was impossible for them to reform a law which they did not know.[208]

---

[204]*Liber de vita christiana* 7.1, ed. Ernst Perels, Texte zur Geschichte des römischen und kanonischen Rechts im Mittelalter 1 (Berlin 1930) 233: "Licet enim Roma senior nostris sit partibus constituta, qui nos religiosos esse iactamus, barbaris tamen servit et suis non utitur legibus. Solum nove Rome imperium, Constantinopolitanum scilicet, . . . barbaris . . . Gothis et Normannis . . . usque hodie contradicit. Et . . . licet culpa imperatorum ac sacerdotum ex magna parte quassatum sit Romanum imperium, . . . adhuc christianitatis . . . freno [subditi] reprimuntur. In occiduis vero partibus insolentia regum et superbia et avaritia subditorum Romanum periit imperium."

[205]*Questiones de iuris subtilitatibus* 1.16, ed. Hermann Fitting (Berlin 1894) 56 (= *Questiones* 2.16, ed. Ginevra Zanetti [Florence 1958] 15). Undoubtedly this jurist was referring primarily to Lombard law (n. 144 above). Fitting attributed this work to Irnerius, but cf. H. Kantorowicz (n. 119 above) 181–205 (and 344–46), ascribing it to Placentinus. See now Peter Weimar, in Coing, *Handbuch* 1.224–25, who assigns it to the circle around Roger and Placentinus.

[206]*Questiones* 1.16, ed. Fitting 56–57 (= 2.16, ed. Zanetti 16; n. 205 above).

[207]*Questiones* 4.4, ed. Fitting 58 (= 5.4, ed. Zanetti 22; n. 205 above).

[208]*Questiones* 4.9, ed. Fitting 59 (= 5.9, ed. Zanetti 24; n. 205 above). For a discussion of this passage, see H. Kantorowicz (n. 119 above) 193–94. Here the anonymous author was directing his

By rejecting the axiom of historical continuity with ancient Rome, the Italian jurist rendered a dissenting opinion—and reduced the *dominus mundi* to the status of a "transalpine king."

And yet, in crucial respects the Staufer *renovatio* was Italian in character. That is, Italians—and Germans dealing with Italians or Italian affairs—frequently invoked those general principles of Roman law which defined the imperial office and prerogative. In charters for German recipients, however, Roman law and classical elements in general made less headway. This is scarcely surprising, since—with the exception of the crime of *lèse majesté*—Roman law found virtually no application in twelfth-century Germany. There, charters proclaimed that the ruler's task is to "guard" or "preserve the laws" (*leges custodire*), and only much less often that his duty is to "issue laws" (*leges condere*) in the Roman fashion. Thus in Germany the Romanistic conception of imperial legislative authority failed to displace the Germanic idea of maintaining the "good old law."[209]

In fact, Barbarossa himself once dramatically rejected the principle that his Empire was "Roman." At a moment of crisis, when the Lombard cities revolted in 1167, Frederick wrote to the princes:

This rebellion does not fall only on ourself, because, having thrown off the yoke of our domination, they are trying to resist and destroy the *imperium* of the Germans, which has been bought and preserved till now with great exertion and much expense and with the blood of many princes and illustrious men.[210]

With this summons, Frederick appealed to a "national" pride in the German chivalry. But more lay behind this statement and the unusual expression *imperium Teutonicorum*, which clearly had, in some sense, an anti-Roman cast. Though the chancery had recently used this phrase to indicate the kingdom of Germany,[211] it obviously had a different meaning here. In 1167, *imperium Teutonicorum* meant either the "rule of the Germans" or the monarchy of the three realms subject to the German crown.

Frederick's reign had begun with a quotation from the *Institutes* about the emperor's "arms" and "laws" as the twin foundations of his *imperium*. Here, however, the talk is only of the effort, arms, and sacrifice which have created and maintained the *imperium Teutonicorum*. In other words, Frederick has shifted the foundation of his rule in Italy: it suddenly appears to be the successful "arms" of the Germans, rather than the status accorded to him through the "laws" of his predecessors, the Roman emperors. With North Italy in revolt, there was temporarily no longer an audience for the *renovatio*

---

critique against the German monarchs and Germanic law in general, not merely against "das Zweikampfgesetz Ottos I." (cf. Schramm, *KRR* 1.287).

[209]Fichtenau (n. 94 above) 54–55, 178–79; Koch (n. 25 above) 239.

[210]MGH DD 10.2.486 no. 538 (fall 1167): "Non enim in nostram solummodo redundat rebellio personam, quia iugo dominationis nostre proiecto Teutonicorum imperium, quod multo labore multisque dispendiis ac plurimorum principum et illustrium virorum sanguine emptum et hactenus conservatum refutare et exterminare conantur. . . ."

[211]MGH DD 10.2.406 no. 487 (23 June 1165).

imperii Romani, a concept which carried more authority in Italy than in Germany. Consequently, Barbarossa has dropped the mask of Roman emperor.

Recalling the martial basis of the German Empire, Frederick also invoked a different conception of law, and a notion of legitimacy different from that which had most usually shaped and informed his Italian policy. The idea that conquest confers legitimacy had been a commonplace in Antiquity. Then—curiously, for violence and conquest were familiar enough to the early Middle Ages—it seems to have disappeared by the end of the fifth century in the West, reemerging in the eleventh century. But Frederick was not the only twelfth-century figure to base dominion on conquest as a warrant of legitimacy.[212] Nor was this the first time that Barbarossa had recourse to this argument. In 1155, after the Commune's envoys had addressed him in *Roma*'s name, his reply appealed to this principle: his predecessors, Charlemagne and Otto the Great, had conquered Rome and Italy, and this was the title of his dominion. Deriving his rights from conquest, naturally he did not mention the pre-Carolingian emperors as his predecessors.[213] "I am the legitimate emperor. Let him who can, snatch the club from the hand of Hercules!" Yet even here he was less anti-Roman than in 1167, for his reply to the envoys maintained that since Rome had lost her power, the Germans had become the true Romans. "With us are your consuls. With us is your Senate. With us is your army."[214]

In the long speech to the Roman envoys, Barbarossa invited them to reflect on "the deeds of the *modern* emperors," specifically of Charlemagne and Otto I.[215] Though he occasionally distinguished between the Franks and the Germans in this address and elsewhere, here he fully identifies Franks and Germans, the Frankish Empire and the Empire under the Ottonians, Salians, and Staufer: there is no difference. Thereby, Barbarossa implicitly contrasted the "modern" age—from the Carolingian era till his own time—with the pagan and Christian Roman Empire. On the two occasions when Frederick appealed to the right of conquest, he certainly regarded the Germanic conquest as a glorious achievement rather than a decline, but he otherwise shared with certain enemies of his Empire the idea of historical discontinuity.[216]

---

[212]Since the topic deserves a more extended discussion than this study permits, I hope to return to it in another setting. Some aspects have been treated by Donald Sutherland, "Conquest and Law," *Studia Gratiana* 15 (1972) 33–51.

[213]Addressing his army before the siege of Milan in 1158, Frederick similarly cited only Charles and Otto as his *antecessores* (GF 3.29 pp. 203–04).

[214]Otto, GF 2.30 pp. 136–39.

[215]GF 2.30 p. 137.

[216]See Appelt (n. 124 above) 23, who rightly notes that conquest as a title of legitimacy contradicts the more usual principle of historical continuity by which Frederick considered himself a Roman emperor. In other respects, however, one may argue that there is no contradiction: From an Italian perspective, Barbarossa's monarchy drew on Roman law to justify his rule in Italy, where he was the successor of the ancient Caesars. But from a purely German perspective, his dominion in Italy rested ultimately on the right of conquest. Thus the two doctrines belonged to different spheres. Still, except on the eve of armed conflict—in 1155 or 1167—Frederick sensibly avoided stating the doctrine of conquest as the foundation of his Italian regime.

In short, political struggle and legal thought—not least, disputes over the legacy of ancient Rome's governing authority—led the twelfth century to an intensified consciousness of historical period. For the twelfth century was cultivating a new and sharpened sense of "modernity" (one encounters the term *modernitas* late in the century), of the distance between past and present, as well as between a more remote and a more recent past, or, as we would say, of the break between Antiquity and Middle Ages.

Though many twelfth-century Italian communes became powerful and autonomous without tracing their lineage and their *libertas* to the ancient Roman world, for Rome itself this possibility did not exist. In this regard, the German monarchy was comparable to the City. Certainly from the eighth century, a king who ruled over several peoples could be considered an *imperator* without reference to Rome.[217] English charters occasionally designated William the Conqueror *basileus*, and two twelfth-century Spanish kings bore the title *imperator totius Hispaniae*. In *The Song of Roland*, the poet calls Charlemagne king and *emperere de France*. Though medieval history and literature furnish many more examples of non-Roman emperors, the imperial standing of the twelfth-century German monarchy depended on the widespread conviction that the rulers of Germany were the successors of Augustus, Constantine, and Justinian.[218] Like the Byzantine emperors and like the popes, the German monarchs could not detach their claims from the legacy of Rome.

In the mid-twelfth century, the idea of Rome had a radically different meaning for the Senate's revolution and for the German monarchy's attempts to reform the Empire. Yet these two case-studies form part of a larger story and belong together, for the common pursuit of a Roman *renovatio* links the two programs, and identifies the main conceptual and ideological streams tributary to both. Even if one defines the twelfth-century renaissance simply as a revival of classical letters and thought, the shared ideal of a *renovatio* entitles the Senate and the Staufer equally to a place in the history of that renaissance.

These two political "renewals"—and medieval *renovatio* in general—shared a common style: they appropriated forms from Antiquity, then grafted them onto contemporary institutions. That this applies to the appropriation of Roman law should not surprise us, since law is a matter of logic and form, which must be imposed upon the substance of life. Such major acts of policy as the Roncaglian decrees exemplify this point, but smaller instances may illustrate it more sharply. Under ancient influence, a charter of Otto III had

---

[217]Folz (n. 18 above) 39–44, 53–58; Kienast (n. 113 above) 2.262–63, 3.712–15, and elsewhere.

[218]As we have seen, the events of 1155 and 1167 stood as isolated exceptions. But even in 1155, Frederick argued that since Rome had declined, and since the Franks (Germans) exemplified the old Roman virtues and *virtus*, by conquest the Franks (Germans) became the new Romans.

assigned him the title *Romanus Saxonicus et Italicus*. Although in the ancient world such titles would have indicated peoples whom the emperor had conquered, here—corresponding to the early medieval notion of emperorship as a hegemony over several *nationes*—they simply listed the peoples over whom Otto ruled.[219] In Lothar III's law prohibiting the alienation of fiefs, he bore titles drawn from Roman Antiquity, but no ancient emperor could have grasped the substance of this law, which was solidly feudal.[220] And when a twelfth-century artist depicted an ancient emperor, he represented him with the costume and the insignia—crown, sword, orb, and throne—typical of a contemporary monarch.[221]

Here one will recall the argument that in the arts, the Middle Ages took over both the forms and the substance of the classical tradition, but never succeeded in uniting the two.[222] Art historians may wish to dispute about the radical disjunction between classical form and classical content in medieval art. But the dictum largely holds true for the political "renewals" of the twelfth century, since twelfth-century people perceived ancient Rome through the prism of their own ideas, assumptions, and hopes. Even apart from their perceptions of Antiquity and their limited knowledge about it, however, they faced limited possibilities in the world around them. In the twelfth century, politics and government were not merely a game for the learned. Rather, they were the responsibility of rulers and statesmen, who sought a certain legitimacy in ideal models from Antiquity but had to govern within the reality of living institutions.

Bibliographical Note

Haskins scarcely touched on the themes treated in this essay (*Ren* 118–19, 207–08), nor has anyone else devoted a general study entirely to Antiquity's role in twelfth-century political thought. Various aspects, however, have been perceptively discussed by Robert Folz, *L'idée d'Empire en Occident du Ve au XIVe siècle* (Paris 1953), trans. Sheila A. Ogilvie, *The Concept of Empire in Western Europe from the Fifth to the Fourteenth Century* (New York 1969). Though different in emphasis, the essay by Ernst H. Kantorowicz, "Kingship under the Impact of Scientific Jurisprudence," *Twelfth-Century Europe* 89–111 (repr. in his *Selected Studies* [Locust Valley, N.Y. 1965] 151–66), comes closer than any other study to charting the boundaries and the topography of this topic. See also, in general, the posthumously published book by a young historian of the Ger-

---

[219]MGH DD 2.2.821 no. 390; Schramm, *KRR* 1.283.

[220]MGH DD 8.170 no. 105 (above, at n. 175).

[221]See the portrait of Augustus by Lambert of St Omer (ca. 1120) in the facsimile of the autograph (Ghent, Bibliothèque Universitaire, MS 92 fol. 138v): *Liber floridus*, ed. Albert Derolez (Ghent 1968) 280; and in BN lat 8865 fol. 45r, from the later thirteenth century (*Liber floridus Colloquium: Papers Read at the International Meeting Held in the University Library, Ghent, on 3–5 September 1967*, ed. Albert Derolez [Ghent 1973] fig. 43).

[222]Panofsky, *Ren & Ren* ch. 2.

man Democratic Republic: Gottfried Koch, *Auf dem Wege zum Sacrum imperium: Studien zur ideologischen Herrschaftsbegründung der deutschen Zentralgewalt im 11. und 12. Jahrhundert,* Forschungen zur mittelalterlichen Geschichte 20 (Vienna 1972) esp. ch. 6–7; my disagreements with this book must not obscure my debt to and respect for it, not least because its author died in 1968, before he could revise the two chapters which principally concern this study.

This essay has relied heavily on two sources: the universal history by bishop Otto of Freising, *Chronica sive Historia de duabus civitatibus,* 2nd ed. Adolf Hofmeister, MGH SS rer Germ (Hanover 1912), and especially the contemporary history by Otto (bks. 1–2) and his continuator Rahewin (bks. 3–4), *Gesta Friderici I. imperatoris,* 3rd ed. Georg Waitz and Bernhard von Simson, MGH SS rer Germ (Hanover 1912). These editions remain generally preferable to the more recent ones in the Freiherr vom Stein-Gedächtnisausgabe by, respectively, Walther Lammers (Darmstadt 1960) and Franz-Josef Schmale (2nd ed. Berlin 1974), both of which also have German translations. Charles Christopher Mierow has translated *The Two Cities: A Chronicle of Universal History to the Year 1146 A.D.* (New York 1928) and *The Deeds of Frederick Barbarossa* (New York 1953) into English.

Beginning in the last two decades of the eleventh century, Roman law increasingly furnished both impetus and substance to the political *renovatio* of Roman Antiquity. Though canon law contributed much less than Roman law to this *renovatio,* with the diffusion of Gratian's *Decretum* canon law began to exert an even greater influence than Roman law on the development of political thought in general. Consequently, the *renovatio Romae* cannot be approached without constant and careful attention to the two laws. For a valuable guide to the writings and doctrines of the Roman lawyers during the twelfth century, with excellent bibliographies, see Coing, *Handbuch* 1, and especially the section by Peter Weimar on ''Die legistische Literatur der Glossatorenzeit'' (129–260). On canon law during this period, Knut Wolfgang Nörr's contributions to Coing's *Handbuch,* ''Die kanonistische Literatur'' and ''Die Entwicklung des Corpus Iuris Canonici'' (1.365–82, 835–46), and Stephan Kuttner's essay in the present volume evaluate the scholarly literature.

For brief accounts of a topic that deserves a monograph, see Eva M. Sanford, ''The Study of Ancient History in the Middle Ages,'' *Journal of the History of Ideas* 5 (1944) 21–43, and the more specialized discussion by Heinrich Fichtenau, ''Vom Verständnis der römischen Geschichte bei deutschen Chronisten des Mittelalters,'' *Festschrift Percy Ernst Schramm,* ed. Peter Classen and Peter Scheibert (2 vols. Wiesbaden 1964) 1.401–19 (repr. in his *Beiträge zur Mediävistik: Ausgewählte Aufsätze* [2 vols. Stuttgart 1975–77] 1.1–23). Though there is no adequate study of the relation between twelfth-century historical conceptions of Antiquity and contemporary political thought, certain aspects of twelfth-century historical and political thought are treated by Werner Goez, *Translatio imperii: Ein Beitrag zur Geschichte des Geschichtsdenkens und der politischen Theorien im Mittelalter und in der frühen Neuzeit* (Tübingen 1958) esp. ch. 5–7, 9.

THE ROMAN REVOLUTION: On many questions about the Commune in the mid-twelfth century, the scanty sources will never permit a fully satisfactory answer. The crucial letters were preserved in the letter collection assembled by Wibald of Corvey (Jaffé, *Bibl* 1.76–609, and now being reedited by Timothy Reuter for the Monumenta Germaniae historica); some are also available in Franco Bartoloni, ed., *Codice diplomatico del Senato Romano dal MCXLIV al MCCCXLVII* 1, Fonti per la storia d'Italia 87 (Rome 1948). Eugenio Dupré Theseider, *L'idea imperiale di Roma nella tradizione del medioevo* (Milan 1942) 37–49, 124–72, furnishes an excellent analysis with many relevant texts. For a critical study of the sources, see Arsenio Frugoni, *Arnaldo da Brescia nelle fonti del secolo XII,* Istituto storico italiano per il medio evo, Studi storici 8–9 (Rome 1954), and for a brief summary, his "Arnaldo da Brescia," *Dizionario biografico degli italiani* 4 (1962) 247–50. Most histories of the medieval papacy give some attention to Arnold and the Commune. The best general history of Rome during this period is by Paolo Brezzi, *Roma e l'impero medioevale, 774–1252,* Storia di Roma 10 (Bologna 1947) esp. 317–46. On various points, these works have superseded the biography by George W. Greenaway, *Arnold of Brescia* (Cambridge 1931), which nonetheless remains useful.

ANTIQUITY AND THE EMPIRE: For the prehistory of this topic, the fundamental inquiry is by Percy Ernst Schramm, *Kaiser, Rom und Renovatio: Studien und Texte zur Geschichte des römischen Erneuerungsgedankens vom Ende des karolingischen Reiches bis zum Investiturstreit,* Studien der Bibliothek Warburg 17 (2 vols. Leipzig 1929); a second edition of the first volume (Darmstadt 1957) has a supplement with more recent bibliography (339–60). Though this work provides indispensable background, it gives—as the subtitle suggests—only a sketchy view of the twelfth century. Some of Schramm's articles illuminate questions relevant to this study; the articles (also the appendices constituting the second volume of *KRR*) have been reprinted, often with addenda, in his *Kaiser, Könige und Päpste* (4 vols. in 5 Stuttgart 1968–71). For an appreciation mainly on other aspects of Schramm's achievement, see J. M. Bak, "A Medieval Symbology of the State: Percy E. Schramm's Contribution," *Viator* 4 (1973) 33–63.

Though the rich documentation in Otto's and Rahewin's narrative remains the main source on the many echoes of and borrowings from Antiquity during the opening years of Barbarossa's reign, this must be supplemented with Frederick's charters. Covering the years 1152–67, the first two of four projected volumes in Heinrich Appelt's edition of *Die Urkunden Friedrichs I.,* MGH DD (Hanover 1975–79), much simplify the task. On this theme and related topics, one may consult: idem, "Friedrich Barbarossa und das römische Recht," *Römische historische Mitteilungen* 5 (1961–62) 18–34; idem, "Friedrich Barbarossa und die italienischen Kommunen," MIÖG 72 (1964) 311–25; idem, *Die Kaiseridee Friedrich Barbarossas,* SB Vienna 252.4 (1967) 1–32; Rainer Maria Herkenrath, *Regnum und Imperium: Das "Reich" in der frühstaufischen Kanzlei (1138–1155),* SB Vienna 264.5 (1969) 1–62.

Res Gestae, Universal History, Apocalypse

Visions of Past and Future

Peter Classen

The longest of the twelve chapters in Haskins's *Renaissance* bears the title "Historical Writing." My task is broader: to deal not only with historiography but also with the interpretation of universal history, which developed more from theology than from empirical history and which Haskins did not discuss.

In sheer quantity, historical writing—like all other written manifestations of intellectual life—increased enormously during the twelfth century. The Rolls Series alone, for example, contains some thirty volumes of narrative sources from the twelfth century, and they do not even exhaust the English sources. To these must be added those of other European countries, among them some that only began to contribute to historiography during the period in question. This discussion can do no more, therefore, than offer a few examples of the ways history was viewed and presented. The theme will be divided into three parts. The first will consider narrative works, *res gestae*, from England, Normandy, and Italy. The second will examine three works produced within the Holy Roman Empire which attempt to present a universal history from the Creation to their own time, or even to the end of the world. The third will be devoted to the theologians who, rather than narrating the course of history, sought to grasp its universal meaning, endeavoring thereby to establish the position of the present and to venture a glimpse into the future.

I. *RES GESTAE*

Historical writing in the twelfth century directly and uninterruptedly continued the historiography of the early Middle Ages, the origin of which goes back not to classical Antiquity but to early Christianity. Even in the twelfth century, the relationship to early Christian historiography lives on, while the classical authors—as in earlier periods—prove to be little more than stylistic models. All of this was already shown by Haskins and needs no further discussion here.

Great historical writing has always arisen from the experience of specific events. In the late eleventh and early twelfth centuries, historiography was given a great impetus chiefly by three historic phenomena: the founding of an Anglo-Norman state by William the Conqueror and his successors; the crusades; and the rise of the communes, at first primarily in Italy.[1]

ORDERIC VITALIS

The most outstanding of the Norman historians was Orderic Vitalis (1075–ca. 1142).[2] The work he himself described as an *historia ecclesiastica* is generally considered an excellent source as well as a good story, although its plan is "rather confused and badly arranged."[3] In fact, the organization of its contents is not easy to grasp; but it reflects the genesis of the work and, inherently, the history of the Normans as it gradually revealed itself to the author.[4] Orderic was not himself a Norman. The son of a French priest who came to England with William, and an Anglo-Saxon mother, he was born in the neighborhood of Shrewsbury on the Welsh border, and at the age of ten was taken by his father to the monastery of St Evroul in southern Normandy (near L'Aigle). He spent the rest of his days there as a Benedictine, with no change in his outward life; from time to time he visited places in Normandy and Lorraine as well as Cluny and once, later, saw England again. "I was brought here as a ten-year-old Englishman from the outermost boundaries of Mercia, placed as a barbarian and ignorant foreigner among the clever inhabitants; now, with God's help, I have undertaken to try to record in writing the deeds and history of the Normans for the Normans."[5] At the beginning of the twelfth century, probably it was only from a Norman monastery that one could turn his gaze in ever-widening circles to new lands almost without having to travel.

Orderic began by expanding and revising the history of the Normans written by William Calculus of Jumiège. Then in 1115 his abbot put him to the task of writing the history of St Evroul (which had been founded only in 1050).

[1]Other events could of course also be mentioned, in particular the founding of the Norman state in Sicily. The concept of "Staufer historiography," on the other hand, seems more problematic, since it actually boils down to Otto of Freising and Rahewin, who had no true followers. The poets of the *Carmen de gestis Frederici in Lombardia* and the *Ligurinus*, as well as Godfrey of Viterbo, can be counted as historians only with some reservations, and after Frederick I, court historiography and historiographical court poetry ceased altogether. The poetry at the court of Frederick II was not really historiographic.

[2]The new critical edition of Orderic, with an English translation, is now complete: *The Ecclesiastical History of Orderic Vitalis*, ed. and trans. Marjorie Chibnall (6 vols. Oxford 1969–81).

[3]Austin Lane Poole, *From Domesday Book to Magna Carta, 1087–1216*, The Oxford History of England 3 (2nd ed. Oxford 1955) 494.

[4]On Orderic and his work see Léopold Delisle in Auguste Le Prévost et al., eds., *Orderici Vitalis Historiae ecclesiasticae libri tredecim*, Société de l'histoire de France 13, 22, 39, 69, 79 (5 vols. Paris 1838–55) 5.i–cvi; Hans Wolter, *Ordericus Vitalis: Ein Beitrag zur kluniazensischen Geschichtsschreibung* (Wiesbaden 1955); Antonia Gransden, *Historical Writing in England c. 550 to c. 1307* (London 1974) 151–65; and the introductions to the volumes of Chibnall (n. 2 above), esp. on the chronology of the composition of the individual books.

[5]"Tandem ego de extremis Merciorum finibus decennis Angligena huc aduectus, barbarusque et ignotus aduena callentibus indigenis admixtus, inspirante Deo Normannorum gesta et euentus Normannis promere scripto sum conatus," *Ecclesiastical History* 5.1, ed. Chibnall (n. 2 above) 3.6.

He worked on it for decades, until shortly before his death, the last recorded event falling in 1141. But the work did not remain a mere history of a monastery, like so many written in the twelfth century. The very first decades of the monastery's existence forced Orderic to broaden his scope: abbot Robert of the noble family of Grandmesnil had been driven out by duke William, finding refuge with Robert Guiscard in Apulia, and monks had been leaving St Evroul for England since 1066; the monastery acquired rich possessions there, and it sent abbots to English monasteries and received English oblates, like Orderic himself, in Normandy. His report of these events was consistently set into a more general context, and the work rapidly expanded to become a history of the Normans in all countries without appropriating the literary tradition of the histories of the Germanic peoples—a tradition that extended from Jordanes and Isidore to Bede, Paul the Deacon, and Widukind of Corvey.

Orderic enlarged the spatial and temporal boundaries of his work in concentric circles, as it were. Book 5 looks back over the ecclesiastical history of Normandy since the first mission in northern Gaul. Epitaphs of bishops and abbots—some handed down, others composed by Orderic himself—adorn the work, which is written largely in the rhymed prose favored since the tenth century and so completely foreign to antique stylistic sensibility. Following the monastic and ecclesiastical history of Normandy, France, and England, book 7 makes a fresh start[6] with Henry IV's expedition to Rome, moves quickly to the more important Robert Guiscard and his wars against Byzantium, then returns once more to the political history of England up to the death of William II. The horizon is expanded again with the history of the first crusade in book 10. The last four books, written about 1135–38 with supplements dating to 1141, relate in essentially chronological order the events of the first decades of the twelfth century, primarily in England, France, and the Holy Land; book 13 adds information on the beginning of the Reconquista in Spain.

Only after the work had gradually been turned into a universal history by tracing the steps of the Normans did Orderic finally set his world chronicle of books 1 and 2 at the head of the whole. Here he explicitly drew upon the literary tradition of Christian historiography, citing Eusebius, Jerome, Isidore, and Bede. But his own conception is highly individual. A detailed *Vita Jesu Christi* is followed by a chronicle of emperors that includes East and West, Byzantium and the Franks, but also mentions West Frankish, Anglo-Saxon, and other kings. The second book begins with the Lives of all the Apostles, leading us to various parts of the world as far as India and Ethiopia, and continues with a brief chronicle of the popes up to the present. Thus, not only emperors but the kings of many nations are placed in the line of succession from Christ, while the popes are given first place among the successors of the Apostles.

---

[6]For opposition to the older opinion that book 7 was not written until later, see Chibnall's introduction (n. 2 above) 4.xix–xxv.

In order to understand this work one must recall its genesis. It is not the chronology, the order of events, that is essential, but the narration itself, which leads inevitably from one theme to another—whether on the basis of written or of oral sources—because relationships and associations are found to exist everywhere. What ultimately results is an "ecclesiastical history" that is truly a universal history of a new and original kind, arising more from the historical experience and the narration itself than from a literary form and tradition or a theoretical conception. Comparatively often—and very characteristically for this self-aware twelfth-century author—Orderic speaks of himself. He mentions all the important dates in his life; we are told what he has seen with his own eyes, and a brief autobiography with a prayer (following the model of Bede) concludes his work.

WILLIAM OF MALMESBURY

Orderic gained a wealth of knowledge from his reading of historical literature, but he did not carry on its traditions. It was quite different with his younger contemporary, William of Malmesbury (ca. 1090–ca. 1142).[7] He too was half continental—in fact, Norman—and half Anglo-Saxon in origin; but he lived in an English monastery, and Bede became his great model. English history seemed to have died with Bede: "Almost all knowledge of history up to our own time was buried with him."[8] To William, the Anglo-Saxon chronicles barely suffice to prevent the obliteration of several centuries, but he feels it better to remain silent about their Latin version. Even Eadmer reported only briefly about the time from the accession of Edgar to the conquest of William; for the time from Bede's death to Edgar—223 years, as William calculates it—no historiographic presentation whatever existed.[9] And so William felt called upon to renew an intellectual tradition interrupted 400 years before; and it must be acknowledged that he succeeded. His history of the English kings begins with the Anglo-Saxon immigration; the first book takes us as far as Edgar, the second to the battle of Hastings, the last three treat the first three Norman kings. The *Historia novella* carries events down to the civil war of 1142.

William studied every field of learning:

I have devoted my efforts to many *litterae*, though to each in a different way. For logic, which arms eloquence, I have only sampled, through lectures. Medicine, which heals the ailing body, I have taken in somewhat more fully. But into the fields of ethics I have

---

[7]William of Malmesbury, *De gestis regum Anglorum libri quinque* and *Historiae novellae libri tres*, ed. William Stubbs, RS 90 (2 vols. London 1887–89); *De gestis pontificum Anglorum libri quinque*, ed. Nicholas E. S. A. Hamilton, RS 52 (London 1870); *The Historia novella*, trans. and ed. Kenneth Reginald Potter (London 1955). On William, see Gransden (n. 4 above) 166–85; Manitius 3.466–73; and esp. the introductions by Stubbs in *Gesta regum* 1 and 2.

[8]"Sepulta est cum eo gestorum omnis pene notitia usque ad nostra tempora." *Gesta regum* 1.62 (n. 7 above) 1.66.

[9]*Gesta regum* 1 prologus (1.1–3).

penetrated very deeply, and I rise to its majesty, because it is accessible of itself to one who studies it and it prepares the mind for living well: history in particular, which through welcome knowledge of deeds develops manners and morals and through examples incites the reader to do good and avoid evil.[10]

William accordingly attributed his effort, his entire work, to ethics, and while he could believe himself on the strength of his origin to be a neutral judge between the Normans and the Anglo-Saxons,[11] he nonetheless considered the fall of the Anglo-Saxon kingdom to have been the direct result of a decline in morals and religion and the Norman victory to have been morally deserved.[12] The religious decay of the Anglo-Saxons had however gone hand in hand with the decline of education: "In the course of time, the striving for knowledge and theology had declined, . . . the clerics contented themselves with a superficial education and could scarcely babble the words of the sacraments. If, for a change, someone really knew Latin well, he was considered a miracle by the others and aroused astonishment."[13] Education together with piety provided a standard; William made literary demands even on the king, and with Henry I he believed them to have been fulfilled. Under Henry, the Platonic maxim, Happy the state when the philosophers rule or the kings philosophize, came true; in the presence of his conqueror-father the young Henry (more insolent than philosophical) is said to have uttered the proverb, "An illiterate king is a crowned ass."[14] Not even Cicero in prose or Vergil in verse, William believed, would have dared to describe such a king as Henry I.[15]

To be sure, remarks of this kind reveal the historian's own limitations as well; nevertheless, William was constantly striving for something higher. He worked hard to acquire a literary education, copying manuscripts of the ancient historians and even of the *Breviarium Alaricianum.*[16] The chronological flow of events and deeds in his history of the English kings is interrupted time

---

[10]"Multis quidem litteris impendi operam, sed aliis aliam. Logicam enim, quae armat eloquium, solo libavi auditu; physicam quae medetur valitudini corporum, aliquanto pressius concepi; iam vero ethicae partes medullitus rimatus, illius maiestati assurgo, quod per se studentibus pateat, et animos ad bene vivendum comparat: historiam praecipue, quae, iocunda quadam gestorum notitia mores condiens, ad bona sequenda vel mala cavenda legentes exemplis irritat." *Gesta regum* 2 prologus (1.103).

[11]*Gesta regum* 3 prologus (2.283).

[12]*Gesta regum* 3.245–46 (2.304–06).

[13]Ibid. (2.304): "Veruntamen litterarum et religionis studia aetate procedente obsoleverunt. . . . Clerici litteratura tumultuaria contenti, vix sacramentorum verba balbutiebant: stupori erat et miraculo ceteris qui grammaticam nosset."

[14]"Rex illitteratus, asinus coronatus," *Gesta regum* 5.390 (2.467). See Vivian H. Galbraith, "The Literacy of the Medieval English Kings," *Proceedings of the British Academy* 21 (1935) 201–38; Herbert Grundmann, "Litteratus–Illitteratus," *Ausgewählte Aufsätze*, MGH Schriften 25 (3 vols. Stuttgart 1976–78) 3.1–66 at 11–13.

[15]*Gesta regum* 5 prologus (2.465).

[16]See the introduction by William Stubbs in *Gesta regum* 1.cxxxi–cxlvii; Manitius 3.468–69. For a comprehensive analysis of the numerous works with which William was familiar, as well as of the codices used by him, see Rodney M. Thomson, "The Reading of William of Malmesbury," *Revue bénédictine* 85 (1975) 362–94, with corrections and additions ibid. 86 (1976) 327–35 and 89 (1979) 313–24.

and again by anecdotes and tales of magic, not a few taking place in Rome and some connected with the history of such popes as Gerbert and Gregory VI.[17] By no means all of them have a recognizable moral; often the report of their strangeness is an end in itself. Not only does William make room for Berengar of Tours, he also includes Hildebert's verses on the allegedly converted heretic.[18] Significantly, however, the longest digression from the history of England is occasioned by the crusade of Robert, duke of Normandy. Robert passed through Rome, giving William the opportunity to include Hildebert's great poem, *Par tibi Roma nihil*, to which he appends a description of the twelve city gates.[19] There follow excursuses on Constantinople, Antioch, and Jerusalem, lists of the Byzantine emperors and the patriarchs of Jerusalem,[20] and finally the history of the first kings of Jerusalem.

William is only one of several English historians of the time. Besides him we find Eadmer, Simeon of Durham, and Henry of Huntingdon, and in the following generations English historiography reached its first high point with William of Newburgh and Roger of Hoveden. It should also be mentioned that Geoffrey of Monmouth presented his *Historia regum Britanniae*[21] to that same Robert earl of Gloucester, son of king Henry I and patron of the young Henry II at the time of the civil war, to whom William dedicated his *Gesta regum* and *Historia novella*.[22] In their saga of the ancient chivalric kings, Britons and Welshmen competed with the heirs of Bede, who, without questioning Arthur's standing as a historical figure, kept a suspicious distance from the *nugae Britonum* and *antiquitas naeniarum* regarding his return.[23] The British king met with unprecedented favor in the chivalric and courtly world, and fifty years after Geoffrey had completed his work, a grandson of king Henry II and presumptive claimant to his throne was christened Arthur.

---

[17]*Gesta regum* 2.169 (1.196ff.) on Gerbert's discovery of the treasures of Octavianus (*sic!*), followed by additional stories about treasures, magic, and the like. A miracle that occurred at the death of Gregory VI (2.203 [1.253]) occasioned the report on the witch of Berkeley, followed (2.206 [1.258–59]) by the story of the discovery of the body of Pallas, son of Evander, in Rome and by other memorabilia.

[18]*Gesta regum* 4.284 (2.338–40).

[19]*Gesta regum* 4.351 (2.402–08).

[20]*Gesta regum* 4.355–56, 359, 367–68 (2.411–13, 415–16, 422–25).

[21]Geoffrey's *Historia* is available in several editions: Edmond Faral, *La légende Arthurienne* (3 vols. Paris 1929) vol. 3; Acton Griscom, *The Historia regum Britanniae of Geoffrey of Monmouth* (London 1929; Latin and Welsh); Jacob Hammer, *Geoffrey of Monmouth, Historia regum Britanniae, a Variant Version*, Mediaeval Academy of America Publication 57 (Cambridge Mass. 1951). On this see Robert W. Hanning, *The Vision of History in Early Britain* (New York and London 1966), Gransden (n. 4 above) 200–09, and C. N. L. Brooke, "Geoffrey of Monmouth as a Historian," *Church and Government in the Middle Ages: Essays presented to C. R. Cheney on His 70th Birthday*, ed. C. N. L. Brooke et al. (Cambridge and New York 1976) 77–91. with additional bibliography.

[22]*Gesta regum* (n. 7 above), dedicatory letter following book 3 (2.355–56); epilogue following book 5 (2.518–21); dedication of the *Historia novella* (2.525–56, = ed. Potter [n. 7 above] 1).

[23]William of Malmesbury, *Gesta regum* 1.8 (1.11–12), 3.287 (2.342).

ITALIAN URBAN ANNALISTS

We first encounter urban historiography in the Italian communes of the twelfth century, where lay education was very highly developed. The northern cities on the Scheldt, Meuse, and Lower Rhine could not yet compete with Italy in this area, and even Galbert of Bruges, who gives a stirring, graphic account from his own experience of the murder of count Charles the Good of Flanders and the subsequent civil wars cannot, for all his openness to the participation and interests of the citizens of Bruges, qualify as an historian of the town and its citizenry;[24] he remains a notary in the entourage of the count, and a man of clerical status.[25]

As in other episcopal towns, historiography in Milan during the eleventh and early twelfth centuries was still entirely in the hands of the clergy.[26] To be sure, strong bonds between the clergy and the ruling class are unmistakable, and in the episcopal towns it was only a small step from the history of a bishopric or bishop to the history of a town. Still, it took the war of the Lombards against Frederick Barbarossa to inspire the new kind of annal writing by the unknown layman who depicted the Lombard struggle for liberty.[27] After the Romans (!), Goths, "Winili" (that is, Langobards), Franks, and Hungarians—so reads the introduction—the Germans have now invaded Lombardy: this should serve as a warning to the reader of the book against future danger and make him politically wise.[28]

Milan at that time was ruled by an annually changing collegium of consuls,[29] among them several judges who were intellectual and political leaders; the most prominent were Oberto de Orto and Girardo Cagapisto. These jurists were famous in their time as outstanding authorities in feudal law and made a decisive contribution to the codification which was later put together as the *Libri feudorum* and which united with their writings the laws of their adver-

---

[24]Galbert of Bruges, *Histoire du meurtre de Charles le Bon, comte de Flandre (1127–1128)*, ed. Henri Pirenne (Paris 1891); also useful are the translation by James Bruce Ross, with a detailed introduction and commentary: *The Murder of Charles the Good, Count of Flanders* (rev. ed. New York 1967), and various essays in Heinrich Sproemberg's posthumous book, *Mittelalter und demokratische Geschichtsschreibung: Ausgewählte Abhandlungen* (Berlin 1971). Not only is the concept of "democratic historiography" anachronistic when applied to the twelfth century, but the idea it seems to imply—that Galbert is a representative of the bourgeoisie—is, I believe, erroneous.

[25]On Galbert's position see Ross (n. 24 above) 65–66; Sproemberg (n. 24 above) 240–41, 248–50.

[26]On Arnulf, Landulf the Elder, and Landulf the Younger see Walther Holtzmann's summary in Wattenbach-Holtzmann (see the Bibliographical Note to this essay, below) 3.918–22.

[27]*Gesta Federici I. imperatoris in Lombardia auct. cive Mediolanensi*, ed. Oswald Holder-Egger, MGH SS rer Germ (Hanover 1892).

[28]*Gesta Federici* prologus (14–16).

[29]The best description of Milan's constitution in the twelfth century is to be found in the introduction to Cesare Manaresi, *Gli atti del Comune di Milano fino all'anno MCCXVI* (Milan 1919).

saries, the emperors.[30] The language and method of Oberto's writings are based on Roman law, though we do not know whether or not he studied in Bologna; his son Anselmo, in any case, lived there for some time but lost his political influence in Milan after collaborating with the Germans.[31]

The anonymous annalist was close to the milieu of these Milanese jurists, but neither his language nor any other clues suggest that he had a legal training. He was a sober, pragmatic thinker. The Church makes its appearance on the edge of political events—as when an archbishop promises God's help and urges war—but he shows no traces of clerical thinking. The wars and politics of his time are the subjects of his narrative; of the author's own involvement we learn only that during the siege of Milan he helped to ration out food.[32]

At the same time as the Milanese annalist, Otto Morena, a judge in the neighboring town of Lodi, began a work dealing with the same material, but from the opposite political point of view.[33] For Lodi, Frederick I was a savior in a time of need resulting from Milan's oppression of neighboring cities. With the emperor's help Lodi was restored after its destruction, and in Morena's eyes the brutal demolition of Milan in turn was only deserved punishment. Otto Morena and his son Acerbo, who continued his work, bore the title of *iudex et missus imperatoris* and sometimes appeared as consuls. In other words, they belonged to the same class in Lodi as Oberto and Girardo in Milan, but their literary achievement lies in the field of historiography: they were the first jurists among the Lombard city historians, yet their subject was more *gesta imperatoris* than urban history. It has been observed that their style adopted turns of phrase used by jurists and in charters but was also influenced by Sallust, who was widely read during the Middle Ages.[34] Acerbo weaves in stylistically skillful portraits of German military commanders.[35]

Even before the start of the crusades, Pisa could boast of great naval victories over the Saracens, who nevertheless remained her partners in trade. Her triumph over Palermo is glorified by an inscription in twenty-five leonine hexameters on the façade of the new cathedral, financed in 1063–64 by the spoils of the war.[36] An adjacent inscription places the victory within the tradition of

---

[30]Karl Lehmann, *Das langobardische Lehnrecht* (Göttingen 1896), repr. with his *Consuetudines feudorum* and new intro. by Karl August Eckhardt, Bibliotheca rerum historicarum (Aalen 1971).

[31]*Gesta Federici* (n. 27 above) 50 for Anselmo's peace negotiations; 58 on the collaboration.

[32]*Gesta Federici* 48; see introduction 5–6. There the earlier opinion is refuted that the writer was called Sire Raul (even today the text is sometimes still cited under this name); he was, instead, the copyist of a 13th-c. manuscript.

[33]*Das Geschichtswerk des Otto Morena und seiner Fortsetzer über die Taten Friedrichs I. in der Lombardei*, ed. Ferdinand Güterbock, MGH SS rer Germ n.s. 7 (Berlin 1930); on the authors see the introduction, ix–xvii.

[34]Ibid. xvi: "In der Form der Darstellung können sich diese Laienschriftsteller mit gleichzeitigen geistlichen Geschichtsschreibern nicht entfernt messen."

[35]Acerbo, ibid. 166–71.

[36]Giuseppe Scalia, "Epigraphica Pisana: Testi latini sulla spedizione contro le Baleari del 1113–15 e su altre imprese anti-saracene del secolo XI," *Miscellanea di studi ispanici dell'Istituto di letteratura spagnola e ispano-americana della Università di Pisa* (Pisa 1963) 234–86 at 253–64 (text 263–64) and pl. 2.

the naval campaigns that took place in 1006, 1016, and 1033, the last advancing as far as Bona in Africa.[37] A poem in seventy-three rhythmic strophes on the expedition of 1087 against Al-Mahdija strikes a new note by comparing Pisa to Rome:

> In writing the history of the illustrious men of Pisa,
> I renew the memory of the ancient Romans:
> For now Pisa continues the splendid renown
> Which Rome once gained by conquering Carthage.[38]

An otherwise unknown consul from the beginning of the twelfth century is celebrated in an inscription on the cathedral:

> Here indeed you had a second Cato, Hector, Cicero—
> In mind, in strength, in eloquence, one man the equal of three.[39]

A few decades later a poet has the town speak as follows:

> I am customarily called a second Rome,
> I who am rich in charters from Frederick
> Because of the barbarian peoples I have defeated everywhere.[40]

Meanwhile, the war against Majorca in 1114–15 was extolled in an epic poem of more than 3500 hexameters.[41] In these and related testimonies scholars have recognized a Pisan tradition of historico-political poetry which links the crusading theme to the idea of an *altera Roma* precisely on the basis of naval dominance.[42] Not a single author is known by name, nor can we say whether this poetry, composed entirely in the service of the city and its naval wars, was in all cases written by clerics or was possibly the work of laymen.

The annals of Pisa are quite different. From a meager collection of brief notes they developed after 1136 into an impressive work giving precise reports

---

[37]Ibid. 235–53, text 252–53.

[38] Inclitorum Pisanorum   scripturus istoriam
antiquorum Romanorum   renovo memoriam
nam extendit modo Pisa   laudem admirabilem
quam recepit olim Roma   vincendo Carthaginem.

Giuseppe Scalia, "Il carme pisano sull'impresa contro i Saraceni del 1087," *Studi di filologia romanza offerti a Silvio Pellegrini* (Padua 1971) 565–627, text 597–627; stanza 1 quoted here (597).

[39] Hic tibi nempe Cato fuit, Ector, Tullius alter
mente manu lingua, par tribus unus homo.

Giuseppe Scalia, "'Romanitas' Pisana tra XI e XII secolo: Le iscrizioni romane del duomo e la statua del console Rodolfo," *Studi medievali* 3rd ser. 13 (1972) 791–843 at 808.

[40]Ibid. 805: Ego Roma altera iam solebam dici
que sum privilegiis dives Friderici
propter gentes barbaras quas ubique vici.

[41]*Liber Maiolichinus de gestis Pisanorum illustribus*, ed. Carlo Calisse, Fonti per la storia d'Italia 29 (Rome 1904). On this see Giuseppe Scalia, "Per una riedizione critica del 'Liber Maiorichinus,'" *Bullettino dell'Istituto storico italiano per il Medio Evo* 71 (1960) 39–112.

[42]See especially the works by Scalia cited in the preceding notes. See also Craig B. Fisher, "The Pisan Clergy and an Awakening of Historical Interest in a Medieval Commune," *Studies in Medieval and Renaissance History* 3 (1966) 143–219.

of military campaigns, legations, and other political affairs of the city; beginning in the 1150s, lists were added of the consuls and in part of other officials, particularly judges.[43] The author of these annals was Bernardo Maragone, a jurist from the group called in Pisa *de usu scientes* and consequently eligible for election as *previsores*, judges at the court of customary law (*curia usus*), as distinguished from the *legis periti*, authorities in Roman law working at the *curia legis*.[44] Bernardo's son Salem, who prided himself on being an expert in Roman law, continued the annals after 1182.[45] The work thus arose in that circle of prominent Pisan jurists to which the translator Burgundio—a *legis peritus*—belonged[46] and which also produced the great statute book of 1160, the *Constituta legis et usus*.[47] Maragone considered it his main task to record the officeholders of the city and their official acts in chronological order, objectively and impersonally including his own name, sometimes as a *previsor*, elsewhere as an envoy to the Roman senate.[48] Strangely enough, the years are quite often repeated and occasionally even confused; it would appear that Maragone initially collected his material on slips of paper. But these annals do not yet constitute an official work.

It was in Genoa, rather, that this final step was taken. There, for the first time, a history of the city was written by a layman with the highest political responsibilities and was then given official status by the commune.[49] In 1152 Caffaro placed in the hands of the ruling consuls his record of Genoa's history

---

[43]*Gli Annales Pisani di Bernardo Maragone*, ed. Michele Lupo Gentile, Rerum italicarum scriptores 6.2 (Bologna 1936). The work survives only in an abridged Latin version in which many of the lists of officeholders are omitted; there exists, besides, a 17th-c. Italian translation of the complete text, which in this edition—deficient in many other respects as well—is cited incompletely and confusingly. On Maragone see the introduction, v–ix.

[44]Gioacchino Volpe, *Studi sulle istituzioni comunali a Pisa: Città e contado, consoli e podestà, secoli XII–XIII*, new ed. with intro. by Cinzio Violante (Florence 1970) 146–50. Peter Classen, "Gesetzgebung im 12. Jahrhundert: Die *Constituta usus et legis* von Pisa," *Recht und Schrift im Mittelalter*, ed. Peter Classen, Vorträge und Forschungen 23 (Sigmaringen 1977) 311–17.

[45]*Annales* (n. 43 above) 73, for the year 1182 Pisan style (1181 *stili communis*), which survives only in the Italian version: "Infino a qui ha fatto Bernardo di Maragone, homo buono savio et pronto in dicti et facti et in ogni opera per honor della città in terra et in mare, il quale visse anni octanta in bona vecchiaia et vide e' figloli de sua figlioli, infino in terza et quarta generatione et tutte queste cose vidde et cognove per grazia et misericordia dello omnipotente Idio, et compose et fece questo registro insieme con Salem, suo figlolo, homo dottor in legge et savio buono, et pronto in praticar et giudicar, il quale Salém tenne le vestigie di suo padre et tanto più che lui era doctor di legge, pieno di scienzia, homo di bona progenia nato et nobile cittadino della città di Pisa. Et da qui inanzi farà solo esso Salem, aiutandolo Idio il quale vive et regna per infiniti secoli Amen."

[46]Peter Classen, *Burgundio von Pisa: Richter, Gesandter, Übersetzer*, SB Heidelberg, Philos.-hist. Kl. 1974 no. 4.

[47]Classen (n. 44 above).

[48]Maragone, *Annales* (n. 43 above) 13, 17 (codex A in footnote), 22, 31, and 32 (text, and additional comment from codex **A** in footnote) names himself in different offices as judge and envoy in 1151, 1159, 1161, and 1165.

[49]*Annali Genovesi di Caffaro e de' suoi continuatori dal MCXIX al MCCXCIII*, ed. Luigi Tommaso Belgrano and Cesare Imperiale di Sant'Angelo, Fonti per la storia d'Italia 11–14bis (5 vols. Rome 1890–1929).

from the year 1100. Caffaro had recorded "the names of the consuls, and the times and successions of the consulates and companies, and the victories, and the changes in coinage that occurred during each consulate."[50] The public scribe was now instructed by the consuls "to make a [fair] copy of the book compiled and annotated by Caffaro and to place it in the public archives, so that henceforth for all time the victories would be known to the people of the city of Genoa."[51]

Caffaro was born in 1080 and took part in the Genoese crusade to the Holy Land in 1099–1101. Already at that time, when the first *compagnia* was formed and its consuls chosen, he began on his own initiative to record the names and deeds of the consuls.[52] In his record, the crusade, the creation of an association that became the nucleus of the city commune, and the first rudiments of urban historiography coincide. Simple lists of the companies (each sworn in for a term of four years) and their consuls form the early framework; beginning in 1112 these were replaced by lists of the annual consulates, in which Caffaro himself appears among the governing officials. Between 1122 and 1147 he was *consul communis* at least five times and *consul de placitis* twice; in other years he served the city as an envoy, ultimately in 1154 and 1158 to Barbarossa.[53] The skeleton of lists of officeholders was fleshed out—probably at a later date—by vivid recollections of such events as the vindication of the crusade in a dialogue with the Saracens[54] or the embassy to pope Calixtus II, who deprived the Pisans of their ecclesiastical supremacy over Corsica;[55] here, to be sure, Caffaro is silent about the payments to pope and cardinals which he himself had negotiated and for which we have exact documentary evidence.[56]

Caffaro's originally private records, later rendered official by the consuls, initiate a new form of historical writing. It is not known how much the details and especially the language of the work in its present form are due to the city scribes who set it down. From 1154 on, continuations were added every year; these seem to have been read or explained by Caffaro to the city authorities before they were approved and incorporated into the official text. In the introductory phrases to each year's additions the notarial style is unmistakable.[57]

[50]"Nomina eorum [*scil.* the consuls] et tempora et uarietates consulatuum et compagniarum, et uictorias, et mutationes monetarum in eodem consulatu factas, sicut subtus legitur, per semet ipsum dictauit, et consulibus . . . in consilio pleno scriptum istud ostendit," *Annali Genovesi* 1.3.

[51]"Consules uero . . . publico scribano preceperunt, ut librum a Cafaro compositum et notatum scriberet et in comuni cartulario poneret, ut deinceps cuncto tempore futuris hominibus Ianuensis [ciuitatis] uictorie cognoscantur," *Annali Genovesi* 1.3–4.

[52]See the note on 1160, *Annali Genovesi* 1.59.

[53]On Caffaro's life see Belgrano's introduction, *Annali Genovesi* 1.lxix–xc.

[54]*Annali Genovesi* 1.9–12, for 1101.

[55]*Annali Genovesi* 1.18–20, for 1122.

[56]See the document in *Annali Genovesi* 1.20–21 n. 1.

[57]See the supplements to 1154–63, *Annali Genovesi* 1.38, 41, 46, 48, 49, 53, 61, 63–64, 66–67, 74. On this see Girolamo Arnaldi, "Uno sguardo agli Annali Genovesi," in his *Studi sui*

The author himself was apparently neither a notary nor even trained in jurisprudence; not until the next generation did members of these professions, to which Caffaro's assistants belonged, assume the task of writing the history of their city. Caffaro made his last entry in 1163; in 1166 he died, and it was not until 1169 that the ruling consuls instructed the chancellor and former consul of the town, Oberto, to continue the work. From then until 1293 the annals of Genoa constituted an official work of urban historiography.

The Genoese annals certainly do not belong in the literary tradition stemming from Antiquity; they owe their origin not to scholarship and literature but to politics. And yet they deserve our attention here, for they have elements that recall the earliest historiography of Rome, with its *fasti consulares*, and because they offer the first significant example of the urban historiography that gradually began to spread over the whole of Europe in the twelfth century.

The examples from Milan, Lodi, Pisa, and Genoa show how the educational monopoly of the clergy was broken in the communes. In addition to their political and administrative duties, the officials—notaries, judges, and sometimes the ruling consuls themselves—took over the recording and transmitting of *acta* and *gesta* in the Italian communes; in Genoa this actually became one of their public functions. The present was consciously being made a monument for the future, but inevitably linked with this was the question of the past, its models, and its traditions. History and reflection on history could thus become a theme of political ideas and actions. Pisa's politico-historical poets adopted Roman tradition; Milan kept to its own past. A relief of about 1171 on the Porta Romana in Milan depicts the reentry of the citizens into the city after its rebuilding in 1167 under the protection of the confederated communes; beside it, however, appears a representation of St Ambrose and his struggle against the Arians.[58]

II. UNIVERSAL HISTORY

Virtually all the works discussed in part I take their point of departure from the experience of political actions in the authors' own time. The great world chronicles, on the other hand, were based far more on literary tradition, even though their authors certainly dealt with contemporary politics—in some cases, indeed, rather polemically. Two works from the turn of the eleventh and twelfth century may serve as examples. Significantly, both were written within the Empire, whose self-conception offered the most fertile soil for the literary composition of a universal history: the Salian emperors and their Staufer suc-

---

cronisti della Marca Trevigiana nell'età di Ezzelino da Romano, Studi storici 48–50 (Rome 1963) 225–45.

[58]Illustrations of the remarkable sculptures of the Porta Romana, which are now in Castel Sforza and have accompanying verse inscriptions, can be found throughout vol. 4 of the *Storia di Milano* (16 vols. Milan 1953–62); I know of no historical or art-historical interpretation of them.

cessors were looked upon, after all, as emperors of the Romans and the successors of Augustus.

SIGEBERT OF GEMBLOUX

Sigebert (ca. 1030–1112), a monk in the Benedictine monastery of Gembloux in the diocese of Liège—and therefore a Walloon-speaking inhabitant of the Empire—shared the allegiance to the Empire of many of his peers during the Investiture Controversy.[59] His world chronicle goes back directly to Jerome and, drawing on many sources, attempts to expand the synchronization of reigns in the manner of Eusebius.[60] For the fourth and fifth centuries he was able to record eight or nine simultaneous *regna*; in the following periods some of these collapsed and the others were scarcely mentioned in the sources. For the early ninth century he names only Romans (= Frankish emperors), Franks (= West Frankish kings), Constantinopolitans, Saracens, and Bulgarians. The latter two disappear after 821, and after 977 the Byzantines as well, due quite simply to lack of information; so that eventually *Romani* and *Franci*, that is to say Germans and French, are all that remain—a rather sad remnant that seems to reflect a provincialism in the "world chronicle" of late Salian times. In 1067 the English are added and in 1100 the Jerusalemites, but neither the Spanish kingdoms nor the Scandinavians, Poles, or Hungarians appear in Sigebert's field of vision; information on the Byzantine emperors does not reappear even for the time of the crusades. Was Sigebert unaware that a universal history of his own time restricted to the Empire could no longer fulfill its purpose?

FRUTOLF OF BAMBERG

Sigebert continued the work of Jerome, beginning with the year 381. His presumably younger contemporary, Frutolf (d. 1103), a Benedictine of Michelsberg Abbey in Bamberg, was more ambitious: he reexamined everything, beginning with the Creation, and filled in the chronological framework—which seemed less important to him—with quantities of material of all kinds.[61] The libraries of Bamberg were no less rich than those of Liège. Frutolf

---

[59]On Sigebert see most recently Jutta Beumann, *Sigebert von Gembloux und der Traktat de investitura episcoporum,* Vorträge und Forschungen, Sonderband 20 (Sigmaringen 1976). Her edition of the treatise, which she ascribes to Sigebert, is in DA 33 (1977) 37–83.

[60]*Sigeberti Gemblacensis chronica cum continuationibus,* ed. Ludwig K. Bethmann, MGH SS 6 (1844) 268–474; text of Sigebert's chronicle (up to 1111) 300–74. The supplements were in part separately edited. On Sigebert as a chronicler see Heinrich Sproemberg in Wattenbach-Holtzmann (see Bibliographical Note) 2.727–37.

[61]Frutolf's chronicle, together with Ekkehard's continuations, were edited by Georg Waitz under Ekkehard's name: *Ekkehardi Uraugiensis chronica,* MGH SS 6 (1844) 1–267. That its core was the work of Frutolf was first recognized by Harry Bresslau, "Die Chroniken des Frutolf von Bamberg und des Ekkehard von Aura," *Neues Archiv* 21 (1896) 197–234. New edition of the section from 1001 on in Franz-Josef Schmale and Irene Schmale-Ott, *Frutolfs und Ekkehards Chroniken und die anonyme Kaiserchronik,* Freiherr vom Stein-Gedächtnisausgabe 15 (Darmstadt 1972); the introduction includes a summary of recent scholarship on the versions and authors of the chronicle, but essentially with reference only to the closing section. See also Wattenbach-Holtzmann (see Bibliographical Note) 2.491–506.

tried to make his chronicle readable by incorporating stories from various sources. When introducing a new people, he adds a comprehensive *origo gentis*—as for the Franks, Goths (among whom, following Jordanes, he includes Huns and Amazons), Lombards, and Saxons. Great rulers such as Alexander, Theodosius, Charlemagne, and Otto the Great are given extensive *vitae* taken more or less verbatim from the sources. But Frutolf was also interested in intellectual achievements: for the year 365 A.U.C., for example, he inserts information (taken essentially from Augustine) on Socrates, Plato, and Pythagoras; and wherever his sources permit, he names poets, Church Fathers, and saints, and occasionally uses their *vitae*. Probably more than any other medieval author before or after him, Frutolf made an attempt to describe in detail and bring together in a comprehensive presentation covering the entire course of time every conceivable piece of historical information known to him—a kind of universalism that marks an end rather than a beginning. Frutolf's work found continuators in Germany, and Sigebert's in France and the Netherlands; but no truly new world chronicles were composed. Otto of Freising's great work attempted to reshape the traditional material of world history intellectually, rather than to enlarge it.

OTTO OF FREISING

With the title *Historia de duabus civitatibus*, bishop Otto of Freising (ca. 1112–58), the French-educated half-brother of king Conrad III, directly linked his work to that of Augustine;[62] but this should not blind us to the fact that the connection is in one particular idea only—and even that received a different accent—not in the substance of the work itself. The chance events of human history had never particularly attracted Augustine; he left this theme to his pupil Orosius, with whom Otto is really more closely linked as a writer of history. Otto's division of history into three parts—*exortus, procursus, et debiti fines*—was taken over from Augustine; but Augustine had devoted to the *procursus* only a third of his narrative (*De civitate Dei*, books 15–18), and thereby restricted himself almost exclusively to depicting the first phase of the heavenly *civitas* named in his title. In contrast, Otto's true theme is the *progressus*:[63] it fills seven of the eight books, with the earthly *civitas* and its *regna* clearly in the foreground. Otto conceives the *civitates* as visible communities

---

[62]*Chronica sive Historia de duabus civitatibus*, ed. Adolf Hofmeister, MGH SS rer Germ (2nd ed. Hanover 1912), cited from this; on the title see Hofmeister, introduction x–xii. Edited by Walther Lammers, with German trans. by Adolf Schmidt, Freiherr vom Stein-Gedächtnisausgabe 16 (Darmstadt 1960); trans. Charles Christopher Mierow, *The Two Cities: A Chronicle of Universal History to the Year 1146 A.D., by Otto, Bishop of Freising* (New York 1928). The literature is extensive, especially in German; for a summary see now Wattenbach-Schmale (see Bibliographical Note) 1.48–55.

[63]Otto writes *progressus* (prologus to book 1 [9]) instead of Augustine's usual *procursus* or *excursus*. However, Otto does not mean a qualitative "progress" but—like Augustine—only a temporal progression.

and consequently can describe two separate *civitates*—the chosen people of the Old Testament and the Church of Christ on the one hand, and the heathen kingdoms on the other—only in the first three books; that is to say, up to the turning point under Constantine. With Constantine, or definitively with Theodosius, begins the history of the one *civitas Christi*, called *ecclesia* and embracing both *imperium* and *sacerdotium*—a *civitas permixta*, to be sure, combining both wheat and chaff. This means, however, that the two *civitates* were no longer a true subject of discussion since they no longer stood in opposition to each other—until the conflict between Henry IV and Gregory VII, when they again threatened to separate.[64]

Besides the image of the *civitas* we find other principles of theoretical order, based only in part on a chronological structure of world history. Again and again Otto deplores the *mutabilitas rerum*—from which, after all, the historian gets his material—as *miseriae mutationum;*[65] in long *exclamationes* he contrasts the changeable world of human miseries with the unchangeable heavenly goal. The books are divided primarily according to the low points in the history of human events: the destruction of Babylon, the death of Caesar, the end of the Roman Empire in the West, the collapse of the Frankish empire, and the death of Gregory VII. Otto recognizes various classifications of change: the coordination of the seven *aetates* with the days of Creation, with the Apocalyptic trumpets, or with the gifts of the Holy Spirit;[66] the three ages *ante gratiam, tempus gratiae, post praesentem vitam;*[67] and the four persecutions that mark the history of the Church ("cruenta sub tyrannis, fraudulenta hereticorum, ficta hypochritarum, ultima tam violenta quam fraudulenta fictaque sub Antichristo").[68] All this serves primarily to identify the end of the world as history's main objective. Earthly history is in turn presented as the history of the four universal empires and of the "transfers" (*translationes*) from one to the next. Otto of course was acquainted through Jerome with the visions of Daniel and their significance; but he observed history too closely to place much value on the quadripartite scheme. What is important is that the empires change, that the first empire in the East, Babylon, was the beginning and that Rome in the West is the end. They are the *potentissima regna;*[69] how one organizes the intervening empires of the Chaldeans, the Persians, the Medes, and the Greeks is a secondary problem, one which Otto solves inconsistently.[70] The element of change, the *translatio*, is more important than the number of *regna*. In the case of the first *translatio*, for instance, Otto sur-

---

[64]For Otto's chief references to the *civitates* in their historical manifestation see *Historia* (n. 62 above) 1.1 (38), 4.4 (188–90), 5 prologus (228), and 7 prologus (308–10).

[65]On the *miseriae mutationum* see e.g. *Historia* 1.5 (43), 1.32 (66), 2 prologus (67–68), 2.51 (128–29), 4.4 (189–90), and 4.31 (222–24).

[66]*Historia* 8.14 (411–12).

[67]*Historia* 8 prologus (391).

[68]*Historia* 8.1 (393).

[69]See Augustine, *De civ. Dei* 18.2.

[70]*Historia* (n. 62 above) 2.12–13 (80–82).

mounts the problem of several *regna* by assuming that the empire remains "in name" (*nomine*) with Babylon, but is transferred "in fact" (*re*) to the Chaldeans and "in authority" (*auctoritate*) to the Medes.[71] It is even more complicated when we reach the continuing Roman Empire: Constantine transferred only the *sedes regni* to the Greeks,[72] or else the empire was transferred *sub Romano nomine ad Graecos,*[73] and later *sub Romano nomine ad Francos.*[74] After the decline of the Franks the Roman Empire went to the Lombards (that is, Berengar and his successors) and to the Germans—or else back to the *teutonici Franci*. Thus, just as Babylon had once succumbed to the Medes and Chaldeans, Rome was now succumbing to inferior peoples, to Greeks and Franks.[75]

We sense Otto's efforts to preserve the theory of the *regna* without doing violence to the facts. The direction of movement, to be sure, is set; it goes from East to West, toward the end of time. But now, parallel to the *regna, sapientia* or *scientia* also moves from Babylon and the Chaldeans to Egypt, to the Greeks and the Romans, and most recently to Gaul and Spain in the far West.[76] Finally *religio* takes the same path, from the Egyptian monastic fathers to Gaul.[77]

The *translatio* of knowledge and wisdom to the far West, to Spain and Gaul, is evidenced by the names of Berengar (of Tours), Manegold (of Lautenbach), and Anselm (of Laon): they were the teachers of those Gallic teachers whose lectures Otto himself had heard. That the far West, the ends of the earth, had been reached indicated to Otto that the end of time was now also at hand. To be sure, he was more disturbed by the conflict between *regnum* and *sacerdotium* which was dividing the *ecclesia* and threatening to separate the *civitates*, united since Constantine; and not least troubling was the accompanying decline of the "Roman" Empire, ruled at the time by Otto's own brother, king Conrad, who was never to win the imperial title.[78] This point of view certainly shows no understanding for the multiplicity of European *regna*: they were marginal phenomena, not the representatives of universal history, even though their right to exist was in no way contested.

At the end of his seventh book Otto explains that the spiritual renovation of the much-subdivided monastic and religious orders is the only force that can still assure the survival of the morally fallen world.[79] The eighth book, with the continuation of history to its *debiti fines*, is modeled on the works of

[71]*Historia* 1.32 (66); cf. p. 13.
[72]*Historia* 4.5 (191). Cf. the inexact rendering, p. 10.
[73]*Historia* 5 prologus (227).
[74]*Historia* 5.31 (256–57); 5.36 (260–61).
[75]*Historia* 6.22 (285); cf. 1 prologus (7).
[76]*Historia* praefatio (8); 5 prologus (226–28).
[77]*Historia* 7.35 (372).
[78]Anxiety about the present permeates the entire book; it is especially apparent in the famous chapter 6.35 on the excommunication of Henry IV and in the following conclusion to book 6 and prologue to book 7 (304–10).
[79]*Historia* 7.34–35 (368–74).

theologians since Augustine; among the chroniclers only Bede had been courageous enough to draw the logical conclusion and to include in his narrative not only the beginning of universal history but also its end.[80]

No historical work before Otto (and very few after him) combined theoretical reflection and the narration of the actual course of events with such keen penetration. We have seen that his basic ideas were borrowed from Christian Antiquity, although they were independently reworked in accordance with the requirements of the material itself: unlike Augustine and Orosius, who wrote scarcely a century after the reconciliation of the Empire with the Church, he was writing more than eight hundred years after the event. Added to this, however, was his intensely personal experience of the historical present, his pessimism born from the conflict between *regnum* and *sacerdotium* as well as from the decline of the Empire in the war between the Staufer and Guelphs.

Whereas Sigebert's and Frutolf's works could at least be continued, if not enlarged upon, to continue Otto's *Historia* was scarcely conceivable. Indeed, he began anew when he wrote his *Gesta Friderici* in a more positive mood—despite the failure of the crusade—and even before the accession of his nephew, Frederick, whom he could afterwards celebrate as the bringer of peace.[81] The Hippocratic principle "better in the climb than on the summit"[82] could now serve as theoretical basis for an account that began with the low point reached under Henry IV and had as its object the ascent that became fully apparent under the youthful emperor Frederick I. But even in this work, whose subject is the *gesta imperatoris*, Otto wanted to do something for the philosophically inclined reader. For this reason he combined the judicial trials of theologians in France with the history of the emperor in an essentially superficial union of *res gestae* and *subtilitatis sublimitas*.[83] For the problem of universal history, the second work of the bishop of Freising, however instructive it may be as an example of *gesta*, offers no new point of view.

III. APOCALYPSE

No other historian of the twelfth century so imbued the stuff of world history with theology as Otto of Freising did. In spite of this, however, he remained a historian who took as his point of departure the historical (and in particular the political) facts, narrating, connecting, and interpreting them. But he and

---

[80]Bede, *Chronica* 68–71, ed. Theodor Mommsen, MGH AA 13.322–27.

[81]Otto, GF (see list of Abbreviations for this volume), cited from this; ed. Franz-Josef Schmale with German trans. by Adolf Schmidt, Freiherr vom Stein-Gedächtnisausgabe 17 (Darmstadt 1965); trans. Charles Christopher Mierow, *The Deeds of Frederick Barbarossa, by Otto of Freising and His Continuator Rahewin* (New York 1953). On this see Wattenbach-Schmale (see Bibliographical Note, below) 1.56–60, with bibliography.

[82]"Melius est ad summum quam in summa," GF 1.4 (16); Josef Koch, "Die Grundlagen der Geschichtsphilosophie Ottos von Freising," *Geschichtsdenken und Geschichtsbild im Mittelalter,* ed. Walther Lammers, Wege der Forschung 21 (Darmstadt 1965) 321–49.

[83]"Sic enim non solum hi, quibus rerum gestarum audiendi seriem inest voluptas, sed et illi, quos rationum amplius delectat subtilitatis sublimitas, ad eiusmodi legenda seu cognoscenda trahuntur." GF prologus (12); cf. Vergil, *Eclogue* 2.65: "trahit sua quemque voluptas."

other thinkers cannot be understood without taking theology into consideration. Even if early scholasticism proceeded from the habit of distinguishing, from dialectic, and strove toward systems that were not primarily historical in structure, the biblical, Augustinian view of salvation as an historical interaction between God and man was never lost and can be recognized even in the structure of Peter Lombard's *Sentences*. Every church offered pictorial representations of the principal stations on the way to human salvation: from the creation of Adam to the Incarnation as shown in the Annunciation to Mary, and from Christ's redemptive death on the Cross to the Last Judgment. In the twelfth century the question concerning the place of the present in the history of salvation was posed more emphatically than ever; to the point where Joachim of Fiore believed that the very end of the age initiated by the New Testament had been reached. We will begin with a look at two theologians of an earlier generation whose methodology was influential: abbot Rupert of Deutz (ca. 1070–1129) and Hugh of St Victor (ca. 1096–1141).

RUPERT OF DEUTZ

Rupert was the great exegete who brought the tradition together and deepened it through meditation; the "fondateur de la théologie biblique"[84] whose works were widely disseminated, especially in Germany, the Netherlands, and France. In recent scholarship Rupert, who made the ambitious claim that he was digging fountains in the field of Holy Scripture "with the plowshare of my own talent" (*proprii vomere ingenii*),[85] has been wrongly characterized as a conservative theologian. In spite of the fact that his method borrowed much from and continued earlier biblical scholarship, and as much as the new schools, especially in Laon, displeased him, he still dared to question the authority of Augustine and bravely defended his point of view against the masters of Laon even when he was threatened with a trial for heresy.[86]

---

[84]Ceslaus Spicq, *Esquisse d'une histoire de l'exégèse latine au moyen âge*, Bibliothèque thomiste 26 (Paris 1944) 117. Rupert's numerous works are printed in PL 167–70. Eight volumes of the new edition by Rhaban Haacke are now available: CCL cm 7, 9, 21–24, and 26, as well as *De victoria verbi Dei*, ed. Haacke, MGH Quellen zur Geistesgeschichte des Mittelalters 5 (Weimar 1970). Of the recent wealth of literature on Rupert the following may be mentioned: Mariano Magrassi, *Theologia e storia nel pensiero di Ruperto di Deutz* (Rome 1959); Horst Dieter Rauh, *Das Bild des Antichrist im Mittelalter: von Tyconius zum deutschen Symbolismus*, BGPTMA n.s. 9 (Münster 1973) 178–235; Herbert Grundmann, "Der Brand von Deutz 1128 in der Darstellung Abt Ruperts von Deutz," DA 22 (1966) 385–471. On the question whether Rupert wrote an early historical work see John Van Engen, "Rupert von Deutz und das sog. *Chronicon S. Laurentii Leodiensis*: Zur Geschichte des Investiturstreites in Lüttich," DA 35 (1979) 33–81; Van Engen is preparing a biography. On the wide dissemination of Rupert's writings see Rhaban Haacke, "Die Überlieferung der Schriften Ruperts von Deutz," DA 16 (1960) 397–436 and "Nachlese zur Überlieferung der Schriften Ruperts von Deutz," DA 26 (1970) 528–40. Rupert's influence on other 12th-c. authors has been little investigated. Gerhoch was certainly highly dependent on him, as were other South German 12th-c. authors; see Classen (n. 107 below) in the Index s.v. Rupert. But it is still uncertain whether Rupert influenced Hugh of St Victor, Bernard of Clairvaux, and other authors living in France.

[85]Dedication of the commentary on the Apocalypse to archbishop Frederick of Cologne, PL 169.825–26.

[86]Commentary on the *Regula S. Benedicti*, book 1, PL 170.492–98.

Nowhere in his writings does Rupert enter into a theoretical discussion of the historical interpretation of salvation, but it is taken for granted throughout his exegesis. Again and again his exegetical works address major theological themes; for instance, his commentary on St John's Gospel treats the Incarnation and the sacrament of the Eucharist.[87] Rupert's most comprehensive exegetical work, *De sancta trinitate et operibus suis,*[88] treats the greater part of the Bible, associating the Three Persons of the Trinity with the principal epochs of history: the Father with Creation, the Son with Redemption (which begins already with the expulsion from Paradise and culminates in the Incarnation), the Holy Spirit with the history of the Church. In the thirty-two books devoted to the Old Testament, for example, the exegesis of the Psalms establishes historical connections with David and the Books of Kings. Only one book deals with the Gospels, on which Rupert had written separate commentaries; the last nine books deal with the seven gifts of the Holy Spirit in descending order, and only at this point is the history of the Church included, in an allegorical exegesis of the Bible, its epochs organized in accordance with the seven gifts of the Holy Spirit:[89]

prudentia	the Passion
intellectus	Pentecost
consilium	the Gathering of the Apostles at Jerusalem, admission of the heathens
fortitudo	the Martyrs
scientia	the Doctors of the Church
pietas	the conversion of the Jews at the end of Time
timor	the Last Judgment

Typology traditionally establishes links between the Old and the New Testaments, but also between the Bible and the institutions, sacraments, and liturgy of the Church. Rupert, however, constructs a succession of epochs—though indeed he only manages to illuminate the early period on one side and the end of time on the other: the vast period between the patristic age and the present remains undifferentiated. Taking up where Rupert left off, Gerhoch of Reichersberg and Anselm of Havelberg went further along this path. In comparison, Rupert himself was very cautious in his interpretation of more recent Church history. His discussion of the liturgy, for example, recognizes typological relationships to the Bible and genetic explanations taken from the history of the Church,[90] but does not become involved with interpretations of the history of the Church as such or even with interpretations of the present.

[87]Rhaban Haacke, ed., CCL cm 9 (1969).
[88]Rhaban Haacke, ed., CCL cm 21–24 (1971–72).
[89]Synopsis of *De sancta Trinitate* 34.31, = *De operibus Spiritus Sancti*, 1.31, CCL cm 24.1860–61; details in the following books.
[90]For example, *De divinis officiis* 2.21, 5.16, 8.2, 9.5, ed. Rhaban Haacke, CCL cm 7 (1967) 50–52, 170, 263, 311–12.

HUGH OF ST VICTOR

Like the exegete Rupert of Deutz, the teacher and systematic theologian Hugh of St Victor also based his scheme of theology on a historical concept. Widely disseminated, his principal work, *De sacramentis*, is divided into two books, in analogy to the Holy Scriptures: one on the *opus conditionis*, the other on the *opus restaurationis*. The first runs *a principio mundi usque ad Incarnationem Verbi*, the second *ab Incarnatione Verbi usque ad finem et consummationem omnium*.[91] A glance at the systematic works from Abelard's theological treatises and Peter Lombard's *Sentences* to the *summae* of high scholasticism reveals how far from self-evident such a historical division is, in a work that seeks to represent the totality of Christian doctrine. It hardly does justice to Hugh's point of view, however, to maintain that Hugh the chronicler was an influence here on Hugh the scholastic.[92] Hugh was never a chronicler, even when he collected historical material. It served him as a basis for exegetical theology and for theology in general; for Hugh's systematic theology develops from his exegesis. His basic pedagogical work, the *Didascalicon*, thus argues emphatically that every hasty allegory must fail if it lacks a basis in historical exegesis. "The basis and beginning of the holy doctrine is history. . . . When you begin to build, first lay the historical foundation, then erect the spiritual structure through typological meaning into a citadel of the Faith, lastly decorate the building by painting it with glorious color, so to speak, through the grace of moral sense."[93] These are the rules of biblical exegesis which were pointedly directed against the arrogant despisers of history and of the literal or historical sense—against hasty and unreliable allegorical interpretation. "I do not believe that you can achieve perfect subtlety in allegory if you have not first found a basis in history. Do not despise this."[94] The diligent pursuit of small, seemingly unimportant and contingent matters precedes the erection of the lofty edifice. "Learn everything; you will see later that nothing is superfluous. Limited knowledge is unsatisfactory."[95]

Hugh intended his (still largely unpublished) work *De tribus maximis circumstantiis gestorum, id est personis, locis, temporibus* to be a great collection

[91]PL 176.173–618; cf. bibliography, cols. 173–74 and prologus 2, col. 183. Of the extensive literature on Hugh, especially noteworthy for our subject is Joachim Ehlers, *Hugo von St. Viktor: Studien zum Geschichtsdenken und zur Geschichtsschreibung des 12. Jahrhunderts* (Wiesbaden 1973).

[92]Cf. Martin Grabmann, *Die Geschichte der scholastischen Methode* (2 vols. Freiburg 1909–11; repr. Berlin 1956) 2.256, giving in general a very good introduction to Hugh's method.

[93]"Fundamentum autem et principium doctrinae sacrae historia est. . . . Aedificaturus ergo primum fundamentum historiae pone; deinde per significationem typicam in arcem fidei fabricam mentis erige; ad extremum vero per moralitatis gratiam quasi pulcherrimo superducto colore aedificium pinge." *Didascalicon* 6.3, PL 176.801C–D, and ed. Charles Henry Buttimer (Washington D.C. 1939) 116.

[94]"Neque ego te perfecte subtilem posse fieri puto in allegoria, nisi prius fundatus fueris in historia. Noli comtemnere minima haec!" *Didascalicon* 6.3, PL 176.799C, Buttimer 114.

[95]"Omnia disce, videbis postea nihil esse superfluum. Coarctata scientia iucunda non est." *Didascalicon* 6.3, PL 176.801A, Buttimer 115.

of historical material, which—though destined ultimately to serve theological allegory and morality—must initially be learned.[96] His program reads: "But we now have history in our hands, like a foundation of all learning that must first be imprinted on the memory."[97] The reader of this preamble then finds himself rather helplessly confronted by seventy-five closely written pages filled with lists of names and numbers—did Hugh really intend them all to be memorized? Not only are there curiosities such as the names of the seventy fathers who accompanied Jacob to Egypt (Gen. 46), but also the first attempt, to the best of my knowledge, at a synchronized table of the Merovingian kings residing in Soissons, Paris, Metz, and Orléans; the successions of Vandal, Visigothic, Lombard, and Norman rulers; and the up-to-date list of the emperors of Constantinople that Sigebert had not succeeded in compiling. The work thus evidences both a collector's zeal and assiduous research. To be sure, all this becomes history only when the three questions it deals with—by whom, where, and when (*a quibus, ubi, quando*)—are accompanied by a fourth, *quid gestum sit*, what happened, which in the *Didascalicon* appears as the first question of history.[98] In the last pages of his tabular synopsis Hugh does, it is true, include annual lists with dates from imperial and papal history, but this does not make him a chronicler.

It is Hugh's didactic and theological works and not this "chronicle" that make him one of the outstanding teachers of his century: the theory and practice of his allegorical and typological interpretation of the Church, its sacraments, institutions, and liturgy were widely disseminated and imitated. But unlike Rupert of Deutz, Hugh never thought of articulating the history of the post-Pentecostal Church according to typologically determined periods.

ANSELM OF HAVELBERG

In his *Liber de una forma credendi et multiformitate vivendi*, which introduces his dialogue with the Greeks written in 1151,[99] bishop Anselm of Havelberg

[96]The introduction is found in William M. Green, "Hugo of St. Victor, *De tribus maximis circumstantiis gestorum,*" *Speculum* 18 (1943) 484–93; part of the text ed. Georg Waitz, MGH SS 24 (1879) 90–97; I have used BN lat 15009 fols. 1–40. See Ehlers (n. 91 above) 53–55; Grover A. Zinn, Jr., "Hugh of Saint Victor and the Art of Memory," *Viator* 5 (1974) 211–34.

[97]"Sed nos hystoriam nunc in manibus habemus, quasi fundamentum omnis doctrinae primum in memoria collocandum," Green (n. 96 above) 491. This is preceded by statements on the value of memory and the technique of memorizing, and is followed by a rationalization for the tabular brevity of the ensuing work: that way the material can be learned by heart!

[98]*Didascalicon* 6.3, PL 176.799, Buttimer (n. 93 above) 114. Here *negotium* is discussed in addition to *persona, tempus,* and *locus.*

[99]The work, entitled *Anticimenon* (ἀντικείμενον), still must be used in the edition of PL 188.1117–1248; text of the first book, with French translation and short commentary, ed. Gaston Salet, *Anselme de Havelberg, Dialogues, Livre 1: Renouveau dans L'Eglise,* Sources chrétiennes 118 (Paris 1966). On the preparation of a new edition see Johann Wilhelm Braun, "Studien zur Überlieferung der Werke Anselms von Havelberg, I: Die Überlieferung des Anticimenon," DA 28 (1972) 133–209, where the important recent literature is cited (134 n. 3), including Kurt Fina, "Anselm von Havelberg," *Analecta Praemonstratensia* 32 (1956) 69–101, 33 (1957) 5–39

(ca. 1095–1158) sought to prove that the diverse styles of life among the
religious orders, especially the new ones, did not contradict the unity of the
faith and consequently did not split the Church but rather enriched it. This
gave him a basis for his discourse with the Greeks, whose deviations from the
forms of the Latin Church created no obstacles, Anselm believed, to a unified
faith. He justified the "innovations that enter in everywhere in the course of
time"[100] by pointing to the advances made by the faith in Old Testament
times, especially in the great *transpositiones* from idolatry to the Law, and
from the Law to the Gospel.[101] "The wisdom of God gradually brought about
a great change. . . . By removing, transforming, and organizing little by little,
it furtively, as it were (*quasi furtim*), led away pedagogically and medicinally
(*paedagogice et medicinaliter*) from idolatry to the Law, and from the Law,
which, after all, did not yet create perfection, to the perfection of the
Gospel."[102] Now, these sentences were taken verbatim from Gregory of Nazianzus's *Orationes theologicae,*[103] which Anselm also used in other parts of
his work; but so far scholars have not been able to determine which Latin
translation was available to him.

The education of mankind continued after the Pentecost. The Old Testament had presented the Father overtly, the Son in veiled form; the New Testament revealed the Son and intimated the divinity of the Holy Spirit.
This pattern continues throughout the history of the Church: "Afterward the
Holy Spirit is preached, bestowing upon us a clearer manifestation of its God-
liness."[104] However, Anselm does not expect this revelation of the
Spirit—which goes beyond the New Testament—in the future but recognizes
it in the past history of the Church. Using the images of the seven seals and the
four Horsemen of the Apocalypse, he interprets the epochs of mankind: the
white horse represents Christ and the first growth of the Church, the red horse

---

and 268–301, and 34 (1958) 13–41; Wilhelm Berges, "Anselm von Havelberg in der Geistesgeschichte des 12. Jahrhunderts," *Jahrbuch für die Geschichte Mittel- und Ostdeutschlands* 5 (1956)
39–57; and the titles given in n. 103 below. For a survey of Anselm's life and works see now
Johann Wilhelm Braun in *Die deutsche Literatur des Mittelalters: Verfasserlexikon* 1, ed. Kurt
Ruh et al. (2nd ed. Berlin 1978) 384–91.

[100]"Novitates passim ubique per successiones temporum," *Liber de una forma* prologus, PL
188.1141B–42A. Polemics against *novitates* were also popular in the 12th c. in reference to 1 Tim.
6:20, "devitans profanas vocum novitates."

[101]"Duae transpositiones factae sunt . . . ab idolis ad legem . . . a lege ad Evangelium,"
Liber de una forma 1.5, PL 188.1147B.

[102]"Divina sapientia tanta varietate paulatim usa est . . . ; paulatim subtrahendo, et
transponendo, et dispensando, quasi furtim ab idolorum cultura ad legem, a lege autem, quae
quidem ad perfectum non duxit, ad perfectionem Evangelii paedagogice et medicinaliter
deduxit," *Liber de una forma* 1.5, PL 188.1147C–D.

[103]Established by M. van Lee, "Les idées d'Anselme de Havelberg sur le développement des
dogmes," *Analecta Praemonstratensia* 14 (1938) 5–35. On this see Salet (n. 99 above) 58; Amos
Funkenstein, *Heilsplan und natürliche Entwicklung: Formen der Gegenwartsbestimmung im Geschichtsdenken des hohen Mittelalters* (Munich 1965) 65–67, 183–86.

[104]"Praedicatur postea Spiritus sanctus, apertiorem nobis tribuens suae Deitatis manifesta-
tionem," *Liber de una forma* 1.6, PL 188.1147D–48A.

the era of the martyrs, the black that of the heretics, and the dun-colored that of the hypocrites. The Church survived each of these three crises and in the process not only grew outwardly but gained *patientia, sapientia,* and *tolerantia.* Anselm associates the fifth seal with an indeterminate time of waiting, the sixth with the Antichrist, the seventh with the end of the world, and an eighth with eternal bliss.[105]

The unfolding of the Spirit and the progress of the Church down to the present and beyond—these are novel ideas that contrast sharply with the almost contemporaneously expressed fears of the bishop of Freising; common to both is the positive evaluation of the diversity of religious orders in present times. But Anselm's work seems to have aroused little interest: his manuscripts began to be copied only in the fifteenth century.[106]

GERHOCH OF REICHERSBERG

A few words about Gerhoch, the willful, prolific provost of Reichersberg (1093–1169), must suffice.[107] He tried to force the whole world to lead a regulated monastic life and fought stubborn battles with the new French schools, especially with Abelard and Gilbert but also with Peter Lombard. In this connection his talent for historical and philological criticism is particularly noteworthy: entirely for polemical reasons he managed to distinguish the Ambrosiaster (so called since Erasmus) from St Ambrose;[108] to interpret correctly from their context disputed passages in Hilary, which were quoted from collections of sentences;[109] and, by consulting his *codices emendatiores,* to correct an Augustinian text that Peter Lombard had quoted as incorrectly as had all those before and after him who relied on such collections—from Alger of Liège and Ivo of Chartres to Gratian and Thomas Aquinas.[110]

Gerhoch's theology of history depended on Rupert for its methodology and for many of its details. Rupert's division of Church history into seven periods is repeated in Gerhoch's *Libellus de ordine donorum Spiritus sancti* (1142) with a more concise, and above all more incisive, emphasis on the present.[111] His last work, written in 1167, is based on a four-part typological division in accordance with the four vigils of Matthew 14:25.[112] It recognizes four

[105]*Liber de una forma* 1.6–12, PL 188.1148–60.

[106]See Braun, "Studien" (n. 99 above) 136–37.

[107]On Gerhoch and his work see: Erich Meuthen, *Kirche und Heilsgeschichte bei Gerhoh von Reichersberg* (Leiden 1959); Damien van den Eynde, *L'oeuvre littéraire de Géroch de Reichersberg* (Rome 1957); Peter Classen, *Gerhoch von Reichersberg: Eine Biographie mit einem Anhang über die Quellen, ihre handschriftliche Überlieferung und ihre Chronologie* (Wiesbaden 1960).

[108]Classen (n. 107 above) 94–96.

[109]Ibid. 173.

[110]Ibid. 173, 261–62.

[111]*Gerhohi praepositi Reichersbergensis opera inedita,* ed. Damien and Odulphe van den Eynde and Angelin Rijmersdael (2 vols. in 3 Rome 1955–56) 1.63–165; interpretations are found in Meuthen (n. 107 above) 120–30 and Classen (n. 107 above) 108–14.

[112]*De quarta vigilia noctis,* ed. Ernst Sackur, MGH LdL 3.503–25; on this see Classen (n. 107 above) 292–97.

Antichrists, as had Otto of Freising before him.[113] In complete contrast to Anselm, but in agreement with Rupert—and in part with Otto—Gerhoch sees a decline in the Church, rather than progress, from early Christianity to the present. Most important for our discussion is his work on the detection of the Antichrist (1160–62).[114] Here Gerhoch primarily tries to show that all biblical predictions about the Antichrist *might* be considered as already fulfilled and that we have to reckon today, without any further precursors, with the Second Coming and the Last Judgment.[115] Of course, Gerhoch does not maintain that the predictions *have* been fulfilled; he is interested only in offering an interpretation—based on a comparison of scriptural evidence with the history of the Church—that could be correct but does not claim to be the only possible one. The important thing is man's readiness here and now for the end. Gerhoch's method consists in comparing the biblical prophecies with history, in particular the history of the preceding century with Henry IV, who is conceived in apocalyptic terms.

The book on the Antichrist offers the most concentrated example of an exegetical method that Gerhoch applies throughout his writings: allegorical-typological and moral exegesis relating the history of the Church, and particularly its most recent phases, to the Bible. Thus the Bible becomes the instrument for a criticism of his own time. In the second book of *De investigatione Antichristi*, moreover, Gerhoch devises two great systems of typological triads, the first dealing with Christ as *via, veritas*, and *vita*, and the second with the Persons of the Trinity. He concludes with a discussion of the divine verdicts pronounced *ante legem, post legem*, and *sub gratia*. In the first of these periods the Father passes judgment with the Flood, the Son with the confusion of languages, and the Holy Spirit with the burning of Sodom; in the period *sub lege* the Father judges the Egyptians in the Red Sea, the Son judges Israel through its partition, and the Holy Spirit judges Jerusalem through its captivity. Finally, in the period *sub gratia*, the Father judges the persecutors of the Church and the Son the heretics. All this lies in the past. Gerhoch does not mention the judgment of the Holy Spirit, but his system demands the expectation in the near future of such a judgment over the contemporary unclean Church of the simoniacs—apparently, he did not dare to express his anticipation of an approaching judgment of the Spirit.[116] The association of the

---

[113]See above at n. 68.

[114]Franz Scheibelberger, ed., *Gerhohi Reichersbergensis praepositi opera hactenus inedita*, vol. 1: *De investigatione Antichristi* (Linz 1875); book 1 only, ed. Ernst Sackur, MGH LdL 3.305–95.

[115]*De investigatione Antichristi* 1, praefatio, MGH LdL 3.307–08; see Classen (n. 107 above) 222–23, 228–29, in part interpreted differently from Rauh (n. 84 above) 446–67, who gives no evidence for his opinion (448) that Gerhoch expected a personal Antichrist.

[116]*De investigatione Antichristi* 2 and 3 passim, ed. Scheibelberger (n. 114 above) 186–373; the conclusion of the work either has not survived or was never written. Most important to our discussion are the chapters on the judgments, 2.29–30 and 3.3–7; on this see Classen (n. 107 above) 229–34.

judgments with the Persons of the Trinity is abandoned in Gerhoch's late work on the vigils. Here he presents a quaternary rhythm; but here too it is evident that while the schism continues Gerhoch expects no earthly improvement or help for the Church, but only the end and the conquest of Christ's enemies through his return.[117]

JOACHIM OF FIORE

Gerhoch's ideas were not widely influential, but they show how allegorical and typological interpretations of history could serve the criticism of present times, help to determine the place of the present, and indicate the future. With his anticipation of a judgment by the Spirit—and with the help of a similar methodology—Gerhoch came closer than any other theologian to the conclusions drawn by Joachim of Fiore. Unlike Joachim's, however, his picture of history remains unqualifiedly Christocentric.

Haskins did not mention Joachim of Fiore, who represents an area until his time studied only, if at all, by theologians.[118] And yet Joachim's influence on the future was like that of no other author of the twelfth century. He has been acclaimed as a prophet of religious movements and eschatological, revolutionary visionaries; and even in our own century—or, rather, once again—he has been alluded to as the herald and "leader" of a mystical "third empire"[119] on the one hand and the discoverer of a "new law" of revolution on the other.[120] This history of Joachimism, important and rich in conse-

---

[117]See n. 112 above.

[118]In this context we can take only a brief look at Joachim's principal works: *Concordia Novi ac Veteris Testamenti* (Venice 1519), *Expositio in Apocalypsim* (with *liber introductorius*) (Venice 1527), and *Psalterium decem cordarum* (Venice 1527), all reprinted (3 vols. Frankfurt 1964–65); cited according to the pagination of this edition. The *Liber figurarum* must be omitted here.

Modern Joachim scholarship began with a book published in the same year as Haskins's *Ren*: the dissertation by Herbert Grundmann, *Studien über Joachim von Fiore*, Beiträge zur Kulturgeschichte des Mittelalters und der Renaissance 32 (Leipzig 1927; repr. Darmstadt 1966). Only a few titles from the vast literature will be cited: Ernst Benz, *Ecclesia spiritualis: Kirchenidee und Geschichtstheologie der franziskanischen Reformation* (Stuttgart 1934); Herbert Grundmann, *Ausgewählte Aufsätze* (n. 14 above) vol. 2, *Joachim von Fiore*; Marjorie Reeves, *The Influence of Prophecy in the Later Middle Ages: A Study in Joachimism* (Oxford 1969); Delno C. West, ed., *Joachim of Fiore in Christian Thought: Essays on the Influence of the Calabrian Prophet* (2 vols. New York 1975); Bernhard Töpfer, *Das kommende Reich des Friedens: Zur Entwicklung chiliastischer Zukunftshoffnungen im Hochmittelalter* (Berlin 1964) 48–103. The change in direction in modern scholarship initiated by Grundmann's dissertation is partially responsible for the present paper's divergence of approach from that of Haskins's comparable chapter.

[119]"Joachim ist sich durchaus bewusst, dass er selber in der Linie Benedikt-Bernhard und des kommenden Dux, des geistigen Führers der neuen Zeit, in der Vorbereitungszeit des dritten Reiches steht." Alois Dempf, *Sacrum Imperium: Geschichts- und Staatsphilosophie des Mittelalters und der politischen Renaissance* (Munich 1929) 271, without reference to sources. Dempf consistently translates *status* as "Reich." Joachim mentions the *novus dux* who will appear in the coming 42nd generation in reference to Apoc. 7:2 (*Concordia* 4.31 [n. 118 above] fol. 56b), without giving special or repeated emphasis to this idea.

[120]Eugen Rosenstock-Huessy, *Die europäischen Revolutionen und der Charakter der Nationen* (Stuttgart 1951) 21: "Joachim de Fiore hat mit seiner Lehre vom Weltalter nachkirchlicher Erfüllung einfach recht. Er hat das neue Gesetz, dessen letzter Vollstrecker Lenin hat werden

quences though it is, lies outside the scope of our discussion, for it begins only decades after Joachim's death (about 1240) and bears a highly ambivalent and not easily perceived relationship to Joachim himself.

Joachim worked with a method of typological exegesis that does not differ in principle from those of Rupert, Anselm, and Gerhoch. Whether he was directly inspired by one of these, or by other theological interpreters of history, has so far not been established with any certainty. The only author—indeed, the only twelfth-century figure of historical importance—whom he mentions specifically by name and with emphasis is Bernard of Clairvaux,[121] not, however, as an exegete or theologian but as an outstanding leader of monasticism.

Joachim's advance over his predecessors lies in his having systematically extended typology beyond the New Testament to the history of the Church after Pentecost, an extension only intimated by Rupert and expanded upon by Anselm and especially by Gerhoch. In general, Joachim built his typological edifice in a more consistent and methodical manner than did the earlier exegetes, ultimately serving a single, often-revised and repeated idea: the doctrine of the three "conditions" or *status*, which in the long run only derives its meaning and fulfillment from the expectation of the third *status*.[122]

No one in the twelfth century was so vividly aware of the impending end as Joachim. To be sure, he expected not the end of the world but the end of the present *status*.[123] Hugh of St Victor had spoken of various *status* of mankind before and after the Fall and before and after Redemption;[124] Anselm of Havelberg, of the *status ecclesiae*;[125] and Otto of Freising, of the *status civitatis*.[126] Joachim speaks of *status mundi* or simply *status*. The triad is derived from the Trinity and is a principle immanent in the deity and all its creation. Joachim tries again and again to reveal the typological concordance of the first two *status*. Not only does he discover the rhythm of the forty-two generations in the first *status* (from Abraham to John the Baptist or Christ) and in

---

müssen, erkannt. Er hat dabei die erste Revolution notwendig mit dem ganzen Jahrtausend revolutionärer Dialektik identifiziert. . . . Neben seiner grossen Geistestat verblasst der moderne Streit über den Beginn der Renaissance."

[121]*Concordia* 4.38 (n. 118 above) fols. 58d–59c. The analysis of the separate generations (4.21–23, fol. 53b–c) is of course also accompanied by references to the popes of the 12th c. as the representatives of generations 38 to 40, but they are conspicuously brief.

[122]The principal places where the *status* doctrine is summarized are *Concordia* 2.1.4–5 (fol. 8a–d), 5.84 (fol. 112a–d), and *Intro. in Apoc.* 5 (n. 118 above) fols. 5b–6b.

[123]This has rightly been emphasized by Grundmann (n. 118 above) 56–59 and passim. One should not overlook the fact that the third *status* is apparently something quite different from the "world" experienced so far and that even Joachim occasionally moves the end of the world very near to the transition to the third *status*, e.g. at the place quoted in n. 134 below.

[124]E.g., *De arca Noe mystica*, PL 176.684–86, and *De sacramentis* 1.8.11, PL 176.313.

[125]In the *Anticimenon*, 1.6–13, PL 188.1148–59, Anselm divides the history of the Church into seven successive *status*.

[126]E.g., *Historia* (n. 62 above) book 4 prologue (183); 4.4 (189), summary discussion of the *civitas Christi* and *civitas perversa* in each of three successive *status: ante gratiam, sub gratia, post praesentem vitam*; book 8 prologue (390–91).

the second (every thirty years from Christ to about 1260)—each *status* preceded by a period of preparation that causes the two to overlap and the second to overlap the anticipated third—but he also compares each generation in the first and second *status*.[127] There are other divisions besides, related to the seven days of Creation, the trumpets of the Apocalypse, and other images.[128] But the temporal typologies are carried through only in the two-part cycle of the first two *status*; they extend to the third *status* only insofar as they apply to the preparatory period initiated by Benedict of Nursia.

The third *status* anticipated by Joachim was to begin, according to the law of numbers, after the forty-second, thirty-year generation, that is, in the year 1260. But Joachim repeatedly gives reasons for combining the last three generations and thus for expecting the new *status* to begin in the forty-first generation, about the year 1200: the change was at hand, even if an exact computation of the time was not possible.[129] The third *status* relates to the Holy Spirit. Following the *coniugati* of the first and the *clerici* of the second, the *monachi* have preeminent standing in the third.[130] This *status* would begin after the *plenitudo gentium* (*et conversio Israel*) had brought the present (second) *status* to a close as foretold by Paul (Rom. 11:25–26).[131] Above all, true understanding, *spiritualis intelligentia*, not one bound to the letter of the Scriptures, was to reveal God to mankind—which, however, was not to entail a change in doctrine or an advance in faith.

In all of this, Joachim tells us nothing about the temporal passage of the third *status*. Whereas the typological relationships in the history of the first two *status* are discussed in great detail, the actual duration of the third—which had to begin at the latest in 1260—is never even hinted at. One may well ask if changes, history, generations, states, organized Church, or sacraments will then exist at all.[132] Does Joachim believe that this *status* will not endure for

---

[127]*Concordia*, book 4 (n. 118 above) fols. 42d–53c.

[128]*Concordia* 3.2.1–7 (fols. 39a–42a), and often in *Expositio in Apocalypsim* (n. 118 above).

[129]*Intro. in Apoc.* 7 (fol. 9c), *Expos. in Apoc.* (fol. 57c), and *Concordia* 4.31 and 33 (fol. 56b–d), 5.20 (fol. 70a–b), and passim.

[130]*Concordia* 2.2.5 (fol. 21c), 4.33 (fol. 56d), and passim.

[131]*Intro. in Apoc.* 5 (fol. 6b). The conversion of the Jews is one of the biblical prerequisites for the end of the world which became part of the medieval literature on the Apocalypse and the Antichrist. Cf. the place in Rupert cited in n. 89 above.

[132]The debate over this question was prompted by Grundmann (n. 118 above) 113–18 and later was stimulated especially by the discovery of the *Liber figurarum*. See the detailed discussion by Töpfer (n. 118 above) 52–81 with the conclusion (80) that the third *status* "is a monastic Church, blessed by a degree of understanding surpassing everything that came before, in which there is no longer any papacy and probably also no clergy, and in which the hermits hold the leading position . . ." ("eine mit allem alles Bisherige übertreffenden Erkenntnisgrad begnadete Mönchskirche, in der es kein Papsttum und wohl auch keinen Klerus mehr gibt und in der Eremiten die führende Stellung innehaben"). Peace and justice will reign, the power of the state will vanish altogether, etc. At issue is also whether, according to Joachim, marriage—and consequently the natural propagation of mankind—will still exist. In various works Marjorie Reeves has accepted as Joachim's image of the third *status* a purely spiritual change without direct consequences for the institutions of the Church, e.g. *Prophecy in the Later Middle Ages* (n. 118 above) 126–32.

any appreciable length of time,[133] or has the category of time and history lost its relevance in this perfect state? Joachim's basic concept is not *aetas* but *status*, which is independent of time. At any rate, the final end of the world—the *consummatio seculi*—and the *vera contemplatio* will only come after the third *status*.

"One must change one's life, because the *status mundi* will inevitably change, so that after the journey through the desert, as it were, we can attain to that godly rest which those who do not believe the teachers and claim that anyone who speaks of the end of the world is totally mad do not deserve to enter."[134] The coming of the third *status* certainly does not mean a revolution. When Joachim demands a change in one's life he means a personal, spiritual consecration, which he expects his monks of Fiore to carry out more strictly than was usual in the Cistercian Order. For the law of history is not determined by mankind but by God; mankind becomes aware of it, can recognize it perhaps through a study of the Scriptures, but can in no sense control it.[135]

We have been able to give only a few examples of historical thought and writing in the twelfth century. In retrospect, the reader may be particularly struck by the omission of the history of the crusades. Almost every historian and theologian mentioned here probably in one way or another included in his thought and writings the collective experience of western Christendom struggling to free the Holy Sepulchre. Not only did it open new dimensions in *gesta*, in war, and in adventures undertaken for a holy cause, but suddenly Christians could feel themselves, in a way previously unknown, to be the representatives and executors of divine action in history. Any disappointments or setbacks they experienced were rationalized as punishment for sins. Strange lands were described with amazement; but only slowly and much later were men's eyes opened to the peculiar character of distant countries and people of a different faith through the historiography of the crusades. The adventures of Alexander the Great may have particularly inspired some poets of the age of the crusades, but in the last analysis this merely heroic conqueror of distant lands remains completely foreign to the protagonists of the concept of waging war by God's orders for the Holy Sepulchre and Holy City. It is precisely the crusades which show most clearly how far removed the twelfth century was from Antiquity— even from Christian Antiquity.

[133]Thus, I think correctly, Töpfer (n. 118 above) 83–88.

[134]"Oportet ergo mutare vitam, quia mutari necesse est statum mundi, ut quasi per transitum deserti perveniamus ad illam requiem Dei nostri, quam intrare non sunt digni, qui non credunt dicentibus [*read* docentibus?], qui loquentes de fine mundi putant omnino deinsanire," *Concordia* 2.2.5 (n. 118 above) fol. 21c.

[135]The difference between *oportet* and *necesse est* in the preceding note should be heeded: one means man's obligation, especially the monk's, the other the divine law of history, which is not in human hands.

Let us look back, therefore, and ask once again, summarily, about the motifs of a "renaissance." Throughout the literature surveyed here—with the sole exception of the histories of the communes—the tradition of Antiquity lives on. It may sometimes grow stronger but it never differs essentially from what it had been in the eleventh century. Rome was the model for cities; the Roman Empire was the bearer of universal history; and Cicero, Sallust, Suetonius, Vergil, Ovid, and Lucan were the much-read, often-cited models for literary style. All this and much more does not, essentially, take us beyond the previous century. When a relationship to Antiquity was consciously established, it was always to Christian Antiquity, which offered continuity and models. Eusebius—as he was transmitted to the histories of the Church and to world chronicles through Rufinus and Jerome—Orosius and Cassiodorus, Augustine and Bede were the literary predecessors and true teachers of our writers, historians as well as theologians. The humanism of the fourteenth and fifteenth centuries has been explained as a return to Jerome and Augustine;[136] this cannot be discussed here, but certainly twelfth-century historical thought grew up entirely on the ground plowed by Augustine, and historical narrative writing remained equally close to him. Only that Italian city historiography which was written by laymen for laymen, totally in the service of the political present and future, is different in character, and precisely in this respect it is remarkably reminiscent of early Roman historiography.

Bibliographical Note

The writing and the interpretation of history have seldom been undertaken by the same person. As a result, medieval historical writing and the interpretation of medieval history have consistently been treated in different books, even though in more recent years not only theologians (and philosophers) but historians as well have concerned themselves with theological views of history. Since the imaginative but problematic work of the philosopher Alois Dempf, *Sacrum Imperium: Geschichts- und Staatsphilosophie des Mittelalters und der politischen Renaissance* (Munich 1929; 2nd ed. Darmstadt 1954), which spans the long period from early Christian times to the sixteenth century and focuses primarily on the Empire as the bearer of history, only one book on the twelfth century has appeared, to the best of my knowledge, that consciously compares theologians and historians: Johannes Spörl, *Grundformen hochmittelalterlicher Geschichtsanschauung: Studien zum Weltbild der Geschichtsschreiber des 12. Jahrhunderts* (Munich 1935). Spörl devotes one chapter each to Anselm of Havelberg (under the title "Entwicklungsgedanke"), Otto of Freising ("Reichsmetaphysik"), Orderic Vitalis ("Nationalstaat"), and John of Salisbury ("Humanismus und Naturalismus"). Under the general title "Aspects of the European Tradition of Historical Writing," Richard W. Southern's presidential addresses to the Royal Historical Society form a series of short but valuable essays on conceptions of history and historiography: "The Classical Tradition from Einhard to Geoffrey of Mon-

---

[136]Giuseppe Toffanin, *Geschichte des Humanismus*, trans. Lili Sertorius (Amsterdam 1941) of *Storia del umanesimo* (Naples 1933).

mouth," TRHS 5th ser. 20 (1970) 173–96; "Hugh of St Victor and the Idea of Historical Development," 21 (1971) 159–79; "History as Prophecy," 22 (1972) 159–80; and "The Sense of the Past," 23 (1973) 243–63.

The literature on medieval historiography is vast, but to date almost no one has dared to present all the available material as a related whole. The only attempt at a comprehensive picture known to me is volume 1 of the American historian James Westfall Thompson's *A History of Historical Writing* (2 vols. New York 1942). Herbert Grundmann presents a brief but thorough survey, well worth reading: *Geschichtsschreibung im Mittelalter: Gattungen, Epochen, Eigenart* (2nd ed. Göttingen 1965). In 1853 the Gesellschaft der Wissenschaften zu Göttingen arranged a competition for a critical history of historiography in Germany. The prize was won by Wilhelm Wattenbach, the successive revised editions of whose book (which first appeared in 1858) are still today the foundation for any study of German medieval historiography. His book includes valuable chapters on Italy, England, France, and other neighbors of the Holy Roman Empire, but it is an introduction to the historical sources rather than a history of historiography, as Wattenbach was well aware. The following are now standard for the twelfth century: Wilhelm Wattenbach and Robert Holtzmann, *Deutschlands Geschichtsquellen im Mittelalter: Die Zeit der Sachsen und Salier*, new ed. Franz-Josef Schmale, volumes 2 (Darmstadt 1967, unrevised repr. of nos. 3 and 4, which first appeared in 1940–43) and 3 (Darmstadt 1971, containing supplements to the earlier volumes, as well as chapters on Italy and England); Wilhelm Wattenbach and Franz-Josef Schmale, *Deutschlands Geschichtsquellen im Mittelalter: Vom Tode Kaiser Heinrichs V. bis zum Ende des Interregnums* 1 (Darmstadt 1976); volume 2, in preparation, will contain chapters on the neighboring countries and Lower Lorraine. Besides these studies of source material it is useful to consult Manitius, volume 3, which offers a wealth of relevant material from all over Europe. An extremely helpful, complete survey of English historiography that has appeared in recent years is Antonia Gransden's *Historical Writing in England c. 550 to c. 1307* (London 1974), a work which can be compared in some respects to Wattenbach's. The author writes (p. xi): "My approach to each author is pragmatic, not theoretical." One of the more prominent works dealing with specific forms of historiography is Anna-Dorothee von den Brincken's valuable study of universal history: *Studien zur lateinischen Weltchronistik bis in das Zeitalter Ottos von Freising* (diss. Münster; Düsseldorf 1957).

Among authors who have written about the interpretation of history should be mentioned in particular the notable philosopher Karl Löwith, *Meaning in History* (Chicago 1949; German ed. *Weltgeschichte und Heilsgeschehen*, Stuttgart 1953), who begins with Burckhardt, Marx, and Hegel, then takes us back to Joachim, Augustine, and Orosius. A selection of more recent essays on medieval historical thought by various authors is found in *Geschichtsdenken und Geschichtsbild im Mittelalter*, ed. Walther Lammers, Wege der Forschung 21 (Darmstadt 1961). The early Christian origins and medieval influence of the theological doctrine of the ages of the world have been investigated by Roderich Schmidt in "*Aetates mundi*: Die Weltalter als Gliederungsprinzip der Geschichte," *Zeitschrift für Kirchengeschichte* 67 (1955–56) 288–317. For the theological interpreters of history prior to Joachim of Fiore who focused their attention on the end of the world, see Wilhelm Kamlah's *Apokalypse und Geschichtstheologie: Die mittelalterliche Auslegung der Apokalypse vor Joachim von Fiore*, Historische Studien 285 (Berlin 1935) and Horst Dieter Rauh's *Das Bild des Antichrist im Mittelalter: Von Tyconius zum deutschen Symbolismus*, BGPTMA n.s. 9 (2nd ed. Münster 1979), which, despite its title, is overwhelmingly devoted to the German theologians of the twelfth century. Bernhard Töpfer's *Das kommende Reich des Friedens: Zur Entwicklung chiliastischer Zukunftshoffnungen im Hochmittelalter* (Berlin 1964) is an historical study of the social and political implications of chiliastic expectations. In his introduction Töpfer discusses the twelfth century, but the main stress of his book is on Joachim and the time following. A brilliant but difficult book concerning the theological and philosophical place of the present in the works of medieval theologians and historians is Amos Funkenstein's *Heilsplan und natürliche Entwicklung: Formen der Gegenwartsbestimmung im Geschichtsdenken des hohen Mittelalters* (Munich 1965); of primary relevance to our subject are its sections dealing with Frutolf, Otto of Freising, and Anselm of Havelberg.

From the abundant literature available on individual writers and problems only a few titles of particular importance to the present study have been cited in the notes.

V

PHILOSOPHY AND SCIENCE

Translations and Translators

Marie-Thérèse d'Alverny

One of Haskins's most important contributions to the advancement of medieval studies was his series of articles collected under the title *Studies in the History of Mediaeval Science*.[1] Several chapters were devoted to the translations from Greek and Arabic executed in the twelfth century and the first half of the thirteenth, and to the translators themselves. Even in chapters apparently concerning other topics, translations and translators reappeared in the text or footnotes; furthermore, notwithstanding the title of the book, Haskins had noted not only the scientific translations but also versions of texts related to philosophy and theology. He had realized the impact of translations on the development of learning during that period, and he endeavored to set them in their historical background.

It was an arduous task. Many texts were either unpublished or carelessly edited, and good catalogues of manuscripts were few. Haskins had the spirit of a discoverer, as befits a good historian, and spared no pains as he patiently investigated many European libraries, examining manuscripts, transcribing relevant data and extracts, and trying to collect evidence on the translators. In his articles he often reproduced the prefaces in which the translators—conscious that they were offering precious gems from Eastern treasures to the poor Western scholars—explained their aims and motives and sometimes gave details concerning the circumstances under which they worked. Although he found little biographical information, he could easily recognize that the favorable places and milieux for translations were Italy and Constantinople for Greek, Spain and the Latin kingdom of the crusaders for Arabic, Sicily for both. A final task was to try to follow the track of the translations as they penetrated among Western European scholars.

So, when he came to write a chapter on translations for his *Renaissance of the Twelfth Century*,[2] Haskins could draw a synthetic picture of one of the most typical elements of twelfth-century culture. This picture could not—as it still cannot—be complete, but he was able to draw a fairly clear outline. It is characteristic of Haskins's point of view that the title of his chapter dedicated

[1] Cambridge Mass. 1924; 2nd ed. 1927; repr. 1960.
[2] Chapter 9, "The Translators from Greek and Arabic" (278–302).

to the foreign sources of intellectual life was "The Translators." The translators were conscious instruments of the recovery of Greek science, with its Arabic additions, and of much of Greek philosophy; in this sense, they were active participants in and even initiators of a "renaissance." In their prefaces or dedications, the translators usually stress that the text they offer either is the work of a famous man of Antiquity or can be considered a commentary on or enlargement of such a work. The desire to recover Plato, Aristotle, Euclid, Galen, and Ptolemy was the main incentive that provoked the flood of translations from Greek and Arabic into Latin. The "Arabic additions," important as they might be, were frequently presented as commentaries derived from the main stream of Greek ancestors. The Arabic medical treatises were dependent on Galenic teaching; Arabic astronomy and astrology relied on Ptolemy, even when his theories were disputed.

THE FORERUNNERS

These intentions were already expressed by the great initiators of the translation movement, in the second half of the eleventh century: Constantine the African and his contemporary, archbishop Alfanus of Salerno.[3] They were in motive and in deed among the leaders of the revival of Galenic medicine and philosophy; their respective translations had a broad impact on the "naturalists" in the twelfth century.

Constantine's life and works have been much discussed, but the result of the preliminary studies is still far from satisfactory. The biographical sketch presented in the *Chronicon Casinense,* though compiled in the monastery where Constantine lived and worked, arouses some suspicion.[4] It reports that he left his native "Carthago" to study in "Babilonia" (probably Fustat, Old Cairo) for thirty-nine years, and there learned the arts and sciences of the Oriental world: "gramatica, dialectica, geometria, arithmetica, mathematica, astronomia nec non et phisica, Chaldeorum, Arabum, Persarum, Saracenorum, Egiptiorum, ac Indorum." He came back to his country but was compelled to flee and took refuge in Salerno, where he was received with honor by duke Robert. He must have found favor too with Richard, count of Aversa and prince of Capua, for when he entered Monte Cassino he offered to the monastery the church of St Agatha of Aversa, with which he had been endowed.

The subsequent redaction of the biography in *De viris illustribus Casinensibus*[5] is enlarged and embellished: the record of Constantine's travels to far-

---

[3]Haskins, *Ren* 22–23, "The Historical Background" (ch. 1) gives a very summary account of Constantine and Alfanus.

[4]*Chronica monasterii Casinensis,* PL 173.439–990 at 767–68; *Continuatio Petri Diaconi,* MGH SS 7.728–29. Peter the Deacon is not a reliable chronicler, but the main points—that Constantine came from Africa, was a monk in Monte Cassino in the time of abbot Desiderius, and wrote many books there—have a good chance of being true.

[5]PL 173.1003–50 at 1034–35, also ascribed to Peter the Deacon.

off India and Ethiopia is hardly credible, and "necromancia" and "musica" are added to the list of his achievements. The "Glosula magistri Mathei F.," discovered in an Erfurt manuscript[6] containing a commentary on the *Dietae universales*, produces another and still more fanciful tale; according to this note, Constantine was a Saracen merchant in his earlier life. The fact that Constantine came from North Africa and knew Arabic does not necessarily imply that he was a converted Moslem. There is no hint of such a remarkable circumstance in the Monte Cassino sources; and small Christian communities are known to have existed in Africa in the eleventh century.[7] That Constantine was from Carthage and studied with Arabic masters seems likely, however; among the authors whose works he adapted are three famous physicians of Kairouan: Ishāq b. ʿImrān, Ishāq b. Sulayman al-Isrāili, and Abū Jaʿfar Ahmad . . . al-Jazzār.[8]

The list of Constantine's works written at Monte Cassino, appended to the biography in the *Chronicon Casinense* and the *De viris* (with some variants and additions), is more reliable than the biography itself, but is probably incomplete.[9] In this list, the fact that most of the titles, if not all, are translations from Arabic is not specified, with the exception of the "liber febrium quem de arabica lingua transtulit." The early manuscripts, however, often bear titles indicating that Constantine is a "translator."[10] What matters for our present

[6]MS Erfurt, Amplon. oct. 62a, fols. 49v–50. Text edited by Rudolf Creutz, "Die Ehrenrettung Konstantins von Afrika," *Studien und Mitteilungen zur Geschichte des Benediktiner-Ordens und seiner Zweige* 49 (1931) 25–44 at 40–41 and facsimile. Creutz identifies "magister Matheus F." with Matheus Ferrarius, supposed to be a Salernitan master of the 12th century. Against this identification see Paul O. Kristeller, "The School of Salerno: Its Development and Its Contribution to the History of Learning," *Bulletin of the History of Medicine* 17 (1945) 138–94 at 151; repr. with additions in his *Studies in Renaissance Thought and Letters*, Storia e letteratura 54 (Rome 1956) 495–551. I cannot share the opinion of Michael McVaugh, who thinks that this account of Constantine's early life is more reliable than the other one: see "Constantine the African," DSB 3 (1971) 393–95.

[7]See Christian Courtois, "Grégoire VII et l'Afrique du Nord: Remarques sur les communautés chrétiennes d'Afrique au XIe siècle," *Revue historique* 195 (1945) 97–122 and 193–226, concerning the correspondence of pope Gregory VII with the Christian communities in North Africa; Charles-Emmanuel Dufourcq, "Le christianisme dans les pays de l'Occident musulman, des alentours de l'an mille jusqu' aux temps almohades," *Etudes de civilisation médiévale, IXe–XIIe siècles: Mélanges offerts à Edmond-René Labande* (Poitiers 1974) 237–46, esp. 241–42 on the discovery of an 11th-c. Christian inscription at Kairouan.

[8]See Fuat Sezgin, *Geschichte des arabischen Schrifttums* (7 vols. Leiden 1967–79) vol. 3, *Medizin* 266, 295–97, 304–07, on these North African physicians, with reference to Constantine's translations.

[9]For instance, the translation of the *Isagoge in medicinam*, from the Arabic of Hunain ibn Ishāq, "Iohannicius," is not on the list. It is one of the most widely diffused early translations of Arabic medicine; this version is incomplete, translated freely, with many lacunae. Two copies can be dated late 11th century and are in Beneventan script; one of them is still at Monte Cassino, so there is little doubt concerning their origin, though the manuscripts do not mention Constantine. See Augusto Beccaria, *I codici di medicina del periodo presalernitano (secoli IX, X e XI)*, Storia e letteratura 53 (Rome 1956) 181, 304–05; E. A. Lowe, *The Beneventan Script: A History of the South Italian Minuscule* (Oxford 1914) 19, 346.

[10]This is noted by Heinrich Schipperges, *Die Assimilation der arabischen Medizin durch das lateinische Mittelalter*, Sudhoffs Archiv für Geschichte der Medizin und der Naturwissenschaften, Beiheft 3 (Wiesbaden 1964) 17–54. Schipperges made a large use of Sudhoff's previous studies

topic is that Constantine's avowed authorities are the great masters of the medical art, Hippocrates and Galen. In the preface of the *Pantegni*, an adaptation of ʿAli ibn ʿAbbas's Kunnash al-Maliki,[11] addressed to the abbot of Monte Cassino, Desiderius, Constantine says that he has examined the best authors in the medical art, ancient and modern—and he names only the Greek physicians quoted by ʿAli ibn ʿAbbas.[12] He refers to the ultimate source, and does not mention the intermediary. When he attempts to translate the *Aphorisms* of Hippocrates with Galen's commentary,[13] he tells his disciple Atto that he hesitated for a long while to comply with his request to translate some of Galen's tracts into Latin, for he had a feeling of awe: "hesitans tanti transferre opera physici."

Constantine was severely criticized, first for assuming an undeserved fame in appearing as an author when he was merely compiling and adapting. This is partly unfair. The prefaces addressed to abbot Desiderius and to his disciples Atto and Iohannes show no undue boasting; he wished to translate useful books of medicine for the benefit of the Latins, who were sorely in need of them. He was also criticized, already in the twelfth century, as incompetent and careless. Stephen of Pisa, treasurer of Antioch, decided to make a new translation of Ibn ʿAbbas's Kunnash al-Maliki, because Constantine's version was incomplete and inadequate.[14] According to the few modern scholars who

and of Creutz's articles on Constantine and his disciples Atto and Iohannes Afflacius, surnamed Sarracenus, who may have continued his master's translations; cf. Rudolf Creutz, "Der Arzt Constantinus Africanus von Montekassino: Sein Leben, sein Werk und seine Bedeutung für die mittelalterliche medizinische Wissenschaft," *Studien und Mitteilungen zur Geschichte des Benediktiner-Ordens und seiner Zweige* 47 (1929) 1–44; idem, "Der Cassinese Iohannes Afflacius Saracenus, ein Arzt aus 'Hochsalerno,'" ibid. 48 (1930) 301–24; idem, "Additamenta zu Konstantinus Africanus und seinen Schülern Johannes and Atto," ibid. 50 (1932) 420–42. Manuscripts containing Constantinian translations are noted, passim, by Hermann Diels, *Die Handschriften der antiken Ärzte* (Leipzig 1970; repr. from Abh Berlin, Philos.-hist. Kl., 1905–07). Lists of manuscripts of the Constantinian translation of Hippocrates's *Aphorisms* by Pearl Kibre, "Hippocrates latinus: Repertorium of Hippocratic Writings in the Latin Middle Ages [II]," *Traditio* 32 (1976) 257–92.

[11]On this work, see Sezgin (n. 8 above) 320–22.

[12]"Unde ego Constantinus tantam huius artis utilitatem perpendens Latinorumque volumina percurrens, cum licet multa essent, non tamen introducendis ea sufficere viderem, recurri ad nostros veteres sive modernos. Revolvi etiam Hippocratem in hac arte maximum, revolvi et Galenum et de novis Alexandrum, Paulum quoque et Oribasium. . . ." Quoted from MSS BN lat 6887, fol. 1; 7042, fol. 1v; and 11223, fol. 1; see also *Omnia opera Ysaac in hoc volumine contenta cum quibusdam aliis opusculis*, Pars II: *Liber Pantegni Ysaac Israelite . . .* quem Constantinus Aphricanus monachus Montis Cassinensis sibi vendicavit (Lyon 1515) fol. 1. The Basel edition of "Opera Constantini" (1536–39) is unreliable; the preface of the *Pantegni*, pars II, fol. a² has been altered by a humanistic rewriting. Constantine's preface is a rather clumsy adaptation of ʿAli ibn ʿAbbas's introduction concerning the works of the great physicians; he leaves out the names of the Syriac and Arabic authors quoted as "modern," but adds the name of Alexander and a list of Galen's main tracts. On this Arabic introduction see Sezgin (n. 8 above) 320–22 and MS Paris, Nat. Arabe 2871, fol. 3.

[13]Kibre, who published a list of manuscripts containing this translation (n. 10 above), noted in a private communication that the preface is not present in the earliest manuscripts; however, the style and manner agree with Constantine's other prologues.

[14]On Stephen of Antioch, see Haskins, *Science* 131–35; this must be supplemented by Richard W. Hunt, "Stephen of Antioch," *M&RS* 2 (1950) 172–73.

have tried to compare his works with an Arabic original, Constantine did not endeavor to produce literal translations: he avoids the difficult points, cuts out sentences and even whole passages; in most cases, his works must be considered adaptations rather than translations.[15]

Constantine may have his faults, but he was a pioneer: his "bad" translations introduced a new medical corpus to the West. The contents of the pre-Constantine medical library are now fairly well known, thanks to recent studies and catalogues of early medieval manuscripts.[16] With the exception of Hippocrates's *Aphorisms* and some Galenic tracts, these texts, consisting mostly of translations from the Greek executed from the fifth to the seventh century, chiefly in Ravenna, were related to the *practica* rather than to the *theorica*; such was the case for early Salernitan medicine. The Constantinian corpus, which offered the *theorica* as well as the *practica*, took some time to influence Salernitan teaching, but it penetrated into more remote countries: William of Conches used the *Pantegni* in his *Philosophia* and Glosses on the *Timaeus*, circa 1130.[17]

Galenic doctrine revived with another translation also used by William of Conches: a treatise by Nemesius of Emesa on the nature of man, combining patristic doctrine and theories of Greek philosophers, especially Galen.[18] It was

---

[15]When Max Meyerhof edited *The Book of the Ten Treatises on the Eye ascribed to Hunain ibn Ishāq* (809–877 A.D.) (Cairo 1928), he remarked (p. vii) that the Latin translation was very badly made. Constantine had translated nine of the ten treatises with the title *Liber de oculis*. Meyerhof later described Constantine's Latin versions as "corrupt, confused, full of misunderstood Arabic terms," in "Science and Medicine," *The Legacy of Islam*, ed. Thomas W. Arnold and Alfred Guillaume (Oxford 1931) 311–55 at 345. It is difficult to appreciate adequately Constantine's faults and merits. There are few modern editions of his works which include a comparison with the Arabic original. See however Ishāq ibn ʿImrān, *Maqāla fīʾl-Mālīhūliyā* (*Abhandlung über die Melancholie, und Constantini Africani Libri duo de Melancholia*), Vergleichende kritische arabisch-lateinische Parallelausgabe, deutsche Übersetzung des arabischen Textes, ausführliche Einleitung und arabischer wie lateinischer drogenkundlichen Apparat von Karl Garbers (Hamburg 1977). An edition is announced for the translation of *Liber febrium*; see J. D. Latham, "Isaac Israeli's 'Kitāb al-ḥummayāt' and the Latin and Castilian Texts," *Journal of Semitic Studies* 14 (1969) 80–95. Comparison of Constantine's version with the Arabic shows that this one is a modified abridgment, the differences residing more in the omission of material than in distortions and inaccurate renderings.

[16]See Beccaria (n. 9 above). In his introduction, Beccaria gives a good survey of the medical texts in circulation during the early Middle Ages. His subsequent studies describe the early translations from the Greek, made mostly at Ravenna: "Sulle tracce di un antico canone latino di Ippocrate e di Galeno [1, 2, and 3]," *Italia medioevale e umanistica* 2 (1959) 1–56; 4 (1961) 1–75; and 14 (1971) 1–23. See also Ernest Wickersheimer, *Les manuscrits latins de médecine du haut moyen âge dans les bibliothèques de France* (Paris 1966), and Henry E. Sigerist, "The Latin Medical Literature of the Early Middle Ages," *Journal of the History of Medicine and Allied Sciences* 13 (1958) 127–46.

[17] See Edouard Jeauneau, ed., *Guillaume de Conches: Glosae super Platonem*, Textes philosophiques du moyen âge 13 (Paris 1965). The introduction contains a tentative chronology of William's works and remarks concerning the quotations of the *Pantegni*.

[18]Karl I. Burkhard, ed., *Nemesii episcopi Premnon physicon; sive* Περὶ φύσεως ἀνθρώπου *liber a N. Alfano, archiepiscopo Salerni in latinum translatus* (Leipzig 1917). On Alfanus, see Rudolf Creutz, "Erzbischof Alfanus I, ein frühsalernitanischer Arzt," *Studien und Mitteilungen zur Geschichte des Benediktiner-Ordens und seiner Zweige* 47 (1929) 413–32 and 48 (1930) 205–08; idem, "Der frühsalernitaner Alfanus und sein bislang unbekannter 'Liber de pulsibus,'"

translated from the Greek by Alfanus, who had been a monk at Monte Cassino before becoming archbishop of Salerno. He expounds his intentions in the preface: In this small book, I shall contribute to learning. I was urged to translate this tract, containing the sayings of many authors, chiefly those that Mother Greece educated, because I felt the penury of the Latins (*Latinorum cogente penuria*—a topical formula of many translators). On the difficult points, he continues, the teachings of Pythagoras, Plato, Aristotle, Hippocrates, and Galen, and of other philosophers not less numerous nor less important than these, will be offered in convenient form. It is clear that Alfanus is consciously initiating a revival of natural science as it was taught by "Mother Greece"; the title that he coined for the text of the unnamed author was "Premnon physicon, hoc est stipes naturalium; quia sicut ab uno stipite multi ramusculi pullullant, sic ex eius fonte doctrinae plurimi scientiae naturalis rivuli exuberabunt."[19]

THE TWELFTH CENTURY

These preliminary signs of a renaissance in the second half of the eleventh century were followed by a much more extensive effort to acquire the learning hidden behind the barrier of a foreign language. It would be premature to undertake a full survey, for we must confess our ignorance on many points; we shall only try to sketch the *status quaestionis* for the history of translations in the twelfth century. What progress has been made since Haskins's time is in large part due to him: not only did he offer a rich harvest of information, he stimulated research and showed how the scanty documents at our disposal could be cautiously used and cleverly interpreted. There are three ways of progressing in our specific topic: by discovering new documents, by carefully studying the manuscript tradition, and by comparing the version or translation with the original text—when it is available—in order to evaluate the skill or inadequacy of the translator, his methods and peculiar habits, and his vocabulary. Such close examination sometimes results in identifying the translator of an anonymous version. Recent publications mark a great improve-

---

Archiv für Geschichte der Medizin 29 (1936) 57–83; Nicola Acocella, "La figura e l'opera di Alfano I di Salerno (sec. XI)," *Rassegna storica salernitana* 19 (1958) 1–74 and 20 (1959) 17–90; Anselmo Lentini, "Sul viaggio Constantinopolitano di Gisulfo di Salerno con l'archivescovo Alfano," *Atti del III. Congresso internazionale di studi sull'Alto Medioevo, 1956* (Spoleto 1959) 437–43; idem, "Alfano," *Dizionario biografico degli Italiani* 2 (1960) 253–57.

[19]On the influence of Alfanus's version, particularly the chapter on the elements, in the 12th century, see Theodore Silverstein, "Guillaume de Conches and the Elements: *Homiomeria* and *Organica*," *Mediaeval Studies* 26 (1964) 363–67; idem, "Guillaume de Conches and Nemesius of Emessa: On the Sources of the 'New Science' of the Twelfth Century," *Harry Austryn Wolfson Jubilee Volume on the Occasion of his Seventy-fifth Birthday* (3 vols. Jerusalem 1965) 2.719–34 at 722ff. Another translation of Nemesius's chapter on the elements was discovered in MS BL Cotton Galba E.IV (from Bury St Edmunds) and edited by Richard C. Dales, "An Unnoticed Translation of the Chapter *De Elementis* from Nemesius' *De natura hominis*," *Mediaevalia et humanistica* 17 (1966) 13–19. The MS, which also contains Alfanus's usual version, dates from the last quarter of the 12th century; the "other translation" may be a revised version.

ment in our knowledge, due to the systematic exploration of the second and third ways—the first, the discovery of new documents, as well as of an original Greek or Arabic text, being partly subject to circumstances and chance.

The research initiated by Haskins and carried on since has produced a more adequate picture of the transmission of Greek philosophy and science, a picture formerly blurred by nineteenth-century historians who focused on the Arabic tradition. The importance of the Greco-Latin versions has been stressed; their number increased in the twelfth century thanks to the developing relations between the Western world and the Byzantine empire, and to the presence of Greek or Greek-speaking scholars in Italy and Sicily. The most competent translators—Burgundio, Hugo Etherianus, his brother Leo Tuscus—visited Constantinople and spent a part of their lives there; Greek manuscripts were brought to Italy, Sicily, and even France from the Byzantine area. If Sicily was such a favorable place, it was not only because the chancery was trilingual, but because intercourse with the Byzantines was uninterrupted.[20] In such places, a man brought up in the Latin West could learn Greek; only rarely was it possible to study with a Greek master visiting France or England.[21] Men born and bred in a bilingual country were apparently in a privileged position, if their Latin was sufficient. Such presumably was the Greek interpreter whom John of Salisbury consulted when he visited Apulia, "qui Latinam linguam commode nouerat."[22]

TRANSLATIONS FROM HEBREW

Science and philosophy were the main objects of Western curiosity; other motives, however, inclined scholars to require translations of other kinds of texts, and even to learn a foreign language themselves. Translators and teachers were certainly required for Hebrew. The search for the *Hebraica veritas* in biblical studies and curiosity about Jewish exegesis and tradition form part of the general movement of translations in the twelfth century.[23] The study of Hebrew is a kind of revival, for the courageous men who undertook to learn the sacred language had in mind the example of St Jerome. The wish to obtain a more adequate text of the Old Testament was the original motive of scholars who began to consult Jewish rabbis. A remarkable

[20]See Haskins, *Culture* ch. 8, "Contacts with Byzantium," 160–69; Milton V. Anastos, "Some Aspects of Byzantine Influence on Latin Thought," *Twelfth-Century Europe* 131–87; Robert Browning, "Courants intellectuels et organisation scolaire à Byzance au XI siècle," *Centre de recherche d'histoire et civilisation de Byzance, Travaux et mémoires* 6: *Recherches sur le XIe siècle* (Paris 1976) 219–22; Michel Balard, "Amalfi et Byzance (Xe–XIIe siècles)," ibid. 85–95, on the Amalfitans' role in the diffusion of Byzantine works.

[21]Bernhard Bischoff, "Das griechische Element in der abendländischen Bildung des Mittelalters," *Mittelalterliche Studien* (2 vols. Stuttgart 1966–67) 2.246–75; idem, "The Study of Foreign Languages in the Middle Ages," ibid. 2.227–45 at 232–35.

[22]John of Salisbury, *Metalogicon* 1.15, ed. Clement C. J. Webb (Oxford 1929) 37.25–26.

[23]See Smalley, *Study*, a fundamental work for the history of Hebraic studies among Christian biblical scholars; and Aryeh Grabois, "The *Hebraica veritas* and Jewish-Christian Intellectual Relations in the Twelfth Century," *Speculum* 50 (1975) 613–34.

testimonial is presented by Stephen Harding, third abbot of Cîteaux. Wondering at the discrepancies in the biblical text transcribed in the manuscripts of the Vulgate version that he had collected as a preliminary to making a monumental copy of the Bible ("nos multum de discordia nostrorum librorum quos ab uno interprete suscepimus admirantes"), and after having perused the prefaces of St Jerome, he sought the help of learned Jewish rabbis to elucidate and correct the difficult passages.[24] The discussion was carried on in the common medium, *lingua romana*, a method frequently used for translations from Hebrew and especially from Arabic, with an interpreter who did not know Latin fluently but spoke a shared vernacular language.

Other scholars, more ambitious, even wanted to become acquainted with Jewish exegesis. Some probably did as Stephen Harding and questioned the neighboring Jews; the best endeavored to learn Hebrew and work on their own. This rare kind of achievement seems to have been realized mainly in England or by Englishmen. The best representatives of the new way of commenting on the Bible with glosses noting the Hebraic tradition are Andrew of St Victor and Herbert of Bosham.[25] We must name too Nicholas Manjacoria, a Cistercian in the monastery of Tre Fontane, near Rome, who learned Hebrew with a Jewish master and later consulted him in order to produce a good recension of the Psalter.[26]

Information from Jewish sources might be sought for controversial purposes. Quotations from the Talmud are found in the *Dialogus* of Peter Alfonsi, a converted Jew from Huesca, who wrote this defense of the Christian faith in the first quarter of the twelfth century, and subsequently in Peter the Venerable's *Contra Iudaeos*; the abbot of Cluny apparently used the material collected by the Spaniard, who had a first-hand knowledge of the Hebraic tradition.[27]

[24]*Censura de aliquot locis Bibliorum*, PL 166.1373–76 at 1375A. The monumental Bible in four volumes is still extant in Dijon, Bibl. mun. MSS 12–15; see C. Oursel, "La Bible de saint Etienne Harding et le scriptorium de Cîteaux (1109–vers 1134)," *Cîteaux* 10 (1959) 34–43 + plate.

[25]Smalley, *Study* 149–72 on Andrew of St Victor, 186ff. on Herbert of Bosham. The achievements of Herbert and the English Hebraists were subsequently stressed by Raphael Loewe, "The Mediaeval Christian Hebraists of England: Herbert of Bosham and Earlier Scholars," *Transactions of the Jewish Historical Society of England* 17 (1951–52) 225–49, and idem, "Herbert of Bosham's Commentary on Jerome's Hebrew Psalter," *Biblica* 34 (1953) 44–77, 159–92, 275–98; see also G. I. Lieftink, "The 'Psalterium hebraycum' from St Augustine's Canterbury Rediscovered in the Scaliger Bequest at Leyden," *Transactions of the Cambridge Bibliographical Society* 2 (1954–58) 97–104. We must note the quotations in Hebrew of biblical texts in the *Ysagoge in theologiam* addressed by an English "Odo" to Gilbert Foliot, ed. Artur M. Landgraf, *Ecrits théologiques de l'école d'Abélard: Textes inédits*, Spicilegium sacrum Lovaniense, études et documents 14 (Louvain 1934) 61–289; Johann Fischer, "Die hebräischen Bibelzitate des Scholastikers Odo," *Biblica* 15 (1934) 50–93; and David E. Luscombe, "The Authorship of the *Ysagoge in theologiam*," AHDLMA 35 (1968) 7–16.

[26]On Manjacoria, see Smalley, *Study* 79–81.

[27]Peter Alfonsi, *Dialogi Alphonsi conversi cum Moyse Iudaeo*, PL 157.535ff., esp. 542–43, 549, 564–67; Peter the Venerable, *Tractatus adversus Iudaeorum inveteratam duritiem* 5, PL 189.602–50. The Rev. Manfred Kniewasser (Vienna), who is studying the knowledge of the

APOLOGETICS

Other translations were made for religious motives, to secure authentic documentation. This spirit inspired Peter the Venerable when he decided to sponsor a collection of texts related to the Moslem faith. Although the final aim was apologetic, the abbot of Cluny intended as a first step to provide Christian theologians with a true account of the Law of the Saracens and their prophet Mohammed's life. This great enterprise was carried on very rapidly by the translators Peter enlisted when he visited Spain in 1142: the two scientific scholars, Robert of Ketene and Herman Sclavus of Carinthia; master Peter of Toledo, associated with the abbot's secretary, Peter of Poitiers; and a "Saracen" named Mohammed, most likely associated with Robert for the version of the Koran.[28] The desire to obtain reliable documents rather than indulge in foolish legends concerning Mohammed, in order to establish a firm basis for study and discussion, is a good sign of a renaissance of learning; the abbot must be excused for accepting among the texts offered by the translators three small tracts of certain Arabic origin, but of a legendary nature.[29]

Don Mauricio, archdeacon of Toledo and bishop-elect of Burgos, was still more daring when he sponsored the translation of the profession of faith of Ibn Tūmart, the Mahdi of the Almohads, done by canon Mark of Toledo in 1213.[30] Mark had previously translated the Koran, at the request of don Mauricio and the archbishop of Toledo, don Rodrigo Jimenez, who was himself to use Arabic sources to write the life of the Prophet in his *Historia Arabum*.[31] Like Peter the Venerable, the Spaniards wished to build the defense of the Christian faith on solid ground.

Other information on the prophet Mohammed and Islam, some of it more or less fanciful, is contained in various works of the twelfth and early

Talmud among Christian authors in the Middle Ages, has noted Peter the Venerable's apparent dependence on the *Dialogus*. This is not surprising, considering the early diffusion of Peter Alfonsi's works in France and England; it seems, however, that the *Contra Iudaeos* contains Talmudic quotations not present in the *Dialogus*. In other cases, information was probably obtained by oral intercourse; see Gilbert Crispin, *Disputatio Iudaei et Christiani et anonymi auctoris*, ed. Bernhard Blumenkranz, Stromata patristica et mediaevalia 3 (Utrecht 1956).

[28] Marie-Thérèse d'Alverny, "Deux traductions latines du Coran au moyen âge," AHDLMA 16 (1947–48) 69–131.

[29] These tracts are (1) a *Cronica Saracenorum*, from the creation of the world to the successors of Mohammed, translated by Robert of Ketene; (2) *Liber generationis Mahumet*, a story of Mohammed's birth and wondrous childhood, translated by Hermannus Sclavus (of Carinthia); the Arabic original was identified by James Kritzeck, *Peter the Venerable and Islam* (Princeton 1964) 84–88; (3) a supposed dialogue between the Prophet and a Jew who professes Islam after this interview; it was translated with the title *Doctrina Mahomet* by the same Herman. It would have required a remarkable insight to realize that these tracts were not worthy of consideration, compared with the important pieces of the collection, the Koran and the pseudo-Kindi, a Christian apology of Eastern origin.

[30] Marie-Thérèse d'Alverny and Georges Vajda, "Marc de Tolède, traducteur d'Ibn Tumart," *Al-Andalus* 16 (1951) 99–140 and 259–307, and 17 (1952) 1–56. See below at n. 150.

[31] Mme Gracia Ferré, who studied the *Historia Arabum* under the direction of Prof. Claude Cahen, found that Rodrigo had used the *Sirat Rasul Allah* of Ibn Isḥāq for his account of the Prophet's life.

thirteenth century; its origin and inspiration are difficult to trace. Some is more accurate, such as Peter Alfonsi's account of Islam in his *Dialogus*, immediately derived from Arabic sources. A genuine translation of a Syriac Christian version of the so-called Bahira legend has been published;[32] it offers an apocalyptic development of the story of the Christian monk Bahira-Sergius, who was linked with Mohammed in Eastern Christian tradition. This text was probably translated from Arabic during our period, but the translator and place of translation are unknown.

CHURCH FATHERS

An increased regard for the teachings of the Greek Church Fathers provoked new translations. A number of texts translated into Latin were available in late Antiquity and the early Middle Ages, but they seem to have been more closely read and appreciated in the twelfth century.[33] Even laymen were interested: among other projects thwarted by his premature death, the Sicilian Henricus Aristippus, archdeacon of Catania, planned to translate the *opuscula* of St Gregory of Nazianzus, at the request of king William of Sicily.[34] The judge Burgundio of Pisa translated Chrysostom's homilies on Matthew, to comply with the wish of pope Eugene III, who had acquired a manuscript of Chrysostom from the patriarch of Antioch. In a lengthy introduction to his translation of the homilies on John, finished long after Eugene's death, Burgundio expounded his views concerning the right method of translation, *de verbo ad verbum*, a rule he attributed to Boethius; he gave moreover a very interesting survey of Greco-Latin versions from Antiquity to his own times.[35] Pope Eugene's eagerness was perhaps influenced by the preference shown by St Bernard for the spiritual teachings of the Greek Fathers. Eugene had also requested a complete translation of John of Damascus's *De fide orthodoxa*, some chapters of which Cerbanus, in Hungary, had previously turned into Latin.[36]

---

[32]J. Bignami-Odier and G. Levi della Vida, "Une version latine de l'Apocalypse syro-arabe de Serge-Bahira," *Mélanges d'archéologie et d'histoire de l'Ecole française de Rome* 62 (1950) 125–48. The editors had only one manuscript, transcribed in the 15th century, and did not propose a date for the translation. We discovered a 13th-c. copy at Bourges, Bibl. mun. MS 367 (306). We suggest tentatively that this version may have been executed in Syria or Palestine.

[33]Albert Siegmund, *Die Überlieferung der griechischen christlichen Literatur in der lateinischen Kirche bis zum zwölften Jahrhundert*, Abh Bayerischen Benediktiner-Akademie 5 (Munich 1949) must be consulted, particularly for the hagiographical translations made during the 11th century.

[34]Preface to his translation of the *Meno*, ed. Victor Kordeuter and Carlotta Labowsky, Plato latinus 1 (London 1940) 6. In the same preface, Henricus Aristippus says that he had been asked by the great admiral Maio and by the archbishop of Palermo, Hugo, to translate Diogenes Laertius.

[35]See Peter Classen, *Burgundio von Pisa: Richter, Gesandter, Übersetzer*, SB Heidelberg, Philos.-hist. Kl. 1974 no. 4, with a full survey of the documents concerning Burgundio's life and career, and a complete edition of the introduction to the translation of Chrysostom's homilies on John.

[36]Cerbanus dedicated a translation of Maximus the Confessor's *De caritate* to David, archimandrite and abbot of the monastery of St Martin "in S. Monte Pannoniae," Pannonhalma in Hungary. The translation of several chapters of John of Damascus's *De fide orthodoxa* is found in the same manuscripts; though anonymous, it has been assumed to be due to the same translator:

The full version which Burgundio completed after the pope's death rapidly became an important element of renovation in Western theology. Peter Lombard, who had used the Cerbanus version in his exposition of Christology, revised some of his quotations from the Burgundio text.[37] When Burgundio dedicated his translation of Nemesius to Frederick Barbarossa, he believed that he was offering the emperor a work of St Gregory of Nyssa; it was under the name of St Basil's brother that the manuscripts of Burgundio's version circulated in the West.[38]

Gilbert of Poitiers had a special reverence for the Greek Fathers; he and his followers were active agents in the revival of Eastern patristics.[39] One of his disciples, Hugh of Honau, visited Constantinople and became acquainted there with a Pisan, Hugo Etherianus. Etherianus, who later became a cardinal, had spent part of his life in the imperial city and was a remarkable Hellenist. From him, after an exchange of letters and with the intervention of a friend, Peter of Vienna, Hugh of Honau obtained two treatises compiled by Etherianus from the writings of the Greek Fathers: *De differentia naturae et personae* and *De sancto et immortali Deo*.[40] Etherianus had translated extracts from the Greek Fathers and from Byzantine theologians, including the Syrian Theodore Abu Qurra. The motives stressed by Hugh of Honau for urging Etherianus to fulfill his promise to confirm the documents possessed by the Latins concerning the doctrine of *persona* and *natura* in Christ, and to produce authorities from the Greek doctors concerning the procession of the Holy Spirit, show a great regard for the teachings of the Greeks: "Because from the Greeks has flowed the source of all wisdom, . . . I ask you to remove these

see *Translatio latina sancti Maximi confessoris (De caritate ad Elpidium, L. I–IV) saeculo XII. in Hungaria confecta*, ed. Andronicus B. Terebessy (Budapest 1944); *Translatio latina Ioannis Damasceni (De orthodoxa fide, L. III, c. 1–8) saeculo XII. in Hungaria confecta*, ed. Remigius L. Szigeti (Budapest 1940). On the character of the two versions, see Iván Boronkai, "Übersetzungsenfehler in Cerbanus' lateinischer Version von Johannes Damascenus und Maximus Confessor," *Philologus* 115 (1971) 32–45. Cerbanus's version was reedited by E. M. Buytaert with Burgundio's full translation: *De fide orthodoxa: Versions of Burgundio and Cerbanus*, Franciscan Institute Publications, Text Series 8 (St Bonaventure N.Y. 1955). Burgundio seems to have finished his task just after pope Eugene's death: "Iohannis presbyteri Damasceni . . . liber . . . a Burgundione iudice cive Pisano de graeco in latinum Domino tertio Eugenio beatae memoriae papae translatus" (11). A new manuscript was discovered later: E. M. Buytaert, "Another Copy of Cerbanus' Version of John Damascene," *Antonianum* 40 (1965) 303–10.

[37] Peter Lombard quotes extracts from *De fide orthodoxa* in books 1 and 3 of the *Sentences*, in his *Glossa in Romanos*, and in *sermo* 18: see *Magistri Petri Lombardi Parisiensis episcopi Sententiae in IV. libris distinctae*, ed. Ignatius Brady, Spicilegium Bonaventurianum 4 (Grottaferrata 1971) *Prolegomena* 63*–64*, 105*, 121*.

[38] Nemesius of Emesa, *De natura hominis: Traduction de Burgundio de Pise; édition critique avec une introduction sur l'anthropologie de Nemesius*, ed. Gérard Verbeke and J. R. Moncho, Corpus latinum commentariorum in Aristotelem graecorum, Supp. 1 (Leiden 1975).

[39] Nikolaus M. Häring, "The Porretans and the Greek Fathers," *Mediaeval Studies* 24 (1962) 181–209.

[40] See Antoine Dondaine, "Hugues Ethérien et Léon Toscan," AHDLMA 19 (1952) 67–134; Nikolaus M. Häring, "The 'Liber de Differentia naturae et personae' by Hugh Etherian and the Letters Addressed to him by Peter of Vienna and Hugh of Honau," *Mediaeval Studies* 24 (1962) 1–34.

dangerous doubts of the Latins . . . by means of the authority of the Greek
doctors, who have spoken more clearly than ours about these matters, and with
their teachings to put an end to this quarrel."[41] Hugh expressed the same feelings in a second letter to Etherianus: "I beseech your kindness in these matters, . . . to relieve, from the riches of the Greeks, not so much my own poverty
as that of all the Latins."[42] Hugh of Honau used the *De differentia naturae et
personae* to write a kind of adaptation, *De diversitate naturae et personae*,
contained, with other theological works, in a Cambridge manuscript.[43]

Hugo Etherianus wrote other tracts containing translations of Greek "authorities." Haskins drew attention to the activity of Etherianus and his brother
Leo Tuscus, and documents discovered subsequently have made it possible to
give a more complete account of the life and work of the two brothers and to
determine Hugo's role in discussions with Greek theologians.[44] Hugo had even
translated a Greek tract against the Latins: *De haeresibus quas in Latinos
Graeci devolvunt.* Theological debates are a permanent feature in Christendom and can hardly be considered as a revival; the efforts of Etherianus to produce genuine patristic texts and to render faithfully the opponents' arguments
show not only a great regard for Greek doctrine, but an earnest desire for full
documentation.[45]

[41]Dondaine (n. 40 above) 130, Häring (n. 40 above) 18: "quia a Graecis sapientiae totius fons
emanavit . . . rogo ut has Latinorum periculosas dubitationes . . . Graecorum doctorum auc-
toritatibus qui de his expressius quam nostri locuti sunt, amputes et huic liti sententiis illorum
finem imponas."

[42]Dondaine (n. 40 above) 131, Häring (n. 40 above) 19: "deprecor tuam bonitatem ut in his
quaestionibus . . . de Graecorum opulentia penuriam non tam meam quam omnium Latinorum
adiuves."

[43]MS Univ. Ii.iv.27. See Nikolaus M. Häring, "The *Liber de diversitate naturae et personae*
by Hugh of Honau," AHDLMA 29 (1962) 103–216. Häring edited two other treatises contained
in the same manuscript, first described by Haskins, *Science* 209–12: "The *Liber de homoysion et
homoeysion* by Hugh of Honau," AHDLMA 34 (1967) 129–253 and 35 (1968) 211–95. He edited
the last tract of this Cambridge manuscript, *Liber de ignorantia*, and ascribed it to Hugh of
Honau; the text is chiefly remarkable for the extensive use of Nemesius. The author knew the two
Latin versions; the fact that he attributes the original to Gregory of Nyssa comes from the Burgundio version: "sicut ait Gregorius episcopus Nyssae, frater magni Basilii Capadoceni episcopi in
libro *De natura hominis.* De Graeco in Latinum translationem duplicem inveni. Quarum alterius
auctorem non reperi, alteram Burgundio Venecianus [*sic*] edidit atque eam Friderico gloriosissimo
Romanorum Imperatori . . . dicavit"; see Nikolaus M. Häring, "Hugh of Honau and the 'Liber
de ignorantia,'" *Mediaeval Studies* 25 (1963) 209–30 at 220.

[44]MSS Colmar 188 and Seville, Colombina 5-1-24 and Tarragona 92 (from the monastery of
Santes Creus) yielded new texts and information. See Dondaine (n. 40 above); idem, "Hugues
Ethérien et le concile de Constantinople de 1166," *Historisches Jahrbuch* 77 (1958) 473–83 at
473–76 (concerning MS Tarragona 92); Peter Classen, "Das Konzil von Konstantinopel 1166 und
die Lateiner," *Byzantinische Zeitschrift* 48 (1955) 339–68.

[45]We should not leave out one of the most famous Hellenists in 12th-c. Italy, Moses of
Bergamo, who in 1136 attended a theological disputation at Constantinople in the company of
Burgundio and James of Venice—even though his translation of Greek extracts does not seem to
have had much impact. In the prologue of his version, *Exceptio compendiosa de divinitus inspirata
scriptura*, Moses explains that he learned Greek in order to offer the Latins useful knowledge:
"cum presertim grecas litteras propter id potissimum didicisse me sim sepe testatus, ut ex eis in
nostras siquid utile reperirem quod nobis minus ante fuisset debita devotione transverterem"
(Haskins, *Science* 201, from MS Nîmes 52); see also Giovanni Cremaschi, *Mosè del Brolo e la*

A legitimate craving for information, and perhaps some curiosity, incited Raymond of Moncada, a Catalan visitor at the court of basileus Manuel Comnenus, to ask Leo Tuscus for a translation of the liturgy ascribed to St John Chrysostom.[46] This version was supplemented some time later by a translation of the liturgy of St Basil (used during Lent by the Orthodox Church), done by Nicholas of Otranto at the request of archbishop William of Otranto, who had brought the Chrysostom version from the East.[47]

It seems appropriate to consider as a revival the increasing impact of the pseudo-Dionysian writings in the twelfth century. A new manuscript had been brought from Constantinople to St Denis by William Le Mire, who knew Greek and himself produced versions of the *Vita Secundi philosophi* and of Greek prologues to the Pauline Epistles, this last at the request of Herbert of Bosham.[48] Another William, also a monk at St Denis, translated the *Laudatio sancti Dionysii* of Michael Syncellos contained in the new Dionysian manuscript.[49] The most important enterprise was the revision of Eriugena's version of pseudo-Dionysius by John Sarrasin, who had learned Greek in the East and who was consulted by John of Salisbury to elucidate difficult Greek terms. He used a Greek manuscript in order to produce a more accurate text, and sought to improve its intelligibility by replacing John the Scot's sophisticated vocabulary with normal Latin terms.[50]

TRANSLATIONS IN SICILY

The acquisition of Greek learning was the obvious motive for the translation of philosophical and scientific texts. The importance of Sicily, endowed with learned men and linguists, and the circumstances making that country so well

cultura a Bergamo nei secoli XI–XII, Collezione storica bergamasca 3 (Bergamo 1945), emending Haskins's account of Moses on several points. Cremaschi later edited the full text: "La 'Exceptio compendiosa de divinitus inspirata scriptura' de Mosè del Brolo," *Bergomum* (Bollettino della Civica Biblioteca di Bergamo) 48 (1953) 29–69.

[46] André Jacob, "La traduction de la Liturgie de saint Jean Chrysostome par Léon Toscan: Edition critique," *Orientalia christiana periodica* 32 (1966) 111–62; Anselm Strittmatter, "Notes on Leo Tuscus' Translation of the Liturgy of St. John Chrysostom," *Didascaliae: Studies in Honor of Anselm M. Albareda, Prefect of the Vatican Library*, ed. Sesto Prete (New York 1961) 409–24.

[47] André Jacob, "La traduction de la Liturgie de saint Basile par Nicolas d'Otrante," *Bulletin de l'Institut historique belge de Rome* 38 (1967) 49–107. On the translator Nicholas, see Johannes M. Hoeck and Raimund J. Loenertz, *Nikolaos-Nektarios von Otranto, Abt von Casole: Beiträge zur Geschichte der ost-westlichen Beziehungen unter Innozenz III. und Friedrich II.*, Studia patristica et byzantina 11 (Ettal 1965). A manuscript preserved in Paris, BN n.a. lat. 1791, 12th c., contains an anonymous version of the liturgy of St Basil and of the liturgy of John Chrysostom; see Anselm Strittmatter, "'Missa Grecorum', 'Missa Sancti Iohannis Crisostomi': The Oldest Latin Version Known of the Byzantine Liturgies of St. Basil and St. John Chrysostom," *Traditio* 1 (1943) 79–137 (with an edition of the text).

[48] Beryl Smalley, "A Commentary on the *Hebraica* by Herbert of Bosham," RTAM 18 (1951) 29–65 at 38, 40.

[49] Haskins, *Science* 146–47; Robert Weiss, "Lo studio del greco all'abbazia di San Dionigi durante il Medioevo," *Rivista di storia della Chiesa in Italia* 6 (1952) 426–36 at 430ff.

[50] Gabriel Théry, "Jean Sarrazin, 'traducteur' de Scot Erigène," *Studia mediaevalia in honorem . . . Raymundi Josephi Martin* (Bruges 1948) 359–81; idem, "Documents concernant

situated for acquiring Greek books and transmitting their contents, have been often described, but obscure points remain.

The revival of Plato is marked by the translation of the *Meno* and *Phaedo* by Henricus Aristippus, archdeacon of Catania and for a while a member of the royal curia. This remarkable translator brought back from a legation to Constantinople a manuscript of Ptolemy's *Mathēmatikē Syntaxis*, the precious *Almagest*. He did not translate the book himself; that was done by an anonymous scholar who had learned some Greek and rushed from Salerno to Sicily when he heard the news. He prefaced his translation of the *Almagest*, for which he required the advice and help of admiral Eugene, with a prologue which has been much discussed.[51] He seems to have tried his Hellenist's skill first on less difficult texts: Euclid's *Data*, *Optica*, and *Catoptrica*, and Proclus's *Elementatio physica*. This valuable collection of physics and astronomy texts has been enlarged by a Greco-Latin translation of Euclid's *Elements* discovered recently; the most notable addition to Haskins's picture of the Sicilian translations, it may be attributable to the anonymous translator of the *Almagest*.[52] Critical editions of the *Meno* and *Phaedo*[53] and of the *Elementatio physica*[54] have thrown much light on Aristippus's methods, and on the vocabulary used by the anonymous translator of Proclus. Some doubts remain concerning the extent of the versions done by the amateur of the *Almagest*, though Haskins was inclined to take his words at face value.[55]

Jean Sarrazin, reviseur de la traduction Erigénienne du *Corpus Dionysiacum*,'' AHDLMA 18 (1950–51) 45–87. Théry's hypothesis that Jean Sarrasin probably learned Greek in England is very unlikely.

[51]Prologue edited by Haskins, *Science* 191–93 and discussed in the preceding chapter, 157–63 and 178–81. The Greco-Latin translation of the *Almagest* was discovered by Dean P. Lockwood and Axel A. Björnbo in two manuscripts; soon afterward Haskins himself found a third one. Haskins noted moreover the existence of another version from the Greek contained in MS Dresden Db. 87 (four books only).

[52]John E. Murdoch, "Euclides graeco-latinus: A Hitherto Unknown Medieval Latin Translation of the *Elements* Made Directly from the Greek," *Harvard Studies in Classical Philology* 71 (1966) 249–302. This version includes books 1–13 and book 15, with a compendium of books 14–15. Murdoch suggested that the translator was probably the man who had already translated the *Almagest* previously, but the question is still open.

[53]*Meno, interprete Henrico Aristippo* (n. 34 above); *Phaedo, interprete Henrico Aristippo*, ed. Lorenzo Minio-Paluello and H. J. Drossaart-Lulofs, Plato latinus 2 (London 1950). Minio-Paluello made a very important point, showing that there were two redactions of the *Phaedo* translation and that the revised redaction also had been done by Aristippus.

[54]Helmut Boese, ed. *Die mittelalterliche Übersetzung der Στοιχείωσις φυσική des Proclus: Procli Diadochi Lycii Elementatio physica*, Deutsche Akademie der Wissenschaften zu Berlin, Institut für griechisch-römische Altertumskunde, Arbeitsgruppe für hellenistisch-römische Philosophie, Veröffentlichungen 6 (Berlin 1958). After a comparative study of the method of translation in the *Elementatio* and *Almagest*, the editor found no serious objection to attributing both works to the same translator.

[55]To the list of mathematical versions done in Sicily during the second half of the 12th century could be added, according to Axel A. Björnbo, a short treatise *De isoperimetris*, translated from Greek: "Die mittelalterlichen lateinischen Übersetzungen aus dem Griechischen auf dem Gebiete der mathematischen Wissenschaften," *Archiv für die Geschichte der Naturwissenschaften und der Technik* 1 (1909) 385–94 at 393–94; cautiously, Marshall Clagett suggests that this text was translated from the Greek sometime before the middle of the 13th century: "Archimedes in the

What is important from our point of view is the eagerness of scholars to obtain and share the best authors of Greek Antiquity. Though the Sicilians could have translated from Arabic, they did so only when they could not succeed in finding a Greek original. This was the case for admiral Eugene, who knew the three languages used in the *Trinacria* but was most familiar with Greek; since he had Ptolemy's *Optics* only in Arabic, he resigned himself to making a version from an imperfect text: the two manuscripts that he used lacked the first book. He explained the circumstances and difficulty of his enterprise in a preface, with interesting remarks on the characteristics of the Greek and Arabic languages.[56]

ARISTOTELES LATINUS

Charting the history of the medieval translations of Aristotle is among the best achievements of recent scholarship. The work had not begun when Haskins wrote his *Renaissance*. For him, James of Venice was "only a name," a translator of the "New Logic." Now, thanks to the efforts of the pioneers and of new collaborators who described the manuscripts, examined the texts, and undertook critical editions, the list of the Greco-Latin translations of Aristotle available at the end of the twelfth century is fairly well established.[57] "Iacobus Veneticus grecus" now has a less meager historical background;[58] he is credited not only with translations of the New Logic—a version of the *Analytica posteriora*, with fragments of a commentary by Alexander Aphrodisias, and a partial version of the *Sophistici elenchi*—but also with translations of the "Libri naturales": *Physica, De anima*, part of the "Parva naturalia" (*De memoria, De iuventute, De longitudine vitae, De vita, De respiratione*) and of the so-called "Metaphysica vetustissima" including books 1–4.4 in the extant manuscripts.[59] A close study of Henricus Aristippus's methods of translation inclined the general editor of "Aristoteles latinus" to deprive him of credit for

Middle Ages: The *de mensura circuli,"* *Osiris* 10 (1952) 587–618 at 596. In a forthcoming study, "Über das isoperimetrische Problem im Mittelalter," H.L.L. Busard shares Björnbo's opinion (private communication).

[56]Albert Lejeune, ed., *L'Optique de Claude Ptolemée dans la version latine d'après l'arabe de l'émir Eugène de Sicile*, Recueil de travaux d'histoire et de philologie 4th ser. 8 (Louvain 1956); see also Wilfred R. Theisen, "The Medieval Tradition of Euclid's Optics" (diss. University of Wisconsin 1972). On Eugene's career, works and translations see Evelyn M. Jamison. *Admiral Eugenius of Sicily, His Life and Work, and the Authorship of the Epistola ad Petrum, and the Historia Hugonis Falcandi Siculi* (London 1957).

[57]The general plan was prepared by Aleksander Birkenmajer, *Classement des ouvrages attribués à Aristote par le moyen âge latin: Prolegomena in Aristotelem latinum* (Cracow 1932), repr. in his *Etudes d'histoire des sciences et de la philosophie du moyen âge*, Studia Copernicana 1 (Wrocław 1970) 53–71. A detailed survey of the Latin translations of Aristotle and Averroes, and descriptions of the manuscripts, were undertaken by George Lacombe and others: see the Bibliographical Note, s.v. *Aristoteles latinus Codices*.

[58]Lorenzo Minio-Paluello, "Iacobus Veneticus grecus, Canonist and Translator of Aristotle," *Traditio* 8 (1952) 265–305, repr. in his *Opuscula: The Latin Aristotle* (Amsterdam 1972) 189–228.

[59]*Metaphysica Libri I–IV, 4. Translatio Iacobi sive 'Vetustissima' cum scholiis et translatio composita sive 'Vetus,'* ed. Gudrun Vuillemin-Diem, Aristoteles latinus 25.1-1a (Brussels 1970).

the early version of *De generatione et corruptione*,[60] but the translation from the Greek of book 4 of the *Meteora* is firmly ascribed to him in the manuscript tradition.

A number of anonymous translators have been dated in the twelfth century and placed most likely in Italy, where a knowledge of Greek and an interest in Aristotle were converging. James of Venice did not translate or retranslate all the treatises constituting the New Logic; an anonymous scholar worked on the *Analytica priora* and the *Topica*.[61] The translator of a version of the *Analytica posteriora* discovered in the Toledo chapter library, first described as "an anonymous reviser" of the version by James of Venice, is probably a "Ioannes," of whom nothing is known yet.[62] Another anonymous scholar translated *De generatione et corruptione* and probably also the "Ethica vetus," including books 2–3 of the *Nicomachean Ethics*.[63] Probably in the late twelfth century, an almost complete translation of the *Metaphysics* (books 1–10 and 12–14), generally known as "Metaphysica media,"[64] was made by the same man who translated book 1 and part of book 2 of the *Physica*, the so-called "Physica Vaticana."[65] The "Parva naturalia" that were not translated by James of Venice are credited to two anonymous scholars: *De somno et vigilia* to one, *De sensu et sensato* and *De divinatione per somnum* to the other.

By about 1200, a large part of the "Libri naturales" existed in Greco-Latin versions;[66] other parts, in Arabo-Latin translations. Aside from these

[60]This question was discussed and settled by Lorenzo Minio-Paluello: "Henri Aristippe, Guillaume de Moerbeke et les traductions latines médiévales des 'Météorologiques' et du 'De generatione et corruptione' d'Aristote," *Revue philosophique de Louvain* 45 (1947) 206–35, repr. in idem, *Opuscula* (n. 58 above) 57–86.

[61]The Logic translations have now been completely edited. Lorenzo Minio-Paluello gives a list of eight translators, six of them anonymous, from Greek into Latin in the 12th century, in the preface to his edition of the *Analytica priora*, Aristoteles latinus 3 (Bruges 1962).

[62]Lorenzo Minio-Paluello and Bernard G. Dod, eds., *Analytica posteriora*, Aristoteles latinus 4.1–4 (2nd ed. Bruges 1968); in the preface the editors ascribe the so-called "translatio anonyma Toletana" to "Iohannes."

[63]René A. Gauthier, ed., *Ethica Nicomachea*, Aristoteles latinus 26.1–3 (5 vols. Leiden 1972–74) vol. 2, *Translatio antiquissima libr. II–III sive 'Ethica vetus' et translationis antiquioris quae supersunt sive 'Ethica nova,' 'Hoferiana,' 'Borghesiana.'*

[64]*Metaphysica Lib. I–X, XII–XIV: Translatio anonyma sive 'media,'* ed. Gudrun Vuillemin-Diem, Aristoteles latinus 25.2 (Leiden 1976).

[65]Auguste Mansion, ed., *Physica: Translatio Vaticana*, Aristoteles latinus 7.2 (Bruges 1957). This translation is preserved in a unique manuscript, Vat Reg lat 1855, signaled and described by Haskins, *Science* 224–25. There is some debate concerning the date of this codex; Gudrun Vuillemin-Diem, in the preface to the edition of the "Metaphysica media" (n. 64 above) reproduced with a charming irony the various opinions of famous scholars. Minio-Paluello was the first to note a close resemblance of vocabulary between the "Physica Vaticana" and the "Metaphysica media"; see his "Note sull'Aristotele latino medievale II: Caratteristiche del traduttore della 'Physica Vaticana' e della 'Metaphysica media,'" *Rivista di filosofia neo-scolastica* 42 (1950) 226–31, repr. in idem, *Opuscula* (n. 58 above) 102–07. Vuillemin-Diem developed the comparison in "Die Metaphysica media: Übersetzungsmethode und Textverständnis," AHDLMA 42 (1975) 7–69.

[66]Concerning this recovery of Aristotle it must be noted that the ignorance of the "Libri naturales" and "Metaphysica" during the early Middle Ages was not as complete as is frequently

translations, there are traces of fragmentary versions of Aristotelian and pseudo-Aristotelian works—one of the many questions scholars have still to elucidate. Some physicians or "naturalists" quote Aristotle and their quotations do not coincide with the known versions; moreover, they allude to or quote texts translated only in the thirteenth century, such as the *Libri de animalibus* and *Problemata*. The most interesting of these outsiders is David of Dinant, whose *Quaternuli* were condemned by a synod in 1210: "Quaternuli magistri David de Dinant infra natale episcopo Parisiensi afferantur et comburantur."[67] Fragments of the *Quaternuli* (later quoted by Albertus Magnus as *De tomis*) were discovered among the manuscripts investigated and described on behalf of the "Aristoteles latinus."[68] These fragments are a kind of "Florilegium aristotelicum": the authority of Aristotle in the "Libri naturales" is constantly invoked, and there are long quotations from *On Animals* and the *Problemata*, translated directly from the Greek. David says that he had visited Greece; a prologue addressed to a certain "Aptideni commilitoni meo in gimnasio greco" seems to imply that he had studied the language seriously.

OTHER TRANSLATIONS FROM THE GREEK IN ITALY

The Greco-Latin versions of Galen and of the *Geoponica* executed by Burgundio did not interest historians much until recently. We need a "Galenus latinus": recension and description of manuscripts and critical editions that would enable us to appreciate the importance of the great physician and philosopher. There is hope that this wish will be realized, particularly for the Burgundio versions,[69] and that the revival of Galen in Italy will be described by competent specialists.[70] We do not know if, or to what extent, translations

---

assumed. Theodore Silverstein observed that a number of philosophical treatises, for instance Calcidius's commentary on the *Timaeus* and the *Solutiones ad Chosroem* of Priscianus Lydus, contained quotations or allusions; see his "Adelard, Aristotle, and the *De natura deorum*," *Classical Philology* 47 (1952) 82–86.

[67]Heinrich Denifle and Emile Chatelain, eds., *Chartularium universitatis Parisiensis* (4 vols. + supp. Paris 1889–97, 1937–64) 1.70.

[68]The discovery was made by A. Birkenmajer, "Découverte de fragments manuscrits de David de Dinant," *Revue néoscolastique de philosophie* 35 (1933) 220–29, repr. in his *Etudes* (n. 57 above) 11–20. The fragments discovered by Birkenmajer were edited by Marian Kurdziałek, *Davidis de Dinanto quaternulorum fragmenta*, Studia mediewistyczne 3 (Warsaw 1963). Previously, Gabriel Théry had published a study on David and his theories, using the quotations contained in Albertus Magnus's works: *Autour du décret de 1210*, vol. 1: *David de Dinant: Etude sur son panthéisme matérialiste* (Kain [Belgium] 1925).

[69]Burgundio, who was a judge and not a physician, was incited to translate Galen's tracts by the reverence surrounding the Galenic tradition and by specific requests. A "translatio antiqua" of the *Technē* (*Ars medica*) was completed by Burgundio for master Bartholomew of Salerno; see Richard J. Durling, "Corrigenda and Addenda to Diels' Galenica, 1: Codices Vaticani," *Traditio* 23 (1967) 463–76 at 463. A Greco-Latin translation of Hippocrates's Aphorisms with the commentary of Galen was partly translated by Burgundio; the second part was translated much later, by Nicholas of Reggio in the 14th century: see Kibre (n. 10 above).

[70]Richard J. Durling initiated a survey of the early editions and the manuscript tradition: "A Chronological Census of Renaissance Editions and Translations of Galen," JWCI 24 (1961)

were made at Salerno. A saying of Stephen of Antioch, often quoted, would suggest that Greek and Arabic were known at Salerno, but no precise documents can corroborate this assertion.[71]

Curiosity about Greek occult science and oneiromancy is an aspect of twelfth-century culture that cannot be overlooked, nor did it fail to interest Haskins. He tentatively ascribed the translation of the *Kyranides*,[72] a curious miscellany of hermetism and folklore, to Pascalis Romanus, an Italian settled at Constantinople; he noted that this man's treatise on the interpretation of dreams, *Liber thesauri occulti*, was apparently derived from Greek sources.[73] The recent editor of this work has indeed shown that the second book and the first part of the third were translated or adapted from Artemidorus and from the so-called "Achmet," a Byzantine compilation under an assumed name, probably in homage to Arabic oneiromancy.[74] A complete version of "Achmet" was executed ten years later (about 1175–76) by Leo Tuscus; this translation was used in the last part of the *Liber thesauri occulti*, perhaps completed or revised later. It must be noted that in the first part of his treatise, Pascalis Romanus quotes Aristotle "in libro de naturis animalium"—another instance of a direct knowledge and free translation of the "Libri naturales."

THE NEAR EAST

The Latin kingdom of the crusaders was not a very favorable place for translating activity. Adelard's alleged experience seems an isolated case;

230–305; see also his "Corrigenda" (n. 69 above) 463–76. He has inaugurated a "Galenus latinus" with a critical edition of one of Burgundio's translations: *Burgundio of Pisa's Translation of Galen's De complexionibus*, Galenus latinus, Ars medica, Abt. 2, Griechisch-lateinische Medizin 6.1 (Berlin 1976).

[71]This occurs in the prologue of the *Breviarium medicaminum* compiled by Stephen: "Medicaminum omnium breviarium subdimus . . . collatis et arabicis et grecę scriptis Diascoridis libris . . . quoniam latinorum nobis nominum ad liquidum peritia non est. qui ad nostrum accesserit opus studiosus lector de incognitis quos possit consulere habeat. Nam et in Sicilia et Salerni ubi horum maxime studiosi sunt et Greci habentur et lingue gnari arabice quos qui voluerit consulere poterit"; see Valentin Rose, *Verzeichniss der lateinischen Handschriften der Königlichen Bibliothek zu Berlin* 13.2.3 (Berlin 1905) 1063, *Codices latini electorales* no. 898 (lat. fol. 74 [12th c.]). Sentence partially quoted by Haskins, *Science* 132–33.

[72]Haskins, *Science* 219–21. Louis Delatte, ed., *Textes latins et vieux français relatifs aux Cyranides* (Liège 1942), an edition, from a limited number of manuscripts, of the Latin translation made at Constantinople in 1169.

[73]S. Collin-Roset, "Le *Liber thesauri occulti* de Pascalis Romanus (Un traité d'interprétation des songes du XIIe siècle)," AHDLMA 30 (1963) 111–98. The treatise in its primitive form was written at Constantinople in 1165; it was probably not completed by Pascalis himself. Collin-Roset confirms Haskins's suggestion concerning the attribution of the version of the *Kyranides* to Pascalis Romanus; she adds a list of manuscripts supplementing Delatte's list. Pascalis's version of Epiphanios's Life of the Virgin was edited by Ezio Franceschini, *Studi e note di filologia latina medievale*, Pubblicazioni della Università Cattolica del Sacro Cuore 4th ser., Scienze filologiche 30 (Milan 1938) 109–28.

[74]See Toufic Fahd, "L'oniromancie orientale et ses répercussions sur l'oniromancie de l'Occident médiéval," *Oriente e Occidente nel medioevo: Filosofia e scienze*, Accademia Nazionale dei Lincei, Convegno 13, 1969 (Rome 1971) 347–71 on the *Oneirocriticon* ascribed to "Achmet b. Sirin," translated from the Greek by Leo Tuscus; Franz Drexl, ed., *Achmetis Oneirocriticon* (Leip-

scholars did not normally travel to Syria or Palestine to get acquainted with Arabic science. The clerics who settled in the East made little use of their opportunity, though a few texts circulating among Eastern Christians may have been translated or excerpted for apologetic purposes.[75] Haskins could name only one man with scientific interests: Stephen, treasurer of Antioch, who had probably studied medicine.[76] Besides his new translation of ꜥAli ibn ꜥAbbas and a *Breviarium medicaminum* compiled from Greek and Arabic sources, we should probably accept the ascription of a treatise contained in MS Cambrai 930: "Liber Mamonis in astronomia a Stephano philosopho translatus." Despite the heading, it is not a translation but a sharp criticism of the old cosmography current in the Latin West, represented by Macrobius, which is contrasted with the Ptolemaic-Arabic system of the nine spheres. Since the peculiar system of dating "a Passione Domini" used by Stephen in his translation is found in this tract, Haskins's doubts concerning the authorship seem unfounded.

TRANSLATIONS FROM ARABIC

Most of the twelfth-century translation from Arabic to Latin was done in Spain, with an occasional extension to Languedoc, and most of the texts chosen were scientific and philosophical. As in Italy, signs of a new era appeared long before the twelfth century. It was probably during the second half of the tenth century that Arabic tracts on the use of the astrolabe and quadrant were translated or adapted in Catalonia, perhaps by Mozarabs coming from Al-Andalus: a remarkable acquisition for the benefit of astronomy—and astrology. Early copies and the use of the tracts by Herman of Reichenau in the eleventh century are witnesses of their diffusion.[77] A strange compilation

---

zig 1925) vi–ix, prolegomena to the edition of the Greek text. The choice of this name by a Byzantine was inspired by the fame of Muh. b. Sirin (d. 728), legendary master of dream interpretation; see A. Abdel Daim, *L'oniromancie arabe d'après Ibn Sirin* (Damascus 1958).

[75]See n. 32 above, and Norman Daniel, *Islam and the West: The Making of an Image* (Edinburgh 1960) 230–31, concerning a "Syrian Apology" quoted by Godfrey of Viterbo and a "Libellus de partibus transmarinis" reproduced in the *Speculum historiale* of Vincent of Beauvais. The most important Eastern Christian Apology, the "Risala" of the so-called pseudo-Kindi, was translated in its full form by Peter of Toledo for Peter the Venerable.

[76]See n. 14 above. The most important translation produced in the East, the version of the "long form" of the pseudo-Aristotelian *Secretum secretorum* by Philip of Tripoli, probably was made in the first half of the 13th century: see Haskins, *Science* 137–40.

[77]José M. Millás Vallicrosa, *Assaig d'història de les idees físiques i matemàtiques a la Catalunya medieval* (Barcelona 1931) 150–212. A series of tracts contained in MS Ripoll 225 (now in the Archivio de la Corona de Aragon, Barcelona) were described and partly edited by Millás. They concern mostly the use of the astrolabe and quadrant. Several are apparently direct translations from Arabic; others are adaptations. Most of these tracts are found in other early manuscripts described previously by Nikolai M. Bubnov, ed., *Gerberti opera mathematica (972–1003)* (Berlin 1899). Millás later supplemented his first study, in *Nuevos estudios sobre historia de la ciencia española* (Barcelona 1960) chs. 4 and 5, "Los primeros tratados de astrolabio en la España arabe" and "Las primeras traducciones cientificas de origen oriental hasta mediados del siglo XII," 61–78 and 79–115 at 93–104. See also Juan Vernet, "Les traductions scientifiques dans l'Espagne du Xe

known as the *Liber Alchandrei* or *Mathematica Alhandrei* circulated too during that period, the oldest copy being late tenth century; it contained a chapter on Arabic lunar mansions and their influence, linked to the Cordova calendar of 961.[78] Why this promising prelude was not followed immediately by an increasing stream of translations during the eleventh century is a question still unsolved. It may simply be due to our ignorance, for an Andalusian Moslem of the late eleventh century, Ibn ʿAbdun, alludes to the translating activity going on in Spain with a warning addressed to the faithful: "You must not sell books of science to Jews and Christians, . . . because it happens that they translate these scientific books and attribute them to their own people and to their bishops, when they are indeed Moslem works."[79]

From what we know now, the great movement of translations followed the progress of the Reconquista. Men born in Spain, who spoke Arabic and the Romance vernacular, sometimes knew Latin if they were clerics, and many scholars coming from far-away countries tried to extract the treasures of science from the books of the Saracens.

ADELARD OF BATH AND PETER ALFONSI

There is a notable exception to this general statement: Adelard of Bath.[80] He says that he visited Salerno and "Graecia maior" (probably including Sicily as well as southern Italy); he dedicated his tract *De eodem et diverso* to William, bishop of Syracuse (ca. 1105–15). He could have picked up some Arabic there, but he mentions only a Greek philosopher and physician in *De eodem et diverso*. He went to the East for several years to study Arabic wisdom and science: he names Tarsus in Cilicia and Antioch in Syria in his *Quaestiones naturales*. The nature and extent of his Arabic studies is obscure; the *Quaestiones naturales* contain vague allusions rather than specific teaching from

---

siècle," *Cahiers de Tunisie* 18 (1970) 47–59 at 56–57. On the same topic with a different point of view, cf. André Van de Vyver, "Les premières traductions latines (Xe–XIe siècles) de traités arabes sur l'astrolabe," *Premier Congrès international de géographie historique* (3 vols. Brussels 1931–35) vols. 2, *Mémoires*, 266–90; idem, "Les plus anciennes traductions latines médiévales (Xe–XIe siècles) de traités d'astronomie et d'astrologie," *Osiris* 1 (1936) 658–91 at 665. On the diffusion of these texts, see James W. Thompson, "The Introduction of Arabic Science into Lorraine in the Tenth Century," *Isis* 12 (1929) 184–93, and Mary C. Welborn, "Lotharingia as a Center of Arabic and Scientific Influence in the Eleventh Century," *Isis* 16 (1931) 188–99 and 17 (1932) 260–63.

[78]On the *Liber Alchandrei* see Millás, *Assaig* (n. 77 above) 246–59; Van de Vyver, "Les plus anciennes" (n. 77 above) 666–84; and Lynn Thorndike, *A History of Magic and Experimental Science* (8 vols. New York 1923–58) 1 710–19.

[79]Evariste Lévi-Provençal, ed., "Un document sur la vie urbaine et les corps de métiers à Séville au début du XIIe siècle: Le traité d'Ibn ʿAbdūn publié avec une introduction et un glossaire," *Journal asiatique* 224 (1934) 177–299 at 248; Spanish translation by E. Lévi-Provençal and E. García Gómez, *Sevilla a comienzos del siglo XII* (Madrid 1948) 173: "No deben venderse a judíos ni a cristianos libros de ciencia, salvo los que tratan de su ley [sharīʿa], por que luego traducen los libros científicos y se los atribuyen a los suyos y a sus obispos, siendo así que se trata de obras musulmanas," quoted by Juan Vernet, "La ciencia en el Islam y Occidente," *L'Occidente e l'Islam nell'alto Medioevo*, Settimane 12 (2 vols. Spoleto 1965) 2.537–72 at 568.

[80]On Adelard of Bath, the most recent and accurate survey is by Marshall Clagett, "Adelard of Bath," DSB 1 (1970) 61–64, but Haskins, *Science* 20–42 is still fundamental.

Arabic "masters."[81] We do not know whether he began his translator's career in the East; possibly he brought back to England some books that he later endeavored to translate into Latin. His translations include two short astrological texts, *Ysagoge minor Iapharis*, a compendium of Abū Maʿshar's great introduction to astrology, and probably a tract on engraved astrological images.[82] His more important contributions to the development of astronomy and mathematics are the translations of the introduction and tables of al-Khwārizmī in the recension of Maslama al-Majriti for the meridian of Cordova, and the version, or versions, of Euclid's *Elements*. The fact that Adelard used the Maslama tables inclined some historians to suppose that he had visited Spain,[83] though (despite a tendency to boast) he never mentions that he had traveled or studied in the Peninsula.

Another suggestion was cautiously offered by Haskins: Adelard may have collaborated with Peter Alfonsi, after this converted Spanish Jew had become king Henry's physician; or he may have used documents left by that learned man. This hypothesis was based on three points: (1) the heading in a manuscript of Peter Alfonsi's *Disciplina clericalis* (a collection of sentences and tales translated or adapted from Arabic), "Dixit Petrus Amphulsus servus Christi Ihesu Henrici primi regis Anglorum medicus compositor huius libri. . ." (MS Cambridge, Univ. Ii.vi.11); (2) a tract on the lunar nodes, dated 1120, presented as a translation into Latin of Peter's teachings by Walcher, prior of Malvern: "Sententia Petri Ebrei cognomento Anphus de Dracone quam Dominus Walcerus prior Malvernensis ecclesie in latinam transtulit linguam"; (3) still more important, an Oxford manuscript (Corpus Christi Coll. 283) containing a partial copy of the long introduction and a peculiar redaction of the Khwarizmian tables with references to Peter Alfonsi, followed by chapters on the various eras, introduced by a prologue due to Peter himself.[84] The subsequent publication of the *Sententia de dracone* and of the prologue, and later of the material contained in the Oxford manuscript, reinforced the

[81]Brian Lawn, *The Salernitan Questions: An Introduction to the History of Medieval and Renaissance Problem Literature* (Oxford 1963) 20–30, denies any Arabic influence on the *Quaestiones naturales*; we should rather say that it is not obvious.

[82]This translation is ascribed to Adelard of Bath in MS Lyon 328 (261), quoted by Haskins, *Science* 30: "Liber prestigiorum Elbidis secundum Ptolomeum et Hermetem per Adhelardum bathoniensem translatus." Lynn Thorndike found another manuscript, anonymous (Vat Pal 1401, fols. 39v–41v), and gave an analysis of the text, "Traditional Medieval Tracts concerning engraved astrological images," *Mélanges Auguste Pelzer: Etudes d'histoire littéraire et doctrinale de la scolastique médiévale offertes à Monseigneur Auguste Pelzer* (Louvain 1947) 217–74 at 227–29. See also Francis J. Carmody, *The Astronomical Works of Thabit b. Qurra* (Berkeley 1960) 178, adding another anonymous manuscript, Vat lat 10803, fols. 62v–66v.

[83]Franz P. Bliemetzrieder, *Adelhard von Bath: Blätter aus dem Leben einer englischen Naturphilosophen des 12. Jahrhunderts und Bahnbrechers einer Wiedererweckung der griechischen Antike* (Munich 1935) 58–59 and 87, is rather cautious.

[84]Haskins's suggestions (*Science* 115–19) were much reinforced by José M. Millás Vallicrosa, "La aportación astronómica de Pedro Alfonso," *Sefarad* 3 (1943) 65–105, which includes an edition of the *Sententia de dracone*, of a "prooemium ad scolares," and of the prologue to the astronomical tables. The introduction was reproduced in his *Estudios sobre historia de la ciencia española* (Barcelona 1949) 197–218.

hypothesis.[85] The editor of the Oxford redaction of the tables proposed the date of 1 October 1116 for the work of Peter Alfonsi; the recension ascribed to Adelard was dated 1126 or later.[86] Probably this last work was preceded by at least a fragmentary text linked with Peter Alfonsi; such an assumption agrees with what his other works, especially the cosmological parts of the *Dialogus*, reveal about his astronomical interests and competence. The *De dracone* contains a specific reference to the astronomical tables: "secundum tabulas Petri Anfulsi." The "translation" of this tract by Walcher—in fact a free interpretation of the master's sayings, probably uttered in a vernacular—is a clear witness of Peter's presence in England during the first quarter of the twelfth century. The formula gives a clue to interpreting the peculiar presentation of Peter's works: they begin in Arabic fashion, "Dixit Petrus Alphunsus," and the headings refer to the "compositor libri." We may strongly suspect that Peter required help for the final redaction of the *Dialogus* and *Disciplina clericalis*.[87] A learned Jew could learn Latin, but he could not easily write a correct prose fluently, especially when he learned the language only late in life.[88] Did Adelard collaborate directly with Peter Alfonsi, or did he use an existing version made by the king's physician?[89]

There is no hint of an outside collaborator for Adelard's translation of Euclid's *Elements*, except perhaps a student of his, Iohannes O'Creath. This is the most widely diffused of Adelard's versions, found in three successive forms

[85]Otto Neugebauer, ed., *The Astronomical Tables of Al-Khwārizmī*, Historisk-filosofiske Skrifter udgivet af Det Kongelige Danske Videnskabernes Selskab 4.2 (Copenhagen 1962) includes the edition of Peter Alfonsi's prologue and of four chapters concerning the Arabic, Persian, Christian, and Egyptian calendars.

[86]Heinrich Suter, ed. (continuing work begun by Axel A. Björnbo and Rasmus O. Besthorn), *Die astronomischen Tafeln des Muhammed ibn Mūsā al-Khwārizmī in der Bearbeitung des Maslama ibn Ahmed al-Madjrītī und der latein.Uebersetzung des Athelhard von Bath*, Det Kongelige Danske Videnskabernes Selskabs Skrifter 7th ser., Historisk og filosofisk afdeling 3.1 (Copenhagen 1914).

[87]Peter Alfonsi presents the *Disciplina clericalis* as his own compilation of Arabic tales and sentences that he then translated into Latin: "Deus . . . michi sit in auxilium qui me librum hunc componere et in latinum transferre compulit," Alfons Hilka and Werner Soderhjelm, eds., *Die "Disciplina clericalis" des Petrus Alfonsi* (Heidelberg 1911) 1.15–17. The manuscript tradition of the *Disciplina clericalis* as well as of the *Dialogus* (n. 27 above) rather favors a final Latin redaction executed in England and/or France; see Manitius 3.276–77.

[88]Peter Alfonsi's age when he was christened is not specified in the genuine text of the *Dialogus* (n. 27 above). The mention of the Spanish era, added after the Christian year (1106) in the manuscripts—"era M^{ma}. C^{ma}. XL^{ma}. IIII^{ta}."—was unduly transformed in the printed editions into "aetatis meae anno quadragesimo quarto"; see C. Nedelcou, "Sur la date de la naissance de Pierre Alphonse," *Romania* 35 (1906) 462–63.

[89]There are some remarkable common points between Peter Alfonsi's cosmography, set forth in the scientific digressions of the *Dialogus*, and Adelard's teachings in the prologue of the Khwarizmian tables and in his still unpublished "Libellus de opere astrolapsus": (1) *Arin* as the center of the world (*Dialogus* 562; Adelard, Prologue, ed. Suter [n. 86 above] 1); (2) the ten spheres of Ptolemaic-Arabic astronomy, the zodiac being ascribed as a sphere (*Dialogus* 562; "Libellus de opere astrolapsus," MS Cambridge, Fitzwilliam Museum McClean 165, fol. 81–81v); (3) the first climate described as an earthly paradise (*Dialogus* 547; "Libellus" fols. 82v–83). An edition of the "Libellus" is being prepared by Bruce Dickey, Pontifical Institute of Mediaeval Studies, Toronto, from the three extant manuscripts of the work.

usually termed "Adelard I, II, III."[90] Recently historians of mathematics have tried to disentangle its complex manuscript tradition, to describe the three versions, and to determine their nature. A treatise derived from a Khwarizmian arithmetic, "Liber Ysagogarum Alchorismi in artem astronomicam a magistro A. compositus," is not a translation, though an Arabic background is presumed; Adelard's eventual authorship of it is very doubtful.[91] No inscription or reference permits crediting to Adelard the translation of a compendium of Khwarizmian arithmetic preserved incomplete (the last quires are missing) in a single manuscript copied in the early thirteenth century.[92] This tract, *De numero Indorum*, appears to be a version from Arabic, presumably executed in the twelfth century.

An interesting case of collaboration between a learned wandering Jew and Western scholars is Abraham ibn Ezra.[93] Like Peter Alfonsi, he was from Spain. Like his contemporary Abraham bar Hiyya, he decided to write scientific works, chiefly astrological, in Hebrew; since astrology requires a sound basis in astronomy, he translated into Hebrew a commentary by Ibn al-Muthannā on the tables of al-Khwārīzmī, adding a preface concerning the introduction of Hindu science among the Arabs.[94] In the mid-twelfth century (ca. 1140–67), he traveled all over Europe, staying successively in Rome, Salerno, Lucca, Pisa, Mantua, Verona, Béziers, Narbonne, Bordeaux, Angers, Dreux, London, and Winchester; it seems that his main occupation was to establish astronomical tables according to the meridian of various cities. One tract extant in Latin has been edited, *Fundamenta tabularum*.[95] Two smaller

[90]Marshall Clagett, "The Medieval Latin Translations from the Arabic of the *Elements* of Euclid, with Special Emphasis on the Versions of Adelard of Bath," *Isis* 44 (1953) 16–42 at 27ff.; John E. Murdoch, "The Medieval Euclid: Salient Aspects of the Translations of the *Elements* by Adelard of Bath and Campanus of Novara," *Revue de synthèse* 89 (1968) = *XIIe Congrès international d'histoire des sciences*, Actes IA (Paris 1968) 67–94; and idem, "Euclid: Transmission of the Elements," DSB 4 (1971) 437–59 at 447.

[91]André Allard, *Les plus anciennes versions latines du XIIe siècle issues de l'arithmétique d'Al-Khwārizmi: Histoire des textes suivie de l'édition critique des traités attribués à Adélard de Bath et Jean de Séville et d'un remaniement de ce dernier* (Louvain 1975; in press, Corpus scriptorum latinorum Paravianum [Turin]).

[92]Edited, with a facsimile of the manuscript (Cambridge Univ. Ii.6.5), by Kurt Vogel, [Muḥammad ibn Mūsā al-Khuwārizmī], *Algorismus, das früheste Lehrbuch zum Rechnen mit indischen Ziffern* (Aalen 1963) and by A. P. Juschkewitsch, "Ueber ein Werk des Abu ʿAbdallah Muḥ. ibn Mūsā al-Huwarizmī al-Maǧusi zur Arithmetik der Inder," *Beiheft zur Schriftenreihe für Geschichte der Naturwissenschaften, Technik und Medizin, herausgegeben zum 60. Geburtstag von Gerhard Harigs* (Leipzig 1964) 21–63. See also Adolf P. Youschkevitch, *Les mathématiques arabes: VIIIe–XVe siècles*, trans. M. Cazenave and K. Jaouiche (Paris 1976) 15–20.

[93]Moritz Steinschneider, "Abraham ibn Esra," *Gesammelte Schriften*, ed. Heinrich Malter and Alexander Marx (Berlin 1925) 407–506; José M. Millás Vallicrosa, "El magisterio astronómico de Abraham ibn ʿEzra en la Europa latina," *Estudios* (n. 84 above) 289–347.

[94]*Ibn al-Muthannā's Commentary on the Astronomical Tables of al-Khwârizmî: Two Hebrew Versions*, ed. and trans. with an astronomical commentary by Bernard R. Goldstein, Yale Studies in the History of Science and Medicine 2 (New Haven 1967). The editor shows convincingly that one of the versions (unfortunately incomplete in a Parma manuscript) can be ascribed to Ibn Ezra. The Latin translation of Ibn al-Muthannā's work is by a contemporary, Hugh of Santalla; see n. 117 below.

[95]José M. Millás Vallicrosa, *El libro de los fundamentos de las Tablas astronómicas de R. Abraham ibn Ezra* (Madrid 1947).

tracts, one on the astrolabe, the other an almanac, exist in Latin form.[96] That he probably had around him friends and local helpers who interpreted his words and were able to produce a version in more or less correct Latin can be inferred from a sentence in the tract on the astrolabe: "ut ait . . . Abraham magister noster egregius quo dictante et hanc dispositionem astrolabii conscripsimus." It is quite possible that other Spanish Jews visiting France, England, and Italy had a similar role and transmitted some Arabic science to local amateurs. But the serious amateurs went to Spain and often endeavored to learn Arabic themselves.

TRANSLATIONS IN SPAIN

One chapter in the traditional account of twelfth-century translations in Spain needs to be emended: the legend of the Toledo school of translators supposedly initiated under the patronage of archbishop Raymond (1125–52). It began when John of Seville, a translator active in the second quarter of the twelfth century, was misidentified with a supposed "Iohannes Avendauth." The latter was presented as the collaborator of an archdeacon Dominicus in translating Avicenna's *De anima*, dedicated to Raymond and offered as a compendium of Aristotelian teaching: "in quo quidquid Aristoteles dixit in libro suo *de anima* et *de sensu et sensato* et *de intellectu et intellecto*, ab auctore libri scias esse collectum."[97] As a consequence, a collection of philosophical translations—of Avicenna, Algazel, and Ibn Gabirol (Avicebron)—was ascribed to the collaboration of "Iohannes Avendauth" with Dominicus Gundi-

[96]José M. Millás Vallicrosa, "Un nuevo tratado de astrolabio, de R. Abraham ibn ʿEzra," *Al-Andalus* 5 (1940) 1–29 at 28; according to Millás this tract was written in England ca. 1160. Idem, "Un tratado de almanaque probablemente de R. Abraham ibn ʿEzra," *Studies and Essays in the History of Science and Learning Offered in Homage to George Sarton*, ed. M. F. Ashley Montagu (New York 1946) 419–32.

[97]Amable Jourdain, *Recherches critiques sur l'âge et l'origine des traductions latines d'Aristote et sur les commentaires grecs ou arabes employés par les docteurs scolastiques*, ed. Charles Jourdain (Paris 1843; repr. 1960; orig. ed. 1819) 107–20, 449. Jourdain, editing the prologue of the translation of *De anima*, mixed up the text offered by two manuscripts of the Bibliothèque du roi, BN lat 6443 and 8802. The latter's rubric (an isolated case) "ad archiepiscopum Toletanum Reimundum" contradicted the text that followed: "Reverentissimo Toletane sedis archiepiscopo . . . Iohanni Avendehut israelita philosopho"; MS lat 6443 presented the abbreviation "Io.," followed by "israelita philosophus." Jourdain interpreted "Iohannes" and suggested that the man was a converted Jew and might be the "Iohannes Hispalensis" or "Hispanus" who had offered a translation to archbishop Raymond. Jourdain's suggestion was transformed into assertion by Moritz Steinschneider, *Die hebraeischen Übersetzungen des Mittelalters und die Juden als Dolmetscher* (Berlin 1893; repr. Graz 1956) 981–84, 259–61, 281–83, 582; see also his *Die europäischen Übersetzungen aus dem Arabischen bis Mitte des 17. Jahrhunderts*, SB Vienna, Phil.-hist. Kl. 149.4 and 151.1 (2 vols. Vienna 1904–05; repr. Graz 1956) n. 68, 40–50. Such is the strength of old habits that when A. Birkenmajer discovered and edited, from MS Bruges 510, the preliminary chapters of Avicenna's *Liber Asschiphe* (Kitāb al-Shifaʾ), in a Latin version known as *Sufficientia*, he assumed that the very important but unnamed dedicatee was archbishop Raymond and that the speaker "Avendeuch israelita" was Iohannes Hispalensis: "Avicennas Vorrede zum 'Liber sufficientiae' und Roger Bacon," *Revue néoscolastique de philosophie* 36 (1934) 308–20, repr. in his *Etudes* (n. 57 above) 89–101.

salvi; these texts, and a collection of astrological translations in which appeared the name of "Iohannes Hispalensis" or "Hispanus" or "Hispaniensis," were situated in Toledo during Raymond's episcopate, in the second quarter of the century. Then, Daniel of Morley's enthusiastic description, in his *De naturis superiorum et inferiorum*,[98] of his studies in Toledo under master Gerard of Cremona, who had just translated Ptolemy's *Almagest* from Arabic, was projected back onto the earlier period to justify viewing Toledo as the main center of translations during the twelfth century.[99]

Haskins did not follow in his predecessors' tracks without some reserve. He expressed doubts about "Iohannes Avendauth," and concerning the "school of Toledo" he remarked, "Of a formal school the sources tell us very little." He pointed to translators active during the first half of the century who worked far from Toledo: Plato of Tivoli in Catalonia, Herman of Carinthia and his friend Robert of Ketene (or Chester) in northern Spain, Hugh of Santalla in Aragon, and later Herman in Languedoc.[100] And documents from the well-preserved Toledo archives have revealed no trace of any organized *studium* or school of translators.

A closer examination of the manuscripts and documents published from the archives has, however, yielded evidence that the flourishing period for translations in Toledo was later than Raymond's episcopate—rather, the second half of the twelfth century, beginning with Raymond's successor, Iohannes (1152–66). It was to him, in fact, that the translation of Avicenna's *De anima* was addressed;[101] similarly, the *floruit* of archdeacon Dominicus Gundisalvi, the Latin collaborator of the Jewish scholar "Avendauth," has been shifted by documents which place him in Toledo as late as 1178–81.[102] He had another collaborator, "magister Iohannes," possibly a member of the Toledo

---

[98]Valentin Rose published extracts in "Ptolomaeus und die Schule von Toledo," *Hermes* 8 (1874) 327–49. The full text was edited later: Karl Sudhoff, "Philosophia magistri Danielis de Merlai ad Iohannem Norwicensem episcopum," *Archiv für die Geschichte der Naturwissenschaften und der Technik* 8 (1917) 6–40; A. Birkenmajer, "Eine neue Handschrift des 'Liber de naturis inferiorum et superiorum' des Daniel von Merlai," ibid. 9 (1920) 45–51, repr. in his *Etudes* (n. 57 above) 45–51. A new edition has recently been published by Gregor Maurach: "Daniel von Morley, 'Philosophia,'" *Mittellateinisches Jahrbuch* 14 (1979) 204–55.

[99]The notion of a "school" originated not with Rose (n. 98 above) but with Jourdain (n. 97 above) 119: "il n'en reste pas moins certain que Raymond est le créateur d'un collège de traducteurs."

[100]Haskins, *Science* 12–13.

[101]H. Bédoret, "Les premières traductions tolédanes de philosophie: Oeuvres d'Avicenne," *Revue néoscolastique de philosophie* 41 (1938) 374–400. A full study of the existing manuscripts confirmed Bédoret's remarks; see Simone van Riet, ed., *Avicenna latinus: Liber de anima seu Sextus de naturalibus I–II–III*, Edition critique de la traduction latine médiévale (Louvain and Leiden 1972) 91*–105*.

[102]Manuel Alonso Alonso, "Notas sobre los traductores toledanos Domingo Gundisalvo y Juan Hispano," *Al-Andalus* 8 (1943) 155–88; idem, "Traducciones del arcediano Domingo Gundisalvo," *Al-Andalus* 12 (1947) 295–338. Alonso, who wrote many studies concerning the Toledo translators and translations, was the first to remark the important data contained in the Mozarabic Toledo cartulary edited by Angel González Palencia, *Los Mozárabes de Toledo en los siglos XII y XIII* (4 vols. Madrid 1926–30) 1.Document no. 141, dated 1178; no. 154, dated 1181.

chapter, for the translation of Algazel and Ibn Gabirol;[103] this man cannot be assimilated to "Avendauth," whose name appears alone in the manuscripts and who is described as "israelita philosophus."[104] The identity of "Avendauth" is still a matter of discussion.[105]

As for the tradition of archbishop Raymond's patronage, it is barely justified by a single dedication from John of Seville,[106] who offered the translation of Costa ben Luca's De differentia spiritus et animae "Raimundo Toletano archiepiscopo." This prolific translator may have spent part of his life in Toledo; some of his translations, however, are said to have been executed in "Limia" or "Luna." His dated versions and his treatise Epitome totius astrologiae indicate that he was active mainly between 1133 and 1142; two short tracts, De regimine sanitatis (extracts from Secretum secretorum), offered to a queen of Spain difficult to identify, and Costa ben Luca's De differentia, might be earlier. These widely diffused tracts are found in a mid-twelfth-century manuscript brought to England by a physician, master Herbert, who bequeathed his books to the Durham chapter.[107]

---

[103]New data were produced by Juan Francisco Rivera Recio from the Latin documents preserved in the Archivio Capitular of Toledo: "Nuevos datos sobre los traductores Gundisalvo y Juan Hispano," Al-Andalus 31 (1966, issued 1970) 267–80. He reproduced the lists of subscriptions of three deeds: one, dated 1162, has the names of "Dominicus Colerar. archidiaconus" and "magister Iohannes"; another, dated 1174, has "D. Colerar. archidiaconus"; a third, dated 1176, has "Girardus dictus magister, Iohannes magister scolarum, D. Colerar. archidiaconus." He explains that the archdeaconate of Cuellar belonged to the diocese of Segovia, linked with the archdiocese of Toledo; this is why "Dominicus" could be qualified as "archidiaconus Segobiensis apud Toletum" in the inscription of MS BN lat 6552. Rivera presents further information on one of Dominicus's successors as archdeacon of Cuellar, a "Iohannes" surnamed "Hispanus," "Ospinel" in the Arabic documents, who appears as dean of the Toledo chapter in 1194 and 1198: La iglesia de Toledo en el siglo XII, 1086–1208, Publicaciones del Instituto español de historia ecclesiastica, Monografias 10.1 (Rome 1966) esp. 198–99.

[104]See Marie-Thérèse d'Alverny, "Notes sur les traductions médiévales d'Avicenne," AHDLMA 19 (1952) 339–58 for a detailed account of the sections of the Kitāb al-Shifaʾ translated in Toledo during the second half of the 12th century and of their ascriptions to "Avendauth" alone, to "Avendauth" and "Dominicus," or to "Gundissalinus" (Dominicus Gundisalvi) alone; some are anonymous.

[105]See, however, Marie-Thérèse d'Alverny, "Avendauth?" Homenaje a Millás-Vallicrosa (2 vols. Barcelona 1954–56) 1.19–43, concerning the possible identification of "Avendauth israelita philosophus" with the Jewish philosopher Abraham ibn Daud, who lived in Toledo ca. 1148–80.

[106]There are two surveys of John of Seville's works and translations: Manuel Alonso Alonso, "Juan Sevillano, sus obras proprias y sus traducciones," Al-Andalus 18 (1953) 17–49, includes some erroneous or incautious ascriptions; Lynn Thorndike, "John of Seville," Speculum 34 (1959) 20–38, basing himself on extensive firsthand experience with manuscripts, decided that there are no grounds for identifying Iohannes Hispalensis with Avendauth, nor with a Iohannes Toletanus who translated Abu ʿAli, De nativitatibus, in 1153. Richard J. Lemay proposed to identify John of Seville with a bishop of Seville who left his seat and came to Talavera in 1145: "Dans l'Espagne du XIIe siècle: Les traductions de l'arabe au latin," Annales E.S.C. 18 (1963) 639–65; against this hypothesis, see Claudio Sánchez Albornoz, "Observaciones a unas paginas de Lemay sobre los traductores Toledanos," Cuadernos de historia de España 41–42 (1965) 313–24.

[107]MS Edinburgh, Nat. Libr. of Scotland Advocates 18.6.11. On this volume, which I have examined, see R. A. B. Mynors, Durham Cathedral Manuscripts to the End of the Twelfth Century (Oxford 1939) 62. The extract from the Secretum secretorum has the name "Iohannes Yspalensis" in the preface; the De differentia ends, "interpretatus a Iohanne Hispalensi et Limiensi." The

The main interest of Iohannes Hispalensis was the science of the stars. He translated al-Farghānī's *Scientia astrorum* and a number of astrological treatises by the best authors in that field: Messahala, Zael (Sahl ben Bishr), Albumasar (Abū Maʿshar),[108] Omar (ʿUmar al-Ṭabarī), Thābit ibn Qurrah on astrological images, and probably Alcabitius (al-Qabīṣī). John of Seville cites Azarquiel (al-Zarqālī), the great Toledan astronomer of the eleventh century, in a short astronomical tract, recently edited;[109] he may also have translated the Toledan tables, long before Gerard of Cremona.[110] The Toledan tables were circulating in southern France before 1141, when Raymond of Marseille's *Liber cursuum planetarum* introduced the Marseille tables.[111]

John of Seville is a very honest translator; his intelligent remarks on the method of translation, in the preface to the *De regimine sanitatis*, show that he understood the difficulty of his task. His literary culture is limited, and his Latin is not elegant, mostly because he follows the Arabic closely, to the point of reproducing the ritual eulogies. It seems likely from this preface that he was a Mozarab, with a sufficient knowledge of Latin to translate directly from Arabic.

Haskins dedicated a whole chapter to Hugh of Santalla, with excerpts from the eloquent prefaces addressed to his protector Michael, bishop of

---

same name and epithets appear in the early manuscripts of his numerous translations; in later manuscripts Limia or Luna disappears and the cognomen frequently becomes Hispaniensis or Hispanus.

[108]The most important of the Albumasar translations is the *Introductorium maius*, in 1133. A critical edition is being prepared by Richard J. Lemay, who published a preliminary study on the translations by John of Seville and Herman and on the impact of the text: *Abū Maʿshar and Latin Aristotelianism in the Twelfth Century: The Recovery of Aristotle's Natural Philosophy through Arabic Astrology* (Beirut 1962). On the translation of Abū Maʿshar's *Flores astrologiae*, see Paul Kunitzsch, "Abū Maʿsar, Johannes Hispalensis und Alkameluz," *Zeitschrift der deutschen Morgenländischen Gesellschaft* 120 (1970) 103–25; the Arabic original was discovered by Juan Vernet, "Cuestiones catalográficas referentes a autores orientales: Problemas bibliográficos intorno a Albumasar," *Biblioteconomía* 9 (1952) 12–17.

[109]José M. Millás Vallicrosa, "Una obra astronómica desconocida de Johannes Avendaut Hispanus" (from MS Madrid Bibl. Nac. 10053), *Osiris* 1 (1936) 451–75, repr. in his *Estudios* (n. 84 above) 263–88. The name inscribed by Millás is his own doing; the Madrid MS (late 13th c.) has "Ioannes Ispanus"; an earlier (13th c.) MS, Oxford St John's Coll. 188, has the correct form: "Iohannes Yspalensis." It is in this tract that John mentions having translated from the Arabic a treatise on astronomy, probably al-Farghānī's *Numerus mensium Arabum*, for two Englishmen: "in libro quem ego Iohannes Yspalensis interpres existens rogatu et ope duorum Angligenarum, Gauconis scilicet et Willelmi, de arabico in latinum transtuli," noted by Haskins, *Science* 13, and by Thorndike (n. 78 above) 2.73–78; this sentence shows John in the capacity of professional translator.

[110]On the early translation of the Toledan tables, circulating in the first half of the 12th century, see José M. Millás Vallicrosa, *Estudios sobre Azarquiel* (Madrid 1950 [1943]) 365–73.

[111]See Emmanuel Poulle, "Le traité d'astrolabe de Raymond de Marseille," *Studi medievali* 3rd ser. 5 (1964) 866–900 at 866–73, on the precise date of the *Liber cursuum planetarum*. The *Liber cursuum* was discovered by Pierre Duhem, who described the Marseille tables from the anonymous MS BN lat 14704: *Le système du monde: Histoire des doctrines cosmologiques de Platon à Copernic* (10 vols. Paris 1913–59) 3.201–26; later, Thorndike discovered another manuscript and Haskins (*Science* 96–98) a third one in which the author's name appeared. I am preparing with Emmanuel Poulle an edition of the *Liber cursuum planetarum* and of the recently discovered *Liber iudiciorum*.

Tarazona (1119–51).[112] Not much is known of Hugh's career.[113] Probably he was from northern Spain: Arabic was for him an acquired language, whereas his Latin is good, even sophisticated. Unlike John of Seville's, his versions are sometimes free: he does not slavishly follow the Arabic word order, and the choice and variety of terms show that he had a good classical background. This is particularly obvious in his version of a hermetic work, the *Liber Apollonii de secretis naturae et occultis rerum causis*, preserved in a unique but fortunately early manuscript.[114] This long treatise ends with the famous revelation of the ultimate secrets of nature which circulated independently under various forms as *Tabula smaragdina*, the fundamental text of alchemy.[115]

The interests of Hugh and his protector, if we can trust the prefaces, were astronomy and astrology, plus several kinds of divination, geomancy, and spatulomancy. The Arabic original of the first translated tract of spatulomancy mentioned by Haskins can be ascribed to al-Kindī.[116] Hugh gave a free version of the author's prologue, suppressing the dedication to the physician Yaḥyā ibn Māsawayh (Mesue). The second tract of spatulomancy described by Haskins was probably translated from an Andalusian author, judging by the contents. Hugh's version of a commentary on al-Khwarīzmī by an Andalusian author, Ibn al-Muthannā,[117] and two Hebrew translations of the same work[118] allow us to appreciate this translator's way of working. In a preface addressed to the bishop, Hugh intermingles al-Muthannā's own prologue, freely adapted, and personal remarks, mentioning for instance that he has not followed the dialogue form of the original. The Latin text generally agrees with the anonymous Hebrew version. Hugh has transcribed some Arabic technical terms; he alters the word order and sometimes leaves out sentences or adds an explanation; he warns once that he has omitted a useless digression concerning angels.

[112]*Science* 67–81.

[113]His name was found in a Tarazona document dated 1145, among the clerics of the cathedral: José Maria Lacarra, "Documentos para el estudio de la reconquista y repoblación del Valle del Ebro," *Estudios de etad media de la corona de Aragón* 5 (1952) 511–668 nos. 357, 358.

[114]MS BN lat 13951. Some fragments of the Latin translation were edited by F. Nau, "Une ancienne traduction latine du Bélinous arabe (Apollonius de Tyane) faite par Hugo Sanctelliensis et conservée dans un MS. du XIIe siècle," *Revue de l'Orient chrétien* 12 (1907) 99–106. I am preparing an edition of this version with F. Hudry; the Arabic text has been edited by Ursula Weisser, *Buch über das Geheimnis der Schöpfung und die Darstellung der Natur (Buch der Ursachen) von pseudo-Apollonios von Tyana*, Sources and Studies in the History of Arabic Islamic Science, Natural Sciences series 1 (Aleppo 1979) with introduction in German.

[115]Julius F. Ruska, *Tabula smaragdina: Ein Beitrag zur Geschichte der hermetischen Literatur* (Heidelberg 1926) 107–80.

[116]Marie-Thérèse d'Alverny, "Trois opuscules inédits d'al-Kindī," *Akten des vierundzwanzigsten internationalen Orientalisten-Kongresses, München, 28. August bis 4. September 1958*, ed. Herbert Franke (Wiesbaden 1959) 301–02. Haskins, *Science* 79; MS BN lat 4161.

[117]Eduardo Millás Vendrell, ed., *El comentario de Ibn al-Mutannā a las tablas astronómicas de al-Jwārizmī: Estudio y edición crítica del texto latino, en la versión de Hugo Sanctallensis* (Madrid 1963).

[118]Goldstein (n. 94 above).

Other translators working in Catalonia and northern Spain during this period were of foreign origin: Plato "Tiburtinus" was presumably from Italy; Robertus Ketenensis or Cestrensis came from England; his friend Herman "Sclavus" was from Carinthia. These last two were studying in the Ebro Valley, searching for the *Almagest*, when they were enlisted by Peter the Venerable in 1142 to contribute to his great plan of translations; later they separated. Robert was appointed archdeacon of Pamplona, more precisely of the Valdonsella. New data from Spanish archives record his ecclesiastical career; he seems also to have been attached to the king of Navarra, Garcia Ramirez.[119] Considering his active role in Spanish affairs, Robert must have visited England only briefly during that period of his life, if at all. A revision of the Khwārizmī-Maslama tables translated by Adelard is ascribed to "Robertus Cestrensis"; it is undated, but a treatise on the astrolabe is dated London 1147; canons "ad meridiem urbis Londiniarum" derived from the Azarquiel tables are calculated for 1149 according to the Toledo meridian, and in a second part according to the London meridian for 1150. That Robert was at Segovia in 1145, when he translated al-Khwārizmī's Algebra, is more likely.[120] No additional documents have been discovered to correct or enlarge the list of his translations given by Haskins, although a recent editor of the alchemical *Liber Morieni* considers that its ascription in two manuscripts to "Robertus Cestrensis" is unjustified.[121] The translations —of Euclid and Theodosius, and a *Liber proportionum*—mentioned by "Robertus de Ketene" in his preface to a version of al-Kindī's *Iudicia*, addressed to his friend Herman, have not been recovered.

The Spanish archives have not yielded Herman's name; the presence of this wandering scholar in Toulouse and Béziers circa 1143 had no great chance of being recorded. Perhaps more important were his relations with other scholars and translators.[122] Besides his friend Robert, Herman had some con-

[119]The text of a peace treaty between this prince and the count of Barcelona, Ramon Berenguer IV, dated July 1149, was drawn up by the learned archdeacon: "Magister Rodebertus, ecclesie Pampilonensis archidiaconus et regis Garsie principalis capellanus ac comitis predicti clericus fecit hanc cartam." Robert appears in deeds dated 1145, 1147, and 1149; ca. 1151, as delegate of the bishop of Pamplona; at Barcelona, in 1152, as witness of the countess's testament; and finally at Tudela, as canon of this church. Angel J. Martin Duque, "El inglés Roberto, traductor del Coran," *Hispania* 22 (1962) 483–506 at 496; José M. Goñi Gaztambide, "Los obispos de Pamplona del siglo XII," *Antologia annua* 13 (1965) 135–358 at 254–64. I am grateful to Juan Paniagua for sending me this information.

[120]Louis C. Karpinski, ed. and trans., *Robert of Chester's Latin Translation of the Algebra of al-Khowarizmi* (New York 1915).

[121]Haskins, *Science* 121–23. Lee Stavenhagen, "The Original Text of the Latin *Morienus*," *Ambix* 17 (1970) 1–12; idem, ed. and trans., *A Testament of Alchemy; Being the Revelations of Morienus, Ancient Adept and Hermit of Jerusalem, to Khālid ibn Yazīd ibn Muʿāwiyya, King of the Arabs, of the Divine Secrets of the Magisterium and Accomplishment of the Alchemical Art* (Hanover N.H. 1974); cf. the review by Barbara B. Kaplan, *Isis* 67 (1976) 119–21.

[122]On the relations between Robert of Ketene, Herman, and Hugh of Santalla, see Charles S. F. Burnett, "A Group of Arabic-Latin Translators Working in Northern Spain in the Mid-12th

nection with Hugh of Santalla: in his treatise *De essentiis* he quotes "Apollonius in Secretis Naturae," the hermetic tract translated by Hugh, and the twelfth-century manuscript of this work is in the same rather peculiar type of hand as a twelfth-century copy of Herman's *De essentiis* and translation of Abū Maʿshar; moreover, Herman and Hugh often use the same scientific vocabulary. A complete survey of Herman's works and translations, including the planned or lost items, has recently been published.[123] An interesting suggestion in this new study concerns a version of books 1–12 of Euclid's *Elements*, ascribed to "Hermannus secundus" in the *Biblionomia* of Richard of Fournival and preserved in a manuscript from Fournival's library:[124] it may be a kind of new edition of the version termed "Adelard II," realized with the help of an Arabic text;[125] if so, Herman was aware of Adelard's work. Several of his translations are dated: the version of Zael (Sahl ben Bishr)'s *Fatidica*, 1148; Albumasar's *Introductorium*, 1140; the tracts offered to Peter the Venerable were completed in 1142, one in León. The following year Herman was in Toulouse, where his translation of Ptolemy's *Planisphere* is dated June 1st;[126] later in the same year he finished the treatise *De essentiis* at Béziers. Two compilations of Arabic astrology have been identified, *De occultis* and *Liber imbrium*, but date and place are unknown. We have no precise details concerning his subsequent career.

Plato of Tivoli[127] collaborated at Barcelona with Abraham bar Hiyya "Savasorda," one of the first Jewish scientists to write his own works in Hebrew. He was however a good Arabist and a great scholar; he must have helped Plato both with interpreting the language and understanding mathematics and astronomy, especially al-Battānī. Recent translations and commentaries on bar Hiyya's works now enable historians of science to appreciate this Barcelona master's importance.[128] His disciple Plato, who besides versions of

---

Century," *Journal of the Royal Asiatic Society of Great Britain and Ireland* (1977) 62–108. Burnett notes similarities of style and vocabulary between Hugh and Herman.

[123]Charles S. F. Burnett, "Arabic into Latin in Twelfth Century Spain: The Works of Hermann of Carinthia," *Mittellateinisches Jahrbuch* 13 (1978) 100–34; idem, "The *De essentiis* of Hermann of Carinthia and Twelfth Century Thought" (Ph.D. thesis Cambridge 1976).

[124]MS BN lat 16646. Cf. A. Birkenmajer, "La bibliothèque de Richard de Fournival, poète et érudit français du début du XIIIe siècle et son sort ultérieur" (trans. of Polish text orig. publ. 1922), *Etudes* (n. 57 above) 117–210 at 162; Richard H. Rouse, "Manuscripts Belonging to Richard de Fournival," *Revue d'histoire des textes* 3 (1973) 253–69.

[125]H. L. L. Busard, ed., *The Translation of the Elements of Euclid from the Arabic into Latin by Hermann of Carinthia (?)* (2 vols. Leiden 1968 [books 1–6], Amsterdam 1977 [books 7–12]; cf. Murdoch, "Euclid: Transmission" (n. 90 above) 447.

[126]The translation of the *Planisphere* is dedicated to Thierry of Chartres in very eloquent and laudatory terms: "diligentissime preceptor Theoderice"; so it seems that Herman had studied with Thierry.

[127]The most accurate and up-to-date survey is by Lorenzo Minio-Paluello, "Plato of Tivoli," DSB 11 (1975) 31–33, with a list of translations and editions.

[128]José M. Millás Vallicrosa, "La obra enciclopedica de R. Abraham bar Ḥiyya," *Estudios* (n. 84 above) 219–62; on his collaboration with Plato of Tivoli, and a list of Plato's translations 258–62. Millás translated and commented on several tracts, including *La obra "Forma de la tierra"* de Abraham bar Ḥiyya ha-Bargeloni (Barcelona 1956) and *La obra Séfer Ḥešbón mahlekot ha-*

Arabic astronomy and astrology transmitted Savasorda's geometry, the *Liber embadorum,*[129] has not been so well treated: modern editions of his translations are scarce, and a study of his methods is needed.[130] There is no doubt about Plato's enthusiasm for a renaissance of science in the West, for in his prologue to al-Battānī he eloquently contrasts the wealth of Greek knowledge preserved by the Arabs with the poverty of the Latins.[131]

The first generation of translators from Arabic had exclusively scientific interests, with mathematics and astronomy/astrology heavily predominant; even occult science was accepted. (The only exception was the collection of religious texts made by Robert, Herman, and Peter of Toledo for Peter of Cluny, who said that he had to use both persuasion and money to induce the two friends to set aside for a while their search for the *Almagest.*) The Toledan translators were searching for Aristotle as well as for Ptolemy. When "Avendauth" and his collaborator Dominicus Gundisalvi undertook the version of Avicenna's philosophical encyclopedia, Kitāb al-Shifaʾ, they intended to provide Western scholars with a commentary on Aristotle's works. In fact, it seems that these versions, especially the *De anima,* circulated first under Aristotle's name.[132] The shorter tracts of the Arabic philosophers al-Kindī and al-Fārābī

kokabim (Libro del cálculo de los movimientos de los astros) de R. Abraham bar Ḥiyya ha-Bargeloni (Barcelona 1959).

[129]The Latin translation ed. Maximilian Curtze, "Der 'Liber embadorum' des Savasorda in der Übersetzung des Plato von Tivoli," *Urkunden zur Geschichte der Mathematik im Mittelalter und der Renaissance,* Abh zur Geschichte der mathematischen Wissenschaften 12 (2 vols. in 1 Leipzig 1902; repr. New York 1968) 1.1–183; trans. into Catalan from the Hebrew by Millás, *Llibre de Geometria Hibbur hameixihā uehatixbōret,* Biblioteca Hebraico-Catalana 3 (Barcelona 1931).

[130]José M. Millás Vallicrosa partially edited the translation of the tract *De horarum electionibus* by ʿAli b. Aḥmad al-ʿImrānī, *Las traducciones orientales en los manuscritos de la Biblioteca Catedral de Toledo* (Madrid 1942) 328–39. He also identified the real author of the tract on the astrolabe translated by Plato: Abūʾl Qāsim ibn al-Ṣaffār, 11th-c. Andalusian astronomer. A recent study on the "Almansor" reproduces the old Pruckner edition: Jean-Claude Vadet, "Les Aphorismes latins d'Almansor, essai d'interprétation," *Annales islamologiques* 5 (1963) 31–130. Marshall Clagett edited a version of Archimedes's *De mensura circuli* from the Arabic, which he ascribed tentatively to Plato: *Archimedes in the Middle Ages,* vol. 1: *The Arabo-Latin Tradition* (Madison Wisc. 1964) 16–27.

[131]"Quo magis latinitatis ignorantie cecitas deploranda magisque desidie negligentia redarguenda est. . . . Roma . . . in artium vero gimnasiis, in disciplinarum speculationibus . . . non tantum Egipto vel Grecia sed etiam Arabia longe inferior extitit. Hoc, cum in ceteris artibus facile deprehendi possit, quas si habent Latini, non a se sed aliunde mutuati sunt, tum vel maxime in prememorata astrorum scientia declaratur, cuius non dico auctorem, sed ne interpretem quidem quo se iactet audet ostentare latinitas. . . . Nostri auctorem quidem nullum, pro libris deliramenta, sompnia, fabulas aniles. Hac causa permotus ego Plato Tiburtinus nostre lingue angustias, qua maxime deficiebat ex aliene lingue thesauris pro ingenii facultate ditare constitui." Quoted from MSS BN lat 7266, fol. 48; 16657, fol. 1; and *Mahometis Albatenii de scientia stellarum liber* (Bologna 1645) fol. b.

[132]See Richard W. Hunt, "The Preface to the 'Speculum Ecclesiae' of Giraldus Cambrensis," *Viator* 8 (1977) 189–213. Gerald refers to "libri quidam tanquam Aristotilis intitulati Toletanis Hispanie finibus nuper inventi et translati," and shortly afterward quotes the preface to the version of Avicenna's *De anima:* "super librum Aristotilis quendam De anima intitulatum." John Blund, probably the first Western master of Paris and Oxford to make a large use of Avicenna's *De anima,* considered it a "commentum" on Aristotle; see his *Tractatus de anima,* ed. D. A. Callus and Richard W. Hunt, Auctores Britannici Medii Aevi 2 (London 1970) xi.

and of the Greek Alexander Aphrodisias appeared as reflections of Aristotelian teachings, as in part they were.

In the second half of the twelfth century, Gerard of Cremona was the most prolific translator from Arabic working in Toledo. According to the Eulogium written shortly after his death (1187) by his former students and disciples, he came to Toledo for the love of Ptolemy's *Almagest*, settled there, and decided to devote his life to translating Arabic books, for he pitied the penury of the Latins—as had Alfanus of Salerno a century before. Preceding the Eulogium is a methodical list of his translations which has been edited several times—not very satisfactorily, for the manuscripts are late and corrupt; the succession of unknown Arabic names was obviously an enigma for the scribes.[133] Under such conditions identifying the original texts is frequently a problem; various scholars have tried to solve the riddles, but all suggestions are tentative as long as an Arabic original is not available.[134] It is possible, on the other hand, to identify versions as Gerard's. Several manuscripts offer a kind of anthology of Gerard's translations, for instance BN lat 9335, a remarkable collection of mathematical and physical tracts.[135] Other smaller collections of Gerard's mathematical versions must derive from the same archetype, for the contents are in the same order.[136] The same remark applies to a smaller collec-

[133]This Eulogium, and/or the list of translations, has been published several times, from various manuscripts: Baldassare Boncompagni, "Della vita e delle opere di Gherardo Cremonese, traduttore del secolo duodecimo e di Gherardo Sabbionetta astronomo del secolo decimoterzo. Notizie raccolte da Baldassare Boncompagni," *Atti dell'Accademia Pontificia de' Nuovi Lincei* 4 (1851) 387–493; Ferdinand Wüstenfeld, *Die Übersetzungen arabischer Werke in das Lateinische seit dem XI. Jahrhundert,* Abh Göttingen, Hist.-philol. Kl. 22 (1877) 58–77; Lucien Leclerc, *Histoire de la médecine arabe* (2 vols. Paris 1876; repr. New York 1961) 2.403–06; Karl Sudhoff, "Die kurze 'Vita' und das Verzeichnis der Arbeiten Gerhards von Cremona," *Archiv für Geschichte der Medizin* 8 (1914) 73–82. We found another manuscript: Paris, Fac. de médecine 2046, fol. 388, but it is as bad as the others. Steinschneider, *Europäischen Übersetzungen* (n. 97 above) 16–32, gave a list of Gerard's translations, enlarging the primitive one, with tentative identifications and references; so did George Sarton, *Introduction to the History of Science* (3 vols. in 5 Baltimore 1927–48) 2.2.339–44. The most recent surveys were published by Edward Grant, *A Source Book in Medieval Science* (Cambridge Mass. 1974) 35–39 and by Richard Lemay, "Gerard of Cremona," DSB 15 (1978) 173–92.

[134]Heinrich Suter, "Über die im 'Liber augmenti et diminutionis' vorkommenden Autoren" and "Über einige noch nicht sicher gestellte Autorennamen in den Übersetzungen des Gerhard von Cremona," *Bibliotheca mathematica* 3 (1902) 350–54 and 4 (1903) 19–27. Sezgin (n. 8 above) vol. 5, *Mathematik,* questioned Suter's tentative identifications (388–89). A. I. Sabra, "The Authorship of the *Liber de crepusculis,* an Eleventh-Century Work on Atmospheric Refraction," *Isis* 58 (1967) 77–85 showed that the real author of this treatise (ascribed wrongly to Ibn al-Haytham) was an Andalusian, Ibn Muʿadh, who also revised astronomical tables translated by Gerard; see Heinrich Hermelink, "Tabulae Jahen," *Archive for History of Exact Sciences* 2 (1964) 108–12.

[135]Axel A. Björnbo, "Über zwei mathematische Handschriften aus dem Vierzehnten Jahrhundert," *Bibliotheca mathematica* 3 (1902) 63–75; detailed description of MS BN lat 9335, 67–75.

[136]H. L. L. Busard, "Die Vermessungstraktate *Liber Saydi Abuothmi* und *Liber Aderameti,*" *Janus* 56 (1969) 161–74, esp. 163–64, notes manuscripts containing 5 tracts on mathematics translated by Gerard, in the same order: BN lat 9335, BN lat 7377A (14th c.), and Cambridge Univ. Libr. Mm.2.18. Another manuscript, Dresden Sächs. Landesbibl. C.80, contains only 4 tracts. We must add that MS BN lat 7377A, of Italian origin, presents in the first part (fols. 1–70v) a com-

tion of medical translations ascribed to Gerard, the opuscula of Rāzī.[137] Another rewarding method of investigation is the study of Gerard's peculiar mannerisms in translating, and of his typical expressions, such as "et illud est quod declarare (or demonstrare) voluimus" at the end of a demonstration, or "quod est quia" rendering "wa dhaliqa ann." The two approaches have permitted suggesting that pseudo-Euclid's De speculis, contained in BN lat 9335 and offering characteristic peculiarities of Gerard's style, might be added to the official list.[138]

Gerard did not work alone to produce such a large number of translations, covering almost every field of knowledge: philosophy, with Aristotelian and pseudo-Aristotelian works plus some Arabic philosophers; mathematics, geometry,[139] optics, catoptrics, and the science of weights; astronomy and astrology (though Gerard was an adept of astrology he did not add much to the large collection made by his predecessors); medicine,[140] with Galenic and pseudo-Galenic tracts, several treatises of Rāzī, the surgery manual of Abuʾl-Qāsim al-Zahrāwī, the huge Canon (Qānūn) of Avicenna; alchemy, geomancy and other types of divination;[141] and finally, the Liber Anoe, the so-called Calendar of Cordova, a mixed monument of Arabic and Mozarabic culture and tradition. According to Daniel of Morley, the great translator was helped by a Mozarab named Galib, with whom Daniel used to chat: "Galippo mixtarabe interpretante, Almagesti latinavit."[142] This information fits rather well Gerard's style of translation, very literal and with stereotyped renderings. He had learned Arabic, but was probably not proficient enough to fulfill such an ambitious program by himself; it is likely that he enlisted not only Galib but other interpreters to hasten the work. Gerard and "Dominicus archidiaconus" (Gundisalvi) are both named in a document from the Toledo chapter's ar-

plete counterpart of BN lat 9335, fols. 92v–133v. Björnbo noted MS Milan Ambrosiana T.100 sup. (13th c.), containing translations of optical tracts corresponding with the contents of BN lat 9335, fols. 75–92. Another collection of some of Gerard's translations is contained in MS Madrid Bibl. Nac. 10010; see Millás (n. 130 above) no. xliv, 208–11. H. L. L. Busard, ed., The Latin Translation of the Arabic Version of Euclid's Elements commonly ascribed to Gerard of Cremona (Leiden 1980).

[137]Lynn Thorndike, "Latin Manuscripts of Works by Rasis in the Bibliothèque Nationale, Paris," Bulletin of the History of Medicine 32 (1958) 54–67.

[138]Axel A. Björnbo and S. Vogl, Alkindi, Tideus und pseudo-Euklid: Drei optische Werke, Abh zur Geschichte der mathematischen Wissenschaften 26.3 (Leipzig 1912) 3ff. See also the remarks of Clagett (n. 130 above) 1.30, 232–33; Ilona Opelt, "Zur Übersetzungstechnik des Gerhard von Cremona," Glotta 38 (1959) 135–70; Paul Kunitzsch, Der Almagest: Die Syntaxis mathematica des Claudius Ptolemäus in arabisch-lateinischer Überlieferung (Wiesbaden 1974) 83–112.

[139]On the translation of the Greco-Arabic "intermediary" books (between geometry and astronomy), see Juan Vernet, La cultura hispanoárabe en Oriente y Occidente (Barcelona 1978) 142–43. Edition of the "Liber mensurationum" by H. L. L. Busard, "L'algèbre au moyen âge: Le 'Liber mensurationum' d'Abû Bekr," Journal des savants (1968) 65–124.

[140]On Gerard's medical translations, see Schipperges (n. 10 above) 85–103.

[141]On a translation of occult science on Gerard's list, see Paul Kunitzsch, "Zum 'Liber Alfadhol,' eine Nachlese," Zeitschrift der deutschen Morgenländischen Gesellschaft 118 (1968) 297–314. Kunitzsch found two Latin versions and wonders which one is Gerard's.

[142]Sudhoff (n. 98 above) 39–40.

chives, dated 1176—just after Gerard had completed his translation of the
Almagest.[143] Their simultaneous presence in Toledo suggests the possibility of
connections between the two translators, or, more exactly, between the two
teams of translators.

Gerard's contribution to "Aristoteles latinus" are versions of *Analytica
posteriora, Physica, De caelo, De generatione et corruptione,* and *Meteora* (in
part),[144] plus the pseudo-Aristotelian *Liber de bonitate pura,* known later as
Liber de causis. The only versions widely diffused and included in the "Corpus
vetustius" are *De caelo* and *Meteora*: for the first no direct translations from
the Greek were available before the second half of the thirteenth century
(Grosseteste's version is fragmentary). The *Meteora* is only in part Gerard's
work: when he was well advanced in his task, he discovered a previous version,
from the Greek, by Henricus Aristippus and did not go further. Gerard had
finished books 1–3 and seems to have started on book 4 when he found out
about Henricus's version, for a translation from Arabic of the first chapter of
book 4 still exists. This is a very rare instance of a connection between the
Greco-Latin translators and the Arabo-Latin translators studying in Spain, due
possibly to the fact that Gerard had attracted to Toledo some of his countrymen, or kept links with his native country.

An addition of three short chapters translated from Avicenna's *Meteora* by
Alfred of Sareshel is normally found in the manuscripts of the "Corpus
vetustius," as if it were a part of the Aristotelian treatise. The full *explicit*
presented in early copies states clearly the share of the three contributors, but
Avicenna is not mentioned.[145] If Alfred is responsible for this kind of standard
edition, he may have visited Toledo. He does not however mention where he
studied Arabic and translated Avicenna's extracts and the pseudo-Aristotelian
De plantis (Nicholas of Damascus), but in his gloss on *Meteora* he refers to his
teacher and probable helper, "magister meus Salomon Avenraza."[146] This
learned Jew has not yet been identified, but in the late twelfth century it is
mostly in Spain that Arabic-speaking Jews could be found. Alfred's "Cas-

[143]Rivera Recio, "Nuevos datos" (n. 103 above) 273.

[144]See *Aristoteles latinus: Codices* (n. 57 above) vol. 1, preface, passim; Lorenzo Minio-
Paluello, "Aristotele dal mondo arabo a quello latino," *L'Occidente e l'Islam nell'alto Medioevo,*
Settimane 12 (n. 79 above) 2.603–37; idem, "Note sull'Aristotele latino medievale, IV. La tradi-
zione semitico-latina del testo dei 'Secondi Analitici,'" *Rivista di filosofia neo-scolastica* 43 (1951)
97–124, repr. in *Opuscula* (n. 58 above) 127–54 with a note on the translation of book 4.1 of the
Meteora by Gerard.

[145]The earliest manuscript, Oxford Bodl. Selden supra 24, contains the following explicit:
"Completus est liber Metheororum Aristotilis cuius tres libros transtulit magister Giraldus Lumbardus sum(m)us philosophus de arabico in latinum; quartum transtulit Henricus Aristippus de
greco in latinum; tria ultima capitula transtulit Aurelius Anglicus Sarulensis de arabico in
latinum." This long note is found in several other manuscripts.

[146]See George Lacombe, "Alfredus Anglicus in Metheora," *Aus der Geisteswelt des Mittelalters: Studien und Texte Martin Grabmann . . . gewidmet,* BGPTMA supp. 3 (2 vols. Münster
1935) 1.463–71; James K. Otte, "The Life and Writings of Alfredus Anglicus" and "The Role of
Alfred of Sareshel (Alfredus Anglicus) and His Commentary on the *Metheora* in the Reacquisition
of Aristotle," *Viator* 3 (1972) 275–91 and 7 (1976) 197–209.

tilianisms" have been pointed out; the study of his version of *De plantis* also reveals Hebraisms that might come from master Salomon.[147]

Three translations bear the name of Salio, a canon of Padua who worked in Toledo about 1218. A fragment of an astrological geomancy ascribed to "Salcharie Albassarith" is said to have been translated from Hebrew into Latin on February 27th in Toledo; a tract *On Nativities* by Abū Bakr al-Ḥasan ibn al-Khaṣīb (Albubecri Alkasibi), translated from Arabic with the help of a learned Jew named David, was completed on 29 December 1218 "in barrio Iudeorum" (a typical Spanish expression); the Arabic original of his third (un-dated) translation, "Liber Hermetis de stellis fixis que dicuntur beybenie,"[148] was recently identified.[149] Salio's case is another instance of the use of Jewish interpreters.

Mark of Toledo did not need help, for he had a fluent knowledge of Arabic and could translate closely and accurately. This young Toledan left his country to study medicine; entreated by his masters and fellows to translate from Arabic Galenic treatises still unknown in the West, he hastened back to Toledo and complied with their wishes. This seems to have happened during the last quarter of the twelfth century, for Mark appears in Toledo deeds among members of the chapter from 1191 onward; his medical studies must have been earlier. After having contributed to the revival of Galen, he notably enlarged the field of Islamic studies with his versions of the Koran and Ibn Tūmart.[150]

Haskins was particularly interested in Michael Scot, whom he included among the agents of a renaissance of studies despite his late appearance on the scene.[151] Michael made a very important contribution to the "Aristoteles latinus": a translation of *De animalibus* in nineteen books, according to the Arabic tradition. It was probably done while he was in Spain. His only transla-tion dated from Toledo, in 1217, is a version of al-Biṭrūjī's *De motibus*

[147]This was noted by H. J. Drossaart-Lulofs, who is preparing the edition of Alfred's transla-tion of pseudo-Aristotle, *De plantis*.

[148]Lynn Thorndike, "A Third Translation by Salio," *Speculum* 32 (1957) 116–17, signaled the fragment found in MSS BN lat 10270 and Venice, San Marco VI.108 and gave some data and references on the other two translations; Francis J. Carmody, *Arabic Astronomical and Astrological Sciences in Latin Translation* (Berkeley 1956) 55 and 136 described the two translations from Arabic and gave lists of manuscripts and early editions. Lynn Thorndike and Pearl Kibre incor-porated Carmody's material in *A Catalogue of Incipits of Mediaeval Scientific Writings in Latin* (2nd ed. Cambridge Mass. and London 1963) 152, 486, 665, 789, 1111. A manuscript must be added to the lists: Oxford, Corpus Christi Coll. 101; see Henry O. Coxe, *Catalogus codicum ma-nuscriptorum qui in collegiis aulisque Oxoniensibus hodie asservantur* (2 vols. in 1 Oxford 1852) 2.35–36. See also Steinschneider, *Europäischen Übersetzungen* (n. 97 above) no. 107.

[149]Paul Kunitzsch, "Zum 'Liber hermetis de stellis beibeniis'" and "Neues zum 'Liber her-metis de stellis beibeniis,'" *Zeitschrift der deutschen Morgenländischen Gesellschaft* 118 (1968) 62–74 and 120 (1970) 126–30.

[150]D'Alverny and Vajda (n. 30 above) 99–140 (introduction).

[151]Haskins, *Science* 272–98; idem, "Michael Scot in Spain," *Estudios eruditos in memoriam de Adolfo Bonilla y San Martín (1875–1926)* (2 vols. Madrid 1927–30) 2.129–34; idem, *Culture* 128, 148–59. Lynn Thorndike, *Michael Scot* (London 1965) 22–31 gave a tentative outline of Michael's translations.

caelorum, executed with the help of "Abuteus levita," but a document from
the chapter's archives, concerning the Fourth Lateran Council in 1215, lists
"magister Michael Scotus" among the "testes de Yspania" who accompanied
the archbishop of Toledo.[152] So he was not a newcomer at that time, and it is
accordingly possible that several translations were completed or begun while he
was in a city where Arabic manuscripts were available in plenty and where it
was not difficult to find help. Haskins proposed tentatively to identify
"Abuteus" with a "magister Andreas," a canon of Palencia who was praised
in 1229 by pope Gregory IX for his knowledge of Hebrew and Arabic, this
identification being suggested by some naughty remarks of Roger Bacon, who
accused Michael Scot of pretending to know Arabic when a Jew named Andrew
had the chief merit of the translations. It is possible indeed that Michael Scot
enlisted not only "Abuteus" but other acolytes; none however are mentioned
in the manuscripts of his works.

Another obscure point is the extent of Michael Scot's share in the translation of the huge Averroes corpus that began to circulate in the second quarter
of the thirteenth century.[153] The only version formally inscribed with his name
is the translation of Averroes's commentary on *De caelo*, with a dedication to
Stephen of Provins; it is not dated, but Michael alludes to the previous version
of al-Biṭrūjī. It seems likely that the Averroes translations were begun in
Toledo. The intellectual connections between Christian Spain and Al-Andalus
were apparently close, though the political circumstances were not favorable;
Averroes's works, banned by the Almohads at the end of the philosopher's
life, were appreciated by their neighbors and enemies.

Did Michael Scot bring many books with him when he moved to Italy
about 1220? How many parts of the *corpus averroisticum* were translated
either by him or by others in Spain or when he was Frederick's astrologer?
Frederick was certainly interested in Arabic science and philosophy, for he
sponsored translations from Arabic. A famous member of the Tibbonide family, Jacob Anatoli, collaborated with Michael Scot under Frederick's aegis;[154]
we do not know in what capacity, but as Anatoli translated into Hebrew the
commentaries of Averroes on Aristotle's Logic, he may also have had a hand in
the translation of some of Averroes's works.

The translation of Avicenna's *De animalibus*, solemnly dedicated to the
emperor, must date from the Italian period of Michael's career; Frederick himself sponsored a kind of standard edition in 1232.[155] This section of the Kitāb

152Juan Francisco Rivero Recio, "Personajes hispanos asistentes en 1215 al IV Concilio de
Letrán," *Hispania sacra* 4 (1951) 335–55.

153See R. de Vaux, "La première entrée d'Averroës chez les latins," *Revue des sciences philosophiques et théologiques* 22 (1933) 193–245.

154See Giuseppe Sermoneta, *Un glossario filosofico ebraico-italiano del XIII secolo*, Lessico in-
tellettuale europeo 1 (Rome 1969) 33–36 on the collaboration of Michael and Jacob Anatoli, who
refers to "the great philosopher Mikhael with whom I was associated for a long time," in the
preface of his tract *Malmad ha-thamidim*. This had been quoted already by Moritz Steinschneider.

155Marie-Thérèse d'Alverny, "L'explicit du 'De animalibus' d'Avicenne traduit par Michel
Scot," *Bibliothèque de l'Ecole des Chartes* 115 (1957) 32–42.

al-Shifaᵓ is an abridgment of Aristotle, and often circulated with the *corpus aristotelicum*. Another addition to "Aristoteles latinus" is more questionable: a translation of the *Ethica Nicomachea*, from the Greek, is ascribed to Michael Scot. The editor of the *Ethica nova* is inclined to accept this ascription, however, and it is not impossible that when Michael was with Frederick in southern Italy or Sicily he managed to learn some Greek and find a Greek-speaking assistant.[156]

DIFFUSION OF THE TRANSLATIONS

The history of the twelfth-century translations from Greek and Arabic is incomplete, and their diffusion and impact on twelfth- and early thirteenth-century learning require much further investigation to be adequately appreciated. The lists of versions that can safely be ascribed to a given known translator are still tentative, even in the most favorable cases, such as Gerard of Cremona. Worse, a number of versions, especially of alchemical tracts, are anonymous, and we do not know their origin and date. It is likely that some, at least, were executed during the twelfth century, and the same can be assumed for tracts of magic, more rightly than alchemy considered an occult science. Still other texts are circulating under an assumed Greek or (mostly) Arabic patronage, and are presented as translations when they are actually only more or less fanciful compilations realized by Westerners. The same kind of fraud was common in the Arabic world, with the ascription of alchemical traditions to Hermes or ancient sages.

The agents of transmission were frequently the wandering scholars, either translators themselves or in occasional or permanent contact with the translators. Many among them were probably physicians who studied in Salerno or Montpellier but traveled further because they were amateurs of mathematics, astrology, and physics.[157] The great *studia*, Bologna and Paris, were centers of meeting and exchange. Arabic science came to England thanks to a brilliant succession of traveling scholars—Adelard and Peter Alfonsi, Robert of Ketene, Daniel of Morley, Alfred of Sareshel—and to the receptivity of other scholars—Roger of Hereford, bishop John of Norwich, and Alexander Neckam.[158] In northern France, the best men must have been aware of new discoveries, for Herman of Carinthia dedicated his version of Ptolemy's *Planisphaera*, completed at Toulouse in 1143, to Thierry of Chartres; shortly

[156]Gauthier, *Ethica Nicomachea* (n. 63 above) vols. 1 (*Praefatio*) cxxxv–cxxxviii and 2.95.

[157]This had been sketched by our late friend A. Birkenmajer, who unfortunately did not live long enough to complete his outline: "Le rôle joué par les médecins et les naturalistes dans la réception d'Aristote au XIIe et XIIIe siècles," *La Pologne au VIe Congrès international des sciences historiques, Oslo 1928* (Warsaw 1930) 1–15, repr. in his *Etudes* (n. 57 above) 73–87.

[158]Haskins, *Science* 113–29; Richard W. Hunt, "English Learning in the Late Twelfth Century," TRHS 4th ser. 19 (1936) 19–42, repr. in *Essays in Medieval History Selected from the Transactions of the Royal Historical Society on the Occasion of Its Centenary*, ed. Richard W. Southern (London and New York 1968) 106–28 at 109–13, 121–22.

before, Abelard seems aware of the progress, or rather abuse, of astrology;[159] later on, Alan of Lille names Euclid, Ptolemy, and Albumasar in the *Anticlaudianus*; Bernard Silvester in his *Cosmographia* as well as the same Alan in his *De planctu Naturae* are witnesses to the influence of the science of the stars.[160] At the end of the century, a certain Odo of Champagne offers a tract in defense of astrology to king Philip's uncle William, archbishop of Reims.[161]

It is however in southern France that a link between translators and local scholars can be seen at an early date. Raymond of Marseille wrote a tract on the astrolabe before 1141, then in 1141 the Marseille tables with his long introduction, the *Liber cursuum planetarum*, and later a *Liber iudiciorum* of which many copies exist; he knew Azarquiel and Arabic astrologers, and was perhaps in touch with John of Seville. It is in Toulouse and Béziers that Herman is found in 1143, probably attracted by the presence of Occitan amateurs. Abraham bar Hiyya and Abraham ibn Ezra visited successively the numerous Jewish communities in Languedoc and Provence. And the Tibbonide family, forming a nucleus of translators from Arabic into Hebrew, settled in southern France before the end of the century.

Italy was the privileged land for Greco-Latin translations and relations with Byzantium. What is less known is that translations from Arabic executed in Spain appeared in Italy at an early date, before Michael Scot's arrival. We may suppose that among the students attracted to Toledo by Gerard of Cremona and who scattered after his death some were his countrymen; they may have carried the master's works back with them. A commentary on Galen's *Microtegni* written by a master Urso Laudensis who was teaching at Cremona in 1198 uses the "old version," but he knows Gerard's new translation and appreciates it.[162] A genuine interest in Gerard's and other interpreters' translations coincided a little later with Frederick II's drive to develop science. The anthology of Gerard's translations noted previously (BN lat 9335) was copied in Italy. This fine volume (wrongly dated to the fourteenth century in the *In-*

[159]Marie-Thérèse d'Alverny, "Abélard et l'astrologie," *Pierre-Pierre* 611–30. Abelard's allusions to astrology are found in his *Expositio in Hexaemeron*, perhaps written ca. 1136–39.

[160]A compilation of *sortes* known as *Experimentarius* was ascribed to Bernard Silvester, who was even presented as a translator of the work. It was edited by Mirella Brini Savorelli, "Un manuele di geomanzia presentato da Bernardo Silvestre da Tours (XII secolo): l'*Experimentarius*," *Rivista critica di storia della filosofia* 14 (1959) 283–342. A recent study suggests that Bernard's links with this curious tract, inspired by Arabic astrology but not a translation, are rather tenuous; see Charles S. F. Burnett, "What is the *Experimentarius* of Bernardus Silvestris? A Preliminary Study of the Material," AHDLMA 44 (1977) 79–125.

[161]Marie-Thérèse d'Alverny, "Astrologues et théologiens au XIIe siècle," *Mélanges offerts à M.-D. Chenu* (Paris 1967) 31–50 at 39–50; the text was edited by Małgorzata H. Malewicz, "Libellus de efficatia artis astrologice: Traité astrologique d'Eudes de Champagne, XIIe siècle," *Mediaevalia philosophica Polonorum* 20 (1974) 3–95. The treatise of this "Odo Campanus" is known through extracts quoted by Hélinand of Froidmont in his *Chronicles*, book 6.

[162]"Non fuit intentio nostra addere verbum nec diminuere huic translationi quamvis in translatione magistri Girardi propter hoc quod invenit in arabico quandoque augeatur vel diminuatur ab hac; nos autem non exposuimus hanc translationem novam, sed veterem hanc et consuetam." MS Venice, Bibl. Marciana 2023 (olim Z.L.512; Valentinelli XIV.8), fol. 43, "Lectura magistri Ursi Laudensis super microtegni Galieni."

ventaire sommaire) was written and decorated during the first half of the thirteenth century; the text is excellent, the geometrical figures carefully drawn.
This manuscript has two closely related codices, with the same type of script
and the same color of rubrics and decoration.[163] One contains Gerard's version
of Euclid's *Elements*; the other perhaps belonged to the celebrated thirteenth-
century collector Richard of Fournival. Although the last one does not contain
any of Gerard's translations, a Spanish model can be assumed. It includes a
calendar preceding a treatise of computus compiled in the twelfth century
(tables dated 1143–59), and the list of saints marks this calendar as Spanish,
more precisely Toledan: on February 13 is noted the "translatio s. Eugenii
episcopi," his "dies natalis" on November 15.[164] We may cautiously infer
that manuscripts originating from Spain, particularly from Toledo, were carried to Italy and copied with care.

These manuscripts are silent witnesses to the important role of Italian
scribes and scholars in the diffusion of scientific translations, chiefly in the
field of medicine. Avicenna's Canon was extensively reproduced in Italy, enriched with glosses; later, when it became the basic text for teaching in the
Italian schools, commentaries were regularly added.

It was indeed for a renewal of learning in the Latin world that the translators
had worked in the late eleventh and twelfth centuries. Their aim was progressively fulfilled. If individual amateurs quickly welcomed the translations,
appreciation of the versions of Greek and Arabic science and philosophy developed more slowly in the organized *studia* and universities. In the course of the
thirteenth century, however, the program of studies came to rely largely on the
fruit of the translators' labor.

Bibliographical Note

The works listed here are not limited to the twelfth century. Several have been superseded, but can still offer useful information if they are used with caution. Caution is required too for recent works of large scope; limited studies, where the author has a first-
hand knowledge of the topic, tend to be more reliable. The most interesting and accurate remarks concerning the translations either from Greek or from Arabic are
presented in the introductions to critical editions, such as those in the *Aristoteles latinus*.

[163]MSS Vat Ross lat 579 and BN 15461. The similarity between Vat Ross lat 579 and BN 9335
was noted by Clagett (n. 130 above) 228 n. 1. I have examined the three manuscripts and share his
opinion.

[164]In the same part of the manuscript is transcribed the "Liber alchorismi de pratica arismetice
qui editus est a magistro Iohanne"; this would perhaps be an argument for the authorship of a
Spanish "John." On this treatise see Allard (n. 91 above).

GENERAL

Catalogus translationum et commentariorum: Mediaeval and Renaissance Translations and Commentaries. Washington D.C. 1960–   . Vol. 1, ed. Paul O. Kristeller (1960); vol. 2, ed. Paul O. Kristeller and F. Edward Cranz (1971); vols. 3, 4, ed. F. Edward Cranz and Paul O. Kristeller (1976, 1980). Annotated lists and guides; includes the works of Greek authors translated into Latin, directly or with an Arabic intermediary.

Haskins's *Science* is still one of the best sources of information for the twelfth and early thirteenth centuries, giving first-hand data on translators and on the manuscripts of their works.

Muckle, J. T. "Greek Works Translated Directly into Latin before 1350," *Mediaeval Studies* 4 (1942) 33–42; 5 (1943) 102–14.

Sarton, George. *Introduction to the History of Science*. 3 vols. in 5 Baltimore 1927–48. Systematic chronological survey of translations; includes philosophical translations; see vol. 2, parts 1–2 for the twelfth century.

Steinschneider, Moritz. *Die europäischen Übersetzungen aus dem Arabischen bis Mitte des 17. Jahrhunderts*. SB Vienna, Phil.-hist. Kl. 149.4 and 151.1. 2 vols. Vienna 1904–05; repr. Graz 1956.

_____. *Die hebraeischen Übersetzungen des Mittelalters und die Juden als Dolmetscher*. Berlin 1893; repr. Graz 1956.

ARISTOTELES LATINUS AND PHILOSOPHY

Aristoteles latinus: Codices. George Lacombe, with Aleksander Birkenmajer, Marthe Dulong, and Ezio Franceschini. Vol. 1 (Rome 1939). The preface presents a survey of the medieval translations, emended and supplemented by Lorenzo Minio-Paluello in vol. 2 (Cambridge 1955) and *Supplementa altera* (Bruges and Paris 1961). (All 3 vols. repr. Leiden 1979).

Franceschini, Ezio. "Studi sull' 'Aristoteles latinus,'" in his *Scritti di filologia latina medievale*, Medioevo e umanesimo 26–27. 2 vols. Padua 1976. Vol. 2, pp. 377–692.

Minio-Paluello, Lorenzo. *Opuscula: The Latin Aristotle*. Amsterdam 1972. Collected essays on the medieval translations of Aristotle.

d'Alverny, Marie-Thérèse. "Les traductions d'Avicenne (Moyen Age et Renaissance)," *Avicenna nella storia della cultura medioevale*, Accademia dei Lincei, Quaderno 40. Rome 1957. Pp. 71–87.

_____. "Avicenna latinus, I–XI," AHDLMA 28–37, 39 (1961–70, 1972). Systematic descriptions of manuscripts containing translations of Avicenna's and other Arabic philosophers' works.

SCIENCE

Björnbo, Axel A. "Die Mittelalterliche Übersetzungen aus dem Griechischen auf dem Gebiete der mathematischen Wissenschaften," *Archiv für die Geschichte der Naturwissenschaften und der Technik* 1 (1909) 385–94.

Björnbo, Axel A., and S. Vogl. *Alkindi, Tideus und pseudo-Euklid: Drei optische Werke*. Abh zur Geschichte der mathematischen Wissenschaften 26.3. Leipzig 1912. With a bibliography of Björnbo's studies, important for the history of translations.

Carmody, Francis J. *Arabic Astronomical and Astrological Sciences in Latin Translation*. Berkeley 1956. Lists of Latin manuscripts and early editions with reference to the Arabic original when it is known.

Clagett, Marshall. *Archimedes in the Middle Ages.* Vol. 1, *The Arabo-Latin Tradition* (Madison Wisc. 1964); vol. 2, *The Translations from the Greek by William of Moerbeke* (2 vols. Philadelphia 1976); vol. 3, *The Fate of the Medieval Archimedes 1300–1565* (3 vols. Philadelphia 1978); vol. 4, *A Supplement on the Medieval Latin Traditions of Conic Sections (1150–1566)* (2 vols. Philadelphia 1980).

Kunitzsch, Paul. *Arabische Sternnamen in Europa.* Wiesbaden 1959.

Lindberg, David C. *A Catalogue of Medieval and Renaissance Optical Manuscripts.* The Pontifical Institute of Mediaeval Studies, Subsidia Mediaevalia 4. Toronto 1975. Translations are listed among medieval tracts on optics and ophthalmology.

Millás Vallicrosa, José Maria. *Las traducciones orientales en los manuscritos de la Biblioteca catedral de Toledo.* Madrid 1942.

_____. *Estudios sobre historia de la ciencia española.* Barcelona 1949. *Nuevos estudios sobre historia de la ciencia española.* Barcelona 1960. Two volumes of essays concerning mostly translators and translations from Arabic.

Revue de synthèse 89 (1968) = *XIIe Congrès international d'histoire des sciences, Paris 1968: Colloques, Textes des rapports.* Paris 1968. Colloque 2, Fautes et contresens des traductions scientifiques médiévales: John E. Murdoch, "The Medieval Euclid: Salient Aspects of the Translations of the *Elements* by Adelard of Bath and Campanus of Novara," 67–94; Richard Lemay, "Fautes et contresens dans les traductions arabo-latines médiévales: L'*Introductorium in astronomiam* d'Abou Maʿshar de Balkh," 101–23; Marie-Thérèse d'Alverny, "Les traductions d'Aristote et de ses commentateurs," 125–44; Guy Beaujouan, "Fautes et obscurités dans les traductions médicales du Moyen Age," 145–52; and Jerry Stannard, "Medieval Reception of Classical Plant Names," 153–62.

Thorndike, Lynn, and Pearl Kibre. *A Catalogue of Incipits of Mediaeval Scientific Writings in Latin.* 2nd ed. Cambridge Mass. and London 1963. Contains a great amount of material concerning the translations, with references to manuscripts and early editions.

Wüstenfeld, Heinrich Ferdinand. *Die Übersetzungen arabischer Werke in das Lateinische seit dem XI. Jahrhundert.* Abh Göttingen, Hist.-philol. Kl. 22, 1877.

MEDICINE

Diels, Hermann. *Die Handschriften der antiken Ärzte.* Abh Berlin, Philos.-hist. Kl. 1905–07; repr. Leipzig 1970.

Durling, Richard J. "Corrigenda and Addenda to Diels' Galenica, 1: Codices Vaticani," *Traditio* 23 (1967) 463–76.

_____. "A Chronological Census of Renaissance Editions and Translations of Galen," JWCI 24 (1961) 230–305. Includes Renaissance editions of early translations.

Kibre, Pearl. "Hippocratic Writings in the Middle Ages," *Bulletin of the History of Medicine* 18 (1945) 371–412.

_____. "Hippocrates latinus: Repertorium of Hippocratic Writings in the Latin Middle Ages," *Traditio* 31 (1975) 99–126; 32 (1976) 257–92; 33 (1977) 253–95; 34 (1978) 193–226; 35 (1979) 273–302; 36 (1980) 347–72. This repertory includes translations from Greek and Arabic.

Leclerc, Lucien. *Histoire de la médecine arabe: Exposé complet des traductions du grec; les sciences en Orient, leur transmission à l'Occident par les traductions latines.* 2 vols. Paris 1876; repr. New York 1961.

Schipperges, Heinrich. *Die Assimilation der arabischen Medizin durch das lateinische Mittelalter*, Sudhoffs Archiv für Geschichte der Medizin und der Naturwissenschaften, Beiheft 3. Wiesbaden 1964.

The following works, concerning Arabic texts, contain references to Latin translations:

Peters, Francis E. *Aristoteles Arabus: The Oriental Translations and Commentaries on the Aristotelian Corpus*. Leiden 1968.

Sezgin, Fuat. *Geschichte des arabischen Schrifttums*. 7 vols. Leiden 1967–79. Vol. 3 (1970) *Medizin*; vol. 4 (1971) *Alchimie*; vol. 5 (1974) *Mathematik*; vol. 6 (1978) *Astronomie*; vol. 7 (1979) *Astrologie-Meteorologie*.

Ullmann, Manfred. *Die Medizin im Islam*. Handbuch der Orientalistik, 1. Abt.: Der Nahe und der Mittlere Osten. Erganzungsband 6.1. Leiden 1970.

_____. *Die Natur- und Geheimwissenschaften im Islam*. Handbuch der Orientalistik, 1. Abt.: Der Nahe und der Mittlere Osten. Erganzungsband 6.2. Leiden 1972.

The Transformation of the Quadrivium

Guy Beaujouan

The very title of this chapter provokes doubt: development, transformation, . . . or the beginning of the death throes of the quadrivium? The last formulation may seem paradoxical, when one ponders the fascinating representation of the liberal arts on the royal portal at Chartres,[1] and, more generally, the iconographic destiny of the quadrivium throughout the Middle Ages.

Conventional as it was, however, the structure of the quadrivium could not remain completely fixed.[2] Boethius equated the quadrivium with the division of mathematics into four parts, according to whether quantity is or is not discontinuous and immobile; thus, arithmetic, music, geometry, and astronomy followed one another in the order established by the combination of these criteria. More or less the same arrangement of the quadrivium is found in the twelfth century in William of Conches, Hugh of St Victor, and Geoffrey of St Victor.[3] In Isidore of Seville, however, and many others after him,[4] the intent to link the arts of the quadrivium to physics can be discerned: geometry then preceded music. This rejection of the purely mathematical status of music and astronomy reappears in the twelfth century, for example in Abelard and Bernard Silvester. It is only later that, in a larger context, Thomas Aquinas will speak of *scientie medie*: of sciences intermediate between mathematics and physics.

A related order of ideas governs the twelfth-century subdivision of the arts of the quadrivium into theory and practice. Certainly, under the stimulus of Aristotle, Macrobius, or Boethius, many medieval authors had distinguished, within the whole of philosophy, a theoretical or speculative sector and a practical or active domain. The novelty in the twelfth century was the application of this distinction to specific disciplines. In medicine, already by 1085, *theorica* and *practica* were clearly differentiated in the *Pantegni* of ʿAli ibn ʿAbbās, translated

[1] Adolf Katzenellenbogen, "The Representation of the Seven Liberal Arts," *Twelfth-Century Europe* 39–55.

[2] *Arts libéraux et philosophie au moyen âge*, Actes du quatrième Congrès international de philosophie médiévale (Montreal and Paris 1969) at 36–70 (esp. Manual C. Díaz y Díaz) and 959ff. (esp. Jean Gagné [n. 3 below]).

[3] Jean Gagné, "Du *quadrivium* aux *scientiae mediae*," ibid. 975–86 at 976.

[4] James A. Weisheipl, "Classification of the Sciences in Medieval Thought," *Mediaeval Studies* 27 (1965) 54–90.

into Latin by Constantine the African. Music offered the traditional contrast between the theoretician *musicus* and the performing *cantor*.[5] The case of geometry is particularly characteristic of the change that took place in the twelfth century. Hugh of St Victor was the first in Christendom (about 1125–30) to apply the theoretical-practical dichotomy to geometry.[6] Let us overlook the fact that this distinction is not found in Hugh's *Didascalicon*, and even that his authorship of the *Practica geometrie*[7] has not always been acknowledged: the interesting thing is to see how this idea, apparently born in the Latin West, merged with a purely Arabic classification of knowledge.

According to al-Fārābī, *scientia doctrinalis* was composed of seven branches, four of which constituted the quadrivium; each of these disciplines was then subdivided into theory and practice. Al-Fārābī's "Catalogue of Sciences" was translated literally by Gerard of Cremona, and Dominicus Gundisalvi also made an adaptation of it. (In the latter, the passage on the division of geometry differs from the Arabic original, and appears to borrow expressions from Hugh of St Victor.)[8] Taken up by Gundisalvi himself in his *De divisione philosophie*, and later by Vincent of Beauvais and many others, al-Fārābī's classification is much closer to the organization of the exact sciences found in twelfth-century Arabo-Latin translations than the old quadrivium was. Here, each is divided into theory and practice: arithmetic, geometry, *scientia de aspectibus* or optics, the science of the stars, music, *scientia de ponderibus*, and lastly *scientia de ingeniis* or engineering science, for which, oddly enough, the theoretical partner was algebra.

The Arabic contributions clearly broke up the quadrivium, but there is a marked difference between the early infiltrations from Gerbert's time and the great outpouring of translations during the twelfth century. Some years ago I made a statement that may appear surprising at first.[9] In eleventh-century schools, instruction in science was rather like an actual apprenticeship: it used the pupil's hand to teach calculation and musical harmony (figs. 12 and 13), and such concrete pedagogical tools as the monochord for music, the *rithmomachia* game for theoretical arithmetic, the abacus for calculation, the sphere and the astrolabe for astronomy (figs. 14–16). The first infiltrations of Arabic science were closely linked to working with the astrolabe and the *apices* on the abacus, and these early handbooks were little more than instructions (very imperfect) for their use. Change took place exactly to the extent that twelfth-century humanism attached more importance to the form of texts. The

---

[5]Guy Beaujouan, "Réflexions sur les rapports entre théorie et pratique au moyen âge," *The Cultural Context of Medieval Learning*, Proceedings of the First International Colloquium on Philosophy, Science, and Theology in the Middle Ages, ed. John E. Murdoch and Edith D. Sylla, Boston Studies in the Philosophy of Science 26 (Dordrecht and Boston 1975) 437–84.

[6]Roger Baron, "Sur l'introduction en Occident des termes *geometria theorica et practica*," *Revue d'histoire des sciences et de leurs applications* 8 (1955) 298–302.

[7]Hugh of St Victor, *Opera propaedeutica*, ed. Roger Baron (Notre Dame 1966) *Practica geometrie*.

[8]Dominicus Gundisalvi, *De scientiis*, ed. Manuel Alonso Alonso (Madrid 1954) 89 and 177.

[9]Guy Beaujouan, "L'enseignement du *quadrivium*," *La scuola nell'Occidente latino dell'alto medioevo*, Settimane 19 (2 vols. Spoleto 1972) 2.639–723.

great era of translation began with Adelard of Bath, and, in the quadrivium, was marked by an increased emphasis on the use of books.

The translations have been studied in an earlier chapter. Little by little, the long list of works translated from Arabic during the twelfth century, in the fields of mathematics, astronomy, and astrology, took shape.[10] But one could also look at the situation in a negative way, and wonder why *other* texts remained unknown during the Latin Middle Ages: the *Arithmetica* of Diophantus, the *Conica* of Apollonius,[11] Arabic theories on Euclid's parallel postulate, Omar Khayyām's treatises—especially his resolution of third-degree equations—and the works of al-Bīrūnī.[12]

The failure to appropriate higher mathematics seems self-explanatory; Latin Christendom, however, was not directly responsible for this. Having found its principal Arabic sources in Spain, medieval Western science obviously reflected, at the start, the choices of the Hispano-Moslem culture. The lack of interest in abstract mathematics, the predominance of astronomy and astrology in the early translations, the relatively late date of the Arabo-Latin versions of Aristotle's natural philosophy, the failure to use important works by eastern Arabic scholars: all are explained by the evolution of Arabic science in the Iberian peninsula, with its peculiarities of history and geography, its particularist pride within the Islamic world, its conditioning by the oppressive domination of the Malikite *fakihs*.[13]

The influx of Arabic science profoundly altered the equilibrium of the quadrivium. Music, which had remained an important branch of the quadrivium, received nothing from the Arabic translations and so, in a sense, withdrew from it. The theory-practice coupling was applied to geometry, and then to the other mathematical disciplines. Henceforth, the two branches of knowledge dealing with the stars, the "mathematical" and the "judicial," were irrevocably linked: astronomy, at the time the most perfected of the sciences, played a supporting role to astrology, which actually enjoyed a kind of hegemony.

THE QUADRIVIUM OF THE SPECIALISTS

THE SECESSION OF MUSIC[14]

The monastic schools had produced teachers of the quadrivium who strove to reconcile, on the monochord, the rules of Gregorian chant with the theories of

[10]See the bibliography at the end of this chapter, and also the papers presented at the Dumbarton Oaks Colloquium on the Transmission and Reception of Knowledge in 1977 (in press).
[11]Except for a brief passage linked to the tradition of Alhazen.
[12]Haskins, *Science* 74, attributed to al-Bīrūnī a commentary that must be restored to Ibn al-Muthannā.
[13]Guy Beaujouan, *La science hispano-arabe et les modalités de son influence*, Rapport au XIIIe Congrès international d'histoire des sciences (Moscow 1971); Juan Vernet, *La cultura hispanoárabe en Oriente y Occidente* (Barcelona 1978) and chapter 3 of his *Historia de la ciencia española* (Madrid 1975). See also Dominique Urvoy, *Le monde des ulémas andalous du V/XIe au VII/XIIIe siècle* (Geneva 1978).
[14]Being an amateur in the field of musicology myself, I warmly thank Michel Huglo, maître de recherche at the C.N.R.S., for his help. During the summer of 1978, he presented lectures at

Boethius, the latter descended from Greek instrumental music. In the areas of notation and mode, the crowning achievement and best expression of such efforts was the *Micrologus* of Guido of Arezzo, about 1020–30. As episcopal schools took over from monastic teaching, however, music drifted away from its sisters of the quadrivium. A case in point is the work of John of Affligem (Cotton) between 1089 and 1121.[15] More or less connected with the school of Liège, he produced a synthesis of his predecessors' works, with a certain historical perspective—but without, it seems, being fully aware that his work marked a turning point.

The study of music was already beginning to shift from its theoretical and mathematical orientation to focus on the concerns of artistic practice.[16] Within the liberal arts, music was increasingly regarded as a language, and hence comparable to grammar and dialectic.[17] Music indeed remained linked to the quadrivium, and always profited from the great dignity conferred on it by a philosophical context predominantly Platonic. But, within this framework, it did not inspire such masters as Adelard of Bath, Hugh and Richard of St Victor, William of Conches, John of Salisbury, Honorius Augustodunensis, or Alan of Lille to noteworthy technical reflections; they remained content with generalities. Thierry of Chartres included in his *Heptateuchon* some fairly long excerpts from the *De musica* of Boethius, but limited himself to the first two of this work's five books (a significant limitation, doubtless, since it recurs 140 years later in Jacques of Liège).

John of Affligem stated sorrowfully that instruction in music was tending to abandon the monochord,[18] a teaching tool which had earlier seemed a noteworthy link between theory and practice. What was happening at the beginning of the twelfth century? Up until then, the single-stringed monochord had permitted testing the solfeggio of pieces written in the monochordal alphabetic notation (see the *Dialogus de Musica* of pseudo-Odo). Much of its instructional value was lost for those who, in the future, sight-read melodies written on the colored staff advocated by Guido of Arezzo.[19] Similarly, the practical usefulness of the tonaries dwindled during the twelfth century: people were no longer willing to memorize psalmodic differences that could henceforth be read directly from the antiphonary.[20]

Any history of twelfth-century music must include the Cistercian reform of religious chant (1134). The theoretical foundation of this reform appeared

---

Poitiers on "Les procédés nouveaux de composition musicale au XIIe siècle: Théorie et pratique," to be published in CCM. In the meantime M. Huglo has kindly lent me his notes, which I have used extensively here.

[15]Iohannes Affligemensis, *De musica cum tonario*, ed. Joseph Smits van Waesberghe (Rome 1950). Michel Huglo, "L'auteur du traité de musique dédié à Fulgence d'Affligem," *Revue belge de musicologie* 31.3–4 (1977) 5–19.

[16]Francisco J. León Tello, *Estudios de historia de la teoría musical* (Madrid 1962).

[17]Iohannes Affligemensis (n. 15 above) 51.

[18]Ibid. 65.

[19]Huglo (n. 15 above) 11.

[20]Michel Huglo, *Les tonaires: Inventaire, analyse, comparaison* (Paris 1971).

in 1132, in the *Regulae de arte musica* by Guy of Eu.[21] But with Guy, and still more with St Bernard's recommendations for the liturgical repertory,[22] we are moving away from the mathematical and cosmological concerns which bound music to the quadrivium.

When musicologists study the books on liturgical practice or anthologies of twelfth-century profane poetry, they witness the liberation from the constraints imposed by "Gregorian" church music. This emancipation took four main directions:

(1) expansion of the range of intervals allowed in the Gregorian chant;

(2) a search for new and more expressive musical formulas, by drawing on secular song;

(3) creation of "rhythmic modes,"[23] made necessary by the development of the *organum* and the descant (the first mention of these rhythmic modes does not, however, appear until 1199, in Alexander of Villedieu's *Doctrinale*);

(4) the introduction of musical instruments of eastern, mainly Arabic, origin.

Histories of music characterize these developments, which took place principally at Notre-Dame in Paris during the twelfth and thirteenth centuries, as what would later be called *ars antiqua*. The autonomy of music was, as it were, confirmed when, in the cathedral schools, training in chant was detached from general studies and entrusted to a special master.

Not until the fourteenth century, with the *ars nova*, did music once more become a specialization of masters of arts interested in mathematics. Then, the vocalistic freedom and complex dislocation of rhythm required a more sophisticated musical notation,[24] and new theoretical research was done by scholars such as John of Murs, Philip of Vitry, and Simon Tunstede. Around 1320, as a result, after a 200-year eclipse, the *De musica* of Boethius was studied with renewed interest.

ALGORISMUS

The twelfth-century renaissance marks an important stage in the diffusion of calculation with so-called Arabic numerals. The abacus of Gerbert's pupils was a tablet with columns for using *apices*, or counters, each marked with one of the nine "ghubār" numerals; even without a zero, these columns gave the numbers a positional value. This type of calculation seems to have spread mainly through practical training. True, there exist numerous treatises on the

[21]Claire Maître is currently preparing a thesis on the Cistercian reform of liturgical music.

[22]"Prologus in antiphonarium," *Sancti Bernardi Opera*, ed. Leclercq 3.515–16; "De revisione cantus cisterciensis," ed. Francisco J. Guentner, *Corpus scriptorum de musica* 24 (1974) 21–22.

[23]William G. Waite, *The Rhythm of Twelfth-Century Polyphony: Its Theory and Practice* (New Haven 1954). See also studies on rhythm in the works of the troubadours and trouvères.

[24]Jacques Chailley, *Histoire musicale du moyen âge* (2nd ed. Paris 1969) 243–44.

abacus, but they are often difficult to understand, and none gained authoritative standing.

The twelfth century saw a decisive change. Henceforth calculations would be done in sand or dust, using a zero and thus without columns, but with the possibility of erasing certain numbers and replacing them with others. Except in Italy, this new type of calculation was no longer called *abacus*, but *algorismus*. This term contains an express reference to al-Khwārizmī, the authority on the subject.[25] This great scholar of the first half of the ninth century wrote a treatise on calculation, the original Arabic version of which is believed lost; thanks to recent work, however, its introduction into the Latin world is now better understood.

The text is found in three main versions. Of the most accurate one there is but a single manuscript—which is, unfortunately, incomplete; it is generally thought to be closest to the Arabic original, but even so it represents a reworking. Of the other two twelfth-century adaptations, one is attributed to Adelard of Bath, the second to John of Seville.[26] The attribution to Adelard remains conjectural, since it rests on the rubric of MS BN lat 16208, "Liber ysagogarum alchorismi in artem astronomicam a magistro A compositus." Though not the best by far, this manuscript appears to be a reworking with significant additions. In the Milan manuscript, the work is rather judiciously entitled "Liber ysagogarum alchoarismi ad totum quadrivium." The adaptation of al-Khwārizmī's treatise provides only the first three books of a set whose last two parts are still unedited (*De musicis ac geometricis rationibus* and *De temporibus et motibus*). In addition to the fact that Euclid's *Elements* (translated by none other than Adelard) is unknown to it, the mention of the Spanish era, the interest in the reciprocal conversion of Arabic and Hebrew years, and finally the table referring to October 1116, are noteworthy. It would not be at all surprising if the converted Jew Peter Alfonsi played a central role in elaborating this "Adelardian" version.[27] John of Seville's version, finally, is much clearer and more detailed, and was much more influential.

As interesting as the detailed comparison of the earliest algorismic treatises is,[28] it is advisable to consider the physical modes of calculation as a

[25]G. J. Toomer, "al-Khwārizmī," DSB 7 (1973) 358–65. Fuat Sezgin, *Geschichte des arabischen Schrifttums* (7 vols. Leiden 1967–79) vol. 5, *Mathematik* 228–41.

[26]The first version was edited from the Cambridge MS by Kurt Vogel, [Muḥammad ibn Mūsā al-Khuwārizmī] *Algorismus, das früheste Lehrbuch zum Rechnen mit indischen Ziffern* (Aalen 1963); the other two 12th-c. adaptations have been edited by André Allard, *Les plus anciennes versions latines du XIIe siècle issues de l'arithmétique d'al-Khwārizmī: Histoire des textes suivie de l'édition critique des traités attribués à Adélard de Bath et Jean de Séville et d'un remaniement de ce dernier* (Louvain 1975; in press, Corpus scriptorum latinorum Paravianum [Turin]).

[27]José M. Millás Vallicrosa, *Estudios sobre historia de la ciencia española* (Barcelona 1949) 197–218, esp. 214–15. Richard J. Lemay supports the attribution to Peter Alfonsi; André Allard voices serious doubts on this score. No decision can be made until the nonalgorismic portions of the text are edited and the astronomical elements are analyzed in comparison to the manuscript of Petrus Anfulsus (Oxford, Corpus Christi 283).

[28]Suzan R. Benedict, *A Comparative Study of the Early Treatises Introducing into Europe the Hindu Art of Reckoning* (diss. University of Michigan 1914; Concord N.H. 1916) offered a useful

whole. We have seen that algorism was conditioned by the possibility of proceeding by means of successive corrections made by erasing: this limited its demands on the memory, and, above all, simplified positional calculation by shifting certain numbers. Through the handbooks of Alexander of Villedieu and John of Sacrobosco, this system persisted in university teaching throughout the Middle Ages. Conversely, written calculation without erasures prevailed in business arithmetic of the late Middle Ages. But this technique, much closer to our own, was the one advocated by Leonardo of Pisa in his *Liber abbaci* (1202). However, concurrently with erasable calculation in sand, written calculation in ink had already been taught by various Arabic authors such as al-Uqlīdisī,[29] then Abuʾ-l-Wafāʾal-Būzjānī, and others.[30]

New theories, more or less fantastic, frequently surface concerning the origin of Arabic numerals and the links between their different known forms,[31] but one can safely say that the very reasonable conclusions reached by Smith and Karpinski's classic study (1911) remain plausible.[32]

Despite the algorismic treatises that did in fact use them for transitory calculations, the use of Arabic numerals for giving data and results spread only slowly during the twelfth century. New figures were sometimes used to compensate for the weaknesses of the Roman system:[33]

$$\tau = 0 \text{ or } 30 \quad \gamma = 4 \quad S = 6 \quad O = 8 \quad \psi = 9 \quad \chi = 40$$

Only recently have paleographers become interested in the forms of these strange symbols, which appear to be derived from the first letter of the number in question:

t = *terminus* (the boundary of a sign of the zodiac being 0 or 30 degrees)

q = 4   Q = 5   s = 6   S = 7   O = 8   N = 9

χ or $\chi = XL$ or 40

comparison of the oldest algorismic treatises. This work was taken up again by André Allard, *Le grand calcul selon les Indiens de Maxime Planude, sa source anonyme de 1252* (5 vols. thèse Louvain 1972) vol. 5.

[29]A. S. Saidan, *The Arithmetic of Al-Uqlīdisī* (Dordrecht 1977) part 4.

[30]André Allard, "Ouverture et résistance au calcul indien," *Colloque d'histoire des sciences: Résistance et ouverture aux découvertes et aux théories scientifiques dans le passé* (March 1972), Université de Louvain, Recueil de travaux d'histoire et de philologie 6th ser. 9 (Louvain 1976) 87–100.

[31]For example, Karl W. Menninger, *Zahlwort und Ziffer* (Göttingen 1957), trans. (without bibliography) Paul Broneer, *Number Words and Number Symbols* (Cambridge Mass. 1969); Abdelhamid I. Sabra, "ʿilm al-ḥisāb," *Encyclopaedia of Islam*, new edition (1970); Georges Ifrah, *Histoire universelle des chiffres* (Paris 1981).

[32]David E. Smith and Louis C. Karpinski, *The Hindu-Arabic Numerals* (Boston and London 1911); Adolf P. Youschkevitch, *Les mathématiques arabes: VIIIe–XVe siècles*, trans. M. Cazenave and K. Jaouiche (Paris 1976).

[33]Emmanuel Poulle and Richard J. Lemay, "Traductions médiévales," *Actes du XIIe Congrès international d'histoire des sciences* (1 vol. in 2 Paris 1970–71) 1B.104–08, colloque 2.

This system seems to have originated in Spain, and it may be related to the Visigothic script.[34] It is tempting to think that this explains certain differences between true Arabic numerals:

and the Western numerals of the twelfth century:[35]

I find the explanation of 8 by  (*octo*) particularly tempting. For the others, we must bear in mind the forms attested from 976:

In this area, one who is not a paleographer risks being fooled by misleading resemblances. It is not the form of the figures which is essential, but the motions of the hand writing lightly on sand. It was under these specific conditions that the Arabic *ductus* (from right to left) gave way to the Western left-to-right movement:  written from right to left on sand readily gives ; when the latter figure is written from left to right, the final stroke tends to disappear, whence . Again, for the five,  and  seem irreconcilable, but both could be derived from the form  attested to by Kūshyār ibn Labbān.[36] It is easy to see how the lightly written form  could give from right to left , and from left to right .[37]

This discussion is still open, but one can see that paleographic analysis of twelfth-century manuscripts is far from complete in this area.

THEORY AND PRACTICE IN GEOMETRY

The concept of theoretical geometry did not acquire its full meaning until the rediscovery of Euclid's *Elements* and their rigorous sequences of proofs—quite unimaginable to a reader of Boethius's apocryphal geometries.[38] In the second of Adelard of Bath's three versions, however, the statement of each proposition is not followed by Euclid's actual proof, but by a simple orientation with a view to eventually giving a proof, with a certain emphasis on constructions and also on considerations which have sensibly been called "meta-mathematical." The third version, with proofs, also contains, along with borrowings from Boethius's *Arithmetic*, sections approaching philosophy, and, more generally,

[34]Richard J. Lemay, "The Hispanic Origin of Our Present Numeral Forms," *Viator* 8 (1977) 435–62.

[35]Forms retained by André Allard in his edition of the version attributed to Adelard of Bath (n. 26 above).

[36]Kushyār ibn Labbān, *Principles of Hindu Reckoning*, ed. and trans. Martin Levey and Marvin Petruck (Madison Wisc. 1965).

[37]Rida A. K. Irani, "Arabic Numeral Forms," *Centaurus* 4 (1955–56) 1–12 at 4.

[38]For the reemergence of Euclid—now much better known, thanks to research during the last thirty years—see the essay by Mlle d'Alverny in this volume. A remarkable study where one least expects it: John E. Murdoch, "Euclid," DSB 4 (1971) 437–59.

an attempt to render the reasoning less abstract.[39] Despite the multiplication of translations of Euclid (Adelard I, II, and III, Herman of Carinthia, Gerard of Cremona, and a Greco-Latin version), no true commentary was composed before the middle of the thirteenth century; Albertus Magnus himself depended on the commentary by Anaritius (al-Nayrīzī, early tenth century) translated by Gerard of Cremona.[40]

By the end of the tenth century, the teaching of practical geometry had added, to the old land-surveying texts of the *agrimensores*, elements borrowed from Arabic rules for using the astrolabe. Typical of this combination was the treatise called *Geometria incerti auctoris*, which seems to have made an important contribution to the three twelfth-century practical geometries edited since Haskins's time: Hugh of St Victor's *Practica geometrie*,[41] the *Artis cuiuslibet*,[42] and the *Geometrie due sunt partes principales*.[43]

The *Artis cuiuslibet* is anonymous, but is known to have been written in Paris in 1193. A knowledge of Euclid is barely perceptible in it, but the Arabic influence is manifest in the relatively well-assimilated elements of astronomy, and above all in the addition of a fourth book devoted to fractions (the tradition which made the art of calculation part of geometry, independent from theoretical arithmetic, persisted). A particularly surprising error is that this treatise advocates the formula of polygonal numbers according to Boethius's *Arithmetic* for computing the area of a polygon.

ASTRONOMICAL INSTRUMENTS[44]

Often linked, it appears, to Arabic instruments imported by the Christian world, the treatises on the astrolabe of the tenth and eleventh centuries are characterized by terminological uncertainty and deficiencies of content (certain elements missing, faulty methods of construction, a misunderstanding of some of its uses).

In this area too a profound change took place during the second quarter of the twelfth century, especially with the translations by Iohannes Hispalensis. But paralleling the reception of texts newly rendered into Latin (those of Messahala, Maslama, and al-Ṣaffār), various authors devoted original treatises to

---

[39]John E. Murdoch, "The Medieval Euclid: Salient Aspects of the Translations of the *Elements* by Adelard of Bath and Campanus of Novara," *Revue de synthèse* 89 (1968) 67–94, esp. 72.

[40]Paul M. J. E. Tummers, "The Commentary of Albert on Euclid's Elements of Geometry," *Albertus Magnus and the Sciences: Commemorative Essays, 1980*, ed. James A. Weisheipl, Pontifical Institute of Mediaeval Studies, Studies and Texts 49 (Toronto 1980) 479–99.

[41]See note 7 above.

[42]Stephen K. Victor, ed. and trans., *Practical Geometry in the High Middle Ages: "Artis cuiuslibet consummatio" and the "Pratike de geometrie,"* Memoirs of the American Philosophical Society 134 (Philadelphia 1979).

[43]See below at notes 48 and 49.

[44]Emmanuel Poulle, "Les instruments astronomiques de l'Occident latin aux XIe et XIIe siècles," CCM 15 (1972) 27–40.

the astrolabe: Raymond of Marseille (before 1141),[45] Adelard of Bath (ca. 1158–61), and John of Seville himself. These texts, as much because of their clarity as for their scientific value, represent significant progress over the preceding century.

The statement that "the ancient quadrant was a typical product of twelfth-century science"[46] refers to the astronomical quadrant known at the end of the thirteenth century as *vetus*, as opposed to the astrolabe quadrant then called *novus*. The astronomical quadrant has a *cursor*, a sort of zodiacal calendar showing the declination of the sun according to the date. When the equinox of the cursor was placed facing the graduation of the quadrant indicating the colatitude of the place of observation, the meridian height of the sun on any given date could be determined without calculations; then, having correctly placed a bead, one could read directly on the instrument the unequal hour corresponding, on that day, to a given observation of the sun's height (fig. 17).

Although it was formerly believed that this *quadrans vetus* went back to the time of Gerbert, it has now been shown that the eleventh-century quadrant (the *vetustissimus*) did not contain the diagram of unequal hours, but a trigonometric graph consisting of lines parallel to one of the sides.[47] Now, the history of the quadrant is linked to that of the astrolabe, because on the back of the latter appear reversed but almost identical graphs (fig. 16). The hour-lines of the *quadrans vetus* were thus marked, before 1141, on the back of the astrolabe described by Raymond of Marseille, and they are also found in an addition to the most widely known Latin version of Messahala's treatise.

All this does not, however, prove that during the twelfth century the *quadrans vetus* had spread in the form later to be popularized in the university world by the *Tractatus quadrantis* attributed to Robertus Anglicus (but more probably by a certain John living in Montpellier).[48] The geometrical part of the *Tractatus quadrantis* consists essentially of a *Practica geometrie* dating from the twelfth century, the *Geometrie due sunt partes principales* mentioned above;[49] the astronomical constituents of the quadrant, on the other hand, seem to have been borrowed from an Arabic text very close to one included in the *Libros del saber* of Alfonso X of Castile.

THE MOVEMENT OF THE STARS

If we leave aside the computus tables, whose inaccuracy was remarked with growing frequency, the earliest trace of astronomical tables in the Latin Middle Ages is found in the *Preceptum canonis Ptolomei*, beginning "Intellectus

[45]Emmanuel Poulle, "Le traité d'astrolabe de Raymond de Marseille," *Studi medievali* 3rd ser. 5 (1964) 866–900.

[46]Poulle (n. 44 above) 36.

[47]Millás Vallicrosa (n. 27 above) 65–110 = "La introducción del cuadrante con cursor en Europa," *Isis* 17 (1932) 218–58.

[48]Frances N. L. Britt, "A Critical Edition of *Tractatus quadrantis*" (diss. Emory University 1972).

[49]Edited, following *Tractatus quadrantis*, by Britt, ibid. 208–55.

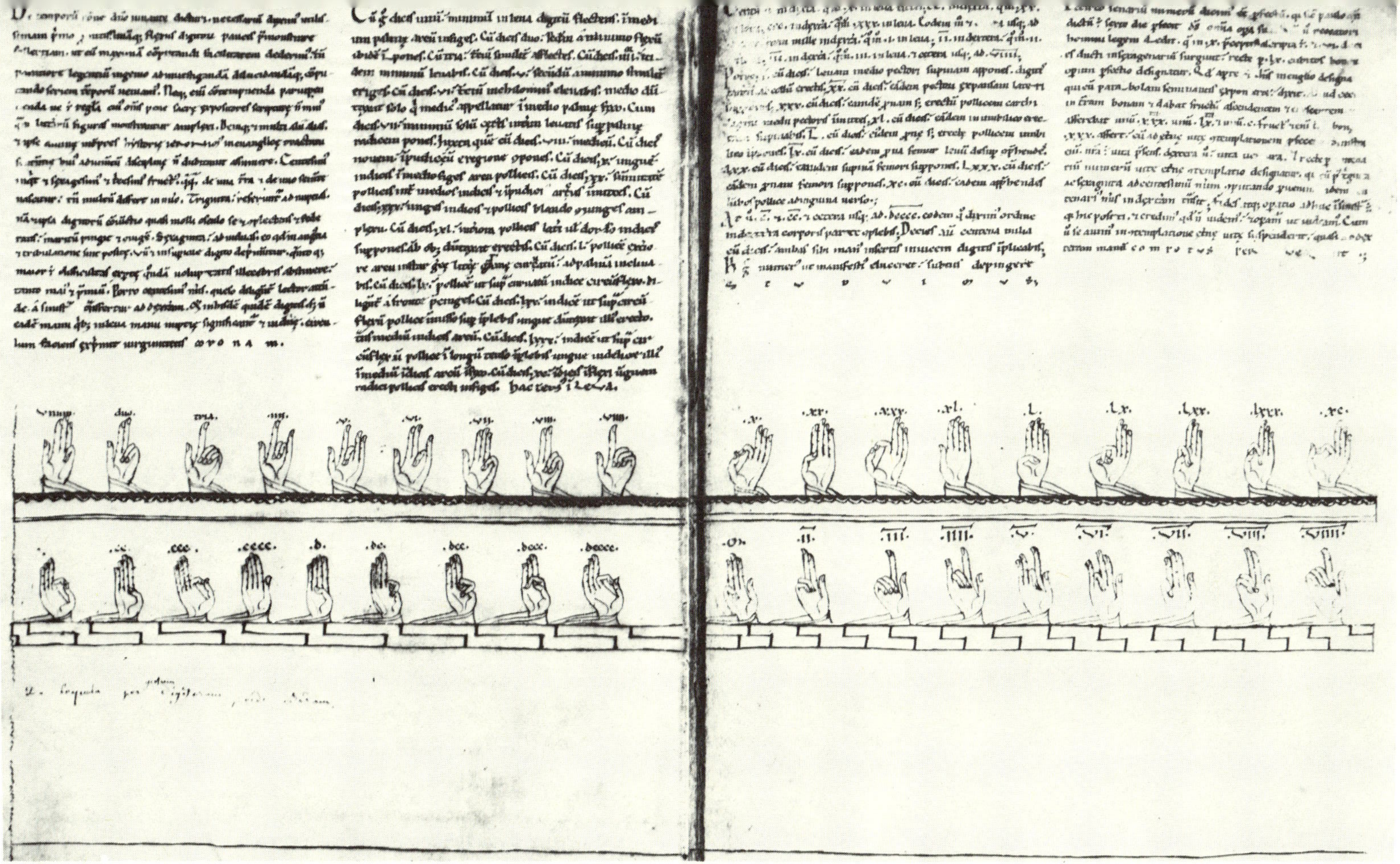

Fig. 12. Rouen. Bibliothèque municipale, MS 3055 (thirteenth century). Bede, *De temporum ratione*, fols. 3v–4r: system for counting by finger signs, showing digits, tens, hundreds, and thousands. Photo courtesy of the Bibliothèque municipale, Rouen.

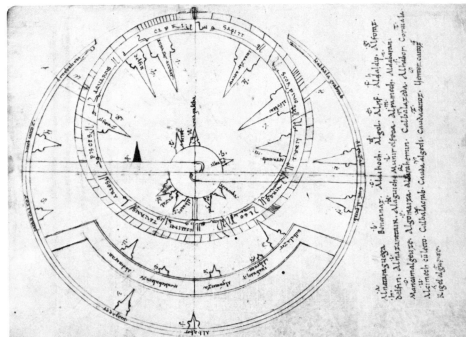

Fig. 14. Paris. Bibliothèque nationale, MS lat 7412 (eleventh century). Diagram of a hispano-arabic astrolabe, fol. 19v: rete. The rete is a pierced-metal projection of the apparently moving celestial sphere. One sees here the circle of the zodiac and pointers marking the positions of certain important stars. Photo: Bibl. nat. Paris.

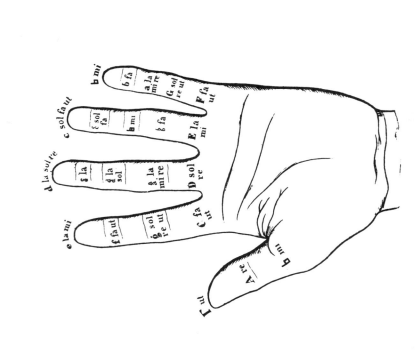

Fig. 13. Guido of Arezzo's "harmonic hand." Each note is assigned to a position on the hand; the scale begins with Γ at the tip of the thumb and runs spiral fashion across the upper palm and around the finger joints. ("C sol fa ut" at the tip of the third finger is the modern middle C.) The choir master would teach a melody by holding up his left hand and pointing to the appropriate joints in sequence with his right. After *Scriptorum de musica medii aevi*, ed. Edmond de Coussemaker (4 vols. Paris 1864–76) 1.21.

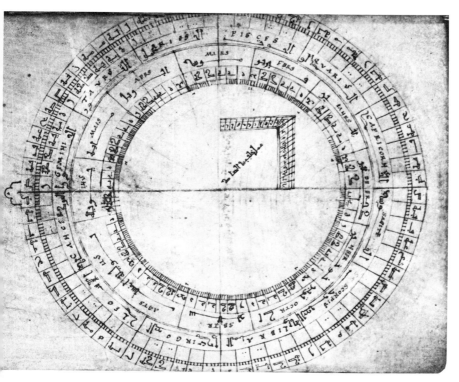

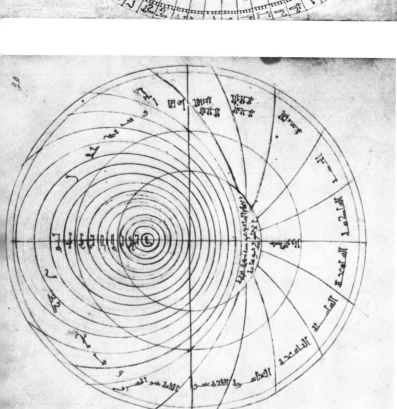

Fig. 15. Paris. Bibliothèque nationale, MS lat 7412 (eleventh century). Diagram of a hispano-arabic astrolabe, fol. 20r: plate for 49° latitude. The plate is a projection of the celestial sphere, fixed in reference to a given observer (horizon, azimuth, almucantar). On the face of the astrolabe, the rete can be turned around the projection of the world's axis onto the plate corresponding to a particular place of observation (here: 49° latitude). Thus the daily movement of the celestial vault is perfectly represented in relation to the observer. Photo: Bibl. nat. Paris.

Fig. 16. Paris. Bibliothèque nationale, MS lat 7412 (eleventh century). Diagram of a hispano-arabic astrolabe, fol. 23v: back of the astrolabe, with its square of umbrae, zodiac calendar, and scale of degrees. Photo: Bibl. nat. Paris.

Fig. 17. Diagram of a *quadrans vetus*. On a particular day, if one has moved a bead along a plumb line to the intersection of the plumb line and Arc VI, thus marking the point corresponding to the sun's culmination, one can at any moment, by sighting the height of the sun, read the hour from the location of the bead: in this illustration, 3⅓ hours before or after high noon. Adapted from Emmanuel Poulle, "Les instruments astronomiques de l'Occident latin aux XIᵉ et XIIᵉ siècles," CCM 15 (1972) 37 fig. 3.

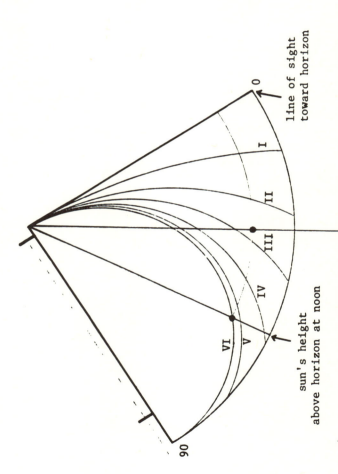

climatum poli.''[50] It offers a set of rules for using Ptolemy's manual tables. The first book seems to be related to Theon of Alexandria, and the second must have been written in North Africa at the beginning of the sixth century;[51] both must have been translated from Greek into Latin in Rome around 535. The oldest preserved manuscript dates from about 1000, and from then on the text enjoyed a certain popularity. It was still used by Hugh of St Victor, and it represents astronomy in Thierry's *Heptateuchon*.[52] We may, however, doubt whether such canons were much used, since they spread without the tables whose use they were supposed to teach.

An unusual document from the eleventh century makes quite clear how astral observation was conducted in the absence of any mathematical model and lacking even the elementary astronomical knowledge that spread with the astrolabe. This curious *horologium stellare* was the work of a monk who recorded, for certain dates, at clearly specified times and from a precise location, the positions of certain stars relative to various architectural features of his monastery (dormitory windows, bell tower, and so on).[53]

Only with the renaissance of the twelfth century, in fact, did the Christian West learn how to calculate the positions of the planets correctly. What happened in this area is strikingly similar to what we have observed concerning algorisms. Here too the authority responsible for transmitting Indian influences is al-Khwārizmī; here too the original work has vanished and is known only through adaptations; here too the new technique was introduced by Adelard of Bath, who doubtless took it from Peter Alfonsi.

If, since the time of Haskins's work, our knowledge of twelfth-century Western science has made some progress through the discovery and study of Latin manuscripts, our perspective has been expanded above all by the contributions of historians of Arabic, Jewish, and Hindu astronomy: a much more technical analysis of the numerical contents of the tables has deepened our understanding. The case of al-Khwārizmī's astronomical tables is typical in this regard.[54]

Originally, an Indian *siddhānta* (probably the *Mahāsiddhānta*), adapted into Arabic by al-Fazārī,[55] inspired al-Khwārizmī's *Zīj-al-Sindhind*—a set of

---

[50]André Van de Vyver, "Les plus anciennes traductions latines médiévales (Xe-XIe siècles) de traités d'astronomie et d'astrologie," *Osiris* 1 (1936) 658-91.

[51]A critical edition of *Preceptum canonis Ptolomei* is to be published by David Pingree and Noel M. Swerdlow. The conclusions presented here are those summarized by Pingree, "Translation and the Progress of Astronomy," Dumbarton Oaks Colloquium (n. 10 above).

[52]On the identification of portions included in the *Heptateuchon*, see Jeauneau, "Note sur l'Ecole de Chartres," *Lectio* 5-49 at 36, 37, and 49 (= *Studi medievali* 3rd ser. 5 [1964] 821-65). The author refers, for the mathematical portions, to N. Bubnov. The ancient descriptions are more uncertain for the astrological part.

[53]Giles Constable, "Horologium stellare monasticum (saec. XI)," *Consuetudines benedictinae variae (saec. XI-saec. XIV)*, Corpus consuetudinum monasticarum 6 (Siegburg 1975) 1-18.

[54]In recent years the study of al-Khwārizmī's tables has been energetically renewed, thanks mainly to the re-edition and splendid technical commentary, with an English translation of the canons, by Otto Neugebauer, *The Astronomical Tables of Al-Khwārizmī* (Copenhagen 1962).

[55]David Pingree, "The Indian and Pseudo-Indian Passages in Greek and Latin Astronomical and Astrological Texts," *Viator* 7 (1976) 141-95 at 151-69.

astronomical tables the original Arabic of which has been lost except for some small fragments—at the beginning of the ninth century. A reading of an extraordinary history of science, the famous *Categories of Nations* written in 1068 by Ibn Ṣāʿid of Toledo, suggests it was a peculiarity of Hispano-Arabic astronomy that a large number of scholars remained attached, even at a late date, to the methods of the *Sindhind* (an attachment which had as a corollary a certain distrust of Ptolemy). Indeed, al-Khwārizmī's astronomical tables had been reworked by Maslama of Madrid, and doubtless by his disciple Ibn al-Ṣaffār. It was this revision, also lost, that Adelard of Bath translated.[56] The desire to recover the original form of these tables led researchers to the tenth-century commentary by al-Muthannā. Haskins studied the translation by Hugh of Santalla, but unfortunately he believed that it was a commentary by al-Bīrūnī on al-Farghānī.[57] Duly restored to al-Muthannā, the Latin version was published;[58] but it is also necessary to refer to two Hebrew versions, one of them by Abraham ibn Ezra.[59]

Insofar as we are able to know them, and even though their general structure is close to Ptolemy, al-Khwārizmī's tables include a number of parameters and procedures borrowed from India.[60] It was because Indian astronomy had Mesopotamian, Greco-Babylonian, and Greek sources that Islam could try to harmonize it with Ptolemy's teaching. In a text which had undergone a long series of revisions—as for example the Latin tables of al-Khwārizmī—it was difficult, in the twelfth century, to recognize and distinguish clearly the contribution of each tradition. Abraham ibn Ezra, however, in the Latin text of his *Book on the Principles of Astronomical Tables*, displays a critical mind; he seems unusually aware of the heterogeneity of the currents—that of India in particular—which meet in Arabic astronomy.[61]

[56]Heinrich Suter, ed. (continuing work begun by Axel A. Björnbo and Rasmus O. Besthorn), *Die astronomischen Tafeln des Muhammed ibn Mūsā al-Khwārizmī in der Bearbeitung des Maslama ibn Ahmed al-Madjrītī und der latein. Uebersetzung des Athelhard von Bath*, Det Kongelige Danske Videnskabernes Selskabs Skrifter 7th ser., Historisk og filosofisk afdeling 3.1 (Copenhagen 1914).

[57]See note 12 above.

[58]Eduardo Millás Vendrell, ed., *El comentario de Ibn al-Muṭannā a las tablas astronómicas de al-Jwārizmī: Estudio y edición crítica del texto latino, en la versión de Hugo Sanctallensis* (Madrid 1963).

[59]Bernard R. Goldstein, *Ibn al-Muthannā's Commentary on the Astronomical Tables of al-Khwārizmī* (New Haven 1967).

[60]See Pingree (n. 55 above). They have no equant; the longitudes of the higher planets are calculated according to a typically Indian approximation which transfers to the mean *centrum* a part of the correction which must be applied to the equation of the anomaly according to the distance from the earth of the center of the epicycle—hence the recourse to the famous *sublimatio examinata* obtained by taking the longitude of the apogee of the deferent and subtracting half of the equation of the anomaly. See Neugebauer (n. 54 above) 22–29 and 98–99. This Indian approximation treats a small arc of the deferent near the center of the epicycle as if it were a straight segment. The clearest and best explanation is that of Otto Neugebauer, "The Transmission of Planetary Theories in Ancient and Medieval Astronomy," *Scripta mathematica* 22 (1956) 165–92, especially the appendix "Hindu Planetary Theory," 174–88.

[61]José M. Millás Vallicrosa, *El libro de los fundamentos de las Tablas astronómicas de R. Abraham ibn Ezra* (Madrid 1947).

Al-Khwārizmī's astronomical tables were rapidly supplanted by a better tool, the tables of Toledo. These were the fruits of a collective endeavor, put in order by a Hispano-Moslem astronomer of the eleventh century, al-Zarqālī (or perhaps al-Zarqiyāl, "the small blue-eyed one").[62] Unfortunately the original of the Toledo tables is lost. We know them mainly through Gerard of Cremona's version, which, except for the trigonometric section, remains unedited. The Toledo tables combine different sources.[63] The table of mean motions is a surprising arrangement of elements borrowed from al-Khwārizmī, al-Battānī, and Ptolemy's *Almagest*; in Gerard of Cremona's version, the supposed oscillating motion of the equinoctial points (*accessio et recessio octavi circuli*) is taken into account, following Thābit ibn Qurra.[64] Despite the difficulty of using them, these tables were enthusiastically received by the most competent astronomers. Well before Gerard of Cremona's classic translation, another version of the Toledo tables existed, probably made by John of Seville; Raymond of Marseille probably used this first adaptation in setting up the tables for the coordinates of his town.[65]

Much research remains to be done on the tradition of astronomical tables and their use during the twelfth century.[66] Scholars then did not hesitate to blend, more or less successfully, heterogeneous ingredients. It has recently been pointed out, for example, that at the end of the twelfth century the tables of London sometimes refer directly to Ptolemy instead of relying on Azarquiel.[67]

ASTROLOGY[68]

We know very little about astrological practices during the early Middle Ages. For the era of Gerbert and his disciples, we have information about the *Mathematica Alhandrei summi astrologi* and related texts in a series of manuscripts going back to the tenth century.[69] It seems that despite these

[62]José M. Millás Vallicrosa, *Estudios sobre Azarquiel* (Madrid 1950 [1943]).

[63]G. J. Toomer, "A Survey of the Toledan Tables," *Osiris* 15 (1968) 5–174.

[64]But the movement of *accessus* and *recessus* does not appear either in the first version (attributed to John of Seville) or in Raymond of Marseille.

[65]Emmanuel Poulle, "Raymond of Marseilles," DSB 11 (1975) 321–23. An edition of the *Liber cursuum planetarum* of Raymond of Marseille will be published by Marie-Thérèse d'Alverny and Emmanuel Poulle.

[66]One should think of the London tables, the Pisan tables, and especially of the mysterious Toulouse tables, the precise dating of which near the end of the 12th century or the beginning of the 13th is still uncertain.

[67]Joshua D. Lipton, "The Astronomer of BN 16208," Dumbarton Oaks Colloquium (n. 10 above).

[68]Joshua D. Lipton, "The Rational Evaluation of Astrology in the Period of Arabo-Latin Translation, ca. 1126–1187 A.D." (diss. University of California, Los Angeles 1978). Although I first saw this excellent thesis in August 1978, I have modified my text only slightly as a result, since I had already had lengthy discussions with Mr. Lipton in 1977, while he was preparing his thesis in Paris.

[69]José M. Millás Vallicrosa, *Assaig d'història de les idees físiques i matemàtiques a la Catalunya medieval* (Barcelona 1931); idem (n. 27 above) pls. 5–6 and *Nuevos estudios sobre la historia de la ciencia española* (Barcelona 1960) 101–03; Van de Vyver (n. 50 above).

texts, and despite the knowledge of abridged canons of Ptolemy's manual tables (see above at note 50), no Latin astrologer was able, before the end of the eleventh century, to make predictions based on calculating the position of the planets. Setting aside predictions based on the visible course of the moon, the numerical components of the subastrology of this period were supplied by adding up the numerical value of the letters of a name, or by other superstitious plays on numbers (for example, the sphere of Pythagoras or pseudo-Apuleius, the letter of Petosiris, and so forth).

It has thus been possible to speak of the quasi-nonexistence of astrological treatises after the time of Firmicus Maternus—that is, between the fourth and the twelfth centuries. Some historians maintain that astrology was then eradicated by the Western Church's continually renewing the condemnations by St Basil, St Augustine, and St Gregory.[70] But if, after what might better be called a lengthy hibernation, astrology was reborn suddenly and with such profusion in the twelfth century, it was not because the attitude of the ecclesiastical authorities had changed. What had changed was that, thanks to the Arabs, Latins had learned to use astronomical tables and to calculate the longitude of the planets for any time whatever, past, present, or future—the precondition of an astrology which truly believed in itself.

Raymond of Marseille perfectly illustrates this interdependence between astronomy and astrology. The same purpose motivates his treatise on the astrolabe, his astronomical tables of 1141, and his *Liber iudiciorum*.[71] Sure of his Christian faith, Raymond vigorously attacked his adversaries who were ignorant of astral science. Raymond's *Liber cursuum planetarum*, read in a copy without the author's name, had a great impact on the legitimization of astrology put forth by Eudes of Champagne at the very end of the twelfth century.[72] The original of this apology is lost, but the contents are well known through Hélinand of Froidmont's refutation of it.

Arabic astrology (the *Introductorium maius* of Abū Maʿshar above all) has been proposed as the intermediary through which Aristotle's natural philosophy was rediscovered by Christianity.[73] The basic connection is doubtless through Peripatetic concepts borrowed from the Sabaeans of Harran by Abū Maʿshar.[74] Here we have astrology promoted to a natural science[75] and conveying—well beyond the old limits of the quadrivium—reflections on causality, on the elements and the quintessence, on matter and form, on generation and corruption.

[70]Małgorzata H. Malewicz, "Libellus de efficatia artis astrologice: Traité astrologique d'Eudes de Champagne, XIIe siècle," *Mediaevalia philosophica Polonorum* 20 (1974) 3–95 at 7–10.

[71]See notes 65 and 80, and Marie-Thérèse d'Alverny, "Astrologues et théologiens au XIIe siècle," *Mélanges offerts à M.-D. Chenu* (Paris 1967) 31–50.

[72]Malewicz (n. 70 above) 25.

[73]Richard J. Lemay, *Abū Maʿshar and Latin Aristotelianism in the Twelfth Century: The Recovery of Aristotle's Natural Philosophy through Arabic Astrology* (Beirut 1962).

[74]David Pingree, "Abū Maʿshar," DSB 1 (1970) 32–39 at 33–34.

[75]Richard Lemay has assembled a small team to study the tradition of the *Centiloquium* incorrectly attributed to Ptolemy. This text too carries a number of philosophical concepts.

Of central importance here is the *De essentiis* composed in Béziers in 1143 by the same Herman of Carinthia who, in 1140, made the second translation of Abū Maʿshar's *Introductorium*.[76] In the *De essentiis*, better than anywhere else, one can discern how the heterogeneous currents of Arabic astrology and Chartrian Platonism mingled together. Notable are, for example, the originality of the concept of *medium*, the philosophical use of Boethius's *Arithmetic*, and the curious modifications to the old theme of celestial music. In addition to the *Introductorium*, Herman used another (now lost) treatise by Abū Maʿshar, the *Kitāb al-Ulūf* or Book of Thousands;[77] he thus borrowed, apparently at second hand, from Arabic texts which at the time had not yet been translated (alchemical literature, the *De radiis* of al-Kindī, and so on).

Is the model which so perfectly fit Herman of Carinthia transferable to other twelfth-century thinkers? One risks seeing the influence of astrology and of Abū Maʿshar everywhere. On this point the controversy about the origin of the word *elementatum* is revealing: was it invented by William of Conches, or borrowed by him after 1153 (therefore quite late) from John of Seville's translation of Abū Maʿshar?[78] Similar hesitations arise when studying the *Cosmographia* of Bernard Silvester (1145–53). It is true that astrology plays an important role in this difficult and fascinating work: it helps explain the order of the universe and the course of events. But the most recent analyses have found it very difficult to determine, in this astrological context, which elements possibly belong to the new Arabic current (for example Abū Maʿshar), and which (more likely) derive from Latin sources then being consulted with renewed interest (Asclepius, Firmicus Maternus, Macrobius, Calcidius).[79]

NONSCIENTIFIC APPLICATIONS OF THE QUADRIVIUM

Whether one listens to Adelard of Bath, Raymond of Marseille, or Daniel of Morley, the metaphor is the same: compared to the adepts of Arabic science, the masters who have remained faithful to the traditional knowledge are nothing more than cattle.

Abelard, though he claimed to have heard, in his youth, "multas ab arithmeticis solutiones," recognized his own lack of mathematical competence, and the most that can be said is that "doubtless he had occasion to

[76]Filling in the gaps of the defective and unobtainable publication of the *De essentiis* by P. Alonso (Comillas 1946), Charles S. F. Burnett has now completed the critical edition of this important text. I have used a typed copy of his carefully annotated edition of the first book.

[77]Charles S. F. Burnett, "The Legend of the Three Hermes and Abū Maʿshar's *Kitāb al-Ulūf* in the Latin Middle Ages," JWCI 39 (1976) 231–34.

[78]Peter Dronke, "New Approaches to the School of Chartres," *Anuario de estudios medievales* 6 (1969) 117–40 at 128–30, on *elementatum*.

[79]Bernard Silvester, *Cosmographia*, ed. Peter Dronke (Leiden 1978); Winthrop Wetherbee, trans., *The Cosmographia of Bernardus Silvestris*, Columbia University Records of Civilization 89 (New York 1973). See the important review of the latter by Charles S. F. Burnett in *Medium Aevum* 44 (1975) 167–71. See also Wetherbee's *Platonism and Poetry in the Twelfth Century* (Princeton 1972).

meet clerks full of curiosity about the new developments in the science of the stars."[80] The quadrivium evidently had a much more important place for those traditionally linked to the school of Chartres.[81] What John of Salisbury said of Gilbert of Poitiers applies equally to them: "He believed that all disciplines were interdependent, and he made them serve theology." Hugh of St Victor declared, more radically still, "Learn everything, and afterward you will see that nothing was superfluous."

Recent studies have sought to evaluate more precisely the use made of mathematics in nonscientific works, notably by Abelard, Thierry of Chartres, Gilbert of Poitiers, and William of Conches.[82] The store of mathematical knowledge displayed is very small, consisting chiefly of commonplaces (definition of number, inequality arising from equality, indivisibility of the point, and so on). Of some interest, however, are the vaguely mathematical reflections on the concept of quantity provoked by Boethius's commentary on book 6 of Aristotle's *Categories*, especially concerning the continuous line consisting of indivisible points. Also singled out was the argument in Boethius's *Arithmetic* (2.4) according to which a point superimposed on another point results in only one point; this argument was to enjoy great favor for explaining how the Holy Trinity could exist at the center of the Unity.

Indeed, the *De Trinitate* of Boethius inspired Thierry of Chartres and his school to write a series of commentaries.[83] The dossier is not yet complete, since one commentary, apparently by Thierry of Chartres, on Boethius's *De institutione arithmetica* has not yet been edited.[84] One should not, when speaking of the twelfth century, revel in the word "rational." The *arithmeticae probationes* applied by Thierry to theology did not claim to be compelling proofs; they were simply, somewhat in the spirit of St Anselm, an intellectual step toward consolidating the Faith.[85]

The study of number symbolism enjoyed great popularity during the twelfth century.[86] Hugh of St Victor applied an almost scientific method to the

[80]Marie-Thérèse d'Alverny, "Abélard et l'astrologie," *Pierre-Pierre* 611–30 at 627. See also note 71 above.

[81]Nikolaus M. Häring, "Chartres and Paris Revisited," *Essays in Honour of Anton Charles Pegis*, ed. J. Reginald O'Donnell (Toronto 1974) 268–329. See also Dronke (n. 78 above).

[82]Gillian R. Evans, "The Influence of Quadrivium Studies in the Eleventh- and Twelfth-Century Schools," *Journal of Medieval History* 1 (1975) 151–64; idem, "*More geometrico*: The Place of the Axiomatic Method in the Twelfth-Century Commentaries on Boethius' Opuscula Sacra," *Archives internationales d'histoire des sciences* 27 no. 101 (1977) 207–21; idem, "Introductions to Boethius's 'Arithmetica' of the Tenth to the Fourteenth Century," *History of Science* 16 no. 31 (1978) 22–41.

[83]See the magnificent edition by Nikolaus M. Häring, *Commentaries on Boethius, by Thierry of Chartres and His School* (Toronto 1971).

[84]Incipit: "Ea quorum doctrinam artem extrinsecus maiores nostri appellaverunt. . . ." MSS Bern 633, 538, 371, and Leiden Voss. lat. F 70 (information supplied by Margareta Fredborg and Charles Burnett).

[85]Jeauneau, "Mathématiques et Trinité chez Thierry de Chartres," *Lectio* 93–99 (= *Die Metaphysik im Mittelalter: Ihr Ursprung und ihre Bedeutung*, ed. Paul Wilpert, Miscellanea mediaevalia 2 [Berlin 1963] 289–95).

[86]Guy Beaujouan, "Le symbolisme des nombres à l'époque romane," *CCM* 4 (1961) 159–69. Ernst Hellgardt, *Zum Problem symbolbestimmter und formalästhetischer Zahlenkomposition in*

allegorical interpretation of numbers found in Scripture, attempting to explicate them according to nine criteria: *ordo positionis, qualitas compositionis, modus porrectionis, forma dispositionis, computatio, multiplicatio, partium aggregatio, multitudo, exaggeratio.* These speculations were taken up and expanded by a group of Cistercians whose arithmetical writings have only been partially published: *Analytica numerorum* by Odo of Morimond (on the numbers 1 and 2 in 1147–48, on 3 in 1153); *De sacramentis numerorum* by William of Auberive for numbers 3 to 12 (about 1164, I believe);[87] and numbers 13 to 20 by Geoffrey of Auxerre (between 1165 and 1170).[88]

William of Auberive was well acquainted with Boethius's *De arithmetica.* He sought to surpass it through research, particularly on perfect numbers. He introduced some concepts that were apparently new: if the sum of *aliquot* parts of a number was greater than that number, then the excess was called *fructus*; if the sum of the *aliquot* parts of two numbers was the same, this sum was called "number of love." This sequence of efforts led to the teachings of Thibaut of Langres,[89] who seems to have been a secular schoolmaster and possibly a canon at the end of the twelfth century. His style is certainly drier, but his aim was to elaborate even more systematically a general theory of numerical symbolism.

Remarkably, in all this literature on the mysteries of numbers, no mention is made of Arabic numerals, *apices*, or *figure algorismi.*

This survey has emphasized arithmetic because, among the branches of the traditional quadrivium, arithmetic was indeed the one that could most readily be applied to theology. But that perspective deserves to be expanded to include, for example, the geometrical digressions inspired by Noah's ark (Hugh of St Victor), the Tabernacle, the Temple of Solomon, or Ezekiel's vision (most notably in Richard of St Victor).[90] Historians of science find it hard to reconcile their knowledge with the often controversial revelations of various

mittelalterlicher Literatur (Munich 1973)—a good study of St Augustine's thought, but without reference to the 12th-c. Cistercian texts: see Hanne Lange's review in *Revue romane* 11 (1976) 201–08. Heinz Meyer, *Die Zahlenallegorese im Mittelalter* (Munich 1975). The fundamental study is now that by Hanne Lange, *Les données mathématiques des traités du XIIe siècle sur la symbolique des nombres,* CIMAGL 32 (Copenhagen 1979).

[87]Jean Leclercq, ''L'arithmétique de Guillaume d'Auberive,'' *Analecta monastica* 1, Studia anselmiana 20 (1948) 181–204. I have used the text according to the unpublished edition by Jean Taccetti; see *Ecole nationale des chartes: Positions des thèses* (1967) 151–53. William says that the troubles of the Jews began 1131 years ago. This must refer to the death of Christ, since the text must date from before 1165–70; thus: 1131 + 33 = 1164.

[88]Ferruccio Gastaldelli, ''L'Esegesi biblica secondo Goffredo di Auxerre,'' *Salesianum* 37 (1975) 219–50. Geoffrey's texts have now been published: Hanne Lange, *Traités du XIIe siècle sur la symbolique des nombres: Geoffroy d'Auxerre et Thibault de Langres,* CIMAGL 29 (Copenhagen 1979) 1–28.

[89]Hanne Lange and René Deleflie have, independently from each other, prepared a critical edition of Thibaut de Langres's text: Lange (n. 88 above) 29–108, with arithmological commentary in *Les données mathématiques* (n. 86 above); Deleflie, *Thibaut de Langres, Traité sur le symbolisme des nombres* (Langres 1978, published by the Société historique et archéologique de Langres). A. Garnier, ''Thibaut de Langres et la symbolique des nombres,'' *Cahiers Haut-Marnais* 136 (1979) 35–39.

[90]Victor (n. 42 above).

art historians concerning the geometrical traditions that governed the architecture and sculpture of the Romanesque era.[91] Here we are approaching the immense problem of the mathematical substratum of beauty.[92]

The domain of the quadrivium ends where astronomy becomes cosmology, where mathematics gives way to physics. It would require a separate essay to discuss what the twelfth-century rationalization of the world-picture entailed.[93] For the scientific thought of the twelfth century—obviously a renaissance, made possible by access to new sources of information—is now being interpreted by some historians as a genuine conceptual revolution.[94]

The notes to this study have mentioned many texts which are not yet published,[95] poorly studied,[96] or accessible only in typescript.[97] Other difficulties arise from the very nature of the renaissance of the twelfth century. Certainly, in all eras there are distinctions to be made between advanced research and the more popular representations of the world. But in the twelfth century, the relationship between the scholastic heritage of the early Middle Ages and the new Arabic science was like the confluence of two water currents of different salinity which do not mix well. This situation lasted throughout the entire century; the genuine homogenization of these two currents began only with the rise of the universities and the subsequent appearance of new basic teaching manuals—notably, the corpus of works by Alexander of Villedieu, Sacrobosco, and Messahala, the *Theorica planetarum*, and so on.

Again, the cultural panorama of the twelfth-century renaissance contains fascinating ambiguities: which changes were caused by outside influences, which by a sort of internal fermentation? Other contributors to this volume have briefly sketched the changes in this setting—the demographic and economic expansion and the resulting growth of the towns that led to the relative secularization of teaching in schools which were already livelier. This dynamism in Christian society thus often contributed to the same developments as did Arabic science.

[91] Alain Sené, *Recherches sur la composition des tympans (XIe–XIIIe siècles): Les traditions géométriques* (Paris 1979); Beaujouan (n. 5 above).

[92] Edgar De Bruyne, *Etudes d'esthétique médiévale* (3 vols. Bruges 1946) vol. 2, *L'époque romane*.

[93] I am thinking of Tullio Gregory's work, notably "La nouvelle idée de nature et de savoir scientifique au XIIe siècle," *Cultural Context* (n. 5 above) 193–218.

[94] Tina Stiefel, "The Heresy of Science: A Twelfth-Century Conceptual Revolution," *Isis* 68 (1977) 347–62. The thesis of this article seems to me somewhat excessive.

[95] Not yet published: astronomical and astrological texts from the 10th and 11th centuries (see notes 50 and 69 above); nonarithmetical portions of the *Liber ysagogarum* attributed to Adelard of Bath; the Adelardian versions of Euclid (edition being prepared by H. Busard and M. Folkerts); the Toledan tables (except the trigonometric part); the two texts of Raymond of Marseille (an edition of which has been announced by Marie-Thérèse d'Alverny and Emmanuel Poulle); Thierry of Chartres's commentary on Boethius's *Arithmetic* (see above at n. 84); Odo of Morimond on number symbolism.

[96] On the *Heptateuchon* of Thierry of Chartres, see n. 52 above.

[97] See notes 26 (algorisms), 48 (practical geometry), and 87 (William of Auberive).

Considered as veiled by *integumentum* in Plato's *Timaeus*, the idea that the stars act as secondary causes led to convergence with Arabic astrology.[98] For the concept of nature as a book written in symbolic language, twelfth-century schools tended to substitute the view of a series of phenomena, each of which was susceptible to a rational explanation. Here too the schools seemed predisposed to accept the elements of natural philosophy which Arabic astrology transmitted, while they awaited the new Aristotle. Even on the question of future contingents, the thoughts inspired by Arabo-Latin translations of Abū Maʿshar were not very different from those stimulated by Calcidius or Nemesius of Emesa.

The same predisposition to Arabic influences is seen in the complementary nature of thought and action. In this feudal civilization, seeking better ways to acquire and use energy, the *ingeniator*, the military and architectural engineer, appeared from 1086 on (in the Domesday Book)—before Dominicus Gundisalvi, popularizing al-Fārābī, integrated the *scientia de ingeniis* into his classification of the sciences. We noted earlier a similar convergence of theory and practice in the field of geometry.

To evoke the cultural dynamism of the twelfth century, it is traditional to quote Bernard of Chartres's remark, as related by John of Salisbury around 1159. The moderns were compared to dwarfs standing on the shoulders of the ancients, described as giants, "so that we can see more and farther than they could, not indeed by the keenness of our vision or the size of our bodies, but because we are raised high up and elevated by the greatness of giants." In its context, however, this metaphor is not a scientist's profession of faith.[99] In a grammatical and literary context, William of Conches says it well, in the first redaction of his glosses on Priscian: "moderni perspicaciores sunt quam antiqui, sed non sapientiores." Alexander Neckam thinks of the fable of the eagle and the wren.[100]

Whatever the merits of this exegesis, it is indisputable that the idea of progress was not totally foreign to twelfth-century thought.[101] In 1020–30, Guido of Arezzo was plainly aware of progress in music: "usque in hunc diem ars paulatim crescendo convaluit." In the twelfth century, Arabic science revealed methods of calculation (arithmetic, trigonometry, and algebra) manifestly unknown to the ancients. In the midst of doubts concerning the precession of equinoxes or the obliquity of the ecliptic, it was obvious that Ptolemaic astronomy could not be adopted whole.

More widespread during the twelfth century was a concept that seems opposed to the idea of progress: that the scholar discovered hidden treasures,

[98]Jeauneau, "L'usage de la notion d'*integumentum* à travers les gloses de Guillaume de Conches," *Lectio* 127–92 at 172–75 (= AHDLMA 24 [1957] 35–100 at 80–83).

[99]John of Salisbury, *Metalogicon* 3.4, ed. Clement C. J. Webb (Oxford 1929) 136, cited by Jeauneau, "'*Nani gigantum humeris insidentes*': Essai d'interprétation de Bernard de Chartres," *Lectio* 53–73 (= *Vivarium* 5 [1967] 79–99).

[100]Ibid. 58 (William) and 64 (Alexander) (= *Vivarium* 84, 90).

[101]Alistair C. Crombie, "Some Attitudes to Scientific Progress, Ancient, Medieval, and Early Modern," *History of Science* 13 (1975) 213–30.

pierced the mystery of the *integumenta*, shared in a certain esotericism, and even (as he sometimes believed) clarified what the Arabs had deliberately made obscure.[102]

These two concepts are contradictory only in appearance. Progress is manifested more clearly through one's work than in being a progressionist. The men of the twelfth century worked.

Bibliographical Note

On the history of the exact sciences during the twelfth century, the two principal works are Haskins, *Science*, and George Sarton, *Introduction to the History of Science* (3 vols. in 5 Baltimore 1927–48) vol. 2 pt. 1. For the quadrivium in particular, see *Arts libéraux et philosophie au moyen âge*, Actes du quatrième Congrès international de philosophie médiévale (Montreal and Paris 1969).

To situate the twelfth century in relation to the whole of medieval scientific thought: Alistair C. Crombie, *Augustine to Galileo: The History of Science, A.D. 400–1650* (2nd ed. 2 vols. London and Cambridge Mass. 1961), and *The Cultural Context of Medieval Learning*, Proceedings of the First International Colloquium on Philosophy, Science, and Theology in the Middle Ages, ed. John E. Murdoch and Edith D. Sylla, Boston Studies in the Philosophy of Science 26 (Dordrecht and Boston 1975). Excellent information, notably on Arabic scholars and their influence, may be found in the *Dictionary of Scientific Biography*, ed. Charles C. Gillispie et al. (14 vols. + supp. New York 1970–78).

That there is no real history of Western science of the twelfth century yet is partly explained by the fact that scholars have devoted their main attention to the problems of the transmission of knowledge. Only recently has the rationalization of the world-image in the twelfth century been emphasized: Tina Stiefel, "The Heresy of Science: A Twelfth-Century Conceptual Revolution," *Isis* 68 (1977) 347–62.

The tools for locating texts and editions have greatly improved since Haskins's time, mainly with the *Introduction* of Sarton (see above) and Manitius, *Geschichte*. The bibliography can be brought up to date thanks to the reworking of the list of abbreviations used in the "new Du Cange": the *Index scriptorum novus* to the *Novum glossarium mediae latinitatis ab anno DCCC usque ad annum MCC* (Copenhagen 1973); see André Vernet's addenda and corrections in Ecole pratique des Hautes Etudes, IVe Section: Sciences historiques et philologiques, *Annuaire 1974–75*, 576–81. But, for the sciences, the richest source of references is Lynn Thorndike and Pearl Kibre, *A Catalogue of Incipits of Mediaeval Scientific Writings in Latin* (2nd ed. Cambridge Mass. and London 1963), with supplements in *Speculum* 40 (1965) and 43 (1968) 78–114.

Given the importance of the Iberian peninsula in the transmission of Arabic science, there is much to draw upon in José M. Millás Vallicrosa, *Estudios sobre historia de la ciencia española* (Barcelona 1949) and *Nuevos estudios sobre historia de la ciencia española* (Barcelona 1960), and most recently in Juan Vernet, *La cultura hispanoárabe en Oriente y Occidente* (Barcelona 1978). There are excellent studies also in *Oriente e Occidente nel medioevo: Filosofia e scienze*, Accademia Nazionale dei Lincei, Convegno 13, 1969 (Rome 1971).

---

[102]Hugo Sanctallensis, ed. Millás Vendrell (n. 58 above) 95. Raymond of Marseille speaks of "dolositas"; see Lipton (n. 67 above) note 67.

On mathematics: Adolf P. Youschkevitch [Juschkewitsch], *Geschichte der Mathematik im Mittelalter* (Leipzig 1964); partial French translation, revised and corrected, *Les mathématiques arabes: VIIIe–Xve siècles* (Paris 1976). Fuat Sezgin, *Geschichte des arabischen Schrifttums* (7 vols. Leiden 1967–79) vol. 5, *Mathematik*.

Concerning the teaching of music and its relationship to the history of science, see Joseph Smits van Waesberghe, *Musikerziehung: Lehre und Theorie der Musik im Mittelalter* (Leipzig 1969).

For astronomy, useful bibliographic information is contained in Francis J. Carmody, *Arabic Astronomical and Astrological Sciences in Latin Translation* (Berkeley 1956). José M. Millás Vallicrosa, *Estudios sobre Azarquiel* (Madrid 1950 [1943]). See also Sezgin (above) vol. 6, *Astronomie*, and the more technical studies cited in the notes to this essay.

The only unified work on astrology during the twelfth century is a Ph.D. dissertation not yet published: Joshua D. Lipton, "The Rational Evaluation of Astrology in the Period of Arabo-Latin Translation, ca. 1126–1187 A.D." (University of California, Los Angeles 1978). See also Richard J. Lemay, *Abū Maʿshar and Latin Aristotelianism in the Twelfth Century: The Recovery of Aristotle's Natural Philosophy through Arabic Astrology* (Beirut 1962).

The Culmination of the Old Logic in Peter Abelard

Norman Kretzmann

The term 'renaissance' as Haskins used it was a conscious, pointed borrowing—the refutation of Burckhardt in a word. No doubt it was partly because of that provenance of the term that Haskins devalued it even as he was adopting it.[1] Still, 'renaissance' can be used precisely, to designate a cultural *revival*, the focusing of widely shared interest or intellectual or artistic activity on some feature of past culture discontinuous with or lost sight of in the culture of the period during which the revival takes place. And Haskins, having declared that he has no special stake in the merely convenient, allusive word 'renaissance', goes on to make frequent, signal use of 'revival', regarding which he makes no such disarming remarks. In his four chapters on "The Revival of the Latin Classics," ". . . of Jurisprudence," ". . . of Science," and ". . . of Philosophy," we may take him to be offering literal, precise descriptions, particularly since he expressly distinguishes "a revival" from "a new birth" in cultural development (17). But the four revivals he alludes to in those chapter headings are, if not the only, at least the most important genuine *revivals* contributing to the renaissance of the twelfth century; and that is another reason (in addition to those offered by Haskins and eloquently seconded by Southern)[2] for taking the term 'renaissance' loosely in 'the renaissance of the twelfth century'.

Two of the four revivals recognized by Haskins pertain to the subject matter of my contribution: "The Revival of the Latin Classics" is related to devel-

I am grateful to John Boler, who offered me detailed philosophical criticisms that led me to rethink a good deal of this paper; to Jan Pinborg, who corrected some mistaken interpretations and generously pointed out valuable references that I would otherwise have missed; and to Eleonore Stump, whose careful reading and discussion of earlier drafts helped to shape this paper from the beginning.

[1]Haskins, *Ren* 5.

[2]Richard W. Southern, "The Place of England in the Twelfth-Century Renaissance," *History* 45 (1960) 201–16 at 201; the article was first presented as a paper in 1953. Referring to William A. Nitze's article, "The So-called Twelfth-Century Renaissance" (*Speculum* 23 [1948] 464–71), Southern says, "I have no wish to enter into this controversy, which in any case seems to attach too much importance to a mere term of convenience which can mean almost anything we choose to

opments in grammar, and "The Revival of Philosophy" has mainly to do with dialectic, or logic. And those two revivals either are less important for my subject matter than we might be led to think from their having been assigned chapters of their own in *The Renaissance of the Twelfth Century* or are ambiguously described as revivals.

The revival of the Latin classics proved to be a growth too delicate to flourish as dialectic proliferated in the schools. Cicero's and Ovid's time in the twelfth-century sun was not long enough to deflect the course of medieval grammar toward an association with literature, away from its already well-established association with dialectic and hence with philosophy generally.[3] The revival of the Latin classics contributed significantly to the culture of the twelfth century, but it did not markedly affect grammatical theory.

As for what Haskins called "The Revival of Philosophy," we can recognize two historically independent developments under that description: first, the resurgence of philosophical activity; second, the recovery of the works of Aristotle (in Latin). For the five hundred years between Boethius and Anselm the history of philosophy is, except for Eriugena, essentially devoid of activity above the custodial level;[4] consequently the first of those two developments is a phenomenon of the greatest importance, as dramatic a change as any of those that make up the twelfth-century renaissance. My historical interests are, however, too narrow to enable me to offer useful explanatory hypotheses for a development of such broad cultural scope. On the other hand, the recovery of the works of Aristotle, beginning around the middle of the century, is strictly relevant to my subject matter, particularly since the first treatises to become available were those *logical* works that had not been transmitted to the early Middle Ages. These treatises—the *Prior* and *Posterior Analytics*, the *Topics*, and the *Sophistical Refutations*—were consequently called the "New Logic."[5] Here is a revival in the strictest sense (as the resurgence of philosophical activity was not) and a historical development of great consequence (as the recovery of

---

make it mean: all I wish to refer to is the large and complex activity in literature, learning and the arts which drew on many sources, yet expressed an outlook which one feels at once to be new and subtly yet unmistakably coherent. As a portmanteau description of this activity I would stand by Haskins in believing that the term 'Renaissance' is no more misleading than any other word. It achieves indeed the sort of sublime meaninglessness which is required in words of high but uncertain import" (201).

[3]The close association of grammar with logic pervades the Middle Ages as thoroughly as does any defining characteristic of medieval thought. Perhaps the basis of the association, although certainly not its full explanation, is the fact that the only texts of ancient philosophy to have been transmitted intact to the early Middle Ages are Aristotle's *Categories* and *On Interpretation*, treatises concerned with the linguistic elements of logic and hence of a distinctly grammatical cast.

[4]I do not mean to denigrate the efforts of Cassiodorus, Isidore, Alcuin, Rabanus Maurus, and the others. And no doubt we have more to learn about those five hundred years; particularly where dialectic is concerned, there is likely to have been some as yet unappreciated contribution to the evolution of concepts between Boethius and Abelard.

[5]On the recovery of Aristotle in the West, see Mlle. Marie-Thérèse d'Alverny's "Translations and Translators" in this volume.

the Latin classics was not, at least not immediately).[6] It is, nevertheless, not the development on which I mean to concentrate. The enormous riches recovered in the logical and other works of Aristotle naturally took time to assimilate and exploit, and so the account of the transforming effect of the new Aristotle is a story of the thirteenth century, not of the twelfth.

Besides these authentic revivals, twelfth-century grammar and logic include developments which surely qualify (as much as intellectual developments ever qualify) as instances of "new birth." In grammar there were the first uncertain stirrings of *grammatica speculativa*,[7] and in logic the clearly discernible beginnings of terminism.[8] Both these original developments, but especially the latter, have very great consequences not only for grammar and logic but for medieval philosophy generally; and so these new births are undeniably attractive as focal points for a discussion of grammar and logic in the twelfth century. All the same, accounts of twelfth-century speculative grammar and terminist logic are accounts of immature stages of intellectual growths that flowered only after the century that saw their origins. I have, therefore, resisted the temptation to deal with them and have turned my attention instead to Peter Abelard and the Old Logic.[9]

Concentrating on Abelard, whom Haskins rightly calls "one of the first philosophical minds of the whole Middle Ages" (351), needs no justification; if Anselm is assigned to the eleventh century, Abelard is *the* philosopher of the twelfth century. But why focus on the Old Logic, which had been the main secular source of intellectual sustenance since the earliest Middle Ages and which therefore scarcely qualifies as the stuff of a renaissance? Because the Old Logic is all that Abelard had,[10] and because in many respects Abelard's philosophical accomplishments are a worthy culmination of the half-millennium of

[6]That the revival of the Latin classics was less successful than it might have been is largely a consequence of the revival of philosophy. The excitement over the newly available Aristotelian treatises on logic is the historical development which goes furthest toward explaining the loss of interest in the literary classics.

[7]See G. L. Bursill-Hall, *Speculative Grammars of the Middle Ages* (The Hague and Paris 1971), esp. 28–29. Cf. Jan Pinborg, *Die Entwicklung der Sprachtheorie im Mittelalter*, BGPTMA 42.2 (Münster 1967), esp. 19–59.

[8]See L. M. de Rijk, *Logica modernorum: A Contribution to the History of Early Terminist Logic* (2 vols. in 3 Assen 1962–67). For a synopsis of the historical developments covered in de Rijk's indispensable study and collection of texts, see my review of it in *The Philosophical Review* 79 (1970) 262–68. The rise of terminist logic is viewed against a broader background in my "History of Semantics" in *The Encyclopedia of Philosophy* (8 vols. New York 1967) 7.358–406; see also Jan Pinborg's more detailed survey in his excellent *Logik und Semantik im Mittelalter: Ein Überblick* (Stuttgart and Bad Canstatt 1972).

[9]Abelard's last and presumably definitive work on logic is his *Dialectica*, ed. L. M. de Rijk (2nd ed. Assen 1970). And his sources in the *Dialectica* are limited to the collection of texts later to be known as the Old Logic: Aristotle's *Categories* and *On Interpretation* (in Latin), Porphyry's *Isagoge* (in Latin), Boethius's commentaries on those three works, and Boethius's own logical treatises. For details, see de Rijk's Introduction to his edition, xiv–xvi.

[10]Abelard was evidently at least acquainted with some treatises of the New Logic (de Rijk's ed., Introduction, xvi–xviii), but his surviving work is in no important way influenced by the recovery of Aristotle, still far from complete when Abelard died in 1142.

the Old Logic. Abelard's contribution to the twelfth-century renaissance, the single most important philosophical contribution, is not that of a sower nor that of a reviver, but the contribution of a harvester. Some of the glory of the twelfth century is not vernal but autumnal.

UNIVERSALS AND PREDICATION IN ABELARD'S LOGIC

Abelard's philosophical fame rests today, as it did when Haskins wrote, primarily on his theory of universals, "a doctrine," Haskins says, "which he worked out with his usual brilliancy and which we have just begun to understand with the publication, now proceeding, of his *Glosses on Porphyry*" (352–53).[11] The problem of universals was the foremost philosophical problem of the twelfth century; and it is so paradigmatically a metaphysical problem that it may not be immediately apparent that it is also well suited to serve as a focal point for considering grammar and logic in the twelfth century, particularly Abelard's handling of it. Aristotle had defined a universal as "that which is naturally suited to be predicated of more than one thing,"[12] and so the traditional concept of a universal essentially involves a grammatical concept; for whatever may be the nature of predication in its details, it seems *prima facie* certain that language is a necessary condition for predication's occurring at all. And so when Abelard took up the problem of universals (in commenting on Boethius's commentary on Porphyry's introduction to Aristotle's *Categories*), he presented its basic issue as the question whether universals have to do "with words *only* or with real things *as well*";[13] that they do have to do with words is never in question.

After criticizing in detail several things-as-well theories, Abelard concluded that we have no recourse but "to ascribe universality of this sort to words alone."[14] As might be expected of someone with that point of view, Abelard's theory of universals was worked out in a context that may be accurately if anachronistically characterized as linguistic philosophy. The books

[11]Haskins is referring to Bernhard Geyer's edition of the *Logica "Ingredientibus"* in *Peter Abaelards philosophische Schriften*, BGPTMA 21.1–3 (3 vols. Münster 1919–27). The *Glosses on Porphyry* are in fact the first of three parts of the *Logica "Ingredientibus"* and had been completely published in 1919. Since the publication of Haskins's book, a great deal more work has been done on Abelard's logical—i.e., philosophical—treatises. Besides the especially valuable edition of the *Dialectica* already mentioned, there are Geyer's edition of the *Logica "Nostrorum petitioni sociorum,"* completing the collection referred to earlier in this note (21.4, Münster 1933); Mario dal Pra's editions published as *Pietro Abelardo: Scritti di logica* (2nd ed. Florence 1969), containing the *Introductiones dialecticae* and the *Super Topica glossae* of the *Logica "Ingredientibus"*; and Lorenzo Minio-Paluello's *Twelfth Century Logic: Texts and Studies* (2 vols. Rome 1956–58) vol. 2, *Abaelardiana inedita*, containing *Super Periermenias* 12–14 and *Sententie secundum M. Petrum*.

[12]*De interpretatione* c. 7, 17a39–40.

[13]*Logica "Ingredientibus"* (n. 11 above) 9.16–17.

[14]*Logica "Ingredientibus"* 16.21–22. For reasons that will very soon appear, it is not now my business to expound Abelard's theory of universals as such; but, of course, this remark must not be interpreted out of context in a way that associates Abelard with the extreme nominalism (of Roscellinus) which he opposed.

in which the work gets done are nominally treatises on logic,[15] although from our point of view their subject matter is not much more recognizably formal logic than it is analytical metaphysics or philosophical grammar. Abelard is the unrivaled master of that twelfth-century amalgam of logical, metaphysical, semantical, and grammatical theory out of which the characteristically thirteenth-century speculative grammar and terminist logic evolved; and Abelard's theory of universals is his masterwork in that medium. It has, consequently, received a good deal of scholarly attention as more material has become available over the last fifty years,[16] although it is still not fully understood.

For all its intimate ties with linguistic issues, Abelard's theory of universals considered as a whole involves too much that is only remotely associated with twelfth-century grammar and logic. But, as we have seen, predication—unmistakably a linguistic concept, or at least immediately dependent on linguistic concepts—is likewise an essential ingredient in the traditional concept of a universal. I have, therefore, selected Abelard's theory of predication as my particular topic. Predication, the connection (the precise nature of which is a disputed point) which converts a string of independent words such as 'Socrates', 'is', and 'white' into the unified proposition 'Socrates is white',[17] is the single linchpin of several sorts of relationships: the grammatical relations among the proper name 'Socrates', the verb 'is', and the adjective 'white'; the logical relations among the subject term, the copula,[18] and the predicate term; and the metaphysical relation (any illustration of which involves giving expression to one or another *theory* of universals) between a particular, Socrates, and a universal, whiteness.[19] And because of this manifold function of predication, Abelard's theory of predication constitutes an obvious and crucial link between

[15]The *Introductiones dialecticae* (or *parvulorum*), the *Logica "Ingredientibus,"* the *Logica "Nostrorum petitioni sociorum,"* the *Dialectica*, and the *Sententie secundum M. Petrum* (apparently a fragmentary compilation from the lost *Libri fantasiarum*). For details, see de Rijk's edition of *Dialectica* (n. 9 above) Introduction, xi–xiii.

[16]See, for example, John F. Boler, "Abailard and the Problem of Universals," *The Journal of the History of Philosophy* 1 (1963) 37–51; Maria Teresa Beonio-Brocchieri Fumagalli, *The Logic of Abelard*, trans. Simon Pleasance (Dordrecht 1969), esp. ch. 3; and Martin M. Tweedale, *Abailard on Universals* (Amsterdam 1976). I had not seen Tweedale's book when I first wrote this paper; to take full account of its many relevant discussions would have required not merely a revision of the draft prepared for the conference but an entirely new paper. I have therefore decided, regretfully, simply to call the reader's attention to its importance for the subject of my paper.

[17]I use the word 'proposition' in this paper as the medievals used '*propositio*', to refer not to a propositional content but to a propositional sign, written or spoken or mental.

[18]In his very valuable article "On the Terminology for *Copula* and *Existence*," *Islamic Philosophy and the Classical Tradition*, ed. Samuel M. Stern, Albert Hourani, and Vivian Brown (Oxford 1972) 141–58, Charles H. Kahn offers new evidence to support Prantl's view that "Abelard is the first extant Latin author to use *copula* as a technical term for *est* in the categorical proposition *homo est mortalis*" (142). See also Kahn's "On the Theory of the Verb 'To Be'," *Logic and Ontology*, ed. M. K. Munitz (New York 1973) 1–20, esp. 10.

[19]Admittedly this third relationship seems nonlinguistic; but a good part of the difficulty in the problem of universals is represented in, not merely historically started by, Aristotle's ambivalence in *Categories* and *On Interpretation* regarding the distinction between linguistic and extralinguistic entities.

grammar and logic as well as between those two *artes sermocinales* on the one hand and metaphysics on the other.[20]

Predication itself is unquestionably a relationship of some sort; its *relata* are uncontroversially designated the subject and the predicate, and 'Socrates is white' is incontrovertibly an instance of predication.[21] Three approaches to predication that figure in Abelard's work may be sorted out as sets of answers to three basic questions about these elements:[22] What is the predicate? What is the nature of the relationship of predication? What is the subject? (1) *Conjunction*—The predicate is *the adjective* 'white', and it *is conjoined with* the subject, *the proper name* 'Socrates' (by means of the verb 'is'). (2) *Identity*—The predicate is *a thing* that is white, and it *is identical with* the subject, *the individual* Socrates. (3) *Inherence*—The predicate is *the characteristic* whiteness, and it *inheres in* the subject, *the individual* Socrates.[23]

At various times in his career Abelard adopted one or another of these approaches, singly or in combination, with results that we shall sample. There are fairly obvious flaws or disadvantages in each approach, and each has a tendency to lead to other difficulties that are not so apparent. But the only difficulties relevant to our purposes here are those that occur in Abelard's employment of them, and so we may postpone criticism.

I want to examine three Abelardian theories of predication. The first occurs in an original version and a revision, and the third is no more than a suggestion. I have chosen these examples not only because they are intrinsically interesting and instructive, but also because they seem to represent stages in Abelard's attempts to explain predication.[24] Broadly speaking, he began by undertaking to explain all predication entirely in terms of the ordinary semantic and syntactic characteristics of verbs, and so an understanding of his

[20]In these preliminaries it is convenient to speak as if Abelard had only one theory of predication. As we shall see, the case is not so simple.

[21]The choice of a paradigm of predication influences the exposition of predication. This discussion would have had to be organized otherwise if I had chosen, say, 'Every philosopher is wise', or 'Loons dive'. But my choice of 'Socrates is white' avoids certain difficulties irrelevant to my purposes in this paper and helps to bring out certain features of predication that will prove to be important to Abelard's approach. Moreover, his own paradigms are always of these two forms: 'Socrates is white' and 'Socrates reads'.

[22]These "approaches" certainly do not exhaust the possibilities. None of them constitutes a theory of predication as it stands, but any of them might serve as the leading idea in the formation of such a theory. I have introduced these three here only because they present basic notions that will come into my discussion. For that reason I have omitted any consideration of class membership or class inclusion, even though those approaches, too, were known to Abelard.

[23]The three approaches are obviously not on a par with one another. (2) and (3) are concerned with *what is said* in predication, while (1) is concerned with *how* what is said in predication gets said.

[24]I will call these stages (in what I take to be their chronological order) the *Ingredientibus* Theory, the *Dialectica* Revision (of the *Ingredientibus* Theory), the *Dialectica* Theory, and the *Dialectica* Suggestion. I have to emphasize the conjectural nature of my account of Abelard on predication. The amount of relevant material in Abelard's writings is vast, and I have studied by no means all of it. Even the chronology of his works is uncertain; see de Rijk's edition of *Dialectica* (n. 9 above) Introduction, xi–xiii. On some special difficulties regarding the *Dialectica* Suggestion and its place in the development of Abelard's thought, see n. 62 below.

theories of predication requires an acquaintance with some of the elements of his theory of meaning.[25]

NAMING, DETERMINING, CONSIGNIFYING, AND COPULATING

Abelard thought of many, if not all, words as having acquired their signification somewhat as a sound becomes established as a proper name in a christening ceremony.[26] For a medieval philosopher this doctrine of the "imposition" or "invention" of words could have had the status of a historical fact, grounded in the story of Adam's naming of every living creature (Gen. 2:19–20).[27] The sort of signification an utterance acquires in a christening ceremony is *naming*: 'Peter', which had not named this individual, now names him, as a result of the ceremony. The imposition of ordinary proper names is at best only a crude model in this context, however; the bestowing of descriptive proper names ('Walks-Like-A-Bear') or nicknames ('Shorty') comes closer to what is wanted. Our interest is in the sort of imposition that might be imagined as taking place in some such declaration as "I hereby name this thing *and all things like it in the relevant respects* 'lion'," or ". . .'tawny'."[28] And the italicized phrase in this formula of imposition introduces a second sort of signification in addition to naming—*determination*—just as essential as naming in Abelard's account of the meaning of common names. When I say truly of some animal that it is tawny, 'tawny' *names* something tawny—in this case the animal I am talking about—and *determines* its tawniness.[29]

The application of the doctrine of imposition moves by easy stages from proper names through common names, both "substantival" ('lion') and "adjectival" ('tawny'). Its application to verbs is less straightforward, but essential

---

[25] Abelard discusses problems of meaning at many points, but perhaps the best presentation of his views is in the *Dialectica*, Tractatus primus, Volumen III—Postpredicamenta—De vocibus significativis, ed. de Rijk (n. 9 above) 111–42. See also Beonio-Brocchieri Fumagalli (n. 16 above) ch. 2, "The Problem of Meaning."

[26] We need not raise here the obvious embarrassing questions about the imposition of syncategorematic words or of names for imaginary entities; Abelard does address himself to such questions, however.

[27] The roots of the doctrine of imposition are no doubt to be found in the ancient grammarians, but the place of the doctrine in the *logica vetus* is established by the way Boethius writes near the beginning of his commentary on Aristotle's *Categories*: "Rebus praeiacentibus, et in propria principaliter naturae constitutione manentibus, humanum solum genus exstitit, quod rebus nomina posset imponere" (*In Categorias*, PL 64.159A9–12; cf. esp. 159C2–7). (I am grateful to Jan Pinborg for supplying this reference.)

[28] The Adamic imposition, after all, must have been of this form; he wasn't just naming his pets: "and whatsoever Adam called *every* living creature, that was *the name* thereof."

[29] Naming and determining are obviously at least to some extent analogous to "denotation" and "connotation" in traditional logic (and to similar pairs in other semantic theories). In introducing this distinction between "connotative and non-connotative" names, John Stuart Mill says that "a connotative term is one which denotes a subject, and implies an attribute" (*A System of Logic* 1.2.5), as 'tawny' names a subject and determines an attribute. It is not clear to me, however, and it need not be decided for my purposes here, whether Abelard takes naming and determining to be functions of words in isolation as well as in propositions.

to Abelard's treatment of the problems of predication.[30] Consider the propositions (A) 'Elizabeth reigns' and (B) 'Elizabeth is regnant'. (A) and (B) are instances of what we may call two-piece and three-piece predication respectively.[31] The verb 'reigns' in (A) is obviously doing things other than naming a regnant thing and determining the characteristic reigning—the things done by the adjective 'regnant' in (B)—but, according to the doctrine of imposition, it is doing those things as well. The naming and determining effected by a verb are called by Abelard its "principal signification"; as far as naming and determining are concerned, a verb is just a peculiar sort of common name.[32] The semantic and syntactic functions *distinctive* of a verb are its "consignification" of a time and its "copulation" of its principal signification to a subject.[33] In proposition (A) the thing named and the characteristic determined by 'reigns' are copulated to the individual named by 'Elizabeth', and the time of that individual's being that named thing and having that determined characteristic is consignified as the present. In the context of the proposition, the form of the verb effects both the copulating (third person, indicative mood, active voice) and the consignifying (present tense).

Solely in order to focus attention on what I consider to be the philosophically and historically most interesting features of Abelard's work on predication, I shall proceed on the supposition that the theory of meaning just sketched can provide a satisfactory account of two-piece predication. There is, however, an evident difference between the mechanisms of two-piece and of three-piece predication, and even if the former is in some respect more fundamental than the latter, it is the latter with which logicians and metaphysicians have been primarily concerned, ever since Aristotle.[34] Any theory of

[30]Some forms of verbs may be considered just substantival or adjectival names—e.g., infinitives and participles ('to paint', 'painting', 'painted')—and they, of course, pose no special difficulties of any kind for the doctrine of imposition.

[31]Abelard has technical terms (adapted from Aristotle) for these two sorts of predication, at least in his *Dialectica* Theory; but those terms suggest some features of that theory, and we need neutral terms for our discussion. The simple designations I have chosen are derived from the medieval distinction (also adapted from Aristotle) between 'is' as *secundum adiacens* and as *tertium adiacens*.

[32]"When uttered just by themselves, verbs are names and signify something," Aristotle, *De interpretatione* c. 3, 16b19–20.

[33]Both these *differentiae* are already recognized in Aristotle's chapter on the verb (*De int.* c. 3). The first is obviously a feature of a finite verb form even outside any propositional context—e.g., 'ran'—but since such a form without context is obviously an *incomplete* symbol (*who*, or *what*, ran?), copulation, too, might be said to be a feature of the verb considered even in isolation. Aristotle certainly seems to have thought so: "[a verb] is *always* a sign of what holds, that is, holds of a subject" (*De int.* c. 3, 16b9–10); and Abelard is inclined to agree: "a verb can be pronounced by itself, without copulating anything; still, it is always copulative as regards its invention [or imposition]" ("Potest enim verbum per se proferri nec aliquid copulare; semper tamen secundum inventionem suam copulativum est," *Dialectica* [n. 9 above] 129.25–26).

[34]When Aristotle compares, e.g., 'A man walks' and 'A man is walking', he always says that it makes no difference which form we use; see *De int.* c. 13, 21b9, *An. pr.* 51b13ff., and *Met.* 1017a27–30 (references from Kahn, "On the Terminology" [n. 18 above] n. 7). Abelard, however, seems to rank two-piece and three-piece predication differently in different respects.

predication worth taking seriously must include a special account of predication involving 'is' as the copula.

THE SUBSTANTIVE VERB AND THE COPULA

The Abelardian theories with which I am here concerned are theories of three-piece predication. In his earlier attempts to explain three-piece predication Abelard based his account of 'is' as the copula squarely on his understanding of the role of verbs generally in predication. A passage from the *Logica "Ingredientibus"* (written before 1120)[35] shows him doing so:

> It is essential to know that all personal verbs,[36] [the verbs] which can be predicated, can, no matter what their signification, copulate themselves. For example, if one says 'Socrates is' [or] 'Socrates reads', 'to be' and 'to read' are themselves predicated by means of themselves.[37] And those verbs perform a dual function, for they have the force both of the predicate and of the copulant, so that they simultaneously both are predicated and copulate themselves. For to say *'currit'* ('[he] runs') is tantamount to saying *'est currens'* ('[he] is running', or '[he] is [a] running [thing]'). There are said to be only two verbs that can copulate utterances different from themselves—the substantive and the nuncupative—as when one says 'He is Socrates' [or] 'He is named Socrates'. (359.23–30)

There are, then, three classes of verbs that can produce predication. By far the largest class comprises the verbs that typically enter into two-piece predica-

---

Since every instance of two-piece predication may be analyzed as an instance of three-piece predication but not conversely (within ordinary Latin or English), three-piece may be considered analytically more fundamental than two-piece. The analytical priority of three-piece predication is brought out in this passage, which is illuminating for our discussion in other respects as well: "The same is true as regards other verbs, which also contain the copulation of the substantive verb. For whoever says 'Peter runs' frames the proposition that Peter is one of those running" ("Sic quoque et in ceteris verbis que etiam substantivi verbi copulationem continent—qui enim dicit *'Petrus currit'*, id quod Petrus sit unus de currentibus proponit," *Dialectica* [n. 9 above] 132.6–8). But in another and ultimately more important respect Abelard takes two-piece to be more fundamental than three-piece predication. As we shall see, he tries to account for three-piece in terms of two-piece, and he proposes complex verbs that would dispense with the need for the copula.

[35]See Beonio-Brocchieri Fumagalli (n. 16 above) 4–6.

[36]I.e., those which take genuine subjects, unlike, e.g., 'rains'. Abelard's examples always involve personal verbs that are, if not strictly intransitive, at any rate capable of forming a complete proposition without the addition of a direct object—e.g., 'reads', 'runs'. Such verbs are undeniably more amenable to Abelard's treatment of predication than strictly transitive personal verbs would be. If the relative clause immediately following this comma is taken as a modifying clause—perhaps the more natural way in which to take it—then it may be that the personal verbs that can be predicated are the intransitive (or semi-transitive) personal verbs, those that can constitute complete predicate terms on their own.

[37]There is a temptation (and some license) to read these infinitives as if they were participles, and to write them without quotation marks. Such a move would make the passage read more smoothly through "are themselves predicated" but would not suit "by means of themselves." Abelard's casualness or ambivalence toward the distinction between linguistic and extralinguistic entities is typical of philosophers, beginning with Aristotle, in their discussion of predication. As Peter Geach observes (after making some stipulations regarding the terminology of predication), for lack of such stipulations "logicians as distinguished as Aristotle and Russell have fallen into almost inextricable confusions, so that you just cannot tell whether a predicate is something within language or something represented by means of language," *Reference and Generality* (Ithaca N.Y. 1962) 23.

tion, those that Abelard elsewhere calls "accidental."[38] The nuncupative verbs[39] play a somewhat larger part in Abelard's theories of predication than they will play in this discussion.[40] The substantive verb[41] is, of course, unique and much the most important for our purposes. In the passage just quoted we have seen it displayed both as an ordinary verb in two-piece predication, where it is said to occur as the second piece (*secundum adiacens*), and as the copula in three-piece predication, where it is called the third piece (*tertium adiacens*). The crucial instance of Abelard's general undertaking to explain all predication in terms of the ordinary characteristics of verbs is his attempt, in the first theory we will look at, to base his account of 'is' as the third piece on his account of 'is' as the second piece.

It seems that we could readily construct the latter sort of account on the model of what we have already seen: The verb in 'Socrates is' names something existent and determines its existence; it copulates that named thing and that determined characteristic (which together constitute its primary signification) to the individual named by 'Socrates', and it consignifies the time of the individual's being that named thing and having that determined characteristic as the present. Abelard's own account follows this pattern, but with at least one significant difference in content. He rejects any suggestion that a thing's existence might be considered one of its characteristics, essential or accidental. Even if all other verbs are associated with the characteristics of things, 'is' "is called the substantive verb because it has been imposed on all things in accordance with their *essentia*, and not in accordance with the adjacence of anything."[42] As 'runs' has been imposed on certain things in accordance with their running, a characteristic, so '*est*' has been imposed on *all* things in accordance with their *essentia*, which is *not* a characteristic. 'Is' names every thing (what is not is nothing) and determines its *essentia*. '*Essentia*' may mean no more than existence, or independent, substantial existence. It is hard to see how the doctrine of imposition would warrant its meaning any more than that;

---

[38]*Logica "Ingredientibus"* (n. 11 above) 352.20–22, where he says that 'reads' and 'teaches' are "accidental verbs—i.e., derived from reading and from teaching, which are accidents" ("legit et docet et cetera talia, quia sunt accidentalia verba, id est sumpta a lectione et a doctrina quae sunt accidentia"). Notice the parallel with the Aristotelian categories: the substantive verb corresponds with the first category, substance; the accidental verbs with the other nine categories, the accidents.

[39]De Rijk lists '*nuncupari*', '*nominari*', '*vocari*', '*appellari*' in the Introduction to his edition of *Dialectica* (n. 9 above) xli. Because English has allowed its only nuncupative verb—'hight'—to lapse, propositions involving Latin nuncupatives have to be translated into English misleadingly, as if they contained an occurrence of the substantive verb: '*nominatur*', 'is named'.

[40]Abelard's fullest discussions of the nuncupative verbs and their relationship with the substantive verb apparently occur in *Logica "Ingredientibus"* (n. 11 above) 359.28–360.12 and *Dialectica* (n. 9 above) 134.3–27.

[41]On the designation 'substantive', see de Rijk's edition of *Dialectica* (n. 9 above) Introduction, xli n. 4.

[42]". . . ut '*est*', quod substantivum verbum dicitur, eo videlicet quod omnibus secundum essentiam suam sit impositum, non secundum alicuius adiacentiam," *Dialectica* (n. 9 above) 131.4–6; I suggest reading '*verba*' for '*nomina*' earlier in line 4. For our purposes Abelard's terms 'adjacence' (*adiacentia*) and 'inherence' (*inhaerentia*) may be considered synonymous.

but because the precise nature of the determination of 'is' is problematic in a way that affects Abelard's account of three-piece predication, I will cautiously retain '*essentia*' as a term of convenience.[43] In any case, Abelard believes that the role of the copula is to be explained on the basis of the imposition of the substantive verb. Immediately following the passage quoted just above there is the explanation that it is "for that reason [that 'is'] can copulate all sorts of *essentiae* of things equally as far as inherence is concerned" (131.6–7).

In two-piece predication, then, the substantive verb copulates an existent thing together with *essentia* to the individual named by the subject term. And when the substantive verb occurs as the third piece in predication, its capacity for copulating "all sorts of *essentiae* of things equally" is derived from the original imposition of the verb. But these relatively clear claims give rise to at least two questions: (1) How, exactly, does its role as copula derive from its ordinary signification and copulation? and (2) Does it retain its ordinary signification and copulation when it is used to copulate something else to the subject? In his *Logica "Ingredientibus"* Abelard gave a clear affirmative answer to the second of these questions in his attempt to answer the first.[44]

THE *Ingredientibus* THEORY

But the substantive [verb], which does its job (*convenit*) not [like the nuncupative verbs, discussed immediately before] on the basis of naming (*appellatione*) but on the basis of the very *essentia* of a thing, can be conjoined with all predicates—not merely with names, but also with pronouns, participles, or even whole phrases. And because it signifies anything whatever in *essentia*, the copulation of *essentia* is never absent from it; for by its means one invariably frames the proposition that one thing *is* another (*aliquid aliud esse*),[45] even when it is adjoined to adjectives, as when one says 'He is white'. For as far as the intention of the framer of the proposition is concerned, whiteness alone is copulated, and so it alone can be predicated. Nevertheless, as a consequence of the force of the substantive verb, the substantive '*album*' ('white [thing]')[46] is conjoined

[43] It may help to remember that '*essentia*' might have looked to Abelard and his contemporaries as if it had been derived from '*esse*' for the purpose of presenting the primary signification of the substantive verb.

[44] There are many difficulties in the passage I am about to quote, but some of them seem to be gratuitous, particularly those brought about by apparently incongruent uses of '*album*' where '*albus*', '*albedo*', or '*albedinem*' would have been expected. In two places I suggest alternative readings, but very hesitantly. The uncertainties are made worse by the fact that a few of the occurrences of '*album*' are plainly just what is wanted.

[45] The Latin here is ambiguous, I think. If it were not for a parallel and unambiguous expression in the *Dialectica* Revision (see below at n. 53)—"*hoc illud esse*"—I would be inclined to translate "*aliquid aliud esse*" as "something or other *is*," which strikes me as all that Abelard is entitled to by the doctrine of imposition, even though the context strongly suggests that he wants the A = B sort of identity claim. (The Latin word-order warrants the emphasis on 'is', I believe, even in the identity claim.) I can see that the imposition of the substantive verb might entitle Abelard to say that "by its means one invariably frames the proposition that a thing is whatever it is"—A = A—but what he does say, both in "*aliquid aliud esse*" and in "*hoc illud esse*," seems too strong.

[46] The neuter form of the adjective can, of course, be understood as a substantive. I am not certain that this passage *must* be read as a claim about the conjunction of a substantive *locution* with the *man* Socrates; it would be easier to understand if "*ipsum substantivum album*" could be interpreted as "the white thing itself," but I think the Latin cannot bear that interpretation.

with Socrates in respect of *essentia* (*essentialiter Socrati coniungitur*); for in virtue of the force of the substantive verb Socrates himself is presented as being (*ipse Socrates esse ponitur*), because it retains the signification of *essentia*.

And so two things are conjoined with Socrates by means of the predicate 'white' (*album*): whiteness in adjacence, and a white thing (*album*)—that is, the very thing affected by the whiteness—in *essentia*. All the same, it is whiteness alone that is predicated, for it alone is what is intended to be conjoined. For not everything that is conjoined is predicated, but only that which is intended to be conjoined by means of the proposition. For whoever frames the proposition 'Socrates is white' declares (*ostendit*) that whiteness alone is in Socrates; and if he had a verb by means of which he could copulate whiteness [reading *albedinem* for *album*] to Socrates directly (*simpliciter*), so that he would have no need of the substantive [verb], he surely would do so. But because there is no verb by means of which that is done, he turns to the substantive [verb], which, because it has only the signification of *essentia*, cannot be uttered without the conjunction of *essentia*. But whiteness [reading *albedo* for *album*] cannot be truly copulated to Socrates in *essentia*—as if one were to say, for example, 'Socrates is whiteness'. (*Logica ''Ingredientibus''* 360.13–34)

There are indications in this passage that Abelard wished he could rid himself of the special problem of the role of the substantive verb in three-piece predication, and he eventually undertook to fulfill that wish, I think, in a radical suggestion he put forward. But at this stage of his thought (which I am designating the *Ingredientibus* Theory) he apparently accepted, as an inescapable feature of the language he had to work with, the use of the substantive verb as the copula. His wistful remark about lacking the sort of verb that would transform 'Socrates is white' from three-piece to two-piece predication certainly suggests that he considered this role for the substantive verb to be only a feature of (certain) languages and not grounded in the nature of reality.[47] Still, he might have remained faithful to the externals of his language and nevertheless avoided or at least reduced the difficulty by distinguishing, as many philosophers after him were to do, between the 'is' of existence (the fully significant verb occurring as the second piece) and the 'is' of predication (the merely functional copula). In the *Ingredientibus* Theory he is obviously and emphatically set against doing any such thing, although, as we shall see, he subsequently changed his mind.

I do not know of any place where he offers a detailed reason against adopting such an expedient, but I think I can see why the proponent of the *Ingredientibus* Theory would reject it. If 'Socrates is white' is to be a proposition and not merely a string of words, then 'is' must retain its copulative function. But it has that function just because it is a verb; and because it is a verb, it has a signification. Since we need the copulative function of the substantive verb when we employ it as the copula, we must accept its inevitable concomitant, the verb's signification. And so we have the affirmative answer to question (2) above: when 'is' occurs as the copula, it does retain its primary signification

[47]Abelard displays unusual insight here, I think, especially considering that he almost certainly knew of no language (such as Russian) which does dispense with the copula, and that he makes this remark in the context of a theory in which he is trying to provide a semantic (or metaphysical) explanation for the use of 'is' as the copula.

and copulation. Of course Abelard's willingness to put up with the inconvenient device he finds in his language, and his reasoning against stripping the copula of its signification (whether or not I have reconstructed it correctly), would weigh a great deal less in his considerations if he did not believe that he had an explanation of the function of the copula *in terms of* the signification and copulation of the substantive verb. The explanation offered in the *Ingredientibus* Theory is unsatisfactory, and was later revised and finally abandoned by Abelard; but it contains some insights, and its flaws are instructive.

The most novel element of the theory is its distinction between conjunction and predication.[48] This is an unusual distinction, even for Abelard, and I am not sure we have evidence enough for a reliable interpretation; but I think we can make some progress in the right direction. If we temporarily revert to 'connection' as our most general term (roughly on a par with 'predication' as I have been using it so far), then it seems that *conjunction* is the connection(s) *effected, intentionally or not, simply* in virtue of the syntactic and semantic character of a proposition and its components, and *predication* is the connection(s) *not only effected* in virtue of the syntactic and semantic character of the proposition and its components *but also intended* by the framer and utterer of the proposition. As Abelard's terminology suggests (more transparently in Latin), predication is concerned with what is said, while conjunction has to do with relations among the parts of the linguistic apparatus by means of which what is said is said.

Aside from the conjunction/predication distinction, the elements of the *Ingredientibus* Theory are those already encountered in our discussion of Abelard. To begin with what is plainest in the theory's explanation of three-piece predication, a person who uses the proposition 'Socrates is white' as such a proposition would ordinarily be used, at least by an Aristotelian, intends simply to ascribe the quality whiteness to the individual Socrates. His language has no verb for carrying out this intention (as it has for ascribing the status of reigning to Elizabeth), and so he carries out his intention with the apparatus afforded by his language for that purpose: the name of the individual, plus the substantive verb, plus the adjective corresponding to the name of the quality. Since all that the utterer means by the proposition is that whiteness inheres in Socrates, whiteness is all that is *predicated* of Socrates.

But what takes place in the linguistic apparatus by means of which this "predication" is effected? To begin, again, with what is plainest, (a) *Socrates is presented as existing.* The signification and copulation of the substantive verb are fully in force, and so 'Socrates is' is really, and not only apparently, an ingredient in 'Socrates is white'. The presentation of the subject as existing is a troublesome feature of the theory, as we shall see, but it should come as no surprise, given Abelard's project of explaining the copula as a special occurrence of the full-fledged substantive verb.

---

[48]Copulation, the third relationship which plays an essential role in the theory, seems to be used here as we have already seen Abelard using it in dealing with verbs generally.

In the second place, (b) *a white thing is conjoined with Socrates in essentia*. This conjunction seems somehow to be brought about both (i) *by "the force of the substantive verb"* and (ii) *"by means of the adjective 'white'."* At this critical juncture the theory seems confused. The force (*vis*) of the substantive verb I take to be the ordinary signification and copulation of 'is', but that force has apparently already been fully, straightforwardly utilized in (a). What is it to conjoin a white thing with Socrates in *essentia*? If it is, not implausibly, to present Socrates as existing *and*, at the same time, to present a white thing as existing, no relevant connection between the two has been brought about. In these circumstances one is bound to think of the "Identity" approach to predication (see above), but our question here is how, if at all, identity can be established on the basis of the force of the substantive verb, or whether the "Identity" approach is warranted. We have been focusing on (b)(i); perhaps (b)(ii) is intended as its complement. The adjective 'white' names every white thing; if Socrates = a white thing, then 'white' and 'Socrates' name one and the same thing. Very well, but how is that relationship presented by means of the force of the substantive verb? By inserting an appositive into 'Socrates is' to form 'Socrates, a white thing, is'? I believe that such an interpretation of 'Socrates is white' is what the *Ingredientibus* Theory leads to, and I suspect that Abelard would endorse it, although—perhaps significantly—I have not found him doing so explicitly. Many serious objections could and should be raised against a theory that transforms at least every proposition of three-piece predication into an existential proposition with an appositive,[49] but because such objections are not the ones that seem to have led Abelard to revise and then abandon this theory, I will forego raising them here.

In the third place, (c) *whiteness is conjoined with Socrates in adjacence by means of the adjective 'white'*. Abelard has based "predication" on inherence and has described "predication" as that portion of the "conjunction" which the utterer intends to express. He is thus bound to provide inherence somewhere in his account of conjunction, and he does so here. Notice that he leaves the substantive verb altogether out of this part of the account. It copulates only *essentia*, and whiteness, Abelard would emphatically agree, has (or is) no *essentia*. We can certainly accept Abelard's observation at the end of the quoted passage: whiteness cannot be conjoined with Socrates simply by sticking 'whiteness' on the other end of 'is'. How, then, is the adjective 'white' supposed to conjoin whiteness with Socrates "in adjacence"? Abelard must be relying on the concept of determination: 'white' determines whiteness in virtue of its imposition on white things. But since the connection between 'Socrates' and 'white' has been left hopelessly obscure despite the efforts made in this theory to clarify it, we cannot acknowledge that we have been shown

---

[49]Particularly in view of Abelard's claim that other verbs "contain the copulation of the substantive verb" (n. 34 above), there is some reason to think that the *Ingredientibus* Theory would have the same effect on two-piece predication, interpreting 'Socrates runs' as 'Socrates, a running thing, is'.

the way in which the linguistic apparatus connects whiteness with Socrates in adjacence.

From Abelard's own point of view, it seems, the most important shortcoming of the *Ingredientibus* Theory occurs in this attempt to explain the "predication" of inherence simply by including inherence within the "conjunction" which underlies the "predication." I believe we have good evidence that considerations of this sort were influential in Abelard's *revising* the *Ingredientibus* Theory, but his eventual replacement of it with quite a different theory may well have been motivated by considerations of another sort. For although the difficulties associated with grounding "predication" in "conjunction" are more fundamental, they are less apparent than the difficulties over nonexistent entities which mortified, or ought to have mortified, the *Ingredientibus* Theory almost immediately.

AN EMBARRASSMENT OF CHIMERAS

A theory committed to accounting for the copula on the basis of the original imposition of the substantive verb is obviously headed for trouble over propositions whose subject terms are names of nonexistent entities. The interpretation of all such propositions will reveal them to be false, no matter how self-evidently true they may appear to be, if the standard interpretation of 'x is A' amounts to an expanded version of, or merely includes, 'x is'. Abelard tries to face up to this trouble very soon after completing his presentation of the *Ingredientibus* Theory.

But if the conjunction of *essentia* is never absent from the substantive verb, how is it conjoined truly with the names of nonexistents—as, for example, when one says 'A chimera is a chimera' or 'A chimera is a non-man'? . . . if the proposition is true, it must be that 'is' and 'chimera' signify the same; but, of course, 'is' contains only existents.

We maintain, therefore, that if we want to preserve the truth of the proposition, then the verb 'is' in this context is interpreted (*transferri*) in a nuncupative sense, as if we were to say, 'A chimera is called a chimera' (*Chimaera vocatur chimaera*) or 'A chimera is called a non-man'—that is, those are names of it. For just as we say that 'A chimera is thinkable' (*est opinabilis*) or 'A chimera is conceived of' (*excogitatur*) is significant—not, indeed, attributing anything to a chimera, but understanding rather that a person thinks of one—so there is nothing to prevent this [reading *hanc* for *haec*] [other sort of] significant [proposition] from being interpreted in another sense. (*Logica "Ingredientibus"* 361.12–14, 16–20)

The very condition laid down as the basis for the opening question in the passage is enough to show that this attempt to overcome the embarrassment of chimeras is a hopeless failure. If, as the *Ingredientibus* Theory plainly claims, the conjunction of *essentia* is *never* absent from the substantive verb, the advent of a convenient "nuncupative sense" will only veil the embarrassment, and pretty thinly at that.[50] And, anyway, if it is open to us to import conve-

---

[50]The illegitimacy of thus importing a nuncupative sense for 'is' seems especially clear in the light of the care with which this theory initially distinguishes the substantive verb from the nuncupative verbs.

nient senses of 'is' or to understand as suits us best, propositions in which the substantive verb occurs as the copula, the complexity and subtlety of the *Ingredientibus* Theory are worse than pointless. It seems unlikely that a mind as sharp as Abelard's would not have noticed these fatal flaws even as he was writing or speaking these lines, and there is evidence that he did see them sooner or later, especially in connection with the new theory he adopted afterwards.

THE *Dialectica* REVISION

In Abelard's *Dialectica*, his last treatise on these subjects,[51] I find not only a theory of the copula very different from the *Ingredientibus* Theory but also what appears to be a revision of the earlier theory. And although the *Dialectica* Theory seems to have been motivated primarily by difficulties over nonexistent entities, some features of the *Dialectica* Revision strongly suggest that it was undertaken in order to avoid the problems generated by the relations between "predication" and "conjunction."

The *Dialectica* Revision is embedded in Abelard's discussion of the views held by some "others"[52] regarding the nature of the substantive verb. These men apparently agree with Abelard about the original imposition of the verb, but

although they concede that that sort of verb is imposed on things themselves in accordance with *essentia* only and not in accordance with the adjacence of anything, they sometimes reduce its copulation to the predication of adjacence only. (Linguistic devices [*vocabula*] of adjacence are used in this way: 'Peter is white', 'Peter is rational'.) For they maintain that whiteness or rationality alone is attributed to me as adjacent, because whoever frames the proposition that I am white says that I am informed by whiteness and declares that it is adjacent to me.

It is my judgment, however, that the predication which pertains to the sense of the proposition and to the function of the substantive verb is certainly the predication of *the subject* of the whiteness—that which is *named* by 'white'—rather than the predication of its adjacence—that which is *determined* by 'white'. For when we say that someone is white—when, that is, we frame the proposition that he is one of those that are informed by whiteness—what is strictly predicated by means of the verb 'is' in accordance with the copulation of *essentia* is that which is said *to be*—that is, the thing informed by the whiteness. But since [the expression] "the name 'white' itself is attributed" is used to show that [the name] is imposed on that thing on the basis of the adjacent whiteness, the inherence of the adjacent whiteness is also implied by the proposition itself. Therefore the predication of *essentia*, which consists in the fact that this is said *to be* that (*hoc illud esse*),[53] is expressed properly by the words of the proposition; but the predication which is the attribution of adjacence is somehow implied (*quodammodo innuitur*). (*Dialectica* 131.23–132.6)

[51]Only the third and final redaction of the *Dialectica* survives; it seems to have been written between 1135 and 1137. But even this late redaction contains material very likely written at the same time as or even earlier than the *Logica "Ingredientibus."* I know of no reason to think that the material we are concerned with here belongs to the earlier drafts, however. On the tangled chronology, see de Rijk's edition (n. 9 above) Introduction, xxii–xxiii, and Beonio-Brocchieri Fumagalli (n. 16 above) 6–7.

[52]These "others" are first alluded to in this context in 130.1; I cannot identify them.

[53]See n. 45 above.

However this revision is to be assessed philosophically,[54] it would be churlish not to acknowledge Abelard's intellectual fortitude in attempting it. Those against whom he is inveighing appear to have evaded the difficulties of accounting for the role of the substantive verb as the copula simply by fiat; and, indeed, if Abelard reports them correctly, their position is flatly inconsistent. Abelard, by contrast, will not—at least, not yet—abandon the attempt to frame a unified theory of the substantive verb and the copula. In the face of all the difficulties, he continues to maintain that the full status of the substantive verb persists in its role as the copula, and he goes on trying to wring identity between subjects out of the original imposition of 'is' in order to provide the basic conjunction of the subject with the predicate. But notice the differences between the original *Ingredientibus* Theory and this revision, all in the direction of fudging troublesome details. Gone is the promising but difficult technical distinction between conjunction and predication; gone, too, is the insupportable claim that whiteness is conjoined in adjacence with the subject of the proposition by means of the linguistic apparatus itself. And the most dramatic falling-off appears in the concluding clause. Abelard's efforts to explain the predication of inherence on the basis of the copulation of *essentia* have dwindled to this: "the predication which is the attribution of adjacence is somehow implied" by the words of the proposition.

THE *Dialectica* THEORY

If my conjectures about the development of Abelard's thought on predication lie close to the truth, an outcome so unsatisfying as that of the *Dialectica* Revision may have helped to lead him away from the project of a unified theory. The difficulties dealt with in the revision, however, are not the ostensible grounds for Abelard's taking a very different tack in the *Dialectica* Theory.

As I see it, this new theory begins with the familiar distinction between two-piece and three-piece predication; but on this occasion the distinction is drawn in significantly different terms.

Now it must not be overlooked that verbs used in statements are said to be predicated *properly* on some occasions and *incidentally* (*per accidens*) on others. They are predicated properly in this way: 'Peter is', 'Peter runs'. For here they are engaged with a double force: they have not only the function of copulating but also the signification of the predicated reality (*rei*). The verb is said to be predicated incidentally and not properly, however, when it is set beside the predicate for the sole purpose of copulating it, as in 'Peter is a man'. For in this case the interposed [verb] does not also contain the predicated reality—then 'man' would be supplied superfluously—instead it merely copulates that which is subjoined as the predicate.[55]   (134.28–37)

---

[54] It is not sufficiently different from the *Ingredientibus* Theory itself—at least not in ways that look promising—to warrant its own assessment here, particularly since we are about to consider a theory that seems to have superseded even this revised version of the *Ingredientibus* Theory.

[55] It is reasonably clear that this passage bears some relationship to *De int.* c. 12, 20b31–21a33, but just what that relationship is not clear to me. In that portion of c. 12, especially in 21a7 ff., Aristotle discusses predication *per accidens*, and in 21a25 ff. he introduces the Homer example

Although the division is between two-piece and three-piece predication generally, it may for our purposes be considered as a distinction between the occurrences of 'is' as the second piece and as the third piece. In 'Peter is' the substantive verb is predicated "properly," while in 'Peter is a man' it is predicated only "incidentally." Even the terminology of this version of the division suggests a drastic reappraisal of the copula's relationship to the full-fledged substantive verb, especially because 'properly' (*proprie*) in the usage of medieval logicians and grammarians frequently means *literally*. But the more substantial indications of a change in Abelard's account of three-piece predication are the claims that 'is' is interposed as the copula "for the *sole* purpose of copulating" the predicate beside which it is placed, that it "*merely* copulates" the predicate, and, perhaps most important of all, that it "does not also contain the predicated reality." Abelard of course would never have described the copula as containing the reality contained in *the predicate* in three-piece predication, but according to the *Ingredientibus* Theory the copula contained (and predicated, or copulated) its own reality, *essentia*, whatever else it did by way of connecting the predicate to the subject. The evidence in this passage is not yet conclusive, but it looks as if Abelard is putting forward a pure-copula theory of three-piece predication.

In the light of everything we have seen him maintaining so far—not only the *Ingredientibus* Theory itself but the semantic doctrines on which that theory was based—such a development is astonishing; and yet as he goes on in this portion of the *Dialectica* it becomes certain that that astonishing development is indeed taking place. In three-piece predication, he says, the substantive verb

is set beside the predicate for the sole purpose of copulating it; it is not used for the purpose of predicating for an underlying reality (*subiecta re*), but only in order to copulate that which is predicated. When, on the other hand, it is used (*dicitur*) *properly*, it contains the predicated reality as well and indeterminately attributes one of the things that exist, as when one says 'Peter is'—that is, Peter is one of the things that exist. (135.4–8)

The primary motivation for this development in Abelard's thought is evidently the embarrassment of chimeras. In the passage immediately following the one just quoted, Abelard observes that

sometimes, indeed, it is *necessary* that the predication be derived from what is incidental (*ex accidentali necesse est consequi*), because ['is'] often copulates words belonging to

---

which is going to figure prominently in Abelard's discussion (see below). Moreover, Aristotle says that in 'Homer is something' "(say a poet)," "the 'is' is predicated *per accidens* of Homer; for it is because he is a poet, not in its own right, that the 'is' is predicated of Homer" (21a26–28). But Aristotle's predication *per accidens* is the predication of accidents and is contrasted with what might be called essential predication, and Abelard's distinction is plainly not founded on that principle. According to Abelard, but definitely not according to Aristotle, 'Peter runs' is not *per accidens*; 'Peter is a man' is *per accidens*. For that reason I have adopted 'incidentally' as a less misleading translation of '*per accidens*' than 'accidentally' would have been here.

nonexistent entities, as when one says 'A chimera is thinkable' or '[A chimera is] nonexistent'. There is nothing strange about this, since the interposed ['is'] has no signification of *essentia* but, as has been said, only exercises the function of copulation.[56]   (135.9–13)

Meager though these statements are, they present all that is essential to the *Dialectica* Theory: when used as the copula, the substantive verb has no signification of *essentia* (or, presumably, of anything else) but serves as a merely syntactic device to indicate that the terms of the proposition stand in the subject-predicate relationship to each other.[57]

As far as I can see, Abelard did not offer positive support for this theory; instead, his arguments in its defense consider the disadvantages in retaining all or even part of the signification of the substantive verb in three-piece predication. He himself puts the main issue as forcefully as any opponent might have done.

The verb 'is' was said above [for example, in the *Dialectica* Revision] to copulate among all *essentiae* because it signifies all things in *essentia*. How, then, can it copulate things the signification of which it does not contain, such as a non-being, or what is [only] thinkable? . . . Or how can it preserve the special character (*proprietas*) of the grammatical construction unless it is also intransitively conjoined with the things it copulates?[58]   (135.18–21; 22–23)

In abandoning the signification of the substantive verb in order to achieve the advantages of the pure copula, must one not also forfeit the concomitant (and presumably still essential) copulative function of the verb? Abelard does not answer these hard questions directly. Some people, he suggests, want somehow to allow the verb to retain its signification, even in 'A chimera is thinkable'; "they want the interposed [verb] 'to be' to be accepted also in the designation of nonexistents. But then," Abelard asks, "what being does one deny them [reading *eis* for *ea*], if one accepts this same being which indicates (*demonstrat*) nonexistents?" (135.26–28). And that question seems reasonable. One good reason for adopting a pure-copula theory, other things being equal, is that without it one seems forced to countenance (as Meinong did)[59] the being of objects that do not exist.

[56]On the concept of the substantive verb's copulative function in medieval grammarians before Abelard see K. M. Fredborg, "The Dependence of Petrus Helias' *Summa super Priscianum* on William of Conches' *Glose super Priscianum*", CIMAGL 11 (1973) 1–57, esp. 27.

[57]As far as I can see, nothing in the *Dialectica* Theory requires that that relationship be depicted in one way rather than another. This bare conjunction of the terms might be taken to express identity, inherence, or even class-membership.

[58]On one view Abelard takes of the nature of predication, it is essential that what is conjoined with the subject *name* the very thing named by the subject, and he describes such conjunction or copulation as "intransitive"; see, e.g., *Dialectica* 166.16–19; also de Rijk's Introduction to his edition (n. 9 above) xliii–xliv. If the substantive verb is used as a pure copula, it does not name anything and yet is conjoined with the subject, which (presumably) names something. Thus this pure-copula theory appears to violate one fundamental principle of predication.

[59]"The two basic theses of Meinong's theory of objects . . . are (1) there are objects that do not exist and (2) every object that does not exist is yet constituted in some way or other and thus may be made the subject of true predication." R. M. Chisholm, "Meinong, Alexius," *Encyclopedia of Philosophy* (n. 8 above) 5.261.

There is a subtler way of attempting to preserve the status of the copula as the fully significant substantive verb, a way which we have seen Abelard himself adopt or at least allude to in his earlier struggles with chimera-propositions. Instead of claiming bluntly that the interposed 'is' must somehow signify being, one takes such propositions as having a logical form quite different from the grammatical form they appear to have and, in particular, as having some subject other than their apparent nonexistent subject. Abelard now considers this maneuver, reporting that "our Master"[60] used to say that in such propositions

the predication was incidental not because of the verb, but because of the figurative and improper speech characterizing the entire grammatical construction, the composite whole of which has to be explicated with reference to some sense other than the one the words (*verba*) seem to have.   (135.29–32)

After discussing at some length Aristotle's example, 'Homer is a poet',[61] which was apparently a paradigm for "our Master," Abelard returns to 'A chimera is thinkable'. Of course it is correct to deny that Homer, who no longer exists, is (136.21–22); it is likewise correct to deny that a chimera, which never existed, is. But when Homer or a chimera is the subject of a three-piece predication, the nonexistence of the subject is circumvented by this maneuver. For

when one considers the meaning of the entire grammatical construction and at the same time joins the words together in the sense of the other [actually intended] statement, then it is not the signification of the individual words that must be attended to; rather, the whole meaning of the expression must be understood. And the grammatical construction of the expression is called improper in that its meaning does not come from the signification of its parts. . . . Thus 'A chimera is thinkable' also is called a figurative and improper locution because as regards its sense the words propose something other than what appears in the utterance. For it is not that by means of 'thinkable' one attributes a property to a chimera (which does not exist), but rather that one attributes a thought of a chimera to someone's mind. It is as if we were to say 'Someone's mind has a thought of a chimera'.   (136.22–26; 32–36)

Abelard's fundamental objection to this maneuver seems to be that it is only a maneuver. It preserves the full signification of 'is' as the copula only by removing it from view. What is the point of insisting, as "our Master" did, that the "impropriety" is *not* to be attributed to the verb if the original three-piece predication involving the verb cannot bear scrutiny? (The Master's reworking of 'Homer is a poet' seems to have been 'The fame of Homer lives on in our memory because of the poem he composed' [135.25].) And so Abelard returns to the heart of the matter.

But *every* such predication of the verb seems to me to be incidental and improper, *whenever* it is interposed as a third piece, as has been said. For, as has been said, it does

[60]De Rijk (n. 9 above) thinks Abelard may be referring to William of Champeaux (Introduction, xxi).
[61]*De int.* c. 12, 21a25 ff. See n. 5 above.

not contain the predicated reality but has the function of the copula only, as it does also in 'Peter is a man' or 'Peter is white'.   (136.37–137.3)

Characteristically, Abelard reaches out to accept the hard consequences of his position; the third piece is a pure copula not only in 'Homer is a poet' and 'A chimera is thinkable', where a pure copula is only convenient, but also in altogether ordinary three-piece predications with existent subjects. And now Abelard reveals the first advantage of the *Dialectica* Theory that does not seem to be entirely *ad hoc*; for it turns out that on this theory, too, 'Peter is' may be inferred from 'Peter is a man', despite the fact that the copula has been stripped of signification.

The fact that from what is said in 'Peter is a man' one can infer 'Peter is' pertains not so much to the interpretation of it [viz., the verb] as, perhaps, to the predication of 'man', which is the name of an existent entity only.   (137.3–6)

Assigning to the imposition of the predicate-term the implication of the subject's existence means that, on this pure-copula theory, 'A chimera is thinkable' is true while 'Homer is a poet' is (now) false, as Abelard goes on to point out (137.6–26).

   The *Dialectica* Theory is undeniably attractive, at least superficially; it does avoid the difficulties that plagued the *Ingredientibus* Theory. But it achieves this result simply by declaring that the copula is not what it appears to be, an occurrence of the substantive verb; and so this theory, too, has the look of a mere maneuver. Moreover, it marks the abandonment of any attempt to produce a theory that will save the appearances, providing, as the *Ingredientibus* Theory sought to do, an account of the single verb 'to be' that will explain its efficacy in expressing (at least) existence, inherence, and identity. Whether or not these latter characteristics of the *Dialectica* Theory are objectively lamentable, it would be strange if a philosopher with Abelard's grounding in the Old Logic were not to lament over them. And, indeed, when he has expounded and exercised this theory, he does seem to revert momentarily to the Abelard of the *Ingredientibus* Theory.

But how is one to call a locution *proper* in which the predication of the verb is *improper* and [the verb] does not retain the signification with respect to which it was invented? For [the substantive verb] was invented not with regard to the function of copulation alone but simultaneously, as has been said, with regard to the signification of existents. For, as has been said, it can copulate anything to anything because it has been imposed on things [reading *rebus* for *nominibus*] in accordance with their *essentia*. But why is it used also in connection with the inherence of things that *are not* and that are not contained in it?   (138.5–11)

This unabashed reintroduction of the doctrine of the imposition of 'is' and the question raised on the basis of it come into the text at this point quite as if the *Dialectica* Theory had not immediately preceded them. The passage has the look of an objection raised by a reactionary and rather inattentive auditor, but I think it is Abelard's lament. Whatever the advantages of a pure-copula theory may be, it does fly in the face of the semantic theory which Abelard had developed out of the materials of the Old Logic. It is as if he had done all he could to come to understand and to explain the copula and has found all the results unsatisfactory in one way or another. And my view of this passage as a lament is reinforced by the fact that it is followed immediately by a really radical suggestion regarding the copula.

THE *Dialectica* SUGGESTION

Therefore, if I may dare to say so publicly, it seems to me more reasonable that we be able to satisfy reason. . . . Thus when one says 'is a man' or 'is thinkable' or 'is white', let us understand it as a verb—'to-be-a-man' [reading *homo* for *hominem*] or 'to-be-white' or 'to-be-thinkable'.[62]   (138.11–12; 15–17)

Here, I believe, we see Abelard making a tentative move in the direction of a goal he had only glanced at wistfully while laying out the *Ingredientibus* Theory: the transformation of all three-piece predication into two-piece predication, ridding our language and our thought of the perplexing copula. He cannot be said to have produced a full theory of predication along these lines, but he did try out the new idea, showing how it might be used to clear up one familiar difficulty and how it might help the logician to deal with tenses—a feature of language which most logicians then as always would rather ignore.[63]

One result of the *Dialectica* Theory, as we have seen, was that 'Homer is a poet' had to be declared false. But, Abelard now suggests, that is "because 'to be a poet' is *not* a single word" (138.20–21), and so we have to take separate

[62]Needless to say, nothing paralleling my hyphenation can be found in Abelard's own text. But many of the things he says in this portion of the *Dialectica* show that he was indeed after some such device. See, for instance, the passage quoted at the end of this paper. Jan Pinborg has called my attention to a passage in *Logica "Ingredientibus"* (n. 11 above, 348.15–350.39) that contains some of the same considerations as are introduced in the *Dialectica* Suggestion. The location of that interestingly similar passage could raise further questions about the chronology of Abelard's writings or about the historical development of his thought. But I think it is most naturally interpreted as an earlier expression of a desideratum whose importance became clearer to him after he had seen the problems generated by his theories of the substantive verb as the copula.

[63]Cf. Otto Jespersen's remarks in *The Philosophy of Grammar* (London and New York 1924): "Logicians are fond of analyzing all sentences into the three elements, subject, copula, and predicate; *the man walks* is taken to contain the subject *the man*, the copula *is*, and the predicate *walking*. A linguist must find this analysis unsatisfactory, not only from the point of view of English grammar, where *is walking* means something different from *walks*, but also from a general point of view. The analysis presents some difficulties when the present tense is not used: *the man walked* cannot be dissolved into anything containing the form *is*, but only into *the man was walking*—but then logicians move always in the present of eternal truths! The copula is so far from being the typical verb, that many languages have never developed any copula at all, and others dispense with it in many cases" (131). It is anachronistic but perhaps instructive to suggest that in his attempt to do away with the copula and transform all three-piece predication into a new sort of two-piece predication, Abelard was moving in the direction of the *functional* analysis of predication which revolutionized logic after it was introduced by Frege more than seven hundred years later. And Abelard's preferred examples—proper name, copula, adjective—lend themselves to this sort of development much more readily than the standard categorical propositions of syllogistic would have done—e.g., 'Every man is mortal'.

account of the verb and of the predicate, with implausible results. But, "on the contrary, 'to be' is *part* of the predicate" (138.22); " 'to be' is not predicated in its own right but makes a *single* predicate with 'poet' " (138.24–25). And, presumably, the doctrine of imposition would raise no barrier to our considering the verb 'is-a-poet' to be applicable also to people who have died.

As if considering this present-tense proposition about the poet of the distant past had caused him to think of it, he goes on abruptly to say "Indeed, true statements of the past and of the future can be propounded in no other way."

For when we say 'He will be sitting' of someone who is not yet sitting (or frame the proposition 'He was sitting' [of someone who is no longer sitting]), the statements seem entirely false if 'will be' (*erit*) and 'sitting' (*sedens*) remain unaffected words and preserve their own invention [or imposition]. For since 'sitting' is in the present tense and was imposed on the basis of present sitting, whoever says 'will be sitting' propounds this: 'will be one among the things that have sitting now'. But that of course is false regarding the man who, not yet sitting, is going to sit.   (138.30–34)

Abelard's solution, expressed in terms of another example of the same sort, is to insist that 'will-be-sitting' "must be accepted as nothing other than the single word of a verb; otherwise it would not produce a true future-tense statement" (139.1–3). He justifies the compression of '*erit sedens*' into a one-word verb on the grounds that that phrase is, after all, accepted as a standard equivalent of the one-word verb '*sedebit*' (138.36–139.1). And he promises that "once this interpretation of compound verbs has been attended to, future-tense or past-tense propositions can also enter into the moods of syllogisms" (139.29–30), sketching a much more flexible syllogistic than had been dreamed of by logicians before him.

In the graceful placatory remarks he makes after having outlined the *Dialectica* Suggestion, Abelard shows that he realized how far he had gone beyond the recognized bounds of the Old Logic.

Do not shudder because in our efforts to expose the correct meaning of statements we seem to go against the grammarians' rules, in putting together many verbs or substantives—'to-be-a-man', for instance—or [compound verbs] that are derived from things other than actions or passions, such as 'to-be-white'. For, out of their consideration for the capacity of the young, those who are in the first rank of the discipline left many things to be corrected, or to be studied by advanced students. On these things one must exert the subtlety of dialectic.   (140.23–29)

An essay devoted to the consideration of 'is', even a longish essay, can only hint at Abelard's achievements in logic and grammar; still less can it do justice to the twelfth-century *artes sermocinales* generally. But often we can most effectively enhance our appreciation of a broad canvas, particularly one familiar to us in outline, by focusing on a detail.

Bibliographical Note

The most significant development since Haskins appended the "Bibliographical Note" to chapter 11 of his book has been the appearance of systematic, topically indexed bibliographies of philosophy, including the history of philosophy. For a full survey of the literature of the last fifty years on twelfth-century philosophy, logic, and grammar, and on Abelard in particular, the reader should consult G. A. de Brie, *Bibliographia Philosophica, 1934–1945* (2 vols. Brussels 1950–54); Fernand van Steenberghen, *Philosophie des Mittelalters*, Bibliographische Einführungen in das Studium der Philosophie 17 (Bern 1950); *Répertoire bibliographique de la Philosophie* (published quarterly at Louvain since 1949); and *Philosopher's Index* (published quarterly at Bowling Green, Ohio, since 1967). Rather full bibliographies on Abelard are available in David E. Luscombe, *The School of Peter Abelard: The Influence of Abelard's Thought in the Early Scholastic Period* (Cambridge 1969) and Leif Grane, *Peter Abelard*, trans. Frederick and Christine Crowley (London 1970).

Bibliographical information regarding editions of Abelard's work relevant to my paper may be found in notes 9 and 11 above. But for an admirably thoroughgoing survey of the status of the manuscripts and editions of all of Abelard's writings see Nikolaus M. Häring, "Abelard Yesterday and Today," *Pierre-Pierre* 341–403.

A few of the specifically relevant secondary sources are mentioned in my note 16 above. The single most important of these is Martin Tweedale's book, *Abailard on Universals*, which came my way too late to be taken into account in my paper. In addition to the books and articles cited in the notes, see Jean Jolivet, *Arts du langage et théologie chez Abélard*, EPM 57 (Paris 1969), and, in *Pierre-Pierre*, Paul Vignaux, "Note sur le nominalisme d'Abélard" (523–27), Jean Jolivet, "Notes de lexicographie abélardienne" (531–43, esp. 538–43, on 'essentia'), and L. M. de Rijk, "La signification de la proposition (*dictum propositionis*) chez Abélard" (547–55).

Platonism—Neoplatonism—Aristotelianism

A Twelfth-Century Metaphysical System
and Its Sources

Stephen Gersh

The medieval history of the Platonic tradition has been substantially reinterpreted during the last fifty years.[1] Regarding the twelfth century, recent scholarship has demonstrated that while earlier views of the extent to which Plato was known directly require little modification, considerably more attention should be paid to the indirect sources of Platonism. This latter perspective could be expanded in three ways.

First, the total impact of Platonism should be rated more highly. Of the Platonism found in Latin writers of late Antiquity, only that of Augustine and to a lesser extent Boethius have been investigated. Considerably more work needs to be done on the influence of Calcidius, Macrobius, and Martianus Capella, and we still only dimly understand the impact of that Latin Hermetic work known as the *Asclepius*. The Platonism available through translations from the Greek, especially in the form of Eriugena's version of Pseudo-Dionysius but also in renderings of significant texts from the Eastern patristic tradition generally, represents a potentially profitable field of future endeavor, and similar remarks could be made about the Platonism accessible through translations of Arabic material at the end of the twelfth century.[2]

Second, we need to make a clearer distinction among different varieties of Platonism. The sources available in the twelfth century stem mostly from late Antiquity and represent different stages in the evolution of Platonic thought. Thus the *Asclepius* represents the so-called "Middle Platonism"; Augustine, Macrobius, and probably Calcidius's *Commentary on the Timaeus* reflect the Neoplatonism of Plotinus and Porphyry; Boethius that of the fifth-century Alexandrian school; and Pseudo-Dionysius that of the Athenian school in the

---

[1] Among the stimuli to scholarly reevaluation have been Raymond Klibansky's important monograph *The Continuity of the Platonic Tradition during the Middle Ages* (2nd ed. London 1950), the gradual publication under the auspices of the Warburg Institute of the *Corpus Platonicum Medii Aevi*, and several critical editions.

[2] Much of the still prevailing obscurity regarding the "sources" of medieval Platonism results from the hesitance of many classically trained scholars to explore in depth the data provided by late Antiquity. Thus, at least one prominent historian of ancient philosophy whose major work is still in process of publication intends to terminate his survey with the Stoics and Epicureans.

same period.[3] On many questions, these writers teach conflicting doctrines, and the type of Platonism which emerges at different periods of the Middle Ages often results from predominant or exclusive reliance upon one particular source or else from a specific combination of sources. On this basis one might compare the Platonism of the twelfth century with that of Eriugena, or the various twelfth-century schools with one another.

Finally, through studying the indirect sources we should develop a clearer appreciation of the relationship between Platonism and Aristotelianism. In the past, the two schools of thought have been contrasted by historians of philosophy far too rigidly, because the indirect sources often reflect the tendency prominent in late Antiquity to assume that Plato and Aristotle, although specializing in different areas of knowledge, are not fundamentally in disagreement. This approach had become prevalent by the time of the Middle Platonists whose doctrine is reflected in the *Asclepius* and, although less obvious in the more Plotinian thought of Augustine, it returns with renewed vigor in all those Latin writers who follow the Neoplatonic tradition after Porphyry. Boethius's declared aim to translate the whole of Aristotle and Plato and show that the two philosophers were essentially in agreement is, of course, well known.[4]

A few recent scholarly works have made significant advances in these three areas. In general, however, they have aimed only at brief surveys and, although dealing satisfactorily with Augustine and Boethius, have done perhaps less justice to the Platonism transmitted through other sources.[5] It therefore seems appropriate to analyze in detail one especially important twelfth-century Platonic text in order to demonstrate how the writer integrated the different traditions of Platonism to which he had access, paying special attention to those sources which he used but did not care to name.

THE "LIBRUM HUNC"—ITS BOETHIAN FRAMEWORK

Known for a long time by its incipit as "Librum hunc," the twelfth-century commentary on the *De Trinitate* of Boethius is a work of Thierry of Chartres or at least was written under his influence.[6] The editor of the recent critical edi-

---

[3]The Platonisms of late Antiquity are also notable for the greater or lesser degree to which they assimilate material from other philosophical traditions—especially the Stoic—as well as doctrines derived from Near Eastern religions.

[4]Boethius, *Commentarii in librum Aristotelis* Περὶ ἑρμηνείας, ed. Karl Meiser (2 vols. Leipzig 1877–80) vol. 2, *In De interpretatione, editio secunda* 79.9.

[5]Even such a distinguished work as Chenu's *Théologie* is somewhat deficient in these respects. See Bibliographical Note.

[6]In the past, this text has been studied principally by Wilhelm Jansen, *Der Kommentar des Clarenbaldus von Arras zu Boethius De Trinitate* (Breslau 1926). Among more recent discussions dealing with aspects of the work are Joseph Marie Parent, *La doctrine de la création dans l'Ecole de Chartres*, Publications de l'Institut d'études médiévales d'Ottawa 8 (Paris and Ottawa 1938); Eugenio Garin, *Studi sul platonismo medievale* (Florence 1958); and Fernand Brunner, "Deus forma essendi," *Entretiens* 85–116.

tion has accepted Thierry's authorship on the basis of textual comparisons with
the treatise *De sex dierum operibus*, whose attribution cannot be disputed,
and with the smaller commentary on the *De Trinitate* by Thierry's pupil Clarembald of Arras.[7] However, the existence in one manuscript containing this
work of a note attributing it to another writer must cast some doubt on the
question.[8] I shall therefore simply refer to "the writer," with the tacit assumption that the commentary is probably, if not indisputably, by Thierry. The
same editor dates the treatise by its quotation of a Sibylline prophecy circulated shortly before the departure of the Second Crusade and by a veiled reference to Gilbert of Poitiers's suspect doctrine of the Trinity examined at the
consistory of Reims.[9] This would place its *terminus a quo* at 1148.

As one might expect in a commentary on the *De Trinitate*, the philosophical doctrine of Boethius functions as a framework for the author's own
speculation, and the prologue and first chapter consist of further expansions
and clarifications of the Boethian text in a manner not obviously inconsistent
with the original writer's intentions. The second chapter is the first of two sections in which the twelfth-century writer considerably expands the scale of
discussion, especially in the later part, as a development of Boethius's pro-
nouncement "everything owes its being to form" (*omne namque esse ex
forma est*).[10] Here, under the influence of a combination of unnamed sources,
the commentary elaborates radically new lines of thought. Much of this
chapter, however, is a routine explanation of Boethian doctrines such as that of
the classification of scientific knowledge into the realms of physics, mathematics, and theology, each associated with a specific methodology;[11] and that
of the nature of God—the proper object of the third scientific method—as
pure Form and as "being itself" (*esse ipsum*).[12] The third chapter is again very
short and returns to closer dependence upon the Boethian text, although it
contains at least one radical deviation from the teaching of the original *De
Trinitate* which has in the past received less attention than it deserves.

Boethius argues, against Arian or subordinationist views of the Trinity,
that God cannot differ from God either by accidents or by substantial differences and that, since there are no differences in God, he must be a unity.[13]
His triune nature is explained by Boethius with the aid of a distinction between two types of number: (1) that "by which we count" (*quo numeramus*),

---

[7]Nikolaus M. Häring, *Commentaries on Boethius by Thierry of Chartres and His School*
(Toronto 1971) 19–24.

[8]MS Oxford, Bodleian Lyell 49 carries an apparent attribution to Peter Helias first noted by
Häring. See Edouard Jeauneau, "Note sur l'Ecole de Chartres," *Studi medievali* 3rd ser. 5 (1964)
821–65 (= *Lectio* 5–49).

[9]Häring (n. 7 above) 24. Cf., however, the same writer's remarks in *Life and Works of
Clarembald of Arras* (Toronto 1965) 28.

[10]*Commentum* 2.18–49 (74.89–84.88). All references in this essay are to the text edited in
Häring, *Commentaries* (n. 7 above).

[11]*Comm.* 2.8–16 (70.82–73.72), to Boethius, *De Trinitate* 2.5–21 , ed. and trans. Hugh F.
Stewart and Edward K. Rand, LCL (1918).

[12]*Comm.* 2.17 (73.73–74.88), to Boeth. *De Trin.* 2.20.

[13]Boeth. *De Trin.* 3.1–12.

for example unity or duality, and (2) that "which occurs in countable objects" (*qui in rebus numerabilibus constat*), for example one or two.[14] In the former case, continues Boethius, repetition creates plurality, but in the latter no plurality results, as when we say "one sword, one brand, one blade."[15] The latter, of course, illustrates the only type of number which can be held to apply to the Trinity, for the analogous formula "Father, Son, Holy Spirit" constitutes the reiteration of one thing rather than the enumeration of a plurality.[16] Boethius's conclusion is not the obvious Platonic one, which may well go some way toward explaining the departures from his text made by the author of the commentary; for here we read not only that number is twofold: (1) that by which we count, and (2) that which occurs in countable objects,[17] but also that the former is constituted by the "repetition of the same unit" (*unitatis eiusdem repeticio*) while the latter represents the "countable reckoning of different things or rather the addition of units" (*rerum est discretarum numerosa conputatio siue mauis dicere unitatum aggregatio*).[18]

This is quite contrary to Boethius, whose own discussion went on to stress that it was a number of type (2) which involved the repetition of the same unit, and not of type (1) as the commentary argues.[19] Two further assumptions have evidently crept into the argument. In the first place, Boethius's type (2) appears to have been taken generally according to its definition—that "which occurs in countable objects"—rather than according to Boethius's actual example—"one sword, one brand, one blade" (which is not the most obvious illustration of the definition)—so that the commentator perhaps justifiably expands upon it by saying that it is exemplified in the normal arithmetical process of addition. Obviously in this case the repetition of units *does* generate a plurality, and so the commentator has to find a new place in the classification for that repetition of units which involves no multiplication.

This leads to the commentator's second assumption, namely that Boethius's type (1) can be interpreted as performing just such a role, in other words that the number by which we count can—contrary to Boethius's own opinion—be held to consist of units which, when repeated, generate no plurality.[20] There is one obvious reason why Boethius's cryptically concise text

[14]*De Trin.* 3.13–18.
[15]*De Trin.* 3.19–28.
[16]*De Trin.* 3.29–40.
[17]*Comm.* 3.4 (90.26–27).
[18]*Comm.* 3.4 (90.28–36).
[19]For a Platonist it is normally the *abstract* (as exemplified in number by which we count) which is held to be incapable of multiplication, and not the *concrete* (as in the case of number which occurs in countable objects). The commentator is therefore reinstating normal Platonism as found in the writings of Augustine. See, for example, Augustine, *De Genesi ad litteram* 4.7 (13), PL 34.301. Possibly a slight complication was created in Boethius's mind by his recollection of the (non-Platonic) treatment of number in Aristotle's *Physics*.
[20]The same exegetical problems are reflected in the other extant 12th-c. commentaries on *De Trinitate*. Thus the "Lectures" of BN lat 14489 attempt to resolve some of the ambiguities by distinguishing *three* types of number (Häring [n. 7 above] *Lectiones* 3.5–7 [178.44–179.62]). However, despite the relative clarification which this produces, the fact still remains that Boethius's original argument has been turned upside-down.

should have given rise to a doctrine taking up a standpoint opposite to that of the original argument: elsewhere the commentary sets forth an arithmetical interpretation of the Trinity according to which the Father is represented by unity, the Son by "equality of unity" (*equalitas unitatis*), and the Holy Spirit by the "connection" (*conexio*) between the two.[21] This arithmetical interpretation accounts for the Trinity of the Persons while safeguarding the unity of the Godhead because, as the commentator argues, "unity multiplied by itself generates equality, since 1 X 1 = 1" (*unitas ergo ex se per semel equalitatem gignit. Unitas enim semel unitas est*).[22] Obviously the theory provides an example of the way in which the repetition—in the specific sense of a multiplication—of a unity by which we count does not produce a plurality, and it is tempting to ask whether the Boethian text had to be reinterpreted to make room for such a theory or whether the genesis of the theory itself owed something to this reading of Boethius's text.[23]

In the fourth chapter of the commentary the writer again considerably expands the scale of the Boethian discussion, this time as a means of providing background to the notion that the ten Aristotelian categories change their meaning when applied to God.[24] The remainder of the chapter, however, resumes commentary on a more modest scale and discusses in a relatively uncontroversial way various Boethian arguments, namely that when the notion of substance is applied to God it really signifies a substance which is "beyond substance" (*ultra substantiam*);[25] that the categories of substance, quantity, and quality are, when used in theology, predicated in such a way that they become actually identical with the subject of predication;[26] that the categories of place, time, condition, and activity are all predicated externally of God;[27] and finally that the notions of situation and passivity are inappropriate for use in the science of theology altogether.[28] The fifth chapter concentrates on the way in which the category of relation plays a role in Trinitarian doctrine, and the sixth is for Boethius and commentator alike a brief review of the results achieved in the whole treatise.

---

[21] *Comm.* 2.30–35 (77.92–79.46).

[22] *Comm.* 2.30 (78.96–97).

[23] This same Trinitarian doctrine is repeated or alluded to in a number of other philosophical works produced in the Charttrian milieu. Apart from the various commentaries on the *De Trinitate*, it is found in the *De sex dierum operibus* of Thierry of Chartres (in incomplete form), the *De septem septenis* formerly attributed to John of Salisbury, and the *Regulae* of Alan of Lille. See Jansen (n. 6 above) 119–24, Parent (n. 6 above) 76–79, Nikolaus M. Häring, "The Creation and Creator of the World according to Thierry of Chartres and Clarenbaldus of Arras," AHDLMA 22 (1955) 157–64, and Edouard Jeauneau, "Mathématiques et Trinité chez Thierry de Chartres," *Miscellanea mediaevalia* 2 (1963) 289–95. A number of sources have been suggested for the doctrine since Jansen's time, and most favored have been the Augustinian texts *De quantitate animae*, PL 32.1043–44, *De ordine* 2.18, PL 32.1017, and *De doctrina christiana* 1.5, PL 34.21.

[24] *Comm.* 4.13–23 (99.28–102.37), to Boeth. *De Trin.* 4.1–9.

[25] *Comm.* 4.24 (102.38–54), to Boeth. *De Trin.* 4.9–16.

[26] *Comm.* 4.26–34 (102.55–105.41), to Boeth. *De Trin.* 4.16–44.

[27] *Comm.* 4.35–45 (105.42–107.30), to Boeth. *De Trin.* 4.44–77.

[28] *Comm.* 4.46–51 (108.31–109.79), to Boeth. *De Trin.* 4.78–98. Certain minor deviations from the Boethian text found in this discussion of the categories, e.g. the notion that the category

NEOPLATONIC ELABORATIONS OF THE TEXT

So much for the Boethian framework of the commentary. The additions made by the twelfth-century writer to the various Boethian formulae and arguments are of comparatively minor philosophical significance, and we might well be pardoned for spending no more time on the text were it not for the two chapters (the second and the fourth) which contain very important digressions where the original Boethian context seems to have been temporarily forgotten. In neither of these are we given much information about the sources of the elaborations—in the second there are only some passing references to Pythagoras, Plato, and Aristotle,[29] while the fourth, although listing as authorities the Fourth Gospel, "quod quidem in *Trimegistro* Mercurius asserit," Boethius on spirit, and Augustine on the six days,[30] provides little explanation of how these sources come together to produce the finished doctrine—and so we might feel justified in attributing the philosophical ideas in these digressions entirely to the commentator. However, I believe that most of the doctrine is at least partially dependent upon two earlier sources with which he was clearly very familiar: Calcidius, who is not mentioned by name anywhere in the commentary, and the Hermetic *Asclepius*, which is cited but not for the doctrine really central to the argument.

The earlier of the two digressions[31] begins with a brief treatment of some side issues which are perhaps most significant because they reveal the first influence of Calcidius's *Commentary on the Timaeus* clearly identifiable in the present text: the relationship between potency and act;[32] the existence of two distinct methods of philosophical argument: "resolution" (*resolutio*), leading to a knowledge of matter, and "composition" (*conpositio*), leading to a knowledge of God;[33] the relationship between Platonic and Aristotelian views of matter;[34] and the fourfold structure of reality, consisting of "act without possibility" (*actus sine possibilitate*), forms, "actual things" (*actualia*), and matter.[35] This should alert us to the possibility of a similar background for the arguments dealing with the Trinity to which the commentator now proceeds.

Initially, the nature of the Trinity is explored by using the mathematical method characteristic of Thierry of Chartres, which owes something to Augustine[36] and perhaps also—as I have argued above—to Boethius. All this

---

of relation is "partly in substance . . . partly outside substance" (*partim in substantia . . . partim extra substantiam*) at *Comm.* 4.16 (99.53–55), can be explained by the influence of a source in addition to Boethius, namely the *De categoriis decem* believed by 12th-c. writers to be a work of Augustine (see *Aristoteles latinus* 1.1–5, ed. Lorenzo Minio-Paluello [Bruges 1961] 129–75).

[29]For Pythagoras, see *Comm.* 2.28 (77.78–79), for Plato, *Comm.* 2.22 (75.22), 2.27 (76.62), and 2.28 (77.76); for Aristotle, *Comm.* 2.27, 29 (77.67, 85).

[30]For St John, see *Comm.* 4.8 (97.81); for "Mercurius," *Comm.* 4.8 (97.89); for Boethius, *Comm.* 4.9 (98.93); and for Augustine, *Comm.* 4.11 (98.12).

[31]*Comm.* 2.18–49 (74.89–84.88).

[32]*Comm.* 2.19–23 (74.96–75.28).

[33]*Comm.* 2.23–26 (75.29–76.61).

[34]*Comm.* 2.27 (76.62–77.69).

[35]*Comm.* 2.28–29 (77.70–91).

[36]See n. 23 above.

concerns the "holy and highest Trinity" (*sancta et summa Trinitas*). The more striking elaborations in this section, however, come in the next passage, which speaks of "a certain trinity of perpetual things" (*quedam perpetuorum trinitas*) descending from the higher Trinity.[37] This turns out to be a kind of reflection of the highest Trinity in the created world, where the unity of the Father is represented by matter, the equality of the Son by the forms, and the connection of the Holy Spirit by a created spirit operating as the force responsible for the combination of matter and form.[38] The function of the created spirit falls slightly into the background now, and the writer proceeds to explore the nature first of form and then of matter.

Rightly, then, the forms of all things are said to emanate from that simple divine Form, since beside that divine Form each thing has its own equality of being. Just as the divine Form is the equality of being and even the completeness and perfection of all things, so also, in order that there might be a descent to an exemplar, "humanity" is a specific equality and the completeness of being a man. Therefore, humanity is a certain image of form, while that divine Form is the true one.[39]

This argument contains two striking notions which cannot exactly be paralleled in earlier medieval Platonism: first the idea that a single divine Form gives rise by an emanation[40] to the forms of created things traditionally postulated by Platonic philosophy, and secondly the notion that this plurality of emanating forms is one not of real forms but of images.

---

[37]*Comm.* 2.39–40 (80.82–81.99). The notion of two trinities, one of which "descends" (*descendit*) from the other, occurs also in the anonymous *De septem septenis*, PL 199.961C, and in virtually identical wording. The doctrine functions to safeguard the distinction between divine transcendence and the mere reflection of the divinity in the created world. In the context of our *De Trinitate* commentary, the care with which this distinction is established is striking, since in many writings of the period the status of the Trinity is left ambivalent. In particular, the Son is frequently treated as equivalent to a formal cause and (more notoriously) the Holy Spirit as coextensive with a world spirit or soul. On the whole problem see Tullio Gregory, *Anima mundi: La filosofia di Guglielmo di Conches e la Scuola di Chartres* (Florence 1955) 133–54. Whether the distinction between the two trinities is a cogent defense against the theological criticism such a doctrine elicited depends upon the status of the "descent" linking the two groups of terms. On this question see n. 40 below.

[38]The notion of a "connection" (*conexio*) appears to go back to two sources: the Hermetic *Asclepius*, in *Corpus Hermeticum*, ed. Arthur D. Nock, trans. André-Jean Festugière (4 vols. Paris 1945–54) 2.319.12–320.1, and Macrobius, *In Somnium Scipionis* 1.14.15, ed. James A. Willis (2nd ed. Leipzig 1970) 58. Both refer to the concept of a continuity of natural forms as the philosophical expression of Homer's "golden chain."

[39]*Comm.* 2.41 (81.1–7): "Merito ergo ab illa simplici forma diuina rerum omnium forme emanare dicuntur quia iuxta formam illam diuinam unaqueque res suam habet essendi equalitatem. Sicut enim forma diuina equalitas essendi est sicut etiam integritas et perfectio omnium rerum ita quoque, ut ad exemplum descensus fiat, humanitas equalitas quedam et integritas essendi hominem est. Quare humanitas imago quedam forme est. Illa uero diuina uere forma est."

[40]The notion of "emanation" (*emanare*) is quite explicit and apparently performs the same philosophical function as the "descent" (*descensus*) mentioned a few lines further on. Emanation represents the dynamic relationship between cause and effect in both the pagan and the Christian Neoplatonic traditions, although it naturally becomes more problematic in the latter on account of its connotations of causal automatism. The notion continues to be common in 12th-c. Platonism, and in our commentary it is represented by the occurrence of the following terminology: (1) *defluere* ("flow down"): *Comm.* 2.63, 64 (88.5–6, 9–10) (forms–images); (2) *descendere* ("des-

Regarding the former point, one should recall that, although Boethius had described God as Form, in accordance with orthodox Aristotelian principles, he had not specified his relationship to the plurality of forms in Platonism.[41] The notion that there is an emanation linking the supreme Form with the others is therefore an addition by the commentator, and it is interesting to speculate how he arrived at this conclusion. The answer can be found, I believe, by examining carefully some texts of that Latin Platonic writer whose influence began to show itself earlier, for in Calcidius we read that the first cause is an ineffable God who gives rise to a second principle called "Providence," "Mind," or "Nous" equivalent to the world of forms.[42] Calcidius's account of the causal process is very sketchy—he mentions merely that the second principle draws off goodness from the first and engages in a tireless reversion upon it—but no doubt the scheme was sufficiently reinforced

---

cend"): *Comm.* 2.28 (77.73–74), 2.41 (81.4–5) (God–forms); 4.24, 25 (102.41–42, 53–54) (God–substance); 2.28 (77.77–78, 81–82) (God–matter); 2.39 (80.82–83) (higher–lower trinities); 2.39, 43 (81.86–87, 89–90, 82.21–22) (unity–otherness); 2.40 (81.93) (unity–matter); 2.36 (79.49–50) (equality–inequality); (3) *emanare* ("emanate"): *Comm.* 2.41 (81.1–2) (God–forms). In addition to these, the pair *manere-provenire* ("remain–proceed") at *Comm.* 2.55 (85.30–36) (God–forms) represents the two inseparable moments of an effect's identity and difference in relation to its cause, standard in the Neoplatonic tradition. Finally, *relabi* ("flow back") at *Comm.* 2.44 (82.25–27) and 2.66 (88.27–29) (forms–God) signifies the reverse process in which the emanated plurality is reabsorbed into the unity. Among these terms (1) is a Boethian usage and apparently occurs only as part of the exegesis of *De Trin.* 2.48–53, although the actual terminology comes not from this text but from Boethius, *De hebdomadibus* (= *Quomodo substantiae* in Stewart-Rand ed. [n. 11 above]) lines 98, 120, 133, and 159 (see Lane Cooper, *A Concordance of Boethius* [Cambridge Mass. 1928]). The expressions *manere-provenire* are more problematic and seem superficially to recall Eriugena's habitual rendering of μένειν–προϊέναι in his translation of Pseudo-Dionysius. Although one could not categorically exclude such influence, a more likely source—in view of the extensive Calcidian influence to be discussed below—is probably Calcidius, *In Timaeum*, ed. Jan H. Waszink, Plato latinus 4 (Leiden and London 1962) 329 (323.11–16). Parallels for the use of terminology (1) and (2) and for *relabi* in other 12th-c. commentaries on the *De Trinitate* are listed in the index to Häring's edition.

[41]*De Trin.* 2.29–31. Boethius probably understood the relationship between the divine Form and the other forms along the lines of contemporary Athenian Neoplatonism, where God (treated provisionally as Intellect) could be termed "Form of forms" (εἶδος εἰδῶν). As in the twelfth-century theory, the supreme Form gives rise by emanation to the others, but in contrast to the later theory, the various forms are not dependent upon matter for their ontological distinction.

[42]Calc. *In Tim.* 176 (n. 40 above, 204.5–205.3): "First, all things that exist and the world itself are sustained and administered principally by the highest God, who is the supreme Good beyond all substance and all nature. He is superior to thinking and intelligence, and is sought by all things, while he is himself filled with perfection and dependent upon no relationship to another. . . . Next, [all things are ruled by] Providence, who holds the second position after that supreme God and is called 'Nous' by the Greeks. She is an intelligible being with a goodness derived from her tireless reversion upon the supreme God. And she draws off goodness from this source, by which she is as much adorned as those other things that are rendered good by the source itself." ("Principio cuncta quae sunt et ipsum mundum contineri regique principaliter quidem a summo deo, qui est summum bonum ultra omnem substantiam omnemque naturam, aestimatione intellectuque melior, quem cuncta expetunt, cum ipse sit plenae perfectionis et nullius societatis indiguus. . . . Deinde a prouidentia, quae est post illum summum secundae eminentiae, quem noyn Graeci uocant; est autem intelligibilis essentia aemulae bonitatis propter indefessam ad summum deum conuersionem, estque ei ex illo bonitatis haustus, quo tam ipsa ornatur quam cetera quae ipso auctore honestantur.") For the identification of Providence or Mind with the totality of forms see *In Tim.* 188 (212.21–213.6), 273 (278.4–7), 304 (305.21–306.7), and 339 (332.5–14).

by other texts.[43] Thus, the twelfth-century writer has a reasonably clear picture of the process by which the One or Good produces the second hypostasis or Intellect in Neoplatonic thought. He integrates it into his own system by combining two somewhat contradictory notions: (1) of a God equivalent to Form, a doctrine in which Boethius followed Alexandrian Neoplatonism of the fifth century in expounding a cautious theology in Aristotelian terms, and (2) of a God who transcends form but gives rise by an emanation to a second form-giving principle, a notion characteristic of Plotinian and Porphyrian Neoplatonism.[44] The commentator's response to the conflict in his sources is his own unique doctrine that God as a single Form produces by emanation a multiplicity of forms.

The second unusual feature of the argument was the notion that the emanating plurality of forms does not consist of real forms at all but only of

[43]Cf. Macr. *In Somn. Scip.* 1.14.6–7 (n. 38 above) 56: "God, who both is and is called the first cause, is the single principle and origin of all things which are and seem to be. He created Mind from himself with the superabundant fertility of his majesty. This mind, which is called 'Nous,' preserves the complete likeness of its source inasmuch as it looks upon its father. But when it looks toward lower things it creates from itself Soul." ("Deus qui prima causa et est et vocatur, unus omnium quaeque sunt quaeque videntur esse princeps et origo est. hic superabundanti maiestatis fecunditate de se mentem creavit. haec mens, quae voῦς vocatur, qua patrem inspicit, plenam similitudinem servat auctoris, animam vero de se creat posteriora respiciens.") This passage contains two points of interest: (1) It provides more detail regarding the actual process of causation than the Calcidian passages quoted above, e.g. the first hypostasis causes the second through its outpouring fertility, the second hypostasis is engaged in a continuous act of contemplation, etc. (2) It deviates in its description of the second hypostasis from the Plotinian text—*Enneades*, ed. Paul Henry and Hans-Rudolf Schwyzer (Paris 1951–73) 5.2.1.1–22—upon which it is based (as noted by Paul Henry, *Plotin et l'Occident: Firmicus Maternus, Marius Victorinus, saint Augustin et Macrobe* [Louvain 1934] 188), since Macrobius specifies that Intellect creates Soul by turning away from the One. Plotinus speaks thus of Soul's productivity but not normally of Intellect's, for the latter gives rise to its consequent by turning *toward* the One. Macrobius, in short, introduces into the creation of Soul an ethically negative element quite absent from the original, and in that way possibly limits the usefulness of the whole scheme for Christian Platonists such as the 12th-c. Chartrians. It is interesting to observe in this connection that there is no full account of the mechanism of the pure pagan Neoplatonic emanative system available to the Latin West prior to the translations of Avicenna and the *Liber de causis*. In both Augustine and the Pseudo-Dionysian (Eriugenian) tradition, the original process is already transformed radically to fit in with a primarily Christian view of creation. Other important texts dealing with the Neoplatonic hypostases are Macr. *In Somn. Scip.* (n. 38 above) 1.2.13–15, 1.6.8–9, 1.17.12–13, and Boethius's hymn *O qui perpetua* at *De consolatione Philosophiae* 3.IX, ed. Ludwig Bieler, CCL 94 (1957) 51.

[44]The connection between the problem of the unity or multiplicity of form and Calcidius is made abundantly clear in two other passages from Chartrian commentaries on the *De Trinitate*. Thus in the "Lectures" 2.66 (Häring [n. 7 above] 176.48–50) we read: "Plato says in the *Parmenides*, according to Calcidius, that there is one archetype of all things and a plurality of archetypes." ("Plato dicit in *Parmenide* Calcidio testante quod unum est exemplar omnium rerum et plura exemplaria.") Even more explicit is the remark in the "Glosses" 2.35 (Häring [n. 7 above] 276.34–37): "And this is why Plato declares in the *Parmenides* that all forms inasmuch as they are form and have no distinction from one another are the Form of forms. They are not a plurality of forms but one Form which, because it is not joined to any mutability, cannot become materiate." ("Inde est quod Plato in *Parmenide* ait quod omnes forme in eo quod sunt forma et sine discretione sunt forma formarum. Nec sunt plures forme sed una forma que quia mutabilitate adiuncta non est inmateriari non potest.") This statement goes beyond the Calcidian passage (*In Tim.* 272 [n. 40 above, 276.15–277.3]) under discussion and already presupposes the argument of synthesis worked out in our commentary.

their images. This departure from tradition can, I suspect, likewise be explained as an attempted rapprochement between the official object of commentary and unstated doctrines, for the later writer is clearly aware of Boethius's argument that pure forms cannot function as substrates but only those which reside in bodies, the latter being more correctly termed "images."[45] Boethius's intention was simply to distinguish the transcendent forms from the immanent forms dependent upon them by saying that the latter alone function as substrates, but the commentator alters this position radically by contending that all forms other than the single divine Form itself are images. The origin of this change of position also seems to be Calcidius, who had developed a theory according to which pure forms function as substrates owing to their presence in a certain intelligible if not sensible matter.[46] Thus, Calcidius argues that the ultimate elements in the universe are matter and form, and that from these, intelligible fire and the other pure substances are composed. He goes on to state, as we might already have expected from his reference to *intelligible* fire, that these substances are not the physical elements of the universe but forms prior to them upon which they depend. The argument must have been puzzling to a twelfth-century writer who had no text available to him containing an account of the pagan Neoplatonists' doctrine of intelligible matter,[47] and so he once more attempts a reconciliation between two contradictory notions: (1) that forms functioning as substrates can only be those residing in bodies, a notion which Boethius would defend when arguing in an Aristotelian context, and (2) that intelligible forms can function as substrates, a doctrine characteristic of Plotinus and his followers.[48] In fact, the commentator has no alternative, in the face of a

---

[45]Boeth. *De Trin.* 2.42–46. The argument is that if a form, e.g. "humanity," becomes a substrate for accidents it does not receive them "because of its essence" (*eo quod ipsa est*), but "because of the matter which is its substrate" (*eo quod materia ei subiecta est*). We might expect Boethius to continue by arguing that no form can be a substrate, but in fact he admits that one type can be: those which are more correctly termed "images" (*imagines*) in matter.

[46]Calc. *In Tim.* 272 (n. 40 above, 276.10–15): "The first element of the universe is unformed and unqualified matter, which, so that there might be a world, is molded by the intelligible form. From these two—matter and form—pure and intelligible fire and the other of the four genuine substances [arise], and from these in turn our sensible varieties of matter: the fiery, the watery, the earthy, and the airy. But the pure fire and the other genuine and intelligible forms of substance are the archetypes of corporeal things which are known as 'ideas'." ("Quippe primum elementum uniuersae rei silua est informis ac sine qualitate quam, ut sit mundus, format intellegibilis species; ex quibus, silua uidelicet et specie, ignis purus et intellegibilis ceteraeque sincerae substantiae quattuor, e quibus demum hae materiae sensiles, igneae aquatiles terrenae et aereae. Ignis porro purus et ceterae sincerae intellegibilesque substantiae species sunt exemplaria corporum, ideae cognominatae.") The actual expression "intelligible matter" (*intellegibilis silua*) does not occur in the passage above but elsewhere, at *In Tim.* 278 (283.8–11).

[47]As elaborated by Plotinus at *Enn.* (n. 43 above) 2.4. Calcidius's argument is quoted as part of a longer passage by Tullio Gregory, *Platonismo medievale* (Rome 1958) 118, who, however, draws no attention to the status of the intelligible matter.

[48]That the background to this argument is the said Calcidian passage is confirmed by the fact that the discussion of the unity of form (see n. 44 above) follows on immediately in Calcidius's text from the discussion of the four pure substances. Clearly this whole section in Calcidius lies behind the twelfth-century commentator's own doctrine of matter and form.

contradiction between two such eminent authorities, to the abolition of the distinction between transcendent and immanent forms itself.

This concludes the study of form. The argument continues with a discussion of the second aspect of the trinity of perpetual things or the matter.

Let us assume as a hypothesis—it is in fact impossible—that matter does not exist. The forms of all things, as I would stoutly maintain, will return to a single Form. There will only be one simple Form, the divine Form which is the only true one. Thus, there is no plurality in matter insofar as it is matter. Nor is there any plurality in form insofar as it is form. Plurality arises from the conjunction of the two, that is to say, form and matter.[49]

This argument is also without parallel in earlier medieval Platonic texts and provides certain useful clarifications of the previous discussion of form. In the first place, we can now understand more easily the contrast between the single divine Form and the plurality of forms dependent upon it: the divine Form alone is totally independent of matter, while all the others depend to some degree upon the presence of individuals which embody them. There are no *forms* (plural) without matter. Second, the argument clarifies the question of the relationship between transcendent and immanent forms, for henceforth all forms except the single divine Form are simultaneously transcendent and immanent. They retain the paradigmatic role of the transcendent forms, yet technically all forms except the first are images and partially dependent upon matter.[50]

When we come to consider the sources of this doctrine, our path seems to lead once more to Calcidius, with the difference that here the problem does

[49]*Comm.* 2.44 (82.25–31): "Ponamus enim per ipothesin materiam non esse—quod tamen fieri non potest—ad unam, ut uerum fatear, formam omnes rerum omnium forme relabentur. Nec erit nisi una et simplex forma: diuina scilicet que una uere forma est. Non igitur in materia quantum in se est ulla est pluralitas: nec in forma quantum in se est. Pluralitas tamen ex coniunctione utriusque prouenit: forme uidelicet et materie."

[50]It must be admitted that the doctrine expressed in this passage is not adhered to absolutely during the remainder of the text, since at *Comm.* 2.64 (88.8–17) the writer distinguishes two levels of forms: (1) "those in the divine mind" (*que in mente diuina sunt*), which truly deserve the appellation "forms," and (2) "those which inform matter and produce bodies" (*iste que materiam informant et corpora efficiunt*). The latter are said to flow down from the former. In this passage we find a return to the more conventional view of the theory of forms—a plurality of entirely transcendent forms is affirmed—presumably necessitated by the specific Boethian text (*De Trin.* 2.51–56) under discussion at this point. A hesitation between these two versions of the theory characterizes much Chartrian philosophy and results not only from the conflict of authorities discussed above but also from the long-standing philosophical problem of explaining how the forms can be eternal and yet still causally dependent upon (and therefore ontologically inferior to) God. This last aspect of the doctrine is brought out in John of Salisbury's well-known account of the teaching of Bernard of Chartres (*Metalogicon* 4.35, ed. Clement C. J. Webb [Oxford 1929] 204–07), where three principles are postulated: God, forms, matter. The forms are eternal but not coeternal with God. Incidentally, this report suggests that Bernard taught the theory of forms in its Boethian rather than Boethian-Calcidian interpretation (as in our commentary), i.e., he stipulated a plurality of transcendent forms from which the images in matter descended by emanation. It is therefore premature on the basis of this text to argue, with Garin (n. 6 above) 52, from the *duplex opus diuine mentis* to a "doppia funzione delle idee." The latter phrase might fairly characterize the doctrine expounded in our commentary, where the forms maintain a deliberately ambivalent status, but John of Salisbury's account does not in itself give us any cause to attribute the same view to Bernard. Quite possibly he was the first to teach the doctrine, but we cannot assume this on the strength of John's report.

not seem to be one of reconciling Calcidius with Boethius—who, if he provided any teaching at all on this question, has not left a doctrine which would be a potential source of conflict—but rather of expanding the Calcidian interpretation of matter in accordance with the Boethian and Calcidian treatment of form set forth earlier in the commentary. The quintessence of Calcidius's teaching on matter is perhaps found in a passage where he distinguishes two phases: before and after it has been endowed with qualities. In the former phase, matter is neither at rest nor in motion, although it has the ability to receive these qualities, while in the latter it assumes the tasks of motion and rest which it performs at different times.[51] Calcidius elaborates Plato's illustration of casting pebbles into water—the surface of the stagnant pool is motionless until an object is thrown into it—but adds one crucially significant corollary: not only, he argues, is the water moved by the pebble cast into it, but the water then itself moves the pebble. It is not difficult to detect the impact of this last illustration upon the twelfth-century writer, for applied in the context of his metaphysical argument it would signify not only that the form is imposed upon the matter by the external cause or God, but that matter in its turn determines the form. Obviously such a theory functions as the perfect complement to the interpretation of form expounded earlier, and a doctrine evolved by a fourth-century Latin writer to reconcile the Aristotelian notion of unformed matter with the Platonic concept of a matter containing disorderly and vestigial qualities becomes in the hands of a later expositor of the Boethian text an ingredient in a revolutionary theory of form.[52]

[51]Calc. *In Tim.* 352 (n. 40 above, 342.15–343.2): "Now, as if with the creator God removed, he [Plato] looks at matter alone and in itself from a twofold viewpoint: first, as not yet subject to qualities, and secondly after the acquisition of qualities. Before the coming together of the qualities it was, I think, neither at rest nor in motion, although there was in it a certain natural tendency to the reception of motion or rest. But after the coming together of the qualities, having been adorned and made a complete body by God, it undertook the duties of motion and rest which it might discharge at different times." ("Nunc iam ueluti separato opifice deo solam per semet ipsam siluam intuetur duplici consideratione, una nondum susceptis qualitatibus, altera post qualitates. Et ante consortium quidem qualitatum neque stabat, opinor, neque mouebatur, erat tamen quaedam in ea naturalis opportunitas ad motus stationisque perceptionem; post qualitatum porro consortium exornata et perfectum corpus a deo facta motus stationisque sumpsit officia, quibus diuersis temporibus uteretur.") The argument is a very neat piece of Platonic and Aristotelian syncretism, as can be shown by comparing *In Tim.* 283 (286.1–287.6), 301 (302.17–303.8), and 344–53 (336.4–344.17).

[52]Most importantly it heralds a change in the theory of universals, for, since the immanent form functions as a particular, it will henceforth be true not only that universals determine particulars but also that particulars determine universals reciprocally. There is only one earlier thinker in the Middle Ages in whom this radical modification of the orthodox Platonic theory is also evident, namely Eriugena. Historically the whole concept probably has its origins in Plotinus, e.g. at *Enn.* (n. 43 above) 2.9.3, where it is argued that each hypostasis would not achieve its true nature if a lower one were not produced after it. Thence the doctrine appears to have influenced the anthropology of Gregory of Nyssa and become elevated by combination with the Chalcedonian Christology into a general cosmological principle in Maximus the Confessor. Eriugena takes it from both Gregory and Maximus, and it becomes one of the primary ingredients in his idealistic philosophy of nature. A similar doctrine now appears in our commentary, and it is no doubt one of the reasons why earlier writers have suspected Eriugenian influence here and in similar Chartrian texts. See M. Jacquin, "L'influence doctrinale de Jean Scot au début du XIIIe siècle," *Revue des sciences philosophiques et théologiques* 4 (1910) 104–05. Of course, such influence cannot be ex-

At this point the commentary develops a further argument to illustrate the peculiar relationship between the unity of form and the unity of matter by examining the genesis and function of a specific transcendent-immanent form, namely "humanity." The writer asks: is the divine Form equivalent to humanity? The reply is that to be "this form" (*forma hec*) requires the presence of matter, but "to be form" (*quod autem forma est*) does not require the presence of matter.[53] Thus the divine Form is equivalent to all the forms in the latter sense but by no means in the former. He then proceeds to demonstrate the point with an interesting argument based on the grammatical use of demonstrative pronouns which seems to be another original contribution; but, since our present concern is only with the knowledge of earlier Platonism enjoyed by a twelfth-century writer, we may perhaps leave the discussion here. The argument continually reaffirms the intrinsic unity of the divine Form which is reflected into multiplicity by things participating in it, just as a single face can be multiplied by reflection in a number of mirrors.[54]

The first digression now ends with a brief examination of a few outstanding issues: for example, how we can arrive at an understanding of matter by "induction" (*inductio*);[55] how the divine Form itself never becomes materiate, since all multiplicity is derived from the mutability of unformed matter;[56] and how the nature of God cannot be subject to accidents.[57] Finally, a brief summary of the results achieved concludes a section throughout which we can once again detect the crucial influence of Calcidius's commentary.

The second of the two digressions in this commentary on the *De Trinitate* is considerably shorter but certainly as interesting for the way it reveals the author's intimate knowledge of the earlier Latin Platonic tradition. Before introducing the actual words Boethius used to begin his discussion of the modes in which the ten Aristotelian categories apply to God, the twelfth-century writer makes various prefatory remarks designed to exclude erroneous interpretations of the Trinity. He states that all the categories except relation—here he anticipates the distinction made later in the text by Boethius—apply to the Trinity as a whole;[58] that God is not to be considered wise according to his possession of wisdom, as a man is human according to his possession of

---

cluded and does not even require the actual availability of texts of the *Periphyseon* but merely of Eriugenian-influenced scholia to the works of Pseudo-Dionysius. However, if my own arguments above are valid, one of the main points of similarity between the Chartrians and Eriugena can be explained adequately in terms of the reconciliation of Boethius and Calcidius, two writers whose influence at Chartres has never been in dispute. Naturally, such developments in our commentary and similar works would have helped to create an intellectual climate in which Eriugena's works could be revived and read with a new understanding and sympathy. This seems to be precisely what happened toward the end of the twelfth century.

[53]*Comm.* 2.46 (82.45–83.69).
[54]*Comm.* 2.48 (83.70–74).
[55]*Comm.* 2.50–53 (84.89–85.19).
[56]*Comm.* 2.54–59 (85.20–87.72).
[57]*Comm.* 2.60 (87.73–80).
[58]*Comm.* 4.1 (95.10–12).

humanity, since God is rather equivalent to Wisdom itself;[59] and that the Father and Son are conceived as males not only because the male sex is worthier and God must receive the most worthy appellation but also because maleness is attributed to the odd number, and the odd number, since it is not divisible into equal parts, reflects the undivided nature of the Trinity.[60] At this point a brief anticipatory list of the ten Aristotelian categories heralds the beginning of the main part of the digression: an account of the five modes in which all things may be understood.

Now that these matters have been concisely and briefly expounded, I think one should add that the totality of things can be considered in five ways, for the totality is in God, it is in the created spirit, in numbers, in matter, and in actuality. This is namely because God is all things, the created spirit all things, nature also all things, matter once again all things, and finally nobody doubts that *actualia* are all things.[61]

In this classification two of the terms used are perhaps slightly ambiguous, although their meaning is clarified by the writer's elaboration of the scheme in the next few paragraphs: that is to say, the numbers or natures and the actualia. The former should probably be understood to signify types of things, and we might translate them as "genera and/or species." The latter clearly correspond to individual created things—the Aristotelian first substances—in which a particular potency has been actualized. We therefore have a fivefold scheme consisting of the totality considered (1) in God, (2) in created spirit, (3) in genera and species, (4) in individuals, and (5) in matter.[62]

What is the origin of this scheme? At least two aspects require specific explanation when one compares the earlier Platonic tradition: the fact that the scheme is a fivefold one, and the uncompromising statements that God is equivalent to his creation.

Turning first to the scheme itself, the most obvious place to look for its source is in the works of the three writers actually mentioned in this passage: Augustine,[63] "in *Trimegistro* Mercurius," and Boethius. It is not difficult to see the parallels between Augustine's cosmological speculations and the argument of our commentary; one has only to think of Augustine's well-known argument that for man and other creatures there are four modes of existence: (1) eternally in the Word of God (where they cannot really be said to be created), (2) in the elements of this world in which everything was created together by God at the beginning of time, (3) in the individual things which come into being each at its proper time in accordance with the causes created

---

[59]*Comm.* 4.2 (95.13–20).

[60]*Comm.* 4.4 (96.34–48).

[61]*Comm.* 4.7 (97.75–80): "Quibus strictim ac breuiter expositis addendum illud estimo quod quinque modis rerum consideratur uniuersitas. Est enim rerum uniuersitas in deo, est in spiritu creato, est in numeris, est in materia, est etiam rerum uniuersitas in actu ita uidelicet quod deus est omnia, spiritus creatus omnia, natura quoque omnia, materia iterum omnia, actualia quoque nemo dubitat esse omnia."

[62]I have arranged the last two classes in what is—aside from the requirements of a specific argument—the natural descending order from God to matter.

[63]*Comm.* 4.11 (98.12–16).

together, and (4) in the seeds of these creatures (which function as a kind of repetition of the primordial causes).[64] If we allow that the seeds in Augustine's scheme perform a role somewhat analogous to that of the genera and species in the twelfth-century work, we can see that four of the five categories are aligned: the eternal reasons in the divine mind with the totality in God, the seeds with the totality in numbers, the individual things with the totality in actuality, and the elements created together with the totality in matter.[65] Only one aspect is missing from the Augustinian scheme—the created spirit—and so we must look for it elsewhere.

The second source cited by the twelfth-century writer with the strange wording "in *Trimegistro* Mercurius"[66] introduces a slight problem because the passage from the Hermetic *Asclepius* here quoted is not in fact crucial for our understanding of the fivefold cosmological scheme. The commentator clearly has in mind, however, the classification of reality into the things in God whence the world has taken its origin, the spirit accompanying matter or in matter, and matter itself, a classification which occurs later in the Hermetic text and which we know to have been influential elsewhere in the writings of the Chartrian philosophers.[67] This passage is obviously of special importance for our present argument, since two elements in the Hermetic cosmology parallel those in the Augustinian scheme, and no doubt the commentator has these correspondences very much before his mind. In the first place, the things in God clearly perform the same role for the Hermetist as Augustine's eternal

[64] Augustine, *De Genesi ad litteram* 6.10 (17), PL 34.346: "But these things are in one manner in the Word of God where they are not made but eternal; in another in the elements of the world where all things that were to be were created together; in another in the things which, according to those causes established together, are now created not together but each at its proper time, as Adam was fashioned from the dust and animated by the divine breath, just as the grass sprang up; and in another in the seeds in which the primordial causes are in a way repeated and which are produced from things arising in accordance with the causes God originally established." ("Sed haec aliter in verbo dei, ubi ista non facta, sed aeterna sunt; aliter in elementis mundi, ubi omnia simul facta futura sunt; aliter in rebus quae secundum causas simul creatas, non iam simul sed quo quaeque tempore creantur, in quibus Adam iam formatus ex limo, et dei flatu animatus, sicut faenum exortum; aliter in seminibus, in quibus rursus quasi primordiales causae repetuntur, de rebus ductae quae secundum causas, quas primum condidit, exstiterunt.")

[65] The other Chartrian commentaries on the *De Trinitate* operate simply with this fourfold scheme. Cf. the "Lectures" 2.9 where we find (1) "absolute necessity" (*absoluta necessitas*), (2) "necessity of combination" (*necessitas conplexionis*), (3) "determinate possibility" (*determinata possibilitas*), and (4) "absolute possibility" (*possibilitas absoluta*) (Häring [n. 7 above] 157.86–91). The repetition of this scheme in the "Little Treatise" of Clarembald of Arras is coupled with a discussion showing how the four classes align with the Augustinian system (Häring, *Clarembald* [n. 9 above] 236.7–14).

[66] *Comm.* 4.8 (97.88–90).

[67] *Asclep.* (n. 38 above) 313.4–7: "And there was God and 'Hyle' which is, I believe, the Greek word for matter. Spirit accompanied matter or was inherent in it, but not in the way that it is present to God nor as those things from which matter arises are present to God." ("Fuit deus et ὕλη, quem Graece credimus mundum, et mundo comitabatur spiritus uel inerat mundo spiritus, sed non similiter ut deo nec deo haec de quibus mundus.") Part of this passage is quoted by Thierry of Chartres in *De sex dierum operibus* 26 (Häring [n. 7 above] 566.32–34), where the notion of spirit is brought into conjunction with the World Soul described in Plato's *Timaeus*. On this combination see n. 37 above.

reasons, and secondly the Hermetic notion of matter is very close, especially on account of its Stoic leanings, to the Augustinian elements created together. What the *Asclepius* provides which is absent from Augustine's scheme is the notion of spirit, and what the Augustinian account supplies which is absent from the Hermetist are the notions of seeds and individuals respectively. The schemes therefore supplement each other and together provide the twelfth-century writer with the five classes constituting his own cosmological scheme.

Of course there is still more, and we must consider the third source cited in our commentary: Boethius. The twelfth-century writer here cites not one of Boethius's theological treatises but the *De consolatione Philosophiae*,[68] and quotes enough of the wording to enable us to identify the original passage with virtual certainty. It is a poem which attacks the Stoic epistemological doctrine that the mind is completely subject to external sensory impressions, and attempts to establish the presence of an *a priori* element by distinguishing a certain force of the mind which awakens inner forms and applies them to the images coming in from the external world.[69] Boethius does not actually employ the word "spirit" here but, since this force of the mind's function coincides precisely with a well-known use of the notion of spirit in the Latin philosophical tradition and undoubtedly known to Boethius and his commentator, we can unhesitatingly supply it at this point.[70] The notion of such a spirit as a psychic force connecting the intelligible forms with the reflections in the sensible world clearly supplements the two earlier cosmological schemes, for the inner forms of Boethius correspond approximately to the Augustinian eternal reasons and the things in God described by the Hermetist. Furthermore, the two notions of spirit in the *Asclepius* and in Boethius's argument could reasonably be held to coincide—although the former represented a life-force while the latter implies more precisely a cognitive aspect of soul, they agree in performing an intermediate function between the sensible and intelligible worlds. Finally the Boethian images are for most purposes equivalent to Augustine's individual things. In other words, Boethius follows the Augustinian scheme with his forms and images but supplements it with the notion of spirit, while he agrees with the Hermetist in postulating forms and

---

[68]*Comm.* 4.9 (98.93–96).

[69]Boeth. *De consol. Philos.* 5.IV.35–40 (n. 43 above) 99: "Then the awakened force of the mind summons those forms which it holds within to similar motions. It relates them to the external stimuli, blending the images with forms concealed within."

> Tum mentis uigor excitus
> Quas intus species tenet
> Ad motus similes uocans
> Notis applicat exteris
> Introrsumque reconditis
> Formis miscet imagines.

[70]Cf. Augustine, *De civitate Dei* 10.9, PL 41.286–87. Etienne Gilson, *The Christian Philosophy of Saint Augustine*, trans. L. E. M. Lynch (New York 1960, London 1961) 269 n. 1 characterizes this as the "Porphyrian meaning" of spirit in contrast to its "Scriptural meaning" in which it corresponds strictly to the soul's rational part.

spirit but adds his images. He therefore completes and connects the two earlier systems. In short, we have no reason to doubt that this combination of sources underlies the twelfth-century writer's fivefold scheme, which can reasonably be viewed as an amalgam of almost all the Platonic cosmological knowledge accessible through Latin sources.[71]

The second aspect of the cosmological scheme which caught our attention was the notion that God is somehow equivalent to his creation. Of course, statements that God is all things, the created spirit all things, nature all things, and so on are held by the commentator to be alternative expressions of the notions that all things are in God, that all things are in the created spirit, and so on. Further, no theological problems are raised by the conversion of most of these statements from the one form to the other. However, to change from the viewpoint that all things are in God (which is Augustine's frequent way of referring to the dependence of all creatures upon their eternal reasons)[72] to that in which God is all things (Augustine would probably condemn this view as a kind of Manichaeism) is to move onto theologically much more dangerous ground. The next paragraph of the text reveals that the source of this radical position is once more the *Asclepius*, where one may read the unequivocal statement that God is all things.[73] It is interesting to speculate how the author of the commentary could justify the use of a text teaching such a doctrine.

This question can, I believe, be answered in two ways. In the first place, the integration of the Hermetic doctrine into the Augustinian and Boethian framework helps to safeguard it from misinterpretation, for one has only to align the respective cosmological schemes to see that all things are causally dependent upon God, since their appropriate reasons are contained in the divine mind. In other words, read in the context of the other authorities—and no doubt this was why the writer establishes the context of these other authorities so carefully at this point, as he does nowhere else in the text—the Hermetic statement is acceptable. Second, one must always be sensitive to the belief common among Chartrian writers that truth is approachable from a

---

[71]It may be useful to add a table showing the approximate interrelation of the three cosmological schemes discussed above:

AUGUSTINE	"ASCLEPIUS"	BOETHIUS
1. things in the Word of God (= "eternal reasons")	things from which the world arises	forms within
2. ———	spirit	force of the mind
3. seeds	———	———
4. things created according to the causes established together	———	images
5. things in the elements (= "seminal reasons")	world	———

[72]See n. 64 above.
[73]*Asclep.* (n. 38 above) 298.1–2.

number of perspectives each of which illuminates the others although none is completely self-contained. A model for this approach in a cosmological context can be found in Calcidius, where it is suggested that form is an intelligible thing from our point of view, a thought or idea from God's, a measure of bodily things from the point of view of matter, and so on.[74] None of these viewpoints is more correct than any of the others, but each reflects a different aspect of a dynamic truth. The doctrine is moreover not peculiar to Calcidius, but an essential ingredient in the Neoplatonic tradition as a whole, and it finds a special expression in the twelfth-century use of "integuments" (*integumenta*).[75]

Having said something of the origins and nature of the fivefold scheme, we should return briefly to the text and see how the commentator expands and clarifies his analysis. He begins by supporting the idea that God is all things with an argument which appeals to Scripture and rejects in advance possible pantheistic misinterpretations: God is everything, but he is not, of course, a stone or a block of wood.[76] Next, he elaborates upon the notion that the created spirit is all things because it contains both the forms and the images of all things: not simply the images of things as some might argue.[77] At this point we are cautioned that the subject of the variability of predication is too complex to be pursued further in the present context,[78] and it looks as though the writer were going to break off his account having discussed only two of the five classes in his cosmological scheme. Fortunately, however, it becomes clear that the highly compressed remarks in the next paragraph offer a complete survey of the other three classes. All we need to know for the present, he says, is that predications vary according to different views of the totality because words relate both to various natures and to the "motion of reason" (*rationis motus*); and that words signify both common and individual natures like "man" and "Plato," and both natures and potencies like "living creature" and "egg".[79] Clearly this passage gives us illustrations of all the remaining types, since man signifies the species, Plato and the creature which has emerged from the egg are individuals, and the egg represents the potency or material substratum. Finally, the commentator concludes his argument by comparing Augustine's exegesis of *Genesis*—here we find the necessary support of authority—where the statement "in the beginning God created heaven and earth" signifies one thing alone: the totality contained within matter.

It remains for the author simply to make a transition back to the Boethian text. This he achieves by briefly summarizing his purpose in constructing the

[74]Calc. *In Tim.* (n. 40 above) 339 (332.5–14).
[75]See Edouard Jeauneau, "L'usage de la notion d'*integumentum* à travers les gloses de Guillaume de Conches," AHDLMA 24 (1957) 35–100 (= *Lectio* 127–92).
[76]*Comm.* 4.8 (97.81–90).
[77]*Comm.* 4.9 (97.91–98.96).
[78]*Comm.* 4.10 (98.97–98.3).
[79]*Comm.* 4.10–11 (98.4–11).

rather complicated foregoing argument as a preamble to Boethius's account of
the categories. It was to demonstrate the variability of predication which one
must grasp before applying categories such as quantity (in saying that God is
"great") or quality (in saying that he is "just") to the Creator.[80] All these
terms change their meaning, and what is predicated accidentally of things
must be understood substantially of God. It is easy enough to go along with
the twelfth-century writer in seeing the logical connection between the doctrines of the digression and of Boethius's main argument, but it is also apparent that the climate of thought in the pages which follow will be very different
from that in the earlier pages.

THE "LIBRUM HUNC" AND MEDIEVAL PLATONISM

We are now in a position to make some general observations about the
Platonism of this twelfth-century commentary. Our primary conclusion must
be that the writer utilizes Platonic material to a much greater extent than his
actual citation of sources by name would suggest. The use of Plato himself—
made through the translation of Calcidius—is not particularly significant, and
so it is with the employment of doctrines derived from later Platonists that we
are mainly concerned. Those cited by name are Boethius, Augustine—here we
must also include the pseudo-Augustinian work on the categories—and "Mercurius," while the uncited ones are represented by Calcidius and possibly
Macrobius.[81] Perhaps the most significant fact of all regarding the range of
Platonic sources is the extent of the writer's use of Calcidius's *Commentary on
the Timaeus*, for it supplies important aspects not only of the doctrine of matter—this has always been well-known—but also of that regarding form.

Our investigation has also revealed interesting facts about the relationship
between the different types of Platonism accessible to this twelfth-century
writer. Of particular importance is the conflict between Boethian and Calcidian Platonisms. It may now be instructive to summarize the doctrinal tensions
to which the commentator, laboring to reconcile his various Platonic sources, is
clearly subject.

The sources used most frequently can be classified into roughly three
types, depending upon their historical point of origin. The first represents the
"Middle Platonic" stage in the history of philosophy, during which the belief
that the transcendent or Platonic forms are equivalent to thoughts contained
within the Intellect of God is considered to be fundamental. It is expressed,
together with doctrines of different origins, in the Hermetic text.[82] The second
type of Platonism to which the twelfth-century writer has access consists of the

---

[80]*Comm.* 4.12 (98.17–99.27).

[81]Martianus Capella may also have influenced the speculation about numbers in our commentary, although it is difficult to isolate any specific points.

[82]It is also clear that Calcidius was very much influenced by Middle Platonic material, and
some scholars have been led by the presence of such doctrine to deny the Plotinian or Porphyrian
influence. A recent supporter of this viewpoint has been John M. Dillon, *The Middle Platonists: A
Study of Platonism, 80 B. C. to A. D. 220* (London 1977) 360–64. But a combination of influ-

Neoplatonism of Plotinus and Porphyry, characterized principally by its assigning the primary place in the universe to an ineffable One which generates by emanation a second hypostasis consisting of a self-reflective Intellect embracing the totality of the forms. The doctrine is present in two versions within the Platonic material available: in a more or less pagan manner in Calcidius,[83] where the ineffable God is elevated above his Providence—equivalent to the world of forms—which functions as a second hypostasis derived from and returning upon its first principle, and also in a version fully accommodated to Christianity in Augustine,[84] who combines the first two hypostases to produce the notion of an ineffable God to whom are present the forms or eternal reasons of all things, thereby returning in effect if not in actual intent to something like the Middle Platonic position. The third type of Platonism to which the writer had access was the Alexandrian Neoplatonism which, whatever its implicit assumptions may have been, for practical purposes confined its theological speculation within the limits of the original Aristotelian view of God as a pure Form. This doctrine is available to the commentator through the writings of Boethius.[85] Thus three (or four) distinct types of Platonism are represented in the same philosophical work: Middle Platonism and various types of Neoplatonism. Together they furnish a metaphysical doctrine of unparalleled richness, while their inherent contradictions provide a fruitful spur to fresh philosophical reflection.

Finally, our survey has been most informative regarding the function of Aristotelianism within the doctrinal complex. Here we see nothing of the tendency to place Plato and Aristotle in antithetical positions, since the Middle Platonists had already set the pattern of combining the two philosophies into a coherent whole. This is demonstrated especially in their postulation at the same time of transcendent (Platonic) and immanent (Aristotelian) forms. The double theory of forms recurs in post-Plotinian Neoplatonism and was transmitted to the Latin world by no fewer than three of the Platonic sources utilized by our twelfth-century writer (the *Asclepius*, Calcidius, and Boethius), so

---

ences from different styles or periods of Platonic exegesis is quite probable in Calcidius's case and, as Jacob C. M. van Winden, *Calcidius on Matter: His Doctrine and Sources* (Leiden 1959; repr. 1965) 243–47 has argued, the appearance of Middle Platonic doctrines in a writer under the influence of Porphyry would be very likely since the latter is well known for his sympathy with many Middle Platonic views.

[83]Even if Calcidius was a Christian, as seems likely on the strength of his presumed association with a Christian bishop, his sympathetic treatment of the Old Testament, and the absence of indisputably pagan religious elements in his commentary, his philosophy in its fundamentals remains aligned with pagan Platonic tradition.

[84]To this extent, Augustine's approach is in line with that of the other great Christian Platonist influential in the early Middle Ages, Pseudo-Dionysius the Areopagite. In this writer, the combination of the first two hypostases of the Plotinian system is achieved by means of the contrast between the Negative and Affirmative Theologies.

[85]The historical evidence suggests that notable philosophers of the Alexandrian Neoplatonic School such as Ammonius accepted the full pagan theology of late Antiquity but refrained in deference to Christian political authority from expounding it in their works. These Neoplatonists are in fact largely known today as Aristotelian commentators and Boethius, whether or not he was ever physically present in Alexandria, follows in their footsteps on many questions.

that in this respect he follows them. One should also remember that even in Plotinus, who among the Platonists of Antiquity was most overtly critical of Aristotle, much is traceable ultimately to Peripatetic sources. Indeed, the central doctrine of the self-reflective hypostasis of Intellect is a piece of Platonic and Aristotelian syncretism. This notion was transmitted to the West by Augustine and Macrobius, among the sources readily accessible to the commentator, and his dynamic view of reality clearly indicates this debt.[86]

In conclusion, then, we can say that the philosophical background of this text encompasses not only a wide variety of Platonisms but also much Aristotelian doctrine.[87] This gives the philosophy expressed there a richness surpassing that of earlier times. Even if, considered in absolute terms, the writer's real achievements fall below the standard of some earlier work—one thinks here of Eriugena three centuries before—in his wide-ranging use of material and exegetical inventiveness he commands a unique position.

Bibliographical Note

For a general survey of the various philosophical schools of late Antiquity which directly or indirectly influenced twelfth-century Platonism, see Arthur Hilary Armstrong, ed., *The Cambridge History of Later Greek and Early Medieval Philosophy* (Cambridge 1967). Most parts of this composite product are adequate, although all suffer from the brevity dictated by the encyclopedia form. The sections by Armstrong, Robert A. Markus, Inglis P. Sheldon-Williams, and Hans Liebeschütz can be recommended as representing contributions by the best scholars in their respective fields. The section on post-Plotinian Neoplatonism—which treats the entire period as though it were simply the history of one or two developments in logic—is perhaps the least satisfactory.

As stated in note 1 above, the study of the medieval Platonic tradition was elevated to a new level by Raymond Klibansky's monograph *The Continuity of the Platonic Tradition during the Middle Ages* (2nd ed. London 1950). Since that time, among works of general relevance to the subject might be mentioned Tullio Gregory, *Platonismo medievale: Studi e ricerche* (Rome 1958), and a useful collection of essays edited by Werner Beierwaltes, *Platonismus in der Philosophie des Mittelalters*, Wege der Forschung 197 (Darmstadt 1969). The two Platonic dialogues which gave rise to the most important developments in medieval thought were the *Timaeus* and (until the thirteenth century via indirect tradition only) the *Parmenides*. For the influence of the former see Margaret Gibson, "The Study of the 'Timaeus' in the Eleventh and Twelfth Centuries," *Pensamiento* 25 (1969) 183–94, and for that of the latter, Raymond Klibansky, "Plato's *Parmenides* in the Middle Ages and the Renaissance," M&RS 1 (1941–43) 281–330.

On the transmission of Greek Neoplatonic doctrine to the West in general there are two outstanding studies: Paul Henry's *Plotin et l'Occident: Firmicus Maternus,*

[86]See n. 40 above (and my argument in general).
[87]Similarly Haskins, *Science* 90 quite correctly noted the Aristotelian physics in Thierry of Chartres's *De sex dierum operibus*, which is derived through Macrobius.

Marius Victorinus, saint Augustin et Macrobe (Louvain 1934) and Pierre Courcelle's *Les lettres grecques en Occident de Macrobe à Cassiodore* (2nd ed. Paris 1948), translated by Harry E. Wedeck as *Late Latin Writers and Their Greek Sources* (Cambridge Mass. 1969). Progress of research into the influence of specific transmitters of Platonic doctrine has been more uneven, but the following works—most of which deal to some extent with the impact upon the twelfth-century—are significant:

 (a) For the *Asclepius*, see Arthur D. Nock, ed., and André-Jean Festugière, trans., *Corpus Hermeticum* (4 vols. Paris 1945-54) 2.259-95, which contains a good survey of the medieval influence.

 (b) For Calcidius, Jan H. Waszink, *Studien zum Timaioskommentar des Calcidius* 1, Philosophia antiqua 12 (Leiden 1964) and Jacob C. M. van Winden, *Calcidius on Matter: His Doctrine and Sources* (Leiden 1959; repr. 1965) are the most important basic studies. Among more recent works on specific problems should be mentioned J. den Boeft, *Calcidius on Fate: His Doctrine and Sources*, Philosophia antiqua 18 (Leiden 1970). Unfortunately, there is as yet no adequate survey of Calcidius's influence during the Middle Ages.

 (c) A convenient introduction to Macrobius is the survey by William Harris Stahl, trans. and ed., *Macrobius, Commentary on the Dream of Scipio*, Columbia University Records of Civilization 48 (New York 1952) 3-65, while a full-scale study has recently appeared in the form of Jacques Flamant's *Macrobe et le néo-platonisme latin, à la fin du IVe siècle* (Leiden 1977). Several short studies of specific problems have also been published, including Meine Adriaan Elferink, *La descente de l'âme d'après Macrobe*, Philosophia antiqua 16 (Leiden 1968) and Herman de Ley, *Macrobius and Numenius* (Brussels 1972). Concerning the extent of Macrobius's later influence see Matthaeus Schedler's old but still useful account *Die Philosophie des Macrobius und ihr Einfluss auf die Wissenschaft des christlichen Mittelalters*, BGPTMA 13.1 (Münster 1916) and Edouard Jeauneau, "Macrobe, source du platonisme chartrain," *Studi medievali* 3rd ser. 1 (1960) 3-14.

 (d) The bibliography on Augustine is too large to list here, but of special relevance to the "Augustine" influential at Chartres (i.e. the cosmologist) are Katharina Staritz, *Augustins Schöpfungsglaube dargestellt nach seinen Genesisauslegungen* (Breslau 1931); Jean Guitton, *Le temps et l'éternité chez Plotin et saint Augustin* (3rd ed. Paris 1959); Christopher O'Toole, *The Philosophical Theory of Creation in the Writings of St. Augustine* (Washington D.C. 1944); Jean de Blic, "Le processus de la création d'après saint Augustin," *Mélanges offerts à F. Cavallera* (Toulouse 1948) 179-89; William A. Christian, "Augustine on the Creation of the World," *Harvard Theological Review* 46 (1953) 1-25; Paul Bissels, "Die sachliche Begründung und philoso-phiegeschichtliche Stellung der Lehre von der 'materia spiritualis' in der Scholastik," *Franziskanische Studien* 38 (1956) 241-95; Marie-Thérèse d'Alverny, "Les anges et les jours," *Cahiers archéologiques* 9 (1957) 271-300; Günther Koch, *Augustins Lehre von der Teilhabe: Untersuchungen zur Bedeutung des participatio-Begriffes im Werke des Hl. Augustinus* (diss. Freiburg i. Br. 1958); Ernest W. Ranly, "St. Augustine's Theory of Matter," *The Modern Schoolman* 42 (1964-65) 287-303; and Joseph Moreau, "Le temps et la création selon saint Augustin," *Giornale di metafisica* 20 (1965) 276-90.

 (e) For general orientation in the philosophy of Boethius one may turn to Antonio Crocco, *Introduzione a Boezio* (Naples 1970; 2nd ed. 1975), while the more specialized reader now also has the benefit of Luca Obertello's extensive study *Severino Boezio* (2 vols. Genoa 1974). On the problems arising from the theological tractates, Konrad Bruder, *Die philosophischen Elemente in den "Opuscula sacra" des Boethius*, Forschungen zur Geschichte der Philosophie und der Pädagogik 3/2 (Leipzig 1928), and Hermann Josef Brosch, *Der Seinsbegriff bei Boethius, mit besonderer Berücksichtigung der Beziehung von Sosein und Dasein* (Innsbruck 1931), though old, are still useful.

Concerning Boethius's influence, see especially Pierre Courcelle, *La Consolation de Philosophie dans la tradition littéraire: Antécédents et postérité de Boèce* (Paris 1967) for Boethius's most celebrated work, and Gangolf Schrimpf, *Die Axiomenschrift (De hebdomadibus) als philosophisches Lehrbuch des Mittelalters*, Studien zur Problemgeschichte der antiken und mittelalterlichen Philosophie 2 (Leiden 1966) for the theological tractates.

(f) For Martianus Capella, see William Harris Stahl, Richard Johnson, and E. L. Burge, *Martianus Capella and the Seven Liberal Arts*, Columbia University Records of Civilization 84 (2 vols. New York 1971–77) on the trivium and quadrivium material and Fanny Le Moine, *Martianus Capella: A Literary Re-evaluation* (Munich 1972) and Luciano Lenaz, *Martiani Capellae De nuptiis Philologiae et Mercurii liber secundus*, Introduzione, traduzione e commento (Padua 1975) on the cosmological myth. Regarding his influence, see the important study by Claudio Leonardi, "I codici di Marziano Capella," *Aevum* 33 (1959) 443–89, 34 (1960) 1–99, 411–524.

(g) For Pseudo-Dionysius, see René Roques, *L'univers dionysien: Structure hiérarchique du monde selon le Pseudo-Denys* (Paris 1954), and, with reference to his later influence, René Roques, *Structures théologiques de la Gnose à Richard de Saint-Victor* (Paris 1962) and Stephen Gersh, *From Iamblichus to Eriugena: An Investigation of the Prehistory and Evolution of the Pseudo-Dionysian Tradition*, Studien zur Problemgeschichte der antiken und mittelalterlichen Philosophie 8 (Leiden 1978).

On twelfth-century Platonism in general and especially the "School of Chartres," the following works—in addition to Chenu's *Théologie*—are of primary importance: Etienne Gilson, "Le platonisme de Bernard de Chartres," *Revue néoscolastique de philosophie* 25 (1923) 5–19; Heinrich Flatten, *Die Philosophie des Wilhelm von Conches* (Coblenz 1929) and "Die materia primordialis in der Schule von Chartres," *Archiv für Geschichte der Philosophie* 40 (1931) 58–65; Gérard M. Paré, A. Brunet, and P. Tremblay, *La renaissance du XIIe siècle: Les écoles et l'enseignement*, Publications de l'Institut d'études médiévales d'Ottawa 3 (Paris and Ottawa 1933); Maurice de Wulf, "Le panthéisme chartrain," *Aus der Geisteswelt des Mittelalters*, BGPTMA Supp. 3 (1935) 282–86; Joseph Marie Parent, *La doctrine de la création dans l'Ecole de Chartres*, Publications de l'Institut d'études médiévales d'Ottawa 8 (Paris and Ottawa 1938); Tullio Gregory, *Anima mundi: La filosofia di Guglielmo di Conches e la Scuola di Chartres* (Florence 1955); Heinrich Schipperges, "Die Schulen von Chartres unter dem Einfluss des Arabismus," *Sudhoffs Archiv für Geschichte der Medizin und der Naturwissenschaften* 40 (1956) 193–210; Edouard Jeauneau, "L'usage de la notion l'*integumentum* à travers les gloses de Guillaume de Conches," AHDLMA 24 (1957) 35–100 (= *Lectio* 127–92); Eugenio Garin, *Studi sul platonismo medievale* (Florence 1958); Edouard Jeauneau, "Note sur l'Ecole de Chartres," *Studi medievali* 3rd ser. 5 (1964) 821–65 (= *Lectio* 5–49); and Ludwig Ott, "Die platonische Weltseele in der Theologie der Frühscholastik," *Parusia: Festgabe für Johannes Hirschberger*, ed. Kurt Flasch (Frankfurt 1965) 307–31.

On the specific problems raised by the commentary on the *De Trinitate*, see Wilhelm Jansen, *Der Kommentar des Clarenbaldus von Arras zu Boethius De Trinitate* (Breslau 1926); Nikolaus M. Häring, "The Creation and Creator of the World according to Thierry of Chartres and Clarenbaldus of Arras," AHDLMA 22 (1955) 137–216 (still the best general introduction to the doctrine of Thierry and his followers); Edouard Jeauneau, "Mathématiques et Trinité chez Thierry de Chartres," *Die Metaphysik im Mittelalter: Ihr Ursprung und Ihre Bedeutung*, ed. Paul Wilpert, Miscellanea mediaevalia 2 (1963) 289–95 (= *Lectio* 93–99); Nikolaus M. Häring, *Life and Works of Clarembald of Arras* (Toronto 1965); Fernand Brunner, "*Creatio numerorum, rerum est creatio*," *Mélanges offerts à René Crozet* (2 vols. Poitiers 1966) 2.719–25 and "Deus forma essendi," *Entretiens* 85–116; and Nikolaus M. Häring, *Commentaries on Boethius by Thierry of Chartres and His School* (Toronto 1971).

VI

LITERATURE

Classicism and Style in Latin Literature

Janet Martin

The vitality of the twelfth-century renaissance is revealed nowhere more clearly than in the quality and abundance of its Latin literature. The revived classicism that characterizes part (though only part) of this large production is manifested both thematically and formally; the formal aspect is the subject of this chapter, which focuses on certain stylistic features of twelfth-century Latin prose and poetry while largely ignoring theme and content. "Style" here will be applied to the selection and ordering of language.[1] The chief questions to be addressed are two. What is a classicizing style? Can style be considered a criterion of renascence? In order to answer the first question, I attempt to characterize the elements of style common to writers of Latin from about 1070 to shortly after 1200 and to identify the distinctive elements of classicizing style. The investigation is carried out primarily through analysis of exemplary texts, with some attention to contemporary theoretical works dealing with prose and poetic composition. The ways of writing Latin in the twelfth century are then related to the broader concept of renascence.

Analysis of style raises difficult theoretical questions of definition and method, questions that seem little closer to resolution for having been the subject of vigorous scholarly debate in recent decades.[2] Quite apart from other difficulties, there is the problem of selecting representative examples. Possibly my conclusions would be different if based on more or different cases. But however provisionally, these soundings of twelfth-century Latin literature attempt to characterize important aspects of Latin style as they illuminate the twelfth-century renaissance.

---

[1]Nils Erik Enkvist, "On Defining Style: An Essay in Applied Linguistics," *Linguistics and Style*, ed. John W. Spencer, Language and Language Learning 6 (London 1964) 1–56 at 15–20; Jules Marouzeau, *Traité de stylistique latine*, Collection d'études latines, Série scientifique 12 (3rd ed. Paris 1954) xi–xxi, 337–43.

[2]Brief introductions to the issues are provided by Graham Hough, *Style and Stylistics* (London 1969); Pierre Guiraud, *La stylistique*, Que sais-je? 646 (rev. ed. Paris 1975); Enkvist (n. 1 above). For a detailed survey, see Wolfram Ax, *Probleme des Sprachstils als Gegenstand der lateinischen Philologie*, Beiträge zur Altertumswissenschaft 1 (Hildesheim and New York 1976).

LITERARY THEORY IN THE TWELFTH CENTURY

Though literary theory in every period is notoriously inadequate to describe literary practice, the theoretical treatises on prose and poetic composition that proliferated in the twelfth century require some attention as a preliminary to examination of the literary texts. Classical works on rhetoric continued to be influential, particularly Cicero's *De inventione*, the anonymous *Ad Herennium* attributed to him, and Horace's *Ars poetica*.[3] Perhaps the most influential rhetorical legacy of Antiquity was Augustine's *De doctrina christiana*, particularly the fourth book, which radically adapts Ciceronian theory to the needs of the Christian orator and writer.[4] Beginning in our period, new theoretical manuals of letter-writing and poetic composition appear that draw both on ancient theory and on a long medieval tradition of teaching composition. The increasingly utilitarian application of rhetoric to letter-writing, largely a consequence of the growth of governmental administrations, brought forth in the late‧eleventh century "the discipline known as the *dictamen* or *ars dictandi*, with teachers (*dictatores*), text-books (*artes* or *summae dictaminis*), and collections of model letters (formularies)."[5] One aspect of *dictamen* was concerned with the form and arrangement of the letter as a whole; the other dealt with the choice and arrangement of words, often including the practice (called *cursus* by modern scholars) of ending sentences and clauses in certain accentual rhythms.[6] The earliest extant medieval works dealing in some detail with letter-writing are the *Flores rhetorici* (or *Dictaminum radii*) and *Breviarium de dictamine* of Alberic of Monte Cassino (fl. 1079).[7] The subsequent history of *dictamen* is of great interest but cannot be followed here.

---

[3] Richard McKeon, "Rhetoric in the Middle Ages," *Speculum* 17 (1942) 1–32; Franz Quadlbauer, *Die antike Theorie der Genera dicendi im lateinischen Mittelalter*, SB Vienna 241.2 (1962) 7–17; John O. Ward, "From Antiquity to the Renaissance: Glosses and Commentaries on Cicero's *Rhetorica*," *Medieval Eloquence: Studies in the Theory and Practice of Medieval Rhetoric*, ed. James J. Murphy (Berkeley 1978) 25–67, with references to recent work.

[4] Erich Auerbach, "*Sermo humilis*," in *Literary Language and Its Public in Late Latin Antiquity and in the Middle Ages*, trans. Ralph Manheim, Bollingen Series 74 (New York and London 1965) 25–66, esp. 33–39; Quadlbauer (n. 3 above) 8–9; Henri-Irénée Marrou, *Saint Augustin et la fin de la culture antique* (4th ed. Paris 1958) 505–40.

[5] Giles Constable, *Letters and Letter-Collections*, Typologie des sources du moyen âge occidental 17 (Turnhout 1976) 34; Haskins, *Culture* 1–35, 170–92; Franz-Josef Schmale, "Die Bologneser Schule der Ars dictandi," *DA* 13 (1957) 16–34; William D. Patt, "The Early 'Ars Dictaminis' as Response to a Changing Society," *Viator* 9 (1978) 133–55, with good bibliography; Charles B. Faulhaber, "The *Summa dictaminis* of Guido Faba," *Medieval Eloquence* (n. 3 above) 85–111.

[6] Giles Constable, ed., *The Letters of Peter the Venerable*, Harvard Historical Studies 78 (2 vols. Cambridge Mass. 1967) 2.29–35; to the bibliography there cited add Tore Janson, *Prose Rhythm in Medieval Latin From the 9th to the 13th Century*, Studia latina Stockholmiensia 20 (Stockholm 1975) 7, 66.

[7] Carol D. Lanham, "*Salutatio*" *Formulas in Latin Letters to 1200: Syntax, Style, and Theory*, Münchener Beiträge zur Mediävistik und Renaissance-Forschung 22 (Munich 1975) 94–97; Dietrich Lohrmann, "Die Jugendwerke des Johannes von Gaeta," *Quellen und Forschungen aus italienischen Archiven und Bibliotheken* 47 (1967) 355–445 at 360–68 and passim; Herbert Bloch, "Monte Cassino's Teachers and Library in the High Middle Ages," *La scuola nell'Occidente latino dell'alto medioevo*, Settimane 19 (2 vols. Spoleto 1972) 2.563–605 at 587–601.

The exact influence of the dictaminal manuals on literary composition is not easy to determine, nor is it clear that their increasingly formalized rules and model letters have much to offer this study. For one thing, the manuals are an imperfect guide to existing practice.[8] More importantly, there is reason to suppose that imitation of other literary texts was at least as significant in the teaching and learning of composition as were the formal rules and model letters of the *dictatores*. The accomplished writer Peter of Blois (d. 1212) tells us that he benefited from having been required as a youth to memorize the letters of Hildebert of Le Mans (1056–1133), letters that he describes as "outstanding for their stylistic elegance and pleasing refinement."[9] But Hildebert's letters, thus praised as models of artistic prose, show little influence of the emerging discipline of *dictamen*. Though he uses the *cursus*, the organization and often the language of his letters owe more to traditional ways of writing sermons.[10] At least one *dictator* explicitly acknowledged the limitations of formal rules. The anonymous author of the highly influential *Rationes dictandi* (ca. 1140), formerly attributed to Alberic of Monte Cassino, remarks that a flowing and sonorous arrangement of words is achieved by following the judgment of one's ear and by practice in writing rather than through application of precise rules; nonetheless he will provide some rules for the benefit of the inexperienced (*rudes*).[11] If the precepts of the *dictatores* were incomplete as instruction, clearly they are even less to be regarded as adequate categories for stylistic analysis of literary texts, except possibly the stereotyped products of the chanceries.[12] But some aspects of *dictamen*, notably the *cursus*, became almost universal in epistolary and other prose by the end of the twelfth century. The precepts of the *artes dictandi* will be cited occasionally when they throw light on literary practice.

If the *artes dictandi* represent the systematization of epistolary rhetoric, the new arts of poetry apply rhetoric to verse composition. The earliest extant

[8]Lanham (n. 7 above) 96, 105–09.

[9]Peter of Blois, *Epist.* 101, PL 207.314A: "Profuit mihi, quod epistolas Hildeberti Cenomanensis episcopi styli elegantia, et suavi urbanitate praecipuas firmare, et corde tenus reddere adolescentulus compellebar"; cited and discussed by Peter von Moos, *Hildebert von Lavardin, 1056–1133: Humanitas an der Schwelle des höfischen Zeitalters,* Pariser historische Studien 3 (Stuttgart 1965) 42; Richard W. Southern, "Peter of Blois: A Twelfth-Century Humanist?" *Humanism* 105–32 at 117–18. This and other translations quoted are my own. Imitation played an important role also in the teaching of Bernard of Chartres (d. ca. 1130), as described by John of Salisbury, *Metalogicon* 1.24, ed. Clement C. J. Webb (Oxford 1929) 55–57.

[10]Janson (n. 6 above) 72–74, 113; von Moos (n. 9 above) 47–50, 67–80.

[11]Anonymous, *Rationes dictandi* 13, ed. Ludwig Rockinger, *Briefsteller und Formelbücher des eilften bis vierzehnten Jahrhunderts,* Quellen und Erörterungen zur bayerischen und deutschen Geschichte 9.1–2 (2 vols. Munich 1863–64; repr. New York 1961) 1.9–28 at 26: "Quam uidelicet appositionem oportet fieri quasi currentem, et sonoram, et diligenti sermonum positione fulgentem. Quod utique licet aurium potius iuditio et dictandi exercitio quam certissima qualibet doctrina conparetur, quedam tamen artificia rudibus ministrare satagemus"; discussed by Marian Plezia, "L'origine de la théorie du *cursus* rythmique au XIIe siècle," *Archivum latinitatis medii aevi (Bulletin Du Cange)* 39 (1974) 5–22 at 6–7.

[12]Hans Martin Schaller, "Die Kanzlei Kaiser Friedrichs II. Ihr Personal und ihr Sprachstil, 2: Der Sprachstil der Kanzlei," *Archiv für Diplomatik* 4 (1958) 264–327, esp. 295–325.

treatise is Matthew of Vendôme's *Ars versificatoria* (before 1175), an introductory schoolbook on versification that resulted probably from his teaching at Orléans.[13] More advanced instruction was provided in two influential works of Geoffrey of Vinsauf, the *Poetria nova* (completed probably between 1200 and 1215) in hexameters, and the closely related prose treatise *Documentum de modo et arte dictandi et versificandi*, which as its title indicates treats both prose and poetic composition.[14] Following the usual divisions of the art of rhetoric, the *Poetria nova* presents instruction on invention, arrangement (natural and artificial order), style (amplification and abbreviation, difficult and easy ornament), memory, and delivery. The title *Poetria nova* echoes the titles of two of Geoffrey's major sources, the *Ad Herennium* (called in the Middle Ages the *Rhetorica nova* to distinguish it from *De inventione*, known as the *Rhetorica vetus*) and Horace's *Ars poetica* (often called his *Poetria*). With this title Geoffrey announces his new poetics.[15] Two other important works are Gervase of Melkley's *Ars poetica*, written between 1208 and 1216, and John of Garland's *Parisiana poetria de arte prosaica, metrica, et rithmica*, originally composed about 1220 and revised between 1231 and 1235.[16]

As with prose composition, some important elements of instruction on verse composition may be unrepresented in the *artes*, in part because much instruction was based directly on the study and imitation of works of literature rather than on the *artes'* formal precepts.[17] But one pervasive notion in the arts of poetry that aids stylistic analysis of medieval literature is their view of literary composition as the ordering of preexisting, often traditional *materia*. *Materia* does not mean theme or raw material but the content of the poem, not matter as the opposite of expression but matter already laid out in words.[18] On one level the revision of the *materia* is part of rudimentary instruction, in prose as well as poetry. Thus Alberic of Monte Cassino advised his students first to compose in simple and artless language, then to elaborate section by section according to the precepts of his *Breviarium*. Like a painter, the writer first draws a bold outline "in ugly charcoal, as it were," then lays on a suitable

[13]Faral, *Les arts poétiques* 1–14, text 106–93; partial translation by Ernest Gallo, "Matthew of Vendôme: Introductory Treatise on the Art of Poetry," *Proceedings of the American Philosophical Society* 118 (1974) 51–92.

[14]Faral, *Les arts poétiques* 15–33, text of *Poetria nova* 194–262, text of *Documentum* 263–320; trans. Margaret F. Nims, *Poetria nova of Geoffrey of Vinsauf* (Toronto 1967) and Roger P. Parr, *Geoffrey of Vinsauf: Documentum de modo et arte dictandi et versificandi (Instruction in the Method and Art of Speaking and Versifying)*, Mediaeval Philosophical Texts in Translation 17 (Milwaukee 1968).

[15]Curtius 153–54; Ernest Gallo, ed. and trans., *The "Poetria Nova" and Its Sources in Early Rhetorical Doctrine* (The Hague 1971).

[16]Faral, *Les arts poétiques* 34–37, 40–46; *Gervais von Melkley: Ars poetica*, ed. Hans-Jürgen Gräbener, Forschungen zur romanischen Philologie 17 (Münster 1965) xxviii; *The "Parisiana Poetria" of John of Garland*, ed. and trans. Traugott Lawler, Yale Studies in English 182 (New Haven and London 1974) xv.

[17]Douglas Kelly, "The Scope of the Treatment of Composition in the Twelfth- and Thirteenth-Century Arts of Poetry," *Speculum* 41 (1966) 261–78 at 276.

[18]Kelly (n. 17 above) 268 n. 26; Quadlbauer (n. 3 above) 68–70; Douglas Kelly, "Topical Invention in Medieval French Literature," *Medieval Eloquence* (n. 3 above) 231–51; Per Nykrog, in this volume, passim.

array of colors (*colores*, "rhetorical figures").[19] Matthew of Vendôme seems to have furnished his young students with *materia* ready for ornamentation.[20]

The notion of preexisting *materia* is central to the sophisticated description of composition offered by Geoffrey of Vinsauf. He postulates three steps in composition: "(1) determination of the scope and order of the *materia*; (2) disposition of the *materia*; (3) embellishment and ornamentation of the *materia*."[21] Only the last step involves actually writing out words. The first two stages, the determination and disposition (or in other terms the "invention" and "arrangement") of the content or *materia*, take place in the mind of the poet and are of primary importance since the success of the completed poem will depend largely on its content: poetic art (*poesis*) is the handmaiden of *materia*.[22] Though clearly Geoffrey does not subordinate content to verbal expression, it is the latter to which he devotes the great part of his works. The elaborate doctrine of verbal art that results is rhetorical and rational, presupposing a conscious control over style that moderns associate rather with the process of revision.[23]

EPISTOLARY PROSE

PETER THE VENERABLE

Let us turn to some examples of twelfth-century prose. The letters of Peter the Venerable, abbot of Cluny (d. 1156), are characteristic of much prose. Peter's sentences typically are long, with main clauses placed early and numerous subordinate clauses following one upon another, the somewhat rambling whole interrupted and further complicated by parenthetical insertions. The sentences are given shape and symmetry by the use of clauses that are of equal length (a figure called *isocolon* in rhetorical theory), or are syntactically parallel, or both. Often this structural parallelism is accompanied by parallelism of sound, produced by repetition of the same word at the beginning of successive clauses or phrases (*anaphora*), by end-rhyme, and by other rhetorical devices. Another frequent figure is *antithesis*, the conjoining of contrary words or ideas.[24]

[19]Alberic of Monte Cassino, *Breviarium de dictamine* 2, ed. Rockinger (n. 11 above) 29–46 at 30: "in primis quod dictandum assumit de industria et de data opera sermone simplici et inculto debeat conponere, et post editiones singulas iuxta documentum breuiarii uariare, atque pingentis emulus prius quasi carbone tetro utcunque insignire imaginem, post quasi per insignitas lineas congruentem colorum superducere uarietatem"; discussed by Quadlbauer (n. 3 above) 57–58.

[20]Kelly (n. 17 above) 268.

[21]Kelly (n. 17 above) 272–75 at 272.

[22]Geoffrey of Vinsauf, *Poetria nova* vv. 43–70, ed. Faral, *Les arts poétiques* 198–99; similarly *Documentum* 2.3.2, ibid. 284–85; cited by Nims (n. 14 above) 10.

[23]Louis T. Milic, "Rhetorical Choice and Stylistic Option: The Conscious and Unconscious Poles," *Literary Style: A Symposium*, ed. and trans. Seymour Chatman (London and New York 1971) 77–94.

[24]For definitions and examples, see *Ad Herennium* 4.13.19 (anaphora); 4.15.21, 45.58 (antithesis); 4.20.27–28 (isocolon and rhyming figures), ed. and trans. Harry Caplan, *Ad C. Herennium De ratione dicendi (Rhetorica ad Herennium)*, LCL (1954) 274–77, 282–83, 376–77, 298–301.

The following typical sentences are from a widely circulated letter, addressed to a hermit named Gilbert, on the singular perfection of the solitary
life; here Gilbert is urged to refuse the gifts of well-meaning admirers. Instances of anaphora and end-rhyme are italicized:

> Quod si institerint,
> *dent* si ita uolunt priori tuo,
> *dent* fratribus tuis,
>   ut   uel ad proprios usus ab ipsis *retineantur*,
>   aut per manus eorum aliis *distribuantur*.
> Sed etsi ipsi fratres tui
>   institorem talium te esse   praecaeperint,
>   et   de paupertate tua sibi negotiari,
> non adquiescas,
> meamque auctoritatem coactioni eorum obice,
>   licet   in his nullum sit periculum *inobaedientiae*
>   in quibus ratio contradicit *iustitiae*.
> Sit cella tua   uacua *pecunia*,
>   repleta *iustitia*,
>   indigens *opibus*,
>   referta *uirtutibus*,
>   ut   quia non est "conuentio Christi ad Belial,"
>   ita exinaniatur rebus *terrenis*,
>   ut possit in ea caelestibus locus esse *thesauris*.

(But if they insist, let them give to your prior if they wish, let them give to your
brethren, so that [the gifts] may be retained by them for their use or else be distributed
through them to others. But even if your brethren should order you to be a broker in
such things and to traffic in your poverty for their gain, do not assent; oppose my
authority to their urging; it is unlawful for there to be any risk of disobedience where
business transactions clash with justice. Let your cell be empty of money but filled with
justice, lacking in wealth but stuffed with virtue, so that since there is no "concord of
Christ with Belial," it may be emptied of the things of earth in such wise that there can
be in it room for the treasures of heaven.)[25]

The first sentence consists (after the introductory *quod*-clause) of two
pairs of clauses that are syntactically and formally parallel. The symmetry is
marked by anaphora of *dent* in the first pair of clauses and by isocolon and
end-rhyme in the second pair. The next sentence is less symmetrical. The syntactically parallel phrases *institorem talium te esse* and *de paupertate tua sibi
negotiari* lack formal parallelism. The three clauses, dissimilar in length and
syntax, are arranged in order of increasing magnitude (a figure called *tricolon
abundans*) as a means of emphasis. The negative thought of the first clause (*non
adquiescas*) is recast positively in the second (*meamque auctoritatem coac-
tioni eorum obice*); the third clause, containing two members, closes the
sentence with parallelism of structure (including approximate isocolon) and
sound (end-rhyme of *inobaedientiae* and *iustitiae*). The third sentence, which
concludes this section of Peter's letter, gains suitable prominence through
studied rhetorical stylization. It begins with four short phrases of equal length

---

[25]Constable (n. 6 above) 1.35 no. 20.

arranged in antithetical pairs with end-rhyme. A parenthetical *quia*-clause citing a biblical authority (2 Cor. 6:15) provides an element of irregularity, to be followed at once by corresponding *ita . . . ut* clauses with end-rhyme. The artful word order of the conclusion, *caelestibus locus esse thesauris*, is notable. The placement of *thesauris* ("treasures") at the end of the sentence, the most prominent position, contributes to its strong emphasis; and the artificial separation (*hyperbaton*) of the modifier *caelestibus* ("heavenly") from its noun gives *caelestibus*, too, prominence. Thus by expert ordering of clauses and words Peter concludes his treatment of the proper use of worldly wealth for otherworldly ends with the key words *caelestibus thesauris* ("the treasures of heaven") thrown into prominence.

These sentences do not represent the full range of structural variety in Peter's letters, but they demonstrate many of his techniques for providing his sentences with a more or less symmetrical structure—at times so regularly that his style approaches true rhymed prose, more often less systematically. This parallelism of structure and sound, which goes back ultimately to the famous Gorgianic figures, is perhaps the chief element of elevated medieval prose.[26]

Another important element in medieval practice and theory is prose rhythm, manifested by attention both to harmony and balance among members of the sentence and to accentual rhythmical patterns ending sentences and clauses. Addressing prose rhythm in the first (and larger) sense, Augustine analyzed biblical passages into their rhetorical members; and the *artes dictandi* taught, for example, that artistic prose should have sentence-members of approximately equal length.[27] That Peter was concerned with rhythm in the larger sense, the harmonious articulation of sentence-members, is evident from the exemplary passage. Less immediately evident is the influence of the *cursus*, the practice of ending sentences and clauses in certain accentual rhythms. Analysis of twenty letters, including the letter excerpted above, shows that Peter used the preferred rhythms in 61 percent of his sentence endings. His usage contrasts both with the pedantic observance of *cursus* by his contemporary Bernard Silvester (96 percent) and with the conservatism of his friend Peter of Celle, who does not observe *cursus* at all.[28] Of our three sentences, the first has an irregular cadence; but the other two end, respectively, with a *cursus tardus* (*contradícit iustítiae*) and a *cursus planus*

---

[26]Eduard Norden, *Die antike Kunstprosa vom VI. Jahrhundert v. Chr. bis in die Zeit der Renaissance* (4th ed. 2 vols. Leipzig 1923) 2.760–63. For the Gorgianic figures in Roman rhetorical theory, see Karl Polheim, *Die lateinische Reimprosa* (Berlin 1925) 158–72.

[27]Augustine, *De doctrina christiana* 4.7.11–13; discussed by Norden (n. 26 above) 2.503–10, 526–28. On the *artes dictandi*, see Marian Plezia, "*Quattuor stili modernorum*: Ein Kapitel mittellateinischer Stillehre," *Orbis Mediaevalis: Festgabe für Anton Blaschka*, ed. Horst Gericke, Manfred Lemmer, and Walter Zöllner (Weimar 1970) 192–210 at 203–05; Plezia (n. 11 above) 6. For brief treatments of classical theory and practice, see Leonard R. Palmer, *The Latin Language* (London 1954; corr. repr. 1961) 115–18, 129–34; Anton D. Leeman, *Orationis Ratio: The Stylistic Theories and Practice of the Roman Orators, Historians and Philosophers* (2 vols. Amsterdam 1963) 1.149–55.

[28]Janson (n. 6 above) 75, 113.

(*ésse thesaúris*). And in the last sentence, which is the most stylized of the three, most of the smaller segments end with favored rhythms as well. Though the *cursus* had a long tradition reaching back to late Antiquity, it attained its full development in the twelfth century. By the end of the century, its influence on artistic prose was all but universal.

A third outstanding characteristic of much medieval prose, in addition to parallelism and rhythm, is frequent use of vocabulary, images, and quotations from the Bible and the Fathers. This habit comes particularly easily to monastic writers like Peter, who were steeped in the sacred text through the liturgy and through *lectio divina*, the ruminative reading of the Bible and its commentaries that was the basis of private prayer and meditation.[29] The sacred texts and the commentaries expounding their spiritual sense provided a rich vocabulary of images. The tropological or moral sense was easily adapted to satire, that "consuming and universal passion of the twelfth century," by extension to the behavior of groups or types and to religious and social abuses.[30] Upon occasion Peter, too, uses biblical texts satirically, within ten lines comparing corrupt monks to the Israelites perversely turning back to Egypt, dogs returning to their vomit, mud trampled in the street, gold become dim, the stones of the sanctuary scattered, and "the precious sons of Zion" now "reckoned as earthen pots."[31] Scriptural diction, though particularly congenial to monastic authors, is not limited to them. The bishop Hildebert of Le Mans, considered by modern scholars a leading representative of medieval humanism, cites the Bible and the Fathers in his prose writings much more often than pagan authorities, so often that frequently his style is very biblical.[32]

The essential characteristics of this elevated prose style—parallelism and antithesis, sound-figures, rhythm, and biblical diction—are found in purest form in the medieval sermon. They resemble and in fact descend from salient features of the "new Christian style" of the Fathers.[33] The dominant patristic style affected elaborate rhetorical ornamentation and stylization, especially in sermons. It also abandoned classical canons in vocabulary and syntax as well as the periodic sentence structure associated with classical and more particularly Ciceronian prose. The essential element of a periodic sentence is suspense, the retarding of the movement of the sentence, usually through interlocking of modifying clauses and participial phrases, so as to secure dramatic focus for the end of the sentence, which typically contains information essential to the

[29]Leclercq, *Love of Learning* 18–22, 89–99, 287–99.

[30]Smalley, *Study* 245. For the use of the imagery of *lectio divina* in contemporary religious poetry, see Peter Dronke, *The Medieval Lyric* (2nd ed. London 1978) 51–63.

[31]For text and biblical references, see Constable (n. 6 above) 1.128 no. 38.

[32]Von Moos (n. 9 above) 61–63.

[33]Palmer (n. 27 above) 200–05; Polheim (n. 26 above) 210–325; Christine Mohrmann, "Saint Augustin écrivain," *Etudes sur le latin des chrétiens*, Storia e letteratura 65, 87, 103, 143 (4 vols. Rome 1958–77) 2.247–75; and particularly Edith Schuchter, "Zum Predigtstil des hl. Augustinus," *Wiener Studien* 52 (1934) 115–38.

meaning.[34] The medieval sentence, as can be seen from Peter the Venerable's examples, has a very different movement. Typically the essential meaning is stated early, then elaborated: the movement is analytic and cumulative rather than synthetic and climactic. Climax in the medieval sentence is that of heightened rhetorical patterning, not that of important syntactical elements or information hitherto withheld. In this fundamental stylistic feature the "loose" medieval sentence, with its main clause often seeming to serve largely as a hook for a succession of elaborate subordinate clauses, clearly shows its patristic origins.

The new Christian style was itself an adaptation of the "modern" style of the post-Augustan period, which had as its ideals poetic color and "rapid sentences exploding in epigram" in which periodicity was rejected. Seneca was "at once its prophet and its first great exponent," affecting "a sententious brevity—*plus significas quam loqueris*—in which antithesis was the chief effect."[35] It is not surprising, given this family resemblance between Senecan and patristic prose, that Seneca was much admired in the twelfth century. His reputation and popularity had to do both with his moral earnestness and with the compression and point of his style. Both qualities are exemplified in a Senecan passage frequently quoted in our period:

> aliquis vir bonus   nobis diligendus est,
> ac   semper ante oculos habendus,
>   ut sic   tamquam illo spectante   vivamus
>   et omnia   tamquam illo vidente   faciamus.

(We should esteem some virtuous man and have him ever in view, so that we may live as though he were watching and do everything as though he saw [us].)[36]

Of pagan prose writers, Seneca may well have been the most influential model in our period (closely rivaled by the historian Sallust, as will be seen), notwithstanding the special reputation of Cicero and Quintilian as the masters of rhetoric.[37] Both Seneca and Sallust were noted for their brevity—a frequently cited stylistic ideal in the Middle Ages.[38]

[34]Walter R. Johnson, *Luxuriance and Economy: Cicero and the Alien Style*, University of California Publications: Classical Studies 6 (Berkeley 1971) 23–30, 42–56.

[35]Palmer (n. 27 above) 141. See also Norden (n. 26 above) 1.299–313; Michael von Albrecht, *Meister römischer Prosa von Cato bis Apuleius: Interpretationen* (Heidelberg 1971) 138–51.

[36]Seneca, *Epistulae morales* 11.8, paraphrasing Epicurus; quoted by Leighton D. Reynolds, *The Medieval Tradition of Seneca's Letters* (Oxford 1965) 114 n. 1. On Seneca's stylistic reputation and influence, see also Geoffrey of Vinsauf, *Poetria nova* vv. 1833–36, ed. Faral, *Les arts poétiques* 253; Plezia (n. 27 above) 210 n. 47; Klaus-Dieter Nothdurft, *Studien zum Einfluss Senecas auf die Philosophie und Theologie des zwölften Jahrhunderts*, Studien und Texte zur Geistesgeschichte des Mittelalters 7 (Leiden and Cologne 1963) 42–43, 147; Peter von Moos, "Literarkritik im Mittelalter: Arnulf von Lisieux über Ennodius," *Mélanges offerts à René Crozet*, ed. Pierre Gallais and Yves-Jean Riou (2 vols. Poitiers 1966) 2.929–35.

[37]Haskins, *Ren* 112, 139; Constable (n. 6 above) 2.38–39; Ludwig Gompf, "Der Leipziger 'Ordo artium,'" *Mittellateinisches Jahrbuch* 3 (1966) 94–128 at 119, citing Isidore, *Etymologiae* 2.2.1, ed. W. M. Lindsay (2 vols. Oxford 1911) and a late 12th-c. poem on the seven liberal arts.

[38]Curtius 487–94 ("Brevity as an Ideal of Style"); on "epistolary brevity," see Constable (n. 5 above) 18–20.

To be sure, Cicero was not without medieval imitators. Meinhard of Bamberg (d. 1088) rejected some un-Ciceronian stylistic features fashionable in his day (notably prose rhyme and the *cursus*) and wrote an ample prose with traces of Ciceronian vocabulary and other elements suggesting a conscious striving for Ciceronian copiousness.[39] But his sentence structure remains characteristically medieval. Indeed, it has been said that authentic periodicity, an earmark of Ciceronian style, is all but unexampled in the Middle Ages.[40] This and other assumptions regarding the stylistic influence of specific ancient models can be tested only by full-scale stylistic investigation of a wide range of medieval authors.

The elevated, sonorous, sermonlike style characterized above was not appropriate to all recipients and all situations. Peter the Venerable, like other medieval writers, also wrote Latin in another style, equally artistic but less solemn. One instance is a letter sent to his secretary from Peter's retreat in the forests near Cluny. "Weary of cities," the abbot writes, "we cherish the country (*Pertesi urbium, rura amamus*). To add something in verse: 'Not turbulent Rome, but quiet Tibur and peaceful Tarentum please me now.'" The quotation is from Horace, whom Peter quotes again later in the same letter:

Ego tamen quod imputas ocium non prorsus ociosum esse uolui. Et ut iterum uerbis illius cuius supra utar, "Me doctarum hederę pręmia frontium diis miscent superis; me gelidum nemus," taceo reliqua, "secernunt populo." Nosti quantum me pigeant falsa in ęcclesia Dei cantica, quantumque "nugę canorę" michi odibiles sint. Inter quas (nam plurimę sunt) cum nuper in festo magni patris Benedicti hymnum preter sententias, metricam legem, seriemque uerborum peroptimum et cantari audirem et cantare cogerer, nimium (sed non tunc primum) egre tuli, et tanti uiri ueras laudes mendaciter proferri erubui.

(I have not wished my alleged idleness to be completely idle. To use again the words of the same poet: "Me the ivy, reward of learned brows, unites with the gods above; me the cool grove"—I omit what follows—"sets apart from the crowd." You know how much I dislike faulty hymns in God's church, and how odious I find "droning nonsense." As one example of many, when recently on the feast of St Benedict I heard and was required to sing a hymn truly excellent save for content, versification, and style, I was indignant—not for the first time—and I was embarrassed that the veracious praises of so great a man were offered mendaciously.)[41]

With the letter Peter sends two hymns of his own composition in honor of St Benedict. The letter itself is conspicuously less stylized, in spite of occasional end-rhyme, than the letter to the hermit Gilbert. Here and elsewhere in

[39]Carl Erdmann, *Studien zur Briefliteratur Deutschlands im elften Jahrhundert*, MGH Schriften 1 (Leipzig 1938; repr. Stuttgart 1959) 55–116.

[40]Aldo D. Scaglione, *The Classical Theory of Composition from Its Origins to the Present: A Historical Survey*, University of North Carolina Studies in Comparative Literature 53 (Chapel Hill 1972) 73, 360–63, 404.

[41]*Peter the Venerable: Selected Letters*, ed. Janet Martin with Giles Constable, Toronto Medieval Latin Texts 3 (Toronto 1974) 67–68 no. 124; the text is available also in Constable (n. 6 above) 1.317–18 no. 124; discussed by Leclercq, *Love of Learning* 299. The quotations are adapted from Horace, *Epistulae* 1.7.44–45; *Carmina* 1.1.29–32, omitting "and nimble bands of Nymphs with Satyrs"; *Ars poetica* 322.

Peter's letters these superficially more classical sentences probably do not reflect an attempt to imitate classical models, but rather constitute a less elevated, less solemn style appropriate to the recipient and the occasion. It is otherwise with the Horatian quotations, which evoke a specifically Roman literary context for Peter's poetic criticism and composition. The classical allusions would have been second nature to Peter; for monastic education used pagan authors such as Vergil and Horace, along with Christian writers, as models of good style.[42]

HILDEBERT OF LE MANS

A similar distinction in practice between an elevated, sermonlike style and a less solemn, though equally artistic, style can be discerned in the letters of Hildebert of Le Mans. Some of his letters are in effect epistolary sermons and exhibit features similar to those of Peter's letter to Gilbert.[43] But Hildebert also wrote a number of letters, usually rather brief, whose style is characterized by relatively terse sentence-structure, sententious abstractness of expression, and pointed word-play. This letter is typical:

Commeantium raritas facit ut rariores inter nos epistolae discurrant. Illa nobis et obsequium salutationis invidet, et amica colloquia. Caeterum epistolarum raritatem pagina potest supplere prolixior. Memineris igitur invigilare aliquid, quod et solatium tuae sit absentiae, et oculos meos diutius remoretur. Odi verba, quae, cum delectare incipiunt desinunt. Tuam vero prolixitatem sic amplector, ut epistolas longiores, et occupatus suscipiam, et invitus deponam. Illae quidem me otiosum non inveniunt, sed faciunt. Vale, atque id potius age, ut aliquando obliviscaris me, quam ut aliquando cogites de me.

(The fewness of travelers means that few letters hurry to and fro between us. It begrudges us loyal greeting and friendly conversation. But a more copious page is able to compensate for fewness of letters. Remember therefore to compose something to serve as consolation for your absence and to detain my eyes a while. I hate words that end just when they begin to delight. I so welcome your wordiness that I pick up your long letters even when I am busy, and I put them down reluctantly. They do not find me at leisure, to be sure; but they make me so. Farewell, and see to it rather that you now and then forget me than that you now and then remember me.)[44]

These terse, pointed sentences with their abstract diction and antithetical word-play may well reflect the influence of Seneca; Hildebert praised the "brevity without obscurity" (*brevitas non obscura*) of his treatise *De clementia.*[45]

In the letters of Hildebert and Peter, then, two kinds or levels of prose style can be distinguished (apart from plain prose with little pretension to artistic style): a more elevated style marked chiefly by parallelism of structure

[42]Leclercq, *Love of Learning* 139–84.

[43]An example is Hildebert's *Epist.* 1.10, PL 171.162B–68B; cited and discussed by von Moos (n. 9 above) 70–71.

[44]Hildebert, *Epist.* 3.6, PL 171.287A–B; cited and discussed by von Moos (n. 9 above) 46–47.

[45]Hildebert, *Epist.* 1.3, PL 171.145A; cited by von Moos (n.9 above) 31 n. 23.

and sound, and a less elevated, though equally artistic, style.[46] The latter can become classicizing in effect, and probably in intention, when accompanied by features such as Horatian allusion (in the example from Peter) or quasi-Senecan brevity, antithesis, and epigram (in the example from Hildebert).

HISTORICAL PROSE

WILLIAM OF POITIERS

One form that medieval classicism does not take, as a rule, is close imitation of one model to the exclusion of others. Some elements of the rhetorical tradition, for one thing, warned against slavish imitation of a single model and recommended instead a judicious blending of features from various models.[47] A partial exception to the rule is the "History of William the Conqueror" (*Gesta Guillelmi*) written by William of Poitiers in 1073–74. In a valuable comment that throws light also on medieval notions of imitation, the later historian Orderic Vitalis (1075–ca. 1142) wrote that in the *Gesta* William had "subtly and eloquently disclosed the deeds of the Conqueror, imitating the style of Sallustius Crispus."[48] The modern critic, though noting Sallustian influence on William's speeches and military terminology, tends to disagree. Sallust's archaizing vocabulary and studied asymmetry of expression, regarded by modern scholars as distinguishing features of his style, have no counterpart in the *Gesta Guillelmi*; and the vocabulary of the latter is influenced by authors other than Sallust, notably the epic poets.[49] But a closer look may indicate the grounds for Orderic's view.

The beginning of the speech put in the mouth of the Conqueror just before the battle of Hastings will serve as an example of the "Sallustian" style of William of Poitiers:

Commonuit Normannos, quod in multis atque magnis periculis victores tamen se duce semper extiterint. Commonuit omnes patriae suae, nobilium gestorum, magnique nominis. Nunc probandum esse manu, qua virtute polleant, quem gerant animum. Iam non id agi, quis regnans vivat, sed quis periculum imminens cum vita evadat. Si

---

[46]For medieval theory of kinds of style, see especially Quadlbauer (n. 3 above); also Plezia (n. 27 above) and Ernst Robert Curtius, "Die Lehre von den drei Stilen in Altertum und Mittelalter," *Romanische Forschungen* 64 (1952) 57–70.

[47]For example, Seneca the Elder, *Controversiae* 1.preface.6; Quintilian, *Institutio oratoria* 10.2.23–26; Geoffrey of Vinsauf, *Poetria nova* vv. 1837–41, ed. Faral, *Les arts poétiques* 253. But cf. Cicero, *De oratore* 2.21.89–23.96.

[48]"Huc usque Guillelmus Pictauinus historiam suam texuit, in qua Guillelmi gesta Crispi Salustii stilum imitatus subtiliter et eloquenter enucleauit," *The Ecclesiastical History of Orderic Vitalis* 4, ed. and trans. Marjorie Chibnall (6 vols. Oxford 1969–81) 2.258; cited and discussed by Beryl Smalley, "Sallust in the Middle Ages," *Classical Influences on European Culture A.D. 500–1500*, ed. R. R. Bolgar (Cambridge 1971) 165–75 at 173–75.

[49]Raymonde Foreville, ed. and trans., *Guillaume de Poitiers: Histoire de Guillaume le Conquérant*, Les classiques de l'histoire de France au moyen âge 23 (Paris 1952) xxxviii–xliii. On Sallust's style, see Norden (n. 26 above) 1.200–04; Palmer (n. 27 above) 135–37; von Albrecht (n. 35 above) 90–109; Ronald Syme, *Sallust*, Sather Classical Lectures 33 (Berkeley 1964) 256–73, 305–12.

more virorum pugnent, victoriam, decus, divitias habituros. Alioquin aut otius trucidari, aut captos ludibrio fore hostibus crudelissimis.

(He reminded the Normans that amid many great dangers they had been ever victorious nonetheless under his leadership. He reminded all of their native land, noble deeds, and great renown. Now they must prove by force of arms the courage with which they are endowed, the spirit they possess. It is no longer a question of who lives as master, but who escapes the imminent danger with his life. If they fight like men, they will have victory, glory, treasure. If not, they will either be butchered swiftly, or else as captives be ridiculed by a cruel enemy.)[50]

Some verbatim reminiscences point to a speech of Catiline to his troops in Sallust's *Catilina* as a specific literary model for this passage—not surprisingly, for Sallust was a school author, his speeches quoted by the theorist and imitated by the historian.[51] Similarity of content and occasion, underlined by verbatim borrowings, could well have made the passage seem Sallustian to the medieval reader familiar with the Roman historian. More to our point, further support for Orderic's opinion comes in William's style narrowly defined, his way of writing sentences. They are antithetical and terse, with frequent asyndeton. End-rhyme is avoided. Sections of narrative end with pithy, sententious sayings. All things considered, William's prose, with its brevity and avoidance of rhyme, *is* Sallustian—relative to Orderic's own regularly rhymed, rather ponderous prose and to much other prose familiar to him.[52]

The distinctive features of classicizing prose are, then, avoidance of the parallelism of structure and sound generally characteristic of elevated patristic and medieval style, the conspicuous use of classical allusion and vocabulary instead of (or, frequently, in addition to) biblical allusion and vocabulary, and often a relative compression and brevity. It can be added that some authors appear consciously to favor classical rather than nonclassical syntax where medieval grammatical rules allowed a choice of construction. Both Meinhard of Bamberg (d. 1088) and John of Gaeta (d. 1119), for example, strongly favor the classical accusative-and-infinitive construction to express indirect statement rather than the distinctively medieval clause introduced by *quod* or *quia*.[53]

---

[50]Foreville (n. 49 above) 182.

[51]Sallust, *Catilina* 58; cited by Foreville (n. 49 above) xxxix, 184 n. 1. For Sallust's influence, see Smalley (n. 48 above) 168–70; Richard W. Southern, "Aspects of the European Tradition of Historical Writing: 1. The Classical Tradition from Einhard to Geoffrey of Monmouth," TRHS 5th ser. 20 (1970) 173–96; Johannes Schneider, *Die Vita Heinrici IV. und Sallust: Studien zu Stil und Imitatio in der mittellateinischen Prosa*, Deutsche Akademie der Wissenschaften zu Berlin, Schriften der Sektion für Altertumswissenschaft 49 (Berlin 1965).

[52]On Orderic's style, see Chibnall (n. 48 above) 2.xix–xxi; Hans Wolter, *Ordericus Vitalis: Ein Beitrag zur kluniazensischen Geschichtsschreibung* (Wiesbaden 1955) 118–26.

[53]Erdmann (n. 39 above) 57–58; Lohrmann (n. 7 above) 405. This distinction has been detected within a single author's (poetic) production. Though Hildebert of Le Mans normally uses the accusative and infinitive, on five occasions he uses *quod* with the indicative; significantly, these instances are limited to poems on religious subjects: A. Brian Scott, "A Critical Edition of the Poems of Hildebert of Le Mans" (diss. Oxford 1960) 33–34; on Hildebert's prose syntax, see von Moos (n. 9 above) 52–53. For Augustine's syntactic usage before and after his conversion, see Mohrmann (n. 33 above) 2.248–49.

In what sense can twelfth-century prose style, and particularly classicizing style, be seen as part of the twelfth-century renaissance? First, the generally high level of Latin prose in our period attests to the revival of learning. Visible as early as the middle of the eleventh century, the new stylistic sureness contrasts with the ineptitude, lack of complication, and indifference to rhetorical rules that characterize some earlier production.[54] In this development, revived classicism is only one of several stylistic currents.

On the one hand, utilitarian claims made themselves felt. Letter-writing came increasingly under the influence of the *artes dictandi*; by the end of the century epistolary style is noticeably more mechanical and impersonal than it had been at the beginning of the century.[55] Similarly, by 1200 the increasingly specialized preoccupations of scholarship and learning had elicited a simpler way of writing than in the past, with technical vocabulary and with argumentation that conformed to the rules of dialectic.[56]

On the other hand, classicizing style found another powerful rival in the systematic affectation of rhetorical devices now labeled "mannerism." A constant in medieval Latin literature, mannerism came to be perhaps the salient stylistic tendency in our period. "The mannerist wants to say things not normally but abnormally. He prefers the artificial and affected to the natural. He wants to surprise, to astonish, to dazzle."[57] Medieval mannerism, which exaggerates qualities found already in the stylistic theory and practice of classical Latin, is manifested particularly in elaboration and exaggeration of the traditional *ornatus* (embellishment) recommended by ancient theory. Thus hyperbaton, the separation of words belonging together grammatically, is a normal feature of literary Latin; but its exaggerated use becomes manneristic. Peter the Venerable, who used a short and normal hyperbaton (*caelestibus locus esse thesauris*) in his letter to Gilbert, offers an instance of extended hyperbaton (*tali . . . conuersatione*) in the following description of Peter Abelard, the hyperbaton only slightly mitigated by the repetition of *tali*:

Tali nobiscum uir "simplex et rectus, timens Deum et recedens a malo," tali inquam per aliquantum temporis conuersatione ultimos uitae suae dies consecrans Deo . . .

---

[54]Karl Pivec, "Stil- und Sprachentwicklung in mittellateinischen Briefen vom 8.–12. Jh.," MIÖG Ergänzungsband 14 (1939) 33–51 at 38–39; Constable (n. 5 above) 31–32; and especially the Latinity and style of a group of ambitious but often clumsy 8th-c. texts: *Salzburger Formelbücher und Briefe aus Tassilonischer und Karolingischer Zeit*, ed. Bernhard Bischoff, SB Munich 1973 no. 4; see also Bengt Löfstedt and Carol D. Lanham, "Zu den neugefundenen Salzburger Formelbüchern und Briefen," *Eranos* 73 (1975) 69–100.

[55]Constable (n. 5 above) 36–38; Lanham (n. 7 above) 53–55.

[56]M. Hubert, "Quelques aspects du latin philosophique aux XIIe et XIIIe siècles," *Revue des études latines* 27 (1949) 211–33. For the earlier ideal, derived largely from Cicero, of union between reason and eloquence, philosophy and rhetoric, see John of Salisbury, *Metalogicon* 1.1 and 1.4 (n. 9 above) 7, 14–15; Curtius 76–77; Panofsky, *Ren & Ren* 68–69, 102–03; Birger Munk-Olsen, "L'humanisme de Jean de Salisbury, un Ciceronien au 12e siècle," *Entretiens* 53–69 at 56–59; Gabriel Nuchelmans, "Philologia et son mariage avec Mercure jusqu'à la fin du XIIe siècle," *Latomus* 16 (1957) 84–107 at 101–04.

[57]Curtius 282. On mannerism in 10th-c. writers, see Auerbach (n. 4 above) 85–179 at 133–67.

(In this way of life with us the man "blameless and upright, fearing God and turning from evil," in this way of life, I say, for some little time consecrating the last days of his life to God . . .)[58]

Similarly with the figure called *annominatio* or *paronomasia*, denoting various sorts of punning word-play. The *Ad Herennium* recommends sparing use of annominatio in serious speeches, for overuse of the device strikes listeners as childish.[59] But accumulated annominatio abounds in late antique and medieval literature, and the new arts of poetry in our period enthusiastically commend the device without the reservations expressed by the author of *Ad Herennium*. Perhaps the extreme of twelfth-century manneristic prose style is reached in the letters of Guy of Bazoches (d. 1203), every page of which displays rhetorical art at its most flamboyant.[60]

Both stylistic developments—the utilitarian and technical, on the one hand, and the manneristic, on the other—made significant contributions, both in quantity and in quality, to twelfth-century prose, which therefore cannot be understood exclusively in terms of its classicizing component. Classicizing prose style, indeed, declined in importance relative to its rivals in the course of the twelfth century.

QUANTITATIVE VERSE

These issues and currents can be clarified further through attention to the large production of Latin poetry in the twelfth century. The treatment here, necessarily very selective, will concentrate on quantitative rather than rhythmical poetry in order to permit comparison with ancient verse technique. The principal exemplary texts, which span our period, are the shorter poems of Hildebert of Le Mans (1056–1133), an early thirteenth-century anthology of rhetorical poems, and the bucolic poems of the so-called "Marcus Valerius," tentatively dated in the second half of the twelfth century.[61] Particular attention will be given to some features of form and verse technique—rhyme, elision, and the treatment of the line-ending—that are significant for the study of classicism and poetic style.

HILDEBERT OF LE MANS AND MARBOD OF RENNES

The choice of a classical theme and the construction of larger effects of structure and organization on a classical model serve to link the medieval poem and

---

[58]Martin (n. 41 above) 65 no. 115; text also in Constable (n. 6 above) 1.307 no. 115. The allusion is to Job 1:1. On hyperbaton see Curtius 274–75.

[59]*Ad Herennium* 4.22.32, ed. Caplan (n. 24 above) 308; Curtius 278–80.

[60]*Liber epistularum Guidonis de Basochis*, ed. Herbert Adolfsson, Studia latina Stockholmiensia 18 (Stockholm 1969); important additions and corrections in the review by Bengt Löfstedt, *Gnomon* 44 (1972) 34–41.

[61]*Hildeberti Cenomannensis episcopi carmina minora*, ed. A. Brian Scott (Leipzig 1969); *A Thirteenth-Century Anthology of Rhetorical Poems: Glasgow MS Hunterian V.8.14*, ed. Bruce Harbert, Toronto Medieval Latin Texts 4 (Toronto 1975); *M. Valerio: Bucoliche*, ed. Franco Munari (2nd ed. Florence 1970) xliv–1.

poet to the classical tradition. A poem by Ovid addressing a ring sent as a gift to his lover may well have inspired verses written by Hildebert of Le Mans probably to accompany the gift of a ring to Odo of Bayeux.[62] In Hildebert's poem the jewel, morose and clouded in its box, begins to sparkle on hearing that it will adorn the finger of the bishop of Bayeux. The educated audience's recognition of the Ovidian model, perhaps only a secondary consideration in this poem, is of primary significance in Hildebert's long elegy lamenting his banishment to England, which is modeled on Ovid's elegiac poems *Tristia* and *Ex Ponto*, written from exile on the shores of the Black Sea.[63] The medieval writer's intended parallel between himself and the ancient poet would have been made clear to his medieval audience by the elegiac form and the subtle but pervasive verbal echoes. Allusions to Ovid's complaints against Fortune and his description of voyage into exile on the Black Sea run through the bishop's account of his own downfall and his crossing to England. In the last part of the poem a paraphrased quotation from the book of Job and similarities in thought and phrasing to Boethius's *Consolation of Philosophy* would have evoked Job and Boethius as further examples from Antiquity of virtuous men tried by temporal suffering. To the medieval audience, responding to the original connotations of these verbal echoes, Hildebert's experience became a modern instance of virtue tested by hardship, and his long elegy a modern counterpart and successor to Ovid's poems written from exile.

Even a single word can effect a link with the classical past. The poet Marbod of Rennes (d. 1123) closes his rhymed hexameter poem to the Virgin with the prayer that on the day of judgment she "banish the torments of hell and grant to the blessed an eternal dwelling in the Elysian fields (*Elisios*)":

> Supplicium post iudicium removeto gehennae,
> Elisios concede pios habitare perenne.[64]

One of very few classical borrowings in the poem, *Elisios* is given prominence by its emphatic position at the beginning of its line and by antithesis in thought to the immediately preceding *gehennae*, "hell." With skilled economy Marbod has placed his poem firmly in the classical tradition. To be sure, his use of "Elysian fields" belongs to a poetic tradition of assigning classical names to Christian theological concepts, at times almost as a matter of habit. But here the expression has a classicizing intention and effect.[65]

---

[62]"Anulus hic nuper," ed. Scott (n. 61 above) 45 no. 54. Cf. Ovid, *Amores* 2.15.

[63]"Nuper eram locuples," ed. Scott (n. 61 above) 11–15 no. 22. On evocative allusion, see Peter Dronke, "Functions of Classical Borrowing in Medieval Latin Verse," *Classical Influences* (n. 48 above) 159–64; on poetic allusions to Ovid's exile, see Winfried Offermanns, *Die Wirkung Ovids auf die literarische Sprache der lateinischen Liebesdichtung des 11. und 12. Jahrhunderts*, Beihefte zum Mittellateinischen Jahrbuch 4 (Wuppertal, Kastellaun, and Düsseldorf 1970) 94–97.

[64]"Stella maris," ed. Guido Maria Dreves and Clemens Blume, *Analecta hymnica medii aevi* (55 vols. Leipzig 1886–1922; repr. New York, London, and Frankfurt 1961) 50.393 no. 302 (4) vv. 21–22.

[65]An instructive parallel is the specifically pagan context of Bernard of Cluny's sole use of *Elysios*—a rebuke of Vergil for his erroneous description of the lower world: *De contemptu mundi* 1.641–44, ed. Herman C. Hoskier, *De contemptu mundi: A Bitter Satirical Poem of 3000 Lines Upon the Morals of the XIIth Century by Bernard of Morval, Monk of Cluny (fl. 1150)* (London

Some twelfth-century poems evoke their classical models so convincingly that they have been thought products of Antiquity. A number of Hildebert's poems belong to this group: his two elegies on Rome, his epigrams on Roman historical and mythological themes, and his satirical and moralizing epigrams in the manner of Martial.[66] Printed in nineteenth-century anthologies of ancient verse are these lines lamenting the venality of the times, which the editors did not recognize as part of an elegy published earlier with correct attribution to Hildebert; one editor suggested Petronius as their author:

> hinc est quod populus aurum quasi numen adorans,
>   audet in ignotum sepe venire nefas,
> speque lucri totiens excedere ius et honestum
>   sustulit, ut gratis iam iuvet esse reum.
> ius ruit, ordo perit, sceleri placet ora manusque
>   vendere, quamque inopem tam pudet esse probum.

(Hence it is that the people worship gold as a god / and dare to enter upon many a new wickedness; / and in hope of gain they have endured so often to exceed right and honor / that now they delight in playing the criminal gratuitously. / Right is fallen, order perishes. A rogue is pleased to sell both speech and deed, / and he finds virtue as disgraceful as poverty.)[67]

The mistaken attribution to Antiquity has some justification. The theme (familiar in Roman poetry), the restraint in vocabulary and rhetorical embellishment, the Ovidian diction of the fourth and sixth lines, and the classical, unrhymed elegiac verse form—all contribute to the classicizing effect.

But in Hildebert's poetry as in medieval Latin literature generally, these classicizing episodes are the exception. The pervading stylistic tendency is the mannerism described above, with its predilection for the artificial and the affected, for accumulated and exaggerated ornament, for far-fetched metaphor and pointed and surprising ideas. An exemplary text is provided by the first lines of Hildebert's poem on his exile. After a classicizing opening couplet modeled on some lines of Ovid, the poem continues with a manneristic description of Hildebert's former prosperity that employs verse-filling asyndeton (piling up words with omission of conjunctions) and zeugma (the use of one verb with several nouns):

> Nuper eram locuples, multisque beatus amicis,
>   et risere diu fata secunda mihi.
> larga Ceres, deus Archadie, Bachusque replebant
>   horrea, tecta, penum, farre, bidente, mero.
> hortus, apes, famule, pulmento, melle, tapetis,
>   ditabant large prandia, vasa, domum.

<hr/>

1929) 22. For Bernard's hostility to "the heathen and poetic style" (*stylus ethnicus atque poeticus,* 3.318), see Panofsky, *Ren & Ren* 75–76.

[66]Scott (n. 61 above) xxxvii–xli and notes to nos. 7, 9, 16, 17, 19, 23, 33, 36, 38, 47, and 48.

[67]"Moribus, arte, fide," ed. Scott (n. 61 above) 6–7 no. 17 vv. 15–20. These lines are printed and tentatively attributed to Petronius in *Poetae latini minores,* ed. Emil Baehrens (5 vols. Leipzig 1879–83) 5.412 no. 106. Cf. Ovid, *Ex Ponto* 2.3.14: "non movet, et gratis paenitet esse probum."

(Once I was prosperous and endowed with many friends, / and favorable fortune long smiled upon me. / Bountiful Ceres, the god of Arcady, and Bacchus once filled / barns, folds, and stores with grain, sheep, and wine. / Garden, bees, and serv-ingwomen with food, honey, and tapestries / enriched bountifully meals, jars, and dwelling.)[68]

To be sure, both asyndeton and zeugma occur in classical poetry: the theorist Matthew of Vendôme (fl. 1175), in recommending zeugma as a way of begin-ning a poem, will cite examples not only from his own poetry but also from Ovid and Statius.[69] It is the accumulation of these figures in Hildebert's poem that is manneristic, though he and his contemporaries would not have made the distinction between classicizing restraint and manneristic exaggeration. Probably they saw these conceits merely as going Ovid one better.

Together with mannerism of form the Middle Ages inherited from late Antiquity a taste for mannerism of thought, a playing with pointed and sur-prising ideas. Mannerism of thought is illustrated by a poem of Hildebert's that has been mistaken for an outstanding product of Antiquity by some Re-naissance and modern scholars. The poem concerns the fulfillment of three contradictory predictions of the Hermaphrodite's manner of death: stabbing, hanging, and drowning. The unfortunate Hermaphrodite relates how, while climbing a tree that stretched over a river, it slipped on its sword and fell head down into the stream with its foot caught in the branches: "Man, woman, neither, I suffered flood, sword, gibbet."[70] A longer and more elaborate poem on the same theme by the virtuoso Peter Riga (d. ca. 1209) forms part of the celebrated collection of his early poems titled *Floridus aspectus*, which he dedicated to Samson, archbishop of Reims (1140–61).[71] Peter's version clearly is an imitation and amplification of Hildebert's poem.

MATTHEW OF VENDÔME

In the course of the twelfth century poetic expression became, if anything, even more ingenious and more involved. The commendations of elaborate decoration and far-fetched metaphor found in the arts of poetry of the late

[68]"Nuper eram locuples" (n. 63 above) vv. 1–6. Cf. Ovid, *Ex Ponto* 2.3.25–26: "en ego, non paucis quondam munitus amicis, / dum flavit velis aura secunda meis."

[69]Matthew of Vendôme, *Ars versificatoria* 1.4–12, ed. Faral, *Les arts poétiques* 111–12. The grammatical dovetailing exhibited by the so-called *versus rapportati* (two examples are in Hildebert's poem on his exile, vv. 35–38) is a formal mannerism that seems not to occur in classical poetry but is common in medieval Latin texts: Curtius 286–87; Edmond Faral, "Sidoine Apollinaire et la technique littéraire du moyen âge," *Miscellanea Giovanni Mercati*, Studi e testi 121–26 (6 vols. Vatican City 1946) 2.567–80 at 578–80.

[70]"Tulique / vir, mulier, neutrum, flumina, tela, crucem": "Dum mea me mater," ed. Scott (n. 61 above) 15–16 no. 23 vv. 9–10; von Moos (n. 9 above) 237; E. H. Alton, "Who Wrote the *Hermaphroditus*?" *Hermathena* 46 (1931) 136–48. On mannerisms of thought, see Curtius 292–93.

[71]Peter Riga, "Uxor Thyresiae," PL 171.1445D–46A, attributed to Hildebert. On Peter's life and works, see now Paul E. Beichner, ed., *Aurora: Petri Rigae Biblia versificata*, University of Notre Dame Publications in Mediaeval Studies 19 (2 vols. Notre Dame Ind. 1965) 1.xx–1v; to the

twelfth and early thirteenth centuries reflected contemporary taste and in turn encouraged a large production of highly manneristic verse. A poem attributed to Matthew of Vendôme that recounts the classical myth of Deucalion and Pyrrha is characteristic of much of this verse in its conceits and punning word-play. A kindly Jupiter, surveying his earthly realm, looks upon a world (*orbis*) that is bereft (*orbus*) of virtue. Among the people (*populis*) every kind of impiety burgeons (*pullulat*). Jupiter decides to remove this stain (*labem*) but wavers (*labat*) in indecision about the method. As recommended in Matthew's own *Ars versificatoria*,[72] the poem begins with a sententious generality, in this case a threefold statement that crime incites its own punishment:

> Supplicium delicta uocant; uindicta scelestos
>   expectat; scelerum crimina pena manet.
> Sors melior dedit astra Ioui qui, cuncta cohercens
>   imperio, stringit sceptra potente manu.
> Hic orbis pastor, pater et capud, ergo tuetur
>   pastor ouile, pater pignora, membra capud.
> Sed gregis hunc delicta mouent, et cogitur orbi
>   pastoris pietas esse nouerca suo.
> Indulget penitus uitiis uirtutibus orbis
>   orbus, et in populis pullulat omne nephas.
> Ergo libet labem detergere, sed labat anceps
>   cura—quod abstergat crimina tanta malum?

(Transgressions provoke punishment; vengeance watches for the wicked; expiation awaits the reproach of impious actions. / A favorable destiny gave the heavens to Jupiter, who, curbing all things by his authority, presses the scepter with mighty hand. / He is the world's shepherd, father, and head: therefore the shepherd protects his fold, the father his children, the head the members. / But the transgressions of his flock move him, and the shepherd's loving-kindness is compelled to be a stepmother to his own world. / The world, bereft of virtue, is given wholly to vice, and among the people flourishes every impiety. / Therefore he is disposed to purge this stain, but his hesitant solicitude wavers: which punishment is to expel such crimes?)[73]

Jupiter decides to send a great flood, which destroys all humankind save for Deucalion and Pyrrha, through whom the earth was later repopulated.

One extreme of formal mannerism in twelfth-century Latin poetry is reached in a poem by Peter Riga, from his verse commentary on the Bible titled *Aurora*. This is his "lipogrammatic" ("letter-dropping") allegorical catalogue of persons of the Old Testament in twenty-three chapters: in the first

---

bibliography there cited add André Boutemy, "Recherches sur le *Floridus Aspectus* de Pierre la Rigge (I)," *Le moyen âge* 54 (1948) 89–112; "Recherches sur le 'Floridus Aspectus' (II)," *Latomus* 8 (1949) 159–68.

[72]Matthew of Vendôme, *Ars versificatoria* 1.16–29, ed. Faral, *Les arts poétiques* 113–16. The opening couplet is quoted as an example of *interpretatio* (repetition of the same idea in different words) by Geoffrey of Vinsauf, *Summa de coloribus rhetoricis*, ed. Faral, *Les arts poétiques* 325 and by Gervase of Melkley, *Ars poetica*, ed. Gräbener (n. 16 above) 39; the latter denies that the device exemplifies perissologia (the rhetorical fault of "excess").

[73]"Supplicium delicta uocant," ed. Harbert (n. 61 above) 63–64 no. 49 vv. 1–12. Cf. Ovid, *Metamorphoses* 1.177–415.

chapter the letter *a* does not appear, in the second the letter *b* does not appear, and so on throughout the rest of the alphabet.[74]

"MARCUS VALERIUS"

In sharp contrast to these manneristic poems is the classicizing bucolic poetry of the so-called "Marcus Valerius."[75] Consisting of a prologue in elegiac distichs followed by four hexameter poems closely modeled on Vergil's *Eclogues*, the poems seemingly were not widely read, since they survive in only one medieval manuscript, written in a French hand about 1200, and one humanistic copy of this manuscript. Valerius's language in his bucolics lacks almost entirely the stereotyped vocabulary and the manneristic rhetorical artifices recommended by the theorists and met with in much twelfth-century poetry.[76] Although this restrained and distinctive style reflects his imitation of his model, Valerius's poems are not, and were not intended to be, slavish imitations. For one thing, the medieval author has not restricted himself to Vergilian vocabulary, as he easily could have done, but draws also on Ovid, Horace, and other poets and even prose writers of classical and late Antiquity. And there are slips in morphology, syntax, and prosody attributable in part to lack of modern tools of scholarship. But taken as a whole the poems represent conscious, multifaceted imitation of a single work of pagan Antiquity—a rare circumstance in our period.

This poetic program is made all the more conspicuous by the radically different style of part of Valerius's brief prologue in elegiac distichs. In a manneristic tour de force that employs such artifices as hexameters and pentameters containing only three or even two words, he describes the poets of old (*maiores*):

> Fortunatorum diffamavere trophea
> Indelimatis plurima carminibus,
> Commemoraverunt pretermittenda frequenter,
> Pretermiserunt commemorabilia,
> Decantaverunt inconsummabiliora
> Formidandorum prelia celicolum.

(They maligned the many victories of the fortunate in unpolished verse; / often did they recount things best omitted and omit things worth recounting; / they chanted over and over again the unending battles of dreaded gods.)[77]

---

[74]Peter Riga, *Recapitulationes*, ed. Beichner (n. 71 above) 1.xviii–xix, 2.605–25; also PL 212.31D–42C; discussed by Curtius 282–83. For the enduring popularity in the later Middle Ages of poems by Hildebert, Matthew of Vendôme, Peter Riga, and other 12th-c. poets, see A. George Rigg, "Medieval Latin Poetic Anthologies (I)," *Mediaeval Studies* 39 (1977) 281–330; "Medieval Latin Poetic Anthologies (II)," *Mediaeval Studies* 40 (1978) 387–407; Franz Brunhölzl, "'Florilegium Treverense' [I, II]," *Mittellateinisches Jahrbuch* 1 (1964) 65–77 and 3 (1966) 129–217.

[75]Munari (n. 61 above) xliv–1; Helen Cooper, *Pastoral: Mediaeval into Renaissance* (Ipswich Eng. and Totowa N.J. 1977) 19–24, 102–03.

[76]Munari (n. 61 above) l–lxiv, lxxviii–lxxxi.

[77]Prologus 13–18, ed. Munari (n. 61 above) 4.

Though hexameters of three words and pentameters of two words were not entirely unknown in Antiquity, hexameters of only two words are unexampled in ancient Latin poetry. Like other twelfth-century poets, "Marcus Valerius" delighted in outdoing the ancients.[78] This passage of his prologue could hardly contrast more strongly with the bucolics that follow. By demonstrating his ability to write in two very different styles, he draws all the more attention to the classicizing and specifically Vergilian style of his bucolics, whose first lines vividly evoke the world, by turns idyllic and harsh, of their Vergilian model:

> Cidne, sub algenti recubas dum molliter umbra
> Nec nova mutato perquiris pascua colle,
> Segnis et exesis miserum pecus afficis herbis,
> Nos patimur solem et nullo requiescimus antro,
> Dum fastiditi mutamus gramina campi
> Et pudet has saturas non semper cernere fetas;
> At tu lascivis victus dum pasceris umbris,
> Heu macie siccantur oves, heu decipis agnos.

(Cidnus, as languidly you lie in the chilly shade, / nor seek new pasturage on another hill, / and lazily afflict your wretched flock with well-nibbled grasses, / I endure the sun, and in no hollow do I take my ease, / as I forsake the turf of a rejected field / and am ashamed not to see these new-delivered ewes always sated; / but while you feast, vanquished by the easeful shade, / alas! your sheep are withered and thin, alas! you cheat the lambs.)[79]

VERSE TECHNIQUE

RHYMED AND UNRHYMED DACTYLIC VERSE

All the poetic texts examined above are written in quantitative verse, whose rhythm is determined not by word accents but by the patterned succession of long and short syllables.[80] This was the principle of verse composition that predominated in classical and late Antiquity, and quantitative Latin verse continued to be written in large amounts throughout the Middle Ages. Some features of form and verse technique are highly significant for the study of classicism and poetic style.[81] For the twelfth-century poet one important choice was between classical, unrhymed dactylic verse and any of a variety of inge-

[78]Munari (n. 61 above) xxxviii–xliv.

[79]*Bucolica* 1.1–8, ed. Munari (n. 61 above) 5. Contrast the explicitly Christian orientation of Metellus of Tegernsee's Vergilian bucolics (ca. 1165), which celebrate the miracles of St Quirinus involving cattle: *Die Quirinalien des Metellus von Tegernsee: Untersuchungen zur Dichtkunst und kritische Textausgabe*, ed. Peter C. Jacobsen, Mittellateinische Studien und Texte 1 (Leiden and Cologne 1965); Cooper (n. 75 above) 19, 22–24.

[80]Good introductions to quantitative verse are: James W. Halporn, Martin Ostwald, and Thomas G. Rosenmeyer, *The Meters of Greek and Latin Poetry* (Indianapolis and New York 1963); David S. Raven, *Latin Metre: An Introduction* (London 1965); Hans Drexler, *Einführung in die römische Metrik* (Darmstadt 1967).

[81]See Dag Norberg, *Introduction à l'étude de la versification latine médiévale*, Studia latina Stockholmiensia 5 (Stockholm 1958), which emphasizes the period before 1100; Munari (n. 61 above) lxiv–lxxviii; and especially Paul Klopsch, *Einführung in die mittellateinische Verslehre* (Darmstadt 1972).

niously rhymed dactylic verse forms. Though rhyming lines occur sporadically in classical poetry, the systematic and regular use of assonance first appeared in Christian writers of late Antiquity. Already in the mid-fifth century, assonance is a pronounced tendency in Caelius Sedulius's influential *Carmen Paschale*, written in hexameter verse. Many lines fall into the rhyming pattern that later will be called "leonine" (*versus leonini*), in which assonance or rhyme links the syllable of the first half of the third foot (less often the fourth foot) of a verse with the last syllable of that verse. In other cases a series of two or more lines is linked by end-rhyme (*versus caudati*):

> Qui diuersa no*uam*   formasti in corpora te*rram*
> Torpentique solo   uiuentia membra dedis*ti*,
> Qui pereuntem hominem   uetiti dulcedine po*mi*
> Instauras   meliore cibo . . .

(You who have shaped the new earth into different bodies / and have bestowed living members upon the sluggish soil, / You who with better food restore humankind perishing from the sweetness of the forbidden apple . . .)[82]

In the Carolingian period, rhyme is the exception; most Carolingian poets followed the practice of Vergil, Ovid, and classicizing Christian authors such as Prudentius. But in the tenth and eleventh centuries the use of rhyme in dactylic verse becomes widespread, and the rhyme patterns increasingly intricate.

The various combinations of internal and end-rhyme in this medieval transformation of the dactylic line were named by thirteenth-century theorists.[83] The hexameter lines by Marbod of Rennes quoted above (at note 64) are of a fairly common type sometimes called *versus trinini salientes*, in this case linked in couplets by end-rhyme. Some varieties of rhymed hexameter amount to a new kind of verse, as in the *versus tripertiti dactylici* in which Bernard of Cluny (fl. 1140) wrote his long and celebrated poem on the evils of the times (see note 65 above). The line is divided into three equal parts; word-accent almost invariably coincides with the quantitative verse-accent (*ictus*); and other fundamental departures from classical practice make this in effect a new verse form even though it retains the succession of long and short syllables belonging to dactylic hexameter.

In the twelfth century rhymed dactylic verse became controversial as emphasizing sound over sense. Marbod of Rennes in his old age criticized the rhymed hexameter forms he once had favored, on two grounds: the labor

---

[82]Sedulius, *Carmen Paschale* 1.68–71, ed. Johann Hümer, *Sedulii opera omnia*, Corpus scriptorum ecclesiasticorum latinorum 10 (Vienna 1885) 20–21. On rhyme, see Norberg (n. 81 above) 38–41, 64–69; Klopsch (n. 81 above) 38–49, 76–79. At least one 12th-c. poet adapted leonine hexameters occurring in Vergil to his own rhyming hexameter verse; see Levi Robert Lind, "Reginald of Canterbury and the Rhymed Hexameter," *Neophilologus* 25 (1940) 273–75.

[83]E.g., Eberhard the German, *Laborintus* vv. 705–33, 775–816, ed. Faral, *Les arts poétiques* 362–65. For a useful modern classification, see Wilhelm Meyer, "Radewin's Gedicht über Theophilus und die Arten der gereimten Hexameter," *Gesammelte Abhandlungen zur mittellateinischen Rythmik* (3 vols. in 2 Berlin 1905–36) 1.59–135 at 82–98.

spent in contriving elaborate rhyme schemes was misplaced, and the rhyming lines themselves were monotonous and lacked variety.[84] The most strident attack appears in the *Ars versificatoria* of Matthew of Vendôme, who condemns leonine verses that lack content: such lines have no beauty (*venustas*) save that little derived from their windiness (*ventositas*).[85]

The context of twelfth-century production, therefore, is heightened awareness of the range of effects available in rhymed and unrhymed dactylic verse. For the twelfth-century poet the use or avoidance of rhyme became increasingly a significant stylistic choice. At the beginning of the century, the fifty-seven shorter poems of Hildebert of Le Mans are in a variety of forms, with nearly two-thirds in classical, unrhymed elegiac distichs.[86] The rest are in rhymed or unrhymed hexameters, with the exception of four short poems in rhymed elegiacs and one long poem and part of another in rhythmical verse. Hildebert used the quantitative forms for the themes with which they had traditionally been associated in ancient and medieval practice: hexameter for didactic themes, elegiac distich for epigram, reflection, and lament. Though there is little evidence that his choice of the unrhymed, classical form or the rhymed, medieval form was conditioned by choice of subject (for Hildebert as for other medieval poets unrhymed elegiac distich was an all-purpose meter), it may be significant that his four elegiac epigrams on subjects from classical history and myth—Lucretia (no. 19), the Hermaphrodite (no. 23), and Ganymede (nos. 33 and 48)—are in unrhymed elegiacs and that the few rhymed epigrams are on sacred and aphoristic themes.

In the course of the century two trends become clear. On the one hand, the manneristic poetry commended and composed by the theorists and associated with their treatises in the manuscripts shows a marked reduction in formal variety relative to Hildebert's collection. Of the forty-nine quantitative poems in the early thirteenth-century rhetorical anthology cited above, forty-six are in unrhymed elegiac distichs, two in unrhymed hexameters, and one (the much copied and imitated "Pergama flere uolo," written about 1080) in rhymed elegiac distichs.[87] The marked preference for elegiac carries further a tendency already evident in Hildebert's poetry, and the avoidance of rhyme recalls contemporary reservations regarding leonines expressed by Matthew of Vendôme and others.

[84]Marbod of Rennes, *Liber decem capitulorum* 1.16–35, ed. Walther Bulst, Editiones Heidelbergenses 8 (Heidelberg 1947) 5; also PL 171.1693B–C; discussed by Bulst, "Studien zu Marbods Carmina varia und Liber decem capitulorum," Nachrichten Göttingen philol.-hist. Kl. n.s., Fachgruppe 4: Neuere Philologie und Literaturgeschichte 2 (1937–39) 173–241 at 212–18.

[85]*Ars versificatoria* 43–45, ed. Faral, *Les arts poétiques* 166–67; discussed by Klopsch (n. 81 above) 45.

[86]Scott (n. 61 above) 63.

[87]Harbert (n. 61 above) 34–37 no. 30: found also in *Carmina Burana*, ed. Alfons Hilka, Otto Schumann, and Bernhard Bischoff (1 vol. in 3 parts (Heidelberg 1930–70) 1.2.139–60 no. 101. See André Boutemy, "Le poème *Pergama flere uolo* . . . et ses imitateurs du XIIe siècle," *Latomus* 5 (1946) 233–44.

On the other hand, rhymed dactylic verse continued to be written, the strictures of the theorists notwithstanding. Indeed, it shows renewed vitality in the works of Hugh Primas (fl. ca. 1150), the Archpoet (d. ca. 1165), and Serlo of Wilton (d. 1181) as a vehicle for witty word-play and verbal juggling. Primas chose rhythmical verse and rhymed (but not unrhymed) dactylic verse for his varied themes—satirical, erotic, and classical. His creative use of rhyme is evident particularly in humorous contexts such as his dialogue with his cloak. The garment, which has no lining, replies to his pleas for warmth:

> Conpatior certe,   moveor pietate super te
> et facerem iussum;   sed Jacob, non Esau sum.

(Assuredly I sympathize, I am moved by affection for you, and I would like to do what you ask: but I am only a Jacob, not an Esau.)[88]

Perhaps the most extravagant developments of rhymed quantitative verse in our period are found in Serlo of Wilton's poetry. The literary possibilities of punning leonine hexameters are revealed in his tour de force, a poem of over a hundred lines of the sort

> Vobis thus, dii, do: redimi me vult mea Dido.

(To you incense, O gods, I give: my Dido wills that I be redeemed.)[89]

Serlo is "a virtuoso delighting in language for its own sake," whose use of puns belongs to a realm "where words, not ideas, reign supreme."[90]

Perhaps it was the preeminence of sound over sense in the work of Serlo and his imitators that inspired Matthew of Vendôme's censure. In any case, a tendency for poets to write *either* rhymed *or* unrhymed verse almost exclusively develops in the twelfth century. One group of writers, whose tastes are reflected in the arts of poetry, rejected rhymed dactylic verse in favor of classical, unrhymed verse, with a strong preference for elegiac distich. Another group of writers, exemplified by Hugh Primas and Serlo of Wilton, pushed the medieval rhymed forms to their limits. These poets used rhymed verse for many themes; but the salient qualities of their work are wit and humor, produced in part by ingenious and sometimes outrageous word-play.

---

[88]"Pauper mantelle," ed. Wilhelm Meyer, "Die Oxforder Gedichte des Primas (des Magisters Hugo von Orleans)," Nachrichten Göttingen 1907 (separately repr. Darmstadt 1970) 75–175 at 115–16 no. 2C vv. 22–23; text with German translation by Karl Langosch, *Hymnen und Vagantenlieder: Lateinische Lyrik des Mittelalters mit deutschen Versen* (Basel 1954; rev. ed. Darmstadt 1961) 184–85. The allusion is to Gen. 27:11. On the theme see Anne Betten, "Lateinische Bettellyrik: Literarische Topik oder Ausdruck existentieller Not? Eine vergleichende Skizze über Martial und den Archipoeta," *Mittellateinisches Jahrbuch* 11 (1976) 143–50, with references to earlier studies.

[89]"Cipri, timent dii," ed. Jan Öberg, *Serlon de Wilton: Poèmes latins*, Studia latina Stockholmiensia 14 (Stockholm 1965) 96–100 at 99 no. 18 v. 101; ed. and trans. with commentary by Peter Dronke, *Medieval Latin and the Rise of European Love-Lyric* (2nd ed. 2 vols. Oxford 1968) 1.239–43, 2.497–503. See also Jan Öberg, "Einige Bemerkungen zu den Gedichten Serlos von Wilton," *Mittellateinisches Jahrbuch* 6 (1970) 98–108.

[90]Dronke (n. 89 above) 1.240–41.

ELISION

Of other formal aspects of versification in addition to rhyme, two in particular help to reveal the stylistic choices available to twelfth-century writers: elision and the treatment of the line-ending. Elision is the suppression of a final vowel, or a vowel plus *m*, before another vowel (or *h*) beginning the next word, as in this hexameter written by Hildebert: "res homin(um) atqu(e) homines levis alea versat in horas."[91] The history of Latin verse shows less and less frequent use of elision, a trend that emerges clearly in percentages indicating the number of elisions in a hundred lines of Vergil's *Aeneid* (52.8 percent) and the much reduced frequency in Ovid's *Metamorphoses* (19.7 percent). From late Antiquity through the earlier ninth century, elision continues to be employed with more or less the same frequency as in such model authors as Ovid and Sidonius Apollinaris.[92] But from the end of the ninth century lower incidences of elision become more common, and from the eleventh century there are authors who plainly attempt to avoid elision. The anonymous author of the *Ruodlieb* (ca. 1050) permitted *no* elisions in over 2000 leonine hexameters; and in the next century the more polished rhymed hexameters of Hugh Primas show a very low incidence of elision (0.9 percent). Avoidance of elision is evident also in unrhymed verse, such as the mid-century *comediae* written in elegiac distichs (for example, *Geta* 5.7 percent, *Alda* 4.9 percent) and two long hexameter poems of the early 1180s: the *Architrenius* of John of Hanville, completed in 1184 (7.2 percent), and Alan of Lille's influential philosophical poem *Anticlaudianus*, completed in 1182 or 1183 (0.2 percent). In striking contrast is the high frequency of elision shown in the bucolics of "Marcus Valerius" (18.4 percent) and in two celebrated epics on classical themes: the *Alexandreis* of Walter of Châtillon, completed about 1182 (15.8 percent), and the *Ylias* or *De bello Troiano* of Joseph of Exeter, completed in 1188–90 (21.0 percent).[93] The verse technique of these three authors in its free use of elision represents a rejection of current norms and practice and a return to ancient models.

The theorists Matthew of Vendôme, Geoffrey of Vinsauf, and John of Garland give cautious approval to elision but in practice all but avoid using it.[94] Alexander of Villedieu's influential *Doctrinale*, a versified summary of

[91]Scott (n. 61 above) 12 no. 22 v. 21. On elision, see Raven (n. 80 above) 27; Halporn et al. (n. 80 above) 64. Aphaeresis (elision of *es* or *est*) will be disregarded.

[92]Klopsch (n. 81 above) 79–87; Munari (n. 61 above) lxix–lxxii. All percentages quoted in this paragraph represent the number of occurrences of elision in 100 lines and come from Klopsch, except for *Architrenius* and "Marcus Valerius," for which see Munari lxx–lxxi.

[93]But the two epics differ greatly in other aspects of style: the *Alexandreis* is "antique," the *Ylias* ingeniously manneristic. See Fritz Peter Knapp, *Similitudo: Stil- und Erzählfunktion von Vergleich und Exempel in der lateinischen, französischen und deutschen Grossepik des Hochmittelalters*, Philologica Germanica 2 (Vienna and Stuttgart 1975) 222–67 (*Alexandreis*), 334–72 (*Ylias*); Heinrich Christensen, *Das Alexanderlied Walters von Châtillon* (Halle 1905); Walter B. Sedgwick, "The *Bellum Troianum* of Joseph of Exeter," *Speculum* 5 (1930) 49–76, 338.

[94]The texts are cited and discussed by Klopsch (n. 81 above) 82 and Munari (n. 61 above) lxx. See also Lawler (n. 16 above) 92, 253; Walter B. Sedgwick, "The Style and Vocabulary of the Latin

grammar written in 1199, condemns elision as "mean" (*vilis*, line 2434). The early thirteenth-century theorist Gervase of Melkley recommends complete avoidance of the varieties of elision (which he calls "licenses of the *auctores*"), not as being bad in themselves but because they "somehow offend the ears of moderns."[95] The rejection of elision as a license unacceptable to modern taste is one of the tendencies of the polished, exaggeratedly "correct" dactylic verse that emerged in the course of the century.

TREATMENT OF LINE-ENDINGS

A third technical aspect of versification that serves as a gauge of verse technique is treatment of line-endings.[96] In the classical Latin hexameter a word-ending was not allowed to fall at the end of the first long syllable of the fifth foot: that is, the line-ending could not consist of a word or word-group of four syllables (though a quadrisyllabic ending was not quite so strictly forbidden if a monosyllable preceded, as in a line ending *di genuerunt*). These rules were strictly observed by early medieval poets of the seventh, eighth, and early ninth centuries. But in the course of the ninth century the fifth-foot caesura without preceding monosyllable becomes more frequent; and by the end of the ninth century it is a deliberately sought feature of style in the long *Bella Parisiacae urbis* by Abbo of St Germain, where it appears in 28.5 percent of the lines.[97] The fully developed medieval hexameter is exemplified by the eleventh-century *Ruodlieb*, in leonines, whose author freely uses the fifth-foot caesura without preceding monosyllable (19.0 percent) and completely avoids elision.

The conditions of twelfth-century poetic production were technical mastery, increased awareness of the esthetic implications of different verse forms, and a sharpening of distinctions. By the end of the twelfth century, writers of dactylic verse fall, roughly, into three categories. One group—Hugh Primas is an example—continued to write the medieval line (often rhymed) that had become common in the tenth and eleventh centuries, with its tolerance of the fifth-foot caesura and its avoidance or sparing use of elision. Two

Arts of Poetry of the Twelfth and Thirteenth Centuries," *Speculum* 3 (1928) 349–81, 615.

[95]"Caveamus ad plenum illas auctorum licentias, sinalimpham scilicet et elipsim. . . . Caveamus, inquam, non propter turpitudinem sed propter usum, quia nescio qua iniuria eis aures modernorum leduntur. Sciatis quod istas licentias apud meam conscientiam non condempno": *Ars poetica* 2C, ed. Gräbener (n. 16 above) 207–08; cited and discussed by Munari (n. 61 above) lxx n. 70. Gervase's examples of this "license" are taken from the spurious but ancient verses prefixed to the *Aeneid* in some manuscripts and from Statius's *Achilleis*, a popular school text.

[96]Klopsch (n. 81 above) 68–74, 85–87; Munari (n. 61 above) lxxvi–lxxvii; Raven (n. 80 above) 99–101; Louis Nougaret, *Traité de métrique latine classique*, Nouvelle collection à l'usage des classes 36 (2nd ed. Paris 1956) 42–49.

[97]Abbo of St Germain, *Bella Parisiacae urbis*, ed. Paul von Winterfeld, MGH Poetae 4.1.72–122; Jean Soubiran, "Prosodie et métrique des Bella Parisiacae urbis d'Abbon," *Journal des Savants* (1965) 204–331; cited by Klopsch (n. 81 above) 71. Cf. the attribution of these and related Carolingian innovations to imperfect imitation of ancient models, as argued by Norberg (n. 81 above) 64–65. The percentages are from Klopsch.

groups rejected this medieval development. The verse technique of a few poets—notably ''Marcus Valerius,'' Walter of Châtillon, and Joseph of Exeter—affects a self-conscious and remarkably bold classicism in its threefold imitation of the *auctores*: avoidance of rhyme and of the forbidden caesura and imitation of the *auctores'* free use of elision. This classicizing versification resembles that of early Carolingian poets. The other group, the modernists who emerged in the twelfth century, were a new phenomenon in medieval Latin poetry. They went even farther than the classicizing poets in the direction of ''correctness'' by rejecting not only rhyme (as a rule) and the fifth-foot caesura but also the ''license'' of elision.[98] The result is the modernists' polished, exaggeratedly ''correct'' line that opposes itself both to recent medieval developments and to the ancient *auctores*. The modernists' consciousness of correcting and improving on the *auctores* is revealed explicitly by the remarks of the theorists.

STYLISTIC ISSUES AND THE TWELFTH-CENTURY RENAISSANCE

Classicism was only one of many stylistic currents in twelfth-century Latin literature. In the sphere of poetry, then as now more receptive than prose to precise stylistic analysis and imitation, the twelfth century offers striking examples of classicizing style. The classicizing features range from stylistically significant use of a single word, to larger effects of structure and pervasive verbal reminiscence, to (rarely) a multifaceted imitation. Rigorously classicizing verse techniques develop in the course of the century, but are used by relatively few authors. Most twelfth-century dactylic verse is either medieval in technique or, from the second half of the century, smoothly ''modern.'' From the point of view of technique the closest approach to classical models and norms occurs also in the second half of the century, but varieties of classicizing poetry are found throughout our period.

''THE FOUR STYLES OF THE MODERNS''

The distinctive features of classicizing prose seem to have been avoidance of the parallelism of structure and sound characteristic of sermons and related genres, the affectation of classical allusion and diction, sometimes the use of classical rather than nonclassical syntax where medieval usage allowed a choice, often a relative compression and brevity, rarely a quasi-Ciceronian copiousness. Under the influence of specific classical models, the prose style of some writers approached classical modes of expression without losing essential characteristics, largely of sentence-structure, that reveal the descent of medieval prose style from the ''new Christian style'' of the Fathers. In the latter half of the twelfth century, classicizing prose style recedes in importance relative to other stylistic

---

[98]For the theorists' prescriptions and practice regarding line-endings, see Klopsch (n. 81 above) 73–74; Sedgwick (n. 94 above) 360–64; Lawler (n. 16 above) 96.

tendencies. The traditional elevated style with its parallelism, sound-figures, and rich biblical imagery found remarkable success, notably in the works of one of the outstanding stylists of the Middle Ages, Bernard of Clairvaux (d. 1153).[99]

This variety of stylistic practice was given new theoretical recognition and formulation at the end of our period in the doctrine of "the four styles of the moderns" that originated probably in French rhetorical teaching around 1200. As found in a longer redaction of Geoffrey of Vinsauf's *Documentum* (attributable to Geoffrey himself or perhaps to Gervase of Melkley) and in John of Garland's *Parisiana poetria*, the theory uses accentual prose rhythm as the essential criterion in distinguishing four styles.[100] One is the "Tullian style," in which no attention is paid to accentual rhythm; its characteristic features are gravity of thought and abundant rhetorical embellishment. According to the theorist, the practitioners of the Tullian style were "the ancient writers in prose and poetry"; as examples he lists Sallust, Quintilian, Seneca, Martianus Capella, Sidonius Apollinaris, Vergil, Varro, Horace, Ovid, Lucan, Statius, Claudian, "and many others whom their eminent authority recommends."[101] The three other styles are the "Gregorian," used at the papal Curia; the "Hilarian," which imitates the rhythmical form of Ambrosian hymn-strophe; and the "Isidorian," characterized by parallelism of structure, isocolon, and end-rhyme and which has the power to move the reader "to piety or to joy."

The doctrine of the four styles requires further study and should be treated skeptically. Still, apart from the *stilus Hilarianus*, which seems to have had little vogue (though both authors claim that it was held in high regard), the categories have a tenuous relation to the principal varieties of prose written in the twelfth century: classicizing prose (*stilus Tullianus*), chancery prose observing the rules of *dictamen* (*stilus Gregorianus*), and the elevated rhymed prose of sermons and related genres (*stilus Ysidorianus*). In assigning the names of the Fathers to the three nonclassical styles, the theory at least by implication places them on a par with the classical *stilus Tullianus*; for in medieval literary canons the ancient *auctores* included pagan and Christian writers alike.[102] The important but restricted role of revived classicism in our period is well illustrated by this new theory of Latin style. From the vantage

[99]Christine Mohrmann, "Le style de Saint Bernard," *Etudes* (n. 33 above) 2.347–67, and "Observations sur la langue et le style de saint Bernard," *Sancti Bernardi opera*, ed. Leclercq 2.ix–xxxiii; Jean Leclercq, *Recueil d'études sur saint Bernard et ses écrits*, Storia e letteratura 92, 104, 114 (3 vols. Rome 1962–69) particularly vol. 3.

[100]Lawler (n. 16 above) 104–09, 256–58, 327–30; to the bibliography there cited, add the important article by Plezia (n. 27 above).

[101]"In stilo Tulliano non est attendenda dictionum cadencia sed sola sentencie grauitas et verborum florida exornacio, qua vtuntur antiquiores tam prosaice quam metrice scribentes, sicut Salustius, Quintilianus, Senica, Marcianus, Sidonius, Virgilius, Varro, Oracius, Ouidius, Lucanus, Stacius, Claudianus, et plures alii quos celsa commendat auctoritas"; cited from the longer redaction of the *Documentum* by Lawler (n. 16 above) 328–29 and by Plezia (n. 27 above) 196.

[102]Curtius 48–51; Günter Glauche, *Schullektüre im Mittelalter: Entstehung und Wandlungen des Lektürekanons bis 1200 nach den Quellen dargestellt*, Münchener Beiträge zur Mediävistik und Renaissance-Forschung 5 (Munich 1970).

point of the late twelfth-century theorist, the varieties of (nonpatristic) Latin prose and poetry written in Antiquity collapse into a single stylistic category that is only one of several giving theoretical recognition to the range of Latin prose written in the twelfth century.

REVIVAL AND INNOVATION

The stylistic qualities of Latin literature in the period extending roughly from 1070 to shortly after 1200 offer evidence of revival and innovation in several respects that illuminate the twelfth-century renaissance. Generally speaking, the level of grammatical correctness, formal control, and stylistic flexibility is higher in a wider range of authors and genres than in the past. Further, though examples of classicizing style are found in most medieval centuries, certain advances are visible in our period as regards technical precision, largeness and ambition of scale (notably in the epics on classical themes), and intelligent receptivity to new and direct stylistic influences from a variety of ancient models, both pagan and patristic.

Stylistic issues play a role too in the consciousness of the dawn of a new era that characterizes the twelfth-century renaissance, and more particularly in the literary quarrel between "ancients and moderns" in the second half of the century.[103] Though Alan of Lille's scornful dismissal of the classicizing epics of Joseph of Exeter and Walter of Châtillon is sufficiently accounted for by differences of content (given Alan's sweeping claims for the philosophical epic as represented by his own *Anticlaudianus*), it is reasonable to suppose that the equally marked differences of style and verse technique contributed to his hostility toward the rival epics.[104] The sharp divergence in ways of writing Latin, particularly verse, that develops in the course of the century and the explicit remarks of theorists show clearly an awareness of the differences between the stylistic norms of the ancients (*ueteres, antiqui*) and those of the twelfth-century *moderni*. Gervase of Melkley's reluctant rejection of elision, as being offensive to modern taste, is rare evidence of contemporary awareness that changes in taste presented an esthetic and literary problem. In the view of an assertive modernist like Matthew of Vendôme, the new way of writing Latin represents progress as well as change. Repeatedly he points to (allegedly) faulty

[103]Curtius 119–20, 154, 251–55, 490; Elisabeth Gössmann, *Antiqui und Moderni im Mittelalter: Eine geschichtliche Standortbestimmung*, Veröffentlichungen des Grabmann-Institutes zur Erforschung der mittelalterlichen Theologie und Philosophie n.s. 23 (Munich 1974) esp. 81–101; Wilfried Hartmann, "'Modernus' und 'Antiquus': Zur Verbreitung und Bedeutung dieser Bezeichnungen in der wissenschaftlichen Literatur vom 9. bis zum 12. Jahrhundert," and Elisabeth Gössmann, "'Antiqui' und 'Moderni' im 12. Jahrhundert," *Antiqui und Moderni: Traditionsbewusstsein und Fortschrittsbewusstsein im späten Mittelalter*, ed. Albert Zimmermann, Miscellanea mediaevalia 9 (Berlin and New York 1974) 21–39, 40–57.

[104]Alan of Lille, *Anticlaudianus* 1.165–70, ed. Robert Bossuat, Textes philosophiques du moyen âge 1 (Paris 1955) 62; also PL 210.492A; cited and discussed by Curtius 119–20; Panofsky, *Ren & Ren* 76–77. On Alan's style, see Guy Raynaud de Lage, *Alain de Lille, poète du XIIe siècle*, Université de Montréal, Publications de l'Institut d'études médiévales 12 (Montreal and Paris 1951) 131–63.

usages in the ancient poets that "are not permitted to moderns." Using language reminiscent of Isidore of Seville's distinction between the Old Testament and the New, he says that "the old has given way, outstripped by the new." In such matters "moderns should excuse the ancients, not imitate them."[105] The practice and theory of Latin style in our period thus participate not only in those aspects of the twelfth-century renaissance characterized by revival of the antique but also in those other aspects, equally significant, of sharpened self-definition and increased self-assertion relative to Antiquity.

Bibliographical Note

For details on individual works and authors of the twelfth century, see Manitius, volume 3; Joseph de Ghellinck, *L'essor de la littérature latine au XIIe siècle* (2nd ed. Brussels 1955); F. J. E. Raby, *A History of Christian-Latin Poetry from the Beginnings to the Close of the Middle Ages* (2nd ed. Oxford 1953; repr. 1966) and *A History of Secular Latin Poetry in the Middle Ages* (2nd ed. 2 vols. Oxford 1957). The edition of "Marcus Valerius" by Munari cited below includes an excellent bibliography of twelfth-century poetry, primarily quantitative verse.

Critical editions, the necessary basis for stylistic study, have been provided for many important authors. To those cited in the footnotes can be added editions of the epic poems of the 1180s: *Galteri de Castellione: Alexandreis*, ed. Marvin L. Colker, Thesaurus mundi: Bibliotheca scriptorum latinorum mediae et recentioris aetatis 17 (Padua 1978); *Alain de Lille: Anticlaudianus*, ed. Robert Bossuat, Textes philosophiques du moyen âge 1 (Paris 1955); *Johannes de Hauvilla: Architrenius*, ed. Paul G. Schmidt (Munich 1974); Joseph of Exeter, *Ylias*, in *Joseph Iscanus: Werke und Briefe*, ed. Ludwig Gompf, Mittellateinische Studien und Texte 4 (Leiden 1970). Especially welcome are editions with detailed indexes of the author's grammatical and rhetorical practice; an example is *Liber epistularum Guidonis de Basochis*, ed. Herbert Adolfsson, Studia latina Stockholmiensia 18 (Stockholm 1969).

The indispensable general study of medieval Latin style, though outdated in many details, remains the second volume of Eduard Norden, *Die antike Kunstprosa vom VI. Jahrhundert v. Chr. bis in die Zeit der Renaissance* (4th ed. 2 vols. Leipzig 1923). Perceptive remarks on individual texts, mostly early medieval, are to be found in Erich Auerbach, *Literatursprache und Publikum in der lateinischen Spätantike und im Mittelalter* (Bern 1958), trans. Ralph Manheim, *Literary Language and Its Public in Late Latin Antiquity and in the Middle Ages*, Bollingen Series 74 (New York and London 1965). Important remarks on many aspects of patristic and medieval Latin can be found throughout Christine Mohrmann's *Etudes sur le latin des chrétiens*, Storia e letteratura 65, 87, 103, 143 (4 vols. Rome 1958–77).

Perhaps the single most important study of medieval style to have been published within the last fifty years is Ernst Robert Curtius, *Europäische Literatur und lateinisches*

---

[105]*Ars versificatoria* 4.5, "Hoc autem modernis non licet. Vetera enim cessavere novis supervenientibus"; 4.8, "Sunt etiam huiusmodi infinitae abusiones, quae tantum attendendae sunt, sed non extendendae. In hoc autem articulo modernis incumbit potius antiquorum apologia quam imitatio"; ed. Faral, *Les arts poétiques* 181. Cf. Isidore, *Etymologiae* 6.1.1 (n. 37 above) citing 2 Cor. 5:17: "Vetus Testamentum ideo dicitur, quia veniente Novo cessavit. De quo Apostolus meminit dicens: 'vetera transierunt, et ecce facta sunt nova'"; cf. also Lev. 26:10, "Vetera novis supervenientibus proicietis."

Mittelalter (Bern 1948), trans. Willard R. Trask, *European Literature and the Latin Middle Ages*, Bollingen Series 36 (New York 1953). By demonstrating the rhetorical orientation of much medieval writing, the work has corrected decisively an earlier perception that medieval literature was the product of untutored spontaneity. Recently some aspects of Curtius's approach have been questioned, notably by Peter Dronke, *Poetic Individuality in the Middle Ages: New Departures in Poetry, 1000–1150* (Oxford 1970) 1–32.

Detailed studies of authors' stylistic practice are few. Notable exceptions include Carl Erdmann, *Studien zur Briefliteratur Deutschlands im elften Jahrhundert*, MGH Schriften 1 (Leipzig 1938; repr. Stuttgart 1959) 55–116, on Meinhard of Bamberg; Peter von Moos, *Hildebert von Lavardin, 1056–1133: Humanitas an der Schwelle des höfischen Zeitalters*, Pariser historische Studien 3 (Stuttgart 1965) 38–93; Dietrich Lohrmann, "Die Jugendwerke des Johannes von Gaeta," *Quellen und Forschungen aus italienischen Archiven und Bibliotheken* 47 (1967) 355–445; Jean Leclercq, *Recueil d'études sur saint Bernard et ses écrits*, Storia e letteratura 92, 104, 114 (3 vols. Rome 1962–69), particularly volume 3; Ernst Voigt, ed., *Ysengrimus* (Halle 1884) xxvi–lxxii; Heinrich Christensen, *Das Alexanderlied Walters von Châtillon* (Halle 1905) 14–101; Franco Munari, ed., *M. Valerio: Bucoliche* (2nd ed. Florence 1970) l–lxxxi. Some basic studies of medieval Latinity and of the practice of individual authors have been reprinted in *Mittellateinische Philologie: Beiträge zur Erforschung der mittelalterlichen Latinität*, ed. Alf Önnerfors, Wege der Forschung 292 (Darmstadt 1975), including a useful bibliography.

Specific features of medieval prose and poetic style have been studied. For prose rhyme, the standard work remains Karl Polheim, *Die lateinische Reimprosa* (Berlin 1925). Prose rhythm, especially the *cursus*, has received much attention. A methodological model and recent bibliography are provided by Tore Janson, *Prose Rhythm in Medieval Latin from the 9th to the 13th Century*, Studia latina Stockholmiensia 20 (Stockholm 1975). Recent studies of medieval versification include Dag Norberg, *Introduction à l'étude de la versification latine médiévale*, Studia latina Stockholmiensia 5 (Stockholm 1958) and Paul Klopsch, *Einführung in die mittellateinische Verslehre* (Darmstadt 1972). The functions of classical allusion have been clarified by Winfried Offermanns, *Die Wirkung Ovids auf die literarische Sprache der lateinischen Liebesdichtung des 11. und 12. Jahrhunderts*, Beihefte zum Mittellateinischen Jahrbuch 4 (Wuppertal, Kastellaun, and Düsseldorf 1970); Paul G. Schmidt, "Das Zitat in der Vagantendichtung: Bakelfest und Vagantenstrophe cum auctoritate," *Antike und Abendland* 20 (1974) 74–87.

Stylistic analysis of literary texts is assisted in important ways by consideration of medieval literary theory, which not only illuminates the effects of stylistic theory on practice but also suggests how the original audience responded to the texts. Some of the *artes dictandi* have been printed by Ludwig Rockinger, *Briefsteller und Formelbücher des eilften bis vierzehnten Jahrhunderts*, Quellen und Erörterungen zur bayerischen und deutschen Geschichte 9.1–2 (2 vols. Munich 1863–64; repr. New York 1961). Some important arts of poetry have been edited by Faral, *Les arts poétiques*. Special mention can be made of the useful edition, translation, and notes by Traugott Lawler, *The "Parisiana Poetria" of John of Garland*, Yale Studies in English 182 (New Haven and London 1974). A guide to other editions and to other bibliography is provided by James J. Murphy, *Medieval Rhetoric: A Select Bibliography*, Toronto Medieval Bibliographies 3 (Toronto 1971).

The nature and significance of medieval theory of kinds or levels of style have been examined by Franz Quadlbauer, *Die antike Theorie der Genera dicendi im lateinischen Mittelalter*, SB Vienna 241.2 (1962) and Marian Plezia, "*Quattuor stili modernorum*: Ein Kapitel mittellateinischer Stillehre," *Orbis Mediaevalis: Festgabe für Anton Blaschka*, ed. Horst Gericke, Manfred Lemmer, and Walter Zöllner (Weimar 1970) 192–210. Medieval theory of metaphorical language has been studied by Ulrich Krewitt, *Metapher und tropische Rede in der Auffassung des Mittelalters*, Beihefte zum Mittellateinischen Jahrbuch 7 (Ratingen, Kastellaun, and Wuppertal 1971). Unfortunately, medieval literary theory usually has been studied in isolation from literary practice. Some productive attempts to apply theory to practice are found in the works of von Moos and Lohrmann cited above.

The literary criticism in commentaries, treatises, and the casual remarks of medieval writers awaits definitive treatment; two studies are: Berthe M. Marti, "Literary Criticism in the Mediaeval Commentaries on Lucan," *Transactions and Proceedings of the American Philological Association* 72 (1941) 245–54 and Peter von Moos, "Literarkritik im Mittelalter: Arnulf von Lisieux über Ennodius," *Mélanges offerts à René Crozet*, ed. Pierre Gallais and Yves-Jean Riou (2 vols. Poitiers 1966) 2.929–35.

Profane Elements in Literature

Peter Dronke

A number of phenomena that historians associate particularly with twelfth-century literature can be seen as showing "profane" elements and impulses. The idealizing of human love in poetry (an exaltation and refinement of sexual emotion that has even led some scholars to speak of a "heresy" or "rival religion" here); the range of protest against aspects of the religious world (satires irreverently mocking or fervently attacking corruption in the Church, parodies and burlesques of the Church's rites, affirmations of ir-religious pleasures—all that tends to be grouped as "goliardic" in spirit); the divergent attitudes to sensuality (earthy and often cynical in fabliaux, golden and seemingly guilt-free in a series of lyrical celebrations)—all these can be seen as manifestations of the profane in the twelfth century. Traditionally, most of these manifestations have been discussed separately: thus for instance there is a vast literature on *The Meaning of Courtly Love*, there are specialist studies of *Les fabliaux*, of *Kirchenkritik in der lateinischen Lyrik*, and of *Die Parodie im Mittelalter*.[1] Yet it may be illuminating to reorient some of the specialized questions, to look at the varied profane elements in conjunction and in relation to one another.

Two areas of meaning of "profane" that are noted in the *Oxford English Dictionary* have a bearing on such an enquiry: the one, "not pertaining or devoted to what is sacred or biblical; . . . secular, lay, common"—the other, "characterized by disregard or contempt of sacred things; . . . irreverent, blas-phemous, ribald." These two semantic fields have no strict border, but, for

I am grateful to Robert L. Benson and Georges Duby for their comments on this paper, and for some valuable references.

[1] Francis X. Newman, ed., *The Meaning of Courtly Love* (Albany N.Y. 1968); Per Nykrog, *Les fabliaux* (2nd ed. Geneva 1973); Helga Schüppert, *Kirchenkritik in der lateinischen Lyrik des 12. und 13. Jahrhunderts* (Munich 1972); Paul Lehmann, *Die Parodie im Mittelalter* (2nd ed. Stuttgart 1963). Among more recent work relating to courtly love poetry, see especially Pierre Bec, *La lyrique française au moyen âge (XIIe–XIIIe siècles)*, vol. 1: *Etudes* (Paris 1977); Anna Maria Clausen, *Le origini della poesia lirica in Provenza e in Italia*, Revue Romane, numéro spécial 7 (Copenhagen 1976); Joan M. Ferrante and George D. Economou, eds., *In Pursuit of Perfection: Courtly Love in Medieval Literature* (Port Washington N.Y. 1975); Jean Frappier, *Amour courtois et Table Ronde* (Geneva 1973); W. D. Paden Jr. et al., "The Troubadour's Lady: Her Marital Status and Social Rank," *Studies in Philology* 72 (1975) 28–50; Marcelle Thiébaux, *The Stag of Love: The Chase in Medieval Literature* (Ithaca 1974); Peter Wapnewski, *Waz ist minne* (Munich 1975); Horst Wenzel, *Frauendienst und Gottesdienst: Studien zur Minne-Ideologie* (Berlin 1974).

practical reasons, the second will be my chief concern. Confronted with the wealth of twelfth-century literature that is secular, not sacred, in orientation, I shall focus especially on examples where we can see a deliberate disregard or deliberate flouting of an acknowledged sacred order of things. And I think that a consideration of profane impulses in this more limited sense may also cast some light on the more comprehensive range of secular impulses in the literature of the time, and indicate at least one striking feature that distinguishes many of the secular manifestations.

Two wider questions are particularly awkward, yet they must be faced and an assessment—however provisional—attempted. First, to what extent are the profane elements in twelfth-century literature new, and characteristic of that century? And second, can we observe any significant changes or developments in the uses of the profane as the century advances? Are there, for instance, in the period around 1200, any aspects of imaginative literature that would have been inconceivable a hundred, or even fifty, years earlier?

Though the literary evidence for the twelfth century, vernacular as well as Latin, is relatively large, it has serious limitations. It can tell us—directly at least—only something about the social milieux in and for which this literature was composed, not about twelfth-century society as a whole. Comparisons and contrasts with earlier centuries are peculiarly hard to attempt because so much more has come down to us in writing from the twelfth century than from the preceding ones. This imbalance is more glaring for the vernaculars than for Latin, since before the twelfth century a vernacular reading-public was rare, and always (even in Anglo-Saxon England) extremely small.

Thus any claim that something is new in the twelfth century must be qualified by attempts to fathom the lost literature—and even more, the lost oral compositions—of the earlier periods, and by efforts to read the Latin imaginative literature, especially from the ninth century to the eleventh, not only for itself but for what it may be able to tell us indirectly about earlier vernacular compositions that have not survived. Yet even for the twelfth century the amount that is lost is considerable, and among the losses, the profane compositions will have suffered far more than the edifying ones. Even if the extant profane literary sources could be surveyed exhaustively, our evidence would remain in important ways imperfect. And in any case in this attempt to adumbrate the problems briefly, the focus must be highly selective. I shall try to illustrate a variety of imaginative uses of profane elements, which include such intentions as to arouse laughter, or to shock the audience, or to express a defiant protest, but which can also include a whole range of more subtle intentions and effects. I shall hazard some suggestions, too, about the wider implications of these profane elements and their functions.

With most of the examples alluded to, a dozen others could equally well be chosen to signal the same problems. If I have illustrated to a large extent from lyrics, it is because these often allow a more succinct consideration of evidence than is possible with examples from epic or romance, prose fiction or drama.

A group of nine secular Latin poems copied in France at the beginning of the thirteenth century contains a woman's lament that (on grounds both of versification and of the date of several pieces alongside it) I would place around 1100:

In me, dei crudeles nimium,	Against me, too cruel gods,
totum vestrum vertistis hodium!	you have turned all your hate!
Miserorum hec potest omnium	This my calamity can afford solace
calamitas esse solatium.	to all others who are wretched.
Successisse mihi crediderant	They thought things had gone well for me,
qui me viro potenti vinxerant;	they who yoked me to a man of power,
sed non ita dei providerant,	but the gods did not foresee it thus:
qui iam viro lepram comparserant.	for my husband they'd stored up leprosy.
Non accuso fratris infantiam	I don't reproach my brother's youth
sive fictam parentum gratiam—	or my parents' semblance of favour—
sed erravi concedens veniam:	yet I am wrong in pardoning:
dei tandem causo sevitiam!	in the end I accuse God's savageness!
Ut tot claustra possim evadere	Even if I could escape my prison,
et custodes et virum fallere,	outwit the watchmen and my husband,
quis me demens dignetur tangere,	who would be so mad as deign to touch me,
nisi lepram velit incurrere?	unless he wanted to become a leper?
Qui, si tutus a lepra affuerit,	Who, if he came near me, safe from leprosy,
me prorutam per stupra noverit?	would couple with me who have been abased?
Sed amare quo pacto poterit	How could he love a woman if he took her
quam post tantam labem susceperit?[2]	after so great a degradation?[2]

[2]Text from MS Florence, Bibl. Laur. Aedil. 197, fol. 130r. Previously printed by Maurice Delbouille, "Trois poésies latines inédites," *Mélanges Paul Thomas* (Bruges 1930) 176 (though with three misreadings—*hic patet* in the third line, *iunxerant* in the sixth). On the date of the lament of Oedipus, *Diri patris infausta pignora*, which is in the same meter as this lyric and follows it immediately on fol. 130v, see Peter Dronke, *Fabula* (Leiden 1974) 128 n. 2 (though the phrase used there, "consistent lack of strong rhyme," should read "lack of consistent strong rhyme"). On fol. 131v comes the lyric *Parce continuis*, which also survives—already in a corrupt text—in the MS Augsburg, Bischöfl. Ord. 5, in a hand of the late eleventh century (Benedikt Kraft) or the first years of the twelfth (Bernhard Bischoff): see Peter Dronke, *Medieval Latin and the Rise of European Love-Lyric* (2nd ed. 2 vols. Oxford 1968) 2.553.

Several points of interpretation remain problematic, and the translation suggests only a possible way of construing the whole. Thus for instance in the third strophe *fratris infantiam* could also refer literally to the brother's silence, or unwillingness to speak out, rather than to his being too young to intervene, and *concedens veniam* might refer to the woman's granting her assent to the match, rather than pardoning what was done to her. In this line, I render *erravi* in the present tense in my translation, in order to suggest that the reference is to the thought of the preceding moment, and not to a more distant past. The poet's use of tenses is throughout unorthodox by classical norms.

Apart from the analogues discussed below, there is one particularly striking parallel in the *Emblematum liber* of Andrea Alciati, which was adapted and became influential in the European vernaculars. Emblem 197 (ed. Lyon 1548, and included in most later editions, both Latin and vernacular: see Henry Green, *Andreae Alciati Emblematum Flumen abundans* [Manchester and London 1871] 20) is entitled NVPTA CONTAGIOSO, and reads:

It is possible to see this song in terms of the genre well known especially from Old French: the *chanson de mal mariée*.³ There often a young wife laments that her family have married her off to a *vilain*, because of his wealth:

> A curse on him who had me given to a churl!
> I'd rather have a little joy to keep
> than have a thousand silver marks, and weep!⁴

The joy the *mal mariée* envisages is, traditionally, a handsome lover. What makes the Latin song so harrowing is the woman's recognition that for her such a dream of liberation is impossible. Her situation is fated: others can take solace that their misfortunes are as nothing compared with hers.⁵ That she alludes to "gods" in the first two strophes may suggest this song is "distanced" by being placed in a pagan realm (as are the two lyrical *planctus* alongside it in the manuscript—a lament of Oedipus, and one of Orpheus). Or again *dei* can—as in Adelard of Bath or Bernard Silvester⁶—mean the "lesser" gods, the planetary intelligences, who transmit destinies to the mortal world. I am inclined to take it that way, for in this song the vivid contemporary (rather than classicizing) quality of the situation evoked—the arranged marriage, before which no one in the bride's family had seen the bridegroom— is unmistakable. But it is the third strophe that stands out by its "profane" moment: her outcry is, in the last resort, not against her family, who had failed to protect her, but against the savageness of God—of the Christian God. Heloise, in her letter of lament, was to write: "O, si fas sit dici, crudelem mihi per omnia deum!"⁷ In the lyric the accusation is unqualified—with not even

---

> Dii meliora piis, Mezenti, cur age sic me
>   Compellas? Emptus quod tibi dote gener;
> Gallica quem scabies, dira et mentagra perurit:
>   Hoc est quidnam aliud, dic mihi saeve pater,
> Corpora corporibus quam iungere mortua vivis,
>   Efferaque Etrusci facta novare ducis?

I am indebted to Dr Aurora Egido for pointing this Emblem out to me.

   Saul N. Brody, *The Disease of the Soul: Leprosy in Medieval Literature* (Ithaca and London 1974), discusses a wide range of poetic as well as other texts; the lyric *In me dei* stands apart from the texts cited by Brody in that there is no suggestion of a moral stigma in the husband's leprosy. Peter Richards, *The Medieval Leper and His Northern Heirs* (Cambridge and Totowa N.J. 1977), presents chiefly late medieval and early modern historical evidence, with special reference to Scandinavia.

   ³Delbouille (n. 2 above) 176–78.
   ⁴"honis soit qui a vilain me fist doner!
      j'aim mult mels un poi de joie a demener
      que mil mars d'argent avoir et puis plorer."

(Karl F. Bartsch, *Altfranzösische Romanzen und Pastourellen* [Leipzig 1870] 87). Delbouille (n. 2 above) 177, allegedly citing from Bartsch's text of this song, prints "Que mil mars *d'or* avoir et *plus* plorer," though these variants are not to be found in Bartsch's apparatus (353).

   ⁵Compare Peter Abelard, *Historia calamitatum*, ed. Jacques Monfrin (Paris 1959) 63: "ut in comparatione [calamitatum] mearum tuas aut nullas aut modicas temptationes recognoscas et tolerabilius feras."

   ⁶Bernard Silvester, *Cosmographia*, ed. Peter Dronke (Leiden 1978) 104 (Megacosmus 3.7–8): "Dico deos quorum ante deum presentia servit, / Quos tenet in vero lumine vera dies." Cf. Adelard of Bath, *Quaestiones naturales* 76 (cited ibid. 71).

   ⁷In the appendix to *Historia calamitatum* (n. 5 above) 119.

"if it were lawful for it to be spoken" to mitigate it. From this the heroine's mind turns to the thought of escape, and at once to the hopelessness of that thought. There is no "conclusion"—only the continuing knowledge that she will never be lovable, never be loved again.

The surviving French and Provençal *chansons de mal mariée* do not have this degree of seriousness: they engage stock motifs and stock figures—the contemptible *vilain* or *jaloux*, the father, the lover, the sensual woman, unhappy but not numbed or inexorably crushed. The Latin poet, by contrast, is unflinchingly specific: he creates a concrete tragic situation, and a woman characterized simply and with total authenticity. Where an audience might have smiled at many a *mal mariée* recounting her woes, this cry at the harshness of fate—and of God, the author of fate—must have moved its first audiences, not just entertained them.

The woman's lament is a traditional type of song: we have evidence for this earlier in medieval Europe from the Mozarabic *kharjas*,[8] as well as from a range of elegiac women's monologues in Anglo-Saxon, Norse, and Celtic poetry.[9] Undoubtedly vernacular *chansons de mal mariée* existed that were known to this Latin poet. But if the genre in the eleventh century was at all like what the surviving later examples suggest, we can say that he transformed the genre, and that a passionately serious use of the profane was an essential element in that transformation.

The same is true of an even earlier woman's lament in Latin, the eleventh-century lyric *Plangit nonna fletibus*.[10] Again we have a group of Old French songs of this type from the twelfth and thirteenth centuries. The Latin song gives a painfully graphic description of the grimness of a nun's existence for one who has no vocation for it—the squalor of her bed and clothing, the lice and the mud—a woman who resolves, if she cannot enjoy a man's love, to kill herself. The French lyrics, by contrast, tend to be piquant and flirtatious in tone. The nun sings "je sant les douls mals / leis ma senturete," or "se plus suis nonette, / ains ke soit li vespres, / je morai des jolis malz"[11] (the diminutives help to lighten the effect). In the Latin lyric the use of a profanity once more plays a distinctive role in the poet's modification of a genre: the

[8]See especially the fine recent account by Margit Frenk Alatorre, *Las jarchas mozárabes y los comienzos de la lírica románica* (Mexico City 1975), and Richard Hitchcock, *The Kharjas: A Critical Bibliography* (London 1977).

[9]Some of the principal Anglo-Saxon, Norse, and Celtic references are indicated in my *Poetic Individuality in the Middle Ages: New Departures in Poetry, 1000–1150* (Oxford 1970) 27–28. While the *kharjas* often evoke the sorrows of a young girl in love, the Germanic and Celtic laments more often concern the misfortunes of a woman married to a man she does not love.

[10]Ed. in Dronke, *Medieval Latin* (n. 2 above) 2.357–60. (I would now, however, date this song somewhat later than *Foebus abierat* [ibid. 2.334–41], of which the first extant copy is from shortly after the year 1000. The techniques of rhyme in *Plangit nonna* suggest the eleventh century, the handwriting in the MS is early twelfth; the song was probably composed in the later eleventh century. A valuable range of further references to nuns' laments can be found in María Rosa Lida de Malkiel's "Nuevas notas para la interpretación del *Libro de Buen Amor*," *Nueva revista de filología hispánica* 13 (1959) 17–82 at 65–67.

[11]Bartsch (n. 4 above) 28–29. ("I feel the sweet pain next to my little girdle"; "If I remain a little nun till vespers, I'll die of the tender pangs.")

opening words, "Plangit nonna, fletibus / inenarrabilibus" ("a nun is lamenting, with unutterable tears"), will by their echo of Romans 8:26 have brought to the audience's mind both the Pauline context—nature groaning with the hope of deliverance—and its misapplication to the human moment here. It is parody, though (I believe) with poetically serious intent. At the same time, it should perhaps be stressed that the evocations in this poem are realistic art, not naked reality. The song still has its music, and was meant for performance in company—that is, it is not a *confessio* but an artistic projection. And the girl's account of her sorrows is not tragedy of the same order as that of the leper's wife: with her fastidious disgust goes a naive desire for the luxuries of married women of her class—wistfully she dreams of ermine furs and a tiara. The incongruities between her mortal longings and the religious life raise a challenge to the audience that admits of more complex responses than compassion (or, for that matter, sentimental acquiescence, or scorn).

The conflicting claims of God and of human love often play a crucial role in a group of twelfth-century songs known as *chansons de croisade*. Once more the earliest testimony is one of the most individual (and in this case, also one of the most widely discussed): Marcabru's *A la fontana del vergier*.[12] While we cannot rule out that comparable songs may have been composed at the time of the First Crusade, I suspect that here, with Marcabru, we may be able to observe the birth of a new kind of lyric, the evolution of a *chanson de croisade* out of an older, traditional kind of *chanson d'aventure* or *pastourelle*.[13] For, with the setting Marcabru evokes at the opening of this song, it is clear that he awakens certain expectations in his audience. He plays on these, yet he does not fulfill them: the thoughts take a wholly different turn.

Beside the fountain in the orchard—in an Arcadian setting—this poet-narrator encounters not an unknown pretty girl but *selha que no vol mon solatz*—her who does not wish to give him joy: that is, a woman whom he knows and cares for, but whose melancholy, withdrawn state he has already experienced. And, unlike the girls in most such lyrical love-adventures, she is no shepherdess or country lass, but of high birth—*filha d'un senhor de castelh*. With her there is no trace of Arcadian joy. From the start we see her weeping, with a sorrow larger than life: "her tears streamed even to the fountain's

[12]Martín de Riquer, ed., *Los trovadores: Historia literaria y textos* (3 vols. Barcelona 1975) 1.203–05. To the fine recent bibliography on this song given there I would add only Alberto Limentani, "A la fontana del vergier," *Annali della Facoltà di lingue e letterature straniere di Ca' Foscari* 11 (1972) 361–80. I follow Riquer in his subtle interpretation of the line *Dels huelhs ploret josta la fon* ("Sus lagrimas llegaron hasta la fuente").

For the Old French texts and melodies, see Joseph Bédier and Pierre Aubry, eds., *Les chansons de croisade* (Paris 1909). Particularly relevant to the conflict of human and divine love are nos. 8–12, 16–19, and 25–28. In only two of the Old French songs (10, 26) is the speaking persona a woman; one song (28) is a dialogue between a man and a woman.

[13]I have discussed the evidence for older traditions of *chanson d'aventure* and *pastourelle* in "Poetic Meaning in the 'Carmina Burana,'" *Mittellateinisches Jahrbuch* 10 (1975) 116–37, and in "The Song of Songs and Medieval Love-Lyric," in *The Bible and Medieval Culture*, ed. W. Lourdaux and D. Verhelst, Mediaevalia Lovaniensia 7 (Louvain 1979) 236–62.

edge.'' They overflow into her reckless lament: it is "Jesus, king of the world,'' who is increasing her grief, the Crusade which is confounding her, by taking her friend away and leaving her to her suffering. A curse on King Louis, on his commands and on the sermons, that have brought such pain into her heart!

In the *chansons d'aventure* too a girl often weeps that her lover has left her, but then the poet tries to console her by offering her his own love. Here, by contrast, Marcabru consoles the lamenting one with the thought of God's love as a source of joy, counterbalancing human unhappiness.[14] And yet—this is Marcabru's final twist—his spiritual consolation is as unavailing as the offer of erotic solace is in many other songs of such encounters:

"Senher,'' dis elha, "ben o cre	"Sir,'' she said, "I do believe
que Dieus aia de mi merce!	that God will have mercy on me—
En l'autre segle per jasse . . . ,	forever, in the other world . . . ,
quon assatz d'autres peccadors . . . ,	as on many other sinners . . . ,
mas sai mi tolh aquelha re,	yet here he robs me of the one
qui joi mi crec, mas pauc mi te,	who raised my joy—nothing matters to
que trop s'es de mi alonhatz.''	me now,
	for he has gone too far from me.''[15]

Relentlessly she shows that the divine consolation is no consolation: it is powerless against so deep a human longing. It is not that she disbelieves in a life after death, but that in her numb anguish the idea is meaningless and useless to her.

In a world where the sublimation of human love came easily to many poets, Marcabru stands out as a poet who never accepts the premises of sublimation: for him, as for the heroine in this lyric, the human and divine loves are not reconcilable. And—as the close of *A la fontana* suggests—if we feel the tension and opposition of these two loves, how can we, being human, admit that the human is less important and should give way to the divine? Marcabru's song is not only a threnody but a probe of conscience.

[14]This in my view is not only the ostensible but the primary meaning of the lines "que Selh qui fai lo bosc fulhar / vos pot donar de joi assatz" (Riquer [n. 12 above] 1.205 st. 5). It is also the way the girl interprets the narrator's words, in the strophe cited below, where she refers them exclusively to the otherworld, seeing no hope before that. I do not think it can be maintained that the God-given joy and consolation promised by the narrator mean that he himself wants to make her happy by becoming her new lover, as several scholars (under the influence of *pastorela* motifs) have argued. Nonetheless there is a hint of an erotic connotation in the words, or (to put it in terms of the dramatic interplay) the narrator's compassion for the girl includes a strong element of erotic attraction to her (*selha que no vol mon solatz*)—even though he knows from the outset that she is no *pastorela*, and that he has no chance of enjoying a love-adventure with her during the absence of her friend.

[15]Ibid. st. 6. The phrase *mas pauc mi te* has been much discussed (for a summary of the diverse views, see François Pirot, *Mélanges de linguistique française et de philologie et littérature médiévales offerts à M. Paul Imbs* [Strasbourg 1973] 639–42); I believe that the interpretation "rien ne me touche plus," proposed by Dejeanne and upheld by Jeanroy and Berry, may still have most to commend it poetically.

A lyrical dialogue (*Wechsel*) of the end of the century, by the Minne-singer Otto von Botenlauben,[16] seems at first sight still more daring by its pro-fane use of sacred hyperbole: the poet, about to leave for the Fourth Crusade, says of his beloved "she indeed can be my heavenly kingdom" (*sie mac vil wol mîn himelrîche sîn*). Yet at once he goes on to implore God's help, that he may win divine mercy both for himself and for her. Her answering strophe out-does his in a profanity of love-worship:

Sît er giht ich sî sîn himelrîche,   Since he affirms I am his heaven,
sô habe ich in zuo gote mir erkorn,   I've chosen him to be my God,
daz er niemer fuoz von mir entwîche.   so that he never take a step away
                                                  from me.

But this too resolves itself into prayer: "Lord God, let this not anger you" (*herre got, lâ dirz niht wesen zorn*). Here the hyperboles are, in the last resort, meant as make-believe: the poet-crusader knows he must depart, and her glorious fantasy—that he need never leave her, just as God never leaves his heaven—returns to sad reality with the last lines of the song, where she voices her fear that he might never come back from Jerusalem alive. The moments of unbridled exaggeration are possible in terms of an outlook that can see human and divine love harmonizing—an outlook that Marcabru's heroine could not bring herself to accept.

What is beginning to emerge from these examples is not a simple or tidy picture, enabling us to say that this or that was possible in the twelfth century and not in the eleventh, but rather that a number of traditional types of poetry could be transformed in individual ways, in the eleventh century as in the twelfth, by gifted poets. I believe that—with certain qualifications—the same holds true of the idealizing or courtly love-poetry which has far more often been supposed an early twelfth-century innovation. I have set out and treated evidence relating to this elsewhere;[17] here it is perhaps enough to recall that, even with the scanty surviving testimonies of secular European love-poetry from the tenth and eleventh centuries, one can see in it clear traces of some of the characteristic impulses of the twelfth-century poetry. Thus for instance with the exaltation of the woman who is loved: in a lyric copied shortly after 900,[18] we encounter a girl who is celebrated as radiant and gracious (*claram et benivolam*), noble of mind (*mente nobilis*) and faithful to her "ami" (*amico fidelis*), who prevails on earth as the moon does in the heavens, and who—like Dante's Beatrice—is loved by the saints: *amant illam sancti*. So, too, with the notion of a lady being served by her lover: in a Latin-German love-dialogue copied ca. 1050,[19] the knight who is trying to persuade a nun to leave her con-

---

[16]*Deutsche Liederdichter des 13. Jahrhunderts*, ed. Carl von Kraus (2 vols. Tübingen 1951–58) 1.314, 2.376–80.

[17]*Medieval Latin* (n. 2 above), esp. chs. 1 and 5.

[18]*Deus amet puellam*, ibid. 1.264–68.

[19]*Suavissima nunna*, ibid. 1.277–81, 2.353–56.

vent for his love's sake twice implores her, with the strikingly courtly expression, "put my love to test" (*coro miner minna*). Again, with the motif of the lady as a source of virtue for her devotee: how is it that the Provençal poet who composed the fragmentary *Boecis* (most probably around 1070, according to the latest researches)[20] was able to elaborate the portrait of a lady whose radiant beauty holds a promise of paradise, who demands a love that is no quick desire for possession but a constant service—a service through which her lover gains in worth, in generosity (*largetat*), and in joy (*alegretat*)?[21] Assuredly the vernacular poet did not find this in his Latin text of Boethius; rather, he was transforming the Boethian *Philosophia* in terms of an already existing language of exalted human love, which was familiar to him.

What, then, are the particular contributions of the twelfth century to such love-poetry? I do not think the sheer abundance of testimonies from the twelfth, compared with the two preceding centuries, can be entirely due to accidents of preservation. Rather, the new abundance itself suggests the extent to which, in the course of the twelfth century, this love-language became "institutionalized" in literary modes and fashions. Far more than before, the motifs of ideal love find social expression in the courts in new "life styles," as well as in new developments of literary forms, such as the first vernacular romances in octosyllabic couplets.

Increasingly, in the century, one can perceive a certain refining and enriching of the language of high love. To illustrate briefly with the help of one motif: the sense that God is on the lover's side, that he can pray to God for happiness in his human love, can be traced from a relatively swift and incidental use in a love-poem by Marbod of Rennes near the close of the eleventh century:[22]

> Inferior tandem,   quia flammam sencio grandem,
> Supplico ne miserum   perdas, pulcherrima rerum.
> Perdis enim plane,   si tam cito vis remeare.

[20]Maurice Delbouille, "Les plus anciens textes romans," in *Grundriss der romanischen Literaturen des Mittelalters*, ed. Hans Robert Jauss, Erich Köhler, et al. (Heidelberg 1968–   ) 1.605–06.

[21]Bella's la donna—e-l vis a ta preclar . . .
Ella metesma—ten claus de paradis,
Quoras que-s vol, laínz col sos amigs. . . .
"Molt me derramen—donzellet de jovent,
Que zo espéren—que faza a lor talen." . . .
Mas cil qui poden—montar . . .
Ab la donzella—pois an molt gran amor.
Cals es la schala?—de que sun li degrat? . . .
Contra perjúri—de bona feeltat.
Contr' avarícia—sun fait de largetat,
Contra tristícia—sun fait d'alegretat . . . .

(*Boecis*, ed. René Lavaud and Georges Machicot [Toulouse 1950] vv. 170, 184–85, 195–96, 213–21).

[22]Walther Bulst, ed., "Liebesbriefgedichte Marbods," in *Liber Floridus: Mittellateinische Studien Paul Lehmann gewidmet*, ed. Bernhard Bischoff and Heinrich Suso Brechter (St Ottilien 1950) 289–90.

> Non precor ut patrias   sedes omnino relinquas—
> Quamvis o utinam   sortem michi det deus illam,
> Sedibus ut patrie   possim tibi carior esse.

> Now cast in the inferior role,   because of the great flame I feel,
> I beseech you, loveliest one,   let me not, wretched, be undone.
> For you destroy me utterly   if you mean to return home so quickly.
> It's not that I am begging   that you reject your parents' dwelling—
> though if only God   would grant me so happy a lot
> that to you I could be   dearer than your own country!

(Note also how the lover here characterizes himself as *inferior*, and as suppliant to his beloved.) A generation later, the troubadour Cercamon (fl. 1137–49) declares, in more extravagant tones:

> Quan totz lo segles brunezis   When the whole world grows dark,
> delai on ylh es si resplan.   where she is, there is resplendence.
> Dieu prejarai qu'ancar l'ades   I'll pray to God I may still touch her
> o que la vej' anar jazer!   or see her lying down to rest![23]

More astonishingly, in another song, Cercamon moves through a cycle of borrowed moral attitudes: threatening *fals amador*—the philandering husbands, the men and women who betray each other in love—with hell-fire, as implacably as does his contemporary Marcabru, reflecting harshly that his own beloved, too, is promiscuous, and yet concluding with a prayer:

> Saint Salvador,   fai m'alberguan   Holy Savior, let me be lodged
> lai el renh on midonz estai,   there in the kingdom where *midonz* dwells,
> ab la genzor,   si q'en baizan   with her, the noblest, so that, kissing,
> sien nostre coven verai   our covenant may be fulfilled
> e qe·m do zo que m'a promes;   and she give me what she has promised me.
> pueis al jorn s'en ira conques,   Then at daybreak she will leave, vanquished,
> si be l'es mal al gelos brau!   even if it hurts the rude jealous one![24]

Yet it is still a long way from Cercamon to the refinements of profanation that we encounter in the songs of Raimbaut d'Orange (fl. 1147–73),[25] where again and again God is brought into the erotic context: when the beloved laughs, it seems the laughter of God (XXXV); prayer to God can be accomplished only by praying to her (XXVI); the thought of holding her is as of holding God (XXII). At moments God is imagined as a potential rival who might want this matchless lady for himself (XV, XXII), at others it is he who has appointed her as sovereign over the world (XXX), or who has given her to the poet as his way to heaven (XXIX).

[23]*Quant l'aura doussa s'amarzis*, ed. Alfred Jeanroy, *Les poésies de Cercamon* (Paris 1922) 2. The expression *que la vej'anar jazer* is in my view a discreet but unmistakable allusion to the wish for complete sexual union.

[24]*Ab lo Pascor*, ibid. 13–14. The envoy follows:

> Amics, diguas li·m, can la ves,   Friend, tell her when you see her,
> Si passa·l terme q'avem pres,   if she lets the term we have agreed go by,
> Q'ieu soi mortz, per sain Nicolau!   I am dead, by Saint Nicolas!

[25]*The Life and Works of the Troubadour Raimbaut d'Orange*, ed. Walter T. Pattison (Minneapolis 1952).

Other troubadours enrich the idealizing love-motifs with new imagery drawn from older sources—from a bestiary by Rigaud de Barbezieux (fl. 1141–60) in his *Atressi con l'orifanz,*[26] or from the Bible by Peire Vidal (fl. 1183–1204) in *Be·m pac d'ivern e d'estiu.*[27] At the same time one can observe, especially in Latin lyrics, refinements of a more openly sensual language of love: thus for instance in the mimetic rhythmic subtlety of Peter of Blois's *Grates ago Veneri*[28] (ca. 1160?), where the ardent drinking of kisses from the girl's weeping eyes

> flentis bibo lacrimas
> dulcissimas . . .
> plus haurio fervoris

and the description of her eyes half-closed and tremulous, as she drowses languorously after love-play

> et subridens tremulis
> semiclausis oculis . . . sopita

may well be inspired, I believe, by the eroticism (and the rhythmic prose) of Apuleius, rare author though he was at this time:

> oculos Photidis meae
> udos ac tremulos
> et prona libidine marcidos
> iamiamque semiadopertulos
> adnixis et sorbillantibus saviis
> sitienter hauriebam.[29]

When we turn to the sphere of satire and parody, determining the specific twelfth-century contributions raises problems of a different kind. To begin with fabliau: here I believe we must recognize that the commonest mode of existence of this genre in most periods and places is not literary at all; rather, there is a continuing "underground" tradition of telling fabliaux, which are seldom committed to writing, and even more rarely transmuted, by writers of unusual talents, into works of high art. When this does happen, the choice of form and artistic means may vary widely: lyrical lay, sustained verse narrative, exemplum, novella, and fictive autobiography are among the possibilities.

[26]*Rigaut de Berbezilh, Liriche*, ed. Alberto Varvaro (Bari 1960) 106–34.

[27]*Peire Vidal, Poesie*, ed. D'Arco Silvio Avalle (2 vols. Milan 1960) 2.310–16.

[28]*Carmina Burana* 1.2: *Die Liebeslieder*, ed. Otto Schumann (Heidelberg 1941) 41–43. On the authorship, see Peter Dronke, "Peter of Blois and Poetry at the Court of Henry II," *Mediaeval Studies* 38 (1976) 185–235, esp. 216–22.

[29]"The eyes of my Photis, moist and tremulous, languescent with the onset of desire and now only half-open, I drained thirstily with pressing, lapping kisses" (Apuleius, *Metamorphoses* 3.14, ed. and [German] trans. Edward Brandt and Wilhelm Ehlers [2nd ed. Munich 1963] 100–02). While in this passage Apuleius uses *semiadopertulus*, he has the equally rare *semiclausus* at *Metamorphoses* 10.10. It is this latter passage that Manitius (3.880) saw as the source for Petrus Pictor's poem *De illa quae impudenter filium suum adamavit*: see also *Petri Pictoris carmina*, ed. L. Van Acker, CCL cm 25 (1972) 108.

From the tenth and early eleventh centuries we still possess a group of seven fabliaux in lyrical forms, copied in the *Cambridge Songs* collection;[30] their themes—amusing trickery, pranks, outwitting, and sexual deception, as well as jests at the expense of priests and nuns—are closely comparable in scope to those in the fabliaux of a poet such as Jean Bodel (d. 1210),[31] composed in French octosyllabic couplets nearly two centuries later. In the eleventh-century Latin verse romance *Ruodlieb*, two fabliau episodes are developed as longer narrative intrigues, with keen imaginative penetration of the characters.[32] Of the artistic formations of vernacular fabliaux before the twelfth century, no direct evidence survives—though a fabliau-like interlude of seven strophes in an Eddic poem which in substance is prior to the year 1000 (*Hávamál*, stanzas 96–102)[33] shows that a succinct lyrical mode of telling amusing episodes of amatory deceit not only existed in the Germanic world but could already be handled with pointed skill, even elegance. As the god Óthinn in *Hávamál* recounts ruefully, in the first person, how he was tricked and humiliated by the (human) girl whom he desired, the author of our earliest extant fabliau in a Romance tongue, William IX, tells—again in a lyrical-narrative mode—a tale in which he himself plays the hero-victim. This poem, *Farai un vers, pos mi sonelh*,[34] with its sharply individual mastery, is clearly no first attempt at an artistic vernacular fabliau, but presupposes a tradition; the poet indeed enriches his tradition by including swift echoes of several other types of lyric—*gab*, *plazer*,[35] and especially the poetic debate about the rival claims of clerk and knight as lovers:

[30]Nos. 6, 14, 15, 20, 24, 35, and 42 in the edition of Karl Strecker, *Die Cambridger Lieder*, MGH (2nd ed. Berlin 1955). All except no. 42 can likewise be found, with a still indispensable commentary, in *Denkmäler deutscher Poesie und Prosa aus dem VIII.–XII. Jahrhundert*, ed. Karl Müllenhoff and Wilhelm Scherer (3rd ed. Berlin 1892). I have discussed these poems in "The Rise of the Medieval Fabliau: Latin and Vernacular Evidence," *Romanische Forschungen* 85 (1973) 275–97. The summary of this article by Luciano Rossi in *Cultura neolatina* 34 (1974 [1976]) 379 unfortunately betrays alarming carelessness. As the references given in my article make clear, the relation between the Latin and Old French versions of the "snow-child" fabliau, far from being "una scoperta" or alleged as such, has been well known to medieval Latinists for nearly a century. Where Signor Rossi claims to be amazed ("stupisce") that I do not cite Edmond Faral's essay "Le fabliau latin au moyen âge," he need only have looked at p. 288 of my article to find there the full reference to Faral—*Romania* 50 (1924) 231–85—as well as others to more recent work on the *comoediae*. For work since 1973, see now *Commedie latine del XII e XIII secolo*, Pubblicazioni dell' Istituto di filologia classica e medievale dell' Università di Genova 48, 61 (2 vols. Genoa 1976–80), and Peter Dronke, "A Note on *Pamphilus*," JWCI 42 (1979) 225–30.

[31]*Jean Bodel, Fabliaux*, ed. Pierre Nardin (Paris 1965). Because of the striking resemblances between the repertoire of tales in the Cambridge Songs and that of a major fabliau poet such as Jean Bodel, I believe it would be misleading to limit the term "fabliau" to Old French compositions of the later period (see my "Fabliau" [n. 30 above] 275–78).

[32]*Ruodlieb*, fragments 6–8, 16–18; see most recently the fine discussion by Walter Haug, in the introduction to his facsimile edition, *Ruodlieb* (Wiesbaden 1974) 23–30, 46–55.

[33]*Eddadigte*, ed. Jón Helgason (2nd ed. Copenhagen–Oslo–Stockholm 1955–) 1.28–29.

[34]Ed. in Riquer, *Los trovadores* (n. 12 above) 1.133–38 (with references to the most recent studies). In the strophe cited below, it seems possible, though not certain, that there is a coarse sexual allusion underlying the expression *cremar ab un tezo*: for Old French, Tobler-Lommatzsch record the verb *tisoner* with the sense "reizen, placken, geschlechtlich erregen," but there are no decisive parallels in the Provençal dictionaries of Raynouard or Levy.

[35]See Nicolò Pasero, ed., *Guglielmo IX [d'Aquitania]: Poesie* (Modena 1973) 121; but on *plazer* cf. also O. Gsell, "Les genres médiévaux de l'enueg et du plazer," *Actes du 5e Congrès in-*

Donna non fai pechat mortau	A lady commits no deadly sin
que ama chevaler leau;	if she loves a loyal knight;
mas s'ama monge o clergau	but if she loves a monk or clerk,
non a raizo:	that is not right:
per dreg la deuria hom cremar	with justice she would then be burnt
ab un tezo.	with a firebrand.

It is a gruesome jest and sophistry. In the earlier eleventh century the countess of Monteforte had been burnt as a heretic by the archbishop of Milan—the first instance I know of a well-born lady being the victim of such atrocities.[36] That countess had followed an ascetic ideal, strange and high. But, for the grim humor of this troubadour, a lady's "heresy" is—to be on the wrong side when choosing her lover![37] In telling his fabliau (the plot is in essence that of *Decameron* III.1, of the man who, pretending to be deaf-mute, is greedily enjoyed by lustful women), William combines the shock of such profanity with light, sardonic moments and with grotesque sexual imaginings, till all is at last resolved—if, as I believe, the *envoi* is genuine[38]—with a flourish of elegant wit. In the narrative fantasy, to test if the mute is only feigning, the women sentence him to "more than a hundred wounds" from the claws of their ferocious cat; now at the close the poet sends his *joglar* to deliver the song to the two ladies,

e diguas lor que per m'amor	and tell them, for the love of me,
aucizo·l cat!	to kill the cat!

In the later twelfth century in northern France, and towards the mid-thirteenth in Germany, it became most fashionable for poets to tell fabliaux in octosyllabic couplets; yet no poet of this later period, to my mind, quite attains the deftly individual shaping of motifs from the common fabliau stock which we find with the author of *Modus Liebinc* in the tenth century,[39] the *Ruodlieb* poet in the eleventh, or the duke of Aquitaine in the early twelfth. In short, the artistic formations of fabliau are unpredictable, and depend at any time on the decisions—and the genius—of particular authors.

---

ternational de langue et littérature d'Oc et d'études franco-provençales [Nice 1967] (Paris 1974) 420–28.

[36]See esp. Herbert Grundmann, *Ketzergeschichte des Mittelalters*, Die Kirche in ihrer Geschichte 2 (Göttingen 1963) 8–9, and the penetrating recent discussion by Huguette Taviani, "Naissance d'une hérésie en Italie du Nord au XIe siècle," *Annales E.S.C.* 29 (1974) 1224–52. About the countess, Taviani concludes (1248) that "Son arrestation par les chevaliers d'Aribert s'explique aisément par le fait qu'il lui revenait de dénoncer et de châtier les hérétiques, comme le font les grands de Milan. Au contraire elle a laissé se développer, dans sa *districtio*, un groupe dissident, par sa foi et ses moeurs, de la société chrétienne. . . ."

[37]For the notion that a woman should be burnt for her wanton behavior, compare *Ruodlieb* (n. 32 above) 14.28–29: "ut eripiatur / A scorto turpi, digne satis igne cremari," or *Carmina Burana* (n. 28 above) 1.2 no. 126, where the pregnant girl laments: "Nutibus me indicant, / dignam rogo iudicant, / quod semel peccaverim."

[38]See Riquer, *Los trovadores* (n. 12 above) 1.138, and Rita Lejeune, "L'extraordinaire insolence du troubadour Guillaume IX d'Aquitaine," *Mélanges de langue et littérature médiévales offerts à Pierre Le Gentil* (Paris 1973) 485–503 at 488–92.

[39]For reasons for this dating, and a reconsideration of the readings in the MSS, see Dronke, "Fabliau" (n. 30 above) 278–79.

In the realm of ecclesiastical satire and parody, on the other hand, I believe distinctive changes in the course of the twelfth century can be traced, and that these can be explained at least in part in terms of social and economic changes.

To signal some broad contrasts swiftly to begin with: I have the impression that in the twelfth century anticlerical satires become not only far more numerous, but often less good-natured, more pressing and more violent than before. Already in Merovingian Gaul Fortunatus mocks a cleric who schemed to usurp a bishop's see,[40] and the rhymed letters of bishops Frodebertus and Importunus,[41] with their high-spirited reciprocal lampooning and abuse, foreshadow later forms of stylized invective such as *tenso* and *flyting*. Yet neither in these nor in the exposures of the human frailties of the clerical world, such as we find in the *Cambridge Songs*,[42] is humor ever eclipsed: there is nothing of the bitterness and fatality of Walter of Châtillon fearing that the ship, Ecclesia, will now be wrecked or sunk at last;[43] Walter who sees black night covering the hills and mountains and about to engulf the whole world;[44] or again, who asks with an ironic insolence born of despair, what's the use of religious knowledge, if it leaves you starving? isn't life in bed with a girl in one's arms safer than a life devoted to learning?[45] So, too, we can see something of the twelfth-century "goliard" poet in the Carolingian Sedulius Scotus—in his enjoyment of writing parody and drinking-songs, in his vivacious begging-poems to his patron, chagrined complaints about draughty lodgings and poor ale, and in his consciousness of his own identity as poet, with a half—but only half—jesting pride.[46] Yet I know no earlier parallels to the darker moments evoked in the poetry of Hugh Primas, moments that dwell painfully on sordidness and viciousness, or where the poet sees himself as "cast out even by the outcasts" (*a deiectis sum deiectus*),[47] as a Lazarus from whose wounds the pus streams (*sanies manat*—Primas's expression outdoes the biblical ones in physical revulsion).[48]

The harsher pictures of those that have not in the clerical world, the fiercer denunciations of those that have, reflect a new historical situation. The demographic explosion of the eleventh century went with the expansion of the temporal power of the Church, from the time of Gregory VII—an expansion

[40]Venantius Fortunatus, *Opera poetica*, ed. Friedrich Leo, MGH AA 4.1.19–21.

[41]*Les cinq épîtres rimées dans l'appendice des Formules de Sens*, ed. Gérard J. J. Walstra (Leiden 1962).

[42]*Die Cambridger Lieder*, ed. Strecker (n. 30 above) nos. 20, 24, 35, 42.

[43]*Propter Sion non tacebo*, ed. Karl Strecker, *Moralisch-satirische Gedichte Walters von Châtillon* (Heidelberg 1929) 17–33.

[44]*Versa est in luctum*, ibid. 147–52; a better text, with fine discussion, by Francisco Rico, *On Source, Meaning and Form in Walter of Châtillon's "Versa est in luctum"* (Barcelona 1977).

[45]*Missus sum in vineam* (esp. sts. 10–12), ed. Strecker (n. 43 above) 80–89.

[46]Sedulius Scotus, *Carmina*, ed. Ludwig Traube, MGH Poetae 3.151–240, esp. the poems 2.4, 9, 41, 49, 58.

[47]"Die Oxforder Gedichte des Primas (des Magisters Hugo von Orleans)," ed. Wilhelm Meyer, Nachr. Göttingen 1907 (separately repr. Darmstadt 1970) 158 no. 23.6.

[48]Ibid. 126 no. 5.3; compare Luke 16:20–21. The poet's identification with Lazarus is not made explicit, yet the implication—especially in the light of Primas's other poetry—seems clear.

for which a growing centralized administration (naturally susceptible to charges of venality) was needed. So, too, the secular courts and the towns increasingly required literate men in administrative positions. But after only a short time-lag the schools, which expanded and became more numerous to meet those needs, and which were fed by increasing numbers of young men from the landed classes who could not inherit land, turned out far more clerks than there were posts available. In the towns a clerical proletariat arose—an unparalleled number of educated men who, at the end of their studies, faced the prospect of unemployment. They were at the mercy of patronage, of favor from highly placed clergy or laity. Even if they obtained an appointment, it seldom implied security. It is this situation that gives a particular edge to the twelfth- (and thirteenth-) century moral satires.

The Spanish *Tractatus* by Garsias of Toledo, also called the *Garsuinis* ("Garsineid"), composed in 1099, represents a turning-point in the satiric tradition.[49] It has the literary verve of the finest twelfth-century satires, and is a headlong attack on the avaricious, gluttonous pope and cardinals—yet its joyous exuberance links it rather with some of the Carolingian *caritas*-songs and drinking-songs[50] than with the sombre indignation of a Walter of Châtillon. Moreover, the protests of Garsias have a specific cause in wounded local pride, in the Toledo Chapter's resentment that Urban II had appointed a foreigner—a fellow-Frenchman and fellow-Cluniac—as their archbishop, showering him with a host of other favors and other sees in Spain.[51] It is not Walter's vision of corruption bringing the world to its ultimate doom; essentially the *Garsuinis* remains a comedy, rich in exhilarating parody of Scripture and liturgy, bringing together litanies of the Church and rigmaroles of the fairground, moments of ancient satire (Horace, Juvenal) and above all the comic modes of Terence.[52] The *Garsuinis* indeed, I would suggest, is shaped as

[49]The most recent edition is by Rodney M. Thomson, *Tractatus Garsiae* (Leiden 1973); the fundamental study remains that of María Rosa Lida de Malkiel, "La *Garcineida* de García de Toledo," *Nueva revista de filología hispánica* 7 (1953) 246–58; some perceptive comments on the historical background in Richard W. Southern, *The Making of the Middle Ages* (London 1953) 151–54.

[50]Bernhard Bischoff, "Caritas-Lieder," *Mittelalterliche Studien* (2 vols. Stuttgart 1966–67) 2.56–77. These songs seem to me to show a spectrum of attitudes that moves from a sense of mirth arising out of the sacred itself to a mischievous parody of the sacred. Thus the *caritas*-song *Hic sistimus cum precibus* (Bischoff 2.69–70) has an unbridled element that suggests a sacred parody of the pagan custom of *Minnetrinken*, while in *O veni, veni, vinum* (ibid. 72) the wine is praised in the language used of the beloved in the Song of Songs. Here we are not far from that unseemly mirth *inter epulas* which was censured by Rabanus Maurus (ibid. 65 n. 35), and which finds perhaps its most vivacious ninth-century expression in the song *Andecavis abbas esse dicitur* (ed. Karl Strecker, MGH Poetae 4.591).

For the range of attacks on Rome, particularly in the earlier period, see Josef Benzinger, *Invectiva in Romam: Romkritik im Mittelalter vom 9. bis zum 12. Jahrhundert*, Historische Studien 404 (Lübeck 1968).

[51]Francisco Rico, "Las letras latinas del siglo XII en Galicia, León y Castilla," *Ábaco* 2 (1969) 9–91 at 41–50.

[52]Lida de Malkiel (n. 49 above) has given an admirable conspectus of the biblical and liturgical echoes (252–53), as well as of the classical, especially from Juvenal and Horace (254–55)

a Terentian comedy: there is a marked sense of five "acts" in the whole,[53] and in the last act Garsias himself, the lowliest of those present at the papal court, but the one who, by his asides, can puncture all the pretensions of the pope and the mighty ones, becomes strikingly like a Terentian comic character.

To return to the problem of profanity. The *Garsuinis* is dominated by an extended conceit: silver and gold are "canonized" as the two saints, Albinus and Rufinus, whose relics are translated to Rome, and every possibility of seeing the veneration of silver and gold in terms of the cult of saints is then exploited. The procedure is similar in other twelfth-century parodies, such as those that feature the god Wine (Lieus), or the god Money (Nummus). A piece such as the mock-sermon *De diligendo Lieo*,[54] for instance, works by way of a "philosophy of as-if"—if wine were really a god, we could preach and proclaim and invoke him with all the language of the Christian cult. The mocking fantasy is teased out in detail as though it were reality. And yet—this is essential to the fantasy—the Christian God and his cult remain. The playful assumption is meaningful, and possible as play, only if there is a Christian God, if there is a frame of reference in relation to which such parody is parody. (So, too, we might say, the outcry of the leper's wife in her *planctus* was meaningful in that she assumes there is a divine power in the universe, a divine framework against which—however hopelessly—a human being can protest.) Nor is this situation essentially different in the invectives and satires of Walter of Châtillon: even if nothing seems safe for the Church, even if the ship is mortally imperiled by sirens and pirates, by Scylla and Charybdis,[55] this sense of danger itself presupposes a horizon—a divine plan for earthly existence. Thus far, at least, parody and satire do not question a certain established sacred order of things.

Yet there are other profane impulses in the goliardic tradition which either disregard that established order or (at least temporarily) escape from it. Thus Peter of Blois, who at times can be a passionate moralist, can at others escape into a sensual, hedonistic realm. Walter of Châtillon too can escape into Arcadian fictions—into a world where Glycerium comes to a rendezvous,[56] where a pretty shepherdess is only pretending that she will not yield in love-

---

and from Terence (255–57). Her observations entail that Garsias's "curtain-line"—*vos valete et plaudite*—and his burlesque of the ancient editor's *auctoritas*—*ego Calliopius recensui*—both relegated by Thomson to the notes in his edition (56), must be restored at the close of the text (44), as must the preceding words in Thomson's codex A: *At illi obdormierunt.*

[53] I would see the structure as follows: Act 1, the scene of the bribe; Act 2, the reading of the lesson; Act 3, the ceremony of translation; Act 4, the pope's address; Act 5, the orgy. On the ancient traditions concerning the five-act structure which were known to the Middle Ages, see Thomas W. Baldwin, *Shakspere's Five-Act Structure* (Urbana 1947) 1–96.

[54] Ed. in Lehmann, *Die Parodie* (n. 1 above) 231–32.

[55] *Propter Sion non tacebo* (n. 43 above) sts. 4–14; on the traditions behind Walter's imagery here, see Hugo Rahner, *Symbole der Kirche* (Salzburg 1964) esp. 306–13.

[56] *Declinante frigore*, ed. Karl Strecker, *Die Lieder Walters von Châtillon in der Hs. 351 von St. Omer* (Berlin 1925) 29–31.

making (*quam mire simulantem*),[57] where Niobe may be amorous, or flighty, or even mercenary[58]—but at least is not tormented by moral problems.

So, too, Marbod and Hildebert in the late eleventh century compose openly profane poems as well as moralistic and religious ones; Marcabru composes not only *A la fontana* but songs of moral fervor and even a renowned summons to the crusade;[59] Cercamon appears to combine a shout of moral indignation and an avowal of sexual enslavement within the same poem. In all these poets secular and spiritual elements coexist, and there is no sense of a decisive rejection of the ones in favor of the others; diverse notions of felicity are held in tension; there are impulses towards profanity and impulses towards piety, and it is their conjunctions that we must accept and try to understand. It would be too simple to say "this is basically a worldly poet," or "basically a spiritual poet," or to assume that such poets moved conclusively from one "phase" to another—in some cases such a supposition would indeed do violence to the known chronology of their works.

Yet there were still other kinds of challenge to an established sacral order possible in the twelfth century. The Archpoet's piece *Lingua balbus, hebes ingenio*[60] contains a sermon on Christ's death, the Redemption and the Judgment, which is indeed not parodistic in the sense that *De diligendo Lieo* is. The sermon as such is moving and magnificent—if its twenty-one quatrains had survived on their own, they would be acknowledged as a summit in twelfth-century religious lyric. It is the use to which this sermon is put that is subversive. The poet uses all his art to cause *compunctio*, to stab the conscience of his listeners. Then comes the peripety: he exploits that compunction with a witty selfishness, for himself, and for purely this-worldly purposes.

Ipse deus est in pauperibus:[61] overtly it is an expression of the Gospel ideal—"whatever you have given to the least of these my brothers, you have given to me." But implicitly the poet is saying to his audience, if you are moved by Christ's being poor and rejected on earth, you should be moved by my condition too. And what is his condition? That of one who is "not wicked" (*non sum nequam*), but who cannot love his neighbor as himself

---

[57]*Sole regente lora*, ibid. 59–61.

[58]Walter's three "Niobe" songs—*Autumnali frigore, Dum queritur michi remedium*, and *Dum flosculum tenera*—ibid. 34–41.

[59]*Pax in nomine Domini!* ed. Riquer, *Los trovadores* (n. 12 above) 1.206–10. Can we go so far as to say that, among the authors who composed both profane and spiritual works, two realms of values are implicitly relativized? With the Archpoet (see below) and Peter of Blois (see my study, n. 28 above), the answer may be affirmative: such ambivalence may have been an essential part of their intellectual makeup. With other authors I think it is more a matter of their participating in different literary contexts and inheriting diverse literary traditions—juxtaposing, rather than clashing, disparate thoughts.

[60]*Die Gedichte des Archipoeta*, ed. Heinrich Watenphul and Heinrich Krefeld (Heidelberg 1958) 47–52 no. 1. I have offered a new text, with detailed literary commentary, in "The Art of the Archpoet: A Reading of *Lingua balbus*," *The Interpretation of Medieval Lyric Poetry*, ed. W. T. H. Jackson (New York 1980) 22–43.

[61]Watenphul and Krefeld (n. 60 above) st. 31 (50).

(*plus mihi quam fratri cupio*):[62] the answer is both self-mockery and a sardonic look at the Gospel's counsel of perfection. At the close comes a burlesque blessing and prayer: for his imperial audience—the high prelates and judges of the earth—the poet prays that God give them ''the pitcher of the oil of charity, the wine of hope, the corn of faith, and life after death''; but for himself he prays that they give him, ''me who enjoy the world . . . and die if I have no wine, lots of money for my huge expenses—amen!''[63]

The climax of the sermon proper had been the thought, if you give to the poor, you are giving to Christ; the oil of charity—refused by the wise virgins to their foolish sisters, but given by the poor widow to Elijah—had been an image used almost as a musical motif in the poem. Now at the close a new *vates*, a new Elijah, begs, and (the Archpoet suggests to his audience), by giving to him, as the widow gave to the prophet of old, they can win spiritual sustenance that never runs dry. Within the parodistic prayer, that is, there lurks a multiple allusion—almost a summation of the poem—which is serious.

Another challenge that the Archpoet sets, one that occurs as a motif in his most celebrated song, *Estuans intrinsecus*, lies in the assessment of sensual desires.[64] *Iuvenes non possumus legem sequi duram*: we who are young cannot follow a harsh law. To follow that (divine) law would be ''to vanquish nature'' (*vincere naturam*), to attempt something most arduous, even impossible. ''Who, if placed in the fire, would not be burnt?'' Are the longings of this world not the natural, the essentially human ones? And if so, how can they be suppressed? For the Archpoet, this aspect of his attitude to earthly existence goes with a deeper, more philosophical strand of pessimism. He is at times overwhelmed by the sense of transience, of his own transience—a leaf that is the plaything of the wind, a gliding stream, a ship without helmsman (*folio sum similis de quo ludunt venti . . . , fluvio labenti . . . , sine nauta navis*). And this prompts the conclusion, if there's only one life and it passes so swiftly, let us at least make it a sweet life, let us make the dying a dying in love, no mere destruction—*morte bona morior, dulci nece necor*. Implicitly, these affirmations of transience deny the Christian otherworld; and yet (a further irony) the language of the Archpoet's nihilism is deeply biblical: it is the bleak moments of Job and of the Book of Wisdom that echo in it.[65] So, too, another poet, Bernard Silvester, writing some fifteen years earlier (ca. 1147), as he presents an unending, purposeless cycle of generation and decay, can scarcely help echoing the nihilistic note in Ecclesiastes. *Generatio praeterit et generatio advenit—terra vero in aeternum stat* (Eccl. 1:4): it is this contrast that dominates the close of Bernard's *Cosmographia*.

---

[62]Ibid. st. 37 (51).

[63]Ibid. sts. 44–45 (52).

[64]Ibid. 73–83 no. 10; I refer especially to sts. 1–8. There is a more recent edition by Bernhard Bischoff, *Carmina Burana* 1.3 (Heidelberg 1970) no. 191.

[65]See esp. the parallels cited by Watenphul and Krefeld (n. 60 above) for no. 10, sts. 1–3 (140–41).

The nature of the universe is in a sense permanent: it survives itself and feeds on its own flux. For whatever is spent reverts to the sum of things: it decays or "dies" often, yet never dies totally:

> Influit ipsa sibi mundi natura, superstes,
> Permanet et fluxu pascitur usque suo:
> Scilicet ad summam rerum iactura recurrit,
> Nec semel—ut possit sepe perire—perit.[66]

But for mankind, the fight against transience is of a different order: man—*sibi deficiens*[67]—is not self-sufficient, like the macrocosm. The only freedom from decay and death, the only hope of perpetuity, that human beings can have, is achieved through human love: it lies in their children.

Earlier in his poem Bernard had evoked an otherworldly goal, in terms of the Timaean and Boethian myth of souls rejoining the stars when they leave their bodies.[68] But at the close he seems to leave otherworldly immortality wholly out of account: the only immortality in question now is that which human beings can attain through sexual love. It is the genitals that "repair nature and perpetuate the race, and do not allow what is mortal to die."[69] The act which is so often a source of ribald amusement in fabliaux is here seen as humanity's only resource against fate. The power of generation (Fetura) makes the battle of love-play into a battle against death, and Natura's craft is to form the sperm in such a way that parents can live on, even in looks, in their descendants:

> Format et effingit sollers Natura liquorem,
> Ut simili genesis ore reducat avos.[70]

For Bernard it would seem (in the words of the *Asclepius*—a text he cherished) "that man is mortal, humanity immortal" (*ut homo mortalis sit, inmortalis humanitas*).[71]

---

[66]*Cosmographia*, Microcosmus 14.171–74 (ed. Dronke [n. 6 above] 154–55).
[67]Ibid. 14.177.
[68]Ibid. 10.51–54 (ed. Dronke 141–42):

> Set cum nutarit, numeris in fine solutis,
> Machina corporee collabefacta domus,
> Ethera scandet homo, iam non incognitus hospes
> Preveniens stelle signa locumque sue.

[69]Ibid. 14.162–64 ("Naturam reparant, perpetuantque genus. / Non mortale mori . . . sinunt").
[70]Ibid. 14.169–70.
[71]*Asclepius* 4, ed. Arthur D. Nock, trans. André-Jean Festugière, *Corpus Hermeticum* (2nd ed. 4 vols. Paris 1960) 2.300. On the wider political and legal implications of this conception in the Middle Ages, see Ernst H. Kantorowicz, *The King's Two Bodies: A Study in Mediaeval Political Theology* (Princeton 1957) 277–84. In the fourteenth century, Baldus de Ubaldis was to apply the Aristotelian-Averroist notion of the eternity of the species to the continuity of the *populus*, "because the people does not die" (ibid. 295), or of the *respublica*, "for the commonweal cannot die" (ibid. 299).

These examples are of necessity brief and allusive. Yet it is clear that certain poets of exceptional stature, such as the Archpoet and Bernard Silvester, are enquiring into profane goals and spiritual goals, into this-worldly and otherworldly hopes, in ways that are too complex and too individual to be reduced to a formula—but also, I would add, in ways to which I can see no close parallels in the poetry of 1100 or of the tenth and eleventh centuries.

I think that such poetic enquiry may imply an even more radical kind of questioning in a famous literary work which the most recent scholarship places either just before or shortly after 1200: *Aucassin et Nicolette*[72]—a work that most scholars have sheltered (perhaps too comfortably) under the umbrella, parody. To recall one of the best known scenes: when the viscount tells Aucassin that he must give up Nicolette and his love for her, the climax of his speech is:

Above all, what do you think you would have gained if you made her your mistress and took her to your bed? You'd have gained precious little, for all the days of the world your soul would be in hell for it, so that you'd never enter paradise.

And Aucassin replies:

In paradise, what's there for me to do? I don't want to enter it save to have Nicolette, my sweetest friend, whom I so love. For into paradise only those people go—I'll tell you which: the old priests and cripples and the one-armed folk who crouch before the altars in the old crypts night and day, and those with old threadbare capes and old tattered clothes, who are naked and unhosed and bare-buttocked, who die of hunger and thirst and cold and diseases; they go to paradise—I've nothing to do with them. Rather I want to go to hell, for into hell go handsome clerks and fair knights who are killed in tournaments and noble wars, good soldiers and free men; I want to go with these. And there go the lovely courtly ladies who have two lovers, or three, besides their husband, and there go gold and silver and vair and grey fur, harpers and minstrels and the kings of the world: with them I want to go, as long as I have Nicolette, my sweetest friend, with me.[73]

[72]Jean Dufournet, ed. (Paris 1973). To Dufournet's bibliography (35–36) may be added, among recent studies, June Hall Martin, *Love's Fools: Aucassin, Troilus, Calisto and the Parody of the Courtly Lover* (London 1972) esp. 23–36; John A. Rea, "The Form of *Aucassin et Nicolette*," *Romance Notes* 15 (1973–74) 504–08; Mariantonia Liborio, "*Aucassin et Nicolette*: I limiti di una parodia," *Cultura neolatina* 30 (1970) 156–71, who gives (162–63) a different interpretation of the passage discussed below.

[73]Dufournet (n. 72 above) 56–58:
Enseurquetot, que cuideriés vous avoir gaegnié, se vous l'aviés asognentee ne mise a vo lit? Mout i ariés peu conquis, car tos les jors du siecle en seroit vo arme en infer, qu'en paradis n'enterriés vo ja.
— En paradis qu'ai je a faire? Je n'i quier entrer, mais que j'aie Nicolete ma tresdouce amie que j'aim tant, c'en paradis ne vont fors tex gens con je vous dirai. Il i vont cil viel prestre et cil viel clop et cil manke qui tote jor et tote nuit cropent devant ces autex et en ces viés croutes, et cil a ces viés capes ereses et a ces viés tatereles vestues, qui sont nu et decauc et estrumelé, qui moeurent de faim et de soi et de froit et de mesaises. Icil vont en paradis: aveuc ciax n'ai jou que faire. Mais en infer voil jou aler, car en infer vont li bel clerc, et li bel cevalier qui sont mort as tornois et as rices gueres, et li buen sergant et li franc home: aveuc ciax voil jou aler. Et s'i vont les beles dames cortoises que eles ont deus amis ou trois avoc leur barons, et s'i va li ors et li argens et li vairs et li gris, et si i vont herpeor et jogleor et li roi del siecle: avoc ciax voil jou aler, mais que j'aie Nicolete ma tresdouce amie aveuc mi.

Evidently there are multiple ironies at work here. At moments we can read the scene almost in a Walter of Châtillon key, the author contrasting the rich and the poor, the exploiters and exploited of this world, with a cool satiric gaze akin to that of Walter's in *Missus sum in vineam*. But beyond that, we must at least ask, did the author of *Aucassin et Nicolette* believe that there existed a heaven and hell—a real otherworld—such as the Church taught him to believe in? Or had he reduced heaven and hell to a fiction, by which he could obliquely and humorously cast light on the human condition, on what is heavenly or hellish on earth? I am inclined to think this is nearer the truth—that, whatever the precise scope of the humor, the author's intention was to undermine the complacency of an accepted framework.

Towards 1200, in Paris, a radical Aristotelian, David of Dinant, expounded for the first time a world-picture in which the traditional antinomies—this-worldly and otherworldly, body and soul, matter and mind—were overcome.[74] He speaks of *yle* (matter as a principle, that is, not as realized in material objects), of *mens* (or *ratio*, or *nois*), and of God; but he will not admit an ultimate opposition:

I maintain that there is only one mind (*mens*), but many souls; and only one matter (*yle*), though there are many bodies. For, since only received attributes (*passiones*), that is, accidents or properties, differentiate things from one another, there is necessarily only one that is not subject to any received attribute. Mind and matter are of this kind. . . .
Yet it must be asked whether these are one, or are diverse. But since only the things that are receptive differ from one another, it seems that mind and matter differ in no way, since neither of them is subject to any received attribute. . . .
From this it can be inferred, then, that mind and matter are the same. Plato seems to assent to this, when he says that the world is the perceptible God. If, then, the world is God outgoing himself, perceptible to sense . . . , the world's matter is God himself, and the form that comes to matter is nothing other than God's making himself into what is perceptible. . . . It is manifest, therefore, that God is the reason of all souls and the matter of all bodies.[75]

[74]On David of Dinant see most recently Marian Kurdziałek, "L'idée de l'homme chez David de Dinant," in *Images of Man in Ancient and Medieval Thought: Studia Gerardo Verbeke . . . dicata* (Louvain 1976) 311–22. Kurdziałek is also the editor of *Davidis de Dinanto quaternulorum fragmenta*, Studia Mediewistyczne 3 (Warsaw 1963), from which the citations below are taken.

[75]*Davidis . . . fragmenta* 70–72:
Dico autem, quod una sola est mens, multe vero anime; et una sola yle et multa vero corpora. Cum enim sole passiones, hoc est accidencia sive proprietates, faciant differenciam rerum ad se invicem, necesse est unum solum esse id, quod nulli passioni subiectum est; cuiusmodi sunt mens et yle. . . .
Querendum autem, utrum mens et yle unum sint, aut diversa. Cum igitur sola passiva differant ad se invicem, videtur mentem et ylen nullo modo differe, cum neutrum eorum sit subiectum passioni. . . .
Ex hiis ergo colligi potest mentem et ylen idem esse. Huic autem assentire videtur PLATO, ubi dicit mundum esse <Deum> sensibilem. . . . Si ergo mundus est ipse Deus preter se ipsum perceptibile sensui . . . , yle igitur mundi est ipse Deus, forma vero adveniens yle nil aliud quam id, quod facit Deus sensibile se ipsum. . . . Manifestum est ergo Deum esse racionem omnium animarum et yle omnium corporum.

I do not believe that either "pantheism" or "materialism"—two terms that have often been applied[76]—are really apt for characterizing David's thought. Clearly in the main his emphasis throughout his work is this-worldly and not otherworldly: he wanted to explain alleged miracles as a scientist, alleged psychic phenomena as a biologist.[77] Yet the cornerstone of his thought (as far as this can be ascertained from the extant fragments) would seem to have been the insight that the opposition between this-worldly and otherworldly can never be absolute, and is—at least for the philosopher who can truly grasp the meaning of "matter" and "mind," of "body" and "soul"—surmountable. For David there was no longer a "higher" and a "lower" realm.

It is such a relativization of this-worldly and otherworldly that I would see in *Aucassin et Nicolette*—or even, by an extended irony, the complete reversal of these concepts: just as this poet deliberately reverses the commonly accepted roles of the sexes in love and in war. In the later thirteenth century, Jean de Meun's part of the *Roman de la Rose* provides, one might almost say, a poetic *summa* of ways in which a commonly accepted order of things—with its "higher" and "lower" aspects—can be relativized. It is in the light of these developments that certain manifestations in twelfth-century literature—the affirmations of what is this-worldly in profane poetry of every kind, and the questioning of the otherworldly, especially in parody and satire—take on a particular significance.

Bibliographical Note

For the historical and literary background of twelfth-century profane literature, the third part of Reto R. Bezzola's *Les origines et la formation de la littérature courtoise en occident (500–1200), La société courtoise: littérature de cour et littérature courtoise* (2 vols. Paris 1963), is rich in materials and insights. As regards the transmission of this literature, the second volume of *Geschichte der Textüberlieferung der antiken und mittelalterlichen Literatur* (2 vols. Zurich 1961–64) includes chapters on medieval Latin, French, Provençal, Italian, Spanish, English, German, and Norse. For twelfth-century works in the Romance languages, the new *Grundriss der romanischen Literaturen des Mittelalters*, ed. Hans Robert Jauss, Erich Köhler, et al. (Heidelberg 1968–) offers a survey and a bibliography that will gradually extend to all the principal genres. So far, the sections *La littérature didactique, allégorique et satirique* have appeared (2 vols. 1968–70), besides an introductory volume, *Généralités* (1972). Twelfth-century Latin secular literature (which the *Grundriss* excludes) is treated succinctly in Joseph de Ghellinck's *L'essor de la littérature latine au XIIe siècle* (2nd ed. Brussels 1955), the poetry more fully in the second volume of F. J. E. Raby, *A History of Secular Latin Poetry in the Middle Ages* (2nd ed. 2 vols. Oxford 1957). Specific aspects are covered by

[76]See for instance Gabriel Théry, *Autour du décret de 1210*, vol. 1: *David de Dinant: Etude sur son panthéisme matérialiste* (Kain [Belgium] 1925).

[77]*Davidis . . . fragmenta* (n. 74 above) esp. 51, 57, 59–61, 63–64, 76, 88; Kurdziałek, "L'idée de l'homme" (n. 74 above) 316–19.

Paul Lehmann, *Die Parodie im Mittelalter* (2nd ed. Stuttgart 1963) and by Winthrop Wetherbee, *Platonism and Poetry in the Twelfth Century* (Princeton 1972). Especially for the Latin prose works, however, the third volume of Manitius must still be consulted.

Some of the more recent histories of medieval vernacular literatures devote a substantial section to the twelfth century: the first volume of Martín de Riquer's *Història de la literatura catalana* (Barcelona 1964); Alan D. Deyermond's volume, *La Edad Media*, trans. Luis Alonso López, in the *Historia de la literatura española* (2nd ed. Barcelona 1973, revised and enlarged from the English ed., London 1971); M. Dominica Legge's *Anglo-Norman Literature and Its Background* (Oxford 1963; corr. repr. 1971); the first two volumes of Helmut A. W. de Boor and Richard Newald's *Geschichte der deutschen Literatur*, vol. 1: *770–1170* (8th ed. Munich 1971), vol. 2: *1170–1250* (9th ed. Munich 1974); and Ewald Erb's corresponding volumes in the East German *Geschichte der deutschen Literatur*, 1.1–2: *Von den Anfängen bis 1160*, and 2: *Von 1160 bis 1230* (2nd ed. 2 vols. Berlin 1976). Some valuable new perspectives for the twelfth century also emerge in Karl Bertau, *Deutsche Literatur im Europäischen Mittelalter* (2 vols. Munich 1972–73). For French literature of the period, the most valuable reference work is perhaps the *Dictionnaire des lettres françaises*, part 1: *Le Moyen Age*, ed. Robert Bossuat, Louis Pichard, and Guy Raynaud de Lage (Paris 1951–64). For the literatures not specifically touched on in this essay, I would signal at least the succinct bibliographic guides by Rachel Bromwich, *Medieval Celtic Literature*, Toronto Medieval Bibliographies (Toronto 1974) and Hans Bekker-Nielsen, *Old Norse-Icelandic Studies* (Toronto 1967), and the new standard work by Herbert Hunger, *Die hochsprachliche profane Literatur der Byzantiner*, Handbuch der Altertumswissenschaft 12.5 (2 vols. Munich 1978), complementing Hans-Georg Beck's *Geschichte der byzantinischen Volksliteratur* (Munich 1971). On the Hispano-Arabic side, Samuel Miklos Stern's posthumous papers, *Hispano-Arabic Strophic Poetry* (Oxford 1974), include the fundamental essay "Literary Connections between the Islamic World and Western Europe in the Early Middle Ages: Did They Exist?" (204–30).

Among works treating particular aspects and genres of twelfth-century profane literature, I would mention especially, for narrative art of various kinds, Hans Robert Jauss, *Alterität und Modernität der mittelalterlichen Literatur* (Munich 1977); Max Wehrli, *Formen mittelalterlicher Erzählung* (Zurich 1969); Eugène Vinaver, *A la recherche d'une poétique médiévale* (Paris 1970) and *The Rise of Romance* (Oxford 1971); Marc-René Jung, *Etudes sur le poème allégorique en France au moyen âge* (Bern 1971); Horst Baader, *Die Lais* (Frankfurt 1966); for secular drama: Richard Axton, *European Drama of the Early Middle Ages* (London 1974), and the first part of Robert Weimann's *Shakespeare und die Tradition des Volkstheaters* (Berlin 1967); for lyric, Martín de Riquer's *Los trovadores: Historia literaria y textos* (3 vols. Barcelona 1975); Hans W. H. Fromm, ed., *Der deutsche Minnesang* (4th ed. Darmstadt 1969); Pierre Bec, *La lyrique française au moyen-âge (XIIe–XIIIe siècles)*, vol. 1, *Etudes* (Paris 1977); and my own *Medieval Latin and the Rise of European Love-Lyric* (2nd ed. 2 vols. Oxford 1968) and *The Medieval Lyric* (2nd ed. London 1978). For the "matter of Tristan," Friedrich Ranke's collection and discussion of evidence, *Tristan und Isold* (Munich 1925), remains unsurpassed. It is now complemented by Álfrún Gunnlaugsdóttir's *Tristán en el Norte* (Reykjavík 1978), where the reconstruction of Thomas's *Tristan* in particular is advanced by substantially new use of the Norse evidence.

Much stimulating discussion of works in the twelfth-century Romance literatures can be found in the volumes of collected essays by four major scholars: Erich Auerbach, *Gesammelte Aufsätze zur romanischen Philologie* (Bern 1967); Philipp August Becker, *Zur romanischen Literaturgeschichte* (Munich 1967); Ernst Robert Curtius, *Gesammelte Aufsätze zur romanischen Philologie* (Bern 1960); Leo Spitzer, *Romanische Literaturstu-*

dien, 1936–1956 (Tübingen 1959). Hugo Kuhn's *Dichtung und Welt im Mittelalter* (Stuttgart 1959) and *Text und Theorie* (Stuttgart 1969) include remarkable essays on aspects of twelfth-century German poetry. To conclude with four works, very different from one another in their aims and methods, that should not be overlooked: Ernst Bloch's *Avicenna und die Aristotelische Linke* (2nd ed. Frankfurt 1963), a brief but fascinating attempt to suggest the wider implications of one of the earliest currents of Aristotelian influence; Ramón Menéndez Pidal's superbly documented *Poesía juglaresca y orígenes de las literaturas románicas* (6th ed. Madrid 1957); Hans Spanke's pioneering work *Beziehungen zwischen romanischer und mittellateinischer Lyrik*, Abh Göttingen 3rd ser. 18 (Berlin 1936); and the "Das Hochmittelalter im Anfang" volumes (3.1–2) in Georg Misch's *Geschichte der Autobiographie* (4 vols. in 8, Frankfurt 1949–69), profound in reflection and meticulous in analysis.

The Rise of Literary Fiction

Per Nykrog

The story-teller's art is the most ancient and beloved of all arts. And therefore: *literary fiction (or fictional literature) naturally occupies a predominant position among the artful uses of language.* So much so, in fact, that the more adventurous student of comparative literature is surprised to realize that the predominance of literary fiction is not the effect of some law of nature, but rather a characteristic of European civilization, and consequently that *literary fiction has come into existence through a specific creative process, by a creation of form.*

The three italicized statements can all be challenged successfully. Actually, they depend upon how the speaker defines the concepts of *literary*, of *fiction*, and of *form*. *Literary* should be used in the sense "essentially in writing" (as opposed to oral); *fiction* should be used in the sense of "narrative acknowledged by narrator and by public essentially as a product of creative imagination"; and *form* should be used in the very vague sense of "precedent for shaping a narrative in a certain characteristic way."

The three concepts are hardly controversial as such, but each of them invites some considerations that may help to visualize the rise of literary fiction in the French-speaking regions around the middle of the twelfth century, and to suggest some of its implications.

To put it crudely, the initial distribution, at the beginning of the century, opposes *literary* to *fiction*. The written word, almost exclusively Latin, is reserved for scholarly (ecclesiastical, administrative) uses, and is thus restricted to the pursuit or propagation of what is considered and presented as *truth* (including traditional narrative). On the other hand, one of the basic possibilities of language is that of taking liberties with actual fact, in other words of spreading fictive information, from the simplest lie to the anecdote to elaborate fictional narrative. The opening statement of this essay (actually borrowed from Isak Dinesen) reflects the conviction that mankind has always taken pleasure in exploiting this fascinating possibility.

But the crude distinction between (literary) writing on one side and (fabulous) fiction on the other is more than just a joke. Writing is costly and rare, and it seems that civilizations have to reach a certain level of technology and productivity before downright and avowedly first-hand fiction can be put into writing. (Fiction that has been consecrated as truth after a long life in oral tradition is of course a different matter.) Actually, the oldest text extant that qualifies as literary fiction (or *roman*) seems to be Petronius's *Satiricon*, followed by a relatively sparse production of other Greco-Roman texts from the first centuries A.D.(Apuleius, Longus, etc.). Chinese, Indian, and Japanese literary fiction seem to start from the sixth century A.D. onward, and to become relatively well established only about the year 1000.

With the rise of literary fiction comes into existence a specific human type: the *author*. The oral storyteller may be a beloved and justly admired creator, and his work may be relatively well fixed in metrical formulation; still, he possesses his work only as long as he himself is the performer. As soon as someone else memorizes and tells the story, *he* becomes the authority, *he* is the one who is in possession of the tale, and *his* version is the only one that exists at the moment of each performance. The *author* is in a different position. He produces his tale as an object existing outside himself and his mind, and in the shape of that object he will be present whenever and wherever it is "performed." The person who does the actual reading is a mere handyman: the only qualification he needs is to know how to read. A creator who commits his work to oral tradition vanishes as an individual. The author who produces a written text remains as an individual person, as the one who left his mark on this text, from the level of more or less artfully calculated, more or less complex composition, down to the level of more or less subtle stylistic detail in the wording of the single sentence. He will remain in control, by means of the written text, even after he is dead and gone.

The writer-author's experience of himself as a person will be further strengthened if he is a writer of fiction, one who freely invents and shapes the life and destiny of a human character for purely esthetic purposes. This is a type of activity very different from that of a man who devotes himself to continuing a tradition, to propagating what he considers as truth, or to preaching the Word of God. The author-writer is a free and independent person who takes command and who intends to stay in control. That is not a simple thing to do. It requires either a precedent, a *form*, or an act of creative innovation (which of course does not have to be a creation *ex nihilo*).

This figure of the author-writer came into existence in the years around 1170 after a gestation that had lasted several decades. It is a remarkable fact that he did not spring directly from the flourishing oral traditions, Germanic, French, or Celtic, and their precedents for fictional narrative: it was the scholarly writer who groped his way toward fiction, not the oral storyteller who simply resorted to writing.

The French tradition of the *chanson de geste* was fully developed, and several "songs" had been taken down in writing during the first half of the twelfth century. But that does not make them literary, for evident and illuminating reasons: the epic was firmly established as a world in itself, having its characteristic form, subject-matters, carriers, performance-situations, and public; and this whole syndrome was, if not exclusively popular, at least strongly conservative. That some of the songs were taken down in writing could only be secondary and accidental, compared to "the real thing": the oral performances. The early author-writers were familiar with the *chansons de geste*, and to some extent influenced by them, but the ample flow of epic tradition did not merge with the scarcer flow of literary fiction until a later stage, toward the end of the century, when author-writers in full possession of their form were looking eagerly in various directions for new types of narrative material to be cast in the by then established form of the *roman*.

The same thing must be true for the Germanic and Celtic epic traditions, but it is difficult to form a clear picture, precisely for lack of extant written material. One thing seems certain, though: the Germanic and the Celtic (continental and insular) situations were deeply different. The Germanic traditions were supported by large populations in unbroken cultural development, and so can be supposed to have been preserved relatively well. The carriers of Celtic traditions, by contrast, had been subjected to successive flows of invasions, to such a point that even their language was disappearing on the continent and severely receding in England, so that their cultural tradition was in a state of decomposition.

But decomposition made possible a secondary, creative re-composition, involuntarily freed from the bonds of respect that an undisturbed ethnic identity will normally impose on the bearers of its traditions, narrative as well as social and behavioral. Eventually, European literary fiction was to spring from the decomposition and a secondary, momentary recomposition of Celtic narrative traditions. The fabulous figure of king Arthur himself was elaborated by the Celtic Britons during the bitter centuries of defeat, under Anglo-Saxon and Viking domination, as a sort of ethnic self-assertion through fantastic wish-fulfillment in retrospect. About the year 1000 he appears, fully developed into a sort of king of kings according to traditional Celtic conceptions, cultural and narrative, in the Welsh tale of *Culhwch and Olwen*.[1] About two generations after the Norman conquest, he was confiscated for the profit of the new invaders and transferred from the historical backwaters of the subjected Celts into the prestigious mainstream of Latin literature by Geoffrey of Monmouth in his *Historia regum Britanniae*.

Historians are ill at ease with Geoffrey, for as a source to "wie es eigentlich gewesen," he is worse than spurious. Folklorists and students of ethnic traditions also frown on him, for he is too evidently a man of imagination, an artist who tells tall tales freely, as he pleases, in his own sophisticated way. So both groups tend to push him into *literature*, and with good reason, for he must certainly have experienced himself as an author-writer of the type described above. But literature refuses to take him in, too, for all his stylistic

[1]English translation in *The Mabinogion* (see Bibliographical Note below).

merits and fictional creativity, on the grounds that his *form*—the precedent for writing the way he does—is that of chronicle. His more or less fabulous biographies are inserted into a framework of national history, and his models are Livy (and derivatives) or, more remotely, the historical books of the Old Testament. And as a historian he was accepted—and indignantly rejected—from the twelfth to the sixteenth century.

Like Livy, Geoffrey writes for the greater glory of his nation, but unlike Livy, he glorifies a borrowed national past. He could not very well bring his "history" up to present times, since his "nation," the Anglo-Norman kingdom, was barely seventy years old: had he gone closer to the present day, he would have clashed with the two main challengers to the upstart he wanted to provide with an age-old mythical and ethnic dignity. He wrote against the Anglo-Saxon (and Viking) populations in England, and against the French kingdom on the continent. Politically, the Arthur story in Geoffrey's *Historia* prefigures and prepares the vast ambitions of the "Angevin Empire" of the Plantagenets, some twenty years before the coronation of Henry II.

The king of France is the successor to Charlemagne, and the self-understanding of his vassals, their system of values, and their ideology are expressed by and reflected in the *chansons de geste*. To compete with this well-established system, Geoffrey's narration delineates a new type of kingly glory, combining the absolute king in continental tradition, Charlemagne, with the absolute princely glory as witnessed in a tradition going back to Antiquity: Alexander.

Alexander, not Caesar: Caesar had been ingloriously murdered at the peak of his glory, and besides, he was too well known from his own minute accounts of his life and deeds. Alexander had not had a historian of his own, so myth could grow freely and abundantly around his fabulous figure. It had grown with particular profusion in the Orient, but the West was familiar with the outlines and essentials: what the archpriest Leo discovered in the tenth century was merely a lush completion of a tantalizing story that had been known since the age of Charlemagne at least.[2]

Geoffrey's Arthur is a medieval king like Charlemagne, leading his vassals in war and in peace. But unlike Charlemagne, Arthur is a thoroughly secular figure: he conquers for the glory of himself, and to enrich his men, not for the glory of God. The Arthur of *Culhwch and Olwen* had been in India and in Africa with his armies, so the comparison was near at hand. Like Alexander (in the versions current at the time), Arthur was born under somewhat reprehensible circumstances involving magic and immorality, and like Alexander (but unlike Charlemagne), he is a youthful, enterprising conqueror, himself

---

[2]For a diplomatic mission, the masters of Naples selected "Leonem archipresbiterum valde fidelem. Quo pergente in eandem Constantinopolitanam urbem coepit inquirere libros ad legendum. Inter quos invenit historiam continentem certamina et victorias Alexandri regis Macedoniae. Et nullam negligentiam vel pigritiam habendo sine mora scripsit et secum usque Neapolim deduxit ad suos predictos excellentissimos seniores. . . ." *Der Alexanderroman des Archipresbyters Leo* prologus c.2, ed. Friedrich Pfister, Sammlung mittellateinischer Texte 6 (Heidelberg 1913) 45.

foremost in battle. Above all, Geoffrey's narrative (in accordance with *Culhwch and Olwen*) persistently praises Arthur for the typical Alexandrian virtue of lavish generosity, in war after victory, and in peace at his brilliant and festive court.

It is a new conception of ideal man. Not a wise and prudent instrument in the hands of Providence, ready to endure hardship and abnegations for a higher cause, as was Charlemagne, but a secular man, active and self-asserting, ever in search of wealth and glory. And it is an updated conception of chivalry, glorified as a purpose in itself, as a splendid way of life, not as a road to self-sacrifice in the transcendental service of God or of justice.

An early precedent for long and complex narrative writing in French (*romanz*) was given by the anonymous cleric who composed the *Roman de Thebes*, probably in England around 1150. It is not a translation of Statius, but a long narration (10,000 verses) in which the dramatic life-stories of "Edyppus" and his sons by incest are staged—after Statius—with feudal knights of the twelfth century in all the parts. The elaboration of each episode is very free, and so the work could be considered as fiction. But since the plot-outline is fixed by tradition, it should not be (according to the definition used here): the authority for the ultimate shaping of the destinies is in the source, which is respected. The writer tells the story of "Edyppus" briefly, as an explanation of the situation the two brothers find themselves in. But apart from that, he merely develops each episode after Statius, insisting on politics and warfare, two fields in which he could lean comfortably on the *chanson de geste* tradition (in spite of the fact that he writes in rhymed octosyllables, as is usual in a literary adaptation in French—the predominant meter in oral tradition being the assonanced decasyllable).

But why Thebes, when there was abundant narrative material at hand that should have a more direct appeal to a twelfth-century audience? The answer is concealed in the question, and the anonymous writer states it bluntly in the opening verses of his tale: he refers to "sir Homer and sir Plato and Vergil and Cicero" (*danz Omers et danz Platons et Virgile et Quicerons*), praising the use they made of their learning. He, too, will show his: "and now everybody should remain silent concerning this matter, unless they are clerics or knights, for no one else can appreciate it any better than a donkey appreciates harp music."[3] This is the reason: it is a rare and strange tale, exotic and not for the *profanum vulgus*. The prologue is a sally directed against the narrative matters which are at hand: let the unsophisticated enjoy their simple

---

[3]Or s'en tesent de cest mestier,
se ne sont clerc ou chevalier,
car ausi pueent escouter
conme li asnes a harper.

Le Roman de Thèbes, ed. Guy Raynaud de Lage, Les classiques français du moyen âge 94, 96 (2 vols. Paris 1966–68) 1.1.

pleasures, what I write is only for those who are discriminating and culturally adventurous. All the early writers of literary narrative take pains to keep at a distance from the reigning narrative form, the age-old, popular, and well-established epic. The best way to keep that distance is to avoid any thematic material connected with that form, and to look for a different material, remote and unknown, therefore new, distinctive, distinguished.

The *Roman de Brut* by Wace (about 1155, based on Geoffrey's *Historia*), and his later *Roman de Rou* (a history of the dukes of Normandy) are more or less in the same vein: for all the narrative imagination displayed in the details (this is where the Round Table appears for the first time), this is not fiction but translation (adaptation) in the formal framework of history or chronicle, setting forth respectively the more remote past of the land and the recent glory of the reigning dynasty. But both these works contribute to the formation of a literature—or of a library—of *romans*, of literary texts in the vernacular meant to be read aloud in the aristocratic circles at Henry's and Eleanor's court, for the enjoyment of learned clerics and distinguished nobles alike and together.

The equally Norman, and equally anonymous, adaptor of the *Aeneid* (about 1160?) starts out as his predecessor (or alter ego?) had done with the *Thebaid*: fixing it up considerably, simplifying, making changes to help an unprepared audience understand the plot, restating freely, abbreviating, expanding. But Vergil's epic is different from that of Statius: it is the biography of a single individual hero, not the development of a political situation, and this hero has a propensity for getting himself involved in far-reaching sentimental love affairs. The ''translator'' gets carried away toward the end, to such a degree that it upsets the balance of his reformulation: the last fourth of his *roman* (vv. 7725–10,156) corresponds to the twelfth book of the *Aeneid*, because of an ample and independent development of the story of Lavinia, a minutely detailed psychological study in the effects of burgeoning illicit love.

A considerable number of scholarly studies in recent decades have shown the influence of the *Eneas* on early French *romans* of all types.[4] The initiative taken by the anonymous cleric who adapted the *Aeneid* to the taste of a non-Latinist audience around 1160 was a momentous one: he turned the modest figure of Lavinia into something that did not exist before, a new and vivid character, torn between duty and a feeling which is new to her, which grows in her to great strength during a sleepless night, and which finally she decides to obey.

Throughout the following ten years or more, the vein that consists of reformulating striking tales from antique sources seems to have been exploited quite consistently. A big monument is the *Roman de Troie* (based on late summaries—about 1165?). A minor one (but heralding a favorite to come) is the decasyllabic *Alexander*, written in Poitou at about the same time. The most characteristic approach, however, seems to have centered on short stories

---

[4]For example, Helen C. R. Laurie, *Two Studies in Chrétien de Troyes* (Geneva 1972) 57–102 and passim.

or episodes: from the *Metamorphoses* of Ovid (*Pyramus and Thisbe, Philo-mena, Narcissus*), a *Hero and Leander* (lost), an *Orpheus* (lost), and even a (partial?) translation of the *Ars amatoria* (lost).

The characteristic thing about the Ovidian tales is that, like the Lavinia episode, they are set in the framework of a striking individual biography, and that the main concern is neither political nor military, but psycho-logical—dealing with the feelings that lead to dramatic, tragic, or rare events, rather than with those events themselves. The focus is on subjective personal experience—characteristically rendered in the form of lengthy interior mono-logues—more than on objective conduct. Parallel to the development of the author-writer, who transforms his independent imagination into objective, fac-tual and permanent *text*, runs an interest in the characters as independent be-ings, who shape their destinies, for the better or for the worse, according to their inner psychological imperatives.

In a famous and often quoted passage of the prologue to the *Lais*, Marie de France says that, wanting to make public use of her talents and knowledge (the standard introduction), she considered translating some good story from Latin into French, "but so many others have done that," and so she came to think of the Breton lays and the stories that go with them.[5]

Marie lived in England, at the royal court, and so it must be expected that she was very well informed about the state of contemporary avant-garde literature. It is evident that she is alluding to the vogue of the "matter of Anti-quity"—a vogue centered around the English court—and it is equally evident that the subject matter she chose to use must have been a novelty in her con-text. She presents herself as an innovator, and, considering her audience, she could not have expected to get away with that claim had it not been true. The date must be sometime in the late 1160s.

All her lays have rather strongly the same character as the *Ovidiana*: a dramatic individual destiny, seen through the mentality of the characters and told in a way which pays attention to their inner experience more than to outer event. Is she a writer of fiction? She might have imagined the stories to go with the lyric lays herself, but the odds are that she did not, that she is another translator-adaptor obedient to and bound by preexisting narrative tradition. In the first place, this is how she introduces herself. (But so do they all: invention and personal imagination are not things to boast of.) More important, the *Lais* form a very motley collection, thematically, and even more so ideologically. An analysis of the system of values in her tales will reveal almost systematic

---

[5]Pur ceo començai a penser
D'aukune bone estoire faire
Et de latin en roumaunz traire;
Mais ne me fust guaires de pris:
Itant s'en sunt altre entremis!
Les Lais de Marie de France, ed. Jean Rychner, Les classiques français du moyen âge 93 (Paris 1966) 2.

contradictions: passions, marriage, resignation, transgression, and so on, are all valued by some stories, condemned by others. And what is worse, the only element that is constantly presented with positive valuation is non-Christian supernatural otherworldliness (even the werewolf!), an element that could hardly have been an intimate personal favorite of the pious Marie's. The discordant chorus of contradictory voices that is heard throughout the collection of her *Lais* strongly indicates that this is not the making of one single person: Marie merely relays what comes to her from a variety of different emitters.

All of Marie's stories first introduce their characters, and then tell the story about them. All, except one—the *Chevrefueil*, which is just a tiny poetical episode, a non-plot involving two persons whom everyone can be expected to know: Tristan and Isolt. The very special treatment that Marie gives to the famous lovers is justified by the exceptional importance of the Tristan story in the courtly universe. As Marie does, so does everyone else in medieval French literature; a rapid allusion is enough, one can count on the reader to know the rest. With the possible exception of Roland at Roncevaux, the Tristan story must be the one most frequently alluded to—and always correctly.

The *Tristan* is intriguing from almost all points of view. It is by far the best known of early romances, it was put into French in two distinct, almost contemporary versions (which tell basically the same story), and yet not a single complete copy of either is extant. Logically, we should have had at least a dozen manuscripts of this all-important tale. And the scholarly efforts to determine the origins of the narrative material have given both overwhelming and disconcerting results.

The hero seems to derive from a king Drust who reigned about 780 over the Picts, a Scottish people that disappeared less than a century later. The story about him seems to be that he delivered a princess from robbers, that others took credit for the deed, but that the princess recognized the true hero by a bandage she had put on his wounds. The triangular story about the lovers eloping into the forest is Irish: the magic (but initially chaste) love between Diarmaid, nephew of Finn, and Finn's wife Grainne. The Cornish king Mark is a different character, with different stories attached to him. Other elements are continental Breton, others Indian, others Arabic. Even seasoned hunters for thematic sources seem impressed when they unravel this extraordinary tangle. Yet the motley mixture of heterogeneous themes may not be what is most extraordinary about it. More than one *chanson de geste* can lead to similar results under thematic analysis, but these *chansons* vary markedly from one version to another, and the public of the times does not seem to have been as intimately familiar with them as with the *Tristan*. The most distinctive thing about the *Tristan* may be not the international bric-a-brac used for its various episodes, but the clear and powerful overall narrative structure that binds this complex multiplicity together and turns it into a monolithic whole that can be mentally grasped and retained as a unity.

The keystone is, of course, the "love-drink."[6] Before, Tristan's childhood and youth, the Morholt, the wooing, the dragon. After, the lovers in court, the exposure, the forest, the reconciliation, the separation, Tristan's empty marriage, the double death. In this clear-cut and mighty structure, each detail inserts itself naturally and satisfactorily with dependent independence. You hear that story once, and you are not likely to forget it, not even to get mixed up in the essentials.

There is considerable evidence for the activities of Celtic—Welsh and Breton—storytellers and their popularity from about 1100 onward. Wace says that they tell many tales, and reports that he took a trip to the forest of Broceliande but came back wiser: he met no fays.[7] But there is no clear evidence of any particular story that compares to the *Tristan*, nothing as firmly established, nothing as widely known. Actually, most of the early allusions to the Celtic storytellers are rather disparaging, with one striking exception—the mysterious Welshman Bleheris, *fabulator famosus* according to Giraldus Cambrensis, the same, probably, as the Breri who is quoted by Thomas in the final fragment of his poem as the one true authority on Tristan: others have told the story in various ways, "but from what I have heard, they do not tell it according to Breri, who knew all the stories about the kings and dukes of Britain."[8]

The *Tristan* did not exist in the tenth century, not even in embryonic form: that is the date of the last allusion to the Pictish Drust, in the *Wooing of Emer*. It existed fully articulated before 1160. We will never know what happened in between, only that this is a typical example of crystallization in an oral tradition—but an oral tradition which was in the state of decomposition described above. In a solidly established culture guiding the life of an autonomous ethnic group, the traditions are carefully preserved by the norm-bearers: cosmological myths and legends about the tribal forefathers are the vital

---

[6]Seignors, du vin de qoi il burent   Mais ne savez, ce m'est avis,
Avez oï, por qoi il furent   A conbien fu determinez
En si grant paine lonctens mis;   *Li lovendrins*, li vin herbez. . . .

Béroul: Le Roman de Tristan, poème du XIIe siècle, ed. Ernest Muret, Les classiques français du moyen âge 12 (Paris 1913), 4th ed. rev. L. M. Defourques (Paris 1947) 66.2133–38.

[7]Wace reports that in the forest of "Brecheliant" is "la fontaine de Berenton." There, in hot weather, the Bretons pour water over themselves so that it also falls on the "perron"; this provokes rainfall. There are fays, too, according to the Bretons. What he describes is evidently the prototype of the adventure of "the Lady of the Fountain" in *Yvain*. He himself was less favored:

La alai jo merveilles querre   fol m'en revinc, fol i alai;
vi la forest e vi la terre,   fol i alai, fol m'en revinc,
merveilles quis, mais nes trovai,   folie quis, por fol me tinc.

Roman de Rou (see Bibliographical Note) 2.122.6393–98.

[8]Entre ceus qui solent cunter   Mès sulun ço que j'ai oï,
E del cunte Tristan parler,   Nel dient pas sulun Breri
Il en cuntent diversement: Ky solt les gestes e les cuntes
Oï en ai de plusur gent.   De tuz les reis, de tuz les cuntes
Asez sai que chescun en dit   Ki orent esté en Bretaingne.
E ço qu'il unt mis en escrit,

Le Roman de Tristan par Thomas, ed. Joseph Bédier, Société des anciens textes français 46 (2 vols. Paris 1902–05) 1.377.2113–23.

backbone of ethnic identity and self-understanding. Along with this vital traditional material, a narrative tradition will normally carry a different flow, a carefree and noncommittal stream of folktale for entertainment and curiosity. In the case of the Celtic narrative lore, solemn myth and vital ethnic tradition seem to have broken down as such, and fallen into the domain of folktale as a floating magma of thematic raw material, drifting to and fro, changing and amalgamating freely, according to the wills and whims of the storytellers. Many of them seem to have been wandering professionals who catered to the non-Celtic populations on the continent.

The powerful and deep-rooted compositional structure of the *Tristan* may have been elaborated piecemeal, by agglutination of theme after theme around a central nucleus. The specific contribution (if any!) of the mysterious Bleheris—who seems to have been active at the court of Poitou, probably in the 1130s—will never be identified. But with Thomas's reference in mind, one is tempted to fasten on the one storyteller famous among all as the mastermind who organized the one story famous among all. The dates do not speak against it. There is no Tristan in Geoffrey's *Historia*.

This was a flashback into Celtic (Welsh, Breton) oral narrative tradition (often from Irish sources), an impression of what it was Marie de France introduced into French literature with her *Lais*. They are, precisely, floating and isolated single narratives, relatively short, both in comparison with the early French *romans* (normally some 10,000 verses) and with the monumental structure of the *Tristan* ("according to Breri"?). The combination of Marie de France in the present, and the *Tristan* in the past, with the precedent of the *romans antiques* as backdrop, sets the stage for Chrétien de Troyes.

Chrétien must have been a native of Champagne, and he seems to have spent his active years at the courts of Champagne and Flanders; with him, the scene shifts from England to the continent. He started out as a writer in the (late?) 1160s, contributing to the wave of "antique" literature with adaptations of Ovid. He also wrote an *Art of Love* and a story about Mark and Isolt, but with one exception these early texts of his are lost. The chronology of his five famous *romans* is most recently reconstructed thus: *Erec*, ca. 1170; *Cligès*, ca. 1175; *Yvain* and *Lancelot*, simultaneously up to about 1180; *Perceval*, from 1181 until death interrupted his writing.[9]

---

[9]For editions, see the Bibliographical Note. The introductory verses to *Cligès* list Chrétien's earlier writings:

> Cil qui fist *d'Erec et d'Enide*,   Del roi Marc et *d'Ysalt la blonde*,
> Et *les comandemanz d'Ovide*,   Et *de la hupe et de l'aronde*
> Et *l'art d'amors* an romans mist,   Et *del rossignol la muance*,
> Et *le mors de l'espaule* fist,   Un novel conte rancomance. . . .

Thus *Erec* is earlier than *Cligès*, and the other *romans* must be posterior. Of the other stories mentioned, only the last has been identified (*Philomele*). A consensus has been reached on the chronology of the others, after discussions by Stefan Hofer and Anthime Fourrier; see Jean Frappier, *Chrétien de Troyes, l'homme et l'oeuvre*, Connaissance des lettres 50 (Paris 1957) 12.

The prologue to *Erec* is interesting. Chrétien says that "some things are despised which are much more valuable than people think," and therefore it is a good thing to put an effort into improving them. For his part, he has taken a "conte d'avanture" and turned it into a "molt bele conjointure." Usually, the professional storytellers make a mess of the story about Erec; he will tell this story in such a way that it will always remain in memory, as long as Christianity will last. This is Chrétien's proud declaration![10] Chrétien does not claim that he has had access to the original, unadulterated form (as does Thomas in his *Tristan*). He says that he has worked on a tale which is held in contempt, and that he has made something beautiful out of it. It is *his* story that is going to last forever in memory, not the story "in itself."

This is the proud language of a creative author-writer whose "hard work" and "learning" will make the story live forever. But this assertion of his own originality brings up the crucial (and classic) problem of Chrétien's models or sources. It can be approached from various angles.

One is the "R. S. Loomis technique," which isolates each narrative element and traces it back to the mythological or legendary form, or (if the element is not to be found in a convincing, archaic form) takes the bearings of what may or must have existed, on the faith of later more or less corrupted forms. The idea is to get back to ancient and authentic, not decayed, Celtic myth and legend, moving upstream against the chaotic flow of disintegrating myth that has fallen into the folkloric state of inorganic narrative themes. This method gives excellent and illuminating results, though it does not contribute very much to the understanding of Chrétien's work in itself. It merely confirms what the author-writer says himself, and nowhere more explicitly than in the prologue to *Erec*: that he draws heavily on thematic material taken from the Celtic storytellers. The Loomis technique positively invites the modern reader to view this material as an unstructured magma of floating, isolated thematic elements.

An approach that tries to arrive at Chrétien from Geoffrey of Monmouth (or Wace) is immediately and decisively discouraged. The Arthur part of the *Historia* leaves no room, chronologically or culturally, for the Arthurian court as depicted in Chrétien. The concerns are different, the style is different. In the *Historia*, the only events recorded are the military and political adventures of Arthur himself, not the personal adventures of his knights. The names are different: Gauvain is in the *Historia*, different but recognizable, and Kei, in a totally different character. Yvain is mentioned marginally. Conversely,

[10]Li vilains dit an son respit   depecier et corrompre suelent
    que tel chose a l'an en despit   cil qui de conter vivre vuelent.
    qui molt valt mialz que l'an ne cuide;   Des or comancerai l'estoire
    . . . .   qui toz jorz mes iert an mimoire
    d'Erec, le fil Lac, est li contes   tant con durra chrestïantez;
    que devant rois et devant contes   de ce s'est Chrestïens vantez.

Erec et Enide (see Bibliographical Note) 1.1–3, 19–26.

Bedoer, considerable in the *Historia*, is mentioned in Chrétien, but marginally. In that connection it is worth noticing that all the early allusions to the "matter of Britain" in the first half of the twelfth century refer to tales about Arthur, not about his men. (Of course that may be an ellipsis: Wace does mention "many tales" told about the [knights of the] Round Table.)

Moving closer to the problem: even Chrétien does not seem to know who were the greatest heroes of the Arthurian reign until he has told their stories himself. In *Erec*, he gives a list of Arthurian knights (vv. 1671–1706): Gauvain, Erec and Lancelot come at the top, Perceval is not there (of course he was a latecomer), and Yvain is listed (with his namesake, and Tristan) among the twenty-odd who come indiscriminately after the first ten. (It can be objected here that Chrétien did know who Tristan is, and yet just put him in the rank and file.) More significantly, in *Cligès* (vv. 4583–4894), the hero fells Sagremor (who personifies the honorable average of knights), Lancelot, and Perceval, before he fights even with Gauvain. Nothing in that text—or any other—makes the reader suspect that Lancelot and Perceval are the two all-important roles in the most essential and significant adventures of the Arthurian world. It is true that they are singled out, Lancelot lower than Perceval, and both superior to Sagremor but inferior to Gauvain and Cligès (Erec is nowhere mentioned in that tale), but certainly not as the greatest of the great. And there is no allusion to any personal adventure of theirs.

In that respect, Chrétien himself is no exception: there is no allusion to four of his five heroes prior to his *romans* (Yvain had been mentioned, but with no story attached to the name). All suppositions about stories prior to his *romans* are based on later stories that might (and might not) go back to a source that might also have been Chrétien's. That is especially the case of the three "pseudomabinogion," *Geraint* (parallel to *Erec*), the *Lady of the Fountain* (or *Owein*, parallel to *Yvain*), and *Peredur* (parallel to *Perceval*).[11] The oldest extant manuscript of any of these, a fragment of *Geraint*, is from about 1275, but all three may have been taken down in writing around 1200.

Even the titles show that there are discrepancies between the narrative in these "Welsh romances" and those of Chrétien: the names are different, the style is completely different of course, the telling and the developments are different, even completely so (for example, what corresponds to the Grail in *Peredur* is a salver containing a human head swimming in blood). Yet there is no doubt that they are the same stories. The succession of analogous episodes shows it, and this general outline also proves that the Welsh tales are not autochthonous: they are stories about knights of courtly continental type maneuvering bizarrely in a traditional Celtic fable-world. The relationship could easily be explained by the hypothesis that Chrétien's stories have gone back into Welsh oral tradition: during fifteen years of going from mouth to ear many things can happen to a story. The argument against this explanation is

---

[11]English translations in *The Mabinogion* (see Bibliographical Note).

based on certain traits that are found in the Welsh versions and in other tales as well, but these traits seem somewhat too slight to make the introduction of an intermediate version inescapable.

Two of Chrétien's tales—*Lancelot* and *Perceval*—have had an impressive posterity. So impressive, in fact, that it is difficult, nowadays, to "see" Chrétien's stories as they are, uninfluenced by the elaborate wilderness of the later versions. Characteristically, they are the two open-ended ones: *Perceval* because Chrétien left his story unfinished, *Lancelot* because the hero's love for the queen could not very well end in the lovers' lifetime. Unlike the *Tristan*, a Chrétien narrative does not end with tragic death.

At the point where Chrétien's *Perceval* is interrupted, a French "First Continuator" ("Pseudo-Wachier") adds 10,000–20,000 verses (there is a short and a long version), after which a "Second Continuator" adds 13,000 more, without bringing the story to an end and explanation. An end is not written until the 1230s (drawing on the *Quête du Saint Graal* written in the 1220s). Neither continuator knows what to do with the mystery. At the point where the continuations begin, the Welsh tale runs absolutely wild, and the line taken by Wolfram von Eschenbach in his *Parzifal* (early thirteenth century) is completely discordant with the others. Not until Robert de Boron identified the Grail as the dish from the Last Supper (around 1200) did any two people agree on what it was all about, and even after that the stories are far from being in accordance. The conclusion seems inescapable: the myths, themes, and stories that Chrétien utilized to make up his enthralling Grail mystery were either very secret or very vague, too vague for anyone else to make use of them to complete the interrupted tale in a convincing way.

The case of *Lancelot* is different. The theme of the queen abducted and freed is extremely old. It is the basic plot in the Indian *Ramayana*, and it is found in well-preserved form in the Greek myths about Persephone (there may even be a humoristic derivative in Scandinavian mythology): it must be a fundamental Indo-European myth, about the fertility of the land and the cycle of seasons. The story is well attested in relatively early Arthurian tradition (it is not in Geoffrey, though), especially in the form of a relief sculpted on an archivolt in Modena (before 1120). Among the "many tales" told about Arthur in the first half of the century, this is certainly one. In the Modena version, Arthur himself attacks the castle of the abductor, seconded by his best men: Isdernus, Walwaginus (Gauvain), and Che. But where, when, and how did Lancelot get into the story, and how did he become the lover of the queen in a Tristan-like plot? Lancelot appears for the first time in *Cligès*, as one of the best knights. A German *Lanzelet* from the early thirteenth century has no such thing as that love story in it. The problem is the same as for the Grail: unless it was the countess of Champagne who imagined an extramarital passion behind the abduction-and-rescue story—which is very probable, considering the prologue and her ideas about love—one seems to be left with the two possibilities of either Chrétien himself or an agent unknown who has left no other trace.

The reluctance to credit Chrétien with the invention of his most famous stories is a habit of thought from the romantic nineteenth century, lingering on in a modified form with the scholarly students of folklore and myth: in that field the hypothesis of a creative mind is an admission of the scholar's impotence, it is a dead end in research. *Cligès*, however, is rather shallow, from a narrative point of view, and so no one has ever refused Chrétien the authorship of that plot: it is an answer to—at moments one would prefer to say a parody of—the *Tristan*, and no other source is needed. But then again, that means admitting that Chrétien was capable of creating from something only very vaguely similar to what he eventually produced himself.

The reluctance lingers on in modern scholarship from the time before 1930 or so, when the reputation of Chrétien was rather low. To Gaston Paris, he was a brilliant but mundane person who distorted the precious and folk-grown mythic material in order to make it palatable to blasé men of the world.[12] In an important book from 1931, Gustave Cohen rehabilitated him as a conscious and intelligent *romancier*—the creator of the French, and therefore the European, *roman*—emphasizing the character of his tales as *romans à thèse* in an approach that has been adopted in numerous critical studies since then.[13] Speculations about Chrétien's identity as an author-writer have turned around his use of the words "story" (*conte*) versus "composition" (*conjointure*) (*Erec*, prologue), thematic "material" (*matière*), and "meaning" (*san*) (*Lancelot*, prologue). It seems evident that the *romans* have an ideological dimension relative to love, chivalry, and morality, an ideology which contrasts—except in the special case of *Lancelot*—with that inherent in the *Tristan* and professed by Marie de Champagne (according to Andreas Capellanus). Like most of his contemporaries, Chrétien does not favor the disruptive, antisocial forces of extra-marital love-passion. But does that mean that his stories are *romans à thèse*?

It is easy to see how they can be considered as such. Each *roman* has a central hero whose life is dominated by a problem to which he reacts. Erec has to disprove the talk that his marital bliss has reduced his prowess as a warrior-knight (and during their double quest for dangerous adventure, Enid proves that she can second him in a way honorable to both). Cligès and especially his Fenice want to live out their love-passion in personal moral integrity in spite of the emperor who has usurped the throne and legally married Fenice. Lancelot faces the double problem of his illicit love and the imperiousness of his lady-love, both of which go contrary to his personal moral integrity as a vassal and as a knight. Yvain has forfeited the love of the woman he loves and who had had justified scruples in accepting him. Perceval has failed fatally in the most decisive test he was put to (whether the reason was his heartlessness toward his

---

[12]Gaston Paris, *Mélanges de littérature française du moyen âge*, ed. Mario Roques (Paris 1912) 244–68; *La littérature française au moyen âge* (2nd ed. Paris 1890) 95–98; and *Esquisse historique de la littérature française au moyen âge* (Paris 1907) 110–13.

[13]Gustave Cohen, *Un grand romancier d'amour et d'aventure au XIIe siècle: Chrétien de Troyes et son oeuvre* (Paris 1931; rev. ed. 1948).

mother or his adoption of the courtly decorum of discreet good manners, in place of his original spontaneity).

However, the word *sans* appears in the prologue to *Lancelot* in a context which seems to indicate that Chrétien declines personal responsibility for the ideology of the story.[14] Though even this consideration does affirm that he was conscious of the significance conveyed by his stories, the above list of moral squeezes does not seem very satisfactory as a list of explicit moral teachings, even less so when one considers how the heroes tackle their problems and get out of them. But the problems become very satisfactory if they are put under the heading of another key notion mentioned by Chrétien, the *conjointure*, understood as construction or (inner) composition: these personal problems of the heroes provide an overall plot which organizes the episodic complexity of each narrative in one firm structural unity.

The thing is very clear in *Erec* and in *Yvain*. In both, the hero sets out for mysterious adventure, and after a series of memorable deeds he finds himself happily married. At this point there is a technical reflection in *Erec: Ici fenist li premiers vers* (v. 1796), meaning that here ends the first part or section. The personal problem arises after this point, as a circumstance that dispels the happiness obtained through the initial exploits. In *Lancelot*, things are somewhat different, but there is a marked transition halfway, from the active liberation adventure to Lancelot's hard lot as the lover of the liberated queen. In *Cligès*, things are different again: considerably more than one third of the story is about the hero's parents, explaining how he came into the unenviable position of an heir presumptive to a throne usurped by an uncle who should remain unmarried (hence childless), but who decides to marry a princess the nephew himself falls in love with.

But whatever the proportions, the basic compositional scheme is the same. The hero sets out for adventure, not knowing what he will meet, except that it is a serious challenge. After an ascending movement, he reaches a (provisional) high-point of harmony, or even bliss. At this point arises *the problem*, bringing about a downfall; and the rest of the hero's deeds and movements are guided and determined by this downfall until the final restoration of renewed harmony and conciliation (provisional and relative in the hopeless case of Lancelot).

In this respect, the compositional structure of Chrétien's *romans* differs from many others. The Greco-Roman romances of Antiquity tell of a separation, and the lovers' long search for each other through the world. In the *Chanson de Roland*, and the *Roman de Thebes* too, drama and tragedy loom from the outset. But the compositional and organizational pattern in Chré-

---

[14]Del chevalier de la charrete   la contesse, et il s'antremet
comance Crestïens son livre;   de panser, que gueres n'i met
matiere et san li done et livre   fors sa painne et s'antancïon.

Lancelot (see Bibliographical Note) 24–29. "Penser" refers to careful handling, "peine" and "attention" refer to hard concentrated work, to craftsmanship.

tien's stories follows more or less closely that of the *Tristan*: youth and initial exploits up to a state of harmony where Tristan is the favorite of Mark, then the catastrophe, the love potion, whose immediate and remote consequences form the backbone of the complicated web of subsequent episodes. In *Tristan* and with Chrétien, the *problem* is located as a sort of keystone at the precise point where the ascent toward harmony is broken by a decline into confusion and torment. On the level of human interest, the problem raised by the catastrophe gives to the hero's destiny its character, its profile and its meaning, its *san*. On the level of narrative literary technique, the same problem gives an overall constructional unity to the multiplicity of more or less disparate narrative elements that make up the main part of the *roman*.

The same technique can be seen at work in the second *roman* by Chrétien's contemporary (and lesser rival?) Gautier d'Arras. His first work, *Eracle*, is a rambling tale located in the the Orient of Antiquity and partly based on the fabulous traditions about Apollonius. In *Ille et Galeron* (from the 1170s?), he turns to a more modern, Western European stage, with a story that does not have the artistic merits of Chrétien's Arthurian tales, but which is historically interesting because its sole and unique source is known, so that it is possible to study how a *romancier* of the first generation turned Marie de France's lay *Eliduc* into a full-size *roman*.

Marie's story (1200 verses) is about a married knight who falls in love with a young princess while in exile. After an animated sequence of realistic and fabulous events (such as a Snow White-like false death and resurrection), the wife voluntarily withdraws to a monastery, leaving the lovers to each other. Gautier turns this into a *roman* (7000 verses) by doubling and reversing the original plot, by padding the story with various nondescript materials, and by forging it into a unity by means of a catastrophe of his own invention, located after the first third of the tale.

His "first part" is made up of two main elements: heroic deeds out of the epic tradition (the young hero avenges his slain father and regains his usurped lands), and a conversion of his immediate source (hero falls in love with sister of his liege the duke of Normandy, but—this is new—is able to marry her thanks to the friendly affection of the duke). Then comes the catastrophe: he loses one eye in combat, and as he feels that a duke's daughter cannot love a simple knight who is disfigured, he takes to voluntary exile, incognito. This is where Marie started, but the situation is now different, and therefore the love affair in exile, with the daughter of the Roman emperor, cannot be mutual, as in the original: the mutual love story was told in the first part. Faithful to his beloved wife, the hero declines the flattering offer of becoming son-in-law and heir to the emperor. Further complications arise. The wife has disappeared and is believed to be dead. Actually, she had set out in affectionate search for her desperate lover-husband, and so the dramatic meeting of the three—high point in both stories—occurs under radically different circumstances, and with the opposite result: the hero opts for the wife and leaves the princess to her grief. It takes another long sequence of adventurous imbroglios to bring about the union of hero and princess (the wife having resigned for reasons alien to the princess's love for her husband).

This is unquestionably the work of a freely creating writer, unbound by any respect for his thematic model. A comparison between final result and starting point gives a unique opportunity to study the author's conception of his *form*, and makes it evident that he conceives the *roman* very much the way Chrétien must have conceived it, in terms of constructional technique. (There are important differences in other respects.) The use of the catastrophe as a keystone is particularly noteworthy: the loss of the eye—which could be inspired from a problem considered by a "cour d'amour" according to Andreas Capellanus[15]—has the typical function comparable to the love potion in the *Tristan* (even though the actual outcome is opposite).

In his famous and influential *Theory of the Novel* (1916) Georg Lukács opposes epic (he thinks of Homer and maybe *Roland*) to novel (he thinks of nineteenth-century literature), and characterizes the tragic hero of the epic, who still lives in a meaningful world despite his adverse destiny, as opposed to the "problematic" hero of the novel, who is personally degraded and who lives in a degraded universe in search of authentic values that have been lost.[16] It is interesting to try his analyses (continued and updated by Lucien Goldmann)[17] on the very first *romans*, created in direct proximity with—and in opposition to—living contemporary epic. But for some reason, the abundant literature theorizing about the *roman* pays scant attention, if any, to the work of the very first European *romanciers*.

For the systematic use of personal catastrophe in the *romans* of the 1170s has strong, if not absolute, resemblances to the personal "degradation" in more recent novels: it leads to the hero's more or less desperate, more or less blind search for reintegration into his world of values, also in cases (Yvain, Ille) where the immediate objective willfully sought is self-destruction. It is not that man's relation to the world or to society has been destroyed; final harmony can be established, except in cases of hopeless adulterous passion. It is the hero's personal (existential) relation to himself, his self-image, that has become provisionally problematic.

This observation gains increased significance when one realizes that this way of constructing a *roman* on the hero's self-image in conflict with itself— and the hero's reaction to that conflict—is characteristic of the first generation of original author-writers exclusively. The following generations of writers happily compose either confused and rambling tales, focusing on unusual event rather than on psychology and reaction, or they build economically constructed

---

[15]*De amore libri tres* 2.7 (*De variis iudiciis amoris*) 15, ed. Emil Trojel (Copenhagen 1892; repr. Munich 1964) 287.

[16]Georg Lukács, *Die Theorie des Romans* (Berlin 1916; numerous translations and reeditions).

[17]Lucien Goldmann, *Pour une sociologie du roman* (Paris 1965).

tales upon a catastrophe brought about by mere unfortunate coincidence or by the mischievous deeds of wicked people (Jean Renart is an example).

It is not unreasonable to think of the personal situation of a pioneer in free writing of fictional literature—creating a character and organizing a destiny out of a more or less embryonic thematic material—as comparable to that of the heroes of these same pioneers, who, at the moment of the catastrophe, find themselves with a life more or less in shambles, and facing the existential task of realizing, with whatever remains, a coherent and acceptable self. Both faces of the phenomenon point to an experience of man's situation as an individual with responsible freedom to form his destiny and direct his activity, an experience that constitutes the essence of what is called *humanism*.

The sources of inspiration for this momentous creative activity were partly autochthonous: the concept of the hero-warrior, themes from degraded myth, and the rambling fabulation characteristic of oral narration. And they were partly learned, drawn from scholarly classical tradition: the process of writing, the use of written texts, the artfulness in style and in construction of plot, but also the psychological humanism of the Augustan poets, mainly Vergil and Ovid. Of course these sources continued to flow around Chrétien and Gautier, and before long merged between them and with the new tradition (*form*) sprung from the pioneer authors, in a way that has a different character, less humanistic, in the sense delineated above.

On the one hand, the tradition from the *romans antiques* continued abundantly. The Alexander material was picked up around 1170, and in the 1180s it was brought to glorious bloom. Material borrowed from saints' lives (an important reservoir of narrative tradition) was developed in tales like the pseudo-Chrétien's *Guillaume d'Angleterre*. A long (and unstructured) mock epic in the form of the *roman* was initiated with the *Renart* (is Renart's abduction of Hersant the she-wolf reminiscent of the adventure of Guenevere?). The enormous tale of *Partenopeus de Blois* used the story of Amor and Psyche as a plot model for its *premier vers* in a Byzantine setting. Soon the narrative material from the *chansons de geste* merged with that of the early *roman* into a composite universe that ultimately led toward the *Orlando furioso*. Chrétien's open-ended stories were continued endlessly, developed and meditated upon (Robert de Boron) in a way that led rather much away from the origins. The trend is away from tightly knit, progressive self-realization of an individual, toward infinite expansion of plot, through accumulation of strange episodes (repeating certain types of adventures), interlacing of various adventures (a technique already used by Chrétien in his *Perceval*), catering to a taste that could be labeled gigantophilia, compared to which Chrétien's esthetics— however disconcerting that may appear to the newcomer—stand out by their clear-cut and organized soberness.

It is as if literary fiction, brought into existence as a specific and intelligent form by the writers of the 1170s, were immediately taken over by others whose thinking was more akin to that of the storytellers of oral tradition than to that of the meticulously constructing pioneers, with their interest in the subtleties of human problems. Strangeness and unheard-of-ness became the focus of interest, more than concise analysis. Cyclic development and enlarging systematization took over the Arthurian world of fiction as they had done with the epic.

But as the pedantic epigones took over where Chrétien left off, the shock waves of the creative achievement of the 1160s and 1170s spread over Europe. German, Norse, Spanish, and Italian literatures in their early phases sought decisive inspiration from there. The French *Alexander* was recreated in Latin, in a vast composition that was to be listed among the great Latin epics by the following generations. Provençal literature picked up the northern fictional narrative to which it had no counterpart. Even prestigious Constantinople underwent the influence. Until the sixteenth century (and well beyond) the echoes from the literary workshops of the twelfth century are heard distinctly.

Bibliographical Note

Attention has been drawn to the specific character of oral composition and tradition by Albert B. Lord in his influential book *The Singer of Tales* (Cambridge Mass. 1960). Jean Rychner has demonstrated the mark of oral tradition on the French epic in *La chanson de geste: Essai sur l'art épique des jongleurs* (Geneva 1955).

A good general introduction to Arthurian literature is Roger S. Loomis, ed., *Arthurian Literature in the Middle Ages: A Collaborative History* (Oxford 1961). The understanding of Chrétien de Troyes in this essay is very close to that expressed by Jean Frappier in various publications, e.g. *Chrétien de Troyes, l'homme et l'oeuvre*, Connaissance des lettres 50 (Paris 1957) and *Chrétien de Troyes et le mythe du Graal* (Paris 1972); see also his articles collected in *Amour courtois et Table ronde* (Geneva 1973). It leans strongly on the work of Roger S. Loomis, e.g. *Arthurian Tradition and Chrétien de Troyes* (New York 1949) and *The Grail: From Celtic Myth to Christian Symbol* (Cardiff and New York 1963). An important historical and literary study of the early *romanciers* is Anthime Fourrier, *Le courant réaliste dans le roman courtois en France au moyen âge: Les débuts (XIIe siècle)* (Paris 1960).

A more detailed analysis of *Ille et Galeron* (and parts of *Perceval*) is presented in Per Nykrog, "Two Creators of Narrative Form in Twelfth Century France: Gautier d'Arras—Chrétien de Troyes," *Speculum* 48 (1973) 258-76.

TEXTS (in order of appearance in this essay):
The Mabinogion, translated with an introduction by Gwyn Jones and Thomas Jones, Everyman's Library (London and New York 1949).
Le Roman de Brut de Wace, ed. Ivor Arnold, Société des anciens textes français (2 vols. Paris 1938-40); *Le Roman de Rou de Wace*, ed. A. J. Holden, Société des anciens textes français (3 vols. Paris 1970-73).
Eneas, roman du XIIe siècle, ed. J.-J. Salverda de Grave, Les classiques français du moyen âge 44, 62 (2 vols. Paris 1925-29).

Les romans de Chrétien de Troyes édités d'après la copie de Guiot, Les classiques français du moyen âge 80 (*Erec et Enide*, ed. Mario Roques, 1952), 84 (*Cligès*, ed. Alexandre Micha, 1957), 86 (*Le Chevalier de la Charrete* [Lancelot], ed. Mario Roques, 1958), 89 (*Le Chevalier au Lion* [*Yvain*], ed. Mario Roques, 1960), and 100, 102 (*Le Conte du Graal* [*Perceval*], ed. Felix Lecoy, 2 vols. 1972–75).

Gautier d'Arras, *Ille et Galeron*, ed. Frederick A. G. Cowper, Société des anciens textes français (Paris 1958).

VII

THE ARTS

The New Fascination with Ancient Rome

Herbert Bloch

The visible remains of Antiquity were an ever-present potential reminder of Rome's past greatness. From the very beginning of the Middle Ages, pagan monuments were ruthlessly plundered to provide columns and decorative elements for Christian churches. It was the easy availability of often priceless building material, not admiration for ancient Rome, that accounts for this practice.

In similar fashion, ancient literature had been studied primarily for didactic purposes, not for its intrinsic value. The Carolingian renaissance—the importance of which is regularly underrated by classicists and not sufficiently appreciated by many medievalists—drastically altered this situation, with lasting effects on the intellectual history of the Middle Ages. Most of all it salvaged the bulk of what now survives of ancient Latin texts, and it permanently improved the level of literature in the centuries that followed.

To speak of a renaissance of the *twelfth* century may, therefore, seem at first blush a misnomer. And yet, what we recognize as a new awareness of ancient Rome in all its manifestations provides a compelling vindication of Haskins's title. This awareness did not grow slowly over decades. It arose rather suddenly, though certainly not in the year 1100.

Haskins wisely warned (8–9) that "history cannot remain history if sawed off into even lengths of hundreds of years"; he was equally right when he pleaded for using "the word 'century' . . . very loosely." "For the movement as a whole," he continued, "we must really go back fifty years or more" (10). These strictures apply to architecture and other arts as well as to literature. While Haskins deliberately excluded the figurative arts, they are here deliberately taken into account, because without them this particular aspect of the renaissance of the twelfth century cannot be understood, even in a sketch which must be limited to few topics and examples.

BEGINNINGS: MONTE CASSINO AND ROME

The new fascination with ancient Rome manifests itself first in Italy—but not in Rome. The crucial figures, closely linked in lifelong friendship, are Alfanus

May I express my thanks to the editors, and especially to Carol D. Lanham, for many helpful suggestions and improvements in the text of my manuscript.

of Salerno and Desiderius of Monte Cassino. Alfanus, a scion of the highest nobility, received an excellent education in Salerno which, significantly, included medicine. He became a monk at Monte Cassino and later abbot of its dependency St Benedict in Salerno; he was archbishop of Salerno from 1058 until his death in 1085. Probably the outstanding poet of Italy in the eleventh century, he was imbued with the greatness of ancient Rome. Close to the men of the Church of the Reform, he addressed his most famous poem to its leader, archdeacon Hildebrand himself, and daringly likened him to the illustrious names of pagan Rome—Marius, Julius Caesar, the Scipios—only to credit him with surpassing them all by accomplishing with one word (the *vis anathematis*) what they had achieved *maxima nece militum* ("at the price of the slaughter of countless men"). However great their merits, Alfanus said, Hildebrand's are greater and will be rewarded with eternal life; and he will be compared to the apostles, his fellow citizens (we are to remember St Paul's "civis Romanus sum"):

> Te quidem potioribus
> praeditum meritis manet
> gloriosa perenniter
> vita, civibus ut tuis
> compareris apostolis.

The claim of the papacy to the throne of the Roman Empire is enunciated here in the eloquent words of the poet.[1] Eighty years later the people of Rome themselves were to rise against the pope and usurp that very claim to worldly power.

Alfanus's grasp of the aspirations of men such as Hildebrand and cardinal Humbert of Silva Candida, aspirations which he enthusiastically embraced, was only one aspect of his yearning to bring back the glory of ancient Rome. And here his younger friend Desiderius (1027–87) becomes equally significant, for their thinking was much alike and found expression in works of art first in Monte Cassino and subsequently in Salerno.

Desiderius, of princely Beneventan lineage, had chosen the monk's calling against the strenuous opposition of his family; after entering Monte Cassino in 1055, he succeeded abbot Frederick (pope Stephen IX) as abbot in 1058. His complete rebuilding of the monastery, and above all of its church, is a landmark in the history of art, not alone because of his deliberate return to early Christian forms. The influence of this church on ecclesiastical architecture, especially in southern Italy, is immense.[2] Leo Marsicanus, a highly intel-

[1] See now the new (and only complete) edition of Alfanus's poems by Anselmo Lentini and Faustino Avagliano, *I Carmi di Alfano I*, Miscellanea Cassinese 38 (Monte Cassino 1974) 155–57 no. 22. The poem had been printed before, e.g. in F. J. E. Raby, ed., *The Oxford Book of Medieval Latin Verse* (Oxford 1959) 192–94 no. 139. For a discussion from the point of view of *renovatio*, see Schramm, *KRR* 1.248–50. These aspects of Alfanus's poetry are treated in my forthcoming *Monte Cassino in the Middle Ages* (2 vols. Rome and Cambridge, Mass.) 1.94–96.

[2] The reconstruction of the basilica of Monte Cassino is discussed in detail in my book (n. 1 above) 1.40–70, 87–92, and 120–24, with ample references to the earlier literature. Among them

ligent eyewitness, entered the monastery under Desiderius, whom he greatly admired; he became bibliothecarius of Monte Cassino and, between 1102 and 1107, rose to be cardinal bishop of Ostia. Leo has left us a detailed description of the basilica in his chronicle of Monte Cassino, written under Desiderius's successor Oderisius I. His description is a most unusual feat in the history of medieval historiography.[3] There was a simple reason for including such an account in his chronicle: a church of comparable grandeur had not been erected in Italy within living memory.

Soon after 1066, Desiderius went to Rome, where he had had many influential friends ever since he had been consecrated cardinal priest of Santa Cecilia by Nicholas II early in 1059, and bought at great expense "huge quantities of [ancient] columns, bases, epistyles, and marbles of different colors."[4] But when it came to hiring workmen "who were experts in the art of laying mosaics and pavements," Desiderius sent his emissaries to Constantinople.[5] Why did he not use his Roman connections for that purpose also? Are we to believe that he was too disdainful of the Roman *marmorarii* to avail himself of their services—if, indeed, *marmorarii* of acceptable skill practiced their craft there? Is it by an oversight that modern writers on the marble workers of Rome (during the thirteenth century most impressively represented by the Cosmati) begin their story with the reign of Paschal II and the year 1109?[6]

Just as there then existed no Italian artist who could fashion monumental bronze doors of the kind that have survived in Amalfi or San Paolo fuori le mura (both imported from Constantinople),[7] so it must be concluded that for

see Richard Krautheimer, "San Nicola in Bari und die apulische Architektur des 12. Jahrhunderts," *Wiener Jahrbuch für Kunstgeschichte* 9 (1934) 5–42 at 16–19; Angelo Pantoni, "Opinioni, valutazioni critiche e dati di fatto sull'arte benedettina in Italia," *Benedictina* 13 (1959) 111–58; Ernst Kitzinger, "The Gregorian Reform and the Visual Arts: A Problem of Method," TRHS 5th ser. 22 (1972) 87–102; idem, in this volume, 639–41.

[3] *Chronica Monasterii Casinensis* 3.18, 26–29, and 32–33, ed. Wilhelm Wattenbach, MGH SS 7 (1846) 711, 716–27. This edition, admirable for its time, will be replaced by a new one by Hartmut Hoffmann, now in press; it has been preceded by a number of outstanding papers in which Hoffmann has contributed greatly to the understanding of many problems connected with the chronicle and its authors. The passages describing the rebuilding of the church have been translated and interpreted by Bloch (n. 1 above). [Hoffman's edition has subsequently appeared: *Chronica monasterii Casinensis*, MGH SS 34 (1980).]

[4] *Chron. Cas.* (n. 3 above) 3.26, p. 717.9–15. Cf. Arnold Esch, "Spolien: Zur Wiederverwendung antiker Baustücke und Skulpturen im mittelalterlichen Italien," AKG 51 (1969) 1–64 at 21–22. Bloch (n. 1 above) 1.71.

[5] *Chron. Cas.* (n. 3 above) 3.27, p. 718.18–21: "Legatos interea Constantinopolim ad locandos artifices destinat, peritos utique in arte musiaria et quadrataria, ex quibus videlicet alii absidam et arcum atque vestibulum maioris basilicae musivo comerent, alii vero totius ecclesiae pavimentum diversorum lapidum varietate consternerent." Cf. Bloch (n. 1 above) 1.45–46.

[6] Antonietta Maria Bessone Aurelj, *I marmorari romani* (Milan 1935) 1–12; Edward Hutton, *The Cosmati: The Roman Marble Workers of the XIIth and XIIIth Centuries* (London 1950) 3–6; Karl Noehles, "Die Kunst der Cosmaten und die Idee der Renovatio Romae," *Festschrift Werner Hager*, ed. Günther Fiensch and Max Imdahl (Recklinghausen 1966) 17–37, esp. at 32 n. 3; Kitzinger, in this volume, 640.

[7] The Byzantine bronze doors of Italy have been treated by Bloch (n. 1 above) 1.138–66. For the probable influence of Desiderius's Monte Cassino doors on the doors of San Paolo—and therefore on Hildebrand—see Kitzinger, this volume, n. 47.

the work Desiderius envisaged he had to turn to Constantinople, as he also did for the bronze doors of his church. Although at least one art historian has ascribed all the marble and stone work of Desiderius to Roman *marmorarii*,[8] the Byzantine origin of the pavement is now established beyond any doubt. Parts of it were rediscovered after the War (fig. 18),[9] and analogies neglected or newly brought to light have further strengthened this view.

Leo of Ostia and Alfanus expressed in similar words their keen awareness of the true *renovatio* which the program of Desiderius represented, words which clearly reflect the abbot's thinking:

And since Roman mastery of these arts [such as the laying of mosaics or pavements] had lapsed for more than five hundred years and deserved to be revived (*recuperare*) in our time through his efforts, with the inspiration and the help of God, the abbot in his wisdom decided that a great number of young monks should be thoroughly trained in these very arts (*eisdem artibus erudiri*), lest this knowledge be lost again in Italy.[10]

Alfanus in his poem on Monte Cassino says: "Four hundred and fifty years have passed during which this kind of art has been excluded from the cities of Italy; something that had been alien to us for a long time has now become our own again."[11]

It logically follows, then, that in Italy during the second half of the eleventh century there existed no workshops which were able to create pavements such as the one in Monte Cassino, and the inescapable conclusion is that early twelfth-century pavements in Roman churches such as Santa Maria in Cosmedin (fig. 19) and San Clemente represent a new departure. The key monument linking Monte Cassino with these Roman churches is the church of St Mennas in Sant'Agata de' Goti (province of Benevento), which was closely tied to Monte Cassino and which was dedicated in 1110 by pope Paschal II. Its pavement is a simplified copy of the pavement at Monte Cassino (fig. 20).[12]

[8]Hans Wentzel, "Antiken-Imitation des 12. und 13. Jahrhunderts in Italien," *Zeitschrift für Kunstwissenschaft* 9 (1955) 29–72; on p. 62 he writes, about my earlier views on (in this study) fig. 18: "die von ihm aufgestellte Annahme, der Mosaikboden sei byzantinisch, ist durch die Beispiele aus der Hagia Sofia und von Chios, Abb. 223, keineswegs ausreichend begründet. Man kann von den von ihm angezogenen Texten ebenso gut auf eine Anti-Byzanz-Tendenz und damit auf eine Pro-Rom-Tendenz schliessen." Wentzel totally misses the point, because he did not read or understand the crucial description of Leo of Ostia of which n. 5 above gives only a particularly significant sentence.

[9]For the rediscovered pavement see Angelo Pantoni, *Le vicende della Basilica di Montecassino attraverso la documentazione archeologica*, Miscellanea Cassinese 36 (1973) 101–37, 180–93, figs. 52–75; part of the plan of the pavement at the end of the volume is reproduced here as fig. 18. The whole problem is treated in Bloch (n. 1 above) 1.44–52.

[10]*Chron. Cas.* (n. 3 above) 3.27, p. 718.24–28.

[11]"Lustra decem novies redeunt, / quo patet esse laboris opus / istius urbibus Italiae / illicitum; peregrina diu / res, modo nostra sed efficitur." *I Carmi di Alfano I* (n. 1 above) 176; also, e.g., *Alphani Salernitani archiepiscopi carmina*, PL 147.1237B–C. In the verses Alfanus composed in the name of Desiderius for the apse of St Martin, also at Monte Cassino, he uses the figure 500 (*post centum lustra*): *Chron. Cas.* (n. 3 above) 3.33, p. 725.41.

[12]Bloch (n. 1 above) 1.49–50 and 91. On the pavement of Santa Maria in Cosmedin see Giovanni Battista Giovenale, *La basilica di S. Maria in Cosmedin* (Rome 1927) 25–26, 177–78, the plans on 21 fig. 8 and pl. II, and pls. LI, XXIII–XXV.

Alfanus was a conscious and enthusiastic believer in and proponent of *renovatio*. What he, Desiderius, and Leo of Ostia had in mind, in bringing back what had disappeared for more than five hundred years, was a revival of the early Christian art (obviously not of that of the Roman Republic or the time of Augustus), many more examples of which were then still extant than now.[13] Alfanus showed the same concern for the lack of Latin counterparts to Greek models in the preface to his translation (an extraordinary undertaking for his time) of Nemesius of Emesa's Περὶ φύσεως ἀνθρώπου.[14] It is important to remember that Alfanus, as archbishop of Salerno, recommended to his friend Desiderius the Saracen student of medicine Constantine the African, who became a monk at Monte Cassino and translated numerous medical treatises from the Arabic into Latin, the most influential interpreter of ancient Greek medicine to the West in centuries.[15]

When Alfanus built the cathedral of Salerno, after the conquest of that city by Robert Guiscard,[16] it was natural that he followed the example of Desiderius's basilica to such an extent, including the magnificent atrium, that even today the cathedral of Salerno, of all extant buildings of the period, comes closest in suggesting how the basilica of Monte Cassino looked. Alfanus, we may be sure, supervised all phases of its construction. A most outstanding example of re-creation of ancient art is found in one feature of this cathedral: the architrave of the main doors of the church (fig. 22) proves to be a Roman soffit from the Macellum (the so-called Temple of Serapis) in Pozzuoli (ancient Puteoli); another one is still preserved in Pozzuoli itself (fig. 21). But its sculptured face, which of course decorated the underside of the piece in its original site, has been turned ninety degrees, and reliefs representing a palm tree and a bird were added at either end to fill the blank spaces which had lain atop the capitals.[17]

[13]Hélène Toubert, "Le renouveau paléochrétien à Rome au début du XIIe siècle," *Cahiers archéologiques* 20 (1970) 99–154; Kitzinger (n. 2 above) 95 and "The First Mosaic Decoration of Salerno Cathedral," *Jahrbuch der österreichischen Byzantinistik* 21 (1972) 149–62, esp. 158–60 (= *The Art of Byzantium and the Medieval West*, ed. W. Eugene Kleinbauer [Bloomington Ind. 1976] 280–82).

[14]*Nemesii episcopi Premnon physicon, sive* Περὶ φύσεως ἀνθρώπου *liber a N. Alfano archiepiscopo Salerni in latinum translatus*, ed. Karl I. Burkhard (Leipzig 1917). In his preface (Prologus 9) he refers to authors "whom mother Greece educated" and to being forced to undertake this task "by the lack of Latin writers." Cf. Bloch (n. 1 above) 1.98.

[15]See the Bibliographical Note.

[16]Arturo Carucci, in "Le lapidi di Alfano I in Salerno," *Benedictina* 21 (1974) 29–52, has published some very important inscriptions of Alfanus, found in the cathedral, all dated in 1081. His attempt to prove that work on the new cathedral started as early as 1078 does not convinced me. The two doors and their lintels discussed here cannot be earlier than 1080, the year in which Desiderius brought about peace between Robert Guiscard and prince Jordan of Capua.

[17]The brilliant discovery is owed to Max Wegner, who discussed it twice: *Ornamente kaiserzeitlicher Bauten Roms. Soffitten*, Münstersche Forschungen 10 (Cologne 1957) 96–98 and pl. 31 a and b, and "Spolien-Miszellen aus Italien," *Festschrift Martin Wackernagel zum 75. Geburtstag* (Cologne 1958) 1–16 at 6–8 and figs. 4–6. Cf. Esch (n. 4 above) 15–18, 20. But Wegner's emphasis on Robert Guiscard's part in building the cathedral cannot be accepted, however much he undoubtedly contributed materially to that project.

Alfanus must have taken a special interest in this lintel, because it bears verses composed by him,[18] as were the verses inscribed on the architrave of the doors which lead to the atrium (the Porta dei Leoni).[19] It shows his respect for a choice piece of Roman architectural sculpture, and his determination to live up to the program of Desiderius, that Alfanus himself ordered his workmen to create for the atrium doors a copy of the architrave of the church doors. The artist carried out this assignment freely, transforming objects such as the two vases, out of which tendrils grow, into pure ornaments which seem to be influenced by motifs found in illuminated manuscripts. He even took over—elegantly, to be sure, but quite unnecessarily—the two palm trees with the feeding birds: not a slavish imitation, but an imaginative use of a Roman model (fig. 23).[20]

In this context must also be mentioned the most important ornament that has come down to us from the Desiderian basilica: the frame of its main doors, which survived the earthquake of 1349 intact and the bombardment of 1944 in severely damaged condition. As in the lintel of the doors to the atrium of the cathedral of Salerno, an artist was here at work who made use of classical decor—above all, the coffer motif—in a highly original form: whereas the coffer normally adorns the underside, mostly of ceilings, here it forms the dominant ornament of the jambs and lintel of the main doors (figs. 24–25).[21]

It may be appropriate at this point to return to Santa Maria in Cosmedin, where Roman *marmorarii* were employed by another Alfanus, *camerarius* of pope Calixtus II, who consecrated its main altar on 6 May 1123.[22] The pavement essentially belongs to this reconstruction, as does the episcopal throne. In the atrium of the church stands the tomb of Alfanus, a classicistic monument, obviously the work of the *marmorarii* who had served him so well. About the same time, Alberada, Robert Guiscard's first wife, died. Her tomb in the Chiesa Vecchia of the abbey of Santissima Trinità in Venosa in Apulia bears a remarkable resemblance to the tomb of Alfanus. A comparison of illustrations brings that out better than a detailed description (fig. 26). Clearly the two monuments are works of the same school.[23]

[18]*I Carmi di Alfano I* (n. 1 above) 216 no. 53.7–8.

[19]Ibid. vv. 9–10. Cf. on both inscriptions also Bloch (n. 1 above) 1.86–87; and on the two lintels, 73. Photographs of both doors ibid. figs. 95–96.

[20]Wegner, *Festschrift Wackernagel* (n. 17 above) 7.

[21]Cf. Pantoni (n. 9 above) 166–73; his figs. 86–88, 94, and 96 are pictures of the frame in its present condition. Bloch (n. 1 above) 1.72–73.

[22]Paul F. Kehr, *Italia pontificia* 1 (Berlin 1906) 114 no. 1; Giovenale (n. 12 above) 63 nos. 9–10 and pl. XXb and a; Angelo Silvagni, *Monumenta epigraphica christiana* 1 (Vatican City 1943) pls. 24.2, 25.1.

[23]The most fruitful treatment of the two monuments is found in Josef Deér, *The Dynastic Porphyry Tombs of the Norman Period in Sicily*, Dumbarton Oaks Studies 5 (Cambridge Mass. 1959) 29–30, figs. 6 and 2. Cf. for the inscription on the tomb Giovenale (n. 12 above) 64 no. 11; it is not dated, contrary to Giovenale's indication. See also Wentzel (n. 8 above) 60 and Esch (n. 4 above) 18. For Alberada see Raoul Manselli, *Dizionario biografico degli Italiani* 1 (1960) 614, who reports doubts about the identity of Alberada, as expressed by Giovanni Antonucci. They do not affect the approximate date of her tomb. For the throne of Santa Maria in Cosmedin see Kitzinger, in this volume, 640 and 647–48 and fig. 31; for the tomb of Alfanus, ibid. 641 and fig. 32, which latter should be compared with my fig. 26.

One leading figure of the Desiderian period must still be mentioned, not only because of his own importance but even more because of the far-reaching influence he had on posterity. This is the great teacher Alberic, whose main work, the *Breviarium de dictamine*, is unfortunately known only in part. Haskins repeatedly referred to that eloquent proponent of classical style, and a disciple of Haskins, Henry M. Willard, published a portion of this work.[24] It was Alberic's pupil at Monte Cassino, John of Gaeta, the later pope Gelasius II (1118–19), who as chancellor of the Roman Church since 1089 reformed the style of papal documents by introducing quantitative *clausulae* and the Leonine *cursus*. In his biography of pope Gelasius II, Pandulf of Pisa expressed it very well by saying, Urban II made John his chancellor "in order that, through the eloquence bestowed on him by the Lord, he might revive the *ancient* graceful and elegant style, which had been lost entirely in the Apostolic See, and that he might bring back the Leonine *cursus* with brilliant dispatch, at the order of the Holy Spirit and by the grace of God."[25] Hence it is clear that contemporaries were aware of his harking back to ancient models in his reform of the Curial style.

FRANCE

At the end of his life, in the eighties of the eleventh century, Alfanus of Salerno had introduced into the cathedral of his city a case of imitation which seemed to demonstrate his ardent wish to bring back to Italy the arts of ancient Rome. In France, half a century later, the architect of St Lazare, the cathedral of Autun, let himself be inspired even more boldly by the still-surviving city gate of Roman Augustodunum, the Porte d'Arroux. The small arcades of triforia above the great arches of the nave of the cathedral are unthinkable without that model, which he used with remarkable ingenuity (figs. 27–28).[26]

In the field of literature, two different but highly significant examples may serve to illustrate the same spirit in France. Baudri of Bourgueil (1046–1130; 1089 abbot of Bourgueil, 1107 archbishop of Dol in Brittany) was not the most outstanding poet of his time, nor was his love of Ovid unusual. In fact, his older contemporary Marbod of Rennes (d. 1123) in his youth wrote light verse with an Ovidian flavor in the form of letters addressed to girls at the

---

[24]*Ren* 23, 28, 140–41. D. Mauro Inguanez and Henry M. Willard, eds., *Alberici Casinensis flores rhetorici*, Miscellanea Cassinese 14 (1938).

[25]*Liber pontificalis prout exstat in codice manuscripto Dertusensi*, ed. José Maria March (Barcelona 1925) 163, reprinted in *Le Liber pontificalis*, ed. Louis Duchesne, 2nd ed. rev. Cyrille Vogel (3 vols. Paris 1955–57) 3.158: "ut per eloquentiam sibi a Domino traditam antiqui leporis et elegantie stilum, in sede apostolica iam pene omnem deperditum, sancto dictante Spiritu, Iohannes Dei gratia reformaret ac leonianum cursum lucida uelocitate reduceret." On Alberic and John of Gaeta, see the Bibliographical Note.

[26]Denis Grivot and George Zarnecki, *Gislebertus, sculpteur d'Autun* (Paris 1960) 19 fig. 67 and pl. 8. See also Christopher N. L. Brooke, *The Twelfth Century Renaissance* (London 1969) 93, 118, figs. 53–54. Cf. Sauerländer's interpretation in this volume, 674, and, in the same connection, his remarks (677) on ancient influences in St Remi in Reims, which appear in the time of abbot Peter of Celle, the friend of John of Salisbury.

convent of Le Ronceray at Angers—poetry for which he expressed remorse as an old man at the beginning of his *Liber decem capitulorum*.[27] Baudri was especially taken with the *Heroides*, so much so that he composed a counterpart to Ovid's *Paris Helenae* and *Helena Paridi* letters (*Heroides* 16 and 17), in which he showed surprising independence. It is amusing how Paris, in describing the attractions of Troy, singles out its wine as surpassing that of Praeneste and of the area of Orléans; no river resembles Simois and Xanthus except the Loire and "the happy Changeon (Cambio) which waters the gardens of Bourgueil." Even more original is an exchange of letters in which Florus, a friend of Ovid, offers to join the poet in his exile and is asked instead, in Ovid's reply, to bring his influence to bear on the emperor for his return.[28] Pseudo-ancient literature is precisely what works of this sort are, analogous in this way to certain phenomena that could be observed in the figurative arts. The creative influence of the *Heroides* is visible in an exchange of poetic epistles between Baudri and the nun Constance, and it does not matter here whether Constance's reply is genuine (Dronke), or fictitious in the manner of the *Heroides* (Schumann).

Perhaps half a century later, a greater French poet, Hugh Primas of Orléans, who hailed from the same district as Baudri, demonstrated in three well-known poems a rare empathy with Greek mythology known to him from Ovid's *Metamorphoses* 10, Horace's *Sermones* 2.5, and the second book of the *Aeneid*.[29] In the first of these poems, Orpheus addresses the Lord of the Underworld like a minstrel who asks for a *merces*, a small *munus* only: the return of his wife. Much more impressive is what Hugh has done—without access to Homer's *Odyssey*—with Horace's savage satire on legacy-hunters. The third

[27]Marbod of Rennes, *Liber decem capitulorum* 1.1–13, ed. Walther Bulst, Editiones Heidelbergenses 8 (Heidelberg 1947) 5; Walther Bulst, "Liebesbriefgedichte Marbods," *Liber Floridus: Mittellateinische Studien Paul Lehmann gewidmet*, ed. Bernhard Bischoff and Heinrich Suso Brechter (St Ottilien 1950) 287–301. Peter Dronke, *Medieval Latin and the Rise of European Love-Lyric* (2 vols. Oxford 1965–66; 2nd ed. 1968) 1.213–14.

[28]Paul Lehmann printed the four texts in his *Pseudo-antike Literatur des Mittelalters*, Studien der Bibliothek Warburg 13 (Leipzig 1927) 65–87; see also the edition by Phyllis Abrahams, *Les oeuvres poétiques de Baudri de Bourgueil (1046–1130)* (Paris 1926). In Ovid's reply to Florus, verses 155–58 now read as follows (Lehmann 87, Abrahams 150 no. 160):

> O michi si sanctum detur spectare senatum,
>   si reliquos patres sique tuam faciem,
> proruerem supplex in quelibet oscula patrum,
>   in tua flore [Flore *Abrahams*] magis oscula proruerem!

Verse 158 must be corrected to: "in tua, Flore, magis oscula proruerem!" See on these poems Otto Schumann, "Baudri von Bourgueil als Dichter," *Studien zur lateinischen Dichtung des Mittelalters: Ehrengabe für Karl Strecker*, ed. Walter Stach and Hans Walther (Dresden 1931) 158–70, esp. at 162. There also his view of the possible fictitious character of Constance's letter (no. 239 Abrahams): cf. for Dronke's dissent (n. 27 above) 217 n. 1. See also in general Franco Munari, *Ovid im Mittelalter* (Zurich 1960) 13–14.

[29]See the edition of Wilhelm Meyer, "Die Oxforder Gedichte des Primas (des Magisters Hugo von Orleans)," *Nachr Göttingen* 1907 (separately repr. Darmstadt 1970) 120–23 no. 3; 139–45 no. 10, and 231–34; 136–38 no. 9; cf. Karl Langosch, *Hymnen und Vagantenlieder: Lateinische Lyrik des Mittelalters mit deutschen Versen* (Basel 1954; rev. ed. Darmstadt 1961) 205–17.

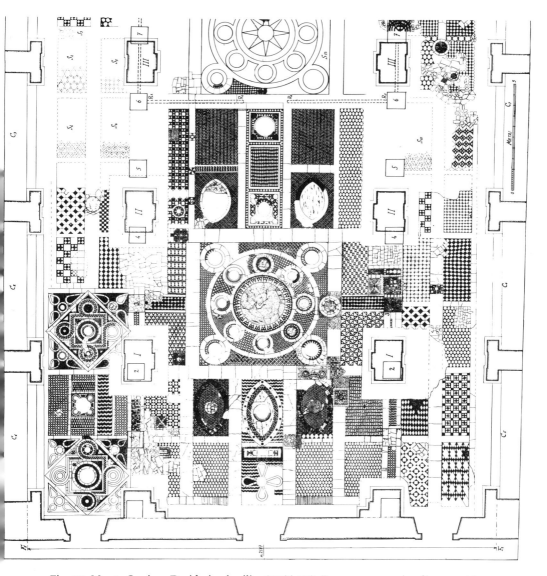

Fig. 18. Monte Cassino. Desiderian basilica (1066–71). Pavement: remains discovered in 1951. Detail of reconstruction. After Angelo Pantoni, *Le vicende della Basilica di Montecassino attraverso la documentazione archeologica*, Miscellanea Cassinese 36 (1973). Reproduced courtesy of Angelo Pantoni.

Fig. 19. Rome. Santa Maria in Cosmedin (ca. 1123). Pavement. Photo: Archivio Fotografico Nazionale.

Fig. 20 (opposite page). Sant'Agata de' Goti. St Mennas (1110). Pavement. Photo: Hutzel 1966, reproduced courtesy of the Biblioteca Hertziana.

Fig. 21. Pozzuoli (Puteoli). Macellum. Detail of soffit. After Max Wegner, "Ornamente kaiserzeitlicher Bauten Roms: Soffitten," *Münstersche Forschungen* 10 (1957) fig. 31a.

Fig. 22. Salerno. Cathedral. Entrance to nave: lintel above the doors. Photo: Bildarchiv Foto Marburg.

Fig. 23. Salerno. Cathedral. Entrance to atrium: detail of lintel above the doors. After Adolfo Venturi, *Storia dell'arte italiana* 3: *L'arte romanica* (Milan 1904) 541 fig. 502.

Fig. 24. Monte Cassino. Desiderian basilica (1066–71). Main doors: 1712/13 engraving. After
Erasmo Gattola, *Historia abbatiae Cassinensis per seculorum seriem distributa* . . . (2 vols.
Venice 1733) 1. pl. 1 = Herbert Bloch, *Monte Cassino in the Middle Ages*, vol. 2 fig. 15a.

Fig. 26 (right). Venosa. Santissima Trinità, Chiesa Vecchia. Tomb of Alberada (after 1111; or after 1122?). After Arthur E. G. Haseloff, *Die Kaiserinnengräber in Andria: Ein Beitrag zur apulischen Kunstge-schichte unter Friedrich II.* (Rome 1905) 50 fig. 20.

Fig. 25. Monte Cassino. Desiderian basilica (1066–71). Main doors: the architrave used as a soffit. Pre-war photograph. Photo: Instituto Centrale per il Catalogo e la Documentazione, Rome, E17661.

Fig. 28. Autun. Cathedral. Choir (second quarter of twelfth century): view from southwest. Photo: Bildarchiv Foto Marburg.

Fig. 27. Autun. Roman city gate ("Porte d'Arroux"). Photo: Neurdein.

poem is the doleful report, by a Greek, of Troy in ruins. The fall of the once proud and powerful city and the contrast between its past glory and its present reversion to nature form the dominant theme. In the last part, Hugh dwells on Troy's sins, sins for which she has paid the penalty. And yet the narrator ends with the confession that when he thinks of Troy's destruction and speaks of her, he cannot suppress his grief.

There is a kinship between this poem and the famous Rome poems of Hildebert of Lavardin, with which Hugh most likely was familiar. Written after Hildebert's trip to Rome in 1100, these two poems were already renowned in the twelfth century. To understand fully their meaning, it is necessary to look at them together, because—with all his admiration for pagan Rome, great even in ruins—for Hildebert the cross contributed more than the eagle, Peter more than Caesar. This contrast was vividly present in Alfanus's ode to Hildebrand, together with praise of the ancient Romans. But new is the nostalgic longing for the physical grandeur of the pagan past, irretrievably lost; all of its achievements are freely admitted by Hildebert, without in the least impairing his Christian thinking. Without qualms he says of Rome that human efforts could create what the efforts of the gods were not able to destroy, that the gods themselves admire their own statues and wish to resemble them. "Nature could not create gods with such faces as those which men created in admirable statues of gods"; the gods of old were revered more because of the accomplishments of artists than because of their own divinity (no. 36 vv. 33–36). With all his sincere and unshakable faith in Christianity, Hildebert has here gone farther than anyone before him in experiencing and expressing a new fascination with ancient Rome.[30]

MIRABILIA URBIS ROMAE

Sometime later, in the second half of the twelfth century (rather than early in the thirteenth), an otherwise unknown English traveler, the "magister Gregorius," was so profoundly affected by the sight of Rome as he approached from the Monte Mario that, urged by his friends, he wrote a brief treatise "de mirabilibus urbis Rome."[31] So overwhelming was his impression that the two

[30]The two Rome poems of Hildebert have often been printed. See now *Hildeberti Cenomannensis episcopi carmina minora*, ed. A. Brian Scott (Leipzig 1969) 22–27 nos. 36 and 38. Among earlier discussions, Haskins, *Ren* 163–65 and Schramm, *KRR* 1.296–304 stand out; the latter also contains the text of the poems, augmented in the 1957 edition by the translation of Wolfram von den Steinen (304–05). The most important treatment of the poems within the framework of Hildebert's entire *oeuvre* is by Peter von Moos, *Hildebert von Lavardin, 1056–1133: Humanitas an der Schwelle des höfischen Zeitalters*, Pariser historische Studien 3 (Stuttgart 1965) 240–58: "Christliches und Heidnisches waren bei ihm problemlos vereinbar" (247). See also Peter Classen, this volume, at n. 19. For the theme of Christian exploits surpassing those of the Romans in the early Middle Ages, see Ernst H. Kantorowicz, *Laudes regiae: A Study in Liturgical Acclamations and Mediaeval Ruler Worship* (Berkeley 1946) 58 and esp. n. 152.

[31]Preserved only in MS Cambridge, St Catherine's Coll. 3 (late thirteenth century). The most recent editions are: *Codice topografico della Città di Roma* 3, ed. Roberto Valentini and Giuseppe

opening lines of Hildebert's first Rome poem, *Par tibi, Roma, nihil*, came immediately to his mind. He scorns the fantastic accounts of the pilgrims and the Romans in favor of information given him by cardinals (cc. 4 and 15), although he does not spurn the anonymous treatise *De septem miraculis mundi*—a source of less than doubtful value. Like Hildebert, Gregorius does not find fault with pagan statues; on the contrary, he repeatedly berates pope Gregory the Great for his alleged iconoclasm (cc. 4, 6, 12) and the Roman people for their greed in supposedly stealing the golden roof tiles of the Pantheon. He singles out a statue dedicated by the Romans to Venus, which shows her naked as she is said to have been during the judgment of Paris. This statue of Parian marble was so perfect a work of art that it seemed to him "rather a living creature than a statue"; "because of its striking beauty and a sort of magic attraction I was compelled to visit it three times, although it was two stadia away from my hostel" (c. 12). In the baths of Diocletian, he reports, there are columns so tall that one cannot throw a small stone as high as the capital. It took a hundred men one year, according to the cardinals, to cut one column into slices (a rare glimpse of the working habits of the *marmorarii*) (c. 15).[32]

Master Gregory was not the only member of the English clergy enamored of Roman statuary. John of Salisbury in the *Historia pontificalis* tells how Henry of Blois, bishop of Winchester, the brother of king Stephen, during a stay in Rome to promote his own interests, bought ancient statues and had them transported to Winchester. This act of buying up idols made by heathens contrasted with the long beard and the "philosophi gravitas" with which Henry tried to outdo everyone at the Curia and inspired "quidam grammaticus" to apply some witty verses of Horace's Damasippus satire to him: "Insanit ueteres statuas Damasippus emendo" ("Buying old statues is Damasippus's folly") (*Sermones* 2.3.64).[33]

John of Salisbury himself revealed, in the prologue to the *Policraticus* of 1159, an unusual awareness of the monuments of ancient Rome. For he did not limit himself to a simple reference to the arch of Constantine as an example of triumphal arches which spread the glory of great men through their in-

---

Zucchetti, Fonti per la storia d'Italia 90 (Rome 1946) 137–67 (critical edition with introduction and commentary) and *Magister Gregorius (12e ou 13e siècle), Narracio de mirabilibus urbis Rome*, ed. R. B. C. Huygens (Leiden 1970) (critical edition of the text with the addition of the excerpts from Gregorius in Ralph Higden's *Polychronicon* and the passages in *De septem miraculis mundi* used by Gregorius).

[32]See on these episodes James B. Ross, "A Study of Twelfth-Century Interest in the Antiquities of Rome," *Medieval and Historiographical Essays in Honor of James Westfall Thompson* (Chicago 1938) 302–21 at 316–20. Gregorius's treatise is entertaining and valuable as a historical document, but I must take exception to its description as "archäologisch sachkundig und gewissenhaft" in Michael Seidlmayer's article "Rom und Romgedanke im Mittelalter," *Saeculum* 7 (1956) 395–412 at 407.

[33]John of Salisbury, *Historia pontificalis (Memoirs of the Papal Court)*, ed. and trans. Marjorie Chibnall (London and New York 1956) 79.

scriptions: "The beholder recognizes the 'liberator of the fatherland', the 'founder of peace' only when the inscription indicates the triumphant Constantine, to whom our Britain gave birth." The words "Liberatori urbis" (not "patriae") and "fundatori quietis" are actually to be found above the two reliefs decorating the main passageway of the arch.[34]

Some years before Henry of Winchester's visit, a canon of St Peter's named Benedict had been commissioned by the cardinal priest of San Marco, Guido of Città di Castello, to write the *Liber politicus*. A kind of handbook for the administration of the Curia, it also contained a new and detailed account of the route which the papal processions had to take. In writing this account, known as the *Ordo romanus*, Benedict took advantage of the topographical studies which had been his avocation, and tried to identify Roman sites of his time with ancient monuments. The work on the *Ordo* inspired him to write an independent treatise on the topography of ancient Rome which goes under the name *Mirabilia urbis Romae*. It is incorporated in the *Liber politicus* but without the name of its author.[35]

Benedict used the ancient compendiary descriptions of the *regiones* of Rome, *passiones* of martyrs, the *Fasti* of Ovid, and the *Liber pontificalis*. He thus was a man of learning who also had some knowledge of Roman history, derived from the usual late Roman compendia. It was not his fault that with this background his efforts to identify the numerous ancient buildings he mentions were not very successful. His attempts often rest on speculations—his own and, we may assume, those of other men of learning. As in his *Ordo*, he follows a certain route, for this book was meant to be used by pilgrims. It is therefore all the more remarkable that he dwells at such length on ancient monuments. His account is punctuated by what one might call etiological tales, such as the story about the origin of "Sancta Maria Ara Coeli" (c. 11), or of the two colossal statues of the Dioscuri on the Piazza del Quirinale (c. 12), or of the alleged statue of Constantine in front of the Lateran palace (actually the statue of Marcus Aurelius now on the Capitoline) (c. 15). That the treatise is full of mistakes does not diminish its author's merit as an innovator.

Benedict found at least one imitator in the twelfth century. Peter the Deacon of Monte Cassino, in his chronicle of Atina, used the same method of

[34]"Liberatorem patriae, fundatorem quietis, tunc demum inspector agnoscit, cum titulus triumphatorem, quem nostra Britannia genuit, indicat Constantinum." *Policraticus*, ed. Clement C. J. Webb (2 vols. Oxford 1909) 1.13.3. The "quotation" from the real inscription (*CIL* VI.1139 = Dessau, *ILS* 694) was apparently not noticed by Webb, Ross (n. 32 above) 312, or Eva M. Sanford, "The Study of Ancient History in the Middle Ages," *Journal of the History of Ideas* 5 (1944) 21–43 at 42 n. 56. But see Roberto Weiss, *The Renaissance Discovery of Classical Antiquity* (Oxford 1969) 11 (with mistaken reference).

[35]Benedict's identity was established in 1904 by Louis Duchesne, "L'auteur des *Mirabilia*," *Mélanges de l'Ecole française de Rome* 24 (1904) 479–89, and is now generally accepted. The basic edition of the *Mirabilia urbis Romae* is found in *Codice topografico della Città di Roma* 3 (n. 31 above); all references here are to the earliest version, ibid. 3–65. On Guido's connections with Abelard see particularly David E. Luscombe, *The School of Abelard: The Influence of Abelard's Thought in the Early Scholastic Period* (Cambridge 1969) 20–21.

identifying the ancient remains in Atina with buildings allegedly erected by Roman emperors, so much so that one might call the work *Mirabilia urbis Atinae*.[36]

It is one of the ironies in which history abounds that only a few years after Benedict of St Peter's work became known, the archeological interest which inspired it, and which in turn aroused in the Romans a new enthusiasm for the remains of ancient Rome, undoubtedly helped to bring about that unique Roman revolution which led to the reestablishment of the Senate on the Capitoline, "the true *caput mundi* where the consuls and senators used to meet to rule the world"—thus begins the *Mirabilia*'s glowing description (c. 23).[37] The new regime had started in the last months of Innocent II's reign in 1143, although the new era of the Senate began in the fall of the following year after the brief pontificate of Celestine II—the former cardinal Guido, who had been the patron of Benedict of St Peter.[38] Already Celestine was challenged by the new regime, and his successor Lucius II, according to one source, met his death in a siege of the Capitoline. The self-assurance of the new rulers has been immortalized by Otto of Freising in the address by the Senate's envoys to Frederick Barbarossa on the road from Sutri to Rome.[39]

Never before had the longing for *renovatio* under Rome's auspices been expressed more ardently. The Senate was eager to protect ancient monuments such as the Column of Trajan (1162) or the Aurelian Walls, as an inscription of 1157 proudly proclaims without any reference to the pope: *SPQR hec menia vetusta et dilapsa restauravit. Senatores:* (they are listed by name).[40] Two centuries later, Colá di Rienzo tried to realize a more ambitious goal in different ways, but there we are on the threshold of the Renaissance, with Petrarch himself deeply involved, and the differences between the two movements must not be overlooked. Still, the precedent of 1143/44 should not be underrated either.

[36]Schramm, *KRR* 2.46. See, for the time being, Erich Caspar, *Petrus Diaconus und die Monte Cassineser Fälschungen* (Berlin 1909) 128–48, esp. 141–48. Peter's chronicle reflects an earlier treatise, entitled apparently *Libellus de excidio civitatis Atinae*, the only surviving copy of which was destroyed during the battle of Cassino in 1943–44. But it was possible to reconstruct much of the lost work from quotations in the unedited *Ecclesiae Atinatis historia* of Marcantonio Palombo (d. 1640); a critical edition of this work, with a commentary, was submitted as a Ph.D. thesis at Harvard University by Carmela V. Franklin in 1977. Professor Franklin is preparing it for publication; and the entire Atina dossier of Peter the Deacon will be edited by the present writer.

[37]"Capitolium, quod erat caput mundi, ubi consules et senatores morabantur ad gubernandum orbem, cuius facies cooperta erat muris altis et firmis diu super fastigium montis, vitro et auro undique coopertis et miris operibus laqueatis" (*Codice topografico* [n. 31 above] 3.51).

[38]For the Roman revolution of 1143–44 and especially its political significance, for the "mystique" of the Capitoline and the role of Arnold of Brescia, see the detailed treatment in the first section of Robert L. Benson's essay in this volume.

[39]Otto of Freising, GF 2.29–30 (135–39). Cf. Seidlmayer (n. 32 above) 405–06.

[40]For the Senatorial *investimentum* of 1162 (which is preserved in the original) see *Codice diplomatico del Senato Romano dal MCXLIV al MCCCXLVII* 1, ed. Franco Bartoloni (vols. 2 and 3 have not been published), Fonti per la storia d'Italia 87 (Rome 1948) 25–27 no. 18; for the inscription of 1157 see Silvagni (n. 22 above) pl. 25.5.

THE NEW INTEREST IN ROMAN HISTORY

It would be surprising if the new interest in ancient Rome did not affect the attitude of the educated men of that time toward ancient historiography. Throughout the Middle Ages even the greatest historians, when they dealt with Roman history, were content with poor compendia such as Paul the Deacon's modernized and Christianized Eutropius or Orosius's *Historia adversus paganos*, that rather pitiful companion volume to St Augustine's grandiose *De civitate Dei*. Even a man of such learning and rare intellectual curiosity as Bede relied in the first book of the *Historia ecclesiastica* on sources of this kind. Flodoard of Reims, who in the tenth century made intelligent use of Livy and of Caesar's *Gallic War* in the first book of his *Historia Remensis Ecclesiae*, remains an exception. Most historians who betray a knowledge of, say, Sallust—Widukind and Richerius come to mind—merely exploited their model, sometimes by transferring the main ideas of entire speeches to situations of contemporary or recent history.[41] For them the ancient historian was nothing but a stylistic exemplar.

Lampert of Hersfeld does not merely *seem* to use Livy, as Haskins says (225), he was steeped in Livy to such an extent that he must have known large portions of Livy by heart.[42] The unusually high literary level of Lampert's work may owe something, perhaps a great deal, to his intimate familiarity with Livy. It is inconceivable that Lampert would have studied Livy with such intensity had he not had an interest in the *contents* of Livy's work. Still, there is a vast difference between a primarily stylistic relationship to an ancient historian, such as Lampert's, and a true interest in Roman history per se, an interest which in the long run cannot be satisfied with the compendia of late Antiquity or of the early Middle Ages.

It will be a touchstone of the genuine involvement of the twelfth century with the classics if it is possible to demonstrate that such involvement did indeed exist. Achieving this end remains a task for further investigation. But it can now be seen that the new interest in ancient Rome provides the most persuasive evidence for understanding that Haskins's "renaissance" actually began thirty to forty years before the dawn of the twelfth century.

Bibliographical Note

The literature on the new awareness of ancient Rome in the last third of the eleventh century and throughout the twelfth is by necessity diffuse, especially if the figurative

[41] Beryl Smalley, "Sallust in the Middle Ages," *Classical Influences on European Culture A.D. 500–1500*, ed. R. R. Bolgar (Cambridge 1971) 165–75, is only a sketch.

[42] His debt to Livy has been shown by Otto Holder-Egger, ed., *Lamperti monachi Hersfeldensis opera*, MGH SS rer Germ (1894) 399–489 and Guido Billanovich, *Lamperto di Hersfeld e Tito Livio* (Padua 1945).

arts are included. By coincidence the most trenchant book on the subject was in preparation when Haskins's work appeared, Percy Ernst Schramm's *Kaiser, Rom und Renovatio* of 1929. Schramm referred to Haskins's title once (1.297), but without using the book itself, and did not include it in the "Nachträge" to his second edition of 1957, as it had been published before 1929. Schramm devoted to the twelfth century only his last chapter, which represents a very small fraction of his entire text. And this in spite of his interest in the *Mirabilia*, a version of which forms the second part of the *Graphia aureae urbis Romae*. The last portion of this treatise, the so-called *Graphia-Libellus*, dated by him around 1030, occupies a central position in Schramm's work; see his edition in the second volume of *KRR* (1929; not reprinted in 1957) 68–111 (and the excursuses 34–44) and in *Kaiser, Könige und Päpste* (*KKP*) 3.313–59, 4.1.22–42. Fedor Schneider in his impressionistic *Rom und Romgedanke im Mittelalter* (Munich 1925; repr. Darmstadt 1959) also gave the twelfth century short shrift. Robert L. Benson's penetrating analysis of the *Mirabilia* and the *Graphia* in the first section of his contribution to the present volume is, therefore, all the more welcome.

The importance of Monte Cassino for the renaissance of the twelfth century and the idea of *renovatio* was recognized implicitly by both Haskins and Schramm. Both scholars contributed to a better understanding of the role which the monastery played in this movement generally and in that particular aspect of it. My forthcoming book on Monte Cassino (n. 1 above) deals with some of the pertinent problems in more detail than other publications. Its first part, entitled "Monte Cassino, Byzantium, and the West in the Early Middle Ages," supersedes the paper by the same title which appeared in *Dumbarton Oaks Papers* 3 (1946) 164–224 and is almost three times the size of the earlier version. Corresponding references to the earlier study, where at all applicable, would be, for n. 1: 218–19; nn. 2–3: 193–200; n. 5: 198; n. 9: 196–98; n. 11: 198 n. 110; n. 12: 197; n. 14: 220; n. 15 (and the next paragraph): 220–22. It goes without saying that the objective of the present essay differs from that of my book.

For Constantine the African see especially Heinrich Schipperges, *Die Assimilation der arabischen Medizin durch das lateinische Mittelalter*, Sudhoffs Archiv, Beiheft 3 (Wiesbaden 1964) 17–54, and Marie-Thérèse d'Alverny's notable contribution to the understanding of his background and of his significance in her essay in this volume. My own treatment (*Monte Cassino* [n. 1 above] 1.98–110 and "Petrus Diaconus on the Life and Works of Constantinus Africanus," ibid. 125–34) attempts to clarify the tradition about Constantinus Africanus, particularly in his relationship to Monte Cassino, and to offer a catalogue of his works with as complete a bibliography as possible. An article on him, to appear in the *Dizionario biografico degli Italiani*, is being prepared by Vera von Falkenhausen.

For the art of Monte Cassino and southern Italy, Emile Bertaux's *L'Art dans l'Italie méridionale* (Paris 1903; repr. in 3 vols. Rome 1968) is a classic, which even after seventy-five years has not been, and will not be, replaced.[43] While studies that have been discussed in the notes are in general not cited again here, Arnold Esch's article "Spolien" of 1969 (n. 4 above) should be singled out as by far the most complete, critical, and easy to use "Materialsammlung" in existence. The pertinent articles cited in notes 6 and 8 are specialized and do not aim at completeness. The study by Richard M. L. Hamann-MacLean, "Antikenstudium in der Kunst des Mittelalters," *Marburger Jahrbücher für Kunstwissenschaft* 15 (1949–50) 157–250, largely concerned with sculpture and architectural sculpture of France, deals in part with the effect of the study of ancient works of art on those of the Middle Ages and, more subjectively, with "Geistesverwandtschaft" between ancient and medieval art. These are approaches worth

---

[43]The reprint edition has recently been augmented by vols. 4–6, *Aggiornamento dell'opera di Emile Bertaux, sotto la direzione di Adriano Prandi* (3 vols. Rome 1978).

pursuing, but not in the province of the present paper. Jean Adhémar's important book *Influences antiques dans l'art du moyen âge français*, Studies of the Warburg Institute 7 (London 1939) must be mentioned in this context.

The emphasis on Santa Maria in Cosmedin was intentional. Its well-established date, its connections with John of Gaeta (who from 1089/1101 to 1118 was cardinal deacon of that church) and with Calixtus II, and the close link of its pavement with Monte Cassino and St Mennas, made it a particularly suitable example. For a survey of medieval art in Rome (with well over 320 illustrations) see Federico Hermanin, *L'arte in Roma dal sec. VIII al XIV*, Storia di Roma 23 (Bologna 1945); the *marmorarii* are treated at 59–83 (pavements at 80–83, less than three pages). For the revival of the arts in Rome and Italy during the eleventh and twelfth centuries, see above all Ernst Kitzinger's study in this volume. See now also Richard Krautheimer, *Rome: Profile of a City, 312–1308* (Princeton 1980), esp. 161–202.

Alberic and John of Gaeta are discussed, in part at least from the point of view taken here, in Herbert Bloch, "Monte Cassino's Teachers and Library in the High Middle Ages," *La scuola nell'Occidente latino dell'alto medioevo*, Settimane 19 (2 vols. Spoleto 1972) 2.563–605 at 587–601 (with references to earlier literature). On John of Gaeta as cardinal deacon of Santa Maria in Cosmedin see now Rudolf Hüls, *Kardinäle, Klerus und Kirchen Roms, 1049–1130*, Bibliothek des Deutschen historischen Instituts in Rom 48 (Tübingen 1977) 231–32, 42–44. For Hildebert's Rome poems see also Walther Rehm, *Europäische Romdichtung* (Munich 1939) 38–54 (the second edition of 1960 was not accessible to me).

The only special treatment of medieval interest in ancient history that is known to me is Eva M. Sanford's article of 1944 cited in n. 34.[44] This is a subject I have been studying in some detail and hope to bring to publication in the near future, in a work which will also deal with the various twelfth-century versions of the *Mirabilia*.

[44]Heinrich Fichtenau's "Vom Verständnis der römischen Geschichte bei deutschen Chronisten des Mittelalters," *Festschrift Percy Ernst Schramm*, ed. Peter Classen and Peter Scheibert (2 vols. Wiesbaden 1964) 1.401–19 (repr. in Fichtenau's *Beiträge zur Mediävistik: Ausgewählte Aufsätze* [2 vols. Stuttgart 1975–77] 1.1–23), to which Robert Benson has called my attention, has objectives quite different from my own and is limited in its scope to Germany alone.

The Arts as Aspects of a Renaissance
Rome and Italy

Ernst Kitzinger

"The renaissance of the twelfth century might conceivably be taken so broadly as to cover all the changes through which Europe passed in the hundred years or more from the late eleventh century to the taking of Constantinople by the Latins in 1204 . . . ; but such a view becomes too wide and vague for any purpose save the general history of the period. More profitably we may limit the phrase to the history of culture in this age—*the complete development of Romanesque art and the rise of Gothic*; the full bloom of vernacular poetry, both lyric and epic; and the new learning and new literature in Latin."[1] Haskins's book, of course, deals only with the last of these three subjects. But evidently he thought of "the complete development of Romanesque art and the rise of Gothic"—or, in other words, all Western art of the period—as an integral part of the twelfth-century renaissance. Indeed, in the passage quoted he gives it pride of place.

For the art historian in turn, however, such a view is "too wide and vague." It makes sense only if the term "renaissance" is used in the loosest sense of a "flowering," a quickening of pace, a concentration of creative effort. Unquestionably these terms do apply to the art of the twelfth century. But both the phenomena involved and their roots and causes are so manifold that the scholar in his effort to explain everything would in the end explain nothing.

Haskins's own study is keyed to revival phenomena, and the revival of the ancient classics in particular. Citing Henry Osborn Taylor's statement that each medieval century "endeavored to reach back to the remote past for further treasure," he sees as the distinctive trait of the twelfth-century renaissance that

In preparing this paper for publication I received valuable criticism and useful references from Robert L. Benson and Richard Krautheimer. I wish to thank them as well as Natasha Staller, to whom the text owes a good many improvements. This essay was completed in the summer of 1978, and subsequent literature has not been taken into account. The study referred to in note 23 has now been published: "A Virgin's Face: Antiquarianism in Twelfth-Century Art," *Art Bulletin* 62 (1980) 6–19.
[1]Haskins, *Ren* 6. Italics in the quotation are mine.

it "reached out more widely and recovered more."[2] This is certainly true in art, and it is under this aspect that twelfth-century art will be examined in the pages that follow. One can, indeed, learn a great deal that is central to the art of the period by asking what got recovered when; in what manner the recovered "treasures" were used; and what motivated those who did the recovering.

My study will be confined to Italy, where the "reaching out" was more intense and more varied than anywhere else—with consequences that were of considerable importance for the art of the other countries of Western Europe. The focus will be on Rome, because successive phases of the process can be traced—and underlying motivations discerned—more clearly in Rome than elsewhere. "Renaissance" initiatives in other regions will be reviewed very briefly in the last part of the paper.

I. THE ARTISTIC REVIVAL IN ROME

Rome saw a dramatic burst of artistic activity in the first half of the twelfth century. After two hundred years barren of major enterprises, there was, above all, an extensive building and rebuilding of churches.[3] This in turn gave new and massive scope to the "decorative arts," to sculpture, mosaic, and fresco painting. There was also a new flowering of book illumination, centered in Benedictine houses.[4]

The patronage, then, was primarily ecclesiastic. First and foremost it was the papacy—still locked in the struggle over investiture during the first two decades of the century and emerging from that struggle in the third—which was responsible for the new initiatives. The Church of the Gregorian Reform by this time already had a tradition of "reaching out widely" in matters of art. These antecedents are of great importance, as we shall see. But for the present what concerns us is that the papacy adopted the tradition, gave it a powerful impetus, and channeled it in new directions.

Let us briefly survey the highlights of artistic achievement in the various media, and more specifically their indebtedness to the past. In architecture, what stands out is a revival of the basilica of Early Christian times. The new Romanesque style of the north never found favor among papal patrons. Im-

---

[2]Ibid. 16.

[3]The principal church buildings of this period are: Santi Quattro Coronati, rebuilt by Paschal II (1099–1118) and consecrated in 1116 (*Le Liber pontificalis*, ed. Louis Duchesne, 2nd ed. rev. Cyrille Vogel [3 vols. Paris 1955–57] 2.305, 310 n. 67, 3.135); Santa Maria in Cosmedin, dedicated by Calixtus II (1119–24) in 1123 (Giovanni B. Giovenale, *La basilica di S. Maria in Cosmedin* [Rome 1927] 63); San Clemente, rebuilt during the first quarter of the twelfth century (see Toubert [n. 19 below] esp. 100 n. 4); San Crisogono, rebuilt 1123–29 (see n. 6 below); Santa Maria in Trastevere, rebuilt by Innocent II (1130–43) in 1140–43 (*Liber pontificalis* 2.384 with n. 1, 3.138); Santa Croce in Gerusalemme, rebuilt by Lucius II (1144–45) before he became pope (ibid. 2.385); the abbey church of Tre Fontane, built in the 1140s (n. 56 below).

[4]Edward B. Garrison, *Studies in the History of Mediaeval Italian Painting* (4 vols. Florence 1953–62) 2.30.

portant precedents for an Early Christian revival had been set by abbot Desiderius in his rebuilding of the abbey church of Monte Cassino (1066–71), and even earlier by the spurt of church building in Florence that began in the middle of the eleventh century.[5] But it was left to Rome to achieve as pure a recreation of an Early Christian church as the interior of Santa Maria in Trastevere (1140–43), with its straight entablature resting on columns with Ionic capitals and its rich and ornate sculptural detail (fig. 29). Such architecture had not been built since a similarly classicizing vogue had created the nave of Santa Maria Maggiore in the fifth century.[6]

Much of the interior detail—the column shafts, most of the capitals, and nearly all of the elaborately carved cornices—is actually ancient (fig. 30).[7] The reuse of ancient decorative pieces was a time-honored practice in Rome, where the decaying or disused buildings of imperial times offered a virtually inexhaustible supply of such material. But in this period the recovery of spoils gained particular momentum.[8] The demand came not only from local builders and patrons but from distant ones as well.[9] A regular trade in antiques developed, no doubt greatly stimulated by its ability to provide prefabricated pieces for architecture and decoration in the antique style. Among medieval buildings in Rome, the one which displays spoils most self-consciously is not a church but a rare relic of domestic architecture, the so-called Casa dei Crescenzi. Though this curious exercise in nostalgic *renovatio* has been attributed by some scholars to the eleventh century, a date in the twelfth century seems more likely.[10]

It was in the furnishing of the newly built or rebuilt churches with pulpits and episcopal thrones, with altar canopies, paschal candelabra, and tombs that

[5] See below, p. 651. Throughout this essay the term "Early Christian" will be used in a loose sense to denote Christian art from the early fourth to the late sixth century. In the perspective of the twelfth century, church art from the time of Constantine to the time of Gregory the Great clearly was a distinct and unified entity.

[6] Actually, among twelfth-century basilicas in Rome, San Crisogono (rebuilt 1123–29) precedes Santa Maria in Trastevere in having a straight entablature supported by columns with Ionic capitals. The church was drastically restored in the seventeenth century, but the basic twelfth-century order survives (see Maurice Mesnard, *La basilique de Saint Chrysogone à Rome*, Studi di antichità cristiana 9 [Vatican City 1935] 132–34, 153–54, and fig. 66). For Santa Maria Maggiore see Richard Krautheimer, "The Architecture of Sixtus III: A Fifth-Century Renascence?" *De artibus opuscula XL: Essays in Honor of Erwin Panofsky*, ed. Millard Meiss (2 vols. New York 1961) 1.291–302.

[7] It was presumably the Baths of Caracalla—not extensively used as a source of *spolia* in medieval times—which supplied the magnificent capitals in the nave adorned with heads of Egyptian divinities (Christian Hülsen, *Architektonische Studien von Sergius Andrejewitsch Iwanoff* 3 [Berlin 1898] 77, with illustrations on p. 8). Not until the restoration of the church in the nineteenth century were some of these heads removed! An exhaustive study of the building in all its aspects is being prepared by Dale Kinney. See also R. E. Malmstrom, "The Colonnades of High Medieval Churches at Rome," *Gesta* 14.2 (1975) 37–45, esp. 42.

[8] See the article by Malmstrom cited in the preceding note, and, in general, Arnold Esch, "Spolien: Zur Wiederverwendung antiker Baustücke und Skulpturen im mittelalterlichen Italien," AKG 51 (1969) 1–64.

[9] Ibid. 21, 29–30; see also below at n. 99 (Henry of Winchester).

[10] See notes 58 and 64 below; and for an illustration, Federico Hermanin, *L'arte in Roma dal sec. VIII al XIV*, Storia di Roma 23 (Bologna 1945) pl. 24, 2.

the classicizing taste of the period found some of its fullest and freest expression. The first half of the twelfth century saw the rise of the ateliers of the Roman *marmorarii*, which would then continue to flourish for many generations, indeed through most of the thirteenth century.[11] From the outset these famous craftsmen made brilliant and varied use of the stones they recovered from the ruins of ancient Rome. Most often, and particularly in the polychrome mosaic inlay that adorns so much of their work, they used them simply as raw material. But there are also instances where an ancient—or Early Christian—piece of sculpture was left intact and allowed to speak for itself, albeit perhaps "updated" by a judicious application of mosaic work.[12] There is some evidence also of ancient statuary having been set up in the workshops of the *marmorarii* to serve as models.[13] Indeed, these craftsmen became extremely adept in their imitations, with the result that in some instances modern scholarship is divided as to whether a given piece of work is ancient or medieval. The armrests of the episcopal throne in Santa Maria in Cosmedin—a church rebuilt and refurnished by pope Calixtus II (1119–24) and Alfanus, his chamberlain—are a case in point (fig. 31): though I have no doubt that these armrests with their magnificent lion protomes are, in fact, spoils, some scholars have considered them to be twelfth-century work.[14] The most important aspect

[11]Antonietta Maria Bessone Aurelj, *I marmorari romani* (Milan 1935); Edward Hutton, *The Cosmati* (London 1950). There is no full and adequate study of this important subject. See also Herbert Bloch's essay in this volume.

[12]An example of a pagan piece of sculpture thus "modernized" by the *marmorarii* is the circular relief in the Capitoline Museum with the story of Achilles, originally the raised border of a table top, the center of which has been filled with polychrome inlay (G. A. S. Snyder, "The So-called Puteal in the Capitoline Museum at Rome," *Journal of Roman Studies* 13 [1923] 56–68). A relief with the story of Jonah from the lid of a fourth-century sarcophagus is an example of an Early Christian relief similarly refurbished; see Wolfgang Stechow, "Selected Acquisitions of European Art, 1947–1948," *Bulletin of the Dudley Peter Allen Memorial Art Museum of Oberlin College* 5 (1948) 25–45, esp. 26–27. It should be noted, however, that there is no evidence of such a practice as early as the *first half* of the twelfth century. The date when the Jonah relief was reemployed by a *marmorarius* is not known. The Achilles relief comes from Santa Maria in Aracoeli and may have been put to use there in the late twelfth century. It seems to have been in some relationship to the ambo (see P. F. Casimiro Romano, *Memorie istoriche della chiesa e convento di S. Maria in Araceli di Roma* [Rome 1736] 127–28), which bears the signature of two *marmorarii* who are known to have worked sometime before 1210 at Città Castellana. The ambo has not survived in its original form (see Hutton [n. 11 above] 18–19, 35; Bessone Aurelj [n. 11 above] 20; R. E. Malmstrom, "The Twelfth Century Church of S. Maria in Capitolio and the Capitoline Obelisk," *Römisches Jahrbuch für Kunstgeschichte* 16 [1976] 1–16, esp. 11 with fig. 14).

[13]Rodolfo A. Lanciani, *Storia degli scavi di Roma* (4 vols. Rome 1902–12) 1.10, 12.

[14]For the view that the armrests were made for the throne in 1123, see especially Giovenàle (n. 3 above) 31, 174–76, and Hans Wentzel, "Antiken-Imitationen des. 12 und 13. Jahrhunderts in Italien," *Zeitschrift für Kunstwissenschaft* 9 (1955) 29–72, esp. 40. On the other hand, the armrests were considered spoils by Karl Noehles ("Die Kunst der Cosmaten und die Idee der Renovatio Romae," *Festschrift Werner Hager* [Recklinghausen 1966] 17–37, esp. 24) and Arnold Esch (n. 8 above, 29). A weakness of this latter thesis has been that the suggestions made by its proponents regarding the original context and use of the pieces do not make sense in terms of the physical shape of the armrests. This difficulty has been resolved in a recent article in which they are interpreted as having been originally supports of a throne. The throne on which Christ is seated in the central scene of the sarcophagus of Junius Bassus provides a convincing parallel (Francesco Gandolfo, "Reimpiego di sculture antiche nei troni papali del XII secolo," *Rendiconti della Pontificia Accademia Romana di Archeologia* 47 [1976] 203–18, esp. 204). It should be noted also that on

of the *marmorarii*'s work, however, is not their skill at imitation but their ability to enter into the spirit of ancient art without copying a specific model; witness the tomb of Alfanus in the vestibule of Santa Maria in Cosmedin, with its severe lines, restrained ornamentation, harmoniously balanced proportions, and classical pediment which screens a painted arcosolium arch (fig. 32).[15]

The polychrome mosaic inlay which is a distinctive feature of so much of this decorative marble work is an inheritance from the *opus sectile* of late Antiquity. The craft tradition was never entirely lost in Rome.[16] But its dramatic flowering in our period was due to influence from Monte Cassino and indirectly from Byzantium, whence abbot Desiderius had imported specialists to make the pavement for his new church. In the richly inlaid pavements of the Roman twelfth-century basilicas, the links with Monte Cassino—and via Monte Cassino with Constantinople—are evident.[17] As this study proceeds we shall frequently encounter cases in which Byzantium was the source of a renewed flowering of ancient forms and techniques in Italy, though in this instance, as in others, artists in the Greek East were instrumental not only in preserving an ancient tradition but also in transforming and developing it.

The most important and the most distinctive element of the Roman churches is the pictorial decoration of their walls. In the apse of the church of San Clemente, rebuilt in the first quarter of the twelfth century, mural mosaic—an eminently "Early Christian" medium—made its triumphant reappearance in Rome after a virtual lapse of some 250 years (fig. 33). Within two decades there followed pope Innocent II's equally sumptuous decoration of the apse of Santa Maria in Trastevere.[18] It is certain that here again Monte Cassino, and indirectly Byzantium, stand behind the revival.[19] But Byzantine artists had been called in by Desiderius mainly because the technical know-

---

the inside of both armrests are slots, evidently stemming from an earlier employment in a different context; and that the marble of the (indubitably medieval) back of the throne is of a different color. Thus it should no longer be doubted that the armrests are spoils. But in other instances uncertainty remains; see in general Esch (n. 8 above) 37–41.

[15] Giovenale (n. 3 above) 9, 118–19, 172–74; Josef Deér, *The Dynastic Porphyry Tombs of the Norman Period in Sicily*, trans. G. A. Gillhoff, Dumbarton Oaks Studies 5 (Cambridge Mass. 1959) 30 and fig. 6. See also the study by Herbert Bloch in the present volume.

[16] Guglielmo Matthiae, "Componenti del gusto decorativo cosmatesco," *Rivista dell'Istituto nazionale d'archeologia e storia dell'arte* n.s. 1 (1952) 249–81, esp. 250–56.

[17] Ibid. 256ff. For the Monte Cassino pavement see now Angelo Pantoni, *Le vicende della Basilica di Montecassino attraverso la documentazione archeologica*, Miscellanea Cassinese 36 (Monte Cassino 1973) 101–37, 180–93; also Herbert Bloch's paper in this volume and his forthcoming work on Monte Cassino, which will include a revised version of his observations on the pavement, "Monte Cassino, Byzantium, and the West in the Early Middle Ages," *Dumbarton Oaks Papers* 3 (1946) 196–97. A monograph on the *opus sectile* pavements of the Roman twelfth- and thirteenth-century churches by Dorothy Glass is awaiting publication; meanwhile see her article "Papal Patronage in the Early Twelfth Century: Notes on the Iconography of Cosmatesque Pavements," JWCI 32 (1969) 386–90.

[18] Guglielmo Matthiae, *Mosaici medioevali delle chiese di Roma* (Rome 1967) 279–304 with pls. XLVIII–LIII, 228–59 (San Clemente); 305–14 with pls. LIV, LVII, 229, 260–68 (Santa Maria in Trastevere).

[19] Hélène Toubert, "Le renouveau paléochrétien à Rome au début du XIIe siècle," *Cahiers archéologiques* 20 (1970) 99–154, esp. 152. Ernst Kitzinger, "The First Mosaic Decoration of Salerno Cathedral," *Jahrbuch der österreichischen Byzantinistik* 21 (1972) 149–62 (reprinted in idem,

how had been lost in Italy. His purpose had been to recreate mosaic in the Early Christian manner. This Early Christian revival did, indeed, quickly take root in the south, and the newly established tradition was taken up—and pushed to the limit—by papal patrons in twelfth-century Rome, where suitable models were, of course, readily at hand. The fourth-, fifth-, and sixth-century models on which the Roman apse decorations are based have been fully identified in recent studies.[20] But these studies have also made it clear in what a free and sovereign manner the models were handled by the medieval artists. Motifs gleaned from disparate sources were imaginatively combined; and, what is most important, the designers for all their "pédanterie archéologique"[21] used the ancient vocabulary to convey new and highly topical messages.

Interestingly enough, in both of these mosaic decorations a composition based on an early model was enriched at its very center by images quite foreign to the Early Christian tradition. At San Clemente, the magnificent rinceau which fills the entire conch (and which is modeled on a fifth-century mosaic still extant in the nearby Lateran—see fig. 34) shows, sprouting from its core, a cross with an explicit crucifixion scene. Along with other motifs this scene helps to make palpable the vision of the "vine" as Christ's living Church, proclaimed in the accompanying inscription. At Santa Maria in Trastevere, the composition is basically faithful to a time-honored scheme of which the sixth-century mosaic of Santi Cosma e Damiano is the classical prototype. But the center of this composition is occupied by a highly innovative grouping, based on the liturgy and ceremonial of Assumption Day (and indirectly on the Song of Songs), whereby Christ shares his glory with the Virgin and thus, at least implicitly, with his Church.[22] Even in this central group, however, the antiquarian bent of the period's patrons and artists comes to the fore. Indeed, it here serves to make a very specific and very telling point. For the countenances of Christ and the Virgin were modeled after two famous and ancient Roman icons whose encounter and throne-sharing was a climactic event in the solemnities of Assumption Day.[23]

In both churches the mosaic on the wall surrounding the apse is based once again on a famous prototype from early times: the mosaic which pope Leo I had had made for the basilica of San Paolo fuori le mura. But other elements

The Art of Byzantium and the Medieval West [Bloomington and London 1976] 271–89). For this and what follows see also idem, "The Gregorian Reform and the Visual Arts: A Problem of Method," TRHS 5th ser. 22 (1972) 87–102.

[20]For San Clemente see Toubert (n. 19 above) 122–54; for Santa Maria in Trastevere, Matthiae (n. 18 above) 306–07, 309–10.

[21]The phrase is Hélène Toubert's (n. 19 above, 105).

[22]G. A. Wellen, "Sponsa Christi: Het Absismozaïek van de Santa Maria in Trastevere te Rome en het Hooglied," *Feestbundel F. van der Meer* (Amsterdam 1966) 148–59.

[23]I presented the evidence for this statement in a lecture delivered at the University of Pittsburgh in 1976 which will be published in due course. [See introductory note above.—eds.] In general terms, the suggestion that the central group of the mosaic of Santa Maria in Trastevere refers to the annual procession on August 15, in which the venerable icon of Christ from the Lateran was carried, has been made repeatedly; see, most recently, Philippe Verdier, "Suger a-t-il été en France le créateur du thème iconographique du couronnement de la Vierge?" *Gesta* 15 (1976) 227–36, esp. 230.

are also included—particularly at San Clemente, where certain features seem to hark back to the mosaic in a corresponding position in the triclinium of pope Leo III in the Lateran, a major monument of a preceding "Early Christian Renaissance" which Roman art had experienced at the time of Charlemagne.[24]

In the fresco decorations of the period, it is the settings—the framework and its ornament—which provide the most tangible evidence of intensive and loving study of ancient models, pagan as well as Christian. The principal extant examples—in the lower church of San Clemente (ca. 1100), in the nave of Santa Maria in Cosmedin (ca. 1123), and the fragments recovered from the crypt of San Nicola in Carcere (1128)—have been thoroughly discussed elsewhere, in an excellent study in which the ornamental repertory has been traced to its ancient sources.[25] The figure-subjects which the fresco painters were commissioned to represent are extremely varied but all the more interesting for that reason. Outright revivals of Early Christian compositions are rare, though the roundel with Christ's Baptism from San Nicola in Carcere clearly harks back to fifth- and sixth-century renderings of that subject.[26] The famous frescoes in the lower church of San Clemente, depicting events in the life of the titular saint, reflect in their stylistic rendering the influence of Byzantine painting—miniature painting in particular—but cannot be traced to any specific models.[27] The poorly preserved cycles in the nave of Santa Maria in Cosmedin followed in a general way a traditional Roman basilican scheme, in that they included both Old and New Testament sequences. But at least the selection of subjects from the Old Testament seems to have been unusual. Those on the left-hand wall—long mistaken for episodes from the life of Charlemagne—illustrate the early chapters of the Book of Ezekiel, while those on the wall opposite are thought to depict episodes from the Book of Daniel.[28]

The paintings of Santa Maria in Cosmedin undoubtedly belong to the renovation of the church under pope Calixtus II (1119–24).[29] This pope also

[24]Toubert (n. 19 above) 150–51. For the Carolingian revival in Rome, see the recent volume *Roma e l'età carolingia* (Rome 1976), including, with particular reference to the triclinium mosaic of Leo III, the contribution by Hans Belting ("I mosaici dell'aula leonina come testimonianza della prima 'renovatio' nell'arte medievale di Roma" 167–82). See also n. 63 below.

[25]Toubert (n. 19 above) 101–12 and passim.

[26]Ibid. 118–19 and fig. 28.

[27]Garrison (n. 4 above) 2.173–80. Otto Demus, *Romanesque Mural Painting*, trans. Mary Whittall (London and New York 1970) 84, 299–300, pls. 47–49 and on p. 43.

[28]The correct identification of the Ezekiel sequence is due to Ian Short, who has refuted point by point the interpretation of these scenes as precociously early illustrations of the *chansons des gestes*, an interpretation originally proposed by Giovenale and repeated by many scholars since ("Le pape Calixte II, Charlemagne et les fresques de Santa Maria in Cosmedin," CCM 13 [1970] 229–38). It should be noted that of the so-called Daniel cycle—again an interpretation proposed by Giovenale—only seven scenes have survived (out of an original twelve) and that some of the identifications are by no means certain. If one accepts them all, one must conclude that the order of the episodes did not strictly follow the biblical text; see Giovenale (n. 3 above) 199–206. As for the New Testament scenes in the lower register, they are very fragmentary and there are large gaps. Only five scenes remain on the left-hand wall and four on the right. Here too the sequence of subjects as identified by Giovenale (ibid. 235–40) raises problems.

[29]See notes 3, 14, 15, and 28 above.

initiated an ambitious project of fresco decoration in the Lateran palace, which extolled as a great triumph the conclusion of the Investiture Controversy through the Concordat of Worms in 1122.[30] Unfortunately these frescoes were destroyed in the eighteenth century and are known only from descriptions, drawings, and engravings made before that time. The project involved two interiors in the papal residence, the Chamber for Secret Councils and the adjacent sanctuary of St Nicholas built by Calixtus as a palace chapel. The pope had the text of the *privilegium* granted by the emperor to the Roman Church monumentally displayed on the walls of the Chamber. He also had his and his predecessors' triumphs over their respective adversaries graphically represented on these walls. In the apse of the chapel, which was decorated some ten years later by antipope Anacletus II,[31] the Reform papacy's self-image as a restorer of the ancient past was proclaimed with all possible concreteness and emphasis (fig. 35). Portraits of the popes of the Investiture Controversy were displayed in the company of the greatest among their predecessors of the fourth, fifth, and sixth centuries; and the centerpiece of the composition was a replica of the venerable ancient icon of the Virgin from Santa Maria in Trastevere (Anacletus's titular church), an instance of studied antiquarianism (fig. 36) which anticipates the "citing" of ancient icons by Innocent II a few years later.[32] Innocent in turn made a further addition to this triumphal imagery in the Lateran by commissioning for another chamber, built by him near the chapel of St Nicholas, a series of scenes depicting his reception and crowning of the German emperor Lothar III. These paintings with their provocative verse inscription (which said that the pictures showed the emperor becoming the pope's vassal) touched off a furor in the following decade when Frederick Barbarossa sought to have them removed. They survived, however, at least in part, until the sixteenth century, when they were recorded by Panvinio in a rough sketch.[33]

Only dimly known to us in their visual aspect, these papal triumphal paintings of the 1120s–40s are difficult to evaluate in art-historical terms. It has been plausibly suggested that those of Calixtus II must have looked somewhat like the frescoes in the lower church of San Clemente.[34] Certainly, except for its frames and settings, and except also for the occasional antiquarian "quotation" in the imagery itself, this propaganda art was not archaizing in

[30]Gerhart B. Ladner, *Die Papstbildnisse des Altertums und des Mittelalters* (2 vols. Vatican City 1941–70) 1.192–218 and pls. 19, 20; Herbert Bloch, "The Schism of Anacletus II and the Glanfeuil Forgeries of Peter the Deacon of Monte Cassino," *Traditio* 8 (1952) 159–264, esp. 178–80; Christopher Walter, "Papal Political Imagery in the Medieval Lateran Palace," *Cahiers archéologiques* 20 (1970) 155–76 and 21 (1971) 109–36. On the political motivation of Calixtus's paintings see Robert L. Benson, *The Bishop-Elect* (Princeton 1968) 304.

[31]I follow Herbert Bloch (see preceding note) in attributing this composition in its entirety to Anacletus II.

[32]See above at n. 23. For the relationship of the central group in the Lateran fresco to the icon of Santa Maria in Trastevere, see Carlo Bertelli, *La Madonna di Santa Maria in Trastevere* (Rome 1961) 22–23; also Toubert (n. 19 above) 154.

[33]Ladner (n. 30 above) 2.17–22 and pl. 3; Walter (n. 30 above) 20.166–69, 21.123–33.

[34]Walter (n. 30 above) 21.109 with fig. 15a; Toubert (n. 19 above) 108.

the same way as were the mosaics of the period. It has also been shown, however, that much of the iconography was ultimately of Roman imperial parentage; and some of it may have been mediated by Byzantium.[35]

Byzantine influence definitely played a part in the revival of miniature-painting in Rome in the early twelfth century. The upturn in both the quality and the quantity of illustrated manuscripts at precisely the moment in which new initiatives began in architecture and the other arts is striking. There is no doubt that this craft, too, received a major impetus from Monte Cassino, though Byzantine influence must have reached the Roman scriptoria also from other sources.[36]

Chief products of the Roman ateliers are the monumental and richly illustrated "Giant Bibles," members of a large family of such Bibles which proliferated in France and Italy in the late eleventh century and which owe their existence to the Reform movement.[37] The group as a whole is considerably indebted to Carolingian antecedents.[38] On the other hand, the rich cycle of scenes with which the Book of Genesis is illustrated in some of the Roman Giant Bibles is certainly derived from a local Early Christian tradition.[39]

II. METHODS AND MOTIVATIONS OF THE ROMAN REVIVAL

It is time to recapitulate. Rome in the first half of the twelfth century harbored a true revival of the arts, dramatically sudden and broad in scope, with new departures in almost every artistic medium. It was not merely a new flowering but specifically a resurrection of the distant past.

Artists drew on a great variety of sources. Primarily, of course, they reappropriated and emulated Rome's own artistic heritage; no sharp distinction was made between what was pagan and what was Christian.[40] Within the Christian artistic patrimony of the city, the first great flowering of church art in

[35]Walter (n. 30 above) 21.109–36; see also Toubert (n. 19 above) 154 with n. 211.

[36]Garrison (n. 4 above) vols. 2–4 passim, esp. 2.24–38, 3.17, and 4.120. New Byzantine influence on Roman painting toward the middle of the twelfth century is evidenced also by the frescoes of Santa Croce in Gerusalemme. A master who was abreast of Byzantine developments worked there side by side with others who were perpetuating the tradition of San Clemente; see Demus (n. 27 above) 85, 301 and pl. 54; Carlo Bertelli, "Un problema medioevale 'romano,'" *Paragone (Arte)* 20 no. 231 (1969) 3–14.

[37]Heinrich Fichtenau, "Neues zum Problem der italienischen 'Riesenbibeln,'" MIÖG 58 (1950) 50–67. P. H. Brieger, "Bible Illustration and Gregorian Reform," *Studies in Church History* 2, ed. G. J. Cuming (London and Edinburgh 1965) 154–64. For the Roman group of manuscripts see Garrison (n. 4 above) vols. 2–4 passim, esp. 4.117–52.

[38]No attempt was made, though, to establish a single standard edition of the entire Bible, as under Charlemagne. Brieger (n. 37 above, 162) has suggested that the Italian production of Giant Bibles was stimulated by the example of the lavishly illuminated Bible of Charles the Bald, allegedly donated to the monastery of San Paolo fuori le mura by Gregory VII and still preserved there today. There is, however, no trace of any influence having been exerted on the twelfth-century illuminators by this particular codex.

[39]Garrison (n. 4 above) 4.201–10.

[40]This important point was rightly made by Hélène Toubert at the outset of her excellent study (n. 19 above, 99 n. 2). For the ideological background, see my remarks in "The Gregorian Reform" (n. 19 above) 97–102.

the fourth, fifth, and sixth centuries was of particular interest. Much also was absorbed from the Greek East. Byzantine elements were mediated by Monte Cassino, where a planned and purposeful revival had taken place some forty years earlier, but there are also indications of direct influence from the Greek sphere. This influence in turn meant a further strengthening of the antique element, since so much of what Byzantine art had to offer was ultimately Hellenistic or Roman. Finally, certain works of the Carolingian period also seem to have attracted the attention of patrons and artists, a phenomenon no doubt due to the fact that Carolingian art itself was saturated with antique—and especially Early Christian—elements. Indeed, in its Roman version that art anticipated in many ways the revival movement of the early twelfth century.[41]

The methods whereby the ancient heritage was assimilated and used range over a wide spectrum—from physical appropriation, via literal copying and free combination, to sovereign and imaginative re-creation, often with new accents and new messages. Literal copying, of course, entailed a particularly close study of the models used. This occurs most commonly in ornamental art—in the decorative framework of mosaics and frescoes and in the sculptured ornaments of buildings and church furnishings. While in some instances from the latter sphere a purely materialistic interpretation of copying activities might suffice—craftsmen might be said to have resorted to faithful imitation of cornices, moldings, and so on, when prefabricated material extracted from ancient ruins gave out—the lavish use of the ancient ornamental repertory in painting certainly indicates that these forms were of intrinsic interest. Instances of free combination of motifs, to say nothing of new creations in the classical spirit, further bear this out.

Slavish copying is much less evident in the great figure-compositions in painting and mosaic. Even when the Early Christian source is obvious—as, for instance, in the great rinceau in the apse of San Clemente—the rendering is not so close to the model that anyone might be deceived and take this for Early Christian work (figs. 33, 34). The heavy linear style of the figures in the mosaic of Santa Maria in Trastevere is unmistakably Romanesque. In these works, stylistic independence from the models that furnished so much of the iconography goes hand in hand with the new content which that iconography was made to convey. At the same time, the Trastevere mosaic provides a case (so far, unique in all twelfth-century art) where advantage was taken of the artist's imitative skill to single out by stylistic means just one element, an element which thus became an (eminently meaningful) "quotation" of a much earlier image.[42]

As for the historical forces that generated this entire revival movement in Rome, undoubtedly central were the purposes and aspirations of the papacy.

---

[41]In the period of Leo III, as in the early twelfth century, the return to Early Christian pictorial models went hand in hand with extensive physical restoration of early churches (Belting [n. 24 above] 175–76). There are analogies also in the manner in which early pictorial models were modified so that they became vehicles for new messages (ibid. 174).

[42]See above at n. 23.

Not only did the popes provide much of the patronage, but often we see a clear reflection of, or even a direct reference to, the contemporary political and ideological scene, a scene dominated by the last phase of the Investiture Controversy and by what the papacy saw—or, at any rate, wished to be seen—as its triumph in that struggle. Nevertheless, it is an oversimplification to speak of the art of the Roman "protorenaissance" as an "art monarchique."[43] Distinctions need to be made.

The initial phase, associated largely with pope Paschal II (1099–1118), is a continuation of the revivals of Early Christian art that had taken place in other centers in Italy in the eleventh century, most notably the Desiderian revival at Monte Cassino. That enterprise had been motivated by the ideas and purposes of the Gregorian Reform. What might crudely be called its propaganda element was, however, only implicit and would have been lost on a beholder who could not make the association with the prototypal monuments of the Early Christian period.[44] The same is true of the remarkable series of church buildings in Florence that were erected or renovated in an extraordinarily classicizing style during the eleventh century under the impulse of the Reform movement.[45] And the same is true also of the Roman revival in its first phase. *Ecclesiae primitivae forma*[46] is most palpably evoked, but the message is not spelled out. The links with the antecedent initiative at Monte Cassino are tangible; and the time lag, customarily attributed to the troubles that beset the papacy during the last decades of the eleventh century, ultimately remains puzzling.[47] In Rome one can properly speak only of a "Paschalian revival."[48]

In the twenties and thirties, papal art becomes more explicit in its messages. Anacletus II, the last "Gregorian" on the throne of St Peter, spells out the linkage with the heroic age of the papacy from Sylvester to Gregory the Great.[49] But the principal theme now is victory and the subjugation of all adversaries, proclaimed with the help of ancient pictorial formulae.[50] These propagandistic works usher in the truly monarchic phase of papal art. Already the

---

[43]André Grabar, "La décoration des coupoles à Karye Camii et les peintures italiennes du Dugento," *Jahrbuch der österreichischen byzantinischen Gesellschaft* 6 (1957) 111–24 at 117; reprinted in idem, *L'art de la fin de l'antiquité et du moyen age* (3 vols. Paris 1968) 2.1055–65 at 1060.

[44]See my paper "The Gregorian Reform" (n. 19 above) passim, esp. 100.

[45]See below, p. 651.

[46]For this term, see Giovanni Miccoli, *Chiesa gregoriana: Ricerche sulla riforma del secolo XI*, Storici antichi e moderni n.s. 17 (Florence 1966) 84, 225–99.

[47]The puzzle is heightened rather than lessened by the fact that in one isolated instance Monte Cassino's lead was followed in Rome quite promptly and by none other than Hildebrand himself. In 1070, Hildebrand, with the help of Pantaleone of Amalfi, procured from Constantinople a magnificent bronze door for the basilica of San Paolo fuori le mura, in evident imitation of what Desiderius had done at Monte Cassino four years earlier. See [Enrico Josi, et al.], *La porta bizantina di San Paolo* (Rome 1967); Herbert Bloch, "L'ordine dei pannelli nella porta della Basilica di S. Paolo," *Rendiconti della Pontificia Accademia Romana di Archeologia* 43 (1971) 267–81.

[48]Garrison (n. 4 above) 2.80.

[49]See fig. 35 and above at n. 31.

[50]Above at n. 35.

throne of Calixtus II in Santa Maria in Cosmedin, with its lions as armrests and its ornate "halo" as a foil for the occupant's head, is the seat of a temporal ruler (fig. 31).[51] But it was Innocent II who went farthest in emphasizing the imperial theme. In the inscription of his paintings in the Lateran he proclaimed himself the German emperor's feudal overlord.[52] And the meaningful use of ancient spoils reached its high point when Innocent appropriated for his own tomb the porphyry sarcophagus of the emperor Hadrian.[53] It is thus no accident that the church building which was the major object of his artistic patronage is the most classical of all medieval architectural interiors in Rome and the one most lavishly and conspicuously adorned with true antiques (figs. 29–30).[54] Nor is it pure chance that what has been aptly called "political archeology" reached its full literary expression during Innocent's pontificate: it was during his brief final years of undisputed power—after the death of the antipope Anacletus II and before the revolt of the Roman Commune in 1143—that the *Mirabilia urbis Romae*, the first guide to the antiquities of Rome, was composed.[55]

The revival of Antiquity has at this point become a glorification of empire. It is a far cry from the idealization of the early Church that had motivated earlier art patrons from Desiderius to Paschal II. The "renaissance" in Roman art thus ends up serving ideas and interests quite distinct from those of the Reform which had provided so much of the original impetus. To what extent the revival has here parted ways with "reform" is brought home forcefully to anyone who after visiting Innocent's basilica in Trastevere proceeds to the abbey of Tre Fontane outside the walls not far from San Paolo. The monastery was given by Innocent to St Bernard as a house for his order and taken over by Cistercian monks in 1140. Its new church was built soon thereafter and is thus an almost exact contemporary of Santa Maria in Trastevere. But the only feature of the building which conforms with Roman tradition is its basilican nave. Otherwise the church is a pure representative of French Cistercian architecture at its most austere (fig. 37).[56] It is an admonition in stone, a mute yet eloquent counterpart to the treatise which St Bernard addressed to the disciple he had installed as the first abbot of Tre Fontane when a few years later that disciple ascended the papal throne as Eugene III. By its very contrast to prevailing papal fashion the architecture of the abbey underscores St Bernard's point: the pope had become the heir of Constantine more than the successor of Peter.[57]

[51]Above at n. 14; see Giovenale (n. 3 above) 174; Deér (n. 15 above) 140–42.

[52]Above at n. 33.

[53]Deér (n. 15 above) 146–54.

[54]Above at nn. 6–7.

[55]Roberto Valentini and Giuseppe Zucchetti, eds., *Codice topografico della Città di Roma* 3, Fonti per la storia d'Italia 90 (Rome 1946) 3–65; for the date of composition see 5–6. For the term "politische Archäologie" see Schramm, *KRR* 1.215.

[56]Hanno Hahn, *Die frühe Kirchenbaukunst der Zisterzienser* (Berlin 1957) 171–73 and figs. 162–64.

[57]"Petrus hic est, qui nescitur processisse aliquando vel gemmis ornatus, vel sericis, non tectus auro, non vectus equo albo, nec stipatus milite, nec circumstrepentibus saeptus ministris. . . . In

Nowhere else has the twelfth-century renaissance in art so evident and tangible an ideological background as in Rome between 1100 and 1150. Yet it may be asked whether this essentially political background is by itself altogether sufficient to explain the artistic achievement embodied in the monuments. When a church was adorned with classical carvings, when holy figures or scenes from the Bible or from a saint's life were surrounded by motifs borrowed from imperial Roman wall decoration, the antique flavor of these elements, their associative value, was certainly important. It was meant to convey a message. But there is good reason to believe that it was also enjoyed.[58] The very fact that the classicizing taste comes to the fore most strongly in incidentals—in frames and accessories—suggests an element of play, of sheer esthetic pleasure. In some way that is difficult to define and impossible to document, both artists and beholders must have found these ancient forms life-enhancing. We shall find more evidence of this less strict, less solemn aspect of the revival in the second half of the century, though not so much in Rome as in other parts of Italy.[59]

In Rome, the second half of the century is in fact strikingly poor in artistic achievement compared with the first. No major church was newly built, and even major restorations were few. The only mosaic of the period is that of Santa Maria Nova, one of the principal churches in the domain of the Frangipani, and it is an oddly provincial work compared with the mosaics of San Clemente and Santa Maria in Trastevere, from which part of the imagery was derived.[60] The only important fresco cycle is that executed toward the end of the century at San Giovanni a Porta Latina, a cycle which, interestingly enough, harks back once again to fifth-century prototypes.[61] The work of the *marmorarii* continued, but unresolved questions of chronology make it difficult to measure their accomplishment during this period.[62]

There was a new spurt of activity—particularly marked in the output of the *marmorarii*, but also in other arts—at the turn of the century and lasting well into the thirteenth. Due primarily to papal patronage, this new flowering is once again both strongly classicizing and keyed to themes of power and

---

his successisti, non Petro, sed Constantino." *De consideratione ad Eugenium papam* 4.3.6, *Sancti Bernardi opera*, ed. Leclercq 3.453.

[58]The wordy inscription which accompanied the display of ancient spoils on the exterior of the so-called Casa dei Crescenzi—remarkable enough for the articulate expression it gives to the sentiments which inspired the architecture of the building—is doubly interesting for making a fine distinction between "vana gloria" and "Romae veterem renovare decorem." The former is disclaimed, of course, and only the latter counts as a motivation. For the inscription see Vincenzo Forcella, *Iscrizioni delle chiese e d'altri edificii di Roma dal secolo XI fino ai giorni nostri* (14 vols. in 7 Rome 1869–84) 13.535–38. See also n. 10 above and n. 64 below.

[59]Below at notes 92–93.

[60]Matthiae (n. 18 above) 315–21 and figs. 269, 271–77.

[61]Guglielmo Matthiae, *Pittura romana del medioevo* (2 vols. Rome 1966) 2.102–16 and figs. 85–96; Demus (n. 27 above) 85.

[62]Opinions concerning the date of the paschal candlestick at San Paolo fuori le mura, the principal sculptural work of the period, range from ca. 1170 to the early thirteenth century. See Hjalmar Torp, "Monumentum Resurrectionis," *Acta ad archaeologiam et artium historiam pertinentia* 1 (1962) 79–112, esp. 89 with n. 3; Noehles (n. 14 above) 26.

triumph[63] (e.g., at Città Castellana—fig. 38). It reflects the renewed ascendancy of the popes in the age of Innocent III, and thus serves to confirm how intimately the artistic revivals in Rome were linked to the shifting fortunes and aspirations of the Church. The communal power that had arisen at the very end of the pontificate of Innocent II and had cut short the papacy's open pursuit of secular dominion was slow in giving artistic expression to its own program. For all its self-conscious and at times grandiloquent attachment to the remote past, the newly resurrected *sacer senatus* did not during the twelfth century become a major sponsor of an artistic revival, though the conspicuous and articulate display of antiques in the façade of the so-called Casa dei Crescenzi may date from this period.[64]

III. ITALY OUTSIDE OF ROME

We leave Rome to cast rapid glances at other parts of Italy. To deal with each region *in extenso* is patently impossible. The sole aim of the remarks which follow is to place the renaissance in Roman twelfth-century art in a broader perspective.

Once we enlarge our field of vision, it immediately becomes apparent that in launching a major artistic revival about 1100 A.D. the Eternal City was decidedly a late-comer. Of special importance are the substantially earlier revivals in Monte Cassino, Florence, and Venice.

[63]Noehles (n. 14 above) 30–31. Note particularly the triumphal arch added to the façade of the cathedral of Città Castellana in 1210 (our fig. 38); its inscription proclaims peace in the same triumphant words from Luke 2:14 that had previously been inscribed in mosaic on the apsidal arches of the Lateran triclinium at the end of the eighth century and of the church of San Clemente in the early twelfth century. The erection of the Capitoline obelisk, which Noehles attributed to the initiative of the Roman Commune in the 1250s (ibid. 18–23), is also likely to have taken place about 1200 and under ecclesiastical auspices; that is to say, it probably was a monument of the same period and conceived in much the same spirit as the Città Castellana arch. See Malmstrom (n. 12 above) 12–16.

[64]See notes 10 and 58 above. I agree with W. S. Heckscher ("Relics of Pagan Antiquity in Mediaeval Settings," JWI 1 [1937–38] 204–20, esp. 207) and Umberto Gnoli ("La casa di Nicola di Crescente o Casa di Pilato," *L'Urbe* 5.10 [Oct. 1940] 2–10, esp. 8) that the communal movement of the twelfth century provides a plausible context for this bizarre creation. Ferdinand Gregorovius aptly compared the tenor of the inscriptions with that of the speech addressed by the emissaries of the Roman Senate to Frederick Barbarossa at Sutri in 1155 (*History of the City of Rome in the Middle Ages*, trans. Annie Hamilton [8 vols. in 13 London 1903–12] 4.2.688). There seems to be no cogent reason to accept the identification of Nicholas, who built the house and had himself commemorated in its inscriptions, with the *magister sacri palatii* who figures prominently in Benzo of Alba's account of the events of 1062 (see Carlo Cecchelli, *I Crescenzi, I Savelli, I Cenci* [Rome 1942] 19–22, 33. Fedele's study of 1940, to which Cecchelli refers, and his own earlier studies, which he also cites, were not accessible to me). However, I am informed by Richard Krautheimer that on epigraphical grounds the inscriptions perhaps should be attributed to the late eleventh or early twelfth century rather than to the middle of the twelfth century. The problem requires further study. The only definite evidence within the twelfth century linking the Roman Commune with activities of an architectural or antiquarian nature is provided by documents which indicate its concern with monuments of Antiquity; see the essays by Robert L. Benson and Herbert Bloch in the present volume.

The initiative undertaken at Monte Cassino by abbot Desiderius has already been referred to at several points.[65] As we have seen, the new departures in Rome were heavily indebted to this earlier effort, which had sought to resurrect the art of the early Church and had drawn strength from the artistic resources of Byzantium. It was the spirit and the program of the Gregorian Reform which had motivated Desiderius, the future pope Victor III; and in due course the momentum he had purposefully generated in matters of art was taken up by his like-minded successors on the papal throne.

Florence experienced a remarkable "protorenaissance" in architecture in the eleventh century.[66] A period of extensive building and rebuilding of churches began with the installation in 1045 of bishop Gerard, a Cluniac monk who later became pope as Nicholas II (1059–61). While the Romanesque elements in this architecture are unquestionably strong,[67] what gives many of these buildings their specific character is the highly imaginative use made of classical and Early Christian forms, most conspicuously in the famous marble incrustations of exterior and interior walls and in decorative detail. The affinities of the Florence Baptistery (fig. 39) with the Roman Pantheon were recognized as early as the fourteenth century; and the question of whether the existing structure is an altogether new creation of the eleventh and twelfth centuries or the restoration of an Early Christian building has not been entirely settled to this day.[68] The heaviest concentration of new initiatives occurred in the late 1050s, when Florence was for a time the headquarters of the Reformers. Three or four churches were consecrated by, or in the presence of, pope Nicholas in one period of a little over two months (1059–60). One of these was the rebuilt church of San Lorenzo, whose fourth-century predecessor had been consecrated by St Ambrose. And it is worth noting that not only Hildebrand and Peter Damiani were present on this occasion but also Desiderius of Monte Cassino.[69] The grandiose project launched at Monte Cassino six years later may well owe something to what its abbot had seen in Florence.

Venice stands somewhat apart. The most important patronage here was secular, and the region possessed a strong and highly visible Early Christian artistic heritage dating back to the fifth and sixth centuries. There is evidence in Venice and in the North Adriatic area of artists in the eleventh century go-

[65]Above at notes 17, 19, and 44.

[66]See in general Walter Paatz, "Die Hauptströmungen in der Florentiner Baukunst des frühen und hohen Mittelalters und ihr geschichtlicher Hintergrund," *Mitteilungen des kunsthistorischen Institutes in Florenz* 6 (1941) 33–72; Walter Horn, "Romanesque Churches in Florence," *Art Bulletin* 25 (1943) 112–31.

[67]Paatz (n. 66 above) 43–49; Horn (n. 66 above) 124–30. Recent excavations beneath the cathedral have revealed for the eleventh-century rebuilding of the church of Santa Reparata a plan that exhibits Cluniac features; see Franklin Toker, "Excavations below the Cathedral of Florence, 1965–1974," *Gesta* 14.2 (1975) 17–36, esp. 32–34.

[68]Franklin Toker, "A Baptistery Below the Baptistery of Florence," *Art Bulletin* 58 (1976) 157–67.

[69]JL 1.557, 562 no. 4429. See also Paatz (n. 66 above) 68.

ing back to models of that period.[70] But Venice also had its eyes fastened intently on the Byzantine East. It was a complicated power game that prompted the rising Republic to construct its principal religious shrine after the model of Justinian's church of the Holy Apostles in Constantinople.[71] As in Monte Cassino, pictorial mosaic was considered an essential and integral feature of the prototypal architecture; and the Venetians, too, procured for the purpose specialized craftsmen from Greek lands. Indeed, here again a precedent may already have been set when Desiderius took a similar action in the late 1060s. There is good reason to believe that by that time Byzantine mosaicists had been at work in the Veneto for a number of years.[72] And the Venetian initiative, too, had important long-term effects. A course was set for developments that were to continue in the Veneto through the twelfth century and well into the thirteenth.

Haskins, speaking of the forces that brought on the twelfth-century renaissance, stressed the need to push back the inquiry into the eleventh century, "that obscure period of origins which holds the secret of the new movement."[73] The examples just cited show that this statement is eminently true for the revival of the arts in Italy. The roots of this revival lie indeed in the initiatives taken in various parts of the peninsula during the eleventh century.

Within the twelfth century, the most concentrated and sustained initiative in the realm of the visual arts undertaken anywhere in Italy outside Rome was that of the Norman kings in Sicily. Begun on a grand scale by Roger II in the 1130s, the Sicilian artistic enterprise exceeded even that of the popes in comprehensiveness. It involved secular as well as ecclesiastical art; it employed a very wide range of media; and it drew on an extraordinary variety of sources. King Roger collected skills and materials as systematically and purposefully as abbot Desiderius had done two generations earlier, though—alas—no chronicler set down for posterity a detailed account of his patronage.

[70]H. Stern, "Le pavement de la basilique de Pomposa (Italie)," *Cahiers archéologiques* 18 (1968) 157–69 (floor mosaics); Otto Demus, *The Church of San Marco in Venice*, Dumbarton Oaks Studies 6 (Washington D.C. 1960) 115, 117 (sculpture). For wall mosaics see n. 72 below.

[71]Demus (n. 70 above) Book One, History, passim, esp. 45–46, 88–100. The dependence on the Constantinopolitan model is spelled out in sources that are almost contemporary with the construction of the church, which began in 1063 (ibid. 90). It is now believed, however, that the first church of San Marco, built in the early ninth century, already followed the same model in its general layout (ibid. 65–66).

[72]The chronology of the Veneto mosaics is at present being reassessed as a result of the detailed photographic recording and thorough investigation of them being carried out by Otto Demus and Irina Andreescu under the auspices of Dumbarton Oaks. Even prior to this campaign, Demus had proposed a date around or just before the middle of the eleventh century for part of the mosaics in the main apse of the cathedral of Torcello ("Zu den Mosaiken der Hauptapsis von Torcello," *Starinar* [СТАРИНАР] n.s. 20 [1969] 53–57). For the Torcello mosaics, see now the articles by Irina Andreescu in *Dumbarton Oaks Papers* 26 (1972) 183–223 ("Torcello I. Le Christ inconnu; II. Anastasis et jugement dernier: Têtes vraies, têtes fausses") and 30 (1976) 245–341 ("Torcello III. La chronologie relative des mosaïques pariétales"), esp. 30.249–50 for the dating of the earliest phase, and 26.192–93, 30.257 for the revival of the Early Christian heritage of Ravenna.

[73]Haskins, *Ren* 16.

Fig. 29. Rome. Santa Maria in Trastevere (1140–43). Interior. Photo: Alinari.

Fig. 30. Rome. Santa Maria in Trastevere. Below, ancient capital of nave column; right, ancient capital and cornice supporting triumphal arch. Photos: Anderson.

Fig. 32. Rome. Santa Maria in Cosmedin. Tomb of Alfanus (ca. 1123). Photo: Anderson.

Fig. 31. Rome. Santa Maria in Cosmedin. Episcopal throne (1123). Photo: Alinari.

Fig. 33 (above). Rome. San Clemente. Apse mosaic (first quarter of twelfth century). Photo: Gabinetto Fotografico Nazionale.

Fig. 34 (below). Rome. Lateran Baptistery. Apse mosaic (fifth century). Photo: Alinari.

Fig. 35. Rome. Lateran Palace. St Nicholas chapel (1130–38): apse. 1638 engraving of lost painting. After Gerhart B. Ladner, *Die Papstbildnisse des Altertums und des Mittelalters* (2 vols. Vatican City 1941–70) vol. 1 pl. 20a.

Fig. 36. Rome. Santa Maria in Trastevere. Icon of the Madonna and Child with angels and pope John VII (705–07). Photo courtesy of Carlo Bertelli.

Fig. 38. Cività Castellana. Cathedral. "Triumphal Arch" added to façade in 1210. Photo: Alinari.

Fig. 37. Rome. Abbey of Tre Fontane (ca. 1140–50). Interior. Photo courtesy of the Biblioteca Hertziana, Rome.

Fig. 39. Florence. Baptistery (eleventh–twelfth century). Interior. Photo: Alinari.

Fig. 40. Palermo. Cappella Palatina. Interior view to west, showing mosaics (ca. 1145–70) and Fatimid ceiling (ca. 1140–50). Photo: Anderson.

Fig. 41 (above). Palermo. Cappella Palatina. Mosaic in nave (ca. 1160): the Tower of Babel. Photo: Anderson.

Fig. 42 (left). Monreale. Cathedral. Mosaic in nave (ca. 1180–90): the Tower of Babel. Photo: Anderson.

Fig. 43. Palermo. Cathedral. Porphyry tomb from Cefalù (1145; since 1215 the tomb of emperor Henry VI). Photo: Anderson.

Fig. 44. Monreale. Cloister. Capital (west, no. 17; ca. 1180–90) with nudes perched on floral decoration. Photo: Austin.

Fig. 45. Monreale. Cloister. Capital (south, no. 22; ca. 1180–90) with "Mithras slaying the bull." Photo: Austin.

Fig. 46. Lucca. Palazzo Mazzarosa. Relief by master Biduinus (late twelfth century): the Entry into Jerusalem.

Fig. 47. Pisa. Baptistery. East portal (ca. 1160): detail showing column shaft. Photo: Anderson.

In its secular sponsorship the Sicilian flowering is comparable to that which had begun earlier in Venice. But it lacked almost entirely the consciously retrospective element that was central to the doges' effort. Roger sought to bring together what was best and most serviceable in the art of his own time. He looked to Norman England and Fatimid Egypt, to Comnenian Byzantium, papal Rome, and Benedictine Monte Cassino. He vied with the great powers of his day, but he did not in his artistic endeavors set out to recover the past.

Thus the revival elements that appear in his monuments are incidental and, as it were, secondhand. For instance, it was presumably from Monte Cassino that the rich cycle of Old Testament scenes in Roger's court chapel (a cycle subsequently repeated in enriched form at Monreale) was derived (figs. 40–42).[74] But this south Italian source was permeated with Early Christian elements, to say nothing of the very idea of giving so much prominence to an Old Testament cycle—itself an Early Christian tradition.[75] Similarly—this has already been mentioned—the adoption of Byzantine forms always brought with it elements that were ultimately antique. Since the execution of the famous mosaic decorations in the churches and palaces of the dynasty was from the outset, and remained throughout the Norman era, essentially in the hands of Byzantine craftsmen, a good deal of what might be called latent classicism was thus automatically imported. In a sense there is more of an "antique" element in the mosaics of Monreale—the creation of William II, Roger's grandson—than in the mosaics of the first generation. Figures and scenes are more animated; there is a great deal of swift narrative action; and the whole conveys an impression of intense agitation (fig. 42). This, however, should not be taken as a sign of a "human awakening" in Sicily. Rather it reflects an important development which took place during this period in Byzantine art.[76] Sicily did, however, play a role in mediating this Byzantine "dynamic" style to the transalpine countries.[77]

The most palpably "antique" of the art forms adopted by Roger and then continued by his successors was the porphyry sarcophagus that became the dynasty's preferred type of funerary monument (fig. 43). Only in recent decades has a full understanding of these monuments been achieved; and it has been plausibly argued that in adopting this form in 1145 Roger was emulating pope Innocent II, who had been buried in Hadrian's porphyry

[74]Ernst Kitzinger, *The Mosaics of Monreale* (Palermo 1960) 60.

[75]Ernst Kitzinger, "The Mosaics of the Cappella Palatina in Palermo," *Art Bulletin* 31 (1949) 269–92, esp. 270–71 (reprinted in his *Art of Byzantium* [n. 19 above] 290–319).

[76]Otto Demus, *The Mosaics of Norman Sicily* (London 1949) 418–42; Kitzinger, *Mosaics* (n. 74 above) 74–84, 98–105; see also idem, "The Byzantine Contribution to Western Art of the Twelfth and Thirteenth Centuries," *Dumbarton Oaks Papers* 20 (1966) 25–47, esp. 30–31, 38–40 (reprinted in his *Art of Byzantium* [n. 19 above] 357–88).

[77]Ernst Kitzinger, "Norman Sicily as a Source of Byzantine Influence on Western Art in the Twelfth Century," *Byzantine Art, an European Art: Lectures* (Athens 1966) 121–47. Otto Demus, *Byzantine Art and the West* (New York 1970) 146–61, 180–81. Larry M. Ayres, "The Work of the Morgan Master at Winchester and English Painting of the Early Gothic Period," *Art Bulletin* 56 (1974) 201–23, esp. 215–21.

tomb just two years earlier.[78] Again, the "antique" form was not in itself a primary concern. The Sicily of Roger II would have to be credited with a more deliberate and direct revival of Antiquity if certain works of glyptic art could be attributed conclusively to that region and period,[79] but this is still a matter of controversy.[80] There are indeed conspicuous instances of a direct use or imitation of antiques in sculptural decorations dating from the last phase of Norman patronage; this, however, is a development which should be viewed in a broader context, as will be seen presently.

Nowhere in twelfth-century Italy were any artistic initiatives taken that can compare with those in Rome and Sicily in range and purposefulness. In both centers a great deal was "recovered" from the past, though, as we have seen, Rome far outstripped Sicily in this regard. In Rome, the main effort was concentrated in the first half of the century, while in the second half the city was relatively unproductive. Precisely in the latter period, however, one finds a scattering of revival phenomena in many places throughout the rest of Italy. Together, they amount to a development of considerable importance, though the time is hardly ripe for a valid synthesis.

Sculpture is the medium of principal interest here. In Sicily, the foremost example of the antique forms and motifs which now gained prominence is the sculptural decoration of the cloister of Monreale. It includes a profusion of classical foliate ornament, a great many nudes in a variety of poses and activities (fig. 44), and such motifs from ancient art as the *spinario* (the boy drawing a thorn from his foot) and "Mithras slaying the bull" (fig. 45).[81] Classical themes, classicizing figures, and extraordinarily faithful imitations of classical ornament also appear during this period in sculptures in Campania, Umbria, and Tuscany (figs. 46, 47).[82] In Lombardy, the rebirth of monumen-

---

[78]Deér (n. 15 above) passim; see esp. 152–54.

[79]See Josef Deér, "Die Basler Löwenkamee und der süditalienische Gemmenschnitt des 12. und 13. Jahrhunderts: Ein Beitrag zur Geschichte der abendländischen Protorenaissance," *Zeitschrift für schweizerische Archäologie und Kunstgeschichte* 14 (1953) 120–58, esp. 145.

[80]Panofsky, *Ren & Ren* 64 n. 1 (with references to Wentzel).

[81]Roberto Salvini, *Il chiostro di Monreale e la scultura romanica in Sicilia* (Palermo 1962). See also Carl D. Sheppard, Jr., "Iconography of the Cloister of Monreale," *Art Bulletin* 31 (1949) 159–69; idem, "A Stylistic Analysis of the Cloister of Monreale," *Art Bulletin* 34 (1952) 35–41. The prominent use at Monreale of a splendid series of Roman capitals (many with human heads) for the columns in the nave of the cathedral should also be noted here; see Wolfgang Krönig, *The Cathedral of Monreale and Norman Architecture in Sicily* (Palermo 1965) 40–43, 181–89, and figs. 28–31, 49–52.

[82]For Campania, see the literature cited by Dorothy Glass, "Romanesque Sculpture in Campania and Sicily: A Problem of Method," *Art Bulletin* 56 (1974) 315–24; for Umbria, Karl Noehles, "Die Fassade von S. Pietro in Tuscania: Ein Beitrag zur Frage der Antikenrezeption im 12. und 13. Jahrhundert in Mittelitalien," *Römisches Jahrbuch für Kunstgeschichte* 9–10 (1961–62) 13–72; for Tuscany, Carl D. Sheppard, Jr., "Classicism in Romanesque Sculpture in Tuscany," *Gesta* 15 (1976) 185–92 (for the Pisa Baptistery east portal—our fig. 47—see 185–88 and fig. 4). Some of the sculptures in question hark back to Christian rather than pagan Antiquity—proving once again that in the twelfth century the revival of the latter went hand in hand with a revival of the former. See, e.g., ibid. 189 with fig. 7 = our fig. 46 (Biduinus); also Dorothy Glass, "Sicily and Campania: The Twelfth-Century Renaissance," *The Twelfth Century*, ed. Ber-

tal sculpture that came early in the twelfth century with the rise of Roman-esque architecture had from the outset entailed a certain amount of borrowing from antique sources, particularly in the work of Wiligelmus of Modena.[83] But in this region, too, a new interest in Antiquity and extensive contacts (albeit more often indirect than direct) with antique models become apparent in the last decades of the century, most notably in the sculptures of Benedetto Antelami and his circle.[84]

A correct evaluation of these scattered phenomena depends to no small extent on an understanding of their art-historical affiliations and interrelation-ships. There is no doubt, for instance, that Antelamesque sculpture is heavily indebted to the "protorenaissance" art of St Gilles and Arles. In southern Italy, on the other hand, basic questions such as the relative priority of classicizing sculpture in different regions remain to be settled.[85] The degree to which southern ateliers during this period underwent influences from the north and from beyond the Alps is another unsolved problem. In the cloister capitals of Monreale, for instance, there is unmistakably a French element; and it is probably true to say that this remarkable series is altogether inexplicable without a transalpine contribution.[86] On the other hand, Rome, with its *mar-morarii* workshops established at least two generations earlier, also should be taken into account, the more so since an early dependence of Sicilian "classicism" on Rome has been conclusively demonstrated in the matter of porphyry monuments.[87]

With so many elementary problems unsolved, the art historian must hesi-tate to pronounce on the meaning of these revival phenomena and the

nard Levy and Sandro Sticca, The Center for Medieval and Early Renaissance Studies, State University of New York at Binghamton, Acta 2 (1975) 130–46, esp. 142–44 (Joseph cycle in the reliefs at Santa Restituta, Naples).

[83]René Jullian, "Les survivances antiques dans la sculpture lombarde au XIIe siècle," *Etudes italiennes* n.s. 1 (1931) 131–40, 217–28; idem, *L'éveil de la sculpture italienne* (Paris 1945) 50–56.

[84]Géza de Francovich, *Benedetto Antelami, architetto e scultore, e l'arte del suo tempo* (2 vols. Milan 1952) passim, esp. figs. 228–31, 255–57 (Parma Baptistery) and 387–88 (Borgo San Donnino); see also Jullian, "Les survivances" (n. 83 above) passim, esp. 224–26, and *L'éveil* (n. 83 above) 236–37.

[85]A monument important for this question is the episcopal throne in San Nicola at Bari. The date of 1098, to which it has been traditionally assigned and which appeared to be well documented, has always been hard to reconcile with the bold and free conception of the seminude caryatids supporting the seat. The validity of this date has now been seriously questioned and the throne has been attributed to the period following the destruction of Bari in 1156. See Pina Belli D'Elia, "La cattedra dell'Abate Elia: Precisazioni sul Romanico Pugliese," *Bollettino d'arte* 5th ser. 59 (1974) 1–17.

[86]Panofsky, *Ren & Ren* 64.

[87]See above at n. 78. A key role in setting off the production of classicizing sculpture in the south was attributed to the Roman *marmorarii* by Wentzel (n. 14 above) 56–68. See also Glass, "Romanesque Sculpture" (n. 82 above) 323, on the puzzling inscription "Ego Romanus filius Constantinus marmararius" (*sic*) on one of the Monreale capitals. On the other hand, it must be pointed out that the evidence particularly for *figure* sculpture produced by the Roman workshops during the first half of the twelfth century is weak, to say the least. Even in the second half of the century the pace of progress of the Roman ateliers in this respect is problematic. The key monu-ment here is the paschal candlestick of San Paolo fuori le mura, for which see above, n. 62.

motivating forces behind them. It may well be doubted, however, that whenever a classical motif was taken up by any of these sculptors it was always done with a profound and solemn purpose. The principle of "iconological usability" has been proclaimed as an essential condition for such revivals, at least in Rome.[88] The well-known *interpretatio christiana* of the "Mithras" motif on one of the Monreale capitals (fig. 45) is in line with this principle.[89] Yet, when a decoration such as that of the Monreale cloister is viewed in its entirety, doubts must arise. Fantasy is rampant in the display of images on these capitals. Even the selection made from biblical subjects appears "arbitrary and capricious."[90] The antique element is one among others, and the whole ensemble is totally unsystematic. A lack of strong ideological motivation is generally characteristic of the art produced under the patronage of William II, in contrast to that of Roger II, William's revered model.[91] One is tempted to agree with those who see in the cloister capitals simply a product of an "eminently sophisticated decorative taste."[92]

Of course, there are intermediate possibilities. A classical theme may be taken up, or a classical work physically reused, with a new interpretation supplied as an *ex post facto* justification. But in an ensemble such as the Monreale capitals the element of "play" is clearly important. Such elements seemed to be marginally present even in the earlier classical revival in Rome.[93] Some of the scattering of antique motifs in Italian sculpture from the second half of the twelfth century certainly should be understood in these terms. It is no less interesting for that reason. The classicizing efforts of this period lack the purposefulness of the movements which had gone before and in which some of them were undoubtedly rooted. It was only in the early thirteenth century—with the patronage of Innocent III in Rome, of Frederick II in the south, and of the doges after their triumph of 1204 in Venice—that such purposefulness returned. In part the new initiatives arose out of the diffuse activities and trends of the latter half of the twelfth century. But in each instance there emerged a new kind of retrospective art with a distinct identity and a sharp ideological focus of its own.[94]

Initiatives taken by powerful and clearsighted patrons in the pursuit of great causes thus become crucial once more. Indeed, such initiatives—by leaders

[88]Noehles (n.14 above) 31 ("ikonologische Verwertbarkeit").

[89]Panofsky, *Ren & Ren* 96–100.

[90]Sheppard, "Iconography" (n. 81 above) 160.

[91]Kitzinger (n. 74 above) 116–17.

[92]Wilhelm Paeseler, "Gedanken zu Monreale und zur Monrealeser Bauplastik," *Aachener Kunstblätter* 41 (1971) 48–59, esp. 54.

[93]See above at notes 58–59.

[94]For Innocent III, see above at n. 63. For Frederick II, see the remarks by Wentzel (n. 14 above) 68–72 and Panofsky, *Ren & Ren* 65–67. For the new initiative in Venice in the early thir-

of the monastic reform, by the papacy, by the new powers of Sicily and Venice—formed the backbone of the entire medieval renaissance in Italian art. But our brief glance at classical revivals in the second half of the twelfth century shows that an essentially "political" interpretation is ultimately not sufficient to explain the phenomenon. Esthetic impulses were released which found an evidently quite disinterested satisfaction in the art of the distant past. These impulses can be explained, if at all, only in a broader context of cultural and intellectual history.

To this end it is important to bear in mind also what was *not* recovered by the retrospective efforts we have surveyed. By and large these efforts were concerned with externals. They created architectural settings with an antique or Early Christian flavor; they revived "historical" media; they concentrated heavily on accessories, furnishings, and framework; and they were much concerned with ornament. By the same token, when an ancient pictorial theme was taken up, there was not necessarily a concomitant effort to recapture the spirit or the style of the model—be it the *spinario* or an Early Christian apse composition. And Italian art was slow in coming to grips with that key element in ancient art, the autonomous human figure conceived in the round.[95]

Panofsky has drawn an important distinction between "surface classicism" and "intrinsic classicism."[96] The phenomena we have surveyed belong largely in the former category. It was left to the transalpine countries to evolve an art to which the latter term can properly be applied. It was in the Meuse valley, in northern France, in the Rhineland and in England—areas with relatively little direct access to true antiques—that artists ultimately came closest to recapturing the monumentality and poise, the animation and serenity of the classical human figure.[97] Theirs is the art that forms the true visual equivalent to the intellectual movement which Panofsky calls "protohumanism" and which had its geographic base in the same regions.[98]

This "intrinsic classicism" of northern art, however, could not have come to fruition without the Byzantine models which the revivals in Italy helped to

teenth century, see Otto Demus, "A Renascence of Early Christian Art in Thirteenth Century Venice," *Late Classical and Mediaeval Studies in Honor of Albert Mathias Friend, Jr.*, ed. Kurt Weitzmann (Princeton 1955) 348–61; also idem, *San Marco* (n. 70 above) 57–60, 101–05, 165–80, and passim.

[95]On the emergence of that concept in the context of the nascent Gothic art of the north, see Panofsky, *Ren & Ren* 60–63.

[96]Ibid. 62. Essentially the same distinction was also made, apropos of the art of Nicholas of Verdun, by Demus in a passage I cited in "The Byzantine Contribution" (n. 76 above) 43 n. 68.

[97]This is the stylistic phenomenon which the exhibition *The Year 1200* held in New York in 1970 was intended to illustrate. Konrad Hoffmann's introduction to the catalogue summarizes pertinent literature (*The Year 1200: A Centennial Exhibition at the Metropolitan Museum of Art*, Cloisters Studies in Medieval Art 1 [New York 1970] xxxiii–xliii). But cf. the critical review by Willibald Sauerländer in *Art Bulletin* 53 (1971) 506–16.

[98]Panofsky, *Ren & Ren* 68–81. Panofsky himself did not explicitly correlate his "intrinsic classicism" in art with his "protohumanism." Such a correlation, however, seems to me legitimate, especially when the geographic framework of the two movements is taken into account (see ibid. 58–65, 71). See also Hoffmann's introduction to *The Year 1200* (n. 97 above) xxxv.

make available, or without the ancient models which these same revivals brought to the fore. To become aware of the European significance of the twelfth-century renaissance in Italian art we need only think of Henry, bishop of Winchester, buying antique statues in Rome for shipment to his distant see, or of that other English traveler, magister Gregorius, enraptured by a statue of Venus he saw in Rome. These are telling examples of a "proto-humanist" esthetic sensibility aroused by the Italian artistic scene.[99]

[99]Bishop Henry: John of Salisbury, *Historia pontificalis* (*Memoirs of the Papal Court*) c. 40, ed. and trans. Marjorie Chibnall (London and New York 1956) 79–80. Magister Gregorius: *Narracio de mirabilibus urbis Rome* c. 12, ed. R. B. C. Huygens (Leiden 1970) 20. See also Herbert Bloch's essay in this volume.

Architecture and the Figurative Arts
The North

Willibald Sauerländer

An art historian given the task of discussing a renaissance in the architecture and figurative arts of the twelfth century is faced with a dilemma peculiar to his discipline. "Renaissance" was, after all, originally an art-historical concept, used in Paris already before 1830 to designate a specific artistic epoch: the fifteenth and sixteenth centuries in Italy.[1] Attempts were made as early as the nineteenth century to extend this concept to specific periods and phenomena in medieval art. Burckhardt, writing of the Florentine Baptistery, spoke of a medieval protorenaissance;[2] Dehio characterized twelfth-century Provençal architecture as "Romanesque renaissance."[3] More such examples could be cited. For a long time, however, objections have been raised against simply transferring the concept "renaissance" to the Middle Ages. In 1948 Paatz proposed the term *renovatio*, but the suggestion has not been widely accepted.[4] Then, Panofsky devoted first an imaginative article and later an entire book to the distinction between the Renaissance of the fifteenth and sixteenth centuries in Italy and the "renascences" of the Middle Ages.[5]

From the very beginning, art historians would do well to keep in mind the structural differences between *borrowing* from Antiquity in the visual arts and antique *tradition* in other areas of intellectual life. When ancient authors were read in schools, a more or less complete tradition (if I understand rightly) was available. When, however, we find ancient motifs in the architecture of the twelfth century, we discover that only isolated forms from Antiquity have been

[1]On the origin of the term "renaissance" see Johan Huizinga, *Wege der Kulturgeschichte* (Munich 1930) 89–139. See also Wallace K. Ferguson, *The Renaissance in Historical Thought: Five Centuries of Interpretation* (Boston 1948).

[2]Jakob Burckhardt, *Die Kunst der Renaissance in Italien*, ed. Heinrich Wölfflin (Berlin and Leipzig 1932) 23ff.

[3]Georg Dehio, "Romanische Renaissance," *Jahrbuch der königlich preussischen Kunstsammlungen* 7 (1886) 129–40.

[4]Walter Paatz, "Renaissance oder Renovatio? Ein Problem der Begriffsbildung in der Kunstgeschichte des Mittelalters," *Beiträge zur Kunst des Mittelalters: Vorträge der ersten deutschen Kunsthistorikertagung auf Schloss Brühl, 1948* (Berlin 1950) 16–27.

[5]Erwin Panofsky, "Renaissance and Renascences," *Kenyon Review* 6 (1944) 201–36; *Ren & Ren*.

applied, that the total effect is in no way antique. Cicero's writings could be taken whole into the pedagogical tradition of the Middle Ages, but the works of ancient architecture—temples, triumphal arches, and theaters—could not be copied in toto, if for no other reason than because the needs they served belonged to the pagan past. Ovid and Suetonius were read, but neither an antique statue of Venus nor a Roman portrait bust could fulfill any particular function in the medieval context. Words had greater license than images.

We must thus define precisely what we mean when we speak of a "classical revival" in connection with the buildings and images of the twelfth century.[6] To a period which felt an awakening urge for a more realistic and sensuous representation, ancient buildings and statues, separated from their original meaning, could offer examples of formal perfection or "preformed pieces of nature."[7] Only in a few fields was antique content taken over as well, and these were usually illustrated not *all'antica* but in the formal language of the time.

The many borrowings from Antiquity in the art of the twelfth century cannot be reduced to a common denominator. In a few pages it is not even remotely possible to show the entire spectrum of adoptions from Antiquity in the art of England, France, and Germany. It is perhaps more important to emphasize some pertinent aspects of the historical picture. The present discussion will therefore be divided into three parts: (1) borrowings from Antiquity in architecture; (2) the imitation of antique form in the figurative arts; (3) antique images and subjects in twelfth-century art.

BORROWINGS FROM ANTIQUITY IN ARCHITECTURE: MONUMENT, ORNAMENT, MEANING

All medieval stone structures follow Roman tradition. This is obvious in such Carolingian monuments as the gatehouse at Lorsch and the basilica of Einhard in Steinbach in the Odenwald. Even the forms of the "premier art roman" stem from late Antiquity.[8] Continuity and return to the past, "survival and revival," must be carefully distinguished.

From the middle of the eleventh century on, we observe a return to ancient building techniques. The rubble or small blocks resembling *opus incertum* in general use before this time were supplanted by regularly worked ashlar in even courses—*opus isodomum* or *pseudisodomum*.[9] This technical revolution in medieval architecture brought with it the development of skills

---

[6]For this term see T. S. R. Boase, *English Art, 1100–1216*, The Oxford History of English Art 3 (Oxford 1953) 272.

[7]On the concept of "preformed nature" (*vorgeformte Natur*), see the report of the discussion on the lecture by Walter Paatz cited in n. 4 above, p. 26. The speaker was presumably K. H. Usener.

[8]See José Puig y Cadafalch, *Le premier art roman: L'architecture en Catalogne et dans l'Occident méditerranéen aux Xe et XIe siècles* (Paris 1928).

[9]The Latin terms are taken from Vitruvius, *De architectura* 2.8.

necessary for the widespread adoption of Roman architectural ornamentation that occurred between about 1090 and the end of the twelfth century. The likely assumption that these technical innovations were inspired by the study of Roman buildings can be confirmed only in certain cases. Provence offers classic examples, since ancient and medieval buildings have survived there side by side to the present day. In the abbey church of St Gilles, the dome of Notre-Dame-des-Doms in Avignon, the cathedral of Nîmes, and the abbey church of Montmajour, the masonry of Roman monuments in Nîmes and Arles was imitated down to the preparation of the stone.[10] Further examples are offered by the Staufer palaces and fortresses, which were built with rusticated building blocks unknown in the early Middle Ages but familiar from utilitarian Roman buildings.[11] Thus it can safely be said that, at least in individual cases, the massive enlargement of masonry which marked the beginning of so-called Romanesque architecture embodies Roman features.

To a lesser extent this holds true also for a second technical innovation that decisively changed church architecture after the middle of the eleventh century: the introduction of stone vaulting over all parts of the building. In this case the Orient played an important role, and we also have to deal with an independent development going back to the early Middle Ages. It would seem, however, that Roman prototypes made a contribution too, at least to the widespread use of barrel vaulting in all of southern Gaul.[12] In Provence, direct relationships can be traced between extant vaulted Roman buildings and medieval architecture of the region. The asymmetric, rampant vaults over the side aisles of the cathedral of Vaison and in the cloisters of many Provençal cathedrals and monasteries (for example, St Trophime at Arles: fig. 48) are modeled on the substructure of the amphitheater in Arles. There, they supported the sloping tiers of seats; in the medieval buildings they correspond to the slope of the lean-to roofs and serve as lateral buttressing.[13] Such adoptions from the past thus have nothing to do with the esthetic aspect of the ancient structures. They were exclusively practical and belong to the history of technology.

From the time that regular ashlar began to be used in medieval architecture, antique architectural ornament also began to reappear. A wealth of evidence, from Santiago de Compostela to Lund and southern Italy, survives even today. Churches, monasteries, and probably also the (now almost totally destroyed) secular buildings were decorated with ancient Roman forms. This borrowing from Antiquity began in the last third of the eleventh century and

[10]On this see now Victor Lassalle, *L'influence antique dans l'art roman provençal* (Paris 1970).

[11]See Fritz Viktor Arens, "Buckelquader," *Reallexikon zur deutschen Kunstgeschichte* 3 (1954) 44–47.

[12]Only isolated references to this appear in the literature. See, however, Georg Dehio and G. von Bezold, *Die kirchliche Baukunst des Abendlandes* (2 vols. + atlas Stuttgart 1887–1901) 1.322; Eugène Viollet-le-Duc, *Dictionnaire raisonné de l'architecture française du XIe au XVI siècle* (10 vols. Paris 1854–68) 9.488.

[13]On this see Lassalle (n. 10 above) 46–47.

continued with offshoots until the end of the twelfth, though it had passed its peak by about 1160. Regions where such borrowing abounded exist side by side with countries and areas where none at all occurred. England, which played such a central role in the renaissance of the twelfth century, was architecturally one of the most productive countries in twelfth-century Europe, but had no tradition of borrowing from ancient architecture. The opposite is true of Provence, which stood, instead, at the periphery of the twelfth-century renaissance but was a showplace for the most pronounced borrowing from ancient architecture in Europe. In France borrowings from ancient architecture occur primarily in the regions lying between the Mediterranean coast and the northern boundary of the duchy of Burgundy: its most important centers were Arles, Avignon, Vienne, Lyon, and Cluny; its furthest outpost to the north was Langres, and to the east, Geneva and Lausanne. In contrast, the regions north of the Loire, where the important schools of learning—Orléans, Chartres, Paris, and Laon—were located, can virtually be excluded from consideration.

This geographical distribution alone should make us proceed with caution. The return to Antiquity in architecture seems to have had other causes and to have run a different course than the "renaissance of the twelfth century" described by Haskins. In many cases architectural borrowing from Antiquity was prompted solely by the availability of nearby ancient monuments. The latter were to be found in Nîmes and Arles, but those cities had no John of Salisbury. In contrast, ancient buildings were more or less lacking in Laon, Chartres, and Paris, where the literary tradition handed down from Antiquity played a far greater role.

Let us take a closer look at the nature of this borrowing from Antiquity, using as our point of departure the well-known Burgundian cathedral of Autun (fig. 49), initially a pilgrimage church for the relics of Lazarus. In elevation a barrel-vaulted basilica, it is richly decorated with forms taken from Roman architecture. Its cruciform piers are faced with fluted pilasters, and the forms of the triforium are copied from the attica of ancient city gates.[14] But these emulations of ancient pilasters are crowned by capitals depicting biblical events in a totally unantique style and carry pointed arches not found in any Roman building. Fronting the piers toward the nave, they function as responds for the vaulting, are inordinately elongated, and follow no canon of proportions. Below the triforium stretches a frieze of rosettes. The motif is found in antique Roman architecture, but principally on coffered or vaulted ceilings. It underwent strange migrations in twelfth-century Burgundy; at Vézelay and Avallon it appears on portal arches. In churches related to Autun we find peculiar modifications of this system of architecture imitating the antique. At Cluny, horseshoe arches having nothing to do with Antiquity are

[14]See Dehio and von Bezold (n. 12 above) 1.394.

placed between the fluted pilasters of the triforium. At Langres, Lyon, and Geneva the antique trappings of Autun and Cluny are combined with Gothic responds and rib vaults.

If such catch phrases as "Romanesque renaissance" and "protorenaissance" are to be introduced for this kind of borrowing from Antiquity, they must be more precisely defined. Relative to eleventh-century Burgundy—to such churches constructed in *opus incertum* as Tournus, Chapaize, and Farges—Cluny and Autun show unquestionable borrowing from Antiquity. But if we look back with the architecture of the modern Renaissance era in mind, the picture changes: we see clearly that the ancient forms were borrowed by twelfth-century Burgundian architects without commitment to canons or norms. Nothing is more revealing than the fact that the theme of the classical orders, so fundamentally important in the architectural theory and practice of the modern era, was never appropriated during this "Romanesque renaissance." Individual antique elements were introduced into contexts in no sense antique—Roman details applied to a medieval wall articulation. No doubt both Vitruvius and the theorists of modern Renaissance architecture would have characterized this arbitrary application of antique elements as a violation of correct usage.

Even in Provence this medieval manner of borrowing from Antiquity changed only gradually. The point of departure differed from that in Burgundy, for Provençal architecture—as can still be seen today—took over the forms of local Roman monuments, with results which were unknown in Burgundy. The portico of Notre-Dame-des-Doms in Avignon (fig. 50), with its fluted engaged columns beneath an entablature with fascias, astragals, and egg and dart moldings is unequaled as an example of antique imitation in twelfth-century architecture.[15] But once again we find such borrowed motifs undergoing curious migrations. Fluted engaged columns of the same sort decorate the thoroughly unantique transept tower of the Avignon church; they appear in a peculiar chapel choir built over a triangular foundation at St Quenin in Vaison; and they are used in the former cathedral of St Véran in Cavaillon for the thoroughly Romanesque blind arcade of an apse (fig. 51).[16] The façade of the chapel in St Gabriel (fig. 52) has an aedicula with engaged columns and a classicizing pediment, like the Roman triumphal arch in Orange; but in a manner completely unantique, the aedicula is set within an overarching niche and frames a Romanesque church portal. The most exquisite antique ornamentation—egg and dart, astragals, rosettes, and acanthus motifs—frames figural reliefs of a startling primitivism. Even if these pieces were actually taken from older buildings and reused, it is nevertheless significant that this juxtapo-

<hr />

[15]See Alan Borg, *Architectural Sculpture in Romanesque Provence* (Oxford 1972) 37. For illustrations see J. M. Roquette, *Provence Romane: La province rhodanienne*, La nuit des temps 40, Zodiaque (1974) pls. 45 and 46.

[16]For illustrations see Roquette (n. 15 above) figs. 37 and 44, and Borg (n. 15 above) fig. 76.

sition of classical and barbaric forms was not felt to be disturbing.[17] The "Romanesque renaissance" had its limits even in Provence.

The best-known work of the so-called "Provençal protorenaissance," the façade of the abbey church of St Gilles, does nothing to change this impression. A medieval triple-portal structure with numerous antique motifs interspersed, a mixture of church entrance and triumphal arch, it testifies both to the attraction exerted by the local Roman monuments and to the arbitrary, piecemeal way their forms were taken over. The many scholarly studies to which this particular façade has given rise have been undertaken not least in the hope of explaining this apparently senseless mustering of antique forms.[18] One might ask whether they may not have proceeded from a false expectation, an inadequate understanding of what one might describe as the fragmentizing, spoliating manner of borrowing from Antiquity which occurred here just as it did in Burgundy.

No other areas of France, Spain, or Germany borrowed to a comparable extent from ancient architecture. To be sure, capitals and architectural ornaments imitating antique forms are found throughout southern France in the twelfth century. For the most part they are scattered among motifs of extremely disparate origin. In an attempt to trace the genesis of this repertoire, scholars have suggested a great variety of sources, from prehistorical goldsmiths' work and Eastern textiles and ivory carvings to the initials of contemporaneous manuscripts.[19] To some extent, all of these motifs also contain bastardized antique elements. But instances of direct borrowing from Antiquity are rare—an occasional capital in the crypt of St Eutrope in Saintes; a decorated column shaft on the façade of Pont l'Abbé d'Arnoult in Saintonge; or masks in St Julien at Brioude in the Auvergne.[20] Under these circumstances, one can hardly speak of a "renaissance." The literature concerning these "survivances antiques" suffers from a failure to distinguish between unequivocal

[17]For illustrations of the chapel in St Gabriel see Roquette (n. 15 above) color pl. preceding 241 and figs. 56–62.

[18]On this see esp. Walter Horn, *Die Fassade von St. Gilles: Eine Untersuchung zur Frage des Antikeneinflusses in der südfranzösischen Kunst des 12. Jahrhunderts* (Hamburg 1937); Richard Hamann, *Die Abteikirche von St. Gilles und ihre künstlerische Nachfolge* (Berlin 1955); Whitney S. Stoddard, *The Façade of Saint-Gilles-du-Gard: Its Influence on French Sculpture* (Middletown Conn. 1973); Léon Pressouyre, review of Stoddard in *Zeitschrift für Kunstgeschichte* 39 (1976) 74–82; Willibald Sauerländer, "Das 10. internationale Colloquium der Société française d'archéologie: Die Fassade der Abteikirche in Saint-Gilles-du-Gard," *Kunstchronik* 31 (1978) 45–55; Dorothea Diemer, *Untersuchungen zu Architektur und Skulptur der Abteikirche von Saint-Gilles* (Stuttgart 1978); Carra Ferguson O'Meara, "Saint-Gilles-du-Gard: The Relationship of the Foundation to the Façade," *Journal of the Society of Architectural Historians* 39 (1980) 57–60; idem, *The Iconography of the Façade of Saint-Gilles-du-Gard* (New York and London 1977).

[19]See, e.g., Emile Mâle, *Religious Art in France: The Twelfth Century*, trans. M. Mathews, ed. H. Bober (Princeton 1978).

[20]On St Eutrope in Saintes see René Crozet, *L'art roman en Saintonge* (Paris 1971) 25, 175; François Eygun, *Saintonge Romane*, La nuit des temps 33, Zodiaque (1970) fig. 5. On Pont l'Abbé d'Arnoult see ibid., fig. 74; René Crozet, "Survivances antiques dans le décor roman du Poitou, de l'Angoumois et de la Saintonge," *Bulletin monumental* 114 (1956) 7–33. On St Julien in Brioude see Zygmunt Świechowski, *Sculpture romane d'Auvergne* (Clermont-Ferrand 1973) 257ff.

recourse to Antiquity and that stock of ancient forms which streamed in from every conceivable source and flooded the Romanesque architectural ornamentation of southern Gaul and northern Spain, proliferating with wild arbitrariness.[21]

Things were different north of the Loire. Imitations of ancient forms on so-called Early Gothic buildings are rare; but in return, the acanthus leaves that we find on the portals of St Denis and Mantes (fig. 53) and the fluted responds in Reims and Châlons-sur-Marne are purer.[22] The situation was different again within the Empire. Here, where Romanesque architecture failed to develop a rich architectural ornamentation, the solitary acanthus capitals (fig. 54), denticulated moldings, and parts of friezes on the cathedral of Speyer unquestionably represent direct recourse to Antiquity.

The example of Speyer raises the question of possible meaning in adoptions of ancient architectural motifs. It is attested that Henry IV took a personal interest in the rebuilding of the cathedral at the end of the eleventh century—Roman architectural ornamentation in the circle of the Roman emperor? May this not have had a concrete, explicit meaning? Are these motifs perhaps architectural symbols of imperial status? This has been repeatedly conjectured, but no source seems to support this speculation.[23] That such suppositions are built on shaky ground is shown by the striking fact that the same Roman forms at Cluny have been interpreted as symbols of the Reform.[24] It could, of course, also be argued that the antique spoils and imitations of antique forms in St Remi in Reims are significant, because they appeared during the reign of abbot Peter of Celle, who is known to have been a friend of John of Salisbury.[25]

But at this point the problem becomes more interesting for our discussion. Isolated borrowings from Antiquity are found in the architecture of the twelfth century in many different areas. Elsewhere—indeed, in many more places—they are not found at all. In twelfth-century philosophy and literature, protohumanistic tendencies are regarded as widespread. If we now conclude that these two phenomena are intentionally related, we must assume that the builders or architects of Cluny, Autun, and Avignon took over fluted pilasters and acanthus rosettes with an awareness that these ornaments were the archi-

[21]This is true for e.g. Marie Durand-Lefèbvre, *Art gallo-romain et sculpture romane* (Paris 1937); Jean Adhémar, *Influences antiques dans l'art du moyen âge français*, Studies of the Warburg Institute 7 (London 1939); Richard H. L. Hamann-MacLean, "Antikenstudium in der Kunst des Mittelalters," *Marburger Jahrbuch für Kunstwissenschaft* 15 (1949–50) 157–250.

[22]On St Denis and Mantes see Hamann-MacLean (n. 21 above) 171–72 with illustrations. On Reims see Willibald Sauerländer, "Beiträge zur Geschichte der 'frühgotischen' Skulptur," *Zeitschrift für Kunstgeschichte* 19 (1956) 1–34. On Châlons see Ernst Gall, *Die gotische Baukunst in Frankreich und Deutschland* (Leipzig 1925) 275.

[23]See Willibald Sauerländer, "Cluny und Speyer," *Investiturstreit und Reichsverfassung*, ed. Josef Fleckenstein, Vorträge und Forschungen 17 (Sigmaringen 1973) 9–32.

[24]See Werner Weisbach, *Religiöse Reform und mittelalterliche Kunst* (Zurich 1945) 65. He believes that the turn to Antiquity which occurred in Florence and Campania had the same basis as that in Burgundy later, namely the stream of ideas set into motion by the Reform.

[25]For the building history of St Remi in Reims see Anne Prache, *Saint-Remi de Reims: L'oeuvre de Pierre de Celle et sa place dans l'architecture gothique* (Geneva 1978).

tectural counterparts of the authors read in the renaissance of the twelfth century. We would thus assume that they were proceeding in the same manner as did Alberti in fact three hundred years later. There is of course the alternative, admittedly sobering, assumption that the two phenomena—protohumanism in philosophy and literature and survivals from Antiquity in architecture—were not directly related. We would then have to agree that when monumental vaulted structures were commissioned, architects in the majority of cases looked to Roman monuments for purely technical and artistic reasons. There are grounds for preferring the second alternative. It is true that the answer may vary from case to case, but since, so far as I can tell, the sources offer no information, the controversy all too quickly becomes speculative and hence indeterminable.

THE IMITATION OF ANTIQUE FORM IN THE FIGURATIVE ARTS

A study of twelfth-century English art used the term "early Renaissance" and devoted an entire chapter to currents hailed as "the classical revival."[26] This revival is understood not as an adoption of ancient subject matter but as an attempt to emulate ancient form and style: "A classical, idealized naturalism, humanity noble and serene, becomes the artist's aim."[27] The idea, mentioned earlier, of ancient art as "preformed nature" points in the same direction. From such phrases it should already be clear that the inspiration received from ancient models for representing figures, faces, or folds of drapery was not at all comparable to the copying of an ancient text. The aim of such borrowing was not to copy ancient models but rather to remodel a contemporary style under the stimulus of ancient models. It is thus impossible, or possible only to a very limited extent, to apply philological methods to the investigation of borrowings from Antiquity in representational art. A text can be spoiled; pictures are transformed.

As a consequence, Antiquity could inspire the representational arts in many different ways. A Byzantine miniature or an ivory carving of the tenth, eleventh, or twelfth century could serve as a trigger for the "classical revival" as well as—indeed occasionally even more effectively than—a draped Roman statue from imperial times or a provincial Roman tombstone. Here, too, reigned an untrammeled freedom quite unknown to the textual tradition. Boase spoke of a "classical revival," referring to English art of the late twelfth century; yet revivals of Antiquity in the figurative arts can be found throughout the century and in many places.

On old Roman soil, especially in ancient Gallia Narbonensis, borrowing from Antiquity resulted from the study of local Roman monuments, as it did in architecture. The stone consoles with animal heads (fig. 55) found in Provençal cloisters and also on the upper moldings of churches such as St Paul in

---

[26]See Boase (n. 6 above) 272–96 (ch. 10).
[27]Ibid. 276.

Lyon can be traced directly to Roman prototypes. But, it is significant that later, about 1180, they also came to be used beneath rib vaults where they were exaggerated in a manner not found in any ancient prototype.[28] In short, here too we have a transformation rather than simple copying. On the capitals and exterior walls of churches in Geneva, Lyon, Vienne, and Avignon (fig. 56) we find the most varied imitations of antique masks, with foliated heads and satyr faces as favorite motifs.[29] In St Martin d'Ainay in Lyon, foliated and animal heads fill the corners of the great pier capitals—obviously motifs taken over from Roman stone altars.[30] Such examples still fall more or less within the category of nonfigural architectural ornamentation, and the manner of their borrowing is no different from that of architecture. It is thus significant that they come from the region where the influence of Roman architecture was strongest. But interesting variations occur: although Burgundy took over structural forms from Roman architecture, and with them Corinthian and Composite capitals, animal consoles or masks are found in that region very rarely if at all. The style of Burgundian architectural sculpture in the vicinity of Cluny has no relation to that of Antiquity.

It was different in Languedoc. The Romanesque sculpture of Toulouse and Moissac (as well as of Spain: Jaca, León, and Santiago de Compostela) indicates attentive study of Early Christian images of a kind still visible in Toulouse today. One must, however, be careful in drawing any broad conclusions. The one useful study available on the subject presented concrete evidence for the imitation of Early Christian prototypes only in the case of certain heads in Toulouse and Moissac.[31] These results seem characteristic of the manner of borrowing in this region: it concentrated particularly on details and techniques. In general, the stylization is no more antique than the walls of vaulted Romanesque basilicas decorated with pilasters in imitation of Antiquity.

In Provence, borrowing from ancient sculpture was again quite different. The statues on the façades and in the cloisters of St Gilles and Arles show a wealth of details taken from Antiquity: drilling is frequently used in the carving of folds; the motif of loose, fluttering drapery has been taken over; and faces take on freer, less forced expressions due to their antique modeling. Nevertheless, the influence of Antiquity is held in check by the Christian subject matter. Some drapery motifs of the statues of the apostles may possibly

[28]See H. A. von Stockhausen, "Die romanischen Kreuzgänge der Provence," *Marburger Jahrbuch für Kunstwissenschaft* 8/9 (1936) 89–171; Willibald Sauerländer, "Löwen in Lyon," *Kunsthistorische Forschungen: Otto Pächt zu seinem 70. Geburtstag*, ed. Artur Rosenauer and Gerold Weber (Salzburg 1972) 215–24.

[29]See the head in the Musée d'art et d'histoire in Geneva, Collection lapidaire 262. On Lyon, Lucien Bégule, *Monographie de la cathédrale de Lyon* (Lyon 1880). On Vienne see idem, *L'église Saint-Maurice, ancienne cathédrale de Vienne en Dauphiné* (Paris 1914) 1, 47. On Avignon, von Stockhausen (n. 28 above) n. 32 and 92, 95.

[30]On St Martin d'Ainay in Lyon see André Chagny, *La basilique Saint-Martin d'Ainay et ses annexes* (Lyon 1935); J. Birot, "Les chapiteaux des pilastres de Saint-Martin d'Ainay à Lyon," *Congrès archéologique de France* 74 (1908) 527–36.

[31]See Friedrich Gerke, *Der Tischaltar des Bernard Gilduin in Saint Sernin in Toulouse*, Abh Mainz 1958 no. 8 (Wiesbaden 1958).

have been taken from an ancient *maenad;*[32] but for all the details they borrow from Antiquity, these apostles retain a linear stylization which is completely medieval. They are "Romanesque with an almost baroque liveliness in the treatment of surfaces."[33] On the frieze of the portal at St Gilles (fig. 57), the animated, three-dimensional portrayal of the scenes indicates the influence of Roman reliefs and Early Christian sarcophagi; but again, the pictorial program of the Passion cycle they depict is entirely medieval, not Early Christian. In them too, imitation of antique form has been inhibited by the unantique subject matter. It is in the light of such examples that Panofsky spoke of a "principle of disjunction," according to which the forms and subjects taken into medieval art from Antiquity were always kept fundamentally separate.[34] This thesis is certainly drawn too sharply, but it is nonetheless true that in twelfth-century art, forms resembling those of Antiquity do indeed appear in different, less consistent guises than they do in the literary "renaissance of the twelfth century."

Borrowings from Antiquity in Gallia Narbonensis must be appraised as a series of attempts to broaden the means and technique of sculptural representation through the study of local Roman and Early Christian monuments. Details taken from Antiquity were incorporated into totally different contexts, usually completely unantique. Only in this very limited sense, therefore, can one speak here of a "renaissance" or "protorenaissance." St Gilles, St Sernin in Toulouse, San Isidoro in León, and Santiago de Compostela were pilgrimage churches. In Moissac around 1100, monastic reform played a role.[35] At St Gilles a relationship has been seen—perhaps somewhat hastily—between the program of the portal and the rejection of the heretical teachings of Peter of Bruys.[36] Be that as it may, in the very narrowest sense this southern French protorenaissance took place in an ecclesiastical setting. Without drawing premature conclusions, one may well say that it stands rather closer to the Reform than to the protohumanism described by Haskins in his *Renaissance of the Twelfth Century*.

It is a different matter when we turn to the "classical revival" of northern France, the Empire, and England. Only in exceptional cases were antique influences in these areas due to the presence of Roman monuments.[37] Borrowing from Antiquity took place at a greater distance and involved different media: medieval sculpture did not borrow from ancient sculpture. Instead, particular

[32]See the comparison in Hamann (n. 18 above) 112.

[33]Ibid.

[34]*Ren & Ren* 85.

[35]On Moissac see Marcel Durliat, "Les origines de la sculpture Romane à Toulouse et à Moissac," CCM 12 (1969) 349–64 at 358–59.

[36]See Marcia L. Colish, "Peter of Bruys, Henry of Lausanne, and the Façade of St.-Gilles," *Traditio* 28 (1972) 451–60. For an entirely different, though hardly convincing, iconographic explanation of the façade of St Gilles, see O'Meara, *Iconography* (n. 18 above).

[37]For example, in the case of a 13th-c. capital in the cathedral of Reims, for which a figure on the Jovinus sarcophagus then located in St Nicaise in Reims was apparently taken over and changed into a centaur. See Panofsky, *Ren & Ren*, figs. 38 and 39. In the north such examples are exceptions.

characteristics of antique figures—or more often only of figures executed under antique influence—were adopted, and in a variety of artistic media (goldsmiths' work, book illumination, stained glass, wall painting, and finally also architectural sculpture) were incorporated into an independent style striving for a new naturalism and animation. It was in these areas, where proto-humanistic features in the sense of Haskins's "renaissance" were generally present in other fields of intellectual life as well, that the encounter with ancient art, or with imitations of ancient art, led to that so-called "classical, idealized naturalism, humanity noble and serene."[38]

This "classical revival" made its appearance in the late twelfth century. It reached its zenith at a time when the "protorenaissance" in the region of ancient Gallia Narbonensis was already over or survived only in late offshoots. Its most important centers were: (1) the land along the Meuse and adjacent areas as far as Cologne, Verdun, and northeastern Champagne, where the most productive workshops for bronze casting, champlevé enamel, and goldsmiths' work were located; (2) the French royal domain, the territory of the counts of Champagne, and the adjoining regions to the north as far as French Flanders—it is in these areas that we find the first Gothic buildings, on which architectural sculpture and stained glass in an antique style appear from 1180–90 on; and (3) the primarily monastic scriptoria in the northern half of France and southern England where psalters and bibles with miniatures belonging to the late phase of the so-called "Channel Style" were produced.[39] For shorter or longer periods Liège, Cologne, Chartres, Paris, Laon, Reims, Winchester, and Canterbury were the centers of such an art based on Antiquity. This list of cities makes clear that, at least on a local level, there was no split between a renaissance in other areas of intellectual life and borrowing from Antiquity in the arts, such as we observed in the Romanesque imitation of ancient architecture. But still there is no justification for concluding that the recovery of the classical tradition expressed a common intention or program shared equally by philosophy, the *artes*, jurisprudence, poetry, and the figurative arts. Here too, antique form or antique-like form was rather a stimulus for the medieval artist than a canonical model; we are not in fifteenth-century Florence. Let us briefly survey those monuments which imitated ancient style in the areas just mentioned.

(1) The Meuse Valley, and particularly Liège, as we can still see today, was in the twelfth century the center of a continuous production of metalwork in which specific stylistic formulas were constantly used.[40] Scholars have attributed an antique character to this production from its beginnings, regarding

---

[38]Boase (n. 6 above) 276.

[39]For the not very satisfying term "Channel Style" see Walter Cahn, "St. Albans and the Channel Style in England," *The Year 1200: A Symposium* (New York 1975) 187–211, and Larry M. Ayres, "English Painting and the Continent during the Reign of Henry II and Eleanor," *Eleanor of Aquitaine: Patron and Politician*, ed. William W. Kibler (Austin 1976) 115–46.

[40]See the thorough summary by Dietrich Kötzsche, "Zum Stand der Forschung der Goldschmiedekunst des 12. Jahrhunderts im Rhein-Maas-Gebiet," *Rhein und Maas: Kunst und Kultur 800–1400* (2 vols. Cologne 1972–73) 2.191–236.

the baptismal font cast in Liège under abbot Hellinus for Notre-Dame-aux-Fonts (1107–18) as its earliest work.[41] One can scarcely deny that this font—with its loose and free composition of scenes, the naturalness of the forms and movements of its figures, and its inclusion of nudes (fig. 58) (which, to be sure, are required by its subject)—is surprising for the early twelfth century. It is open to question, however, whether, when we assume it to be a case of direct borrowing from Antiquity, we are proceeding from a stereotyped view of the antique—that is, from the rough equation of three-dimensionality, liveliness, and nudity with Antiquity—or from independent observation. It seems to me that evidence for a direct relationship to Antiquity is still lacking.[42] The same must be said for the famous reliquary head in which Wibald of Stavelot placed relics of Alexander in 1145 (fig. 59). Though it is an indisputable fact that all medieval busts descend from Antiquity, to suggest that this head was modeled on imperial portraiture would be, in my opinion, to confuse ancient descent with an ad hoc return to the past—"survival" with "revival."[43]

Above all, it would weaken the historical significance of the true, unmistakable return to Antiquity that began in the Meuse region about 1180. We observe this revival in an ambo, firmly dated 1181, from the abbey of Klosterneuburg in Lower Austria. The goldsmith signed the work "Nicolaus Virdunensis" and thus came from the upper Meuse.[44] We observe it as well in the embossing and champlevé enamels of a shrine made for the relics of the Three Kings that Rainald of Dassel brought to the cathedral of Cologne from Milan in 1164. And we see it once again in the cast figures and crests of a shrine made in Siegburg for the mortal remains of archbishop Anno of Cologne, canonized in 1183.[45] The enamels in Klosterneuburg and the metalwork in Cologne (fig. 60, left) depict biblical figures clothed in drapery with natural, realistic folds that follow Roman prescriptions with greater empathy and consequently with a far more sensuous effect than had the marble sculptors of Provence. The richly modeled, portrait-like heads of the apostles and prophets on the Cologne Shrine of the Three Kings reveal direct study of busts from the Roman imperial era. Its relationship to Antiquity is most apparent in the comparably modeled heads in medallions arranged in ornamental bands (fig. 60, right); the champlevé enamels imitate antique gems.[46] The crests from the Anno Shrine show equally tangible evidence of direct

[41] See Kötzsche (n. 40 above) 194–95.

[42] On the assumption that there was a definite antique influence, see most recently Anton Legner, "Die Rinderherde des Reiner von Huy," *Rhein und Maas* (n. 40 above) 2.237–50.

[43] For the Alexander reliquary and possible antique influences, see esp. K.-H. Usener, "Le Chef-Reliquaire du Pape Saint Alexandre," *Bulletin des Musées royaux d'art et d'histoire* 3rd ser. 6 (1934) 57–63.

[44] For the inscription see Floridus Rörig, *Der Verduner Altar* (2nd ed. Klosterneuburg 1955) 16.

[45] For the Anno Shrine see *Monumenta Annonis: Köln und Siegburg, Weltbild und Kunst im hohen Mittelalter*, ed. Anton Legner (Cologne 1975) 185–215, "Reliquienschreine."

[46] To date there is no extensive, summarizing work on the Shrine of the Three Kings. A bibliography up to 1972 is in Kötzsche (n. 40 above) 226–29.

recourse to Antiquity; they depict nude figures wearing the winged cap of Mercury (fig. 62). It is only here in the Meuse region after 1180 that we can properly speak of a "classical revival" in the full sense of this phrase.

(2) Neither the cathedrals and monastic churches erected in the French royal domain after 1135, and today called Gothic or proto-Gothic, nor the figures carved for those churches show any certain evidence of a return to Antiquity. Yet in the stamp of physiognomy and the rendering of costume, these figures reveal a surprisingly accurate observation of nature and reality, despite their overall unnaturalistic stylization. The empiricism which this suggests may, indeed, have made the sculptors receptive to Roman sculpture as a kind of "preformed nature." However, works of an antique character do not appear in this region before 1190, and then they were more probably inspired by medieval goldsmiths' work or paintings than by a direct study of ancient sculpture, though the latter may conceivably have exerted a direct influence in one place or another. In Laon and Sens, Chartres and Paris, a sculptural style with antique characteristics gained acceptance about 1190–1200. This is evident in a new, comparatively realistic rendering of drapery and in the modeling of heads (fig. 63).[47] But the sculpture never took on the pronounced character of the Mosan goldsmiths' work mentioned above. A glance at the trumeau of the main portal of Sens cathedral reveals the true nature of this stylization all'antica of prophets, apostles, and saints. A figure of St Stephen (fig. 61), which imitates Antiquity in the most general sense, is placed on the front; on the sides, however, are grapevine tendrils and birds taken not from Antiquity but from nature. Obviously it was not an antique or classical appearance as such that mattered, but to make the church sculpture more natural and more animated by borrowing from Antiquity.

(3) A similar process can be observed in the late phase of the "Channel Style" in book illumination. If we compare the so-called last copy of the Utrecht Psalter, made in Canterbury about 1200 (BN lat 8846) with the Eadwine Psalter (Cambridge, Trinity College, MS R.17.1) made in Canterbury half a century earlier and also believed to be a copy of the Utrecht Psalter, our immediate impression is that the illustrations of the later manuscript have acquired new antique traits and are consequently both livelier and more sensuous.[48] If, in the famous Bible that probably traveled back and forth from Winchester to Witham under Henry II of England between 1180 and 1186, we compare the oldest pages—the work of the "Master of the Leaping Figures" (fig. 64, below)—to the later initials of the "Master of the Morgan Leaf" or

[47]See Willibald Sauerländer, *Gotische Skulptur in Frankreich 1140–1270* (Munich 1970) 48–54, trans. Janet Sondheimer, *Gothic Sculpture in France 1140–1270* (New York 1972) 50–56.

[48]On BN lat 8846 see Victor Leroquais, *Les psautiers manuscrits des bibliothèques publiques de France* (2 vols. Mâcon 1940–41) 2.78–99; Boase (n. 6 above) 289–90; Adelheid Heimann, "The Last Copy of the Utrecht Psalter," *The Year 1200* (n. 39 above) 313–38. On Cambridge, Trinity College, MS R.17.1, see Claus M. Kauffmann, *Romanesque Manuscripts, 1066–1190* (London 1975) 96–97 with bibliography.

those of the "Master of the Genesis Initial" (fig. 64, above), we can observe how the figures were humanized by recourse to classicizing, presumably Middle Byzantine, sources.[49] In the famous psalter of Queen Ingeborg of France we encounter pictures with a stylized drapery that must go back, through intermediate sources, to Roman sculptural models.[50] But these pictures, too, remain completely within the tradition of medieval iconography. Only their appearance has been changed by their antique characteristics: they are more beautiful, more three-dimensional, and more natural.

This brings us once more to the two questions: what role did this artistic "classical revival" play in the general culture of the twelfth century? and what was its relationship to the renaissance described by Haskins? The history of art can do no more than demonstrate the presence of various antique currents during the late twelfth century, chiefly in northwest Europe. Some fields—book illumination and stained glass, for example—have not even been fully inventoried. In isolated cases we think we can trace the routes along which the influence of ancient art traveled, the clearest of these being between Sicily and England.[51] Henry of Blois, bishop of Winchester and brother of king Stephen, had "veteres statuas" sent to him from Rome.[52] John of Salisbury's report of the event betrays an ambivalent attitude toward this attempt to rescue heathen idols,[53] but we know nothing about the artistic effect the figures may have had on twelfth-century Winchester. Ancient cut gems introduced on the Shrine of the Three Kings were immediately imitated.

The coincidence in time and place between the classical revival in the arts and aspects of the twelfth-century renaissance might, of course, lead us to conclude that the two phenomena were the result of related processes arising from similar intentions. The sources cannot help us to resolve the issue, but the monuments suggest that there is no basis for assuming that Nicolaus Virdunensis, the "Master of the Genesis Initial," and the sculptor working at the cathedral of Laon were striving for a renaissance of classical Antiquity. It is more likely that they were looking to Antiquity as a stimulus and for ways of improving their own representations by a greater naturalism and animation. What the antique exempla or their imitations offered was preformed nature—mimesis. And once again we come to the realization that the study of

[49]Still important for the Winchester Bible is Walter F. Oakeshott, *The Artists of the Winchester Bible* (London 1945). Bibliography in Kauffmann (n. 48 above) 108–11. See also Larry M. Ayres, "The Work of the Morgan Master at Winchester and English Painting of the Early Gothic Period," *Art Bulletin* 56 (1974) 201–23. On the Morgan Master, see the more recent article by Ayres (n. 39 above).

[50]See Florens Deuchler, *Der Ingeborgpsalter* (Berlin 1967); Reiner Haussherr, "Der Ingeborgpsalter: Bemerkungen zu Datierungs- und Stilfragen," *The Year 1200* (n. 39 above) 231–44.

[51]On this see Boase (n. 6 above) 188–90.

[52]John of Salisbury, *Historia pontificalis (Memoirs of the Papal Court)* c. 40, ed. and trans. Marjorie Chibnall (London and New York 1956) 79–80. See also Lena Voss, *Heinrich von Blois, Bischof von Winchester (1129–71)*, Historische Studien 210 (Berlin 1932) and Panofsky, *Ren & Ren* 72–73.

[53]See Otto Lehmann-Brockhaus, *Lateinische Schriftquellen zur Kunst in England, Wales und Schottland vom Jahre 901 bis zum Jahre 1307* (5 vols. Munich 1955–60) 2.667 no. 4760.

Fig. 48. Arles. St Trophime. Cloister (second third of twelfth century): north wing. Photo: Austin.

Fig. 49. Autun. Cathedral. Nave (1125–40): piers, triforium, and vault. Photo: Bildarchiv Foto Marburg.

Fig. 50. Avignon. Notre-Dame-des-Doms. Portico (last third of twelfth century). Photo: Bildarchiv Foto Marburg.

Fig. 51. Cavaillon. St Véran. Apse (third quarter of twelfth century): exterior. Photo: Bildarchiv Foto Marburg.

Fig. 53 (right). Mantes. Collegiate church. Detail of door post (ca. 1180). Photo: Monuments Historiques, Paris.

Fig. 52 (below). St Gabriel. Chapel (third quarter of twelfth century): façade. Photo: Austin.

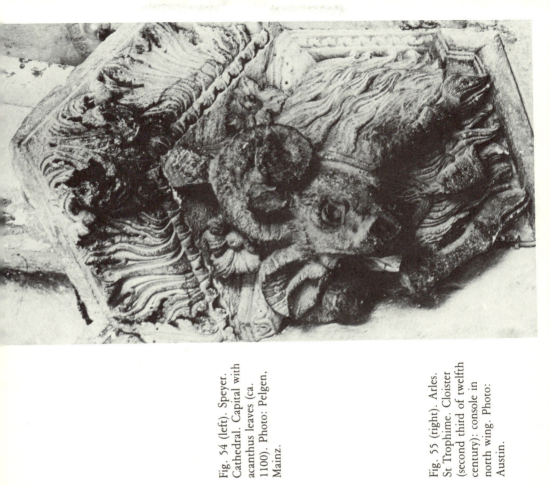

Fig. 54 (left). Speyer. Cathedral. Capital with acanthus leaves (ca. 1100). Photo: Pelgen, Mainz.

Fig. 55 (right). Arles. St Trophime. Cloister (second third of twelfth century): console in north wing. Photo: Austin.

Fig. 56. Avignon. Musée Calvet. Capital from Notre-Dame-des-Doms (second half of twelfth century). Photo: Bildarchiv Foto Marburg.

Fig. 57. St Gilles. Abbey church. West facade portal frieze (second third of twelfth century): the Betrayal of Christ. Photo: Austin.

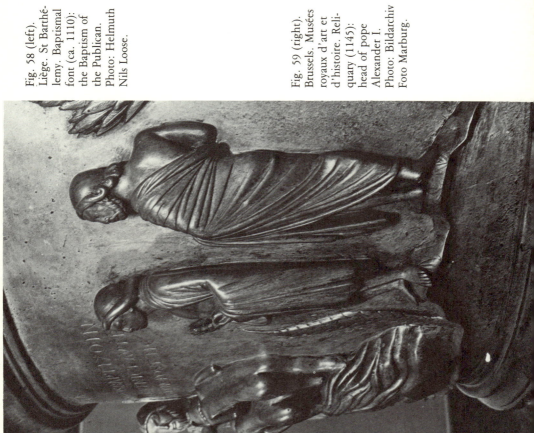

Fig. 58 (left).
Liège. St Barthé-
lemy. Baptismal
font (ca. 1110):
the Baptism of
the Publican.
Photo: Helmuth
Nils Loose.

Fig. 59 (right).
Brussels. Musées
royaux d'art et
d'histoire. Reli-
quary (1145):
head of pope
Alexander I.
Photo: Bildarchiv
Foto Marburg.

Fig. 60. Cologne. Cathedral. Shrine of the Three Kings (ca. 1190): left, Moses; right, ornamental enamels. Photos: Rhein. Bildarchiv.

Fig. 61 (left). Sens. Cathedral. Trumeau of main portal (ca. 1190–1200): St Stephen. Photo: Hirmer Fotoarchiv.

Fig. 62 (below). Siegburg. St Servatius. Shrine of St Anno (ca. 1185): detail of ornamented gable. Photo: Bredol-Lepper.

Fig. 63. Sens. Palais Synodal. Head of apostle or prophet (ca. 1190–1200). Photo: Hirmer Fotoarchiv.

Fig. 64. Winchester. Cathedral Library. "Winchester Bible." Above, fol. 1r: brother Ambrose bringing a letter to Jerome; below, fol. 148r: the inspiration of Jeremiah. Photos: Warburg Institute, London.

Fig. 65. Stuttgart. Württembergische Landesbibliothek, MS Hist. folio 415 (ca. 1160–70). Zwiefalten choir book for Prime, fol. 17v: *Annus*. Photo: Bildarchiv Foto Marburg.

Fig. 66. Munich. Bayerisches Nationalmuseum. Bronze statuettes (Mosan region, ca. 1180): the Four Elements. Photo: Bayerisches Nationalmuseum.

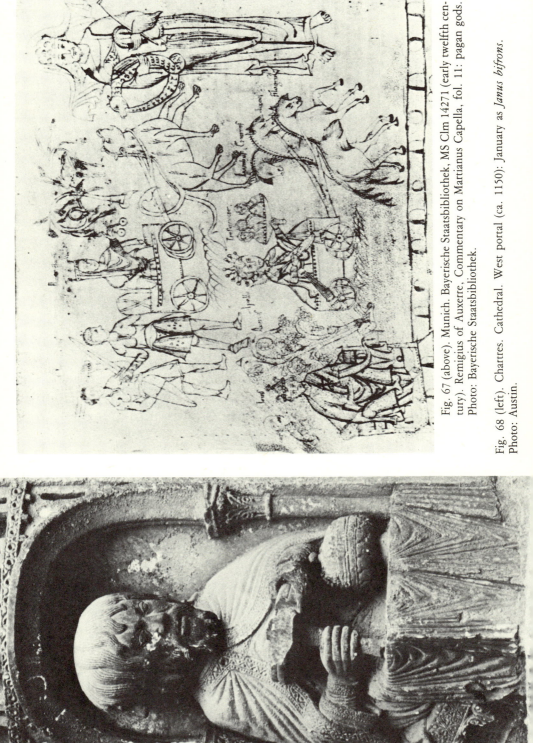

Fig. 67 (above). Munich. Bayerische Staatsbibliothek, MS Clm 14271 (early twelfth century). Remigius of Auxerre, Commentary on Martianus Capella, fol. 11: pagan gods. Photo: Bayerische Staatsbibliothek.

Fig. 68 (left). Chartres. Cathedral. West portal (ca. 1150): January as *Janus bifrons*. Photo: Austin.

Fig. 69 (left). Munich. Bayerische Staatsbibliothek, MS Clm 21563 (late twelfth century). Horace, *Epistolae*, fol. 1v: Horace. Photo: Bildarchiv Foto Marburg.

Fig. 70 (below). Strasbourg. Bibliothèque publique. Herrad of Landsberg, *Hortus deliciarum* (late twelfth century), fol. 221v: Ulysses and the Sirens. The library and codex were destroyed in the 1870 fire; figure after *Herrade de Landsberg: Hortus deliciarum*, ed. Alexandre Straub and Gustave Keller (Strasbourg 1901) pl. 58 (= Paris, Bibliothèque nationale, Cabinet des Estampes, Ad. 144 a. Fol.). Photo: Zentralinstitut für Kunstgeschichte, Munich.

Fig. 71. Chartres. Cathedral. West portal (ca. 1150): *Musica* and *Grammatica* with authors. Photo: Austin.

Fig. 72. Ghent. Bibliothèque universitaire, MS 92 (ca. 1120). Lambert of St Omer, *Liber floridus*, fol. 153v: Alexander. Photo: Bildarchiv Foto Marburg.

Fig. 73 (opposite page). Cappenberg. Parish church of St John the Evangelist. The so-called Barbarossa head (third quarter of twelfth century). Photo: Schmidt-Glassner.

Antiquity in the schools of the twelfth century and the tendencies toward the imitation of Antiquity in twelfth-century art were at most very indirectly linked. In one respect alone were imitations of the antique in the figurative arts and the renaissance in other fields of intellectual life more closely related, and only in that did they correspond in a manner which can be historically ascertained: namely, in the depiction of ancient subjects.

ANTIQUE IMAGES AND SUBJECTS IN THE FIGURATIVE ARTS

From the start there were a number of pictorial conceptions which belonged to the ancient heritage handed down to the Middle Ages, including the personifications and images representing *mundus* and *annus*: the elements, seasons, zodiac, months, and winds. For the most part they were adopted during the Carolingian renaissance, were already modified occasionally then, and continued to be available, so to speak, throughout the following centuries. Even though they appear rather more frequently during the twelfth century than they do, say, in Ottonian times, it is nevertheless more accurate to speak of a "survival" than a "renaissance." The art historian should also stress that pictorial imagery apparently was almost never renewed by going back directly to Antiquity; on the contrary, it departed increasingly from the antique through changes effected within the medieval tradition itself.

Carolingian representations of the elements, especially of *terra* and *mare*, are sometimes still very close to their antique prototypes. The four well-known twelfth-century Mosan bronze statuettes (fig. 66) in the Bayerisches Nationalmuseum in Munich retain the ancient attributes—a snake for *terra* and an urn for *aqua*—but their appearance as a whole (indeed, even the manner in which these attributes are held) is not antique.[54] Panofsky's "principle of disjunction" holds for them as well:[55] the ancient conception of the personified elements has survived but has assumed medieval form. This is equally true of the seasons. As they appear in the twelfth century—in medieval garb with attributes modeled on medieval implements (for example, on a well-known *annus* page from a choir book in Zwiefalten [fig. 65] and on the portal of Autun)—the antique personifications have been almost totally transformed into medieval images.[56] Representations of the months retain isolated antique motifs, as when January appears on the portals of St Denis and Chartres in the form of a "janus bifrons" (fig. 68); but more generally these images are

[54]On the representation of the elements, see most recently Gerhard Frey and Ellen J. Beer, "Elemente," *Reallexikon zur deutschen Kunstgeschichte* 4 (1958) 1256–88 and U. Nilgen, "Elemente, Vier," *Lexikon der christlichen Ikonographie* 1 (1968) 600–06.

[55]*Ren & Ren* 85.

[56]On the iconography of the seasons, see (among others) James Fowler, "On Mediaeval Representations of the Months and the Seasons," *Archaeologia* 44 (1873) 137–44; Arduino Colasanti, "Le stagioni nell'antichità e nell'arte cristiana," *Rivista d'Italia* 4 (1901) 669–87; Géza de Francovich, *Benedetto Antelami, architetto e scultore, e l'arte del suo tempo* (2 vols. Milan 1952) 1.233–42.

marked by realistic elements which had been in wide use since the early Middle Ages and have little to do with ancient tradition. In the twelfth century they occur on such a large scale that regional variations reflecting climate and tillage become recognizable.[57] For obvious reasons the representation of the winds was comparatively more constant; realistic elements could hardly be used for images of the ancient wind gods. As late as 1170, in a well-known illustration of *Aer* from a *Liber pontificalis* made in Reims, they live on as winged heads with wind-blown hair such as are occasionally encountered already in Antiquity.[58]

Such foreign—to us legendary—peoples as the Panotii, Cynocephali, Sciopodes, and Hippopodes found on capitals, portals, and columns during the twelfth century (chiefly in Burgundy and the Nivernais) are antique in origin. But just as these ethnographic traditions were already well known in medieval encyclopedic literature as early as Isidore and Rabanus, so their representations did not originate in the twelfth century but go back to the early Middle Ages. Once again we are dealing with a "survival" rather than a "revival."[59] This is true also for the hybrid creatures—sirens, griffins, winged horses, centaurs, and sphinxes—that proliferated during the twelfth century, especially in the architectural sculpture of France. The motifs are of antique or ancient Oriental origin. For the most part, however, they had entered the medieval tradition long before the twelfth century and became established with specific meanings, often of a highly complex, moralizing nature.[60] Thus they too are not peculiar to the twelfth century. Long before the twelfth century, moreover, ancient fables about animals appeared in medieval art. When, however, in the architectural sculpture of the time we encounter such themes as the wolf teaching or the donkey playing the lyre (the latter most memorably

[57]On the representation of the months, see esp. Olga Koseleff, *Die Monatsdarstellungen in der französischen Plastik des 12. Jahrhunderts* (Marburg 1934); James C. Webster, *The Labors of the Months in Antique and Mediaeval Art to the End of the Twelfth Century* (Princeton 1938); Léon Pressouyre, "'Marcius Cornator': Note sur un groupe de représentations médiévales du mois de mars," *Mélanges d'archéologie et d'histoire de l'Ecole française de Rome* 77 (1965) 395–473.

[58]On the representation of the winds, see now the lengthy and important article by Thomas Raff, "Die Ikonographie der mittelalterlichen Windpersonifikationen," *Aachener Kunstblätter* 48 (1978–79) 71–218; and, among older works, H. Steinmetz, "Windgötter," *Jahrbuch des kaiserlich deutschen archäologischen Instituts* 25 (1911) 35–55.

[59]On these ethnographic representations, see among others Mâle (n. 19 above) 322–32; Jean Adhémar in Francis Salet, *La Madeleine de Vézelay* (Melun 1948) 124–29; Rudolf Wittkower, "Marvels of the East: A Study in the History of Monsters," *JWCI* 5 (1942) 159–97; Salome Zajadacz-Hastenrath, "Fabelwesen," *Reallexikon zur deutschen Kunstgeschichte* 6 (1973) 739–816.

[60]The extensive literature on this theme which has accumulated since the 19th century has never been brought together. Richard Bernheimer, *Romanische Tierplastik und die Ursprünge ihrer Motive* (Munich 1931) and esp. Victor H. Debidour, *Le Bestiaire sculpté du Moyen Age en France* (Paris 1961) are rather disappointing. On sirens see W. Deonna, "La Sirène, femme poisson," *Revue archéologique* 5th ser. 27 (1928) 18–25. On centaurs, Jean Bayet, "Le symbolisme du Cerf et du Centaure à la porte rouge de Notre-Dame de Paris," *Bulletin de la Société nationale des Antiquaires de France* [82] (1952–53) 177–80. On both subjects see also Adhémar (n. 21 above) 179–86.

at Chartres), we can scarcely fail to notice a connection with the schools that played so important a role for the "renaissance of the twelfth century."[61] But in these cases, too, the manner of depiction is in no way antique; the "principle of disjunction" obtains here as well.

The relatively rare twelfth-century representations of ancient gods are no different. An established tradition for the depiction of ancient divinities as constellations existed during the Middle Ages from the ninth century on.[62] Yet when we look at twelfth-century examples we find that they have been either so barbarized that they are far removed from the classical originals, as in the Ghent *Liber floridus*,[63] or completely transformed, as in an English astrological manuscript of the early twelfth century, where Hercules looks like a "Romanesque Saint Michael fighting the dragon or a decorative figure on a contemporary capital."[64] The written tradition and the pictorial tradition are not on an equal level; the pictures have changed more than the words.

This is even more striking in cases where the twelfth-century artist tried to depict the ancient gods on the basis of descriptions—that is, without a pictorial model. These attempts to depict the gods of Antiquity (if the supposition is true that no pictorial model was available) would seem to have been inspired by newly awakened literary interest. In the opinion of scholars, such attempts did not take place before the twelfth century. We are thus dealing here with a "renaissance" phenomenon in Haskins's sense. But the results are curious indeed! A page in an early twelfth-century manuscript of Remigius of Auxerre's commentary on Martianus Capella (fig. 67) shows Apollo, Mars, and Saturn, among others; but the Roman god of war looks like a knight in chain mail, and Saturn resembles a biblical prophet with rather odd attributes. In other words, the artists knew Mars as a god of war and Saturn as a bearded old man with scythe and sickle, but they no longer had any idea what these gods had looked like in the art of Antiquity.[65] In a Saxon manuscript of St

---

[61]On these themes in 12th-c. art in general, see Mâle (n. 19 above) 333–40 and Adhémar (n. 21 above) 223–30. On the donkey playing the lyre, see Volker Plagemann, "Esel," *Reallexikon zur deutschen Kunstgeschichte* 5 (1967) 1484–1528 at 1498–1501.

[62]On this see the fundamental compilation by Fritz Saxl, *Verzeichnis astrologischer und mythologischer illustrierter Handschriften des lateinischen Mittelalters*, vol. 1: *Die Handschriften in römischen Bibliotheken*, SB Heidelberg 6.6–7 (1915); vol. 2: *Die Handschriften in der Nationalbibliothek in Wien*, SB Heidelberg 16.2 (1925–26); and, with Hans Meier, *Catalogue of Astrological and Mythological Illuminated Manuscripts of the Latin Middle Ages*, vol. 3: *Manuscripts in British Libraries* (2 vols. London 1953); continued by Patrick McGurk, vol. 4: *Astrological Manuscripts in Italian Libraries (Other than Rome)* (London 1966); Jean Seznec, *Les survivances des dieux antiques*, Studies of the Warburg Institute 11 (London 1940), trans. Barbara F. Sessions, *The Survival of the Pagan Gods* (New York 1953).

[63]For the illustrations for "De Ordine et positione signorū" in the *Liber floridus*, see Lambert of St Omer, *Liber floridus*, ed. Albert Derolez (Ghent 1968) 181–86 (fols. 89r–91v). For the English manuscript Oxford, Bodl. MS 614, see Saxl and Meier, *British Libraries* (n. 62 above) 1.313–16. See also Albert Derolez, ed., *Liber floridus Colloquium: Papers Read at the International Meeting Held in the University Library, Ghent, on 3–5 September 1967* (Ghent 1973).

[64]See Erwin Panofsky and Fritz Saxl, "Classical Mythology in Mediaeval Art," *Metropolitan Museum Studies* 4 (1932) 228–80 at 238.

[65]For this page, see among others Erwin Panofsky, *Studies in Iconology: Humanistic Themes in the Art of the Renaissance* (2nd ed. New York 1962) 24–25 and 78.

Augustine's *Civitas Dei* we find no fewer than twenty medallions with busts, half-figures, and full figures of ancient deities surrounding a picture of the "civitas terrena." But Mercury looks more like an angel than an ancient god, and in another context Apollo might readily be confused with an Elder of the Apocalypse, or Juno with a noble twelfth-century lady holding a peacock feather as an attribute. The painter obviously had some idea of the specific identifying marks of individual deities but could not imagine their classical appearance. He depicted them in the way he customarily depicted rulers, biblical figures, saints, and virtues.[66] There is just as little evidence here of a renaissance of ancient images of deities as in the preceding manuscript.

One final example is even more instructive. The basin of a fountain erected in the cloister of St Denis at the end of the twelfth century shows images of antique gods in medallions, executed in the antique-like style of the late twelfth century discussed in the preceding section. Is this, then, an instance of borrowing both form and content from Antiquity; has the "principle of disjunction" for once been violated? The iconography of these deities disproves the assumption. Jupiter's head sports enormous wings, Neptune wears a fish as a headdress, and Venus has a wreath of roses in her hair. Again, the artist had knowledge only of certain attributes, which he presented in his pictures in a completely unantique manner.[67] The fountain basin in St Denis undoubtedly belongs to the intellectual ambience of the twelfth-century renaissance. Some elements of twelfth-century encyclopedic book learning are evident in its program. But despite their antique characteristics, the pictorial conceptions bear little relation to Antiquity.

Ancient poetry was, apparently, scarcely ever illustrated during the twelfth century. Now and then we encounter depictions of ancient authors. But here too we can hardly speak of antique appearance when we discover, in a late twelfth-century manuscript from Freising, Horace or Vergil decked out in astonishing, largely medieval robes, with Phrygian-type caps, scepters, and banderoles (fig. 69). The headdress and attributes indicate that if an antique model was used, it was more likely the image of a ruler or a soldier than of a poet; and this prototype was then distorted through intermediate changes to the point where it was no longer recognizable.[68] Again, a manuscript in Le Mans has a picture of Pliny presenting his *Naturalis historia* to Vespasian. Wearing chain mail and carrying a shield and a lance with a banner, he resembles a knightly vassal of the twelfth century appearing before his lord.[69]

[66]For the Augustine manuscript in Schulpforta, see A. Haseloff in *Meisterwerke der Kunst aus Sachsen und Thüringen*, ed. Oscar Doering and Georg Voss (Magdeburg 1905) 94–95, and Alexandre de Laborde, *Les manuscrits à peintures de la Cité de Dieu de saint Augustin* (3 vols. Paris 1909) 1.218–25, 3 pl. 3.

[67]For the fountain basin in St Denis, see Willibald Sauerländer, "Art antique et sculpture autour de 1200," *Art de France* 1 (1961) 47–56, and idem (n. 47 above) 103.

[68]On this manuscript, see Sigrid von Borries-Schulten, "Eine Bildhandschrift aus Weihenstephan in der Vaticana," *Studien zur Buchmalerei und Goldschmiedekunst des Mittelalters: Festschrift für Karl Hermann Usener*, ed. Frieda Dettweiler et al. (Marburg 1967) 201–08.

[69]See Hanns Swarzenski, *Monuments of Romanesque Art* (Chicago 1954) pl. 129.

And, in a manuscript of about 1200, presumably from northern France, the death of Seneca has been used as an author portrait. Evidently no model was available to the painter. He illustrated the death of the philosopher by analogy with the scenes of Christian martyrdom familiar to him—John in the cauldron of oil, for example.[70] To be sure, all these depictions show evidence of the same lively interest in ancient literary tradition that prevailed in the schools and libraries of the twelfth century, but at the same time they reveal the complete breakdown of an antique pictorial tradition. We have again reached a "disjunction."

On the few occasions when we encounter illustrations of, or for, ancient poems, their appearance is no less remote from Antiquity. Even when ancient iconography has been assiduously retained—as in certain manuscripts of Terence—the style becomes increasingly medieval from the ninth to the twelfth century. Illusionistic effects and mobility are sacrificed to a linear, ornamental stylization.[71] But, whereas the Terence miniatures at least retain ancient iconography, the picture in the *Hortus deliciarum* of Odysseus rowing past the sirens with his companions (fig. 70) apparently belongs to a thoroughly medieval tradition. Odysseus, tied to the mast, resembles a knight from the time of Barbarossa, the helmsman wears a hooded medieval garment, and even the sirens retain only the claws and wings of their original ancient guise.[72] In such scenes as those from the *Achilleis* of Statius represented on the sides of a twelfth-century bronze bowl in the Paris Cabinet des Médailles, or from the story of Pyramus and Thisbe depicted on a capital in the choir of the cathedral in Basel, we invariably find an interest in antique subject matter—combined with no understanding of antique form.[73] To the extent that this can be called a renaissance, it is one of literary content and does not extend to the realm of art.

It has been suggested that the depiction of the liberal arts and the authors representing them on the Royal Portal of Chartres cathedral (fig. 71) may have been inspired by Thierry of Chartres, who compiled one of the great presentations of the seven liberal arts in his (still unprinted) *Heptateuchon*.[74] If the suggestion should prove valid, it would be a verified example of a connection between one of the great cathedral schools of the twelfth century and a

[70]See Konrad Hoffmann, ed., *The Year 1200: A Centennial Exhibition at the Metropolitan Museum of Art*, Cloisters Studies in Medieval Art 1 (New York 1970) no. 255.

[71]Leslie W. Jones and Charles R. Morey, *The Miniatures of the Manuscripts of Terence prior to the Thirteenth Century* (2 vols. Princeton 1930–31).

[72]Herrad of Landsberg, *Hortus deliciarum*, ed. A. Straub and G. Keller (Strasbourg 1901) 44 and pl. LVIII. See now also *Herrad of Hohenbourg, Hortus deliciarum*, ed. Rosalie Green, Studies of the Warburg Institute 36 (2 vols. London and Leiden 1979) *Reconstruction* 365–67, *Commentary* 202.

[73]For the Achilles bowl, see Josepha Weitzmann-Fiedler, "Romanische Bronzeschalen mit mythologischen Darstellungen," *Zeitschrift für Kunstwissenschaft* 11 (1957) 1–34 at 5–13. For the Pyramus and Thisbe capital in the Basel Minster, see Hans Reinhardt, *Das Münster zu Basel* (Burg bei Magdeburg 1928) 22–23 and fig. 67.

[74]See Adolf Katzenellenbogen, *The Sculptural Programs of Chartres Cathedral: Christ, Mary, Ecclesia* (Baltimore 1959) 18, 19.

monumental pictorial program. But once again the representations of the *artes* are not conceived in an ancient manner. The instruments of *Musica* are medieval, the fasces of *Grammatica* realistic. More important still, the ancient authors who represent the various *artes*, and whose identities remain uncertain, look no more antique than the poets, philosophers, and scholars pictured in twelfth-century manuscripts. They simply follow the relatively uniform scheme generally used in the twelfth century for the depiction of learned writers. Even in this case, where the images appear to have a direct connection with protohumanism, "disjunction" between ancient subject matter and medieval form still exists.

Finally, a brief look at medieval representations of ancient rulers. On fol. 153v of the *Liber floridus* is a picture of Alexander the Great on horseback (fig. 72). The painter apparently had no model to follow, and so his ancient emperor is made to look something like the counts of Flanders as they appear on equestrian seals.[75] Augustus, on fol. 138v of the same manuscript, looks entirely like a medieval ruler, from his folding chair to his clothing and raised sword. Only the name—the "word"—and not the image, is antique. But a famous counter-example may close this survey. If the bust at Schloss Cappenberg in Westphalia (fig. 73), preserved there as a reliquary of St John, is indeed identical with a "silver head made in the image of the emperor" ("caput argenteum ad imperatoris formatum effigiem") mentioned in documents, then we are confronted with a most exciting and instructive example of a return to Antiquity.[76] So far as we know, the depiction of the *Imperator* in the form of an imperial bust was unusual in the Middle Ages. If such is the case with the reliquary, it can only be understood as a conscious revival of Roman imperial portraiture and so constitutes pictorial proof of a "renovatio." It would be the exceptional case of a return to Antiquity gaining what might be called institutional significance. In all likelihood, this could probably occur only within the immediate circle of the emperor.

It is true that in purely quantitative terms there was an increase during the twelfth century of individual examples of borrowing from Antiquity in architecture and in the figurative arts. When we make this statement, however, we must keep in mind that our map of monuments is generally more crowded now than it was during the early Middle Ages. The various borrowings from Antiquity during the twelfth century cannot, apparently, be ascribed to a single, conscious motivation, as they can for the Renaissance of the modern

[75]See Lambert, ed. Derolez (n. 63 above) 310 (fol. 153v). For the equestrian seals of the counts of Flanders, see Rainer Kahsnitz, *Die Zeit der Staufer: Geschichte, Kunst, Kultur*, Württembergisches Landesmuseum, Katalog der Ausstellung, ed. Reiner Haussherr et al. (5 vols. Stuttgart 1977–79) 1.45 nos. 67, 68.

[76]On this see Herbert Grundmann, *Der Cappenberger Barbarossakopf und die Anfänge des Stiftes Cappenberg* (Cologne 1959).

era. The imitation of Antiquity in medieval architecture had purely practical or artistic reasons. In the figurative arts imitation of Antiquity was part of a general striving for a more natural, a more effective—physically and psychologically—method of representation. No bridge links this striving with the schools, jurisprudence, and philosophy of the twelfth century. While the depiction of ancient subject matter was undoubtedly in some cases connected with the "renaissance of the twelfth century," the art historian must qualify the conclusions that might be drawn from those depictions by noting that the connection resulted in the most unantique images imaginable. A close examination of individual cases could refine such propositions, but in the light of our present knowledge one may venture to predict that the picture would not change essentially.

Survival, Revival, Transformation

The Dialectic of Development in

Architecture and Other Arts

Walter Horn

It has become increasingly clear that the medieval response to Antiquity was governed by a developmental dialectic that led from the revival of classical ideas in art and literature through processes of transformation to successively higher levels of revival. Revival and transformation have sometimes been simultaneous and sometimes sequential, but in their effect on the shaping of medieval art and architecture they were interdependent.

This view was first expressed by Erwin Panofsky in 1924 and recurs as a leitmotif in much of his later writing about the medieval response to Antiquity. In 1924, he wrote:

The Hegelian idea that the historical process passes through a sequence of thesis, antithesis, and synthesis proves true in the development of art as well, to the extent that each stylistic advance, that is each discovery of new artistic values, has to be purchased with a partial abandonment of values already at hand. But in general the subsequent development seeks to retrieve, and make subservient to new artistic goals, those elements which in the first approach had been discarded.[1]

I should like to support this view with new material, but to do so I must extend the inquiry beyond the bounds of the century to which this volume is devoted. This seems to me justifiable, for if a historical analysis overlooks or undervalues any phase of these dialectical cycles, or equally, if the subject is studied within a span of history too short to exhibit all these interacting forces, the resultant picture may well be distorted.

[1]Erwin Panofsky, *Die deutsche Plastik des elften bis dreizehnten Jahrhunderts* (2 vols. Munich 1924) 1.28: "Der Hegelsche Gedanke, dass der historische Prozess in einer Abfolge von Thesis, Antithesis und Synthesis sich vollziehe, scheint sich auch an der Entwicklung der Kunst insofern zu bewähren, als jeder stilistische 'Fortschritt', d.h. jede Entdeckung neuer künstlerischer Werte, zunächst durch eine partielle Preisgabe der jeweils vorhandenen erkauft werden muss; die weitere Entwicklung aber zielt gewöhnlich darauf ab, das im ersten Ansturm Beiseitegeworfene von Neuem (und unter neuen Gesichtspunkten) wiederaufzunehmen und den veränderten künstlerischen Absichten dienstbar zu machen."

Confined to the fields of architecture and sculpture, my analysis considers painting only insofar as new concepts of portraying spatial depth on a two-dimensional plane emerged from concepts first developed in architecture. Still, I believe that the theories set forth here apply to all the visual arts of the Middle Ages, and that aspects of them may also be traced in the development of other disciplines such as literature, scholastic thought, and music.

THE CAROLINGIAN MODULE

The revival of the T-shaped Early Christian basilica of Rome is one of the main accomplishments of the "Carolingian renascence." It found its most powerful expression in three churches built or conceived after Charlemagne's coronation in Rome: the abbey church of Fulda, the cathedral of Cologne, and the church of the famous Plan of St Gall. The last of these was never built. It was delineated on a master plan for a monastic settlement, worked out during the reign of Louis the Pious and known to us through a contemporary copy now in the archives of the Stiftsbibliothek of St Gall.[2]

The Early Christian prototype of these churches is the Constantinian church of Old St Peter's in Rome (figs. 74 and 75). The Carolingian architects who designed and built them (some of whom may have knelt in Old St Peter's when Charlemagne received his imperial crown) did not confine themselves simply to borrowing the scheme of their model—they reshaped it by introducing into the dimensional organization of its component spaces a geometricity that was not part of the original concept.

In the Early Christian tradition of this building type, the relationship of nave to transept, and nave to aisles, was not governed by any given set of proportions but varied from building to building. As the T-shaped basilica was resurrected in Fulda, Cologne, and the Plan of St Gall (figs. 76–78), the dimensions of the constituent spaces were gradually standardized. The transept was given the same width as the nave. This established at the crucial intersection of nave and transept a square which was used as a module for the dimensional organization of the other spaces. Followed in all three of these Carolingian churches, this principle reached its apogee in the Plan of St Gall (fig. 78), in which a modular grid was applied not only to the basilica itself but also to the layout of the cloister, and in fact to the entire monastery.

This is what Panofsky (had the analyses shown in figs. 76–78 been known to him) would have referred to as *estrangement:*[3] that is, the creation, within

---

[2]On the Carolingian architectural revival in general see Richard Krautheimer, "The Carolingian Revival of Early Christian Architecture," *Art Bulletin* 24 (1942) 1–38, repr. in *Studies in Early Christian, Medieval, and Renaissance Art* (New York and London 1969) 203–56; on the specific subject of modules in Carolingian architecture see Walter Horn and Ernest Born, *The Plan of St. Gall: A Study of the Architecture and Economy of, and Life in a Paradigmatic Carolingian Monastery* (3 vols. Berkeley 1979) 1.217–23.

[3]On the use of the terms *estrangement* (occasionally supplanted by *alienation*) and *rapprochement*, see Erwin Panofsky, "Renaissance and Renascences," *The Kenyon Review* 6 (1944) 201–36 at 208, 223, and 225, and *Ren & Ren* 42.

an organism borrowed from Antiquity, of a new esthetic concept that was not part of the original scheme—a *rebirth* in a new cultural context. But this one had extraordinary consequences, because it carried within itself the possibility of the entire architectural development that followed.

FROM MODULE TO BAY-DIVISION

In very abstract and simple terms, the development from Carolingian to Gothic architecture could be characterized as a gradual but consistent transference of the modular principle adopted for the ground plan in the great Carolingian churches to the vertical parts of the structure, until modular organization permeated the space in all three dimensions.[4]

The Constantinian transept basilica (figs. 74, 75, and diagram at upper left in fig. 85) was a composition of large spaces without interior subdivisions, spaces which were placed either side by side or at right angles to one another, each a block by itself and the whole a composite of the simplest imaginable spatial volumes. The Romanesque and Gothic churches that descend from this prototype (the two lower diagrams of fig. 85), by contrast, are bay-divided churches: that is, churches whose volumes are conceived as multiples of a common spatial unit either square or oblong in plan. In the fully developed Romanesque and Gothic (figs. 81, 82, 95, 96), this division is accomplished by an all-pervasive skeleton of shafts and arches that penetrate the space in all directions.

Intermediate steps between the modular geometricity of the great Carolingian churches and the skeletal bay-division of the Romanesque and Gothic are taken in such Ottonian churches as Gernrode, 961–65, and Hildesheim, 1010–33 (fig. 79). In them, the Carolingian principle of constructing the overall dimensions of the component spaces of the church as multiples of a basic unit gained momentum with the introduction of the "alternating support system" (pier–column–pier, or pier–column–column–pier). This carried into the elevation of the church a rhythm of alternating accents that mirrored, in the varying shapes of the columns, modular prime relationships heretofore encountered only in the floor plan. This step was followed by three further innovations crucial for the emergence of the medieval bay-system: the attachment to the nave walls, at regular intervals, of shafts rising from floor to clerestory level (Speyer I, 1030–61); the interconnection of these shafts by means of diaphragm arches that carry the modular division transversely across the nave, a stage reached at Jumièges, shortly after 1052 (fig. 80); and the construction of boundary arches connecting the shafts both longitudinally and transversely, a stage first reached in Speyer II, 1082–1106 (figs. 81 and 82).

[4]On the Carolingian module as a developmental precursor of the medieval bay-system, see Walter Horn, "On the Origins of the Mediaeval Bay System," *Journal of the Society of Architectural Historians* 17 (1958) 2–23, and "On the Selective Use of Sacred Numbers and the Creation in Carolingian Architecture of a New Aesthetic Based on Modular Concepts," *Viator* 6 (1975) 351–90; and of course the work by Horn and Born quoted in n. 2 above.

As soon as this point was reached, the churches could be vaulted; and since by now all load-bearing functions had been transferred to an all-pervasive skeleton of structural members (fig. 82), the masonry between the rising shafts and arches could be perforated, to be replaced eventually by stained-glass windows. Thus the Early Christian basilica with its aggregate of adjacent monolithic spaces separated by rigid walls (figs. 74 and 75) was transformed into that intensely skeletal and bay-divided system of the Romanesque (figs. 81 and 82; fig. 85 diagrams below) and Gothic (figs. 95 and 96).

One of the cultural sources of this crucial architectural concept was the vernacular timber architecture of northern Europe, where bay-division made its appearance as early as the fourteenth century B.C. and became widely diffused during the Iron Age and throughout the entire Middle Ages.[5] A typical example of the earlier phases of this tradition is seen in the plan and axonometric reconstruction of a Germanic cattle barn of the third century B.C., excavated in 1936 (fig. 83). In this structure, the roof rests on a frame of slender timbers, whose supporting members rise from the floor at modular intervals and are tied together at the head by cross beams and long beams that divide the interior into a continuous sequence of rectangular bays. Numerous subsequent excavations have established that this type of timber building—previously almost unknown—was a standard form of house construction in all the territories occupied by Germanic peoples during prehistoric, protohistoric, and medieval times. In all these periods its primary function was to serve as dwelling for the farmer, accommodating, often under a single roof, both his family and his cattle. Used as a barn, it stored the harvest. In medieval England it became a standard form for rural manor halls and, on higher social levels, even for royal audience halls. It reached its peak of constructional beauty, both in England and on the continent, in the great monastic tithe barns, one outstanding example of which is shown in fig. 84; and it was used in France from the twelfth century onward as the standard form for urban market halls.[6] It was thus a building type known to everyone in the transalpine territories of medieval Europe.

[5]The case for the influence of vernacular timber architecture on the development of the medieval bay-system was first strongly urged by Walter Horn in "Origins" (n. 4 above) and in "Selective Use" (n. 4 above) 374–86, and vigorously reiterated by Horn and Born, *Plan of St. Gall* (n. 2 above) 1.217–23 and 2.23–114. The first and third of these three studies also contain brief summaries of the development of bay-divided timber architecture from the Bronze Age to the Middle Ages, as well as demonstrations that the guest and service structures of the Plan of St Gall are part of this building tradition.

[6]Monographic studies of two outstanding medieval monuments of this building tradition, both of the thirteenth century, are presented in Walter Horn and Ernest Born, *The Barns of the Abbey of Beaulieu at Its Granges of Great Coxwell and Beaulieu-St. Leonards* (Berkeley 1965). For good examples of medieval market halls see Walter Horn and Ernest Born, "Les Halles de Crémieu," *Evocation*, Bulletin du Groupe d'études historiques et géographiques du Bas-Dauphiné 17 (1961) 66–90; Walter Horn, "Les Halles de Questembert (Morbihan)," *Bulletin de la Société polymathique du Morbihan* (1963) 1–16; and Walter Horn and Ernest Born, "French Market Halls in Timber: Medieval and Postmedieval," *The Shape of the Past: Studies in Honor of Franklin D. Murphy*, ed. Giorgio Buccellati and Charles Speroni (Los Angeles 1981) 195–239.

From the mid-eleventh century on, these timbered halls began to exercise a powerful influence on church construction. The strength of that influence becomes apparent as one glances from the plans and elevations of Speyer cathedral (figs. 81 and 82) back to its two disparate cultural prototypes, the church of Old St Peter's in Rome (figs. 74 and 75) and the examples of vernacular northern timber architecture shown in figs. 83 and 84.

In advancing the claim that the medieval bay-system had one of its roots in the bay-division of vernacular northern timber structures, I do not mean to imply that the Romanesque and Gothic architectural systems emerged mechanically from the simple superimposition or interpenetration of two formerly separate building traditions, that of the Early Christian stone basilica and that of the medieval timber house. Primarily and above all, of course, those systems reflect metaphysical postulates and have their origins in the fact that in the Middle Ages, bay-division was as much an intellectual and cultural concept as it was a principle of architectural composition.

Sometime between 1230 and 1236, William of Auvergne put the finishing touches to a book that dealt with the structure of the universe (*Liber de universo*)[7] and sought to integrate all metaphysical concepts prevailing in his time into a comprehensive cosmological and metaphysical system. In it the universe is envisaged as a triad of structurally related hierarchies (fig. 86), each reflecting the other as well as the system as a whole, with its identically structured subdivisions into triads of triads of ranks; in each of these triads, each subordinate rank corresponds in substance to its equivalent part in every other triad. The architectural plan that underlies this metaphysical scheme displays astounding analogies with that of the Gothic bay-system. In both cases, the whole "is arranged according to a system of homologous parts and parts of parts"—if I may apply to the substance of a metaphysical concept a definition that Panofsky coined with regard to the formal layout of the scholastic treatise.[8]

[7]For William of Auvergne the reader may wish to consult Berthold Vallentin's analysis of the *Liber de universo* in a study entitled "Der Engelstaat: Zur mittelalterlichen Anschauung vom Staate (bis auf Thomas von Aquino)" in *Grundrisse und Bausteine zur Staats- und zur Geschichtslehre*, gathered in honor of Gustav Schmoller (Berlin 1908) 41–120.

For a sensitive definition of the high medieval concept of the universe as "an intelligible and coherent cosmos in which man could distinguish one area from another by clear conceptual boundaries reflected in the structure of life as well as thought" and the shattering effect the breakdown of this system had in creating cultural anxieties subsequently in Western life, see William J. Bouwsma, "Anxiety and the Formation of Early Modern Culture," in *After the Reformation: Essays in Honor of J. H. Hexter*, ed. Barbara C. Malament (Philadelphia 1980) 215–46, esp. 228ff.

[8]On intrinsic analogies between Gothic architecture and scholastic thought, see Erwin Panofsky, *Gothic Architecture and Scholasticism* (New York 1957). One component of this concept—the parallelism of secular and ecclesiastical institutions—is Early Christian, for by the fourth century the Church had modeled its administrative structure largely after that of the Empire. Carolingian awareness of this parallelism is most elaborately attested in Walafrid Strabo's *Liber de exordiis et incrementis rerum ecclesiasticarum*, written between 840 and 842; for a brief account, see Charles E. Odegaard, *Vassi and Fideles in the Carolingian Empire*, Harvard Historical Monographs 19 (Cambridge Mass. 1945) 20–21. Dionysius the Pseudo-Areopagite (fifth/sixth c.), with

THE EMERGENCE OF LIFE-SIZE ARCHITECTURAL STATUARY

The revival of the T–shaped Early Christian basilica in the Carolingian age was
an expression in architecture of the cultural and political aspirations that led in
751 to a new alliance between north and south, the Frankish state and the
Roman Church, culminating in Charlemagne's coronation as emperor of the
Romans in the year 800. It was accompanied by an astonishing revival of narrative art in book illumination and ivory carving, but it did not lead as well to a
resurrection of life-size stone statuary. That had to wait for another great wave
of resurgent classicism three centuries later. Significantly for the developmental dialectic being discussed here, it is precisely when medieval architecture, in creating the Gothic cathedral, had attained its maximum point of
"estrangement" from the original concept of the Early Christian basilica that
the north gave birth to life-size statuary, in which classical concepts of unprecedented richness and vigor emerged.

Why did this occur in the north, within the context of the Gothic cathedral, and not in Rome or elsewhere in Italy, where life-size statues were still to
be seen in many places? For the simple reason that transalpine architecture, in
its development from Romanesque to Gothic, had provided a new architectural device: the recessed Gothic portal (fig. 87), which permitted the incor-
poration of life-size sculpture into the design of the church while at the same
time setting clear and definite boundaries for the display of sculpture within
that context. This setting of boundaries was an essential precondition for the
emergence within the organism of the Gothic cathedral of such intensely
classicizing pieces of sculpture as the Visitation Group in the right jamb of the
central portal of Reims (fig. 92), the classicizing statues and carving of Strasbourg cathedral, or—in a different yet equally protective architectural context—
the famous figures of Mary and Elizabeth in the cathedral of Bamberg, not to
mention the matchless monumental statuary addorsed to the choir piers of
Naumburg cathedral.

The south of France had experimented with the idea of life-size sculpture
in a number of germinal and transitional forms. Nearly life-size reliefs carved
in niches or framed by arcades appear in the ambulatory of St Sernin in
Toulouse and the pier reliefs of the cloister of Moissac (fig. 88) as early as
around 1100; shortly thereafter, they are found attached to the jambs of portals, in the portal under the porch of Moissac and in the cloister of St Etienne
in Toulouse, both roughly around 1135. But Languedoc and Provence were

his growing influence in Carolingian Francia, may have contributed to these tendencies by viewing
the heavenly hierarchies as parallel to the orders of the Church.

   An earlier version of the diagram in fig. 86 appeared in my paper "Origins" (n. 4 above) 19
fig. 42, but I did not then know that in the early twelfth century, bishop Gilbert of Limerick illustrated graphically the parallelism of lay and ecclesiastical hierarchies, from priest to pope and from
knight to emperor; see his treatise *De statu ecclesiae* (PL 159.995–1004 at 999), and the accompanying diagrams reproduced in R. A. B. Mynors, *Durham Cathedral Manuscripts to the End of
the Twelfth Century* (Oxford 1939) 41–42 and pl. 32. Robert L. Benson called my attention to
Gilbert's theory, on which he is preparing a study.

not capable of offering any appropriate architectural matrix within which to accommodate life-size statuary. The most outstanding example of the twelfth-century classical revival in Gallia Narbonensis, the façade of St Gilles—a "mixture of church entrance and triumphal arch"[9]—was a pseudo-façade attached to the exterior of the church like a relief, but it was neither structurally nor stylistically an integral part of its fabric. Some of the figures are draped like Roman senators and displayed in Roman niches, manifestations of an important local revival nourished by the proximity of a rich repertoire of surviving Roman statues; yet they were not within the mainstream of the medieval development. The St Gilles figures may have had a stimulating effect on the north in posing the problem of life-size statuary, but they did not solve it.[10]

The solution was found in the north with the invention of the columnar statue. The idea for it came, surprisingly enough, in a context where it might least have been expected: in the field of book illumination, where figures of saints were attached to long initial letters such as I (fig. 89) in the same manner in which statues were subsequently attached to the columns in the façades of St Denis and Chartres (figs. 87, 90, and 91). The primary condition for the sudden acceptance and phenomenal propagation of the columnar statue was the production in the Ile de France, within an architectural context wholly unclassical, of the recessed Gothic portal, which permitted life-size sculpture to develop more freely and with vastly superior opportunities for imitating the classical treatment of body and drapery than was possible in the south, where such an architectural matrix was wanting.

The steps leading to the concept of the columnar statue within the context of the recessed Gothic portal have been brilliantly described by Erwin Panofsky.[11] First, the frontal Romanesque pier or jamb figure (fig. 88) was converted into a figure placed diagonally within the block (fig. 90) out of which it was hewn. Next came the separation, in the "diagonalized" Early Gothic jamb figure, of both the figure and the residual mass of the block into two basically cylindrical units, the statue and colonette (compare figs. 87, 90, and 91). Finally, the colonette was absorbed within the mass of the figure, which could thus become completely detached (fig. 92) and yet still remain firmly integrated with the architectural structure by means of a bracket beneath and an elaborate canopy above.

It is at this point—within the context of an architectural system intrinsically northern and lacking any antecedents or parallels in the classical

---

[9]See Willibald Sauerländer, in this volume, p. 676.

[10]It is again Panofsky who must be credited with having defined, with unsurpassable succinctness, this antithetical interdependence between classical resurgence and Gothic art: "In France, then, mediaeval art came closest to the Antique when a proto-Renaissance movement born in the Romanesque South was drawn into the orbit of the Gothic style developed in the Royal Domain and Champagne; and we can understand that in Italy a like stage was not reached until, conversely, the Gothic style developed in the Royal Domain and Champagne had interpenetrated with, and in a sense transformed, the indigenous proto-Renaissance" (*Ren & Ren* 64).

[11]In *Deutsche Plastik* (n. 1 above) 25–28 and *Ren & Ren* 60–62.

world—that medieval statuary attains its greatest strength in reviving classical forms. This seemingly paradoxical yet (in terms of the underlying cultural dialectic) extremely logical response to Antiquity holds true as well for another important medieval innovation.

FROM TIMBER ROOF TO MASONRY VAULT

The diffusion throughout the entire Mediterranean world of public buildings of unprecedented dimensions, composed of massive blocks of masonry and covered with monumental groin and barrel vaults, constituted one of Rome's most significant contributions to the architecture of the Western world. This accomplishment was predicated by the invention of concrete, which enabled the Romans to construct walls of sufficient thickness and strength to take the load and thrust of vaults rising to considerable heights, and in this manner to construct such vast interiors as the halls of the baths of Caracalla and Diocletian and the even more overwhelming basilica of the emperor Maxentius—not to speak of that dome of incomparable perfection that covers the Roman Pantheon (figs. 99 and 100), or the mile of barrel vaults, superimposed one upon the other, tier after tier, that support the seats of the Roman Colosseum.

When Constantine the Great elevated the Christian faith to the status of the officially favored religion, he found himself compelled to sponsor the erection in every major Roman town of places of worship capable of accommodating large crowds. Had Constantine selected for this purpose a masonry structure covered with monumental groin and barrel vaults—of the kind then preferred for buildings of state, as strikingly exemplified in the heroic basilica begun by his imperial rival and predecessor Maxentius a decade earlier—he would have bankrupted the empire. He chose instead a thin-walled structure (figs. 74 and 75) composed of a nave and aisles and roofed with timber, prototypes for which could be found in Roman market and audience halls. The medieval conversion of this building-type into an all-masonry structure was accomplished not in the homeland of Roman masonry tradition, but north of the Alps, surprisingly enough under the influence of barbarian wood construction.

Even after the collapse of the Roman Empire and the conquest of its former provinces by Germanic tribes whose peoples by tradition built in timber, the art of constructing groin and barrel vaults never died out entirely (not at all in Spain or on the French side of the Pyrenees); but in the earlier Middle Ages, it generally remained confined to subterranean or semisubterranean parts of churches, such as crypts (fig. 93) or the lower stories of Carolingian westworks (fig. 94), which because of their limited heights were relatively easy to vault. This continuity of Roman building methods, practiced on a limited scale, clearly must be classified as *survival*.

The transfer, however, of such masonry vaults from the crypts and ground floor of westworks to the principal body of the church, with its large and more steeply ascending spaces—first to the aisles (Speyer I and Jumièges, fig. 80) and then to nave and transept (Speyer II, figs. 81 and 82)—cannot possibly be interpreted as survival but is clearly a return to Roman imperial concepts that antedate the Constantinian invention of the Early Christian basilica. This harking back to a more classical phase of Antiquity was made possible by the evolution, under the influence of northern wood construction, of building methods that allowed the church to be divided into sequences of relatively narrow spaces—sufficiently narrow to be vaulted in masonry at breathtaking heights (figs. 95 and 96).

The basic model on which this was accomplished remained that of the Early Christian basilica (figs. 74, 75, and 97), but so reshaped, across the development that led from its Carolingian revival to the emergence of the Romanesque, as to constitute a new form of Romanization—sufficiently so to justify the term Romanesque. It is paradoxical yet highly symptomatic of the underlying cultural dialectic that the transformation of the timber-roofed Early Christian basilica into an all-masonry structure depended on its encounter with a transalpine tradition of vernacular timber architecture which changed the flat load-bearing walls of the Early Christian prototype into an armature of shafts and arches capable of supporting masonry vaults on every level of the structure.[12]

The nature of this dialectical interaction between north and south, the Middle Ages and Antiquity, becomes especially apparent by comparison with other attempts to invoke the memory of the classical past that lack one of these contributing forces. This I believe to have been the case in the "twelfth-century renaissance" of the city of Rome.

REVIVAL OF THE EARLY CHRISTIAN BASILICA IN TWELFTH-CENTURY ROME

If viewed within the entire framework of medieval revivals of Antiquity—the relation of the so-called renascences to one another, and of their aggregate to the Italian Renaissance of the fifteenth and sixteenth centuries—the Roman renascence of the twelfth century appears to me to be the least important. It lacks one of the two intrinsic ingredients of all developmentally productive medieval renascences, in that it was limited merely to borrowing esthetic formulas from the past without reshaping them.

The church of Santa Maria in Trastevere (fig. 98) is an outstanding work of architecture, as distinguished in its own terms as its Early Christian prototype, the church of Santa Maria Maggiore in Rome (fig. 97); but there is nothing innovative in either its style, the shaping of its spaces, the concept of its walls, or the design of its roof. It does not even have a Latin-cross plan, and in the absence of projecting transept arms and a fore-choir lacks architectural

---

[12]In his courses on Gothic architectures, offered at the University of Hamburg in the second decade of this century, Panofsky referred to this process with the term *Vergliederung* (membrification)—without, however, relating it to any influences exerted by vernacular timber architecture on the development of church construction. The existence of this vernacular building tradition was not known in those days.

components that by geometrical interaction with nave and presbytery played a primary role in the creation of the Carolingian modular grid (figs. 76–78).[13] It is the absence of any such innovative response that distinguishes this Roman twelfth-century resurrection of the Early Christian basilica from the revival of that same building tradition three centuries earlier on the other side of the Alps—with, as we saw, tremendous effects on subsequent developments. I would be inclined to define Santa Maria in Trastevere as a simple attempt to retrieve the memory of past grandeur, undertaken primarily in the pursuit of political goals—but not as a renascence in the medieval sense of that term.

In the field of sculpture, also, twelfth-century Rome was surprisingly uncreative. The great twelfth-century revival of classicizing life-size statuary occurred not in Rome but north of the Alps, and within the context of an architectural system as wholly un-Roman as it was intrinsically medieval and northern. It is symptomatic of this categorical lack of interaction with northern esthetic concepts in twelfth-century Rome that Innocent II, in a symbolic act designed to bolster the unique traditional sovereignty of the Roman See (in the face of similar claims being made by the neo-Roman senate), ordered his mortal remains to be placed not in a coffin carved by a contemporary sculptor, but in the monumental porphyry sarcophagus that had once enshrined the body of the emperor Hadrian.[14] This too was revival without transformation: a case of borrowing, not a rebirth or recreation.

The absence of any dialectical interaction between two disparate esthetic traditions, such as that which governed the development of architecture and life-size architectural sculpture in the north, may well be why twelfth-century Rome's fascination with ancient Rome had so little, if any, effect on the Italian Renaissance of the fifteenth century. The lifeline that leads from the Pantheon to Bramante's and Michelangelo's New St Peter's does not run through twelfth-century Rome but through eleventh-century Florence, and, on its way from ancient Rome to Florence, through Charlemagne's Palace Chapel at Aachen. This process could not possibly be understood if its analysis were confined to only a part of the developmental dialectic connecting these monuments.

MEDIEVAL SEGMENTATION OF SPACE

Buildings of circular plan were not in the mainstream of medieval architectural development in Western Europe. They remained confined to secondary structures such as palace chapels and baptisteries, plus a few isolated churches. The

---

[13]Since these lines were written, Richard Krautheimer has addressed himself in unequivocal language to the question of the inhibiting burden which Rome had to face with the weight of her own past. Roman church planning of the twelfth century, he states in *Rome: Profile of a City, 312–1308* (Princeton 1980) 176, ''is unexciting when viewed in the context of the great Romanesque churches that in these same years, and often one or two generations before,'' rose elsewhere in Europe; ''Rome was weighed down by her history; and the weight she carried kept her out of Europe'' (177).

[14]See the discussion of this event by Ernst Kitzinger in this volume, p. 648.

reason is simple: by the nature of its design, a building of circular plan is a nondirectional structure. It does not guide the eye, or for that matter the entering worshipper, to any particular point unless it is modified for that purpose; and it does not lend itself as readily as do churches of longitudinal plan to internal subdivision into altar- or keystone-oriented aggregates of modular and hierarchically ordered spaces. Yet even with their natural typological limitations, the only two medieval buildings of central plan in the West that may lay claim to true historical distinction—the Palace Chapel at Aachen and the Baptistery at Florence—cannot escape the impact of that powerful medieval urge to break up and compartmentalize the corporeal spaces inherited from late Antiquity.

The conceptual archetypes and prototypes of the Palace Chapel at Aachen and the Baptistery of Florence were the Roman Pantheon (figs. 99 and 100) and the early Byzantine church of San Vitale in Ravenna (figs. 101 and 102)—each in its own terms a prime example of the classical concept of spatial corporeality. The main characteristic of this concept—whether embodied in a unitary structure such as the Pantheon or in a composite building such as San Vitale—is that their masonry shells bound the space they enclose, as the skin of a man bounds the mass of his body. In either case, the movement of the enclosing masonry is encircling, not divisive, and the enveloped space, uninvaded by any of the surrounding features, is undisturbed in the full corporeal unity of its spatial mass. The Pantheon is a body of space of globular perfection cast within a masonry shell of simple cylindrical shape, whose surfaces merge in unbroken continuity with those of its superincumbent dome. San Vitale is a composite space, formed by an octahedron that is encircled by a double-storied perimeter of outer spaces of lesser width and height. The shell that bounds the center space (fig. 102) is perforated by a double tier of arches corresponding to the two levels of the peripheral spaces. Despite this intensive perforation, the masonry shell that encircles the inner space is so designed as to give the appearance of a coherent, undulating shell that envelops without in any way fragmenting the encircled space. This is sculpture in space, springing from a concept of spatial mass akin in spirit to the blocklike self-containedness of the component spaces of the Early Christian basilica.

By contrast, the design of the Palace Chapel at Aachen (figs. 103 and 104), and that of the Baptistery of Florence (figs. 105–107), are based upon the concept of spatial divisibility. Instead of billowing niches swinging inward and outward yet never losing their encircling hold, we find straight surfaces, separated by sharp lines rising from the corners of the octagon and ascending in an uninterrupted flow from the ground floor to the apex of the cloister vault that covers them. The emphasis has shifted from connecting surfaces to separating lines. For this reason, both the Palace Chapel at Aachen and the Baptistery of Florence convey the feeling of being composed of wedges of space, rather than forming an internally undivided and indivisible whole. Each building could be thought of as an aggregate of triangular prisms, with their sharp inner edges meeting at the vertical center axis (somewhat like the segments of an orange). This is medieval modular articulation versus nonsegmental classical composition of space—the conceptual equivalent in a building of central plan to the modular square division of the Carolingian basilica and the modular bay-division of the Romanesque and Gothic.[15]

The Florentine Baptistery has other features even more distinctly medieval: its enclosing wall, including even the lower half of its dome (fig. 105), is double-shelled, and the residual slice of space between these shells is subdivided into sequences of narrow compartments by means of transverse walls that transmit the thrust of the dome through the entire lower portion of the building—a principle of active resistance copiously used in Romanesque and Gothic architecture beyond the Alps, and successfully reemployed in Brunelleschi's dome of Santa Maria del Fiore in Florence and Michelangelo's dome of New St Peter's in Rome. It is vastly different from the principle, employed in Roman architecture, of neutralizing the thrust of superincumbent vaults by a massive thickening of the supporting walls. It is medieval, moreover, in the sense that the profiles of pilasters, columns, architraves, and blind arches displayed in relief on the inner and outer shells of the building are not only in essence identical (as they never were in classical buildings) but also are so closely aligned with the buttress-system located between these shells as to appear to be surface projections of this interior structural system. Yet the design of these relief elements (figs. 106 and 107) is so classical that Filippo Brunelleschi and all other Florentines of his period were convinced that the Baptistery was a Roman temple.[16] It is one of the great but significant paradoxes in the history of Western art that a building more classical in design than any of the surviving Early Christian baptisteries is not an ancient but a medieval structure, the product of the most ingenious, most successful, and most deceptive medieval synthesis of Antiquity and the Middle Ages.

FROM BAY-DIVISION TO VANISHING-POINT PERSPECTIVE

The Baptistery of Florence played a crucial role in shaping the architectural philosophy of the man generally acknowledged as the founder of the fifteenth-century Italian Renaissance, Ser Filippo Brunelleschi. Yet Brunelleschi's most significant contribution to Western art was not in the field of architecture. It was in painting. He is the inventor of modern central-vanishing-point perspective, which he developed by examining, from the steps of the cathedral of

[15]For these distinctions between Roman and Early Christian corporeality of space and medieval segmentation of space, see Walter Horn, "Das Florentiner Baptisterium," *Mitteilungen des Kunsthistorischen Institutes in Florenz* 5 (1938) 100–51 (reprinted by the Department of History of Art, University of California at Berkeley, 1974), and idem, "Romanesque Churches in Florence: A Study in Their Chronology and Stylistic Development," *Art Bulletin* 25 (1943) 112–31; and "Selective Use" (n. 4 above) 377–79.

[16]An opinion shared even in modern times, by such distinguished scholars as Nardini, Venturi, Rupp, Toesca, and Anthony. For references see Horn, "Das Florentiner Baptisterium" (n. 15 above) 102.

Florence, the linear deflection that the octagonal form of the adjacent Baptistery underwent when reflected on the flat surface of a mirror.[17]

Central-vanishing-point perspective is a system of linear coordinates (orthogonals and transversals) that define with mathematical precision the dimensional changes to which images are subjected according to their position in the space that extends from the frontal plane of a picture to its point of infinity (fig. 108). The formulation of such a system of linear coordinates, pervading, dividing, and encompassing the visible world in all directions, would have been unthinkable without the premise of medieval modularity, whether embodied in the bay-division of the Romanesque and Gothic (figs. 81–82) or in the philosophy of the hierarchically ordered universe envisaged by such men as William of Auvergne (fig. 86) and Thomas Aquinas. It is classical corporeality reborn within the framework of a system of invisible all-pervasive and all-inclusive linear coordinates, and its net product is an intellectually ordered and mathematically controllable spatial continuum.

This synthesis could only have been accomplished south of the Alps, where the concept of spatial corporeality, never entirely suppressed, shared in a cultural ambience sensitive to linear control and modular divisibility. Florence with its Baptistery was such a place.

The Romans had struggled with the problem of linear perspective but did not solve it (fig. 109). Byzantine painters and mosaicists transmitted the problem to the Middle Ages. Increasing interest in a perspective interpretation of space can be observed in the work of such painters as Duccio (ca. 1255–1319) and Giotto (1267?–1337), and it spread throughout Europe in the course of the fourteenth century.[18] The solution was found by Brunelleschi—an architect, not a painter—as he strove to make accurate architectural drawings of a building that, because of its octagonal shape, was extremely difficult to portray on a flat surface. He discovered that this could be done by means of a linear system that defined the visible outer world of space as an aggregate of mathematically controllable units of space (figs. 108 and 110).

The impact of this discovery was overwhelming. It enabled painters to depict man and his physical environment with a degree of realism never attained in any earlier age, and it allowed them to incorporate in this new spatial continuum a wealth of classical imagery that lay beyond the grasp of any previous renascence of Antiquity. It is obvious that this transfer of the concept of measurability from architecture to environmental space was associated with a crucial change in metaphysical thought. In the cosmological scheme of William of Auvergne and other scholastics of the twelfth and thirteenth cen-

[17]For graphic reconstructions of precisely how this might have been done, see Richard Krautheimer and Trude Krautheimer-Hess, *Lorenzo Ghiberti* (Princeton 1956) 235ff; Samuel Y. Edgerton, Jr., *The Renaissance Rediscovery of Linear Perspective* (New York 1975) 143–53; and, concerning symbolic implications of this epochal discovery, Erwin Panofsky, "Die Perspektive als 'Symbolische Form,'" *Vorträge der Bibliothek Warburg* (1924–25) 258–330.

[18]See the chapter "*I Primi Lumi*: Italian Trecento Painting and Its Impact on the Rest of Europe" in Panofsky, *Ren & Ren* 114–61.

turies, God was outside and above all material substances. The fourteenth and fifteenth centuries brought a more sympathetic attitude toward nature. More and more voices could be heard describing God as immanent in the universe of finite things—an idea that made the physical world and physical space a subject worthy of exploration in the arts as well as in intellectual analysis. Nature and the variety and contrariety of material substances thus having been ennobled in a metaphysical sense, the time had come for sculpture to step out of its architectural confinement into the reality of open, but by now mathematically controlled space.

A direct developmental line thus leads from Carolingian modular control of architectural space, through its structural and spatial elaboration in the bay-divided churches of the Romanesque and Gothic, to Brunelleschi's portrayal of man's spatial environment as a void composed of a multitude of accurately measurable, modular units of space. In its ultimate form this amounted to nothing less than a total integration of northern linear control with the Roman concept of spatial corporeality and pictorial illusionism.

The road that led to this synthesis was by no means straight. By origin diametrically opposed to one another, these two converging cultural traditions—one by origin abstract and antifigurative, the other inherently figurative and deeply interested in the pictorial conquest of space—fell under each other's spell because they were in essence supplementary, and because in merging each had the capacity to reinforce the other's intrinsic strength. They managed to reconcile their conflicts in a process of dialectical interaction which, over a period of no less than seven hundred years, passed from *revival* through intermittent phases of *transformation* to successively higher and *more comprehensive stages of revival.* A prime characteristic of this dialectic is the extraordinary self-restraint with which the nascent medieval world approached Antiquity. It rarely reached out for more than was compatible with its own esthetic and intellectual imperatives, and when in moments of exuberant fascination with classical ideas this principle was violated, incompatible elements were quickly and invariably sloughed off, to be reconsidered under more favorable conditions in a subsequent phase.[19]

During the first successful revival of classical concepts, in the age of Charlemagne, sculpture was categorically rejected, except for some interesting

[19] An outstanding example of this occasional urge to reach for more than can profitably be absorbed is the portraits of the Evangelists in the Vienna Treasury Gospels, one of the principal manuscripts of the so-called Palace School at the court of Charlemagne, with illuminations so deceptively antique in style that they were credited by some scholars to a Byzantine artist. The reaction came quickly in the manuscripts of the so-called Court School, in a stylistic reorganization that emphasized linear and planimetric control (main example: Lorsch Gospels, ca. 820). This trend was further strengthened in the manuscripts of the Ottonian schools of book illumination, which produced a style so firm and self-assured as to admit in the periods that followed a strong wave of new and richer inspirations from the classical past (Nicholas of Verdun and his school) that exercised a strong influence on the nascent Gothic portal sculpture.

experiments in the minor arts. It began to assert itself cautiously in the second half of the eleventh century as an integral part of the architectural mass of churches, but it did not secure a firm and legitimate base of existence prior to the twelfth century, when architecture, in the form of the columnar statue, had established for it a slot in a structural system that had no parallels in Roman architecture. Sculpture developed great strength in this context (in some places even great "classical" strength—see fig. 92), but it had to wait for the passage of another three hundred years to break out of its architectural captivity into the reality of open space—which by now had become an all-embracing and mathematically controllable entity, a new yet broader form of containment. The creation of this new concept of space was the work of a man whose love for classical form was as abiding as his commitment to medieval geometricity.[20]

The fullness and complexity of the synthesis thus attained between Antiquity and the Middle Ages was in direct proportion to the strength of the differences that originally divided them. It has been said that in Byzantine art "there was too much survival of classical traditions to admit of full-scale revivals."[21] The north did not suffer from any such hereditary burdens. It was just because the initial differences were so great, the approach so slow and guarded, that the resulting synthesis proved to be so penetrating.

Performing this feat of integration in what Panofsky liked to refer to as an "undulating curve of alternate estrangements and rapprochements,"[22] the West finally evolved a cultural structure that had the strength of two civilizations wrapped into one. It did not entail suppression of one by the other, but complete absorbtion *of each in the other*. And, in the end, it turned out to be, not a return to Antiquity, but a breakthrough to modern forms of art and thought.

Bibliographical Note

For general orientation on the development of European architecture from late Antiquity to the end of the Middle Ages: Nikolaus Pevsner, *An Outline of European Architecture* (7th ed. Harmondsworth 1963) chs. 2–3; Richard Krautheimer, *Early Chris-*

[20]Brunelleschi did not accomplish in architecture the same consummate synthesis between medieval and classical concepts of space that he achieved with his invention of central-vanishing-point perspective. The floor plans of his basilican churches of San Lorenzo and Santo Spirito at Florence are a fifteenth-century revival of the square schematism of the Romanesque. The classical elements of his architecture were inspired primarily by the Baptistery of Florence, which he and his contemporaries thought to be antique but which in fact was medieval. In architecture the great synthesis between Antiquity and the Middle Ages was struck two generations later by such men as Bramante, Michelangelo, and Vignola, with the replacement of Old St Peter's by New St Peter's. This work is characterized by the same dialectical interaction between medieval and classical concepts of mass, structure, and space that activated earlier renascences.

[21]Panofsky, "Renaissance and Renascences" (n. 3 above) 204.

[22]Panofsky, *Ren & Ren* 42, or, as he put it in "Renaissance and Renascences," "a cyclical succession of assimilative and non-assimilative phases" (225).

tian and Byzantine Architecture, Pelican History of Art (2nd ed. Harmondsworth and Baltimore 1975); Kenneth J. Conant, *Carolingian and Romanesque Architecture, 800 to 1200*, Pelican History of Art (3rd ed. Harmondsworth and Baltimore 1973); Hermann Fillitz et al., *Das Mittelalter* I, Propyläen Kunstgeschichte 5 (Berlin 1969); Otto von Simson et al., *Das Mittelalter* II: *Das Hohe Mittelalter*, Propyläen Kunstgeschichte 6 (Berlin 1972). In each of these last two works the reader will find magnificent bibliographical records of all aspects, regions, and periods of medieval art and architecture.

Fundamental for medieval revivals of Antiquity and their underlying developmental dialectic are Erwin Panofsky's "Renaissance and Renascences," *The Kenyon Review* 6 (1944) 201–36 and *Ren & Ren*.

Works dealing with Carolingian art in general: Jean Hubert, Jean Porcher, and W. F. Volbach, *The Carolingian Renaissance* (New York 1970 [published in London as *Carolingian Art*]); Wolfgang Braunfels, *Die Welt der Karolinger und ihre Kunst* (Munich 1968); *Karl der Grosse, Lebenswerk und Nachleben*, ed. Wolfgang Braunfels et al. (5 vols. Düsseldorf 1965–68) esp. vol. 3. Indispensable for the study of Carolingian architecture: *Vorromanische Kirchenbauten: Katalog der Denkmäler bis zum Ausgang der Ottonen*, ed. Friedrich Oswald, Leo Schaefer, and Hans Rudolf Sennhauser, Veröffentlichungen des Zentralinstitut für Kunstgeschichte 3 (1 vol. in 3 Munich 1960–71). On the Carolingian architectural revival specifically, see Richard Krautheimer's masterly study, "The Carolingian Revival of Early Christian Architecture," *Art Bulletin* 24 (1942) 1–38, reprinted in his *Studies in Early Christian, Medieval, and Renaissance Art* (New York and London 1969) 203–56. On the concept of modularity in Carolingian architecture (not dealt with by Krautheimer), see Walter Horn, "On the Selective Use of Sacred Numbers and the Creation in Carolingian Architecture of a New Aesthetic Based on Modular Concepts," *Viator* 6 (1975) 351–90, and Walter Horn and Ernest Born, *The Plan of St. Gall: A Study of the Architecture and Economy of, and Life in a Paradigmatic Carolingian Monastery* (3 vols. Berkeley 1979) 1.217–23. The appearance of modular concepts in Carolingian literature and music has been dealt with in two articles: Charles W. Jones, "Carolingian Aesthetics: Why Modular Verse?" *Viator* 6 (1975) 309–40, and Richard L. Crocker, "The Early Frankish Sequence: A New Musical Form," ibid. 341–49; to which must now be added Crocker's book, *The Early Medieval Sequence* (Berkeley 1977).

For Ottonian architecture, see Louis Grodecki, *L'architecture ottonienne* (Paris 1958). For Early and High Romanesque architecture: Hans Erich Kubach and Peter Bloch, *Früh- und Hochromanik*, Kunst der Welt ser. 2: Die Kulturen des Abendlandes (Baden-Baden 1964); Hans Erich Kubach and Albert Verbeek, *Romanische Baukunst an Rhein und Maas: Katalog der vorromanischen und romanischen Denkmäler*, Deutscher Verlag für Kunstwissenschaft (3 vols. Berlin 1976). A magnificent visual record of Romanesque architecture in France is contained in the collection "La nuit des temps" (94 vols. Paris 1954–78).

Outstanding recent studies dealing with Gothic architecture are: Robert Branner, *Gothic Architecture* (New York 1961); Louis Grodecki et al., *Gothic Architecture*, trans. I. Mark Paris, History of World Architecture Series (New York 1977); and Jean Bony, *French Gothic Architecture of the Twelfth and Thirteenth Century*, California Studies in the History of Art 20 (in press). On Gothic sculpture, see the essay by Willibald Sauerländer in this volume and the literature cited there.

Concerning sculpture as an integral part of architectural mass (in the Romanesque period) and architectural structure (in the Gothic period), see Erwin Panofsky, *Die deutsche Plastik des elften bis dreizehnten Jahrhunderts* (2 vols. Munich 1924). Intrinsic analogies between Gothic architecture and scholastic thought were studied by the same author: *Gothic Architecture and Scholasticism* (New York 1957).

The conception of space, its mass and the structural treatment of it, was of course a central part of the developmental dialectic. On the distinction between Roman and Early Christian corporeality of space on the one hand and medieval segmentation of architectural space on the other, see the articles cited in note 15 above, and the literature quoted under "Zum Problem der Zentralbauten," on page 301 of the work by Fillitz listed above.

The study of the vernacular architecture of the Middle Ages is in a pitiful state. The rich and exemplary literature available on proto- and prehistoric as well as early medieval house construction of northwestern Europe (where spectacular discoveries have been made during the last three decades) apparently lies outside the reading of most scholars studying medieval architecture. Worse, the surviving medieval buildings of the European countryside—many of outstanding beauty—remain unsurveyed, while fire diminishes their number at an alarming rate. Such neglect has retarded our understanding of this building tradition's impact on shaping two of the great ecclesiastical styles of the West, Romanesque and Gothic. My own attempts (notes 5 and 6 above) to correct these shortcomings summarize the development of bay-divided timber architecture from the Bronze Age to the Middle Ages.

Those interested in the prehistoric and medieval archeology of this architectural tradition will find surveys of recent excavations in *Neue Ausgrabungen in Deutschland*, ed. Werner Krämer, Deutsches Archäologisches Institut, Römisch-Germanische Kommission (Berlin 1958); and *Ausgrabungen in Deutschland: Gefördert von der Deutschen Forschungsgemeinschaft, 1950–1975*, Römisch-Germanisches Zentralmuseum zu Mainz, Forschungsinstitut für Vor- und Frühgeschichte (Mainz 1975) vol. 1, *Vorgeschichte und Römerzeit*; vol. 2, *Römische Kaiserzeit im Freien Germanien, Frühmittelalter I*; vol. 3, *Frühmittelalter II, Archäologie und Naturwissenschaften, Karten und Modelle*; vol. 4, *Beilagen 1–50*. For England, see *The Archaeology of Anglo-Saxon England*, ed. David M. Wilson (London 1976).

On the origins and development of modern vanishing-point perspective: Erwin Panofsky, "Die Perspektive als 'Symbolische Form,'" *Vorträge der Bibliothek Warburg* (1924–25) 258–330 has studied the symbolic and general cultural implications of its discovery. For graphic reconstructions of how Brunelleschi actually might have gone about demonstrating the underlying mathematical principles involved, see Richard Krautheimer and Trude Krautheimer-Hess, *Lorenzo Ghiberti* (Princeton 1956) 235ff. John E. C. T. White, in *The Birth and Rebirth of Pictorial Space* (London 1957), is concerned not so much with the discovery of the laws of perspective as such, as with how Renaissance artists manipulated perspectival methods in pictorial representation. By contrast, Samuel Y. Edgerton, Jr. builds his book *The Renaissance Rediscovery of Linear Perspective* (New York 1975) around the drama of Brunelleschi's discovery, looking back at medieval optics as a theoretical and intellectual background of Renaissance perspective. Magnificent drawings giving the illusion of elaborate, often deep architectural space as employed in theatrical stage design of the seventeenth and eighteenth centuries will be found in Dunbar H. Ogden, ed. and trans., *The Italian Baroque Stage: Documents by Giulio Troili, Andrea Pozzo, Ferdinando Galli-Bibiena, and Baldassare Orsini* (Berkeley 1978).

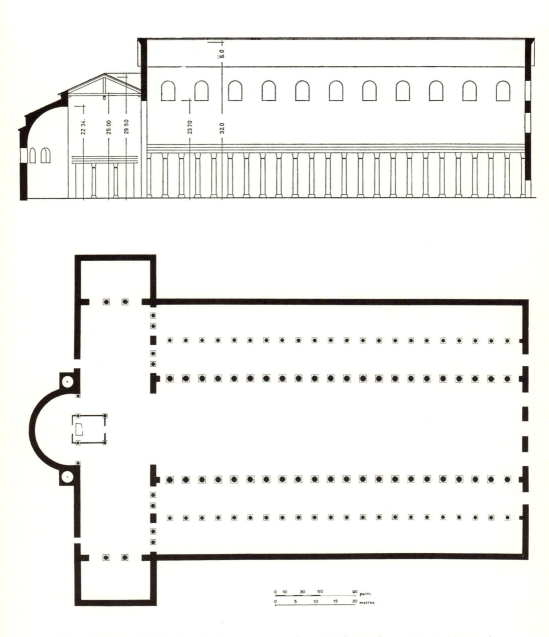

Fig 74. Rome. Old St Peter's (begun shortly after 324; finished ca. 337). Section and plan. Section after Jürgen Christern and Katharina Thiersch, "Der Aufriss von Alt-St.-Peter," *Römische Quartalschrift für Christliche Altertumskunde und Kirchengeschichte* 64 (1969) 1–34 at 24 fig. 7; plan after Jan H. Jongkees, *Studies on Old St. Peter's,* Archaeologica Traiectina 8 (Groningen 1966) pl. 1.

Fig. 75. Rome. Old St Peter's. Interior, looking toward altar. Reconstruction by Turpin C. Bannister, "The Constantinian Basilica of Saint Peter at Rome," *Journal of the Society of Architectural Historians* 27 (1968) 3–32 at 26 fig. 26.

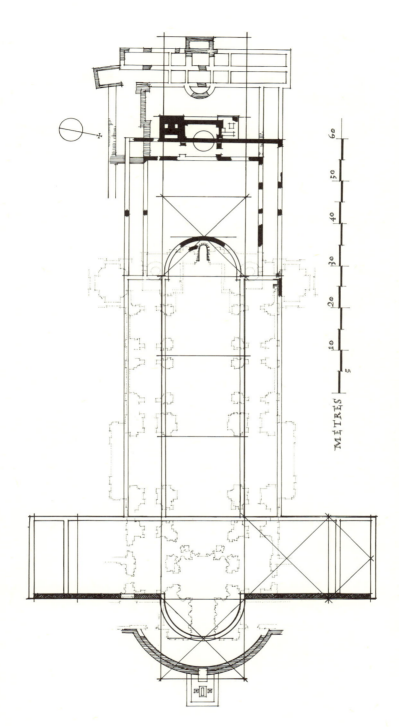

Fig. 76. Fulda. Abbey church. Plan of the form it had attained under abbot Ratgar (802–17). Redrawn (with square grid super-imposed) by Ernest Born, after *Vorromanische Kirchenbauten: Katalog der Denkmäler bis zum Ausgang der Ottonen*, ed. Friedrich Oswald, Leo Schaefer, and Hans R. Sennhauser (1 vol. in 3 Munich 1966–71) pt. 1 pl. following p. 80.

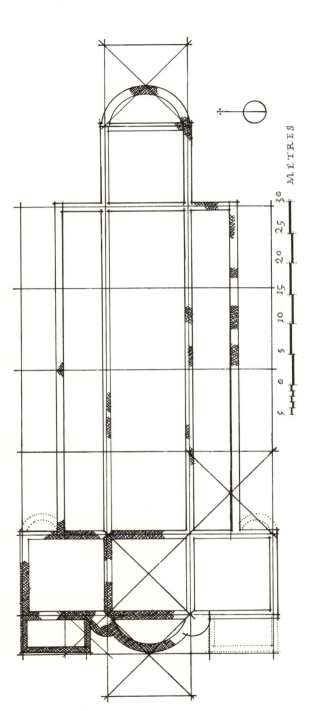

METRES

Fig. 77. Cologne. Cathedral (founded by bishop Hildebold, d. 819). Plan. Redrawn (with square grid superimposed) by Ernest Born, after Willy Weyres, "Der karolingische Dom zu Köln," *Karl der Grosse: Lebenswerk und Nachleben*, ed. Wolfgang Braunfels et al. (5 vols. Düsseldorf 1965–68) vol. 3, *Karolingische Kunst*, 384–423 at 410 fig. 11.

Fig. 78 (below). Plan of St Gall (ca. 820). Plan of church and claustrum. Redrawn by Ernest Born with superimposed 40-foot square grid (Carolingian feet).

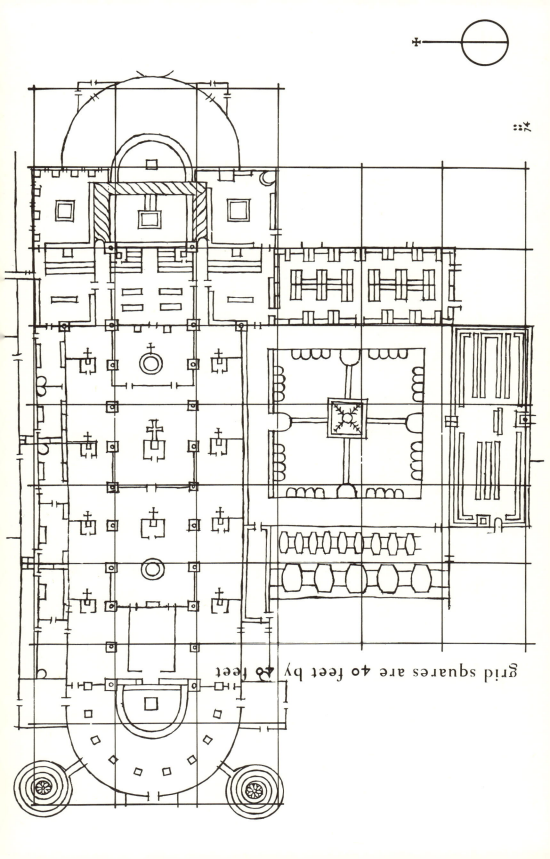

grid squares are 40 feet by 40 feet

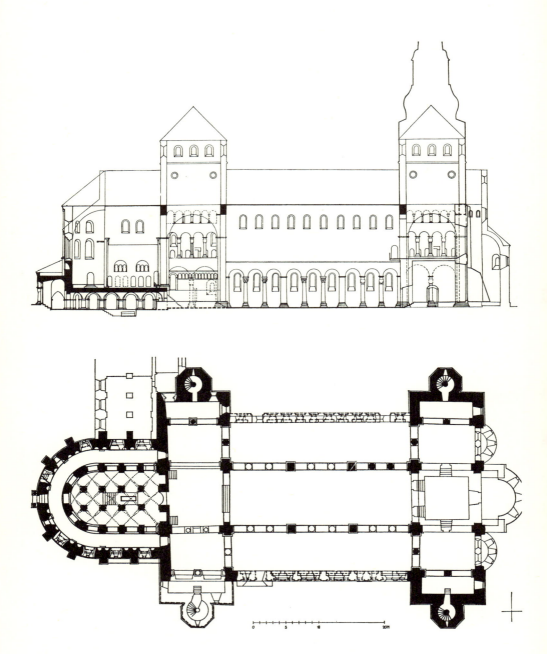

Fig. 79. Hildesheim. St Michael's (1010–33). Section and plan. Alternating piers and columns at modular intervals is a leitmotif of Ottonian architecture, but it has sporadic antecedents in Carolingian architecture (Reichenau-Mittelzell, Werden, Solnhofen). After *Vorromanische Kirchenbauten: Katalog der Denkmäler bis zum Ausgang der Ottonen*, ed. Friedrich Oswald, Leo Schaefer, and Hans R. Sennhauser (1 vol. in 3 Munich 1966–71) pt. 1, 119 and 120.

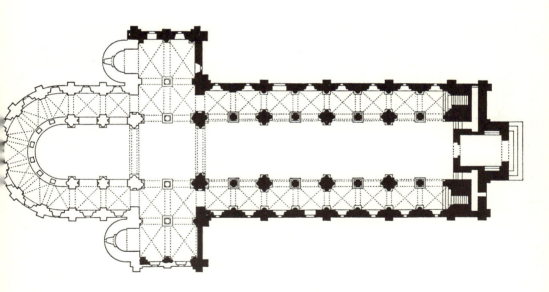

Fig. 80. Jumièges. Abbey church (1040–67). Section and plan. After Georges Lanfry, *L'abbaye de Jumièges: Plans et documents* (Rouen 1954) pls. 4 and 5, with diaphragm arches superimposed by Ernest Born. For justification of these arches see Walter Horn and Ernest Born, *The Plan of St. Gall: A Study of the Architecture and Economy of, and Life in a Paradigmatic Carolingian Monastery* (3 vols. Berkeley 1979) 1.234–38.

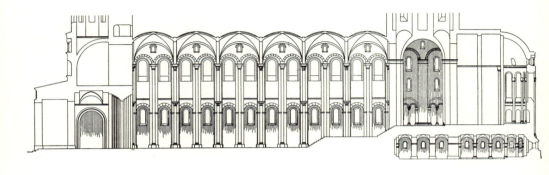

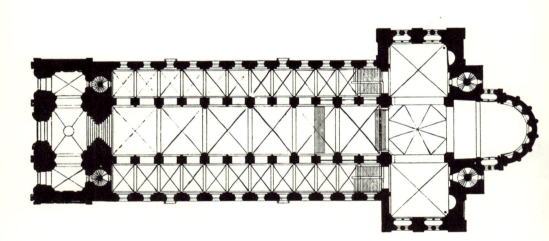

Fig. 81. Speyer. Cathedral. Section and plan of the form it had attained in 1082–1106 (Speyer II). The great conceptual leap from Early to High Romanesque was made by introducing continuous sequences of arch-framed vaults springing from shafts that reached from floor to head of clerestory walls. Modularity, now embodied in an armature of architectural members pervading and framing space in all directions, thus acquired its full medieval form. After Georg Dehio, *Geschichte der deutschen Kunst* (4th ed. 4 vols. + 4 pl. vols. Berlin and Leipzig 1930–34) pl. vol. 1 figs. 59 and 60.

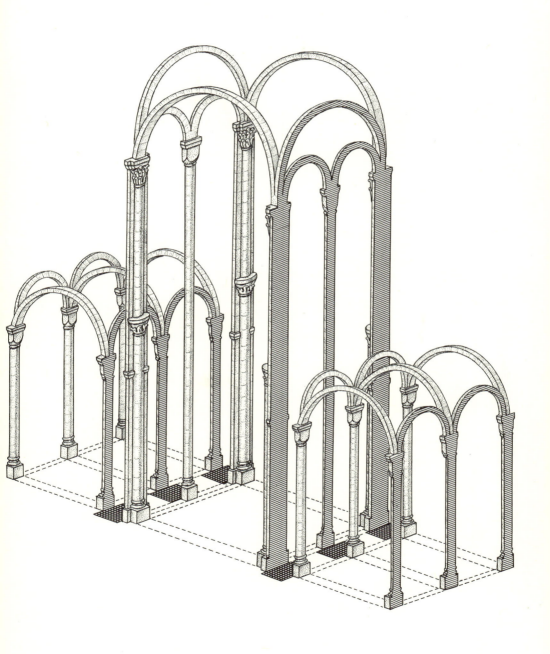

Fig. 82. Speyer. Cathedral (1082–1106: Speyer II). Bay-framing armature of shafts and arches with masonry removed. Drawn for author by Walter Schwarz.

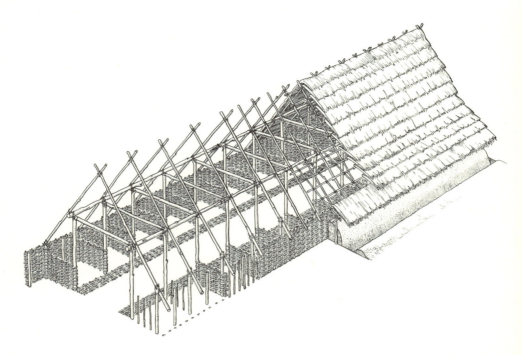

Fig. 83. Ezinge. Cattle barn (third century B.C.). Author's reconstruction, drawn by Walter Schwarz. This type of timber architecture, making use of modular principles of spatial composition long before any such tendencies emerged in medieval church construction, was common in territories occupied by Germanic peoples in prehistoric times and can now be traced back to the fourteenth century B.C. It remained a standard form of manorial architecture throughout the Middle Ages. For the Bronze Age origins of this house type, see H. T. Waterbolk, "The Bronze Age Settlement of Elp," *Helinium* 4 (1964) 97–131. For other prehistoric and medieval examples see Walter Horn, "On the Origins of the Mediaeval Bay System," *Journal of the Society of Architectural Historians* 17 (1958) 2–23, and (with Ernest Born) *The Plan of St. Gall* (3 vols. Berkeley 1979) 2.23–77 and 88–114.

Fig. 84. Peterborough. Tithe barn (early fourteenth century). After *Country Life* 5 no. 122 (May 6, 1899) 556.

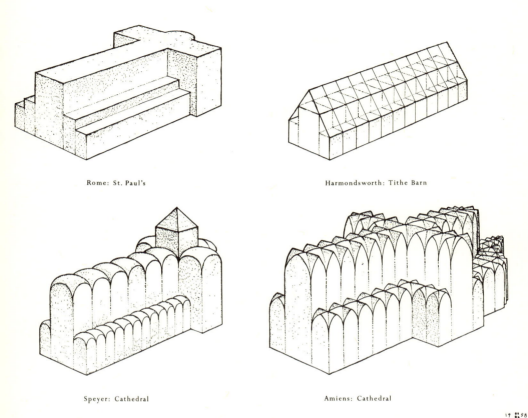

Rome: St. Paul's

Harmondsworth: Tithe Barn

Speyer: Cathedral

Amiens: Cathedral

17 ⁑58

Fig. 85. Diagram illustrating the Early Christian concept of shaping basilicas by ag-
gregating internally undivided (''monolithic'') spaces, and the fundamentally different
principle of composing space as an aggregate of bay-divided, modular spatial units,
prevailing in the Germanic all-purpose house as well as in Romanesque and Gothic
churches. For the schema of the Early Christian basilica of San Paolo fuori le mura in
Rome (upper left), compare figs. 74 and 75 (Old St Peter's). Redrawn by Ernest Born
after construction of William Hill.

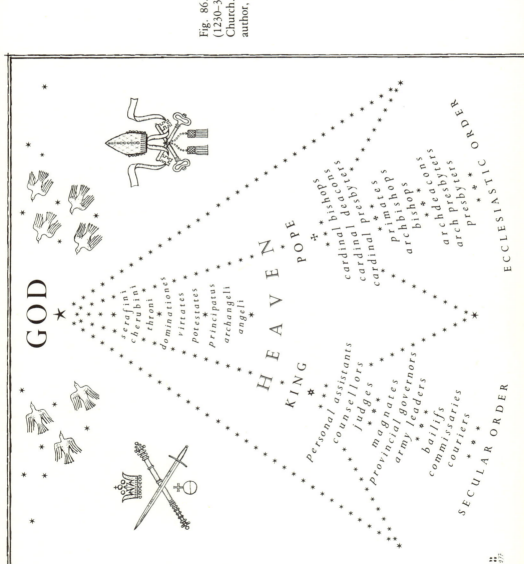

Fig. 86. William of Auvergne, *Liber de univeso* (1230–36). The hierarchies of Heaven, State, and Church. A diagrammatic interpretation by the author, drawn by Ernest Born.

GOD

HEAVEN

serafini
cherubini
throni
dominationes
virtates
potestates
principatus
archangeli
angeli

POPE

cardinal bishops
cardinal deacons
cardinal presbyters
primates
archbishops
bishops
archdeacons
arch Presbyters
archpresbyters
presbyters

ECCLESIASTIC ORDER

KING

Personal assistants
counsellors
judges
magnates
provincial governors
army leaders
bailiffs
commissaries
couriers

SECULAR ORDER

Fig. 87. Chartres. Cathedral. Recessed Gothic portal with columnar statues (1145–50). One of the first examples of this type of architectural sculpture. Photo: Hirmer Fotoarchiv.

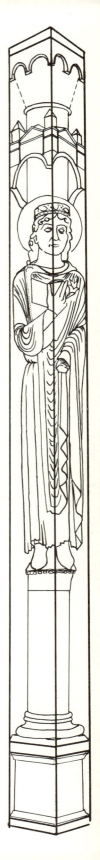

Fig. 88 (left). Moissac. Abbey church. Pier in cloister walk (ca. 1100) showing SS Peter and Paul, in bas-relief framed by arcades. Redrawn by Tom Yamamoto from a photograph in the Bildarchiv Foto Marburg.

Fig. 89 (center). Dijon. Bibliothèque municipale, MS 641 vol. IV (ca. 1135). *Légendaire de Cîteaux*, fol. 18r: initial "I" with byzantinizing figure of saint attached to two columnar shafts. Photo courtesy of the Bibliothèque municipale.

Fig. 90 (right). Chartres. Cathedral. West façade (ca. 1145): columnar statue. Diagram showing how statue is carved out of and remains confined to a tall block of stone that faces the spectator with one of its edges and is conceptually divided into two prisms, the forward one containing the statue, the rearward one the column to which it is attached. Drawn for author by Tom Yamamoto.

Fig. 91. Chartres. Cathedral. West façade, right jamb of center portal (ca. 1145–50): columnar statues of Old Testament queen, king, and prophet. Photo: Bildarchiv Foto Marburg.

Fig. 92. Reims. Cathedral. Center portal, right jamb (ca. 1235): Visitation Group. Photo: Austin.

Fig. 93. Reicheanu-Oberzell.
St George. Crypt (890–96).
Photo: Th. Keller,
Reichenau.

Fig. 94. Corvey. Abbey church.
Westwork (873–85): ground
floor. Source of photo
unknown.

Fig. 95. Diagram of arches, ribs, and supporting shafts in a Gothic cathedral, showing the skeleton framework of ribs over a nave bay. *A*, transverse rib; *B*, diagonal rib; *C*, cross ridge; *D*, longitudinal ridge; *E*, wall or longitudinal rib. This also shows the stonework filling between ribs in a finished vault. After James W. Thompson and Edgar N. Johnson, *An Introduction to Medieval Europe, 300–1500* (New York 1937) 817.

Fig. 96 (opposite page). Amiens. Cathedral. Vaults at the intersection of nave and transept (1220–36). Photo: Clarence Ward Medieval Archive, Courtesy of the Photographic Archives, National Gallery of Art, Washington, D.C.

Fig. 97. Rome. Santa Maria Maggiore (432–40). Interior. Despite its coffered Renaissance ceiling (substituted in 1500 for the original open-timbered roof), Santa Maria Maggiore conveys persuasively the stylistic quality of the great Early Christian basilicas composed of huge, block-shaped, internally undivided voids. Photo: Alinari.

Fig. 98. Rome. Santa Maria in Trastevere (1140–43). Interior. Photo: Alinari.

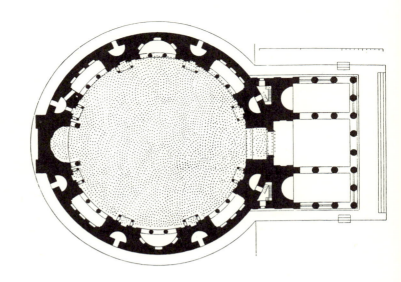

Fig. 99. Rome. Pantheon (110–25 A.D.). Plan, with stippling added to stress the classical corporeality of space. After Georg Dehio and G. von Bezold, *Die kirchliche Baukunst des Abendlandes* (2 vols. + 5 pl. vols. Stuttgart 1887–1901) pl. vol. 1, pl. 1 fig. 12.

Fig. 100. Washington, D.C. National Gallery of Art, Kress Collection. Interior of Pantheon (110–25 A.D.), Rome. Painted by Giovanni Paolo Pannini (ca. 1750). Photo courtesy of the National Gallery of Art.

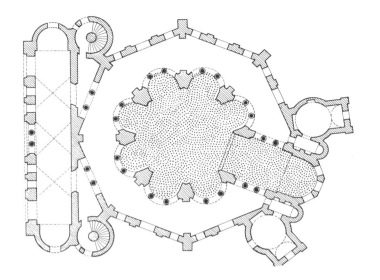

Fig. 101. Ravenna.
San Vitale (532–46).
Plan, with stippling
added to stress the
Early Byzantine
corporeality of space.
After *Enciclopedia
dell'arte antica,
classica e orientale* 6
(1965) 630 fig. 730.

Fig. 102. Ravenna.
San Vitale (532–46).
Interior, looking
north. Photo:
Vincent.

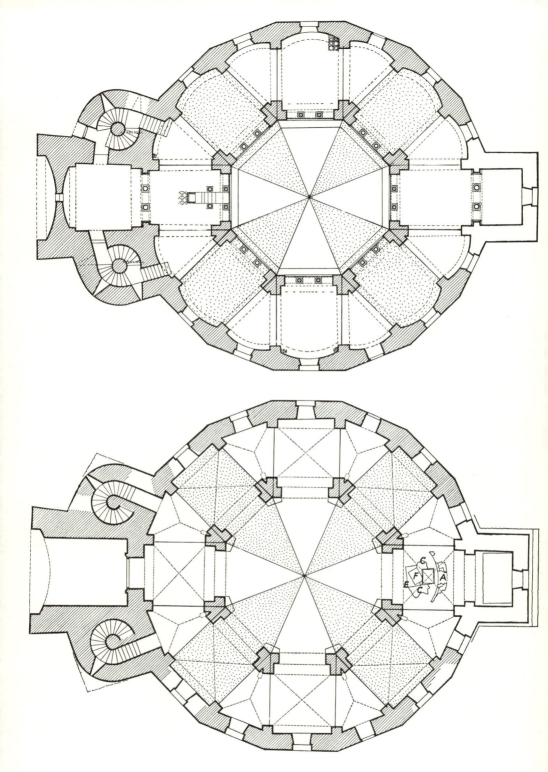

Fig. 103. Aachen. Palace chapel (796–804). Above, plan of gallery level; below, plan of ground floor. Stippling added to stress the medieval modular organization of space. After Felix Kreusch, "Kirche, Atrium und Portikus der Aachener Pfalz," *Karl der Grosse: Lebenswerk und Nachleben*, ed. Wolfgang Braunfels et al. (5 vols. Düsseldorf 1965–68) vol. 3, *Karolingische Kunst*, 466–67 fig. 3.

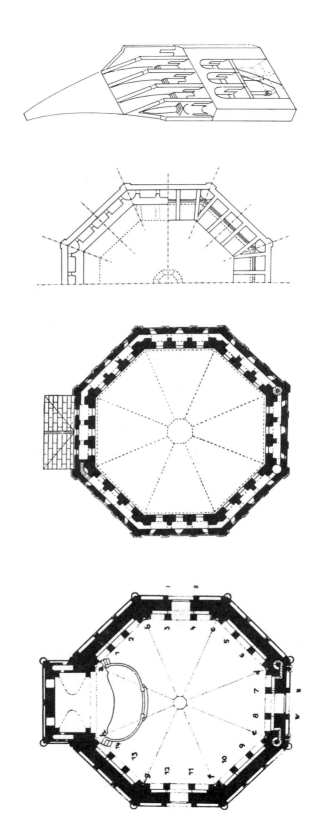

Fig. 105. Florence. Baptistery (1059–1150). Left to right: plan of ground level; plan of second story; horizontal section through dome; scheme of wall construction. After Walter Horn, ''Das Florentiner Baptisterium,'' *Mitteilungen des Kunsthistorischen Institutes in Florenz* 5 (1938) 118–19.

Fig. 107. Florence. Baptistery (1059–1150). Exterior, from southeast. Photo: Alinari.

Fig. 106. Florence. Baptistery (1059–1150). Interior. Photo: Alinari.

Fig. 109. Naples. Museo Nazionale. Pompeiian fresco (late first century B.C.): landscape and architectural scene. Photo: Anderson.

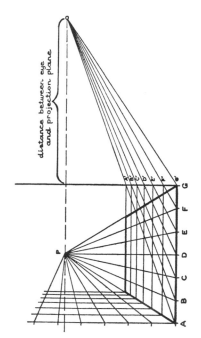

Fig. 108. Modern vanishing-point perspective. Linear system used in construction of a rectangular space box. After Samuel Y. Edgerton, Jr., *The Renaissance Discovery of Linear Perspective* (New York 1975) 95 fig. 2.

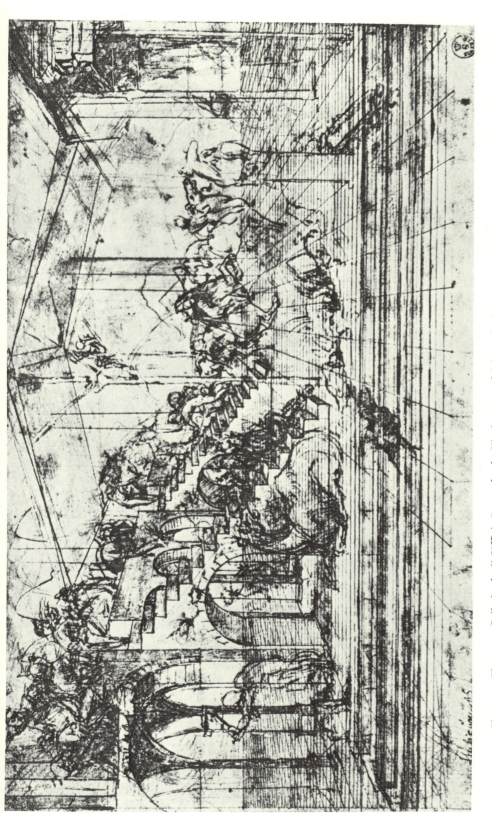

Fig. 110. Florence. Galleria degli Uffizi. Leonardo da Vinci: pen-and-ink study for the unfinished *Adoration of the Magi* (1481–82).

Contributors

MARIE-THÉRÈSE D'ALVERNY: Directeur de Recherche (hon.), Centre National de la Recherche Scientifique (Paris)

JOHN W. BALDWIN: Professor of History, The Johns Hopkins University

GUY BEAUJOUAN: Directeur d'Etudes à la IVe Section de l'Ecole Pratique des Hautes Etudes, Sorbonne (Paris)

ROBERT L. BENSON: Professor of History, University of California (Los Angeles)

JOHN F. BENTON: Professor of History, California Institute of Technology

HERBERT BLOCH: Pope Professor of the Latin Language and Literature, Harvard University

PETER CLASSEN: late Professor für Mittelalterliche und Neuere Geschichte, University of Heidelberg

GILES CONSTABLE: Director, Dumbarton Oaks Research Library and Collection; Professor of History, Harvard University

PETER DRONKE: University Reader in Medieval Latin Literature, Cambridge University

GEORGES DUBY: Professeur au Collège de France

STEPHEN GERSH: Associate Professor, The Mediaeval Institute, University of Notre Dame

NIKOLAUS M. HÄRING: Professor emeritus, Theologische Hochschule (Vallendar am Rhein, Federal Republic of Germany)

WALTER HORN: Professor emeritus of History of Art, University of California (Berkeley)

ERNST KITZINGER: Arthur Kingsley Porter University Professor emeritus, Harvard University

NORMAN KRETZMANN: Susan Linn Sage Professor of Philosophy, Cornell University

STEPHAN KUTTNER: Professor emeritus, School of Law, University of California (Berkeley)

GERHART B. LADNER: Professor emeritus of History, University of California (Los Angeles)

JEAN LECLERCQ, O.S.B.: Professor at the Gregorian University (Rome)

JANET MARTIN: Associate Professor of Classics, Princeton University

JOHN HINE MUNDY: Professor of History, Columbia University

KNUT WOLFGANG NÖRR: Professor, University of Tübingen

PER NYKROG: Professor of Romance Languages and Literatures, Harvard University

MARY A. ROUSE: Managing Editor of *Viator*, Center for Medieval and Renaissance Studies, University of California (Los Angeles)

RICHARD H. ROUSE: Professor of History, University of California (Los Angeles)

WILLIBALD SAUERLÄNDER: Director, Zentralinstitut für Kunstgeschichte (Munich)

R. W. SOUTHERN: President of St John's College, Oxford

CHRYSOGONUS WADDELL, O.C.S.O.: Monk of Our Lady of Gethsemani Abbey (Trappist, Kentucky)

Acknowledgments

For the editors of this volume, it is a pleasant duty to thank cordially the institutions and persons who helped—with financial support, wise counsel, hard work, and important skills—from the inception of the book to its publication.

Before recounting this indebtedness, however, we want first to express gratitude to the authors, not only for the scholarship of their essays, but also for their good-natured acceptance of editorial suggestions and various delays. Here we must mention, with grief, the loss of a cherished friend and colleague, Peter Classen, who died on 23 December 1980. His contribution to this volume reflects the distinction of his scholarly career, much of it devoted to the twelfth century—a career too short in years, but richly illuminating the many problems which interested him.

The universities cosponsoring the conference, Harvard and UCLA, contributed funds as well as their facilities. A generous grant from the National Endowment for the Humanities enabled the planners to hold the conference without reducing its scale or limiting its value. The travel expenses of European scholars were covered principally by the American Council of Learned Societies, with additional support from the Deutsche Forschungsgemeinschaft. Finally, a further grant from the National Endowment for the Humanities helped substantially to defray the cost of photocomposition.

The list of individual benefactors must begin—as the volume began—with the preparations for the conference from which it grew. Apart from the editors, the planning committee included: John F. Benton (Caltech), Morton W. Bloomfield (Harvard), Fredi Chiappelli (UCLA), Paul J. Meyvaert (Mediaeval Academy of America), John E. Murdoch (Harvard), and Lynn White, jr. (UCLA).

At the conference itself, the participants and auditors played a crucial role, in informal conversations as well as the formal discussions. We owe particular thanks to those participants whose prepared comments introduced the sessions and effectively sparked the discussion: Morton W. Bloomfield, Caroline W. Bynum, John E. Murdoch, and Brian Stock.

Though only a few names can be noted, the staffs of UCLA's Center for Medieval and Renaissance Studies and of Harvard's Committee on Medieval Studies did much to make the conference a success. Moreover, since the detailed work of editing was largely done at the UCLA Center, many members of the Center's staff—again, too numerous to be thanked individually—were charged with various tasks in preparing this volume for publication. Both in the planning of the conference and in the initial stages of editing, Abigail Bok worked devotedly. With able assistance from the staff at UCLA's University Research Library, Steven J. Livesey and others verified the accuracy of virtually all citations—and more than 2,500 works are cited in this volume. Deborah Crawford prepared the composition of the illustrations and edited their captions.

Cynthia Craig translated the essays presented in French (Beaujouan, Duby, Leclercq), and Renate Franciscono those in German (Classen, Nörr, Sauerländer). Alison P. Seidel compiled the index. Further, we are grateful to the many libraries, institutes, and publishers who gave permission to reproduce illustrations; the sources of individual illustrations are named in the captions.

Two debts remain. First, Fredi Chiappelli supported and encouraged us enthusiastically from the initial conception of this volume. As Director of the UCLA Center, further, he unstintingly placed the Center's staff and resources at our disposal. Finally, Carol D. Lanham contributed indispensably to the editing of this volume. Though her duties as Senior Editor of the Center included responsibility for copyediting and for coordinating the staff's efforts, in her execution of those duties she went far beyond what one expects, or could reasonably hope, from a copyeditor. As her name on the title page indicates, she has been throughout—to us as editors, and individually to many authors in this volume—an invaluable scholarly colleague.

RLB   GC

Index

Manuscripts are listed under "Manuscripts cited," alphabetically by location.

Maragone, Bernardo, 396
Maragone, Salem, 396
Marbod of Rennes: 59, 577–78, 585, 621–22;
  Liber decem capitulorum, 559*n*, 622; on
  Robert of La Chaise Dieu, 65; *Stella maris*,
  552, 558
Marcabru, 574–78, 585
Marcus Valerius, 551, 556–57, 561, 563
Maria, widow of Raymond Faber, 237
Marie de Champagne, 606
Marie de France, 81, 599–600, 602, 608
Marius, 616
Mark, kg. of Cornwall, 600, 602
Mark of Toledo, 429, 455
Marmoutier, abbey of, 259
Marseille, tables of, 447
Marsh, Richard, 156
Martial, 553
Martianus Capella, 512, 330*n*, 564, 706
Martin (Martinus Gosia), *doctor* of Bologna,
  363, 375
Martin, master at Paris, 168
Martin of Tours, St, 292
Martinus Polonus, 204*n*
Marx, Karl, 75, 76, 240*n*
Mary, Virgin: 11, 642; Anselm on, 46; Benedict
  on, 354; in worship, 107, 404; Marbod on,
  552
Maslama, 441, 449, 471, 478
Master of the Genesis Initial, 684
Master of the Leaping Figures, 683–84
Master of the Morgan Leaf, 683–84
Matheus Ferrarius, 423*n*
Matthew of Albano, 42, 91
Matthew of Angers, 146
Matthew of Vendôme: 145, 165, 285–86; *Ars
  versificatoria*, 540, 541, 559, 560, 561, 565–
  66; poems by, 554, 555
Matthew Paris, 238*n*
Maurice, emp., 347
Maurice of Sully, bp. of Paris, 131, 133, 255
Mauricio, archdeacon of Toledo, 429
Maximus the Confessor, 430*n*, 523*n*
Meaux, 50*n*
Meinhard of Bamberg, 546, 549
Meinong, Alexius, 506
Meludinenses, 114